NEW TESTAMENT APOCRYPHA

II

NEW TESTAMENT APOCRYPHA

Revised Edition
of the Collection initiated by
Edgar Hennecke

edited by
Wilhelm Schneemelcher

English translation edited by
R. McL. Wilson

II

WRITINGS RELATING TO THE APOSTLES
APOCALYPSES AND RELATED SUBJECTS

James Clarke & Co
Westminster/John Knox Press

Published in Great Britain by
James Clarke & Co Ltd
P. O. Box 60
Cambridge CB1 2NT

Published in the United States by
Westminster/John Knox Press
Louisville, Kentucky 40202-1396

British Library Cataloguing-in-Publication Data
A catalogue record for this book is available from the British Library

ISBN 0-2276-7917-2

Library of Congress Cataloguing-in-Publication Data
(Revised for vol. 2)

New Testament apocrypha

Translation of: Neutestamentliche Apokryphen.
Includes bibliographical references and indexes.
Contents: Gospels and related writings - v. 2. Writings related to the apostles; apocalypses and related literature.
I. Schneemelcher, Wilhelm, 1914- II. Wilson, R. McL. (Robert McLachlan).
BS2832.S3 1991 229'.92052 90-23504
ISBN 0-664-21878-4 (v. 1)
ISBN 0-664-21879-2 (v. 2)

Printed in the United States of America
2 4 6 8 9 7 5 3 1

Table of Contents

Foreword

The present Volume II completes the revised edition of the collection *Neutestamentliche Apokryphen in deutscher Übersetzung*, founded in 1904 by Edgar Hennecke. As with the first volume of the collection (NTApo[5] I, 1987,[6] 1990; ET 1991), this volume too had to be thoroughly revised and brought up to date with the present state of research. In the process, some texts could be taken over from the previous edition after revision and correction. The introductions have been largely written afresh. Those texts from the Nag Hammadi library which from their literary character belong in this collection have been included. For good counsel in this matter I thank H.M. Schenke.

Particular store has been attached to the bibliographies. They are intended to put the reader in a position to follow up the problems which specially interest him, beyond the necessarily compressed presentations in such a collection. Here the reader will certainly be struck by many a difference in the assessment of the texts. These differences (e.g. on the question how the apocryphal Acts are to be judged) have been quite deliberately accepted. The editor neither could nor wished to prescribe to the contributors any uniform line. In the present state of research that simply was not possible.

In this volume too I have had the advantage of help from many sides. I would mention only R. Kassel, H.J. Klimkeit, W.D. Lebek, R. Merkelbach and G. Wirth. A. de Santos Otero has once again given much good advice. K. Schäferdiek was for this volume also a true and reliable helper. G. Ahn assisted with the editing and proof-correction, and also prepared the index. To all those named, but above all to all the contributors who placed their work at my disposal, I would express my hearty thanks. Finally, a word of thanks is due also to the publisher, Herr G. Siebeck, and his assistants (especially Herr R. Pflug) for their valuable collaboration.

Bad Honnef, 31 May 1989 Wilhelm Schneemelcher

Preface to the English Edition

Over the past thirty years or so 'Hennecke-Schneemelcher' has become a standard tool for those working in the field of the NT Apocrypha. Much has happened, however, in these three decades, and the time was ripe for a revision and up-dating, to bring it abreast of recent research. The two German volumes have now been completely revised, and it is appropriate that the English edition also should be updated to bring it into line.

The policy adopted in this book is that which governed the first volume, and indeed right back to the two volumes of the previous English edition: to present the work of our German colleagues in an English version, checked and corrected to make it in every way possible an adequate tool for the English-speaking reader. The several introductions are straight translations from the German; the texts have been checked against the originals in Latin, Greek or Coptic, to ensure that they are truly English translations and not merely versions at second or third hand.

The extent of the revision varies: some parts are entirely new, in some cases by new contributors, and these have been translated from scratch. In other cases, particularly where the older texts are concerned, it has been possible to retain much from the earlier edition, and here due acknowledgement must be paid to my collaborators in that earlier volume, Professors Ernest Best and G. C. Stead, Dr David Hill, and the late Dr George Ogg. The whole has however been very thoroughly checked and revised, and the translation editor must now accept full responsibility.

The production of such a book as this involves the work of many hands, not only the editors and contributors and the translators but also the staff of the publishers, who often are not accorded the credit which they deserve. I can name only two, with whom I have been in more direct contact: Miss Jane K. Hodgart, the copy editor, and Miss Sarah Brierley, the desk editor who saw this volume through the press. To them and to their colleagues the reader and the translation editor are much indebted.

R. McL. Wilson

Abbreviations

For abbreviations of the titles of journals or series, the lists of Schwertner (*Theologische Realenzyklopädie, Abkürzungsverzeichnis*, 1976) and RGG³ (1957) have generally been used. For the texts from Nag Hammadi reference may be made to the list of abbreviations in *The Nag Hammadi Library in English* (General Editor: James M. Robinson), 1988, pp. xiii-xiv. A few abbreviations frequently used are adduced below.

Aa	*Acta apostolorum apocrypha* I, ed. Lipsius, 1891; II 1 and 2, ed. Bonnet, 1898 and 1903 (reprint 1959)
AGG	*Apokryphe Apostelgeschichten* (= Apocryphal Acts)
AnalBoll	*Analecta Bollandiana*
ANRW	*Aufstieg und Niedergang der Römischen Welt*
Apa	*Apocalypses Apocryphae*, ed. C. Tischendorf, 1866
BHG	Bibliotheca hagiographica graeca, ³1957
BHL	Bibliotheca hagiographica latina, ²1949
BHO	Bibliotheca hagiographica orientalis, 1910
CChrSL	Corpus Christianorum, Series latina, 1953ff.
CChrSG	Corpus Christianorum, Series graeca, 1976ff.
CChrSA	Corpus Christianorum, Series Apocryphorum, 1983ff.
CSCO	Corpus scriptorum Christianorum orientalium
CSEL	Corpus scriptorum ecclesiasticorum latinorum
DACL	*Dictionnaire d'archéologie chrétienne et de liturgie*
Ea	*Evangelia apocrypha*, ed. C. Tischendorf, ²1876
Erbetta	Mario Erbetta, *Gli Apocrifi del Nuovo Testamento*, I-III, 1966-1981
FS	Festschrift
GCS	Die griechischen christlichen Schriftsteller der ersten drei Jahrhunderte Berlin
GKT	Grundkurs Theologie, Stuttgart 1989ff.
GTA	Göttinger Theologische Arbeiten 1975ff.
Graf	G. Graf, *Geschichte der christlichen arabischen Literatur*, 1-5, 1944-1953
Harnack, *Lit. gesch.*	Adolf Harnack, *Geschichte der altchristlichen Literatur bis Eusebius*, ²1958
James	M.R. James, *The Apocryphal New Testament*, 1924 (reprint 1955)
KIT	Kleine Texte für Vorlesungen und Übungen
Lipsius, *Apostelgesch.*	R.A. Lipsius, *Die apokryphen Apostelgeschichten und Apostellegenden*, 2 vols., 1883f.; supplement 1890
McNamara	Martin McNamara, *The Apocrypha in the Irish Church*, Dublin 1975

B. Writings Relating to the Apostles

Michaelis	*Die Apocryphen Schriften zum Neuen Testament,* Übers. und erl. von W. Michaelis, ²1958
Moraldi	Luigi Moraldi, *Apocrifi del Nuovo Testamento,* 2 vols., 1971
NHC	Nag Hammadi Codex
NHLE	*The Nag Hammadi Library in English,* ed. James M. Robinson, 3rd ed., Leiden 1988
NHS	Nag Hammadi Studies
NTApo¹	*Neutestamentliche Apokryphen in deutscher Übersetzung,* ed. Edgar Hennecke, 1904
NTApo²	id., 2nd edition 1924
NTApo³	id., 3rd edition, ed. W. Schneemelcher, 2 vols. 1959/64 (reprint ⁴1968; ET 1963, 1965; reprinted 1973, 1974)
NTApoHandb	*Handbuch zu den Neutestamentlichen Apokryphen,* ed. Edgar Hennecke, 1904
PG	Patrologiae cursus completus, accurante J.P. Migne, Series Graeca
PL	id., Series Latina
PO	Patrologia orientalis, Paris
PTS	Patristische Texte und Studien, 1964ff.
PWRE	*Realencyclopädie der classischen Altertumswissenschaften.* Neue Bearb. (Pauly-Wissowa)
RE	*Realenzyclopädie fur protestantische Theologie und Kirche,* ²1896ff.
RGG³	*Die Religion in Geschichte und Gegenwart,* ³1956ff.
de Santos	Aurelio de Santos Otero (ed.), *Los Evangelios Apócrifos* (BAC 148), ⁴1984, ⁶1988
de Santos, *Überlieferung*	Aurelio de Santos Otero, *Die handschriftliche Überlieferung der altslavischen Apokryphen* I (PTS 20), 1978; II (PTS 23), 1981
TDNT	*Theological Dictionary of the New Testament,* tr. G. W. Bromiley (ET of *Theologische Wörterbuch zum Neuen Testament,* 1933ff.)
TRE	*Theologische Realenzyklopädie,* 1976ff.
TU	Texte und Untersuchungen zur Geschichte der altchristlichen Literatur
Vielhauer, *Lit. gesch.*	Philipp Vielhauer, *Geschichte der urchristlichen Literatur,* ³1981
VigChr	*Vigiliae Christianae,* 1947ff.

B. WRITINGS RELATING TO THE APOSTLES

Introduction

Wilhelm Schneemelcher

The texts brought together in Part B of the present collection do not by any means constitute a uniform literary *Gattung*. They are rather very diverse works, which however because of their concern with one or more apostles may be included under the very general heading of 'apostolic'.

Certainly the apostles to some extent also play an important role in the 'gospel literature' assembled in volume I, as guarantors of the true tradition, which is intended to be attested as old and genuine by the fact that an apostle is named as its authority. But these texts in volume I relate almost exclusively to the life, work and preaching (before and after the resurrection) of Jesus. The texts which here follow have the apostles as the subject of their presentation in a different way. Here the boundaries cannot always be sharply drawn. This is clear, for example, with the Coptic 'Acts of Peter and the Twelve Apostles' (see below, pp. 412ff.). But on the whole the division of the material over the two sections is probably justified.

To the sphere of the 'apostolic' (in the sense of this distinction) there belong in the first place some texts which are described as apostolic pseudepigrapha. These are writings which were published under the name of an apostle.

Then those works are presented in which one or more apostles take the central place. The five great acts of apostles from the 2nd and 3rd centuries, which are the most important representatives of this group, portray the career and the fate of the apostles, linking up with the ancient romance (and frequently also drawing upon other literary traditions of antiquity); here it can be seen from the speeches inserted that they are not merely 'fictional prose narratives', but are intended to serve for proclamation, or better for missionary propaganda, as well as for the edification of the reader. The Pseudo-Clementine literature also belongs in this context. The texts then exercised an influence in manifold revisions in the later acts of apostles, which however in part already represent the transition to the hagiographical literature of late antiquity and the Middle Ages.

This whole very diverse literature can only be understood when it is set in its proper place in the development of Church history. Thus an account of the way in which the concepts 'apostle' and 'apostolic' were shaped and developed, and what significance they took on in the course of the 2nd century (see below, pp. 5ff.), is the necessary presupposition for an appropriate interpretation of the texts. For pseudapostolic literature in its diverse forms could indeed only come into being after a definite opinion had been formed as to what was meant by 'apostle' and 'apostolic'. It is therefore not surprising that this literature came into vogue in the 2nd century, thus in the period in which - as W.A. Bienert shows below (pp. 25ff.) - the idea of the 'apostolic norm' was developing. In this period, in which the solid structures of later centuries still did not exist, the efforts of the Church to create for itself some security in faith and life by appeal to a witness from the beginning, who still stood in close association with Jesus, finally led to the writings in which old traditions were frequently combined with newer tendencies. This holds for all groups in Christendom, whether they must now be described as 'catholic' or as 'gnostic'. The boundaries in the 2nd century are in any case not so clear as a later period was to think.

The intentions which brought about this literature were certainly not uniform. Thus the 'Teaching of the Lord for the Gentiles through the Twelve Apostles' (the so-called Didache) is concerned for conduct of life and church order. In the Pastoral Epistles the aims of 'Church law' emerge still more clearly, but combined with demarcation over against 'heretics'. This antiheretical tendency occurs to some extent also in works which owe their origin to an increased interest in the person and work of individual apostles (so for example in the five great acts of apostles), but there it is probably not the chief motive.

Luke already in his Acts took up several legends about the apostles which correspond to a concern of this sort (Acts 5:15; 19:11f.). However, he did not regard the popular narratives about the miraculous powers of the apostles as the main theme, but used them sporadically, to underline the edifying character of his work. There was a danger here, that the apostles might become miracle-workers such as the environment of early Christianity also knew, a danger which in later works was further enhanced.

In the 2nd century, as already indicated, people in the different Christian groups appealed to the apostles as guarantors for the correct doctrine and preaching. With this is bound up the attempt to report something more about the life of the apostles. Here many factors may have played a part: the diffusion of Christianity, the conflict over the correct doctrine, the rise of the veneration of martyrs, etc. It was probably important that ideas about the 'apostolic norm' required, as it were, a sub-structure which would not only set forth the 'apostolic doctrine' but also give to the figures of the apostles a concrete form.

In the process, not only were literary models taken over from the surrounding world, but non-Christian ideas also flowed in. Thus we can demonstrate from the apocryphal acts of apostles not only the use of pre-Christian and non-Christian *Gattungen*, but also the taking-over of the image of the θεῖος ἀνήρ. Here the apostles become figures which often correspond to ancient phenomena.

This is not surprising when we consider that in the 2nd century the Church had to begin to come to terms with the world in which it was growing up. In this process influences from outside also penetrated into the Church's thinking. We can thus set the apocryphal acts in place in the manifold process of the interaction of antiquity and

Christianity (as we can on another level with the Apologists of the 2nd century).

The relation of this literature to the canon cannot be described in a single sentence, but must be clarified for each individual document separately. Thus the Letter to the Laodiceans (see below, pp. 42ff.) is nothing but a compilation of quotations from Pauline letters, hence pre-supposes the canon and is intended to fill an alleged gap in it. The acts of apostles on the other hand are not shaped after the pattern of the canonical Acts, even though knowledge of it cannot be excluded.

With regard to this question it must be observed that the canon of the NT only developed in the course of the 2nd century (cf. vol. I, pp. 15ff.), and that for a long time its limits were still uncertain. Also we can scarcely assume that all communities immediately possessed a complete exemplar of the NT; probably only separate writings, which were regarded as authoritative, were available. Whether and to what extent Acts belonged to these is an open question.

For our literature we may at any rate determine that for the most part it originated without any reference to a canon of the NT. Also we should probably not assume a wish to replace canonical writings. This does not exclude the possibility that the motive of supplementation played a role in several writings. Certainly more important, however, were the tendencies for the dissemination of certain opinions and doctrines, to some extent combined with the aims of entertainment and 'edification'. Here people turned back to material from older tradition (local and personal legends) and made use of literary *Gattungen* from the surrounding world, in order to link the most diverse things in manifold ways with the names and figures of the apostles. Dogmatic, polemic and apologetic intentions were brought into the literary form appropriate to the ends in view, just as were projects of Church law or aims at edification and entertainment.

In connection with this literature we should probably also bear in mind that not only does it derive from different communities with distinct traditions, but also we can identify considerable differences with regard to spiritual and theological level. It is not a question of witnesses to an elevated theological reflection; the popular elements preponderate. This however gives to our literature its special importance: here the 'apostolic norm' is not established in systematic or theological fashion, but the apostles, their life, their preaching and their death, are brought before the community in a comprehensible manner, be it that in the pseudepigraphical texts and in the speeches inserted into the narrative works the apostles themselves are made the spokesmen, or that their figures are delineated in a graphic and popular way. Thereby these works are in a certain fashion a parallel phenomenon - on another level indeed, but of considerable influence - to the theological development of the 'apostle' concept and the idea of the norm that belongs to it in the 2nd century.

Reference has already been made to the fact that the texts have frequently taken up traditions which were alive in individual communities, worked them in, and probably also to some extent reshaped them. This however means that we cannot assess them in the same way as other literary works. The *Sitz im Leben* is an important aspect not only for judgment about a work as a whole, but also for evaluation of the traditions worked up in it, and for many traditions this *Sitz im Leben* is public worship or report by word of mouth.

B. Writings relating to the Apostles

This literature bears witness that, alongside the theological reflection which later led in the Church to the norm of the 'apostolic', there was also a broad tradition about the apostles, nurtured also in special groups. Much of it was soon condemned as 'heretical' and 'apocryphal', and excluded from the use of the churches. But certain elements survived in modifications and reworkings of various kinds, and contributed to the consolidation of the 'apostolic norm'. They are also still operative in the later hagiography of the 'catholic Apostolic Church'.

XIII. The Picture of the Apostle in Early Christian Tradition

Wolfgang A. Bienert

1. The concept of the apostle in primitive Christianity

Literature (with special consideration of more recent works): K.H. Rengstorf, art. ἀπόστολος, TDNT I, 407-447 (fundamental). H. von Campenhausen, 'Der urchristliche Apostelbegriff', in StTh 1, 1947/48, 96-130; id., *Kirchliches Amt und geistliche Vollmacht in den ersten drei Jahrhunderten* (BHTh 14), [2]1963 (ET *Ecclesiastical Authority and Spiritual Power*, 1969); B. Rigaux, 'Die "Zwölf" in Geschichte und Kerygma', in H. Ristow/K. Matthiae (eds.), *Der historische Jesus and der kerygmatische Christus*, [2]1962, 468-486. G. Klein, *Die zwölf Apostel. Ursprung und Gehalt einer Idee* (FRLANT 77), 1961; W. Schmithals, *Das kirchliche Apostelamt. Eine historische Untersuchung* (FRLANT 79), 1961 (ET *The Office of the Apostle*, 1969); J. Roloff, *Apostolat - Verkündigung - Kirche*, 1965; G. Schille, *Die urchristliche Kollegialmission* (AThANT 48), 1967; S. Freyne, *The Twelve Disciples and Apostles*, London 1968; H. Kasting, *Die Anfänge der urchristlichen Mission* (BEvTh 55), 1969; K. Kertelge, 'Die Funktion der "Zwölf" im Markusevangelium', TThZ 78, 1969, 193-206; id., 'Das Apostelamt des Paulus, sein Ursprung und seine Bedeutung', BZ 14, 1970, 161-181; G. Schneider, 'Die zwölf Apostel als "Zeugen"' (1970), in id., *Lukas, Theologe der Heilsgeschichte* (BBB 59), 1985, 61-85; R. Schnackenburg, 'Apostel vor und neben Paulus' (1970), in id., *Schriften zum NT*, 1971, 338-358; G. Schmahl, *Die Zwölf im Markusevangelium* (TThSt 30), 1974 (Lit.); F. Hahn, 'Der Apostolat im Urchristentum', KuD 20, 1974, 54-77; F. Agnew, 'On the Origin of the Term Apostolos', CBQ 38, 1976, 49-53; K. Kertelge (ed.), *Das kirchliche Amt im NT* (WdF 439), 1977 (Lit.); J.A. Bühner, *Der Gesandte und sein Weg im 4. Evangelium* (WUNT II, 2), 1977; W. Trilling, 'Zur Entstehung des Zwölferkreises', in *Die Kirche des Anfangs* (FS H. Schürmann) (EThSt 38), 1978, 201-222; J. Roloff, art. 'Apostel/Apostolat/Apostolizität I. Neues Testament', TRE 3, 1978, 430-445 (Lit.); D. Lührmann, *Das Markusevangelium* (HNT 3), 1987; K. Haacker, 'Verwendung und Vermeidung des Apostelbegriffs im lukanischen Werk', NT 30, 1988, 9-38. Cf. further the relevant articles in TBLNT, 2 vols., [4]1977 and in EWNT, ed. H. Balz/G. Schneider, 3 vols. 1980-1983 - as well as W. Bauer-Aland, *Wb. z. NT*, [6]1988 and G.W.H. Lampe, *A Patristic Greek Lexicon*, 1961.

The question of the *primitive Christian apostle concept* is closely connected with that of the origin of the Christian Church and the beginning of its offices and norms of faith; it thereby falls of necessity into that 'dangerous thicket of reciprocally contradictory hypotheses' which still surrounds the investigation of the history of primitive Christianity, 'in which indeed a general orientation and isolated vistas are possible, but any definite interpretation of the whole leads immediately into boundless controversies'. This remark by H. von Campenhausen (StTh 1, 1947/48, 96) has lost nothing of its fundamental significance even after forty years, especially since W. Schmithals even in 1961 wrote of the origin of the Church's apostolate (p. 12): 'The debate over our problem is . . . still not approaching conclusion.' Indeed, the solution he proposes, to derive the apostle concept from Jewish or Jewish Christian Gnosis (cf. p. 216), has met with almost unanimous rejection. Its basis in the sources is inadequate, and the argument therefore remains largely hypothetical. His book, however, has drawn attention to a field of problems which is none the less of central importance for the understanding of the early Christian picture of the apostle as a whole, namely the question of its relation to Gnosis and Gnosticism.

In our context it is not possible to give a critical evaluation of recent discussion of the early Christian apostle concept in detail. It can only be a matter of discussing the New Testament conceptual field in its historical context against the background of the results of recent research and naming the areas which are of significance for its understanding and that of the history of its influence, and which contribute to the outcome that what is 'apostolic' finally became the basic norm of Christian faith. Here it already deserves to be noticed that the adjective 'apostolic' (ἀποστολικός) does not occur at all in the New Testament,[1] while the substantive ἀπόστολος appears relatively frequently in the New Testament literature, and that, in contrast to secular Greek, always with reference to persons. In the first place it describes quite generally an envoy, a messenger. Later it is said in Origen (3rd cent.): 'Anyone who is sent by any person is an "apostle" of the one who sent him' (*Comm. in Joh.* 32.17). Its use for the proclaimers of a religious message appears to be a specifically Christian coinage. K. Haacker speaks in this connection of an 'early Christian neologism' (pp. 12f.), a reminting of the concept, which had become necessary, among other reasons, because comparable Greek terms like ἄγγελος or κῆρυξ had already in terms of content become set in other ways. It is at any rate beyond dispute that in Christian usage the term 'apostle' took on a special stamp. And it is certainly no accident that - just like the terms ἐκκλησία or ἐπίσκοπος - it was not translated into Latin, but simply taken over. Nevertheless it is necessary to keep in view the wider linguistic and conceptual field in which it was originally at home. In addition it remains also to be noted that in the New Testament itself the apostle concept is variously interpreted, in Paul otherwise than, for example, in the Lucan writings (cf., e.g., Gal. 1:1 and Acts 1:21f.).

1: Outside of biblical usage the word ἀπόστολος has a wide-ranging and usually technical significance, e.g. 'covering letter', 'bill of lading', 'passport' or the like - often in connection with the language of shipping and navigation, where it can also describe a cargo ship or a naval expedition. Occasionally it is also applied to persons, for example to describe the commander of a fleet. Only rarely does it have the meaning 'emissary' (attested only at two places in Herodotus; cf. W. Bauer, WbNT s.v.). Only in a later period does it appear with this significance in papyri also (cf. F. Agnew), and here the meaning 'authorised agent' is latent, a use rooted in the ancient oriental law regarding messengers (cf. e.g. 1 Sam. 25:40f.; 2 Sam. 10:1ff.), according to which an emissary represents his principal with full authority. In correspondence with the basic rule: 'The agent (*shaluach*) is like the man himself' (Berachoth 5.5) there later developed out of this - in Rabbinic Judaism - the so-called '*shaliach*' institution (named after the Hebrew substantive to the passive participle of the verb *shalach*, which in Greek - e.g. in the Septuagint - is generally rendered by ἀποστέλλειν). The proximity to the New Testament apostle concept is not to be overlooked. However, the conviction that the Christian apostle concept goes back directly to the Jewish institution of the *shaliach* (Rengstorf *et al.*) has proved untenable. Two things above all tell against this assumption: a) as a designation for a particular office-bearer with an official commission, the term *shaliach* is attested in Judaism only after the destruction of the Second Temple (after A.D. 70). Here it is in general a question of an agent authorised by the Great Sanhedrin, who had to carry out visitations or gather in collections. A direct influence on the early Christian apostle concept or upon Paul, who had a fundamental share in coining the term, is on this ground excluded. b) Over and above that, the *shaliach* as a rule is given a clearly delimited and temporally restricted commission by the institution which sends him. On the other hand, he has no divine commission for preaching or even for mission, which for the early Christian apostolate and particularly for Paul is one of the characteristic attributes. Despite these differences, which become all the more clear the more precisely we inquire into the specific religious profile in each case, certain structural similarities still remain recognisable, e.g. the motif of authorisation and of personal representation, which points to common roots which have influenced Jewish and early Christian thought, probably more strongly than has often been assumed in research hitherto. Linguistically at any rate, *shaliach* is beyond doubt the equivalent of ἀπόστολος.

These common roots lie in Old Testament ideas about emissaries and intermediaries, which are just as characteristic for the political and legal life of Israel as for the religious, and here above all for prophecy (cf. e.g. Is. 6:8). In the present context it is not possible to set this out in detail. What is important for our purpose is above all the linguistic bridge of the Septuagint, which made Hebrew and Aramaic thought accessible to the Greek, and recollection of the fact that it became the Bible of the early Christians, just as the Christians in many respects entered into the heritage of hellenistic Judaism. Unfortunately the adjectival noun ἀπόστολος occurs in LXX only in a single passage, and indeed as a translation of the Hebrew *shaluach* (passive participle of *shalach* - 1 Kings 14:6). But it is worthy of note that the person 'commissioned' there, Ahijah, is a prophet, who with his statement to the queen of that time: 'I come to you as a messenger charged with heavy tidings' - 'gives expression to his inner - not his outward! - mission and authorisation from God' (v. Campenhausen, StTh 1, p. 99). This evidence, however, only takes on importance from the fact that in LXX the verb ἀποστέλλειν appears at more than 700 places instead of the Hebrew *shalach*, 'and indeed predominantly in just such a way that it designates a formal commissioning with a message or some other task' (v. Campenhausen, op. cit., 98). More recent investigations have now shown, on the foundation of K.H. Rengstorf's article, that the *shaliach* concept in Judaism was by no means anchored in a juristic or institutional sense, but could also describe prophets like Elijah, Elisha, Ezekiel or even Moses (J.A. Bühner, 281-306, cf. id. in EWNT I, 342ff.), so that the usual separation between legal and prophetic commission (Schmithals, pp. 95f.; cf. Rengstorf, 420) cannot be sustained. But then the proximity between the Jewish *shaliach* and the Christian 'apostle' appears originally even closer than is commonly assumed. It remains however for us to take account of the different linguistic area, which naturally contributed to the particular coining and to the delimitation of one against the other.

2: Of the 80 examples in all for the **apostle concept in the New Testament**, 34 in each case fall to the Pauline (including the Deutero-Paulines and 5 cases in the Pastorals) and to the Lucan writings. With that we can recognise the two - very distinct (see above, p. 6) - centres of gravity for definition of the concept. And it is certainly no accident that the abstract ἀποστολή occurs only in these two bodies of documents, three times in Paul (1 Cor. 9:2; Gal. 2:8; Rom. 1:5) and once in Acts 1:25 - in connection with the election of the apostle Matthias. To clarify things more precisely, but also to differentiate the early Christian picture of the apostle and its development, it is necessary to examine the normal usage of the term in the New Testament and at the same time to take into account the verbal manner of expression so important for the LXX. This is significant for the Gospels as a whole, but above all for the Gospel of John, in which the noun ἀπόστολος occurs only once (as however also in Matt.). Mark on the other hand contains two examples - not, as occasionally alleged, only one: Mark 3:14 is in this respect, with D. Lührmann, 'to be regarded as original' (HNT 3, p. 70).

2.1: The earliest and at the same time the most nuanced general picture of the early Christian apostolate is to be found in **Paul**. For the Deutero-Paulines and especially for the Pastorals, he is quite simply the ideal and epitome of the Christian apostolate, and for them already possesses a normative significance within the Christian tradition (cf. 1 Tim. 2:7; 6:20; 2 Tim. 1:11-14). He himself, however, in his apostolate sees himself exposed to a peculiar pressure for legitimation. He describes himself with perceptible emphasis as 'apostle of Jesus Christ' (2 Cor. 1:1), and stresses that he was called 'not by men or through men, but by Jesus Christ and God' (Gal. 1:1). At the same time he comes to grips with opponents, whom he calls 'false apostles' (ψευδαπόστολος - 2 Cor. 11:13) or even 'super-apostles' (ὑπερλίαν ἀπόστολοι - 2 Cor. 11:5; 12:11) (cf. F. Hahn, p. 60). Everything points to the conclusion that the apostle concept was still not precisely defined in terms of content, but that Paul has taken it over from a tradition existing before him, especially since he himself once speaks of predecessors (οἱ πρὸ ἐμοῦ ἀπόστολοι - Gal. 1:17). Those intended in this connection are the apostles in Jerusalem and Cephas/Peter (Gal. 1:18f.), an evidently closed circle (F. Hahn, p. 58), in regard to which one instinctively thinks - in view of 1 Cor. 15:5 - of 'the Twelve' and in a wider sense also of James the Lord's brother (cf. 1 Cor. 15:7).

If we examine Paul's usage more carefully, we can distinguish in it three levels of significance for the concept, which are however linked with one another and influence one another: a) in a very general and non-specific sense Paul can for example describe Epaphroditus, the emissary of the community in Philippi, as an 'apostle' (Phil. 2:25), just as in 2 Cor. 8:23 he can speak of ἀπόστολοι ἐκκλησιῶν. Here the basic meaning of the term - 'emissary', 'messenger' - is still clearly recognisable. b) Beside this there is another, specifically Christian but likewise not precisely defined, apostle concept, which Paul has evidently taken over; for it occurs also outside the Pauline corpus (e.g. Acts 14:4, 14, where Paul and Barnabas are so named; cf. also Acts 2:2). This is used to describe preachers of the Gospel, who know themselves to be commissioned by the

Holy Spirit or the risen Lord and equipped with special gifts (cf. 1 Cor. 9:5), to work in his name - as missionaries - in the world. To these certainly belong the 'super-apostles' so named by Paul, but ultimately also Paul himself, although for his part he repeatedly has to take issue with their spiritual claims. In a positive sense Paul mentions Andronicus and Junia[2] as his close kindred and fellow prisoners, 'who are eminent among the apostles' (Rom. 16:7). With these 'apostles', in terms of their self-understanding, it is a question of prophets called and sent by God, who speak and act by divine commission and with divine authority. They understand themselves as bearers of the prophetic Spirit promised for the last times (cf. Acts 2 with Joel 3:1-5) and are part of the eschatological community of salvation (ἐκκλησία). What relationship these prophets had to the Jerusalem community, or originally even to the earthly Jesus, and how the formation of the apostle concept came about in this connection, we can no longer discern from our extant sources. It is however highly probable that the apostle concept in the sense of the early Christian missionary derives from Jewish-Christian circles and has its roots in these relationships.[3] In the further development we then come to the formation of the pair of concepts 'apostles and prophets', which is already found in Paul (1 Cor. 12:28) but can be documented also elsewhere in the New Testament. The letter to the Ephesians has a special fondness for it (cf. 2:20; 3:5; 4:11); but Luke 11:49 is also interesting. Outside the New Testament the pair of concepts occurs at Did. 11.3-6, where it is a question of criteria for discrimination between true and false prophets. Here it is worthy of note that it is not 'false apostle' but 'false prophet' (ψευδοπροφήτης) that is chosen as the opposite of 'apostle'. Apostle and prophet are here evidently understood as equivalent. The phenomenon of itinerant Christian prophets can however be documented down to the 2nd century (cf. Celsus in Origen, *c. Cels.* VII 9). c) In so far as the reference to prophets does not relate to Old Testament figures (e.g. Lk. 11:49; cf. also Eph. 2:20), the pair of concepts 'apostles and prophets', by making this distinction and giving precedence to the apostles, also points to that tendency in primitive Christianity which would restrict the apostles to the beginnings of the Church and to a particular circle of witnesses to the resurrection. Paul already encountered this tendency, and basically assented to it (cf. 1 Cor. 15:1-11), but with his understanding of himself as an apostle came nevertheless into conflict with it. In the struggle for the recognition of his apostolate - ultimately a singular one - the criteria at the same time emerge by which for him the apostles in the narrower sense are distinguished from all other groups in the Church. Here the most important criterion is not the commission to preach the Gospel among the nations and to found new communities, but personal encounter with the risen Lord (cf. 1 Cor. 9:1; 15:8). That is, the apostle of Jesus Christ is first and above all a witness to the resurrection of Jesus from the dead. The special precedence accorded to Cephas/Peter and 'the Twelve' (1 Cor. 15:5) is evidently grounded in the fact that they were the first to bear witness to the resurrection of Jesus. But how can anyone who - like Paul - never met the earthly Jesus credibly bear witness to the resurrection of Jesus? On what basis is he to recognise that the risen Lord who reveals himself to him is no other than the crucified? Paul was conscious of the resultant problematic character of his apostolate, and therefore even describes himself as 'the least among the apostles' - not only because he had previously persecuted the Church of God (1 Cor. 15:9).

The apostolate in the narrower sense recalls the necessary connection of the Easter event with the Jesus community before Easter. For this reason Luke could not with consistency describe the Paul whom he admired and revered as an apostle in this sense (otherwise only in Acts 14:4, 14). At any rate Paul had his authority for mission among the Gentiles (ἀποστολή) confirmed by the Jerusalem apostles (Gal. 2:8; cf. Rom. 1:5). But for him that was not the basis for his apostleship. His authorisation and call to be an apostle he owed to God Himself (Gal. 1:1). But this was at the same time the basis for the peculiar freedom of his missionary activity, which gave a special stature to the early Christian apostolate which he helped to shape, so that Paul, although he had not been a disciple of the earthly Jesus, could quite simply become for certain circles *the* apostle of Jesus Christ. This could later - as the example of Marcion shows - also lead to a narrowing-down of the apostle concept.

2.2: The bracketing together of the early Christian apostolate and the **pre-Easter Jesus community** finds its clearest expression in the notion of the **twelve apostles**, a combination of the apostle concept with 'the Twelve'. The two elements appear originally to have been independent; for Paul clearly distinguishes them from one another (1 Cor. 15:5-7) and at the same time lets it be seen that not every witness to the resurrection is also an 'apostle'. The formula 'the Twelve' is for the rest a designation especially favoured by Mark for the narrower circle of the disciples of Jesus (cf. G. Schmahl), but also occurs in the other evangelists - not only the Synoptics, but also in John (Jn. 6:67-71) - and originally probably had its roots in the early community's apocalyptic world of ideas (cf. Mt. 19:28/Lk. 22:28-30 from the Sayings source Q). 'This passage does indeed stand in the context of the Sayings source's polemic against Israel, but nevertheless contains the old motif that the righteous at the end of days will sit in judgment over the unrighteous; the twelve here thus represent that true Israel of the righteous' (D. Lührmann, HNT 3, p. 71) in symbolic contrast to the twelve tribes of Israel, the ancient people of God (cf. also Rev. 21:14). The real historical background of the circle of the Twelve can no longer be discovered with any precision. When Paul travels to Jerusalem for the first time, to seek out 'the apostles' (Gal. 1:17ff. - interestingly he does not speak at this point of 'the Twelve'; these appear only in the traditional formula 1 Cor. 15:5), he meets only with Peter and James the Lord's brother - who did not belong to the circle of the Twelve. It seems as if at this early point the institution of 'the Twelve' already belongs to the past. This impression is strengthened by the fact that the four catalogues of the Twelve (Mk. 3:16-19; Mt. 10:2-16; Lk. 6:14-16; Acts 1:13) present 'problems in the history of tradition which can scarcely be resolved' (J. Roloff, TRE 3, p. 434). The fact that the traitor Judas also belonged to the original circle of the Twelve ('one of the twelve' - cf. Mk. 14:10, 20, 43; Mt. 26:14; Lk. 22:3; Jn. 6:71), and - according to Luke's account - was replaced by Matthias (Acts 1:26), tells against the conjecture (G. Klein) that the circle of the Twelve first arose after Easter. Rather it embodies, as a symbol for the eschatological people of God, the elect, the continuity between the pre-Easter and the post-Easter fellowship with Jesus, the Christ. With the decline of apocalyptic expectations in early Christianity, this circle very soon lost its original significance. In place of the office of judge (cf. Rev. 21:14) the office of apostle now moves into the foreground.

The description of the Twelve as 'apostles' occurs first of all in Mark, where it is said: 'And he [= Jesus] *created* the twelve, whom he also named apostles, that they might be with him and that he might send them out to preach and to have authority to drive out the demons' (3:14f.). It is indeed often assumed that the phrase 'whom he also named apostles' is taken over from Lk. 6:13. Yet this assumption is unfounded, especially since Mk. 6:30 in combination with 6:7 confirms that Mark identifies the Twelve with the disciples (μαθηταί; cf. 6:25) and the apostles, even though as a rule he prefers the formula 'the twelve' (cf. 3:16; 4:10, 6:7 and often), whereas Matthew, who also once uses the phrase 'the twelve apostles' (10:2), readily adds the word 'disciples' (μαθηταί; 10:1; 11:1). Mk. 3:14f. is illuminating to the extent that there an explanation of the title apostle is given, for the Twelve are 'sent out' (ἀποστέλλειν) to preach, and they receive authority over the demons. The introductory formula 'he created the twelve' is also worthy of note. The institution here appears as the work of the earthly Jesus, who however in Mark's theology, conceived in post-Easter terms, is no other than the still hidden Messiah. Here he symbolically lays the foundation for his new people of God, and the apostolate is given a basis in the pre-Easter sending-out of the disciples. It is clear that the creation of the Twelve as apostles is stamped by the theology of Mark, which for its part has influenced Matthew and Luke. This means at the same time that it was not Luke who was the creator of the apostolate of the Twelve, as G. Klein thought (p. 203). Luke does indeed carry the identification of the Twelve with the apostles consistently further, but by no means so strictly as is occasionally affirmed (cf. Acts 14:4, 14 with K. Haacker). For that matter, it is striking that in Luke's work the formula 'the twelve apostles' does not occur at all. Instead there is just once the phrase ἕνδεκα ἀπόστολοι, which indicates that Luke understands the twelve apostles as a historic entity (cf. also Mt. 28:16), as a body which must be appropriately supplemented after the death of a member.

Here the criteria according to which the new apostle is to be chosen are illuminating; for in them it becomes particularly clear how Luke in terms of content understands the apostle concept. In the speech which he places in the mouth of Peter it is said: 'Of the men who were together with us in all the time in which the Lord Jesus went in and out among us - beginning from the baptism of John to the day on which he was taken up from us - one of these men must now become a witness of his resurrection with us' (Acts 1:21f.). For Luke it is thus decisive that an apostle was a companion of the earthly Jesus, from his baptism by John to the day of his ascension. Certainly he is also a witness to his resurrection, as Paul requires - and this is especially singled out, but above all he must have been a companion of the earthly Jesus from the beginning of his activity on. There is no word of a mission and corresponding authorisation from the risen Lord. What Luke is aiming at is clear: he is concerned for a chain of eye-witnesses without any gaps, for historical reliability. On this for him the trustworthiness of the witness (μάρτυς) depends, and he regards the apostles as such witnesses of the first order (cf. G. Schneider). Paul, who was called only after the ascension of Jesus, does not meet the criteria of Luke's apostle concept.

By this binding of the apostle concept to the historical Jesus and not only through concentration on the Twelve, who in Acts are mentioned only once (Acts 6:2 - elsewhere Luke speaks of 'the apostles'), Luke restricted the apostle concept to a particular period in history. And it can be foreseen that the age of the apostles will at some time come to an end. But thereby the apostles and their period - and with them indeed Paul too - are given a special position in the Church. With them its history began, and they vouch for the truth of its origins.

2.3: The two centres of gravity in the Pauline and Lucan writings give each a different stamp to the primitive Christian apostle concept, and this at the same time points to developments and changes in the early Christian picture of the apostle, in which Luke as it were appears as a counterpoint to Paul and marks a provisional terminus for the efforts to delimit the apostle concept, which began very early. Apart from these, the term accurs only sporadically in the New Testament, but sometimes with special accents. The opening formulae of 1 and 2 Peter resemble those of the Pauline and Deutero-Pauline letters, in that in each case they present Peter as 'apostle of Jesus Christ'. Over and above that, 2 Peter shows clear criticism of false prophets and teachers (2:1), and here possibly early Christian itinerant apostles and prophets are meant, for the author refers for the strengthening of orthodoxy not only to the 'holy prophets' of the old covenant but also to 'your apostles' (3:2), without naming the latter more precisely. They appear - in the same way as in Jud. 17 - as reliable mediators of the words and commands of the Lord (Christ). In 2 Peter however Paul is mentioned by name (3:15) and even described as 'beloved brother', which after 1:1 can only mean that he is reckoned to the circle of the apostles (in contrast to Acts!). Here we can already see the effort, which is carried further in the 'Apostolic Fathers' (cf. 1 Clem. 5; Ign. *Rom.* 4.3), to bring Peter and Paul together as the two most important apostolic authorities.

The *Letter to the Hebrews* has an emphasis of its own. Only here is Christ himself described as 'apostle' (3:1), while nothing is said of other apostles. Jesus is apostle and high priest, and as Son of God he is at the same time the sole mediator between God and his community, surpassing Moses. According to 1:4ff. he is even superior to all angels. That this ἀπόστολος appears as a redeemer links him with gnostic ideas. In Mani's Kephalaia 'apostle' is one of the titles of honour of the redeemer, who reveals himself in speeches and dialogues to his disciples (cf. O. Michel, *Hebräerbrief*, KEK 11th ed. *ad loc.*). Yet Hebrews appears to be more strongly indebted to Jewish traditions, above all to the Jewish Wisdom literature (Heb. 1:3, for example, clearly alludes to Wisd. 7:26). However, here the boundaries between Jewish-hellenistic (Wisdom) literature, apocalyptic and Gnosis are notoriously fluid. In our context this can only be referred to in passing. Heb. 3:1 however shows at the same time that the apostle concept in early Christianity was not anchored to one meaning, and could be variously interpreted: it could also be brought into association with the concepts of 'angel' and 'priest' - in the sense of divine mediation of salvation - so that from there it could also penetrate into the early christological terminology. In Justin (d. *ca.* 165) we find it later, likewise in association with a whole range of christological titles. In him Christ is described not only as Logos, Son of God and Teacher, but also as ἄγγελος and ἀπόστολος, (*Apol.* I 63.5; cf. also 12.9).

The ideas about Christ as the one 'sent' by God in the *Gospel of John* move in peculiar proximity to Heb. 1:3 (cf. J.A. Bühner, p. 325). However, the Fourth Gospel in this connection avoids the substantive ἀπόστολος, but rather expresses the sending of the Son by the Father by using verbs (ἀποστέλλειν, πέμπειν), as it does the sending of the disciples by the risen Lord (Jn. 20:21: 'As my Father sent me, so I send you'!).

The formulation ὁ πέμψας με (πατήρ) occurs frequently on the lips of Jesus (5:37; 6:44; 7:49 and often). The only place at which the Gospel of John employs the substantive (13:16) is only indirectly connected with Christ. When Jesus there in connection with the foot-washing emphasises: 'Truly, truly, I say to you: A servant is not greater than his master nor an apostle greater than the one who sent him', this sounds rather like criticism of an apostle concept which is on the point of becoming a special title of honour; for it is striking that John otherwise avoids the term.

3: As a **conclusion**, it remains to hold fast the point that there was not a uniform early Christian apostle concept. As a 'neologism' (K. Haacker), it underwent various mintings - including association with Jewish *shaliach* ideas. For Paul, his encounter with and commissioning by the risen Christ had a constitutive significance for his apostleship. No human institution commissioned him, but Christ himself. Like the Old Testament prophets, he saw himself called through a Christophany before Damascus, and appointed as an apostle (cf. Hahn, p. 68). This links him at the same time with the early Christian itinerant apostles and prophets (cf. 1 Cor. 9:1-6; J. Roloff, TRE 3, p. 437).

The charismatic and pneumatic foundation of his apostleship stands however in tension with that of his predecessors (cf. Gal. 1:17), who as adherents (μαθηταί) and travelling companions of Jesus (cf. Acts 1:21f.) first witnessed to and proclaimed the resurrection of their Lord. Over against them Paul describes himself as the last and least of the apostles (1 Cor. 15:9), and thereby lends support to the tendency to limit the circle of the apostles to the oldest witnesses of the resurrection. These are according to 1 Cor. 15:3-5 Cephas and the Twelve, who are then understood by Luke as the real apostles; that for him means: as 'guarantors of the tradition which founded the Church', and connected with that as 'prototypes of church office-bearers' (J. Roloff, TRE 3, p. 442).

While Ephesians and above all the Pastorals elevated Paul into the prototype and norm of apostolic tradition, he could be that for Luke only in a wider and more general sense (cf. Acts 14:4, 14). 2 Peter then sought to link together the two lines of tradition, which was facilitated by the open manner of speaking of "the apostles" - even in Luke. Here the path is marked out in the early Church which in the end led to the canonisation of both traditions. But this is only to describe the better known part of a path which is altogether very tangled and full of conflict. For the adherents and champions of an apostolate charismatically and pneumatically defined, with whom Paul already had to contend in Corinth and who were certainly present in other places, accompanied the Church's path - sometimes as gnostic or apocalyptically oriented groups - with their own traditions and theological peculiarities (and with their own revelation documents), and caused the Christianity of the early centuries to appear as an extremely variegated movement (cf. for example R.L. Wilken, *The Christians: As the Romans saw them*, 1984)

Notes

1. The concept of the apostle in primitive Christianity

1. The earliest evidence is in the so-called 'Apostolic Fathers': Ign. *Trall.* preface and *Mart.*

Pol. 16.2. See below pp. 25f.
2. In the literature the form is usually the masculine 'Junias'. This is, however, a later alteration aimed at removing the situation, evidently felt offensive, that here a woman is described by Paul as an apostle. But even in John Chrysostom (4th cent.) it is said: 'To be an apostle is something great. But to be famed among the apostles - consider what great praise this is. They [Junia and Andronicus] were prominent because of their works and their activity. How great then must the wisdom of this woman have been, that she was considered worthy of the title of apostle' (*Hom. 32 in Rom.*, PG 60, 669f.). Cf. on this: B. Brooten, '"Junia... hervorragend unter den Aposteln", Röm. 16,7', in E. Moltmann-Wendel (ed.), *Frauenbefreiung*, Munich 1982, 158ff.; G. Lohfink, 'Weibliche Diakone im Neuen Testament', in G. Dautzenberg (ed.), *Die Frau im Urchristentum* (QD 95), Freiburg 1983, 320-338, esp. pp. 327-332; S. Heine, *Frauen der frühen Christenheit*, Göttingen [2]1987, 49f. and 96ff.
3. Cf. W. Schneemelcher in his introduction, NTApo[3] II, p. 29: 'According to the fragmentary information about them which can still be gathered from Acts these Hellenists (cf. Acts 6) were the people who first applied themselves to missionary work. From the term ἀπόστολος it may be supposed that this title came into vogue in this circle and that thus first of all it denoted simply a special group of missionaries.'

2. The apostles as bearers of the tradition and mediators of revelation

Literature: 1. *General:* W. Bauer, *Rechtgläubigkeit und Ketzerei im ältesten Christentum* (BHTh 10), 1934; [2]1964 with appendices, ed. G. Strecker; [3]1971 (ET *Orthodoxy and Heresy in Earliest Christianity*, 1971); H. Koester/J.M. Robinson, *Trajectories through Early Christianity*, 1971; U.B. Müller, *Zur frühchristlichen Theologiegeschichte. Judenchristentum und Paulinismus in Kleinasien an der Wende vom ersten zum zweiten Jahrhundert n. Chr.*, 1976; K. Koschorke, *Die Polemik der Gnostiker gegen das kirchliche Christentum* (NHS 12), 1978; K. Rudolph, *Die Gnosis*, 1978, [2]1980 (Lit.) (ET *Gnosis*, 1983); K.-W. Tröger (ed.), *Altes Testament - Fruhjudentum - Gnosis*, 1980; G. Strecker, *Das Judenchristentum in den Pseudoklementinen* (TU 70), [2]1981 (rev. and enlarged ed.); id., art. 'Judenchristentum', TRE 17, 1988, 310-325; H. Conzelmann, *Heiden - Juden - Christen* (BHTh 62), 1981.

2. *On individual Apostles:* a) *Paul:* E. Aleith, *Das Paulusverständnis in der alten Kirche* (BZNW 18), 1937; W. Schneemelcher, 'Paulus in der griechischen Kirche des 2. Jahrhunderts', ZKG 75, 1964, 1-20 (= id., *Ges. Aufs. z. NT und z. Patristik*, Anal. Vlatadon 22, 1974, 154-181); E.H. Pagels, *The Gnostic Paul. Gnostic Exegesis of the Pauline Letters*, 1975; H.M. Schenke, 'Das Weiterwirken des Paulus und die Pflege seines Erbes durch die Paulus-Schule', NTS 21, 1975, 505-518; A. Lindemann, *Paulus im ältesten Christentum* (BHTh 58), 1979 (Lit.!); E. Dassmann, *Der Stachel im Fleisch. Paulus in der frühchristlichen Literatur bis Irenäus*, 1979; G. Lüdemann, *Paulus, der Heidenapostel* (FRLANT 123), 1980; id., *Antipaulinismus im frühen Christentum* (FRLANT 130), 1983; K. Koschorke, 'Paulus in den Nag-Hammadi-Texten', ZThK 78, 1981, 177-205; J. Jervell, 'Paulus in der Apostelgeschichte und in der Geschichte des Urchristentums', NTS 32, 1986, 378-392; O. Merk, 'Paulus-Forschung 1936-1985', ThR 53, 1988, 1-81.

b) *Peter:* A. v. Harnack, 'Petrus im Urteil der Kirchenfeinde des Altertums', in Festg. f. K. Müller, 1922, 1-6; O. Cullmann, *Petrus. Jünger - Apostel - Märtyrer. Das historische und das theologische Petrusproblem*, [2]1960 (ET *Peter. Disciple - Apostle - Martyr*, 1953); E. Dinkler, 'Die Petrus-Rom-Frage', ThR 25, 1959, 189-230, 289-335 (Lit.); W. Dietrich, *Das Petrusbild der lukanischen Schriften* (BWANT V/14), 1972; R.E. Brown/K.P. Donfried/J. Reumann (eds.), *Peter in the New Testament*, 1973; R. Pesch, *Simon-Petrus. Geschichte und*

Bedeutung des ersten Jüngers Jesu Christi (PuP 15), 1980; K. Berger, 'Unfehlbare Offenbarung. Petrus in der gnostischen und apokalyptischen Offenbarungsliteratur', *Kontinuität und Einheit* (FS F. Mußner), 1981, pp. 261-326; T.V. Smith, *Petrine Controversies in Early Christianity* (WUNT II/15), 1985 (Lit.).

c) *John and others:* W.v. Loewenich, *Das Johannesverständnis im 2. Jahrhundert* (BZNW 13), 1932; E. Ruckstuhl, 'Das Johannesevangelium und die Gnosis', in *Neues Testament und Geschichte* (FS O. Cullmann), 1970, 143-156; O. Cullmann, *Der johanneische Kreis. Zum Ursprung des Johannesevangeliums*, 1975 (ET *The Johannine Circle*, 1976); K. Wengst, *Häresie und Orthodoxie im Spiegel des ersten Johannesbriefes*, 1976; id., *Bedrängte Gemeinde und verherrlichter Christus* (BThSt 5), [2]1983; G. Strecker, 'Die Anfänge der johanneischen Schule', NTS 32, 1986, 31-47. *Andrew:* P.M. Peterson, *Andrew, Brother of Simon Peter, His History and his Legends*, 1958; F. Dvornik, *The Idea of Apostolicity in Byzantium and the Legend of the Apostle Andrew* (DOS 4), 1958 (cf. on this M. Hornschuh, ZKG 71, 1960, 138-142). *Judas Iscariot:* W. Vogler, *Judas Iskarioth. Untersuchungen zu Tradition und Redaktion von Texten des Neuen Testaments und außerkanonischen Schriften* (ThA 42), 1983; [2]1985 (Lit.); G. Schwarz, *Jesus und Judas. Aramaistische Untersuchungen zur Jesus-Judas-Überlieferung* (BWANT 123), 1988 (Lit.). d) *Women:* L. Zscharnack, *Der Dienst der Frauen in den ersten Jahrhunderten der christlichen Kirche*, 1902; R. Albrecht, *Das Leben der heiligen Makrina auf dem Hintergrund der Thekla-Traditionen* (FKDG 38), 1986; S. Heine, *Frauen der frühen Christenheit*, [2]1987.

1. Characteristic features of the understanding of the apostle in early Christianity: The event of Easter is not accessible in any other way than through the testimony of the apostles, the witnesses to the resurrection. For the Christian community and its preaching, just as much depends upon the credibility of these witnesses as upon the event of the resurrection itself, through which the fate of the earthly Jesus, his preaching and his works, and above all his death upon the cross, underwent an interpretation that was repeatedly shaped afresh, that in this Jesus God's salvation for this world lies once and for all determined, that he is the promised Messiah and redeemer of the world. In the apostolic message the preaching of the resurrection of Jesus and the interpretation of this unique event in history as an act of God for the world created and beloved by him belong inseparably together. To this the Church owes its existence, and to hand it on unadulterated is its abiding task in history. This handing on, which aims at acceptance in faith, is however for its part something wrought by God. The risen Lord himself selected his messengers - not only from the circle of his disciples, as the example of Paul shows - invested them with power through the gift of his Spirit, and sent them into the world. The apostles are thus not solely the direct eye-witnesses of a historical event, essential for its reliable transmission, but at the same time ambassadors (cf. 2 Cor. 5:20) and interpreters of this event, which has overpowered them themselves and which they now hand on with the authority of the Spirit of God as a power for bliss (cf. Rom. 1:16). They are messengers of salvation, bearers of divine revelation (cf. 2 Cor. 12:1ff.; Mt. 16:17), and they vouch for the truth of their message with their own persons - not a few at the cost of their lives.

The abundance of apostolic witnesses and testimonies, however, raises the question of the credibility and trustworthiness of individual voices, especially since from the beginning there was dispute over the witness to Christ and the interpretation of the Easter event. Here there already appears within the New

Testament literature a particular tension between the charismatically determined apostolate of Paul and the historically anchored apostolate of Luke, which is bound to the person of the earthly Jesus and understood as eye-witness authority in a historical sense. This tension is already reflected in the conflict between Peter and Paul, the first and the last witnesses to the resurrection of Jesus according to 1 Cor. 15:3ff., in connection with the question of the legitimacy of Paul's apostleship. The tension is further intensified by the fact that Paul previously had persecuted the community of Christ, indeed even Christ himself (Acts 9:5; Gal. 1:13; 1 Cor. 15:9 and often). In the Jewish-Christian literature especially there appears a clear coolness towards Paul - for example among the 'Ebionites' and Encratites (cf. Origen, *c. Cels.* V 65) - which can be aggravated into a vehement anti-Paulinism, as in the pseudo-Clementines (cf. G. Strecker; also E. Dassmann, 283ff.; G. Lüdemann, *Antipaulinismus*). In writings of a Jewish-Christian slant, James the Lord's brother often appears as a special authority alongside Peter and the Twelve, in addition to the apostles proper. On the other hand there were other circles, including gnostic groups, which particularly revered Paul (cf. E. Pagels; K. Koschorke). Marcion sees in Paul *the* apostolic authority *par excellence*, but a 'Paul' who has been 'cleansed of all Jewish falsifications'. His Paulinism is emphatically directed against a combination of the Christian with the Jewish tradition, and thus stands in contrast to the anti-Paulinism of Jewish-Christian or anti-gnostic circles.

The incorporation of Paul into the recognised apostolic tradition, which was understood as normative, was one of the most important decisions of the early Church. The way runs from the so-called Deutero-Paulines through Luke's Acts, the Pastorals and 2 Peter to 1 Clement, in which the two great martyrs Peter and Paul are commemorated side by side (1 Clem. 5); from this, among other things, the special position of the apostolic foundation in Rome was then derived (cf. Irenaeus, *adv. Haer.* III 3.2; Tertullian, *Praescr. haer.* 36). The incorporation of Paul finds its specific expression in the canonising of the Pauline and Deutero-Pauline letters by the Church. In Alexandria Hebrews also was regarded as a work 'of the Apostle' (cf., e.g., Dionysius of Alexandria ap. Euseb. *HE* VI 41.6; also Clement of Alexandria ap. Euseb. *HE* VI 14.2f.).

The mention of Paul in the anti-gnostic Epistula Apostolorum (see vol. I, pp.267f) is worthy of note. His unique position among the apostles is not however passed over in silence - just as in Luke's Acts. Paul is also mentioned in the Acts of Peter (c.1-3), but here he is only a 'fellow-apostle' of Peter (c.10). The unique position of Paul, which E. Dassmann describes as 'a thorn in the flesh' of early Christianity, can already be recognised from the fact that he and he alone is occasionally described as 'the apostle' (cf. G.W.H. Lampe, *Lexicon* 212), whereas by 'the apostles' as a rule 'the Twelve' from the circle of Jesus' disciples are meant, although neither the number nor any definite list of names was settled.

2. The number of the apostles fluctuates in the tradition of the early Church, as already in the New Testament. The figure of twelve, rooted in apocalyptic tradition, occurs frequently in early Christian literature - e.g. Justin, *Dial.* 42; Irenaeus, *Adv. Haer.* I 3.2; 18.4; Tertullian, *adv. Marc.* IV 13.1 and often - even where, from a historical point of view, the reference should be to *eleven* disciples or apostles (e.g. Gos.Peter 59, Asc. Is. 3.17 and often; Kerygma Petri. Cf. Mt 28:16; Acts 1:26 and often). In gnostic and Manichean literature there are references to a Gospel of the Twelve (cf. vol. I, pp.374ff.), where the title is evidently intended to underline the comprehensive revelation content of this document. Epiphanius (*Pan.* 30.13.2f.) quotes from the Gospel of the Ebionites a saying of Jesus, in which after the call of eight disciples who are mentioned by name he says: 'You therefore I will to be twelve apostles for a testimony unto Israel' (see vol. I, p.170). Occasionally there is reference also to seventy apostles (cf. Lk 10:1ff - or to seventy-two); this has left its deposit in a 'Gospel of the Seventy' (see vol. I, p.380).

For outsiders, the number of the apostles of Jesus was by no means fixed. The Platonist Celsus speaks of ten or eleven (cf. Origen, *c. Cels.* II 46 and I 62), and in the Babylonian Talmud five disciples of Jesus are mentioned by name: 'Matthai, Nagai, Nezer, Buni, Thoda' (Sanhedrin 43a). A decisive factor here was certainly which Christian group the respective informants had met with, or what they regarded as representative for Christianity. It is in keeping with the manifold character of early Christian communities that individual apostles enjoyed a special veneration in particular communities; these were, in addition to Peter and Paul, especially John and Thomas. In this connection it deserves to be noted that not all early Christian writers are described as apostles in the narrower sense. The apostles Matthew (= Levi) and John, who was identified with the 'beloved disciple', are indeed considered the authors of the Gospels of Matthew and John, but for Mark and Luke the title is not affirmed. They are simply described as companions and associates of the apostles, Mark as the associate of Peter and Luke as the companion of Paul. Conversely, the title 'gospel' does not by any means guarantee the apostolicity of a revelation document. Rather we hear also of a Gospel of Basilides (see vol. I, pp.397f.) and one of the Persian 'apostle' Mani (see ibid., pp.404ff.,411f.). The gnostic 'Gospel of Truth' (NHC I 3) completely renounces any apostolic legitimation, and indeed any historical anchoring of its message.

In Church tradition the apostles, and above all the special group of the Twelve, rank as guarantors and bearers of reliable revelation. Whether the oldest manual of church order, the Didache, already laid claim to have been written by the apostles we cannot say with any certainty. The Epistula Apostolorum, the Syriac Didascalia and the Apostolic Church Order, however, are all considered as having been composed by the twelve apostles.

3: This does not mean that there was a definite *list of names* to match the number twelve. In the New Testament already the lists of apostles differ (see above, pp. 10f.), not only in the sequence but also in the stock of the names. The difference appears most clearly with the name *Thaddaeus* (Mk. 3:18; Mt. 10:3 with the variant Lebbaeus), in place of which *Judas son of James* appears in Luke (6:16; Acts 1:13). Beyond that there are gradations and differences of rank in the circle of the apostles. Simon - surnamed Peter (or Cephas) - has an exalted position, and not only in Jewish-Christian circles, as the first to be called and the spokesman of the group (cf. Mt. 16:13-29 par.), but also as the first witness to the resurrection (cf. 1 Cor. 15:5). A special position is occupied also by the brothers John and James, the sons of

Zebedee, who are once described as 'sons of thunder' (Mk. 3:17). Together with Peter they are eye-witnesses of the raising of the daughter of Jairus (Mk. 5:37; Lk. 8:51) and of the transfiguration of Jesus (Mk. 9:2 par.). In the garden of Gethsemane they are likewise singled out from the circle of the disciples as the closest associates of Jesus (Mk. 14:35; Mt. 26:37). It is therefore not surprising that their names appear in most apostle lists of the early Church, even the incomplete ones.

There are also, however, notable discrepancies. In contrast to the Synoptics, Andrew is named in the Fourth Gospel before his brother Peter, and after them Philip and Nathanael (Jn. 1:40ff.). In the Epistula Apostolorum (c. 2; see vol. I, p.252) the list begins with the names: John, Thomas, Peter, Andrew, etc., just as in the Apostolic Church Order. In the gnostic Pistis Sophia (c.42-43; GCS 45, pp. 44f.), Philip, Thomas and Matthew are named as the witnesses upon whose testimony the reliability of the revelation of Jesus rests - probably an allusion to the Gospels of Thomas and Philip, treasured and handed down in gnostic circles (see vol. I, pp.110ff.; 179ff.). The Nag Hammadi discovery has brought to light a series of writings which show how much reference there was in gnostic circles to apostolic traditions - or better: revelations. This holds not only for Thomas, who also enjoyed high repute among the Manicheans, and Philip, but also for Peter and Paul (cf. NHC V 2; VII 3 etc.).

4: The apostles however, in the view of the early Church, are not only guarantors of reliable tradition for the life and doctrine of the Church, they are in particular also *bearers of the mission* and exemplary in their life and death. The gnostic Heracleon does indeed point to the fact that four of the disciples did not die as martyrs (cf. Clem. Alex. *Strom.* IV 71.3), but that did not prevent the places of apostolic activity from becoming just as revered (cf. Tertullian, *Praescr. Haer.* 36.1) as the graves of the apostles. In Rome it was the graves of Peter and Paul (cf. Euseb. *HE* II 25.7), in Ephesus that of John and in Hierapolis that of Philip and his two virgin daughters (so Polycrates of Ephesus, end of 2nd cent., in Euseb. *HE* V 24.2f.).

The charge for mission is from the beginning constitutive for the apostolic office, and not only in Paul. The New Testament mission charges (Mt. 28:19f.; Lk. 24:47f.; Acts 1:8; 10:42) are taken up in the early Christian literature and handed on. Thus it is said in the Syriac Didascalia (J. Flemming, TU 25.2, 1904, p. 77): 'Jesus Christ sent us out, the twelve, to teach the (chosen) people and the Gentiles' (cf. also Epist. Apostolorum 30). Note should be taken of the special position of the people of Israel within the universalistically understood mission charge, which preserves the recollection of the charge to the Twelve (cf. Mt. 19:28 = Lk. 22:30; Barn. 8.3), but was variously interpreted in the course of history. In Jewish-Christian circles the priority of Israel was given prominence, in others the mission among the Gentile nations. In the Kerygma Petri (Clem. Alex. *Strom.* VI 5.43) Peter reports about a word of the Lord, that during the first twelve years the apostles should give ear to the desire for repentance and forgiveness in Israel, but then should turn to the 'world'. In an appendix to the Pistis Sophia (GCS 45, p. 254) we find the sentence: 'They went out by threes to the four regions of the heavens and preached the Gospel of the kingdom of God in the whole world' - an indication of how concretely the universal mission charge was understood. The idea was also widely spread that the apostles divided the world into twelve parts (Act. Thomae 1; Syr. Didascalia, J. Flemming, op. cit., p. 120) and apportioned to each a mission sphere of his own. Eusebius (*HE* III 1) reports from Origen's commentary on Genesis (*ca.* 229) that the apostles received these territories by lot: Thomas the land of the Parthians, Andrew Scythia, John Asia, where after a long sojourn he died in Ephesus. It is said of Peter that in Pontus, Galatia, Bithynia, Cappadocia and Asia he preached to the Jews in the Diaspora (cf. 1 Peter 1:1), and then came to Rome where - in accordance with his wish - he was crucified head downwards (one of the oldest testimonies for this tradition). The last to be named is Paul, who 'had preached the Gospel of Christ from Jerusalem to Illyria' (Rom. 15:19) and later suffered martyrdom in Rome under Nero[1].

Three things in particular are worthy of note in this tradition: 1) only five apostles are named, not twelve, without any indication that the list is incomplete. And only with Peter and Paul is there any attempt to link with New Testament writings. 2) It is the same apostles for whom the oldest relatively extensive apostle-romances, the so-called Acts of apostles, have been handed down; through their legendary reports these have impressed the image of these apostles as preachers and wonder-workers in popular piety. Later this left its traces in iconography also. 3) The sequence of the names, finally, is unusual. However, there is a similar series - with Thomas and Andrew at the head - in the Pistis Sophia (c. 136; GCS 45, p. 232). This points to gnostic associations, which are also recognisable in the Acts themselves. These are moreover the same Acts of apostles 'which the Manichees, rejecting the New Testament Acts, incorporated into their canon' (P. Nagel, 'Die apokryphen Apostelakten des 2. und 3. Jahrhunderte in der manichäischen Literatur', in *Gnosis und NT*, ed. K.W. Tröger, 1973, pp. 149-182; quotation from p. 152), and which had been in use among them at least since the 4th century.

It is admittedly not certain whether the note from Origen transmitted by Eusebius reliably reproduces the former's information or has been expanded (cf. A. v. Harnack, TU 42.3, 1918, pp. 14ff.). But it shows the state of Eusebius' information, which was later expanded by two further names by Rufinus in his translation and revision of Eusebius' *Church History* (*HE* I 9f.). According to this Matthew went to Ethiopia and Bartholomew to *India citeriora*. We may also refer to the fact that the apostle Thomas according to Eusebius' account went to Parthia, while in the Acts of Thomas he appears as the apostle of India.

The transmission problems of these acts, the 'travels' (περίοδοι) of the apostles, as Photius calls them (Bibl. cod. 114), can only be hinted at here (see below, pp. 75ff.). They indicate in their own way the difficulties of describing the early Christian picture of the apostle. In these texts, however, we can recognise the picture of the early Christian communities, as it was delineated and further developed in the 2nd and 3rd centuries, the image of the wonder-working and authoritatively preaching itinerant apostle, with sometimes very personal features. Thus according to the Acts of Paul and Thecla Paul travels about with the virgin Thecla, who for her part accomplishes miracles. He himself is there described as 'a man small of stature, with a bald head and crooked legs, in a good state of body, with eye-brows meeting and nose somewhat hooked, full of friendliness' (APlThe, c. 3). It is striking that the descriptions in the Acts of Paul do not draw upon Luke's Acts, and the same holds for the Acts of Peter. Whether and to what extent these Acts report historically reliable material in addition to prodigious legends is often hard to say; and the boundaries between orthodoxy and heresy are likewise fluid. Nevertheless the assessment of these texts in ancient Church literature changed only gradually from benevolent use (Tertullian; Hippolytus - sometimes with certain reservations) through a certain mistrust (e.g. in Euseb. *HE* III 3.5) to rejection after the closing of the canon - probably also because of the partiality of the Manichees for these texts (cf. P. Nagel, op. cit., 154; cf. also Schäferdiek below, pp. 87ff.). At the time of their origin they show clearly how manifold the apostle picture of the early Christian communities was, quite apart from the personal peculiarities of individual apostles. The (ascetic) life here played a role just as important as the (martyr's) death - sometimes depicted in separate Acts. This aspect was in addition a necessary element in the legitimising of the early Christian apostolic tradition.

5. On individual apostles: The apostle picture of the early Church is on the one hand the picture of (twelve) apostles as a fellowship of disciples and messengers of Jesus, with the special charge for mission (among Israel) and for the trustworthy handing-on of the message of the revelation of God in Jesus Christ as the message of salvation for the world. On the other hand, this picture only becomes concrete in the life and work of the individual apostles. In the abundant and many-faceted images of these individual apostles which the early Church created and handed on, the picture of the apostle once again takes on a special stamp. At the same time, in these varied and mutually conflicting images and in the special reverence for particular apostles there is reflected the relationship of the early Christian groups and communites. Here it is also a question of the reception and influence of New Testament traditions, which themselves are not always uniform (cf. the portrait of Paul which emerges from his own letters with the Lucan picture of Paul), together with other Church traditions from the first centuries of Christian history, in a peculiar combination of historical recollection and theological interpretation, which is characteristic for the texts at our disposal. It is not possible here to enter in detail into the developments mentioned, or the different apostle portraits. Not only is our source material too extensive, but its investigation is still only in its beginnings. Even now the boundaries between the canonical writings of the New Testament and the apocryphal and extra-biblical traditions are too sharply drawn for us to be aware of the overlapping and widely influential developments in the early Church and recognise that the process of the formation of the canon and the growth of the Church are connected, taking both theological and historical aspects into account. Only in two areas - apart from single studies - are there major and continued investigations in this direction, namely in the study of Peter and of Paul.

a) In the study of *Peter*, mention should be made above all of the works of R. Pesch (*Simon-Petrus*, 1980) and K. Berger ('Unfehlbare Offenbarung. Petrus in der gnostischen und apokalyptischen Offenbarungsliteratur', 1981). Pesch in his book has not only investigated the development of the picture of Peter in the New Testament writings and inquired into its theological and historical background - in the Synoptics, in John, where Peter appears as subordinated to the beloved disciple, in Paul and in the Petrine letters (pp. 136-152) - but has also followed up the apocryphal traditions (pp. 152-162). The New Testament at various places knows Peter as spokesman of the apostles, but also as the one who denied his Lord, as the 'rock' on which Christ founded his Church, as a witness of the resurrection, but also as one of those who fell asleep in Gethsemane, as ebullient and also as weak in faith. The conflict with Paul also shows him as profoundly a man. This picture - in detail one of many facets - is reinforced by the indication that Peter was married (cf. Mk. 1:29-31 par.; 1 Cor. 9:5) and had children (cf. Mk. 10:29); in the Acts of Peter there is reference to a daughter. Origen however emphasises that Peter after his call forsook his wife and children (*Comm. in Mt.* tom. XV 21 = GCS 40, p. 411). In gnostic literature he appears at times as an outspoken foe of women (Pistis Sophia c. 72, p. 104; Gos. Thom. log. 114), of whom Mary stands in awe.

On the other side - as K. Berger has underlined with extensive source material (cf. the list, pp. 261-265) - Peter does indeed rank as 'a human witness and mediator of revelation' (p. 268), but at the same time he is 'the type *par excellence* of the initiated' (p. 269), who in the course of early Church history is united with the episcopal office in a claim for infallibility over against mere knowledge and discernment. In the New Testament already the first traces can be found of the way in which the reception of revelation and leadership in the Church flowed together in his person (e.g. Jn. 21). In gnostic literature, in contrast, Peter recedes behind Thomas (Gos. Thom., log. 13) or even John. The controversy with Gnosis is reflected, on the basis of popular piety, in the Acts of Peter from the end of the 2nd century. Here Peter appears as a miracle-worker who makes dogs and suckling infants speak, drives out demons, raises the dead, and so on, and in this manner unmasks Simon Magus as a deceiver and messenger of the devil, and overcomes him. The Pseudo-Clementines belong in the same tradition. The gnostics come to terms with Peter in their own way (cf. NHC VII 3; on this see K. Koschorke, *Polemik*, 1978, pp. 32f.). For them Peter is not the beginning of the episcopate, but the origin of true Gnosis, out of which Christian 'brotherhood' develops. The Church's portrait of Peter, in which office and knowledge form a unity, from which springs the authority to forgive a penitent his sins, is for them a false picture. The conflict over the correct portrait of Peter is an expression of the debate about orthodoxy and heresy in this period. And since in the conviction of the Church the apostolic heritage of Peter lived on in the Roman episcopate, Rome became the bulwark of orthodoxy in this debate.

The Petrine tradition found an ally in the Clementine, in that in the Pseudo-Clementines from the 3rd century not only is the struggle against Simon Magus continued, but his person is made the basis - from Jewish-Christian tradition - for the attack against Paul. The title of apostle is already denied to Paul in the Kerygmata Petri, one of the basic documents for the Pseudo-Clementines, because he did not belong to the Twelve. Even his vision of Christ is contested. On the other hand Peter is recognised (*Hom.* XVII 18.1-2; 19.4; cf. also Berger, 307ff.) as a visionary and recipient of divine revelation (Mt. 16:17). It is however to be noted that not only must the gnostic picture of Peter be distinguished from that of the Church; the eastern must also be distinguished from the western (Latin) portrait.

b) Alongside the picture of Peter, that of Paul has been the subject of recent major investigations which also take the extra-canonical tradition into account (esp. E. Dassmann; A. Lindemann). Since Paul never personally saw the earthly Jesus, and before his conversion even persecuted the Christian community, his position among the apostles is disputed from the beginning. In the Jewish-Christian tradition reservations against Paul as apostle to the Gentiles live on (Irenaeus, *adv. Haer.* I 26.2; III 15.1; Origen, *c. Cels.* V 65; Euseb. *HE* III 27.4 and often). The special veneration accorded to him by Marcion probably contributed to the fact that Tertullian described him as 'apostle of the heretics' (*adv. Marc.* III 5.4). The gnostics also, however, esteemed Paul as a visionary and bearer of special revelations. But it is said of Basilides that he 'and his true son and disciple Isidore say that *Matthias* spoke to them secret words which he heard from the Saviour when he was taught privately ' (Hippol. *Ref.* VII 20.1). Of Valentinus however his adherents affirmed that he heard a certain Theudas, a disciple of Paul (Clem Alex. VII 17.106). This does confirm that Paul was recognised as an apostolic authority in gnostic circles. But this holds not for him alone, but also for Peter, John, Thomas, Matthias and other apostles. He plays a special role only with Marcion and his followers.

If in gnostic tradition Paul ranks above all as a bearer and mediator of divine revelations, in the devotional literature of the Gentile Christian communities he appears as a missionary, wonder-worker and martyr, especially in the Acts of Paul. But the author of the Acts of Paul (end of 2nd century) is just as little concerned for the teaching of the apostle, which he set down in his letters, as is the Epistula Apostolorum, which is intended to secure recognition in the Church for the activity of the apostle to the Gentiles, or the Acts of Peter; the concern is rather with his person, which is 'hagiographically taken over for popular piety' (Dassmann, p. 279). It must however, be added that he sets himself against false teachings, above all in a fictitious writing, the so-called 3 Corinthians (Act. Paul., section 8, see below, pp. 254ff.), in which the basic doctrines of the Christian faith, the creation of the world by God, the incarnation of Christ and the resurrection of the flesh, are defended against gnostic and Marcionite views. The preaching of continence and of the resurrection appears already at the beginning of the Acts of Paul (cf. 3.5 with the appended beatitudes) as the core of Paul's doctrine - sometimes linking up with New Testament traditions, but without any need being felt to convey an authentic and historically reliable picture of the apostle to the Gentiles. Paul is here only one of the apostolic witnesses who as a body vouch for the trustworthiness of the Church's doctrine. Irenaeus appears to have been the first to rediscover Paul the *theologian* in his original significance for the Church. In him the Pauline writings attain to canonical rank, and that in their uncut pre-Marcionite form (cf. *adv. Haer.* III 12.12) but at the same time with special consideration of the Pastorals (cf. *adv. Haer.* I 1, preface). By casting back to the original Paul tradition, Irenaeus marks out in advance the way which determined the further development of the canon. The historical beginnings are given a normative significance for the life and doctrine of the Church.

c) It is scarcely possible to obtain an authentic picture of the apostle *John* from the New Testament writings and early Christian literature. Comparison of the Gospel of John, the letters, and the Apocalypse of John led already in the early Church to the conviction that the author of the Apocalypse might indeed be called John, but could not be identical with the author of the other writings (cf. Dionysius of Alexandria ap. Euseb. *HE* VII 25). For the Muratorian Canon however (9ff.) all these writings derive from the same author! Special attention was accorded in the early Church to John the son of Zebedee, who is frequently mentioned in the Synoptic Gospels, in Paul (Gal.

2:9) and in Acts and evidently occupied a prominent role in the early Church, especially after the early death of his brother James (*ca.* 42 A.D.; cf. Acts 12:1f.). Papias of Hierapolis distinguishes from him a presbyter of the same name (Euseb.*HE* III 39.3), and Eusebius traces the tradition of two graves of John in Ephesus back to the two bearers of this name (*HE* III 39.6). The accounts of the death of John the theologian, who generally ranks as author of the Fourth Gospel, are perplexing. Papias reports (according to Philip of Side; cf. U. Körtner, *Papias von Hierapolis*, 1983, 63f.) that like his brother James he was slain by the Jews. Beside this there is a widespread tradition that he died at an advanced age (Tertullian, *de Anima* 50; Clem. Alex. *Quis div. salv.* 42.2; cf. also Iren. *adv. Haer.* II 22.5; III 4; Act. Joh. 115 etc.). Origen speaks of a tradition which knows of an exile of John to Patmos (*Comm. in Mt.* XVI 6), but this is evidently modelled on Rev. 1:9. The gnostic Heracleon however, the earliest commentator on the Gospel of John, evidently knows of a martyrdom of John; for he names four disciples who died a natural death, but not John (cf. Clem. Alex. *Strom.* IV 71.3). Aphraates (417.10) expressly mentions James and John among the apostolic martyrs. Their two names also appear side by side in the Syriac and in the Armenian martyrologium.

Similar difficulty attaches to the problem of the authorship of the Fourth Gospel, of which it was occasionally affirmed that it was composed by the heretic Cerinthus (so the Roman presbyter Gaius; cf. K. Wengst, *Häresie*, 1976; on Cerinthus, esp. pp. 24-34). On the other hand that mysterious figure who in John's Gospel is described as 'the disciple whom Jesus loved' (Jn. 13:21ff.; 19:25ff., 35; 20:21ff.; 21:1ff.) was apparently already identified with John at an early date, and this had a decisive influence on the later canonising of this document.

In the Acts of John it is said that John was called by Jesus while still a young man (113), and his virginity is repeatedly emphasised. In the Pistis Sophia Jesus says: 'Mary Magdalene and John the virgin will be superior to all my disciples' (c. 96, GCS 45, p. 148). And in fact John as a close associate of Jesus enjoys a high esteem in gnostic circles.

On the other side Irenaeus (*adv. Haer.* III 11.1) writes that John composed the Gospel against Cerinthus and the Nicolaitans. In the Muratori Canon (10) it was bishops who induced John to write, while in the *Hypotyposes* of Clement of Alexandria (Euseb., *HE* VI 14.7) it is said: 'Last of all John, knowing that the human nature had (already) been set forth in the Gospels, at the urging of his friends and inspired by the Spirit composed a spiritual Gospel'. Since the traditions attaching to the various bearers of the name John in the early Church have evidently mingled with one another, it is no longer possible to obtain a clear picture of the apostle.

d) In the Pistis Sophia, *Philip*, *Thomas* and *Matthew* (Matthias?) are charged by the risen Lord with the task of writing 'all the words which I shall say and do, and all the things which you shall see' (c. 42, GCS 45, p. 44; cf. c. 43, p. 45). They are to be the officially appointed witnesses of his message. The Gospels of Philip and Thomas then also rank in gnostic circles as central revelation documents. These three are already mentioned by Papias (c. 140) in the preface to his κυριακῶν ἐξηγήσεις as bearers of apostolic tradition (ap. Euseb. *HE* III 39.4). While the fragment from the Gospel of Philip quoted by Epiphanius (*Pan.* 26.2-3; see vol. I, p. 180. This passage is not contained in the Coptic Gospel of Philip from Nag Hammadi [NHC II 3, vol. I, pp. 179ff.]!) shows Encratite features, Philip elsewhere is usually regarded as married and as the father of daughters (cf. Papias ap. Euseb. *HE* III 39.9; Clem. Alex. ap Euseb. *HE* III 30.1). Polycrates of Ephesus mentions Philip, one of the twelve apostles, 'who sleeps in Hierapolis with his two daughters who grew old as virgins, while another daughter, who walked in the Holy Spirit, rests in Ephesus' (ap. Euseb. *HE* III 31.3). The reference to the daughters recalls Acts 21: 8f., but the daughters there are those of Philip 'the evangelist' (cf. Acts 6:5; 8:5ff.). Here evidently a mixing of the traditions has taken place.

The *Thomas* tradition is broader than with Philip, and to some extent is still living in the eastern Churches. Thomas is mentioned not only in Papias and in the Pistis Sophia (see above), but also in the Epistula Apostolorum 2 (13); 11 (22) (see vol. I,, pp. 252f.; 255f.), where he is named with Peter and Andrew (!) as one who doubted the resurrection of Jesus (cf. Jn. 20:20, 27). Over and above that he ranks as the author of the Apocalypse of Thomas (see below, pp. 748ff.) and the Gospel of Thomas (see vol. I, pp. 110ff.). There are extensive reports about him - developed in novellistic fashion - in the Acts of Thomas (see below, pp. 322ff.), where the apostle - as in Syrian tradition generally - is described as *Judas Thomas* and after a gnostic pattern ranks as the bearer and mediator of special secret revelations (Act. Thom. c. 39). In addition he is treated as twin brother of the Redeemer, and therefore bears the nickname Didymus. In the older tradition Thomas is held to be the missionary of Parthia (Origen ap Euseb. *HE* III 1); in the Acts of Thomas he appears for the first time as the apostle of India.

e) *Judas Iscariot* plays a role all his own among the apostles. As 'one of the twelve' he reminds the Christian community of the darker side of the saving events, since the 'traitor' or 'betrayer' also must be counted among the inner circle of the disciples. It is part of the biblical picture of Judas that this disciple is treated as an instrument of Satan (Jn. 13:27), and meets his end - by suicide - in horrible fashion (Mt. 27:3ff.; Acts 1:18; cf. 2 Sam. 17:23). Papias developed this event into a dire warning, according to which Judas' body swelled to such proportions 'that he could no longer pass through where a wagon could easily go', and finally went to a wretched death. He left behind such an offensive odour that the piece of ground on which he died remained waste and uninhabited (transmitted in Apollinaris of Laodicea, cf. U. Körtner, *Papias*, 59ff.). W. Vogler has examined the picture of Judas in the apocrypha also (pp. 127-136). There it is in general expanded as a negative example for the fate of the ungodly, and his parents and his wife are also drawn in (e.g. in the Gospel of Bartholomew, see vol. I, pp. 537ff.). There were however gnostic circles, especially the Cainites, who did not share the general condemnation of Judas, but saw in him an instrument of Sophia. From them comes the so-called Gospel of Judas, which has not indeed survived but is mentioned by Irenaeus (*adv. Haer.* I 31.1), Epiphanius (*Pan.* 38.1.5) and others (cf. vol. I, pp. 306f.).

f) It is striking that there is hardly any mention of female apostles in the early Church, although *women* - e.g. Mary Magdalene - are amply attested as companions of Jesus (Lk. 8:2) and witnesses to the resurrection (Mk. 16; Mt. 28; Lk. 24; Jn. 20) and Paul described *Junia* as 'prominent among the apostles' (Rom. 16:7). Later however she was transformed into a masculine Junias (see above, p. 14 note 2). There is no woman among the 'twelve', and the bishops appointed in succession to them are male (cf. 1 Tim. 3:2). Women were elevated into presbyters and even bishops only by some Montanists (cf. Epiphanius, *Pan.* 49.3). Among them the prophetic tradition was dominant (cf. Maximilla; Priscilla and others), and to this women belonged in the New Testament also (cf. Acts 21:9).

In gnostic circles (contrary to 1 Tim. 2:12) women were allowed to teach and even to administer sacraments (cf. Irenaeus, *adv. Haer.* I 13.1-5; Tertullian, *Praescr. Haer.* 41), which further contributed to the custom that in the catholic communities the offices were held only by men. The conflicts connected with this are still reflected in the New Testament apocrypha. In the Pistis Sophia, Mary Magdalene plays a leading role among the apostles, and once she says: 'I am afraid of Peter, for he threatens me and hates our race' (c. 72; GCS 45, p. 104. Cf. Gos. Thom. log. 114). In gnostic tradition moreover there is in addition to other Mary texts a Gospel of Mary (see vol. I, pp. 390ff.). While Peter in this tradition passes for a foe of women, and for this reason is reproved by Jesus, Paul according to the report of the Acts of Paul and Thecla travels about with the virgin Thecla (see below, pp. 239ff.), and even charges her with the proclamation of the Gospel (c. 40f.). Tertullian does indeed take offence at the fact that the right of women to teach and to baptise was given a foundation by the example of Thecla (*de Baptismo* 17), but it was only the reception of the Acts of Paul by the Manichees and not only its encratite preaching which made it obsolete for the Church tradition as a whole. This moreover holds not only for the Acts of Paul but for all those acts of apostles which towards the end of the 3rd century were accepted into the Manichean corpus of the Acta apostolorum (cf. P. Nagel in K.W. Tröger [ed.], *Gnosis und Neues Testament*, 1973, 149-182; Schäferdiek, below pp. 87ff.)

Notes

2. The Apostles as bearers of the tradition

1. On the division of the lands among the apostles, cf. E. Junod, 'Origène, Eusèbe et la tradition sur la répartition des champs de mission des apôtres (Eusèbe, HE III, 1, 1-3)', in F. Bovon *et al.*, *Les Actes Apocryphes des Apôtres*, 1981, 233-248.

3. 'Apostolic' as a norm of orthodoxy

Literature: C. Andresen, 'Die Anfänge christlicher Lehrentwicklung', in id. (ed.), *Handbuch der Dogmen- und Theologiegeschichte I*, 1982 (= 1988), 1-98; G.G. Blum, art. 'Apostel/Apostolat/Apostolizität II. Alte Kirche', TRE 3, 1978, 445-466 (Lit.); id., *Tradition und Sukzession. Studien zum Normbegriff des Apostolischen von Paulus bis Irenäus* (AGTL 9), 1963; H. von Campenhausen, *Die Entstehung der christlichen Bibel* (BHTh 39), 1968 (ET *The Formation of the Christian Bible*, 1972); R. Schnackenburg, 'Apostolizität: Stand der Forschung', in R. Groscurth (ed.), *Katholizität und Apostolizität* (KuD, Beih. 2) 1971, pp. 51-73.

The New Testament writings do not know the term 'apostolic'. And where it first occurs in early Christian literature, it does indeed refer to the model of the apostles, in that it recalls the character of their letters (Ign. *Trall.*, preface), yet not in the sense of a fundamental feature of the Christian Church, as later in the creed of Constantinople (381). Even at this point, nevertheless, we can recognise the special position which the early Church accorded to the apostles, especially in the so-called Apostolic

Fathers in the first half of the 2nd century (this term derives only from J. Cotelier in the 17th century). Yet in the writings which later attained to canonical status as apostolic witnesses there are already the beginnings of a recognition of a normative significance for the teachings of the apostles. For Luke the apostles are not only the authoritative witnesses of the life, sufferings and resurrection of Jesus, the bearers of the Holy Spirit poured out at Pentecost, with special gifts for preaching and healing, and the first leaders of the Christian community, but their teachings are at the same time fundamental for the community (cf. Acts 2:42), for its worship and also for its social life (cf. Acts 4:32). According to Acts 20:17-38, Paul handed on his charge to the elders in Ephesus, and so established something like an apostolic tradition. The Pastorals attributed to Paul reinforce this feature, in that the tradition of faith which has been 'given in trust' is set over against the 'falsely so called gnosis' (1 Tim. 6:20) and reference is made to 'sound doctrine' (cf. Tit. 1:9). The words of the apostle are also recalled in a similar sense at other points in the late writings of the New Testament (Jud. 17; 2 Pet. 3:2).

It is however not only the writings which later became canonical that refer to the apostles as authorities in questions of doctrine and church practice; Marcion and the gnostics also appeal to them. According to the report of Epiphanius, Marcion called his corpus of Pauline writings 'τὸ ἀποστολικόν' (*Pan.* 42.10, 12), and the Valentinian Ptolemy, who taught in Rome in the 2nd century and *inter alia* debated with Marcion, appealed to 'the apostolic tradition handed down by succession' (τὴν ἀποστολικὴν παράδοσιν ἐκ διαδοχῆς; Ep. ad Floram, in Epiphanius, *Pan.* 33.7). Later it is above all Hippolytus who refers to the *traditio apostolica* (cf. CIG 8613A; also Origen, *de Princ.* I, prooem. 2). Gnostic interest was directed to the apostles above all as bearers of divine revelations and mysteries, which the risen Lord was held to have imparted to his disciples after his resurrection and which then - by way of oral transmission from teacher to disciple - could become tradition. Over against this the Church tradition from Irenaeus on increasingly relied on the written tradition of the oldest historical witnesses.

In the middle of the 2nd century an attempt was made to counter gnostic revelation documents with the Church's own (Epistula Apostolorum). Papias of Hierapolis was still of the opinion that 'book-learning did not profit (him) so much as the (statements of the) living and abiding voice' of the presbyters who had been the direct auditors of the apostles (ap. Euseb. *HE* III 39.4). It is however against gnostic ideas of revelation, in the manner of pneumatic immediacy and visionary intuition, that Irenaeus then directs his anti-gnostic design of giving the concept 'apostolic' a historical anchorage and elevating the *traditio ab apostolis* (*adv. Haer.*III 2.2; III 3.1; IV 26.2) into the source and norm of Christian truth (cf. G.G. Blum, TRE 3, 1978, p.449). The succession of the bishops in the communities founded by the apostles, the *Successio episcoporum* (*adv. Haer.* III 3.1), becomes the guarantor of reliable tradition. The model for this idea was for Irenaeus certainly Bishop Polycarp of Smyrna, whom he had himself known and who is described in the Martyrdom devoted to him (*Mart. Pol.* 16.2) as 'apostolic and prophetic teacher', and by Irenaeus himself once as 'apostolic presbyter' (ap. Euseb., *HE* V 20.7).

While Irenaeus employs the term 'apostolic' relatively seldom and more frequently refers to the apostles as the beginning and origin of Christian tradition, that is, as persons who handed on their teaching to the bishops appointed by them, for Tertullian, Hippolytus and others this becomes the 'apostolic tradition'. Tertullian repeatedly refers to 'apostolic churches' (*Praescr. Haer.* 26; 32; 36) which have exemplary character for all communities, and for the West particular prominence is given to Rome, where the blood of the martyrs Peter and Paul has especially sanctified the place (ib. 36.3). He even speaks of an 'apostolic age' (ib. 32.1) and of 'apostolic men', among whom he counts Polycarp (ib. 32.2). He regards himself as an 'heir of the apostles' (ib. 37.5). The idea of the 'apostolic' thereby becomes more and more the norm of reliable tradition in the Church, which has its origin in the 'apostolic churches'. But while in Irenaeus the handing-on of the apostolic tradition in the Church unites both office and spirit with the Church's apostolic origins, in Tertullian this process takes an independent form as an act of handing on within the communities. Against Marcion it is, however, firmly held that apostolic tradition cannot be narrowed down to the tradition of *one* apostle (such as Paul), especially since the Easter controversy at the end of the 2nd century shows that the tradition of the Fourth Gospel, to which the so-called Quartodecimans in Asia Minor appealed, is in collision with the tradition of the West (cf. Socrates, *HE* V 22), that is, that there were tensions between the tradition of John on the one hand and that of Peter and Paul on the other. Mention should also be made here of the traditions of the apostle Thomas, which went through an independent development in the East.

Such experiences rather strengthened the idea, rooted in apocalyptic tradition, that the twelve apostles symbolically embodied the missionary charge for all peoples, so that at this point apostolicity and catholicity of necessity touched upon and supplemented one another.

Over against Marcion, but also against the gnostics, this harking back to the historical origins of the Church proved to be a necessary and salutary corrective. For not only could Paul thus be restored to the Church in his original form, but Peter too was preserved for the Church in his human, all too human, form. Even the novelistic developments in the apostolic Acts made no difference to that.

At the end of the 4th century the norm of the 'apostolic' gained afresh in interest. This is the period in which the *symbolum apostolorum* underwent its shaping (cf. Rufinus) and the so-called Apostolic Constitutions were created. It is probably no accident that it was also in this period that the canon of the apostolic writings reached its completion. With this the 'apostolic' has finally carried the day as the basic norm of the Church, which with its historical anchoring preserves the memory of the Church's origin, independent of pneumatic and charismatic eruptions.

XIV. Apostolic Pseudepigrapha

Introduction

Wilhelm Schneemelcher

1. Literature: F. Torm, *Die Psychologie der Pseudonymität im Hinblick auf die Literatur des Urchristentums* (Studien der Luther-Akademie 2), 1932; A. Meyer, 'Religiöse Pseudepigraphie als ethisch-psychologisches Problem', ZNW 35, 1936, 262-279; K. Aland, 'The Problem of Anonymity and Pseudonymity in Christian Literature of the First Two Centuries', JTS NS 12, 1961, 39-49 (German version in *Arb. zur ntl. Textforschung* 2, 1967, 24-34); W. Speyer, art. 'Fälschung, literarische', in RAC 7, 1969, cols. 236-277; id., *Die literarische Fälschung im heidnischen und christlichen Altertum. Ein Versuch ihrer Deutung* (Hdb. d. klass. Altert.wiss. I, 2), 1971; id., 'Fälschung, pseudepigraphische freie Erfindung und "echte religiöse Pseudepigraphie"', in *Pseudepigrapha I. Pseudopythagorica-Lettres de Platon - Littérature pseudépigraphique juive* (Fondation Hardt, Entretiens sur l'antiquité classique 18), 1972, 331-368; N. Brox, 'Patristische Pseudepigraphie', in FS A. Rohracher, 1969, 57-61; id., *Falsche Verfasserangaben. Zur Erklärung der frühchristlichen Pseudepigraphie* (Stuttgarter Bibelstudien 79), 1975; M. Hengel, 'Anonymität, Pseudepigraphie und "Literarische Fälschung" in der jüdisch-hellenistischen Literatur', in *Pseudepigrapha I* (see above), 229-308; N. Brox (ed.), *Pseudepigraphie in der heidnischen und jüdisch-christlichen Antike* (Wege der Forschung CDLXXXIV), 1977 (Lit.).

2. In the following pages four writings are brought together under the heading '**Apostolic Pseudepigrapha**'. In their titles or in their subscriptions they make the claim to be composed by an apostle, but in other respects they are of very diverse character.

The title of the *Kerygma Petri* (1) is attested by Clement of Alexandria, but in view of the fragmentary character of the few extant remains its literary *Gattung* eludes any precise definition. We may however conjecture that it was a comprehensive presentation of the Christian proclamation, which was placed under the name of Peter. The proximity to the speeches in Acts is just as little to be overlooked as the connection with the apologetic literature of the 2nd century. That in the Kerygma Petri we are dealing with a pseudepigraphon cannot indeed be proved, but is to be assumed.

The *Letter to the Laodiceans* (2), in itself an altogether insignificant document, is a pseudapostolic epistle which deliberately, on very superficial grounds - the absence of the letter to the Laodiceans mentioned in Col. 4:16 - ties up with the *Gattung* of the New Testament letter and seeks to fill the gap by a combination of individual verses from the Pauline letters (above all from Philippians). In the case of this text we may speak of a literary forgery.

The *Correspondence between Paul and Seneca* (3) is also a pseudapostolic pseudepigraphon. We cannot say whether or not it is a case of a stylistic exercise from a rhetorical school, but it is certain that it is a literary fiction in which, probably in the 4th century, a motif dating back to earlier times (Seneca and Christianity) has been used for the invention of a pseudapostolic exchange of letters.

A theological and ascetic tractate, which probably originated in the 5th century in Priscillianist circles, has been handed down under the title *Epistle of Titus, disciple of Paul* (4). It remains an open question whether the title was bound up with this text from the beginning or given to it only later. In its present form this 'letter' is likewise a pseudapostolic epigraphon, in which the theme of celibacy is dealt with under the name of Titus.

One may well ask whether this selection of writings under the heading of Apostolic Pseudepigrapha is not somewhat arbitrary, and whether this does not conceal the fact that there are other writings in the present collection which ought also to be placed under this designation. In answer to this question, at least brief reference may be made to the problem of pseudepigraphy (and connected with it: anonymity, pseudonymity and 'forgery') in the literature here assembled.

3. It is correct to say that for a long time the **problem of pseudepigraphy**, i.e. that of pseudonymity or forgery in early Christian literature, was not given adequate consideration[1]. This is probably connected with the fact that on the one hand the New Testament writings which are regarded as 'inauthentic' are drawn into the debate, which of necessity poses the question of canonicity, and thus a historical and literary problem is combined with a dogmatic one. On the other hand, any discussion of this theme must define very precisely the terms with which we are working. Otherwise it is all too easy for the emphasis to be wrongly placed. Even W. Speyer, to whom we owe the basic works in this field, did not entirely escape this danger. In his concern to investigate the phenomenon of 'forgery' as comprehensively as possible, he assembled an abundance of material and endeavoured to demonstrate the problems connected with the forgeries in antiquity and late antiquity and contribute to their solution. But to my mind, despite his illuminating definition of the term (*Die literarische Fälschung* 13ff.), he used the concept 'forgery' too extensively. Above all - and this affects the literature with which we are concerned - he probably did not take the literary *Gattungen* sufficiently into account, nor did he adequately consider the historical environment to which a text belongs. The difference between the several epochs of Church history in the early centuries naturally left its deposit in the literature also, and has to be appropriately taken into account in discussing the theme of pseudepigraphy[2].

This is not the place to enter into a detailed discussion with Speyer and Brox. It must suffice to refer to a few points which are important for the apocryphal literature.

a) A large part of the *gospel literature* brought together in volume I cannot be comprehended by the term pseudepigraphy. The older texts especially, of which in any case we sometimes have only fragments extant, are not literary works with (or without) a genuine (or inauthentic) author's name. Rather we must regard them, on the analogy of the canonical Gospels, as the collecting and shaping of traditional material for liturgical, catechetical and missionary purposes, hence not as works of literature, for which the name of an author, whether genuine or false, would be essential[3].

Another group of 'gospels' uses the name of an apostle (or some other prominent person) to bestow upon the collection of traditions the legitimacy of the 'true gospel'. Here it is to be noted that this binding to a tradition linked with a person is often nothing more than the acceptance of a tradition current in a particular circle. Thus, for example, the Coptic Gospel of Thomas is linked with the person of Thomas only in the opening words, but otherwise is a very complex collection of older material for which terms like pseudepigraphy or forgery are scarcely applicable. The same holds also for several other texts of this category, which can be described as revelation documents intended to convey to a community the authentic preaching tradition. They belong to another context than literature in the narrower sense[4].

The Gospel of Peter (cf. vol. I, pp. 216ff.) presents a special problem, since evidently it is meant to be thought of as composed by Peter. At any rate the I-style points to that conclusion.[5] Since however we have only a fragment extant, we must be very cautious in our judgment, as also with the Protevangelium Jacobi. The correspondence with Abgar is certainly to be described as a forgery.

b) The group of writings which are brought together in this volume under the title of 'apostolic' also presents a very varied picture so far as the question of pseudepigraphy is concerned. It is indeed a matter of very diverse kinds of text.

Thus the five great apocryphal acts of apostles are a special form of 'fictional prose narrative'[6]. By the taking over of stylistic elements from the Greek novel a form has been created which has been given some very distinct stamps, but has nothing to do with pseudepigraphy or even with 'forgery'[7]. In these works there are only a few places in which the speaker is an 'I' or a 'we' (AJ c. 19 c. 60 c. 62 c. 110 c. 115; APt c. 4, c. 21; ATh c. 1). These few passages are of no significance for the question of pseudepigraphy, and are probably for the most part traditional material taken over. No author's names have been handed down. Only in the case of APl is it attested by Tertullian that the author was a presbyter in Asia Minor. Despite the assertion repeatedly made that the work was published under Paul's name, it must be firmly stated that the APl and also the other major Acts are not pseudepigrapha, but anonymous 'romances'.[8]

On the other hand we shall have to regard the Pseudo-Clementines as pseudepigraphical. Among the later Acts of apostles also, which cannot be discussed in detail here, there are several examples of pseudepigraphy.[9] They mark the transition to the hagiographical literature, in which there were probably many forgeries.[10] In regard to this literature it should however be pointed out that it had its *Sitz im Leben* in public worship, and therefore certainly links up with older traditions. We must accordingly investigate for each text at what stage of the transmission process the 'false' name became attached to it.

As already said, the pseudepigrapha presented in this section may rightly be so described (despite some doubt regarding the Kerygma Petri). We may observe from these texts how, from traditions fixed in writing about the apostles and their preaching (as in certain gospels and probably also in the Kerygma Petri), a pseudepigraphical literature was now formed.

We need not here discuss the apocalypses. In their case one may probably speak of 'religious pseudepigrapha' (Speyer).[11]

4. Lost Pseudepigrapha: in addition to the texts so far mentioned there are some reports of works which perhaps belong in our context, but of which nothing is known apart from these brief notices.

a) *Letter of Paul to the Alexandrians.* We know of this apocryphon only through the statement of the Muratori Canon (line 64: vol. I, p. 36), which rejects this letter, as also the Letter to the Laodiceans, as Marcionite. Every further discussion of its content or purpose (Harnack: perhaps forged to further Marcionite propaganda in Egypt? *Marcion*², p. 134*) leads us into the domain of phantasy. The conjectures of Th. Zahn (*Gesch. des ntl. Kanons* II, 2, pp. 586ff.) also carry us no farther. The *Lectionarium Bobbiense* mentioned there speaks of an *epistola Pauli ad Colos.*, but denotes by that a section from a later homily. Cf. Harnack, *Gesch. d. altchr. Lit.* I, 1, p. 33; L. Vouaux, *Les Actes de Paul*, 1913, pp. 327-332.

b) *Letter of Paul to the Macedonians.* Clement of Alexandria mentions once such a letter: 'In this sense the apostle of the Lord also exhorted the Macedonians and became an interpreter of the divine word. "The Lord is at hand", he says, "wherefore take care that we be not overtaken empty (in vain)"' (*Protr.* IX 87.4; Stählin I³, p. 65). The citation recalls Phil. 4:5. Since otherwise nothing is known of a Macedonian letter of Paul, either free citation or a mistake can be assumed. Cf. Harnack, *Gesch. d. altchr. Lit.* I, 2, p. 788.

c) *Letter of Peter.* In Optatus of Milevis it is said: 'Since we have read in the Letter of the Apostle Peter: "Judge not your brother according to prejudice"' (*de Schism. Donat.* I, 5; Ziwsa, CSEL 26, p. 7). Harnack conjectures that Optatus combined Jas. 2:1 and 4:11 and then erroneously attributed this saying to Peter (*Gesch. d. altchr. Lit.* I, 2, p. 788). But it is also possible that we are concerned here with a citation from some lost apocryphon of Peter about which we can say nothing at all.

d) A quotation from a *letter of John* is met with in ps.-Cyprian, *de Montibus Sina et Sion*, c. 13: Christ 'instructs and exhorts us in the letter of his disciple John to the people: "So see me in you as one of you sees himself in water or in a mirror."' (Hartel, CSEL III, 3, p. 117). Zahn has maintained that we are concerned here with a quotation from a letter of John which had belonged to the Acts of John (*Forsch. zur Gesch. d. ntl. Kanons* VI, 1900, p. 196, note 1; literature also there). He refers above all to a passage from the hymn of Christ in c. 95 of the Acts of John: 'A mirror am I to thee who perceivest me' (see p. 183 below). Hennecke (NTApo², p. 172, note 1) has recourse to c. 15 of the Acts of Andrew (see p. 133 below) where also a mirror is spoken of. But these are speculations which cannot be proved. Nothing can be learned from ps.-Cyprian about an alleged letter of John. Cf. also Schäferdiek, pp. 152f. below.

e) A *Praedicatio Pauli* (Homily of Paul) is mentioned in ps.-Cyprian, *de Rebaptismate* 17 (3rd cent.?). This is said to have been forged by heretics to give support to their false doctrine: 'In this book one discovers how Christ, who alone had committed no kind of sin, contrary to all (the assertions of) Scripture confessed his own sins and almost against his own will was constrained by his mother to receive the baptism of John. Further (it is related) that when he was baptised, fire appeared upon the water, a thing that is written in no Gospel. And after the agreement regarding the gospel come to in Jerusalem and consultation and debate together and after arrangements had been made as to what was to be done, after so long a time Peter and Paul finally came to know one another in Rome, as it were for the first time. And there are some other things of the kind (it is stated), absurd, improper and fictitious, all of which are found collected in that book.' We shall not here enter into a discussion as to which heretics are referred to and as to whether the statement of ps.-Cyprian that the Praedicatio Pauli was composed by them is true. That ps.-Cyprian had a definite writing before him, seems to me to be certain. It is likewise clear that the Praedicatio mentioned here had nothing to do with the Acts of Paul, as Th. Zahn supposed (*Gesch. d. ntl. Kanons* II, 2, p. 881; against that Dobschütz, *Das Kerygma Petri*, p. 127). The statement that Jesus had received the baptism of John only when constrained, and that at the time of his baptism fire was seen upon the water, is striking. It has rightly been concluded that here our text is connected with a fragment of the Gospel of the Nazaraeans (vol. I, p. 160, no. 2) and another of the Gospel of the Ebionites (vol. I, p. 169, no. 3) (cf. Dobschutz, op. cit., pp. 128ff.). A use of two different Jewish-Christian Gospels in the Praedicatio Pauli is unlikely. But above all hardly more than the possibility of a use of Jewish-Christian Gospels can be made out, the basis for more far-reaching hypotheses being in fact too small. The other statement that Peter and Paul came to know one another properly only in Rome - earlier meetings, it is true, seem according to the text not be altogether excluded (!!) - is singular. Here also the short text allows of no far-reaching conclusion. With regard also to the composition, content and form of this Praedicatio nothing can be said. Only this seems to be certain, that the writing has nothing to do with the Kerygma Petri and nothing with the Acts of Paul.

f) A *Praedicatio Petri et Pauli* (Homily of Peter and Paul) has been inferred from a passage in Lactantius. He writes: 'And he (*sc.* Jesus) has revealed to them (*sc.* the disciples) all the future; Peter and Paul have preached this in Rome and this discourse of theirs remains in writing for a memorial. In it, besides many other wonderful things, it is also said that in the future it would come to pass that after a short time God would send a king who would conquer the Jews, make their cities level with the ground and besiege them themselves, exhausted by hunger and thirst. Then it would come to pass that they would live on the bodies of their own and consume one another. At last they would fall as prisoners into the hands of their enemies and would see before their eyes their wives disgracefully ill-treated, their maidens violated and deflowered, their youths deported, their small children dashed to the ground. Finally everything would be devastated by fire and sword, and they would be exiled for ever as prisoners from their own land because they had gloated over the most beloved and most acceptable Son of God' (Lact. *Divin. Instit.* IV 21. 2-4; Brandt, CSEL 19, p. 367.17ff.; Dobschütz, op. cit., p. 132, translates the conclusion: 'over the (reviled) most beloved Son of God, in whom he is well pleased'). In Lactantius the text stands in the context of the account of the ascension and the command to *praedicatio evangelii*. On this occasion Jesus also revealed the future, and this future is now described more closely in traditional apocalyptic traits (in this connection accounts of the Jewish War may also be used). But with not a single word does Lactantius say that he goes back to a particular writing. In any case all conjectures about such a Praedicatio Petri et Pauli are pure hypotheses without support of any kind. Cf. Dobschütz, op. cit., pp. 131-134.

g) *A Discourse of Simon Kephas in the City of Rome* preserved in Syriac (edited by W. Cureton, *Ancient Syriac Documents*, 1864, pp. 35-41; BHO 936) hardly belongs to our context. It is a late work which is doubtless connected with the Acts of Peter and has been enriched with all sorts of other legends about Peter. The dogmatic statements in this discourse refer it to the 5th or 6th century. Cf. de Santos, below p. 437.

h) Finally it may be noted that some surviving texts which profess to be apostolic letters do not need to be considered more closely here since they belong to another context. This holds for the apocryphal correspondence of Paul with the church at Corinth (III Cor.; cf. below, pp. 254ff.) and for the Epistula Petri in the Pseudo-Clementines (see below, pp. 493f.). The Epistula Apostolorum (see vol. I, pp. 249ff.) and the Epistle of Barnabas also do not belong in the category of the pseudapostolic letters

Notes

Introduction

1. Cf. e.g. Speyer, *Die lit. Fälschung*, foreword; Brox, *Pseudepigraphie*, p. 1.
2. Here we must recall F. Overbeck and his concept of the 'primitive literature', on which see vol. I, pp. 52ff. The deficiencies addressed above are especially clear in the treatment of the apocryphal apostle Acts (Speyer, *Fälschung*, 210ff.) and in the 'forgeries of heretics and schismatics' (ib., 260ff.). When Speyer (309) writes: 'In the Greek East during the sixth to eighth centuries forgery quite expressly belonged to the business of the theologian', that is a foolish slip of the pen, which only shows that a good philologist may not also be by any means a good historian.
3. For details see vol. I, pp. 77ff. On the question of the authorship of the Gospels, cf. M. Hengel, *Die Evangelienüberschriften* (SBHAW 1984, 3), 1984.
4. It is open to doubt whether one can work with the term 'religious pseudepigraphy', which Speyer employs.
5. Cf. Vielhauer, *Lit. gesch.* 644ff.
6. N. Holzberg, *Der antike Roman*, 1986, 29
7. Against Speyer, *Fälschung*, 210ff.
8. Against Speyer, loc. cit. On the problem of the subscription with κατά in the Acts of Paul, cf. below, p. 215.
9. For the Pseudo-Clementines, see below, pp. 483ff. For the later Acts of apostles, see below, pp. 426ff.
10. On the later forgeries see now the congress volume: H. Fuhrmann (ed.), *Fälschungen im Mittelalter* (Schriften der MGH 26), 5 vols., 1988.
11. Cf. on this Vielhauer/Strecker below, pp. 569ff.

1. The Kerygma Petri

Wilhelm Schneemelcher

Introduction

Literature: Texts. E. von Dobschütz, *Das Kerygma Petri kritisch untersucht* (TU XI, 1), 1893; E. Klostermann, *Apocrypha I. Reste des Petrusevangeliums, der Petrusapokalypse und des Kerygma Petri* (KlT 3), 1933, 13-16; M.G. Mara, 'Il Kerygma Petrou', *Studi e Materiali di Storia delle Religioni* 38 (FS Pincherle), Rome 1967, 314-342; English translation: James 16-18.

Studies: Harnack, *Lit. gesch.* I, 25ff.; II 1, 472ff; R. Seeberg, *Die Apologie des Aristides* (Forsch. zur Gesch. des ntl. Kanons V, 2), 1893, 216-220; E.Hennecke, NTApoHdb, 239-247; J.N. Reagan, *The Preaching of Peter: The Beginning of Christian Apologetic*, Chicago 1923; G. Quispel and R.M. Grant, 'Note on the Petrine Apocrypha', *VigChr* 6, 1952, 31f; P. Nautin, 'Les citations de la "Prédication de Pierre" dans Clément d'Alexandrie, Strom. VI.V. 39-41', JTS NS 25, 1974, 98-105; H. Paulsen, 'Das Kerygma Petri und die urchristliche Apologetik', ZKG 88, 1977, 1-37; W. Rordorf, 'Christus als Logos und Nomos. Das Kerygma Petri in seinem Verhältnis zu Justin', in *Kerygma und Logos*, FS C. Andresen, 1979, 424-434.

1. Attestation and time of composition: In Clement of Alexandria we find a series of quotations from a writing κήρυγμα Πέτρου (KP). There can be no doubt that Clement regards this work as composed by Peter. Certainly, without expressing himself more nearly about the origin, genuineness or any other problem of the writing, he quotes from it with the words: 'Peter says in the Kerygma' or the like. Unhappily the contexts in which Clement quotes the writing give only a few clues to its composition and origin (cf. below, pp. 35f.). Origen apparently no longer shares the high opinion that Clement had of the KP. For in his *Commentary on John* (XIII 17) he quotes Heracleon, who had used the KP, but at the same time indicates that he is in doubt as to whether it is 'genuine, not genuine or mixed'. Origen's comments on this passage (see below, p. 41, note 14) allow it to appear questionable whether on the whole he himself had known the KP. It is quite possible that here he merely reproduces what he has found in Heracleon. At any rate the KP for him no longer belongs to the uncontested sources of Christian tradition. On the other hand it is clear from this passage in Origen that the gnostic Heracleon (middle of the 2nd century) made use of it, probably in the conviction that the KP was a genuine work of Peter. The apologist Aristides seems to have used this work, at least considerable connection between his Apology and the KP can be pointed out (cf. R. Seeberg and Dobschütz). Despite a number of topological contacts, one cannot speak of Theophilus of Antioch (*ad Autolyc.* I 10 and II 2) having quoted or used the KP[1]. It is also to be noted that the KP is not named either in Aristides or in Theophilus. In Eusebius (*HE* III 3.2) and Jerome, *de Vir. Ill.* 1) the KP is definitely reckoned to the non-canonical writings.

The attestation and conjectured use of the KP refer this writing to the 2nd century and indeed to its first half. Dobschütz sets it between 80 and 140; Paulsen between 100 and 120. Egypt has doubtless to be accepted as its homeland, even although this conjecture is not strictly demonstrable.

2. Title: The title Κήρυγμα Πέτρου attested by Clement is probably to be understood in the sense that this writing is intended to be a compendium of the preaching of Peter, but that probably means, over and above that, a compendium of the whole apostolic proclamation. Here κήρυγμα is certainly not be be understood as *actus praedicandi*, but is intended to indicate the content: it is a matter of the gospel which was preached by Peter, as the representative of the apostolic activity, and which mediates salvation.[2] Accordingly the title is interpreted too narrowly when it is rendered merely 'The Missionary Preaching of Peter' (so Hennecke, NTApo[2], pp. 144f.). Rather the title that has been handed down is best translated 'The Proclamation of Peter'. By that it is not said that the work claimed to be written by Peter, even if Clement of Alexandria seems to assume this. But the title says nothing about this. It may be that Peter is named in the title merely as authority for the apostolic preaching (at any rate he obviously often discoursed in the plural). The apostle as guarantor of the true preaching of salvation is an idea also attested elsewhere[3]. On the other hand, the possibility that Peter was meant to be regarded as the author is of course not to be excluded. From the title nothing further results that in any way can have a bearing on a relation to the Gospel of Mark. Dobschütz (op. cit., pp. 68ff.) has conjectured that the KP may have been written as a δεύτερος λόγος to the Gospel of Mark. But neither the title nor the contents of the fragments admit such an hypothesis.

3. Composition and contents: The small amount of extant text makes it almost impossible to voice any conjectures about the structure of this work. One can probably demonstrate a connection in terms of content between individual fragments, but a coherent text cannot be reconstructed out of this (*contra*: Nautin). It is also scarcely possible to show the original sequence of the fragments. One may conjecture a certain pattern of arrangement, for which there are parallels in early Christian literature[4], but such a hypothesis is not capable of proof.

For determining the literary *Gattung* of the KP our meagre text material is likewise quite inadequate. Probably this document was a comprehensive presentation of the 'preaching' of Peter (in the sense indicated above). It could have shown a certain proximity to the speeches of Acts and to the AGG, but also have taken over other forms. Fragment 3b for example can to some extent be interpreted as part of a dialogue between Jesus and his disciples after the resurrection (cf. vol. I, pp. 228ff.). But this too is an assumption, for which there is much to be said, but which cannot be proved.

In view of this uncertainty with regard to the original structure and the *Gattung* of the complete KP, it is advisable to attempt an interpretation in terms of content, and its location in the history of theology in the 2nd century, only on the basis of the individual fragments. Such an interpretation of the several pieces leads however to interesting results.

We may first of all mention the themes with which the KP dealt, according to what can be deduced from the fragments. It is a matter of the proclamation of the *one* God, hence of the monotheistic faith (2a). With this is connected the warding-off of heathen polytheism (2b) and of the false Jewish worship of God (2c). The Old Testament is claimed for the Church (2d and 4a). The originality of Christianity (as a 'third race'[5]: 2d) is strongly emphasised. From fragment 3b it seems to follow that the preaching of the KP goes back to the Lord who appointed the apostles. It is not possible to draw out any distinct Christology from these fragments, even though texts 1, 4a and 4b show that this theme probably was not lacking. Finally, warning to repentance and paraenesis evidently played a role in this document.

This catalogue of themes, as already noted, is not intended to be a table of contents of the original text of the KP, but simply to indicate the questions which concerned the author (and probably also his community). With this the problem of the position of the KP within the history of theology in the 2nd century now comes into view. Dobschütz, who has given a detailed commentary on the fragments (op. cit., 27-64), was of opinion that the document 'marks the transition from the early Christian to the apologetic literature' (op. cit., 66). This characterisation, taken over by me in NTApo[3] II, 96f., has in the interval been comprehensively confirmed by the work of Paulsen and Rordorf. We need here only to emphasise that the KP is to be understood as a combination of ideas which also occur in the New Testament (e.g. 1 Thess. 1:9f.; Rom. 1:18ff.; Acts 17) with elements which derive from Jewish apologetic. It cannot be regarded as an apology in the sense of the later Greek apologists of the 2nd century, even though the development in that direction is already marked. The KP is however evidence that we cannot, as so often happens, assume a radical breach between primitive Christian theology and preaching on the one hand and the apologists on the other, but must reckon with connecting lines of many kinds. The significance of the KP seems to lie in the fact that here we have a middle term in the preaching tradition between the early Christian missionary preaching, which has left traces for example in Acts, and the Greek apologetic. It is the more regrettable that so few fragments of this important document have survived.

4. The Kerygma Petri and other apocryphal writings: Attempts have been made to enlarge the number of the fragments of the KP by adding to them some other assumed quotations from this work. Thus in the prologue to his *de Principiis* (preserved only in a Latin translation) Origen mentions a *doctrina Petri*:

> And if any one should confront us with (a section) from that book which is called the 'Doctrine of Peter', in which the Saviour seems to say to the disciples: 'I am not a bodiless daemon', then the answer must be given him, in the first place, that this book is not included among the books of the Church, and further it must be pointed out that this writing comes neither from Peter nor from any other person inspired by the Spirit of God. (Orig. *de Princ.* praef. 8)

Now in the first place it is remarkable that here Origen rejects the work named by him much more decisively than he does in his *Commentary on John*. Further, the question must evidently be asked whether *doctrina* in the translation of Rufinus actually renders the word κήρυγμα or whether διδασκαλία is not rather to be regarded as its Greek equivalent, and whether therefore a writing other than the KP is meant here. Finally, the cited word of Jesus has also been handed down elsewhere: from Ignatius (*Smyrn.* 3.1f.) it reached Eusebius, and Jerome - wrongly - ascribed it to a Jewish-Christian Gospel (cf. Vielhauer, vol. I, pp. 143f.). All this makes it very questionable whether here Origen actually refers to the KP.[6]

The problem is further complicated by the fact that there may possibly have been such a *doctrina Petri*. Certainly in Gregory of Nazianzus and in John of Damascus we come upon quotations from a διδασκαλία Πέτρου. Gregory of Nazianzus twice quotes a logion:

> God is near a soul that toils and moils. (Gregory Naz. Ep. 20; Or. 17.5)

In *Ep*. 20 he adds to this word: 'Peter says somewhere in an admirable way'. Elias of Crete (12th cent.), in commenting on this passage, suggests that it comes from the διδακαλία Πέτρου (PG 36, 395). Now we cannot do much with this 'beautiful, pithy dictum' (Dobschütz, p. 109), and the suggestion of Elias of Crete affords us no further help, since it is not to be assumed that he was at all acquainted with the work which he mentions. To judge then by this quotation, it cannot be said whether the saying belongs to the KP or whether there was a *doctrina Petri* and the sentence comes from it.

In the *Sacra Parallela* of John of Damascus there are two passages which are ascribed in the lemmata to a διδακαλία Πέτρου:

> I, unhappy one, did not reflect that God sees the heart and has regard to the voice of the soul. I consented to sin, saying to myself: God is merciful and will suffer me; and since I was not struck at once, I did not discontinue but still more despised the forgiveness and exhausted the patience of God. (Joh. Dam. in Holl, TU 20.2, 1899, p. 234, no. 502.)

> Rich is that man who has compassion on many and who in imitation of God gives of what he has. For God has given to all all of that which he has made. Understand then (ye) rich men that ye must serve since ye have received more than ye yourselves need. Learn that others lack what ye have in abundance. Be ashamed to retain other people's property. Imitate God's equity, and no one will be poor. (Holl, op. cit., p. 234, no. 503)

Now these two texts are so general - they are exhortations to repentance such as are frequently met with in Christian literature - that it would hardly be possible to assign them to some one particular work. Dobschütz (op. cit., pp. 110-121) has conjectured that they come from a writing of Peter of Alexandria. This hypothesis is, however, just as undemonstrable as the one that the *doctrina Petri* mentioned here is to be identified with the KP of Clement of Alexandria.

Texts

1. a) In the 'Preaching of Peter' we find the Lord called *Law and Word* (*Logos*). (Clem. Alex. *Strom.* I 29.182)

b) In the 'Preaching' Peter called the Lord *Law and Word* (*Logos*). (Clem. Alex. *Strom.* II 15.68)

c) The Lord himself is called *Law and Word* (*Logos*), as Peter says in the

'Preaching' and the prophet: 'For out of Zion will the Law go forth and the Word from Jerusalem'. (Clem. Alex. *Ecl. proph.* 58).[7]

2. a) And that the most notable of the Greeks know (about) God not by positive knowledge, but (only) by roundabout expression, Peter says in the 'Preaching':

Recognize now that there is one God who created the beginning of all things and who has the power to set an end;[8]

and[9]

the Invisible who sees all things; the Incomprehensible who comprehends all things; the One who needs nothing, of whom all things stand in need and for whose sake they are; the Inconceivable, the Everlasting, the Imperishable, the Uncreated, who has made all things by the word of his power[10] [from the gnostic writing], that is his Son.[11]

2. b) Then he proceeds:

Worship not this God in the manner of the Greeks;

by which it is obviously said that the notables among the Greeks also worship the same God as we, but not with perfect knowledge since they have not learned to know what was delivered by the Son. Therefore he says: 'Worship not!' He does not say: 'the God whom the Greeks (worship), but '(worship) not in the manner of the Greeks'. In doing so he gives another direction to the way of worshipping God, but does not proclaim another (God). What now 'not in the manner of the Greeks' means, Peter himself makes clear, adding:

For actuated by ignorance and not knowing God [as we do according to the perfect knowledge][12] they have fashioned into figures that over which he has given them the power of disposal for use, (namely) stocks and stones, brass and iron, gold and silver; and <forgetting>[13] their material and use, have set up and worshipped (as gods) that which should have served them as subsistence. That also which God has given them for food, the fowls of the air and the fishes of the sea, the creeping things of the earth with the four-footed beasts of the field, weasels and mice, cats, dogs and apes; and that which should serve them as food they sacrifice to (animals) that can be eaten up; and offering what is dead to the dead as though they were gods, they are unthankful toward God since thereby they deny his existence.[14]

2. c) And since he thinks that we ourselves and the Greeks know the same God, although not in the same way, he adds the following:

Neither worship him in the manner of the Jews; for they also, who think that they alone know God, do not understand, worshipping angels and archangels, the months and the moon.[15] And when the moon does not shine, they do not celebrate the so-called first Sabbath,[16] also they do not celebrate the new moon or the feast of unleavened bread or the feast (of Tabernacles) or the great day (of atonement).

2. d) He then inserts the keystone to his own inquiry:

Learn then, ye also, holily and righteously what we deliver to you and keep it, worshipping God through Christ in a new way. For we have found in the Scriptures, how the Lord says: 'Behold, I make with you a new covenant, not as I made (one) with your fathers in Mount Horeb.'[17] A new one has he made with us. For what has reference to the Greeks and Jews is old. But we are Christians, who as a third race worship him in a new way. (Clem. Alex. *Strom.* VI 5.39-41).

3. a) For that reason Peter records that the Lord had said to the disciples:

If now any one of Israel wishes to repent and through my name to believe in God, his sins will be forgiven him.[18] And after 12 years go ye out into the world that no one may say, 'We have not heard it.' (Clem. Alex. *Strom.* VI 5.43).

3. b) To adduce an example: In the 'Preaching of Peter' the Lord says to his disciples after the resurrection:

I have chosen you twelve[19] because I judged you worthy to be my disciples [whom the Lord wished].[20] And I sent them, of whom I was persuaded that they would be true apostles, into the world to proclaim to men in all the world the joyous message[21] that they may know that there is (only) one God, and to reveal what future happenings there would be through faith in me [Christ],[22] to the end that those who hear and believe may be saved;[23] and that those who believe not may testify that they have heard it and not be able to excuse themselves saying, 'We have not heard.' (Clem. Alex. *Strom.* VI 6.48).

3. c) But concerning all reasonable souls it has been said from the beginning: All sins which any one [of you][24] has committed in ignorance, because he did not know God accurately, will be forgiven him if he comes to know (God) and repents.[25] (Clem. Alex. *Strom.* VI 6.48)

4. a) Wherefore Peter also in the 'Preaching' speaks about the apostles as follows:

But we opened the books of the prophets[26] which we had, which partly in parables, partly in enigmas, partly with certainty and in clear words name Christ Jesus, and found his coming, his death, his crucifixion and all the rest of the tortures which the Jews inflicted on him, his resurrection and his assumption to heaven before the foundation of Jerusalem,[27] how all was written that he had to suffer and what would be after him.[28] Recognising this, we believed God in consequence of what is written of (in reference to) him.

4. b) And somewhat later he adds the following, stating that the prophecies have taken place through the divine providence:

For we recognise that God enjoined them, and we say nothing apart from Scripture. (Clem. Alex. *Strom.* VI 15.128).

Notes

1. The Kerygma Petri

1. Cf. Paulsen, op. cit., 12.
2. On κήρυγμα cf. G. Friedrich, art. κήρυξ etc., in TDNT III 683ff. (supplement to literature in X/2, 1138 of German edition (supplement).
3. On the AGG cf. below pp. 75ff.; on the apocalypses cf. K. Berger, 'Unfehlbare Offenbarung. Petrus in der gnostischen und apokalyptischen Offenbarungsliteratur', in FS Mussner 1981, 261-326.
4. Cf. Paulsen, op. cit., 4ff., who however rightly formulates his theses very cautiously. It may be noted here that the numbering and therefore also the sequence of the fragments is variously handled.

Dobschutz/Mara	Klostermann	Dobschutz/Mara	Klostermann
I	1	VI, VII, VIII	3
II, III, IV, V	2	IX, X	4

Paulsen takes over Klostermann's numbering, but subdivides the texts and arranges them as follows:

3b	(1)
3a	2a
3c	2b
4	2c
	2d

I take over Paulsen's refinement of Klostermann's numbering, but adhere to the latter's arrangement.
5. Cf. on this Paulsen, op. cit. pp. 20f.
6. I take no notice at all of the passages Origen, *Hom. X in Lev.* and Optatus Mil. *de Schism. Donat.* I 5, discussed in Dobschütz, op. cit., pp. 84-105. They have certainly nothing to do with the KP.

7. Cf. Is. 2:3. On the importance of this passage in early Christian theology see Rordorf, op. cit., 425; Paulsen, op. cit., 24f.
8. Cf. with this Clem. Alex. *Strom.* VI 7.58: 'For truly *one* is God who created the beginning of all things, writes Peter, referring (thereby) to the first-born Son, since he accurately understands the word: In the beginning God created the heaven and the earth (Gen. 1:1).' Clement here is probably quoting the same passage from the KP as in text 2a adduced above.
9. Whether this 'and' should be ascribed to the KP or to Clement remains questionable; cf. Nautin op. cit., 103f.
10. Cf. Heb. 1:3.
11. The text of this passage is much discussed (cf. Stählin-Früchtel, App. ad loc.; Nautin, op. cit., 103; Paulsen, op. cit., 22, note 141; Rordorf, op. cit., 427ff.). Nautin's proposal, to delete the bracketed words as an interpolated gloss, is plausible. The interpretation of the content in Rordorf, who refers especially to the parallel in Justin (*Dial.* 61.1), speaks in favour of the above version.
12. [as we ... knowledge]: regarded by Klostermann and me ($NTApo^3$ II 99) as an addition by Clement, which is contested by Nautin, op. cit., 304.
13. Stählin's conjecture.
14. It is very questionable whether Theophilus of Antioch (*ad Autol.* I 10 and II 2) refers to this passage; see above, p. 34. On the other hand Origen's report of the use of the KP by Heracleon relates to it. Origen writes (*Comm. in Joh.* XIII 17): 'Now there is much to adduce from the words quoted by Heracleon from the so-called Preaching of Peter, and regarding them inquiry has to be made concerning the book, whether it is genuine or not genuine or mixed. But for that very reason we would willingly pass it by and merely refer to the fact that it states that Peter taught: (God) should not be worshipped in the manner of the Greeks, who take material things and serve stocks and stones. Also the Divine ought not to be worshipped in the manner of the Jews, for they, who believe that they alone know God, rather do not know him and worship angels, the month and the moon.'
15. Cf. Gal. 4:10; Col. 2:16, 18.
16. The expression 'first Sabbath' is unusual, and its interpretation debated. Nautin (op. cit., 105) suggests the following: 'Ils ne célèbrent pas le sabbat, qu'ils disent être la première chose (le célébrer).' Rordorf (op. cit., 427) considers this 'a proposal worthy of consideration'. But it can scarcely be proved from the text. Cf. also Paulsen, op. cit., 17, note 5.
17. Cf. Jer. 31 (38):31f.; Deut. 29:1; Heb. 8:8-9.
18. Cf. Lk. 24:47; Acts 5:31; 10:43.
19. Cf. Lk. 6:13; Jn. 6:70.
20. [whom the Lord wished]: an addition by Clement
21. Cf. Mt. 10:5ff.
22. To be deleted.
23. Cf. Rom. 10:14f.
24. [of you] probably does not belong to the KP; cf. Paulsen, op. cit., 32.
25. Cf. Acts 3:17; 17:30.
26. Cf. 1 Pet. 1:10-12.
27. Instead of 'foundation' some would read 'destruction' or 'judgment'. Against this: Mara, op. cit., 342; Paulsen, op. cit., 12; Rordorf, op. cit., pp. 430f. An eschatological interpretation of the transmitted text is perfectly possible.
28. Cf. 1 Pet. 1:11.

2. The Epistle to the Laodiceans

Wilhelm Schneemelcher

Introduction

1. Literature: R. Anger, *Über den Laodicenerbrief. Eine biblisch-kritische Untersuchung*, 1843; J.B. Lightfoot, *St Paul's Epistles to the Colossians and to Philemon*, 1879, 274-300; E. Jacquier, *Le nouveau Testament dans l'église chrétienne* I, 1911, 345-351; L. Vouaux, *Les Actes de Paul et ses lettres apocryphes*, 1913, 315-326; A. von Harnack, *Apocrypha IV. Die apokryphen Briefe des Paulus an die Laodicener und Korinther* (KIT 12), 1931²; id., *Marcion. Das Evangelium vom fremden Gott*, 1924², 134*-149*; K.Pink, 'Die pseudopaulinischen Briefe II', *Biblica* 6, 1925, 179-192; John Knox, *Marcion and the New Testament*, Chicago 1942; G. Quispel, 'De Brief aan die Laodicensen - een Marcionitische vervalsing', *Nederlands Theologisch Tijdschrift* 5, 1950, 43-46; Erbetta, III, 63-67; Moraldi II, 1719-1726 and 1733-1738.

2. Attestation and tradition: in the Muratori Canon (cf. vol. I, p. 36) two Marcionite forgeries, an epistle to the Laodiceans and one to the Alexandrians, are mentioned and rejected. Apart from the suggestion that these books were 'forged in Paul's name for the sect of Marcion' (lines 64f.), the passage provides no sort of clue to any closer identification of this epistle. Tertullian reports (*adv. Marc.* V 11 and 17) that the heretics, i.e. the Marcionites, regarded Ephesians as the Epistle to the Laodiceans and that Marcion himself had made this change in the title. This note is confirmed to some extent by Epiphanius of Salamis (*Haer.* 42.9.4 and 42.12.3), who, it is true, gives no clear information as to whether the source which he copies here (Hippolytus) recognised Ephesians as the Epistle to the Laodiceans or whether in addition to Ephesians an Epistle to the Laodiceans also stood in the Marcionite canon. Filastrius (*Haer.* LXXXIX), who briefly mentions the Epistle to the Laodiceans in the context of his discussion of Hebrews, likewise goes no farther. Other references (assembled in Pink, op. cit.) also contribute little to our knowledge of the Epistle to the Laodiceans. The so-called *Speculum* (ps.-Augustine, *de Divinis Scripturis*, 5th or 6th century) is unambiguous: here verse 4 of the Epistle to the Laodiceans preserved in Latin is quoted (CSEL 12, 516); Gregory the Great must also be reckoned among the positive witnesses for this epistle handed down in Latin (*Moralia* 35.20.48; PL 76, 778C).

This Latin Epistle to the Laodiceans is found in many Bible manuscripts[1], and was evidently widely disseminated in the West. There was also a series of translations into western vernaculars.[2] Whether a Slavonic version existed is very doubtful.[3] This is regrettable, since the existence of a Slavonic version would indicate that the letter 'was also at home in the Byzantine east' (de Santos). But so far no evidence has been found of a Greek text. On the other hand, later Greek sources speak of an epistle to the Laodiceans (cf. the compilation in Pink, op. cit.), so that we must at least assume that the existence of such an epistle was known in the East. The epistle probably came into being in the West (despite verse 5, the corrupt text of which may perhaps be remedied through translation back into Greek).

3. Content, occasion, date: when we consider this small apocryphon, we are amazed that it ever found a place in Bible manuscripts. For this pretended epistle of Paul is nothing other than a 'worthless patching together of Pauline passages and phrases, mainly from the Epistle to the Philippians' (Knopf-Krüger, *Apokr.* 2, p. 150). A suggestive statement of its contents can scarcely be given, and we seek in vain for a definite theological intention. The author seems to have gathered verses from Paul's epistles, worded in as general terms as possible, that with his patch-work he might close a gap in the Pauline corpus, which could indeed be noticed by any Bible reader. There can be no doubt that Col. 4:16 was the occasion of this forgery. There it is said: 'And when this letter has been read among you, have it read also in the church of the Laodiceans, and have the one from Laodicea come to you that you may read it also.' Here we do not need to inquire more closely what is to be understood by the ἐπιστολὴ ἐκ Λαοδικείας. What still lies nearest at hand is that Paul refers to a letter to Laodicea which, however, has not come into the Pauline corpus. This want was to be met by the elaborate work of an unknown person who had a knowledge of the Bible, but in other respects had not exactly had a theological training.

The dating of the Epistle to the Laodiceans is difficult for the reason that it depends on the question of the identity of this apocryphon with the one mentioned in the Muratori Canon, and this again is closely connected with the problem of its Marcionite derivation. Either the Muratori Canon means the Epistle to the Ephesians, the name of which was changed by Marcion into the Epistle to the Laodiceans (so Tertullian) - that, however, is unlikely, since Ephesians is mentioned in the Muratori Canon - or it had actually in view a separate Epistle to the Laodiceans, and then it must be the Latin Epistle to the Laodiceans that has come down to us, if we are not to assume several pseudo-Pauline letters to Laodicea. Certainly the Latin Epistle to the Laodiceans shows no sort of Marcionite character such as ought to be expected according to the statement of the Muratori Canon.

4. The problem of the Marcionite derivation of the Epistle to the Laodiceans: Whilst for a long time it was widely agreed that the Epistle to the Laodiceans was a colourless and dull compilation of Pauline sentences, A. von Harnack put forward the thesis that the Epistle is a Marcionite forgery: 'In the Epistle to the Laodiceans we salute the only complete writing which has been preserved to us from the Marcionite church of the earliest time' (*Marcion*², p. 149*). Harnack would like to see the 'irrefutable' proof of that in the fact that the Epistle to the Laodiceans begins with Gal. 1:1, i.e. with 'monumental, anticatholic words in Marcion's sense' (p. 141*) from the epistle which stood at the head of the Marcionite apostolos. In the departure from Phil. 1:3 (gratias ago *deo* meo; Ep. to the Laodiceans verse 3: *Christo*), in the idea of *veritas evangelii* and in the addition *quod a me praedicatur* (verse 4), in the *ex me* (= οἱ ὄντες ἐξ ἐμοῦ; in Phil. 1:12 we read τὰ κατ' ἐμέ), in the elimination of the ἀπουσία of Phil. 2:12 in Laod. verse 10 and in the twice-repeated appearance of *vita aeterna* (verses 5 and 10) Harnack sees the sagacity and the artfulness of Marcion at work. The Ep. to the Laodiceans must however have come not from the master himself but from a pupil who, between 160 and 190, after the title 'Epistle to the Laodiceans' had again become free (Ephesians had been given back its early name), produced it simultaneously in Latin and Greek. From the same workshop there also came the Marcionite Arguments on the Epistles of Paul.

Now the hypothesis of the Marcionite character of the Prologues to Paul is just as problematic as that of the antimarcionite Prologues to the Gospels.[4] That the Roman church unknowingly took over Marcion's Prologues to Paul into its 'counter-canon' (so de Bruyne and Harnack) is indeed scarcely conceivable. But here it can be left aside; it merely shows us on how precarious ground Harnack's construction stands. Anyhow, it has of itself no convincing power. The passages adduced can be drawn upon only with violence as strict proof of a Marcionite origin of the Ep. to the Laodiceans. That the Marcionite forger - it certainly cannot have been the master himself - satisfied himself with such trifles and did not use the opportunity to give clearer expression to his theology does not speak for his 'sagacity'. Further, from the fact that the epistle begins with Gal. 1:1 no far-reaching conclusions can be drawn. Harnack has here got on to a wrong track.

G. Quispel op. cit. has recently taken up Harnack's hypothesis and attempted to support it from another side. He thinks that the beginning of the Ep. to the Laodiceans (= Gal. 1:1) answers to a stylistic expedient that was conventional in antiquity: in literary counterfeits it was made clear to the readers and hearers through the opening words which model was to be imitated. The beginning of the Ep. to the Laodiceans ought then to draw the reader's attention to the fact that really there speaks here the Paul who - according to Marcion - had expounded in Galatians the decisive points of his theology. Consequently we should here have a case similar to the one in Jn. 1:1, where also a connection is intentionally made with Gen. 1:1. But this reasoning also may hardly carry conviction. For the Ep. to the Laodiceans does not purpose to be a rhetorical performance, and the author had obviously no literary ambitions. Too much honour is done the author of this paltry and carelessly compiled concoction when we judge him by the yardstick of ancient literary practices.

To sum up, it may be said that the Marcionite origin of the Latin Epistle to the Laodiceans is an hypothesis that can neither be proved nor sustained. It is rather a clumsy forgery, the purpose of which is to have in the Pauline corpus the Epistle to the Laodiceans mentioned in Col. 4:16. Whether the Epistle to the Laodiceans mentioned in the Muratori Canon is identical with this apocryphon remains unsettled. With that the possibility of an accurate dating also falls out. As the time of composition there comes into question the period between the 2nd century and the 4th

* *To the Laodiceans*

1. Paul, an apostle not of men and not through man, but through Jesus
Christ, to the brethren who are in Laodicea: 2. Grace to you and peace from God
the Father and the Lord Jesus Christ. 3. I thank Christ in all my prayer that you
are steadfast in him and persevering in his works, in expectation of the promise
for the day of judgment. 4. And may you not be deceived by the vain talk of
some people who tell (you) tales that they may lead you away from the truth
of the gospel which is proclaimed by me. 5. And now may God grant that those
who come from me for the furtherance of the truth of the gospel (. . .) may

be able to serve and to do good works for the well-being of eternal life. 6. And now my bonds are manifest, which I suffer in Christ, on account of which I am glad and rejoice. 7. This ministers to me unto eternal salvation, which (itself) is effected through your prayers and by the help of the Holy Spirit, whether it be through life or through death. 8. For my life is in Christ and to die is joy (to me). 9. And this will his mercy work in you, that you may have the same love and be of one mind. 10. Therefore, beloved, as you have heard in my presence, so hold fast and do in the fear of God, and eternal life will be your portion. 11. For it is God who works in you. 12. And do without hesitation what you do. 13. And for the rest, beloved, rejoice in Christ and beware of those who are out for sordid gain. 14. May all your requests be manifest before God, and be ye stedfast in the mind of Christ. 15. And what is pure, true, proper, just and lovely, do. 16. And what you have heard and received, hold in your heart and peace will be with you. [17. Salute all the brethren with the holy kiss.] 18. The saints salute you. 19. The grace of the Lord Jesus Christ be with your spirit. 20. And see that this epistle is read to the Colossians and that of the Colossians among you.

Notes

2. The Epistle to the Laodiceans

1. Cf. among others Jacquier, op. cit. I, 345ff.; S. Berger, *Histoire de la vulgate*, 341f. We cannot enter here into the question whether Laod. is one of the Old Latin elements by which the Vulgate tradition has in various ways been contaminated. Cf. H.J. Frede, *Einleitung zu Vetus Latina*, vol. 24/2 (esp. pp. 301-303); B. Fischer, *Lateinische Bibelhandschriften im frühen Mittelalter* (Aus der Geschichte der lateinischen Bibel 11), 1985.
2. Cf. Anger, op. cit. and Lightfoot, op. cit.
3. Cf. de Santos, *Überlieferung* I, 147f.
4. Cf. E. Haenchen, *Die Apostelgeschichte*, 1961[3], 8, note 3 (ET *Acts*, 1971, 10, note 1); J. Regul, *Die antimarkionitischen Evangelienprologe* (Aus der Geschichte der lateinischen Bibel 6), 1969.

To the Laodiceans
* The numbers of the notes refer to the verses of the Epistle.
1. Gal. 1:1.
2. Gal. 1:3; Phil. 1:2.
3. Phil. 1:3.
4. Cf. Col. 2:4; Gal. 1:11.
5. Verse 5 has been corrupted in transmission; the translation rests on conjecture; cf. Phil. 1:12.
6. Phil. 1:13, 18.
7. Phil. 1:19f.
8. Phil. 1:21.
9. Phil. 2:2.
10. Phil. 2:12.
11. Phil. 2:13.
12. Cf. Phil. 2:14.

13. Cf. Phil. 3:1.
14. Phil. 4:6; cf. 1 Cor. 15:58; 2:16.
15. Phil. 4:8.
16. Phil. 4:9.
17. Lacking in some MSS; doubtless a secondary addition; 1 Thess. 5:26.
18. Phil. 4:22.
19. Phil. 4:23; Gal. 6:18.
20. The words 'this epistle' and 'to the Colossians' are lacking in some MSS; cf. Col. 4:16.

3. The Correspondence between Seneca and Paul

Cornelia Römer

Introduction

1. Literature: (a) *Editions*: C.W. Barlow, *Epistolae Senecae ad Paulum et Pauli ad Senecam <quae vocantur>* (Papers and Monographs of the American Academy in Rome X), Rome 1938. Reprint of this text in PL Suppl. 1, 673-678. New edition with copious commentary and bibliography by L. Bocciolini Palagi, *Il carteggio apocrifo di Seneca e San Paolo* (Accademia toscana di scienze e lettere 'La Colombaria', Studi XLVI), Florence 1978; with updated commentary and list of literature by the same authoress in the series 'Bibliotheca Patristica', Florence 1985.

(b) There is a complete list of *literature* down to 1938 on the theme 'Seneca and Christianity' in J. Haußleiter, *Bursians Jahresbericht über die Fortschritte der klass. Altertumswiss.* 281, 1943, 172-175. Thereafter: A. Kurfess, 'Der Brand Roms und die Christenverfolgung im Jahre 64 n. Chr.', *Mnemosyne* 3.Ser. 6, 1938, 261-272; H. Leclercq, 'Sénèque et Paul', DACL 15/1, 1950, cols. 1193-1198; A. Momigliano, 'La leggenda del cristianesimo di Seneca', *Rivista storica italiana* 62, 1950, 325-344; E. Franceschini, 'Un ignoto codice delle Epistole Senecae et Pauli', *Mélanges J. de Ghellinck* I, 1951, 149-197; A. Kurfess, 'Zu dem apokryphen Briefwechsel zwischen dem Philosophen Seneca and dem Apostel Paulus', *Aevum* 26, 1952, 42-48; J.N. Sevenster, *Paul and Seneca*, Leiden 1961; W. Trillitzsch, *Seneca im literarischen Urteil der Antike* I, Amsterdam 1971, 170-185.

2. Content and origin: The fourteen letters profess to be a private correspondence between the philosopher and the apostle. In them the two personalities exchange compliments and manifestations of friendship with one another. The Pauline letters, which Seneca is said to have shown to the emperor Nero, also come under discussion. The philosopher censures the style of these letters.

In general the content of the letters may be described as meagre. A certain place apart is occupied by the eleventh letter, which in dealing with the burning of Rome and the persecution of the Christians evidently goes back to a historical source not known to us. The philosophy of the two outstanding personalities of their time does not find expression in a single sentence.

Despite this meagre content, the letters were of great importance for the legend which brought Seneca into connection with Christianity. Down to the beginning of the Renaissance they were regarded as genuine. Today the 4th century A.D. is generally assumed to be the period of their origin. In favour of this are not only linguistic and stylistic considerations (on which see E. Liénhard in *Revue belge de philologie et d'histoire* 11, 1932, 5-32), but above all the mention of the correspondence by Jerome in 392 (*de Vir. Ill.* 12, see below), whereas it is clear from the *Divinae institutiones* of Lactantius (VI 24.13-14) of the year 324 that these letters did not yet lie before him.

It must remain an open question whether we owe the correspondence to some exercise in a rhetorical school (Barlow, 91-92). Certainly all the letters came into being about the same time (against this: A. Kurfess, *Zeitschrift f. Religions- u. Geistesgeschichte* 2, 1949/50, 67-70), the eleventh letter probably a little later than the rest (L. Bocciolini Palagi pp. 35-47).

The origins of the manuscript tradition available to us can be traced back to the 5th century (the oldest codex derives from the 9th century). The great quantity of the manuscripts presents numerous variants and corruptions, so that some passages even today are not certainly cleared up (letter VIII).

3. Witnesses, from which it emerges that people had no doubt of the *authenticity* of the letters. - All the testimonies down to the 13th century are printed in Barlow (110-112). In most manuscripts the passage from Jerome's *de Vir. Ill.* 12 (of the year 392) stands as an introduction to the letters: "Lucius Annaeus Seneca from Cordoba, disciple of the Stoic Sotion and uncle of the poet Lucan, lived a very abstemious life. I would not receive him into the list of the saints were I not made to do so by those epistles which are read by very many, (the epistles) of Paul to Seneca and of Seneca to Paul. In these epistles he who was the teacher of Nero and the most influential man of his time declares that he wishes to occupy among his own people the same place that Paul had among the Christians. This (Seneca) was put to death by Nero two years before the glorious martyrdom of Peter and Paul.'

We may mention further: Augustine, Ep. CLIII 14 (CSEL 44, p. 412); Pseudo-Linus, *Passio Sancti Pauli apostoli* (Bonnet, Aa I, p. 24); Alcuin, dedicatory poem in his edition of the letters (PL 101, 1375C); Peter Abelard, *Sermo* XXIV (PL 178, 535D) and often; Peter of Cluny, *Tractatus adversus Petrobrusianos* (PL 189, 737C); Petrarch, *Ad Annaeum Senecam, Fam.* 24.5.25. From the 15th century people began to doubt the authenticity of the letters.

New aspects for the whole discussion could result from a 'Letter of the high priest Annas to the philosopher Seneca', recently published by B. Bischoff. The correspondence between Seneca and Paul could have originated as a counterblast to this letter of a Jewish author, likewise to be regarded as fictitious, with the aim of making the philosopher appear in association with a representative of the Christian faith (so B. Bischoff, 'Der Brief des Hohenpriesters Annas an den Philosophen Seneca - eine jüdisch-apologetische Missionsschrift (Viertes Jahrhundert?)', in *Anecdota novissima. Texte des vierten bis sechzehnten Jahrhunderts*, 1984, 1-9, esp. p. 5).

I
Seneca greets Paul

I believe, Paul, that you have been informed as to what we discussed yesterday with our Lucilius[1] regarding the hidden things and other matters. For certain friends of your teachings were with me. We had withdrawn into the gardens of Sallust,[2] where those people of whom I have just spoken, although they were going elsewhere, seized the opportunity of our presence and joined us when they saw us. Certainly we longed for your presence, and I wish you to know this: after we had read your little book, that is, some letters out of many which you have directed to some city or chief town of a province and which contain wonderful exhortations to the moral life, we were greatly refreshed. These sentiments, I think, were not spoken by you, but through you,[3] although certainly at some time (both) by you[4] and through you. So great is the majesty of these things, and they shine with such a generosity, that I think that generations of men would scarce suffice to be instructed and perfected in them. Brother, I wish you prosperity.

II

Paul greets Annaeus Seneca

I was happy to receive your letter yesterday. I could have answered it at once if I had had the young man at hand whom I intended to send to you. You well know when and through whom, at what time and to whom something ought to be given for transmission. I beg you therefore not to think yourself neglected, while I have regard to the trustworthiness of the person. But since you write that you are somewhat taken with my letters, I count myself happy in the judgment of so great a man. For you, the censor, philosopher and teacher of so great a prince and indeed of all, would not say this except because you are speaking the truth. I wish you long prosperity.

III

Seneca greets Paul

I have arranged some scrolls and set them in order corresponding to their divisions. These I also intend to read to the emperor. If only fortune smiles, that he shows new interest, perhaps you also will be present; if not, I shall name a day for you at another time, that we may look into this work together. Also I could not read that writing to him unless I first conferred with you, if only it could have been done with impunity. This that you may know that you are not being passed over. Farewell, most beloved Paul.

IV

Paul greets Annaeus Seneca

As often as I hear your letters, I think that you are present, and imagine nothing other than that you are always with us. As soon then as you come, we shall see one another, and that at close quarters. I wish you prosperity.

V
Seneca greets Paul

We are distressed by your all too long staying away. What is it? What keeps you away? If it is the displeasure of the empress[5] because you have departed from the ancient rite and belief (of Judaism) and become a convert elsewhere, there will be opportunity to convince her that this was done from deliberation and not from levity. Farewell.

VI
Paul greets Seneca and Lucilius

Regarding the things which you write to me, it is not right to express oneself with pen and ink[6] - of which the one notes and designs something, the other shows it clearly - especially since I know that there are among you, that is with you and in your midst, those who understand me. Respect is to be shown to all, the more so when they strain after opportunity to express their displeasure. If we have patience with them, we shall overcome them in every way and in every respect, if only they are people who know penitence for their former life. Farewell.

VII
Annaeus Seneca greets Paul and Theophilus[7]

I confess that I was much taken with the reading of your letters which you sent to the Galatians, the Corinthians and the Achaeans,[8] and let us both live in the spirit which with sacred awe you show in them. For the Holy Spirit is in you and above all exalted ones gives expression by your sublime speech to the most venerable thoughts. I could wish therefore that when you express such lofty thoughts a cultivated form of discourse should not be lacking to their majesty. And that I may conceal nothing from you, brother, or burden my conscience, I confess that the emperor was moved by your sentiments. When I had read to him about the origin of the power in you, he said that he could only wonder that a man who had not enjoyed the usual education should be capable of such thoughts. To which I answered that the gods are wont to speak through the mouths of the innocent, not of those who by their education are able to prevaricate.[9] I gave him the example of Vatienus, an uneducated countryman, to whom two men appeared in a field at Reate who afterwards are named as Castor and Pollux;[10] with that he seems sufficiently instructed. Farewell.

VIII

Paul greets Seneca

I am not unaware that our emperor, if ever he is despondent, is a lover of marvellous things; however, he allows himself not to be injured, but only admonished.[11] For I think you have gravely erred that you have wished to bring to his notice what is contrary to his belief and tenets. Since he worships the gods of the nations, I do not see what was your purpose in wishing him to know this, unless I am to think that you are doing this out of undue love for me. I beg you for the future not to do it. For you must beware lest in loving me you cause offence to the empress,[12] whose displeasure will indeed only do harm if it persists, but also will be of no profit if that is not so. Even if as empress she is not affronted, as a woman she will be offended.[13] Farewell.

IX

Seneca greets Paul

I know that you are not so much disturbed for your own sake by the letter which I wrote to you about the giving of your letters to the emperor as by the nature of the things which so hold back the minds of men from all arts and right customs. Today I do not wonder, especially since I now know it well from many documents. Therefore let us make a new beginning, and if in the past anything has been done too lightly, you will grant me forgiveness. I have sent you a book on 'verbosity'.[14] Farewell, most beloved Paul.

X

Paul greets Seneca

As often as I write to you and set my name behind yours, I commit a serious fault which is not congruent with my religion.[15] For I ought, as I have often professed, to be all things to all men,[16] and as concerns your person to observe what Roman law has conceded to the honour of the Senate,[17] namely after perusal of a letter to choose the last place, that I may not with embarrassment and shame seek to do what was within my power. Farewell, my highly revered teacher.

Given on 27 June in the consulship of Nero (for the third time) and Messala.[18]

XI (XIV?)

Seneca greets Paul[19]

Greetings, my dearest Paul! Do you think that I am not saddened and distressed that capital punishment is still visited upon your innocence? And also that all the populace judges you people so hard-hearted and so ready for any crime, believing that whatever happens amiss in the city is done by you? But let us bear with equanimity and make use of the forum which fate provides, until invincible good fortune makes an end of evils. The time of the ancients suffered the Macedonian, the son of Philip, the Cyruses, Darius and Dionysius, our own time also Gaius Caesar (= Caligula), men for whom all that they wished was legitimate. It is clear at whose hands the city of Rome so often suffers burning. But if human humility could declare what is the cause of it, and in this darkness was free to speak with impunity, then all would see everything. Christians and Jews are - forsooth! - executed as fire-raisers, as a matter of common custom. Whoever that delinquent is, who takes pleasure in murder and uses lies as a disguise, his days are numbered, and just as the best is sometimes offered up as one life for many,[20] so also will this accursed one be burned in the fire for all. 132 palaces, 4000 apartment houses were burned in six days; the seventh brought a pause. I wish you good health, brother.

Given on 28 March in the consulship of Frugi and Bassus.

XII (XI?)
Seneca greets Paul

Greetings, my dearest Paul![21] If a man so distinguished as you and in every way beloved by God is I do not say united but of necessity interwoven with me and my name, then it will be for the best with your Seneca. Since you are the crown and peak of all most lofty mountains, do you not wish me to rejoice that I am so close to you that I may be thought your second self? You should therefore not think that you are unworthy to be named in the first place in the letters, that you may not seem to tempt rather than to praise me, especially since you know yourself to be a Roman citizen. For I could wish that my place could be yours in your letters and yours mine.[22] Fare well, dearest Paul.

Given on 23 March in the consulship of Apronianus and Capito.[23]

XIII
Seneca greets Paul

Many things are brought together by you, allegorically and enigmatically, from every quarter, and therefore the great power granted to you, in your material and in your office, ought to be adorned not with verbal trappings but with a certain refinement. Nor should you be afraid - as I recall, I have said this often already - that many who concern themselves with such things may corrupt the sense and weaken the power of the material. Certainly I could wish that you make me the concession to have regard for the Latinity and with noble words find the proper form, that you may worthily fulfil the honorable task entrusted to you. Fare well.

Given on 6 July in the consulship of Lurco and Sabinus.[24]

XIV (XII?)
Paul greets Seneca

In your reflection things have been revealed to you which the Deity has granted only to a few. With assurance therefore I sow in a field already fertile most powerful seed, not indeed matter that seems to be decaying but the firm word of God, the outflow of him who grows and abides for ever.[25] What your discernment has grasped must remain unfailing: that the observances of the Gentiles and the Jews are to be avoided. Make yourself a new herald of Christ Jesus, showing by your rhetorical proclamations the irrefutable wisdom which you have almost attained. This you will teach to the temporal king and his servants and faithful friends. For them persuasion will be hard and above their capacity, for several of them are but little swayed by your expositions. But if the word of God is instilled in them as a vital blessing, it begets a new man without corruption,[26] an animal ever in motion,[27] which hastens hence towards God. Farewell, Seneca most dear to us!

Given on 1 August in the consulship of Lurco and Sabinus.[28]

Notes

3. The Correspondence between Seneca and Paul

1. A friend of Seneca, to whom he dedicated the *Epistulae morales*.
2. A park on the Quirinal, which formerly belonged to the historian Sallust.
3. I.e. from God through you.
4. When Paul is later regarded as an apostle, then 'by Paul' will mean 'by the recognised teacher'.
5. Poppaea Sabina; cf. letter VIII.
6. Cf. 2 Jn. 12; 3 Jn. 13.
7. Luke dedicated his Gospel and Acts to Theophilus. Nothing is known of any relation between Paul and Theophilus.
8. What is meant is 2 Corinthians; cf. 1:1 there.
9. Cf. Mt. 11:25; 1 Cor. 1:26-29.
10. Cf. Cicero, *de Natura Deorum* II 2.6; Valerius Maximus I 8.1; Lactantius, *Div. Inst.* II 7.10.
11. According to another reading the text should run: 'But you will none the less allow that I do not affront you, only warn you'.
12. See note 5.
13. According to the ms. tradition we should have to give a translation here that makes no sense: '. . . whose displeasure will neither harm if it lasts, nor benefit if that is not the case. If she is an empress, she will not be offended, if a woman, she will feel herself attacked'.
14. *De Verborum Copia*: handed down in many MSS under Seneca's name, with a reference to the letter to Paul, cf. J. Fohlen in *Mediaeval Studies* 42, 1980, 139ff.
15. Paul has actually placed his name in the final greetings in three of his letters (1 Cor., Col., 2 Thess.).
16. Cf. 1 Cor. 9:22; 10:33.
17. Nothing is known of any such law.

18. In A.D. 58.
19. This letter is ostensibly written after the burning of Rome in A.D. 64.
20. Cf. Virgil, *Aen.* V 815: *unum pro multis dabitur caput.*
21. This is evidently the answer to letter X.
22. Cf. Gal. 4:12.
23. In A.D. 59.
24. In A.D. 58.
25. Cf. 1 Pet. 1:23; 1:25.
26. *sine corruptela*: cf. 1 Cor. 15:42 according to OL: *seminatur corpus in corruptione, surgit sine corruptela.*
27. *perpetuum animal*: what is continually in motion is according to Platonic and Neo-Platonic doctrine immortal (Phaedrus 245C).
28. In A.D. 58.

4. The Pseudo-Titus Epistle

Aurelio de Santos Otero

Introduction

As the 'Epistle of Titus, the Disciple of Paul, on the State of Chastity' there has survived a noteworthy document which was discovered in 1896 in a Latin manuscript of the 8th century (fols. 84-93v of the 'Codex Burchardi' Mp. th. f. 28 of the University of Würzburg) among the *Homilies* of Caesarius of Arles (cf. D.G. Morin, *Revue Bénédictine* 13, 1896, 97-111). Only in 1925 after lengthy study was this document published in full by D. de Bruyne (*Rev. Bén.* 37, 1925, pp. 47-72; reprinted PL Suppl. II 1522-1542). This 'Epistle' is composed in barbarous language, the solecisms of which are not to be explained simply through the clumsiness of some scribe, but also go back in large part to the author himself. The hypothesis put forward by de Bruyne that we are concerned here with a Latin translation from the Greek, made apparently by a man who knew neither Latin nor Greek sufficiently (*Rev. Bén.* 25, 1908, 150; M.R. James on his part even attempted to restore the presumably original Greek text in the light of some *indicia* of the 'Epistle', cf. *ibid.*, p. 151) is today no longer tenable, especially after the investigations of A. von Harnack (cf. SPAW 17, 1925, 191). To this there has to be added the close connection of our 'Epistle' with other like-minded Latin writings about which we have still to speak.

Since we are dependent on a single manuscript the reading of which presents considerable linguistic difficulties, the last word cannot yet be spoken regarding the origin of the Epistle of Titus. Nevertheless much can already be stated about the character and the content of this 'Epistle'. What is most striking is not only the external apocryphal guise of the 'Epistula Titi', but also the liberal use that is made in it of all sorts of apocrypha, especially of the Acts of Apostles and of some Apocalypses. In the course of half a century these numerous quotations from the apocrypha have most of all aroused the interest of scholars, and they have led to many arguments regarding the origin of the 'Epistle'. But this clue (which is especially valuable for the judgment of a writing which contains no dogmatic statements) ought not to be considered apart from the ostensible aim of the Epistle. The author seems to have had above all a concrete ascetic aim in view, namely to commend the life of chastity. Those whom he addresses belong to a special circle of ascetics of both sexes (*spadones* and *virgines*), who have vowed to live in the state of celibacy, but in whose life several abuses (among them that of 'spiritual marriage') have been naturalised. That he may combat this impropriety and give prominence to the worth of chastity, the author has recourse to all the means that are at his disposal. The mere enlistment of Titus as the reputed author of the epistle (as is well known, his authority in the sphere of ascetic matters was very great because of his close connection with Paul) goes to prove the ascetic interests which Pseudo-Titus wishes to support.

But the wealth of quotations from the Holy Scriptures with which the author accompanies his enthusiastic exclamations on the state of celibacy reveals a distinct leaning on other ascetic writings which originated above all in literary circles about Jerome and Cyprian and pursued a similar aim. Reference may be made among others to ps.-Cyprian, *de Singularitate Clericorum* (ed. Hartel, CSEL 3, 1871) and *de Centesima, Sexagesima, Trigesima* (ed. Reitzenstein, ZNW 15, 1914, 60ff.); Jerome, *Epistula* 117 (ed. Hilberg, CSEL 55, pp. 422ff.); ps.-Jerome, *Epistula* 42 *ad Oceanum* (PL 30, 288ff.); Bachiarius, *de Reparatione Lapsi* (PL 20, 1038-1062).

The fact that Pseudo-Titus also has recourse to apocryphal quotations which are distinguished by their misogamy not only goes to prove his own naive enthusiasm, but also suggests the conjecture that this writing may have originated in an environment where the ascetic life especially flourished and the apocryphal writings (above all the strictly ascetic Acts of Apostles) enjoyed a great reputation. This environment is probably to be sought in connection with the Priscillianist movement in the ascetic circles of the Spanish Church in the course of the 5th century. In favour of that there is first the fact that in this land there was from the beginning a rigorous ascetic tendency, which absorbed with a special enthusiasm both the ascetic writings that have been named and the apocryphal Acts of Apostles. To this there have to be added the official documents of the Spanish hierarchy, which denounce the improprieties combated by Pseudo-Titus as something typically Priscillianist and condemn them in similar terms. In the author of this 'Epistle', however, we certainly do not need to see a Priscillianist. It is quite conceivable that a member of the catholic Church, carried away by his ignorant enthusiasm, composed this document and had it circulated under the banner of Titus.

Among the different contributions to the study of Pseudo-Titus reference may first be made to works which deal on occasion with some of the problems of this 'Epistle' (mainly with the quotations from the apocrypha): E. Schürer, ThLZ 33, 1908, 614; J. Weiss, *Der I Korintherbrief*, 1910, pp. 58ff.; M.R. James, *The Lost Apocrypha of the OT*, 1920, p. 55; id, *The Apocryphal NT*, 1924, pp. 265, 303, 349; Hennecke, NTApo[2] 227-228; C. Schmidt, ZKG 43, 1924, 334ff.

D.G. Morin (*Rev. Bén.* 13, 1896, 97-111) and von Eckhart (*Commentarii de rebus Franciae orientalis* I, 837-847) have described the Würzburg manuscript in detail.

D. de Bruyne first published the quotations made in Pseudo-Titus from the apocrypha (*Rev. Bén.* 25, 1908, 149-160) and then edited the whole text with some corrections and elucidations (see above). The most important contribution to the study of Pseudo-Titus has been made by A. von Harnack in his investigation 'Der apokryphe *Brief des Paulusschülers Titus*', SPAW 17, 1925, 180-213. H. Koch has discovered a partnership in catchwords between Pseudo-Titus and other ascetic writings (ZNW 32, 1933, pp. 131-144). Bulhart has suggested some corrections to the Latin text (*Rev. Bén.* 62, 1952, 297-299). For justification of the views regarding the Epistle of Titus advocated by us in the foregoing introduction, we refer to the article 'Der apokryphe Titusbrief', ZKG 74, 1963, 1-14.

A complete translation of this 'Epistle' was published for the first time in the German edition of NTApo³, and for the present edition this has been thoroughly revised.[1] We have endeavoured to solve as far as possible the linguistic puzzles which crop up again and again, so as to be able to present a readable and coherent text. In so doing we have had regard not only to the corrections suggested by de Bruyne and Bulhart but also to the peculiar style of Pseudo-Titus.

Epistle of Titus, the Disciple of Paul[2]

Great and honourable is the divine promise which the Lord has made with his own mouth to them that are holy and pure: *He will bestow upon them what eyes have not seen nor ears heard, nor has it entered into any human heart.* And from eternity to eternity there will be a race incomparable and incomprehensible.[3]

Blessed then are those who have not polluted their flesh by craving for this world, but are dead to the world that they may live for God! To whom neither flesh nor blood has shown deadly secrets, but the Spirit has shone upon them and shown some better thing so that even in this < . . . > and instant of our <pilgrimage on the earth> they may display an angelic appearance. As the Lord says, *Such are to be called angels.*[4]

Those then *who are not defiled with women*[5] he calls an angelic host. Those who have not abandoned themselves to men, he calls virgins, as the apostle of Christ says: *the unmarried think day and night on godly things*,[6] i.e. to act properly and to please Him alone, and not to deny by their doings what they have promised in words. Why should a virgin who is already betrothed to Christ be united with a carnal man?

It is not lawful to cling to a man and to serve him more than God. Virgin! Thou hast cast off Christ, to whom thou wert betrothed! Thou has separated thyself from Him, thou who strivest to remain united to another! O beauteous maidenhood, at the last thou art stuck fast in love to a male being! O (holy) ascetic state, thou disappearest (when) the saints match human offences!

O body, thou art put to the yoke of the law of God, and ever and again committest fornication! Thou art crucified to this world[7] and continuest to act up to it! If the apostle Paul forbade communion to a woman caught in an adulterous relation with a strange man,[8] how much more when those concerned are saints dedicated to Christ! Thou art caught in the vile fellowship of this world, and yet regardest thyself as worthy of the blood of Christ or as united with his body! But this is not the case: if thou eat of the flesh of the Lord unworthily, then thou takest vainly instead of life the fire of thine everlasting punishment! O virgin: if thou strivest to please (another), then thou hast already committed a sin of volition, for the Evangelist says: *one cannot serve two masters, for he obeys the one, and despises the other.*[9] O virgin! so is it also with thee. Thou despisest God, whilst striving to please a man.

Wherefore contemplate the footprints of our ancestors! Consider the daughter of Jephthah: willing to do what had been promised by her father and vowing her own self as a sacrifice to the Lord, she first manifested her connection with God and took other virgins with her *that in the mountains throughout sixty days they might bewail her virginity.*[10] O luminous secrets which disclose the future in advance! Virgin is joined with virgin, and in love to her she bewails the peril of her flesh until the day of her reward comes! Rightly does he say 'sixty days', since he means the sixtyfold reward of holiness which the ascetic can gain through many pains, according to the teaching of the apostle: *Let us not lose courage*, he says, *in the hardest labours, in affliction, in grief, in suffering abuse: we suffer persecution, but we are not forsaken, because we bear in our body the passion of Christ. Wherefore we are by no means overcome.*[11] And again the same apostle left an example behind him, describing his own disasters and saying: *I have laboured much, I have frequently been imprisoned, I have suffered extremely many floggings, I have often fallen into deadly peril. Of the Jews*, he says, *I have five times received forty stripes save one, three times have I been beaten with rods, once have I been stoned; thrice have I suffered shipwreck, a day and a night I have spent in the depth of the sea; I have often journeyed,*[12] *often been in peril of rivers, in peril of robbers, in peril among unbelievers in manifold ways, in peril in cities, in peril among Gentiles, in peril in the wilderness, in peril among false brethren; in trouble and labour, frequently in sorrow, in many watchings, in hunger and thirst, in many fastings, in cold and nakedness, in inward anxieties, besides the cares which do not have direct reference to my personal suffering. And in all these I have not lost courage, because Christ was and still is with me.*[13]

Oh, through how much trouble does man attain to glory! Besides there is the word of the Lord, who says: *Whom I love*, he says, *I rebuke and chasten*[14] that the righteous man may be tested as gold in the crucible. What bodily joy can there be then in the life to come if the word of the Lord runs: *Oh! as a virgin, as a woman, so is the mystery of resurrection (which) you have shown to me, you who in the beginning of the world did institute vain feasts for yourselves and delighted in the wantonness of the Gentiles and behaved in the same way as those who take delight therein.*[15] Behold what sort of young maidens there are among you! But come and ponder over this, that there is one who tries the soul and a last day of retribution and persecution.

Where then art thou now, thou who hast passed the time of thy youth happily with a sinner, the apostle testifying moreover that *neither flesh nor blood will possess the kingdom of God*?[16]

And again the law runs: *let not a man glory in his strength, but rather let him trust in the Lord,*[17] and Jeremiah says: *Accursed is he who puts his hope in man.*[18] And in the Psalms it is said: *It is better to trust in the Lord than to rely on men.*[19] Why then art thou not afraid to abandon the Lord and to trust in a man who in the last judgment will not save thee but rather destroy? Consider and take note of the happening about which the following account informs us: *A peasant had a girl who was a virgin. She was also his only daughter, and therefore he besought Peter to offer a prayer for her. After he had prayed, the apostle said to the father that the Lord would bestow upon her what was expedient for her soul. Immediately the girl fell down dead.* O reward worthy and ever pleasing to God, to escape the shamelessness of the flesh and to break the pride of the blood! *But this distrustful old man, failing to recognise the worth of the heavenly grace, i.e. the divine blessing, besought Peter again that his only daughter be raised from the dead. And some days later, after she had been raised, a man who passed himself off as a believer*[20] *came into the house of the old man to stay with him, and seduced the girl, and the two of them never appeared again.*[21]

For the man who dishonours his own body makes himself like the godless. And therefore the dwelling-place of the godless cannot be found out, as David says: *I sought him but he was nowhere to be found,*[22] as also in the (mentioned) case of death those two did not dare (to appear) any more. Thou oughtest then, O virgin, to fear the judgment of this law: *If*, says Moses, *a betrothed virgin is caught unawares with another man, let the two of them be brought before the court of the elders and be condemned to death.*[23]

These happenings have been recorded for us on whom the end of this age has come. One thing stands fast: should a virgin who is betrothed to Christ be caught unawares with another man, let them both be committed for final sentence before the court of the elders, i.e. of Abraham, Isaac and Jacob, whose charge it is to investigate the case of their children. Then will the fathers disown their own children as evildoers. And finally the malefactors will cry amidst the torment of their punishment: Hear us, O Lord God, for our father Abraham has not known us, and Isaac and Jacob have disowned us! Thus then let the children conduct themselves that (some day) they may find themselves in the bosom of father Abraham. That is to say, that they may remain praiseworthy in his remembrance and be not as the daughters of Zion whom the Holy Spirit reproaches through Isaiah: *They moved together through the streets, dancing with their heads erect. And they engaged themselves to men in the villages of Jerusalem, and heaped up iniquity to the sky, and the Lord was angry and delivered them up to king Nebuchadnezzar to slavery for seventy years.*[24]

You also are disobedient and undisciplined, you who do something even worse than the first committed. In the end you also will be delivered up to the wicked king Nebuchadnezzar, as he says, i.e. to the devil who will fall upon you. And as they (the Jews), after they had spent seventy years in anguish, returned to their own places of abode, so a period of seven years is (now) appointed under Antichrist. But the pain of these seven years presents eternal anguish. And as, after their return to their homeland, they henceforth experienced much evil, so is it also now with (these): after death the soul of each one will be tormented unto the judgment day. And again, after the slaughter of the beast, the first resurrection will take place; and then will the faithless souls return to their dwellings; and according to the increase of their (earlier) evil-doings will their torment (now) be augmented beyond the first punishment.

Therefore, beloved, we must combat the works of the flesh because of the coming retribution. In order then that ye may escape eternal torment, ye must struggle, daughters, against flesh and blood so long as a period for that continues and a few days still remain wherein ye may contend for life. Why should the man who hast renounced the flesh be held fast in its lust? Why, O virgin, thou who has renounced a man, dost thou hug this physical beauty? Why (ascetic) givest thou up to a strange woman (i.e. one belonging to Christ) thy body which was not made for that? Why strivest thou against thine own salvation to find death in love? Hear the apostle who says to you: *See*, he says, *that ye give not place to the flesh through the liberty of God.*[25] And again: *Fulfil not the lusts of the flesh. For the flesh lusteth against the Spirit and the Spirit against the flesh. These are opposed to one another. Therefore*, he says, *do not what ye would. Otherwise the Spirit of God is not in you.*[26] O inherently false one, to despise the commandments of the holy law and (through) a deceitful marriage to lose in secret the life everlasting! O honeyed cheat, to draw on torment in the future! O unbridled passion for glory, to offend against the devotion that has been vowed to God! O steps that lead astray from the way, that a virgin is fond of the flesh of another! O faith(less) craving, theft of fire, honour entangled in crime![27] O broken promise, that the mind blazes up for a stranger! O pledge of lust, beauty inclined to crime! O alluring symbol of vice that brings disdain! *O seminari da membra vicinacio tenebrarum!*[28] O concealed thievery, to give an appearance of humility and chastity! O gloom of the dark deed which plunders the glory of Christ for ever! O fleeting remembrance of holiness which strives after death in the name of beauty! O *silver that has been refused*, which according to the saying of

Isaiah *is not worthy of God*![29] O dishonoured Sabbath in which the works of the flesh come to light in the last days and times! O foot, that failest on the way to holiness and dost not arrive at a sure habitation! O ship burst open by pirates, thou that gettest away empty and miserable! O house that is undermined by burglars whilst the watchmen sleep and lose the costly treasure! O maidenly youth, thou that fallest off miserably from right conduct! O enlargement of trust in this world which turns into desolation in eternity![30] O consequence of unchastity which brings down upon itself the malady of melancholy! O fountain of sweet poison which springs up from the flesh as inextricable entanglement! O wretched house founded on sand! O despicable crime of (this) time, that corruptest not thine own members but those of a stranger! O fleeting enjoyment on a brink of collapse! O parcel of deceit! O unsleeping ardour for the perdition of the soul! O tower that is in building to be left unfinished! O shameful work, thou art the scorn of them that pass by! Why, O virgin, dost thou not ponder over it and estimate the heavenly charges before laying the foundation? In the beginning thou hast acted too hastily, and before the house was completed, thou hast already experienced a terrible collapse![31] In your case the saying of the law has been fulfilled, the prophecy has come to pass: *Many a tract of land*, it says, *is built upon and soon it grows old; temples and cities are built in the land and soon they are abandoned*![32] O flames of lust! The unclean profane with their lust the temple of God and by Him are condemned to destruction! Oh, a contest is entered upon in the stadium, and when it has hardly come to grappling, the shields fall to the ground! O city captured by enemies and reduced to a wilderness!

Against this whorish behaviour the Lord turns through Ezekiel saying: *Thou hast built thee thy brothel, thou hast desecrated thy beauty and thy comeliness in every by-way, thou hast become an unclean woman, thou who hast heaped up shamelessness for thyself. Thy disgrace in the unchastity which thou hast practised with thy lovers will yet come to light.* And again, *As I live, saith the Lord, Sodom has not so done as thou Jerusalem and thy daughters. But the iniquity of Sodom, thy sister, is fulfilled. For Samaria has not committed the half of thy sins. Thou hast multiplied iniquities beyond thy sisters in all that thou hast done. Wherefore be ashamed and take thy disgrace upon thy head.*[33]

O how frequently the scourgings and beatings of God are not spared, and yet no one takes to heart the word of the Lord to be concerned about the future life! Has not Jerusalem, possessing the law, sinned more than Sodom and Gomorrah, which possessed no law? And have not the crimes of Jerusalem, whose sons and daughters have stood under the banner of faith, outweighed those of Samaria, which already from the beginning was worldly-minded?

On the unprecedented crime of this new people the apostle says: *One hears commonly of unchastity among you and indeed of such unchastity as is never met with among the Gentiles, that one lives with his father's wife. And ye are yet puffed up, and do not rather mourn, that such an evil-doer may be removed from your midst. I am indeed absent in the body, but in the spirit am among you and already, as if I were present, I have passed sentence on the evil-doer: to hand over that man to Satan in the name of Christ.*[34]

O invention of the devil, sport for those about to perish! Oh poison instead of honey, to take a father's wife in the same way as any bride dedicated to Christ whom in thine heart thou hast craved for! O man, thou hast lent no ear to the wisdom that says to thee: the lust of the ascetic dishonours the virgin.[35] So also did the first created man fall because of a virgin: *when he saw a woman giving him a smile, he fell.*[36] His senses became tied to a craving which he had never known before;[37] assuredly he had not experienced earlier its flavour and the sweetness that proved his downfall. O man who fearest not the face of this criminal person, passing by whom many have lost their lives. The disciple of the Lord, Judas Jacobi, brings that to our remembrance when he says: *Beloved, I would bring to your remembrance, though ye know, what happened to them* who were oppressed by the corruption of the flesh, as for instance the genuine persons (*veraces*) *who did not preserve their dignity, but abandoned their heavenly abode* and, enticed by lust, went to the daughters of men to dwell with them.[38]

Today also they forfeit the angelic character who crave to dwell with strange daughters, according to the word of the Lord who proclaimed by Isaiah: *Woe unto you who join house to house and add field to field that they may draw nigh one another.*[39] And in Micah it is said: *Bewail the house which you have pulled on yourselves and endure of yourselves the punishment of indignation.*[40] Does the Lord mean perhaps the house or the field of this time when he warns us against pressing them together? (No) rather it is a matter here of warnings in reference to holiness, in which the separation of man and woman is ordered. So the Lord also admonishes us through Jeremiah, saying, *It is an excellent thing for a man that he bear the yoke in his youth; he will sit alone when his hope is real; he will keep quiet and have patience.*[41] 'To bear the yoke' is then to observe God's order. And in conclusion the Lord says: *Take my yoke upon you.*[42] And further, 'in his youth' means in his hope. Thus he has commanded that salvation be preserved in lonely celibacy, so that each one of you may remain as a lonely tower according to the saying of the Evangelist that house should not remain upon house, but should come down at once. Why then, O man, dost thou make haste to build you a ruin upon a strange house and thus to occasion not only your own destruction but also that of the bride of Christ who is united to you?

And also if thou art free from unchastity, already thou committest a sin in keeping up connections with women;[43] for finally, thus says the Lord in the Gospel: *He who looks upon a woman to lust after her hath committed adultery with her already in his heart.*[44] On this account a man must live for God sincerely and free from all lust. In Daniel also we read: As these false old men, who had craved for the beauty of Susanna, were unable to practise any unchastity with her, they slandered her. Susanna was brought before their court, and these rogues had her stand before them with her head uncovered so that they might satisfy their craving at least in looking on her beauty.[45] And thus they were unable to escape capital punishment. How much more when the last day comes! What, thinkest thou, will Christ do to those who have surrendered their own members to rape? The apostle has already shown the future in advance, saying: *Let no temptation take hold of you*, he says, *save what is human*![46] O temptation to sensuality! Man is not able to control himself, and inflicts on himself the predicted fatal wounds! O exhalations of the flesh! The glowing fire hidden deep in the heart nourishes a conflagration! O ignoble fight, to strike root in a dark night! O tree of seducing fruit that shows thick foliage! O false lips, out of which honey drops and which in the end are as bitter as poison! O charming eloquence, the words of which shoot arrows into the heart! O madness of love: death fetters the young as a chain, whilst wisdom announces the future, that is, what it always orders: *Avoid, my son, every evil and everything that resembles it.*[47] And further: *And every man who takes part in a foot-race abstains from all things that he may be able to obtain the crown that is prepared for him.*[48]

Why takest thou, O man, a woman as a servant? Consider the conduct of (our) holy ancestors. Thus Elias, a noble man who still lives in the body, took a young man as servant, to whom also he left his mantle as a holy keepsake when he was taken up into paradise in a chariot of fire.[49] There Enoch also lives in the body, who was carried away (there) in the first age. O holy dispensation of God, who has provided for the coming age! Enoch, the righteous, from among the first people, was commissioned[50] to commit to writing the history of the first men, and the holy Elias (was given the task) of registering the new deeds of this later people![51]

All that has thus to be construed according to the condition of (our) time: each of the two springs from his own age, Enoch (as a symbol) of righteousness and Elias (as a symbol) of holiness. But we must comply with the rule of our holiness, as the apostle says: *In body and spirit genus must resemble genus and the disciple the master.*[52] And the spirit of Elias rested finally on Elisha. He also begged of him that he might immediately receive from him a double blessing like the one which (later) the Lord gave to his advanced disciples, saying, *He that believes on me will also do the works that I do, and will do greater works than these.*[53] But such grace is granted only to those who fulfil the commandments of the Master. What should we now say? If Elisha served in the house of Elias to comply with the rule of propriety and the boy Gehazi assisted the (prophet) Elisha as Baruch (the prophet) Jeremiah, in order to leave us an (instructive) remembrance, why does a man today take a woman as servant[54] under a semblance of holiness? If it is a matter of a close relative, then that will do; but not if she is a strange woman. After the flood the sons of Noah looked for places for themselves where they might build cities, and they named them after their wives.[55] Precisely so do these (men) now behave who are united (to women).

O ascetics of God who look back at women to offer them gifts, to give them property, to promise them houses, to make them presents of clothes, to surrender to them their own souls and yield to their name all that belongs to them! If thou then, O man, behavest rightly and innocently, why dost thou not take thine own sister with thee? Why doest thou not give her all that belongs to thee, and thou wilt possess every thing? Further and further thou separatest thyself from her: thou hatest her, thou persecutest her. And yet thy greatest safety is in her. Nay, separated from her thou attachest thyself to another. And thus dost thou think to remain wealthy in body and not be controlled by any lust, and dost say that thou possessest the heavenly hope. Hear a word that holds good for thee. Consider what the Lord in the Gospel says to Mary: *Touch me not*, says he, *for I am not yet ascended to my Father*![56] O divine examples which have been written for us! And Paul, the chosen vessel (of the Lord) and the impregnable wall among the disciples,[57] admonishes us when in the course of his mission the virgin Thecla, full of innocent faithfulness to Christ, wished to kiss his chain - mark thou what the apostle said to her: *Touch me not*, he said, *because of the frailty of* (*this*) *time*.[58] Thou dost see then, O young man, what the present Lord and the recorded testament of the disciple have said against the flesh. For they did not order the women to withdraw for their own sakes, for the Lord cannot be tempted and just as little can Paul, his vicar, but these admonitions and commands were uttered for the sake of us who are now members of Christ.

Above all the ascetic should avoid women on that account and see to it that he does (worthily) the duty entrusted to him by God. Consider the rebuilding of Jerusalem: at the time of this laborious work every man was armed and mail-clad, and with one hand he built whilst in the other he held fast a sword, always ready to contend against the enemy. Apprehend then the mystery, how one should build the sanctuary of celibacy: in ascetic loneliness one hand must be engaged in the work that an extremely beautiful city may be built for God, whilst the other grasps the sword and is always ready for action against the wicked devil. That is then to be interpreted in this way: both hands, i.e. the spirit and the flesh, have in mutual harmony to bring the building to completion, the spirit being always on the lookout for the enemy and the flesh building on the bedrock of good conduct. Therefore it is said in the Gospel: *Let your works shine before men that they may glorify your Father in heaven*.[59] Behold what a splendid structure is built in the heavenly Jerusalem. In this city one contends rightly in a lonely position, without any intercourse with the flesh, as it stands in the Gospel: *In the coming age*, says the Lord, *they will neither marry nor be given in marriage, but will be as the angels in heaven.*[60] Thus we must endeavour through blameless conduct to gain for ourselves everlasting honour in the future age. O man, who understandest nothing at all of the fruits of righteousness, why has the Lord made the divine phoenix and not given it a little wife, but allowed it to remain in loneliness? Manifestly only on purpose to show the standing of virginity, i.e. that young men, remote from intercourse with women, should remain holy. And its resurrection points finally to life. In this connection David says in the Psalms: *I will lay me down and sleep in peace for thou, O Lord, makest me to dwell lonesome in hope.*[61] O peaceful rest given without interruption! O great security, when a man lives lonesome in the body! *Thou canst not expect to bind glowing coals on thy garment, and not set the robe alight.*[62] Should you do such a thing, then you will remain naked and your shame will be manifest. Add to this the word of the prophet: *All flesh is grass.*[63] That a man then may not go up in flames, let him keep far from fire. Why exposest thou thine eternal salvation to loss through a trifle? Hast thou not read in the law this word that holds good for thee: *The people sat down to eat and to drink; and they rose to make merry; and of them 23,000 fell there?*[64] For they had begun to have intercourse with the daughters of men, i.e. they allowed themselves to be invited by them to their unclean sacrifices, *and the children of Israel dedicated themselves to Baalpeor.*[83]

Behold, what a godless play it was in which (the children of Israel) allowed themselves to be entangled, and perished! Seeing in advance how such criminal doings would multiply until the end, Christ the Saviour was grieved, and he said: *Woe, woe unto the souls that despise their own judgment! For I see men who delight their souls in vanity and abandon themselves to the unclean world. I see also how all that is for the benefit of the enemy! Therefore I can stand by them and say: O souls that apply yourselves to unchastity and have no fear before God!*[66] The Gibeonites also in the time of the Judges moved the Lord to indignation. Twelve thousand strong men arose to overthrow the city, and only three hundred and two virgins who had had no sexual intercourse with men came forth alive.[67] The name Gibeonites signifies *children of confusion*, who received the body of Christ in the form of a woman, and prostituted it to their amusement, and made it an object of derision and mockery. Dost thou not do likewise in venturing to ridicule the members of Christ with a virgin? For all of us, both men and women, who have been baptised into Christ have put on Christ.[68] It is then a matter of the violation not of earthy flesh but of the body of Christ. And rightly was that city taken by the attacking twelve legions, which were a symbol of the twelve apostles. Rightly have they sprung from a strong race, for they are called sons of thunder.[69] In the last judgment they will appear, equipped with might, to perform miracles against the Gentiles. And they will judge the twelve tribes of Israel, sitting on twelve thrones. And no one from the church will then be able to get away, apart from the virgins dedicated to God, whose members have not been defiled by the enemy with the infection of his evil will. The number also suggests the sign of the cross: for 300 is written with the Greek letter T, and T is the figure of the cross, which makes its appearance in the life of virginity. Rightly also is the kingdom of heaven to be arrived at through five virgins, by which he means that the promises can be certain only through purity and wisdom. And therefore the promise was not fulfilled to Abraham through fleshly procreation, but it was through divine inspiration that he received the blessing. What should we then say to this? Can virginity not perhaps itself lead to eternal torment? (Oh yes!), but these five virgins were foolish, precisely as are those who today have not watched over their flesh but have marred their readiness for battle through desire for the male sex. Wherefore also David says in the Psalms: *Those who mounted on horses fell asleep.*[70] In body indeed they went on horseback, but they were unable to persist in their virgin watchfulness, just like the children of confusion who were again thrown from their horses. O dark cringing of the flesh which has turned into torment! Finally they will reprove themselves for their past doings with the following words: O wretched flesh, which has brought us to ruin! Had we not suffered ourselves to be misled by thee, then we also could have been numbered among the saints!

O man, who believest that all these things shall be! Thou knowest that different judgments must be passed on sinners. In the member with which each man has sinned, in the same also shall he be tormented.

The prophet Elias bears witness to a vision: *The angel of the Lord*, he says, *showed me a deep valley, which is called Gehenna, burning with brimstone and pitch. In this place the souls of many sinners dwell and are tormented in different ways. Some suffer hanging from the genitals, others by the tongue, some by the eyes, others head downwards. The women are tormented in their breasts, and the young hang from their hands. Some virgins are roasted on a gridiron, and other souls undergo an unceasing torment. The multiplicity of the torments answers to the diversity of the sins of each. The adulterers and the corrupters of such as are under age are tormented in their genitals. Those who hang from their tongues are the blasphemers and false witnesses. They have their eyes burned who have stumbled through their glances and who have looked at foul things with craving for them. Head downwards there hang those who have detested the righteousness of God, who have been evil-minded, quarrelsome towards their fellows. Rightly then are they burned according to the punishment imposed on them. If some women are punished with torment in their breasts, then these are women who for sport have surrendered their own bodies to men, and for this reason these also hang from their hands.*[71] Solomon took these things into account, saying: *Blessed is the eunuch who has committed no offence with his hands.*[72] And again, *If thou controllest the craving of thy heart, then art thou an athlete.*[73]

And through wisdom he admonishes in the following way: *Of what benefit to an idol is an offering when it can neither taste nor smell it? Just as little does it benefit an eunuch to embrace a virgin. O my son, thou shouldest not make her the object of your pleasure*![74] Thou seest clearly that thou has become a stranger to God.

In another passage we read: *I abhor such sport*, he says, *unclean heresy, lust of the ascetic, bodies entwined in one another*![75] I am ashamed to bring forward the further final doings, which the enemy has instigated and to which the apostle has prudently called our attention, saying: *I am afraid concerning you lest ye be seduced by the enemy, as* (*in those days*) *Eve was cunningly tempted by the serpent.*[76]

Therefore, watching craftily, let us arm ourselves with spiritual weapons that we may be able to defeat the giant, as the discourse of the Lord by his prophet runs: *He who defeats a giant*, says he, *takes his spoil.*[77] That means to bridle the desires of the flesh that, as its spoil, we may be able to carry away the everlasting resurrection. (That can only take place) after we have been renewed to the glory of God. How wilt thou then be capable of defeating a giant if thou art prevented by women? Hear the thanksgiving[78] rendered by John, the disciple of the Lord, when praying before his death: *O Lord, thou who from my infancy until this age hast preserved me untouched by woman, thou who hast kept my body from them so that the mere sight of a woman excites abhorrence in me*. O gift (of God), to remain untouched by the influence of women! By the grace of this holy state thou canst love what is abominable to the flesh. But thou honorary ascetic, how canst thou believe that thou canst remain free from sordid deed if willingly thou hast women always before thee? Does what we teach (here) stand perhaps outside the law? Compare with this what even the demons declared when they made confession before the deacon Dyrus on the arrival of John:[79] *In the last times many will attempt to dispossess us, saying that they are free from women and from craving after them and clean. And yet if we desired it, we could possess even them themselves.*

Thou seest then, O man, how the strange spirits, i.e. the deeds of the devil, testify to thee that one can be overcome by womanly beauty. How then canst thou set free the bodies possessed by them if thou thyself art possessed by them? To conquer them one must have in oneself the necessary power. *Beware then of being possessed by the evil one or of being conquered by the adulterer;*[80] *i.e. keep thyself far from association with women and from pleasantry with them during meal-times*. Thus runs the word of Holy Scripture: *Suffer not thy heart to be enticed by her lest thou also come to death. Thus, my child, beware of her, as of a serpent's head.*[81] Receive into thine heart the admonitions of the blessed John, who, when he was invited to a wedding, came only for the sake of chastity. And what did he say? *Children, while your flesh is still clean and you have a body that is untouched, and you are not caught in corruption nor soiled by Satan, that most adverse and shame<less> (enemy) to chastity, know now more fully the mystery of conjugal union: it is a device of the serpent, a disregard of the teaching, an injury to the seed, a gift of death, a work of destruction, a teaching of division, a work of corruption, a boorish rusticity < . . . >, a second sowing of the enemy, an ambush of Satan, a device of the jealous one, an unclean fruit of parturition, a shedding of blood, a passion in the mind, a falling from reason, a token of punishment, an instruction of pain, an operation of fire, a sign of the enemy, the deadly malice of envy, the embrace of deceit, a union with bitterness, a morbid humour of the mind, an invention of ruin, the desire of a phantom, a converse with matter, a comedy of the devil, hatred of life, a fetter of darkness, an intoxication < . . . >, a derision of the enemy, a hindrance of life, that separates from the Lord, the beginning of disobedience, the end and death of life. Hearing this, my children, bind yourselves each one of you in an indivisible, true and holy matrimony, waiting for the one incomparable and true bridegroom from heaven, even Christ, who is a bridegroom for ever*[82].

If the apostle allowed marriage itself to be dissolved that it might not occasion a heaping up of offences,[83] what should we say of the state of the ascetic, which most of all should be free from fleshly lust? O bodies separated from one another and already dedicated to Christ! O carnal glow of youth, difficult to quench! O dew that, flowing down from heaven, warms the cold vessel! O those who have ventured to call back to life the lost heavenly dignity! O endless glory of the saints, from death set free! O field pleasing to Christ, which brings forth eternal fruits! O denial of the flesh, spiritual nuptials with eternal marriage-ties in the heavenly habitations! O how much one can do in the conflict for chastity when one is discerning!

When finally the apostle Andrew came to a wedding to show the glory of God, he separated the spouses intended for one another, the women and the men, and taught them to remain holy in celibacy.[84] O glory of the one-horned lamb that separates the sheep from the goats, whilst the Lord himself admonishes us: Hear me, my chosen sheep, and fear not the wolf.[85] Not to fear the wolf means to flee from the offence of death. To separate the sheep from the goats means to keep oneself free from foul sins, to live in solitude as one of God's ascetics. So also it is said in Ezra in reference to the future: *Come ye from all cities to Jerusalem to the mount and bring with you cypress and palm leaves and build you detached booths*![86]

Thou seest then, O holy man, that the hope described by the authors named holds good for us that, pure in body, we may live in solitude in our booths and that no one of us suffer himself to be fettered by carnal love. *For*, according to the question and answer of Christ, our Lord, *the cypress is a mystery of chastity*.[87] Its spike on a single stalk rightly aims at the sky. By the palm leaves also he signifies the victory, the glory of martyrdom. Out of these two kinds of trees are the booths built, which are the bodies of the saints. And since he added *out of the mount*, i.e. from the body of Christ, he meant doubtless the *substancia conexa*.[88] Blessed then are those who preserve this *substancia*! These the Lord praises through Isaiah: *Every one that does not profane the Sabbath but keeps it and takes hold of my covenant, them will I bring to my holy mountain and make them joyful in my house of prayer, and their offering and burnt offering will be accepted on my altar*. So saith the Lord.[89] The keeping holy of the Sabbath clearly means not to defile the pure flesh. And therefore was it ordered in the books of the patriarchs that no unprofitable work should be done on the Sabbath.[90] Clearly then it is a positive fact that God forbids the doing of the works of this world in the flesh that is dedicated to Him.

Once upon a time on a Sabbath two men were surprised collecting wood, and God in indignation ordered that the two of them should be put to death.[91] That took place in the past, but it is to be interpreted in the following way: the two collectors of wood signify those who are committing sin, their evil-doings being symbolised by the collected foliage. And therefore the bundle of wood could not be made by one person alone, but it was two together who defiled the Sabbath. Rightly does the Lord give warning by Ezekiel: *Behold the princes of Israel, they have despised my sanctuary and defiled my sabbaths; adulterous men have shed blood in thy midst, O Jerusalem*.[92]

O most beautiful city, in the midst of thy beauty they have exposed their father's nakedness! O priceless holiness of God rejected by all evil-doers! O sabbaths dedicated to Christ, desecrated by burglars! O priceless city, redeemed by the blood of Christ and overwhelmed with most filthy indecencies! The exposing of the father's nakedness means assuredly the violation of the virginity that has been consecrated to God. Finally the Lord urges him on, namely the prophet, to lodge the following reproach: *Each one of you has defiled a wife not his own in shameless act, and each one of you has ravished his father's daughter*.[93] O error of judgment! The devil entices many minds to ravish not their own but the bride of Christ! O imitation of the animal way of life, when a man sleeps with his father's daughter and with one born of the self-same mother!

Therefore, under the inspiration of the Holy Spirit, the voice of the lawgiver sounds:[94] *Cursed be he who lies with his own sister. And the people said, Amen, Amen*.[95] Why art thou not afraid to lie with this sister, daughter of (thy) father and of (thy) mother - here Christ is meant as father and the church as mother - as if thou couldest evade the punishment that is to be imposed by the court? Consider the by-gone doings recorded in the Books of the Kings, e.g. when Adonijah craved for the Shunammite Abishag, his father's girl (*puella*), who was a symbol of the virginity that is dedicated to Christ, (was) he not because of a mere thought <. . . >?[96] And if Adonijah was punished with death without having realised his purpose, how much more today he who is found guilty of such a deed? If Adonijah perished because of a word, what punishment, thinkest thou, will be measured out for the act? It is hard for a man controlled by lust to come forth unsullied, as the word of the Lord through the prophet Haggai indicates, saying: *Ask the priests concerning the law and say: if one bear holy flesh in the skirt of his garment and after that do touch with his skirt bread, wine, oil, or any other food, will it thereby be holy or not? And the priests answered and said, No. And Haggai said: if one who is defiled touches all this, will it thereby be unclean? And the priests answered and said: It will be unclean. Then answered Haggai and said: So is it also with this people and with this nation before me, saith the Lord.*[97] Now it is the sanctified flesh, dedicated to chastity, that was touched by the skirt of the baptismal robe. But he showed that had it come into contact with what is despicable, (this) food would not thereby become holy; for the material food signifies the transient wishes of the human mind. That is carnal food, and it is not pleasing to the Holy Spirit. Therefore he decreed that the king's garment should not be considered as holy thereby. And further he has likewise shown that there is a state of defilement whereby the creature also is defiled. What Moses had already previously said has been made clear to us by the author of (this) saying: *Everything that an unclean person touches shall be unclean.*[98] And what says Haggai (in addition)? *Even so this people and this race, saith the Lord.* The city governor orders that the city dwellers be like him! O thou that turnest far aside from holiness and usurpest honour for thyself, putting thyself on a par with that priest![99] O unreasonable king, thou that exploitest the people to rebellion! O the resemblance of an insincere course of life; many step in and out without justice! O vain, strange prophecy which has no validity for the future! O worldly reckoning which is rejected by Christ! In conclusion he reproves them on the last day with the words: *Depart from me, ye evil-doers, I know you not: so will I speak to those who go into destruction.*[100]

Thou seest how those who counterfeit holy celibacy, the enemies of chastity, the unjust, the <. . . > of belief, the destroyers of the flock of God will be rejected. He shows that no one will escape punishment. Why thinkest thou, O foolish man, that what thou committest in secrecy is not forbidden, when God is Lord of the night and of the day, saying <. . . >. If one knows that it is not lawful to comply with the divers desires of the flesh and does what he regards as contrary to belief, can that not be described as obstinate offence? And it is that even if he does not give a thought to the fact that, although no one is present, contempt of the law weighs more heavily than unchastity. The lusts of the flesh must be deplored; this greediness must be expelled from the mind; but thou repentest not of this offence, and passest thyself off as guiltless when on the threshold of the glory that is due to (guiltlessness), and praisest thyself!

But consider what David prophesies and what the Holy Spirit says through his mouth: *I said*, he says, *ye are gods and altogether children of the Highest, but ye will die like men and perish like one of the princes.*[101] O gods who die a human death! O glory of princes that falls from the height into the depth! That will take place some day, there being a separation between the righteous and the profane, and no fellowship of the believer with the (un)righteous, of death with life. Or else consider what lies between destruction and salvation![102] Today the prophecy of the Lord through Ezekiel has finally come to fulfilment: *My house*, he says, *has for me turned into such dross as brass, iron, tin, lead in the midst of silver.*[103] Into such a mixture have you turned.[104] For in the state of the ascetic, which is silver, there have emerged in the end alloys of different sorts, bad ingredients. Now these are the elements of this mixture. The iron signifies the hardness of the heart in which the wisdom of the spiritual mind has taken no root. Reuben was rightly characterised by Jacob as the hardness of iron, for he is reckoned the hardest among those who belong to the Jewish people[105] The lead signifies the heaviness of the flesh, which is extremely heavy. By this is signified the offence which submerges men in the destruction of death, for the submerging of Pharaoh and his people as lead in the sea according to the account in Scripture[106] was (only) a sign (for us). And similarly we are admonished through Zechariah: *The mouth of a shameless woman is stopped up with lead*,[107] whereby crime is clearly meant. The brass signifes the stench of the sinful flesh, after which the sons of Israel craved in Egypt when they longed for the fleshpots.[108] And on that account they died and were unable to come into possession of the ancestral promises, precisely as those also who suffer themselves to be enticed by the human < . . . > of the flesh will not attain to the possession of the kingdom of God! The interpretation of the tin is this: They are tin who dazzle our eyes with the wisdom of God and who in the matter of chastity exhibit an appearance of polluted silver, but who are in no wise of great value in the church. They will be rejected according to the saying of Solomon: *In secrecy they carry out abortions and at the same time think that they will live for ever.*[109] That is then the mixture that has come to be in the house of God. O seducers of women who concoct new doctrine! Burglars in strange houses, corrupters of maidens, violators of chastity, apostates from belief, resisters of the truth, rebels to the discipline of God! O outrageous mixture! Thou hast turned into silver, i.e. to chastity, and therefore these will be melted in the furnace of burning judgment, and then will the Lord purify for himself precious, pure, sterling, fine silver for that holy Jerusalem with a view to preparing for himself the paternal throne. But the others, of whom we have spoken above, who have apostatized from belief, these will go into eternal torment! *Blessed then are those who have remained holy in body and united in spirit, for they will often speak to God! Blessed are those who have kept themselves from the unchastity of this world, for they will be pleasing to Christ, the Son of God, and to the Father, the Lord! Blessed are those who have kept the baptism of salvation, for they will enjoy eternal delight.*[110] He who has the hearing of the heart, let him hear what God promises: *To the victor*, he says, *will I give to eat of the tree of life which stands in the paradise of my God.*[111] O incorruptible nourishment that comes from the tree of wisdom, the leaves of which are destined for the healing of the nations, where there shall be no curse and where no unclean flesh can enter, where no spite from unrighteous works and no lie will find a place, but only God and the Lamb will be enthroned. Their servants will render them homage for ever and ever![112] These then are the servants of God who always minister to His will and please Him, who live not for the flesh but for the Holy Spirit. These are they who will not be overtaken by the second death and who will eat of the hidden manna, the food of the heavenly paradise.[113] They will receive the white stone, the helmet of eternal salvation, upon which is written the ineffable name of God, which no man knows save he who has received it. O host most white, legions of sanctity, precious to God, to whom Christ the Lord orders royal powers to be given for the judging of all! Like the potter's useless vessels will they smash them! *I will give them*, he says, *the eternal morning star, as I myself received (it) from my Father.*[114] Likewise will he grant those victors to be clad in splendid clothing, nor will their name ever be deleted from the book of life. *I will confess them*, he says, *before my Father and his angels in heaven.*[115] Blessed therefore are they who persevere even unto the end, as the Lord says: *To him that overcometh will I grant to sit at my right hand in my throne, even as I have overcome and sit on the right hand of my Father in his throne to all ages for ever and ever. Amen.*[116]

HERE ENDETH THE EPISTLE OF TITUS, THE DISCIPLE OF PAUL, ON THE ESTATE OF CHASTITY.

Notes

4. The Pseudo-Titus Epistle

1. In recent years several translations of PsT have appeared: NTApo³ II, 141-166, English translation by George Ogg, (reproduced here in revised form); Erbetta III, 93-110 (Italian); Moraldi II, 1757-1788 (Italian). Cf. also H. Chadwick, *Priscillian of Avila*, Oxford 1976, pp. 109-110.
2. In the translating of this difficult text the suggestions of W. Schneemelcher and K. Schäferdiek were of great value to me.
3. This saying, to which Paul himself appeals (1 Cor. 2:9) and which for its part recalls Is. 64:4, has had a great after-effect in later tradition. Origen already discussed the problem of its origin and came to the conclusion that Paul borrowed this sentence from the Apocalypse of Elias, *in nullo enim regulari libro hoc positum invenitur, nisi in secretis Elias prophetae* (*Comm. in Mt.* XXVII 3-10; GCS 38, p. 250). Both the Martyrium Petri (c. 10; cf. Aa I, 98 and 316 below) and the Gospel

of Thomas found at Nag Hammadi (log. 17; cf. vol. I, p. 119) ascribe this saying expressly to Jesus. There is another parallel in the Manichaean Turfan fragment M 789 (cf. vol. I, p. 403). PsT puts the word of this promise into the mouth of the *Lord* and adds to the usual text a concluding sentence, to the affinity of which with Clement of Alexandria (*Protr.* IX 94) Harnack (op. cit., p. 193) has referred. The question to what immediate source this quotation should be carried back is not easy to answer. Resch. (cf. *Agrapha*[1], pp. 102, 154-167, 281) suggested that this saying is to be conceived as a logion; but the assumption that PsT wished in this place to cite nothing other than 1 Cor. 2:9 seems to me much more likely. The naming in both passages of the author of the promise in question also goes to prove that. Cf. NTApo[3] I, 300.
4. Mk. 12:25 par.
5. Rev. 14:4.
6. 1 Cor. 7:34.
7. Cf. Gal. 6:14.
8. This happening is recorded in detail in the Actus Petri cum Simone (c. 2, Aa I, 46, and below, p. 288). The name of the woman concerned is there given as Rufina.
9. Mt. 6:24.
10. Judg. 11:38.
11. 2 Cor. 4:8ff.
12. The correction *in (ex) pedicionibus* instead of *in pedicionibus* proposed by Bulhart is apposite.
13. 2 Cor. 11:23ff.
14. Rev. 3:19.
15. Harnack regards this quotation as a logion of unknown origin (op. cit., p. 195).
16. 1 Cor. 15:50.
17. Jer. 9:23.
18. Jer. 17:5.
19. Ps. 118:8.
20. The text runs: *homo vinctus fidelis*. Our translation is based on Harnack's assumption that a scribe erroneously replaced the original *fictus* by *vinctus*. Ficker (NTApo[2], p. 228) understands the *homo vinctus* as 'the slave of a believer' or 'a bewitched Christian man'.
21. Augustine ascribes this story to the Manichaean apocrypha: *In apocryphis legunt . . . hortulani filiam ad precem ipsius Petri esse mortuam* (*c. Adimantum* 17.5: CSEL 25/1, 170 l.3). Unhappily he does not give the title of this apocryphon. This story is not found in the extant Actus Petri Vercellenses. Ficker (NTApo[2], p. 227) is of opinion that it never belonged to them, even if it be assumed that these Actus are due to mutilations. Cf. pp. 279, 287 below.
22. Ps. 37:36.
23. Deut. 22:23.
24. The source of this apocryphal quotation cannot be traced.
25. Gal. 5:13.
26. Gal. 5:16.
27. The text runs: *O fida cupiditas et ignis praerogativa dignitas sceleris apta*. Bulhart suggests that *fida* and *dignitas* should either be understood ironically or replaced by *(per) fida* and *(in) dignitas*. The present translation, which has as its basis only the correction of the *fida*, seems to me to render clearly the right sense of the sentence. PsT lays emphasis on the worthiness (*dignitas*) of these 'honorary ascetics' in order to describe more realistically the seriousness of their sins.
28. In spite of the correction proposed by Bulhart: *O seminari da(re) membra vicinacio tenebrarum*, the passage remains unintelligible to me.
29. Is. 1:22 or the Apocryphon of Isaiah.
30. The text runs: *O locupletacio secularis fiducia egere in aevo caeleste*. De Bruyne suggests *fiduciae* instead of *fiducia*. Bulhart translates: 'Sinful gain in the earthly life has as its consequence lack of hope for the endless life.'

31. Cf. Lk. 14:28ff.
32. The source of this apocryphal quotation cannot be determined.
33. Cf. Ezek. 16:24, 25, 31, 36, 48, 49, 51, 52.
34. 1 Cor. 5:1ff.
35. Ecclus. 20:4?
36. This allusion to the fall of Adam is regarded by Harnack (op. cit., p. 192) as a remnant of a lost Book of Adam. Since it is the seduction of Adam by a woman that is spoken of, I am inclined to understand the *irrisio* as 'the giving of a smile' rather than as 'derision'.
37. The words *rursus haberet* of the original have been left out in the translation because they seem to have no suitable sense in the context.
38. The allusion to Gen 6:2 (cf. Jud. 1:5f.) is typical of many ascetic writings which deal with the theme of PsT. Cf. *de Singularitate Clericorum* 28 (Hartel, CSEL 3, p. 204.10); Bachiarius, *de Reparatione Lapsi* c. 4 (PL 20, 1059).
39. Is. 5:8.
40. Mic. 1:11 (?)
41. Lam. 3:27-28.
42. Mt. 11:29.
43. The text runs: *Licet inmunis a scelere stupri, et in hoc ipsut peccasti eo quod in conplexum foeminarum teneris.* I do not regard Bulhart's correction *licet a scelere stupri (s)et . . . peccasti* as necessary, since the passage is understandable without it.
44. Mt. 5:28.
45. Cf. Dan. 13:32 ('Susanna' in Apocrypha).
46. Cf. 1 Cor. 10:13.
47. Although this quotation agrees verbally with Didache 3.1, it may yet be asked whether PsT has quoted the Didache itself or one of the sayings of Sirach that are similar in content. The introduction of *prudentia* occurs again and again in this and similar quotations (e.g. lines 109 and 420). Cf. Harnack, op. cit., p. 195.
48. 1 Cor. 9:25.
49. 2 Kings 2:15.
50. This charge to Enoch, unknown in the Bible, forms a kind of leitmotif in the extant Ethiopic and Slavonic versions of the Book of Enoch.
51. Harnack (p. 193) is of opinion that this statement goes back to the Apocalypse of Elias. Bulhart and De Bruyne have proposed many corrections of the text. But the sense of the passage is clear without them.
52. The source of this Paul-saying is unknown.
53. Jn. 14:12.
54. The text runs: *Cur . . . mascel sive vir feminam sumit?* The *sive vir* is regarded by Bulhart as a gloss on the strange *mascel*, which was constantly rejected by the grammarians and is to be found only in the Vetus Latina of the Codex Lugdunensis.
55. In this passage Harnack finds the starting-point for the assumption that an apocryphal History of Noah is the source of these allusions.
56. Jn. 20:17.
57. As a parallel to this passage (*Eciam et vas electionis Paulus, vere datus inexpugnabilis murus ex discentibus, exortatur missus*) Harnack (p. 198) has referred to the Epistula Apostolorum c. 31 (cf. vol. I, p. 267), where it is said: 'And he will be among my elect a chosen vessel and a wall that does not fall.' In view of the numerous parallel passages which the ascetic literature presents (cf. *de Centesima* [ed. Reitzenstein, ZNW 15, 1914] lines 191, 278; Cyprian, *de Habitu Virg*. 23 [ed. Hartel, CSEL 3, p. 204.11]; Jerome, *Ep*. 22.5 [ed. Hilberg, CSEL 54, p. 149.11]; Bachiarus, *de Fide* [PL 20, 1023]), I am inclined to carry back the description of Paul as *vas electionis*, which goes back ultimately to Acts 9:25, to the influences of the ascetic literature just mentioned rather than to the Epistula Apostolorum.

58. The scene is described in the surviving Acta Pauli cum Thecla c. 18 (As I, 247, and see below, p. 242), but there the word of Paul is lacking.
59. Mt. 5:16.
60. Mk. 12:25 and pars.
61. Ps. 4:8.
62. Cf. Prov. 6:27. The use of this metaphor is typical of the anti-syneisactic writings. Cf. *de Singul. Cler.* 2 (ed. Hartel, CSEL 3, p. 175.10); Jerome, *Ep.* 22, c. 14 (ed. Hilberg, CSEL 54, p. 161); Bachiarus, *de Reparatione Lapsi* c. 21 (PL 20, 1060).
63. Is. 40:6.
64. Exod. 32:6, 28.
65. Ps. 106:28.
66. The source of this unknown logion cannot be determined. The words *euge me, euge me contemptores suae sentencia animae* provide a typical example of the grammatical anarchy of the text. Harnack suggests that *sentencia* should be struck out. Bulhart writes, 'Instead of the senseless *sentencia* I suggest *sine paenitencia.*' In spite of the obscurity of the expression the sense can in my opinion be clearly recognised. Harnack finds the expression *et plurimum esse ad inimicum* unintelligible. Bulhart translates it 'to be much with the enemy, to attempt much devil's work'.
67. Cf. Judg. 21:12.
68. Cf. Gal. 3:27.
69. Mk. 3:17.
70. Ps. 76:6.
71. This fragment of the Apocalypse of Elias is not otherwise attested, although texts which engage in descriptions of the torments of hell are very numerous. Above all reference may be made to the Apocalypse b. Dei Genitricis de poenis (ed. M.R. James, *Apocrypha Anecdota*, Cambridge 1893, pp. 115ff.), which circulated particularly in the Slavic area under the name 'Chozdenie Bogorodicy po mukam'. Cf. E. Schürer, ThLZ 33, 1908, 614; M.R. James, *The Lost Apocrypha of the Old Testament*, 1920, p. 55; K.H. Schwarte, TRE III, 1978, 274 (Lit.). Cf. also the Apocalypse of Paul, below, pp.712ff.
72. Cf. Wisd. 3:14.
73. Apocryphon of Solomon?
74. Ecclus. 30:19ff.
75. An apocryphon that cannot be identified.
76. Cf. 2 Cor. 11:3.
77. An apocryphon that cannot be identified. It may perhaps have developed out of Lk. 11:22.
78. This *gratulacio* is to be regarded as a free quotation from the Acts of John c. 113 (ed. Junod-Kaestli, CChrSA 1, 1983, pp. 311-313), cf. below, p. 203f.
79. The text runs: *Aut numquid extra legem est quod docemus ut et ipsi daemones cum confiterentur dyro diacono in adventu Johannis considera quid dixerint.* Bulhart rightly suggests that the words *considera quid dixerint* should be regarded as a dittography. The deacon Dyrus mentioned here is identical with the 'Berus Diakon' who appears in the Acts of John (c. 30) (cf. Junod-Kaestli, op. cit., pp. 181-183, and below, p. 176). But the whole fragment has not survived.
80. An apocryphon that cannot be identified.
81. Ecclus. 9:9; 25:22?
82. The translation of this missing fragment from the Acts of John comes from K. Schäferdiek.
83. The text runs: *Si utique matrimonium deiunxit apostolus ne sit occasio delicti comulando.* Bulhart replaces *comulando* by *copulando.*
84. The sentence probably relates to the Acts of Andrew, although the point of reference cannot be identified from the extant remains of these Acts. Cf. below, p. 103.
85. This logion may be free citation from the Gospels (cf. Mt. 10:16 and Mk. 13:9).

86. Neh. 8:15.
87. The source of this logion is unknown. The cypress must already at this time have counted as a symbol of the ascetic-monastic life.
88. What PsT means by this *substancia conexa* is not clear to me.
89. Is. 56:6, 7.
90. We do not know what books of the patriarchs are referred to here. On this occasion Harnack (p. 193) has referred to the lost work 'τῶν τριῶν Πατριαρχῶν'. Certainly the 'Conversatio trium Patriarchum', composed in the form of a conversation between Basil the Great, Gregory of Nazianzus and John Chrysostom and widely disseminated in the Slavic area (cf. A. de Santos Otero, *Die handschriftliche Uberlieferung der altsl. Apokryphen*, II, 1981, 196-222) hardly comes into question in this connection. Whether instead the reference could be to the 'Testaments of the three Patriarchs' (Abraham, Isaac and Jacob), which have come down to us in separate Greek, Coptic and Arabic versions (cf. J.H. Charlesworth *et al., The OT Pseudepigrapha*, I, London 1983, 869-918), can also scarcely be established for lack of firm points of contact.
91. Cf. Num. 15:32ff.
92. Cf. Ezek. 22:6ff.
93. Cf. Ezek. 22:11.
94. The text runs: *Unde legislatoris vox sancto spiritu cecinitante.* Here (in my opinion without reason) Bulhart reads *cecinit ante.*
95. Deut. 27:22.
96. 1 Kings 2:13-25.
97. Hag. 2:11-14.
98. Num. 19:22.
99. The text runs: *O imper sancto ut aequiperetur illi sacerdoti.* Bulhart gives *imper(are).*
100. Mt. 25:41.
101. Ps. 82:6f.
102. The text runs: *Haec ergo facient cum sit separacio inter iustum et prophanum, nec est participacio inter fidelem et iustum, et nulla sit segregacio inter mortem et vitam, vel considera quid sit inter perditum et saluum.* Harnack suggests *inter fidelem et (in) iustum.* Bulhart thinks 'it should then also read *ut* instead of *et*'.
103. Cf. Ezek. 22:18.
104. According to the text *id ergo commixti estis omnes* the *id* is to be construed as an accusative, and perhaps it ought not to be replaced by *ideo* as Bulhart suggests.
105. Cf. Gen. 49:3.
106. Exod. 15:10.
107. Cf. Zech. 5:8.
108. Cf. Exod. 16:3.
109. According to Harnack's assumption we have to reckon here with a lost Apocryphon of Solomon.
110. Cf. APlThe c. 5 (cf. Aa I, 238 and below, p. 239f).
111. Rev. 2:7.
112. Cf. Rev. 22:2, 3.
113. *Caelestis ortus esca.* De Bruyne has rightly understood *ortus* as the genitive of *hortus* by contamination. But Bulhart thinks that '*ortus* indicates *origin*: one makes do with this interpretation'.
114. Cf. Rev. 2:26-28.
115. Mt. 10:32f.
116. Rev. 3:21.

XV. Second and Third Century Acts of Apostles

Introduction

Wilhelm Schneemelcher

1. Literature: *Texts:* R.A. Lipsius and M. Bonnet (eds.), *Acta Apostolorum Apocrypha* I, 1891; II/1, 1898; II/2, 1903 (reprinted 1959); W. Wright, *Apocryphal Acts of the Apostles, edited from Syriac Mss. in the British Museum and other Libraries* I (Syriac text), II (English trans.), London 1871; I. Guidi, 'Gli Atti apocrifi degli apostoli nei testi copti, arabi ed etiopici' (*Rendiconti della R. Accademia dei Lincei* Note I-VII; vol. III, 1887, I, part 2; II, parts 2, 4, 8, 10, 11; vol. IV, 1888, I, part 2 (text); *Giornale della Società Asiatica Italiana* II, 1888 (Italian trans.); German summary of contents in Lipsius, *Apostelgeschichten*, Erg. 89ff.; A. Smith Lewis, *The Mythological Acts of the Apostles* (Horae Semiticae IV, 1904: Arabic); E.A. Wallis Budge, *The Contendings of the Apostles* I, 1898; II, 1901 (Ethiopic); *Écrits apocryphes sur les Apôtres. Traduction de l'édition arménienne de Venise* (1) par Louis Leloir (CChrSA 3), Turnhout 1986.

On the complete critical edition planned by the *Association pour l'étude de la littérature apocryphe chrétienne* cf. F. Bovon, 'Vers une nouvelle édition de la littérature apocryphe chrétienne: la *Series apocryphorum* du *Corpus christianorum*', *Augustinianum* XXIII, 1983, 373-378.

Translations: Michaelis, 216-438; James, 228-475; Erbetta, II; Moraldi, II, 935-1429.

Studies: Lipsius, *Apostelgeschichten*; H. Ljungvik, *Studien zur Sprache der apokryphen Apostelgeschichten* (Uppsala Univ. Årsskrift 8), 1926; K. Kerényi, *Die griechisch-orientalische Romanliteratur in religionsgeschichtlicher Beleuchtung*, 1927 (reprinted 1962); R. Söder, *Die apokryphen Apostelgeschichten und die romanhafte Literatur der Antike* (Würzburger Studien zur Altertumswiss. 3), 1932; M. Blumenthal, *Formen und Motive in den apokryphen Apostelgeschichten* (TU 48, 1), 1933; C.L. Sturhahn, *Die Christologie der ältesten apokryphen Apostelakten* (Theol. Diss. Heidelberg 1951); L. Fabricius, *Die Legende im Bild des ersten Jahrtausende der Kirche. Der Einfluß der Apokryphen und Pseudepigraphen auf die altchristliche und byzantinische Kunst*, 1956; Vielhauer, *Lit. gesch.* 693-718; E. Plümacher, art. 'Apokryphe Apostelakten', in PWRE, Suppl. XV, 1978, cols.11-70; R. McL. Wilson, art. 'Apokryphen II', in TRE III, 1978, 316-362 (on the AGG: 341-348); F. Bovon *et al.*, *Les Actes apocryphes des Apôtres. Christianisme et monde païen* (Publications de la Faculté de Théologie de l'Université de Genève No. 4), Geneva 1981 (Lit.); *Augustinianum* XXIII, 1983, fasc. 1/2: 'Gli Apocrifi cristiani e cristianizzati'; N. Holzberg, *Der antike Roman* (Artemis Einführungen, 25), 1986 (Lit.); Dennis Ronald MacDonald (ed.), *The Apocryphal Acts of Apostles* (Semeia 38), 1986 (pp. 173-181: Bibliography).

Abbreviations: AGG = apocryphal Acts of apostles; Acts = canonical Acts; AA = Acta Andreae (Acts of Andrew); AJ = Acta Johannis (Acts of John); APl = Acta Pauli (Acts of Paul); APlThe = Acta Pauli et Thecla (Paul and Thecla); APt = Acta Petri (Acts of Peter); ActVerc = Actus Vercellenses (Acts of Peter); ATh = Acta Thomae (Acts of Thomas).

2. General survey: When in this section the five great apocryphal Acts of Apostles (or better: the surviving remains of these AGG) are brought together, the impression could easily arise that we have to do with a corpus of texts which in terms of form and content present a unity. It must however be emphasised from the outset that this impression is deceptive. Rather, the five works were first brought together only in Manicheism; as a result they became widespread in the West also, and were transmitted, probably in single manuscripts, down to the time of Photius.[1] Before that, and also alongside this collection, each of the five AGG had its own history of transmission, which is understandable when we take note of the differences in regard to time and place of origin, as well as in theological tendency.

The question is, however, whether these works are to be regarded as a uniform kind of text, at least on the basis of their literary *Gattung*. This problem will be discussed in detail below. Here it need only be stated in advance, quite generally, that the five great apostolic Acts do not belong together, in literary terms, in any way that can be defined more precisely. They are however also - despite their unmistakable theological differences - to be reckoned to a particular phase in Church history, the 2nd and 3rd centuries, and offer insights into a Christianity which sometimes diverges considerably from 'official' theology and churchmanship.

A further aspect may also be mentioned: the AGG stand apart from the remaining Christian literature of the period by the fact that they do not discuss any theological or ecclesiastical problem theoretically, but that at their centre stands the life of an apostle, his deeds and his teachings. The motifs and stylistic resources are very diverse, and the relation to ancient literary models also cannot be explained in a single sentence (see below). But the central position of the apostle is not to be overlooked.[2] This makes these works a starting-point for the later hagiographical literature, which set in on a grand scale with the rise of the veneration of the saints. The AGG undoubtedly influenced this literature, especially since individual parts (e.g. martyrdoms) were, evidently at an early date, lifted out of the original AGG and circulated separately. It is certainly not altogether easy, but probably rewarding, to follow up the question of when and how the process of transition from the AGG to the legends of the saints came about.

These general remarks are intended in the first place to indicate that the five old AGG here brought together cannot be treated as a self-contained unity. Rather, scientific work on these texts will have to analyse and classify the individual works separately, without prejudice to the fact that there are also elements in common between them.

This means that in this introduction it is possible to give a brief discussion of only a few problems, but that in accordance with the character of the present collection much greater importance attaches to the introductions to the individual AGG. This shift of emphasis is also suggested by the present state of research. In recent years the AGG have again been accorded greater attention by scholars. On the one hand the preparation of a complete critical edition by the 'Association pour l'étude de la littérature apocryphe chrétienne'[3] in the series Corpus Christianorum, Series Apocryphorum has given impetus to the debate about the problems connected with these texts. On the other hand, authors concerned with modern questions (e.g. in sociology) have laid hold of them.[4] However, not all the questions which have been thrown up are so new as some authors think, and the answers are by no means all convincing. The abundant discussion about the AGG has so far not yet led to any agreed picture. The differences between the various trends in scholarship are not to be overlooked.[5] Nevertheless it has become clear that there are some particularly important themes to which pre-eminent attention should be given[6]. Some of these themes may now be briefly discussed in what follows.

3. On the transmission: A manuscript of the corpus of the AGG, such as Photius[7] evidently had before him, has not survived. Rather we must resort, in reconstructing the individual Acts, to a plurality of witnesses, the value of which is however of differing levels. The history of the transmission is at the same time the history of the reception, the redaction and in part also the 'ecclesiasticising' of the AGG.

The *Lipsius-Bonnet* edition,[8] which for its time was an admirable achievement and even today still has its value, rested upon a large number of Greek and Latin manuscripts, mostly of hagiographical content. Through the work of *A. Ehrhard* the number of the hagiographical manuscripts which come into question for the AGG was considerably increased.[9] The full utilisation of Ehrhard's work will certainly also benefit research into the apocrypha. It must however be noted that the extraction of older material from later hagiographical texts is a particularly difficult task. For only when reliable criteria are available can parts of the later texts be entered as constituents of the original Acts. Nevertheless the edition of the Acts of John by Junod and Kaestli (see below, p. 152) shows that along the way we can attain to improvements over against Lipsius-Bonnet.

Today still other materials can be added. On the one hand, papyrus discoveries with parts of AGG have been brought to light (this holds above all for the *APl*). On the other hand the importance which attaches to the many *versions* is becoming ever clearer. It is astonishing how strong an influence this literature had in the different linguistic and cultural areas.[10] In the evaluation of this rich material, as yet not fully opened up, we have to investigate in each individual case whether the translation is a faithful reproduction of a Greek *Vorlage*, or represents a stage of reception marked by redaction and further development of the original tradition. Further, we have to investigate whether the extant manuscripts do not attest a later stage of development within the linguistic area in question. This means that the numerous translations must first so far as possible be examined with regard to their own tradition history, and only then be compared with the Greek tradition.[11] Here one may at first be inclined to accord a greater significance to a Greek or Coptic papyrus from the 4th century than to a manuscript from the 14th. But, as is well known, the age of a manuscript is no indication of the value of its tradition. There is no question that in the present collection these problems cannot be examined in detail. On the other hand there is beyond doubt an important task for scholarship here.

It may also be noted - as Vielhauer rightly emphasises[12] - that this situation of a fragmentary tradition, sometimes extant only in redactions, has its grounds in the history of the canon. While the apocryphal gospels at least in large part sought to present the Gospel in a form independent of the canonical Gospels (see vol. I, p. 77ff.), the AGG were probably never intended to be rivals to the canonical Acts. This emerges just as clearly from their content as from their literary form.

4. The literary *Gattung*: There is still no exact and generally recognised definition of the kind of text to which the apocryphal Acts belong. One of the fundamental difficulties here is the fact that in terms of content the AGG are so varied, but also that several differences appear in their manner of presentation. On the other hand a literary relationship is not to be denied. But how is it to be defined more precisely?

Especially under the influence of *E. Rohde*, these works have been assessed as a Christian form of the hellenistic novel.[13] Now it cannot be disputed that certain elements of the Greek novel also occur in the AGG. The question is, however, whether we may safely draw from this the conclusion that the AGG have accepted and merely Christianised the *Gattung* of the novel. In NTApo² (163ff.), *F. Pfister* maintained the thesis that it was a case of Christian travel and missionary aretalogies which belong to the ancient *Gattung* of the πράξεις literature. Pfister here took up ideas of R. Reitzenstein, who emphasised in particular the model of the 'aretalogies' of prophets and philosophers.[14]

Rosa Söder in 1932[15] examined in particular the individual motifs of the AGG, and endeavoured to draw the connecting lines from there to the hellenistic literature. In her view five main elements can be identified:

1. the travel motif;
2. the aretalogical element, i.e. the emphasis on the ἀρεταί and δυνάμεις, the marvellous aspect of the hero's powers;
3. the teratological element, i.e. the representation of the wonder-world into which the apostles come: cannibals, talking animals, etc.;
4. the tendentious element, especially in the speeches;
5. the erotic element, which finds expression both in the love-motifs proper and also in the ascetic and encratite features.

These motifs appear in various ways in the AGG, but through them also the differences between the individual works become clear. They have their models in various ancient kinds of text.

One cannot in any case simply derive the AGG from the hellenistic novel. Nor have we a mixture of aretalogy (evidently considered by Söder as an independent *Gattung*) and hellenistic or sophistic novel, to which then still other elements have been added. It is likewise clear that the AGG are not fashioned after the model of Luke's Acts, just as they are not simply a continuation of the ancient aretalogies.

It is not in itself out of the question that in early Christianity a new literary form could have been created out of the most diverse elements. But the fact that the AGG differ markedly from one another tells against this. To be able to determine the *Gattung* of the AGG correctly, we must according to Söder set out from their purpose. This may be defined as entertainment, instruction and edification of the people, not so much of the educated. We may thus say that the AGG are 'evidence of ancient popular narratives of the adventures, exploits and love affairs of great men, as now fixed in literary form and in a Christian spirit'.[16] Even if they are defined as popular narrative, that naturally does not exclude the possibility that their authors made use of the stylistic methods which were customary in their time. This explains the connections of various kinds with the hellenistic novel as with the aretalogies of philosophers, which are not, however, sufficient for us to assign the AGG to these stylistic categories.

In NTApo[3] I attempted to draw out the lines on the basis of Söder's investigation of the AGG and to clarify their literary *Gattung*, taking up form-critical aspects.

According to this, the composition of the AGG is to be understood as a literary activity on the part of their authors; they gave their own individual arrangement and form to the material, but in so doing they were frequently able to rely on older traditions. Here there are certain similarities with the process which led to the origin of the Gospels, as it is assumed by Form Criticism. We have thus to do with the fixation in writing of popular tradition. This explains the fact that the AGG are frequently composed of single πράξεις strung together without any apparent connection. One is often led to suspect that the authors have inserted traditions which originally circulated separately (personal legends, local tales etc.) into the framework which they have created.

In discussion of Pfister and Söder, *Vielhauer* has sought in similar fashion to determine the *Gattung* of the AGG, but has placed the accent somewhat differently.[17] First we must mention his criticism of the use hitherto of the term 'aretalogy' as a description of *Gattung*. 'Aretalogy' is a statement of content, but not a characterisation for a kind of text (against Reitzenstein and Pfister). The description of the AGG as popular literature - for the people and not for the educated - tells us nothing for the question of *Gattung* (against Söder). There were considerable differences of level in the Greek novel also.

In terms of literary history, the AGG in Vielhauer's view belong in the context of the ancient novel. Travel reports (περίοδοι) and accounts of exploits (πράξεις) are imitated in various ways. It is to be noted 'that in terms of the history of tradition the individual stories, the Praxeis, are primary and the travel reports, the Periodoi, secondary' (716). Thus the AGG in their present shape are a combination of two literary forms.

The connection with the novelistic literature of the ancient world, and at the same time the difference from the New Testament, is also clear from the individual narrative materials. Thus the tale withdraws behind the legend. Dialogue and monologue (these are something new in Christian literature) correspond to literary patterns.

According to Vielhauer an important motive in the origin of the AGG, in addition to the demand for specifically Christian entertainment literature, was the increased interest in the apostles. Certainly there are already in Luke's Acts traditional reports about the apostles (e.g. in the form of tales) which have been worked into the book. But in the course of the 2nd century the need for more information about the apostles is growing.[18] Here they become more and more θεῖοι ἄνδρες, such as are known in the surrounding world. At the same time however they are put forward as bearers of tradition to support various opinions and doctrines.

The AGG are thus not biographies (birth, childhood etc. are not presented). They rather take up 'the very old idea of the apostles as θεῖοι ἄνδρες, but develop it in literary terms in the form of the novelistic Praxeis and - re-shaping these - in that of the Periodoi. They are evidence for the acceptance of *Gattungen* of secular literature ... into Christianity' (718). Thus far Vielhauer, who in a few pages sets out the most important aspects of this literature, and at the same time indicates the questions which have still to be clarified in further work.

In his fundamental article on the AGG,[19] *E. Plümacher* comes to the conclusion that for various reasons 'they are indeed so close to the *Gattung* of the hellenistic romance that they are scarcely to be understood as other than Christian variants of this *Gattung*' (col. 63). However, they are not simply novels, but represent a special literary *Gattung* which can be understood 'as popular entertainment literature, marked by specific concerns which it seeks to further, a literature which has borrowed numerous elements from the hellenistic novel, especially the love-romance, as well as from the aretalogies of philosophers or of mission' (col. 12).[20]

The AGG stand in the strongest contrast with Luke's Acts 'if one is not prepared to see a certain relationship between Acts and the AGG, albeit a very external one, in "the wish for more precise information about the activity of the other apostles (i.e. those of whom there is little or no mention in Acts) which was aroused by the ideas of the missionary work of the twelve, already enhanced at an early date" (P. Wendland, *Die urchristl. Lit.formen* [1912² ³]' (col. 12).

It is understandable that in the intensive work on the AGG in connection with the planned complete edition the problem of the literary *Gattung* should also be discussed. Both *J.D. Kaestli* and *E. Junod*, the two editors of the AJ, have voiced their opinions on this question.[21] Although minor differences between the members of the Association are not to be overlooked (as the volume edited by Bovon shows), and there may perhaps be some modifications in the course of the work, we may recognise a tendency to place the accent otherwise than has been done in research hitherto.

Thus - in criticism of Söder - the characterisation of the AGG as 'popular literature' is rejected (Kaestli, 66). But also one cannot speak of individual traditions which have been worked into them. They are to be understood as literary works, composed by a single person.

Naturally the connection with the hellenistic novel cannot be denied. But the AGG cannot be defined as a Christian variety of the novel. Thus the miracle-stories of the apostles do not belong to the *Gattung* of the novel (Kaestli, 67). The AGG do not correspond to any *Gattung* of ancient literature, but are rather independent Christian productions under the influence of various *Gattungen*.

The rejection of a view which was stimulated by the form-critical method (cf. NTApo³ pp. 176ff.) is not so clearly expressed by Kaestli as by Junod. He too emphasises the literary character of the AGG, which he calls 'littérature romanesque chrétienne du IIe siècle' (280). A more precise characterisation of the *Gattung* is not however given. For Junod it is more important that we must assume 'traditions ecclésiastiques' about the activity and death of the apostles as the source for the AGG.

In the novel we find stories which the author himself has thought out, but in the AGG the Church traditions taken over by the author (or his group), which are regarded as old and genuine, are remoulded. These traditions, however, cannot be separated out by literary criticism, since the AGG as we now have them are homogeneous creations by the authors concerned. Only parallels from outside this literature might help us further here.

The authors of the AGG availed themselves of the 'Church traditions' in order to create a hearing and gain recognition for their novelistic writings. The scenario and biographical scenes were invented by them, and are not in the nature of isolated traditions which have come down to them. But the 'Church traditions' are, as one might put it, the 'native soil'.

This is not the place for an extended discussion of these theses. In any case the question of the *Gattung* to which the AGG belong is only marginally dealt with by Junod. He contents himself with the term 'novelistic literature'. Kaestli too, however, does not really come to any precise definition of the kind of text. This is somewhat surprising, since the AGG are treated by both as works of literature. It is further not to be overlooked that with their interpretation there is combined a certain aversion to Form Criticism, such as may also be met with elsewhere today. Finally, some people in this circle appear to be concerned for as early a date as possible for the AGG, which probably goes half-way to meet the acceptance of 'Church traditions'. Future research, which has undergone considerable stimulus through the work of the Association, will show whether and how far these theses are tenable.

It is not surprising that it is precisely by members of the Association that considerable doubts have been expressed regarding the hypotheses of some American scholars.[22] The works in question are above all those of *Stevan L. Davies*, *Dennis Ronald MacDonald* and *Virginia Burrus*.[23]

Even if these authors do not form a self-contained group, and there are certainly differences among them, a common tendency can still be identified: the AGG are to be 'explained' with the aid of sociology, psychology and feminist ideology. Somewhat cursorily we may formulate the basic idea thus:

The AGG derive from groups of women who practised sexual continence, as an expression of their emancipation and their resistance to the patriarchal order in marriage, the family, in society and in the state. The AGG are documents of this 'revolt of the widows' (this term including also the young women who renounced marriage). This basic pattern is enriched with various other elements. For one thing it is affirmed, indeed presupposed as certain, that all conventional ties such as marriage, the family, etc. are simply means to the enslavement of women. In early Christianity groups of women freed themselves from this slavery - as a consequence of the proclamation of the Gospel. For another, a literary thesis is also advanced with regard to the AGG: they are oral narratives which were recited and handed on by 'widows' in the women's circles in which they lived (hence to some extent a fixation of the recitation of 'old wives' tales'). The study of folk-lore allegedly provides the necessary comparative material for this.[24]

The contributions by Kaestli and Bovon in the collective volume *Semeia* 38 have already given voice to decisive objections. But one may probably take up position still more clearly against these ahistorical travesties:

a) In these works the AGG are treated as a homogeneous block, without any reflection on the differences between the individual works. Thus in Davies the Acta Xanthippae (6th cent.) can be put on a level with the old Acts of the 2nd and 3rd centuries. Problems of literary history are completely left aside. The relation to the hellenistic novel is not further discussed, it is simply decided in the negative.

b) The analysis of the narrative structure of the abstinence stories by V. Burrus, who adheres to the methods of V. Propp,[25] suffers from the fact that individual scenes are torn from their context, and the application of Propp's categories is very violently done. Above all, the oral character of the original narrative probably cannot be proved from the structure of a story. At many points the parallels from the Greek novel tell against any such assumption.

c) The one-sided interpretation of all abstinence stories as reports about liberated women and their struggle against the patriarchalist authorities manifestly overlooks the fact that the ἐγκράτεια mentioned in the AGG is reported, and required, not only of women but also of men.[26] It also has wholly different spiritual roots from the modern liberation movement.

d) It is a rewarding question, even if not an altogether new one, what historical value legends have.[27] That here the social milieu in which narratives of this kind are to be located should also be taken into account is really self-evident, only one cannot in the process simply bracket out other questions. In our case it should not be overlooked that many features of the AGG are taken over as τόποι from the hellenistic novel (e.g. the heroines are beautiful, rich and belong to the upper classes), and thus are not very appropriate for an analysis of the social structure of the Christian communities in the 2nd and 3rd centuries, about which in any case we do not know so much as is often affirmed today. It may be emphasised once again that the narratives of the AGG are determined by other motives than the social criticism of modern sociologists.

e) We block off any understanding of the AGG when - as manifestly happens in the works under discussion - we isolate them from the total context of Church history in the early centuries. The fact that the heroines as the decisive figures are drawn into the centre of the treatment means that the apostles, with whom the AGG are primarily concerned, withdraw to the margin. But this distorts our view, for the fact is that the AGG are only rightly understood when we set them in place in the history of Church and theology in the 2nd and 3rd centuries. They belong in the discussion of that time, which had such portentous results, regarding 'apostle' and 'apostolic'.

Sociology, psychoanalysis and feminist ideology may be of use in another place. As a basis for the interpretation of Greek Christian texts of the 2nd and 3rd centuries they are scarcely helpful.

This survey of the various attempts to clarify the literary genus of the AGG shows a motley picture. In conclusion a few points may be mentioned which seem to me important for their interpretation. Their literary model was not Luke's Acts - whether it was known to the authors or not. Rather they are connected in various ways with the hellenistic novel. The authors of the AGG used this *Gattung*, and out of it created a Christian text form of their own. Formal elements of the *Praxeis* and *Periodoi* literature are particularly influential. Other motifs (such as R. Söder especially has identified) were likewise taken over from the novels.

The AGG took on their special stamp through the position of the apostles. They (and not the liberated women) stand in the centre of the works, and it was because of them that the AGG were written. They are intended to be the bearers of the message, which is proclaimed in a form which comes close to the novel. So here the aims of entertainment, instruction and religious propaganda are combined into a unique *Gattung*, which represents the starting-point for the later hagiography.

With their works the authors of the AGG created 'without doubt a new type of fictional prose narrative, which could with some justice be called early Christian romance. Certainly one will no longer reckon it to the *Gattung* of the ancient novel, but see here the beginning of the latter's acceptance'.[28]

We probably cannot regard the Vitae of the philosophers as a model for the *Gattung* of the AGG.[29] Biography and the writing of history are remote from these works.

It is a debated question whether the authors of the texts worked to any extent worth mentioning with traditional material which had come down to them, or whether, like the authors of the novels as men of letters, they freely invented all that they wrote. If we decide for the first possibility, then there is the further question, of what nature the traditional material was: popular legends, Church tradition or oral narratives?

In my opinion it is not to be denied that in the AGG personal and local legends have been worked over, which do not seem to have been invented by the author of the work in question. Sometimes it is a matter of popular narrative (e.g. APt 9ff.: the talking dog; APt 13: the dried fish; AJ 37: the destruction of the temple of Artemis; AJ 60f.: the obedient bugs, etc.). Sometimes however it can also be assumed that texts already given a literary form have been worked in (e.g. the Thecla cycle in the APl?). On the other hand the framework and the composition of the several AGG must be regarded as in each case the work of an author about whose person - except with the APl - we know nothing.

The separation of tradition and composition is difficult, and certainly cannot be undertaken in the same way and according to uniform criteria with all the AGG. Here we should not get things out of focus by dating them as early as possible, or attempting to bring their theological statements into a system. Recourse to other disciplines is of only limited assistance.

5. The place of the AGG in theology and Church history: Lipsius' theory that the AGG were of gnostic origin for a long time influenced research.[30] He attempted to explain the fact that in these texts there are many passages which could not be regarded as gnostic by the assumption of 'catholic' redactions (which is partly correct). Over against this C. Schmidt and A. von Harnack affirmed the 'catholic' origin of the AGG.[31] More precisely, they saw in them the products of a 'vulgar catholicism'.

Today a sharp antithesis between 'gnostic' and 'catholic' with reference to the AGG can no longer be maintained. For one thing, the picture of Gnosis has so greatly changed in recent decades, through many new discoveries and intensive research, and above all it has fanned out into a manifold spectrum, so that to declare the AGG 'gnostic' would be to say absolutely nothing. For another, it has become clear that 'Gnosis' and 'early catholicism' cannot simply be set in opposition to one another as fixed quantities. The boundaries in the 2nd century were evidently fluid.[32] It is therefore not surprising that we cannot speak of any uniform theological thrust of the texts. Rather there are considerable differences between the several Acts, and moreover differences can be detected even within a single work. This is probably connected on the one hand with the authors' use of traditions, already mentioned. On the other hand it is to be observed that these writings are intended to propagate the peculiar opinions of the circles in which they arose, and here "Church" material was not excluded as a matter of course. We may concur with Plümacher when he writes: 'The theological ideas which stamped Christian thought in the 2nd and 3rd centuries, as well as the convictions which governed the piety of the individual Christian in this period, have left manifold traces in the AGG, which often enough reveal a remarkable conjunction and co-existence of the most varied ideas, sometimes to be reconciled with one another only with difficulty: consistency and uniformity are remote from the AGG, entirely in conformity with their literary genus, which has no interest in the building of theological systems, so that their classification in the context of the history of early Christian theology and piety is not a simple matter'.[33]

Plümacher himself - with due consideration of the differences between the individual acts - has singled out two aspects, which could not indeed serve as the basis for a theological unity of all the AGG, but which do point to a religious and theological milieu, namely that dogmatically still by no means firmly articulated 'climate' in the Church in the 2nd and 3rd centuries, in which the AGG came into being. For one thing there are the unmistakable 'encratite' features which occur in all the AGG. Here it is above all, but not exclusively, a question of sexual continence. In this respect they are evidence for a tendency widespread in the ancient world and in early Christianity, the motives for which were certainly varied.[34] In the Church from the time of Paul (1 Cor. 7) there was much discussion regarding this ideal. For a long time it stood 'on the border-line between orthodoxy and heresy'.[35] This characterisation probably applies to the AGG both on this point and as a whole.

For another, Plümacher in his cautious survey has also set out the varied relationships of the AGG to Gnosis. This problem too cannot be reduced to any simple formula. There are pieces of tradition influenced by Gnosis (e.g. in the AJ), but there is also anti-gnostic polemic (APl). The variety of the theological statements shows not only the deficient interest of this literature in dogmatic theory, but also that there are no sharp boundaries between Gnosis and 'catholicism' in this period. 'The groups to whom we owe the AGG must at least in part have stood rather on the margin than in the centre of the wide area covered by the term "catholic vulgar Christianity"'.[36]

This means that we cannot characterise the texts as a whole under one comprehensive label. There is no theology of the AGG. Rather we have to work out the specific theological statements and the *Sitz im Leben* for each individual work, and also for the several traditions contained therein.[37] This will frequently lead only to hypothetical results, since the necessary material for comparison is too fragmentary. But only so can we assign the AGG to their place in the history of theology and of the Church.

Here one thing will become clear: just because of the juxtaposition and mingling of very diverse elements the AGG are a valuable corrective to the picture of the Church in the 2nd and 3rd centuries which we can reconstruct from the writings of the theologians. Here marginal groups, with an independent tradition and an often very unreflecting grasp of the faith, find a voice. It can hardly be said to what social stratum we should assign the author and his addressees.[38] For this question it is probably not unimportant that it is not so much systematic theological thinking that is dominant, but rather a multiplicity of themes which interest the ordinary Christian people.

It is common to all the AGG that they accord to the apostle concerned a pre-eminent role. The message which these works are intended to convey to their readers, in the form of a novelistic narrative, is bound up with the person of the apostle and presented in his speeches. The apostle thus - just as in several apocryphal gospels - becomes the bearer of a specific tradition. It is not surprising that the speeches, which are given so great a significance, are in the later revisions largely eliminated or altered.[39]

In the AGG various aims and intentions are combined: the need for entertainment (in place of the 'heathen' novel), interest in the apostles as bearers of special traditions and belief in the power of the θεῖοι ἄνδρες, the apostles, who point the right way to salvation. It is not the thin air of abstraction that is dominant in them, but the massive belief in miracle of the common people, or more accurately of small marginal groups in the Church. For the historian who is concerned with the process of theological clarification in the 2nd and 3rd centuries, and constantly comes across the problem of the 'apostolic tradition', they are an interesting and important source.

Notes

Introduction

1. Cf. on this K. Schäferdiek, below, p. 87ff.
2. Cf. *inter alia* the contributions of Prieur, Bovon and Junod in Bovon *et al.*, *Les Actes apocryphes des Apôtres.*
3. Cf. F. Bovon, 'Vers une nouvelle édition de la littérature apocryphe chrétienne: la *Series apocryphorum* du *Corpus christianorum*', *Augustinianum* XXIII, 1983, 373-378; F. Bovon *et al.*, *Les Actes apocryphes des Apôtres*, 1981. The Acts of John have appeared as the first edition; on this see below, pp. 152ff.
4. Cf. for example Dennis Ronald MacDonald (ed.), *The Apocryphal Acts of Apostles* (Semeia 38) 1986 (literature).
5. They may be readily found in the Semeia 38 volume cited in note 4.
6. Cf. Jean-Daniel Kaestli, 'Les principales orientations de la recherche sur les Actes apocryphes', in Bovon *et al.*, *Les Actes . . .* , 49-67; F. Bovon/E. Junod, 'Reading the Apocryphal Acts of Apostles', in Semeia 38, 161-171.
7. Cod. 114; on this see Schäferdiek, below pp. 87ff.
8. *Acta Apostolorum Apocrypha*, ed. R.A. Lipsius et M. Bonnet, I (1891), II/1 (1898), II/2 (1903); reprinted 1959.
9. A. Ehrhard, *Überlieferung und Bestand der hagiographischen und homiletischen Literatur der griechischen Kirche, von den Anfängen bis zum Ende des 16. Jahrhunderts* (TU 50-52), 1939-1952. As an example we need only refer to the JS text of the Acts of Andrew (see below, p. 105), the manuscript evidence for which is adduced in Ehrhard I, 243[57] and II, 71[37].
10. Cf. the references in vol. I, 62ff.; J.-D. Kaestli, op. cit. (note 6 above), 51ff. The various contributions in *Augustinianum* XXIII, 1983 are important.
11. An exemplary investigation of this kind is A. de Santos Otero, *Das kirchenslavische Evangelium des Thomas* (PTS 6), 1967, on which see vol. I, pp. 439ff.
12. *Lit. gesch.* 693.
13. Cf. E. Rohde, *Der griechische Roman und seine Vorläufer*, 1867 ([5]1974); E. von Dobschütz, 'Der Roman in der altchristlichen Literatur', *Deutsche Rundschau* 28, 1902, 87-106; N. Holzberg (*Der antike Roman. Eine Einführung* (Artemis Einführungen 25), 1986) offers an excellent introduction to the problems of the hellenistic novel from the point of view of present-day research.

14. Cf. R. Reitzenstein, *Hellenistische Wundererzählungen*, 1909. It may be emphasised here - as already in vol. I, p. 86 note 10 - that 'aretalogy' as the description of a literary *Gattung* is problematic, and indeed 'inappropriate' (Vielhauer, *Lit. gesch.* 715).
15. R. Söder, *Die apokryphen Apostelgeschichten und die romanhafte Literatur der Antike*, 1932.
16. Söder, op. cit. 187.
17. *Lit. gesch.* 693ff.
18. Vielhauer does not go into the relation of this tendency to other theological phenomena of the time. However, it is naturally important for the understanding of the AGG. Cf. below, pp. 83ff.
19. PWRE, Suppl. XV, 1978, cols. 11-70.
20. On the problem of aretalogy, see above, pp. 78f.
21. Cf. among others J.-D. Kaestli, 'Les principales orientations de la recherche sur les Actes apocryphes des Apôtres', in F. Bovon *et al.*, *Les Actes* . . . , 49-67, esp. 57ff; E. Junod, 'Creations romanesques et traditions ecclésiastiques dans les Actes apocryphes des Apôtres', in *Augustinianum* XXIII, 1983, 271-285.
22. Cf. the interesting collection of essays, Semeia 38 (above, note 4).
23. Stevan L. Davies, *The Revolt of the Widows: The Social World of the Apocryphal Acts*, New York 1980; id., 'Women, Tertullian and the *Acts of Paul*', in Semeia 38, 139-144; Dennis Ronald MacDonald, *The Legend and The Apostle: The Battle for Paul in Story and Canon*, Philadelphia 1983; id., 'The *Acts of Andrew and Matthias* and the Acts of Andrew', in Semeia 38, 9-26; - Virginia Burrus, 'Chastity as Autonomy: Women in the Stories of the Apocryphal Acts', in Semeia 38, 101-118.
24. Cf. the literature listed in Semeia 38, 173ff.
25. Vladimir Propp, *Morphology of the Folktale*, Austin, [2]1968.
26. Cf. Kaestli in Semeia, 130f., who gives some examples.
27. A. Harnack in 1890, in a lecture still worth reading today, already made some remarks deserving consideration on the theme of 'Legends as historical sources': *Reden und Aufsätze* I, [2]1906, 3-26.
28. Holzberg (above, note 13), 29.
29. On these biographies cf. Richard Goulet, 'Les Vies de philosophes dans l'Antiquité tardive et leur portée mystérique', in Bovon *et al.*, *Les Actes* . . . , 161-208. With this cf. Eric Junod, 'Les Vies de philosophes et les Actes apocryphes: poursuivent-ils un dessein similaire?', in *Les Actes* . . . , 209-219.
30. Cf. Lipsius, *Apostelgeschichten* I, 4ff.; J.-D. Kaestli in Bovon *et al.*, *Les Actes* . . . , 53-57.
31. Carl Schmidt, *Die alten Petrusakten* (TU 24, 1), 1903; A. Harnack, *Lit. gesch.* II 2, 169ff.
32. Cf. above all W. Bauer, *Rechtgläubigkeit und Ketzerei im ältesten Christentum*, [2]1964 (ET *Orthodoxy and Heresy*, 1971).
33. Plümacher, op. cit. (above, note 19), col. 43.
34. On the problem of Encratism cf. in addition to Plümacher's survey (op. cit., cols. 43-48) especially H. Chadwick, art. 'Enkrateia' in RAC V, 1960, cols. 343-365 (Lit.). The question of the encratite origin and stamp of the AGG is dealt with by Yves Tissot, 'Encratisme et Actes apocryphes', in Bovon *et al.*, *les Actes* . . . , 109-119. It may be noted that it will not do to assign the AGG to a sect like the Encratites presented by Epiphanius (*Pan.* 47). In the AGG we should better speak of the predominant role of the 'preaching of continence' (predominant - despite Tissot's disagreement).
35. Chadwick, op. cit., col. 355.
36. Plümacher, op. cit., col. 54.
37. An outstanding example for the work required on the AGG is the essay by K. Schäferkiek, 'Herkunft und Interesse der alten Johannesakten', ZNW 74, 1983, 247-267.
38. A noteworthy contribution on this question is Robert F. Stoops, Jr., 'Patronage in the *Acts of Peter*', in *Semeia* 38, 91-100.
39. Cf. for example the treatment of the Acts of Andrew by Gregory of Tours, see below, pp. 118ff.

The Manichean Collection of apocryphal Acts ascribed to Leucius Charinus

Knut Schäferdiek

Photius in his *Bibliotheca* describes a collection of five apocryphal books of Acts of Apostles:[1] '... a book, the so-called journeyings (περίοδοι) of the apostles, in which are contained the Acts of Peter, John, Andrew, Thomas, Paul. These were written, as the book itself makes clear, by Leucius Charinus. The style is thoroughly uneven and corrupt, for in places it uses well-turned constructions and expressions, but for the most part common and hackneyed ones, while it shows no trace of the plain artless style and native grace which characterises the diction of the evangelists and the apostles. It is stuffed with foolishness, inconsistency and incongruity; for it says that there is One who is God of the Jews, who is evil, whose servant Simon Magus became; and another is Christ, whom it calls good;[2] but it mixes and confuses everything by calling him both Father and Son.[3] It also says that he was not truly made man, but only appeared to be, and that he often appeared to his disciples in many forms, as a young man, as an old man, as a child, as an old man again and again as a child, as larger and smaller and then of great size, so that sometimes his head even reached up to heaven.[4] It also invents many foolish absurdities about the Cross,[5] saying that it was not Christ that was crucified, but another in his place, and that for this reason he derided those who crucified him.[6] It rejects lawful marriages[7] and says that every birth is evil and a work of the evil one;[8] and it absurdly states that the creator of the demons is another,[9] and it concocts senseless and childish (stories about) resurrections of dead men and of cattle and other animals.[10] And the Iconoclasts believe that in the Acts of John there is teaching directed against the (holy) pictures (or icons).[11] In short this book contains innumerable childish, improbable, ill-conceived, false, foolish, self-contradictory, profane and godless things; and if anyone called it the source and mother of all heresies he would not be far from the truth.' The Acts of the second Council of Nicaea (787), which quote from the Acts of John, adduce these not as an isolated writing but as part of a collection of 'pseudepigraphic journeyings of the holy apostles'.[12]

Information provided by Eusebius might give the impression that Origen already knew a similar collection of five apocryphal books of apostolic Acts: in his *Church History*[13] he writes as follows: 'The holy apostles and disciples of our Saviour were dispersed about the whole world. Thomas, as the tradition has it, was allotted Parthia, and Andrew Scythia, and John Asia; and here he remained till he died at Ephesus. Peter must have preached in Pontus, Galatia, Bithynia, Cappadocia and Asia, among the Jews of the Dispersion; and when at last he came to Rome he was crucified head downwards, since he had requested that he might suffer in this manner. What need is there to speak of Paul, who "accomplished the Gospel of Christ from Jerusalem as far as Illyria" (Rom. 15:19) and afterwards was martyred at Rome under Nero? - These are the express terms which Origen uses in the third book of his Commentaries on Genesis.' But the examination of this text by A. von Harnack and E. Junod,[14] however different their results may be in other respects, shows that his notes about Peter and Paul on the one hand and his statements about Thomas, Andrew and John on the other probably go back to different sources, and the last can scarcely rest upon corresponding Acts of apostles. On the other hand the *Manichean Psalm-book* preserved in a Coptic translation, in one of its 'pilgrim psalms' (ψαλμοὶ Σαρακωτῶν), presents within a list of examples for patience in suffering a passage from which it is clear that the author knew the ancient Acts of Peter, Andrew, John, Thomas and Paul. After the example of Jesus and before that of Mani comes the following list of apostles and female pupils of apostles.[15]

"All the apostles who endured their pains:
Peter the apostle, who was crucified head downwards,[16]
how many torments did he suffer . . . with this purity.
Andrew the apostle - his house was set ablaze under him.[17]
He and his disciples - hail to them, they were crucified.[18]
The two sons of Zebedee were made to drink the cup of the . . .
John the virgin - he too was made to drink of the cup,
imprisoned fourteen days, that he might die of hunger,[19]
and also James, he was stoned and slain,
all cast their stones upon him, that he might die under the storm.[20]
This again Thomas endured in his martyrdom (lit.: cross):
four soldiers pierced him at once with the point of their lances,
they encircled him on four sides and let his blood flow . . . [21]
How many mysteries did he accomplish; many a sign did he fulfil.
The apostle Paul - they proceeded against him and caused him to die.
How great is their wrath - he gave up his spirit, he did not escape.
I too have endured what he received, before this present day.
He was put into a basket, which was lowered outside the wall.[22]
All these (sufferings) he bore. He did not weary nor [flinch].
He left the vicinity(?) of his Lord, knowing that . . .
Thecla, the lover of God, was made to mount the pyre.
She received the sign of the Cross, stepped into the fire rejoicing.
Yet she was not put to shame, naked in the midst of the throng.[23]
She was cast to the bears, the lions were started against her.
She was bound on the bulls, the seals were let loose against her.[24]
All these (sufferings) she bore, she did not flinch nor [yield?].
A crown it is that she wishes; purity it is she strives for.
Even so the blessed Drusiana, she too endured the like,
imprisoned fourteen days, like her master, her apostle.[25]
Maximilla and Aristobula - great torment was brought upon them.[26]
What is the profit, that they accepted this? Purity it is, for which they contend.

In the material taken from the Acts named[27] there are inserted, in addition to a line about the psalmist's own experience (142.33), one about the sons of Zebedee, who 'were made to drink the cup' (142.22) and two about the stoning of James (142.55f.), which evidently confuse the Lord's brother with the son of Zebedee. The statement about the sons of Zebedee and the cup is certainly not a reference to any specific incident, but like Mk. 10:38f. par. intended metaphorically, just as at 143.17

the suffering of Mani also is described as being made to drink of the cup. The statement that John was made to drink of the cup (cf. Mk. 10:38f.; Mt. 10:22f.) is also to be understood correspondingly. It is only filled out in terms of content by the following reference to his incarceration. The lines about the sons of Zebedee only form a kind of summary rubric for the statements about John and James. The statement that the latter was stoned supplements the report about John, by association and in correspondence with the immediately preceding treatment of the other apostolic pair of brothers, Peter and Andrew, through some information about his brother James, who was possibly simply taken from some list of apostles[28] handed down in Manichean circles. The statements about Paul are in similar fashion actually expanded by association through a statement about the psalmist himself. There is therefore no reason for not seeing in this enumeration of the apostles who were patient in suffering a reflection of the collection, also attested elsewhere, of the five ancient apostolic Acts.

It has also left traces at another point in the Manichean Psalm-book, in a Psalm of Heracleides which illustrates the parable of the wise and foolish virgins (Mt. 25:1-13) by examples of true watchfulness.[29]. The series begins with Jesus and culminates in Mani. After the example of Jesus there follows first a list of his twelve disciples,[30] which adduces James the son of Alphaeus as Alphaeus and confuses James the son of Zebedee with the Lord's brother. That Judas also appears here, in conflict with the view of the psalm, as a negative example among others wholly positive, points to the conclusion that this list has been taken over as a fixed block. Among the statements about the individual apostles deriving from New Testament or extra-biblical tradition, or from tradition which at any rate cannot be verified elsewhere, there is a reflection of the narratives of the ancient apostle Acts at the most in the report about the activity of Thomas in India, but the description of him as a merchant tells against a direct link with the Acts of Thomas itself.[31] The list of apostles accordingly does not provide any indication either for or, as J.D. Kaestli would assume,[32] against the existence of a clearly defined corpus of apostolic Acts in Manichean use. Then follow as further examples the names of four women from canonical and apocryphal gospel tradition, Mary and Martha, Salome and Arsenoe,[33] and finally as a last group a series of female disciples of apostles is added:[34]

> A despiser of the body is Thecla, the lover of God.[35]
> A shamer of the serpent is the faithful Maximilla;[36]
> A recipient of good news is Iphidama her sister also, imprisoned in the prisons.[37]
> A contender in the fight is Aristobula the steadfast.[38]
> A giver of light to others is the noble Eubula, drawing the heart of the governor.[39]
> A [woman] that loves her master is Drusiana, the lover of God, shut up for fourteen days, seeking after her apostle.[40]
> . . . who was found is Mygdonia in the land of India.[41]

Here too the ancient apostle Acts are again marked off as a closed group, and even if the name of Eubula should not point to the Acts of Peter that cannot with J.D. Kaestli be interpreted as an indication that the five Acts did not form a clearly defined collection in the Manichean tradition;[42] that would be to try the capacity of an *argumentum e silentio* much too far.

Towards the end of the 4th century, finally, the Manichean Faustus of Milevis in his anti-catholic treatise appeals in his discussion of the Manichean attitude to marriage to the report in the Acts of Paul about Thecla's conversion to continence,[43] as well as to the word of the Lord in Mt. 19:12, and then writes that he foregoes citing Peter, Andrew, Thomas and John as further witnesses. 'These rather I pass over, as I said, since you have excluded them from the Canon, and in your blasphemous turn of mind are able to ascribe to them only teachings of the devil'.[44] With this Faustus sums up concretely and precisely the reports found elsewhere about the Manichean use of apocryphal Acts, and there is no ground for calling in question, with J.D. Kaestli, the view that within the Manichean literature they formed a clearly defined collection handed down as such,[45] especially since he confuses this question with the idea that the acceptance of such a corpus of necessity entails its possession of a canonical validity, which in his view was accorded by the Manicheans solely to the canon of Mani's writings. The transmission of the five Acts as a closed collection in itself says nothing whatever about the degree of binding force ascribed to them, while on the other side the Manichean Faustus and also the former Manichean Augustine allow us to see that a certain degree of binding force was definitely accorded to the Acts included in the collection, at any rate in the circle of the Latin African Manicheans: the former implicitly by his statement that on the Church side these writings had been excluded from the Canon, the latter by his use of them to refute Manichean opponents with texts which for them themselves were of binding force.[46]

The first-hand evidence available in the Manichean Psalm-book and in Faustus cannot be discredited by reference to the fact that the patristic testimonies for Manichean use of apocryphal Acts do not mention any collection, and that none of their enumerations includes all five of the Acts in question.[47] The extent to which anti-heretical writers possessed an exact and direct knowledge of the literature of the groups opposed certainly varied from case to case, and also their readiness to provide themselves and their readers with factually accurate and basic information about them is, in view of their preconceived opinions about this literature, frequently limited. Their notices are not a corrective to the Manichean witnesses, but must rather be interpreted on the basis of the latter. The Manicheans, so Philaster of Brescia writes towards 390 in his heresiological compendium,[48] used the report about what the apostle Andrew brought about on his journey from Pontus to Greece, and 'therefore', so it continues, 'the Manicheans also and others have such Acts of the blessed Andrew and the blessed evangelist John and likewise those of the apostle Peter as well as the blessed apostle Paul'. In them the apostles worked 'great signs and wonders, so that (tame) animals (*pecudes*), dogs and (wild) animals (*bestiae*) spoke'. This notice betrays a knowledge, whether acquired by Philaster himself or mediated to him by another source, of the itinerary in the ancient Acts of Andrew as well as of various stories of talking animals, the enumeration of which matches the stock of such stories contained in the extant five ancient Acts. There is mention of a talking dog in the Acts of Peter[49] - the plural may be understood as pure generalisation. In addition talking *pecudes* and *bestiae* are mentioned, and this distinction forbids our thinking solely of the talking lion in the Acts of Paul.[50] Rather the stories about talking asses in the Acts of Thomas[51] are also in view. That the latter

Acts do not appear in the series of the apostolic Acts named by Philaster can then only be the result of a defective or superficial enumeration.

According to Photius, the Manichean Agapius relied upon 'the so-called Acts of the Twelve Apostles and especially those of Andrew'.[52] To judge from Photius' report, Agapius appears to have been concerned in a special degree about the Manichean working-up of Christian tradition, and his *Heptalogos* is named along with the writings of Mani and other Manichean literature in the anti-Manichean *Seven Chapters*,[53] perhaps to be ascribed to Zacharias Rhetor (d. after 536); this is probably an indication that he possessed a certain significance for Manichean canvassing among Christians. In the list of the twelve disciples of Mani handed on by Peter of Sicily (second half of 9th cent.) and Photius he appears in the tenth place,[54] while on the other hand Photius has the impression that he entered into debate with the doctrine of Eunomius (d. 392/5);[55] but neither of these two conflicting reports may offer a reliable fixed point for locating him chronologically. We shall probably not go astray if we assume that the 'Acts of the Twelve Apostles' used by him are the collection of the five ancient Acts, and regard the title as a hyperbolical formulation corresponding to the description of Luke's Acts as 'Acts of the' or even 'of all the apostles' or 'of the twelve apostles'.[56] If the Acts of Andrew had an outstanding significance for Agapius and for Manichean canvassing among Christians,[57] this may provide an explanation for the remarkable collocation in Philaster's report of the Acts of Andrew on the one hand and the collection of Acts including the Acts of Andrew on the other; here evidently two pieces of information have been linked together, one about the use of the Acts of Andrew by the Manicheans and a second about the corpus of apostolic Acts in use among them and others. The latter itself appears not to have remained altogether unnoticed in Greek Christianity also in the 4th century. The Acts of Philip, domiciled in encratite and monastic circles in Asia Minor in this period, apparently hark back to all five of the Acts united in this collection, although this is not equally clear for each of them.[58]

Light is also shed upon a further group of witnesses by the Manichean evidence and the statements of Philaster confirmed by it. In his debate with the Manichean Felix (398), Augustine seeks to smite his opponent with his own weapons by referring to a passage which can no longer be verified from 'apocryphal writings' which are 'in the Acts composed by Leucius (Leutius), which he wrote as alleged apostolic Acts', and some years later Bishop Evodius of Uzala (El Alia in the north of Tunisia), a friend of Augustine's, quotes the same passage with the same indication of its source in his work 'On Faith against the Manichees'.[59] In the same document Evodius further adduces two stories from the Acts of Andrew, which are to be found 'in the Acts of Leucius, which he wrote under the names of apostles'.[60] All three passages presuppose coherent apocryphal apostolic acts, assigned to a common author, as a firmly defined entity in Manichean literature; they do not state its compass, but it is sufficiently clearly and reliably attested by the testimony of Faustus, and they know this collection under the same author's name which Photius four and a half centuries later will take in an expanded form from the Greek exemplar of the five journeyings of the apostles which he examined.

The Manichean Psalm-book goes back to the early period of the formation of the Manichean Church, and hence the collection of the 'Journeyings' which it already presupposes must also have been completed not too late in the third quarter of the 3rd century;[61] on the other hand it can scarcely have come into being very much earlier, in so far as its dissemination points to the conclusion that it was first put together in Manichean circles. In the course of its expansion Manicheism seems then, with its handing-on of this corpus and the creation of a Latin translation, to have imparted to the Church of the West the 'Greek gift' of a knowledge of the Acts of Andrew, John and Thomas, which had their home in Christian splinter groups in the East. These three Acts first appear in western Church witnesses in the late 4th and early 5th centuries, in Philaster, Augustine, Evodius[62] and in Innocent I,[63] while the Acts of Paul were already known in the West around 200, in the time of Tertullian and Hippolytus,[64] and with regard to the earliest western attestation for the Acts of Peter a secure verdict is scarcely to be gained.[65] Philaster already gave an incomplete description of the compass of the whole collection, which however can be corrected from his own statements, and Augustine and Evodius spoke of it only in very general terms. Over and above that, it left no really clear traces in Church reports either in the West, where it was probably taken over by the Priscillianists also, or in the East, apart from the report of Photius. There are only various compilations of some of the five Acts, in which as a rule we find not so much evidence of direct knowledge on the part of the witness concerned, but rather some more or less clear information that has come down to him about their existence. The question moreover remains whether in each case it is a question of information about fragments of the old collection, or fragmentary information about the collection itself, or whether we have to do with witnesses to a tradition independent of it.

In the Latin area, Innocent I in his letter to Exsuperius of Toulouse of 20 February 405 reckons among the non-canonical writings to be rejected 'those under the names of Peter and John, which were composed by a certain Leucius, as well as under the name of Andrew, which (were written) by the philosophers Xenocarides and Leonidas, and under the name of Thomas'.[66] Turribius of Astorga (mid-5th cent.), in a letter to the Spanish bishops Idacius, probably the Galician chronicler of the years 379-479, Hydatius of Chaves and Ceponius, names among the apocrypha in his view composed or redacted by the Manicheans 'especially those Acts which are called the (Acts) of the holy Andrew and those which are described as such of the holy John, which Leucius composed in godless speech, and those which are called the (Acts) of the holy Thomas, and the like (writings), from which the Manicheans and Priscillianists, and whatever other sect is kindred to them, seek to corroborate their whole heresy'.[67] The so-called *Passio Johannis* under the name of a bishop Melito of Laodicea, which hardly came into being before the second half of the 5th century, is extant only in Latin, but probably of Greek origin.[68] Its foreword warns 'against a certain Leucius, who has written Acts of the Apostles, of John the Evangelist and the holy Andrew as well as the apostle Thomas',[69] and taxes them with teaching a consistent dualism such as later Photius also thought he could find in the corpus of 'journeyings' he examined.[70] Even if one certainly cannot without more ado reckon that behind these testimonies there actually stands a direct and independent knowledge of the Acts mentioned in each case, yet one may probably see in their enumerations of such Acts, which at the same time name Leucius as the author for one or more of them, a faint echo of the Manichean corpus. It finally petered out in the West in the vague idea of one Leucius as an author of dangerous apocrypha generally.[71]

On the other hand it must remain an open question whether two lists, each of four of the five ancient Acts, which occur in the later Greek Church tradition should be claimed as faint echoes of the corpus, or rather as chance compilations. In the first half of the 7th century John of Thessalonica composed a homily on the Dormitio Mariae, a revision which seemed to him necessary because he held that this document itself had been corrupted by heretics. In the preface he appeals to similar works: 'We have indeed established that our most recent predecessors and the holy fathers long before them used this procedure - the former with the so-called separate Travels of the holy apostles, Peter, Paul, Andrew and John, the latter with most of the writings about the Christ-bearing martyrs'.[72] This text at any rate does not betray any direct knowledge of the ancient Acts, for which the designation 'Travels' here occurs for the first time.[73] Finally the Stichometry added in one version of the Chronography from the middle of the 9th century placed under the name of Nicephorus of Constantinople (the age of the Stichometry itself cannot be determined) names under the New Testament apocrypha the Travels of Paul, Peter, John and Thomas.[74]

Photius found occasion in the manuscript of the Travels collection which he examined to consider Leucius Charinus as the author of this corpus, and for Augustine and Evodius already Leucius evidently ranks as the author of the collection treasured by the Manicheans, and not merely of individual Acts contained therein, as has occasionally been assumed as a result of an isolated treatment of the individual witnesses apart from the total complex of the source material and also against their actual wording.[75] The surname Charinus adduced by Photius also was possibly not unknown in the West, but in a tradition for which the name Leucius cannot have been saddled with the hypothetical authorship of questionable apocryphal writings; for in the Latin form of the report of Christ's descent to Hell, the origin of which probably falls not before the middle of the 6th century, the sons of the aged Symeon who appear as witnesses to the Descensus (unnamed in the Greek version) bear the names Karinus and Leucius;[76] the question however remains open whether the Latin text here presents an independent addition, or preserves something more original over against the transmitted Greek form. When the Manichean corpus of apostolic Acts was placed under the name Leucius (Charinus) is obscure. However, the evidence of Photius at any rate justifies our starting out, despite the silence of the Greek tradition elsewhere, from the view that it did not first grow up in the West.

Outside of this corpus and the tradition which can be traced back to it of a heretical author of apocrypha named Leucius, and in addition to the use in the Latin Descensus, the name also occurs in the *Panarion* of Epiphanius, written in 375/7, and about the same time in Pacian of Barcelona (d. before 392). Epiphanius writes that Cerinthus and other heretics of the early period had 'often been attacked by the holy John and his companions, Leucius and many others',[77] a later relic of a tradition which already occurs in the 2nd century in the idea that John directed his Gospel against Cerinthus.[78] Pacian again speaks of Montanists 'who falsely claim to have drawn their inspiration from Leucius',[79] and by this formulation at the same time contests their right to appeal to him as a guarantor of authenticity, a guarantor, we may assume, for the Johannine apostolic tradition, which Montanism in particular claimed as its own. Pseudo-

Melito of Sardis in the prologue to his *Transitus Mariae* (5th or 6th cent.) marks a point of intersection of the tradition about a disciple of John named Leucius, contained in these witnesses, and that of Leucius as the composer of apocryphal writings. He introduces himself there as a disciple of the apostles and especially of John, and at the same time speaks of Leucius, 'who with us had been a companion of the apostles', but then departed from the way of righteousness, and combines this statement with the idea evidently taken from the *Passio Johannis*, that this Leucius did indeed in his writings report much of the deeds of the apostles but also inserted into them a false doctrine.[80]

The name of Leucius probably fell into such discredit because he was claimed by the Manicheans as guarantor of tradition for the collection of apocryphal Acts used among them and disseminated by them. It has often been conjectured that he was originally associated with the Acts of John and only from there passed over to the corpus as a whole.[81] It fits well with such an assumption that in Innocent I and Turribius of Astorga, in whose notices the information about the corpus itself has already become uncertain or even been lost, the name of Leucius in any case still attaches to the Acts of John. What above all tells in favour of his original attachment to these Acts is on the one hand the fact that there was a developing tradition about a disciple of John named Leucius, which from the context of its reflection in Epiphanius and Pacian points to the 2nd century and to Asia Minor, and on the other the fact that the Acts of John themselves from the point of view of controversial theology hark back precisely to the tradition which was developing in the 2nd century about John's activity in Ephesus and Asia Minor.[82] They could evidently take from this the name of a putative disciple of John, as they did the geographical framework of their narrative. He does not however appear in the only remains of this text extant today. They stand apart from the other ancient Acts, however, in that to a considerable extent they are written in the 'we' style of a fictional reporter,[83] who moreover also makes use of the first person singular in one of his narratives (AJ 61). This ostensible reporter, presenting himself as an intimate companion of the apostle, must have been introduced in the lost opening section of the document, and in view of the indications given it is certainly no far-fetched conjecture that this was done under the name of the putative disciple Leucius from the John tradition of Asia Minor.

Notes

The Manichean Collection of apocryphal Acts

1. Photius, *Bibl.*, cod. 114, ed. R. Henry, II, 84-86; on this cf. Eric Junod, 'Actes apocryphes et hérésie: Le jugement de Photius', in François Bovon *et al.*, *Les Actes apocryphes des Apôtres* (Publications de la Faculté de Théologie de l'Université de Genève 4), Geneva 1981, 11-24; Eric Junod/Jean-Daniel Kaestli, *L'histoire des Actes apocryphes du IIIe au IXe siècle* (Cahiers de la Revue de Théologie et de Philosophie 7), Geneva/Lausanne/Neuchâtel 1982, 134-137.
2. This statement cannot in this form be documented from the extant remains of the Acts mentioned; for the first part cf. however AJ 94: (the Jews) 'to whom their law was given by a lawless serpent'.
3. Cf. AJ 98: the Cross of Light is called *inter alia* 'sometimes Father, sometimes Son';

also AJ 109; 112.
4. Cf. AJ 87-93; APt (Act. Verc.) 21.
5. Cf. AJ 97-100; APt (Act. Verc.) 37f.; speech of Andrew to the Cross in the martyrdom of the Acts of Andrew: Armenian tradition of the Mart. Andr., ed. K. Tserakian, *Ankanon Girk' arrak' elakank'*, Venice 1904, 154-156; French trans. Louis Leloir, *Écrits apocryphes sur les apôtres* I(CChrSA 3), Turnhout 1986, 241-244.
6. Cf. AJ 97 and 102; however here it is John who laughs at the crowd. The motif that Jesus laughed at his crucifiers, because they were not aware that they were actually nailing another man in his form to the cross, appears in the Second Logos of the Great Seth (NHC VII 2) 55.30-56.19 and in the Nag Hammadi Apocalypse of Peter (NHC VII 3) 81.3-22, ed. and tr. M. Krause in Altheim/Stiehl (ed.), *Christentum am Roten Meer* II, 1973, 119-121; 172-175 (Eng. trans. in NHLE [3]1988, 365, 377); later, in c.5 of the anti-Manichean *Seven Chapters* of the 6th cent. (ed. Marcel Richard in the Introduction to the edition of John of Caesarea, CChrSG 1, Turnhout 1977, XXXIII-XXXX, here XXXVI 132-135; cf. the great Greek abjuration formula, PG 1, col. 1464D), it is also ascribed to the Manicheans (cf. also Samuel N.C. Lieu, 'An Early Byzantine Formula for the Renunciation of Manicheism', JbAC 26, 1983, 152-218, here 208). For the gnostic Basilides the man crucified in Christ's place, according to Irenaeus (*adv. Haer.* I 24.4, ed. Adelin Rousseau/Louis Doutreleau [SC 264], Paris 1979, 328), is identified with Simon of Cyrene. Linked with the scenery of the Acts of John, which make Christ appear on the Mount of Olives at the hour of the crucifixion, this idea occurs once again very much later in anti-heretical polemic in Nicephorus of Constantinople (806-816), who reproaches the iconoclasts who are demonstrably appealing to the Acts of John with dreaming, under the constraints of docetic heresy, 'that the incarnation and crucifixion of the Lord were only in appearance; for they fancy that it was not Christ who was the crucified, rather he took his stand upon the mount and laughed at the Jews, who crucified Simon in the delusion that it was Christ who would be crucified' (*Antirrheticus* II 19, PG 100, col. 369). Perhaps we should not, with E. Junod (see above, note 1), 21f., start out exclusively from the assumption that Photius' report on the basis of heresiological tradition is here distorted, but may also reflect that the version of the corresponding episode from the Acts of John which has come down to us in a single MS. only was possibly not the only one in circulation.
7. This judgment may for Photius have resulted from the encratite features which occur in the Acts mentioned; cf. e.g. AJ 113; APlThe 11; AA, frag. of Cod. Vat. gr. 808, cap. 4-8 (cf. below, pp. 129ff.); ATh 12; 55; 88; a passage from the apocryphal Epistle of Titus, which probably goes back to the Acts of John (see below, pp. 159f.), speaks of an express rejection of marriage; cf. also G. Sfameni Gasparro, 'Gli Atti apocrifi degli Apostoli e la tradizione dell'enkrateia', *Augustinianum* 23, 1983, 287-307.
8. This statement cannot be directly documented from the extant remains of the Acts named; cf. however the apocryphal Epistle of Titus (see below, pp. 159f.)
9. It is difficult to find any basis in the extant remains of the Acts mentioned for this reproach of a consistent dualism raised by Photius.
10. The miracle of raising the dead occurs in all apocryphal Acts; the raising of dead animals is on the contrary not reported in the extant Acts, if we leave aside the resuscitation of a dried sardine in APt (Act. Verc.) 13. In ATh 41 the raising of a dead ass is refused, although it is basically declared to be possible.
11. AJ 26-29.
12. Ed. Eric Junod/Jean-Daniel Kaestli, *Acta Johannis* I (CChrSA 1), Turnhout, 1983, 361.
13. Eusebius, *HE* III 1, ed. E. Schwartz I (GCS 9, 1), 188.1-12.
14. Adolf von Harnack, *Der kirchengeschichtliche Ertrag der exegetischen Schriften*

des Origenes I (TU 42, 3), 1918, 14-16; Eric Junod, 'Origène, Eusèbe et la tradition sur la répartition des champs de mission des Apôtres', *Les Actes apocryphes* (see p. 94, note 1), 233-248.

15. *A Manichaean Psalm-Book*, Part II, ed. C.R.C. Allberry, 1938, 142.17-143.14; cf. Peter Nagel, 'Die Psalmoi Sarakoton des manichäischen Psalmbuchs', *Oriental. Literaturzeitung* 62, 1967, 123-130; id., 'Die apokryphen Apostelakten des 2. und 3. Jahrhunderts in der manichäischen Literatur', *Gnosis und Neues Testament*, ed. Karl-Wolfgang Tröger, 1973, 149-182. The translation above follows Nagel's version, but has been checked against Allberry and the Coptic text. Cf. also J.-D. Kaestli, L'utilisation des Actes apocryphes des Apôtres dans le Manichéisme', *Gnosis and Gnosticism: Papers read at the Seventh International Conference on Patristic Studies*, ed. Martin Krause (NHS 8), Leiden 1977, 107-116; E. Junod/J.-D. Kaestli, *Histoire* (see p. 94, note 1), 73-77.

16. APt (Act. Verc.) 37f.

17. AA: Gregory of Tours, *de Miraculis b. Andr.* 12, ed. M. Bonnet (MG. SSrerMer. I 2, ^{2}1969), 382f.; see below, p. 120.

18. Cf. the martyrdom of the AA (see below, pp. 135ff.); there is however no mention of a crucifixion of his disciples there.

19. AJ; the narrative referred to is not extant, but can be deduced to be part of the ancient Acts of John; see below, p. 179.

20. Cf. Josephus, *Ant.* 20, 200, ed. B. Niese IV, 260.31-261.5; Hegesippus, *Hypomnem.* V ap. Euseb. *HE* II 23.12-18, ed. E. Schwartz (GCS 9, 1), 168.20-170.20 (see vol. I, p. 475ff.); Second Apocalypse of James (= NHC V 4), ed. Wolf-Peter Funk, *Die zweite Apokalypse des Jakobus aus Nag Hammadi Codex V* (TU 119), 44-47; translation in vol. I, p. 339. Not to be overlooked is above all the verbal contact with the note about James in the first of the two apostle lists in the Manichean Psalm-book (Allberry, 192.9). The two passages also correspond in that there is reference only to the stoning, and not as in Hegesippus and Apoc. Jas. to the casting-down from the Temple.

21. ATh 164f.

22. Cf. 2 Cor. 11:33; Acts 9:52; the wording is however not intelligible from these passages alone, but rather seems to presuppose a narrative elaborated from them.

23. APlThe 20f.

24. APlThe 33-35.

25. AJ; the narrative referred to is not extant, but can be deduced to be part of the ancient Acts of John; see below, p. 178f.

26. Maximilla is a prominent figure in the Acts of Andrew (see below, p. 128ff.); Aristobula is mentioned only in passing in AJ 59, but must have played a larger part in the Acts of John; cf. Nagel, 'Apostelakten' (see above, note 15), 168.

27. P. Nagel, 'Apostelakten' (see above, note 15), 154, thinks that of the Acts of Paul the psalmist had only the Acts of Paul and Thecla. If however, as would seem to be the case because of his juxtaposition of *pecudes* and *bestiae*, the talking lion of the Acts of Paul (see above, p. 90) is in mind in the statements of Philaster of Brescia about stories of talking animals in the Acts read by the Manicheans, then the Acts of Paul in the Manichean corpus cannot have contained only the Paul and Thecla complex.

28. See above, note 20, and on the apostle lists further below.

29. Allberry, 191.17-193.12.

30. Allberry, 192.5-20.

31. 'A merchant who finds gain is Thomas in the land of India' (Allberry, 192.15f.). In ATh 2 Thomas is represented as a carpenter who is sold to the merchant Abban.

32. J.-D. Kaestli (see above, note 15), 110f.

33. Allberry, 192.21-24.

34. Allberry, 192.25-193.3. Translation after Nagel (p. 96, note 15), but checked against Allberry and the Coptic text.
35. A summary of the portrait of Thecla in the APlThe.
36. AA; frag. of Cod. Vat. gr. 808, c. 5-8 (see below, p. 129ff.); cf. P. Nagel, 'Apostelakten' (p. 96, note 15), 136.
37. Iphidamia is, alongside Maximilla, an important figure in the Acts of Andrew, and together with her continually seeks out the imprisoned apostle (AA, frag. of Cod. Vat. Gr. 808, c.2; 5; 14; see below, pp. 129ff.); but there is no reference to the fact that she too was imprisoned.
38. See above, note 26.
39. A woman named Eubula appears in each of APt (Act. Verc.) 17 and APl, p. 2-5 of the Hamburg papyrus fragment. P. Nagel, 'Apostelakten' (p. 96, note 15), 158, has sought to relate the statements of the psalm to the Acts of Peter, J.-D. Kaestli (p. 96, note 15), 111, on the other hand, following the example of C.R.C. Allberry (app. ad loc.), to the Acts of Paul. She does not however fit these two narratives very well, and also the description of Eubula as 'noble' (εὐγενής) is of no assistance in deciding between the Eubula of the Acts of Peter, 'a woman of some distinction (*honesta*) in this world', and the freedwoman Eubula of the Acts of Paul, since the reference is probably to qualities of mind rather than to social status.
40. See above, note 25 and for the translation E. Junod/J.-D. Kaestli, *Histoire* (p. 94, note 1), 52.
41. ATh 82-105; 119-137; 157-160; 169.
42. J.-D. Kaestli (p. 96, note 15), 111.
43. APlThe 7.
44. Augustine, *c. Faust.* XXX 4, ed. J. Zycha (CSEL 25), 751.8-752.5.
45. J.-D. Kaestli (p. 96, note 15), 108-112. When in E. Junod/J.-D. Kaestli (p. 94, note 1), 140 it is said that the five Acts did not form 'a corpus in opposition to the canonical Acts', but rather only a 'collection' (*recueil, collection*), one has the impression that the contesting of the assumption of a Manichean 'corpus of Acts' is ultimately simply a quarrel about words, which starts out from too narrow a definition of the term 'corpus'.
46. See above, pp. 90f.
47. J.-D. Kaestli (p. 96, note 15), 108.
48. Philaster, *de Haer.* 88.6, ed. F. Heylen (CChrSL 9), 255f.; on the text-critical problem of this passage cf. P. Nagel, 'Apostelakten' (p. 96, note 15), 159, and E. Junod/ J.-D. Kaestli, *Histoire* (p. 94, note 1), 60; on the composition see above, p. 91f.
49. APt (Act. Verc.) 9; 11f. The Acts of Andrew according to Gregory of Tours (*de Mir. b. Andr.* 6, ed. M. Bonnet, MG.SSrerMer I 2, [2]1969, 380) are of no account here, since it is not dogs that speak but demons in the form of dogs, quite apart from the fact the original form of this demon-expulsion story cannot be reconstructed. Nor can the 'serpent' of ATh 30-33 be included among the talking animals.
50. APl, Hamburg papyrus p. 5 and Kasser's Coptic papyrus.
51. ATh 39f. (ass's colt); 74; 78f. (wild asses become tame).
52. Photius, *Bibl.*, cod.179, ed. R. Henry II, 184-187, here 186.
53. *Seven Chapters* 2, ed. M. Richard (p. 95, note 6) XXXIV 47f.; probably dependent on it the two abjuration formulae, the small (ed. G. Ficker, ZKG 27, 1906, 446-448, here 447.7f.) and great (PG 1, col. 1468A); cf. S.N.C. Lieu (p. 95, note 6), 170f. and 198f.
54. Peter of Sicily, *Hist. Manich.* 67, ed. Ch. Astruc *et al.*, *Travaux et Mémoires* 4, 1970, 3-67, here 31.28; Photius, *Narr. de Manich.* 50, ibid. 99-183, here 137.17; cf. the great Greek abjuration formula, PG 1, col. 1468B.
55. Photius, *Bibl.*, cod. 179, ed. R. Henry, II, 187.
56. Cf. C. Schmidt, *Die alten Petrusakten im Zusammenhang der apokryphen*

Apostelliteratur (TU 24,1), 1903, 30, note 1. On the title of Luke's Acts cf. E. Plümacher, TRE 3, 1978, 483; 'Acts of all the Apostles': Muratori Canon 34f. ed. P. Preuschen, *Analecta* II, [2]1910, 29; 'Acts of the Twelve Apostles': Cyril of Jerus. *Catech.* IV 36, ib. 81.71f. Cf. also Augustine, *c. Felic.* II 6 (see below).

57. Cf also Timothy the Presbyter, *de Recept. Haer.* (1st half 7th cent.), who in referring to the writings of Mani and after the Gospels of Thomas and Philip mentions 'the Acts of the Apostle Andrew' (PG 86 I, col. 21C).

58. E. Junod/J.-D. Kaestli, *Histoire* (p. 94, note 1), 30; François Bovon, 'Les Actes de Philippe', ANRW II 25.6, 1988, 4431-4527 (here 4522f.). The use is less clear for the Acts of Paul and Andrew than for the other three.

59. Augustine, *c. Felic.* II 6, ed. J. Zycha (CSEL 25), 833.8-17, the words quoted from 833.12f; Evodius, *de Fide* 5, ib. 952.16-20; it is not out of the question that Evodius here draws not directly from the source but from Augustine. On the conjecture that the text quoted could derive from the Acts of Andrew, see E. Junod/J.-D. Kaestli, *Histoire* (p. 94, note 1), 65.

60. Evodius, *de Fide* 38, ed. J. Zycha (CSEL 25) 968.24-969.6, the words quoted from 968.24f.; on the two episodes, see below, p. 109.

61. Cf. P. Nagel, 'Apostelakten', 153; J.-D. Kaestli (p. 96, note 15), 144f. and for the dating of the Psalm-book also Torgny Säve-Söderbergh, *Studies in the Coptic Manichean Psalm-book*, Uppsala 1949, 155f.

62. *Acts of Andrew*: Philaster (see above, note 48); Evodius, *de Fide* 38, ed. J. Zycha (CSEL 25), 968.24-969.6; in the 'apocrypha' mentioned by Augustine (*c. Adv. Leg. et Proph.* I 20, PL 42, col. 626), 'which were composed under the names of the apostles Andrew and John', it will also be a case of the corresponding Acts; cf. the statement in the introduction to the report from the Acts of Thomas (*c. Faust.* XXII, p. 79.): '... apocryphal writings ... under the names of apostles'. *Acts of John*: Philaster (see above, note 48); Augustine, *in Joh. tract.* 124.2, ed. R. Willems (CChrSL 36) 681.24-34 (reference to the death of John, AJ 106-115); *Ep.* 237.2 and 5f., ed. A. Goldbacher, IV (CSEL 57), 526.14-24 and 529.3-532.18 (quotations from the hymn in AJ 94-97, see below, p. 206, note 27); on *c. Adv. Leg. et Proph.* see above under Acts of Andrew. *Acts of Thomas*: Philaster implicitly (see above, p. 90); Augustine, *de Serm. dom. in monte* I 26.65, ed. A. Mutzenbecher (CChrSL 35), 75.1628-1637; *c. Adim.* 17, ed. J. Zycha (CSEL 25, 1), 166.6-22; *c. Faust.* XXII 79, ib. 618.6-26 (ATh 6 and 8). Klaus Zelzer (*Die alten lateinischen Thomasakten* [TU 12] 1977, XXIV-XXVI) thinks it possible to date the ecclesiasticising Latin redaction of the Acts of Thomas which we have in the *Passio Thomae* as early as the 4th century. This however stands on a very weak footing. The trinitarian interpolation (*Passio Thomae* 27-29, ed. K. Zelzer, ib. 20.11-22.14) is said to point to the time of the Arian controversy. But anti-Arian polemic still continued in Latin Church literature even in the 5th century; the use of a psychological trinitarian analogy (*Passio Thomae* 28, ed. Zelzer, 21.20-22.3) probably stands under the influence of Augustine, and the parallels from the younger Arnobius (d. after 455) adduced by Zelzer (114) in an appendix point to the 5th century. It is just as difficult to conceive that the fitting of the apostle's martyrdom into the frame of a conflict with the cult of Sol Invictus (*Passio Thomae* 55-60, ed. Zelser, 37.5-40.14) demands a location in the 4th century; apart from the fact that here we have a variation on a hagiographic motif which is not at all time-conditioned, we might also mention the point that even in 451 Leo the Great (*Tract.* 27.4, ed. A. Chavasse (CChrSL 138), 135.83-90) denounces a reversion of Christians to sun-worship. Finally, it is cutting corners to relate Augustine's references to the Acts of Thomas without more ado to one of the Church revisions, be it the *Passio* or the *Miracula Thomae*.

63. On Innocent I see above, p. 92.

64. Tertullian, *de Bapt.* 17.5, ed. J.W.P. Borleffs (CChrSL 1), 291f.; Hippolytus, *Comm. in Dan.* III 29.4, ed. M. Lefevre (SC 14), 254.
65. Commodian (*Carm. apol.* 626 and 628, ed. B. Dombart (CSEL 15), 156) refers to the narratives Act. Verc. 9; 11f. and 15. Assessment of this evidence is however faced not only with the question of Commodian's dating, in regard to which there is much to be said for a location in the 3rd century (cf. Klaus Thraede, 'Beiträge zur Datierung Commodians', JbAC 2, 1959, 90-114), but also with that of his origin; if he derived from the East, then his references would not necessarily attest without qualification a western dissemination of the Acts of Peter. The oldest indubitable western evidence is provided once again by Philaster (see above, p. 97, note 48) and Augustine (*c. Adim.* 17, ed. J. Zycha (CSEL 25), 170.9-13).
66. Innocent I, *Ep.* 6.7, ed. Hubert Wurm in *Apollinaris* 12, 1939, 77f., lines 34-37 (= Denzinger/Schönmetzer 213). The passage about the Acts of Andrew (line 37) is missing in part of the manuscript tradition.
67. Turribius Asturic. *Ep. ad Idac. et Cepon.* 5, PL 54, col. 694. The apocryphal Epistle of Titus witnesses to the dissemination in the Spanish region of the Acts of Paul and Peter also, which Turribius does not mention (see above, pp. 71 note 8 and 73 note 58).
68. Melito (Mellitus, Miletus) of Laodicea, *Passio Johannis*, ed. Franciscus Maria Florentinius, *Vetustius occidentalis ecclesiae Martyrologium*, Lucca 1668, 130-137 (reprinted in Johannes Albert Fabricius, *Codex apocryphus Novi Testamenti* III, Hamburg 1724, [2]1743, cols. 604-623) and (in another text-form) Gotthold Heine, *Bibliotheca anecdotorum* I, Leipzig 1848, 109-117 (reprinted in PG 5, cols. 1239-1250). On its origin and dating cf. Knut Schäferdiek, 'Die Passio Johannis des Melito von Laodikea und die Virtutes Johannis', *AnalBoll* 103, 1985, 367-382.
69. *Passio Johannis*, prol., Fabricius 604, cf. PG 5, col. 1239.
70. See above, p. 87f.
71. Ps.-Gelasius, *Decr. de libris recip.* V 4.4, ed. E. von Dobschütz (TU 38,4), 52: 'All the books which Leucius, the disciple of the devil, has made', where 'disciple of the devil' may indicate that the Manichean literature is in mind.
72. John of Thessalonica, *Koimesis-homily*, ed. M. Jugie (PO 19), 377.5-12.
73. Cf. E. Junod/J.-D. Kaestli, *Histoire* (p. 94, note 1), 117-119, who also think, although with reservations, of Latin writings on which the judgment could rest. On the later apostolic Acts, see below, pp. 426ff.
74. So-called Stichometry of Nicephorus, ed. Th. Zahn, *Geschichte des ntl. Kanons* II 1, Erlangen/Leipzig 1888, 300.63-66; see vol. I, p. 42.
75. On this cf. NTApo[3] II, pp. 182-186.
76. Gospel of Nicodemus 17-27, ed. H.C. Kim, *The Gospel of Nicodemus* (Toronto Medieval Texts 2), Toronto 1973, 35-39 passim (cf. vol. I, pp. 526-530); on the dating cf. G.C. O'Ceallaigh, 'Dating the commentaries of Nicodemus', *Harv. Theol. Review* 56, 1963, 21-58. On the parcelling out of the double name to two persons, cf. Josef Kroll, *Gott und Hölle*, 1932, 86.
77. Epiphanius, *Pan.* 51.6.7-9, ed. K. Holl II (GCS 31) 255.16-24, the words quoted from 255.23f.
78. Irenaeus, *adv. Haer.* III 11.1, ed. A. Rousseau/L. Doutreleau (SC 211), 138f.; cf. also the anecdote reported ib. III 3.4 (SC 211, 40-42), under appeal to Polycarp, about John's encounter with Cerinthus in a bath-house.
79. Pacian of Barcelona, *Ep.* I 2, ed. P.H. Peyrot, Zwolle 1896 = Amsterdam 1969, 4; PL 13, col. 1053B.
80. Ps.-Melito, *de Trans. Mariae*, Prol., PG 5, cols. 1231f.
81. Cf. Isaac de Beausobre, *Histoire critique de Manichée et de Manichéisme* I, Amsterdam 1734, 348-352; Johann Karl Thilo, *Colliguntur et commentariis illustrantur*

fragmenta actuum S. Ioannis a Leucio Charino conscriptorum, Halle 1847, 5, note; Theodor Zahn, *Acta Johannis*, Erlangen 1880 = Hildesheim 1975, LX-LXXXI; Carl Schmidt, *Die alten Petrusakten im Zusammenhang der apokryphen Apostelliteratur* (TU 24,1), Leipzig 1903, 76f. On the other hand the source material offers no support for E. Junod's conjecture (see p. 94, note 1, there p. 17) that the name of Leucius became attached to the Acts as a result of the efforts of Manichean circles to put a name to the author of the Acts of Andrew, who in a still unpublished epilogue speaks anonymously about the aim of his work. Even if Leucius is possibly named in Augustine and Evodius only at quotations from the Acts of Andrew (cf. above, p. 98, note 59), he is there linked not with these Acts but with the Manichean corpus as a whole. In view of this, Junod and Kaestli (*Histoire* [see p. 94, note 1], 137-142, esp. 140) retreat to the assumption that the name of Leucius was first attached to it in circles of Latin African Manicheans, and if Photius found occasion in his manuscript for assigning it to Leucius Charinus, that is possibly a reflection of western tradition (ib., 142f.). Here the question of the Ephesian John legend, in which the Leucius tradition and the Acts of John have a common point of reference, is not taken into consideration.

82. Cf. below, p. 164, and Knut Schäferdiek, 'Herkunft und Interesse der alten Johannesakten', ZNW 74, 1983, 247-267, esp. 261-263.

83. Cf. E. Junod/J.-D. Kaestli, *Acta Johannis* (p. 95, note 12), 530-533.

1. The Acts of Andrew

Jean-Marc Prieur and *Wilhelm Schneemelcher*

Introduction

Jean-Marc Prieur

1. Literature: Texts: Bonnet, Aa II 1,1-64; Acta Andreae Apostoli cum Laudatione contexta, ed. M. Bonnet, *AnalBoll* 13, 1894, 311-352; Martyrium Sancti Apostoli Andreae, ed. M. Bonnet, *AnalBoll* 13, 1894, 353-378; Gregory of Tours, *Liber de miraculis beati Andreae Apostoli*, ed. M. Bonnet (MGH, Script. rerum Merov. I 2), 1885, 821-846; Th. Detorakis, 'Τὸ ἀνέκδοτο μαρτύριο τοῦ 'Αποστόλου 'Ανδρέα', *Acts of the Second International Congress of Peloponnesian Studies 1980*, I, Athens 1981/82, 325-352 (Modern Greek Introd. with Eng. summary, edition of text); J. Barns, 'A Coptic Apocryphal Fragment in the Bodleian Library', JThS NS 11, 1960, 70-76; Martyre d'Andrée (BHO 52), in *Écrits apocryphes sur les Apôtres. Traduction de l'édition arménienne de Venise*, by L. Leloir (CChrSA 3) 1986, 228-257; Moraldi II, 1351-1429; Erbetta II, 395-449g;. new edition of the complete material by J.-M. Prieur: *Acta Andreae* (CChrSA 5: Praefatio, Commentarius; 6: Textus), Turnhout 1989.

Studies: R.A. Lipsius, *Die apokryphen Apostelgeschichten* I, 1883, 543-622; J. Flamion, *Les Actes d'André et les textes apparentés* (Recueil de travaux d'histoire et de philologie 33), Louvain 1911; E. Hennecke, 'Zur christlichen Apokryphenliteratur', ZKG 45, 1926, 309-315; G. Quispel, 'An Unknown Fragment of the Acts of Andrew (Pap. Copt. Utrecht 1)', *VigChr* 10, 1956, 129-148; F. Dvornik, *The Idea of Apostolicity in Byzantium and the Legend of the Apostle Andrew* (Dumbarton Oaks Studies IV), Cambridge/Mass. 1958; P.M. Peterson, *Andrew, Brother of Simon Peter. His History and His Legends* (Suppl. to *Novum Testamentum* I), Leiden 1958; M. Hornschuh, 'Andreasakten', NTApo^3 II 270-297 (ET 390-425); E. Plümacher, art. 'Apostelakten', PWRE Suppl. XV, 1978, cols. 11-70; Jean-Marc Prieur, 'La figure de l'apôtre dans les Actes d'André', in F. Bovon *et al.*, *Les Actes apocryphes des apôtres. Christianisme et monde païen*, Geneva 1981, 121-139; id., 'Découvertes sur les Actes d'André à Patras', *Acts of the Second Internat. Congress of Pelopon. Studies* (see above), 321-324; id., 'Les Actes apocryphes de l'apôtre André. Présentation des diverse traditions apocryphes et état de la question', ANRW II 25/6, 4384-4414; D.R. MacDonald, 'Odysseus's Oar and Andrew's Cross: The Transformation of a Homeric Theme in the Acts of Andrew' (SBL Seminar Papers 25), Atlanta 1981, 309-312.

2. Attestation: a) In the East (4th cent.). The oldest direct mention is in Eusebius of Caesarea (*HE* III 25.6; see vol. I, p. 47), who lists the AA along with the Acts of John among the texts which are to be rejected as absurd and impious.[1]

The Papyrus Copt. Utrecht I, which contains a translation of a section from the AA, confirms that this work was known in Egypt in the 4th century (the papyrus is dated to this period).[2]

In his *Panarion* Epiphanius reports that the AA were used by the Encratites, the Apostolici or Apotactites, and the Origenists.[3]

b) Among the Manicheans. The AA, like the other apocryphal Acts, were in use among the Manicheans (see above, pp. 87ff.), who treasured them because of their dualism and their encratite tendency.

In two Manichean psalms there are clear allusions to events and personalities in the AA.[4] In the 'psalm of endurance' (p. 142) it is said: 'Andrew the apostle - they set fire to the house beneath him. He and his disciples - hail to them, they were crucified.' The AA say nothing about any crucifixion of Andrew's disciples, but they do end with the apostle's death by crucifixion. In addition there is in the *Liber de miraculis* of Gregory of Tours a story of the burning of a house in which Andrew was on the third story (c. 12, 832.41-833.2). In the same psalm (143.13-14) it is said: 'Maximilla and Aristobula - on them was great torture inflicted. What need for them to suffer these things? It is purity for which they contend.' Maximilla appears in the AA. She is the wife of Aegeates, the proconsul of Patras, who applies moral torture to her because after her conversion she denies herself to him.

In the psalm 'There were ten virgins' we find the following lines (192.26-28): 'A shamer of the serpent is the faithful Maximilla. A recipient of good news is Iphidama her sister also, imprisoned in the prisons.' Here again Maximilla appears; her husband, whom she in fact put to shame, is called 'serpent' in the AA, while she receives the designation 'most faithful' (πιστοτάτη). Her companion is called 'sister' by her, and meets with Andrew in the prison. These psalms, translated from Greek into Coptic, probably go back to a Syriac original. The papyrus on which they are handed down derives from the second half of the 4th century, but the texts themselves go back to the end of the 3rd. Even if they do not expressly quote the AA, we have here the evidence for the earliest use of this apocryphon.[5]

In his *Diversarum haereseon liber* (about 390), Philaster of Brescia affirms that the apocrypha, corresponding to the ideas of the Manicheans, have much added or omitted. He expressly names the AA: 'Apocrypha of the blessed Andrew, these are: Acts which he did when he came from Pontus to Greece, and which the disciples who followed the apostle wrote up.'[6] A twofold interest attaches to this testimony. On the one hand it gives us a valuable indication of the content of the AA: Andrew's travels from Pontus to Greece. On the other it suggests the idea that the apocryphon presented itself as the work of eye-witnesses.

Augustine writes in his *Contra Felicem Manichaeum* (404): 'In the Acts composed by Leucius, which he wrote as if they were Acts of the Apostles, you will find these statements: For indeed specious figments, a simulated brilliance and a laying claim through visible things do not proceed from one's own nature, but from that man who through himself has become corrupted, through seduction'.[7] Augustine does not say that this quotation comes from the AA, and we have not been able to find it in any transmitted text. But its content does probably correspond to the world of ideas of the AA described below (see pp. 110ff.). The quotation may then very well have been taken from this apocryphon, and then attests that Augustine knew the AA.

In the 5th century Evodius of Uzala (d. 424), in his work *de Fide contra Manichaeos*, first takes up the quotation from Augustine and then adduces two allusions to the content of the AA which can be verified in the sources available to us. These are not indeed citations of passages from the AA, but the precise statements show that Evodius had an accurate knowledge of the work.

'In the Acts of Leucius, which he composed in the names of apostles, consider what kind of things you accept in regard to Maximilla the wife of Egetes: when she refused to pay the due proper to her husband, although the apostle said: Let the man give what is due to the woman, and so also the woman to the man (1 Cor. 7:3), she foisted on him her maid Euclia, supplying her, as is written there, with enticements and cosmetics, and substituted her in the night for herself, so that he without knowing it slept with her as if she were his wife. There it is also written that when Maximilla and Iphidamia went away together to hear the apostle Andrew, a handsome little boy, whom Leucius would have us understand either as God or at least as an angel, handed them over to the apostle Andrew; and he departed to the Praetorium of Egetes, went into the bedroom and imitated a woman's voice, as if Maximilla were complaining about the suffering of the female sex and Iphidamia were answering her. When Egetes heard this conversation he believed that they were within and went away.'[8]

c) Among the Priscillianists. The AA were also used by the Priscillianists, the ascetic sect which developed from the preaching of Priscillian about 375 in Spain. In his list of the canonical books, drawn up with them in view, Pope Innocent I intimates that the AA belong to the writings to be condemned and rejected. He adds that they were composed by the philosophers Xenocarides and Leonidas.[9] This report is without any parallel. It must however be set in association with Philaster's statement about the disciples of Andrew, and perhaps - as we shall see later - gives a hint as to the identity of the author of the AA.

The Epistle of Pseudo-Titus, which derives from a milieu close to Priscillianism (see above, pp. 53ff.), clearly alludes to an episode in the AA, and in a general way to its encratism: 'When finally the apostle Andrew came to a wedding, to show the glory of God, he separated the spouses intended for one another, the women and the men, and taught them to remain holy in celibacy.'[10]

In the Decretum Gelasianum (cf. vol. I, pp. 38ff.) the AA are expressly adduced among the texts which, as composed and used by heretics and schismatics, are not approved by the catholics.[11]

d) Catholic redactions of the AA. Despite the papal condemnations the AA were widely read and used by catholics. They were however subjected to revision, to make them acceptable for popular piety. The Letter of the Presbyters and Deacons of Achaea, which came into being probably in the 6th century, is the oldest Latin reworking, but contains only the end of the book, i.e. the martyrdom of the apostle.[12] The *Liber de miraculis Beati Andreae Apostoli*[13] was composed by Gregory of Tours shortly before his death (593). In the prologue Gregory explains that he has had the AA in his hands. He has revised them in order - as he says - to remove their prolixity (*verbositas*). Gregory is the last Latin witness for the existence of the complete AA, probably in the form of a Latin version.

e) The AA in the Greek and Byzantine area. After 815 a monk of Kallistratia, Epiphanius, wrote a life of Andrew[14] which extends from the apostle's call, as it is related in the Gospel of John, to his death in Patras. This Life is evidently dependent on the AA, but only towards the end of the book, that is from the report about the arrival in Patras on. This suggests the conclusion that at this time exemplars of the AA were in circulation which contained no more than the concluding part of this apocryphon.[15] Photius (Patriarch of Constantinople 858-867 and 877-886) is the last Greek witness for the existence of the AA. He says that he read them, like the APt, the AJ, the ATh and the APl, in a book which was ascribed to Leucius (cod. 114; cf. above, pp. 87f.).[16] It can no longer be established whether this book contained the AA in full or only the last part of it.

f) The Armenian Martyrdom.[17] This martyrdom, translated from the Greek in the 6th or 7th century, is proof of the dissemination of the AA in Armenia in this period. But since only the text of the final chapters (the martyrdom in Patras and part of the speech preceding it) is reproduced, it is a question whether the Armenian translator had a complete exemplar of the AA in his hands, or only the last part of the work.

g) Summary. Between the 3rd and the 9th century the AA became known and read everywhere, in Africa, Egypt, Palestine, Syria, Armenia, Asia Minor, Greece, Italy, Gaul and Spain. They were particularly successful in circles of a dualistic and ascetic tendency, especially among the Manicheans and Priscillianists. They were repeatedly the subject of condemnations, but this did not result in their disappearance. Rather they lived on in the form of revisions and extracts, as we shall see in the following section. The trail vanishes in the West in the 6th century, in the East in the 9th.

3. Transmission and extant remains: The AA have not come down to us in the primary form of their original Greek text. For their partial reconstruction, five texts or groups of texts of various kinds are at our disposal.

a. *The Liber de miraculis of Gregory of Tours:* This work is a source of inestimable value, for Gregory reports about the AA from beginning to end, and thus makes possible for us an insight into the total plan of the work and the general design of the travel narratives. They run from Pontus to Patras in Achaea, which corresponds with the witness of Philaster of Brescia. A comparison with the sources which have handed on original elements of the AA[18] yields the following results:

1. Gregory has throughout suppressed the speeches;

2. he has probably often thought it necessary to change the structure of the narrative;

3. he has bent the work to a sense acceptable for catholic thinking.

From c. 36 on he reports very concisely about the martyrdom, referring to a Latin Passio which seemed to him worthy of commendation.[19]

b. *The Coptic Papyrus Utrecht 1*: This papyrus contains the translation of an extract from the AA which corresponds to c. 18 of the *Liber de miraculis*. It did not contain the whole book, as is evident from the fact that it ends with the title 'the Act of Andrew'. The extract extends over pages 1-15 of the manuscript. The first eight pages are however lost, and in addition pages 11 and 12 are also missing. The version is in the Sahidic dialect.

c. *The Armenian Martyrdom*: This is a complete translation of the final part of the AA, which contains Andrew's martyrdom in Patras together with the immediately preceding speech of the apostle in the prison. This Armenian version contains passages which are omitted in all the Greek witnesses mentioned further below. The translator has however remoulded the text in the sense of a more strongly 'orthodox' and biblically oriented theology. It is moreover possible that he has added the eagle allegory in c. 12-15.[20]

d. *Five Greek recensions of the final part of the AA*: The concluding part of the AA is extant in Greek in five recensions. These are witnesses which reproduce the original text of the AA, but which do not all transmit the same extent of text and also have not preserved the same elements throughout.

The *Passio Andreae* in Cod. Sinait. gr. 526 (fols. 121v-132v) and Cod. Jerusal. S. Sabas 103 (fols. 155-168v). This text is here designated as JS.[21] It is the most extensive witness to the martyrdom. It begins before the Armenian version, i.e. it reports what Andrew did and said in Patras before the martyrdom, and extends to the end of the AA. Comparison with the Armenian martyrdom and the other Greek witnesses makes it clear that JS has not preserved all the elements of the report. The scribe to whom this recension goes back has made excisions above all in the speeches.

Extract from the AA in Cod. Vatic. gr. 808 (fols. 507-512)[22]. This fragment of the AA is mutilated at the beginning and the end. It belongs within the course of the narrative of JS. The text ends shortly before the beginning of the martyrdom. It reproduces in full the part of the AA which it contains.

The *Passio Andreae* in Cod. Ann Arbor 36 (fols. 60v-66v). This text, as yet unpublished, has for its content the report of the martyrdom of Andrew. It begins immediately after the mutilated end of Vat. gr. 808. Like JS, this witness too has not preserved all the elements of the original text. Thus the speeches have been eliminated. The lacunae are not however the same as in JS. This shows that Ann Arbor 36 is not dependent on JS. Rather the two forms of text go back to a common *Vorlage*: the AA.

The *Passio Andreae* in Cod. Paris. B.N. gr. 770 (fols. 43v-46) and Cod. Jerus. S.Sabas 30 (fols. 154v-156v), known under the title *Martyrium alterum A*.[23] As in Ann Arbor 36, the whole martyrdom is extant in this version, but with numerous important excisions.

The *Passio Andreae* in Cod. Paris. B.N. gr. 1539 (fols. 304-305v), known as *Martyrium alterum B*.[24] As in the two Passions mentioned above, the whole martyrdom is contained in this manuscript, but with even more numerous abbreviations.

e. *Extracts from the AA handed down in Greek revisions*: Three descriptions of the Life or Passion of Andrew which are dependent on the AA have preserved Greek extracts from this apocryphon:

One of the Greek versions of the *Letter of the Presbyters and Deacons of Achaea*. This letter was composed in Latin, and has undergone two Greek translations in particular. One of them, which begins with the words Ἅπερ τοῖς ὀφθαλμοῖς ἡμῶν, has taken over important passages from the original AA in chapters 10-15. These extracts, which occur towards the end of the martyrdom, can be clearly recognised in the other Greek witnesses.

Two reports which are dependent on one and the same revision of the AA: the *Martyrium prius* (8th cent.)[25] and the *Laudatio* of Nicetas of Paphlagonia (9th-10th cent.).[26] The *Laudatio* is a reworking of the Vita Andreae of Epiphanius of Kallistratia (see above, p. 103). It gives its narrative outline as a whole, and has many sections in common with it. But from Andrew's arrival in Patras on (c. 33) the Laudatio inserts additional pieces, several of which also appear in the Martyrium prius, which also begins with the arrival in Patras: the conversion of the town of Patras and of the proconsul Lesbius (Martyrium prius c. 3-8; Laudatio c. 34-37); speech to the cross (Martyrium prius c. 14; Laudatio c. 46). The Laudatio further contains the story of the healing of the servant of the brother of Aegeates, Lesbius' successor (c. 43), which appears in the same wording at the beginning of JS, and also a few lines (c. 48,

p. 348.8-22) which can be found in the Greek witnesses to the martyrdom. Finally there is the story of a healing in Patras (c. 41), which corresponds to c. 33 in Gregory of Tours.

If we compare the corresponding sections of the Martyrium prius and the Laudatio with one another and with the other Greek witnesses of the AA (Greek text and Armenian martyrdom), the result is:

1. The Martyrium prius and Laudatio are not dependent on one another, but rather point back to a common *Vorlage*.

2. This *Vorlage* did not exactly correspond to the original AA.

The Martyrium prius and the Laudatio are thus dependent on a version of the AA which reports only the events in Patras and shows differences as compared with the original version. Despite this the pieces preserved by the two texts are of value for the reconstruction of the AA.[27]

In addition to these five groups of witnesses mention must be made of a further fragment in Coptic (Sahidic), which consists of two poorly preserved leaves (4th cent.).[28] It contains a conversation between Jesus and Andrew in which the latter briefly strikes the balance of his apostolic activity. The editor of the fragment, J. Barns, wanted to assign it to an apocryphal gospel or - better still - to the AA. The assumption that the text belongs to the AA appears to us very probable, even if a firm proof cannot be produced. The forsaking of wife and children, to which there is reference in the text, corresponds well with the thought of the AA. Further, the words 'I came out of the house of my father . . . and I did not lay it down' recall the retrospective prayers in two texts which are close to the AA: AJ c. 113 and ATh c. 144-148. Barns would assign the text to the beginning of the AA. If this were correct, it would mean that the AA, like the ATh (c. 1-3), began with an appearance of Jesus to the apostle.[29] But such an episode may also have been related at other points in the AA, for this apocryphon must often have reported on appearances of Christ. We find a trace of this in Gregory (c. 22), who may moreover have suppressed other reports of the kind. The conversation in the Coptic fragment would fit particularly well in a vision, of which the Martyrium prius (c. 8) and the Laudatio (c. 37) have preserved a trace. This vision notifies Andrew of his imminent death. One could well understand that Andrew should at this point strike a balance of his life, as the apostles do in AJ and ATh. Apart from that, the Coptic fragment and the two Greek revisions contain the theme of cross-bearing and of the imitation of Christ.

4. The possibility of reconstructing the structure and content: If we follow Gregory's reworking of the AA, it consisted of two main parts: 1. a report of the travels which brought Andrew from Pontus by way of Amasia, Sinope, Nicaea, Nicomedia, Byzantium, Thrace, Perinthus, Philippi and Thessalonica to Patras (c. 2-21); 2. the acts of Andrew in Patras and Achaea (c. 22-35). This second part begins with his activity in Patras (c. 22-24). Thereafter Andrew visits several towns in Achaea: Corinth, Megara and perhaps Sparta (cf. the allusion in Gregory c. 29, p. 843.29). Then he returns to Patras, where he resumes his activity (c. 30-35). Finally comes the report about the martyrdom (c. 36).

Gregory's work begins with the episode of the deliverance of Matthias from imprisonment among the cannibals (c. 1). This story has also been handed down in a separate and much more detailed work under the title 'The Acts of Andrew and Matthias.'[30] Several scholars believe that this episode originally belonged to the AA, and was later expanded and made into an independent work. We think on the other hand that the story was not a part of the AA, but has been inserted at the beginning of the Latin version which Gregory had to hand.[31]

Down to Andrew's arrival in Patras, Gregory's *Liber de miraculis* is in fact our only witness for the AA, and despite the modifications introduced by Gregory our best source of knowledge. It does not allow us to reconstruct the text of the AA, but it does convey a very precise idea of the course of the narrative. Some external clues however allow us to restore the original sense of some sections altered by Gregory.

The Acts of John of Pseudo-Prochorus (cf. below, pp. 429ff.), the author of which knew the AA, may clarify some obscurities in c. 4 of Gregory's account, since they report a comparable story. In Gregory there is reference to a mother who betakes herself to the proconsul of the town of Amasia, to lay charges against her son: he has nursed incestuous designs against her, and has then attached himself to Andrew. This arouses the wrath of the proconsul against the apostle. This reaction is surprising, but can easily be explained if - as in the report of ps.-Prochorus - the mother accuses the apostle himself of having put the incestuous attack into her son's mind.[32]

We may further recall that the Letter of Pseudo-Titus, following the AA, reports how Andrew intervenes to prevent the consummation of a marriage. This notice must probably be seen in some connection with Gregory's report (c. 11) about the prevention of an incestuous union between two brothers and their kinswomen. Gregory considers it necessary to make Andrew express himself clearly: 'We do not abhor marriage, nor avoid it, for God has ordained from the beginning that man and wife should unite together. But we reject incest.'[33] Actually the AA must have reported how Andrew stepped in to prevent a perfectly normal marriage, i.e. to preach encratism. Gregory evidently took offence at this episode, and reworked it. The forced explanation which he puts into Andrew's mouth makes it expressly clear that the latter would not wish to expose himself to the reproach of rejecting marriage.

Gregory's report in c. 18 presents some deviations as compared with the text of Pap. Utrecht 1, which belongs at this point. The two reports agree in that a soldier who has been deputed to arrest Andrew falls to the ground, but then is finally healed. Between these two events however the Pap. Utrecht 1 presents a dialogue between Andrew and the demon who has taken possession of the soldier, whereas Gregory tells of a meeting with the proconsul. Now the lost pages of Pap. Utrecht 1 leave no room for the insertion of this official. This will rather have taken place after the healing of the soldier and not before. Gregory has possibly altered this episode because it developed ideas hostile to marriage, or perhaps also because of the example of military disobedience given in it.

The report about Andrew's arrival in Patras in c. 22 of Gregory's account can be clarified through a section transmitted in the monk Epiphanius (PG 120, col. 244) and in the Laudatio (c. 33, p. 335.13-20). The two texts make the precise statement that Andrew on his arrival in Patras lodged with a certain Sozius, whom he had healed. Gregory on the other hand says only that Andrew was received by a man to whose house the proconsul Lesbius sent in search of him, but lets out nothing more precise as to who he was and how it came about. Epiphanius and the Laudatio give this man's name and explain why Andrew went to stay with him.

The beginning of Andrew's activity in Patras is reported by the Martyrium prius (c. 3-7) and the Laudatio (c. 34-36) in two almost identical versions, which go back to a common source. In both texts Andrew performs numerous miracles, so that his fame spreads through the town and the proconsul Lesbius grows suspicious. An angel appears to the proconsul, and informs him that he will remain speechless until he has learned the truth from Andrew. Lesbius has Andrew summoned, and he heals and converts him. The whole town is then also converted and to the proconsul's satisfaction destroys the pagan idols. Shortly thereafter he is released from his command.

In Gregory (c. 22) Lesbius is directly instructed in a dream to have Andrew brought. When Andrew comes to him, he finds him wellnigh dead. He brings him back to health, and Lesbius reports that he had had the intention to exterminate him, but that two Ethiopians appeared to him who smote him with scourges, which explains his present condition.

Gregory need not have invented the intervention of the Ethiopians. That would not be in keeping with the sobriety he shows elsewhere. On the other hand the Martyrium prius and the Laudatio probably adhere exactly to the AA when they report the intervention of an angel. This need not however have come to a conclusion with Lesbius' dumbness, a motif determined by Luke 1:11-20. The suffering from which Andrew heals the proconsul must in fact derive from the scourging by the Ethiopians. For the rest, this course of events will certainly have been reported in the narrative itself, and not by Lesbius. It would be entirely conceivable that it had its place before the appearance of the angel. In that case it would have been made known to Lesbius, after he had already been stricken, that the man who was to heal him was at hand in Patras.

Gregory says nothing about the destruction of the idols by the inhabitants of the town. He contents himself with referring to their conversion. This episode, reported in the Martyrium prius (c. 6) and in the Laudatio (c. 35), was however probably in the AA. Despite Gregory's silence, we may also retain the deposition of Lesbius by the emperor (Martyrium prius c. 7 and Laudatio c. 36) as part of the AA, for it explains why this proconsul was replaced by Aegeates, who brought Andrew to his death.

Gregory's reports about Andrew's activity in Patras (c. 23 and 24) and his journeying through various towns in Achaea (c. 25 to 29) belong at this point. There is no report of these in the Martyrium prius or the Laudatio, but the Laudatio still has a brief allusion (c. 36, p. 337.31-32). The Martyrium prius (c. 8) and the Laudatio (c. 37) then report an appearance of Christ in which Andrew is informed of his impending death and (Laudatio c. 37) receives the charge to return to Patras. This vision, of which Gregory says not a word, must none the less have belonged to the original text of the AA.

For the beginning of the acts of Andrew after his return to Patras we have only the evidence of Gregory at our disposal (c. 30-32). For the healing narrative in c. 33, on the other hand, the much more broadly developed text in the Laudatio (c. 41) is probably to be preferred. Its description of the event does not diverge in any essential features, but probably reproduces the original Greek text.

The text attested by JS begins immediately after this healing narrative (Gregory

c. 34). This is the narrative of the healing of the servant of Aegeates' brother, which is also in c. 43 of the Laudatio.

The two episodes to which Evodius refers can be clearly recognised in the course of the narrative of JS. In the first it is reported that Maximilla, the wife of Aegeates, is no longer willing to have sexual relations with her husband, and has her servant take her place in his bed. This is fully narrated in JS.

In the second episode it is a question of Maximilla and her companion Iphidama having gone to Andrew, to hear him. A handsome little boy hands them over to the apostle and then goes off to the praetorium of Aegeates. There he goes into the women's room and imitates Maximilla's voice, lamenting 'the sufferings of the female sex', to give the impression that the women are there. This story is not in JS, but we can discern there its place in the original text of the AA; for JS relates that at the moment when Maximilla and Iphidama go to Andrew's prison, a handsome little boy receives them and leads them to Andrew. We may assume with good reason that the story reproduced by Evodius had its place at this point. The copyist of JS has then omitted it. This report stood directly before the speech which is transmitted at the beginning of Vat. gr. 808.

Vat. gr. 808 is the most complete Greek witness for the part of the AA contained in this manuscript, more complete than the corresponding section in JS. From the martyrdom on, JS, Ann Arbor 36, Martyrium alterum A and B and also the original elements which are contained in one of the Greek versions of the Letter of the Deacons of Achaea allow us to form a very accurate idea of how the Greek text of the AA looked at this point. It is even possible to reconstruct it almost completely.[34] Comparison of these witnesses with the Armenian Passio, which has translated the whole of the text in question, shows however that some sections have been unanimously omitted by all the Greek witnesses.

The address to the cross, which Andrew delivers immediately before his crucifixion, is the most famous passage in the AA. It was long thought that it is best transmitted in the Martyrium prius (c. 16) and the Laudatio (c. 46). Comparison of these two forms of the text with the Armenian Passio (c. 16-19) shows however that the common source of the Martyrium prius and the Laudatio has not reproduced the speech exactly in its original form, but sometimes abbreviated and sometimes altered it. The Armenian Passio is thus the better witness for this speech. It has preserved it in its full extent, and made only incidental changes. The other Greek witnesses (JS, Ann Arbor 36, Martyrium alterum A and B, Epistula) have preserved only the beginning of the address, and at various points abbreviated it. The Armenian Passio does not contain the speculations about the vertical and horizontal extension of the cross, which are characteristic for the Martyrium prius and the Laudatio. On the other hand its argument rests principally on the fact that the cross is of the same nature as Andrew, who is on the point of uniting with it, and also on the point that it reveals only in part the mystery of which it is the bearer. These ideas agree perfectly with the thought of the rest of the AA.

In JS and Ann Arbor 36 the AA end with a very interesting remark in the first person singular. This is not a colophon; rather the author is here giving a concluding summary. In the form preserved in Ann Arbor 36, which is without doubt very close to the original, the text runs: 'Here I end my salutary report of the deeds and the mysteries, to tell out which is difficult, not to say impossible. May the conclusion end (the work). And I pray first for myself: may I have heard what was said as it was said, and indeed what (was said) openly, as also further that which is not manifest to the understanding; further I pray for all who have been equipped through what has been said: may they all hold fellowship together, while God opens the ears of the hearers, so that all his gifts will be received in Christ Jesus our Lord . . . '.[35]

This final note throws light on the intentions of the author: he wishes to impart to all the knowledge of the mysteries about which he has reported. Here it is clear that he distinguishes two levels of revelation and of knowledge, one which can be expressed and is directly accessible, and another which is not manifest to the intellect.

Furthermore, this final note is in the first person singular. That must be taken together with the fact that in some manuscripts (JS, Martyrium alterum B) it is said in the description of Andrew's death: ' . . . while we wept and were all distressed at this separation'. These two pieces of evidence provide occasion for the assumption that the AA purported to be the work of eye-witnesses.[36] The author would then have written in their name. Possibly he introduced himself at the beginning of the work, in order to announce his undertaking. That would fit with the notice of Philaster of Brescia, according to which the AA were written by disciples who followed Andrew. It is perfectly possible that Philaster, who was well informed about the essential content of the work, read at its beginning these references to its ostensible author.

It is not out of the question that, as Innocent I allows us to conjecture, two of these disciples of Andrew were the philosophers Xenocarides and Leonidas. The philosophical slant of the AA shows that this apocryphon must in fact have been edited by a philosopher. He might have had the idea of ascribing the work to philosophers among Andrew's disciples. But there is no reliable basis for the conclusion that the ostensible authors' names were actually those mentioned by Innocent.

What has been said thus far indicates that the AA were a very detailed report about the apostle's journeyings. He travels from town to town, performs a miracle in each of them, and converts a considerable number of their inhabitants. Two towns in particular adhered to him: Philippi (Gregory c. 11-18, with an excursion to Thessalonica in the middle of the narrative) and Patras. Both places were the scene for comparable actions and entanglements. The speeches occupied a large place, and were artistically and pleasingly arranged. Towards the end of Andrew's life in Patras above all they were numerous and detailed. They contained the essential features of the author's world of ideas.

It appears that the AA were an original and uniform work, i.e. they were written at one stretch by one and the same author, who evidently did not, as was the case for example with the Acts of Thomas or those of Paul, take up literary units already available to him and compile them into a whole.

5. Theological tendency: a. Outline of the theology of the AA. In the speeches which are handed down in the Greek witnesses a clear and self-coherent theological view is developed. It describes essentially a process of salvation, which can be summed up under several heads.

The situation of mankind before revelation. Human existence is determined through the fall of an element related to God into the body. This element is variously called 'soul' (ψυχή), 'spirit' (πνεῦμα), 'understanding' (νοῦς) or 'man' (ἄνθρωπος). It is as it were a captive, subjected to negative entities, to 'time' (χρόνος), 'movement' (κίνησις), 'multiplicity' (τὰ πολλά), 'becoming' (γένεσις). Man is not aware of this situation. This ignorance is the work of demonic powers, who wish to dominate and possess him by deceiving him and pretending that they are his friends.

The revelation. Man cannot escape from this situation except through revelation. It reveals to him both the divine origin of his own true being and also his captivity and the dominance which the demonic powers exercise over him. He is called upon to set an actual spiritual birth in operation, in which knowledge or perception of consciousness (γνωρίζω) play a fundamental role.

This revelation is brought about through the miracles and the speeches of the apostle. The miracles effect a salutary convulsion in the one who participates in them. The speeches are 'of like nature' (συγγενής) with mankind, and act like a mirror in which he recognises his true nature.

The revelation here in question is not reserved to a special class of men, rather it is intended for all who are ready to hear and accept this proclamation.

The revealer.[37] The revealer of this salvation is the apostle Andrew. It is he who does the miracles and delivers the speeches which lead to knowledge of oneself. He accomplishes a work of salvation in the initiate. Through his activity as a 'midwife' (οὐκ εἰμι ἀμύητος μαιευτικῆς ἀλλ' οὐδὲ μαντικῆς) he causes him to gain self-knowledge. Then he fortifies him (στηρίζω) until he attains spiritual maturity and is capable of handing on the message in his turn. During this process Andrew is in a genuine fellowship of destiny with his pupils. His own salvation depends upon them; for so long as they have not attained to spiritual maturity he cannot leave this earthly life behind him and experience the final deliverance. In the moment of his death he opens the way to rest for those who later strike out along the same path.

The apostle's activity as miracle-worker, revealer and spiritual leader endows him with the features of a redeemed redeemer, a divine man and a new Socrates. He is a redeemed redeemer because at the same time he delivers himself from his existence and his own salvation is bound up with that of other men.[38] He proves himself a divine man through the veneration that surrounds him, through the extraordinary and voluntary character of his death, through his ascetic life, his miracles, his power of discernment and his supernatural knowledge, through the special revelations imparted to him, by the fact that he introduces a new religion, converts the masses and forms a circle of disciples around himself.[39]

One may finally call him a new Socrates - even though the AA do not so describe him - on the basis of some comparable features in the life and work of the Greek philosopher. Andrew acts like a master of 'midwifery'. In addition the narrative of his death shows a clear proximity to the account of the death of Socrates in Plato's *Phaedo* (58d-66a and 116a-118a): the bystanders lament; one of them attempts to prevent the death, and thereby shows his lack of understanding of what is happening; on the other hand the man who goes to meet his death rejoices over his end, because it makes possible the separation of soul from body; he remains to the last master of himself, admonishes the others, and speaks with them about fundamental questions; he goes to meet his death calmly and of his own free will.

Man after receiving the revelation. Those who have accepted the revelation imparted by Andrew must earn a spiritual maturity. For this they draw upon sources in themselves, and need not wait to be instructed by others. Their life is determined by an ethic which includes the renunciation of all that belongs to the fleshly body and to the world. Since man has discovered his true being, which is spiritual and of divine origin, he can now only live in a way determined by this being, rejecting all that does not belong to it. Andrew's disciples drive out from themselves all that is 'outside' (ἐκτός). In matters of food they aim at the utmost simplicity. They renounce sexuality and practise encratism. In consequence they also avoid procreation. They give up material riches and all that is worldly, including public office and positions of honour.[40] Finally they prepare themselves, like their master, to suffer martyrdom.

In expectation of the final deliverance these men and women live together in the same simplicity, abandoning all social distinctions and united by the discovery of their common nature (συγγένεια). This common nature distinguishes and separates them from everyone who is opposed and hostile to them (ἀλλότριος, ἐχθρός, ἐνάντιος) and is governed by devilish powers.

Their group does not describe itself as a church. Among themselves they call themselves 'brothers' (ἀδελφοί). These brethren create no institutions for themselves: at no point do the AA allude to any regulation of offices, or even to the celebration of the eucharist.[41] The brethren receive from Andrew a 'seal' (σφραγίς), the actual form of which is difficult to discern, but which is a protective amulet for their ascent after death, to enable them to escape the devilish powers who wish to hold them back. After the apostle's death they continue his work of revelation.

The hope of the faithful. The way of salvation is already opened up here on earth with the acceptance of the saving knowledge and deliverance from earthly contingencies through asceticism. But it finds fulfilment only after death, when the soul, released at last, returns to its origin. Then it comes to know 'rest' (ἀνάπαυσις) and sees God.

This salvation is a matter of a purely individual process: in his own death man experiences deliverance and returns to God. In the AA there is no kind of reference to any global eschatology.

God. God in the AA is a God who is near to the faithful and full of solicitude for them. He intervenes to heal them, to protect them from danger, to notify them of coming events and to lead them. He appears in visions, either in the form of a young boy or in that of the apostle.[42] He is the God of Andrew, the unknown God but now revealed by him.

God is the origin of the knowledge revealed by the apostle. Moreover he allows the hearers to receive this knowledge. Finally he takes the faithful to himself, as soon as after death they return to their origin and there find rest.

Here the saving function of God comes to an end. The AA do not develop any reflection about salvation in Christ. This follows from their understanding of salvation as a perception of his true origin on the part of man, and his return to it. God has nothing more to do than to bring about this perception by commissioning a revealer, and to receive those who have achieved this perception. Consequently there is also no allusion to the earthly life of Jesus. It is indeed without significance for salvation. Jesus, his life, his death, his resurrection (there are no allusions to these events) and his preaching are therefore no part of the apostolic proclamation. Further we find no kind of reference to the creative activity of God. It lies outside the text's area of interest. Everything is focussed upon salvation and the way to attain and to preserve it.

Further, it is not possible to distinguish between the divine persons. The functions linked with different predicates of God are interchangeable. Everything proceeds as if it were the same deity who alternatively receives the predicates 'Lord' (κύριος), 'God' (θεός), 'Jesus', 'Master' (δεσπότης), 'unbegotten' (ἀγένητος), 'light' (φῶς), 'life' (ζωή), 'Father' (πατήρ), 'brother' (ἀδελφός), 'majesty' (μεγεθός), 'above the heavens' (ὑπερουράνιος), 'merciful' (ἐλεῶν), 'compassionate' (ἐλεήμων), 'deliverer' (σώζων), 'the better' (κρείττων), 'the beautiful' (καλός), 'righteous' (δίκαιος), 'the One' (εἷς). It must in addition be emphasised that the AA never bring two divine persons into relationship with one another: God and Jesus. The expression 'Son of God' is completely lacking. This lack of distinction between the divine persons is also connected with the soteriology of the text. If on the one side no attention is given to creation, but only to salvation, and if on the other this salvation does not include the incarnation of a divine redeemer, then it is not necessary to make any distinction between the functions and consequently between the persons who fulfil them.

This conception of the deity and of salvation explains the significance which attaches to the apostle. Andrew as the revealer fills a part of the place which is not occupied by Christ.

b. Assessment of the Theology of the AA. *The purpose of the AA*. The AA are a propaganda document. They were written by an educated author, who very probably had himself been won over to Christianity and found in it what one might call the true philosophy. It is this philosophy which he wishes to convey to his readers.

The AA have an apologetic character. They attack pagan philosophy, yet their author largely uses the linguistic and conceptual methods with which his education provided him. Moreover the religious attitude which he delineates is to a considerable extent determined by the contemporary philosophy.

The author has chosen the literary *Gattung* of a biographical narrative. Yet even if the biographical interest is not entirely lacking, it is by no means pre-eminent. The pre-eminence is rather given to the divine dispensation in favour of mankind. The author has chosen the literary form of a Vita of Andrew, in our opinion, for three reasons:

1. On paedagogical grounds: it is a question of presenting a work that is equally instructive and entertaining. In addition a Vita, through the persons active in it, conveys practical spiritual experiences.

2. The report of the deeds and the speeches of a divine man was a common contemporary way of imparting a religious message.

3. To lend weight to the teachings reported, they are placed under the authority of an apostle.

The gnostic character of the AA. The AA show a clear proximity to Gnosticism.[43] This relates above all to the dualism. The presence of a spiritual element in the fleshly body is contrary to nature: what is fleshly stands in opposition to what is of divine origin.

This closeness to Gnosticism appears also in regard to the question of salvation, which is grounded in the revelation and in becoming aware of the divine element in man himself. Death means deliverance. At this point the soul completes an ascent, which the hostile powers seek to prevent. This process of salvation is a destiny for the individual. All these are gnostic ideas.

The dualism however does not determine human existence in a natural manner. Confronted by the message of salvation, man has the choice of setting himself on the side of the Light or of the Darkness. Over and above that, the AA offer no explanation for the fall of the soul. They do not hark back to the idea of a Pleroma or of aeons, and they offer no gnostic cosmogony. There is nothing in them which could be co-ordinated with any known gnostic system. The AA are therefore not to be described as a gnostic text in the proper sense. They belong rather to a gnosticising way of thinking, such as was widespread in their time.[44]

The Platonism and Neo-Pythagoreanism of the AA. Many features draw the AA into proximity to Platonism: the discovery of the inner man, represented as a spiritual birth; Andrew as a master of 'midwifery', whose death is like that of Socrates; the spiritual mirror-image; the deliverance and ascent of the soul; God as beautiful and good.

We can also demonstrate elements in common with Neo-Pythagoreanism, a philosophical stream in the contemporary environment which stands very close to Platonism: a striving after personal unity with God and a desire for deification; rejection of what has part in plurality and in matter; the soul akin to God, imprisoned in the body; the necessity of living a pure and holy life in order to come again to God; the immortality of the soul which after the dissolution of the body frees itself from its fetters and rises up, to return again to its origin.[45]

The Stoicism of the AA. The AA finally also show Stoic features. They determine the ethic of the apocryphon. Andrew admonishes his hearers not to let themselves be carried away by their emotions, to bring their behaviour and their inward disposition into a unity. He himself before his death is untouched by suffering, not because he could not feel any pain but in the power of his spiritual exaltation. Even if the term ἀπάθεια does not appear in the AA, it is still actually this Stoic ideal which Andrew has attained and to which he would lead his hearers. This does not mean that the author of the AA was an adherent of the Stoic philosophy. Rather he is indebted in his basic ethical standpoint to specific general tendencies in the philosophical and religious environment of his time.

The AA as a reflection of the spiritual attitude of their time. It does not seem possible to assign the AA to any precisely defined philosophical or religious milieu. Various movements of thought have been passed under review, and we can see the AA as in proximity to them, without being able to assign them in a strict sense to any one of them. This makes it necessary to see the AA rather as a witness to a whole period. It is a kind of religious and philosophical climate that makes itself prevalent here, marked by a need to break free from the body and the world and take flight, through striving after union with the deity; in the practical conduct of life it is accompanied by sexual asceticism, a negative attitude towards procreation, a simple mode of diet and the longing for a plain way of life that is not dominated by the passions. In the 2nd and 3rd centuries this spiritual climate, moulded by Platonism and Neo-Pythagoreanism, had reached its full development.[46]

6. Place and date of composition: The Manichean Psalm-book, which contains allusions to the content of the AA, shows that the 3rd century is the *terminus ad quem* for the composition of this apocryphon. But the AA must have been composed earlier, between 150 and 200, probably about 150 rather than about 200. The peculiar Christology of the text, the absence of reference to the historical and biblical Jesus, the remoteness from any kind of institution and church ritual - all this speaks for an early dating. In the same way the quiet and quite unpolemical fashion in which the AA develop heterodox ideas, especially in the area of Christology, shows that we are in a period in which the Christology of the Great Church had not yet taken on any firm outlines.[47] So far as the place of origin is concerned, there is nothing to compel us to decide for one particular region rather than another. The text may have been composed just as well in Greece as in Asia Minor, Syria or Egypt. Alexandria especially could have afforded the spiritual and intellectual surroundings in which a text like the AA could have come into being.[48]

Notes

Introduction

1. In addition to this attestation reference should be made to the indirect evidence of the Acts of Paul and of Thomas. It is very probable that the AA have influenced these two apocrypha.
2. Cf. G. Quispel (*VigChr* 10, 1956, 129-148), who prepared the first English translation and the first study of this text.
3. *Pan. haer*. 47.1.5 (GCS 31, Holl, 216); 61.1.5 (Holl, 381); 63.2.1 (Holl, 399).
4. See C.R.C. Allberry, *A Manichaean Psalmbook* (Manichaean Manuscripts in the Chester Beatty Collection 2), 1938.
5. Hornschuh (ET 391, note 9) thinks it not certain that the Manichean Psalm-book knew the AA in their original form, for the allusions contained in it diverge from the statements of the apocryphon. But in my opinion the authors of these psalms need not without qualification have possessed a direct knowledge of the apocryphal Acts; they could have taken up and remoulded the tradition which had its origin in the Acts. It thus appears to be a case of indirect dependence, which would also explain the divergences.
6. CChrSL 9, 255f.
7. *C. Fel*. II 6 (CSEL 25, 833).
8. *De Fide contra M*. 38 (CSEL 25/2, 968.24-969.6).
9. Edition: H. Wurm, *Apollinaris* 12, 1939, 57-78; the relevant passage p. 78, line 36. Reference should be made to the fact that the note about Andrew is missing in several MSS, which are not however dependent on one another. It could thus be an interpolation.
10. D. de Bruyne, 'Nouveaux fragments des Actes de Pierre, de Paul, de Jean, d'André et de l'Apocalypse d'Élie', *Rev. bénédictine* 25, 1908, 150-160.
11. Ed. E. von Dobschütz (TU 38,4), 1912, 49-52.
12. Ed. Bonnet, Aa II 1, 1-37.
13. Ed. Bonnet, *Monumenta Germaniae Historica. Scriptorum Rerum Merovingicarum* I 2, 1885.
14. PG 120, cols. 216-260.
15. The same phenomenon can be observed with the *Martyrium sancti apostoli Andreae*, known under the title of *Narratio* (ed. Bonnet, *AnalBoll* 13, 1894, 353-372). This text follows the AA only from cap. 9 on, i.e. from the arrival in Patras. But by and large this martyrdom diverges too greatly from the AA to be of service for our reconstruction.
16. Ed. R. Henry (Collection des Universités de France), Paris 1960, II, 84.

17. Ed. Ch. Tchérakian, *Écrits apostoliques non canoniques*, Venice 1904. French trans. by L. Leloir, *Écrits apocryphes sur les apôtres* (CChrSA 3), Turnhout 1986, 228-257.
18. Especially the Coptic Papyrus Utrecht 1, the Laudatio and JS (see below, p. 104ff.).
19. Very probably it is a question of the *Passio sancti Andreae Apostoli*, usually cited under the title *Conversante et docente* (ed. Bonnet, *AnalBoll* 13, 1894, 374-378). This Passion is a revision of the *Letter of the Presbyters and Deacons of Achaea*, which depends on the AA, to which however the author probably had access only through a Latin translation.
20. This section of the Armenian Passion agrees only very poorly with the corresponding Greek witnesses. Moreover it contains views about the resurrection which are influenced by biblical thought and alien to the AA.
21. Ed. Th. Detorakis, *Acts of the Second International Congress of Peloponnesian Studies* I, Athens 1981/82, 325-352.
22. Ed. Bonnet, Aa II 1, 38-45.
23. Ed. Bonnet, Aa II 1, 58-64.
24. Ed. Bonnet, Aa II 1, 58-64; in Bonnet's edition this second text is set beneath the first.
25. Ed. Bonnet, Aa II 1, 46-57.
26. Ed. Bonnet, *AnalBoll* 13, 1894, 311-352.
27. The Laudatio is thus of no assistance in reconstructing all those parts of the AA which precede the arrival in Patras. Even the report of the conflict with the demons in c. 18 does not come from the AA. Gregory certainly had a report about the conflict with demons before him in c. 6, exactly like the Narratio (c. 4) and Epiphanius (col. 232A). But these four accounts are not like one another. Also, in the Laudatio, the Narratio and Epiphanius they appear in parts of these works which are clearly not dependent on the AA. There was rather, in my opinion, a tradition according to which Andrew hunted the demons from Nicaea, a tradition which could have developed on the basis of the AA and which was then taken up by the three authors and written down in their several ways.
28. Edited with an English trans. by J. Barns, 'A Coptic Apocryphal Fragment in the Bodleian Library', JThS NS 11, 1960, 70-76.
29. Gregory to be sure writes nothing about such an appearance. But since the report in question could have stood at the beginning of the AA, and Gregory in any case reworked this beginning (unless it had already been worked over in the Latin exemplar which lay before Gregory), we cannot draw any special conclusions from this evidence.
30. Ed. Bonnet, Aa II 1, 65-116.
31. Since Flamion most scholars are agreed that the story of the freeing of Matthias by Andrew does not belong to the AA. Recently D.R. MacDonald has challenged this view. Cf. on this question our discussion: 'The Acts of Andrew and Matthias and the Acts of Andrew, by D.R. MacDonald; Response by J.M. Prieur; Response by D.R. MacDonald', *The Apocryphal Acts of the Apostles* (Semeia 38), 1986, 9-39.
32. Cf. Zahn (ed.), *Acta Johannis*, 1880, 135 line 12 to 150 line 12.
33. *Liber de miraculis*, cap. 11, 832.20-22.
34. In my study on the AA in the Corpus Christianorum, a single text is presented on the basis of these various Greek witnesses; the result does not claim to reconstruct the text of the AA, but to approximate to it so far as is possible.
35. After these words JS and Ann Arbor 36 close with a trinitarian doxology, which obviously did not belong to the AA.
36. To this it should be added that the Letter of the Presbyters and Deacons of Achaea also purports to be an eye-witness account. It is possible that the author of the letter found the idea in the AA itself.
37. See J.M. Prieur, 'La figure de l'apôtre dans les Actes apocryphes d'André', in F. Bovon *et al.*, *Les Actes apocryphes*, Geneva 1981, 121-139.
38. Cf. the typology of C. Colpe, *Die religionsgeschichtliche Schule. Darstellung und Kritik*

ihres Bildes vom gnostischen Erlösermythos, 1961.
39. Andrew corresponds in many points to the topos of the divine man, as it is described in L. Bieler, ΘΕΙΟΣ ΑΝΗΡ. *Das Bild des "göttlichen Menschen" in Spätantike und Frühchristentum*, 2 vols. 1935/36 (repr. 1976).
40. According to the Coptic Papyrus Utrecht 1, the soldier on whom Andrew performed the exorcism casts away his weapons, and Stratocles, brother of the proconsul Aegeates (beginning of JS), asks the emperor for release from military service to devote himself to philosophy.
41. According to Gregory's *Liber de miraculis*, Andrew establishes a bishopric (c. 6) and holds divine worship (c. 5 and 20). These however will be additions by Gregory. The Greek witnesses make no reference either to the office or to any rite, although the whole report of Andrew's last days offered many opportunities for doing so.
42. On this problem of 'polymorphy' cf. E. Junod, 'Polymorphie du dieu sauveur', *Gnosticisme et monde hellénistique* (PIOL 27), Leuven 1982, 38-46.
43. Lipsius thinks that the AA, like the other apocryphal Acts, are a gnostic writing. Flamion attempted to refute this idea and advocate the view that the author moved in the circles of the Great Church. Quispel starts out from the gnostic character of the AA, but then says more precisely as he goes on that people could have professed the ideas contained in the AA without leaving the ground of Church doctrine. Hornschuh and Plümacher admit gnostic features in the AA, but do not believe they can be assigned to a gnostic system.
44. Hornschuh likewise emphasises that one could not speak of a *praedestinatio physica* for the AA, and that the distinction among mankind is made on the basis of acceptance or rejection of the salvation proclaimed by Andrew.
45. These are the characteristic marks of Neo-Pythagoreanism according to the list drawn up by A. Festugière, *L'idéal religieux des Grecs et l'Évangile*, Paris 1932, 79-84.
46. This spiritual climate is particularly well described in E.R. Dodds, *Pagan and Christian in an Age of Anxiety*, Cambridge 1965.
In Flamion's view the AA contain Neo-Platonic ideas, but that would lead us to think of the 3rd century, which is too late a date as the terminus for such a redaction. Hornschuh for his part drew attention to the closeness of the AA to Middle Platonism on the one hand and (following E. Peterson, 'Bemerkungen zum Hamburger Papyrus-Fragment der Acta Pauli', *Frühkirche, Judentum und Gnosis*, Rome/Freiburg/Vienna 1959, 183-208) the ideas of Tatian on the other. This affinity is evident. Without gainsaying this, we should nevertheless hold firmly that it is necessary to stand aloof from the arguments which Hornschuch develops for a connection between the speculations about the cross in the AA and Platonism (ET 394). For the text on which they are based is precisely the Martyrium prius, which as we have seen does not reliably reproduce the original document, which is better preserved in the Armenian Passion. And the latter makes no connection between Cross and Logos.
47. E. Junod and J.-D. Kaestli (*Acta Johannis*, CChrSA 2, Turnhout 1983, 695) make use of this argument to date the Acts of John to the same period. The Acts of John show a close proximity to the AA in terms both of the structure of their outward form and of their internal content. Also the author of the AA appears to have known the Acts of John.
Various important common features allow us further to conclude that the author knew the Acts of Peter. If however this hypothesis is correct, it is not out of the question that the form of the APt known to the author of the AA was not the same as the one which has survived in the Latin version of the Actus Vercellenses (see below, pp. 287ff.). This actually has as its content a very classical Christology with frequent references to the earthly life of Christ and to his teaching. Over and above that there is reflected here the image of a church organisation which is more strongly developed and therefore even later than that of the AA. Further we must allow for the possibility that the AA were known to the authors of the Acts of Thomas and of Paul.

48. E. Junod and J.-D. Kaestli set the composition of the Acts of John in Alexandria. The AA also show a great closeness in thought to the Authoritative Teaching (or Authentic Logos) and the Teachings of Silvanus, two pieces of Alexandrian origin which date to the 2nd century. Cf. on these R. van den Broek, 'The Authentikos Logos: A New Document of Christian Platonism', *VigChr* 33, 1979, 260-286; J. Zandee, *The Teaching of Silvanus and Clement of Alexandria. A New Document of Alexandrian Theology*, Leiden 1977.

Texts

Wilhelm Schneemelcher

Preliminary note: The comprehensive survey which J.M. Prieur has given in the introduction, of the tradition and of the reworking of the AA which has taken place in the course of the centuries, shows the manifold difficulties presented to the historian by this apocryphon, the original Greek text of which has not survived *in toto*. Certainly, as Prieur has indicated, a considerable part of the ancient AA can be approximately reconstructed. The edition in CChrSA will offer such a reconstruction, and thereby open up new paths for research. This we cannot anticipate in our collection. Rather it seems appropriate to renounce any reconstruction, and instead present a few important texts in the form in which they have been handed down to us.

a) First we offer a comprehensive survey of the *Liber de miraculis* of Gregory of Tours. As already indicated, Gregory had the ancient AA in his hands (in a Latin version), and so reworked them as to make them acceptable in the Church-theological situation of the 6th century. He certainly contributes nothing for a reconstruction of the actual wording of the original AA, but from his revision we can deduce the course of events, and in particular the way followed by the apostle to his various halting-places. The martyrdom is dealt with only very briefly by Gregory, who refers for it to another description (on Gregory cf. above, pp. 106ff.).

b) The fragment of an extract from the AA contained in the Coptic Papyrus Utrecht 1, written in the 4th century, is specially valuable because on the one hand it shows how greatly Gregory altered his *Vorlage* (the text is to be compared with Gregory c. 18), and on the other it offers a part of the AA not extant elsewhere, the text of which may be placed not too far from the original work (cf. above, pp. 104; 107).

c) The fragment handed down in Cod. Vatic. gr. 808 (10/11th cent.) is beyond doubt one of the most important witnesses for the original AA, and its text is therefore here given in full (cf. above, pp. 105; 109).

d) A more extensive part of the AA, the Martyrdom, is contained in two Greek manuscripts (JS, on which see above, pp. 105; 108f.).

Certainly this text too is not completely identical with the original AA, but must be regarded as a revision, in which abridgements have been made in particular in the speeches. Despite this a great significance attaches to this text, and it is therefore here set forth.

1. Gregory of Tours, On the Miracles of the Blessed Apostle Andrew (Summary of contents*)

In the introduction Gregory explains his intentions: out of the Acts of Andrew before him, which some considered apocryphal because of their prolixity, he will bring together in a small book the most remarkable miracles of the apostle.

Gregory begins with a reference to the partitioning of the various regions of the earth among the individual apostles.[1] Andrew is to work as an apostle in Achaea, while Mermidona is assigned to Matthew. Chapter 1 is concerned with Matthew's experiences there.[2] Andrew frees Matthew from his prison, and after he himself had run into danger converts the town.[3]

After these events he now goes 'to his region', i.e. he travels from Mermidona to Achaea (c. 2-21). On the way he heals a blind man (c. 2), although the place is not named. Perhaps this act was already accomplished in Amasia, where Andrew works later (c. 3). He preaches here for a long time, and then raises a dead boy. Many people are converted through his preaching and the miracle.[4] The story of the mother who accused her son of incestuous demands (c. 4) seems also to be enacted in Amasia. The son and the apostle, who accompanies him to the proconsul's tribunal, are condemned. A prayer by Andrew is followed by an earthquake, in which the mother is killed. The proconsul is converted, and is baptised together with his household.[5]

On an appeal for help from an inhabitant of Sinope, Andrew sets out from Amasia to go there (c. 5). He frees this man's son from an evil spirit, and also heals his parents, after reproaching them for their sins. They celebrate the communion together and are converted (in that order!). Gratinus, the citizen of Sinope, offers rich gifts in gratitude, but Andrew declines them.

From Sinope the road leads in c. 6 to Nicaea. There seven demons are up to mischief on a road. At the entreaty of the inhabitants Andrew drives out the demons, and thus frees the whole region from a deadly danger. He then baptises the citizens of Nicaea and gives them a bishop.[6]

The demons expelled from Nicaea are however evidently still active. For when Andrew comes to Nicomedia (c. 7), he meets a funeral procession. According to the report which Andrew hears, the youth who is being borne to his grave was brought to his death by seven hounds, i.e. those very demons from Nicaea. Andrew awakens him to life and takes him into the service of the proclamation. He refuses the gifts offered to him.

On the way to Byzantium, Andrew experiences a storm on the Hellespont, but calms it (c. 8). He continues his journey, to reach Thrace.[7] There is a report, without any precise indication of the place, of an encounter with heavily-armed men, who threaten the apostle. At his prayer an angel intervenes and disarms the group, so that Andrew can continue his journey unharmed (c. 9).

He now arrives in Perinthus (c. 10) and there on the instructions of an angel embarks on a ship for Macedonia, the crew of which he converts. The following chapters (11-20) are devoted to the apostle's activity in Macedonia, that is, in Philippi and Thessalonica. Here the routes are not always clearly marked. The first report (c. 11) is of Andrew's preventing the marriage of two brothers and their cousins.[8]

The next episode also probably takes place in Philippi (c. 12): a young man from Thessalonica attaches himself to Andrew. His parents track him down and attempt to set fire to the house in which the apostle is with their son.[9] When this fails, they want to kill the youth by other means, but are stricken with blindness. The story ends with the conversion of all concerned, apart from the parents, who die fifty days later but leave their son a considerable fortune, which he employs in providing for the poor.

At the young man's request, Andrew goes with him to Thessalonica. There the young man preaches the Gospel. Andrew heals a man who has been crippled for twenty-three years (c. 13). This miracle is surpassed by the resuscitation of a young man done to death by a demon. The whole populace is converted (c. 14). The next episode again takes place in Philippi (c. 15). A man comes for Andrew, to heal his crippled son. When Andrew arrives in Philippi, it becomes known to him that the petitioner holds two people captive (it later turns out that there are actually nine). These are set free and healed from their wounds; then the son to whose aid the apostle was brought is also healed. The people now demand the healing of other invalids also, and with this task Andrew charges the young man. The people thereupon become believers and bring gifts, of which the apostle accepts nothing.

Nicolaus, a citizen of the town, brings to Andrew a gilded carriage with four white asses and four white horses, and begs him to heal his daughter. The apostle answers with a speech in which he points away from the visible to the invisible eternal and spiritual values.[10] The hearers are converted, and Nicolaus' daughter healed. The apostle's fame spreads through all Macedonia (c. 16).

A further exorcism (c. 17) also leads to successful conversions. Even philosophers come for discussions with Andrew.[11] In c. 18 Gregory - in much greater detail than elsewhere - summarises and re-shapes the events narrated also in the Coptic Papyrus Utrecht 1. According to Gregory's report, Andrew is denounced before the proconsul Virinus as destroying the established order, in that he preached that people should worship only one God. The proconsul sends soldiers to arrest Andrew, but this is evidently only achieved after several attempts. Here the story is inserted of one of the soldiers, who is possessed by a demon and falls dead when it leaves him. Andrew brings him back to life, but this does not divert the proconsul from his wrath against the apostle. Rather he organises a fight with wild animals, in which however the animals do nothing to Andrew and a leopard finally kills the proconsul's son, whom Andrew then immediately raises again to life. In the whole scene the people stand on the side of the apostle, and even want to kill the proconsul, but this Andrew prevents.[12]

Andrew performs a further miracle on the estate of a woman whom he had previously converted: a great dragon is destroyed, and a child who had been done to death by the dragon is raised again to life (c. 19).

Chapter 20 prepares for the transition to Patras, and therefore for the martyrdom. The apostle - evidently still in Philippi - has a dream which he reports to the brethren and in which the martyrdom is foretold. After instruction of the brethren, and prayer and communion, Andrew sets off for Thessalonica, where he stays for two days and then continues his journey. During the crossing in two ships, Andrew again stills a storm, and rescues a man who had fallen overboard. Patras is reached after twelve days (c. 21).

At the beginning of the activity in Patras (c. 22) stands the healing and conversion of the proconsul Lesbius. He wanted to persecute the apostle and put him to death, but was smitten in the night by two Ethiopians (demons?). Andrew heals him.[13]

The next chapter (23) is concerned above all with two women: Triphima, the proconsul's former concubine, who has in the interval been converted by Andrew, and her fate in a brothel; and Calisto, the proconsul's wife, who dies with another man in the bath. All the deceased are raised again to life by the apostle, and are reconciled to one another. The proconsul Lesbius, who is growing in faith, takes a walk with Andrew on the shore, and with this the next episode is prepared for.[14] There on the beach the next miracle takes place. A corpse is washed ashore, and Andrew recognises that here the devil has taken a hand in the game and that he must therefore raise up the dead man. He does so, and now learns that the man had heard of him and his message, and was therefore on his way to him. On the voyage he had with thirty-nine companions been the victim of a shipwreck. At the apostle's prayer the other thirty-nine corpses also are washed up on the shore and restored to life.

In the next episode (c. 25) Andrew is summoned to a woman in Corinth, who is having difficulties in the birth of an illegitimate child. The proconsul Lesbius accompanies him. The child is born dead, but the woman is converted.

The events narrated in c. 26 also take place in Corinth. The father of Philopator, the young man raised to life in c. 23, travels after the apostle and finds him in Corinth. He too is won for the faith. The gifts which he brings to Andrew are declined by him.

On a visit to a bath - evidently still in Corinth - an expulsion of demons by the apostle takes place (c. 27). This has for its sequel the story that sick people from the whole region are brought in and then healed. Probably still at the same place (Corinth) a seventy-four year-old man comes to Andrew and confesses that he has led a profligate life and repeatedly fallen into sin, although he manifestly believes in the power of the Gospel. With prayer and fasting Andrew brings about a change. The man is forgiven, and after a six-month fast he dies in peace (c. 28).

While the apostle is staying in Corinth, a man comes from Megara to beg for help against demons who are plying their mischief in his house (c. 29). Andrew sets off for Megara - from or through Sparta[15] - and there overcomes the demons and heals the householder plagued by them. The family in the future helps in the proclamation of the Gospel.

With c. 30 Gregory's report returns to Patras. There Andrew is summoned by Iphidama[16] to the sick Maximilla, wife of the proconsul Aegeates. The latter stands beside his wife's bed, ready to kill himself should Maximilla die. Andrew heals the woman, for which the proconsul wishes to pay with a gift of gold, but the apostle does not accept it.

After a short report about the healing of a cripple (c. 31), Gregory tells of a blind family to whom Andrew restores their sight (c. 32). Then follows the healing of a sick man (probably a leper) outside the city (c. 33).[17]

During these events Stratocles, the brother of Aegeates, has come from Italy to Patras. A boy from his retinue is seized by a demon and falls (evidently dead) to the ground. Maximilla and Iphidama see to it that Andrew can undertake the healing of the boy. Stratocles is converted (c. 34).[18] Maximilla has herself instructed daily - in Aegeates' absence - by Andrew. She has resolved upon continence, which arouses the proconsul's wrath against the apostle. When Aegeates returns to Patras, Andrew sees to it that the Christians assembled in the praetorium may disappear without hindrance (c. 35).

In c. 36 Gregory reports in only a few words - with a reference to the *lectio passionis*[19] - the apostle's death and the burial of his corpse by Maximilla. This is followed by a brief note about the miracles at his grave (c. 37). He adds also the remark that he has not reported the martyrdom of Andrew in detail, because there is another good account of it.[20] Gregory then ends his exposition with a personal closing sentence (c. 38).

Notes

Texts

* After *Gregorii Episcopi Turonensis Liber de miraculis Beati Andreae Apostoli*, ed. M. Bonnet (MGH Script. rerum Merovin. I/2) 1885, 826-846.

1. On the problem of the partition of the mission areas cf. Jean-Daniel Kaestli, 'Les scènes d'attribution des champs de mission et le départ de l'apôtre dans les Actes apocryphes', in F. Bovon *et al.*, *Les Actes apocryphes des Apôtres*, 1981, 249-264.
2. On the 'Acts of Andrew and Matthias among the cannibals' cf. below, pp. 443ff.
3. It is questionable whether c. 1 belonged to the original AA. On this cf. Prieur, above p. 106f. The vague and confused beginning of c. 2, in my opinion, also tells against its belonging there.
4. These conversions resulting from preaching and miracles are repeated in stereotyped fashion by Gregory.
5. Cf. the AJ of Pseudo-Prochorus (Zahn 135.12-150.12). On this see Prieur, pp. 107f. above.
6. The end of this chapter certainly goes back to Gregory. In the original AA there is no reference to church offices. The rest of the story is also reported in the Narratio and Laudatio (cf. Hornschuh, NTApo^3 II, ET 399).
7. Here Gregory has considerably shortened his *Vorlage*.
8. This episode is also mentioned in the Epistle of Pseudo-Titus; cf. Prieur, above p. 103.

9. A Manichean psalm alludes to this; cf. Prieur, above p. 101f.
10. Some formulations in this speech sound as if Gregory had taken them over from the original AA.
11. On the problem of the 'philosophers' cf. Prieur, above pp. 110; 113f.
12. This chapter is particularly instructive for Gregory's way of working. The Coptic text Pap. Utrecht 1 is part of an early version of the original AA. It is however completely different in theological intention from Gregory's report. Evidently Gregory not only revised the episode of the soldier freed from a demon, but also to a considerable extent used other parts of the context. Above all he completely eliminated the speeches, and so totally altered the theological statements of the text. Cf. Prieur, above p. 107.
13. In this chapter also Gregory has compressed and altered his *Vorlage*, as can be seen from parallels in other witnesses; cf. Prieur, above pp. 107f.
14. Here Gregory has probably summarised a fairly extensive text, but not always successfully, as several obscurities show.
15. Here Gregory has evidently alluded simply by the place-names to an episode to which he gave no consideration.
16. The name is not transmitted with any unanimity: Iphidama or Iphidamia.
17. For c. 33-34 there are detailed parallels in the Laudatio, cf. Prieur, above p. 108f.
18. From here on Gregory has summarised in a very compressed form what is reported in JS.
19. As with many apocryphal Acts of apostles, the martyrdom became independent at an early date.
20. Cf. on this Prieur, above p. 116, note 19.

2. Pap. Copt. Utrecht 1

(Text established by *Roelof van den Broek*, translation from the Coptic by *Gilles Quispel* and *R.McL. Wilson*)

(the) apostle. But when Andrew the apostle of Christ heard that they had arrested the (faithful) from the city on his account, he arose and went out into the middle of the street and said to the brethren that there was no reason to pretend anything (ὑποκρίνειν). And while the apostle was yet speaking these words, there was a young man (there), (one) of the four soldiers, in whose body was hidden a demon. But when that young man had come into the presence of the apostle, he cried out and said: 'O Varianus, what have I done to you that you should send me to this god-fearing man?' When the young man had said this, the demon cast him down and made him foam at the mouth. His fellow-soldiers however seized him and attempted <to raise> him <up>. But Andrew pitied the young man and said to his fellow-soldiers: Are you ashamed before me, because you see that your nature (φύσις) betrays you? Why do you take away <from him> the prize, so that he cannot appeal to his king that he may receive help and be able to fight against the demon who is hidden in his limbs? Not only that he is appealing for this, but he is speaking in the language of the palace, so that his king will soon hear him. For I hear him say: "<O> Varianus, what have I <done to you> that you <should send me to this> god-fearing <man>?"' <The apostle An>drew

(*Lacuna of 6 to 8 lines of about 22 letters*)

against me. For this thing which I have done, I have not done it of myself, but I was compelled (to do it). I will tell you of this affair as well as possible. This young man, who is (so) tormented in his body, has a sister, a virgin (παρθένος), who is a great ascetic (πολιτευτής) and champion (ἀθλητής). Truly I say, she is near to God because of her purity and her prayers and her alms. Now, to relate it briefly, there was somebody near to her house who was a great magician. It happened one day thus: at the time of evening the virgin went up on her roof to pray. The young magician saw her praying. Semmath entered into him to contend against this great champion.

The young magician said within himself: “If I have spent five and twenty years under the instruction of my master until I was trained in this skill (τέχνη), this (then) is the beginning of my craft (τέχνη); should I not be stronger than this virgin, I shall not be able for any work.” And the young magician conjured up great powers against the virgin, and sent them after her. But when the demons came to tempt her or (even) to persuade her, they took the form of her brother and knocked at the door. And she arose and went down to open the door, since she thought that it was her brother. But first she prayed earnestly, so that the demons became like [...............] and fled away. [..................] the young <man> [...........................]

(*Lacuna of 4-6 lines of about 22 letters*)

The virgin wept in the presence of Teirousia. Teirousia (Erucia?) however said to the virgin: ‘Why do you weep? Do you not know that those who shall go to this place ought not to weep? For that is the place [......]. Now these powers pursue after you’. Teirousia said: ‘Why do you weep, while sorrow .... Now however, since you are weeping over your brother, because a god ...... with him, tomorrow I will send him to the apostle Andrew, that he may heal him. Not only that I will heal him, but I shall bring it about that he shall gird himself for the palace’. When the demon had said this, the apostle said to him: ‘How did you acquire knowledge concerning the hidden mysteries of

the height? If a soldier is
cast out from the palace, he is not at all
allowed to learn the
mysteries of the palace. How
will he learn the hidden mysteries of the height?'
The demon said
to him: 'I descended
in this night into this
young man, while a power from
the height entered in ......
...... friend of the virgin
in him ...... while she
will go away ....
Her (the virgin's) friend said:
befalls me, because .... For
the great power came down from
the height in this night

(*4 lines mutilated. Lacuna of 3-5 lines of about 20 letters*)

'Why then should you not tremble, since you
speak out the mysteries of the height?
I tremble wholly in all my limbs
and I glorify the receiver (παραλήμπτωρ)
who is coming for the souls
of the saints.
O champions of virtue, not in vain
have you contended: see, the judge of the contest
prepares for you the crown
unfading. O warriors,
not in vain have you
put on weapons and
shields, and not in vain have you
endured wars:
the king has prepared the palace for you.
O virgins,
not in vain have you guarded the purity,
and not in vain have you
persevered in prayers,
while your lamps burned
in the midst of the night, until
the call reached you: "Arise,

go out to meet the bridegroom"'. When the apostle had said this, he turned to the demon and said to him: 'It is now fully time for you to come out from this young man, that he may gird himself for the heavenly palace'. The demon said to the apostle: 'Truly, O man of God, I have never destroyed a limb of his, thanks to the holy hands of his sister. But now I will go out from this young man, to whom I have done not the slightest damage in his members.' And after the demon had said this he came out of the young man. After he <had departed> from the young <man> ....

(*Lacuna of 1-3 lines of about 19 letters*)

of soldiery and (cast it away) before the eyes of the apostle, saying: 'O man of God, I have spent twenty pieces of gold to acquire this ephemeral garment[1] for myself; but now I will give all that I possess that I may obtain for myself the uniform of your God.' His comrades in arms said to him: 'O wretched youth, if you deny the emperor's uniform, you will be punished.' The young man said to them: 'Truly I am wretched because of my former sins. Would that my punishment were only because of this, that I denied the uniform of the emperor,

and that I be not punished
because I have despised the (baptismal)
garment of the immortal King of the ages (αἰών).
O ignorant ones, do you not see
what kind of a man this is?
He has no sword in his hand nor
any weapon of war, and (yet)
these great miracles are
wrought by him.'

The Act (πρᾶξις) of Andrew.

Note

2. Pap. Copt. Utrecht 1

1. σχῆμα (cf. Phil. 2:8): in these lines this word is used both for the transitory uniform of the emperor (6, 13, 19) and for the eternal 'garment' of God (9, 21). In Coptic monasticism it is also used of a monk's habit. [R.M.W.]

3. Codex Vaticanus 808
(Aa II 1, pp. 38-45)

'... is there in you only feebleness? Have you not yet convinced yourselves that you do not yet bear his goodness? Let us reverently rejoice among ourselves in our abundant fellowship with him. Let us say to one another: Happy is our race! by whom has it been loved? Happy is our existence! from whom has it received mercy? We are not cast to the ground, we who have been recognised by such a height. We do not belong to time in order that we may be then dissolved by time. We are not the product (handiwork) of movement, which is again destroyed by itself, (we are) not of (earthly) birth in order to die (again) therein.[1] We are rather those who pursue greatness. We belong <to it> and [probably][2] to him who has mercy on us. We belong to the better; therefore we flee the worse. We belong to the noble, through whom we drive away the mean; to the righteous, through whom we cast away unrighteousness; to the merciful, through whom we reject the unmerciful; to the Saviour, through whom we recognised the destroyer; to the light, through whom we banished the darkness; to the One, through whom we have turned away from the many; to the heavenly, through whom we understood the earthly; to the abiding, through whom we perceived the transitory. If we intend fitly to thank the God who has mercy on us or to acknowledge to him our confidence or to offer him a song of praise or to glorify him, <we can do it on no other basis> than that we have been recognised by him.'[3]

2. When he had thus addressed the brethren he sent them away, each to his own home, saying to them: 'Neither are you ever forsaken by me, you who are servants of Christ on account of the love that is in him, nor again shall I myself be forsaken by you on account of his mediation.' And each went away to his own house. And there was such joy among them for many days during which Aegeates had no thought of pursuing the charge against the apostle. So they were then each confirmed in hope toward the Lord; and they gathered fearlessly with Maximilla, Iphidamia and the others into the prison, protected by the guardianship and grace of the Lord.
3. One day when Aegeates was acting as judge he remembered the affair of Andrew. And just as if he had become mad he left the case with which he was dealing and rising from the bench went at the run into the praetorium and embraced and flattered Maximilla. She, coming from the prison, had entered the house before him; and when he had come in he said to her:
4. 'Thy parents, Maximilla, considered me worthy of marriage with you, and gave you to me as wife, looking neither to wealth nor family nor renown, but perhaps (only) to the good character of my soul. And intending <to pass over> much with which I wished to reproach you, both things which I have enjoyed from your parents and things which you (enjoyed) from me during all our life together, <I have come from the court> to learn this alone from you; <give me therefore> a reasonable <answer>[4]: if you were the person you used to be, living with me in the way we know, sleeping with me, keeping up marital intercourse with me, bearing my children, then I would treat you well in everything; even more, I would release the stranger whom I have in prison. But if you are not willing, I would not do you any harm, indeed I could not; but the one whom you love more than me, I will torture him so much the more. Consider then, Maximilla, which you wish and answer me tomorrow; for I am completely prepared for it.'

5. And when he had said this he went out. But Maximilla went again at the usual time with Iphidamia to Andrew; and laying his hands on her face she kissed them and began to tell him in full of the demand of Aegeates. And Andrew answered her: 'I know, Maximilla my child, that you are moved to resist the whole allurement of sexual intercourse, because you wish to be separated from a polluted and foul way of life. And this (attitude) has governed my mind for a long time; and now I will declare to you my opinion. I earnestly beseech you not to do this; do not give way to the threat of Aegeates; do not be overcome through association with him; do not fear his shameful intention; do not be overcome by his clever flattery; do not consent to give yourself up to his impure spells; but endure all his torments, looking unto us for a short time; and you will see him wholly paralysed and wasting away from you and from all who are akin (by nature) to you.[5] For what I really ought to say to you - for I do not rest in accomplishing the matter seen through you and coming

to pass through you - has eluded me (until now). And I rightly see in you Eve repenting and in myself Adam being converted: for what she suffered in ignorance you to whose soul I direct my words are now setting right again because you are converted: and what the mind suffered which was brought down with her and was estranged from itself, I put right with you who know that you yourself are being drawn up. For you yourself who did not suffer the same things have healed her affliction; and I by taking refuge with God have perfected his (Adam's) imperfection: and where she disobeyed, you have been obedient; and where he acquiesced, there I flee; and where they let themselves be deceived, there we have known. For it is ordained that everyone should correct his own fall.

6. I then said these things as I have said them; and I would also say the following:

Well done, O nature, you who are saved despite your weakness and though you did not hide yourself.

Well done, O soul, you who have cried aloud what you have suffered and are returning to yourself.

Well done, O man, you who are learning what is not yours and desiring what is yours.

Well done, you who hear what is being said. For I know that you are more powerful than those who seem to overpower you, more glorious than those who are casting you down in shame, than those who are leading you away to imprisonment. If, O man, you understand all these things in yourself, namely that you are immaterial, holy, light, akin to the unbegotten, intellectual, heavenly, translucent, pure, superior to the flesh, superior to the world,[6] superior to powers, superior to authorities, over whom you really are, if you perceive yourself in your condition, then take knowledge in what you are superior. And you, when you have looked at your face in your own being and broken every bond, - I mean not only those about birth, but those beyond birth whose exceeding great names we have set out for you - desire to see him who has appeared to you, who has not come into being, whom you alone will recognise with confidence.

7. I have said these things in reference to you, Maximilla, for what has been said in its meaning concerns even you. As Adam died in Eve because of the harmony of their relationship, so even now I live in you who keep the command of the Lord and who give yourself over to the state (dignity) of your (true) being. But scorn the threats of Aegeates, Maximilla, for you know that we have a God who is merciful to us. And do not let his empty talk move you, but remain chaste; and let him not only punish me with tortures and bonds, but let him even throw me to the beasts or burn me with fire or hurl me from a cliff - what does it matter? Let him ill-treat this body as he wishes, it is only one; it is akin (in nature) to his own.

8. My words are intended again for you, Maximilla. I say to you, Do not give yourself over to Aegeates; stand out against his snares, especially since I have seen the Lord (in a vision) who said to me: "Andrew, Aegeates' father, the devil, will release you from this prison." For you, then, keep yourself henceforward chaste and pure, holy, undefiled, sincere, free from adultery, unwilling for relationship with him who is a stranger to us, unbent, unbroken, tearless, unhurt, immovable in storms, undivided, free from offence, and without sympathy for the works of Cain.[7] For if you do not give yourself over, Maximilla, to the things that are the opposites of these, I shall rest, being thus compelled to give up this life for your sake, that is for my own sake. But if I, who am perhaps even able to help other (souls) akin to you through you, am driven away from here and if you are persuaded by your relationship with Aegeates and by the flatteries of his father, the serpent, to return to your earlier ways, know that I shall be punished on your account until you would understand that I had spurned life for the sake of a soul that was unworthy.

9. I beg you, then, the wise man (*sic!*), that your noble mind continue steadfast; I beg you, the invisible mind, that you may be preserved yourself; I exhort you, love Jesus and do not submit to the worse; help me, you, on whose aid as man I call, that I may be perfect; help me, that you may know your own true nature; suffer with my suffering, that you may know what I suffer and you will escape suffering. See what I see and what you see will blind you; see what you ought to see and you will not see what you ought not; hear what I say and what you have not heard reject.

10. I have said these things to you and to everyone who will listen, if indeed he will listen. But you, Stratocles,' he said, looking at him, 'why are you so distressed with many tears and why do you sigh so audibly? Why your despondency? Why your great pain and great grief? You know what has been said, and why then do I beseech you as (my) child to be in control of yourself? Do you understand to whom the words that are said are addressed? Has each gripped your mind? Has it made contact with you in your intellectual part? Have I you as one who hears me? Do I find myself in you? Is there in you someone who speaks to you, whom I see as belonging to myself? Does he love the one who speaks in me and does he desire to have fellowship with him? Will he be made one with him? Does he hasten to be loved by him? Does he strive to be united with him? Does he find in him any peace? Does he have where he may lay his head?[8] Is there nothing there which is opposed to him, which behaves unfriendly, which resists him, which hates him, which flees (from him), which is savage, which withdraws, which has turned away, which rushes away, which is burdened, which fights, which associates with others, which is flattered by others, which combines with others? Are there other things which trouble him? Is there someone within me who is foreign to me? An adversary? a destroyer? an enemy? a cheat? a sorcerer? a corrupted? a man of furtive

character? a deceitful man? a misanthrope? a hater of the word? one like a tyrant? a boaster? an arrogant man? a madman? a kinsman of the serpent? a weapon of the devil? a champion of the fire? a friend of darkness? Is there in you, Stratocles, someone who will not endure me speaking like this? Who is it? Answer! Am I speaking in vain, have I spoken in vain? No, says the man in you, Stratocles, who is again weeping.'

11. And Andrew took the hand of Stratocles and said: 'I have him whom I loved. I will rest on him for whom I waited; your present groans and incessant weeping have become a sign to me that I have already enjoyed rest, that I have not addressed in vain to you these words which are akin to my own nature.'

12. And Stratocles answered him: 'Do not think, most blessed Andrew, that there is anything other than yourself which troubles me: for the words which come forth from you are like fiery arrows piercing into me; each of them touches me and truly sets me on fire. That part of my soul which inclines to the things I hear is being punished because it has a presentiment of the distress that comes after this. For you yourself go away and I know well that you will do it nobly. Where and in whom shall I seek and find hereafter your care and love? When you were the sower I received the seeds of the words of salvation. And for these to sprout and grow up there is need of no other than yourself, most blessed Andrew. And what else have I to say to you than this? I need the great mercy and help that comes from you, to be able to be worthy of the seed I have from you, which will only grow permanently and emerge into the light if you wish it and pray for it and for my whole self.'

13. And Andrew answered him: 'That, my son, was what I myself also saw in you. And I praise my Lord that my opinion of you was not wrong but knows (rather) what it says. And so that you may know: Aegeates will to-morrow hand me over to be crucified. For the servant of the Lord, Maximilla, will enrage the enemy in him, the enemy to whom he belongs, when she refuses to take part with him in those things which are alien to her (to her true nature). And by turning on me he will think to console himself.'

14. While the Apostle was so speaking Maximilla was absent. For when she had heard what he answered her and had been in some way impressed by it and had become what the words signified, she had gone out, neither rashly nor without set purpose, and had gone to the praetorium. And she had said farewell to her whole life in (with) the flesh and when Aegeates brought up the same matter which he had told her to consider, i.e. whether she was willing to sleep with him, she rejected it; from then on he turned his mind to the murder of Andrew and considered in what way he might kill him. And when crucifixion alone of all deaths mastered him he went away with some of his friends and dined. But Maximilla, the Lord going before her in the form of Andrew, went with Iphidamia to the prison. And there she came on him with a great crowd of the brethren discoursing as follows:

15. 'Brethren, I was sent as an apostle by the Lord into these parts, of which my Lord thought me worthy, not indeed to teach anyone, but to remind everyone who is akin to these words that they live in transient evils while they enjoy their harmful delusions. From which things I always exhorted you to keep clear and to press towards the things that are permanent and to take flight from all that is transient. For you see that no one of you stands firm, but everything, even to the ways of men, is changeable. And this is the case because the soul is untrained and has gone astray in nature (φύσις) and retains pledges corresponding to its error. I therefore hold blessed those who obey the words preached to them and who through them see as in a mirror the mysteries of their own nature, for the sake of which all things were built.

16. I therefore command you, beloved children, to build firmly on the foundation[9] which has been laid for you, for it is unshakeable and no evil person can assail it. Be rooted on this foundation. Stand fast remembering what <you saw?>[10] and what happened while I was living among you all. You have seen works take place through me which you have not the power to disbelieve, and signs such that dumb nature would perhaps have cried them out.[11] I have communicated to you words which, I pray, have been received by you in the way the words themselves would wish. Stand fast then, beloved, in everything which you have seen and heard and shared in. And God, whom you have trusted, will have mercy on you and present you acceptable to himself, to have rest for all eternity.

17. Do not be troubled by what is about to happen to me as if it were some strange marvel that the servant of God, to whom God himself has granted much through works and words, should be forcibly expelled from this temporal life by an evil man. For such will happen not only to myself but to all who have been loving him, trusting him and who confess him. The devil, who is utterly shameless, will arm his own children against them, so that they may be his adherents. But he will not obtain what he desires. And I will tell you why he attempts these things: From the beginning of all things, and, if I may so put it, from the time when he who is without beginning came down to be subject to his 'rule', the enemy, an opponent of peace, drives away (from God) whoever does not belong to him but is only one of the weaker and has not attained to full brightness and cannot yet be recognised. And because he did not even know him (the devil), he must for that reason be locked in combat with him. For since he (the devil) thinks that he possesses him and will always rule him, he fights against him so much that their enmity becomes a kind of friendship. In order to subject him he often sketched his own pleasure-seeking and deceitful nature, by which means he thought to dominate him completely. He did <not>[12] therefore show himself openly as an enemy but he pretended a friendship worthy of himself.

18. And he carried on his work for so long that man forgot to recognise it,

whereas he (the devil) knew: that is, on account of his gifts he <was not seen to be an enemy>.[13] But when the mystery of grace was lighted up, and the counsel of (eternal) rest was made known and the light of the word appeared and it was proved that the redeemed race had to struggle against many pleasures, the enemy himself was scorned, and, because of the goodness of Him who is merciful was mocked in respect of his own gifts by which he appeared to triumph over him (man), then he began to plot against us with hatred and enmity and arrogance. And this he practises: not to leave us alone until he thinks to separate us (from God). For then indeed our adversary was without care; and he pretended to offer us a friendship such as was worthy of him. And he had no fear that we whom he had led astray should revolt from him. However the possession of the plan of salvation, which enlightened us (like a light), has <made his enmity> not stronger <but clearer>.[14] For the hidden part of his nature and what appeared concealed he has exposed and prepared it to confess what it (really) is. Since therefore, brethren, we know the future, let us awake from sleep, not being discontented, nor cutting a fine figure, nor bearing in our souls his marks which are not our own, but being lifted up wholly in the whole word, let us all await with joy the end and take flight from him, that henceforth he may be seen as he is, the one who our nature against our . . .

Notes

Codex Vaticanus 808

1. Bonnet already notes at this point: *num sana*? Erbetta (II, 399) translates: *e neppure siamo causa della vita, noi, là cui fine è identica.*
2. τάχα probably does not fit the context.
3. So Hornschuh (NTApo³, ET 409); Bonnet: *videtur aliquid deesse*; Hennecke (NTApo² 252): 'So let us boast of nothing more in him, than that we have been recognised by him.'
4. Restoration after Bonnet.
5. Hornschuh: 'gradually wasting away and leaving you and those who are akin (by nature) to you'.
6. Cf. Col. 1:16.
7. Cf. 1 Jn. 3:12.
8. Cf. Mt. 8:20.
9. Cf. Eph. 2:20.
10. Conjecture by Bonnet.
11. Cf. Lk. 19:40.
12. Conjecture by Bonnet.
13. The text at this point is corrupt; restoration by Hornschuh (NTApo³, ET 416), following Hennecke (NTApo² 254).
14. Conjecture by Bonnet.

4. Martyrdom of the holy and glorious first-called Andrew the Apostle

Translated after Detorakis' edition*

[p. 333] Stratocles, the brother of Aegeates, having asked Caesar for release from military service to turn to philosophy, arrived from Italy in Patras at that time. And a great confusion seized the whole praetorium because of <Stratocles>, who had come to Aegeates after some length of time; Maximilla went out from her bedroom to meet him gladly, and having greeted Stratocles went into the house with him. And when the sky became clear and bright, she was by herself, but Stratocles fulfilled his proper duty to his friends, bearing himself kindly to all and greeting all in gracious and seemly fashion.

While he was about this, a certain slave of the household of <Stratocles>, smitten by a demon, lay paralysed on a dung-heap, one whom he greatly loved. When he saw him, he said: 'Would that I had never come, but had perished in the sea, that this should not have befallen me; for indeed I could not, my friends' - turning to his companions - 'live without him.' And as he said this, he smote his face, being greatly disturbed and unseemly to look upon. And when Maximilla heard it, she came out of her bedroom, herself distressed, and said to Stratocles: 'Have no care, brother, on account of this slave; he will soon be saved. For there is come to dwell in this city a very god-fearing man, who is able not only to put demons to flight, but even if some ill-omened and terrible disease take hold, he will heal it. We have such trust in him, but we say this as having experience of him.' And Iphidama said the same to Stratocles, holding him back lest he venture something terrible, since he was wholly beside himself. And as they were both comforting him, Andrew arrived at the **[p. 334]** praetorium, having arranged with Maximilla to come to her. And when he entered the gateway he said: 'Some power is striving within, let us hasten, brethren.' And without even asking anyone, he immediately entered in at a run where Stratocles' slave was foaming at the mouth, utterly convulsed. All those who had run up at Stratocles' cries were at a loss as to who he might be, when they suddenly saw him smiling and parting the by-standers and making room for himself until he came to the slave lying on the ground. And those who knew him of old and had experience of him, whatever god they feared, made way for him. But Stratocles' slaves, seeing that he was a humble man and meanly clad, tried to strike him; the others, seeing them insulting him, rebuked those who knew not what they were daring. And they, calming down, waited to see the end.

And immediately one told Maximilla and Iphidama that the blessed one had arrived. And they full of joy leaped up from their places and came to Stratocles. 'Come then, and you will see how your slave is made strong.' So he arose and went with them. But when Stratocles saw a very great crowd standing around his slave, he said quietly: 'You have become a spectacle when you came to Achaea, Alcmanes' (for this was the slave's name). And Andrew looked at Maximilla, and with his eyes on her said this: 'What most causes shame, my child, for those who out of much storm and wandering turn to faith in God, is to see sufferings which have been given up as hopeless by the many healed. For see what I say, and now see happening here. Magicians have taken their stand, unable to do anything, who also have given the slave up for lost, and others whom we all in common see as meddlesome because they have not been able to drive out this terrible demon from the unhappy slave, since they are its kinsmen. It was beneficial to say this because of the crowd that is present.' And without delay he rose up and said: 'O God who does not hearken to the magicians, God who does not yield himself to the meddlesome, God who stands apart from the alien, God who ever grants your gifts to your own, grant now that my request be speedily fulfilled before all these in the slave of Stratocles, putting to flight the demon whom his kinsmen could not drive out.' And immediately the demon, speaking with a man's voice, said: 'I flee, servant and man of God, I flee not only from this slave, but also from this whole city.' And Andrew said to him: 'Not only from this city do I command you to take flight, but if anywhere there is even the footprint of a brother of mine, I forbid you to enter upon those places.' And when the demon had departed, Alcmanes rose up from the ground, **[p. 335]** as Andrew stretched out his hand to him; and he sat down with him, sound in mind and tranquil and talking normally, looking happily at Andrew and his master, and asking the cause of the crowd within. And he answered him: 'There is no need for you to learn anything of the alien. It is enough for us who have seen in you what we have seen.'[1]

And while they were about this, Maximilla took the hand of Andrew and of Stratocles and went into the bedroom, and all the brethren who were there went in with them. And when they had sat down they looked towards the blessed Andrew, that he might say something. And Maximilla was eager, for Stratocles' sake, for the apostle to converse, that he might believe in the Lord. For his brother Aegeates was exceedingly blasphemous and very wretched regarding the better course. So Andrew began to say to Stratocles: 'I know well, Stratocles, that you are moved by what has happened. But I know also that it was necessary for the man now slumbering in you to be brought into the open. For to be at once at a loss and to ponder on what has happened, whence or how it came about, is the best proof of the disturbed soul in you; and the perplexity in you, the hesitation, the astonishment, make me well disposed. Bring forth, my child, what you have, and do not only give yourself up to travails. I am not uninitiated in midwifery, but not in the soothsayer's art. It is what you give birth to that I love. It is what you keep silent, but I speak forth, which I will care for even within you. I know him who is silent, I know him who yearns, already your new man speaks to me, already he appeals to me as to what he has ever suffered many a time. He is ashamed at his former religion, grieved at his first way of life, all his former observances he counts as vain, he is at a loss as to what is really piety, silently he reproaches his former vain gods, he suffers, having become a wanderer for the sake of instruction. What was his former philosophy? He knows now that it is vain. He sees that it is empty and dashed to the ground; now he learns that it promises nothing of the things that are necessary, now he confesses that it pledges nothing useful. What then? Does not the man in you, Stratocles, say these things?'

And Stratocles after a great groan answered thus: 'Most prophetic man and truly messenger of the living God, I will not depart from you until I know myself, having condemned all these and the vain things with which you have not reproached me for wearing myself out in them.' And Stratocles was with the apostle night and day, never leaving him, **[p.336]** on the one hand inquiring and learning and being refreshed, on the other silent and glad, having become truly a friend of the hearing of salvation who, having bid farewell to all that was his, wished only to spend his life with the apostle alone. For no longer did he question the blessed one at all in the presence of someone, but while the other brethren were doing something else, he inquired of him privately. When they turned to sleep, he stayed awake, and not even allowing Andrew to sleep he continued rejoicing. But Andrew did not weary of making Stratocles' questions known to the brethren, and said to him: 'Reap your debts twofold, Stratocles, since you both inquire of me privately and also hear the same things in the presence of the brethren. For thus what you desire and seek will be better set in you; it is not right not to set forth your birth-pangs to those who are like you. For as with a woman giving birth, when the pangs take hold of her and the babe strives by some power not to remain within but to struggle to the outside, this too is evident and not obscure to the women present, who have shared in the same mysteries. The child itself cries out after the mother has already screamed. Then after the birth they bring to the child a treatment which they know who are initiated, that so far as in them lies something may become of what is brought to birth - so we also, my child Stratocles, must bring your embryos into the midst and not rest easy, that they may be registered by many kinsfolk (συγγενεῖς) and brought on to the giving of the salutary laws, of which I have found you a partaker.'

Since Stratocles continued happily and was fortified by all his kinsfolk (συγγενεῖς), and had obtained a steadfast soul and a firm and unswerving faith in the Lord, Maximilla and Iphidama rejoiced. And Alcmanes who had been healed no longer stood apart from the faith. Night and day they were glad and fortified in Christ, and having grace Stratocles, Maximilla, Iphidama and Alcmanes, together with many other brethren, were counted worthy of the seal in the Lord. Andrew said to them: 'If you guard this impression (τύπος), my children, which does not admit of other seals that impress the opposite symbols, God will praise you and receive you to his own. When such a vision appears clearly in your souls, especially those that are released from their bodies, the punishing powers and evil authorities and fiery angels and wicked demons and filthy operations which cannot bear to be overtaken by you, since they do not belong to the symbol of the seal which is akin (συγγενοῦς) to light, **[p. 337]** creep away in flight and sink down into the darkness, fire and fog that is akin to them, and whatever meditates promise of punishment. But if you sully the brightness of the grace that is given you, those terrible powers will dance in triumph around you and mock you, dancing in chorus this way and that. For each will demand its own, just like a braggart and a tyrant, and there will be no benefit for you when you call upon the God of your seal, which you defiled when you fell away from him. Let us therefore, my children, guard the deposit that is entrusted to us, let us give it back without spot to him who entrusted it, and let us say to him when we come there: "Behold, we have brought your gift of grace unharmed to you. What of your own will you bestow on us?" Immediately he will answer us: "I will bestow on you myself; for all that I am I give also to my own. If you wish light, I am one whose eyes never close. If life that is not subjected to becoming, it is I; if rest from vain labours, you have me as your rest; if a friend offering things that are not earthly, I am your friend; if a father for those who intercede on earth, I am your father; if a true brother, separated from the brothers who are not true, I am your brother; and if there is anything more dear to you, which you desire and seek, you have me in all that is mine, and all that is mine in you". This, my beloved, our Lord will answer to us.'

And when Andrew said this, some of the brethren wept, but the others rejoiced, but Stratocles especially, the newly converted, was lifted up to the height in his mind, so as to abandon all that was his and pledge himself to the Logos alone. So there was great rejoicing among the brethren night and day, as they came together to Maximilla in the praetorium. On the Lord's day the proconsul arrived, while the brethren were gathered together in his bedroom and listening to Andrew. When it was reported to Maximilla that her husband had come, she was not a little troubled, expecting the outcome that many people would be caught in the room by him. But Andrew, seeing her at a loss, said to the Lord: 'Lord Jesus, let not Aegeates come into this bedroom until your servants have gone out from here without fear, who have come together for your sake and for Maximilla, who ever graciously urges us to gather here. But since you have judged her worthy of your kingdom, let her be fortified the more, together with Stratocles, and quench the rush of the raging lion armed against us, saving us all.' And when the proconsul Aegeates came in, he was troubled by his belly, and sat for many an hour attending to himself. And since all the brethren went out, **[p. 338]** he saw nothing before him. For Andrew, laying his hand on each one, said: 'May Jesus hide what is visible of you from Aegeates, that what is unseen in you may be fortified against him.' Last of all he went out himself, after sealing himself.[2]

Now when such a grace of the Lord had been accomplished, Stratocles went out, took his brother aside, and embraced him, and his other servants and freedmen likewise greeted him. But he (Aegeates) himself pressed on to go into the bedroom, thinking that Maximilla was still sleeping; for he loved her. But she was praying. When she saw him, she turned away and looked to the ground. And he said to her: 'Give me first your right hand to kiss, you whom I shall not address as wife but as my lady, being so greatly refreshed by your prudence and your love toward me.' For the unhappy man thought when he caught her praying that she was praying for him. For as she prayed he was delighted to hear his own name. But what Maximilla said was this: 'And deliver me now from the unclean union with Aegeates and keep me pure and chaste, serving you my God alone.' But as he drew near to her mouth wishing to kiss it, she pushed him away, saying: 'It is not right, Aegeates, for a man's mouth to touch a woman's mouth after prayer.' And the proconsul, amazed at the sternness of her countenance, departed from her and stripping off his travelling clothes rested, and lying down slept after his long journey.

Maximilla said to Iphidama: 'Go, sister, to the blessed one, that he may come here while he (Aegeates) is asleep, and lay his hand on me and pray.' And she without delay went running to Andrew. When she had told him the request of that most faithful Maximilla, Andrew came and went into the other bedroom, where Maximilla was. And Stratocles, who had come with him from the blessed one's lodging, went in along with the apostle. For when he had greeted his brother, he inquired about the lodging where the apostle of the Lord was living. And guided by a certain brother Antiphanes he went in to the blessed one. Laying his hand on Maximilla, Andrew prayed thus: 'I pray you, my God, Lord Jesus Christ, who know what is to be, to you I commend my worthy child Maximilla. May your word (λόγος) and power be strong in her, and may the spirit in her overcome even Aegeates, the insolent and hostile serpent, and may the soul in her remain pure, sanctified by your name; but especially protect her, Lord, from this foul corruption; put to sleep our wild and ever untamed enemy, her visible husband, and unite her with the inner man, whom especially you make known and for whose sake **[p. 339]** the whole mystery of your dispensation was accomplished. That thus possessing a firm faith in you she may grasp her own true kindred (συγγενεία) when she is separated from the pretended, who are actually enemies.' And when he had prayed thus and committed Maximilla to the Lord, he went out again along with Stratocles.

Maximilla now devised the following plan. She summoned her maid-servant, Eucleia by name, very comely and by nature extremely undisciplined, and said to her what pleased the girl herself and she desired: 'You will have me as benefactress for all that you ask, if you will consent with me and keep safe what I propose to you.' And when she had told Eucleia what she wanted and been reassured by her, wishing for the future to lead a holy life, she had such comfort for a considerable time. For as it is customary for one woman to prepare requisites for another, she adorned Eucleia with such things and allowed her to sleep with Aegeates in her stead. And he used her as if she were his own wife, then let her rise and go to her own bedroom. For this was Maximilla's custom. Thus refreshed and rejoicing in the Lord, and not departing from Andrew, she escaped notice for a long time in what she had done.

But when eight months had passed, Eucleia requested of her mistress to obtain her freedom. And on the same day she granted what she asked. Again after a few days she asked for not a little money, and she gave it to her without delay. Then again something of her adornments, and she did not refuse. And to put it briefly, garments, linen, necklaces, which she received each time from Maximilla, did not satisfy her, but she made the affair known to her fellow-slaves, boasting as it were and putting on airs. And they were vexed at Eucleia's boasting, but at first kept their mouths shut, reviling her. But she, laughing, showed them the gifts given to her by her mistress. Angry at this, Eucleia's fellow-slaves were at a loss what to do. But Eucleia, wishing to provide yet more proof of what she said, when her master was drunk set two of them at his head, that they might be persuaded that she really did lie with him as if she were Maximilla herself. For waking him when he was sunk in slumber she with her fellow-slaves who were observing the affair heard him say: 'My lady Maximilla, why slowly?' But she was silent. And those who stood by went quietly out of the bedroom.

Maximilla, thinking that Eucleia was not gossipy but faithful because of the gifts she had given her, **[p. 340]** rested even in the nights beside Andrew, along with Stratocles and all the other brethren. Now Andrew had a dream, and said to the brethren in the hearing of Maximilla: 'Today something new is launched in the house of Aegeates, a contrivance of disturbance and full of wrath.' Maximilla begged to learn what this might be. But he said: 'Do not make haste to learn from me what you will shortly know.' And she, having changed her clothes as her custom was, went out while all looked on, into the vestibule of the praetorium. Those of the household who had learned of the affair, and how every day she went away with Stratocles to Andrew, and at what time she went into her own bedroom, laid hold of her as a stranger when at that hour she came into the praetorium of the proconsul and endeavoured not to be seen. And when on unveiling her they saw their own mistress, some of them wished to make the affair known and tell Aegeates, but others held fast, impelled by affection and dissimulation towards their mistress, shut the mouths of those with them, and beating them as if they were madmen drove them thence. And while they were thus fighting with one another, Maximilla rushed into her bedroom, praying the Lord to turn away all evil from her. And after an hour those who had fought with their fellow-slaves on her behalf burst in on her, speaking flattering words to her and expecting to receive something, as if they were slaves of Aegeates; and the blessed woman did not refuse them what they demanded. Summoning Iphidama, she said: 'Let us give to these what they deserve.' So she commanded that a thousand denarii be given to those who in pretence had professed to love her, and charged them to make the matter known to no one. But they, even after many oaths to keep silent what they had seen, under the guidance of their father the devil immediately hastened to their own master, taking the money with them, and told him the whole story, and how their fellow-slave had informed them of the plan devised by Maximilla when she no longer wished to consort with Aegeates, rejecting union with him as some terrible and shameful deed.

The proconsul took cognizance of everything, and how Eucleia had lain with him as if she were herself his wife, (and then) confessed to her fellow-slaves; when he questioned her also, he learned the whole charge, and under torture she confessed everything that she had received from her mistress to keep her silent. He was greatly enraged with her because she had boasted to her fellow-slaves and said these things, slandering her mistress **[p. 341]** (for being deeply in love with his wife he wished the matter had been kept secret). As for Eucleia, he cut out her tongue and cut off her hands and feet, ordering that she be cast out, and after remaining some days without nourishment she became food for the dogs. His other slaves who had spoken - there were three of them - he had crucified for all that they had said. He remained by himself and ate nothing at all that day because of his anguish, being at a loss on account of the great change in Maximilla from her previous disposition towards him. And after weeping much and reviling his gods, he went to his wife. Falling at her feet, he said with tears: 'I touch your feet, a man who has lived with you as my wife for twelve years now. I have ever treated you as a goddess, and still do, because of your prudence and the rest of your character, which is honourable. Since you too are human, this admits the possibility of some change of mind for a short time. If then there is anything of the sort, which I could not imagine, a preference for some other man over me, I will forgive it, and myself keep it secret, just as you have often borne with me when I was out of my senses. Even if there is something worse than this that separates you from me, confess it and I will quickly heal it, knowing that in nothing at all can I gainsay you.' But she replied to him who entreated and besought at such length: 'I love, Aegeates, I love. And what I love is nothing of the things of this world, so as to become manifest to you; and night and day it kindles and inflames me with love for itself, which you yourself could not see, for it is difficult, nor could you separate me from it, for that is impossible. Leave me then to consort with it, and to find my rest in it alone.'

The proconsul departed from her and was like a madman, he did not know what to do. For he did not dare to do to the blessed one anything that was not fitting, since she was of a much more distinguished family than he. And he said to Stratocles, who was walking with him: 'Brother, my only genuine relative of all our dying race, I do not understand my wife, who has gone off her head or fallen into madness.' And as he began to say something else to his brother in his despair, one of the slaves who were with him said in his ear: 'Master, if you wish to learn of the matter, ask Stratocles, and he will give you rest. For he knows everything that concerns your wife. But if you wish to know the whole matter now, I will reveal it to you.' And drawing him aside privately he said: 'There is a stranger come to stay, who has become notorious not only in this city but in all Achaea. He practises mighty works and healings beyond the power of men, as he himself (*sc.* Stratocles) will testify in part, having been present and seen dead men raised by him. **[p. 342]** In general, that you may know it, he professes piety, and truly he shows it even shining out openly. To this stranger, then, my lady has become known, with Iphidama leading the way, and she has gone to such a length in desire of him as to love no other at all more than him, that I speak not of yourself. Not only is she thus united with the man, but she has also ensnared your brother Stratocles with desire for him, by which he also is bound. They confess one god only, the one made known to them by him, and that there is no other at all on earth. But listen to the most senseless thing of all done by your brother. Being of such a family, bearing the name most glorious in Achaea of brother of Aegeates the proconsul, he brings an oil-flask into the gymnasium; he who has many slaves shows himself a servant, buying vegetables, bread and other necessities, and brings them, walking through the midst of the city, quite unashamed to be seen by all.'

And as the young man told this to his master as he walked, because for many an hour he looked upon the ground, he saw Andrew at a distance and crying out aloud said: 'Master, behold the man by whom your house is now unsettled!' And the whole crowd turned at his shout to see the cause. And without saying more that crafty one who was like him, as it were his brother, not his slave, left the proconsul and going at a run seized Andrew and brought him by force to Aegeates, wrapping about his neck the linen cloth which the blessed one wore. Seeing him, the proconsul recognised him and said: 'You are the man who once healed my wife, on whom I wished to bestow much money, but you refused? What is this rumour about you? Instruct me too. Or this great power of yours, that so poor and mean to see, and already an old man, you have lovers rich and poor, and even infants, as I am told.' The whole crowd present was kindly disposed towards the apostle, and learning that the proconsul was conversing with him ran up in longing where he was talking with him, at a loss as to the reason. And without delay Aegeates commanded him to be shut up, and said: 'You corrupter, for your good deeds to Maximilla these thanks are returned by me.' And after a short interval he went in to Maximilla and found her along with Iphidama, eating bread with olives - for that was their custom at this hour - and said to her: 'Maximilla, I have conveyed your teacher here and shut him up, and am gathering information about him, for he will not escape me but perish in an evil way.' And the blessed one answered him: 'My teacher is not one of those who can be hanged. For he is not capable of being grasped by the senses or perceptible to sight. Since then you have become master of no-one of this kind, Aegeates, **[p. 343]** give up this boasting of yours.' And he, smiling, went out, leaving her eating.

And Maximilla said to Iphidama: 'Sister, we are now eating, and he who after the Lord is our benefactor is imprisoned. Go in the name of the Lord, Iphidama, to the citadel, and find out where the prison is. I believe that when evening comes we shall be able to see the apostle of the Lord, and that not one will see me going off, save only Jesus and you who show me the way.' And Iphidama, changing her accustomed clothing, set off faithfully. So having learned where the prison was and standing at the spot, she saw a great crowd standing in front of the gate of the prison and inquired about this assembling of the crowd, and someone answered her: 'Because of that most godly Andrew, shut up by Aegeates.'

And when she had stood there for an hour, the faithful Iphidama saw the gate of the prison opened, and taking courage said: 'Jesus, go in with me to your servant, I beg of you.' And without being detected by anyone she went in, and found the apostle conversing with those who were imprisoned with him, whom he was already exhorting to faith in the Lord and confirming. And turning round he saw Iphidama, and uplifted in his soul he said to the Lord: 'Glory to you, Jesus Christ, Lord of true words and promises, giving immortality to your fellow-servants, who alone are what all require to overcome their adversaries. Behold, your Iphidama, whom I know kept safe together with her mistress, has come here to us led by her desire for us. Gird her about with your protection now when she departs, and when she comes in the evening with her mistress, that they may not be evident to any of the enemy; for down to now, when I am (in such a condition), they are eager in some way to be bound along with me. Guard them, Lord, yourself, for they are both devoted and God-fearing.' And having prayed over Iphidama Andrew let her go, saying: 'The gate of the prison will be open before you reach it, and when you come in here (again) it will be opened and you will rejoice in the Lord, and again you will go away, that through this you may be confirmed in (faith in) our Lord.'

And immediately Iphidama went out, and found everything even as Andrew told her. And when she came to Maximilla she related to her the noble soul and resolution of the blessed one, because even when imprisoned he was not at rest, but also encouraged those who were imprisoned with him, and that he was magnified in the power of the Lord; and all the other things he said to her within she described to her for both their sakes. And when Maximilla had heard all that Iphidama related to her, as from the apostle, **[p. 344]** she rejoiced in spirit and said: 'Glory to you, Lord, that I am about to see your apostle again without fear. For not even a whole legion could prevail to keep me imprisoned, so as not to see your apostle. For it will be blinded by the radiant vision of the Lord and the confidence which his servant has in God.' And when she had said this, she waited for the lamps to be lit, that she might go forth.

The proconsul said to some of those with him: 'I know Maximilla's boldness, because she is not concerned about me. Therefore let the gates of the praetorium not be guarded thus, but let four of you go to the prison and tell the jailer: "Let the door with which you are entrusted be secured, and see that you do not open it to any influential person, whether you are moved by respect or by cajolery, not even if I myself should come, or you will have no head."' And he commanded four others to take position round her bedroom and watch if she went out.

So the first four hastened to the prison and the rest, according to their orders, did sentry duty in front of the blessed one's bedroom. But the accursed Aegeates turned to his dinner. Maximilla prayed to the Lord for many an hour along with Iphidama, and again said to the Lord: 'It is now the hour, Lord, to go to your servant.' She went out of the bedroom with Iphidama, saying: 'Be with us, Lord, from whom here you are not separated'. And when she came to the gate of the prison she found a small comely boy standing, the gates being open, and he said to them: 'Go in, both of you, to the apostle of our Lord, who has long been expecting you.' And running forward he came to Andrew and said to him: 'Look, Andrew, you have these who rejoice in your Lord; let them be fortified in him as you discourse.' And[3] when he had conversed with them for many hours, at last he sent them away, saying: 'Go in peace. Know well that neither are you ever wholly forsaken of me, handmaids of the Lord through the love that is in him, nor again will I myself be forsaken of you through his mediation.' And there was joy in them over some days, in which Aegeates had no thought to prosecute the charge against the apostle. So the whole multitude of the faithful was confirmed in hope in the Lord, all gathering together without fear in the prison, along with Maximilla and Iphidama.

When Aegeates was acting as judge one day, he remembered the affair concerning Andrew. And like one become mad he left the case which he had in hand, rose up from the tribunal, and went running **[p. 345]** into the praetorium, embracing and flattering Maximilla. Now Maximilla, coming from the prison, had entered the house before him; and rushing in he said to her: 'Your parents, Maximilla, counting me worthy of living with you, pledged to me your marriage, looking neither to wealth nor to family nor to reputation, but perhaps to the prudent character of my soul. And not (to mention) many things which I wished to bring out to reproach you, the kindnesses which I experienced from your parents, the honours and services which you yourself have met with from me, being enrolled as my lady in all our life, this one thing only I have come to learn from you, abandoning the court of judgment and (now) standing before you. If you were the woman you were of old, living with me in the manner we know, sleeping with me, having intercourse, bearing my children, I would treat you well in every way, and yet more, I will set free the stranger whom I hold in the prison. But if you are not willing, to you indeed I would not do any harm, nor can I, but through him whom you love especially, more than me, I will torment you. Consider then, Maximilla, which of the two you wish, and answer me tomorrow. For this alone I am fully armed.' And having said this he went out.

Maximilla again at the usual hour went with Iphidama to Andrew, and laying his hands on her face and bringing them to her mouth she kissed them, and began to tell him the whole of Aegeates' demand. And Andrew answered her: 'I know, my child Maximilla, that of yourself you are moved to resist the whole temptation of sexual intercourse, wishing to separate yourself from a loathsome and unclean life, and this for a long time has dominated my mind. But since you wish (me) to testify to my opinion, I will declare it. Maximilla, do not do this. Do not succumb to Aegeates' threat. Do not be afraid of his hostility and plots. Do not be overcome by his clever flatteries. Do not be willing to give yourself up to his filthy and evil sorceries, but endure all his torture, looking unto us for a short time, and you will see him altogether paralysed and wasting away both from you and from all who are akin (συγγενοῦς) to you. It is with confidence in you, Maximilla, that I say these things. For as Adam died in Eve, consenting to her intercourse, so I now live in you, who keep the commandment of the Lord and bring yourself over to the dignity of (your true) being. Withdraw from the threats of Aegeates, Maximilla, knowing that we have a God who has mercy on us, and do not let his empty talk move you, but remain pure; let him not only punish me with tortures but even cast me to the wild beasts and burn me with fire and hurl me over a cliff. What does it matter? This body is (but) one, to use it as he will, since it is akin to him. But to you again **[p. 346]** I speak, Maximilla. Do not hire yourself out to Aegeates for his plots, and especially since I have seen the Lord saying: "The father of Aegeates, the devil, will release you through him, Andrew, from this prison." Let it be yours henceforth to keep yourself chaste, pure, holy, undefiled, sincere, free from adultery, unwilling for intercourse with the alien, unbent, unbroken. For if you do not yield yourself to the opposite of these, I myself shall rest, being thus compelled to depart this life for your sake, that is for my own. But if I should be driven hence, perhaps I can benefit other kinsfolk (συγγενεῖς) of mine also. Be not therefore persuaded by the speeches of Aegeates and the flatteries of his father the serpent, so as to return to your former works. Know that I am about to be punished there for your sake, until you yourself recognise that it was not for a worthy soul that I spurned this earthly life.'

At this point Stratocles came in to Andrew, weeping and lamenting. So Andrew took Stratocles' hand and said: 'I have what I sought, I have found what I desired, I hold fast him whom I loved, I rest on him whom I awaited. That you groan all the more and weep incessantly is to me a sign that I already have rest, because not in vain have I addressed words to your kinsfolk (συγγενεῖς).' And Stratocles answered him: 'Do not think, most blessed Andrew, that there is anything else that troubles me, other than you. For the words that come forth from you are like fire as they pierce into me, and each of them touches me as if truly kindling and inflaming to love for you; the receptive part of myself that inclines to the things I hear is being punished, divining the distress that is after it. You yourself are departing, and I know well that (you will do it) nobly; but when I seek your care and love hereafter, where or in whom am I to find it? The seeds of the saving words I have received, with you being for me the sower; but for them to sprout and grow up needs no other than you, most blessed Andrew. And what have I to say to you, servant of God, other than this? I need much mercy and help from you, that I may be able to become worthy of your seeds which I have, which I do not otherwise see growing unharmed and emerging into the open, except you wish it. But pray for some of it, and all of me.' And Andrew answered: 'This, my child, (is) what I myself saw in you, and now I congratulate myself, that my opinion concerning you was not in vain, but spoke what I knew. But that you may know: tomorrow Aegeates will hand me over to be crucified. For Maximilla, the handmaid of the Lord, **[p. 347]** will enrage the enemy in him, whose own he is, by not putting her hand to the works that are alien to her. And by turning on me he will think to console himself.'

Maximilla was not present when the apostle said these words. For having heard the words which he directed to her, she was in a way impressed by them and became what the words themselves signified. She set off, not rashly or without set purpose, and came to the praetorium. She bade farewell to her whole life along with evil, mother of the flesh, and to the things of the flesh, and when Aegeates presented to her the same demand which he had previously made known to her, (asking) if she was willing to sleep with him, she refused; and thereafter he turned his mind to the killing of Andrew, and considered to what death he should expose him. And when crucifixion satisfied him most of all, he went off together with his friends and ate greedily like an animal.

And Maximilla, the Lord going before her in the form of Andrew, came again with Iphidama to the prison. And a large crowd of the brethren being inside, she came upon him saying these words: 'I, brethren, was sent by the Lord as an apostle into these regions, of which the Lord counted me worthy, not to teach anyone but to remind every man who is akin (συγγενῆ) to these words, that all men live in transient evils, delighting in their harmful fantasies. But when the mystery of grace was kindled, and the bright ray of rest was made manifest, and the light of the Logos was shown forth, and the race that was being saved was proven, warring against its former pleasures, then the alien, seeing himself despised and his gifts, through which he thought to triumph over the goodness of him that has mercy, made a laughing-stock, then he began to weave together hatred and enmity and uprisings against us; and this he set in operation, not to desist from us until we should dance according to what he thinks. Since then we know what is about to happen, brethren, let us awake from sleep and come to the point of freeing ourselves from him, neither reluctantly nor tossed by storms, nor carrying away in our souls any traces of him that are not our own, but all together lifted up in all the Logos let us all gladly await the end and our flight from him, that he hereafter may display what he is by nature, while we fly up to what is our own.'

After[4] Andrew had spoken thus to the brethren the whole night through and prayed, and they were all rejoicing together and confirmed **[p. 348]** in the Lord, on the next day at dawn Aegeates sent for Andrew from the prison and said to him: 'The end of the judgment concerning you is at hand, you stranger, alien, enemy of my family and corrupter of my whole household. Why did you think fit to rush into alien places and secretly corrupt a woman who has long wholly pleased me and has never consorted with any other, as I have learned for sure from her? Now to you and to your god, farewell. Indeed, enjoy my gifts!' And he commanded him to be scourged with seven scourges. Later he sent him to be crucified, ordering his executioners to leave his sinews uncut in order, as he thought, that he might punish him yet more. And this was manifest to all, for it was given out and spread abroad through all Patras, that the stranger, the righteous one, the man filled with God, was being crucified by the godless Aegeates, although he had done nothing wrong. And they were one and all indignant.

When the executioners brought him to the place and wished to carry out their orders, Stratocles, who had learned what was happening, came running and saw the blessed one being dragged along by force by the executioners, as if he had done something wicked. He did not spare them, but rained blows on each of them, ripped their tunics from top to bottom, and pulled away the blessed Andrew, saying to them: 'In this too give thanks to the blessed one who trained me, and taught me to restrain the violence of my anger, or I would have shown you what Stratocles can do and what the foul Aegeates. But we have learned to bear what befalls us.' And taking the apostle's hand he went away to the place beside the sea where he was to be crucified. But the soldiers went and showed themselves to Aegeates, telling him what had happened. And he answered them: 'Take other clothes and go to the place appointed and carry out your orders; and when the condemned man is disposed to take his departure from you, at that time obey. As for Stratocles, do not let him see you, so far as in you lies, but do not refuse him if he requires anything of you. For I know the nobility of his soul, such that perhaps he will not spare even me should he be provoked.' And they did as Aegeates had told them.

While Stratocles was walking with the apostle on the way to the appointed place, he was at a loss, being embittered against Aegeates and sometimes reviling him in a low voice. And Andrew answered him: 'My child Stratocles, I wish you for the future to possess your mind unmoved and not to wait to be admonished by another, but receive such a thing from **[p. 349]** yourself, and neither let yourself be affected inwardly by what appears evil nor inflamed outwardly. For it is fitting that the servant of Jesus should be worthy of Jesus. But I will say something else to you and to the brethren who are walking with me, concerning the men who are alien to us. So long as the demonic nature does not have its blood-red nourishment, nor draws in the sustenance that comes from it, since animals are not slain, it is weak and comes to nothing, being wholly dead. But when it has what it desires, it becomes strong and expands and rises up, enlarged by the things it delights in. Such, my child, is what happens with the men outside, who die when we do not cleave to what they adhere to. But even in us ourselves the opposing man, when he ventures anything and does not find anyone who agrees with him, is struck and beaten and completely knocked to the ground, because he did not accomplish what he undertook. So, my children, we have this one before our eyes, lest while we sleep he come upon us as our adversary to slay us. But let this for now be the limit of our speaking. For indeed I think this is the place, to which we have come as we conversed; for to me the cross set up is a sign that shows the place.'

And leaving them all Andrew went up to the cross and said to it in a loud voice: 'Hail, O cross, for indeed I know that you may truly rejoice, since now henceforth you rest, when for a long time you have been weary, set up and waiting for me. Wherefore, O cross, pure and shining and full of life and light, receive me, the one greatly wearied.' And having said this the most blessed one, standing on the ground and gazing steadfastly, went up on it, bidding the brethren that the executioners should come and do what they were ordered; for they were standing at a distance. And when they came they only bound his feet and his arm-pits, without nailing him; and they did not cut either his hands or his feet or his sinews, having received this command from the proconsul. For he wished to torture him as he hung, and that in the night he should be eaten alive by dogs. And the brethren who stood round, whose number could not easily be counted, they were so many, saw them going away and that they had not done in the case of the blessed one any of the things which those crucified (usually) suffer; but they were expecting to hear again something from him, for as he hung he moved his head, smiling.

And Stratocles asked him: 'Why do you smile, Andrew, servant of God? Your laughter makes us mourn and weep, because we are being deprived of you.' He answered him: 'Should I not laugh, my child Stratocles, at the empty plot of Aegeates, by which he thinks to take vengeance on us? **[p. 350]** Are you not yet persuaded that we are alien to him and to his plots? He has no sense of hearing, for if he had he would have heard that Jesus is a man who cannot be punished. In the future it will be made known to him.' When he had said this, Andrew addressed a word to all in common, for indeed the heathen were running together, indignant at Aegeates' unrighteous judgment: 'You men who stand by me, and women and children, old men and slaves and freemen, and whoever else will hear, if you consider this the end of this transitory life, (namely) to die, then you are already released from this place. And if you take the coming together of the soul into the body for the soul itself, so that after the departure there is no longer anything, you have the thoughts of animals and must be counted among the wild beasts. And if you love the present delights and pursue after them with all your might, reaping only this of all, you are like robbers. And if you think you are this that is visible only, and that there is nothing else besides, you are slaves of ignorance and stupidity. And if your other possessions exalt you within your own selves, let their transitory character be a reproach to you. For what profit is it to you to have obtained the things without, but not yourselves? What is this exaltation of the soul that is in you which comes from external things, when the soul is sold captive to the desires? Or what is all the rest of your concern for things outside of you, when you thus neglect what you yourselves are? But turn away, I beg you all, from this troublesome life, vain, insane, presumptuous, transitory, and strive to lay hold of my soul as it reaches out to what is above time, above law, above word, and you shall obtain whatever you wish. For such is set within your power.'

And the crowds, hearing the things said by Andrew and in a way taken by them, did not depart from the spot. And the most blessed one went on to say to them yet more than he had said. And it was so much that, as there are those who heard to testify, he discoursed to them for three days and nights, and no one at all grew weary and departed from him, since on the following day also they beheld his nobility, the unswerving character of his mind, the abundance of words, the usefulness of his admonition, the composure of his soul, the wisdom of his spirit, the steadfastness of his mind, the sincerity of his reflections. Indignant at Aegeates, they hastened one and all to the tribunal. And as he sat down they shouted out: 'What is your judgment, proconsul? You have condemned wrongly, you have judged unjustly, your tribunals are unholy! What wrong has the man done? What crime has he committed? The city is in tumult, you wrong us all. Do not **[p. 351]** betray Caesar's city! Grant the Achaeans a righteous man, grant to us a man inspired of God! Do not kill a holy man, do not destroy a pious man. Four days he has hung, and eaten nothing, but he has fed us to the full with his words. Take the man down, and we shall all become philosophers! Set the wise man free, and all Patras will be righteous. Release this man of understanding, and Achaea will again find mercy.'

When Aegeates did not listen, at first signing with his hand to the crowd to depart from the tribunal, they were full of rage and ventured to take action against him; they were about two thousand in number. When the proconsul saw that they had in a way gone mad, he was afraid that he might suffer a riot, and rising from the tribunal he went with them, promising to set the blessed one free. Some ran ahead and told the apostle, and related the reason why they had come to the place. The crowd then rejoiced because the blessed one was about to be released when the proconsul arrived, and all the brethren together with Maximilla were rejoicing; but when Andrew heard he said: 'O the great dullness of those instructed by me! O the cloud that overshadows you after many mysteries! O how much have we spoken to you even till now, and (yet) have not persuaded our own! What is this great love towards the flesh, or this ample intercourse with it? Do you urge me to surrender myself again to what is transient? If you knew that I was freed from fetters but bound to myself, you would yourselves have been eager to be freed from the many but bound to the one. But since Aegeates comes to me, I will say what I must say to him to take my leave. For what reason (do you come) again to us, Aegeates? For what cause does he that is alien to us approach us? What do you wish to venture again, what to contrive, what to say? Do you come to release us, as having repented? But you have not truly repented, Aegeates. I will not come to terms with you; not even if you promised me all that is yours will I depart from myself, nor should you take thought for yourself will I trust myself to you.'

When he heard this the proconsul stood amazed, as it were out of his mind. And looking at him again Andrew said: 'O dreadful Aegeates, enemy of us all, why do you stand calm and quiet when you can do nothing of what you venture? I and those who are akin (συγγενῆ) to me press on to what is ours, leaving you to be what you are, even though you yourself do not know about yourself.' And when he again ventured to draw near to the cross to set Andrew free, the whole city clamouring at him, the apostle Andrew said in a loud voice: 'Lord, do not suffer Andrew who is bound upon your cross to be released again. Let not your adversary release the one who hangs upon your grace, Father, but take me yourself, Christ, whom I desired, whom I loved. Receive me, that through my departure (ἔξοδος) there may be an entry to you for my many kinsfolk (συγγενεῖς), who rest upon your [p. 352] majesty.' And when he had said this and glorified the Lord, the blessed one gave up his spirit.

While we were weeping and were all sorrowful over his passing, after the departure of the blessed apostle, Maximilla without any thought at all of those who were standing by came and unbound the corpse of the blessed one and buried it, giving it the necessary attention. And she was separated from Aegeates because of his savage nature and lawless way of life, and did not approach him at all in the future, although he made hypocritical offers to her; she chose a holy and quiet life, and supplied with the blessed love of Christ spent it along with the brethren. Aegeates strongly urged her, promising that she would be mistress of all that was his, but was unable to persuade her. One night he arose, without any of his household knowing it, and threw himself from a great height and died. Stratocles, Aegeates' brother after the flesh, was unwilling to touch any of the property left by him (for the unhappy man died childless) saying: 'May what is yours, Aegeates, go with you; but may Jesus be my friend, and I his. Casting from me the great multitude of evils without and within, and laying before him what is mine, I reject all that is opposed.'

Here now I would make an end to these blessed narratives and deeds and mysteries hard to tell, that I may not say also too wonderful for words. And I pray first for myself, to hear what was said as it was spoken, and then with all who are impressed by the things said let us send up a common hymn of praise to God, the lover of mankind, with his only-begotten Son and the all-holy and life-giving Spirit, now and for ever and to all eternity. Amen.

Notes

Martyrdom of the holy and glorious
first-called Andrew the Apostle

* On this text see Prieur, above p. 105. We cannot offer a detailed comparison of JS with the other witnesses, since this would exceed the limits of the present work. Reference may be made to Prieur's edition of the AA in CChrSa. A few references only are intended to draw attention to the parallel passages. (The German translation was made by Gregor Ahn. The English version has been modified at a few points in the light of Prieur's edition, but differences remain).

1. The beginning of JS (to this point) is summarised by Gregory of Tours in c. 34.
2. On this section cf. Gregory of Tours, c. 35.
3. From here on the text of Cod. Vat. 808 (see above, pp. 128ff.) should be compared.
4. For the following, Ann Arbor 36, the Martyrium alterum A and B, the Armenian version and to some extent the Letter of the Deacons of Achaea form the parallel tradition (cf. Prieur, above pp. 109f.).

2. The Acts of John

Knut Schäferdiek

Introduction

1. Literature: Standard **edition** (hereafter adduced as 'Junod/Kaestli'): *Acta Johannis*. 1. Praefatio, textus. 2. Textus alii, commentarius, indices, cura Eric Junod et Jean-Daniel Kaestli (Corpus Christianorum, series apocryphorum 1,2), Turnhout 1983, with detailed **commentary.** On the ancient versions see below, pp. 159ff. From the **literature** the following may be mentioned: Eric Junod/Jean-Daniel Kaestli, 'Les traits caractéristiques de la théologie des Actes de Jean', *Revue de Théologie et de Philosophie* 26, 1976, 125-145; id., *L'histoire des Actes apocryphes des Apôtres du IIIe au IXe siècle: le cas des Actes de Jean* (Cahiers de la Revue de Théologie et de Philosophie 7), Geneva/Lausanne/ Neuchâtel 1982; id., 'Le dossier des Actes de Jean. État de la question et perspectives nouvelles', ANRW II 25.6, 1988, 4293-4362; Knut Schäferdiek, 'Herkunft und Interesse der alten Johannesakten', ZNW 74, 1983, 247-267; David R. Cartlidge, 'Transfigurations of Metamorphosis Traditions in the Acts of John, Thomas and Peter', *Semeia* 38, 1986, 53-66; Arthur J. Dewey, 'The Hymn in the Acts of John. Dance as Hermeneutic', *Semeia* 38, 1986, 67-80 and on this J.-D. Kaestli, *ib.* 81-88; Gerlinde Sirker-Wicklaus, 'Untersuchungen zur Struktur, zur theologischen Tendenz und zum kirchengeschichtlichen Hintergrund der Acta Johannis' (Ev.-theol. Diss. Bonn 1988). For further literature reference may be made to the detailed bibliography in the Junod/Kaestli edition, pp. x-xix. Modern **Translations:** *German*: Georg Schimmelpfeng in NTApo[1], 423-459 (in NTApo[2], 175-191 only a selection edited by E. Hennecke, with summaries of contents for the sections omitted); selections in Wilhelm Michaelis, *Die Apokryphen zum Neuen Testament übersetzt und erläutert* (Sammlung Dieterich 129), Bremen 1956; [3]1963, 222-268. *English*: James, 228-270. *French*: André-Jean Festugière, *Les Actes apocryphes de Jean et de Thomas* (Cahiers d'Orientalisme VI), Geneva 1983, 9-37; Junod/Kaestli in their edition, 160-314. *Italian*: Erbetta II, 29-67; Moraldi II, 1131-1151.

2. Attestation and use:[1] It is not possible to demonstrate any use of the Acts of John in the Christian literature of the 2nd and early 3rd centuries. In two of the four extant versions of the Apocryphon of John,[2] already in some form known to Irenaeus (*c*. 180), there is an evidently secondary introduction which recalls the description of the situation at the beginning of the revelation of the mystery of the Cross (AJ 97).[3] The differences are however too great for there to be any question of dependence of the Apocryphon on the Acts of John. Evidently we have here an independent use of the motif of John as an outstanding mediator of revelation and of the mount (of Olives) as a place for the giving of secret revelations.[4] In older research a reference in Clement of Alexandria (c. 200) to 'traditions' was often adduced as the alleged earliest witness for the Acts of John; according to this John when he touched the 'outward body' of Jesus could put his hand right through it.[5] This corresponds to John's statement in the Acts that when he touched Jesus' body it was sometimes solid and material, but sometimes appeared as if without substance (AJ 93). Despite the agreement in content, the differences in formulation are so great[6] that we cannot understand Clement's remark as a reference to the Acts of John. Here too we have to do rather with independent variations on a traditional motif which described John as the guarantor of the tangible reality of Christ's revelation, such as we find also in

1 Jn. 1:1.[7] On the basis of some contacts in form and content with the Acts of Thomas, E. Junod and J.D. Kaestli thought that they could reckon with literary dependence of the latter on the Acts of John.[8] It is much more likely to be a matter of indications of a related milieu and traditional background.[9] Finally a passage in the Pseudo-Cyprianic *de Montibus Sina et Sion*, which originated in Africa before 240, was often claimed in the older literature for the Acts of John. There it is said, in the context of a speculation on Wisd. 7:26: 'For we too, who believe in him, see Christ in us as in a mirror, for he himself instructs and reminds us in a letter of his disciple John to the people: "You see me in yourselves as one of you sees himself in water or in a mirror."'[10] It is however quite arbitrary to ascribe this citation from an ostensible letter of John, or the letter itself, to the Acts of John, and also an alleged reminiscence of a line in the hymn in the Acts (AJ 95.45f.) actually does not exist, since the two texts employ the image of the mirror in different ways and in a different context.

Since Origen also cannot be claimed as a witness for the Acts of John,[11] their use by the Manichean Psalm-book, which probably goes back to the last third of the 3rd century, must rank as the earliest trace.[12] It points to dissemination in the Syrian region and the Syriac language. At the turn from the 4th to the 5th century, the Syriac *Liber Graduum* possibly offers an allusion to this tradition with its remark that it was written of John that he died a natural death,[13] in which we may probably see a reference to the report in these Acts of the apostle's departure (Metastasis), which however was also transmitted independently of the Acts themselves. A further trace in the Syrian area first appears again in Gregory Barhebraeus (1225/6-1286), who however is drawing on a substantially older heresiological source. In his description of the Audian sect he ascribes to them the idea that 'the body of our Lord was heavenly, and that he was struck with the lance and (yet) not struck, and hanged on the tree and (yet) not hanged'.[14] Here two of the antitheses in AJ 101 are clearly taken up, in each case simply expanded by the insertion of an adverbial phrase and transposed from the first person of the revealer into the third person of indirect speech.[15]

In the Greek-speaking area the attestation of the Acts of John begins in the 4th century with their mention by Eusebius, who names them with the Acts of Andrew 'and the other apostles' as examples of apocryphal Acts.[16] According to the *Panarion* of Epiphanius, written in 375/7, the Encratites used 'the so-called Acts of Andrew, of John and of Thomas',[17] and Epiphanius himself possibly once refers to the Metastasis in the Acts of John.[18] Amphilochius of Iconium (d. after 394) discussed the content of the Acts of John in a lost work. In a fragment of it preserved in the Acts of the Nicene Council of 787 there are the words: 'This would not have been said by the apostle John, who wrote in the Gospel that the Lord spoke from the Cross saying, "Behold, thy son" (Jn. 19:26), so that from that day St John took Mary to himself. How then does he say here that he was not present?'[19] He here refers to AJ 97, a reference which is confirmed by the fact that his words were quoted during a discussion in the Council about the Acts of John, in the course of which, *inter alia*, this chapter had been read shortly before. Didymus the Blind (d. 398) refers his readers to the Acts of John for the names of those converted by John.[20] That Pseudo-Macarius (*c*. 400) once uses the description of Christ as 'the doctor who heals for nothing', which otherwise occurs only in the Acts of John, is still no evidence for direct knowledge.[21] On the other hand the author of the Acts of Philip, whose homeland is in encratite and monastic circles in Asia Minor in the 4th century, harks back in a fragment as yet unpublished, preserved in the Athos manuscript Xenophontos 32, to the hymn in AJ 94-96.[22] The Passio Johannis under the name of a bishop Melito of Laodicea,[23] handed down in Latin but presumably originally Greek, which scarcely came into being before the middle of the 5th century, has taken up several narratives from the Acts of John in a considerably revised form: the story of Drusiana and Callimachus (AJ 62-86), of which only the name of Drusiana and her raising up by John have remained in the revision, the story of the destruction of the temple of Artemis (AJ 37-45), and the Metastasis (AJ 106-115), which here has been substantially abridged and transformed into a cultic legend for the alleged tomb of the apostle in the basilica of John at Ephesus.[24] In a foreword the Passio sets itself apart from heretical apostolic Acts. Together with the Acts of John it mentions the Acts of Andrew and of Thomas, all three of which Leucius is said to have composed and which are reproached for a consistent dualism.[25] It is uncertain whether these statements derive from the author's own direct knowledge of these Acts. Also the narrative sections taken up from the Acts of John need not in any case have been drawn directly from the Acts themselves. They could just as well have come to the redactor as isolated pieces of tradition, already separated from their context, hence from a kind of tradition through which practically the whole of the remains of the Acts of John still extant today has been transmitted.

In the Latin area the attestation of the Acts of John begins only with the close of the 4th century. In Philaster of Brescia and Faustus of Milevis they appear as part of the Manichean corpus of apocryphal Acts.[26] Augustine certainly knows of them from the same source. He once expressly names them[27] and another time reports the Metastasis from 'apocryphal writings',[28] while in his letter to Ceretius he adduces some lines from the hymn in AJ 94-96, evidently only from a Priscillianist work sent to him by his correspondent, as deriving from apocryphal writings but without directly mentioning the Acts of John.[29] There is probably an allusion to them in bishop Evodius of Uzala in proconsular Africa,[30] who was friendly with Augustine. On the other side a recast form of the Metastasis in a Latin version appears to have been in circulation independently about the turn of the 5th century: for Chromatius of Aquileia summarises a modified form of the Metastasis story of John's end according to a 'writing which reports of his death'.[31]

The use of the Acts of John by the so-called Monarchian prologue to John probably leads to Spanish Priscillianist circles about 400,[32] and the Epistle of Pseudo-Titus, which also exploited them,[33] points if not to the same milieu at least to its close geographical and spiritual neighbourhood, while Turribius of Astorga about the middle of the 5th century speaks again of their use among the Manicheans and Priscillianists in his field of operation.[34] At the beginning of the 5th century the Acts of John had evidently also made their appearance in Aquitania; for Innocent I names them in his letter to Exsuperius of Toulouse of 20 February 405, which gives judgment in response to his correspondent's inquiries in a list of writings to be rejected.[35] The Pseudo-Gelasian Decree from the beginning of the 6th century does not adduce them by name, but they should possibly be included under the rubric 'all the books which Leucius, the disciple of the devil, has made',[36] so far as the author had any concrete ideas at all about these books. But in the Latin area at this period it was probably only isolated pieces of the Acts of John that were transmitted, which then occasionally found their way into hagiographic descriptions of John, as in the *Virtutes Johannis*,[37] which probably came into being in the late 6th century in Gaul; these however did not stand alone, as the appearance of material from the Acts of John in an Irish text of the 14th century[38] allows us to recognise.

While the chain of the western witnesses breaks off in the 5th century, there are still some later attestations in the east. It is questionable whether we can already count Ephraim of Antioch (Patriarch 527-545) among them. In a fragment preserved by Photius he reproduces briefly the content of the Metastasis, in a form which corresponds to the secondary developed text-form designated as γ by Junod/Kaestli, and names as his source 'the Acts of the beloved John and the Vita, which not a few bring forward'.[39] That the ancient Acts of John are meant is nevertheless doubtful; for recension γ of the Metastasis was combined in the tradition with another text, independent of the ancient Acts, the 'Acts of John in Rome'.[40] The 'travels of John' are at least mentioned, although probably not on the basis of his own direct knowledge, in John of Thessalonica (d. c. 630).[41] The most important evidence of all is provided by the Nicene Council of 787, already mentioned. Its fifth session dealt, among other matters, with the Acts of John, to which the Iconoclastic Council of 754 had appealed. Here AJ 27 and the first half of AJ 28 were read out 'from the pseudepigraphical Travels of the Holy Apostles' as a document hostile to images, together with a large part of AJ 93-98 as a general indication of the book's heretical character.[42] The so-called Stichometry of Nicephorus, a canon catalogue of uncertain age attached to a version of the Chronography handed down under the name of Nicephorus of Constantinople (9th cent.), assigns 2500 lines to the Acts of John (other readings 2600, 3600), the same as for the Gospel of Matthew.[43] Finally Photius in his *Bibliotheca*, the date of which is in dispute (towards 855 or after 873), gives an analysis of the whole Manichean corpus of Acts, which in substance appears to rely primarily on the Acts of John.[44]

The general picture resulting from this attestation may be briefly outlined as follows: the Acts of John first come into view in the last third of the 3rd century as part of the Manichean corpus of apocryphal Acts. Known to the earliest Church authorities only as a sectarian work, they may have belonged to the tradition of Christian splinter groups, probably in Syria and Asia Minor, from which they must have passed to the Manicheans. In the West, where they became known in the 4th century through the Manichean corpus and seem to have met with approval primarily among the Priscillianists and other representatives of rigorous asceticism, especially in Spain, Aquitania and South Gaul, all trace is lost in the 5th century. In the East on the other hand, where the continuous attestation already breaks off in the 4th century, they appear once again in the 8th and 9th centuries. This should not be evaluated without more ado as an indication of an interest in the transmission of this document which continued right down to this period; all that it really attests is simply that zealous collectors among antiquarians and librarians of the time might occasionally come across an exemplar of the ancient Acts on library shelves. This applies not only to the notice in Photius, but also to the use of the Acts of John by the Iconoclasts, which alone brought this document into the range of vision of the second Nicene

Council. The iconoclastic proof from tradition at the time of the council of Hiereia in 754 was faced with the demand that it should be substantiated by witnesses to the tradition fixed in writing,[45] and thus they were positively directed toward the antiquarian lore of the librarians. That it could still be found, however, may perhaps allow us to deduce a certain widespread dissemination of the ancient Acts, or more exactly the ancient corpus of Acts, in earlier centuries. For the rest, at the period of the iconoclastic controversy the handing-on of materials from the Acts of John must long have been limited, in the East as in the West, to those passages which had found entry into the hagiographic tradition.[46] In this medium of transmission the passage hostile to images (AJ 26-29) for a long time held its ground; it was still being copied in the 14th century.[47] Even the completely unorthodox 'preaching of the Gospel' (AJ 87-105) was now and then transmitted at a late date as an isolated piece in some marginal area - perhaps just because it was a marginal area - in the Byzantine Church; at any rate the scribe who in 1319 in the Crimea incorporated it in a hagiographic collection[48] gives us no reason to suppose that in so doing he was drawing directly on the Acts of John.

3. Contents of the tradition: At its fifth session the Nicene Council of 787 pronounced on the Acts of John: 'No one is to copy (this book): not only so, but we consider that it deserves to be consigned to the fire'.[49] In the West, 340 years earlier, Leo the Great had given a similar verdict on the entire compass of the apocryphal literature concerning the apostles which was used by the Priscillianists: 'The apocryphal writings, however, which under the names of the apostles contain a hotbed of manifold perversity, should not only be forbidden but altogether removed and burnt with fire'.[50] These judgments sufficiently explain why the Acts of John have survived only in fragmentary form. According to the statement of the Stichometry of Nicephorus, which assigns to the Acts of John the same compass as to the Gospel of Matthew, the extant fragments amount to some 70% of the whole work. We must however view this statement with some reserve. For deductions as to narrative complexes no longer extant, which are possible on the basis of the remains handed down, arouse the impression that more than just a bare third of the original text has been lost.

3.1. The Greek text: The extant stock of Greek text is almost without exception handed down in hagiographical collections of various types intended for liturgical use, and may be divided into four strands of tradition. **1.** The largest of these includes AJ 18-36; 37-55; 58-86 and 106-115. It is transmitted as an expansion of a recension of the later Acts of John of ps.-Prochorus. **2.** A second fragment, AJ 56f., is transmitted along with the beginning of these Acts of ps.-Prochorus;[51] it also appears in the Armenian translation of the Acts of ps.-Prochorus.[52] **3.** The most widely disseminated complex is AJ 106-115, the so-called Metastasis of the Acts of John. It is preserved not only as part of the first complex mentioned above but also as an independent piece, as well as in connection with forms of the ps-Prochorus Acts and with the 'Acts of John in Rome'. This branching tradition of the Metastasis led to the formation of three distinguishable forms of text, which in the Junod/Kaestli edition (317-343) are reproduced separately by way of appendix, as first steps in the reconstruction of the text. In addition this section is also extant in a series of ancient versions.[53] **4.** The most interesting section from the point of view of the history of religion and theology, but also the most scandalous for Church orthodoxy, 'John's preaching of the Gospel' (AJ 87-105), was incorporated as late as 1319 into a hagiographical collection, as an independent text, under the rubric 'Wonderful report of the deeds and of the vision which the holy John the theologian beheld', by a scribe who was a cleric in the eparchy of Gothia in the Crimea.[54] For some sections of the stock of text thus preserved, namely AJ 27 and part of AJ 28, AJ 93 and part of AJ 94, as well as AJ 97 and part of AJ 98, there is also the parallel tradition of their quotation in the Acts of the second Nicene Council.[55]

In addition to these unbroken complexes of text, two episodes which may be assigned to the Acts of John are preserved in the Greek Papyrus Oxyrhynchus 850;[56] they are also extant in a revised form in an Irish translation from the Latin[57] (the translation of the Greek does not take into account some of the far-reaching attempts at restoration by Junod and Kaestli):

Verso

. . . f>or him < . . .
. . . > groans and < . . .
. . . > but John < . . .
. . . to Zeux>is, having arisen and taken . . < . . .
. . . > who didst compel me . . < . . .
. . . > (him) who thought to hang himself; who the desper<ate
. . . > dost convert to thyself; who what to no one is kno<wn
. . . > dost make known; who weepest for the oppre<ssed
. . . > . . who raisest up the dead . . < . . .
. . . > of the powerless, Jesus, the comforter <of the . . .
. . . > we praise thee and worship thee an<d give
than>ks for all thy gifts and thy present dispensation
and> service. And (after he) to Zeuxis alone of the euchar<ist
. . . > he gave to those who wished to receive < . . .
. . . > . . . they did not dare. But the proconsul < . . .
. . . > . . in the midst of the congregation to <John
. . . > . . (and) s<ai>d: Servant of the Unnameable . < . . .
. . . > . . has brought letters from Caes<ar . . .
. . . > . . and with < . . .

Recto

he went > forth (?).
. . . A>ndronicus and . . < . . . [58]
When a few <days> had passed . . < . . .

. . . > several brethren to < . . . cross> over a bridge, under which a <great> river flowed. And as> John went to the brethre<n a <man> came to him <gar>bed in soldier's clothing and standing before him said: John, if < . . . into my> hands thou wilt shortly come. And John . . < . . . said: T>he Lord shall quench thy threatening and thine anger a<nd thy transgression! And behold, that man disappeared. So when John c<ame>to them whom he was visiting and fou<nd them> gathered together, he said: Ri<se up>, m<y brethren>, and let us bow our knees before the Lord, who the gre<at enemy's un>seen activity has brought to noth<ing . . th>em, he bowed the knee together with th<em . . . . . . > . . . God . . . < . . .

The sequence of verso and recto corresponds to the order of the two episodes in the Irish redaction,[59] and takes account of the fact that the end of the Zeuxis incident on the verso must have been preceded by a longer narrative than could have been accommodated in the few lines missing between the end of the recto and the beginning of the verso if the order were reversed. The name of Andronicus, which belongs to the *dramatis personae* of the Acts (AJ 31, 105, 37, 46, 59, 61-63, 65f., 70, 72-74, 76, 79, 80, 82f., 86), already tells in favour of the view that these episodes belong to the Acts of John. This is further confirmed by Junod/Kaestli (127f.), who have shown a whole series of linguistic and factual common elements. At the same time however they point (128f.) to signs that in the fragment we have to do with a redacted form of the text over against the original form of the Acts of John. Among these are in the first place the use of the term 'congregation' (ἐκκλησία) and the expression 'to bow the knee' for 'to pray'. We therefore cannot without further ado start out from the position that in the original context of the ancient Acts the two episodes followed directly one after the other. On the other side the interpolation of another passage from the ancient Acts of John between the two in the Irish story of John does not necessarily prove the opposite, since it could equally be secondary. In these circumstances it will scarcely be possible to locate the fragment with any confidence in one of the lacunae which can be deduced from the text transmitted. Junod/Kaestli (91f.) suggest for consideration its insertion in the gap between AJ 105 and 37.

The Greek material thus handed down represents the oldest transmitted linguistic form of the Acts of John, but not beyond question their original form. Their use by the early Manichean community suggests the conjecture that there could have been an ancient Syriac version of the document. In addition, we shall also have to ask whether they, or at least parts of the material incorporated in them, were not originally written in Syriac. Indications of this are provided by AJ 97, with its evident use of a Syriac name for a day of the week,[60] and by the almost verbatim quotation from AJ 101 in Gregory Barhebraeus, behind the Syriac wording of which there possibly stands a Syriac version of the text which is more original than the Greek version which has come down to us.[61] The transmitted Syriac version of the Metastasis cannot however be considered as the remains of such a Syriac form of the text, for it shows signs of translation from the Greek.[62] In view of the rich and widely branching separate transmission which this section of the text enjoyed, it cannot by any means rank without more ado as representative for the Acts of John as a whole.

The Armenian version of AJ 56f.,[63] already mentioned, is also a transfer of a piece of Greek hagiographical tradition without evidential value for the transmission history of the ancient Acts. Finally the text which occurs in the Old Slavonic tradition, designated as *de pictore* by Aurelio de Santos Otero and erroneously compared with AJ 26-29,[64] has nothing to to with the ancient Acts of John.

3.2. The ancient versions: 3.2.1. The Latin version: The attestation shows that there was a Latin version of the Acts of John, which was in any case in existence in the late 4th century.[65] The lines from the Hymn of Christ quoted by Augustine from a Priscillianist work certainly derive from it.[66] In addition the apocryphal Epistle of Titus may be regarded as an indirect witness for it. Among its numerous borrowings from apocryphal writings there are three passages which must rank as free and in part also recast quotations from the Acts of John:[67]

Hearken to the thanksgiving of John, the disciple of the Lord, how in the prayer at his passing he said: 'Lord, who hast kept me from my infancy until this time untouched by woman, who hast separated my body from them, so that it was offensive to me (even) to see a woman.'
(Introduction: ll. 436f.; citation: ll.437-440).

Or is it outside the Law, what we teach, as even the demons when they confessed to the deacon Dyrus (= Verus? - see AJ 30; 61; 111) (in regard) to John's coming - consider what they said: 'Many will come to us in the last times to drive us out of our vessels [sc. the demoniacs], saying that they are pure and undefiled by women, and not possessed by desire for them. If we wished, we would gain possession of them also.'
(Introduction : ll. 444-446; citation; ll. 446-449)

Take also to heart the warnings of the blessed John, who when he was called to a marriage went there only for the sake of chastity. And what did he say? 'Children, while your flesh is still clean and you have a body that is untouched, and you are not caught in corruption nor soiled by Satan, that most adverse and shame<less> (enemy) to chastity, know now more fully the mystery of conjugal union: it is a device of the serpent, a disregard of the teaching, an injury to the seed, a gift of death, a work of destruction, a teaching of division, a work of corruption, a boorish rusticity <. . .>, a second sowing of the enemy, an ambush of Satan, a device of the jealous one, an unclean fruit of parturition, a shedding of blood, a passion in the mind, a falling from reason, a token of punishment, an instruction of pain, an operation of fire, a sign of the enemy, the deadly malice of envy, the embrace of deceit, a union with bitterness, a morbid humour of the mind, an invention of ruin, the desire of a phantom, a converse with matter, a comedy of the devil, hatred of life, a fetter of darkness, an intoxication < . . . >, a derision of the enemy, a hindrance of life, that separates from the Lord, the beginning of disobedience, the end and death of life. Hearing this, my children, bind yourselves each one of you in an indivisible, true and holy matrimony, waiting for the one incomparable and true bridegroom from heaven, even Christ, who is a bridegroom for ever.' (Introduction: ll. 458-460; citation: ll. 460-477).

The first of these passages is a shortened paraphrase of the beginning of AJ 113 from John's valedictory prayer. For the other two an origin in the Acts of John cannot be assumed with the same certainty. It is however probable.[68] The name of the deacon Dyrus who appears in the second passage must be a corruption of Verus, the name borne by the 'deacon' who attends the apostle in the Acts of John. The rejection of marriage expressed in the third passage is a feature which Photius noted for the corpus of apostolic Acts which he examined, and evidently for the Acts of John in particular.[69] On the other hand the eschatological motif which is sounded in these two passages is alien to the ancient Acts of John. It may be regarded as a sign of adaptation by the author of the Letter of Pseudo-Titus.

Two passages of the Acts of John are directly transmitted in a Latin translation, the story of Drusiana and Callimachus (AJ 63-86) and the Metastasis (AJ 106-115). They are preserved in the *Virtutes Johannis*, a hagiographical compilation generally dated to the 6th century.[70] It is based on the Passio Johannis of Melito of Laodicea, which it expands by additional material. In the process, the original Drusiana-Callimachus story[71] takes the place of the short and colourless miracle story into which the Passio had transformed it, the Metastasis[72] that of the recasting which was to be found in the Passio, from which however some passages are still retained by the Virtutes.[73] In relation to the Greek the two passages are distinct. The Latin Drusiana-Callimachus story is closer to it than the Latin version of the Metastasis.[74] This suggests the hypothesis that they are also of different origin. While we may see in the Drusiana-Callimachus story of the Virtutes an isolated portion of the Latin translation of the Acts of John as a whole, the version of the Metastasis could derive from a self-contained Latin Metastasis tradition independent of it, such as is attested also in Chromatius of Aquileia.[75]

That still other narrative sequences, in addition to the Drusiana-Callimachus story, were handed on by the Latin version of the Acts of John is shown by the late mediaeval Irish story of John, *Beatha Eoin Bruinne*, only partially extant, which was composed by the Augustinian canon Uighisdin (= Augustine) MacRaighin (d. 1405) on the basis of a Latin *Vorlage*.[76] In addition to apocalyptic material[77] and elements from the Passio Johannis,[78] it contains three passages which go back to the Acts of John. Its story of the priest who has a secret sin which is detected by John, and who repents, is reconciled, and celebrates mass together with John,[79] is to all appearances a heavily revised version, transposed into the colouring of the mediaeval Church, of an episode of which part is preserved on the verso of the Greek Papyrus Oxyrhynchus 850. This fragment tells of a man named Zeuxis, who makes an attempt at suicide but, evidently through the apostle's intervention, is saved and then takes part in a eucharistic service conducted by John. His name may probably be found in that of the priest in the Irish narrative, Eusip, Seusisp, Seuesp or Seusp. In addition there also appears in the Irish text the deacon Birro, in whom we may without doubt recognise the 'deacon' of the Acts of John, the brother who ministered to the apostle (AJ 30; 61; 110), Verus (Βῆρος, Οὐῆρος, Βήρρος, Βίρρος; Byrrus in the Virtutes Johannis). The adjoining section,[80] in which at John's prayer hay is transmuted into gold, which he then throws into the water to demonstrate the worthlessness of earthly goods, apparently preserves an episode to which Evodius of Uzala once alludes. He confronts the Manicheans with a series of arguments against their denial of a bodily resurrection, and then writes: 'And yet, though flesh itself is called grass (*foenum*, lit. "hay") because of its present weakness, you believe that John made gold out of grass, but you do not believe that God the Almighty can make a spiritual body out of a carnal body.'[81] Here he clearly presupposes that the story of the apostle's miraculous deed was generally known at least to the Manicheans who shared his environment. It may therefore be taken as certain that it derived from a source in circulation among them, and such a source would be the Acts of John in the Manichean corpus of apocryphal Acts. The motif of the transformation of worthless material into gold by John does indeed also occur elsewhere, in the Passio Johannis[82] as well as in Symeon Metaphrastes (second half of 10th cent.) and in a hagiographical compilation about John which rests chiefly on Pseudo-Prochorus and is preserved in a Georgian redaction by Euthymius Hagiorites (d. 1028).[83] But the motif of contempt for earthly goods, which corresponds to the tendency of the ancient Acts of John, is dominant only in the Passio Johannis and the Irish text, and over against the Passio the Irish text agrees with Evodius in the detail of the transforming of the hay into gold. Moreover the statements of John which occur in it, about the imperishability of the garment which he put on with his acceptance of apostolic service (c. 13), recall those in AJ 29 about the true shape, form and colour which cannot be caught in a painted picture. Finally, it is not difficult to recognise in a third section of the Irish story[84] John's meeting with a demon, which appears on the recto of POx 850.[85]

3.2.2. Eastern versions of the Metastasis: If we leave aside the question of an ancient Syriac version of the Acts of John,[86] the available material offers no clue to suggest that the document as a whole existed in other translations in addition to the Latin, although this finding, which might rest upon the accidents of transmission history, does not definitively exclude the temporary existence of such translations. In any case the Metastasis underwent a wide transmission of its own, outside of the context of the Acts as a whole, and found its way into almost all the languages of the eastern Church.

A *Syriac* version from the Greek was published by W. Wright (*Apocryphal Acts of the Apostles*, London 1871; reprint Amsterdam 1968, I 66-72; English trans. II 61-68) from what is still the only known manuscript of it. It cannot have been the only one, for there is a secondary Arabic version from the Syriac which presents another form of text (see Junod/Kaestli 43f.).

A fifth-century *Armenian* translation based on a Greek original enjoyed a wide circulation, and found its way into Armenian biblical manuscripts; it has often been printed (survey in BHO, No. 474), *inter alia* in the Armenian Bible edited by Johannes Zohrab (Venice 1805, Appendix 27-29); English translation by S.C. Malan (*The Conflicts of the Apostles*, London 1871); separate edition with Latin translation by Joseph Catergian (*Dormitio b. Ioannis Apostoli. Ecclesiae Ephesinae de obitu Ioannis Apostoli narratio armeniaca saeculi V*, Vienna 1877, 32-51).

A *Coptic* (Sahidic) translation, presumably of the 6th century, is preserved in its full text and in a series of fragments, and has been critically edited in Junod/Kaestli (382-397); unsatisfactory English translation in E.A. Wallis Budge, *Coptic Apocrypha in the Dialect of Upper Egypt*, London 1913, 233-240 (the Coptic basis, ib. 51-58); additional notes on the manuscript tradition by Enzo Lucchesi, 'Contribution codicologique au corpus copte des actes apocryphes des apôtres', in Paul-Hubert Poirier, *La version copte de la prédication et du martyre de Thomas* (Subsidia hagiographica 67), Brussels 1984, 5-24 (esp. 19-21).

A fragment of a free, paraphrastic Coptic (Bohairic) version is preserved in a Cairo manuscript (Coptic Museum 5-6) deriving from the monastery of Macarius in the Wadi 'n-Natrun; in this the Metastasis is linked by an intervening section with the first part of the later Acts of John by ps.-Prochorus, and thus incorporated into an Egyptian collection of later apostolic Acts.[87] The fragment corresponds to AJ 112.3-18 (Junod/ Kaestli 307-9); text with English translation in *The Monasteries of the Wadi 'n Natrun I. New Coptic texts from the Monastery of St Macarius*, ed. H.G. Evelyn White, New York 1926, 36f.

Michel van Esbroeck has published a *Georgian* version, probably of the 6th century, which serves as the conclusion of a Georgian version of the Acts of John of ps.-Prochorus ('Les formes géorgiennes des Acta Johannis', *AnalBoll* 93, 1975, 5-19; esp. 11-19, with a Latin translation), C. Kekelidze a later one revised under Armenian influence and transmitted as an independent text (*Monumenta hagiographica georgica* I 1, Tiflis 1918, 198-201; Latin translation likewise in van Esbroeck).

A version of the Metastasis close to the Greek text form γ, but severely abridged, forms the conclusion of a hagiographical compilation about John resting especially on ps.-Prochorus and preserved in a Georgian revision by Euthymius Hagiorites (d. 1028); its text is published in *At'onis Iveriis monastris 1074 c. helt'naceri agapebit*, Tiflis 1901, 111-176, and Michel van Esbroeck has provided a French translation ('Les Acta Johannis traduits par Euthyme l'Hagiorite', in *Bedi Kartlisa* 33, 1975, 73-109; for the Metastasis, pp. 108f., c. 194-200 of van Esbroeck's division).

In *Arabic*, two secondary versions of the Metastasis have been published with an English translation by Agnes Smith Lewis, *Acta mythologica Apostolorum* (Horae Semiticae III), London 1904 (Arabic text) and *The mythological Acts of the Apostles* (Horae Semiticae IV), London 1904 (English trans.). The first (text op. cit 144-146; trans. 168-171), as a continuation of the later Syriac John story (see Junod/Kaestli 705-717), is translated along with it from the Syriac. The other (text op. cit 46-51; trans. 54-59) rests on the Bohairic Coptic version and belongs to the Egyptian collection of later apocryphal Acts. Finally Georg Graf gives a list of manuscripts containing the Metastasis outside of this collection (*Geschichte der arabischen christlichen Literatur* I [Studi e Testi 118], Rome 1944, 263f.).

Finally, the Metastasis was translated into *Ethiopic* from the Arabic, not before the first half of the 14th century, in association with the Egyptian Arabic collection of apostolic Acts already mentioned; text in E.A. Wallis Budge, *The Contendings of the Apostles* I, London 1899, 214-222; English trans. ib. II, London 1901, 253-263; an older English translation on the basis of one manuscript by S.C. Malan, *The Conflicts of the Holy Apostles*, London 1871, 137-145.

On the other hand a text circulated in the *Old Slavonic* tradition as the 'Death of John the theologian' (*prestavlenie ioanna bogoslava*) rests not on the Metastasis of the ancient Acts of John but on ps.-Prochorus.[88]

4. The structure and unity of the book: Enough of the text of the Acts of John has come down to us to allow its whole structure to be shown in a table; items resting on inference or conjecture are printed in italics; further details are inserted at corresponding points in the translation (but cf. also Junod/Kaestli 76-100).

Introduction and antecedents
- *Introduction of the narrator (Leucius; cf. above pp. 92ff.)?*
- *John's conversion to continence (cf. c. 113)?*
- *Allocation of the mission areas among the apostles?*

First travel-narrative
- Journey *from Jerusalem (?)* to Miletus
- *Stay in Miletus*
- Journey from Miletus to Ephesus (c. 18)

First Stay in Ephesus
- Raising of Cleopatra and Lycomedes (cc. 19-25)
- The portrait of John (cc. 26-29)
- Healing of the old women (incomplete, cc. 30-36)
- *Conversion of Drusiana, conflict with Andronicus, conversion of Andronicus*
- John's Preaching of the Gospel (cc. 87-105)
  - Introduction (cc. 87-88)
  - The Christ of many forms (cc. 88-93)
  - The Hymn of Christ (cc. 94-96)
  - Revelation of the Mystery of the Cross (cc. 97-102)
  - Concluding exhortation (cc. 103-105).
- *Break, whose length and content cannot be determined.*
- Destruction of the Temple of Artemis and conversion of the Ephesians (cc. 37-45)
- Raising of the priest of Artemis (cc. 46-47)
- Conversion of a parricide (cc. 48-54)
- Call to Smyrna (c. 55)

Second travel-narrative
- *Journey from Ephesus to Smyrna*
- Healing of the sons of Antipatros (c. 56-57)
- *Further journey through various towns (probably Pergamum, Thyateira, Sardis, Philadelphia) to Laodicea*
- Departure for Ephesus (c. 58-59)
- The obedient bugs (c. 60-61)

Second Stay in Ephesus and Death of John

Arrival in Ephesus (c. 62)
Drusiana and Callimachus (cc. 63-86)
The Departure (cc. 106-110)
Death of John (cc. 111-115)

The Hymn of Christ (AJ 94-96) and the Revelation of the Mystery of the Cross (AJ 79-102) stand apart from the Acts of John as a whole in form and content, through their special character.[89] They were evidently incorporated into the Acts as a piece already completely formed. Junod and Kaestli assume the same for the eucharistic prayer in the Metastasis (c. 109), since we can detect connections in terminology and in substance between it and AJ 94-102.[90] They further reckon with the possibility that these sections did not belong to the original content of the document, but were inserted only later. They see an indication of this, in addition to the special character of these sections, in an alleged break between AJ 93 and 94.[91] But the last two sentences of AJ 93, which they see as the conclusion of what precedes, are rather to be understood as an introduction to what follows, and thus actually as a connective element, with a parenthetic insertion to explain why in this 'preaching of the Gospel' there is no reference to the miracles of Christ, or to signs as a familiar part of the preaching of Christ.[92] There is no indication at all of a secondary insertion of AJ 109. The passage is formally so firmly bonded into the context that the idea of its later introduction entails the hazardous assumption that it has supplanted an original text with the same function.[93] The redactional integration favours the view that the two passages, AJ 94-102 and 109, despite their special character, belonged from the beginning to the Acts of John.

5. Character: As the frame for their narrative, the Acts of John claim as their own the Church tradition of the activity of John the son of Zebedee in Asia Minor. They make the apostle take up his work in Ephesus, from there undertake a missionary journey to Smyrna, to other towns and finally to Laodicea, which probably means through the seven communities of the Apocalypse of John, and in conclusion find his last rest in Ephesus. The content with which this framework is filled out, however, disputes this John-tradition with the Great Church, and claims it for the Christian groups among whom the Acts had their home.[94] It is from this that the most peculiar section in the document, John's revelation speech in AJ 87-102, derives its specific significance. Seen purely in terms of literary criticism, it brackets together a series of smaller sections, namely John's account of the manifold forms and actual other-worldliness in which the Lord encountered his disciples (AJ 88-93), a revelation hymn of Christ with its own introduction (AJ 94-96), and a revelation discourse of Christ about the mystery of the Cross (AJ 97-102), which redactionally is closely attached to the hymn by a transition in AJ 97 and a reference back in AJ 101, but likewise is provided with its own introduction and conclusion. In terms of its literary form this speech by John can be called a gospel.[95] The Acts make their apostle proclaim this gospel in Ephesus. Thereby they set it, as genuine Johannine proclamation, in opposition to the gospel document of the ecclesiasticised 'Johannine' tradition, the Fourth Gospel, of which church tradition affirmed that John wrote it in Ephesus.

These two sections, the hymn and the revelation discourse about the mystery of the Cross, which to all appearances were taken up into the 'gospel' of the Acts of John as units already given a literary form, have a clearly gnostic character. Junod/Kaestli consider a kinship in motif with Valentinian Gnosticism, which they have thrown into relief, as an indication of origin in a milieu close to the eastern school of Valentinianism.[96] If it is correct that they were inserted into the Acts from the beginning and, as part of John's preaching of the Gospel, in conscious opposition to the Gospel tradition of the Church, then they also define the horizon of interpretation within which the remaining material is to be read. It reflects an understanding of Christian belief ultimately accessible only to an elect circle, within the framework of a dualism of two spheres of life, that of salvation determined by Christ and that of evil dominated by Satan. To this corresponds a 'realised' eschatology. It becomes especially evident in the narratives about raisings of the dead, which should not simply be understood as merely aretalogical, but have the character of signs. Here the unity of faith and possession of life manifests itself in the conjunction of resurrection and conversion (AJ 19-25; 46f.; 48-53; 72-78), so that the lack of a conversion logically makes the resurrection also once more ineffective (AJ 81-86), and the raising of the model Christian Drusiana (AJ 79f.) lets it be seen that the believer has life even in death. Salvation is made accessible through the revelation of Christ. It has no continuity with the Old Testament, as is made clear in a quite non-polemical way, apart from a remark about 'the lawless Jews whose law-giver is the lawless serpent' in the introduction to the revelation hymn (AJ 94), by the simple omission of any Old Testament allusions. This leads to a marked 'Christomonism' against the background of an image of Christ imparted by the 'gospel', the salient feature of which is a polymorphism of Christ which gives expression to his other-worldly character, beyond the grasp of human comprehension.[97] Salvation, as the possession of life, is realised in faith, and there seems to be no need for any sacramental mediation. At any rate there is never any mention of baptism in the conversion stories of the Acts of John. It is mentioned only once, in passing, in an exorcism formula (AJ 84), a text which is possibly traditional material already shaped. The eucharist celebrated without wine as a breaking of bread has the character of thanksgiving and remembrance of Christ for his glorification. The new life manifests itself in, and is to be substantiated by, aversion from all that is earthly and corruptible, in an encratite contempt for worldly goods, in disparagement of the body and in sexual continence.

In relation to the New Testament tradition there is a marked difference between the 'gospel' and the narrative material. In the latter the logion 'Ask, and it shall be given you' is once quoted verbatim in the form which appears also in Mt. 7:7 and Lk. 11:9 (AJ 22), possibly as an element of a petition handed down with its basic features already firmly fixed in the tradition,[98] and in a missionary exhortation there is a passage (AJ 35) which looks like a homiletic application of the pericope about the Rich Man and Lazarus (Lk. 16:19-26). Other contacts in form and substance with individual New Testament passages, indicated in the following translation, are in contrast too general and not significant enough to prove any clear direct relationship. On the other hand the 'gospel', in itself again not homogeneous, echoes in its first part a series both of Synoptic and also of Johannine motifs,[99] which however are used or transformed very freely, and altogether made to serve the author's own theological tendency. At AJ 90 the admonition 'Do not be faithless, but believing' (Jn. 20:27) appears word for word, but directed to John instead of Thomas and expanded by a further phrase. The revelation discourse about the mystery of the Cross presents a string of allusions to the passion story (AJ 97; 101) which with reminiscences of the Gospel of Peter and once perhaps of the Diatessaron contrast with the canonical Gospel tradition.[100] In this section the Revealer's charge 'Know that I am wholly in the Father, and the Father in me' (AJ 100) is closely connected with Jn. 14:10. Further there occur in it the Johannine titles for Christ: Logos, bread, door, way, truth, life, resurrection (AJ 98), some of which also appear in the Hymn of Christ (AJ 95f.), as well as the term 'seed' from the Synoptic parables tradition, used as a predicate of Christ. The hymn again in its introduction evidently links up with Mk. 14:20; Mt. 26:30 (AJ 94), and in one of its couplets (AJ 95) takes up and transforms Mt. 11:17; Lk. 7:32.

6. Circumstances of composition: The earliest attestation, the indications of a bilingual milieu and possibly even of an original Syriac form of at least part of the 'gospel', as well as a background of tradition close to that of the Acts of Thomas, must all make us think of an origin in the region of East Syria for the Acts of John. Junod/Kaestli (692-694) think of an origin in Egypt. The basic presupposition for this is however the not very probable assumption that the revelation of the mystery of the Cross, the Syrian origin of which they do not question, is an element of a secondary interpolation. This passage, especially in association with the other indications mentioned, tells so emphatically in favour of a Syrian origin that in comparison the arguments advanced for an Egyptian origin cannot tilt the balance. That it is possible to adduce parallels in terminology or in ideas for a string of passages in the Acts of John, partly in Clement of Alexandria and Origen, partly in the Hermetic literature, shows only the openness of Alexandrian eclecticism and syncretism for such ideas, motifs and traditions, but not their Egyptian origin or their dissemination exclusively in Egypt. Again, an Egyptian origin for the motif of a deity revealing himself in many forms,[101] which was widely current, is still not an adequate indication of locality for its adoption by the Acts of John, especially in view of the regular traffic between Egypt and the Syrian region. That the term δικρόσσιον, which in the Acts of John describes an undergarment, occurs elsewhere only in the *Periplus maris Erythraei*,[102] in a list of articles exported from Egypt to the Eritrean coast, does not mean that it must be a question of an Egyptian designation for something specially Egyptian; in view of the detailed rewriting of this designation in the Sahidic version,[103] which starts out from the Greek etymology, this seems rather improbable.

The date of the Acts of John is usually placed in the second half of the 2nd century.[104] According to Junod/Kaestli, they were composed at this time by a member of the hellenistic cultivated classes, who drew upon various literary *Gattungen* and in so doing, without any specific attachment to a concrete community, sought to propagate a Christianity as he understood it, as the expression of certain aspirations of a philosophical attitude to the world which he had held even before his conversion.[105] The Acts of John however presuppose the tradition of John's activity in Ephesus and Asia Minor, which was apparently fully developed and brought into general circulation only in the last third of the 2nd century. On the other hand they were already used in the early Manichean Church as part of a corpus of several apostolic Acts. This suggests the first half of the 3rd century for their composition, in which evidently older material, already put into a fixed form (AJ 94-96, 97 and perhaps also 109), was used. The objection raised against so late a date, that the author must then have taken up a stance over against the developing doctrines of the Great Church,[106] is not valid, since the Acts of John as a whole, in their total redactional plan, can be understood as precisely the taking-up of such a stance. They belong in the debate with 'orthodox' claims to tradition, such as made their influence felt in the first half of the 3rd century in the region of East Syria, in Edessa for example with the group of the Palutians.[107] This is at least the pattern of a situation out of which the origin of the document can be made comprehensible. It serves to bring self-assurance to a Christian group which feels itself bound to the apostle John as the guarantor of a tradition of 'Johannine' theology transmuted into gnostic terms, and which certainly must be conceived as only a very small community without any developed institutional forms. The picture conjured up by the Acts themselves, of a primitive Christian house church, may to be sure be an archaising idealisation, just as the picture sketched of John, as an itinerant charismatic preacher accompanied by a changing group of adherents male and female, should not be taken without more ado as a reflection of the actual situation in a specific community at the time when the Acts came into being. They manifest no interest in the legitimising of any institutional office, nor do they share the relegation of women to an inner realm of life in Church and home which was coming into force in the 'orthodox' development. Their author seems to be not unfamiliar with the rules of rhetoric and perhaps also with the dramatisations of the Greek novel, and makes their action take place chiefly in an upper-class milieu. He is probably one of the circle of those who belonged to the cultivated classes of the area of origin, people who with a view to a 'philosophical' life were critical of their times and inclined to withdrawal, and had found in such Christian groups a new orientation.

Notes

Introduction

1. E. Junod and J.D. Kaestli (*Histoire*) offer a detailed examination of the attestation and use of the Acts of John in early Christian literature, with a thorough discussion of the individual witnesses; as a rule, separate reference is not made to this in what follows.
2. On this see vol. 1, p. 387.
3. Apoc. Joh., version of Pap. Berol. 8502, 19.6-19, ed. Walter C. Till/Hans-Martin Schenke, *Die gnostischen Schriften des koptischen Papyrus Berolinensis 8502* (TU60), ^{2}1972, 79-81; version of NHC II 1.5-20, ed. Martin Krause/Pahor Labib, *Die drei Versionen des Apokryphon des Johannes* (Abh. d.dt. archäol. Instituts Kairo, kopt. Reihe 1), 1962, 109-111; not in the NHC IV 1 version, *ib.* 201 (for the version in NHC III and that used by Irenaeus, *ad. Haer.* I 29, comparison is not possible because the beginning is missing).
4. Cf. Manfred Hornschuh in NTApo^3 II (ET), 81f.; Knut Schäferdiek, 'Herkunft und Interesse der alten Johannesakten', ZNW 74, 1983, 247-267, esp. 255f.
5. Clement of Alexandria, *Hypotyp.* fragm. III, ed. Otto Stählin/Ludwig Früchtel III (GCS 17^2), 210.12-15.

6. Cf. on this E. Junod/J.D. Kaestli, *Histoire* 13-16.
7. Cf. also Jn. 20:27; the saying here addressed to Thomas appears in AJ 90, admittedly in another context, as addressed to John.
8. E. Junod/J.D. Kaestli, *Histoire*, 36-40; on the older question of the relation of the Acts of John and the Acts of Peter, see below, pp. 274f.
9. Cf. on this K. Schäferdiek, 'Herkunft' 249-251.
10. Ps.-Cyprian, *de Montibus Sinai et Sion* 13, ed. W. Hartel (CSEL 3.3), 117.2-6.
11. See above, pp. 87f.
12. See above, pp. 88-91. In addition to the passages mentioned there, cf. the mention of Drusiana in another of the 'pilgrim psalms' (ed. Allberry, 180.30); on contacts between the 'Amen psalm' and the hymn of Christ and the revelation of the mystery of the Cross (AJ 94-102) cf. P. Nagel, 'Apostelakten' (p. 96, note 15) 168-171 and Junod/Kaestli, *Histoire* 54-56.
13. *Liber Graduum*, Serm. 30.6, ed. Michael Kmosko (Patrologia Syriaca 3), Paris 1926, 877.14-16.
14. Gregory Barhebraeus, *adv. Haer.* 22, ed. R. Graffin/F. Nau (PO 13), Paris 1919, 260.1f.; cf. on this Junod/Kaestli, *Histoire* 40-42.
15. Cf. on this K. Schäferdiek, 'Herkunft' 251-253.
16. Eusebius, *HE* III 25.6, ed. E. Schwartz I (GCS 9,1), 252.17 (see vol. 1, p. 47).
17. Epiphanius, *Pan.* 47.1.5, ed. K. Holl/J. Dummer II (GCS 31^2), 1980, 216.5f.
18. Epiphanius, *Pan.* 79.5.3, ed. K. Holl III (GCS 37), 480.2-5.
19. Conc. Nic. II, sectio V: Junod/Kaestli 400.9-13.
20. Didymus, *Comm. on Zech.* IV 210, ed. L. Doutreleau III (SC 85), Paris 1962, 910.21f.
21. Ps.-Macarius, *Hom.* I 12.2.4, ed. H. Berthold (GCS), 1973, I 153.4; AJ 22, 56, 108 (cf. also Act. Thom. 20: the doctor who heals 'without reward'); on ps.-Macarius see Junod/Kaestli, *Histoire* 33f.
22. Junod/Kaestli, *Histoire* 30; François Bovon, 'Les Actes de Philippe', ANRW II 25.6, 1988, 4431-4527, esp. 4522.
23. *Passio Johannis*, ed. Johann Albert Fabricius, *Codex apocryphus Novi Testamenti* III, Hamburg 1724, ^{2}1743, 604-623 (after Franciscus Maria Florentinus, *Vetustius occidentalis ecclesiae Martyrologium*, Lucca 1668, 130-137); PG 5, cols. 1239-1250 (after Gotthold Heine, *Bibliotheca anecdotorum* I, Leipzig 1848, 109-117); cf. on this Knut Schäferdiek, 'Die Passio Johannis des Melito von Laodikeia und die Virtutes Johannis', *AnalBoll* 103, 1985, 368-382.
24. *Passio Johannis*, ed. Fabricius, 607; PG 5, cols. 1241C-1242B (Drusiana). Fabricius 616f.; PG 5, col. 1247A-C (temple of Artemis). Fabricius 621-623; PG 5, col. 1249B-1250C (Metastasis).
25. *Passio Johannis*, Prol., ed. Fabricius, 604-606; PG 5, cols. 1239B-1242B.
26. Philaster, *de Haer.* 88.6, ed. F. Heylen (CChrSL 9), 255f.; Faustus of Milevis ap. Augustine, *c. Faustum* XXX 4, ed. J. Zycha (CSEL 25.1), 751.8-752.5; on this see above, pp. 90f.
27. Augustine, *c. Advers. Leg. et Proph.* I 20, PL 42, col. 626.
28. Augustine, In Joh. tract. 124.2, ed. R. Willems (CChrSL 36) 681f.; cf. on this Junod/Kaestli, *Histoire* 81-85.
29. Augustine, *Ep.* 237.2 and 5f., ed. A. Goldbacher IV (CSEL 57), 526.14-24 and 529.3-532.18 (the parts of lines quoted are brought together in note 27 on p. 206 below).
30. Evodius of Uzala, *de Fide* 40, ed. J. Zycha (CSEL 25.2), 971.1; on this see below, p. 161.
31. Chromatius of Aquileia, *Sermo* XXI 4, ed. R. Étaix/J. Lemarié (CChrSL 9A), 99.78-85. Chromatius' report speaks of John's great age, and says that the Lord informed him of the day of his decease. He could also have taken from the same source a reference to the miracles which occurred at the place of his grave (ibid., 99.87f.). In both points his 'Departure of John' is in contact with the form of the Metastasis taken up by the *Passio Johannis* of Melito of Laodicea, but also further developed into the cult legend of the basilica of John in Ephesus in particular (Fabricius 621 and 623; PG 5, cols. 1249B/C and 1250C). It is evidently a case of features of a development of the Metastasis tradition combined with the Ephesian cult of John. The community of Aquileia

also had connections with this cult. It possessed dust from John's grave, and therefore felt itself obliged to impressive celebration of the anniversary of his decease (Chromatius, ibid. 99.91-93).

32. Monarchian Prologue to John, ed. Jürgen Regul, *Die antimarcionitischen Evangelienprologe* (Aus der Geschichte der lateinischen Bibel 6), 1969, 42f.; on place and date of origin, ibid. 212-262. The Prologue takes up (line 1f.) John's own statement from the beginning of AJ 113, and in lines 18-21 reports the essential content of AJ 111f. Certainly the 'Metastasis' (AJ 106-115) had a wide circulation outside of the context of the ancient Acts of John, but in view of the evidence for Priscillianist knowledge of the ancient Acts we need not think of that here.

33. On this see above, pp. 159f., and on the historical place of the Epistle of ps.-Titus Aurelio de Santos Otero, above pp. 53ff.

34. Turribius Asturic. *Ep. ad Idac. et Cepon.* 5 (PL 54, col. 694).

35. Innocent I, *Ep.* 6.7, ed. H. Wurm, *Apollinaris* 12, 1936, 77 line 35; Denzinger-Schönmetzer, [36]1976, No. 213; Mirbt-Aland, 1967, No. 405.

36. Ps.-Gelasius, *de Libris Recip.* V 4.4, ed. E. von Dobschütz (TU 38, 4) 52; see vol. 1, p. 39.

37. Junod/Kaestli (799-834) present a critical edition of the *Virtutes Johannis*, which belong to a larger collection of *Virtutes apostolorum* (in the older literature also described as the ps.-Abdias collection). On the dating, cf. Louis Duchesne, 'Les anciens recueils des legendes apostoliques': *Compte-rendu du IIIe Congrès scientifique international des Catholiques*, Brussels 1895, 69-79, esp. 73f.

38. On this see below, pp. 160ff.

39. Photius, *Bibl.* cod. 229, ed. R. Henry IV, 141; cf. on this Junod/Kaestli, *Histoire* 115f.

40. On the *Acts of John in Rome*, see Junod/Kaestli 836-886; edition of the text there, pp. 881-886.

41. John of Thessalonica, *Koimesis Homily*, ed. M. Jugie (PO 19), 377.5-12.

42. Con. Nic. II, actio V (Mansi XIII, cols. 168D-172C); critical edition of the quotations from the Acts of John in Junod/Kaestli 361-365 (Greek text) and 366-368 (Latin translation of Anastasius Bibliothecarius).

43. Ed. Theodor Zahn, *Geschichte des neutestamentl. Kanons* II 1, 1890, 300.65 (see vol. 1, p. 42; AJ) and 298.25 (Mt.); cf. on this Junod/Kaestli, *Histoire* 126-128. Dependent on this list is the 'Synopsis' handed down under the name of Athanasius among others, a catalogue the age of which likewise cannot be determined, which names the Travels of John beside those of Peter and Thomas (ed. Zahn, op. cit. 317); cf. on this Erich Klostermann, *Analecta zur Septuaginta, Hexapla und Patristik*, 1895, 77-112 and Junod/Kaestli, *Histoire* 127f.

44. Photius, *Bibl.* cod. 114, ed. R. Henry II, 84-86; see above, pp. 87f.; on the date, cf. Junod/Kaestli, *Histoire* 133, note 1.

45. Cf. Stephen Gero, *Byzantine Iconoclasm during the reign of Constantine V* (CSCO 384), Leuven 1977, 32. The members of the Synod of Hiereia themselves could not form any reliable judgment on the theological character of the Acts of John, since they had only an extract at their disposal, as Gregory of Neocaesarea states at the second Nicene Council (Mansi XIII, col. 173E).

46. On the use of such tradition see Junod/Kaestli, *Histoire* 110f.

47. In MS 188 of the monastery of St John on Patmos (R in Junod/Kaestli) and in MS 2 of the monastery of St Mary at Mezzojuso in Sicily (Z in Junod/Kaestli), closely related to it and presumably also deriving from Patmos. That on the other hand this passage lay before the Council of Nicaea in its original context in the Acts of John is shown by its quotation 'from the pseudepigraphical Travels of the holy apostles' (Junod/Kaestli 361) and its association with passages from AJ 93-98.

48. See further below.

49. Conc. Nic. II, actio V (Mansi XIII, col. 176A).

50. Leo the Great, letter to Turribius of Astorga on 21 July 447, c.15 (PL 54, col. 688A).

51. Ps.-Prochorus, *Acta Johannis*, ed. Th. Zahn, 3.1-44.9 (on the *Acts of John* of ps.-Prochorus see below, pp. 429ff.).

52. Ed. K. Tserakian, *Ankanon girk[c] arrak[c] elakank[c]*, Venice 1904, 219-221; French translation by L. Leloir, *Écrits Apocryphes sur les apôtres. Traduction de l'édition arménienne de Venise*,

I (CChrSA 3), Turnhout 1986, 323-325.
53. On this see below, pp. 160ff.
54. Cod. hist. gr. 63 of the Austrian National Library in Vienna (C in Junod/Kaestli); cf. on this Herbert Hunger, *Beschreibung der griechischen Handschriften der Österreichischen Nationalbibliothek*, Teil 1 (Museion NF 4, Reihe I 1), Vienna 1961, 72f. The colophon is printed in Josef Bick, *Die Schreiber der Wiener griechischen Handschriften* (Museion. Abhandlungen 1), Vienna 1920, no. 22 (pp. 33f.), with a false location of the Byzantine eparchy of Gothia also taken over by Junod/Kaestli.
55. See above, p. 155.
56. Oxford, Bodleian Library Gr. th. f.13 (P); Ap 21 in Kurt Aland, *Repertorium der griechischen christlichen Papyri* I (PTS 18), 1976, 383; text in Junod/Kaestli 118-122.
57. See above, p. 160f..
58. Line 21 is marked off as the superscription for what follows.
59. See above, p. 160f.
60. On this see below, pp. 206, note 33.
61. Gregory Barhebraeus, as at p. 168, note 14 above; on this cf. K. Schäferdiek, 'Herkunft' 251-253.
62. Cf. on this K. Schäferdiek, 'Herkunft' 253f.
63. See above, p. 156.
64. Aurelio de Santos Otero, *Die handschriftliche Überlieferung der altslawischen Apokryphen* I (PTS 20), 1978, 98.
65. See above, pp. 154f.
66. See below, p. 206, note 27.
67. Junod/Kaestli 139f.; numbering of lines after Domitien de Bruyne's edition: 'Epistula Titi, discipuli Pauli, de dispositione sanctimonii', *Revue Bénédictine* 27, 1925, 47-72.
68. Cf. Junod/Kaestli 140-145.
69. See above, pp. 87f.
70. See above, p. 155.
71. *Virtutes Johannis* IV (Junod/Kaestli 803-814).
72. *Virtutes Johannis* IX (Junod/Kaestli 827-832).
73. On the relation of the *Passio* and the *Virtutes*, see K. Schäferdiek, 'Passio' (as p. 168, note 23).
74. Cf. Junod/Kaestli 790-793.
75. See above, p. 154.
76. Cf. on this M. McNamara, *The Apocrypha in the Irish Church*, Dublin 1975, 95-98; Junod/Kaestli 109-136. Text: 'Beatha Eoin Bruinne', ed. Gearóid Mac Niocaill, in *Eigse* 7, 1955, 248-253 (= Part II) and 8, 1956, 222-230 (= Part I); translation of the passages which can be traced back to the Acts of John below, pp. 210-213.
77. II 1-9; *Eigse* 7, 249f.
78. I 1-8; *Eigse* 8, 223-225. II 10-19; *Eigse* 7, 250-253.
79. I 9-11; *Eigse* 8, 225f.; see below, pp. 210f.
80. I 12f.; *Eigse* 8, 226f.; see below, pp. 211f.
81. Evodius of Uzala, *de Fide contra Manich.* 40, ed. J. Zycha (CSEL 25.2) 970.31-971.2.
82. *Passio Johannis*, Fabricius 606-616; PG 5, cols. 1243B-1247A; taken up verbatim *Virtutes Johannis* VIf., Junod/Kaestli 816-823: two brothers sell their property for the benefit of the poor and attach themselves to John, but then regret their action. John transforms sticks and stones into gold and jewels for them, but with the support of a dead man raised by him leads them to see that they have thus exchanged the true spiritual riches for worthless earthly goods, and after their repentance changes the gold and jewels back again.
83. Symeon Metaphrastes, *Hypomnem. in Joh. Apost.* VI, PG 116, cols 701d-704A (cf. Menaion for 26 Sept.: Synaxarion Ecclesiae Constantinopolitanae, ed. H. Delehaye, AASS LXII, Propyl. Nov., cols. 81.18-82.10); Michel van Esbroeck, 'Les Acta Iohannis traduits par Euthyme l'Hagiorite', *Bedi Kartlisa* 33, 1975, 73-109, esp. 106-108 (c. 187-192 of van Esbroeck's

division). Here the motifs of the suicide miraculously prevented and the transformation of worthless material into gold are combined into the story of a Christian who in the face of economic ruin seeks to take his life but is delivered (without John's intervention), and then is freed by John from his financial embarrassment also by the changing of grass or hay into gold. We should probably not rule out the possibility that here as in the *Passio Johannis* (see note 82) we have a completely free use of a motif originally deriving from the Acts of John.

84. I 14; *Eigse* 8, 227; see below, p. 212.

85. See above, p. 157f.

86. Cf. above, p. 158f.

87. On this collection see Ignazio Guidi, 'Gli atti apocrifi degli Apostoli nei testi copti, arabi ed etiopici', *Giornale della Società Asiatica Italiana* 2, 1888, 1-66; cf. Françoise Morard, 'Notes sur le recueil copte des Actes apocryphes des Apôtres', *Revue de Théologie et de Philosophie* 113, 1981, 403-413 (without consideration of the Bohairic manuscript).

88. Published from a late manuscript by E.I. Demina, *Tichonravoskij Damaskin* II, Sofia 1971, 81-88; see on this A. de Santos Otero, p. 435 below.

89. Cf. on this Junod/Kaestli 581-586.

90. Junod/Kaestli 586-589.

91 Junod/Kaestli 581; cf. pp. 566f and 198, note 1.

92. See now the examination of the internal structure of the AJ by G. Sirker-Wicklaus.

93. Junod/Kaestli 566f.

94. Cf. on this K. Schäferdiek, 'Herkunft' 256-261.

95. On this passage cf. also D.L. Cartlidge, 'Transfigurations'.

96. Junod/Kaestli 589-632.

97. Cf. on this also Norbert Brox, '"Doketismus" - eine Problemanzeige', ZKG 95, 1984, 301-314, esp. 309-311.

98. Cf. Act. Thom. 53; K. Schäferdiek, 'Herkunft' 250.

99. AJ 88: call of the pairs of brothers, Andrew and Peter, James and John (Mk. 1:16-20; Mt. 4:18-22); AJ 89f.: the disciple whom Jesus loved - identified with John - lying in his bosom (Jn. 13:23, 25; 20:2); AJ 90: the Transfiguration (Mk. 9:2f.; Mt. 7:1f.; Lk. 9.28f.); AJ 93: Jesus invited 'by one of the Pharisees' (cf. Lk. 7:36; 11:37); the motif of the multiplication of the loaves is closely appended, but in a wholly different situation from the corresponding pericopae in the Gospels.

100. AJ 97: '(a) I am being crucified (b) and pierced with lances and reeds (c) and given vinegar and gall to drink.' Here (b) looks like a combination of Jn. 19:34: 'pierced his side with a spear', and Gos. Pet. 9: 'nudged him with a reed' (cf. Mk. 15:19; Mt. 27:30), and (c) corresponds to the Diatessaron text presupposed by Ephraem Syrus (see below, p. 207, note 37); but cf. also Barn. 7.3: 'he was given vinegar and gall to drink', and Gos. Pet. 16: 'Give him to drink gall and vinegar' (the connection here with Ps. 68:22 LXX probably was not noticed by the author of AJ 97 and the redactor of the Acts). Jn. 19:34 appears to have influenced 'that blood flowed from me' in AJ 101.

101. Eric Junod, 'Polymorphie du dieu sauveur': *Gnosticisme et monde hellénistique* (Publications de l'Institut Orientaliste de Louvain 27), Louvain-la-Neuve 1982, 38-46; cf. Junod/Kaestli 469-474.

102. See below, p. 208, note 67.

103. AJ 111.18 of the Sahidic version of the Metastasis, ed. Junod/Kaestli 391: (upper) garment with trimming (or fringes) on both sides.

104. Cf. Junod/Kaestli 694f.

105. Ibid. 682-687.

106. Ibid. 695.

107. Cf. Walter Bauer, *Rechtgläubigkeit und Ketzerei*, 2nd ed. rev. G. Strecker (BHTh 10), 1964, 25f. (ET *Orthodoxy and Heresy*, 1971, 20f.).

The Acts of John[1]

The beginning of the Acts of John is lost. The numbering of the chapters beginning with c. 18 goes back to Maximilian Bonnet's edition (Aa II 1, 1898; reprinted 1959), which set two later texts before the fragments of the ancient Acts of John: first, as cc. 1-14, in two recensions, the 'Acts of John in Rome', which came into being as an independent narrative not before the 4th century (new edition with introduction and French translation in Junod/Kaestli 835-886); and second, as cc. 14 (second recension) - 17* (Bonnet 159.24-30; 160.8-36), a transitional passage between the narrative of the Patmos exile from the later Acts of John of ps.-Prochorus (cf. below, pp. 429ff.) and the 'Metastasis' (cc. 106-115) of the ancient Acts of John.

It must remain an open question whether the lost beginning of the document, in correspondence with the apostle's personal reminiscences in c. 113, went back as far as his call by Christ. In any case it must have reported on his journey - probably from Jerusalem - to Miletus, and his sojourn there, and of the persons named in c.18 at least Demonicus and the wife of Marcellus must have been mentioned. It is not inconceivable that the apostle's departure for Asia Minor was related in the context of a report about an assignment of mission areas.[2] Probably the narrator, who frequently speaks in the 'we'-style, introduced himself at the beginning of the document, presumably under the name of Leucius, a fictitious disciple of John (see above, pp. 92ff.).

From Miletus to Ephesus

18. Now John was hastening to Ephesus, prompted by a vision; so that Demonicus and his kinsman Aristodemus and a very wealthy (man named) Cleobius and the wife of Marcellus prevailed upon him with some difficulty to remain for one day at Miletus and rested with him. And when they departed very early in the morning and some four miles of their journey were already accomplished, a voice came from heaven in the hearing of us all, saying 'John, you shall give glory to your Lord in Ephesus, (glory) of which you shall know, both you and all your brothers that are with you and some of those in that place who shall believe through you.' Then John joyfully considered with himself what was to happen at Ephesus, saying, 'Lord, behold I go according to thy will. Thy will be done.'

First Stay in Ephesus (Chapters 19-55)
Raising of Cleopatra and Lycomedes

19. And as we approached the city Lycomedes met us, a wealthy man who was praetor of the Ephesians; and he fell at John's feet and entreated him, saying 'Is your name John? The God whom you preach has sent you to help my wife who has been paralysed for the past seven days and is lying there unable to be cured. But glorify your God by healing her, and have pity upon

us. For while I was considering with myself what conclusion to draw *from this* someone came to me and said. "Lycomedes, enough of this thought which besets you, for it is harmful. Do not submit to it! For I have had compassion on my servant Cleopatra and have sent from Miletus a man named John, who will raise her up and restore her to you in good health." Do not delay then, servant of God who has revealed you to me; come quickly to my wife, who is only just breathing.' Then John went at once, and the brothers who were with him, and Lycomedes, from the gate to his house. But Cleobius said to his servants, 'Go to my kinsman Callippus and let him give you a comfortable lodging - for I am coming there with his son - so that we may find everything convenient.'

20. But when Lycomedes came with John into the house in which the woman was lying, he grasped his feet again and said 'See, my Lord, this faded beauty; look at her youth; look at the famous flower(-like grace) of my poor wife, at which all Ephesus was amazed! Wretched man, I am the victim of envy. I am humbled, my enemies' eye has fallen upon me! I have never wronged anyone, although I could have injured many, for I had just this in view and was on my guard, so as not to see any evil or misfortune like this. What use then, Cleopatra, was my care? What have I gained by being known as a pious man until today? I suffer worse than an impious (man) seeing you, Cleopatra, lying there so. The sun in its course shall no more see me, if you *are no longer (my) companion*[3]. I will go before you, Cleopatra, and despatch myself from life. I will not spare my vigorous health, though it be still youthful. I will defend myself before Justice,[4] as one that has served (her) justly, for it is permissible to indict her for judging unjustly. I will call her to account when I come (before her) a (mere) phantom of life. I will say to her "You have done violence to my light (of life) by tearing away Cleopatra; you have made me a dead man by bringing this upon me; you have forced me to anger Providence by cutting off my joy."'

21. And Lycomedes still speaking to Cleopatra approached her bed and lamented with a loud voice.

But John pulled him away and said, 'Cease from these lamentations and from these unfitting words of yours. It is not proper to mistrust him who appeared to you. Know that you will receive your consort again. Stand then with us, who have come on her behalf, and pray to the God whom you saw manifesting me through dreams. What is it, then, Lycomedes? You too must wake up and open your soul. Cast off this heavy sleep of yours! Call on the Lord, entreat him for your consort and he will revive her.' But he fell upon the ground and lamented with all his soul.[5]

John therefore said with tears, 'Alas for the fresh betrayal of my vision! Alas for the fresh temptation that is prepared for me! Alas for the fresh contrivance of him that is contriving against me! The voice from heaven that came to me on the way, did it intend this for me? Did it forewarn me of this that must happen here, *betraying* me to this great crowd of citizens because of Lycomedes? The man lies there lifeless, and I know very well that they will not let me leave the house alive. Why tarriest thou, Lord? Why hast thou withdrawn from us thy gracious promise? No, Lord, I pray thee; do not let him exult who delights in the misfortunes of others; do not let him dance who is always deriding us! But let thy holy name and thy mercy make haste! Raise up the two dead who (have brought enmity) against me!'

22. And while John was crying aloud the city of the Ephesians came running together to the house of Lycomedes, (supposing him) dead. But John, seeing the great crowd that had come together, said to the Lord, 'Now is the time of refreshment[6] and of confidence in thee, O Christ. Now is the time for us who are sick to have help from thee, O physican that healest for nothing. Keep thou my entrance to this place free from derision. I pray thee, Jesus, help this great multitude to come to thee who art Lord of the universe. Look at the affliction, look at those who lie here! Do thou prepare, even from those gathered here, holy vessels for thy service, when they have seen thy gracious gift. For thou thyself hast said, O Christ, "Ask, and it shall be given you."[7] We therefore ask of thee, O King, not gold or silver, not substance or possessions, nor any of the perishable things upon earth, but two souls, through whom thou shalt convert <those who shall believe> to thy way (and) to thy teaching, to thy confidence, to thine excellent promise; for some of them shall be saved when they learn thy power through the resurrection of (these) who are lifeless. So now thyself grant hope in thee. I am going, then, to Cleopatra and say, "Arise in the name of Jesus Christ."'

23. And he went to her and touched her face and said 'Cleopatra, he speaks to thee, whom every ruler fears, and every creature, power, abyss and all darkness, and unsmiling death, the height of heaven and the circles of hell, the resurrection of the dead and the sight of the blind, the whole power of the prince of this world and the pride of its ruler: Arise (he says), and be not an excuse for many who wish to disbelieve, and an affliction to souls that are able to hope and be saved.' And Cleopatra cried out at once with a loud voice, 'I arise, Master, save thou thy Cleopatra.'

And when she had arisen after seven days, the city of the Ephesians was stirred at that amazing sight.

But Cleopatra asked after her husband Lycomedes. But John said to her, 'Cleopatra, keep your soul unmoved and unwavering, and then you shall have Lycomedes your husband standing here with you, <. . . > if indeed you are not disturbed nor shaken by what has happened, but have come to believe in my God, who through me shall give him back to you) alive. Come then with me to your other bedroom, and you shall see him dead (indeed), but rising again through the power of my God.' 24. And when Cleopatra came with John into her bedroom and saw Lycomedes dead on her account she lost her voice, and ground her teeth and bit her tongue, and closed her eyes, raining down tears; and she quietly attended to the Apostle.

But John had pity upon Cleopatra when he saw her neither raging nor distraught, and called upon the perfect and condescending mercy, and said, 'Lord Jesus Christ, thou seest (her) distress, thou seest (her) need, thou seest Cleopatra crying out her soul in silence; for she contains within her the intolerable raging (of her sorrow). My soul foretells, Lord; I know that for Lycomedes' sake she will follow him to death.' And she quietly said to John, 'That is in my mind, Master, and nothing else.' Then the Apostle went up to the couch on which Lycomedes lay, and taking Cleopatra's hand he said, 'Cleopatra, because of the crowd that is present, and because of your relatives who have come here also, speak with a loud voice to your husband and say, "Rise up and glorify the name of God, since to the dead he gives (back) the dead."' And she went near and spoke to her husband as she was instructed, and immediately raised him up. And he arose and fell to the ground and kissed John's feet; but he lifted him up and said 'It is not my feet, man, that you should kiss, but those of God in whose power you both have been raised up.'

25. But Lycomedes said to John, 'I beg and entreat you in God's name through whom you raised us up, to stay with us, both you and your companions <. . . >.' Likewise Cleopatra grasped his feet and said the same. But John said to them, 'Tomorrow I will be with you.' And they said to him again, 'There is no hope for us in your God, but we shall have been raised in vain, if you do not stay with us.' And Cleobius together with Aristodemus and also Demonicus in distress of soul said to John, 'Let us stay with them, that they may stay free of offence before the Lord.' And he remained there with the brethren.

The Portrait of John

26. Then there came together a great gathering of people because of John. And while he was addressing those who were present Lycomedes, who had a friend who was a skilful painter, went running to him and said, 'You see how I have hurried to come to you: come quickly to my house and paint the man whom I show you without his knowing it.' And the painter, giving someone the necessary implements and colours, said to Lycomedes, 'Show me the man and for the rest have no anxiety.' Then Lycomedes pointed out John to the painter, and brought him near and shut him up in a room from which the Apostle of Christ could be seen. <And Lycomedes> was with the blessed man, feasting upon the faith and the knowledge of our God, and rejoiced even more because he was going to have him in a portrait.

27. So on the first day the painter drew his outline and went away; but on the next day he painted him in with his colours, and so delivered the portrait to Lycomedes, to his great joy; and he <took it>, put it in his bedroom and put

garlands on it; so that when John later noticed (something), he said to him, 'My dear child, what is it you are doing when you come from the bath into your bedroom alone? Am I not to pray with you and with the other brethren? Or are you hiding (something) from us?' And saying this and joking with him he went into the bedroom; and he saw there a portrait of an old man crowned with garlands, and lamps beside it and altars in front. And he called him and said, 'Lycomedes, what does this portrait mean to you? Is it one of your gods that is painted here? Why, I see you are still living as a pagan!' And Lycomedes answered him 'He alone is my God who raised me up from death with my wife. But if besides that God we may call our earthly benefactors gods, you are the one painted in the portrait, whom I crown and love and reverence, as having become a good guide to me.'

28. Then John, who had never beheld his own face, said to him, 'You are teasing me, child; am I such in form? By your Lord, how can you persuade me that the portrait is like me?' And Lycomedes brought him a mirror, and when he had seen himself in the mirror and gazed at the portrait, he said, 'As the Lord Jesus Christ liveth, the portrait is like me; yet not like me, my child, but like my image in the flesh; for if this painter who has copied this face of mine wants to put me in a picture, *let him break away* <from> colours such as are given to me now,[8] from boards, from outline and drapery (?), from shape <and> form, from age and youth, and from all that is visible.

29. But do you be a good painter for me, Lycomedes. You have colours which he gives you through me, that is, Jesus, who paints us all for himself, who knows the shapes and forms and figures and dispositions and types of our souls. And these are the colours which I tell you to paint with: faith in God, knowledge (*gnosis*), reverence, kindness, fellowship, mildness, goodness, brotherly love, purity, sincerity, tranquillity, fearlessness, cheerfulness, dignity and the whole band of colours which portray your soul and already raise up your members that were cast down and level those that were lifted up, < . . . > which cure your bruises and heal your wounds and arrange your tangled hair and wash your face and instruct your eyes and cleanse your heart and purge your belly and cut off that which is below it; in brief, when a full blend and mixture of such colours has come together into your soul it will present it to our Lord Jesus Christ indelible, well-polished and firmly shaped. But what you have now done is childish and imperfect; you have drawn a dead likeness of a dead man < . . . >.'

Healing of the Old Women

30. Then he commanded Verus, the brother who attended him, to bring the old women (that were) in the whole of Ephesus, and he and Cleopatra and Lycomedes made preparations to care for them. So Verus came and said to

him: 'John, out of the old women over sixty that are here, I have found only four in good bodily health; of the rest, some are paralytic, others deaf, some arthritic and others sick with divers diseases.' And John on hearing this kept silence for a long time; then he rubbed his face and said, 'Oh, what slackness among the people of Ephesus! What a collapse, what weakness towards God! O devil, what a mockery you have made all this time of the faithful at Ephesus! Jesus, who gives me grace and the gift of confidence in him, says to me now in silence, "Send for the old women who are sick, and be with them in the theatre and through me heal them; for there are some of those who come to this spectacle whom I will convert through such healings as have been beneficial."'

31. Now when the whole crowd had come together to Lycomedes on John's account, he dismissed them all, saying, 'Come tomorrow into the theatre, all you who wish to see the power of God!' And on the next day the crowds came together into the theatre while it was still night, so that the proconsul heard of it and came quickly and took his seat with all the people. And a certain Andronicus who was praetor, and was the leading citizen of Ephesus at that time, spread the story that John had promised what was impossible and incredible. 'But if he can do any such thing as I hear', he said, 'let him come naked into the public theatre, when it is open, holding nothing in his hands; neither let him name that magical name which I have heard him pronounce.'

32. So when John heard this and was disturbed by these words, he commanded the old women to be brought into the theatre. And when they were all brought into the midst, some lying on beds and others in a torpor, and when the city had come running together, a great silence ensued; then John opened his mouth and began to say,

33. 'Men of Ephesus, you must first know why I am visiting your city <. . . >, or what is this great confidence of mine towards you,[9] (which is) so great that it is evident to you all in this general assembly. I have been sent, then, on no human mission, nor on a useless journey; nor am I a merchant that makes bargains or exchanges; but Jesus Christ, whom I preach, in his mercy and goodness is converting you all, you who are held fast in unbelief and enslaved by shameful desires; and through me he wills to deliver you from your error; and by his power I will convict even your praetor's disbelief, by raising up these women who are lying before you - you see what a state and what sicknesses they are in. And this is not possible for me now <. . . > if they *perish* (?) < . . . >, and will be removed by healings (?).'

34. But this I wish first to sow in your ears, that you take heed for your souls, which is the reason for my coming to you <. . . >. Do not expect that this time is eternal, which is (the time of) the yoke, nor lay up treasures on earth, where everything withers away <. . . >. Do not think, if children come to you, to rest in them; and do not try for their sakes to rob and to swindle. <. . . > Do not be grieved, you who are poor, if you have not (the means) to serve your pleasures;

for even those who have them, when they fall ill, pronounce (you) happy. And do not rejoice in possessing much wealth, you who are rich; for by possessing these things you provide for yourselves a constant distress if you lose them, and again *while you have them* you are afraid that someone may attack you because of them.

35. But you who are proud of your handsome figure and give haughty looks, you shall see the end of this promise in the grave. And you who delight in adultery, be sure that law and nature alike take vengeance on you, and conscience before these. And you, adulterous woman, who rebel against the law, you know not where you will end. You who give nothing to the needy, although you have money put away, when you depart from this body and are burning in fire, begging for mercy, will have no one to pity you. And you, hot-tempered and savage man, be sure that you are living like the brute beasts. And you, drunkard and trouble-maker, must learn that you are out of your senses when you are enslaved to a shameful and filthy desire.

36. You who delight in gold and ivory and jewels, do you see your loved (possessions) when night comes on? And you who give way to soft clothing, and then depart from life, will these things be useful in the place where you are going? And *let* the murderer *know* that the punishment he has earned awaits him in double measure after he leaves this (world). So also the poisoner, sorcerer, robber, swindler, and sodomite, the thief and all of this band, guided by your deeds you shall come to unquenchable fire[10] and utter darkness and the pit of torments and eternal doom. So, men of Ephesus, change your ways; for you know this also, that kings, rulers, tyrants, boasters and warmongers shall go naked from this world and come to eternal misery and torment.'

So saying, John healed all (their) diseases through the power of God.

* * *

The summary statement of the last sentence of c. 36 covers the disappearance of a considerable section. It must have concluded the story of the healing of the old women. Moreover a fairly lengthy narrative concerned with Drusiana and Andronicus can be inferred to have stood in this lost section. Andronicus is mentioned for the first time in c. 31, where he figures as an unbeliever; he appears next in c. 37, but now as a loyal disciple of John. The lost section, therefore, must have told of his conversion, and indeed in a fairly lengthy narrative, as a number of surviving indications show. A prayer by Drusiana in c. 82 contains some personal reminiscences, including in what is evidently meant to be chronological order: 1) Christ allowed her to see signs and wonders; 2) he made her a partaker of his name; 3) he revealed himself to her as one of many forms, and had mercy on her in manifold ways; 4) he protected her from violence from her consort Andronicus; 5) he made the latter become a brother to her; 6) he has kept her pure since then; 7) he raised her from death through John; 8) he caused Callimachus to undergo a change of heart; 9) he gave to Drusiana the true rest. Points 6-9 in this list relate to the immediate context of c. 82, the story of Drusiana and Callimachus (cc. 63-86), but points 1-5 must refer to something further back. Additional light falls on point 4 through a reference in c. 63. Callimachus, who is seeking to ensnare Drusiana in carnal love, is told by his friends: 'It is impossible for you to win this woman, for she has long ago separated even from her husband for the sake of piety. Are you the only one who does not know that Andronicus, who formerly was not the god-fearing man he is now, shut her into a sepulchre, saying "Either I must have you as the wife whom I had before, or you must die!" And . . . she chose to die, rather than commit that abominable act.' This can be supplemented by three allusions in the Manichean Psalm-book which can be traced back to the Acts of John. In one of the 'Psalms of Heracleides' it is said: 'A [woman] that loves her master is Drusiana, the lover of God, shut up for fourteen days, seeking her apostle',[11] and in one of the 'pilgrim psalms': 'Even so the blessed Drusiana, she too endured the like, imprisoned fourteen days, like her master, her apostle';[12] a few lines earlier it was said of John that he was 'imprisoned fourteen days, that he might die of hunger'.[13] Finally, the 'preaching of the Gospel' in the Acts of John (cc. 87-105) starts with a narrative in which Drusiana says: 'The Lord appeared to me in the tomb like John, and as a young man' (c. 87), a statement which cannot be related to the events in the Drusiana-Callimachus story, which also took place in a sepulchre, but can be linked very well with point 3 of the reminiscences in c. 82. Finally, at the close of the 'preaching of the Gospel' John speaks of God as the one who hears all, 'and now also myself and Drusiana, being the God of those who are imprisoned' (c. 103).

From this we may deduce the following narrative complex, no longer extant: impressed by John's preaching and its powerful signs, Drusiana is converted and turns herself completely to sexual continence, so that she denies herself to her husband Andronicus. He finally shuts her up in a sepulchre, in order to compel her to give up this vow of chastity or leave her to die, and evidently at the same time brings about the imprisonment of John also, with the intention of letting him starve to death. The deliverance of both is brought about in miraculous fashion, after Drusiana at least has experienced an appearance of Christ both in the form of the apostle and in that of a young man. The conversion of Andronicus appears to have taken place in the same context, and he now as Drusiana's 'brother' turns to a life of abstinence in the same way as she does.[14] The 'preaching of the Gospel', which twice refers back to this complex, was then attached directly to it. The numbering as cc. 87-105 comes from M. Bonnet's edition, in which it was erroneously placed after the Drusiana-Callimachus story (cc. 63-86). Despite the necessary alteration in the order of the text, this numbering has been preserved on practical grounds, as already in the third and fourth German editions of this work and the earlier editions of its English translation as well as in the Junod/Kaestli edition.

John's Preaching of the Gospel (cc. 87-105)[15]

Introduction to the Preaching

87. Now those that were present enquired the cause, and were especially perplexed, because Drusiana had said, 'The Lord appeared to me in the tomb like John and as a young man.' So since they were perplexed and in some ways

not yet established in the faith, John *took* it patiently and said, (88) 'Men and brethren, you have experienced nothing strange or incredible in your perception of the <Lord>, since even we whom he chose to be his apostles have suffered many temptations; and I cannot <either> speak or write to you the things which I have seen and heard. Yet now I must adapt myself to your hearing and according to each man's capacity I will impart to you those things of which you can be hearers, that you may see the glory which surrounds him, which was and is both now and evermore.

The Christ of many forms

For when he had chosen Peter and Andrew, who were brothers, he came to me and to my brother James, saying "I need you; come to me!"[16] And my brother <when he heard> this said: "John, what does he want, this child on the shore who called us?" And I said, "Which child?" And he answered me, "The one who is beckoning to us." And I replied: "Because of the long watch we have kept at sea, you are not seeing well, brother James. Do you not see the man standing there who is handsome, fair and cheerful-looking?" But he said to me, "I do not see that man, my brother. But let us go, and we shall see what this means.' And when we had brought the boat *to land* we saw how he also helped us to beach the boat. 89. And as we left the place, wishing to follow him, he appeared to me again as rather bald-<headed> but with a thick flowing beard, but to James as a young man whose beard was just beginning. So we were both puzzled about the meaning of what we had seen. Then as we followed him we became gradually <more> perplexed as we considered the matter.

But then there appeared to me a yet more amazing sight; I tried to see him as he was, and I never saw his eyes closing, but always open. But he sometimes appeared to me as a small man with no good looks, and also as wholly looking up to heaven (?). And he had another strange (property); when I reclined at table he would take me to his breast,[17] and I held <him> to me; and sometimes his breast felt to me smooth and soft, but sometimes hard like rock; so that I was perplexed in my (mind) and said: "What does <*> this mean?" And as I thought about it, he . . .

90. Another time he took me and James and Peter to the mountain where he used to pray, and we saw <on> him a light[18] such that a man who uses mortal speech cannot describe what it was like. Again he took us three likewise up the mountain, saying "Come with me." And again we went; and we saw him at a distance praying. Then I, since he loved me,[19] went quietly up to him, as if he [.] could not see, and stood looking [.] at his hinder parts; and I saw him not dressed in clothes at all, but stripped of those <which> we (usually) saw (upon him), and not like a man at all. (And I saw that) his feet [.] were whiter than snow, so that the ground there was lit up by his feet; and that his head stretched

up to heaven, so that I was afraid and cried out; and he, turning about, appeared as a small man and caught hold of my beard and pulled it and said to me, "John, do not be faithless, but believing,[20] and not inquisitive." And I said to him, "Why, Lord, what have I done?" But I tell you, my brethren, that I suffered such pain for thirty days in the place where he touched my beard, that I said to him, "Lord, if your playful tug has caused such pain, what (would it be) if you had dealt me a blow?" And he said to me, "Let it be your (concern) from now on not to tempt him that cannot be tempted."

91. But Peter and James were vexed as I spoke with the Lord, and beckoned me to come to them, leaving the Lord alone. And I went, and they both said to me "The old man who spoke with the Lord on the (mountain-) top, who was he? For we heard them both speaking." And when I considered his abundant grace and his unity within many faces and his unceasing wisdom that looks after us, I said, "You shall learn this from him if you ask him."

92. And again when we - that is, all his disciples - were sleeping in one house at Gennesaret, I wrapped myself in my cloak and watched by myself (to see) what he was doing. And first I heard him say, "John, go to sleep." Then I pretended to sleep; and I saw another like him [.], and I heard him also saying to my Lord, "Jesus, the men you have chosen still disbelieve you." And my Lord said to him, "You are right; for they are men."

93. I will tell you another glory, brethren; sometimes when I meant to touch him I encountered a material, solid body; but at other times again when I felt him, his substance was immaterial and incorporeal, and as if it did not exist at all.

And if ever he were invited by one of the Pharisees and went (where) he was invited,[21] we went with him; and each one of us received one appointed loaf from those who invited us, and he also would take one; but he would bless his and divide it among us; and every man was satisfied by that little (piece),[22] and our own loaves were kept intact, so that those who had invited him were amazed.

And I often wished, as I walked with him, to see if his footprint appeared on the ground - for I saw him raising himself from the earth - and I never saw it. And (the following) too I tell you, my brethren, so as to encourage your faith in him - for his miracles and wonderful works must not be told for the moment, for they are unspeakable and, perhaps, can neither be uttered nor heard:

The Hymn of Christ[23]

94. Before he was arrested[24] by the lawless Jews, whose lawgiver is the lawless serpent, he assembled us all and said, "Before I am delivered to them,[25] let us sing a hymn to the Father, and so go to meet[26] what lies before (us)." So he told us to form a circle, holding one another's hands, and himself stood in the middle and said, "Answer Amen to me." So he began to sing a hymn and to say,[27]

"Glory be to thee, Father."
And we circled round him and answered him, "Amen."
"Glory be to thee, Logos:
Glory be to thee, Grace." - "Amen."
"Glory be to thee, Spirit:
Glory be to thee, Holy One:
Glory be to thy Glory." - "Amen."
"We praise thee, Father:
We thank thee, Light:
In whom darkness dwelleth not."[28] - "Amen."

"And why we give thanks, I tell you:
"I will be saved,[28a]
And I will save." - "Amen."
"I will be loosed,
And I will loose." - "Amen."
"I will be wounded,
And I will wound." - "Amen."
"I will be born,
And I will bear." - "Amen."
"I will eat,
And I will be eaten." - "Amen."
"I will hear,
And I will be heard." - "Amen."
"I will be thought,
Being wholly thought." - "Amen."
"I will be washed,
And I will wash." - "Amen."

Grace dances.
"I will pipe,
Dance, all of you." - "Amen."
"I will mourn,
Beat you all your breasts (κόπτεσθαι)[29] - "Amen".
"(The) one Ogdoad
sings praises with us." - "Amen."
"The twelfth number
dances on high." - "Amen."
"To the All
it belongs to dance in the height(?)" - "Amen."
"He who does not dance
does not know what happens." - "Amen."

"I will flee,
and I will remain." - "Amen."
"I will adorn (κοσμεῖν),
and I will be adorned." - "Amen."
"I will be united,
and I will unite." - "Amen."
"I have no house,
and I have houses." - "Amen."
"I have no place,
and I have places." - "Amen."
"I have no temple
and I have temples." - "Amen."
"I am a lamp to you (sing.)
who see me." - "Amen."
"I am a mirror to you
who know me." - "Amen."
"I am a door[30] to you
<who> knock on me." - "Amen."
"I am a way[31] to you
<the> traveller." - "Amen."

Now if you follow
my dance,
see yourself
in Me who am speaking,
and when you have seen what I do,
keep silence about my mysteries.
You who dance, consider
what I do, for yours is
this passion of Man
which I am to suffer.
For you could by no means
have understood what you suffer
unless to you as Logos
I had been sent by the Father.
You who saw what I do
saw (me) as suffering,
and seeing it you did not stay
but were wholly moved.
Being moved towards wisdom (?)
you have me as a support (*lit.* couch);
rest in me.

Who I am, you shall know
    when I go forth.
What I now am seen to be,
    that I am not;
What I am you shall see
    when you come.
If you knew how to suffer
    you would be able not to suffer.
Learn how to suffer
    and you shall be able not to suffer
What you do not know
    I myself will teach you.
I am your God,
    not (the God) of the traitor.
I will that holy souls
    be made in harmony with me.
Understand the word
    of wisdom!
Say again to me,
Glory be to thee, Father
    Glory be to thee, Logos,
        Glory be to thee, [.] Spirit." - "Amen."
"As for me,
    if you would understand *what I was*:
By the Logos I [.] made a jest (παίζειν) of everything
    and was not *made a jest*[32] at all.
I exulted: (*lit.* leaped)
    but do you understand the whole,
and when you have understood it, say,
    Glory be to thee, Father." - "Amen."

Revelation of the Mystery of the Cross

97. After the Lord had so danced with us, my beloved, he went out. And we, like men amazed or fast asleep, fled one this way and another that. And so I saw him suffer, and did not wait by his suffering, but fled to the Mount of Olives and wept at what had come to pass. And when he was hung (upon the Cross) on the Friday[33] at the sixth hour of the day,[34] there came a darkness over the whole earth.[35] And my Lord stood in the middle of the cave and giving light to me said: "John, for the people below in Jerusalem I am being crucified and pierced with lances and reeds[36] and given vinegar and gall to drink.[37] But to you I am speaking, and listen to what I speak.[38] I put into your mind to come up to

this mountain so that you may hear what a disciple should learn from his teacher and a man from God."

98.[39]And when he had said this he showed me a Cross of Light brought to a fixed shape, and around the Cross a great crowd, which had no single form; and in it (the Cross) was one form and the same likeness. And I saw the Lord himself above the Cross, having no shape but only a kind of voice; yet not that voice which we knew, but one that was sweet and gentle and truly (the voice) of God, which said to me, "John, there must (be) one man (to) hear these things from me; for I need one who is ready to hear. This Cross of Light is sometimes called Logos[40] by me for your sakes, sometimes mind, sometimes Christ, sometimes a door,[41] sometimes a way,[42] sometimes bread,[43] sometimes seed,[44] sometimes resurrection,[45] sometimes Son, sometimes Father, sometimes Spirit, sometimes life,[46] sometimes truth,[47] sometimes faith, sometimes grace;[48] and so (it is called) for men's sake.

But what it truly is, as known in itself and spoken to you, (is this): it is the the delimitation of all things and the strong uplifting of what is firmly fixed out of what is unstable, and the harmony of wisdom. Now when wisdom is in harmony, there are those of the right and of the left, powers, authorities, principalities [and] demons, activities, threatenings, passions, calumnies, Satan and the inferior root from which <the> nature of transient things proceeded.

99. This Cross then, which has made all things stable through the Logos and separated off what is transitory and inferior, and then has poured itself (?) into everything, is not that wooden Cross which you will see when you go down from here; nor am I the (man) who is on the Cross, (I) whom now you do not see but only hear (my) voice. I was taken to be what I am not, I who am not what for the many I am; but what they will say of me is mean and unworthy of me. Since then the place of rest is neither (to be) seen nor told, much more shall I, the Lord of this (place), be neither seen <nor told>.

100. The multitude around the Cross that is <not> of one form is the inferior nature. As for those whom you see in the Cross, if they do not have a single form, not every member of him who came down has yet been gathered together. But when human nature is taken up, and the race that comes to me and obeys[49] my voice, then he who now hears me shall be united with it and shall no longer be what he now is, but (shall be) above *them*(?) as I am now. For so long as you do not call yourself mine, I am not what I was; but if you hear me, you also who hear shall be as I am, and I shall be what I was, when [. . .]. Therefore ignore the many and despise those who are outside the mystery; for you must know that I am wholly with the Father, and the Father with me.[50]

101. So then I have suffered none of those things which they will say of me; even that suffering which I showed to you and to the rest in my dance, I will that it be called a mystery. For what you are you see, I have shown it to you; but what I am is known to me alone and to no one else. So let me have what

is mine; what is yours you must see through me; but to see me truly is, as I said, not possible, except for what you are able to know, being a kinsman. You hear that I suffered, yet I suffered not; and that I suffered not, yet I did suffer; and that I was pierced,[51] yet I was not lashed; that I was hanged, yet I was not hanged; that blood flowed from me,[52] yet it did not flow; and, in a word, that what they say of me, I did not endure, but what they do not say, those things I did suffer. Now what these are, I secretly show you; for I know that you will understand. You must know me, then, as the *torment* of the Logos, the piercing of the Logos, the blood of the Logos, the wounding of the Logos, the hanging of the Logos, the suffering of the Logos, the fastening of the Logos, the death of the Logos. And so I speak, having made room for the man. The first then (that) you must know (is) the Logos; then you shall know the Lord, and thirdly the man, and what he has suffered."

102. When he had said these things to me, and others which I know not how to say as he wills, he was taken up,[53] without any of the multitude seeing him. And going down I laughed at them all when they told me what they had said about him; and I held this one thing fast in my (mind), that the Lord had performed everything as a symbol and a dispensation for the conversion and salvation of man.

Concluding Admonitions

103. Now, my brothers, since we have seen the grace of the Lord and his affection towards us, let us worship him, since we have obtained mercy from him; not with (our) fingers, nor with (our) mouths nor with (our) tongue nor with any bodily organ at all, but with the disposition of our soul [. . .]. And let us watch, since he is at hand even now in prisons for our sakes, and in tombs, in bonds and dungeons, in reproaches and insults, by sea and on dry land, in torments, condemnations, conspiracies, plots and punishments; in a word, he is with all of us, and with the sufferers he suffers himself. Brethren, if he is called upon by any of us he does not hold out against hearing us, but being everywhere he hears us all, and now also myself and Drusiana, being the God of those who are imprisoned, *bringing* us help through his own compassion.

104. You therefore, beloved, (must) also be persuaded, that it is not a man that I exhort you to worship, but God unchangeable, God invincible, God who is higher than all authority and all power and older and stronger than all angels and (all) that are called (*) creatures and all aeons. So if you hold fast to this and are built up in this, you shall possess your soul indestructible.'

105. And when John had delivered these things to the brethren, he went out with Andronicus to walk. And Drusiana followed at a distance with all <the brethren> to see the things performed by him and to hear his word at all times in the Lord.[54]

* * *

Between c. 105 and c. 37 there is a gap the extent and content of which cannot be determined. Junod/Kaestli (91f.) think that the narratives of which the Oxyrhynchus Papyrus 850 has preserved remains (see above, p. 157f.), and possibly also the episode known from the Irish John story, the transformation of hay into gold (see above p. 161), could have had their place here. But the latter could be assigned at least as well to the travel report which has disappeared between c. 57 and c. 58.

* * *

Destruction of the Temple of Artemis and Conversion of the Ephesians

37. Now the brothers from Miletus said to John, 'We have remained a long time in Ephesus; if you agree, let us go to Smyrna. For already we hear that the great works of God have arrived there also.' And Andronicus said to them, 'When our teacher wishes, then let us go.' But John said, 'Let us first go into the Temple of Artemis; for perhaps if we are seen (there), the servants of the Lord will be found there also.'

38. Now two days later there was the dedication-festival of the idol-temple. So while everyone was wearing white, John alone put on black clothing and went up to the temple;[55] and they seized him and tried to kill him. But John said, 'You are mad to lay hands on me, men, a servant of the only God.' And he went up on a high platform, and said to them,

39. 'Men of Ephesus, you are liable to behave like the sea; every river at its outfall, every spring that flows down, the rains and incessant waves and stony torrents, are all made salt by the bitter brine that is in it. You likewise have remained to this day unchanged (in your attitude) towards the true religion, and are being corrupted by your ancient rituals. How many miracles (and) cures of diseases have you seen (performed) through me? And yet you are blinded in your hearts, and cannot recover your sight. What is it then, men of Ephesus? I have ventured to come up now into this very idol-temple of yours. I will convict you of being utterly godless and dead as regards human reasoning. See, here I stand. You all say that you have Artemis as your goddess [.]; pray to her, then, that I, and I alone, may die; or if you cannot do this, then I alone will call upon my own God and because of your unbelief I will put you all to death.'

40. But since they had long experience of him and had seen dead men raised (by him), they cried out, 'Do not destroy us like that, we implore you, John; we know that you can do it!' And John said to them, 'If you do not wish to die, then your religion must be convicted; and why convicted? - so that you may abandon your ancient error. For now is the time! Either you must be converted by my God, or I myself will die at the hands of your goddess; for I will pray in your presence and entreat my God that you may find mercy.'

41. So saying he uttered this prayer: 'O God, who art God above all that are called gods; yet rejected till this day in the city of the Ephesians; who didst put me in mind to come to this place, of which I never thought; who dost convict every form of worship, by converting (men) to thee; at whose name every idol takes flight, and every demon, <every> power and every unclean nature; now let the demon that is here take flight at thy name, the deceiver of this great multitude; and show thy mercy in this place, for they have been led astray."

42. And while John was saying this, of a sudden the altar of Artemis split into many pieces, and all the offerings laid up in the temple suddenly fell to the floor and *its glory*[56] was shattered, and so were more than seven images; and half the temple fell down, so that the priest was killed at one stroke as *the pillar*[57] came down. Then the assembled Ephesians cried out, '(There is but) one God, (the God) of John!. (There is but) one God who has mercy upon us; for thou alone art God! We are converted, now that we have seen thy marvellous works! Have mercy upon us, O God, according to thy will, and save us from our great error!' And some of them lay on their faces and made supplication, others bent their knees and prayed; some tore their clothes and wept, and others tried to take flight.

43. But John stretched out his hands and with uplifted heart said to the Lord, 'Glory be to thee, my Jesus, the only God of truth, for thou dost gain thy servants by elaborate means.' And having said this he said to the people, 'Rise up from the ground, men of Ephesus, and pray to my God, and acknowledge his invisible power that is openly seen, and the wonderful works that were done before your eyes. Artemis should have helped herself; her servant should have been helped by her, and not have died. Where is the power of the demon (i.e. the goddess)? Where are her sacrifices? Where are her dedication-festivals? - her feasts? - her garlands? Where is all that sorcery and the witchcraft that is sister to it?'

44. And the people rising from the ground went running and threw down the rest of the idol temple, crying out, 'The God of John (is the) only (God) we know; from now on we worship him, since he has had mercy upon us!' And as John came down from that place a great crowd took hold of him, saying, 'Help us, John; stand by us, for we perish in vain. You see our purpose; you see the people following after you, hanging in hope upon your God. We have seen the way which we followed in error (as a false way), *since we have lost (him)*; we have seen that our gods were set up in vain; we have seen their great and shameful derision. But let us, we beg you, come to your house and receive help without hindrance. Accept us, for we are desperate!'

45. But John said to them, 'Friends, you must believe that it was on your account that I remained at Ephesus, although I was eager to go to Smyrna and the other cities, that the servants of Christ who are there may be converted to him. But since I would have departed without being fully at ease about you,

I have waited, praying to my God, and asked him that I should leave Ephesus (only) when I have confirmed you (in the faith); and now I see that this has happened, and indeed is still happening, I will not leave you until I have weaned you like children from the nurse's milk and set you upon a solid rock.'

Raising of the Priest of Artemis

46. So John remained with them and received them [.] in the house of Andronicus. And one of those who were assembled there laid down the dead body of the priest of Artemis before the door [.], for he was his kinsman, and came in quickly with the rest, telling no one. Therefore, John, after he had addressed the brethren, and after the prayer and the thanksgiving (eucharist), and [.] when he had laid hands on each of those who were assembled, said in the Spirit, "One of those present, led to this house by faith in God, has laid down the priest of Artemis before the door and has come in; <and> in the longing of his soul he has put the concern for himself first, reasoning thus with himself; "It is better that I should take thought for the living than for my dead kinsman; for I know that if I turn to the Lord and save my own soul, John will not refuse even to raise up the dead."' And John rising from <his> place went where the priest's kinsman, who had thought this, came in; and he took him by the hand, and said, 'Had you these thoughts when you came in to me, my son?' And he, overcome with trembling and fright, said, 'Yes, my Lord', and threw himself at his feet. And John (said), 'Our Lord is Jesus Christ, and he will show his power on your dead kinsman by raising him again.'

47. And he made the young man rise and took his hand and said, 'It is no great matter for a man who has power over great mysteries to be still concerned with small things. Or is it any great matter if bodily sicknesses are cured? . . .' And still holding the young man by the hand he said, 'I tell you, my son, go and raise up the dead man yourself, saying nothing but only this: "John, the servant of God, says to you, Arise!"' And the young man went to his kinsman and said just this, while a great crowd of people were with him, and came in to John bringing him alive.

And when John saw the man who was raised up, he said, 'Now that you have risen, you are not really living, nor are you a partner and heir to the true life; will you belong to him by whose name and power you were raised up? So now, believe, and you shall live for all eternity.' And then and there he believed on the Lord Jesus, and from that time kept company with John.

Conversion of a Parricide

48. On the next day John saw in a dream that he was to walk three miles outside the gates, and he did not ignore it, but rose up at dawn and started with

the brothers along the road. And (there was) a countryman who was warned by his father not to take to himself the wife of his fellow-labourer, since he threatened to kill him; (but) the young man could not put up with his father's warning, but kicked him and left him speechless. But when John saw what had happened, he said to the Lord, 'Lord, was it because of this that you told me to come here today?'

49. But the young man, seeing (his) sudden death and fearing arrest, took out the sickle that was in his belt and began running towards his cottage; but John met him and said, 'Stand still, you ruthless demon, and tell me where you are running with (that) bloodthirsty sickle.' And the young man in his confusion let his weapon fall to the ground and said to him, 'I have committed a monstrous and inhuman act, and know that I will be arrested, so I resolved to do something worse and more cruel to myself, and to die at once. My father was always urging me to live a chaste and honourable life, yet I could not put up with his reproofs, but kicked him to death. And when I saw what had happened I was hurrying to the woman for whom I murdered my father, and I meant to kill her and her husband and last of all myself. I could not bear the woman's husband to see me suffer the death-penalty.'

50. Then John said to him, 'I will not go away and leave you in danger, or I shall give place to him who would laugh and scoff at you. No, come with me and show me where your father is lying. And if I raise him up for you, will you keep away from the woman who has become (so) dangerous to you?' And the young man said, 'If you raise me up my father himself alive and I see him whole and *continuing* (?) in life, I will keep away (from her) in future.'

51. And as he said this, they came to the place where the old man lay dead, and there were a number of passers-by standing by the place. And John said to the young man, 'You wretch, did you not even spare your father's old age?' But he wept and tore his hair and said he was sorry for it. And John the servant of the Lord said, '(Lord,) who didst show me today that I was to come to this place, who knewest that this would happen, whom nothing that is done in this life can escape, who dost grant me every (kind of) cure and healing by thy will; grant even now that this old man may live, seeing that his murderer has become his own judge. And do thou alone, Lord, spare him, though he did not spare his father, who gave him counsel for the best.'

52. With these words he went to the old man and said, 'My Lord will not be slack to extend his good pity and his condescending heart even to you; rise up and give glory to God for the timely miracle.'[58] And the old man said, 'I arise, my Lord.' And he arose. And seating himself he said, 'I was released from a terrible life (in which) I suffered many grievous insults from my son, and his lack of affection, and you called me back, servant (*lit.* man) of the living God - for what purpose?' <And John answered him, 'If> you are arising to this same (life), you should rather be dead; but rouse yourself to a better (one)!' And

he took him and brought him into the city and proclaimed the grace of God to him, so that before they reached the gate the old man believed.

53. But when the young man saw the unexpected resurrection of his father and his own deliverance, he took <the> sickle and took off his private parts; and he ran to the house where he kept his adulteress and threw them down before her, and said, 'For your sake I became my father's murderer, and of you two, and of myself. There you have the pattern and cause of this! As for me, God has had mercy on me and shown me his power.'

54. And he went and told John before the brethren what he had done. But John said to him, 'Young man, the one who tempted you to kill your father and commit adultery with another man's wife, he has also made you take off the unruly (members) as if this were a virtuous act. But you should not have destroyed the place (of your temptation), but the thought which showed its temper through those members; for it is not those organs which are harmful to man, but the unseen springs through which every shameful emotion is stirred up and comes to light. So, my son, if you repent of this fault and recognise the devices of Satan, you have God to help you in everything that your soul requires.' And the young man kept quiet, repenting of his former sins that he might obtain pardon from the goodness of God; and he would not separate from John.

The Call to Smyrna

55. Now while he was doing these things in the city of the Ephesians, the people of Smyrna sent messengers to him, saying, 'We hear that the God whom you preach is bountiful, and has charged you not to show favour by staying in one place. Since then you are the preacher of such a God, come over to Smyrna and to the other cities, so that we may come to know of your God and knowing him may set our hopes on him.'

* * *

Travel report (cc.56-61)

While c. 55 reports the urgent call which reached John from Smyrna, the episode in c. 56f., transmitted without any connection with other passages from the ancient Acts of John, leads to the beginning of his stay in Smyrna. Accordingly an intervening passage is missing, which must have narrated at least the departure from Ephesus to Smyrna.

Healing of the sons of Antipatros

56. So departing from Ephesus we came to the city of Smyrna. The whole city came together on learning that John was there; and a man named Antipatros, prominent among the Smyrneans, came up to John saying:

'Servant of God, I hear that you have done many good deeds and great miracles in Ephesus. Look, I give you ten thousand gold pieces. I have two twin sons who at the moment of their birth were smitten by a demon, and to this day suffer terribly - they are now thirty-four years old. In one hour they both collapse, at one time seized in the bath, at another while walking, often again at table, and sometimes again in the public assembly of the city. You will see yourself that they are men of goodly size, but wasted by the illness that comes upon them every day. I beg you, help my old age. For I am considering imposing a resolve upon myself; when they were babes, they suffered in moderation, but now that they are grown men they have attracted demons also more full-grown. So have pity on me and on them.' John said to him: 'My physician takes no reward in money, but when he heals for nothing he reaps the souls of those who are healed, in exchange for the diseases. What then are you willing (to give), Antipatros, in exchange for your children? Offer your own soul to God, and you shall have your children healthy by the power of Christ.' And Antipatros said: 'No one have you overlooked until now, do not (neglect) my sons. For <with the consent> of all my kinsfolk I am of a mind, because of the derision (we have experienced), to put them to death by poison. But do you who come as a faithful physician, appointed for them by God, shine upon them and help them.' 57. Thus entreated, John said to the Lord: 'Thou who dost ever comfort the humble[59] and art called to aid, who dost never *need*[60] to be summoned, for you are yourself present before we begin, let the unclean spirits be driven out from the sons of Antipatros!' And immediately they came out from them. But John ordered that the young men should come; and when their father saw them in good health he fell down and did obeisance to John. [And after instructing them in the things concerning the Father and the Son and the Holy Spirit, he baptised them].[61] And John enjoined Antipatros to give money to those who were in need and sent them away praising and blessing God.

* * *

Between c. 57 and c. 58 a fairly long account of a journey by the apostle through various cities of the province of Asia must be missing. In c. 55 he is called not only to Smyrna but also 'to the other cities', and according to the superscription handed down at c. 58 he begins his return journey to Ephesus from Laodicea. The sequence of the stopping-places, Ephesus, Smyrna . . . and Laodicea, may suggest the conjecture that it was a matter of a report of a journey through the seven churches of the Apocalypse of John (Rev. 1:11; 2f.).[62] It is also not out of the question that the episode of the transforming of hay into gold, transmitted by the Irish John-story (see above, p. 161), belonged to this travel narrative. Finally, among the persons named in c. 59 Aristobula, who according to the Manichean Psalm-book appears to have played an important role in the Acts of John (see above, p. 89), Aristippus, Xenophon and the 'virtuous prostitute' must have been introduced in this report.

Departure for Ephesus

(Two manuscripts have the heading: From Laodicea to Ephesus the second time)

58. Now when some considerable time had gone by, and none of the brethren had ever been distressed by John, they were distressed at that time because he had said, 'Brethren, it is now time for me to go to Ephesus; for so I have agreed with those who live there, so that they do not grow slack through having no one to encourage them all this time; and you all must set your minds upon God, who does not desert us.' When the brethren heard this from him they were grieved, because he was parting from them. But John said, 'Even if I am parting from you, yet Christ Jesus is with you always; and if you love him purely, you shall possess continually the fellowship (that comes) from him; for where he is loved, he first (loves) those who love him.' 59. And when he had said this and bidden farewell to them, and had left large sums of money with the brethren for distribution, he set out for Ephesus, to all the brethren's grief and lamentation.

Now there were with him those who were also with him on his journey from Ephesus, Andronicus and Drusiana and the household of Lycomedes and of Cleobius. Also there followed him Aristobula, who had learnt that her husband Tertullus had died on the way,[63] and Aristippus together with Xenophon, and the virtuous prostitute and several others, whom he continually charged to (follow) the Lord Jesus Christ and who would not be parted from him.

The Obedient Bugs

60. And on the first day we arrived at a lonely inn; and while we were trying to find a bed for John we saw a curious thing. There was one bed there lying somewhere not made up; so we spread the cloaks which we were wearing over it, and begged him to lie down on it and take his ease, while all the rest of us slept on the floor. But when he lay down he was troubled by the numerous bugs; and as they became more and more troublesome to him, and it was already midnight, he said to them in the hearing of us all, 'I tell you, you bugs, to behave yourselves, one and all; you must leave your home for tonight and be quiet in one place and keep your distance from the servants of God.' And while we laughed and went on talking, John went to sleep; but we talked quietly and did not disturb him.

61. Now as the day was breaking I got up first, and Verus and Andronicus with me; and we saw by the door of the room a mass of bugs collected; and as we were astounded at the great number of them, and all the brethren had woken up because of them, John went on sleeping. And when he woke up we explained to him what we had seen. And he sat up in the bed and looked at them and said to the bugs 'Since you have behaved yourselves and avoided my

punishment go (back) to your own place.' And when he had said this and had got up from the bed, the bugs came running from the door towards the bed and climbed up its legs and disappeared into the joints. Then John said again, 'This creature listened to a man's voice and kept to itself and was quiet and obedient; but we who hear the voice of God disobey his commandments and are irresponsible; how long will this go on?'

Second Stay in Ephesus (cc. 62-86, 105-115)

Arrival in Ephesus

62. After this we came to Ephesus; and the brethren in that place, learning that John had arrived after all this time, came running to the house of Andronicus, where he was staying, and grasped his feet and laid his hands on their faces and kissed them. And they stretched out their own hands and kissed them, if they touched *<him>*, because they had at least touched his clothes.

Drusiana and Callimachus[64]

63. And while great love and unsurpassed joy prevailed among the brethren, a certain man, an emissary of Satan, fell in love with Drusiana when he saw her, although he knew that she was the wife of Andronicus. And several people said to him, 'It is impossible for you to win this woman, for she has long ago separated even from her husband for the sake of piety. Are you the only one who does not know that Andronicus, who formerly was not the god-fearing man he is now, shut her into a sepulchre, saying "Either I must have you as the wife whom I had before, or you must die!" And she chose to die and not to share with him his ample wealth; she chose to be put to death rather than commit that abominable act. If then she would not consent to union with her lord and husband, but even persuaded him to be of the same mind as herself, will she agree with you who wish to become her lover? Leave off (this) madness, which has no rest in you! Leave off (this) project which you cannot fulfil! Why do you inflame your desire, thinking you can do what you venture?'

64. But his intimate friends could not persuade him with these words, but he had the effrontery to send to her. And having abandoned his attempts on her, lest he should be exposed to many an insult, he spent his life in despair. After two days Drusiana took to her bed with a fever resulting from despondency, saying: 'I wish I had never come to my native town, that I might not have become a stumbling-block to a man uninstructed in religion! If he were a man *filled with <God's> word*, he would not have come to such a pitch of wantonness. So, Lord, since I have been partly to blame for the wounding of an ignorant soul, release me from this bondage and remove me to thee at once!'

And in the presence of John, though he was not fully aware of (the truth of) the matter, Drusiana departed this life, having no joy at all but rather distress because of the spiritual hurt of that man.

65. But Andronicus, troubled with secret sorrow, grieved in his heart and also lamented openly, so that John often quietened him and said to him, 'Drusiana has gone to a better hope out of this unjust life.' And Andronicus answered him, 'Yes, I am convinced (of it), Father John, and have no doubt about faith in my God; and above all I insist that she departed this life in purity.'

66. And when she was brought out (for burying), John took hold of Andronicus; and when he had learned the reason (for what had happened), he grieved (even) more than Andronicus; and he kept quiet, troubled by the machinations of the adversary, and sat (still) for a little. Then, when the brothers had collected to hear what speech he would make about the departed, he began to say,

67. 'When the pilot in his voyage, together with the sailors and the ship herself, arrives in a calm and sheltered haven, then he may say that he is safe. And the farmer who has laid the seed in the earth and has laboured long to cultivate and guard it, may rest from his labours only when he lays up the seed increased many times in his storehouses. The man who enters for a race in the arena should triumph only when he brings back the prize. The man who puts in for a boxing-match should boast only when he gets his crowns. And (so are) all such contests and skills (acknowledged) when they do not fail in the end, but prove to be equal to what they promised.

68. The same I think is the case with the faith which each one of us practises; its truth is decided when it persists unaltered even to the end of life. For many hindrances assail and cause disturbances to the thoughts of men: anxiety, children, parents, reputation, poverty, flattery, youth, beauty, vanity, desire, wealth, anger, presumption, indolence, envy, jealousy, negligence, violence, lust, deceit, money, pretence, and all such other hindrances as there are in this life; just as the pilot sailing on a calm passage is opposed by the onset of contrary winds and a great storm and surge (that comes) out of the calm, and the farmer by untimely cold and mildew and the (pests) that creep out of the earth, and athletes by narrowly failing and craftsmen by falling short (in their crafts).

69. But the man of faith before all else must take thought for his ending and learn how it is to meet him, whether vigilant (?)[65] and sober and unhindered, or disturbed and courting worldly things and held fast by desires. So again one can praise the grace of a body (only) when it is wholly stripped and the greatness of a general (only) when he fulfils the whole promise of the war, and the excellence of a doctor (only) when he was succeeded in every cure, and a soul as <full> of faith and worthy of God (only) when it has performed what agrees with (its) promise; one cannot (praise the soul) which began (well) but slipped down into all the things of this life and fell away; nor the sluggish soul, which made an effort to follow better (examples), but then was reduced to

transitory (pursuits); nor that which desired temporal things rather than the eternal, nor that which exchanged the enduring for the impermanent, nor that which respected what deserves no respect, nor that which esteemed deeds worthy of reprobation, nor that which takes pledges from Satan, nor that which received the serpent into its house, nor that which laughed at what is no laughing matter, nor that which suffers reproach for God's sake and then does not allow itself to be exposed to shame,[66] nor that which consents with its lips but does not show it in practice. But (we must praise the soul) which has had the constancy not to be paralysed by filthy pleasure, not to yield to indolence, not to be ensnared by love of money, not to be betrayed by the vigour of the body and by anger.'

70. And while John was addressing yet more words to the brethren, to teach them to despise transitory things, Drusiana's lover, inflamed by the fiercest lust and by the influence of the many-formed Satan, bribed the steward of Andronicus, an acquisitive man, with a great sum of money; and he opened Drusiana's grave and gave (him) leave to perform the forbidden thing upon (her) dead body. Having not succeeded with her while she was alive, he still persisted with her body after her death, and said, 'If you would not consent to union with me when alive, I will dishonour your corpse now you are dead.' With this design, when he had arranged for his wicked deed through the abominable steward, he burst into the tomb with him; and when they had opened the door they began to strip the grave-clothes from the corpse, saying, 'Miserable Drusiana, what have you gained? Could you not have done this while you were alive? It need not have distressed you, if you had done it willingly.'

71. And when only her undergarment[67] remained about her nakedness, a serpent appeared from somewhere and despatched the steward with a single bite; so it killed him; but it did not bite the young man, but wound itself round his feet, hissing terribly; and when he fell, the serpent mounted (his body) and sat upon him.

72. Now on the next day John came with Andronicus and the brethren to the sepulchre at dawn, it being now the third day[68] (from) Drusiana's (death), so that we might break bread there. And at first when we came the keys could not be found when they were looked for; and John said to Andronicus, 'It is right that they should be lost; for Drusiana is not in the sepulchre. Still, let us go on, that you may not be neglectful, and the doors will open of themselves, just as the Lord has granted us many other things.'

73. And when we came to the place, at John's command the doors came open, and *we saw* by the grave of Drusiana a handsome young man who was smiling. And when he saw him John cried out and said, 'Have you come before us here also, beautiful one? And for what reason?' And he heard a voice saying to him, 'For the sake of Drusiana, whom I will now raise up - for but a short time (only) have I found her mine - and for the sake of the man who has expired by her grave.' And when the beautiful one had said this to John he went up to heaven in the sight of us all.

But when John turned to the other side of the sepulchre he saw a young man, a prominent citizen of Ephesus, Callimachus, and a huge serpent lying asleep upon him, and Andronicus' steward, Fortunatus, (lying) dead. And when he saw them both he stood perplexed, saying to the brethren: 'What is the meaning of this sight? Or why did not the Lord reveal to me what happened here, for he has never neglected me?'

74. And when Andronicus saw them (lying) dead he sprang up and went to Drusiana's grave; and seeing her only in her undergarment, he said to John, 'I understand what has happened, John, blessed servant of God; this Callimachus was in love with my sister; and since he never gained her, though he often ventured upon it, he bribed this accursed steward of mine with a great sum of money, intending perhaps, as now we can see, to execute by means of him the tragedy which he had plotted; for indeed Callimachus avowed this to many and said, "Even if she would not consort with me when living, she shall be violated when she is dead!" And perhaps, John, the beautiful one resolved that her (mortal) remains should not be dishonoured, and this is why the men who ventured on this are (lying) dead. And may it not be that the voice which said to you, "Raise up Drusiana - for but a short time have I known her my own" was foretelling this? For she departed this life in distress, thinking she had become a stumbling-block. But I believe him who said that this is one of the men who were led astray; for you have been bidden to raise him up; as for the other, I know that he is unworthy of salvation. But I make you this one request: raise up Callimachus first, and he will confess to us what has happened.'

75. So John looked at the dead body and said to the venomous reptile, 'Remove from him who shall be a servant of Jesus Christ!' Then he stood up and made this prayer: 'O God, whose name is rightly glorified by us; God, who subduest every harmful influence; God, whose will is performed and who hearest us always; may thy bounty be performed on this young man; and if any dispensation is to be made through him, declare it to us when he is raised up.' And at once the young man arose; and for a whole hour he kept silence.

76. But when he came to his senses, John asked him the meaning of his entry into the sepulchre; and when he heard from him what Andronicus had told him, that he had been in love with Drusiana, John asked him again: 'Did you succeed with your abominable design of dishonouring a corpse full of holiness?' And he answered him, 'How could I then accomplish this, when this dreadful creature struck down Fortunatus with one bite before my eyes? - and rightly so, for he encouraged me in this madness when I had already ceased from this great insanity - and it checked me with fright, and put me in the state in which you saw me before I arose. And I will tell you something else yet more marvellous, which undid me even more and made me a corpse; when my soul gave way to madness and the uncontrollable sickness was troubling me, and I had already stripped off the grave-clothes in which she was clothed, and then

had come out of the grave and laid them down as you see, I returned to my detestable work; and I saw a handsome young man covering her with his cloak. And from his face rays of light shone out on to her face. And he also spoke to me and said "Callimachus, die that you may live!" Now who he was I did not know, servant of God; but now that you have come, I know for certain that he is an angel of God; and I understand this in truth, that the true God is proclaimed by you, and of this I am convinced. But I beg you, do not be slow to deliver me from this calamity and dreadful crime, and present me to your God as a man who was deceived with a shameful and foul deceit. Would that it were given to you to open my breast and show my thoughts! For henceforth this lies upon my soul, a great pain, that once I cherished thoughts which I should not have had, and tempted by an evil disposition brought upon myself the greatest sorrow. So begging your help I clasp your feet, that I may become good [.] like you, since (otherwise) it is impossible for me to belong to God. And nothing lies upon my mind more than this, to have confidence towards your God as a true and genuine son. I entreat you therefore, I wish to become one of those who set their hopes on Christ, so that the voice may prove true that said to me here, "Die, that you may live!" That voice has indeed accomplished its effect; for that man is dead, that faithless, lawless, godless man; and I have been raised at your hands, and will be faithful and Godfearing, knowing the truth, which I beg you may be shown me by you.'

77. And John seized with great gladness and contemplating the whole spectacle of man's salvation said, 'Ah, what is thy power, Lord Jesu Christ, I know not, for I am amazed at thy great compassion and infinite forbearance. O, what greatness came down into bondage! O inexpressible freedom, reduced to slavery by us! O ineffable nobility, taken into captivity! O incomprehensible glory, who art also our advocate! The only king, yet subjected to us; who hast kept even the lifeless frame from dishonour; who hast convicted in this young man the whole unbridled state, and not allowed it to go to the limit; who hast muzzled the demon raging within him, and had pity on the man who was out of his senses! Deliverer of the man who was stained with blood, corrector of him that was entombed; who didst not send away him who scattered his fortune, nor turn thy face from him when he repented! Father who hast shown pity and compassion on the man who neglected himself! We glorify thee and praise and bless and give thanks for thy great goodness and forbearance, holy Jesu; for thou alone art God and no other. To whom is the power beyond all conspiracy, now and for all eternity. Amen.'

78. So saying John took Callimachus and kissed him and said, 'Glory be to our God, my child, Jesus Christ who has pitied you, and counted me worthy to glorify his power, and counted you also worthy by a way that comes from him to desist from that madness and frenzy of yours, and has summoned you to his own rest and renewal of life.'

78. But when Andronicus saw that Callimachus was raised from the dead a believer, he and all the brethren entreated John to raise up Drusiana also, and said, 'John, let Drusiana rise up and spend happily that short space <of life> which she gave up through distress about Callimachus, when she thought she had become a temptation to him; and when the Lord wills he shall take her to himself.' And John made no delay, but went to her grave and took Drusiana's hand and said, 'I call upon thee who art God alone, the exceeding great, the unutterable, the everlasting; to whom every power of principalities is subject; to whom every authority bows; before whom every pride is humbled and is still; before whom every presumption falls down and keeps silence; whom the demons hear and tremble;[69] whom all creation perceives and keeps its bounds; whom flesh does not know and blood does not understand: let thy name be glorified by us, and raise up Drusiana, that Callimachus may be further strengthened <in thee>, who providest what to men is unattainable and impossible, and to thee alone is possible, even salvation and resurrection; and that Drusiana may now be at peace, since now that the young man is converted she has no more with her the least hindrance in her hastening towards thee.'

80. And after these words John said: 'Drusiana, arise.' And she arose at once and came out of the grave; and seeing herself clad only in her undergarment, she was perplexed about what had happened; but when she had learnt the whole truth from Andronicus, while John lay upon his face and Callimachus with (uplifted) voice and with tears gave praise to God, she also rejoiced and gave praise in like manner.

81. Now when she had dressed herself she turned and saw Fortunatus lying, and said to John, 'Father, let this man arise also, for all that he strove to become my betrayer.' And when Callimachus heard her say this, he said, 'No, Drusiana, I beg you; for the voice which I heard took no thought of him, but made mention only of you; and I saw and believed. For if he had been good, no doubt God would have pited him and raised him up through the blessed John. He made it known then that the man had come to a bad end. And John said to him 'My son, we have not learned to return evil for evil.[70] For God also, though we have done much ill and nothing well towards him, has given us not retribution but repentance; and although we knew not his name, he did not forsake but had mercy on us; and though we blasphemed, he did not punish but pitied us; and though we disbelieved, he bore no grudge; and though we persecuted his brethren, he made no (such) return; and though we ventured many abominable and terrible deeds, he did not repel us, but moved us to repentance and restraint of wickedness and so called us to himself, as (he has called) you too, my son Callimachus, and without insisting on your former misdeeds he has made you his servant to serve his mercy. If then you will not allow <me> to raise up Fortunatus, it is a task for Drusiana.'

82. And she made no delay, but rejoicing in spirit and and in gladness of soul she went up to the body of Fortunatus and said, 'O God of (all) ages, Jesus Christ, God of truth, who sufferedst me to see wonders and signs and didst grant me to become partaker of thy name, who didst reveal thyself to me with thy many-formed countenance and hadst mercy on me in every way; who by thy great goodness didst protect me when I suffered violence from my former consort Andronicus; who gavest me thy servant Andronicus as my brother; who hast kept me, thine handmaid, pure until this day; who hast raised me up when I was dead through thy servant John,[71] and when I was raised hast shown me the man who fell (as now) unfallen; who hast given me perfect rest in thee, and relieved me of the secret madness; whom I have loved and embraced; I entreat thee, Jesus Christ, do not refuse thy Drusiana's petition that Fortunatus should rise again, for all that he strove to become my betrayer.'

83. And she grasped the dead man's hand, and said, 'Rise up, Fortunatus, in the name of our Lord Jesus Christ, even though you are in the highest degree an enemy of the handmaid of God.' And Fortunatus rose up, and saw John in the sepulchre and Andronicus and Drusiana, now raised from the dead, and Callimachus, now a believer, and the rest of the brethren glorifying God; and he said, 'O, what end is there to the powers of these terrible men! I did not want to be resurrected, but would rather be dead, so as not to see them.' And with these words he ran away and left the sepulchre.

84. And John, seeing that the soul of Fortunatus was inflexible towards the good, said: 'O nature without natural inclination for the better! What a spring of the soul that persists in defilement! What essence of corruption full of darkness! What a death, dancing among those that are yours! What a barren tree that is full of fire! What a stump that has a demon for reason! What a branch (*lit.* wood) that brings forth coals of fire for fruit! What matter, consorting with the *madness of matter*[72] and neighbour to unbelief! You have convinced (us) who you are; you are convicted for ever with your children. The power of praising better things you do not know; for you do not possess it. Therefore as your way is, so is your root and nature. Be removed then, from those who hope in the Lord; from their thoughts, from their mind, from their souls, from their bodies, from their action, their life, their behaviour, their way of life, their practice, their counsel, from their resurrection to God, from their fragrance in which you can have <no> share, from their fasting, from their prayers, from their holy bath, from their Eucharist, from the nourishment of their flesh, from their drink, from their clothing, from their love-feast (ἀγάπη), from their care for the dead, from their continence, from their justice; from all these, most wicked Satan, enemy of God, shall Jesus Christ our God remove you and those who are like you and follow your ways.'

85. And when he had said this John prayed, and taking bread brought it into the sepulchre to break and said, 'We glorify thy name that converteth us from

error and pitiless deceit; we glorify thee who hast shown before our eyes what we have seen; we testify to thy goodness, in various ways appearing; we praise thy gracious name, O Lord, <which> has convicted those that are convicted by thee; we thank thee, Lord Jesus Christ, that we confide in < . . . >, which is unchanging; we thank thee who hadst need <.> of (our) nature that is being saved; we thank thee that hast given us this unwavering <faith> that thou alone art <God> both now and for ever; we thy servants, that are assembled and gathered with (good) cause, give thanks to thee, O holy one.'

86. And when he had made this prayer and glorified (God) he gave to all the brethren the Lord's Eucharist, and went out of the sepulchre. And he came to the house of Andronicus, and said to the brethren, 'My brethren, some spirit within me has foretold that Fortunatus must shortly turn black and die from the bite of the serpent; but let someone go quickly and learn if this be true.' Then one of the young men ran and found him now swollen up and the blackness spreading and reaching his heart. And he came and told John that he had been dead three hours. And John said, 'Devil, thou hast thy son.'

[For cc. 87-105 see above, pp. 179ff.]

The Departure (Metastasis: c.106-115)
John's Last Act of Worship

106. The blessed John therefore kept company with the brethren rejoicing in the Lord. And on the next day, as it was a Sunday and all the brethren were assembled, he began to say to them, 'My brethren and fellow-servants, joint-heirs and partners with me in the kingdom of the Lord, you know God, how many great works he has granted you through me, how many wonders, how many signs, how many healings, what gifts of grace, (what) teachings, directions, refreshments, services, glories, manifestations of faith, acts of fellowship, graces, gifts, which you have seen with your eyes are given you by him, (though) they are not seen with these eyes nor heard with these ears. Therefore be firmly settled in him, remembering him in all you do, understanding the mystery of (God's) providence that has been accomplished for men, why the Lord has performed it. The Lord himself entreats you through me, my brethren, and makes request, desiring to continue free from distress, free from insult, and from disloyalty, and from injury; for he knows the insult that comes from you, he knows that dishonour, he knows that disloyalty, he knows even injury when you do not obey his holy commandments.

107. So let not your gracious God be grieved, the compassionate, the merciful, the holy, the pure, the undefiled, the immaterial, the only, the one, the unchanging, the sincere, the guileless, the patient, the one that is higher and loftier than every name we can utter or conceive, the God Jesus Christ. Let him rejoice with you because you behave honourably, let him be glad because you

live purely, let him be refreshed because your ways are sober, let him be easy because you live strictly, let him be pleased at your fellowship, let him laugh because you are chaste, let him be merry because you love him. I give you this charge, my brethren, because I am now hastening towards the task that is prepared for me, which is already being perfected by the Lord. For what else could I have to say to you? You have the pledges of your God, you have the securities of his goodness, you have his presence that is inescapable. If, then, you sin no longer, he forgives you what you did in ignorance; but if when you have known him and found mercy with him you resort again to such (deeds), then both your former (sins) will be laid to your charge, and you shall have no part nor mercy in him.'

108. And after speaking these words to them he made this prayer: 'O Jesus, who hast woven this crown with thy weaving, who hast united these many flowers into thine unfading flower, who hast sown these words of thine; thou only protector of thy servants, and physician who healest for nothing; only benefactor, free of arrogance, only merciful and lover of men, only saviour and righteous one; who ever art and dwellest in all and art everywhere present, encompassing all things and filling all things, God, Jesus, Christ, Lord; with thy gifts and thy mercy protect those that hope in thee, who exactly knowest all the devices and the malice of him that is everywhere our adversary, which he contriveth against us; do thou only, O Lord, assist thy servants by thy visitation.'

109. And he asked for bread, and gave thanks with these words: 'What praise or what offering or what thanksgiving shall we name as we break this bread, but thee alone, Jesu? We glorify thy name of Father which was spoken by thee; we glorify thy name of Son which was spoken by thee. We glorify thine entering of the door;[73] we glorify thy Resurrection[74] that is shown us through thee; we glorify thy Way;[75] we glorify thy Seed,[76] the Word,[77] Grace, Faith, the Salt,[78] the inexpressible Pearl,[79] the Treasure,[80] the Plough,[81] the Net,[82] the Greatness, the Diadem, him that for our sakes was called the Son of Man, the truth,[83] repose, knowledge, power, commandment, confidence, liberty and refuge in thee. For thou alone, O Lord, art the root of immortality[84] and the fount of incorruption and the seat of the aeons, who art called all these things on our account, that calling on thee through them we may know thy greatness, which at the present is invisible to us, but visible only to the pure *as it is portrayed* in thy man only.'

110. And he broke the bread and gave it to us, praying over each of the brethren that he would be worthy of the Lord's grace and of the most holy Eucharist. And he partook of it himself and said, 'May there be for me also a part with you', and, 'Peace be with you, my beloved.' After this he said to Verus, 'Take two brethren with baskets and spades, and follow me.' And Verus without delay did what was ordered by John the servant of God.

The Death of John

111. So the blessed John came out of the house and walked outside the gates, having told the greater number that they should leave him; and when he came to a tomb of a brother of ours,[85] he said to the young men, 'Dig, my sons'. And they dug. And he was more insistent with them, and said, 'The digging must go deeper.' And while they were digging he spoke to them the word and encouraged those that had come from the house with him, edifying them and preparing them for the greatness of God and praying for each one of us.

And when the young men had finished the trench as he desired, while we knew nothing (of his intention) he took off the outer clothes which he had on and laid them like a mattress in the bottom of the trench; and standing in his undergarment[86] only he lifted up his hands and prayed thus: 112. 'O thou that didst choose us for the apostolate among the Gentiles; O God who has sent us into (all) the world; who hast shown thyself through thine apostles; who hast never rested, but dost always save those who can be saved; who hast revealed thyself through all nature; who hast proclaimed thyself even among beasts; who hast made even the lonely and embittered soul (grow) tame and quiet; who hast given thyself to it when it thirsted for thy words; who hast speedily appeared to it when it was dying; who hast shown thyself to it as a law when sunk into lawlessness; who hast revealed thyself to it when it was already overcome by Satan; who hast overcome its adversary when it took refuge with thee; who hast given to it thine hand and aroused it from the works of Hades; who hast not suffered it to conform to the body; who hast shown it its own enemy; who hast made knowledge of thee pure, God, Lord, Jesus; Father of beings beyond the heavens, God of those that are in the heavens; Law of the ethereal beings and Path of those in the air; Guardian of beings upon earth, and Terror of those beneath the earth; receive also the soul of thy John which, it may be, is approved by thee.

113. 'Thou who hast kept me also till this present hour pure for thyself and untouched by union with a woman; who when I wished to marry in my youth didst appear to me and say: "John, I need thee"; who when I was about to marry didst prepare for me a bodily sickness; who, though disobeyed, on the third occasion when I wished to marry didst prevent me, and then at the third hour of the day didst say to me upon the sea, "John, if thou wert not mine, I should have allowed thee to marry"; who didst blind me for two years, letting me be grieved and entreat thee; who in the third year didst open the eyes of my understanding and didst give me (back) my eyes that are seen; who when I regained my sight didst disclose to me the repugnance even of looking closely at a woman; who hast saved me from the temporal vision and guided me into that which endureth for ever; who hast rid me of the foul madness that is in the flesh; who hast snatched me from bitter death and presented me only to thee;

who hast silenced the secret disease of my soul and cut off the open deed; who hast weakened and expelled the rebellious (enemy) within me; who hast made my love for thee unsullied; who hast ruled my course to thee unbroken; who hast given me faith in thee undoubting; who hast instructed my knowledge of thee with purity; who givest to each man's works their due reward; who hast inspired my soul to have no possession more precious than thee. So now that I have fulfilled the charge which I was entrusted by thee,[87] Lord Jesus, count me worthy of thy rest and grant me my end in thee, which is inexpressible and unutterable salvation.

114. 'And as I come to thee let the fire retreat and the darkness be overcome, let chaos be enfeebled, the furnace grow dim and Gehenna be quenched; let angels be put to shame and demons be afraid, let the rulers be shattered and the powers fall; let the places on the right hand stand fast and those on the left be removed; let the devil be silenced, let Satan be derided, let his wrath be burned out, let his madness be calmed, let his vengeance be disgraced, let his assault be distressed, let his children be wounded and all his root rejected. And grant me to finish my way to thee preserved from violence and insult, receiving what thou hast promised to them that have lived purely and loved thee alone.'

115. And having sealed himself in every part, standing thus, he said '(Be) thou with me, Lord Jesus Christ'; and he lay down in the trench where he had spread out his clothes; and he said to us, 'Peace (be) with you, my brethren',[88] and gave up his spirit rejoicing.

The Metastasis[89] was subsequently expanded. According to a branch of text-form δ, represented by two manuscripts (RZ), and text-form β (with similar treatment in ps.-Prochorus: Zahn, p. 164.12f.) the apostle's body could not be found on the next day (RZ) or after three days (β; in ps.-Prochorus evidently already on the same day); 'for', RZ add, 'it was removed through the power of our Lord Jesus Christ'. The expansion in text-form γ is more elaborate: the apostle dismisses the brethren, and when they return on the next day they find only his sandals and see the earth pouring out, on which remembering the words of Jesus in Jn. 21:22 they return giving praise. This conclusion, which is also presupposed by Ephraim of Antioch (see above, p. 155), without the detail of the sandals left behind, combines two mutually conflicting traditions, both derived from Jn. 21:22; the one says that John did not die but was transported, while according to the other, reported in detail by Augustine (*in Joh. tract.* 124.2, ed. Willems, CChrSL 36, 681f. 28-37), he is indeed lying in the grave, but is not dead but asleep, so that the earth is shaken by his breathing and dust pours out (further witnesses in Junod/Kaestli, *Histoire*, 116, note 20). The revision of the Metastasis legend in the so-called Passio Johannis of Melito of Laodicea (PG 5, col. 1250C) makes the empty tomb produce manna, and for Ephraim of Antioch also (in office 527-545) it is a holy substance which pours out from the burial place (in Photius, *Bibl.*, cod. 229, ed. Henry IV, 141.4-7). In the 6th century this 'manna', regarded as having miraculous effect, was already the subject of a wide-ranging trade in relics (cf. Gregory of Tours, *in Glor. Mart.* 29, ed. Bruno Krusch, MGH.SSrerMer

I 2, ^{2}1969, 55). Yet in the time of their bishop Chromatius (c. 387-407) the church of Aquileia apparently already possessed such dust as a relic (Chromatius of Aquileia, *Sermo* XXI 4, ed. R. Étaix/J. Lemarié, CChrSL 9A, 99.89-93). As an institutionalised miracle, it was in the course of time restricted to the apostle's commemoration day - in the East September 26 - and the sepulchral area in the church of St John was structurally adapted for its unfolding (cf. J. Hörmann, *Das Johannesgrab: Forschungen in Ephesos IV 3*, published by the Austrian Archaeological Institute, Vienna 1951, 179-185); its gushing from the alleged tomb of John remained of significance for the Ephesian cult of John down to the Turkish conquest of the city in 1304 (cf. ps.-John Chrysostom, *in Laudem s. Joh. Apost.*, PG 61, col. 719 and *in s. Joh. Theol.* IV, Junod/Kaestli 415; Symeon Metaphrastes, *Hypomn. in Joh. Apost.* VII, PG 116, col. 704f.; compilation on John transmitted in a Georgian redaction by Euthymius Hagiorites: Michel van Esbroeck, 'Les Acta Johannis traduits par Euthyme l'Hagiorite', *Bedi Kartlisa* 33, 1975, 73-109, esp. 109, c. 199 of van Esbroeck's division; Ramón Muntaner [*Chronicle* c. 206, trans. by Lady Goodenough II, London 1921, 499f.] presents a particularly vivid portrayal from the period immediately before the Turkish conquest).

Notes

The Acts of John (text)

1. For the following translation those of Schimmelpfeng, James, Festugière and Junod/Kaestli were consulted with advantage. All passages where there is a deviation from the text of Junod/Kaestli are enclosed within *; (*) indicates an omission as compared with this text. Angled brackets < > mark an expansion, square brackets [ ] an omission against the wording of the manuscripts. Assumed lacunae in the text transmitted are indicated by < . . . >. Explanatory additions in the translation stand in round brackets ( ). Conjectures marked by asterisks for which there are no notes are from the apparatus in the Junod/Kaestli edition. Instead of constant single references, a general reference to their Introduction, Commentary and Notes may be given here for all problems of form or substance in the text. The sub-headings in the translation derive from the translator.
2. Cf. ATh 1; Jean-Daniel Kaestli, 'Les scènes d'attribution des champs de mission et de départ de l'apôtre dans les Actes apocryphes', in: François Bovon *et al.*, *Les Actes apocryphes des Apôtres*, Geneva 1981, 249-264.
3. προσομιλούσης is read instead of προσομιλοῦντος of the MSS.
4. Dike: Righteousness personified (as a goddess).
5. In what follows it is presupposed that Lycomedes is dead.
6. Cf. Acts 3:20.
7. Cf. Mt. 7:7; Lk. 11:9.
8. Reading with Festugière (13, note 17): <ἀπὸ>χρωμάτων τῶν δεδομένων μοι (MSS σοι) νῦν ἀπορρῆξαι αὐτόν (MSS ἀπορῆσαι αὐτόν, Junod/Kaestli ἀπορήσει αὐτός).
9. Cf. 2 Cor. 7:4.
10. Cf. Mk. 9:43.
11. *A Manichaean Psalm-Book*, Part II, ed. C.R.C. Allberry, 1938, 192.33-193.1 (cf. above, p. 97, note 34).
12. Allberry 143.11f.
13. Ibid. 142.24.
14. Virginia Burrus ('Chastity as Autonomy. Women in the Stories of the Apocryphal Acts',

Semeia 38, 1986, 101-117) has attempted to find a pre-literary *Sitz im Leben* in a specific early Christian women's milieu for such conversion stories in the apocryphal Acts; but see the criticism of J.-D. Kaestli, ib. 119-131.

15. Superscription in MS C (see above, p. 170, note 54), which contains only the 'Preaching of the Gospel': 'Wonderful report of the deeds and of the vision which the holy John the theologian beheld from our Lord Jesus Christ; how he appeared in the beginning *to Peter* and *James* and in which he recounts the mystery of the Cross.'

16. Cf. Mk. 1:16-20; Mt. 4:18-22.

17. Cf. Jn. 13:23, 25.

18. Cf. Mk. 9:2f.; Mt. 17:1f.; Lk. 9:28f..

19. Cf. Jn. 20:2.

20. Cf. Jn. 20:27.

21. Cf. Lk. 7:36; 11:37; 14:1.

22. Cf. Mk. 6:35-44; Mt. 14:15-21; Lk. 9:12-17; Jn. 6:5-13; Mk. 8:1-10; Mt. 15:32-39.

23. Junod/Kaestli (621-627) think of a possible liturgical *Sitz im Leben* for this so-called 'dance-hymn' in a gnostic initiation ritual; see further on the structure and function of the passage A.J. Dewey, 'Hymn', with the pertinent comments by J.-D. Kaestli. In the 20th century this text has frequently attracted practitioners in the arts: in 1917 the English composer Gustav Holst (1874-1934) set it to music in an English version as the 'Hymn of Jesus' (Op. 37; cf. Imogen Holst, *The Music of Gustav Holst*, Oxford [3]1968, 47-51); the French authoress Marguerite Yourcenar (1903-1987) in her novel *L'oeuvre au noir* (1968; ET *The Abyss*, c. 1976) drew freely upon it to characterise the milieu of occult esoteric circles in the 16th century; the Spanish film director Luis Buñuel (1900-1983) drew upon it, admittedly only according to Augustine (*Ep.* 237), in his film *La Voie Lactée* (*The Milky Way*, 1969), which is critical of the Christian Church, for the representation of a Priscillianist mystery festival (text: *L'Avant-Scène du Cinema* 94/95, July/Sept. 1969, 29f.).

24. Cf. Lk. 22:54; Jn. 18:12.

25. Cf. Jn. 18:36.

26. Cf. Mk. 14:26; Mt. 26:30.

27. Some fragments of the hymn are quoted by Augustine in *Ep.* 237. 5-9 (see above, pp. 154, 168 note 29) and may be collected here; the numbers following them in brackets give the context of quotation in Goldbacher IV, CSEL 57:
I will save, and I will be saved (530.17)
I will loose, and I will be loosed (529.3 and 29)
I will be born (531.4)
I will sing, dance all of you (531.7 and 9)
I will lament, beat you all yourselves (531.12)
I will adorn, and I will be adorned (531.13f.)
I am a lamp to you who see me (531.18)
I am a door to you who knock on me (531.20f.)
You who see what I do, keep silence about my works (531.26)
By the Word I mocked at all things, and I was not mocked at all (532.17f.)

28. Cf. 1 Jn. 1:5.

28a. The word "will" in this and the following verses has its full significance; "it is my will to be saved; not simply "I shall be saved." - G. C. S.

29. Cf. Mt. 11:17; Lk. 7:32.

30. Cf. Jn. 10:9.

31. Cf. Jn. 14:6.

32. MS ἐπαισχύνθην (Junod/Kaestli ἐπῃσχύνθην: 'was put to shame' or 'was in disgrace'); Augustine, *Ep.* 237.9: *sum lusus* (ἐπαίχθην).

33. According to the manuscript tradition of the Council of Nicaea 787 τῷ ἀρουβάτῳ, in

which the Syriac ^{ca}*rubta'*, 'day of preparation, Friday', may lie concealed.
34. Cf. Jn. 19:14 (on Friday about the sixth hour Pilate presented Jesus to the Jews); for the gnostic Marcus of the school of Valentinus, according to Irenaeus (*adv. Haer.* I 14.6, ed. Adelin Rousseau/Louis Doutreleau (SC 264), Paris 1979, 224f.), the sixth hour of the day was by divine dispensation the hour of the Crucifixion. On a different punctuation however the words 'at the sixth hour' could also be related to the onset of the darkness, as in the Synoptic passion story (Mk. 15:33; Mt, 27:45; Lk. 23:44; cf. Gos. Pet. 15).
35. Cf. Mk. 15:33; Mt. 27:45; Lk. 23:44.
36. Cf. Mk. 15:19; Jn. 19:34; Gos. Pet. 9; Second Treatise of the Great Seth (NHC VII 2) 56.8f. (ed. and trans. M. Krause in F. Altheim/R. Stiehl, *Christentum am Roten Meer* II, 1973, 121; Eng. trans. in NHLE 1988, 365).
37. Cf. Ephraem Syrus, Diatessaron Commentary XX 27, tr. Louis Leloir (SC 121), Paris 1966, 362 (' . . . and they gave him vinegar and gall to drink'); Gos. Pet. 16 ('give him to drink gall with vinegar'); but cf. also Barn. 7.3 (' . . . he was given vinegar and gall to drink', according to Helmut Koester [*Synoptische Überlieferung bei den Apostolischen Vätern*, TU 65, 1957, 149-152] from Christian school-tradition); Second Treatise of the Great Seth (NHC VII 2) 56.6f. (see note 36) (' . . . who drank the gall and the vinegar').
38. For the motif of the apparent crucifixion cf. the gnostic Apocalypse of Peter (NHC VII 3) 81.15-21, ed. and trans. M. Krause/Victor Girgis, *Christentum am Roten Meer* II (as note 36) 175 ('He whom you see on the cross, glad and laughing, is the living Jesus. But he into whose hands and feet they drive the nails is his fleshly part, the substitute'; see below, p. 708; Eng. trans. in NHLE 1988, 377); Second Treatise of the Great Seth (as note 36) 55.30-56.13 (the subject of the sufferings in the passion story is [in each case?] someone other than the Saviour, and those who crucify him actually nail 'their man' to the cross); the gnostic Basilides according to Irenaeus (I 24.4 ed. Rousseau/Doutreleau [SC 264] 328: the crucified is not Jesus but Simon of Cyrene). The motif was also taken up later by Mohammed: Koran, Sura 4, 156f. (in a series of charges against the Jews): 'They said (in boast) "We killed Christ Jesus, the son of Mary, the Apostle of God"; - but they killed him not nor crucified him, but so it was made to appear to them' (tr. A. Yusuf Ali, 1977, p. 230).
39. For cc. 98-101 the German translation by Alexander Böhlig, 'Zur Vorstellung vom Lichtkreuz in Gnostizismus und Manichäismus', in *Gnosis* (FS Hans Jonas), 1978, 473-491, was also consulted.
40. Jn. 1:1.
41. Jn. 10:9.
42. Jn. 14:6.
43. Jn. 6:33, 35, 48.
44. Mk. 4:26; Lk. 8:5.
45. Jn. 11:25.
46. Jn. 11:25; 14:6.
47. Jn. 14:6.
48. Cf. Jn. 1:14, 17.
49. Cf. Jn. 10:16.
50. Cf. Jn. 10:38; 14:10f.
51. The wording of the Greek text evidently has Jn. 19:34 in view; but originally it was rather the scourging of Jesus that was meant (Mk. 15:15; Mt. 27:26; Jn. 19:1); cf. Schäferdiek, 'Herkunft' 252f.
52. Cf. Jn. 19:34.
53. Cf. Gos. Pet. 19.
54. Here the text from MS C closes with: 'now and for ever and from everlasting to everlasting. Amen'.
55. The author evidently envisages the temple of Artemis at Ephesus, wrongly, as an elevated

sanctuary, to which he makes the apostle 'go up' (cf. also c. 39: 'I have come up'). Actually it lay on the low ground north-east of the city. It ranked as one of the seven wonders of the world. In 268/9 it was devastated in a raid by the Goths, and thereafter only partly restored. From the beginning of the 5th century it finally fell into ruin (Anton Bammer, *Das Heiligtum der Artemis von Ephesos*, Graz 1984; Clive Foss, *Ephesus after Antiquity*, Cambridge 1979, 86f.).
56. MSS τὸ δόξαν αὐτῷ, 'what seemed good to him', for which Festugière (16 note 26) suggests ἡ δόξα αὐτοῦ, interpreting δόξα (radiance, glory) as the cultic image. Junod/Kaestli (222, note 42.1) conjecture τὸ τόξον αὐτῶν, 'their (= the votive offerings) bow (as an attribute of Artemis)'.
57. MSS τοῦ στυμόνος (lexically not attested); Junod/Kaestli (223, note 42.2) suggest τοῦ στήμονος in a meaning likewise not attested (cross-beam). The homily for St John's day (BHG[3] 927), dependent on the Acts of John and attributed to John Chrysostom, has the priest killed ὑπὸ τοῦ κίονος, by the column or pillar (PG 61, 720), hence the above translation presupposes τοῦ στυλοῦ, a suggestion also made independent of the homily by G.C. Stead ('Conjectures on the Acts of John', JTS 32, 1981, 152-153 at p. 153).
58. MSS τοῦ ἐπιχείρου γεγενημένου ἔργου, corrected to ἐπὶ καιροῦ by J.B. Bauer, Die Korruptel Acta Johannis 52, *Vig. Chr.* 44 (1990) 295-7.
59. Cf. 2 Cor. 7:6.
60. MSS διαμίνος, corrected to δεόμενος by Eric Junod/Jean-Daniel Kaestli, 'Un fragment inédit des Actes de Jean: la guérison des fils d'Antipatros à Smyrne', *Museum Helveticum* 31, 1974, 96-104, (at 104 note 41). In their edition they propose the correction διαμείνας, which however appears difficult in view of the durative significance of διαμένειν ('remain', but taken by Junod/Kaestli in the sense of 'await, expect').
61. This sentence in comparison with the ancient Acts of John is undoubtedly secondary.
62. So Theodor Zahn, 'Die Wanderungen des Apostels Johannes', *Neue kirchliche Zeitschrift* 10, 1899, 191-218; id., *Forschungen zur Geschichte des neutestamentlichen Kanons* VI, 1900, 197-199. The decisive rejection of this conjecture by Junod/Kaestli (93f.) hangs together with a misunderstanding of the functional significance of the narrative framework of the Acts of John for their conception as a whole.
63. Junod/Kaestli (95) understand 'way' here as a metaphor for Christianity; Aristobula has accordingly learned that her husband Tertullus has died as a Christian, i.e. after being converted. In view of the order of resurrection from death and conversion which is characteristic for the Acts of John, a conversion leading to a speedy blissful end is for them not a very likely motif.
64. In the 10th century the episode of Drusiana and Callimachus was made into a drama, *Resuscitatio Drusianae et Calimachi*, after the Latin version of the *Virtutes Johannis*, by Roswitha of Gandersheim (*Hrotsvitae opera*, ed. Helene Homeyer, 1970, 283-297).
65. The translation follows the *Virtutes Johannis* (*vigilantem*); διεργής in the Greek *Vorlage* (with attempts at correction in two MSS) cannot be explained.
66. Text μὴ αἰσχυνομένην. Junod/Kaestli (263) suggest the deletion of μή. Festugière (22): '... qui n'en conçoit pas de honte'. For αἰσχύνεσθαι as describing the condition of being ashamed cf. Bultmann, TDNT I, 189-191.
67. The Greek τὸ δικρόσσιον (literally something doubly equipped with tassels or fringes) evidently means a garment worn directly on the body by both sexes, of the nature of which nothing is otherwise known. The term occurs only in the Acts of John (cc. 71; 74; 80 for Drusiana; c. 111 for John) and in the *Periplus maris Erythraei* (c. 6, ed. Hjalmar Frisk, *Le périple de la mer érythrée* [Göteborgs högskolas årsskrift XXXIII], Gothenburg 1927, 23, 26), the date of which is disputed (the suggestions range between the middle of the 1st and the first half of the 3rd century; cf. Walter Raunig, 'Die Versuche einer Datierung des Periplus maris Erythraei', *Mitteilungen der anthropolog. Gesellschaft in Wien* 100, 1970, 231-241), but which is probably best placed in the middle of the 1st century (cf. G.W. Bowersock, *Roman Arabia*, Cambridge, Mass./London 1983, 70f.).

68. On the 'third day' as the conventional date for a cultic commemoration of the dead, see Franz Joseph Dölger, 'ΙΧΘΥC *II. Der heilige Fisch in den antiken Religionen und im Christentum*, 1922, 555-569.
69. Cf. Jas. 2:19.
70. Cf. Rom. 12:17; 1 Thess. 5:15; 1 Pet. 3:9.
71. The clause 'who hast raised me up . . . ' seems to be an abbreviation of the original text, which is still partly legible in the palimpsest MS H (Istanbul, Patriarchal Library, Monastery of the Holy Trinity [Chalki] 102): ' . . . who when I was dead didst take me <to thyself> because of my affliction; who when I was separated from the body didst say (to me): "For <a short time> you are mine, Drusiana"; who <didst bestow> on John the grace to raise <me> up again, that I < . . . > the short time . . . '
72. The translation follows the reading ὑλημανίας of the palimpsest H (against ὑλομανίας of the other witnesses).
73. Cf. Jn. 10:9.
74. Cf. Jn. 11:25.
75. Cf. Jn. 14:6.
76. Cf. Mk. 4:26.
77. Cf. Jn. 1:1.
78. Cf. Mk. 9:50; Mt. 5:13; Lk. 14:34.
79. Cf. Mt. 13:45f.
80. Cf. Mt. 13:44.
81. Cf. Lk. 9:62.
82. Cf. Mt. 13:47.
83. Cf. Jn. 14:6.
84. Cf. Wisd. 15:3.
85. This evidently presupposes a burial place of John, displayed in Ephesus, as an element of the Ephesian John-legend which is polemically taken up in the Acts, although scarcely in a way to show independent knowledge of the place (cf. also the erroneous ideas of the Acts of John regarding the location of the temple of Artemis, see above, p. 207, note 55). Indeed there was apparently still no unanimous tradition about this burial-place down to the 4th century. Dionysius of Alexandria (d. 264/5) had knowledge of two tombs in Ephesus, which were both described as the grave of John (ap. Euseb., *HE* VII 25.16, ed. E. Schwartz, GCS 9.2, 696.18f.); at the beginning of the 4th century Eusebius accepted his statement as still correct 'even now' (*HE* III 39.6, Schwartz GCS 9.1, 288.6f.). Even in 392 Jerome writes that there were people who spoke of two tombs of John in Ephesus (*de Vir. Ill.* 9, ed. W. Herding, 1924, 15.19-22). But in his time that tradition was certainly already definitive which located the apostle's grave in a burial ground on the hill now called Ayasoluk, north-east of the city, above the temple of Artemis. Here, probably in the Constantinian period, a Martyrium was built, which the pilgrim Egeria in the late 4th century would gladly have visited (*Itinerarium Egeriae* 233.10, ed. A. Franceschini/R. Weber [CChrSL 175], Turnhout 1965, 67.49-53); a large cruciform three-aisle basilica was erected on the site, apparently about 400, and finally in the time of Justinian (527-565) this was replaced by an even more imposing and magnificent building; cf. *Forschungen in Ephesos*, published by the Austrian Archaeological Institute, IV 3, Die Johanneskirche, Vienna 1951; Wilhelm Alzinger, 'Ephesos B (archäol.)' in PWRE, Supplementband XII, 1970, cols. 1588-1704, esp. 1681-1684; Marcel Restle, 'Ephesos', in *Reallexikon zur byzantinischen Kunst* II, 1971, 164-207, esp. 180-192.
86. Cf. above, p. 208, note 67.
87. Cf. 1 Cor. 9:17.
88. Cf. Jn. 20:19; 21:26.
89. On the formation of tradition and legend about John's end, cf. Jean-Daniel Kaestli, 'Le rôle des textes bibliques dans la genèse et le dévelopment des légendes apocryphes: le cas du sort final de l'apôtre Jean', *Augustinianum* 23, 1983, 319-336.

Appendix

Beatha Eoin Bruinne

Ruairi ó hUiginn

Introduction: The text from which the passage below derives (paragraphs 9-14) is to be found on fol. 32ᵛ, col. a - 33ᵛ, col. b (the passage translated: fol. 33ʳ, col. a - 33ᵛ, col. b) of the *Liber Flavus Fergusiorum*, an Irish manuscript of the 15th century, today preserved in the Royal Irish Academy in Dublin (Cod 23 O 48). The *Liber Flavus* contains a large selection of hagiographical texts of Irish and non-Irish origin, many of which derive from the apocryphal tradition, in addition to various other items.

Our text was edited and commented on by Gearóid Mac Niocaill under the title 'Beatha Eoin Bruinne II' in *Eigse* 8, 1956, 222-230 (Text 1). An English translation of paragraphs 9-14 by M. Mac Craith was published in 1983 in the introduction to the Junod/Kaestli edition of the Acts of John (113-116). Mac Niocaill published a related text from the same manuscript (fol. 32ʳ, col. a - 32ᵛ, col. a) under the heading *Beatha Eoin Bruinne* in *Eigse* 7, 1955, 248-253 (Text 2). He was of the opinion that the two texts belong together, and represent fragments, in inverted order, of a fairly long life of John compiled from various sources. In it John is described as Eoin Bruinne, John of the (Lord's) breast. According to the colophon to Text 2, it was translated from the Latin by one Uidhistin Magraighin, whom Mac Niocaill regards as identical with Uighistin Mac Raighin, a member of the community of Augustinian canons of Holy Island, Lough Ree, in central Ireland, whose death the Irish annals mention at the year 1405. There is a detailed discussion of the text and its origin in M. McNamara, *The Apocrypha in the Irish Church*, Dublin 1975, 95-98; cf. also Junod/Kaestli, 109-112; on the position of the three episodes reproduced below in the history of the tradition of the ancient Acts of John, see above, p. 160f.

The language of the text is early modern Irish. It shows the verbose and florid style which marks the Irish prose of that period. It abounds in synonymous and alliterative adjectives and compound substantives. In some cases, which probably go back to imperfect copying, the text appears to be defective, and our translation can therefore only be regarded as an approximation.

Beatha Eoin Bruinne II 9-14

9 Once when Eoin had arisen and had cleaned his bright hands and had washed his fresh face and had celebrated the canonical hours with psalms and had gone into the chapel to hear Mass and the Sacrifice, a gentle, comely, big priest called Eusisp arose and put a smooth, beautiful, richly-embroidered, wonderful prescribed amice of gold thread around his neck, and he put a fine-textured, crafted (?), wonderful (?) alb over his body, and he put the beautiful, golden-threaded maniple on the wrist of his left hand, and he put a silken-laced, compactly fringed, golden-crossed chasuble on top, and began to celebrate Mass. Blue-eyed Eoin of the bright hue was devoutly attending the sacrifice, and he understood, from the holy fine-coloured host and from the lovely, fine, golden-crossed chalice that were in the hands of the priest called Seusisp, that he had a concealed sin.

10 Then Eoin made passionate, pitiful and sad lamentations, and threw himself prostrate on the ground and said:

'O God who has assembled us, do not denounce us again, and
O God who has saved us from the plagues and who has loved us, do not denounce us, and
O God who has sacrificed himself for us, do not avoid us again.
I now beseech you, O God and O Creator, Ruler and Lord, to cleanse the soul of that cleric and priest, that is, Seusisp, from the darkness of evil thoughts and from the suffocation of the great sin which is on him. For he is as one hanging in the Devil's noose, so that he is not fit to make sacrifice nor to do homage to the powerful Lord'.

11 On hearing these holy and proper words, the priest left the sacrifice, fled from the chapel and began to lament his sin in the presence of God the Father, the Creator. Then sweet-worded Eoin Bruinne (i.e. 'of the breast') arose and addressed the sweet-syllabled deacon, Birro, and said to him: 'Go to where Seusp the priest is and tell him to come in'. And as he came in he let out a great cry lamenting his sins and said to everyone: 'Let you pray steadfastly and assiduously to God for the destruction of my sins.' And he lowered himself on to his knees in his presence and said these words:

Fosterling of the Creator,
Fresh, angelic Eoin,
Sedate, with beautiful hair,
Bright, with blue eyes,
Red-cheeked, with a beautiful face,
With bright teeth and brown brows,
Red-lipped with a bright throat,
Skilful, bright-handed,
Long-fingered, fresh-complexioned,
Bright-sided, light of step,
Noble and slender, serene,
Famous, pure and saintly,
Friend of the Christians,
Expulsion of the dark devil (?),
To God he is a good fosterling.

God listened to the prayer of the priest and intervened on his behalf, and noble, refined Eoin the Evangelist took the Sacrifice again and recited the office and mass purely and renewed for ever after it.

12 There were devout old women and widows without offspring (?) and people of equal rank who were spending their lives completely and entirely following Eoin, listening to the pure bright sermons which he used to give to the people,

so that they had no food or sustenance, wealth or means save what Eoin used to get from the Christians; and they complained frequently to Eoin and castigated him many times. For in their opinion the wealth and alms that Eoin received from the people were great, and they deemed their share of it to be paltry, and they said: 'What does he do with it, since we do not get it for food or clothing? For he wishes that he himself should be wealthy and that we should be destitute.'

13 Eoin heard that, but he was not seized by an outburst of anger nor by a fury of rage as a result of it, but was sedate and patient until one day he happened to be on a big wide bridge, and donkeys and beasts were bringing hay to the town; and Eoin took the fullness of his bright hand of the hay and said: 'O God in whom I believe and whom I follow, make gold of it all without delay.' Eoin then said to his attendants: 'Count all of the gold.' And it was counted and was found to consist of one hundred polished rods of beautiful refined gold. And Eoin said: 'Dear sons, take the gold with you to those who know about gold.' And the gold was taken to the nearest workshop, and a fire was set to smelt it, and they said that they had never seen better gold than it. Thereupon the gold was brought to Eoin, and he let it fall into the depths and the rushing torrent that was underneath the bridge; and that amazed everyone. Eoin then said: 'Were I to wish for gold without sparing and wealth without want, I would get it from the Lord himself. For I prefer to be poor and destitute of my own will, since the heavenly kingdom belongs to the spiritually poor, as the Lord said. Tell now those hypocritical widows that all I do with what I get is to give it to the other paupers and to themselves. For neither the colour nor the shape, the material nor the noble edges of the garment I put on when beginning the apostolic work of the Lord have deteriorated, and the shoes (?) are yet no worse and will be no worse as long as I am alive. For Christ intended that we should understand the 72 languages that exist as well as our mother tongue.'

14 One day when Eoin was on his travels he saw approaching him on the road an armoured knight ready to kill the apostle. And as he came up to the apostle he said viciously, threateningly, hostilely and sullenly: 'It will not be long until you are powerless and under my control, and until my hands will kill you in the fashion of a powerful warrior.' Eoin said: 'May God extinguish your barbaric threat and your swift anger and yourself.' Thereupon the knight fled the spot quickly and left, just as smoke goes from a good fire or as ashes go with the wind; for it was the devil who came in the guise of a knight to fight Eoin on account of the number of people he converts to Christianity, and who serve him for his devotion.

Thus far the birth of the Anti-Christ and the life of Eoin Bruinne.

3. Acts of Paul

Wilhelm Schneemelcher

Introduction

1. Literature: *Bibliography*: F. Bovon *et al.*, *Les Actes apocryphes des Apôtres*, Geneva 1981, 295-298; D.R. MacDonald (ed.), *The Apocryphal Acts of Apostles* (*Semeia* 38), 1986, 173-181.

Texts: Lipsius, Aa I, 23-44; 104-117; 235-272; L. Vouaux, *Les Actes de Paul et ses Lettres Apocryphes*, Paris 1913; Carl Schmidt, *Acta Pauli aus der Heidelberger koptischen Papyrushandschrift Nr. 1*, 1904 ([2]1905; repr. 1965)(abbreviated: Schmidt, AP); id., Πράξεις Παύλου, *Acta Pauli*. Nach dem Papyrus der Hamburger Staats- und Universitäts-Bibliothek, unter Mitarbeit von W. Schubart, 1936 (abbreviated: Schmidt, ΠΠ).

Versions: O. von Gebhart, *Die lateinischen Übersetzungen der Acta Pauli et Theclae* (TU NF VII, 2), 1902; W. Wright, *Apocryphal Acts of the Apostles*, 1871, I.126-169; II.116-145 (Syriac and English); F. Nau, 'La version syriaque des martyres de S. Pierre, S. Paul et S. Luc', *Revue de l'Orient chrétien* III, 1898, 39-57; E.J. Goodspeed, 'The Book of Thecla', *The American Journal of Semitic Languages and Literatures* 17, 1901, 65f. (Ethiopic); F.C. Conybeare, *The Apology and Acts of Apollonius and other Monuments of early Christianity*, London 1894, 61f. (Armenian); L. Leloir, *Écrits apocryphes sur les Apôtres. Traduction de l'édition arménienne de Venise*, I: 'Pierre, Paul, André, Jacques, Jean' (CChrSA 3) 1986 (French trans.; 77-86 Martyrium Pauli; 1-34 Acta Petri et Pauli of ps.-Marcellus; cf. below, pp. 440ff.); on the Slavonic tradition cf. de Santos, *Überlieferung* I, 43-51.
On the smaller *papyrus fragments* see below, p. 216. On the correspondence between the Corinthians and Paul (3 Cor.) see below, pp. 217f.

Later texts, in which elements of the ancient APl live on: G. Dagron, *Vie et miracles de Sainte Thècle*. Text grec, traduction et commentaire. Avec la collaboration de Marie Dupré la Tour (Subs. hagiogr. 62), Brussels 1978; A. Vogt (ed.), 'Panégyrique de St Pierre; Panégyrique de St Paul. Deux discours inédits de Nicétas de Paphlagonie, disciple de Photius', *Orientalia Christiana* 23, 1931, 5-97 (Paul: 58ff.); F. Halkin, 'La légende crétoise de saint Tite', *AnalBoll* 79, 1961, 241-256. For other apostolic Acts see below, pp. 439ff.
Translations: English: James 270-299; French: Vouaux (see above); Italian: Moraldi, II 1061-1131; Erbetta, II 243-303.

A complete critical edition of the APl is being prepared for the CChrSA by W. Rordorf.

Studies: Older literature in Lipsius, *Apostelgeschichten*, II/1; Vouaux (see above), 135-140. Schmidt's discussions in AP and ΠΠ (see above) are fundamental. Also important are the collective volumes: F. Bovon, *Les Actes*... (see above); D.R. MacDonald (ed.), *Semeia* 38 (see above); 'Gli Apocrifi cristiani e cristianizzati' (*Augustinianum* 23) 1983.

Ruth Albrecht, *Das Leben der heiligen Makrina auf dem Hintergrund der Thekla-Traditionen*. Studien zu den Ursprüngen des weiblichen Mönchtums im 4. Jh. in Kleinasien (FKDG 38) 1986; F. Bovon, 'La vie des apôtres: traditions bibliques et narrations apocryphes', in: F. Bovon *et al.*, *Les Actes*... (see above), 141-158; V. Burrus, 'Chastity as Autonomy: Women in the Stories of the Apocryphal Acts'; J.-D. Kaestli, 'Response'; V. Burrus, 'Response', in *Semeia* 38 (see above), 101-135; id., *Chastity as Autonomy: Women in the Stories of the Apocryphal Acts* (Studies in Women and Religion 23), Lewiston NY, 1987; E. Dassmann, *Der Stachel im Fleisch. Paulus in der frühchristlichen Literatur bis Irenaeus*, 1979 (esp. 271ff.); S.L. Davies, *The Revolt of the Widows. The Social World of the Apocryphal Acts* (Southern Illinois University Press), 1980; id., 'Women, Tertullian and the Acts of Paul'; T.W. MacKay, 'Response', in *Semeia* 38 (see above), 139-149; P. Devos,

'Actes de Thomas et Actes de Paul', *AnalBoll* 69, 1951, 119-130; R. Kasser, Acta Pauli 1959, RHPR 40, 1960, 45-57; D.R. MacDonald, *The Legend and the Apostle. The Battle for Paul in Story and Canon*, Philadelphia 1983; id. and A.D. Scrimgeour, 'Pseudo-Chrysostom's Panegyric to Thecla: The Heroine of the Acts of Paul in Homily and Art', *Semeia* 38 (see above), 151-159; G. Poupon, 'L'accusation de magie dans les Actes apocryphes', in: F. Bovon *et al.*, *Les Actes . . .* (see above), 71-93; J. Rohde, 'Pastoralbriefe und Acta Pauli', *Studia Evangelica* V (TU 103), 1968, 303-310; W. Rordorf, 'Die neronische Christenverfolgung im Spiegel der apokryphen Paulusakten', NTS 28, 1981, 365-374; id., 'Sainte Thècle dans la tradition hagiographique occidentale', *Augustinianum* 24, 1984, 73-81; id., 'Tradition et composition dans les Actes de Thècle. État de la question', *Theol. Zeitschr. Basel* 41, 1985, 272-283 (Engl. version: *Semeia* 38, 43-52); id., 'In welchem Verhältnis stehen die apokryphen Paulusakten zur kanonischen Apostelgeschichte und zu den Pastoralbriefen?', in: *Text and Testimony*, FS A.F.J. Klijn, Kampen 1988, 225-241; id., 'Nochmals Paulusakten und Pastoralbriefe', in: *Tradition and Interpretation in the New Testament*, FS E. Earle Ellis, 1987, 319-327; id., 'Les Actes de Paul sur papyrus: problèmes liés aux P. Michigan inv. 1317 et 3788', *Proceedings of the XVIII International Congress of Papyrology (1986)*, Athens 1988, 453-460; id., 'Héresie et Orthodoxie selon la Correspondance apocryphe entre les Corinthiens et l'Apôtre Paul' (in the press); id., 'Was wissen wir über Plan und Absicht der Paulusakten?', in *Oecumenica et Patristica*, FS W. Schneemelcher 1989, 71-82; W. Schneemelcher, 'Paulus in der griechischen Kirche des zweiten Jh.', ZKG 75, 1964, 1-20 (= *Ges. Aufsätze* 1974, 154-181); id., 'Die Acta Pauli. Neue Funde und neue Aufgaben', ThLZ 89, 1964, cols. 241-254 (= *Ges. Aufsätze* 1974, 182-203); id., 'Die Apostelgeschichte des Lukas und die Acta Pauli', in: *Apophoreta*, FS E. Haenchen (BZNW 30) 1964, 236-250 (= *Ges. Aufsätze* 1974, 204-222); id., 'Der getaufte Löwe in den Acta Pauli', in: *Mullus*, FS Th. Klauser (JbAC Erg. I) 1964, 316-326 (= *Ges. Aufsätze* 1974, 223-239); Y. Tissot, 'Encratisme et Actes apocryphes', in: F. Bovon *et al.*, *Les Actes . . .* (see above), 109-119; A. Jensen, 'Thekla die Apostelgleiche. Wandlungen einer frühchristlichen Frauentradition' (in the press).

Abbreviations: APl = Acta Pauli (Acts of Paul); AThe = Acta Pauli et Theclae (Acts of Paul and Thecla); MP = Martyrium Pauli; 3 Cor. = Correspondence between the Corinthians and Paul; PH = Hamburg Papyrus; PHeid = Heidelberg Coptic Papyrus; PM = Pap. Michigan 1317 (PM1) + Pap. Berolinensis 13893 (PB) + Pap. Michigan 3788 (PM2); PO = Pap. Oxyrhynchus 1602 (= Pap. Gent. 62); PA = Pap. Antinoopolis; Ry = Fragment in the John Rylands Library (unpublished); PG = unpublished Coptic papyrus (see below, pp. 263ff.). For details on all these witnesses see below, pp. 216f.

2. Attestation: the attestation of the APl is both early and good. Tertullian writes in *de Baptismo* 17 (date uncertain, probably about 200): 'As for those (women) who <appeal to> the falsely written Acts of Paul [example of Thecla] <in order to> defend the right of women to teach and to baptize, let them know that the presbyter in Asia who produced this document, as if he could add something of his own to the prestige of Paul, was removed from his office after he had been convicted and had confessed that he had done it out of love for Paul' (ed. Borleffs, CChrSL 1, 1954, 291f.).

This text presents some difficulties. First it should be mentioned that the *de Baptismo* is extant only in one manuscript and in a printed copy of 1545 which goes back to an old manuscript, so that the text is not completely certain. Points at issue in our passage are whether Tertullian wrote *Acta Pauli* and whether the words *exemplum Theclae* should be deleted[1]. We must hold fast to the reading *Acta Pauli*, but on the other hand have to regard *exemplum Theclae* as questionable. Tertullian thus had the APl before him when in this passage he turned against tendencies to admit women also to teaching and to the administration of the sacraments. It cannot however be determined from the text whether Tertullian knew the whole APl or only the AThe, which reports Thecla's baptism of herself and her being authorised to teach by Paul (AThe 41). But there is much in favour of the view that Tertullian actually means the whole APl and not merely the AThe; for in the AThe Paul really does not occupy the centre of the stage. The assumption that Tertullian's remark relates to a lost pseudo-Pauline letter (so Davies) is pure speculation.

The title *Acta Pauli* (= Πράξεις Παύλου) is confirmed by the subscriptions in PH and PHeid. It remains open to question whether the Coptic colophon was correctly restored by C. Schmidt (AP 50* and 90). Schmidt reads 'The πράξεις of Paul <according to> the apostle'. Of the κατά which Schmidt assumes only one letter (κ) has survived. At all events it cannot be concluded from Tertullian that the author of the APl put out his work as an apostolic pseudepigraphon. We therefore cannot include it in the group of the literary forgeries.

While Tertullian rejects the APl on theological grounds (disapproving of the participation of women in teaching and the administration of the sacraments), but does not attack it as heretical, his contemporary Hippolytus evidently uses the work without hesitation. In his commentary on Daniel, composed probably *c.* 204, he writes: 'If we believe that when Paul was condemned to the circus the lion which was set upon him lay down at his feet and licked him, why should we not also believe what happened in the case of Daniel?' (III 29; Sources chrét. 14, 1947, 254). This passage might refer to AThe c. 28 and c. 33, but only becomes properly intelligible if Hippolytus had also read the scene of Paul's combat with the beasts. We may thus conjecture that Hippolytus knew the whole APl and did not repudiate it, even if he does not name the source for his statement.

Origen on the other hand twice mentions the APl. In his work *de Principiis* he quotes a saying from the Acta Pauli (so in Rufinus' Latin translation): 'This is the Word, a living Being' (*de Princ.* I 2.3; Koetschau, p. 30). It is clear from the context that Origen is here quoting a work under the title Acta Pauli (Πράξεις Παύλου); but so far the quotation has not come to light in any known text of the APl. C. Schmidt conjectured (ΠΠ, p. 128) that the author of the APl borrowed this saying as well as the Quo Vadis scene from the APt, and indeed from Peter's prayer on the cross (APt c. 38, cf. below, p. 315f). But this remains pure conjecture. On the other hand we can now verify Origen's other quotation from the APl. In his commentary on John he says: 'If anyone cares to accept what is written in the "Acts of Paul", where the Lord says: "I am on the point of being crucified afresh" . . . ' (*Comm. in Joh.* XX 12; Preuschen, p. 342). As PH p. 7.39 shows, this is a literal quotation from the APl. Origen thus knew this work, and probably valued it; at least he did not reject it as heretical.

The mention of the lion speaking to the people in Commodian (*Carmen apol.* 627ff.) is not of great importance (on this see below, p. 273).

In Eusebius on the other hand we can see how the attitude to the APl has changed, without the document being yet entirely rejected. In his discussion of the writings of Peter and Paul Eusebius affirms that the Πράξεις (Παύλου) do not belong to the undisputed books (*HE* III 3.5; trans. in vol. I, p. 48). In the summing up of his statement on the Canon Eusebius reckons the AP1 among the spurious writings, and sets them on the same level as the Shepherd of Hermas, the Apocalypse of Peter, etc. (HE III 25; trans. in vol. I, p. 47). Here also it is clear that the APl do not indeed possess any canonical dignity, but that they are distinguished from the inferior heretical works.

The same attitude seems to be reflected in the catalogue of the Codex Claromontanus (4th cent.; trans. in vol. I, p. 37), where the APl stand between Hermas and the Apocalypse of Peter. The note of the number of lines, i.e. of its compass, shows that the APl still lay before the author as part of (or an appendix to?) a biblical manuscript.

On the other hand Jerome reckons the 'περίοδοι Pauli et Theclae and the whole fable of the baptized lion' among the apocryphal writings, and quotes Tertullian on this point (*De vir. ill.* 7). But since in Tertullian nothing is said about a baptized lion, we may assume that Jerome knew the APl and rejected it as apocryphal. In the following period the Church gradually came to the same judgment as Jerome. Thus the APl are rejected as apocryphal in the Decretum Gelasianum (twice: 1. All books which Leucius the disciple of the devil has made; 2. the Book which is called the Acts of Thecla and of Paul), in the Stichometry of Nicephorus, and in the Catalogue of the 60 canonical books (cf. the texts in vol. I, pp. 38-43). The acceptance of the AGG by the Manicheans naturally played a role here (for the use of the APl by the Manicheans cf. the *Manichean Psalm-book* II, ed. Allberry, 143.4ff.).

The APl however evidently did not become altogether extinct. Photius in cod. 114 (ed. Henry II, 84ff.) reports very negatively about the five AGG, and therefore knew them. It is astonishing that Nicetas of Paphlagonia (10th cent.)[2] makes intensive use of the APl in his speech on Paul, and combines their statements with those of the canonical Acts. We cannot here present an analysis of this speech, and show its use of the APl in detail, but we may at any rate refer to the episode in Antioch, which Nicetas transports to Syrian Antioch (see below, p. 219f). Even in the 14th century Nicephorus Callistus (Xanthopulos; *c.* 1256-*c.* 1335) incorporated into his *Church History* a long report about the Ephesian episode in the APl (*HE* II 25; PG 145, col. 821).[3]

3. Extant Remains: In recent decades our knowledge of the APl, a work frequently attested but as a whole lost, has steadily grown. Above all the discovery of the Coptic PHeid in 1894 considerably increased our knowledge of this apocryphon. Since then many other finds have been added, in particular the great Hamburg Papyrus (PH). We must here content ourselves with a brief enumeration of the material.

The following, all unfortunately preserved only in a fragmentary condition, may be regarded as witnesses to the entire APl:

a) The Greek Papyrus of the Hamburg Staats- und Universitäts-bibliothek (PH), 10 leaves of a papyrus book from the period about 300 (description of the manuscript in Schmidt-Schubart, ΠΠ pp. 4-14). This manuscript contains a large part of the Ephesus episode (pp. 1-5), Paul's sojourn in Corinth (pp. 6-7), the journey from Corinth to Italy (pp. 7-8) and a part of the MP (pp. 9-11).

It is supplemented by various fragments: Pap. Berlin 13893, (PB), Pap. Michigan 1317 (PM1) and PM 3788 (PM2) belong to a leaf which offers a parallel to the text contained in PH p. 8.[4] Pap. Oxyrhynchus 1602 is not a papyrus but a leaf from a parchment codex of the 4th/5th cent., which contains the text of PH p. 8.17-26.[5]

b) The Coptic Papyrus No. 1 in Heidelberg (PHeid) contains extensive fragments of the whole APl (description of the manuscript, probably written in the 6th century, in Schmidt, AP pp. 3-20).

The fragment of a Coptic parchment of the 4th century in the John Rylands Library Suppl. 44 (Ry), so far not yet published, presents some lines from the beginning of the APl (cf. Schmidt, ΠΠ, pp. 117f.).

On the Coptic papyrus, likewise not yet published, which contains the Ephesus episode complete (PG), cf. R. Kasser, below, pp. 263ff.

Three complexes of text, which we may assume to have belonged to the ancient APl, have each a separate tradition history. Even if the author found these parts already shaped, and incorporated them into his work, we cannot say anything about their history before their inclusion in the APl.

c) The Acta Pauli et Theclae were edited by Lipsius Aa 1, pp. 235-269) on the basis of 11 Greek manuscripts as well as Latin, Syriac, Slavic and Arabic versions (cf. his Introduction, Aa 1, pp. xciv-cvi). To these may be added a small Greek fragment POx. No. 6 (Grenfell-Hunt I, pp. 9f.) and another fragment from Antinoopolis (PA: Roberts no. 13, pp. 26-28). Important are the Latin translations, of which according to O. von Gebhart TU NF 7.2, 1902) there were at least four, independent of one another. Further information on the tradition in Vouaux, pp. 12-19. The relation of the witnesses to one another and the value of the individual versions probably requires a fresh investigation. Lipsius' text is frequently in need of correction. In this respect a special significance attaches to the Coptic version (see above under *b*), even if it is not of itself decisive.

d) The correspondence between the Corinthians and Paul (3 Cor) in several respects presents considerable problems (cf. below, p. 228). Here it is in the first place only a matter of the questions of its transmission. The correspondence was known through the Armenian Bible and through the commentary of Ephraem Syrus on the Pauline Epistles (also preserved in Armenian). Through PHeid the Coptic text was published as part of the APl. Then gradually there followed the discovery of five Latin manuscripts, some of them admittedly fragmentary: Cod. Ambros. E 53 inf., 10th cent. (M); Cod. Laon 45, 13th cent. (L); Cod. Paris. lat. 5288, 10/11th cent. (P); Cod. Zürich Car. C 14, 10th cent. (Z); Cod. Berlin Ham. 84, 13th cent. (B). While 3 Cor is missing in PH (and also is completely ignored in the remaining text of this witness), we now have for the first time a Greek version in the 3rd-century PBodm X.[6]

The various witnesses differ considerably, especially with regard to their compass. PHeid presents an introduction, through which the correspondence is linked with the rest of the text of the APl. Then follow the two letters, separated by some intervening material. The letters and the intervening material (without the introduction) are handed down by most Armenian MSS and by Ephraem. The letters only (without the intervening section) are to be found in PBodm, M, L and B. Z has only the letter of the Corinthians and the intervening section, while P contains only Paul's letter. The witnesses also differ within the text of Paul's letter, through additions or through omissions.

e) The Martyrium Pauli was edited by Lipsius according to two Greek manuscripts (Cod. Patmiacus 48 (9th cent.) = P; Cod. Athous Vatoped. 79 (10th/11th cent.) = A), as well as a Coptic, a Slavic and an Ethiopic version. Appended is the fragmentary Latin version according to three Munich manuscripts (Lipsius, Aa 1, pp. 104-117; cf. pp. lii-lvii). To these may be added a Syriac version, which Lipsius did not take into account, and above all PH pp. 9-11. Lipsius' text must at many points be corrected on the basis of PH and PHeid.

4. Reconstruction and composition: relation to the Lucan Acts: in what follows, an attempt will be made to bring the material available into a certain order. It should be emphasised that this is really only an attempt. Many questions remain open. Above all, it is not possible to determine the extent of the lacunae with any certainty. Nor can we say with any confidence whether the APl portray *one* major missionary journey by Paul, or whether some places were visited twice by the apostle. Here we can conjecture much, but prove little. The same also holds for other problems.[7]

1. *From Damascus to Jerusalem.* The beginning of the APl has not survived, but C. Schmidt has made the first episode available from some fragments. A small Coptic fragment (Ry) contains some lines of a narrative from the life of Paul. Evidently the appearance of Christ on the way to Damascus was previously reported. In the extant text Paul receives the command to go to Damascus, and from there to Jerusalem; he comes to Damascus to the community there assembled (and fasting!).[8] He seems then to have delivered a sermon in the presence of the Jews.[9] Presumably it was then reported (referring to Acts 9:26?) that Paul journeyed from Damascus to Jerusalem.

Now in a later section of the APl Paul himself speaks of his passage from persecutor of Christians to preacher of Christ (cf. below, p. 264). In this address in Ephesus he recounts that he came to the community in Damascus (Judas, the brother of the Lord, plays a part here), that he was there instructed in the Christian faith and was then himself found worthy to preach the Gospel. The technique of the author of the AGG makes it seem possible that this short and indirect account relates to a preceding longer narrative (cf. for example the Eubula story in the APt; see below, p. 280). We may thus assume that in the context of Paul's sojourn in Damascus a sermon actually was recorded. Paul further relates in Ephesus that he departed from Damascus - the reasons are not stated, but his departure took place by night, cf. Acts 9:25 - and marched in the direction of Jericho. He thus set himself, in conformity with the Lord's injunction (cf. Ry), on the way to Jerusalem. According to the apostle's later speech, the baptism of the lion (see below, p. 264) took place on this journey, and this too will presumably have been related in detail at this point.

For Jerusalem we have no further reports. C. Schmidt however regarded two leaves of PHeid as parts of this episode. These are the pages 60/59 and 61/62, which however are so badly damaged that we can voice little more than a conjecture about their position in the APl as a whole. If on p. 61 it is said: 'Thou findest thyself in sight of Jerusalem', that is no sure indication that the scene took place in Jerusalem. The mention of Peter on p. 59 is also not of much consequence, especially since we do not know who is really speaking at p. 59, lines 8ff. Hence we cannot by any means form so confident a judgment of these pages as Schmidt did (ΠΠ, p. 118). Despite this it remains probable that a certain space in the APl was devoted to Paul's stay in Jerusalem.

2. *Paul in Antioch.* In PHeid pp. 1-6 are preserved the remains of the description of Paul's activity in Antioch. These pages also however have so many gaps that we

can only approximately reconstruct the course of the action. In particular it is not clear how Paul's passage from Jerusalem to Antioch was described in the APl, nor can we determine from the extant fragments whether the author of the APl adhered to the route of the canonical Acts.[10] Again it is not clear which Antioch is meant in PHeid pp. 1-6, the Syrian or the Pisidian. Since reference is made on p. 6 to Paul's flight from Antioch to Iconium, it has been assumed that it is the Pisidian Antioch that is in view (cf. the particulars in Schmidt, ΠΠ, pp. 115ff.). On the other hand it is reported in AThe c. 26 that Paul came to Antioch with Thecla, and Thecla was there embraced by a man Alexander on the open street (see below, p. 243). Now this Alexander is characterised in the greater part of the Greek manuscripts as a Syrian, while one manuscript, which Tischendorf and Lipsius followed, describes him as συριάρχης. Even if this reading were correct,[11] which however can scarcely be the case, it remains questionable whether we may draw from it the conclusion that here the Syrian Antioch is meant.

Reference may be made here to three points:

a) In the Greek Acts of Titus[12] the APl have undoubtedly been used. Now it is said there in c. 4 (Halkin, p. 246): 'When they reached Antioch, they found Barnabas, the son of Panchares, whom Paul had raised up.... Thereafter they journeyed to Seleucia and Cyprus, Salamis and Paphos, and from there to Perga in Pamphylia and *again* to Antioch in Pisidia and to Iconium, to the house of Onesiphorus, to whom Titus had previously related the matter concerning Paul.' Part of this account probably goes back to the canonical Acts, but the name Panchares, the father of Barnabas, takes us beyond Acts. This name and the raising from the dead referred to appear in PHeid pp. 1-6, although admittedly the son is not there called by the name of Barnabas.[13] It is thus fairly clear that the author of the Acts of Titus borrowed from the APl. The Onesiphorus in Iconium and the role of Titus also derive from the APl (cf. AThe c. 2).[14] Now it is said in the Acts of Titus that Paul journeyed again (πάλιν) to Antioch in Pisidia. This can only be understood thus: that the author of the Acts of Titus assumed that the raising of Barnabas took place in Pisidian Antioch, and that Paul after his activity in Cyprus returned thither by way of Perga, and thence came to Iconium. It remains however obscure whether in this interpretation of the Antioch in the Panchares episode as the Pisidian the author of the Acts of Titus could really appeal to the APl, or whether he hit upon exactly the same conclusion as modern scholars.

b) It is not clear what value we should accord to the note in Nicetas of Paphlagonia (see above, p. 216). He reports (ed. Vogt, 70f.) that Paul escaped from Damascus (cf. Acts 9:25) and then continued his journey to Antioch in Syria (which does not agree with Acts 9). There he is at first thrown into prison, but later freed. He then raises from death the son of a high official (Panchares?), and thereafter travels on to Iconium. The report of the episode in Iconium is manifestly dependent on the AThe, which indeed link on to the report of Paul's sojourn in Antioch (see below). It could therefore well be that the mention of Syrian Antioch in Nicetas derives from the APl.

c) Finally it must be observed that we are probably ascribing rather too high an intellectual level to the author of the APl when we expect him to have elaborated all the details of his work consistently and harmonised them one with another, and at the same time also to have sought after the closest possible correspondence with the canonical Acts. Rather is the author of this apocryphal work to a great extent a compiler. He gave a fixed written form to legends which were current and inserted them into a larger composition; many a section he probably invented himself. In the process obscurities, gaps and contradictions have remained. Further it must be emphasised that the dominating factor in the production of the APl was neither a geographical nor a historical interest. The author's purpose is the edification and upbuilding of the community, perhaps also the propagation of a particular 'image' of Paul. We may therefore conjecture that he did not set particular store upon the distinction of the two Antiochs. Naturally he has a definite itinerary for the apostle in view, and sought to present it. So too the model of the canonical Acts may in a certain fashion have influenced him and his work. But how strong this influence was, and whether it determined the itinerary, we do not know. The material is too fragmentary for us to decide with certainty whether Paul in fact appears only once in each place (as C. Schmidt thought, ΠΠΠ 118; this is uncertain for Corinth, see below, p. 229f.). Thus the question which Antioch is here meant does not admit of a definite answer. The Acts of Titus speak for the Pisidian Antioch as the scene for all the events. The text of Nicetas tells against this, and so does the fact that in PHeid only eight pages of text could have preceded, if Schmidt's reconstruction is correct. On these eight pages, then, room must have been found for the events in Damascus, Jerusalem and Antioch in Syria, which is scarcely possible. However that may be: even if the Panchares episode took place in Pisidian Antioch, this does not mean that in the APl there was no reference to Syrian Antioch at all. In particular, we cannot affirm with any certainty that PHeid contained the complete text of the APl. There is indeed much in favour of this view, but we cannot prove it.[15] It is quite possible that the lacuna before the Panchares episode (in Pisidian Antioch?) was greater than has been assumed on the basis of the Coptic manuscript. But this also remains conjecture.

From the fragmentary pages of PHeid 1-6 we can deduce at least in outline what Paul did in Antioch (see below, p. 238).

3. *Acts of Paul and Thecla* (Iconium, Antioch, Myra, Iconium, Seleucia). - The next episode is particularly well known through the fact that it was transmitted as an independent piece (see above, p. 217f). In PHeid it is directly attached to the events in Antioch, and is thus guaranteed by this manuscript as part of the APl. Paul's stay in Myra and Thecla's meeting with him there (AThe c. 40) also link the AThe with the APl.

Since the content of this piece is guaranteed by a wide textual tradition, the reconstruction offers no problem. The composition of the narrative is also clear: Paul comes to Iconium, preaches there (the sermon is summarised, cc. 5f., in the form of blessings), and through this sermon converts Thecla. The consequences correspond to the pattern which occurs also in other apocryphal Acts: the husband (here it is the fiancé), who through the woman's continence has been deprived of her, stirs up the people or the authorities against the apostle. Here Paul is now imprisoned. Thecla visits him by night, but this is discovered and in consequence, after Paul has been expelled from the town, she is condemned to death at the stake. Rain and hail however prevent the execution and Thecla, now set free again, is able to follow Paul, who is staying meanwhile with Onesiphorus and his family in a burial vault on the road to Daphne. Despite serious scruples Paul takes Thecla with him to Antioch (which?), where at once a fresh misfortune comes upon her. A Syrian Alexander (cf. above, p. 219) falls in love with Thecla, but naturally is rebuffed and takes his revenge by having her condemned by the governor to the arena. A woman named Tryphaena, who is later described as a queen and a kinswoman of the emperor, takes her under her protection. This Tryphaena has lost her daughter Falconilla, and begs Thecla to intercede for the deceased. We now come to the fight with the beasts, in the course of which Thecla baptizes herself. As many beasts are set loose against her, she throws herself into a large pit full of water. The seals in it are killed as by a flash of lightning. Since the other animals also do nothing to Thecla, but Tryphaena falls in a swoon and it is feared that she is dead, Thecla is set free. It is characteristic for the entire APl that the detailed description of the fight with the beasts, which owing to the help of a lioness and some marvellous events does not lead to Thecla's death, concludes with the conversion of Tryphaena and part of her household: 'Now I believe that the dead are raised up! Now I believe that my child lives!' (c. 39). The miracles here as always are the proof of the truth of the Christian proclamation.

After Thecla has rested eight days in the house of Tryphaena and has there proclaimed the Word of God, she yearns after Paul. She learns that he is in Myra, and goes after him. After a short time together she goes back to Iconium with the commission to teach the Word of God, finds her fiancé no longer alive, attempts to convert her mother (nothing is reported of any outcome), and then proceeds to Seleucia. There she enlightens many through the Word of God and dies a peaceful death.[16]

This brief account of the contents shows that we have to do with a homogeneous composition. Some questions remain, which are important from the point of view of the composition of the APl as a whole. In the entire section it is not so much Paul as Thecla who stands in the foreground. Certainly there are also reports about Paul: his sermon in Iconium, his defence before the governor, his meetings with Thecla outside Iconium and in Myra. But this in no way alters the fact that here it is more a question of 'Acts of Thecla' than of 'Acts of Paul'. Thus it is striking that Paul, who is the really guilty party, is according to c. 21 expelled from Iconium, but Thecla must suffer death by fire. The apostle is indeed asked by Alexander in c. 26 to help him to win Thecla, but disappears from the ensuing narrative. When Thecla has successfully endured the combat with the beasts, she has to seek after Paul; he thus appears to have set out from Antioch for Myra without leaving any message. All this points to the view that the author of the APl has here absorbed independent Thecla-traditions into his book and worked them up.[17] It will be difficult to disentangle these traditions, which are probably connected with the worship of Thecla in Seleucia (or Iconium), since the linguistic form of the text today before us is the work of the author of the APl.[18] This means that the author has given a stamp of his own to the traditional material which came down to him. Whether the striking double narration of Thecla's deliverance in Iconium and Antioch belonged thereto, or whether here two different and in some respects competing traditions have been used, can scarcely be determined. Nevertheless we may here apply the general observation that the authors of the apocryphal Acts are fond of repetitions of motifs and scenes which to them were especially valuable - in this again a true reflection of popular tradition. Whether we can apply the 'laws' of folk-lore to the AThe (and also to the other parts of the APl) remains however doubtful. Above all we must be very cautious about any combination of these folk-lore hypotheses with the assumption of a liberated women's movement in the Church of the 2nd century as the *Sitz im Leben* for the APl (and the other AGG). On a sober treatment of the evidence, hypotheses of such a kind appear to be largely no more than the products of modern fancy, without any basis in the sources.[19]

If it is correct that the AThe are a collection of oral traditions put into shape by the author of the APl, then the question of historical reminiscences in the Thecla legends, which formerly was accorded such importance,[20] is probably to be answered with an unambiguous negative. Even if there was - as we may presume - a woman named Thecla who was converted by Paul, the attempt to provide historical proof for the actual occurrences is unavailing. Neither 'queen' Tryphaena (who did exist, cf. Rolffs, NTApoHdb 377f.; *Der kleine Pauly* I, 1964, col. 415, s.v. Antonia Tr.) nor the author's alleged knowledge of the roads (cf. Ramsay) are of any assistance here. Nor can Pseudo-Chrysostom's homily on Thecla (BHG^3, no. 1720) be claimed as evidence for an older tradition.[21] Rather this text shows how the legend developed further. We may probably assume that in the process the local cult of St Thecla, which spread very quickly from Seleucia to the East and to the West, played an important role. The wide dissemination of the AThe shows that this part of the ancient Acts, separated off from the APl, was certainly influential.[22]

4. *Paul in Myra.* Already in c. 40 of the AThe it was reported that Paul was in Myra (on the south coast of Lycia). Now on p. 28 of PHeid a new section is attached directly to the conclusion of the AThe. Its superscription was reconstructed by Schmidt (AP, p. 52): '<When he was departed from> Antioch <and taught in My>ra'. This supplement to the seven extant letters may be correct. At any rate the following scene takes place in Myra. Unfortunately the Coptic papyrus has many lacunae, and in particular at least one leaf of the text is missing (cf. Schmidt, AP, p. 9). In spite of this the train of thought can be clearly recognised. During his activity in Myra Paul heals a man suffering from dropsy, named Hermocrates. This man's son Hermippus is but little pleased by the healing, since he had already been counting on the inheritance, while another son, Dion, 'heard Paul gladly'. Unfortunately the following text is not very clear. Dion appears to lose his life through a fall. His father mourns indeed at first, but during Paul's sermon forgets his sorrow, while his mother comes to Paul with her clothes rent, i.e. as one in mourning, and Paul sends young men to bring the dead Dion - probably with the intention of raising him again to life. Unfortunately the text here breaks off; a leaf is missing, on which probably reference was made to the resurrection of Dion. Further there will have been an account of Hermippus' preparations for revenge on Paul. Page 31 at any rate begins with a dream of Paul's, in which he is warned against a great danger. Hermippus comes against Paul with a crowd with a sword and staves, and Paul meets this attack as Christ did in the Garden of Gethsemane. As Hermippus sets upon Paul, he becomes blind and now not only repents of his hostility against Paul but also recognises the vanity of this world's goods. Paul is shaken at the hearing of his prayer and the humbling of the proud Hermippus, but seems to have no intention of helping the blind man. If there is no leaf missing between pages 32 and 33, we must take the sequel to be that Paul goes into the house of Hermocrates, but the young men lay Hermippus down before the door. This however is not a very meaningful sequence of events, since after the

preceding text the action of the young men is superfluous. It seems more natural to assume a lengthy lacuna, probably a whole leaf. On the following leaf we are told how Hermippus lies before the door, and how his parents on the other hand first distribute money and grain, but are then troubled over their blinded son. They pray with Paul, and Hermippus recovers his sight. He relates that Paul laid his hand upon him, which however according to the narrative cannot have been possible; the Lord himself healed him, in the form of Paul. The end of the story cannot be reconstructed, since not only are there lacunae on the extant pages but also there is probably a leaf missing between pages 34 and 35.

We can thus trace at least in outline a large part of this section of Paul's journey. Whether the author of the APl contented himself with a resurrection from the dead and the healing of a blind man, or whether a lengthy sermon by Paul also stood here, we cannot say. The material before us is sufficient only to enable us to recognise various motifs and scenes which are typical for the APl and the other apocryphal Acts. Here it must be said that this section has no detailed reference to the continence which elsewhere is so strongly emphasised; at most one might mention in this connection Hermippus' renunciation of the goods of this world, or the distribution of money and grain to the widows by his parents. But the sexual continence which in other parts of the APl plays so prominent a role is lacking in the extant fragments of this episode. It might in some way have been of importance in the lost sections. We may however also assume that the author wished in this case to display by means of an example the other side of Paul's preaching, the resurrection. But even this is by no means clearly said. However that may be, these considerations lead to the conclusion that here also the author has worked into his composition a tradition which had come down to him.

Here comparison with the canonical Acts is interesting. According to Acts 27:5f., Paul on his journey to Rome only changed ships in Myra. In the APl he works there as a missionary, as always not by word only but also through his acts. We may conjecture that some local legends provided the author with the inspiration and the pattern for this section.

5. *Paul in Sidon.* Paul's activity in Myra is followed in PHeid pp. 35-39, according to Schmidt's reconstruction, by the unfortunately very fragmentary account of his stay in Sidon. This reconstruction, to be sure, is only partially certain. In the first place, it is probably correct that Sidon follows Myra, even if the lemma on p. 35 is not preserved in full: 'When he was departed from Myra and <wished to go to Sidon>'. What now follows however has to a great extent been very uncertainly restored or interpreted by Schmidt (cf. his account of the contents, AP pp. 95ff.). On pp. 35/36 we have first of all a report of Paul's journey to Sidon. Paul is accompanied by a number of brethren from Perga. On the way he appears to have entered into a discussion at a pagan altar with an old man, who quotes examples of the punishment meted out by the gods to those who forsake them. Here already, however, much remains obscure. There follows a gap of at least two leaves. This figure was suggested by Schmidt 'since on p. 37 we are in the middle of the narrative of the events in Sidon'. On this line of argument it might naturally have been four leaves. What was contained in these leaves we do not know. On p. 37 we have first the end of an address by Paul (we may probably assume that it is he who is speaking), in which he seeks to restrain

his hearers from some course of action by referring to Sodom and Gomorrah. The consequence is however that Paul, with the brethren Thrasymachus and Cleon (cf. p. 38.5), is cast into the temple of Apollo where, surprisingly, the people seek to fatten them up with good food (in preparation for sacrifice?). Paul fasts and prays, and at his prayer the half of the temple collapses (probably the part in which the prisoners were not shut up). This occasions considerable alarm, and on the insistence of the people Paul and his companions are brought into the theatre. Here the text breaks off again. Whether here again two leaves only are missing or more, we cannot say. On p. 39 we find the conclusion of the Sidon episode, of which unfortunately only a little is coherently preserved. We can recognise that Paul delivered an address, which possibly won the people over. A certain Theudas appears to have begged for baptism. The page ends with the departure from Sidon for Tyre.

It is thus scarcely possible to give an accurate account of the contents of this section. Many lacunae, obscurities and uncertainties remain. The brief notice in the Acts of Titus c. 3 does not help us very far. After briefly reporting that Paul first preached the word of Christ in Damascus (this may derive from Acts 9:22), the author continues: 'And Apphia, the wife of Chrysippus, who was possessed by a demon, was healed by Paul; and after he had fasted seven days he overcame the idol of Apollo.' Now the names Amphion and Chrysippus appear in PHeid p. 40 (Tyre, see below, p. 250). From this Schmidt (ΠΠ p. 114) concluded that the author of the Acts of Titus has condensed the episode at Tyre, the name Amphion in the Coptic being only a corruption of Apphia.[23] The note about the overcoming of the idol of Apollo in the Acts of Titus would then go back to the Sidon section of the APl. Against this it can hardly be objected that in the Acts of Titus the sequence Sidon-Tyre in the APl is reversed; in so summary a report this can readily be understood. It is more difficult to reconcile the overcoming of the idol with the collapse of the temple (according to Schmidt's reconstruction, p. 98). Even this however would be possible, only it would then have to be assumed that reference was made to it also in the narrative, and not only to the collapse of the temple. In favour of this view is the fact that p. 38. 19f. says: 'The god of the Sidonians, Apollo, is fallen, and the half of his temple.' All this shows however that here we can work only with cautious conjectures.

It may be further noted that the evidently quite detailed portrayal of Paul's experiences in Sidon does not tally very well with the brief mention of this town in Acts 27:3. According to Acts, Paul is brought from Caesarea to Sidon, and there by permission of the 'philanthropic' centurion Julius he is allowed to visit 'his friends', i.e. the Christian community in Sidon, which was either known to Luke or imagined by him. That the narrative of the APl cannot have originated out of this note needs no further proof. Again, the route of the journey does not agree with Acts. Whether this part of the APl goes back to a local legend of the church in Sidon cannot be said, owing to the fragmentary state of the tradition.

6. *Paul in Tyre*. Still more difficult is the reconstruction of the part of the APl in which Paul's sojourn in Tyre is depicted. The lemma on p. 39 of PHeid is well preserved: 'When he was departed from Sidon and wished to go to Tyre.' This makes it certain that, contrary to the account in Acts, Paul travelled from Sidon to Tyre. There, according to PHeid p. 40, he had to deal with Jews. The Apphia and Chrysippus known from the Acts of Titus (cf. above) make their appearance, and

ultimately Paul appears to be active as an exorciser of demons. Schmidt by way of experiment attached some fragments from PHeid here, but it remains questionable whether these (pp. 64, 63, 70, 69, 68, 67, 66, 65) have anything to do with the episode at Tyre, or whether they belong to some other point on the route. It may be correct that a part of these fragments derives from a speech by Paul or from a disputation, but more we cannot say.[24] On pp. 60/59 and 61/62, which Schmidt originally wanted to accommodate here as well, cf. above, p. 218.

We must thus content ourselves with the observation that only PHeid p. 40 belongs to the episode at Tyre, and that here the thread of the narrative breaks off. This is all the more regrettable in that the gap which here opens is very large, and cannot be removed by any kind of conjecture as to what may have stood in the lacuna. Schmidt thought (ΠΠ 119) that Jerusalem could not have been referred to here, since the author has already reported on Paul's stay in this city at the beginning of his work. In this Schmidt presupposes that the APl never make the apostle return to the same place twice. This however, as already noted (see above, p. 220) is a hypothesis incapable of proof. As a further reason for excluding Jerusalem (from the lacuna here), Schmidt assumes that the author deliberately did not wish to take up Paul's journey with the collection and his imprisonment in Caesarea because he did not want 'to set before his readers a Paul transported as a prisoner to Rome' (ΠΠ 119). This argument too may be considered not very convincing.

It is admittedly surprising that according to the APl Paul arrives in Rome as a free man (cf. MP, below, pp. 260ff.). W. Rordorf has attempted to solve this riddle by assuming that the APl reported two different journeys by Paul.[25] The one would correspond to the so-called third missionary journey, the other (after the lacuna in PH pp.5/6) is to be located after the events of Acts 28. Rordorf adduces the Pastorals and the Acts of Titus in support of his thesis. In the Pastorals (according to R.) we meet with traditions which are also taken up in the APl. In the Acts of Titus there is brief mention of activity by the apostle in Seleucia, on Cyprus, in Perga, Antioch (in Pisidia), Iconium, Lystra and Derbe (c. 4; for text see above, p. 219f.). This account is a combination of Acts and the APl. The gap between Tyre and Ephesus could thus be closed, just as on the other side the gap between Ephesus and Philippi - PH leaves out Philippi altogether (see below, p. 227) - also appears in a different light.

This hypothesis, which cannot here be discussed in the detail one would wish, is indeed fascinating, but still leaves some questions outstanding. For one thing, both Schmidt and Rordorf seem to me too much set upon a comparison with Acts. The author of the APl may have known Acts (see below, p. 232), but he did not intend to supply a duplicate of Luke's work; he fashioned a portrait of Paul of his own, rooted in the tradition of Asia Minor, in the form of a 'novel'. For another, the comparison with the Pastorals is rendered questionable by the fact that Rordorf wishes to extract historical information or primeval traditions from these pseudapostolic letters, which derive from the beginning of the 2nd century.

We must therefore for the moment accept that the gap between Tyre and Ephesus cannot at present be filled. Whether Paul went from Tyre to Caesarea[26] or Jerusalem or Crete or Cyprus (Schmidt ΠΠ, p. 119) remains unknown, pending the discovery of new material. That Ephesus was not the only scene of operations in Asia Minor Schmidt (*loc. cit.*) had already conjectured. But here, as we now know, it is a question not of Miletus but of Smyrna. This is shown by the beginning of the as yet unpublished PG (cf. Kasser, RHPR 40, 1960, pp. 45-57, and below, p. 263). But what Paul did in Smyrna, and what stopping-places lay before it, remains uncertain.

7. *Paul in Ephesus*. For Paul's stay in Ephesus we have, in addition to the unpublished PG (see below, pp. 263ff.), the Hamburg Papyrus, which presents this episode on pp. 1-5. This makes it possible to survey the structure of the whole section. Paul comes from Smyrna to Ephesus and there puts up at the house of Aquila and Priscilla. After a vision with the intimation of sorrows to come, Paul delivers a sermon, in the course of which he gives an account of his conversion and of the baptism of the lion. This sermon has the usual result: Paul is brought before the proconsul Hieronymus (PH p. 1.30), and is required to give an account of himself (here PH p. 1 begins). The speech in which he does so is shot through with apologetic motifs. This is all the more striking in that previously there has not been - as Schmidt still conjectured (ΠΠ, p. 87) - any detailed account of an attack by Paul on the statuettes of Artemis. Only in a single sentence is the criticism of idol-worship suggested. We may ask whether the author of the APl did not wish so far as possible to avoid a doublet to Acts 19:23ff. But allusions have not entirely been renounced: in PH 1.28 the χρυσοχόοι, the goldsmiths, appear as the agitators who wish to see Paul condemned. The pro-consul finds nothing at all wrong in Paul's sppech, but bows before the determination of the people, who demand that Paul be thrown to the beasts. After six days there follows the procession of the animals, among whom a lion especially attracts attention. His roaring startles even Paul, who in his prison is deep in prayer. Here is inserted a story about the conversion and baptism of Artemilla, the wife of Hieronymus.[27] Artemilla is informed of Paul's preaching and activity through Eubula, the wife of Diophantes, a freedman of the proconsul, and wishes to make the apostle's acquaintance herself. A short address by Paul, in which he urges flight from and contempt for the world, brings about her desire for baptism, which takes place amid all kinds of wonderful phenomena and with the assistance of Christ himself. After the celebration of the eucharist with bread and water, Artemilla goes back to her house and Paul in prison returns to his prayers.[28] In the whole story Eubula plays no further part. It is a conversion-story, in which a prominent lady comes to the Christian faith. Difficulties are created only by the lines on PH p. 3.1-4, according to which Diophantes informs the proconsul that the women are sitting day and night with Paul. Hieronymus thereupon interrupts his meal in order to hasten on the fight with the beasts. These lines not only break the connection, but do not at all fit what has gone before. The whole story is played out in one night (Saturday to Sunday), while in these lines it is said of the two women that they stayed a longer time with Paul. It is thus possible to take these lines as a secondary insertion, but a better assumption is that the contradiction has arisen from the fact that the author has here worked together two different traditions, but has not quite succeeded. On the one hand he had before him, perhaps in the setting of the Ephesus episode, a story about the occasion for the persecution of the apostle, i.e. about the jealousy of Diophantes (a favourite motif in all apocryphal Acts), on the other he may have lit upon a conversion story linked with the name of Artemilla. At all events I see here again an indication of the author's methods of working, making use in his composition of older traditions.

This is to a certain extent confirmed by some observations on the following text.

Next morning we come to the fight with the beasts, and here Paul meets the lion he had baptized. Since the lion does nothing to harm the apostle, other animals are released. But a violent hailstorm brings to nothing all efforts to make away with Paul. Paul takes leave of the lion, who goes back to the mountains while the apostle mingles with those who are fleeing in terror of the fall of the city, and embarks on a ship for Macedonia. Now in this story notes about Hieronymus and Diophantes, or about Artemilla and Eubula, are interspersed (PH p. 4, 8-11; 4, 14-18), and after Paul's departure we are told how Artemilla and Eubula were in sorrow and mourning for him, but were comforted by an angel (PH p. 5.19ff.). Unfortunately the end of PH p. 5 has come down to us in very bad condition. But it seems to describe how Hieronymus called upon the God of Paul for help for his ear, injured in the hailstorm, and how the ear was then healed. Schmidt has described these last notices as a brief 'Epilogue, concerned with the other leading figures in the Ephesus story' (ΠΠ, p. 94). This is certainly correct if we look at the composition as a whole. The question however remains, whether the author has not here also laid hold of a tradition which he himself was the first to bring into connection with the fight with the beasts in Ephesus. At any rate this conjecture has much in its favour.

The structure of this section is thus clear, but the problem of the use of tradition in its composition is also evident. The inspiration for the formation of this story of Paul's fight with the beasts may be sought in various NT passages: 1 Cor. 15:32; 2 Tim. 4:17; and above all Acts 19:23ff., but in these passages we can see no more than the initial impulse for this episode. The decisive motives were certainly different.[29]

8. *Paul in Philippi*. From Ephesus Paul set out by ship for Macedonia, i.e. probably for Philippi (PH p. 5.15ff.), but curiously we learn nothing from PH about Paul's stay in this city. On the contrary the next episode, 'From Philippi to Corinth', follows directly on p. 6 of PH, i.e. on the back of p. 5. A whole section has thus been omitted in this manuscript. We cannot say why nothing is reported in PH of this station in Paul's journey, nor can we determine the extent of the missing narrative. W. Rordorf[30] assumes a gap of considerable size, and would see here probably the break between the report of APl, which corresponds to the third missionary journey (Acts 19-20), and a renewed missionary journey after Paul's release from prison in Rome (i.e. after Acts 28). This however is scarcely capable of proof, even though some particular arguments deserve consideration (e.g. the differences between PHeid pp. 45-50 and pp. 41-44, and between the persons mentioned in 3 Cor. and those in PH). In view of the author's way of working, these differences are probably not to be taken too seriously. It has already been said above (p. 225) that we must be very cautious in our use of the Pastorals and the Acts of Titus.

For the moment it remains a riddle why Philippi is missing in PH. Various explanations offer themselves for its solution: it could have been external reasons (e.g. the size of the book) that led to the omission. Or the episode was already missing in the *Vorlage* from which PH was copied. It is also possible that offence taken at the contents led to the abbreviation (3 Cor. according to PHeid belongs to this section).

However that may be, we cannot deduce from PH what took place in Philippi. Only a reference in Paul's report in Corinth (PH p. 6.5) indicates that in Philippi the apostle suffered much.

PHeid also, however, allows us to extract only a little for this part of the APl. The beginning of PHeid p. 45 - the page on which 3 Cor. begins with its preamble - is so fragmentary that we can do nothing with it. We learn from the introductory narrative to 3 Cor. that people in Corinth were very anxious about Paul, even though his deliverance had been announced through a special revelation, and that on the other hand there was an urgent need for the apostle's presence to head the resistance to false teachers. Accordingly a letter was written to Paul and brought by Threptus and Eutychus to Philippi, where Paul was a prisoner 'because of Stratonice, the wife of Apollophanes' (3 Cor. 2:2). Evidently events thus took the same course at Philippi as at many other places: the preaching of continence met with success among the women, but aroused the men against the apostle. Paul now answers the Corinthians and attempts to refute the false doctrine, largely, it must be said, in summary and apodeictic fashion and only in his argument on the question of the resurrection in a rather more judicious and lively way.

With the end of 3 Cor. the tradition regrettably once more breaks off, so that we hear nothing of the delivery of the letter and its outcome. The conclusion of the Philippi episode is however extant: PHeid pp. 41/42 and 44. Admittedly these pages also are not preserved complete, but the course of events appears to be as follows. Paul is working in the mines (?), but has apparently still found time to preach. At any rate reference is made to one Frontina who with Paul is to be put to death by her father Longinus, presumably because she has allowed herself to be converted by Paul's preaching. We then come to the execution, which Paul somehow or other escapes, while Frontina dies. In response to Paul's prayer (and that of her mother Firmilla?) Frontina is restored to life again, which occasions great alarm among the inhabitants. Paul leads Frontina to her father's house amid the acclamation of the crowd. In Longinus' house a celebration of the eucharist seems then to have taken place, and thereafter Paul departs for Corinth.

Even if we can conjecture some things on the analogy of other episodes, our knowledge of the narrative of the APl in this area remains on the whole very defective.

This section however presents, through 3 Cor., a particularly difficult problem. The transmission of this complex has already been discussed above (p. 217). The question is how we are to assess this tradition. After the discovery of PHeid it seemed clear that 3 Cor. was unambiguously a part of the APl, and had passed from there into the Syriac and Armenian Bible. From the East the letters somehow found their way to the West (North Italy?). The intervening material survived only in Z as a remnant of the older stage of the tradition. The discovery of PH, in which 3 Cor. together with the whole Philippi episode is missing, could not contribute much for a solution of the problem. Now through PBodm a Greek witness from the 3rd century became known, which presents only the two letters. In itself this could be an early extract from the APl, but there is no kind of evidence for this assumption. The problem of 3 Cor. has been examined afresh in a comprehensive way by A.F.J. Klijn and W. Rordorf.[31] These two scholars think that we must see in 3 Cor. an independent text, which was only subsequently brought into connection with the APl. There are in fact several things which tell in favour of this view (above all differences of substance between 3 Cor. and PH), but we cannot enter into them here. On the basis of the work of Klijn and Rordorf we may assume - with all due caution - that the correspondence between Paul and the Corinthians had an origin all its own. It was then at some point brought into connection with the APl. It may be recalled that PBodm (Greek text of the letters without the intervening material) derives from the 3rd cent.; PH (Greek text of the APl without 3 Cor.) was written in the 4th cent.; PHeid (Coptic text of the APl with 3 Cor.) came into being in the 6th cent.

The differences between 3 Cor. and the other parts of the APl, which Klijn and Rordorf have dealt with in detail, are certainly of varying weight. The identification of the theological fronts and Rordorf's early dating are also not beyond all doubt. But the view that 3 Cor. belonged in origin to the APl can probably no longer be maintained.

It certainly remains enigmatic why the complex turns up in the Coptic PHeid and the letters with the intervening material then appear in A, E and Z, but not in the rest of the tradition. With the material at our disposal an explanation cannot for the present be given for this.[32]

9. *Paul in Corinth.* According to PHeid p. 44 Paul's stay in Corinth follows immediately on the episode at Philippi. That this is correct is evident from the rubric in PH p. 6: 'From Philippi to Corinth'. Although imperfect, the text of the section is well enough preserved for the march of events to be clear: Paul comes in Corinth to the house of Epiphanius, preaches there, and then prepares for his departure for Rome. The community is dismayed at the prospect of this journey to Rome, but is comforted by a Spirit-inspired address by one Cleobius.[33] In the course of a celebration of the eucharist something happens, which is interpreted by a certain Myrta.[34] Thereafter the meal proceeds. On the Day of Preparation Paul sets out and indeed - in contrast to the canonical Acts - as a free man.

This section is striking in the first place through its brevity and also through the absence of any miraculous acts by Paul. Although the apostle stays forty days with the brethren, we are told only of his sermons which, curious to relate, do not appear to enter at all upon the difficulties with the gnostic heretics to which reference was made in 3 Cor., but are dedicated above all to Paul's experiences and to the divine benevolence shown in these experiences. 'The theme of his preaching is perseverance (ὑπομονή)' (Schmidt, ΠΠ, p. 101), but over and above that also the providence of God, who is carrying through His οἰκονομία, i.e. His plan of salvation (PH p. 6.26 and already PH p. 5.27).

The meagre presentation of the apostle's stay in Corinth stands in striking contrast to the significance which Corinth and the Christian community there had for Paul according to Acts and the canonical letters to the Corinthians. The reasons for this can only be conjectured. It could be that in view of the many reports about Corinth in the New Testament the author, who had indeed no intention of providing a substitute for Acts but probably knew it and the Pauline letters, wished to content himself with a brief account. We might see another explanation in the fact that for the presbyter in Asia Minor who composed the APl there was not so much legendary material available for this period in Paul's life as was the case for his own home province. Finally we may also refer to the fact that this section gives the impression of being a transition to the martyrdom in Rome, i.e. in this short passage the author is already steering towards the conclusion of his work.

No matter which of these conjectures accurately describes the reason for this astonishing brevity, one thing is clear: the author does not make Paul come to Corinth for the first time at this point in his work. The apostle indeed (as also in other places) comes upon a Christian community, and thus does not require first to lay the foundation for a community through the conversion of one or more people. Whether there was mention in the APl of an earlier activity of the apostle in Corinth, and in which of the present lacunae such a report might have stood, it is impossible to say. It may be noted further that 3 Cor. speaks unambiguously for an earlier sojourn by Paul in Corinth. The heresy which breaks out in Corinth is characterised by the fact that it is something new, something which the community has not heard from Paul (3 Cor. 1.4f.). But naturally we cannot say whether this statement is formulated on the basis of a report in the APl about Paul's first sojourn in Corinth.

10. *From Corinth to Italy.* The journey from Corinth to Italy is preserved in PH pp. 7-8, to which we may add some fragments in PHeid pp. 72-74. Paul travels to Italy on a ship whose captain Artemon has been baptized by Peter. On the way the Lord appears to him, and his sombre countenance startles Paul. To his question as to the reason, the Lord answers: "I am on the point of being crucified afresh" (ἄνωθεν μέλλω σταυροῦσθαι). Without touching upon Paul's protest, Christ gives to the apostle the injunction to exhort the brethren, and escorts the ship to Italy. The place of landing is not stated; presumably the author himself did not know, or else he assumed Puteoli as a matter of course (cf. Acts 28:13). On landing Artemon is awaited by a man named Claudius, introduces Paul to him, and the two carry the apostle's baggage ashore. In Claudius' house Paul teaches "the word of truth". The sermon here presented contains first of all an Old Testament section, in which God's dealing with Israel is depicted as exemplary of God's faithfulness, while in the second part Christ is spoken of. Unfortunately the text in PH breaks off in the middle of the sermon. The papyrus leaf PM (= PB + PM1 + PM2) and PHeid pp. 79/80 belong in this context. The gap between this section and the report of the martyrdom is probably largely filled up thereby (cf. below, p. 259f.). Paul's speech, which breaks off with PH p. 8 and is continued in the fragments of PM and PHeid, could have been conceived by the author of the APl as a conclusion and at the same time as the transition to the MP. It cannot be said whether Paul's speech in Miletus (Acts 20) provided the impulse. At any rate it looks as if in the APl nothing would have been reported about any further activity of the apostle before his entry into Rome.

The short report of Paul's journey to Italy also presents a problem of its own, in that here we find a doublet to the famous Quo Vadis scene in the Acts of Peter (Mart. Petr. c. 6). With this scene we shall not here deal in detail. In regard to the problem of the composition, however, we must note the following points: The description in the APl shows clearly that it is secondary as compared with the APt. Above all, the reference to the crucifixion is in place in the APt, since Peter too was crucified, but not in the APl, since Paul was beheaded. In addition this scene fits in well in the APt, while in the APl it seems to be a foreign body.[35] At all events the author of the APl has borrowed from the APt. It is therefore not improbable that Schmidt's conjecture is correct, that the captain Artemon is the Theon of the APt (Schmidt, ΠΠ, pp. 128f.).

11. *Martyrdom of Paul.* This part of the APl was probably separated from the work as a whole at an early date, since it was used for reading on the day of commemoration of the apostle. The tradition and also the further use and elaboration (cf. for example Schmidt, AP pp. 118ff.; ΠΠ, pp. 124f.) show the Martyrdom becoming an independent work. The text early ran wild, and this makes reconstitu-

tion difficult. That it originally belonged to the APl is certain from PHeid and PH, although in both witnesses the beginning is unfortunately missing and Paul's progress from Puteoli (?) to Rome has thus not been preserved.

In Rome Paul is awaited by Luke and Titus (in the Acts of Titus c. 6, where again the APl has been used, Timothy also is named). Paul rents a barn and there teaches 'the word of truth' with great success. This introduction was probably shaped with Acts 28:30f. in mind. Then follows the story of the death of Patroclus, an imperial cup-bearer, and his revival.[36] Since Patroclus confesses his Christianity before Nero, persecution breaks out. In the course of it Paul too is brought to trial, and as ringleader is condemned to death by the sword while the other Christians are to suffer death by fire.[37] This is not quite logical, since surely death by decapitation was thought of as the less severe penalty. It was however in the tradition before the author that Paul was beheaded. Nero's fury against the Christians is brought to a check by the protests of the people, but the judgment against Paul is allowed to stand. In prison Paul preaches to the Prefect Longus and the centurion Cestus (in particular about the resurrection), and promises them that they will receive baptism at his grave. After a long prayer by Paul his execution follows, and in the course of it milk spurts on to the soldiers' clothes. Soon thereafter Paul appears to Nero, who in consternation sets the prisoners free. The narrative ends with the scene at Paul's grave: Longus and Cestus go there and meet Titus and Luke, who take to flight but are reassured and then administer baptism to the other two.

By and large, the MP gives the impression of being a uniform work, complete in itself. Some passages admittedly are thoroughly clumsy, and one might conjecture that different traditions which originally had nothing to do with one another have here been brought together (the story of Patroclus, the conversion of Longus and Cestus, the martyrdom of Paul). But whether this was done by the author of the APl or had already been achieved before him we cannot say. The composition of the whole scene probably derives from the author (cf. Schubart, ΠΠ, p. 123), but it must be said that here at the conclusion of his work he has not accomplished any masterly performance. The question how far he was able to rely on local Roman tradition cannot be confidently answered.

Like the author of the APt in his account of Peter's end (cf. below, p. 311ff.), the author of the APl also could in the MP make use of certain models for guidance (Martyrdom of Polycarp, Martyrdom of Peter).

Summary. 1. As already said, the detailed presentation of the composition and structure of the APl on the basis of the extant material can only be an attempt. We can reconstruct particular sections, and also link together a series of halting-places. But great gaps remain, about the extent and content of which we can only advance conjectures. The question can also be raised whether the APl was not already abbreviated (PH) or expanded (3 Cor.) in early times. However, we do not have the necessary witnesses for a history of the transmission of this work. How much of the ancient APl has been lost cannot be exactly determined. According to the Stichometry of Nicephorus the book extended to 3600 lines, the canonical Acts on the other hand only to 2800. Even though we do not know in what version Nicephorus saw the APl, it is still clear that a considerable part of the text is missing.

2. From the extant material the route of Paul's journey in the APl is: Damascus

- Jerusalem - Antioch (which?) - Iconium - Antioch (which?) - Myra - Sidon - Tyre. Here there is a yawning gap which cannot be filled. Then follow Smyrna - Ephesus - Philippi - Corinth - Italy - Rome. The texts before us up to now arouse the impression that the author wished to present *one* great journey by the apostle. Paul appears to have travelled from place to place without any fixed base of operations, such as Antioch was for a time according to Acts. Journey - preaching - persecution - miracle - departure follow one another in almost schematic fashion.[38] In the extant parts there is no mention of a repeated sojourn in any one place. This does not however mean that Paul was not several times at one place (this can be assumed at any rate for Antioch and Corinth); only thus far there are no certain clues for this. Nor can we fill the gaps with the aid of the hypothesis of a twofold imprisonment of the apostle.

3. It is striking that Paul in the APl often finds a community already in existence in the place he is visiting (Iconium, Ephesus, Puteoli, Rome). This probably means that the author has no intention of describing the history of the Pauline mission throughout the world, 'even to the ends of the earth', on the basis of some leading theme (such as Acts 1:8), but that his real interest is in the individual stories. These pieces, gathered and worked up by the author, are held together by his concern to sketch a picture of Paul, in an edifying, instructive and entertaining form and drawing on literary *Gattungen* of the time, which would correspond to Church ideas in the second half of the 2nd century, but not to the reality of the apostle's own lifetime. 'Paul is not theologically assessed, but hagiographically claimed for popular piety.'[39] His activity is set in the frame of the established Church. It is however striking that Church offices or forms of organisation find no mention (only in 3 Cor. is there reference to offices). This may be connected with the fact that the literary genus and the process of tradition lying behind the author's own literary work were determined by the individual narratives; the theological motives, which are not indeed lacking and find expression above all in the speeches, are to be exhibited by way of example in the several destinies of the persons involved. The fact that the debate with Judaism, so important for Paul, does not appear in the APl shows that - despite older tradition which the author has taken up - the work belongs in a later time, and that even the traditions which are worked up in it do not reach back to the period of primitive Christianity.

4. It is understandable that the relation of the APl to Luke's Acts (and to the rest of the NT) has always been the subject of special interest. After all, it is ultimately a question of the apostle Paul, a central figure in the NT. It would be natural to think that the author of this 'romance' joined forces with the Lucan model. After the discovery of PHeid, C. Schmidt expressed himself forcefully in favour of the dependence of the APl upon Acts, then after the appearance of PH somewhat modified this opinion, but still maintained it,despite the arguments of W. Schubart, the co-editor of PH.[40] Against this I have attempted to explain the agreements and the differences between the APl and Acts on the basis that the author of the APl probably did know Acts, but is not literarily dependent on it; rather he used traditions that were in circulation about Paul and his work.[41] W. Rordorf considers this interpretation incorrect, and affirms that the author of the APl did not know Acts. The few parallels which might perhaps be adduced for such knowledge are to be explained on the basis that behind both writings there stands a common tradition. Rordorf would also draw from this interpretation certain consequences for the dating

of the APl (APl: middle of 2nd cent.; Acts: first half of 2nd cent.).[42]

This question cannot be discussed in detail here. It may only be remarked that knowledge of Acts is probably to be assumed in a Church 'novel' writer at the end of the 2nd century (this is to be firmly held as the date for the APl). On the other side the literary genus, the aims in view, and the completely different situation tell in favour of literary independence. In any case knowledge of Acts and independent shaping of the APl are not mutually exclusive.

5. In the APl there are many passages which in vocabulary recall the language of the NT, without being direct quotations. Only in the beatitudes in AThe 5f. are there two sentences which agree word for word with Mt. 5:8 and 5:9. This means that the author of the APl was at home in a community in which a churchly devotional terminology was familiar. This took shape in the course of the 2nd century - not least under the influence of the NT Canon and the liturgy. We find the beginnings of it already in Acts. Now this is of significance for the question of the use of the NT by the APl, because we cannot prove with certainty the use of particular passages; often it is rather only a question of the use of the current devotional language. This naturally does not exclude a knowledge of the NT writings, even though nothing can be said about the extent of the canon known to the author. It is however also clear from the language that the author wanted his work to have an edifying and instructive effect. Finally, it is also difficult to demonstrate on this basis the unity of the work. We may however start out from the position that the APl in their present form (apart from 3 Cor) are linguistically the work of one author.

5. Theological tendency: The APl is not a theological treatise, but a religious tract. The author certainly binds up with it certain definite ecclesiastical and theological purposes, and it is based upon a certain theological knowledge, but it was intended in the first instance for the edifying and entertainment of the community. This means that we do the author an injustice, and put the wrong questions to him, when we seek to extract a theological system from his work. Thus the attempt by Loofs to claim the APl also as a witness for his theory of a Spirit-Christology[43] is extremely questionable. Peterson's attempt to determine the place of the APl in the history of theology also seems to me mistaken.[44] Peterson thinks that the APl, like the other apocryphal Acts, belong to the domain of Encratism which is associated with the name of Tatian. Here however he has in my view attributed to the APl too great a theological significance. Many traits which are interpreted by Peterson as esoteric 'symbolism' admit of a much simpler explanation, as the graphic style of popular narrative (e.g. Artemilla's change of clothing, PH p. 2.16; cf. Peterson, op. cit. 183f.). More recently Han J.W. Drijvers has taken up again and modified Peterson's theses,[45] in an interpretation of the story of the baptized lion. Drijvers would see in the lion (before his baptism) the symbol for death and sexuality. After baptism the lion then represents life, and hence can also save Paul's life in the conflict with the beasts. The APl, Drijvers thinks, are on the one hand a popular devotional book, but on the other hand could also be read 'on a different symbolic level'. Here considerable significance attaches to the connections with the Acts of Thomas, which are not to be interpreted in terms of literary dependence. The question is whether we can draw conclusions so far-reaching from a single episode. It is indeed rather the case that the story of the baptized lion, like many other parts of the APl, belongs to the *Gattung* of popular legend, in which specific practical intentions (here above all the emphasis on continence) are not excluded.

We must therefore, in conformity with the literary peculiarity of the APl, renounce any attempt at illegitimate systematisation, and content ourselves with the indication of certain theological tendencies, which often indeed appear to contradict one another (much material is collected in Schmidt, AP pp. 183ff.).

Christian preaching for the author of the APl is preaching of continence and of the resurrection (AThe 5). In practically every episode the motif of sexual continence plays a dominant role. This demand, and the apostle's success in preaching it, are often the occasion for persecution. The basis of this attitude is the conviction that the goods of this world are worthless and unprofitable, that salvation lies in the world to come, and that all depends on the securing of this other-worldly salvation (which in part appears to be envisaged as the survival of the immortal soul). From the beatitudes in AThe 5f. it is clear how the hope of glory with God is combined with the injunction to sexual purity. The resurrection is held out as the goal and the reward for those who keep themselves pure and set their hope on God and on Christ.

The Christology of the AP can scarcely be set out unambiguously in terms of the later dogmatic decisions. The most important statement for the author is that Christ is Lord, not only the Lord of his Church, but also of the world, of life and death. If these christological statements frequently appear to be in conflict with monotheism, this is not a peculiarity of the APl but belongs to the problem presented by early Christian Christology as a whole. Of a well-marked Logos Christology there is in the APl hardly any trace.

W. Rordorf, without fundamentally calling in question the general characterisation of the APl given here, attempts to work out the 'something of his own' which according to Tertullian the presbyter in Asia Minor wished to add to the prestige of Paul, in order to determine more exactly the place of the APl in Church history.[46] He points to some important features in this work, in which this 'something of his own' stands out particularly clearly. These are: the role of the Holy Spirit and its consequences; the ascetic demands; the uses in Church worship (eucharist with water and bread); the absence of reference to Church offices; the detailed knowledge of the OT, which seems to go back to Jewish-Christian circles. According to Rordorf, all these features point to Montanism. 'Then that "something of his own" which the presbyter in Asia added to the apostolic romance would have to be sought in the Montanist ideas which he sought to disseminate under the cloak of the apostle.' This hypothesis probably still requires a more searching scrutiny. Here it may only be noted: apart from the fact that the problem of Montanism has as yet by no means been unambiguously explained, the similarity which Rordorf has worked out can also be accounted for on the view that particular forms of piety were also represented elsewhere in the Church in the 2nd century, outside of the 'Phrygian prophecy'. It does not seem to me possible to demonstrate specifically Montanist ideas in the APl.

6. Author, date and place of origin: according to the testimony of Tertullian (see above, p. 214) the author of the APl was a presbyter in Asia Minor, who was rewarded for his work by deposition from his office but not apparently by expulsion from the Church. This we can understand if we bear in mind the theological tendencies - which are really not heretical - but on the other hand observe what offence must have been occasioned on a more rigorous examination by certain particular traits in the APl. We need recall only Thecla's baptism of herself and the baptized lion. In addition, comparison with the canonical Acts was very natural, and from this the APl must have come out rather badly. Certainly the author acted in all good faith when 'out of love for Paul' he gathered up whatever legends were in circulation, set them in order, and also surely elaborated and expanded them. For in so doing he wished to confirm the communities in the true Christian faith.

Of the person of the author nothing more can be said. His native land was Asia Minor. This is not only stated by Tertullian, but may also be seen from the work itself. So far as we can see, it is the places visited in Asia Minor about which the author has most to tell, whereas for Corinth he has less to offer and hence in part makes use of the APt. A more precise location is scarcely possible, even though we may be inclined to think of Iconium or Seleucia. But this remains conjecture.

The date likewise cannot be precisely determined. We can only say that the APl must have been written before 200, the approximate date of Tertullian's *de Baptismo*. Since on the other hand it is dependent on the APt, the period between 185 and 195 may be regarded as a possible estimate. An earlier dating (Rordorf) scarcely admits of proof.[47]

Notes

Introduction

1. Cf. S.L. Davies, *Semeia* 38, 139ff., also the response by T.W. MacKay, ib. 145ff.
2. On Nicetas cf. H.G. Beck, *Kirche und theologische Literatur im byzantinischen Reich*, 1959, 548f. - Edition by A. Vogt, 1931 (see Lit. above).
3. On the attestation of the APl cf. also Vouaux 24-69; Schmidt, AP 108-116; ΠΠ 85ff.
4. PB and PM1: H.A. Sanders, 'A Fragment of the Acta Pauli in the Michigan Collection', *Harv. Theol. Rev.* 31, 1938, 70-90; PM2: G.D. Kilpatrick and C.H. Roberts, 'The Acta Pauli: A New Fragment', JTS 37, 1946, 196-199; on this see W.D. McHardy, *Expos. Times* 58, 1947, 279. For these fragments as belonging together cf. W. Rordorf, 'Les Actes de Paul sur papyrus' (see above, p. 214).
5. PO: Sanders, op. cit. (note 4), 79.
6. On 3 Cor. and its transmission cf. A.F.J. Klijn, 'The Apocryphal Correspondence between Paul and the Corinthians', *VigChr* 17, 1963, 2-23; W. Rordorf, 'Héresie et Orthodoxie . . . ' (in the press); there also lit. Particularly important: M. Testuz, *Papyrus Bodmer X-XII*, Geneva 1959, 7-45.
7. I would at this point cordially thank Prof. Rordorf, who has greatly helped me by sending his works (some still not published) produced in connection with the preparation of the new edition of the APl. Even if I cannot follow Rordorf in some points, his contributions and discussion with him have facilitated and advanced my work.
8. Fasting plays a large part in the APl as a whole.
9. The statement in the Acts of Titus c. 3 (Halkin, p. 245) that Paul 'first preached the Word of Christ in Damascus' need not go back to the APl, even if the following sentence derives therefrom. On the Acts of Titus, cf. below, pp. 219f.
10. Acts 9:30: Jerusalem-Tarsus; 11:25f.: Tarsus-Syrian Antioch; 11:27ff.: Paul's journey with Barnabas to Jerusalem; 12:24f.: return; 13: Antioch-Seleucia-Cyprus-Perga-Pisidian Antioch-Iconium.
11. Cf. the variants to this passage in Lipsius, Aa I, 253; Gebhardt xcviii.
12. Ed. F. Halkin, *AnalBoll* 79, 1961, 241-256.

13. The name Panchares is rendered in the Coptic as Anchares, i.e. the Coptic translator regarded the P at the beginning as the article; cf. Schmidt, ΠΠ 115.
14. Τὰ κατὰ τὸν Παῦλον in the Acts of Titus is probably a condensation of ποταπός ἐστιν τῇ εἰδέᾳ ὁ Παῦλος in AThe.
15. It may be recalled that between PH p. 5 and p. 6 a whole episode has evidently been omitted, cf. above, p. 227. PH however bears in the colophon the designation Πράξεις Παύλου, and thus is probably not intended to be an extract.
16. In later legends this conclusion is greatly altered and expanded. Cf. BHG[3] II, 267ff., also the works of G. Dagron and R. Albrecht.
17. Kasser (Acta Pauli 1959, 57) raises for discussion the question whether such sections as the AThe were not originally published independently, and only later joined together with other pieces to make the APl. This is possible, but perhaps is to think too much in modern terms. Cf. Rordorf, 'Tradition et composition . . . ' 279; also above, pp. 231f.
18. Cf. Schubart's demonstration, ΠΠ, 120ff.
19. Cf. the works of R. Albrecht, V. Burrus, S.L. Davies and D.R. MacDonald. Rordorf also considers this position worthy of consideration, e.g. 'Tradition et composition . . . ' 280ff. Only there is unfortunately no evidence from the sources of the period which could be adduced for a 'women's liberation movement' in the Church of the 2nd century.
20. Cf. Th. Zahn, *Geschichte des ntl. Kanons* II 1, 1890, 892ff.; W.M. Ramsay, *The Church in the Roman Empire before A.D. 170*, 1893, 375ff.; Rordorf, 'Tradition et composition . . . ' 275ff.
21. Text: PG 50, cols. 745ff. and M. Aubineau, 'Le Panégyrique de Thècle attribué à Jean Chrysostome (BHG 1720): la fin retrouvée d'un texte mutilé', *AnalBoll* 93, 1975, 349-362. Cf. also D.R. MacDonald and A.D. Scrimgeour, *Semeia* 38, 151ff.; Kasser (Acta Pauli 1959, 49, n. 44) conjectures that the conclusion of the narrative in ps.-Chrysostom reflects the original version of the legend. But this cannot be proved.
22. The cult of Thecla cannot be dealt with here. Cf. already *Peregrinatio Aetheriae* 22f. (CSEL 39, 69f.); BHG[3] II, 267-269 (lists all the relevant texts). Further literature: Leclercq, DACL XV/2, cols. 2225ff.; B. Kötting, art. 'Thecla', LThK 10, 1965, cols. 18f. (Lit.); D.R. MacDonald and A.D. Scrimgeour, *Semeia* 38, 151ff.; R. Albrecht, *Das Leben der Hlg. Makrina*, 239ff.
23. Kasser (Acta Pauli 1959, 54 n. 87) asks whether Apphia may not be connected with Ammia in PG; but this to me is improbable.
24. The fragment p. 68e (Schmidt, AP 65) is interesting: 'That man is <not justified through the law>, but that he is justified <through the> works of righteousness'. This shows clearly how far removed the author is from the historical Paul.
25. Rordorf, 'Nochmals Paulusakten . . . ' 323f.
26. On Caesarea cf. Kasser, Acta Pauli 1959, 50 n. 46 and 51 n. 61. For this question the 'Letter of Pelagia', preserved in Ethiopic, has a certain significance, but into this I cannot enter here. It need only be remarked that this apocryphon, which unfortunately can neither be dated nor localised, made use of the APl. When the meeting between Paul and the lion is there transferred to the region of Caesarea, this probably goes back to the compiler; conclusions as to the composition of the APl cannot be drawn from this. Cf. E.J. Goodspeed, *American Journal of Semitic Languages and Literatures* XX, 1904, 95ff.; English trans. also in Schmidt AP, 2nd ed. xxi-xxv; G. Krüger, ZNW 5, 1904, 261ff.; Schmidt, ΠΠ 87ff.
27. On the baptism of Artemilla cf. G. Poupon, 'L'accusation . . ' (see Lit. above) 86-93.
28. PH 4.2ff. remains obscure: Artemilla goes into the house (which? her house or the prison?). The eucharist probably takes place in the prison.
29. The baptized lion referred to in this story, the baptism of which is reported in PG, naturally enjoyed a special popularity, but also gave offence. Cf, the compilation in Schmidt, ΠΠ 85ff.; B.M. Metzger, 'St Paul and the baptized lion', *Princeton Seminary Bulletin* XXXIX, 1945, 11-21; W. Schneemelcher, 'Der getaufte Löwe . . . ' (see Lit. above). H.J.W. Drijvers, 'Der getaufte Löwe und die Theologie der Acta Pauli' (so far unpublished, to

appear in the Acts of the Carl Schmidt Colloquium, Halle 1988. I thank Prof. Drijvers for making the manuscript available to me).
30. W. Rordorf, 'Nochmals Paulusakten . . . ' 323f.
31. Cf. above, note 6.
32. On the problem how 3 Cor. came into the Syrian Church, cf. W. Bauer, *Rechtgläubigkeit und Ketzerei*, [2]1964, 45-48 (ET 1971, 39-43). Bauer sees 3 Cor. as a fixed element in the APl. In the translation below I have placed 3 Cor. as the text is transmitted in PHeid. The reader is requested to bear in mind the reservations expressed above.
33. One of the false teachers who came to Corinth is named Cleobius (3 Cor. 1.4). Is the Cleobius mentioned in PHeid p. 51.7 - now a speaker filled with the Spirit - the same person?
34. Kasser (Acta Pauli 1959, 52 n. 68): 'une prophétie est exprimée par un rameau de myrte'. This however does not seem to be correct.
35. One should not argue, as Michaelis (327ff.) does, on the basis that πάλιν stands in the APt, whereas in the APl it is ἄνωθεν. On the meaning of the word ἄνωθεν (often equivalent to πάλιν), cf. Bauer-Aland, *Wörterbuch* s.v.
36. Cf. the story of the fall of Eutyches (Acts 20:7-12).
37. W. Rordorf, 'Die neronische Christenverfolgung . . . ' (see Lit. above) has attempted with the aid of MP to bring some light into the reports about the persecution under Nero. I am more sceptical.
38. Kasser (Acta Pauli 1959, 48 n. 31) has rightly drawn attention to a certain schematisation: journey - preaching - persecution - miracle. But whether we are to link with this the other assumption, that Paul never returned to the same place, remains (as already said) questionable.
39. E. Dassmann, *Der Stachel im Fleisch. Paulus in der frühchristlichen Literatur bis Irenäus*, 1979, 279.
40. Cf. the report in my essay: 'Die Apostelgeschichte des Lukas und die Acta Pauli', 238ff. (= *Ges. Aufs.* 207ff.).
41. Cf. the essay mentioned in note 40.
42. W. Rordorf, In welchem Verhältnis . . . (see Lit. above).
43. F. Loofs, *Theophilus von Antiochien adversus Marcionem und die anderen theologischen Quellen bei Irenäus* (TU 46) 1930, 148-157.
44. E. Peterson, 'Einige Bemerkungen zum Hamburger Papyrusfragment der Acta Pauli', *VigChr* 3, 1949, 142-164 (= *Frühkirche, Judentum und Gnosis*, 1959, 183-208). On Peterson, cf. P. Devos, *AnalBoll* 69, 1951, 119-130.
45. H.J.W. Drijvers, 'Der getaufte Löwe . . . ' (see above, note 29).
46. W. Rordorf, 'Was wissen wir über Plan . . . ' (see Lit. above).
47. On the dating of 3 Cor. cf. Rordorf, 'Héresie et Orthodoxie . . ' (see Lit. above). According to Rordorf 3 Cor. belongs in the first half of the 2nd century.

The Acts of Paul *

1

(From Damascus to Jerusalem)
(Ry; PHeid pp. 60/59 and 61/62; cf. PG, p. 000 below)

After his conversion outside Damascus Paul receives the command (from whom?) to go to Damascus and later to Jerusalem. 'With great joy' he enters Damascus, and finds the community in the (observance?) of fasting. Here probably a sermon before the Jews was included.

On Paul's journey from Damascus to Jericho (i.e. probably to Jerusalem) the baptism of the lion took place, according to Paul's later account in Ephesus. Whether the fragments PHeid pp. 60/59 and 61/62 contain remnants of the description of Paul's stay and activity in Jerusalem remains uncertain.

2

(Paul in Antioch)
(PHeid pp. 1-6)

In Antioch (Syrian or Pisidian?[1]) Paul raises up a dead boy. The son of Anchares (Greek Acts of Titus: Panchares) and Phila has died, and Paul has evidently betaken himself to the house of the parents in order to assist, but is prevented by the woman (so Schmidt, AP p. 92). Anchares fasts and prays until the crowd comes to carry out his son (who according to the Acts of Titus was called Barnabas). Then Paul comes in and - the sequel is unfortunately lost - appears to have raised up the boy. How the story proceeded we cannot say. Possibly there was some discussion over the miracle. When at PHeid p. 4. 19f. it is said:

'<We> believe, Anchares . . . , but save the city'

this points to occurrences of some kind which alarm the people. Perhaps Paul has already left the city, and is now to be brought back. At any rate, according to PHeid p. 5, the narrative probably led to a confession by Anchares, which is now followed by the persecution of Paul by the Jews:

'And I <also believe>, my <brethren>, <that> there is no other God save <Jesus> Christ, the son <of the> Blessed, unto whom is the glory <for ever.> Amen.' But when they <observed> that he would not turn to them, they pursued Paul, laid hold of him, and brought him back <into> the city, ill-using (?) him, (and) they cast stones at him, (and) thrust him out of their city and out of their country.[2] But Anchares was not able to requite evil with evil.[3] He shut the door <of his house> (and) <went> in with his wife . . . while he fasted . . .

What follows is so fragmentary that hardly anything can be said about its content. The part of the APl which was also independently transmitted as *Acta Pauli et Theclae* attaches directly to this scene. PHeid p. 6 presents as a sub-heading:

<After the flight from> Antioch when <he> wanted to go up to Iconium.

3

Acts of Paul and Thecla[1]
(Aa 1, pp. 235-269; PHeid pp. 6-28)

1. As Paul went up to Iconium after his flight from Antioch, his travelling companions were Demas and Hermogenes the copper-smith,[2] who were full of hypocrisy and flattered Paul as if they loved him. But Paul, who had eyes only for the goodness of Christ, did them no evil,[3] but loved (p. 236) them greatly, so that he sought to make sweet to them all the words of the Lord, [of the doctrine and of the interpretation of the Gospel],[4] both of the birth and of the resurrection of the Beloved, and he related to them word for word the great acts of Christ[5] as they had been revealed to him.

2. And a man named Onesiphorus,[6] who had heard that Paul was come to Iconium,[7] went out with his children Simmias and Zeno and his wife Lectra[8] to meet Paul (p. 237), that he might receive him to his house. For Titus had told him what Paul looked like. For (hitherto) he had not seen him in the flesh, but only in the spirit. 3. And he went along the royal road which leads to Lystra, and stood there waiting for him, and looked at (all) who came, according to Titus' description. And he saw Paul coming, a man small of stature, with a bald head and crooked legs, in a good state of body, with eyebrows meeting and nose somewhat hooked, full of friendliness; for now he appeared like a man, and now he had the face of an angel.[9] (p. 238)

4. And when Paul saw Onesiphorus he smiled; and Onesiphorus said: 'Greeting, thou servant of the blessed God!' And he replied: 'Grace be with thee and thy house!' But Demas and Hermogenes grew jealous, and went even further in their hypocrisy; so that Demas said: 'Are we then not (servants) of the Blessed, that thou didst not greet us thus?' And Onesiphorus said: 'I do not see in you any fruit of righteousness; but if ye are anything, come ye also into my house and rest yourselves!'

5. And when Paul was entered into the house of Onesiphorus there was great joy, and bowing of knees and breaking of bread, and the word of God concerning continence and the resurrection, as Paul said:

'Blessed are the pure in heart, for they shall see God.[10]
Blessed are they who have kept the flesh pure, for they shall become a temple of God.[11]
Blessed are the continent, for to them will God speak.
Blessed are they who have renounced this world, for they shall be well pleasing unto God.
Blessed are they who have wives as if (p. 239) they had them not, for they shall be heirs to God.[12]

Blessed are they who have fear of God, for they shall become angels of God.
6. Blessed are they who tremble at the words of God, for they shall be comforted.[13]
Blessed are they who have received (the) wisdom of Jesus Christ, for they shall be called sons of the Most High.[14]
Blessed are they who have kept their baptism secure,[15] for they shall rest with the Father and the Son.
Blessed are they who have laid hold upon the understanding of Jesus Christ, for they shall be in light.
Blessed are they who through love of God have departed from the form of this world, for they shall judge angels[16] and at the right hand of the Father they shall be blessed.
Blessed are the merciful, for (p. 240) they shall obtain mercy,[17] and shall not see the bitter day of judgment.
Blessed are the bodies of the virgins, for they shall be well pleasing to God, and shall not lose the reward of their purity.[18]
For the word of the Father shall be for them a work of salvation in the day of his Son, and they shall have rest[19] for ever and ever.'

7. And while Paul was thus speaking in the midst of the assembly in the house of Onesiphorus, a virgin (named) Thecla - her mother was Theocleia - who was betrothed to a man (named) Thamyris, sat at a near-by window and listened night and day to the word of the virgin life as it was spoken by Paul; and she did not turn away from the window (p. 241), but pressed on in the faith rejoicing exceedingly. Moreover, when she saw many women and virgins going in to Paul she desired to be counted worthy herself to stand in Paul's presence[20] and hear the word of Christ; for she had not yet seen Paul in person, but only heard his word. 8. Since however she did not move from the window, her mother sent to Thamyris. He came in great joy as if he were already taking her in marriage. So Thamyris said to Theocleia 'Where is my Thecla, that I may see her?'[21] And[22] Theocleia said: 'I have a new tale to tell thee, Thamyris. For indeed for three days and three nights Thecla has not risen from the window either to eat or to drink, but gazing steadily as if on some joyful spectacle she so devotes herself to a strange man who teaches deceptive and subtle words that I wonder how a maiden [of such modesty] as she is can be so sorely troubled. (p. 242) 9. Thamyris, this man is upsetting the city of the Iconians, and thy Thecla in addition; for all the women and young people go in to him, and are taught by him. "You must" he says, "fear one single God only, and live chastely." And my daughter also, who sticks to the window like a spider, is (moved) by his words (and) gripped by a new desire and a fearful passion; for the maiden hangs upon the things he says, and is taken captive. But go thou to her and speak to her, for she is betrothed to thee.' 10. And Thamyris went

to her, at one and the same time loving her and yet afraid of her distraction, and said: 'Thecla, my betrothed, why dost thou sit thus? And what is this passion that holds thee distracted? Turn to thy Thamyris and be ashamed.' And her mother also said the same: 'Child, why dost thou sit thus (p. 243) looking down and making no answer, but like one stricken?' And those who were in the house wept bitterly, Thamyris for the loss of a wife, Theocleia for that of a daughter, the maidservants for that of a mistress. So there was a great confusion of mourning in the house. And while this was going on (all around her) Thecla did not turn away, but gave her whole attention to Paul's word.

11. But Thamyris sprang up and went out into the street, and closely watched all who went in to Paul and came out. And he saw two men quarrelling bitterly with one another, and said to them: 'You men, who are you, tell me, and who is he that is inside with you, [the false teacher] who deceives the souls of young men and maidens, that they should not marry but remain as they are? I promise now to give you much money if you will tell me about him; for I am the first man of this city.' 12. (p. 244) And Demas and Hermogenes said to him: 'Who this man is, we do not know. But he deprives young men of wives and maidens of husbands, saying: "Otherwise there is no resurrection for you, except ye remain chaste and do not defile the flesh,[23] but keep it pure."' 13. And Thamyris said to them: 'Come into my house, you men, and rest with me.' And they went off to a sumptuous banquet, with much wine, great wealth and a splendid table. And Thamyris gave them to drink, for he loved Thecla and wished to have her for his wife. And during the dinner Thamyris said: 'Tell me, you men, what is his teaching, that I also may know it; for I am greatly distressed about Thecla because she so loves the stranger, and I am deprived of my marriage.' (p. 245) 14. But Demas and Hermogenes said: 'Bring him before the governor Castellius, on the ground that he is seducing the crowds to the new doctrine of the Christians, and so he will have him executed and thou shalt have thy wife Thecla. And we shall teach thee concerning the resurrection which he says is to come, that it has already taken place in the children whom we have,[24] and that we are risen again in that we have come to know the true God.'[25]

15. When Thamyris had heard this from them, he rose up early in the morning full of jealousy and wrath and went to the house of Onesiphorus with the rulers and officers and a great crowd with cudgels, and said to Paul: 'Thou hast destroyed the city of the Iconians, and my betrothed, so that she will not have me. Let us go to the governor Castellius!' And the whole crowd shouted: 'Away with the sorcerer! For he has corrupted all our wives.' And the multitude let themselves be persuaded. (p. 246) 16. And Thamyris stood before the judgment-seat and cried aloud: 'Proconsul, this man - we know not whence he is - who does not allow maidens to marry, let him declare before thee for what cause he teaches these things.' And Demas and Hermogenes said to Thamyris: 'Say that he is a Christian, and so thou wilt destroy him.' But the governor was

not easily to be swayed, and he called Paul, saying to him: 'Who art thou, and what dost thou teach? For it is no light accusation that they bring against thee.'[26] 17. And Paul lifted up his voice and said: 'If I today am examined as to what I teach, then listen, Proconsul. The living God,[27] the God of vengeance,[28] the jealous God,[29] the God who has need of nothing, has sent me since he desires the salvation of men, that I may draw them away from corruption and impurity, all pleasure and death, that they may sin no more. For this cause God sent His own Son, whom I preach and teach that in him men (p. 247) have hope, who alone had compassion upon a world in error; that men may no longer be under judgment but have faith, and fear of God, and knowledge of propriety, and love of truth. If then I teach the things revealed to me by God, what wrong do I do, Proconsul?' When the governor heard this, he commanded Paul to be bound and led off to prison until he should find leisure to give him a more attentive hearing.[30] 18.But Thecla in the night took off her bracelets and gave them to the door-keeper, and when the door was opened for her she went off to the prison. To the gaoler she gave a silver mirror, and so went in to Paul and sat at his feet and heard (him proclaim) the mighty acts of God.[31] And Paul feared nothing, but comported himself with full confidence in God; and her faith also was increased, as she kissed his fetters. (p. 248) 19. But when Thecla was sought for by her own people and by Thamyris, they hunted her through the streets as one lost; and one of the door-keeper's fellow slaves betrayed that she had gone out by night. And they questioned the door-keeper, and he told them: 'She has gone to the stranger in the prison.' And they went as he had told them and found her, so to speak, bound with him in affection. And they went thence, rallied the crowd about them, and disclosed to the governor what had happened.[32]

20. He commanded Paul to be brought to the judgment-seat; but Thecla rolled herself upon the place where Paul taught as he sat in the prison. The governor commanded her also to be brought to the judgment seat, and she went off with joy exulting. (p. 249) But when Paul was brought forward again, the crowd shouted out even louder: 'He is a sorcerer! Away with him!'[33] But the governor heard Paul gladly concerning the holy works of Christ; and when he had taken counsel he called Thecla and said: 'Why dost thou not marry Thamyris according to the law of the Iconians?' But she stood there looking steadily at Paul. And when she did not answer, Theocleia her mother cried out, saying: 'Burn the lawless one! Burn her that is no bride in the midst of the theatre, that all the women who have been taught by this man may be afraid!' 21. And the governor was greatly affected. He had Paul scourged and drove him out of the city,[34] but Thecla he condemned to be burned. And forthwith the governor arose and went off to the theatre, and all the crowd went out to the unavoidable spectacle. But Thecla sought for Paul, as a lamb in the wilderness looks about for the shepherd. (p. 250) And when she looked upon the crowd, she saw the Lord sitting in the form of Paul and said: 'As if I were not able to

endure, Paul has come to look after me.' And she looked steadily at him; but he departed into the heavens. 22. Now the young men and maidens brought wood and straw that Thecla might be burned. And as she was brought in naked, the governor wept and marvelled at the power that was in her. The executioners laid out the wood and bade her mount the pyre; and making the sign of the Cross[35] she climbed up on the wood. They kindled it, and although a great fire blazed up[36] the fire did not touch her. For God in compassion caused a noise beneath the earth and a cloud above, full of rain and hail, overshadowed (the theatre) and its whole content (p. 251) poured out, so that many were in danger and died, and the fire was quenched and Thecla saved. 23. But Paul was fasting with Onesiphorus and his wife and the children in an open tomb on the way by which they go from Iconium to Daphne. And when many days were past, as they were fasting the boys said to Paul: 'We are hungry.' And they had nothing with which to buy bread, for Onesiphorus had left the things of the world and followed Paul with all his house. But Paul took off his outer garment and said: 'Go, my child, <sell this and>[37] buy several loaves and bring them here.' But while the boy was buying he saw his neighbour Thecla, and was astonished and said: 'Thecla, where art thou going?' And she said: 'I am seeking after Paul, for I was saved from the fire.' And (p. 252) the boy said: 'Come, I will take thee to him, for he has been mourning for thee and praying and fasting six days already.' 24. But when she came to the tomb Paul had bent his knees and was praying and saying: 'Father of Christ, let not the fire touch Thecla, but be merciful to her, for she is thine!' But she standing behind him cried out: 'Father, who didst make heaven and earth,[38] the Father of thy beloved Son <Jesus Christ>,[39] I praise thee that thou didst save me from the fire, that I might see Paul!' And as Paul arose he saw her and said: 'O God the knower of hearts,[40] Father of our Lord Jesus Christ, I praise thee that thou hast so speedily <accomplished> what I asked, and hast hearkened unto me.' 25. And within the tomb there was much love, Paul (p. 253) rejoicing, and Onesiphorus and all of them. But they had five loaves, and vegetables, and water, and they were joyful over the holy works of Christ. And Thecla said to Paul: 'I will cut my hair short and follow thee wherever thou goest.'[41] But he said: 'The season is unfavourable, and thou art comely. May no other temptation come upon thee, worse than the first, and thou endure not and play the coward!' And Thecla said: 'Only give me the seal in Christ, and temptation shall not touch me.' And Paul said: 'Have patience, Thecla, and thou shalt receive the water.'

26. And Paul sent away Onesiphorus with all his family to Iconium, and so taking Thecla came into Antioch. But immediately as they entered a Syrian[42] by the name of Alexander, one of the first of the Antiochenes, seeing Thecla fell in love with her, and sought to win over Paul with money and gifts. But Paul said: 'I do not know the woman (p. 254) of whom thou dost speak, nor is she mine.' But he, being a powerful man, embraced her on the open street;

she however would not endure it, but looked about for Paul and cried out bitterly, saying: 'Force not the stranger, force not the handmaid of God! Among the Iconians I am one of the first, and because I did not wish to marry Thamyris I have been cast out of the city.' And taking hold of Alexander she ripped his cloak, took off the crown from his head, and made him a laughing-stock. 27. But he, partly out of love for her and partly in shame at what had befallen him, brought her before the governor; and when she confessed that she had done these things, he condemned her to the beasts, <since Alexander was arranging games>.[43] But the women were panic-stricken, and cried out before the judgment-seat: 'An evil (p. 255) judgment! A godless judgment!' But Thecla asked of the governor that she might remain pure until she was to fight with the beasts. And a rich woman named Tryphaena, whose daughter had died, took her under her protection and found comfort in her. 28. When the beasts were led in procession, they bound her to a fierce lioness, and the queen Tryphaena followed her. And as Thecla sat upon her back, the lioness licked her feet, and all the crowd was amazed. Now the charge upon her superscription[44] was: Guilty of Sacrilege. But the women with their children cried out from above, saying: 'O God, an impious judgment[45] is come to pass in this city!' And after the procession Tryphaena took her again; for (p. 256) her daughter[46] who was dead had spoken to her in a dream: 'Mother, thou shalt have in my place the stranger, the desolate Thecla, that she may pray for me and I be translated to the place of the just.'[47] 29. So when Tryphaena received her back from the procession she was at once sorrowful, because she was to fight with the beasts on the following day, but at the same time loved her dearly like her own daughter Falconilla; and she said: 'Thecla, my second child, come and pray for my child, that she may live; for this I saw in my dream.' And she without delay lifted up her voice and said: 'Thou God of heaven, Son of the Most High,[48] grant to her according to her wish, that her daughter Falconilla may live for ever!' (p. 257) And when Thecla said this, Tryphaena mourned,[49] considering that such beauty was to be thrown to the beasts. 30. And when it was dawn, Alexander came to take her away - for he himself was arranging the games - and he said: 'The governor has taken his place, and the crowd is clamouring for us. Give me her that is to fight the beasts, that I may take her away.' But Tryphaena cried out so that he fled, saying: 'A second mourning for my Falconilla is come upon my house, and there is none to help; neither child, for she is dead, nor kinsman, for I am a widow. O God of Thecla my child, help thou Thecla.' 31. And the governor sent soldiers to fetch Thecla. Tryphaena however did not stand aloof, but taking her hand herself led her up, saying: 'My daughter Falconilla I (p. 258) brought to the tomb; but thee, Thecla, I bring to fight the beasts.' And Thecla wept bitterly and sighed to the Lord, saying: 'Lord God, in whom I trust, with whom I have taken refuge, who didst deliver me from the fire, reward thou Tryphaena, who had compassion upon thy handmaid, and because she preserved me pure'. 32. Then there was a tumult,[50] and roaring of the beasts, and a shouting of the people and of the women who sat together, some saying: 'Bring in the sacrilegious one!' but others: 'May the city perish for this lawlessness! Slay us all, Proconsul! A bitter sight, an evil judgment!' 33. But Thecla was taken out of Tryphaena's hands and stripped, and (p. 259) was given a girdle and flung into the stadium. And lions and bears were set upon her, and a fierce lioness ran to her and lay down at her feet. And the crowd of the women raised a great shout. And a bear ran upon her, but the lioness ran and met it, and tore the bear asunder. And again a lion trained against men, which belonged to Alexander, ran upon her; and the lioness grappled with the lion, and perished with it. (p. 260) And the women mourned the more, since the lioness which helped her was dead. 34. Then they sent in many beasts, while she stood and stretched out her hands and prayed. And when she had finished her prayer, she turned and saw a great pit full of water, and said: 'Now is the time for me to wash.' And she threw herself in, saying: 'In the name of Jesus Christ I baptize myself on the last day!' And when they saw it, the women and all the people wept, saying: 'Cast not thyself into the water!'; so that even the governor wept that such beauty should be devoured by seals. So, then, she threw herself (p. 261) into the water in the name of Jesus Christ; but the seals, seeing the light of a lightning-flash, floated dead on the surface. And there was about her a cloud of fire, so that neither could the beasts touch her nor could she be seen naked. 35. But as other more terrible beasts were let loose, the women cried aloud, and some threw petals, others nard, others cassia, others amomum, so that there was an abundance of perfumes. And all the beasts let loose were overpowered as if by sleep, and did not touch her. So Alexander said to the governor: 'I have some very fearsome bulls - let us tie her to them.' The governor frowning (p. 262) gave his consent, saying: 'Do what thou wilt.' And they bound her by the feet between the bulls, and set red-hot irons beneath their bellies that being the more enraged they might kill her. The bulls indeed leaped forward, but the flame that blazed around her burned through the ropes, and she was as if she were not bound. 36. But Tryphaena fainted as she stood beside the arena, so that her handmaids said: 'The queen Tryphaena is dead!' And the governor took note of it, and the whole city was alarmed. And Alexander fell down at the governor's feet and said: (p. 263) 'Have mercy upon me, and on the city, and set the prisoner free, lest the city also perish with her. For if Caesar should hear this he will probably destroy both us and the city as well, because his kinswoman Tryphaena[51] has died at the circus gates.'

37. And the governor summoned Thecla from among the beasts, and said to her: 'Who art thou? And what hast thou about thee,[52] that not one of the beasts touched thee?' She answered: 'I am a handmaid of the living God. As to what I have about me, I have believed in him in whom God is well pleased, His Son.[53] For his sake not one of the beasts touched me. For he (p. 264) alone

is the goal[54] of salvation and the foundation of immortal life. To the storm-tossed he is a refuge, to the oppressed relief,[55] to the despairing shelter; in a word, whoever does not believe in him shall not live, but die for ever.' 38. When the governor heard this, he commanded garments to be brought, and said: 'Put on these garments.' But she said: 'He who clothed me when I was naked among the beasts shall clothe me with salvation in the day of judgment.' And taking the garments she put them on.

And straightway the governor issued a decree, saying: 'I release to you Thecla, the pious handmaid of God.' But all the women cried out with a loud voice, and as with one mouth gave praise to God, saying: 'One is God, who has delivered Thecla!', so that all the city was shaken by the sound. (p. 265) 39. And Tryphaena when she was told the good news came to meet her with a crowd, and embraced Thecla and said: 'Now I believe that the dead are raised up! Now I believe that my child lives! Come inside, and I will assign to thee all that is mine.' So Thecla went in with her and rested in her house for eight days, instructing her in the word of God, so that the majority of the maidservants also believed; and there was great joy in the house.

(p. 266) 40. But Thecla yearned for Paul and sought after him, sending in every direction. And it was reported to her that he was in Myra. So she took young men and maidservants and girded herself, and sewed her mantle into a cloak after the fashion of men, and went off to Myra, and found Paul speaking the word of God and went to him. But he was astonished when he saw her and the crowd that was with her, pondering whether another temptation was not upon her. But observing this she said to him: 'I have taken the bath, Paul; for he who worked with thee for the Gospel has also worked with me for my baptism.' (p. 267) 41. And taking her by the hand Paul led her into the house of Hermias, and heard from her everything (that had happened), so that Paul marvelled greatly and the hearers were confirmed and prayed for Tryphaena. And Thecla arose and said to Paul: 'I am going to Iconium.' But Paul said: 'Go and teach the word of God!' Now Tryphaena sent her much clothing and gold, so that she could leave (some of it) for the service of the poor. (p. 268) 42. But she herself went away to Iconium and went into the house of Onesiphorus, and threw herself down on the floor where Paul had sat and taught the oracles of God, and wept, saying: 'My God, and God of this house where the light shone upon me, Christ Jesus the Son of God, my helper in prison, my helper before governors, my helper in the fire, my helper among the beasts, thou art God, and to thee be the glory for ever. Amen' (p. 269) 43. And she found Thamyris dead, but her mother still alive; and calling her mother to her she said to her: 'Theocleia my mother, canst thou believe that the Lord lives in heaven? For whether thou dost desire money, the Lord will give it thee through me; or thy child, see, I stand beside thee.'

And when she had borne this witness she went away to Seleucia; and after enlightening many with the word of God she slept with a noble sleep.

4

(Paul in Myra)
(PHeid pp. 28-35)
<When he was departed from> Antioch
<and taught in> Myra

(p. 28) When Paul was <teaching> the word of God in Myra, there <was> a man there named Hermocrates, who had the dropsy. He took his stand before the eyes of all, and said to Paul: 'Nothing is impossible with God,[1] but especially with him whom thou dost preach; for when he came he healed many,[2] he whose servant thou art. Lo, I and my wife <and> my children, (p. 29) we cast ourselves at <thy> feet, < . . . . . > that I also may believe <as> thou hast believed in the living God.'[3] <Paul> said to him: 'I will give thee < . . . . . > without reward, but <through the> name of Jesus Christ shalt thou become <whole in the presence> of all these.'[4]

The following sentences are badly preserved, but probably the healing is described. The man loses a great deal of water, and falls as one dead.

. . . so that some said: '<It is> better for him to die, that he may <not> be in pain.' But when Paul had quietened the crowd he <took> his hand, raised him up and asked him, saying: 'Hermocrates, < . . . . . > what thou wilt.' But he said: 'I wish to eat.'[5] (And) he took a loaf and gave him to eat. He became whole in that hour, and received the grace of the seal in the Lord, he and his wife.

But Hermippus his son was angry <with> Paul, and sought for an appointed time (a good opportunity?) that he might rise up with those of his own age and destroy him. For he wished that his father should not be healed, but (p. 30) die, that he might quickly be master of his property. But Dion, his younger son, heard Paul gladly.

What follows is badly preserved. The content is probably: the friends of Hermippus take counsel as to how to put an end to Paul. Dion has a fall, and dies. Hermocrates mourns deeply but, listening to Paul's sermon, forgets that Dion is dead.

But when Dion was dead, his mother Nympha rent <her> clothing (and) went to Paul, and set herself before her husband Hermocrates and Paul. But when Paul saw her, he was startled and said: 'Why (art thou doing) this, Nympha?' But she said to him: 'Dion is dead.' And the whole crowd wept as they looked upon her. And Paul looked upon the mourning crowd; he sent young men and said to them: 'Go and bring him here to me.' So they went, but Hermippus <caught hold of> the body in the street and cried out . . .

(A leaf missing)

(p. 31) . . . But an angel <of the> Lord had said to him in the night:[6] 'Paul, <there is before thee> today a great conflict <against> thy body (?), but God, <the Father> of his Son Jesus Christ, will < . . . . . > thee.' When <Paul> had arisen, <he> went to his brethren and remained < . . . . . >, saying: 'What means this vision?' But while Paul thought on this, he saw Hermippus coming with a drawn sword in his hand, and with him many other young men with their cudgels. Paul <said to them>: 'I am <not> a robber, nor am I <a> murderer.[7] The God of all things, <the Father> of Christ, will turn < . . . > backwards, and your <sword> into its sheath, and <will transform> your strength into weakness. For I am a servant of God, and I am alone, a stranger, small and of no significance among the heathen. But thou, O God, look down upon <their> plotting (?) and let me not be brought to nought by them.' (p. 32) As Hermippus < . . . . . > his sword < . . . . > against Paul, < . . . . . > he ceased to see, so that <he> cried aloud, saying: '< . . . > comrades, forget not < . . . > Hermippus. For I have < . . . >, Paul, I have pursued after < . . > blood. <Learn>, ye foolish and ye of understanding, <this> world is nothing, gold is <nothing>, all possessions are nothing. I who glutted myself with all that is good am <now> a beggar, <and> entreat you all: Hearken, all ye my companions, and every one who dwells in Myra. <I have> mocked a man <who saved> my father, I have <mocked . . . > raised up my brother < . . . >

Lines badly preserved, which are restored by Schmidt: <I have mocked> a man who <has . . . without> doing me any <evil> (?).

But entreat ye him; for look; <since?> he saved my father and raised up my brother, it is possible for him also to deliver me. But Paul stood there weeping, on the one hand before God (with God in mind), because he had heard him (so) quickly, but on the other also before men (with men in mind), because the proud was brought low. He turned and went up . . .

Probably a leaf is missing.

The upper part of p. 33 is preserved so fragmentarily that while we can indeed reproduce its contents with the help of Schmidt's restorations, a translation is not possible. On the contents cf. above, pp. 222f.

And they saw Hermippus <their> son in the form of < . . . . . >, and how he touched the feet of each one, and also the feet of his parents, praying them like one of the strangers that he might be healed. And his parents were troubled and lamented to every one who went in, so that <some> said: 'Why do they weep? For <Dion is> risen.' But Hermocrates <sold . . . . . > and brought the price to the <widows>, and took it and divided it . . . . .

The following lines are again badly damaged.

But they and Paul <prayed> to God. And when Hermippus recoverd his sight, he turned to his mother Nympha, saying to her: 'Paul came and laid his hand upon me while I wept. And in that hour I saw all things clearly.' And she took his hand and brought <him> in to the widows and Paul.

The last lines of p. 34 are badly damaged. Between pages 34 and 35 a leaf is possibly missing. The end of a speech by Paul appears to have stood on p. 35. The last sentence before the lemma is restored by Schmidt:

<And when> Paul <had confirmed> the brethren who <were in> Myra, he departed for <Sidon>.

5

(Paul in Sidon)
(PHeid pp. 35-39)

When he was departed from Myra
and <would go to Sidon>.

(p. 35) But <when Paul was departed from Myra and wished to go> up to Si<don>, there was great sorrow among the brethren who were in <Pisidia> and Pamphylia, since they yearned <after> his word and his holy presence; so that some from Perga[1] followed Paul, namely Thrasymachus and Cleon with their wives Aline (?) and Chrysa, the wife of Cleon.

The following section is preserved only fragmentarily. On its contents cf. above, pp. 220f. Then at least two leaves are missing, and possibly more (see above, p. 223). Page 37 begins with a speech by Paul in Sidon.

(p. 37) ' . . . <after> the manner of strange men. Why do you presume to do things that are not seemly? Have you not heard of that which happened, which God brought upon Sodom and Gomorrah,[2] because they robbed . . . '

The remainder of the speech is severely damaged.

<But they> did not listen to him, but <laid hold of> them and flung them into <the temple of Apol>lo to keep them secure until <the morning>, in order that they might assemble the city < . . . > Abundant and costly was the food they gave them, but Paul, who was fasting for the third day, testified all night

long, sad at heart and smiting his brow and saying: 'O God, look down upon their threats[3] and suffer us not to fall, and let not our adversary strike us down (?), (p. 38) but <deliver> us by speedily bringing down thy righteousness upon us.'

The following lines are badly damaged. Probably at Paul's prayer a part of the temple collapses, which creates a considerable stir.

They (i.e. those who had seen the fallen temple) went away (and) proclaimed in the city: 'Apollo the god of the Sidonians is fallen, with the half of his temple.' And all the inhabitants of the city ran to the temple (and) saw Paul and those that were with him weeping at this tribulation, that they were to become a spectacle for everyone. But the crowd cried out: 'Bring them to the theatre!' The magistrates came to fetch them; and they groaned bitterly in their soul . . .

Here at least two leaves are missing. On p. 39, which presents the end of the Sidon episode, only a little can be read. Apparently Paul makes a speech, which brings the crowd round. Schmidt restores the conclusion thus:

<But he> commanded <them> to go to Tyre . . . <in> safety (?), and they put Paul <aboard a ship?> and went with him.

6

(Paul in Tyre)
(PHeid p. 40)

When he was departed from Sidon
and would go to Tyre.

(p. 40) But when <Paul> had entered <into Tyre> there <came a> crowd of Jews . . . in to him.

The following lines are damaged. Paul probably preaches and also drives out demons. The names Amphion and Chrysippus can be recognised.

But immediately the demons <fled>. But when the crowd saw <these things in the power> of God, they praised him who <. . . . .> to Paul. Now there was one named <. . . >rimos, who had a <son> who had been born dumb . . .

Here the episode at Tyre breaks off; cf. above, pp. 224f.

7

(Paul in Ephesus)
(PH pp. 1-5)

This was preceded by a stay in Smyrna and the arrival in Ephesus, where Paul preaches in the house of Aquila and Priscilla (cf. PG, below, p. 263). PH begins with the scene before the governor.

(p. 1) But Paul said to him: '< . . . > For thou hast no power <over me except over> my body; but my soul thou <canst> not <slay>.[1] But <hear> in what manner thou must be saved. And taking all <my words> to heart < . . . > and the earth and stars and dominions and < . . . > and all the good things in the world for the sake of < . . . > moulded < . . . > of men < . . . > led astray and enslaved < . . . > by gold < . . . > silver and precious stones < . . . > and adultery and drunkenness. < . . . >, which lead to deception through the afore-mentioned < . . . > went and were slain.[2] Now then, since the Lord wishes us to live in God because of the error in the world, <and not> die in sins, he saves through the < . . . > who preach, that ye may repent and believe < . . . >[3] and one Christ Jesus and no other exists. For your gods are of < . . . > and stone and wood, and can neither take food nor see nor hear, nor even stand. Form a good resolve, and be ye saved, lest God be wroth and burn you with unquenchable fire,[4] and the memory of you perish.'[5] And when the governor heard this < . . . > in the theatre with the people, he said: 'Ye men of Ephesus, that this man has spoken well I know, but also that < . . . > is no time for you to learn these things. Decide now what you wish!' Some said he should be burned < . . . . . >, but the goldsmiths[6] said: 'To the beasts with the man!' And since a great <tumult> broke out Hieronymus condemned him to the beasts, after having him scourged. Now the brethren, since it was Pentecost, did not mourn or bow their knees, but rejoiced and prayed <standing>. But after six days Hieronymus made < . . . >[7] all who saw it were astonished at the size < . . . >[8]

(p. 2) The first lines are imperfect. Paul sits a prisoner, and hears the preparations for the fight with the beasts.

And <when the lion> came to the side door of the stadium, <where Paul> was imprisoned, it roared loudly, so that all < . . . > cried out: 'The lion!' For it roared fiercely and angrily, <so that even Paul> broke off his prayer in terror. There was < . . . > Diophantes, a freedman of Hieronymus, whose wife was a disciple of Paul and sat beside him night and day, <so that> Diophantes became jealous and hastened on the conflict. <And> Artemilla, the wife of Hieronymus, wished to hear Paul <praying>, and said to Eubula, the wife of Diophantes: '<

. . . > to hear the beast-fighter's prayer.' And she went and told Paul, and Paul full of joy said: 'Bring her.' She put on darker clothes, and came to him with Eubula. But when Paul saw her, he groaned and said: 'Woman, ruler of this world, mistress of much gold, citizen of great luxury, splendid in thy raiment, sit down on the floor and forget thy riches and thy beauty and thy finery. For these will profit thee nothing if thou pray not to God who regards as dross all that here is imposing, but graciously bestows what there is wonderful. Gold perishes, riches are consumed, clothes become worn out. Beauty grows old, and great cities are changed, and the world will be destroyed in fire[9] because of the lawlessness of men. God alone abides, and the sonship[10] that is given through him in whom men must be saved.[11] And now, Artemilla, hope in God and he will deliver thee, hope in Christ and he will give thee forgiveness of sins and will bestow upon thee a crown of freedom, that thou mayest no longer serve idols and the steam of sacrifice but the living God[12] and Father of Christ, whose is the glory for ever and ever. Amen.' And when Artemilla heard this she with Eubula besought Paul that he would <forthwith?> baptize her in God. And the fight with the beasts was (arranged) for the next day.

(p. 3) And Hieronymus heard from Diophantes that the women sat night and day with Paul, and he was not a little wroth with Artemilla and the freedwoman Eubula. And when he had dined Hieronymus withdrew early, that he might quickly carry through the beast-hunt. But the women said to Paul: 'Dost thou wish us to bring a smith, that thou mayest baptize us in the sea as a free man?' And Paul said: 'I do not wish it, for I have faith in God, who delivered the whole world from (its) bonds.' And Paul cried out to God on the Sabbath as the Lord's day drew near, the day on which Paul was to fight with the beasts, and he said: 'My God, Jesus Christ, who didst redeem me from so many evils,[13] grant me that before the eyes of Artemilla and Eubula, who are thine, the fetters may be broken from my hands.' And as Paul thus testified (or: adjured God),[14] there came in a youth very comely in grace and loosed Paul's bonds, the youth smiling as he did so. And straightway he departed. But because of the vision which was granted to Paul, and the eminent sign relating to his fetters, his grief over the fight with the beasts departed, and rejoicing he leaped as if in paradise. And taking Artemilla he went out from the narrow and <dark place where the> prisoners were kept.

In the following there are considerable gaps, which Schmidt has meaningfully restored. The subject is Artemilla's baptism at the sea. As Artemilla swoons at the sight of the surging sea, Paul prays:

'O thou who dost give light and shine, <help, that> the heathen may <not> say (p. 4) that Paul the prisoner fled after killing Artemilla.' And again the youth smiled, and the matron (Artemilla) breathed again, and she went into the house as dawn was already breaking. But as he (Paul?) went in, the guards being asleep, he broke bread and brought water, gave her to drink of the word, and dismissed her to her husband Hieronymus. But he himself prayed.

At dawn there was a cry from the citizens: 'Let us go to the spectacle! Come, let us see the man who possesses God fighting with the beasts!' Hieronymus himself joined them, partly because of his suspicion against his wife, partly because he (Paul) had not fled; he commanded Diophantes and the other slaves to bring Paul into the stadium. He (Paul) was dragged in, saying nothing but bowed down and groaning because he was led in triumph by the city. And when he was brought out he was immediately flung into the stadium, so that all were vexed at Paul's dignity. But since Artemilla and Eubula fell into a sickness and were in extreme danger because of Paul's (impending) destruction, Hieronymus was not a little grieved over (his) wife, but also because the rumour was already abroad in the city and he did not have his wife with him. So when he had taken his place the < . . . > ordered a very fierce lion, which had but recently been captured, to be set loose against him.

The following text is very imperfect. It deals with the lion's prayer and its conversation with Paul. The people thereupon cry out:

'Away with the sorcerer![15] Away with the <poisoner!' But the lion> looked at Paul and Paul <at the lion. Then> Paul recognised that this <was the> lion (p. 5) which had come <and> been baptized. <And> borne along by faith[16] Paul said: 'Lion, was it thou whom I baptized?' And the lion in answer said to Paul: 'Yes,' Paul spoke to it again and said: 'And how wast thou captured?' The lion said with one (?) voice:[17] Even as thou, Paul.' As Hieronymus sent many beasts, that Paul might be slain, and against the lion archers, that it too might be killed, a violent and exceedingly heavy hail-storm fell from heaven, although the sky was clear, so that many died and all the rest took to flight. But it did not touch Paul or the lion, although the other beasts perished under the weight of the hail, (which was so severe) that Hieronymus' ear was smitten and torn off, and the people cried out as they fled: 'Save us, O God, save us, O God of the man who fought with the beasts!' And Paul took leave of the lion, without his (i.e. the lion?) saying anything more, and went out of the stadium and down to the harbour and embarked on the ship which was sailing for Macedonia; for there were many who were sailing, as if the city were about to perish. So he embarked too like one of the fugitives, but the lion went away into the mountains as was customary for it.

Now Artemilla and Eubula mourned not a little, fasting and in < . . >[18] as to what had befallen Paul. But when it was night there came <. . . >[19] visibly into the bedroom, where < . . . > Hieronymus was discharging at the ear.

The following lacunae have been so restored by Schmidt that their content becomes clear: the women are comforted as to Paul's fate. Hieronymus prays to

Paul's God for help for his ear.

Through the will of Christ Jesus <heal> the ear!' And it became whole, as <the youth> had commanded him: 'Treat <the ear?> with honey.'

8

(Paul in Philippi)

(PHeid pp. 45-50; 41, 42 and 44; for 3 Cor. see above, pp. 217 and 228[1]

The beginning of the Philippi episode is missing. The first lines of PHeid p. 45 are so fragmentary that no conclusions can be drawn from them.

<For> the Corinthians were in <great> distress <over> Paul, because he was going out of the world before it was time. For men were come to Corinth, Simon and Cleobius, who said that there was no resurrection of the flesh but (only) of the spirit, and that the body of man is not the creation of God; and of the world (they said) that God did not create it, and that God does not know the world; and that Jesus Christ was not crucified, but was only a semblance, and that he was not born of Mary, or of the seed of David.[2] In a word, many were the things which they <taught?> in Corinth, deceiving <many others . . . and> themselves. <Because of this>, when <the Corinthians> heard <that Paul was in Philippi> they sent a <letter to Paul> in Macedonia <by> Threptus <and> Eutychus <the deacons>. And the letter was <in this form>.

(Letter of the Corinthians to Paul)[3]

1. 1. Stephanas and the presbyters who are with him, Daphnus, Eubulus, Theophilus and Xenon, to Paul <their brother> in the Lord, greeting.

2. Two men are come to Corinth, named Simon and Cleobius, who pervert the faith of many through pernicious words, 3. which thou shalt put to the test. 4. For never have we heard such words, either from thee or from other [apostles]; 5. but what we have received from thee and from them, that we hold fast. 6. Since now the Lord has shown mercy to us, that while thou art still in the flesh we may hear such things again from thee, 7. do thou [write to us or] come to us. 8. For we believe, as it has been revealed to Theonoe, that the Lord has delivered thee out of the hand of the lawless one. 9. What they say and teach is as follows: 10. We must not, they say, appeal to the prophets, 11. and that God is not almighty, 12. and that there is no resurrection of the flesh, 13. and that the creation of man is not God's (work), 14. and that the Lord is not come in the flesh, nor was he born of Mary, 15. and that the world is not of God, but of the angels. 16. Wherefore, brother, make all speed to come hither, that the church of the Corinthians may remain without offence, and the foolishness of these men be made manifest. Fare thee well in the Lord!

2. 1. The deacons Threptus and Eutychus brought the letter to Philippi, 2. and delivered it to Paul, who was in prison because of Stratonice, the wife of Apollophanes; and he began to shed many tears and to mourn, and cried out: 3. 'Better were it for me to die and be with the Lord, than to be in the flesh and hear such things, so that sorrow after sorrow comes upon me, 4. and suffering such things to be bound and (have to see how) the tools (intrigues?) of the evil one run their course!' 5. And so Paul in affliction wrote the (following) letter.

(Letter of Paul to the Corinthians)

3. 1. Paul, the prisoner of Jesus Christ, to the brethren in Corinth - greeting! 2. Since I am in many tribulations, I do not wonder that the teachings of the evil one are so quickly gaining ground. 3. For <my> Lord Jesus Christ will quickly come, since he is rejected by those who falsify his words. 4. For I delivered to you in the beginning what I received from the apostles who were before me, who at all times were together with the Lord Jesus Christ, 5. that our Lord Jesus Christ was born of Mary of the seed of David, when the Holy Spirit was sent from heaven by the Father into her, 6. that he might come into this world and redeem all flesh through his own flesh, and that he might raise up from the dead us who are fleshly, even as he has shown himself as our example. 7. And since man was moulded by his Father, 8. for this reason was he sought when he was lost, that he might be quickened by adoption into sonship. 9. For the almighty God, who made heaven and earth, first sent the prophets to the Jews, that they might be drawn away from their sins; 10. for he had determined to save the house of Israel, therefore he sent a portion of the Spirit of Christ into the prophets, who at many times proclaimed the faultless worship of God. 11. But since the prince who was unrighteous wished himself to be God, he laid hands upon them and slew them, and so fettered all flesh of men to the passions <to his will, and the end of the world drew nigh to judgment>. 12. But God, the almighty, who is righteous and would not repudiate his own creation, 13. sent the <Holy> Spirit <through fire> into Mary the Galilean, 14. who believed with all her heart, and she received the Holy Spirit in her womb that Jesus might enter into the world, 15. in order that the evil one might be conquered through the same flesh by which he held sway, and convinced that he was not God. 16. For by his own body Jesus Christ saved all flesh <and brought it to eternal life through faith>, 17. that he might present a temple of righteousness in his body, 18. through whom we are redeemed. 19. They are thus not children of righteousness but children of wrath, who reject the providence of God, saying <far from faith> that heaven and earth and all that in them is are not works of the Father. 20. They are themselves therefore children of wrath, for they have the accursed faith of the serpent. 21. From them turn ye away, and flee from their teaching! <22. For ye are not sons of disobedience but of the Church most

dearly beloved. 23. Wherefore the time of the resurrection is proclaimed>.

24. As for those who tell you that there is no resurrection of the flesh, for them there is no resurrection, 25. who do not believe in him who is thus risen. 26. For indeed, ye men of Corinth, they do not know about the sowing of wheat or the other seeds, that they are cast naked into the ground and when they have perished below are raised again by the will of God in a body and clothed. 27. And not only is the body which was cast (into the earth) raised up, but also abundantly blessed. 28. And if we must not derive the similitude from the seeds alone, <but from nobler bodies>, 29. you know that Jonah the son of Amathios, when he would not preach in Nineveh <but fled>, was swallowed by a whale, 30. and after three days and three nights God heard Jonah's prayer out of deepest hell, and no part of him was corrupted, not even a hair or an eyelid. 31. How much more, O ye of little faith, will he raise up you who have believed in Christ Jesus, as he himself rose up? 32. And if, when a corpse was thrown by the children of Israel upon the bones of the prophet Elisha, the man's body rose up, so you also who have been cast upon the body and bones and Spirit of the Lord shall rise up on that day with your flesh whole.

34. But if you receive anything else, do not cause me trouble; 33. for I have these fetters on my hands that I may gain Christ, and his marks in my body that I may attain to the resurrection from the dead. 36. And whoever abides by the rule which he received through the blessed prophets and the holy Gospel, he shall receive a reward <and when he is risen from the dead shall obtain eternal life>. 37. But he who turns aside therefrom - there is fire with him and with those who go before him in the way, 38. since they are men without God, a generation of vipers; 39. from these turn ye away in the power of the Lord, 40. and peace, <grace and love> be with you. Amen.

Between 3 Cor. and the conclusion of the Philippi episode there is a lacuna, the length of which cannot be determined. Of the first lines on page 41 of PHeid only the names Longinus and Paul can be read. Evidently Longinus, the father of Frontina, is speaking.

(p. 41) . . . nothing good has <befallen> my house.' <And> he advised that <. . . > who <were to throw> down Frontina <his> daughter should <also> throw down Paul alive <with> her. Now Paul knew of the <matter>, but he laboured and fasted in great cheerfulness for two <days> with the prisoners. They <commanded that> on the third day < . . . > bring out Frontina. But the < . . > followed her. And Firmilla and Longinus and the soldiers <lamented>. But the prisoners carried the bier. And when Paul saw a great mourning . . .

Lacuna of about 8 lines

(p. 42) . . . Paul alive <with the> daughter. But when Paul <had taken> the daughter in <his> arms, he groaned to the Lord Jesus Christ because of Firmilla's sorrow; he threw himself on his knees in the mire < . . . > and prayed for Frontina and <her> in one prayer. In <that> hour Frontina <rose up>. And all the <crowd> was afraid and fled. Paul <took> the daughter's hand and < . . . > through the city to the house <of> Longinus. But the whole <crowd> cried with one voice: 'One is God, who has made heaven and earth, who has given life to the daughter < . . . . . > of Paul.'

A few more lines follow on pages 42 and 44, but of these only a few letters or words can be recognised. On the content cf. above, pp. 227f. A new section begins in the middle of page 44 of PHeid. Of the lemma not much is preserved. In accordance with PH it may be restored:

<When he was departed from Philippi>
and would go <to Corinth>.

9

(Paul in Corinth)
(PH pp. 6-7; PHeid pp. 44/43; 51/52)

From Philippi to Corinth

(p. 6) When Paul came from Philippi to Corinth, to the house of Epiphanius, there was joy,[1] so that all our people rejoiced but at the same time wept as Paul related what he had suffered in Philippi in the workhouse[2] and everywhere, what had befallen him, so that further his tears became < . . . >[3] and continuous prayer was offered by all for Paul, and he counted himself blessed that so single-heartedly every day they guided his affairs in prayer to the Lord. Unrivalled therefore was the greatness of the joy, and Paul's soul was uplifted because of the goodwill of the brethren, so that for forty days he preached the word of perseverance,[4] (relating) in what place anything had befallen him and what great deeds had been granted to him. So in every account he praised almighty God and Christ Jesus who in every place had been well pleased with Paul. <But when> the days were ended (and the time drew near) for Paul to depart for Rome, grief came upon the brethren as to when they should see him again. And Paul, full of the Holy Spirit, said: 'Brethren, he zealous about <fasting?>[5] and love. For behold, I go away to a furnace of fire < . . . >[6] and I am not strong except the Lord <grant> me power. For indeed David accompanied Saul[7] < . . . >,[8] for Christ Jesus was with him < . . . >. <The grace of> the Lord will go with me, that I may <fulfil> the < . . . > dispensation with steadfastness.' But they were distressed and fasted. Then Cleobius was filled with the Spirit and said: 'Brethren, now must Paul fulfil all his assignment, and go up to the < . . . >[9] of death < . . . > in great instruction and knowledge and sowing of the word, and (must) suffer envy[10] and depart out of this world.' But when the brethren and Paul heard ,this>, they lifted up their voice and said: 'O God, < . . . > Father of Christ, help thou Paul thy servant, that he may yet abide with us because of our weakness.' But since Paul was cut (to the heart) and no longer fasted with them, when an offering (i.e. Eucharist) was celebrated by Paul . . .

(PH p. 7) The beginning of the page is very imperfect, nor does it admit of any meaningful restoration from PHeid p. 52.

But the Spirit came upon Myrta, so that she said: 'Brethren, why <are you alarmed at the sight of this sign?>[11] Paul the servant of the Lord will save many in Rome, and will nourish many with the word, so that there is no number (to count them), and he (?) will become manifest above all the faithful,[12] and greatly will the glory < . . . come> upon him, so that there will be great grace in Rome.' And immediately, when the Spirit that was in Myrta was at peace, each one took of the bread and feasted according to custom < . . . >[13] amid the singing of psalms of David and of hymns. And Paul too enjoyed himself. On the following day, after they had spent the whole night according to the will of God, Paul said: 'Brethren, I shall set out on the day of preparation and sail for Rome, that I may not delay what is ordained and laid upon me, for to this I was appointed.' They were greatly distressed when they heard this, and all the brethren contributed according to their ability so that Paul might not be troubled, except that he was going away from the brethren.

10

(From Corinth to Italy)
(PH pp. 7-8; PO; PM)

(p. 7) As he embarked on the ship, while they all prayed, Artemon[1] the captain of the ship was there. He had been baptized by Peter, and < . . . . . > Paul, that so much was entrusted to him < . . . . . >[2] the Lord was embarking. But when the ship had set sail, Artemon held fellowship with Paul to glorify the Lord Jesus Christ in the grace of God, since he had fore-ordained his plan for Paul.[3] When they were on the open sea and it was quiet, Paul fell asleep, fatigued by the fastings and the night watches with the brethren. And the Lord came to him, walking upon the sea, and he nudged Paul and said: 'Stand up and see!' And he awakening said: 'Thou art my Lord Jesus Christ, the king < . . . . >, But why so gloomy and downcast, Lord? And if thou < . . . . > Lord, for I am not a little distressed that thou art so.' <And the> Lord said: 'Paul, I am about to be crucified afresh.'[4] And Paul said: 'God forbid, Lord, that I should see this!'

But the Lord said to Paul: 'Paul, get thee up, go to Rome and admonish the brethren, that they abide in the calling to the Father.' And < . . . . . > walking on the sea, he went before them < . . . . . > showed (the way). But when the voyage was ended < . . . > Paul went < . . . . . > with great sadness, and <he saw> a man standing <on> the harbour, who was waiting for Artemon the captain, and seeing him greeted him < . . . (p. 8) . . > and he said to him: 'Claudius, <see here Paul> the beloved of the Lord, who is with me.' < . . . > Claudius embraced[5] Paul and greeted him. And without delay he with Artemon carried the (baggage) from the ship to his house. And he rejoiced greatly and informed the brethren about him, so that at once Claudius' house was filled with joy and thanksgiving. For they saw how Paul laid aside his mood of sadness and taught the word of truth[6] and said: 'Brethren and soldiers of Christ,[7] listen! How often did God deliver Israel out of the hand of the lawless! And so long as they kept the things of God[8] he did not forsake them. For he saved them out of the hand of Pharaoh the lawless, and of Og the still more ungodly king,[9] and of Adar[10] and the foreign people. And so long as they kept the things of God he gave them of the fruit of the loins,[11] after he had promised them the land of the Canaanites, and he made the foreign people subject to them. And after all that he provided for them in the desert and in the waterless (country), he sent them in addition prophets to proclaim our Lord Jesus Christ;[12] and these in succession received share and portion of the Spirit of Christ,[13] and having suffered much were slain by the people. Having thus forsaken the living God according to their own desires, they forfeited the eternal inheritance. And now, brethren, a great temptation lies before us. If we endure, we shall have access to the Lord, and shall receive as the refuge and shield of his good pleasure[14] Jesus Christ, who gave himself for us, if at least ye receive the word so as it is.[15] For in these last times God for our sakes has sent down a spirit of power into the flesh, that is, into Mary the Galilean, according to the prophetic word; who[16] was conceived and borne by her as the fruit of her womb until she was delivered and gave birth to <Jesus> the Christ, our King,[17] of Bethlehem in Judaea, brought up in Nazareth, who went to Jerusalem and taught all Judaea: "The kingdom of heaven is at hand! Forsake the darkness, receive the light, you who live in the darkness of death![18] A light has arisen for you!" And he did great and wonderful works, so that he chose from the tribes twelve men whom he had with him in understanding and faith, as he raised the dead, healed diseases, cleansed lepers, healed the blind,[19] made cripples whole, raised up paralytics, cleansed those possessed by demons . . .

Here the text of PH (p. 8) breaks off. In (the three parts of) PM there follow the fragments of further lines, which however scarcely permit of a coherent translation. Only this much is clear, that there is reference to miracles of Jesus. Probably we have in PHeid p. 79/80 the Coptic version of this part of the AP1, of which only these Greek fragments survive. That the Coptic text is not, as Schmidt thought, the remains of an apocryphal gospel was already conjectured in NTApo[3] (ET 344f.). W. Rordorf ('Les actes de Paul sur papyrus' [see above, p. 214] has confirmed this conjecture. He has further calculated that with the aid of PHeid and the three fragments of PM the lacunae in PH, which begins again on p. 9 with MP c. 3, can largely be filled up.

(p. 79) . . . wondered <greatly and deliberated> in their hearts. <He said to them>: 'Why are you amazed <that I raise up> the dead, or that <I make the lame> walk, or that I cleanse <the lepers>, or that I raise up the <sick, or that I have> healed the paralytic and those possessed by demons, or that I have divided a little bread and satisfied many, or that I have walked upon the sea, or that I have commanded the winds?[20] If you believe this and <are convinced>, then are you great. For truly <I say> to you: If you say to <this mountain>, Be thou removed and cast <into the sea>, and are not doubtful <in your heart>, it will come to pass for you.'[21] < . . . > when <one of> them was convinced, whose name was Simon and who said: 'Lord, truly great are the works which thou dost do. For we have never heard, nor have <we ever> seen (p. 80) <a man who> has raised <the dead>, except for <thee.' The Lord said to him:> 'You <will pray for the works> which I myself will <do . . . . . > But the other works <I> will do at once. For these I do <for the sake of?> a temporary deliverance in the time during which they are in these places, that they may believe in him who sent me.' Simon said to him: 'Lord, command me to speak.' He said to him: 'Speak, Peter!' For from that day he <called? them by name. He said: <'What then is> the work that is greater than these < . . . . . apart from> raising of the dead and <the feeding> of such a crowd?' The Lord said to him: 'There is something that is <greater than this>, and blessed are they who have believed with all their heart.' But Philip lifted up his voice in wrath, saying: 'What manner of thing is this that thou wouldst teach us?' But he said to him: 'Thou . . .

On the lacuna between this speech by Paul and the beginning of the Martyrdom, which is probably not very great, cf. above, p. 230.

11

Martyrdom of the Holy Apostle Paul
(*Aa* 1, pp. 104-117; PH pp. 9-11; PHeid pp. 53-58)

1. There were awaiting Paul at Rome Luke from Gaul and Titus from Dalmatia.[1] When Paul saw them he was glad, so that he hired a barn outside Rome, where with the brethren he taught the word of truth. The news was spread abroad, and many souls were added to the Lord,[2] so that there was a rumour throughout Rome, and a great number of believers came to him from

the house of Caesar,[3] and there was great joy.

But a certain Patroclus, Caesar's cup-bearer, came late to the barn and, (p. 106) being unable because of the crowd to go in to Paul, sat at a high window and listened to him teaching the word of God. But since the wicked devil was envious of the love of the brethren, Patroclus fell from the window and died,[4] and the news was quickly brought to Nero. But Paul, perceiving it in the spirit, said: 'Brethren, the evil one has gained an opportunity to tempt you. Go out, and you will find a youth fallen from a height and already on the point of death. Lift him up, and bring him here to me!' So they went out and brought him. And when the crowd saw (him), they were troubled. Paul said to them: 'Now, brethren, let your faith be manifest. Come, all of you, let us mourn to our Lord Jesus Christ, that this youth may live and we remain unmolested.' But as they all lamented the youth drew breath again, and setting him upon a beast they sent him back alive with the others who were of Caesar's house. 2. When Nero heard of Patroclus' death, he was greatly distressed, and when he came out from the bath he commanded that another be appointed for the wine. But his servants told him the news, saying: 'Caesar, Patroclus is alive and standing at the (p. 108) table.' And when Caesar heard that Patroclus was alive he was afraid, and did not want to go in. But when he had entered he saw Patroclus and, beside himself, cried out: 'Patroclus, art thou alive?' And he said: 'I am alive, Caesar.' But he said: 'Who is he who made thee to live?' And the youth, borne by the conviction of faith, said: 'Christ Jesus, the king of the ages.'[5] But Caesar in perplexity said: 'So he is to be king of the ages, and destroy all the kingdoms?' Patroclus said to him: 'Yes, all the kingdoms under heaven he destroys, and he alone shall be for ever, and there shall be no kingdom which shall escape him.' But he struck him on the face and said: 'Patroclus, dost thou also serve in that king's army?' And he said: 'Yes, lord Caesar, for indeed he raised me up when I was dead.' And Barsabas Justus of the flat feet, and Orion the Cappadocian, and Festus the Galatian, Nero's chief men, (p. 110) said: 'We also are in the army[6] of that king of the ages.' But he shut them up in prison, after torturing dreadfully men whom he greatly loved, and commanded that the soldiers of the great king be sought out, and he issued a decree to this effect, that all who were found to be Christians and soldiers of Christ[7] should be put to death.

3. And among the many Paul also was brought bound; to him all his fellow-prisoners gave heed, so that Caesar observed that he was the man in command. And he said to him:[8] 'Man of the great king, but (now) my prisoner, why did it seem good to thee to come secretly into the empire of the Romans and enlist soldiers from my province?' But Paul, filled with the Holy Spirit,[9] said before them all: 'Caesar, not only from thy province do we enlist soldiers, but from the whole world. For this charge has been laid upon us, that no man be excluded who wishes to serve my king. If thou also think it good, do him service! for neither riches nor the splendour of this present life will save thee,[10] but if thou

submit and entreat him, then shalt thou be saved. For in one day he will (p. 112) destroy the world with fire.'

When Caesar heard this, he commanded all the prisoners to be burned with fire, but Paul to be beheaded according to the law of the Romans. But Paul did not keep silence concerning the word, but communicated it to the prefect Longus and the centurion Cestus.

In Rome, then, Nero was (raging) at the instigation of the evil one, many Christians being put to death without trial, so that the Romans took their stand at the palace and cried: 'It is enough, Caesar! For these men are ours. Thou dost destroy the power of the Romans!' Then he made an end (of the persecution), whereupon none of the Christians was to be touched until he had himself investigated his case. 4. Then Paul was brought before him in accordance with the decree, and he adhered to the decision that he should be beheaded. But Paul said: 'Caesar, it is not for a short time that I live for my king. And if thou behead me, this will I do: I will arise and appear to thee (in proof) that I am not dead, but alive to my Lord Christ Jesus,[11] (p. 114) who is coming to judge the world.'[12]

But Longus and Cestus said to Paul: 'Whence have you this king, that you believe in him without change of heart, even unto death?' Paul communicated the word to them and said: 'Ye men who are in this ignorance and error, change your mind and be saved from the fire that is coming upon the whole world. For we do not march, as you suppose, with a king who comes from earth,[13] but one from heaven, the living God, who comes as judge because of the lawless deeds that are done in this world. And blessed is that man who shall believe in him, and live for ever,[14] when he comes to burn the world till it is pure.' So they besought him and said: 'We entreat thee, help us and we will let thee go.' But he answered and said: 'I am no deserter from Christ, but a lawful soldier of the living God. Had I known that I was to die, I would have done it, Longus and Cestus. But since I live to God and love myself, I go to the Lord that I may come (again) with him (p. 115) in the glory of his Father.' They said to him: 'How then shall we live, when thou art beheaded?' 5. While they were still saying this, Nero sent a certain Parthenius and Pheretas to see if Paul had already been beheaded; and they found him still alive. But he called them to him and said: 'Believe in the living God, who raises up from the dead both me and all who believe in him!' But they said: 'We are going now to Nero; but when thou dost die and rise again, then will we believe in thy God.' But when Longus and Cestus questioned him further about salvation, he said to them: 'Come quickly here to my grave at dawn, and you will find two men praying, Titus and Luke. They will give you the seal in the Lord.'

Then Paul stood with his face to the east, and lifting up his hands to heaven prayed at length;[15] and after communing in prayer in Hebrew with the fathers he stretched out his neck without speaking further. But when the executioner struck off his head, milk spurted upon the soldier's clothing. And when they saw it, the soldier and all who stood by were amazed, and glorified God who had given Paul (p. 116) such glory. And they went off and reported to Caesar what had happened.

6. When he heard it, he marvelled greatly and was at a loss. Then Paul came about the ninth hour, when many philosophers and the centurion were standing with Caesar, and he stood before them all and said:[16] Caesar, here I am - Paul, God's soldier. I am not dead, but alive in my God. But for thee, unhappy man, there shall be many evils and great punishment, because thou didst unjustly shed the blood of the righteous, and that not many days hence!'[17] And when he had said this Paul departed from him. But when Nero heard (it) he was greatly troubled, and commanded the prisoners to be set free, including Patroclus and Barsabas and his companions.

7. As Paul directed, Longus and Cestus went at dawn and with fear approached Paul's tomb. But as they drew near they saw two men praying, and Paul between them, so that at the sight of this unexpected wonder they were astounded, while Titus and Luke were seized with human fear when they saw Longus and Cestus coming towards them, and turned to flight. (p. 117) But they followed after them, saying: 'We are not pursuing you to kill you, as you imagine, ye blessed men of God, but for life, that you may give it to us as Paul promised us, whom we saw but now standing between you and praying.' And when Titus and Luke heard this from them, with great joy they gave them the seal in the Lord, glorifying the God and Father of our Lord Jesus Christ, unto whom be the glory for ever and ever.[18] Amen.

Appendix

The beginning of the stay in Ephesus
(From a Coptic Papyrus not yet published)[1]

(*R. Kasser*)

When Paul had said this, he departed from Smyrna to go to Ephesus. And he went into the house of Aquila and Priscilla, rejoicing to see the brethren whom he, Paul, loved. They also rejoiced, and prayed that they might be found worthy for Paul to set foot in their house (?). And there was joy and great gladness. And they spent the night watching in prayer, examining[2] <the will of God> to strengthen <their> heart and praying with one accord in the same form.

The angel of the Lord came into the house of Aquila, and stood before them all. He spoke with Paul, so that all were troubled: for <this angel> who stood there was indeed visible (*lit.* revealed), but the words which he was speaking to Paul they (the bystanders) did not hear. But after he had stopped speaking with Paul in tongues, they fell into fear and confusion, and were silent. But Paul looked at the brethren and said:

'Men (and) brethren, the angel of the Lord has come to me, as you all have seen, and has told me: There is a great tumult coming upon thee at Pentecost . . . '[3]

But Paul could not be sorrowful (?) because of Pentecost, for it was a kind of festival for (?) those who believe in Christ, the catechumens as well as the believers; but there was great joy and abundance of love, with psalms and praises to Christ, to the confirmation of those who heard. Paul said:

'Men (and) brethren, hearken to what befell me when I was in Damascus, at the time when I persecuted the faith in God. The Spirit which fell <upon me> from the Father, he it is who preached to me the Gospel[4] of his Son, that I might live in him. Indeed, there is no life except the life which is in Christ. I entered into a great church[5] through (?) the blessed Judas, the brother of the Lord, who from the beginning gave me the exalted love of faith.

'I comported myself[6] in grace through (?) the blessed prophet, and <applied myself to> the revelation of Christ who was begotten before <all> ages. While they preached him, I was rejoicing in the Lord, nourished by his words. But when I was able, I was found <worthy> to speak. I spoke with the brethren - Judas it was who urged[7] me - so that I became beloved of those who heard me.

'But when evening came I went out, lovingly (?) accompanied by the widow Lemma and her daughter Ammia(?). I was walking in the night, meaning to go to Jericho in Phoenicia,[8] and we covered great distances.[9] But when morning came, Lemma and Ammia were behind me, they who . . . *agape*, for I (?) was dear <to their hearts (?), so that they were not far from me (?). There came a great and terrible lion out of the valley of the burying-ground. But we were praying, so that through the prayer Lemma and Ammia did not come upon the beast (?).[10] But when I finished praying, the beast had cast himself at my feet. I was filled with the Spirit (and) looked upon him, (and) said to him: "Lion, what wilt thou?" But he said: "I wish to be baptized."

'I glorifed God, who had given speech to the beast and salvation to his servants. Now there was a great river in that place; I went down into it and he followed me. As doves (?) in terror before eagles (?) fly into a house in order to escape, so was it with Lemma and Ammia, who did not cease (?) to pray humbly, until I had praised and glorified God. I myself was in fear and wonderment, in that I was on the point of leading the lion like an ox and baptizing him in the water. But I stood on the bank, men and brethren, and cried out, saying: 'Thou who dost dwell in the heights, who didst look upon the humble, who didst give rest to the afflicted (?), who with Daniel didst shut the mouths of the lions, who didst send to me our Lord Jesus Christ, grant that we . . . escape (?) the beast, and accomplish the plan[11] which thou hast appointed."

When I had prayed thus, I took <the lion> by his mane <and> in the name of Jesus Christ immersed him three times. But when he came up out of the water he shook out his mane and said to me: "Grace be with thee!" And I said to him: "And likewise with thee."'

The lion ran off to the country rejoicing (for this was revealed to me in my heart). A lioness met him, and he did not yield himself to her but . . . ran off . . .

"See now, you also, Aquila and Priscilla, have become believers in the living God; and in that you have been instructed (?) you have preached the Word (?)."

But as Paul said this a great crowd was added to the faith, so that there was jealousy and the ruler[12] of all Asia[13] turned against Paul, that he might die. For there was a woman in the city who did many <good> works for the Ephesians. Her name was Procla. He baptized her with all her household. And there was a fame of the grace and much blessing between . . . and Pentecost. The crown of Christ was multiplied, so that the (heathen) people (?) in the city came to know a high respect (?). <People said>: 'This man has destroyed the gods through his speeches: "You shall see how they are all consumed with fire!"'

But when Paul went out the people belonging to the city (?) seized him outside the prytaneum (?), brought him to the theatre, and called upon the governor[14] to come. But when he came he questioned Paul saying: 'Why dost thou say that and teach the doctrines which are condemned by the kings and rejected by the world and not learned by us? Thou dost exalt (?)[15] thy God, as we (?) have heard (?), in order (?) to destroy the <gods> of the Romans and <of the people here> (?). Repeat[16] <now> what thou hast said when thou didst persuade the multitude!'

Then Paul said: 'Proconsul, do what thou wilt' etc.[17]

Notes

The Acts of Paul

* The following translation of the extant texts cannot be a substitute for a critical edition (such as we await from W. Rordorf in the CChrSA), nor is it intended to be one. In particular it is not possible in the present context to arrange all the fragments meaningfully and restore them, just as the variants which occur in part of the text (e.g. in 3 Cor.) cannot be presented in full. All that is attempted here is to provide a readable text from the material handed down in many forms, and one which in my view allows us to recognise the original structure and content of the APl. That many questions must remain open, and others are still debated, has already been emphasised in the introduction. References are noted only for a selection of allusions to NT passages or ideas. The language of the APl is very close to that of the NT and other early Christian literature. How far we should assume a common devotional language, how far direct influence, is a question that cannot be examined in the notes. The title is attested by the colophons in PH and PHeid; on this see above, p. 215. For the abbreviations, see p. 214.

2. (Paul in Antioch)

1. On the question which Antioch is meant, see above, p. 218f.
2. Cf. Acts 14:19; 13:50(?).
3. Cf. Rom. 12:17.

3. (Acts of Paul and Thecla)

1. In other MSS: 'Martyrdom of the holy proto-martyr Thecla' (or something similar).

2. Cf. 2 Tim. 4:10; 1:15; 4:14 (?).
3. Lat.: 'expected no evil from them'.
4. The words in brackets are missing in part of the tradition, and are probably secondary. Cf. Klijn, *VigChr* 17, 1963, 19f.
5. Cf. Acts 2:11.
6. Cf. 2 Tim. 1:16; 4:19.
7. The following lines are also in Pap. Antinoopolis (PA).
8. PA: 'with his children and Zeno and his wife'.
9. Cf. Acts 6:15.
10. Cf. Mt. 5:8.
11. Cf. 2 Clem. 8.6; 2 Cor. 6:16.
12. Cf. 1 Cor. 7:29; Rom. 8:17.
13. Cf. Mt. 5:4.
14. Cf. Mt. 5:9.
15. Cf. 2 Clem. 6.9.
16. Cf. 1 Cor. 6:3.
17. Mt. 5:7; this beatitude is lacking in PHeid.
18. Cf. Mt. 10:42.
19. Cf. Mt. 11:29.
20. So the Greek MSS.
21. In Greek MSS 'that I may see her' is lacking.
22. The following lines in Pap. Ox. 6
23. Cf. Rev. 14:4.
24. Cf. 2 Tim. 2:18.
25. So with PHeid against Lipsius, to be regarded as original.
26. Cf. Mk. 15:4.
27. Cf. Acts 14:15 *et al.*.
28. Cf. Ps. 94:1.
29. Cf. Exod. 20:5.
30. Cf. Acts 24:25.
31. Cf. Lk. 10:39; Acts 2:11.
32. So E F G Lat. Syr. PHeid.
33. Cf. Lk. 23:18.
34. Cf. Acts 13:50; 14:19.
35. Lat. A: *signum crucis*; B: *extensis manibus similitudinem crucis*.
36. Cf. Mart. Polyc. 15.1.
37. Only in part of the tradition.
38. Cf. Acts 4:24; 14:15.
39. Only in part of the tradition; missing in PHeid.
40. Cf. Acts 1:24; 15:8.
41. Cf. Mt. 8:19.
42. Cf. Gebhardt xcviii; PHeid: 'A Syrian by the name of Alexander, <who> was the great man in Antioch and did much in the city among all the rulers.' On this passage cf. above, p. 219.
43. Omitted in the Greek tradition; cf. Gebhardt xcixf. and PHeid.
44. Cf. Mk. 15:26.
45. 'Judgment' is perhaps secondary; cf. Gebhardt, pp. c f.
46. Lipsius with some MSS: 'daughter Falconilla'.
47. Cf. on the other hand 2 Clem. 8.3.
48. So according to Gebhardt, pp. ci f.
49. Gebhardt (p. ci) would assume as original: 'And when Tryphaena heard this, she mourned.'
50. Cf. Mart. Polyc. 8:3.

51. Lipsius: 'Tryphaena, the queen'. But this is probably a secondary addition, cf. Gebhardt p. civ.
52. Cf. F. Bovon, *Lukas in neuer Sicht* (BThSt 8), 1985, 244, note 56: 'τίνα τὰ περὶ σέ [AAA I 263] - "what is it about thee?" is probably better to be rendered "what surrounds you?". The motif of the protective enfolding deserves closer examination.'
53. Cf. Mk. 1:11 par.
54. Bovon (loc. cit.) translates 'goal, boundary', thus reads ὅρος instead of ὁδός.
55. Cf. 2 Thess. 1:2.

4. (Paul in Myra)

1. Cf. Mk. 10:27 par.
2. Cf. e.g. Mt. 15:29-31.
3. Cf. 1 Thess. 1:9; Acts 14:15, etc.
4. Cf. Acts 3:6.
5. Cf. Mk. 5:43.
6. Cf. Acts 18:9.
7. Cf. Mk. 14:48 par.

5. (Paul in Sidon)

1. Cf. Acts 13:13ff.
2. Cf. Gen. 19.
3. Cf. Acts 4:29.

7. (Paul in Ephesus)

1. Cf. Mt. 10:28.
2. Cf. Rom. 13:13; Gal. 5:20f.; 1 Clem. 30:1.
3. Probably to be restored: 'that there is only one God;' cf. 1 Cor. 8:4ff.; Eph. 4:5, 6; 1 Tim. 2:5; Jas. 2:19; cf. also PHeid p. 5. 11 (above, p. 238): 'There is no other God save Jesus Christ, the Son of the Blessed.'
4. Cf. Mt. 3:12 par.
5. On Paul's sermon cf. the parallel tradition in PG, as yet unpublished; French translation in Kasser, *RHPR* 40, 1960, 55f.
6. Cf. Acts 19:24ff.
7. Restore: 'the display of animals'.
8. Restore: 'of the beasts'.
9. Cf. 1 Cor. 3:13; 2 Pet. 3:7; MP 3 (see above p. 262).
10. Cf. Rom. 8:15, 23; 9:4; Gal. 4:5; Eph. 1:5.
11. Cf. Acts 4:12.
12. Cf. Acts 14:15 etc.
13. Cf. 2 Tim. 3:11.
14. Schmidt ΠΠ, p. 33, ad loc.: 'διαμαρτύρεσθαι strictly "adjure", cf. 1 Tim. 5:21; 2 Tim. 2:14; 4:1 - perhaps "as Paul thus testified", see Acts 20:21, 23, 24; 23:11, etc. AThe 269.5 (Coptic text p. 37.23) or generally "pray in adjuration".'
15. Cf. AThe c. 20; known also elsewhere in descriptions of the baiting of Christians. On this cf. G. Poupon, 'L'accusation de magie dans les Actes Apocryphes', in Bovon *et al.*, *Les Actes apocryphes des Apôtres*, 71-93. Poupon gives an interpretation of the baptism of Artemilla on pp. 86ff.
16. Cf. 2 Pet. 1:21.
17. Schmidt: μιᾷ φωνῇ corrupted from θία = θείᾳ φωνῇ.
18. Perhaps to be restored: 'in anguish'.

19. Schmidt restores: 'a comely youth'.

8. (Paul in Philippi)

1. The introduction, the letters and the intervening material are handed down only in PHeid. The letters and the intervening material are in the Armenian tradition (A) and in Ephraem's Syriac commentary (E). Letter 1 and the intervening material (2) in a Latin version are in the Zürich MS (Z). Letters 1 and 3 without the intervening material are preserved in Greek in Pap. Bodm. and in Latin in the MSS in Milan (M), Laon (L) and Berlin (B). The letter of Paul alone (3) is contained in Latin in the Paris MS (P).
2. It is improbable that this sentence is intended to be direct speech (introduced in the original Greek text by ὅτι?); the Coptic text of 3 Cor. 1:11ff. suggests the contrary.
3. The superscriptions vary in the tradition. The following notes to 3 Cor. 1-3 relate to the verses.

1. MLBA Stephanus. Cf. 1 Cor. 1:16; 16:15-17; 2 Tim. 4:21; Lk. 1:3; Acts 1:1. MBZAE: the brother; PBodm: τῷ ἐν κυρίῳ.
2. Cf. 2 Tim. 2:18.
4. PBodm leaves out 'apostles'; in PB 'other' is missing.
5. Cf. 1 Cor. 11:2.
6. PBodm. omits: 'such'. Cf. Phil. 1:24.
7. and 8. show many variants in the tradition; cf. Klijn, op. cit. 7f., who considers the reading in PHeid as the original. At the end of v.8 PBodm and B add: 'or answer us'.
14. B: our Lord Jesus Christ.
16. Cf. 2 Tim. 4:9.

2. 2. A adds: 'so that he forgot the bonds'.
3. Cf. Phil. 1:23; 2:27.
5. Cf. 2 Cor. 2:4.

3. Superscription after PBodm.
1. Cf. Eph. 3:1; Phm. 9.
2. Cf. 2 Cor. 2:4; Gal. 1:6.
3. PBodm omits: 'my'.
4. Cf. 1 Cor. 15:3; Gal. 1:17; Acts 1:21f.
5. Cf. Rom. 1:3.
6. Cf. 1 Tim. 1:15.
8. Cf. Rom. 8:15, 23; 9:4; Gal. 4:5; Eph. 1:5. After v. 8 in M & P a longer addition, which agrees with v. 15/16.
11. AE: 'he laid hands on them and slew them'. The conclusion of the verse is a secondary addition in MBPA. Cf. 2 Thess. 2:4.
13. <Holy> MPA, but probably secondary. - <through fire> PBodm. Cf. Klijn, op. cit. 8f.
14. The verse only in MBPA.
16. The conclusion is an addition in PA, similarly in B.
19. Cf. Eph. 2:3. - <far from faith> M.
20. 'They are themselves therefore children of wrath': missing in PBodm and PHeid.
22. Cf. Eph. 2:2; 5:6. - V. 22/23 only in MPBA.
26. Cf. 1 Cor. 15:37; Jn. 12:24f. With this verse PHeid breaks off.
28. Conclusion in MPBA.
29. <but fled>: MP. - V. 29/30 cf. Mt. 12:40 par.
31. Cf. Mt. 6:30 par.; Rom. 6:4.
32. Cf. 2 Kings 13:21ff. - After v. 32 in MPA a longer addition (= v. 33).

34. Cf. Gal. 6:17.
35. Cf. Phil. 3:8; Gal. 6:17; Phil. 3:11.
36. Cf. Gal. 6:16; 1 Cor. 3:14. - Conclusion of verse an addition in MPBA.
38. Cf. Mt. 3:7, etc.
40. <grace and love>: MP

9. (Paul in Corinth)

1. PHeid: great joy.
2. Probably in the sense of 'penitentiary'.
3. Schmidt restores: εἰς ἄνεσιν = for relief; cf. 2 Cor. 7:5.
4. Schmidt (ΠΠ, p. 45, n. 11) gathers together the expressions used to describe Paul's preaching in the APl.
5. Schmidt restores νεότητα, which however does not make sense. In his apparatus he suggests νηστείαν, but this does not fit the traces which remain.
6. Restore with Schmidt: <I mean to Rome>'. On the furnace of fire cf. Mt. 13:42, 50; Dan. 3.
7. Cf. 1 Sam. 24.
8. In the lacuna reference is made to Nabal, cf. 1 Sam. 24. On this cf. Schmidt ΠΠ, p. 47: 'In both cases David thus overcame his adversary without any action of his own, since God was with him. So Paul too hopes to master the destiny which threatens him through the power bestowed upon him by the Lord'.
9. Lacuna in PH and PHeid; possibly: into <the city> of death'.
10. On ζηλωθέντα cf. 1 Clem. 3ff.; MP 1 (above, pp. 260f.).
11. Restoration after Schmidt.
12. i.e. he will surpass all the faithful.
13. Schmidt restores PH according to PHeid: 'according to the custom of fasting'. This however would not fill the lacuna, and the expression remains obscure. Probably what is meant is that after the preparation by fasting the Eucharist is celebrated, and to this an Agape is appended.

10. (From Corinth to Italy)

1. Whether the name Artemon is taken from Acts 27:40 remains questionable. The word, which in Acts indicates the foresail, also frequently occurs as a name. Cf. APt 5 (Theon).
2. The meaning is probably: Artemon welcomes Paul, and esteems him as if the Lord himself had embarked on the ship.
3. προοικονομοῦντα is to be understood from p. 7. 14f.: Paul's path, as part of the plan of salvation (οἰκονομία), is predetermined. Cf. 1 Tim. 2:7; 2 Tim. 1:11.
4. ἄνωθεν here = afresh; cf. above, p. 237 note 35.
5. Here PB begins.
6. Cf. 2 Cor. 6:7; 2 Tim. 2:15.
7. Cf. 2 Tim. 2:3.
8. i.e. God's commandments.
9. Cf. Num. 21:33.
10. Cf. Num. 21:1-3; Adar = Arad.
11. PO: 'of the fruit of the power'. On 'fruit of the loins' = posterity, cf. Acts 2:30 (Ps. 132:11). For the author of the APl the expression was probably only a pious phrase.
12. Cf. Acts 7:52.
13. On the whole section cf. 3 Cor. Schmidt (ΠΠ, pp. 57ff.) has indicated the parallels.
14. Here begins PM2, which however contains only 9 lines.
15. The translation follows PB and Sanders. The sense is not quite clear.
16. On the prophetic word cf. 2 Pet. 1:19; κυοφορεῖσθαι occurs also in Ign. Eph. 18.2.

17. 'King' restored after PM, where a ß can be read.
18. Translation after Sanders; cf. Mt. 4:16; Is. 9:2.
19. Here PH p. 8 ends; the following words are from PB. On the enumeration of the miracles cf. Mt. 4:24; 10:8, 11:5, etc.
20. The enumeration of the miracles follows the Synoptics.
21. Cf. Mk. 11:22f. par.

11. Martyrdom of the Holy Apostle Paul

1. Cf. 2 Tim. 4:10.
2. Cf. Acts 2:41.
3. Cf. Phil. 4:22.
4. Cf. Acts 20:9ff.
5. Cf. 1 Tim. 1:17.
6. Cf. 1 Tim. 1:18; 2 Tim. 2:4.
7. Cf. 2 Tim. 2:3.
8. PH begins again here.
9. Cf. Acts 4:8.
10. Here an addition in PH from PH p. 2. 24ff.
11. Cf. Rom. 14:8.
12. Cf. Acts 17:31.
13. Cf. Jn. 18:36.
14. Cf. Jn. 11:25f.
15. Addition in PH, which however is poorly preserved.
16. Addition in PH: 'through the voice of the Holy Spirit'.
17. Acts 1:5.
18. Cf. 1 Tim. 1:17, etc.

Appendix

1. Cf. *RHPR*, 1960, 45ff. The papyrus is in a very poor condition and we can give only extracts. In addition the translation here presented must be considered provisional. The text so far as it is legible, complete and with a more accurate translation, will be supplied in the Editio princeps.
2. Coptic: ἀνακρίνεσθαι.
3. This section is scarcely legible. The substance is: 'Put thy trust in God and Christ; they will support thee in this trial'.
4. Coptic: εὐαγγελίζειν.
5. Coptic: ἐκκλησία.
6. Coptic: πολιτεύεσθαι.
7. Coptic: προτρέπειν.
8. Confusion of 'Phoenicia' and 'palms'.
9. Lit. marches.
10. An obscure passage: 'fell upon'?
11. Coptic: οἰκονομία.
12. Coptic: ἄρχων.
13. Written 'Amia', with one or two letters added as a correction above the line.
14. Coptic: ἡγεμών.
15. Or: 'exaggerate' (?) - *jis[e]*
16. Lit.: 'Say!'
17. What follows is supplied by the Greek text of the Hamburg Papyrus; but cf. RHPhR 40, 1960, 55ff. (the Coptic text diverges from the Greek).

4. The Acts of Peter

Wilhelm Schneemelcher

Introduction

Preliminary note: in this introduction to the ancient Acts of Peter we cannot undertake to discuss the entire Petrine literature of the early Church and its interrelations.[1] We must confine ourselves to the problems of this one particular work, the ancient Πράξεις Πέτρου, and above all discuss the problems connected with the extant texts.

1. Literature: Texts. Lipsius, Aa I, 45-103; L. Vouaux, *Les Actes de Pierre. Introduction, Textes, Traduction et Commentaires*, Paris 1922; C. Schmidt, *Die alten Petrusakten* (TU 24.1), 1903, 3-7 (Coptic text); James Brashler and Douglas M. Parrott, 'The Acts of Peter', BG 4.128. 1-141.7, in *Nag Hammadi Codices V 2-5 and VI with Papyrus Berolinensis 8502.1 and 4* (NHC XI), Leiden 1979, 473-493 (Coptic and English). On the *oriental* versions cf. BHO 933-954; Vouaux, op. cit. 19-22; Poupon, in ANRW (see below); Louis Leloir, 'Martyre de Pierre (BHO 933)', in L. Leloir, *Écrits apocryphes sur les Apôtres. Traduction de l'édition arménienne de Venise* I (CChrSA 3), Turnhout 1986, 64-76 (French trans.). On the *Slavonic* tradition cf. de Santos, *Überlieferung* I, 52-59. A new critical edition is being prepared by G. Poupon for the CChrSA.

Translations: *German:* G. Ficker, NTApo[1], 383-422; NTApo[2] 226-249 (revised for NTApo[3] and NTApo[5] by W. Schneemelcher); W. Michaelis, 317-379. *French:* Vouaux, op. cit. 221-467. *English:* James, 300-336. *Italian:* Erbetta II, 135-168; Moraldi II, 981-1040.

Studies: older literature in Lipsius, *Apostelgeschichten* II/1, 1887 and supplementary volume 1890; Harnack, *Lit. gesch.* I/1, 131-136; A. Baumstark, *Die Petrus- und Paulusacten in der literarischen Überlieferung der syrischen Kirche*, 1902; G. Ficker, *Die Petrusakten. Beiträge zu ihrem Verständnis*, 1903; id. in NTApoHdb, 395-491 (detailed commentary); C. Schmidt, *Die alten Petrusakten*, 1903 (see above); id., 'Studien zu den alten Petrusakten', ZKG 43, 1924, 321-348 [= Studien I]; 45, 1927, 481-513 [= Studien II]; id., 'Zur Datierung der alten Petrusakten', ZNW 29, 1930, 150-155; Th. Nissen, 'Die Petrusakten und ein bardesanitischer Dialog in der Aberkiosvita', ZNW 9, 1908, 190-203, 315-328; J. Flamion, 'Les actes apocryphes de Pierre', RHE IX, 1908, 233-254, 465-490; X, 1909, 5-29, 215-277; XI, 1910, 5-28, 223-256, 447-470, 675-692; XII, 1911, 209-230, 437-450; C. Erbes, 'Ursprung und Umfang der Petrusakten', ZKG 32, 1911, 497-530; L. Vouaux (see above); C.H. Turner, 'The Latin Acts of Peter', JTS XXXII, 1931, 119-133; C.L. Sturhahn, 'Die Christologie der ältesten apokryphen Apostelakten' (Theol. Diss. Heidelberg, 1951, typescript); Vielhauer, *Lit. gesch.* 696-699; E. Plümacher, 'Apokryphe Apostelakten', in Pauly-Wissowa RE. Suppl. XV, 1978, cols. 19-24; Brian McNeil, 'A Liturgical Source in Acts of Peter 38', *VigChr* 33, 1979, 342-346; F. Bovon *et al.*, *Les Actes apocryphes des Apôtres. Christianisme et Monde Païen*, 1981 (cf. index); G. Stuhlfauth, *Die apokryphen Petrusgeschichten in der altchristlichen Kunst*, 1925; G. Poupon, 'Les "Actes de Pierre" et leur remaniement', ANRW II 25.6, 1988, 4363-4383[2]; D.R. Cartlidge, 'Transfigurations of Metamorphosis Traditions in the Acts of John, Thomas and Peter', *Semeia* 38, 1986, 53-66; Robert F. Stoops, Jr., 'Patronage in the Acts of Peter', *Semeia* 38, 91-100.

2. Attestation: the earliest certain direct evidence for the existence of the Acts of Peter (APt) is the notice in Eusebius (*HE* III 3.2; for the text see vol. 1, p. 48).

Eusebius speaks of the ἐπικεκλημέναι αὐτοῦ (sc. Πέτρου) Πράξεις, which means that he knows a work entitled Πράξεις Πέτρου and rejects this work as uncanonical, just as he also rejects the Gospel of Peter, the Preaching of Peter and the Revelation of Peter. However Eusebius tells us nothing about the extent and contents of the APt. Various attempts have indeed been made to establish earlier evidence for the APt. The Muratorian Canon (see vol. I, pp. 34ff. for the text) does not list the APt, but many scholars (e.g. Schmidt, *Petrusakten*, p. 105; cf. also Vouaux, pp. 110ff.) think there is a reference to these Acts in the passage: 'For the "most excellent Theophilus" Luke summarizes the several things that in his own presence have come to pass, as also by the omission of the Passion of Peter he makes quite clear, and equally by (the omission of) the journey of Paul, who from the city (of Rome) proceeded to Spain.' According to Schmidt (*Petrusakten*, p. 105; cf. also 'Studien' II, 495) this is intended to express the view which the author of this table of canonical books takes of events not recorded in the Lucan Acts of the Apostles, namely Peter's death and Paul's journey to Spain: 'he knows them as actual occurrences, and not only on the basis of oral tradition, but of a written work which he has read with interest'. But such an interpretation probably reads too much out of this brief comment. The author of the Canon gives no indication that he had before him any written account of the death of Peter or Paul's journey to Spain. His words must rather be taken to indicate that he did indeed know of these two events, but had not found them in the Lucan Acts because, in his opinion, Luke was not an eyewitness of these events. The source of his information cannot be discovered from his comment. This precludes the possibility of using the Muratorian Canon as a witness to the APt or even for its date. The brief details there given cannot determine whether common traditions are to be assumed for the Muratorian Canon and the APt, or what form they took.

Two passages found in Clement of Alexandria have been connected with the APt. In *Strom.* III 6.52 Clement observes that Peter and Philip produced children, a remark which in no way helps to settle the problem of the APt. In *Strom.* VII 11.63 he relates that Peter encouraged his wife on the way to her martyrdom. This statement also has nothing to do with the APt, but belongs rather to the oral traditions known to Clement.

The same judgment applies to a passage in Hippolytus. In *Ref.* VI 20 he describes the arrival of Simon at Rome: 'This Simon, who perverted many in Samaria by magical arts, was convicted by the apostles and denounced, as is recorded in Acts; but afterwards in desperation he resumed the same practices, and on coming to Rome he (again) came into conflict with the apostles; and as he perverted many by his magical arts Peter continually opposed him. And as his end in Gitta drew near, he sat beneath a plane-tree and taught. And now, being almost discredited, in order to gain time he said that if he were buried alive he would rise again on the third day. And ordering a grave to be dug by his disciples, he made them bury him. So they did as he instructed them, but he has remained (buried) to this day; for he was not the Christ.' (Hipp. *Ref.* VI 20.2f.; Markovich, PTS 25, 228). C. Schmidt says of this passage 'Hippolytus' narrative therefore already has this scene from the APt as its basis' (*Petrusakten*, p. 104). But this assertion is quite groundless. Hippolytus relies primarily on the account given in the canonical Acts, and then gives a tradition of Simon's death which has nothing to do with the APt as we have them (cf. ActVerc c. 32 = Mart. Petr. c. 3). Hippolytus therefore is not a witness for the APt.

Origen in the third book of his *Commentary on Genesis* (according to Eusebius, *HE* III 1.2) relates that Peter was in Rome towards the end of his life: 'He was crucified head-downwards; for he requested that he might suffer thus.' This statement agrees in substance with the account given in the extant APt (ActVerc c. 37 = Mart. Petr. c. 8), but is not a literal citation. It can therefore be only a supposition that Origen, who certainly knew some part of the apocryphal literature, had also read the APt; this point cannot be certainly established. Certainly this statement gives no indication whatever of the form and content of the APt which Origen possibly knew. If he did have the work before him, this would establish the *terminus ad quem*, since the Commentary on Genesis was compiled before 231 (Eusebius, *HE* VI 24.2).

Great importance has often been attached to some lines from the *Carmen apologeticum* of Commodian, which mention the dog who speaks to Simon (v. 626 = ActVerc cc. 9, 11, 12) and the talking infant (v. 629f. = ActVerc c. 15). But even if Commodian's date were accurately known (probably middle of 3rd cent.),[3] these lines again would signify nothing more than that Commodian knew the legends of the speaking animals as they appear in the APt and the APl. They do not prove knowledge of the APt as a whole, and hardly give grounds for more precise inferences about the currency of the APt in the West in the 3rd century.

On the other hand the author of the Didascalia (probably first half of the 3rd century) seems actually to have used the APt. In VI, 7-9 he gives an account of the beginnings of heresy and makes Peter describe his encounters with Simon in Jerusalem and Rome. C. Schmidt has collected the various points which indicate that the APt were the basis for the Didascalia (*Petrusakten*, p. 147; cf. also Vouaux, pp. 119f. and Schmidt, 'Studien' II, 507). Here the most important point is the fact that Simon's first meeting with the apostles takes place in Jerusalem, which disagrees with Acts 8:14ff. We cannot in all points arrive at the certainty which Schmidt displays;[4] but there is plenty of evidence for the truth of the contention that the author of the Didascalia used the APt. Following Harnack's suggestion Schmidt has also attempted to show that Porphyry knew the Acts of Peter (Schmidt, *Petrusakten*, pp. 167ff.). Two passages preserved by Macarius Magnes (II 22 and IV 4)[5] are taken as evidence of this knowledge. The point depends especially on the fact that according to Porphyry - and contrary to the official Roman tradition - Peter was in Rome for only a short time before his death there by crucifixion. But it is hardly possible to prove conclusively that Porphyry derived this assertion from the APt.

Accordingly not much remains of the numerous so-called testimonies to the APt for the period before Eusebius. Only Origen and the Didascalia can be used as witnesses to its existence; and they give no reliable information about the extent and contents of the work.

Now it has been thought that these scant witnesses could be enriched by an assessment of the Pseudo-Clementines. Thus H. Waitz in NTApo² (212-226) sought to reconstruct from the Pseudo-Clementines the Πράξεις Πέτρου, the relationship of which to the remaining Peter texts (i.e. the ActVerc and the Coptic fragment; see below) he defined on the principle that both 'derive from a common tradition, which has survived in its original form in the Pseudo-Clementine Πράξεις Πέτρου' (NTApo² 213).

C. Schmidt, rightly, vigorously contested this hypothesis.[6] He himself sought to show that the author of the source-document underlying the Pseudo-Clementines used the ancient APt. Now the question of the relation of the Pseudo-Clementines to the ancient APt is linked with many others which have by no means been unambiguously settled (date, sources, etc). These Pseudo-Clementine problems cannot be discussed here (see below, pp. 483ff.), but we must give notice that considerable doubts have been raised about Schmidt's theory that the author of the basic document used the APt.[7] It is for example doubtful whether the differences in the localities in which the encounters between Peter and Simon take place, in the APt on the one hand and the basic document of the Pseudo-Clementines on the other, allow of such a simple explanation as Schmidt's (op. cit. 31f.).

All that we can say is that it is perfectly possible that the author of the Pseudo-Clementine basic document, which is to be dated to the period around 260 (see below, pp. 492f.), knew the material which is also used in the APt. It has not yet been possible to determine in what form this material lay before him.

It is particularly difficult to determine the relation of the APt to the Acts of John, especially since this problem is bound up with the whole complex of questions about the dating of the five ancient apostolic Acts and their connections with one another.

It should probably be said to begin with that any attempt at a dating of the individual Acts has to start out from the texts concerned in each case, and such statements contained in them as may offer anything to our purpose. Here we must heed the warning voiced by Junod-Kaestli: when we undertake to date a text in which precise historical statements are lacking, and the reading of which has left no direct traces, extreme caution is called for.[8] This holds also for the chronological and literary relationship of the five Acts to one another. Statements on this subject would indeed only be possible if we had firm clues to work with for the individual works. Except for the APl, such fixed points for the chronology are lacking; and for literary dependence the evidence in general must be called rather meagre.

Junod-Kaestli in their edition of the AJ have investigated the relation of the AJ to the APt in a comprehensive manner.[9] The result is simply the conjecture that some kind of dependence of the APt on the AJ is not to be excluded (here the great age of the AJ is in a certain fashion presupposed). Identity of the author of the AJ with that of the APt, which Zahn in his time affirmed (*Gesch. des ntl. Kanons* II, 860), is to be ruled out. However, there remain similarities, the significance of which must be examined.

First of all there is the phenomenon of polymorphy. In the 'Preaching of the Gospel' (AJ c. 87ff.) John comes to speak about the earthly appearance of Christ, and describes at the outset how he and his brother James were called by Jesus, when James saw the Lord as a boy, while John saw him standing by in the form of a handsome, good-looking man (cc. 88f.). There follows the account of the Transfiguration, a remarkable new version of the story (c. 90), and here too the theme of the Saviour's distinct forms plays an important part.[10] Now in APt 20, Peter likewise tells the congregation assembled to hear the Gospel that Christ was seen by the disciples in the form that each one could comprehend. Here too the story of the Transfiguration is given as an example, but without doubt the author keeps closer to the biblical narrative. Moreover the story in c. 21 about the widows whose sight is restored and who are then made to describe what they have seen is also characterised by the theme of polymorphy: some saw him as an old man, others as a youth, etc.

An accurate interpretation of the two chapters in the APt shows that we can indeed speak of certain polymorphous appearances, about which the author reports, but that the difference from the AJ is considerable. This becomes especially clear in the final sentence of c. 21: 'Certainly God is greater than our thoughts, as we have learned from the aged widows, how they saw the Lord in a variety of forms.' The author has taken up the widespread motif of polymorphy in order to emphasise the limitations of our possible knowledge of God.[11] In the AJ this motif stands in a wholly different context (cf. Schäferdiek above, p. 166). At any rate we cannot deduce from these chapters of the APt a literary dependence on the AJ.

Other passages which have been adduced do not take us any further. Thus in AJ c. 98 various designations for the Cross of Light are listed, so that a series of christological predicates is assembled.[12] In APt 20 we find a similar list of designations for Jesus: in AJ it is *Logos*, Mind (νοῦς), Jesus, Christ, *Door*, *Way*, *Bread*, *Seed*, *Resurrection*, Son, Father, Spirit, *Life*, Truth, *Faith*, *Grace:* in APt it is *Door*, Light, *Way*, *Bread*, Water, *Life*, *Resurrection*, Refreshment, Pearl, Treasure, *Seed*, Abundance, Mustard-seed, Vine, Plough, *Grace*, *Faith*, *Word*.

Comparison of the two lists does indeed show several common features, but the terms also derive from the common Christian tradition. They stand in the two works in a completely different context. As Justin (*Dial.* 100.4) and the Letter to Diognetus (9.6) show, such catalogues occur in other connections as well, and therefore can scarcely be used as evidence for the question of the literary dependence of the APt upon the AJ.

Finally, C. Schmidt (*Petrusakten*, pp. 97ff.) sought to establish that the APt c. 39 (10) are indebted to the AJ cc. 99ff. But this passage likewise does not admit a conclusive proof of dependence.[13] To sum up, the ostensible cases where the APt borrowed from the AJ, which on a different chronology may and indeed must be seen as borrowings by the AJ from the APt, are by no means demonstrable literary plagiarisms. They are in the main to be explained in that the ideas they contain have similar origins, from the historian of religion's point of view, despite their very different theological intention and application.[14] Thus, so far as we can see today, the AJ prove nothing in regard to the attestation, the dating and the sources of the APt.

The case is different with the APl. Here we can put the case more briefly, since C. Schmidt has probably said all that is necessary. Whereas formerly Schmidt strongly upheld the dependence of the APt, he abandoned this view in consequence of the discovery of the Hamburg Papyrus of the APl (cf. pp. 230f. above). In this papyrus there occurs a variant of the famous 'Quo vadis' scene (APt c. 35 = Mart. c. 6), which does not really fit its context. From this and other sections (especially the story of Theon, APt c. 5) Schmidt has rightly concluded that the author of the APl used and transcribed the APt.[15] The significance of this for dating the APt remains to be discussed (cf. p. 283). Here we need only report the APl as being among the few witnesses for the existence of the APt before Eusebius' time.

In the 4th century the sources mentioning the APt become rather more plentiful. This has been pointed out often enough in the relevant literature (especially by C. Schmidt, Vouaux and Flamion) and need not be repeated here. Two facts stand out:

1. The *Manichean Psalm-book* clearly uses the APt among other apocryphal books of Acts (cf. above pp. 87f.).

2. The polemic against the apocryphal Acts of apostles, known to us principally from numerous references in Augustine, led to an almost total disappearance of these

Acts, including the APt.[16]

One of the statements in Augustine is especially important as proving that the Coptic fragment (below, pp. 285f.) belong to the APt. Augustine in his treatise against Adimantus attacks the Manicheans' rejection of the canonical Acts, in which they rely principally on Acts 5:1ff., and says, 'They show great blindness in condemning this since, among the apocrypha, they read and treat as an important work the one which I have mentioned about the apostle Thomas and about the daughter of Peter himself who became paralysed through the prayers of her father, and about the gardener's daughter who died at the prayer of the said Peter; and they reply that this was expedient for them, that the one should be crippled with paralysis and the other die; nevertheless they do not deny that this was done at the prayers of the apostle' (Augustine, *c. Adimantum Man. disc.* XVII; ed. Zycha, *CSEL* XXV 1, p. 170, 9-16). Even if Augustine does not mention the APt directly, it is clear that he knows an apocryphal work, translated into Latin, which contained the story of Peter's daughter. But in fact it can only have been the APt to which the Coptic fragment belonged.

Finally we may note that the scanty attestation of the APt even after Eusebius' time (until Photius, cod. 114, on which see Schäferdiek, above pp. 87ff.) is supplemented through the use of the APt in later Acts of apostles.[17] The texts which are to be mentioned in this connection include some which are important for the textual tradition. In the *Vita Abercii* (4th century; ed. Th. Nissen, 1912) the following passages are taken verbatim from the Acts of Peter:

Act. Verc. c.2 (Lipsius p. 46. 31-47. 11	= Vit. Ab. c. 13 (Nissen, p.11. 12-12.9)
Act. Verc. c. 20 (p. 67. 3-8)	= Vit. Ab. c. 15 (p. 13.7-11)
Act. Verc. c. 20 (p. 67. 26-68. 15)	= Vit. Ab. c. 15 (p. 13.16-15.2)
Act. Verc. c. 7 (p. 53. 20-29)	= Vit. Ab. c. 24 (p. 19.9-20.2)
Act. Verc. c. 21 (p. 68. 17-69. 2)	= Vit. Ab. c. 26 (p. 20.11-23.1)

These passages, of which full use is made in the translation presented below, are of special interest in that they put us in a position to evaluate the Latin translation of the APt given in the Vercelli MS. The Latin translator has obviously followed the Greek text practically word for word. Another instructive feature is that these borrowed sections all consist of speeches; clearly the imagination of the author of the Vita Abercii was not quite equal to composing such occasional speeches and he therefore borrowed from the APt.

The Acts of Philip (see below, pp. 468ff.) are also probably to be counted among the witnesses from the 4th/5th centuries. At three points in this work we may assume knowledge and use of the APt:

Act. Phil. c. 80-85 (Bonnet pp. 32f.)	= Act Verc 28
Act. Phil. c. 140 (p. 74)	= Act Verc 38 (Mart. c. 9)
Act. Phil. c. 142 (p. 81)	= Coptic fragment (Peter's daughter)

It cannot indeed be conclusively proved that the author of the Act. Phil. actually transcribed the APt. But the agreements are so strong that literary dependence has to be suspected.[18] Again, the *Acta Xanthippae et Polyxenae* (ed. M.R. James, *Apocrypha anedocta*, Texts and Studies II.3, 1893, pp. 43-85) seem to have used the APt. Thus following C. Schmidt ('Studien', II, 494f.) we can see in c. 24 an excerpt from the beginning of the Vercelli Acts. Further details, especially the name Xanthippa, indicate a literary connection; indeed the author of these late Acts (probably 6th century) seems in general to have borrowed freely from other apocryphal Acts.[19]

In the *Acta SS. Nerei et Achillei* (5th-6th century; edited by H. Achelis, *TU* XI.2, 1893) at least c. 15 can hardly be thought of without its prototype in the Acts of Peter, which, it is important to note, is the Coptic narrative of Peter's daughter. All sorts of developments must certainly be noted, but the prototype is clearly discernible (cf. Schmidt, 'Studien' I, 342f.; also Vouaux, pp. 155ff.). Finally it should be mentioned that the later Petrine texts (the so-called Linus- and Marcellus-texts) are dependent on the ancient APt (cf. Vouaux, pp. 129ff., 160ff.; Lipsius, *Apostelgeschichten* II; further details below, pp. 436ff.), though probably not directly on the surviving Latin Vercelli Acts.

This later use of the APt demonstrates, what C. Schmidt in particular has repeatedly emphasised, that the APt long continued in use in catholic circles. They 'originated in catholic circles and originally were read with great respect as products of the Great Church'; they fell into disfavour in the time after Nicaea, but nevertheless 'persisted for a long time as favourite reading in good catholic circles, until a substitute had been devised for them in the form of supposedly orthodox revisions' (Schmidt, *Petrusakten*, p. 151). The history of the APt in the early Church allows these facts to be acknowledged, even though much remains obscure, and also reflects the history and development of the Church's doctrine and spirituality.

3. Surviving contents: the following passages of the ancient Acts of Peter are preserved:

a) The so-called *Actus Vercellenses* (Act. Verc.), named after the single Latin MS in which the text has come down to us, a codex at Vercelli (cod. Verc. CLVIII, 6th-7th century). The translation it presents originated according to Turner (*JTS* 32, 1931, 119f.) not later than the 3rd or 4th century. Its contents are not quite correctly represented by the title inferred by Lipsius, 'Actus Petri cum Simone' (cf. Aa I, 45). It is better to assume with C. Schmidt ('Studien', II, 510) that the title read, *Actus Petri apostoli* = Πράξεις Πέτρου τοῦ ἀποστόλου, which indeed would be the title which accords with the contents.

After a short account of the departure of Paul for Spain (cc. 1-3) we read of the arrival of Simon in Rome and of Peter's journey thither prompted by divine instructions (cc. 4-6). There follow the accounts of the recovery of the Roman congregation by Peter, of his controversy with Simon, which reaches its climax in the contest in the forum (cc. 7-29) and finally Peter's martyrdom (cc. 30-41). In the Latin MS one leaf is missing (c. 35-36). This gap is closed by the Greek text of the martyrdom, of which three manuscripts exist. Of these three Greek manuscripts, Bonnet already used two; the third has become known only in recent times. They are:

Cod. Patmiacus 48, 9th cent. = P
Cod. Athous Vatoped. 79, 10th/11th cent. = A
Cod. Ochrid. bibl. mun. 44, 11th cent. = O[20]

Besides the three Greek MSS of the Martyrdom there is further attestation of the Greek text of the APt for the end of c. 25 and the beginning of c. 26 in a papyrus fragment: Pap. Oxyrhynchos 849 (ed. Grenfell and Hunt, Ox. Pap. VI, 1908, pp. 6-12; text also given by Vouaux, pp. 374ff., in his apparatus). Lastly we must recall the passages of the Vita Abercii cited above (p. 276) which, in spite of the slight revision they disclose, agree with the three Greek MSS of the Martyrdom and with the papyrus in showing that the Latin translation given in the cod. Verc. 'is generally reliable, even though it is not free from misunderstandings, eccentricities and inexactitudes. We are also justified in observing that the Latin translator sometimes tries to make the sense clear by adding a few words, but seems nevertheless more anxious to abbreviate than to amplify' (Ficker, NTApo^2, pp. 226f.).

This conclusion rests upon a comparison of the texts available. It shows in fact that in general the Act. Verc. reproduce relatively faithfully a text which is also attested by the Greek witnesses. We may now ask whether this Greek *Vorlage* of the Latin version (the later Greek MSS also go back to this *Vorlage*) presented the original text of the APt, or whether it is already a revision (so G. Poupon). This question will require to be discussed below in connection with the composition of the APt.

That the Act. Verc. do not contain the complete text of the APt is shown by the fact that according to the Stichometry of Nicephorus (cf. vol. I, p.41f.) this work consisted of 2750 lines, and thus was somewhat more extensive than Luke's Gospel (2600 lines). Zahn already calculated that according to this information we must assume the loss of about a third (*Gesch. des ntl. Kanons* II, 841, note 3). Down to today but little has changed.

As the Greek MSS and also the oriental versions show, the Martyrdom was at an early date already transmitted as an independent text. That this text was originally part of the APt can be seen from the fact that the three Greek MSS start at different points: A begins with Act. Verc. 30, and thus contains the narrative about Chryse etc. before the martyrdom proper; P and O (and a series of oriental versions) only begin at Act. Verc. 33.

The many oriental versions show the wide dissemination of the APt, and especially of the Martyrdom. There are Coptic, Syriac, Armenian, Arabic and Ethiopic texts, some of which report the Martyrdom in agreement with the Greek witnesses, while some probably recast material from the APt. The survey which Vouaux presents (op. cit. 19-21) has been supplemented and improved by Poupon (in his contribution to ANRW). An evaluation will follow in his edition of the APt.

In Church Slavonic manuscripts, apart from a 'Vita Petri' which is not directly connected with the APt, there is a text which corresponds to Act. Verc. from c. 7 (so far unpublished; cf. de Santos, *Überlieferung* I, 52-59).

Finally it may be mentioned that among the Sogdian texts from Turfan, which F.W.K. Müller published in 1934, there is a text described by the editor as a 'Simon' fragment (siglum: T II B 15).[21] This fragment is probably connected with the ancient APt (cf. c. 28 and c. 31), but contributes nothing for the reconstruction of the original text.

b) The Story of Peter's daughter, preserved in the Coptic papyrus Berlin 8502.[22] This papyrus, discovered and edited by C. Schmidt (*Petrusakten*, 1903) contains on pp. 128-132 and 135-141 this story, which Schmidt claimed as belonging to the APt; and, after Ficker had contested it, Schmidt finally established his view (cf. esp. Schmidt, 'Studien' I). The reasons adduced by Schmidt are of varying cogency, but are so convincing as a whole that it can no longer be doubted that we have here a fragment of the first part of the APt, which is otherwise lost.

The contents of the story are not especially noteworthy. Peter demonstrates in the case of his daughter that outward suffering can be a gift from God if it has the effect of preserving virginity. This, then, is a miracle-story coloured by encratite sympathies such as we often find in the Act. Verc. The scene of the story is not directly indicated; but since it mentions Peter's going to his house, and since Peter's daughter lives with her father, one must assume that the setting is Peter's home; but this, according to Act. Verc. c. 5, is to be looked for in Jerusalem. But since this story must have belonged to the first section of the APt, which has disappeared, one must suppose that it is in Jerusalem that the events of this section take place. It may be supposed that this first section already described a contest between Peter and Simon; since the fact that Peter when in Rome repeatedly speaks of this earlier contest with the magician is no argument against it (cf. the different accounts of Paul's conversion in Acts 9, 22 and 26). Apart from this, hardly anything can be said about the extent and further contents of this first section. We know of only one other narrative that must have belonged to it.

c) In the apocryphal Epistle of Titus (above, pp. 53ff.) there is found a narrative of a gardener's daughter, who falls down dead at the prayer of Peter, is then restored to life on her father's petition, but a few days later is seduced and abducted. This story, which is hardly misinterpreted by the author of ps.-Titus, has the same (encratite) sympathies as the narrative of Peter's daughter (above): it is better for a man to be dead than to be polluted by sexual intercourse. That this narrative taken from ps.-Titus belongs to the APt is shown by the reference in Augustine (*c. Adimant.* XVII, above, p. 276) where the two events are put side by side, so that they were probably quoted from the same apocryphal work. Certainly we have here a case of parallel narratives. But the Act. Verc. themselves and other apocryphal Acts present us with similar parallel narratives, which soon become tedious to the modern reader.

It is questionable whether the fragment of a speech of Peter edited by de Bruyne belongs to the APt (de Bruyne in *Revue Bénédictine* XXV, 1908, 152f., presenting a fragment of a biblical concordance, Cod. Cambrai 254, 13th century). C. Schmidt connects these words with the narrative of the gardener's daughter: 'It is highly probable that we have here the words spoken by the apostle to the distracted father' ('Studien', I, 336). But this surely says more than can be proved; nothing more than a possibility can be established.

The Coptic gnostic 'Acts of Peter' belonging to the Nag Hammadi library have nothing to do with the ancient APt (see below, pp. 412ff.).

This brief survey shows that for a reconstruction of the APt - even if only a fragmentary one - we must look to the Act. Verc. and the Greek parallel tradition. This naturally does not mean that many a valuable supplement in points of detail may not yet result from an intensive evaluation both of the later Petrine texts (Linus, Marcellus) and of the versions.

4. Composition: it may be inferred from the Act. Verc. that the first section, which apart from a few remnants has disappeared, took place in Jerusalem (cf. Schmidt, 'Studien', II, 497ff.). Here too there evidently occurred the first collision between Peter and Simon, together with the events which we learn from the Coptic account of Peter's daughter and from the fragment of ps.-Titus. It should be noted that the author of the APt, who transferred the first controversy between Peter and Simon to Jerusalem, clearly did so because he was bound by the tradition of Peter's twelve-year stay in Jerusalem (cf. Act. Verc. c. 5). On the other hand he knew of Paul's activity in Rome, and of Peter's martyrdom at Rome, and presumably had information of some kind about operations of Simon in Rome. We cannot say whether he knew Justin's account (*Apol.* 26.2), of the statue of Simon at Rome (cf. Act. Verc. c. 10: Marcellus reports that Simon had persuaded him to set up a statue to him).

The composition of the work was determined by these traditions which the author inherited. First the two scenes of action, Jerusalem and Rome, were determined. Next it had to be explained how the Roman congregation could come into being before Peter's arrival. For this purpose the author inserted the episode concerned with Paul in Act. Verc. c. 1-3. We cannot say with certainty whether, or in what way, the first section of the APt dealt with Paul. But from Peter's observation in Act. Verc. 23 we may assume that Paul was present at his first meeting with Simon. For Peter describes how Simon tried to persuade, not John and himself, as in Acts 8:18ff., but Paul and himself, to sell him the power of working miracles, i.e. the Holy Ghost. It is probable that this fact, which Peter mentions in c. 23, was previously recounted in greater detail in the first section, thus preparing the way for Paul's activity in Rome. On the other hand the corruption of the Roman congregation by Simon can only have gone on in the absence of an apostle; Paul therefore had to leave Rome for Spain. No doubt the author took this journey of Paul's to Spain from his Epistle to the Romans, as he did with a number of names.

While Paul is already at work in Rome but Peter is still bound to Jerusalem by the Lord's command, there intervenes the story of Eubula, which Peter several times afterwards recalls (cf. Schmidt, 'Studien', II, 502ff.). This narrative must have been of some significance to the author, since he so often refers back to it.[23] It is in fact important for him since it is through this event that Simon is exposed as a magician and a villain, and Peter can refer to this exposure.

The contest with Simon, which is indeed the real theme of the story of Eubula, is in every way an especially important element in the whole composition. This clearly appears in the Act. Verc; the controversy with the magician Simon is to some extent the predominant theme to which the other narratives, and also the Martyrdom, are attached and which they supplement. At the same time the Martyrdom is certainly assimilated to definite prototypes which were already known to the author (cf. *inter alia* H. von Campenhausen, *Die Idee des Martyriums in der alten Kirche*, 1936, especially pp. 144ff.). But he has set the narrative of Peter's ending in close connection with the contest against Simon. The controversy between the two fought out in public in the forum certainly goes in Peter's favour, but has no appropriate ending. The author has reserved his account of Simon's ending in order to use it as the introduction to Peter's martyrdom (Act. Verc. cc. 30-32): Simon attempts to ascend into heaven, but falls, breaks his limbs and comes to a miserable end. This is the beginning of the Martyrdom-story, which however displays no further connection with the story of Simon.[24] Probably the author has here adapted well-defined traditions which he found ready to hand.

This attempt to unravel the composition of the APt starts out from the presupposition that the Act. Verc. have preserved the text of the original Acts. Now G. Poupon in his contribution to ANRW (see above, p. 271) has advanced the thesis that the Act. Verc. (or their Greek *Vorlage*) were already an adaptation of the original APt. In particular the inconsistencies which occur in the Act. Verc. are adduced in support of this theory. Thus cc. 1-3, which are only loosely connected with the rest of the text, could be a secondary addition intended to provide a connection with the canonical Acts. The story of Marcellus also shows several absurdities. C. 10 could originally have been a report of the conversion and baptism of a prominent Roman. In its present form the text really indicates that Marcellus is not a baptized Christian. On the other side there are also features which point to a *lapsus*, as indeed in cc. 2 and 30 there is a suggestion of the problem of a second baptism. Poupon conjectures that the reviser who brought the original APt into the form in which we now have them in the Act. Verc. was indebted to Roman local tradition. Within the frame of this introduction it is not possible to examine Poupon's thesis in detail. Many observations are undoubtedly correct, and take us further in our understanding of this work. It is however questionable whether the conclusions which Poupon draws are convincing. To put the question in another way: was an originally self-contained work (focussing on only one apostle) altered by a redactor with specific tendencies? Or are the APt to be understood as a work put together from various sources which the reviser has not always succeeded in co-ordinating? This makes it clear that the interpretation of the inconsistencies and tensions which undoubtedly exist in the Act. Verc. (or its Greek *Vorlage*) hangs together with the problems of the literary form, the intention and the theological tendency of the work.

5. Literary form, intention and theological tendency of the APt: although the contest with Simon is an essential theme of the APt, this does not imply that the work was written as a polemical tract against Simonian gnosis. A cursory reading is enough to show how little the author could relate of Simon's teaching. Again, very little about the career of this character is conveyed to the reader. 'In general the picture of Simon's personality given in the Actus is a remarkably meagre portrayal' (Sturhahn, p. 168). The whole emphasis of this picture rests on the constantly reiterated fact that Simon is nothing but a magician, an evil wizard. But here it is expressed in the phrase that he is an 'expositor of Satan' (Sturhahn p. 170), the ἄγγελος τοῦ διαβόλου (Mart. c. 3). The APt obviously do not intend to conduct a heresy-hunt; their purpose is to demonstrate, in the persons of Simon and his constantly victorious adversary, that God is stronger than Satan, whose service Simon has entered. Hence Peter can ascribe what is almost redemptive significance to this contest (Act. Verc. c. 6). We are dealing, not with the doctrines of Simonian Gnosticism, but with the contest between God and the devil.

Now this picture of Simon in the APt can probably give an important clue to the purpose of the work. As already stated (see above, pp. 76ff.), the AGG are not indeed a unity, either in theological tendency or in literary intention. But they nevertheless belong together, because it is a matter of works intended to entertain, instruct and edify, and in part also to have a propagandist effect. They seek to attain these aims by collecting manifold popular traditions, shaping (or sometimes taking over) speeches with their own tendencies, and so putting together works which do not always possess the form of a literary work of art. This holds for the APt also. This work too is governed by the intention of producing an edifying, instructive and at the same time entertaining effect. The picture of Simon in the APt makes the difference from the anti-heretical literature clear. The doctrine of this arch-heretic is suppressed and instead of it anti-christian objections of a general character are attributed to him.[25] In refuting these objections Peter does indeed make use of scriptural evidence (Act. Verc. c. 24), but achieves decisive success through his miracles, and through his frustrating or out-doing Simon's miracles, whose reality the author in no way denies. The popular character of the APt is also shown in the fact that it is not extensive theological discussions that occupy the central place, but miraculous acts: marvels of all kinds, resurrections, apparitions, etc. Peter's speeches in Mart. cc. 8-10 constitute something of an exception, and in their theological content also they take up a position of their own (cf. Sturhahn, pp. 153ff.). But here the author may probably have modelled himself on an earlier writing of homiletic character. There is nothing here which alters our overall estimate of the character of the work; it only makes clear that the unity of the APt does not depend on a formulated theological programme, but on its purpose of edification and entertainment together with certain moral inclinations.

It is certainly difficult, and would overstep the limits of this introduction, to attempt to indicate in detail how far the author made use of orally transmitted legendary material of various kinds. There are some points at which this combination of traditions becomes evident. We need only recall the Martyrdom; but the legend of Simon also circulated without doubt in the form of single episodes before attaining a fixed form in the APt. The miracle-stories in particular, which indeed are for the most part typical legends, were not combined with the legends about Simon from the outset, but arose and were passed on separately. The author of the APt has collected this material and made of it a comparatively well-knit whole, even if the working up of the tradition has not always been successful.

In so doing, was he aiming at a continuation of the canonical Acts, and was his work intended as an alternative account? This question is not quite correctly posed. Obviously the brief narrative of Acts 8:9ff. gave the impetus for the formation of legends centring on the figure of Simon. But it becomes very clear in the APt that this narrative given in Acts is completely recast. But above all the theological intention, as well as the material which the APt refashions, are different in character from those of the canonical Acts. Thus 'alternative account' and 'continuation' are equally unsuitable descriptions: the APt are rather to be described as an attempt to supplement the canonical Acts with regard to the personal history of Peter. Here as in the other apocryphal Acts it is the interest in individual personalities, about whom the canonical Acts tells us little - and in Peter's case this corresponds with his later destiny - which has given the impetus to this literature.

There remains the question whether we can speak of a consistent theological orientation. The earlier alternative, gnostic or catholic, has already been characterised as questionable (above, pp. 83ff.). The APt certainly are not a gnostic work. One cannot however overlook the fact that at several points statements are made which can be interpreted in a gnostic way (esp. Mart. cc. 8-10). On the other hand attempts have been made to establish docetic and monarchian[26] tendencies also. Thus Sturhahn writes: 'There results . . . the . . . situation that a popular Christian writing, whose non-gnostic character may on other grounds be taken as proved, sees itself driven to answer the question, how we should understand the Saviour's entry into this world, in a docetic sense, and in so doing concerns itself with traditions which in structure are closely related to the gnostic myth of the Redeemer . . . while at the same time the Kerygma of the Virgin Birth lends the docetic solution the appearance of legitimacy' (op. cit. 182f.). Sturhahn himself has tried to define the place of the APt in the history of theology as popular Modalistic Monarchianism.

Some reservations must be intimated against any such systematising of the theological statements of the APt. For example, the passages at which one can speak of polymorphy are not to be described as docetic.[27] We must also in this context deal very warily with the term 'Monarchianism'. Above all, it must once again be emphasised that the APt are not a theological treatise, but belong to popular literature, for which edification and practical effect are of more consequence than theological clarity. This naturally does not mean that we could abandon the highlighting of individual motifs and the verification of their place in the history of religion and theology. But probably we can scarcely present a 'theology of the APt' as a coherent systematic scheme.[28]

The practical aspect of the work certainly includes a certain 'encratite' tendency. This is already visible in Act. Verc. c. 2 in the celebration of the eucharist with bread and water. A more important point is the strong emphasis on sexual continence as a condition of salvation (cf. Mart. c. 4). This motif plays an important role in the Coptic fragment, as in Peter's later preaching in Rome. We may probably say that the circles from which the APt derive were especially interested in precisely this point. It is not surprising that many motifs which might be described as 'gnostic' or 'docetic' could be combined with this ethic. Here the popular piety of the 2nd and 3rd centuries finds a voice. In it, as in every age, many elements which the theologians tend to keep carefully apart have their place side by side.

6. Date and place of writing: The APt, originally composed in Greek, were used by the author of the Acts of Paul, as indicated above, p. 275. The date of his work is fixed by a reference in Tertullian as the end of the 2nd century (cf. p. 235 above). We have here an indication for the Acts of Peter; they must have originated before *c*. 190, perhaps in the decade 180-190.[29]

The place at which the work came into being cannot be certainly determined. Rome or Asia Minor have been suggested. The 'only inexact knowledge of the place' (Plümacher, op. cit. col. 24) tells against Rome. In favour of Asia Minor we may refer to the connection with the APl. But for the present we cannot get beyond conjecture

Notes

Introduction

1. We may refer here only to: A. Rimoldi, 'L'apostolo S. Pietro nella letteratura apocrifa del primi 6 secoli', *La Scuola Cattolica* 83, 1955, 196-224 (a short collection of the relevant texts); K. Berger, 'Unfehlbare Offenbarung. Petrus in der gnostischen und apokalyptischen Offenbarungsliteratur', *Kontinuität und Einheit* (FS Mußner) 1981, 261-326; W.A. Bienert, above pp. 20f.

2. I would very cordially thank G. Poupon for making the proofs of this important essay available to me before its publication.
3. Cf. A. Salvatore, 'Appunti sulla Cronologia di Commodiana', *Orpheus* VII, 1960, 161-187; *Commodiano, Carme apologetico*, ed. A. Salvatore (Corona Patrum), Turin 1977, 5-31.
4. Schmidt relies here mainly on the Coptic fragment, assigning the events it describes to Jerusalem. The place of action is not mentioned in the text, but may be inferred. As regards the Didascalia, however, we cannot say 'but this derives simply and solely from the Acts of Peter' (Schmidt, *Petrusakten*, 147).
5. On the question of Macarius' use of Porphyry cf. Quasten, III, 486-488; and works there mentioned.
6. Cf. C. Schmidt, *Studien zu den Ps.-Clementinen* (TU 46/1), 1929, 1-46.
7. Cf. G. Strecker, *Das Judenchristentum in den Pseudoklementinen* (TU 70), 1981^2, 255.
8. Junod/Kaestli, *Acta Johannis* (CChrSA 2), 694.
9. Op. cit. 694ff.; to this should be added the other passages in the edition to which reference is made in this section.
10. Cf. Junod/Kaestli 466-493; further literature there.
11. Cf. Junod/Kaestli, loc. cit; K. Schäferdiek, 'Herkunft und Interesse der alten Johannesakten', ZNW 74, 1983, 247-267, esp. 266f.
12. Cf. Junod/Kaestli 656-663.
13. Cf. Sturhahn's interpretation, 157ff.
14. For these problems Sturhahn's work is still important, even though one will not always agree with his interpretation. Cf. further: E. Junod, 'Polymorphie du Dieu sauveur', *Gnosticisme et monde hellénistique* (Publ. de l'Institut Orientaliste de Louvain 27), 1982, 38-46. D.R. Cartlidge, *Semeia* 38, 53-66.
15. Cf. above all C. Schmidt, ΠΡΑΞΕΙΣ ΠΑΥΛΟΥ, *Acta Pauli*, 1936, 127ff.
16. It may be noted that this conflict against the apocrypha in the ancient Church led 19th-century scholars, especially Lipsius, on the certainly false trail of 'gnostic' as opposed to 'catholic' Acts of apostles. It is above all thanks to C. Schmidt that this false antithesis is no longer maintained in the sense it then had. We must however proceed cautiously with the term 'vulgar catholic', which Schmidt uses freely. In particular we must probably reckon in most of the AGG with a mixture of diverse elements, which is connected with their literary genus.
17. Cf. below, pp. 436ff. The evaluation of these later texts for the reconstruction of the ancient APt is certainly a difficult undertaking, but will yield many an illuminating insight; cf. G. Poupon in ANRW.
18. Cf. C. Schmidt, 'Studien' I, 329ff; F. Bovon, 'Les Actes de Philippe', ANRW II, 25.6, 1988, 4431-4527 (I thank Prof. Bovon for giving me access to the proofs before publication).
19. Cf. the catalogue in James, op. cit. 47ff.; for the APt we may refer also to Vouaux's commentary (cf. his index s.v. 'Actes de Xanthippe').
20. On the manuscript from Ochrida: F. Halkin, *AnalBoll* 80, 1962, 15.
21. F.W.K. Müller, *Soghdische Texte II*. Aus dem Nachlaß, hrsg. von W. Lentz (SPAW 1934, 504-607). Reprint: *Sprachwissenschaftliche Ergebnisse der deutschen Turfan-Forschung*, part 3, 1985. The 'Simon' fragment on pp. 528-531 (= 334-337); supplement p. 603 (= 409).
22. A description of the papyrus by J.M. Robinson in NHS XI, 1979, 9-45.
23. In c. 17 Peter recapitulates this incident. At one point it is clear that the author is referring back to an earlier report: Aa I, 64.28 has *ad quem Petrus dixit*, whereas previously Peter always speaks in the first person.
24. In part of the tradition cc. 30-32 are missing (see above).
25. E.g. Act. Verc. 23: 'Men of Rome, is God born? Is he crucified? He who owns a Lord is no God!' Cf. Sturhahn, 176ff., including further examples from early Christian literature.
26. So already Schmidt, *Petrusakten*, 24.

27. On polymorphy cf. above, p. 274f. On the problem of Docetism: N. Brox, '"Doketismus" - eine Problemanzeige', ZKG 95, 1984, 301-314.
28. With the AJ and the ATh things are somewhat different; cf. Schäferdiek above, pp. 164ff. and Drijvers below, pp. 322ff.
29. If Poupon's theory outlined above were correct, we should come to an earlier date for the composition of the *Vorlage* of the Act. Verc., and thus for the original APt. Investigation is probably also necessary as to which individual pieces are older traditional material.

*The Acts of Peter**

I. Fragments of the first section

a) Peter's Daughter
(Berlin Coptic Papyrus 8502, pp. 128-132 and 135-141; ed. J. Brashler and D.M. Parrott, pp. 478-493)

(p. 128). But on the first day of the week, which is the Lord's day, a crowd collected, and they brought many sick people to Peter for him to heal them.[1] But one of the crowd ventured to say to Peter, 'Look, Peter, before our eyes you have made many (who were) blind to see, and the deaf to hear and the lame to walk, and you have helped the weak and given them strength.[2] Why have you not helped your virgin daughter, who has grown up beautiful and (p. 129) has believed on the name of God? For she is quite paralysed on one side, and she lies there stretched out in the corner helpless. We see the people you have healed; but your own daughter you have neglected.'

But Peter smiled and said to him 'My son, it is evident to God alone why her body is not well. You must know, then, that God is not weak or powerless to grant his gift to my daughter. But to convince your soul and increase the faith of those who are here' - (p. 130) he looked then towards his daughter, and spoke to her: 'Rise up from your place without any man's help but Jesus' alone and walk naturally before them all and come to me.' And she rose up and went to him; but the crowd rejoiced at what had happened.[3] Then Peter said to them, 'Look, your heart is convinced that God is not powerless in all the things which we ask of him.' Then they rejoiced even more and praised God. (Then) said (p. 131) Peter to his daughter, 'Go to your place, lie down and return to your infirmity, for this is profitable for you and for me.' And the girl went back, lay down in her place and became as she was before. The whole crowd lamented and entreated Peter to make her well.

Peter said to them: 'As the Lord liveth, this is profitable for her and for me. For on the day when she was born to me I saw a vision, and the Lord said to me, "Peter, today there is born for you a great (132) trial; for this (daughter) will do harm to many souls if her body remains healthy." But I thought that the vision mocked me.

'When the girl was ten years old she became a temptation to many. And a rich man named Ptolemaeus, who had seen the girl with her mother bathing, sent for her to take her as his wife; (but) her mother would not agree. He sent many times for her, he could not wait. . . .

(pp. 133 and 134 are missing).[4]

'(The servants of) Ptolemaeus brought the girl and laid her down before the door of the house and went away. But when I and her mother perceived (it), we went down and found the girl, (and) that all one side of her body from her toes to her head was paralysed and wasted; and we carried her away, praising the Lord who had preserved his servant from uncleanness and shame and. . . . This is the cause of the matter, why the girl (continues) in this state until this day.

'Now then it is right that you should know the fate of (p. 136) Ptolemaeus. He went home and grieved night and day over what had happened to him; and because of the many tears which he shed, he became blind; and he resolved to go up and hang himself. And lo, about the ninth hour of that day, when he was alone in his bedroom, he saw a great light which lit up the whole house, and heard a voice which said to him: (p. 137) "Ptolemaeus, God has not given the vessels for corruption and shame; nor is it right for you, a believer in me, to defile my virgin, one whom you are to know as your sister,[5] since I have become for both of you one spirit.[6] But get up and go quickly to the house of the apostle Peter, and you shall behold my glory; he will explain this matter to you.' But Ptolemaeus made no delay, and told his servants (138) to show him the way and bring him to me. And coming to me he told (me) all that had happened to him[7] in the power of our Lord Jesus Christ. Then he did see with the eyes of his flesh and with the eyes of his soul, and many people set their hopes on Christ. He did good to them and gave them the gift of God.

After this Ptolemaeus died; he departed (this) life and went to his Lord. (p. 139) And when he <made> his will, he bequeathed a piece of land in the name of my daughter, because (it was) through her (that) he had believed in God and had been made whole. But I being given this trust, executed it with care. I sold the land, and - God alone knows - neither I nor my daughter kept back any of the price of the land,[8] but I gave all the money to the poor.[9]

Know then, O servant of Jesus Christ, that God (p. 140) cares for his own and prepares good for every one of them, although we think that God has forgotten us. But now, brethren, let us be sorrowful and watch and pray, and God's goodness shall look upon us, and we wait for it.' And Peter continued speaking before them all, and praising the name (p. 141) of the Lord Christ, he gave of the bread to them all; (and) when he had distributed it he rose up and went to his house.

The Act of Peter.

b) The Gardener's Daughter
(Ps.-Titus, *de Dispositione sanctimonii* lines 83ff.; cf. above, p. 57)

Consider and take note of the happening about which the following account informs us:

A peasant had a girl who was a virgin. She was also his only daughter, and therefore he besought Peter to offer a prayer for her. After he had prayed, the apostle said to the father that the Lord would bestow upon her what was expedient for her soul. Immediately the girl fell down dead.

O reward worthy and ever pleasing to God, to escape the shamelessness of the flesh and to break the pride of the blood!

But this distrustful old man, failing to recognise the worth of the heavenly grace, i.e. the divine blessing, besought Peter again that his only daugher be raised from the dead. And some days later, after she had been raised, a man who passed himself off as a believer came into the house of the old man to stay with him, and seduced the girl, and the two of them never appeared again.

c) Fragment of a speech of Peter's
(Cod. Cambrai 254, ed. de Bruyne, *Rev. Bénédictine* XXV, 1908, p. 153.)

Peter, speaking to a (man) who bitterly complained at the death of his daughter, said 'So many assaults of the devil, so many struggles with the body, so many disasters of the world she has escaped; and you shed tears, as if you did not know what you yourself have undergone (i.e. what you have gained).'

II. Actus Vercellenses

(Peter's dealings with Simon)
(Aa 1, pp. 45-103)

1
(Paul's Departure from Rome)

1. While Paul was spending some time in Rome and strengthening many in the faith, it happened that a woman by name Candida, the wife of Quartus, a prison officer, heard Paul speak and paid attention to his words and believed. And when she had instructed her husband also and he believed, Quartus[1] gave leave[2] to Paul to leave the city (and go) where he wished. But Paul said to him, 'If it is God's will, He himself will reveal it to me.' And when he had fasted for three days and asked of the Lord what was right for him, Paul then saw a vision, the Lord saying to him, 'Paul, arise and be a physician to those who are[3] in Spain.' So when he had related to the brethren what God had enjoined,

without doubting he prepared to leave the city. But when Paul was about to leave, great lamentation arose among all the brotherhood because they believed that they would not see Paul again,[4] so that they even rent their clothes. Besides, they had in view that Paul had often contended with the Jewish teachers and had confuted them, (saying) 'It is Christ[5] on whom your fathers laid hands. He abolished their sabbath and fasts and festivals and circumcision and he abolished the (p. 46) doctrines of men and the other traditions.'[6] But the brethren besought[7] Paul by the coming of our Lord Jesus Christ that he should not stay away longer than a year; and they said, 'We know your love for your brethren; do not forget us when you arrive there (in Spain), or begin to desert us like little children without their mother.' And while they continued entreating him with tears, there came a sound from heaven and a great voice which said, 'Paul the servant of God is chosen for (this) service for the time of his life; but at the hands of Nero, that godless and wicked man, he shall be perfected before your eyes.' And great fear fell upon the brethren yet more because of the voice that had come from heaven; and they were much more confirmed (in the faith).

2. And they brought bread and water[8] to Paul for the sacrifice so that after the prayer he should distribute to everyone. Among them as it proved there was a woman named Rufina who indeed[9] wished that even she should receive the eucharist at Paul's hands. But as she approached, Paul, filled with the Spirit of God said to her, 'Rufina, you are not coming to the altar of God like a true (worshipper), rising from beside (one who is) not your husband but an adulterer, yet you seek to receive God's eucharist. For behold Satan shall break your body[10] and cast you down in the sight of all that believe in the Lord, so that they may see and believe, and know that it is the living God, who examines (men's) hearts,[11] in whom they have believed. But if you repent of your action, he is faithful,[12] so that he can wipe away your sins (and) deliver you from this sin. But if you do not repent while you are still in the body, the consuming fire and the outer darkness[13] shall receive you for ever.' And at once Rufina fell down, being paralysed on the left side from her head to her toe-nails. And she had no power to speak, for her tongue was tied.[14] And when the believers in the faith and the newly-converted saw this, they beat their breast remembering their own former sins, lamenting and saying, 'We do not know whether God will forgive us the former sins which we have committed.'

Then Paul called for silence and said, 'Men and brethren, who have now begun to believe in Christ,[15] if you do not continue in (p. 47) your former works, those of the tradition of your fathers, but keep yourselves from all deceit and anger and cruelty and adultery and impurity, and from pride and envy and contempt and hostility, then Jesus the living God will forgive you what you have done in ignorance.[16] Therefore arm yourselves, you servants of God, each one of you in your inner man, with peace, composure, gentleness, faith, love, knowledge, wisdom, fraternal affection, hospitality, compassion, abstinence, purity, kindness, justice; then you shall have as your guide for ever the first-born of all creation[17] and have strength in peace with our Lord.'[18] And when they heard Paul say this, they asked him to pray for them. But Paul lifted up his voice and said, 'O God eternal, God of the heavens, God of unutterable majesty, who has established all things by thy word, who hast <broken> the chain set fast <upon man,> who hast brought <the light>[19] of thy grace to all the world, Father of thine holy Son Jesus Christ, we entreat thee together through thy Son Jesus Christ to strengthen the souls which once were unbelieving but now have faith. I was once a blasphemer,[20] but now I am blasphemed; I was once a persecutor, but now I suffer persecution from others; once an enemy of Christ, but now I pray to be his friend. For I trust in his promise and his mercy; for I think that I am faithful and have received forgiveness for my former misdeeds. Therefore I exhort you also, brethren, to believe in the Lord, the Father almighty, and to put all your trust in our Lord Jesus Christ his Son. If you believe in him, no one will be able to uproot you from his promise. Likewise you must bend your knees and commend me to the Lord, as I am about to set forth to another nation, that his grace may go before me and dispose my journey aright and may be able to gather in his holy vessels, even those that believe, and that they may give thanks to me for my preaching the Lord's word, and be well established (in the faith).' But the brethren continued weeping and entreated the Lord with Paul and said, 'Lord Jesus Christ, be thou with Paul, and restore him to us unharmed; for we know our weakness which is still with us.'

3. And a great crowd of women knelt down and fervently (p. 48) entreated the blessed Paul, and they kissed his feet and escorted him to the harbour, and with them[21] Dionysius and Balbus from Asia, who were Roman knights and illustrious men. And a senator by name Demetrius kept close to Paul on his right hand and said, 'Paul, I could wish to leave the city, if I were not a magistrate, so as not to leave you.' And (so said) some from Caesar's household,[22] Cleobius and Iphitus and Lysimachus and Aristaeus and two matrons, Berenice and Philostrate, with the presbyter Narcissus, after they had conducted him to the harbour. But as a storm at sea was threatening, he (Paul) sent the brethren back to Rome, so that if anyone wished he could come down and listen to Paul till he set sail. The brethren heard this (suggestion) and went up to the city. When they told the brethren that had remained in the city, the word went round at once; and they came to the harbour, some riding, some on foot and others by way of the Tiber; and they were greatly strengthened in the faith during three days, and on the fourth day until the fifth hour; and they prayed together with Paul and brought him gifts and put on the ship whatever he needed; and they delivered to him two young men who were believers to sail with him, and bade him farewell in the Lord and returned to Rome.

2

(Simon's arrival in Rome and his initial success; Peter's journey to Rome)

4. But after some days there arose a great commotion in the church, for (some) said that they had seen miracles done by a man whose name was Simon, and that he was at Aricia. They added further,[23] 'He says that he is the great power of God,[24] and that without God he does nothing. Is he then himself the Christ? But we believe in him whom Paul preached to us; for through him we have seen the dead raised up and (men) delivered from various infirmities. But what this contention is, we do not know.[25] For it is no small excitement that has come upon us. Perhaps he will now enter into Rome; for yesterday he was invited with great acclamations, and they said to him, "Thou art God in Italy, thou art saviour of the Romans: make haste and go quickly to Rome." But he spoke to the people with a tuneful voice, saying, "Tomorrow you shall see me about the seventh hour flying over the city gate in the form in which you now see me speaking with you." So, brethren, if you agree, let us go (p. 49) and carefully await the outcome of (this) matter.' So they all ran together and came to the gate. And when the seventh hour had come, behold suddenly in the distance a cloud of dust was seen in the sky, like a smoke shining from far away with (fiery) rays. And when it approached the gate it suddenly vanished; and then he appeared standing among the people, while they all worshipped him and realised that it was he who had been seen by them the day before. And the brethren were seriously disaffected among themselves, especially because Paul was not at Rome, nor were Timothy or Barnabas, since they had been sent by Paul to Macedonia;[26] and there was no one to encourage us, especially those who were but recently instructed. And Simon's reputation continually increased with those among whom he worked, and some of them in their daily conversations called Paul a sorcerer, others a deceiver; so that out of so great a number that were established in the faith, they all fell away except the presbyter Narcissus and two women in the lodging-house of the Bithynians and four who could no longer go out of their house; and being thus confined they devoted themselves to prayer day and night, and entreated the Lord that Paul might quickly return, or some other who could care for his servants, since the devil in his wickedness had made them unfaithful.

5. But as they mourned and fasted, God was already preparing Peter for what was to come, now that the twelve years in Jerusalem which the Lord Christ had enjoined on him[27] were completed.[28] He showed him a vision of this kind, and said to him 'Peter, the man Simon whom you expelled from Judaea, proving him a sorcerer, has again forestalled you (pl.) at Rome. In short you must know that Satan by his cunning and his power has perverted all those who

believed in me; and (in this way Simon) proves himself his agent. But do not delay; set out tomorrow (for Caesarea), and there you will find a ship ready which is sailing to Italy. And in a few days I will show you my grace which has no bounds.'[29] Peter then, instructed by this vision, related it to the brethren without delay and said, 'I must go up to Rome to overthrow the opponent and enemy of the Lord and (p. 50) of our brethren.'

And he went down to Caesarea and at once boarded the ship, when the gangway was already removed and without embarking any provisions. But the captain, whose name was Theon, looked at Peter and said, 'All that we have here is yours. For what merit is it of ours, if we take on board a man like ourselves who takes his chance, and do not share with you all that we have? Only let us have a prosperous voyage.' And Peter thanked him for his offer, but he himself fasted while aboard the ship, being grieved in mind yet comforting himself again because God had accounted him a worthy servant in his service.

But after a few days the captain rose up at the hour of his dinner, and asked Peter to eat with him, saying to him, 'Sir, (*lit.* O) whoever you are, I hardly know you, whether you are God or man; but in my opinion, I take you for a servant of God. For in the middle of the night while I was steering the ship and had fallen asleep, it seemed that a man's voice said to me from heaven, "Theon, Theon!" It called me twice by my name and said to me, "Of all those who sail with you let Peter be highest in your esteem; for through him both you and the others shall escape uninjured from an unexpected (mis) chance."'[30] Now Peter thought that God wished to show his providence upon the sea to those who were in the ship; so Peter began to relate to Theon the wonderful works[31] of God, and how God had chosen him among the apostles, and for what business he was sailing to Italy. And day by day he imparted to him the words of God. And he considered him and found by conversing with him that he was like-minded in the faith and worthy of (God's) service.[32]

But when the ship met with a calm in the Adriatic, Theon remarked on the calm to Peter and said to him, 'If you will count me worthy to be baptized with the sign of the Lord, you have the opportunity.' For all those aboard the ship were drunk and had fallen asleep. And Peter went down by a rope and baptized Theon in the name of the Father and of the Son and of the Holy Ghost. And he came up out of the water rejoicing with great joy, and Peter also was more cheerful because God had accounted Theon worthy of his name. And it came to pass (p. 51) that at the same place where Theon was baptized, there appeared a young man shining with splendour, saying to them 'Peace (be) with you.'[33] And straightway Peter and Theon went up and entered the cabin; and Peter took bread and gave thanks to the Lord, who had accounted him worthy of his holy service, and because the young man had appeared to them saying 'Peace (be) with you.' (And he said), 'Most excellent, the only holy one, it is thou that hast appeared to us, thou God Jesus Christ; in thy name hath this man been washed[34] and signed with thy holy sign. Therefore in thy name I impart to him thine eucharist, that he may be thy perfect servant without blame for ever.'

And as they feasted and rejoiced in the Lord, suddenly (there came) a wind, not violent but temperate, on the ship's bow and did not slacken for six days and as many nights, until they came to Puteoli.

6. And when they had brought up at Puteoli, Theon sprang down from the ship and came to the lodging-house where he used to say, to prepare it to receive Peter. Now the man with whom he stayed was called Ariston; this man had always feared the Lord, and Theon entrusted himself to him on account of the Name. When he had come to the lodging-house and seen Ariston, Theon said to him, 'God, who counted you worthy to serve him, has imparted his grace to me also through his holy servant Peter, who has just sailed with me from Judaea, being commanded by our Lord to come to Italy.' And when Ariston heard this, he fell on Theon's neck and embraced him and asked him to take him to the ship and show him Peter; for Ariston said that since Paul had set out for Spain, there was no one of the brethren with whom he could refresh himself; and moreover that a certain Jew named Simon had invaded the city - 'and he by incantation and by his wickedness has altogether perverted the entire brotherhood, so that I also fled from Rome, hoping that Peter would come. For Paul had told (us) of him, and I have seen many things in a vision. Now therefore I believe in my Lord that he is rebuilding his ministry, for all deception shall be uprooted from among his servants. For our Lord Jesus Christ is faithful, who can restore (p. 52) our minds.'

Now when Theon heard this from Ariston, who was weeping, his spirit was restored and he was the more strengthened, because he knew that he had believed on the living God.

But when they came together to the ship, Peter looked at them, and being filled with the spirit he smiled; so that Ariston fell on his face at Peter's feet and said, 'Brother and Lord, partaker of the holy mysteries and teacher of the right way which is in Jesus Christ our God; he has openly shown us of your coming;[35] for we have lost all those whom Paul entrusted to us, through the power of Satan. But now I hope in the Lord, who sent his messenger (i.e. angel) and told you to come (quickly) to us, since he has counted us worthy to see his great and wonderful works done at your hands. I beg you, therefore, to go quickly to the city; for I left the brethren who were causing distress, whom I saw falling into the temptation of the devil, and retired to this place and I said to them, "Brethren, stand fast in the faith;[36] for it must be that within two months from now the mercy of our Lord will bring his servant to you." For I had seen a vision of Paul saying to me, "Ariston, retire from the city." When I heard that I believed without delay and departed in the Lord, although I bear great infirmity of the flesh, and I arrived at this place; and day by day I stood by the sea-shore and asked the sailors "Has Peter sailed with you?" But now that the Lord's grace abounds (towards us), I beg you that we may go up to Rome without delay, or the teaching of this most wicked man may prevail yet further.' And as Ariston said this with tears, Peter gave him his hand and raised him up from the ground, and Peter also groaning said with tears, 'He has forestalled us, he who tempts the whole world by his angels;[37] but (God) shall quench his deceits and subdue him beneath the feet[38] of those who have believed in Christ whom we preach, who has power to deliver his servants from all temptation.' And as they went in at the gate, Theon entreated Peter and said, 'You did not refresh yourself on board on any day in all that long sea (voyage); and now will you set out straight from the ship over such a rough road? No, (p. 53) stay and refresh yourself, and then you shall set out. It is a flinty road from here to Rome, and I am afraid you may take some harm from the shaking.' But Peter answered them saying, 'Suppose it should be my fate, like the enemy of our Lord, to have a millstone hung about me, as my Lord said to us, if one should offend (any) of the brethren, and be drowned in the sea?[39] But it might be not only a millstone, but what is worse, it would be far away from those who have believed on the Lord Jesus Christ, that the opponent of this persecutor of his servants would find his end.'[40] And Theon could not induce him by any persuasion to remain there even for a single day. But Theon for his part handed over all his ship's cargo to be sold for its fair price (German: to those who came as buyers) and followed Peter to Rome; and Ariston brought (them) to the house of the presbyter Narcissus.[41]

3

(Peter's first preaching at Rome)

7. Now the rumour flew about the city to the brethren who were scattered that Peter at the Lord's command[42] had come because of Simon, in order to show that he was a deceiver and a persecutor of good men. So the whole multitude collected to see the Lord's apostle establishing (the Church) in Christ. And on the first day of the week, when the multitude came together to see Peter, he began to say with a loud voice. 'You men who are present here, who hope in Christ, you who have suffered temptation for a little, attend! Why did God send his Son into the world,[43] or why did he reveal him through the Virgin Mary,[44] if it were not to effect some grace or means of salvation?[45] For he wished to remove[46] all offence and all ignorance and all activity of the devil, frustrating his designs and his powers through which he formerly prevailed, before our God shone forth in the world.[47] Because (mankind) through ignorance fell into death in their many and varied weaknesses,[48] almighty God, moved with compassion, sent his Son into the world; and I was with him. And I walked on the water,[49] and myself survive as a witness of it;[50] I confess that

I was there when formerly in the world (p. 54) he was at work with the signs and all the miracles which he performed. Dearest brethren, I denied our Lord Jesus Christ, and not once only, but three times.[51] For there were wicked dogs who came about me, as said the prophet of the Lord.[52] But the Lord did not lay it to my charge; he turned to me[53] and had compassion on the weakness of my flesh, so that afterwards I wept bitterly and lamented the weakness of my faith, because I was made senseless by the devil and did not keep my Lord's word in mind. And now I tell you, men and brethren, who have come together in the name of Jesus Christ: Satan the deceiver points his arrows at you too, that you may depart from the way.[54] But do not be disloyal, brethren, nor let your spirit fall, but be strong and stand fast and do not doubt. For if Satan overthrew me, whom the Lord held in such great honour, so that I denied the light of my hope; if he subdued me and persuaded me to flee, as if I had put my trust in a man, what do you expect, you who are new to the faith? Did you expect that he would not subvert you, to make you enemies of the Kingdom of God and plunge you into perdition by the lowest deceit? For whoever he has dislodged from hope in our Lord Jesus Christ, that man is a son of perdition[55] for ever. Change your hearts, therefore, brethen beloved of the Lord, and be strong in the Lord Almighty, the Father of our Lord Jesus Christ, whom no man has ever seen, nor can see, save him who has believed on him.[56] And you must understand whence this temptation has come to you. For this is not only to convince you with words that it is the Christ that I am preaching, but also by deeds and marvellous powers I urge you through the faith in Jesus Christ, that none of you should expect another (saviour) than him who was despised and mocked by the Jews, this Nazarene who was crucified and died and rose again the third day.'

4

(Marcellus. Recovery of the Church of Rome)

8. But the brethren repented and entreated Peter to overthrow Simon, who said that he was the power of God; now he was staying at the house of the Senator Marcellus, who was persuaded by his charms. And they said, 'Believe us, brother Peter; no one was so wise (p. 55) among men as this Marcellus. All the widows who hoped in Christ found refuge with him; all the orphans were fed by him. And what more, brother? All the poor called Marcellus their patron, and his house was called (the house) of pilgrims and of the poor. The emperor said to him, "I am keeping you out of every office, or you will plunder the provinces to benefit the Christians"; and Marcellus replied, "All my goods are yours"; but Caesar said to him, "They would be mine, if you kept them for me; but now they are not mine, because you give them to whom you will[57] and to

I know not what wretches." We have this in view, brother Peter, and warn you that all that man's great charity has turned to blasphemy; for if he had not been won over, we in turn should not have deserted the holy faith in our Lord God. This Marcellus is now enraged and repents of his good deeds, and says, "All this wealth I have spent in all this time, vainly believing that I paid it for the knowledge of God." So much so, that if one of the strangers comes to his house door, he strikes him with his staff and orders him to be driven away, saying, "If only I had not spent so much money on these impostors!" - and yet more blasphemous words. But if there remains in you any of our Lord's mercy or of the goodness of his commandments, give help to this man's error who has so abundantly given alms to the servants of God.'

But Peter perceiving this was struck with sorrow and uttered this reproach:[58] O what manifold arts and temptations of the devil! O what contrivances and inventions of evil! He prepares for himself a great fire in the day of wrath,[59] the destruction of simple men, the ravening wolf,[60] the devourer and waster of eternal life! Thou hast ensnared the first man in lustful desire and bound him by thine ancient wickedness and with the chain of the body; thou art the fruit of the tree of bitterness, which is all most bitter, inducing lusts of every kind. Thou hast made Judas, who was a disciple and apostle together with me, do wickedly and betray our Lord Jesus Christ, who (p. 56) must punish thee. Thou didst harden the heart of Herod and provoke Pharaoh, making him fight against Moses, the holy servant of God; thou didst give Caiaphas the boldness to hand over our Lord Jesus Christ to the cruel throng,[61] and even now thou dost shoot at innocent souls with thy poisoned arrows. Thou wicked enemy of all, accursed shalt thou be from the Church[62] of the Son of holy and almighty God, and like a firebrand thrust out from the hearth thou shalt be quenched by the servants of our Lord Jesus Christ. Upon thee may thy blackness be turned and upon thy sons, that most wicked seed; upon thee be turned thy misdeeds, upon thee thy threats, and upon thee and thine angels be thy temptations, thou source of wickedness and abyss of darkness! May thy darkness which thou hast be with thee and with thy vessels whom thou dost possess. Depart therefore from these who shall believe in God, depart from the servants of Christ and from them who would fight for him. Keep for thyself thy gates[63] of darkness; in vain thou dost knock at the doors of others, which belong not to thee but to Christ Jesus who keeps them. For thou, devouring wolf, wouldst carry off sheep[64] which are not thine, but belong to Christ Jesus, who keeps them with the most careful care.'

9. While Peter said this in great distress of mind, many more were added[65] as believers in the Lord. And the brethren entreated Peter to join battle with Simon and not allow him to vex the people any longer. And without delay Peter left the assembly[66] and went to the house of Marcellus, where Simon was staying; and great crowds followed him. And when he came to the door, he

called the doorkeeper and said to him, 'Go and tell Simon: "Peter, on whose account you fled from Judaea, is waiting for you at the door."' The doorkeeper answered Peter, 'I do not know, Sir, whether you are Peter; but I have an order; for he (i.e. Simon) found out that you came into the city yesterday, and he said to me, "Whether it be by day or by night, at whatever[67] time he comes, tell him that I am not in (the house)."' But Peter said to the young man, 'You were right to say this, and explain what he made you say'; and Peter turned to the people who followed him, and said, 'You shall see a great and marvellous wonder.' And Peter, seeing a great dog (p. 57) tied fast with a massive chain, went up to him and let him loose. And when the dog was let loose he acquired a human voice and said to Peter, 'What do you bid me do, you servant of the ineffable living God?' And Peter said to him, 'Go in and tell Simon in the presence of his company, "Peter says to you, Come out in public; for on your account I have come to Rome, you wicked man and troubler of simple souls."' And immediately[68] the dog ran and went in and rushed into the middle of Simon's companions and lifting his fore-feet called out with a loud voice. '(I tell) you Simon, Peter the servant of Christ is standing at the door, and says to you, "Come out in public; for on your account I have come to Rome, you most wicked deceiver of simple souls."' And when Simon heard it and saw the incredible sight, he lost the words with which he was deceiving those who stood by, and all were amazed.

10. But when Marcellus saw it he went to the door and threw himself down at Peter's feet and said, 'Peter, I clasp your feet, you holy servant of the holy God; I have sinned greatly; but do not punish my sins, if you have any true faith in the Christ whom you preach, if you remember his commandments, not to hate anyone, not to be angry with anyone,[69] as I have learnt from Paul, your fellow-apostle. Do not consider my faults, but pray for me to the Lord, the holy Son of God, whom I provoked to anger by persecuting his servants. Pray therefore for me like a good steward of God, that I be not consigned - with the sins of Simon - to eternal fire; for he even persuaded me to set up a statue to him with this inscription, "To Simon the young God".[70] If I knew, Peter, that you could be won over with money, I would give my whole fortune; I would have given it to you and despised it, in order to regain my soul.[71] If I had sons, I would have thought nothing of them, if only I could believe in the living God. But I protest that he would not have deceived me except by saying that he was the power of God. Yet I will tell you, dearest Peter; I was not worthy to hear you, servant of God, nor was I firmly grounded in the faith of God which is in Christ; and for this reason I was overthrown. So I beg you, do not resent what I am about to say: that Christ (p. 58) our Lord, whom you preach in truth, said to your fellow-apostles in your presence. "If you have faith like a grain of mustard-seed, you shall say to this mountain, Remove yourself, and at once it will remove."[72] But, Peter, this Simon called you an unbeliever, since you lost

faith when upon the water;[73] indeed I heard that he also had said, "Those who are with me have not understood me." Therefore if you (pl.) lost faith, you on whom he laid his hands, whom he also chose, and with whom he worked miracles, then since I have this assurance, I repent and resort to your (sing.) prayers. Receive my soul, though I have fallen away from our Lord and from his promise. But I believe that he will have mercy on me, since I repent. For the Almighty is faithful to forgive me my sins.'

But Peter said with a loud voice, 'To thee, our Lord, be glory and splendour (?), almighty God, Father of our Lord Jesus Christ. To thee be praise and glory and honour, for ever and ever, Amen. As thou hast fully encouraged and established us now in thee in the sight of all beholders, holy Lord, so strengthen Marcellus and send thy peace to him and his house today; but whatever is lost or astray thou alone canst restore.[74] We all beseech thee, O Lord, the shepherd of sheep that once were scattered, but now shall be gathered in one through thee:[75] receive Marcellus again as one of thy lambs and suffer him no longer to riot in error or in ignorance; but accept him among the number of thy sheep. Even so, Lord, receive him, that with sorrow and tears doth entreat thee.'

11. So saying, Peter embraced Marcellus. Then Peter turned to the crowd who stood by him, and saw in the crowd a man half laughing, in whom was a most wicked demon. And Peter said to him, 'Whoever you are, that laughed, show yourself openly to all who stand by.' And hearing this the young man ran into the courtyard of the house, and he shouted aloud and threw himself against the wall and said, 'Peter, there is a huge contest between (p. 59) Simon and the dog which you sent; for Simon says to the dog, "Say that I am not here" - but the dog says more to him than the message you gave; and when he has finished the mysterious work which you gave him, he shall die at your feet.' But Peter said, 'You too, then, whatever demon you may be, in the name of our Lord Jesus Christ, come out of the young man and do him no harm; (and) show yourself to all who stand by!' And hearing this he left the young man;[76] and he caught hold of a great marble statue, which stood in the courtyard of the house, and kicked it to pieces. Now it was a statue of Caesar. And when Marcellus saw that he beat his forehead and said to Peter, 'A great crime has been committed; if Caesar hears of this through some busybody, he will punish us severely.' But Peter answered him, 'I see you are not the man you were just now; for you said you were ready to spend your whole fortune to save your soul. But if you are truly repentant and believe in Christ with all your heart, take (some) running water in your hands and pray to the Lord; then sprinkle it in his name over the broken pieces of the statue, and it will be restored as before.' And Marcellus did not doubt, but believed with his whole heart, and before taking the water in his hands he looked upwards and said, 'I believe in thee, Lord Jesus Christ, for I am being tested by thine apostle Peter whether I truly believe in thy holy name. Therefore I take water in my hands, and in thy name I sprinkle those

stones, that the statue may be restored as it was before. So, Lord, if it be thy will that I remain in the body and suffer nothing at Caesar's hand, let this stone be restored as it was before.' And he sprinkled the water upon the stones, and the statue was restored.[77] So Peter exulted because he had not doubted when he prayed to the Lord, and Marcellus also was uplifted in spirit, because this first miracle was done by his hands; and he therefore believed with his whole heart in the name of Jesus Christ the Son of God, through whom all things impossible are (made) possible.[78]

5

(Peter's miracles and first attacks on Simon)

12. But Simon (was) in (the house, and) said to the dog, 'Tell Peter that I am not in (the house).' And the dog answered him in the presence of Marcellus, (p. 60) 'You most wicked and shameless (man), you enemy of all that live and believe in Christ Jesus, (here is) a dumb animal sent to you and taking a human voice[79] to convict you and prove you a cheat and a deceiver. Have you thought for all these hours, (only) to say, "Say that I am not here"? Were you not ashamed to raise your feeble and useless voice against Peter, the servant and apostle of Christ, as if you could hide from him who commanded me to speak against (you to) your face? And this is not for your sake, but for those whom you were perverting and sending to destruction. Cursed therefore you shall be, you enemy and corrupter of the way to the truth of Christ, who shall prove your iniquities which you have done with undying fire, and you shall be in outer darkness.'[80] Having said these words the dog ran off; and the people followed, leaving Simon alone. (So) the dog came to Peter, who was sitting with the crowd (who had come) to see the face of Peter; and the dog reported his dealings with Simon. So the dog said, 'Messenger and apostle of the true God, Peter,[81] you shall have a great contest with Simon, the enemy of Christ, and with his servants; and you shall convert many to the faith that were deceived by him. Therefore you shall receive from God a reward for your work.' And when the dog had said this, he fell down at the apostle Peter's feet and gave up his spirit. And when the crowd with great amazement saw the dog speaking, some began to throw themselves down at Peter's feet, but others said, 'Show us another sign, that we may believe in you as the servant of the living God; (for) Simon too did many signs in our presence, and therefore we followed him'

13. But Peter turned round and saw (smoked?) fish[82] hanging in a window; and he took it and said to the people, 'If you now see this swimming in the water like a fish, will you be able to believe in him whom I preach?' And they all said with one accord, 'Indeed we will believe you!' Now there was a fish-pond near by; so he said, 'In thy name, Jesus Christ, in which they still fail to believe' (he

said) 'in the presence of all these be alive and swim like a fish!' And he threw (p. 61) the tunny into the pond, and it came alive and began to swim. And the people saw the fish swimming; and he made it do so not merely for that hour, or it might have been called a delusion, but he made it go on swimming, so that it attracted crowds from all sides and showed that the tunny had become a (live) fish; so much so that some of the people threw in bread for it, and it ate it all up.[83] And when they saw this, a great number followed him and believed in the Lord, and they assembled by day and by night in the house of Narcissus the presbyter. And Peter expounded to them the writings of the prophets and what our Lord Jesus Christ had enacted both in word and in deeds.

14. Now Marcellus was being day by day (more) firmly established through the signs which he saw performed through Peter through the grace of Jesus Christ which he had granted him. And Marcellus ran in on Simon as he sat in his house in the dining-room, and he cursed him, saying: 'Most hateful and foulest of men, corrupter of my soul and of my house, who would have had me abandon Christ, my Lord and Saviour!' And he laid hands on him and ordered him to be driven from the house. And now the slaves had (him in their) power, and rained insults upon him, some boxing his face, some (using) the stick and some the stone, while others emptied pots full of filth over his head, those who had offended[84] their master on his account and had long been in chains; and other fellow-slaves (of theirs) whom he had maligned before their master abused him and said to him: 'Now we are repaying you a just reward, through the will of God, who has had mercy on us and on our master.' So Simon was soundly beaten and thrown out of the house; and he ran to the house where Peter was staying; and he stood at the door of the house of Narcissus the presbyter and called out, 'Here am I, Simon; so come down, Peter, and I will convict you of having believed in a (mere) man, a Jew and the son of a carpenter.'[85]

15. Now Peter was told that Simon had said this; (and) Peter sent to him a woman who had a child at the breast, saying to her, 'Go down quickly, and you will see someone looking for me. And you are not to answer him; but keep silent and hear what the child you are holding will say to him.' So the woman went down. Now the child whom she suckled was seven months old; and it took the voice of a man and said to Simon (p. 62): 'You abomination of God and men, you destruction of the truth and most wicked seed of corruption, you fruitless one of nature's fruits! But you appear but briefly and for a minute, and after this everlasting punishment awaits you. Son of a shameless father, striking no roots for good but only for poison, unfaithful creature, devoid of any hope! A dog reproved you, yet you were not shaken; now I, an infant, am compelled by God to speak, and yet you do not blush for shame! But even though you refuse, on the coming sabbath another shall bring you to the forum of Julius to prove what kind of man you are. So get away from the door which the feet (*lit.* footsteps) of the saints are using; for no longer shall you corrupt

the innocent souls which you used to pervert and made them offended at Christ. So now your most evil nature shall be exposed and your contrivance destroyed. This last word I am telling you now: Jesus Christ says to you "Be struck dumb by the power of my name, and depart from Rome until the coming sabbath."' And immediately he became dumb and could not resist, but left Rome until the sabbath and lodged in a stable. The woman went back with her child to Peter, and told him and the other brethren what the child had said to Simon; and they glorified the Lord who had shown these things to men.

6

(Peter's vision and narrative about Simon)

16. But when night came on Peter saw Jesus clothed in a robe of splendour, smiling and saying to him while he was still awake, 'Already the great mass of the brethren have turned back to me through you and through the signs which[86] you have done in my name. But you shall have a trial of faith on the coming sabbath, and many more of the Gentiles and of the Jews shall be converted in my name to me, who was insulted, mocked and spat upon. For I will show myself to you when you ask for signs and miracles, and you shall convert many; but you will have Simon opposing you with the works of his father.[87] But all his (actions) shall be exposed as charms and illusions of magic. But now do not delay and you shall establish in my name all those whom I send you.' And when it was light he told the brethren that the Lord had appeared to him and what he had commanded.

17. 'But believe me, men and brethren, I drove this Simon (p. 63) out of Judaea, where he did much harm by his incantations. He stayed in Judaea with a woman named Eubula, a woman of some distinction in this world, who possessed much gold and pearls of no little value. Simon stole into her house with two others like himself; though none of the household saw these two, but only Simon; and by means of a spell they took away all the woman's gold and disappeared. But Eubula discovering this crime began to torture her household, saying, "You took advantage of (the visit of) this godly man and have robbed me, because you saw him coming in to me to do honour to a simple woman; but his name is <the power of the Lord>."[88]

'Now as I fasted for three days and prayed that this crime should come to light, I saw in a vision Italicus and Antulus, whom I had instructed in the name of the Lord, and a boy who was naked and bound, who gave me a wheaten loaf and said to me, "Peter, hold out for two days and you shall see the wonderful works of God.[89] For the things which are lost from Eubula's house were stolen by Simon and two others, using magical arts and creating a delusion. And you shall see them on the third day at the ninth hour by the gate which leads toward

Naples, selling to a goldsmith named Agrippinus a young satyr made of gold, of two pounds weight, and having a precious stone set in it. Now you are not to touch it, to avoid pollution; but have with you some of the lady's servants; then show them the goldsmith's shop and leave them. For this event will cause many to believe in the name of the Lord. For the things which they have constantly stolen by their cunning and wickedness shall be brought to light." When I heard this I came to Eubula and found her sitting and lamenting with her clothes torn and her hair in disorder; and I said to her, "Eubula, rise up from your bed[90] and compose your face, put up your hair and put on a dress that becomes you, and pray to the Lord Jesus Christ who judges every soul. For he is the Son of the invisible God; in him you must be saved, if indeed you repent with all your heart of your former sins. And receive power from him; for now the Lord says to you through me, 'All that you have lost (p. 64) you shall find.' And when you have received them, be sure that you find[91] <the way>, so as to renounce this present world and seek for everlasting refreshment.[92] Listen then to this: let some of your people keep watch by the gate that leads towards Naples. On the day after tomorrow, about the ninth hour, they will see two young men with a young satyr in gold of two pounds weight set with stones, as a vision has shown me, and they will offer it for sale to a certain Agrippinus, who is familiar with the godly life and the faith in our Lord Jesus Christ. And through him (i.e. Christ) it will be shown you that you must believe in the living God and not in Simon the sorcerer, that inconstant demon, who would have you remain in mourning and your innocent household be tortured, who with his soothing eloquence perverted you with (empty) words and spoke of devotion to God with his lips alone, while he himself is wholly filled with wickedness. For when you meant to celebrate a festival and put up your idol and veiled it and put out all the ornaments upon a stand, he had brought in two young men whom none of you saw; and they made an incantation and stole your ornaments and disappeared. But his plan miscarried; for my God disclosed (it) to me, so that you should not be deceived nor perish in hell, whatever wickedness and perversity you have shown towards God, who is full of all truth and a just judge of the living and the dead. And there is no other hope of life for man, except through him, through whom your lost (possessions) are preserved for you. And now you must regain your own soul!" But she threw herself at my feet, saying, "Sir, who you are I do not know; but I received him as a servant of God, and I gave by his hands whatever he asked of me for the care of the poor, a great deal, and made him large presents besides. What harm has he suffered from me, that he should cause such trouble in my house?" Peter answered her, "We must put no faith in words, but in actions and deeds. So we must go on with what we have begun."

'So I left her and went with two stewards of Eubula, and came to Agrippinus and said to him, "Make sure that you take note of these men. For tomorrow two young men will come to you, wishing to sell you a young satyr in gold set with stones, which belongs to these men's mistress. So you are to take it (p. 65) as if to inspect it and to admire its workmanship. Afterwards these men will come in; (then) God shall bring the rest to the proof." And on the next day the lady's stewards came about the ninth hour, and also those young men, wishing to sell Agrippinus the golden satyr; and at once they were seized, and word was sent to the lady. But she in great distress of mind went to the magistrate, and loudly declared what had happened to her. And when the magistrate Pompeius saw her so distressed, whereas she had never (before) come out in public, he immediately rose up from the bench and went to the guardroom and ordered them to be produced and examined. And they under torture confessed that they were acting as Simon's agents - "who gave us money (to do it)". And when tortured further they confessed that all that Eubula had lost had been put underground in a cave outside the gate, and more besides. When Pompeius heard this, he got up to go to the gate, having those two men bound with two chains each. And there! - Simon came in at the gate, looking for them because they had been so long; and he saw a great crowd coming, and those men held fast in chains. At once he realised (what had happened) and took to flight, and has not been seen in Judaea until this day. But Eubula having recovered all her property gave it for the care of the poor; she believed in the Lord Jesus Christ and was strengthened (in the faith); and despising and renouncing this world she gave (alms) to the widows and orphans and clothed the poor; and after a long time she gained her repose. Now these things, my dearest brethren, were done in Judaea; and so he came to be expelled from there, who is called the messenger of Satan.[93]

18. 'Brethren most dear and beloved, let us fast together and pray to the Lord. He who expelled him from there is able to uproot him from this place also. May he give us power to resist him and his incantations and to expose him as the messenger of Satan. For on the sabbath our Lord shall bring him, even if[94] he refuses to come, to the forum of Julius. So let us bow our knees to Christ, who hears us even if we have not called upon him; it is he who sees us, even if he is not seen with these eyes, but is within us; if we are willing (p. 66) he will not forsake us. Let us therefore cleanse our souls of every wicked temptation, and God will not depart from us; and if we only wink with our eyes, he is present with us.'

7

(Peter's miracles)

19. When Peter had just said this, Marcellus came in and said, 'Peter, I have cleansed my house for you of (all) traces of Simon and removed (all traces) of

his wicked dust. For I took water and calling on the holy name of Jesus Christ, with other servants of mine who belong to him, I sprinkled all my house and all the dining-rooms and all the colonnades right out to the doorway; and I said, "I know that thou, Lord Jesus Christ, art pure and untouched by any impurity; so that my opponent and enemy is driven away from before thy face." And now, most blessed man, I have told the widows and the aged to meet you in my house which is cleansed, that they may pray with us. And each of them shall be given a piece of gold on account of their service (?), so that they may truly be called Christ's servants. And everything else is ready for the service; I beg you therefore, most blessed Peter, to endorse their request, so that you also may grace their prayers for me. Let us go, then, and let us also take Narcissus and all the brethren who are here.' So Peter assented to his simplicty and went with him and the other brethren to do as he desired.

20. So Peter went in and saw one of the old people, a widow that was blind, and her daughter giving her a hand and leading her to Marcellus' house. And Peter said to her, 'Mother, come here; from this day onward Jesus give you his right hand, through whom we have light unapproachable[95] which no darkness hides; and he says to you through me, "Open your eyes and see, and walk on your own."' And at once the widow saw Peter laying his hand on her.

And Peter went into the dining-room and saw that the gospel was being read. So he rolled up (the book) and said, 'You men who believe and hope in Christ (p. 67), you must know how the holy scriptures of our Lord should be declared. What we have written by his grace, so far as we were able,[96] although it seems weak to you as yet, yet (we have written) according to our powers, so far as it is endurable to be implanted in human flesh.[97] We should therefore first learn to know the will of God, or (his) goodness;[98] for when error was in full flood and many thousands of men were plunging to destruction, the Lord in his mercy was moved to show himself in another shape and to be seen in the form of a man, on whom neither the Jews nor we were worthy to be enlightened. For each one of us saw (him) as he was able, as he had power to see. And now I will explain to you what has just been read to you. Our Lord wished me to see his majesty on the holy mountain;[99] but when I with the sons of Zebedee saw the brilliance of his light, I fell as one dead, and closed my eyes and heard his voice, such as I cannot describe, and thought that I had been blinded by his radiance. And recovering my breath a little I said to myself, "Perhaps my Lord willed to bring me here to deprive me of my sight." And I said, "If this be thy will, Lord, I do not gainsay it." And he gave me his hand and lifted me up. And when I stood up I saw him in such a form as I was able to take in. So, my dearest brethren, as God is merciful, he has borne our weaknesses and carried our sins, as the prophet says, "He beareth our sins and is afflicted for us; yet we thought him to be afflicted and stricken with wounds."[100] For "he is in the Father and the Father in him";[101] he also is himself the fullness of all majesty, who has shown us all his goodness. He ate and drank for our sakes, though himself without hunger or thirst, he bore and suffered reproaches for our sakes, he died and rose again because of us. He who defended me also when I sinned (p. 68) and strengthened me with his greatness,[102] will also comfort you that you may love him, this (God) who is both great and little, beautiful and ugly, young and old, appearing in time and yet in eternity wholly invisible; whom no human hand has grasped, yet is held by his servants, whom no flesh has seen, yet now he is seen;[103] whom no hearing has found yet now he is known as the word that is heard; whom no suffering can reach, yet now is (chastened) as we are;[104] who was never chastened, yet now is chastened; who is before the world, yet now is comprehended in time; the beginning greater than all princedom, yet now delivered to the princes; beauteous, yet appearing among us as poor and ugly, yet foreseeing; this Jesus you have, brethren, the door,[105] the light, the way, the bread, the water, the life, the resurrection,[106] the refreshment,[107] the pearl, the treasure, the seed, the abundance, the mustard-seed, the vine, the plough, the grace, the faith, the word:[108] He is all things, and there is no other greater than he. To him be praise for ever and ever. Amen.'

21. And when the ninth hour was fully come they stood up to pray. And now suddenly some of the old blind widows, who still sat there unknown to Peter and had not stood up,[109] called out and said to Peter, 'We sit here together, Peter, hoping in Christ Jesus and believing (in him). So as you have now made one of us to see, we beg you, sir Peter, let us also share his mercy and goodness.'[110] And Peter said to them 'If there is in you the faith which is in Christ, if it is established in you, then see with your mind what you do not see with your eyes; and (though) your ears be closed, yet let them open in your mind within you. These eyes shall again be closed, that see nothing but men and cattle and dumb animals and stones and sticks; but only the inner[111] eyes see Jesus Christ.[112] Yet now, Lord, let thy sweet and holy name assist these women; do thou touch their eyes, for thou art able, that they may see with their own eyesight.'

And when prayer was made by all, the room in which they were shone as if with lightning, such as shines in the clouds. Yet it was not such light as (p. 69) (is seen) by day, (but) ineffable, invisible, such as no man could describe, a light that shone on us so (brightly) that we were senseless with bewilderment, and called upon the Lord and said, 'Have mercy on us thy servants, Lord. Let thy gift to us, Lord, be such as we can endure; for this we can neither see nor endure.' And as we lay there, there stood there only those widows, which were blind. But the bright light which appeared to us entered into their eyes and made them see.

Then Peter said to them, 'Tell (us) what you saw.' And they said, 'We saw an old man, who had such a presence as we cannot describe to you'; but others (said), 'We saw a growing lad'; and others said, 'We saw a boy who gently touched our eyes, and so our eyes were opened.'[113] So Peter praised the Lord, saying, 'Thou alone art God the Lord, to whom praise is due. How many lips should we need to give thanks to thee in accordance with thy mercy? So, brethren, as I told you a little while ago, God is greater[114] than our thoughts, as we have learnt from the aged widows, how they have seen the Lord in a variety of forms.'

22. And he exhorted them all to understand the Lord with all their heart; then he and Marcellus and the other brethren began to attend to the virgins of the Lord and to rest until morning. Marcellus said to them, 'You holy and inviolate virgins of the Lord, give ear; you have a place where you (may) stay. For the things that are called mine, to whom do they belong but you? Do not leave this place, but refresh yourselves; for on the sabbath which comes tomorrow Simon holds a contest with Peter, the holy one of God. For as the Lord has always been with him, so may Christ the Lord stand for him now as his apostle! For Peter has continued (in prayer) tasting nothing, but fasting, that he may overcome the wicked enemy and persecutor of the Lord's truth. For here are my young men who have come with the news that they have seen stands being set up in the forum, and the crowd saying "Tomorrow (p. 70) at dawn two Jews will contend in this place concerning the worship of God."[115] Now therefore let us watch till morning, praying and entreating our Lord Jesus Christ to hear our prayers on behalf of Peter.'

And Marcellus went to sleep for a short time; and when he awoke he said to Peter, 'Peter, apostle of Christ, let us boldly set about our task. For just now as I slept for a little I saw you sitting on a high place, and before you a great assembly; and a most evil-looking woman, who looked like an Ethiopian, not an Egyptian, but was all black, clothed in filthy rags,[116] (was) dancing, with an iron collar about her neck and chains on her hands and feet. When you saw her you said aloud to me, "Marcellus, the whole power of Simon and of his god is this dancer; take off her head!" But I said to you "Brother Peter, I am a senator of noble family, and I have never stained my hands, nor killed even a sparrow at any time." And when you heard this you began to cry out even louder, "Come, our true sword, Jesus Christ, and do not only cut off the head of this demon, but cut in pieces all her limbs in the sight of all these whom I have approved in thy service." And immediately a (man who looked) like yourself, Peter, with sword in hand, cut her all to pieces, so that I gazed upon you both, both on you and on the one who was cutting up the demon, whose likeness caused me great amazement. And now I have awakened, and have told you these signs of Christ.' And when Peter heard this he was the more encouraged, because Marcellus had seen these things; for the Lord is always careful for his own. So cheered and refreshed by these words he stood up to go to the forum.

8

(The Contest with Simon in the Forum)

23. Now the brethren assembled and all those that were in Rome, taking their places and paying a piece of gold for each; and the senators, prefects and officers also collected together. Then Peter came in and took his place in the centre. They all cried, out, 'Show us, Peter, who is your god, or what is his greatness, which has given you such confidence. (p. 71) Do not be ungenerous to the Romans; they are lovers of the gods. We have had evidence from Simon, now let us have yours; convince us, both of you, whom we should truly believe.' And while they said this, Simon also came in; and he stood in confusion at Peter's side and gazed at him closely.

After a long silence Peter said, 'You men of Rome, you must be our true judges. Now I say that I have believed in the living and true God, and I promise you to give evidence of him, such as I have known already, as many among you bear witness. For you see that this man is completely silent, since he has been convicted and I drove him from Judaea because of the impostures which he practised on Eubula, an honourable and most simple woman, using his magic arts. Expelled from there by me, he has come to this place, believing he could hide himself among you; and there he stands face to face with me. Tell me now, Simon, did you not fall at my feet and Paul's in Jerusalem,[117] when you saw the healings which were done by our hands? - and you said, "I beg you, take payment from me as much as you will, so that I can lay hands (on men) and work such benefits." When we heard these words of yours we cursed you (saying) "Do you think you can tempt us to wish for possession of money?" And now are you not afraid? My name is Peter, because the Lord Christ thought fit to call me "prepared for all things".[118] For I believe on the living God, through whom I shall destroy your sorceries. Now let him (Simon) do the marvellous things he used to do, here in your presence. And what I have just told you of him, will you not believe me?'

But Simon said, 'You presume to talk of Jesus the Nazarene, the son of a carpenter and a carpenter himself,[119] whose family comes from Judaea. Listen, Peter, the Romans have sense; they are not fools.' And he turned to the people and said, 'You men of Rome, is God born? Is he crucified? He who owns a Lord is no God!' And as he said this, many answered, 'Well said, Simon!'

24. But Peter said, 'A curse on your words against Christ! Did you presume to speak in these terms, while the prophet says of him, "His generation, who shall declare it?"[120] And another prophet says, "And we saw (p. 72) him and he had no grace nor beauty."[121] And: "In the last times a boy is born of the Holy Spirit; his mother knows not a man, nor does anyone claim to be his father."[122] And again he says, "She has given birth and has not given birth."[123] And again,

"Is it a small thing for you to make trouble . . . ?"[124] (And again) "Behold, a virgin shall conceive in the womb."[125] And another prophet says in the Father's honour, "We have neither heard her voice, nor is a midwife come in."[126] Another prophet says, "He was not born from the womb of a woman, but came down from a heavenly place";[127] and, "A stone is cut out without hands and has broken all the kingdoms";[128] and, "The stone which the builders rejected is become the head of the corner";[129] and he calls him a stone "elect and precious".[130] And again the prophet says of him, "And behold I saw one coming upon a cloud like a son of man."[131] And what more (need be said)? You men of Rome, if you were versed in the prophetic writings I would explain all (this) to you; for through them it had to be (told) in secret (*lit.* in a mystery) and the kingdom of God be fulfilled. But these things shall be disclosed to you hereafter.

'Now as for you, Simon; do one of those things with which you used to deceive them, and I will undo it through my Lord Jesus Christ.' Simon put on a bold front and said, 'If the prefect permits.'

25. But the prefect wished to show impartiality towards both, so as not to appear to act unjustly. And the prefect put forward one of his young men, and said to Simon, 'Take this man and put him to death.' And he said to Peter, 'And you, restore him to life.' And the prefect addressed the people saying, 'It is now for you to judge which of these men is acceptable to God, the one who kills or the one who gives life.'

And immediately Simon spoke in the boy's ear, and made him speechless, and he died. And as a murmuring arose among the people, one of the (p. 73) widows who rested at Marcellus' house cried out from behind the crowd, 'Peter, servant of God, my son is dead, the only one that I had.'[132] And the people made room for her and led her to Peter. But she threw herself down at his feet and said, 'I had only one son; he provided my food with his hands (*lit.* shoulders), he lifted me up, he carried me. Now he is dead, who will lend me a hand?' Peter said to her, 'Take these men for witnesses and go[133] and bring your son, so that these may see, and be enabled to believe that by the power of God he is raised up.' But when she heard this,[134] she fell down. Then Peter said to the young men, 'Now we need some young men, who are also willing to believe.' And immediately thirty young men stood up, who were ready to carry her or to bring her dead son. And when the widow had hardly recovered herself, the young men lifted her up. But she was crying out and saying, 'Look, my son, the servant of Christ has sent for you', and tearing her hair and her face. Now the young men who came examined the boy's nostrils, (to see)[135] whether he were really dead. And seeing that he was dead they comforted his mother[136] and said, 'If you truly believe in Peter's God,[137] we (will) lift him up and bring him to Peter, that he may revive him and restore him to you.'

26. While the young men were saying these things the prefect in the forum looked at Peter and said, 'What say you, Peter? See, the boy lies there dead[138]

- of whom even the emperor thinks kindly - and I have not spared him. Certainly I had many other young men, but I trusted in you, and in your Lord whom you preach, if indeed you are sure and truthful;[139] therefore I allowed him to die." Then Peter said, 'God is not tested or weighed in the balance; but he is to be worshipped by those whom he loves[140] with (all) their heart, and he will listen to those who are worthy.[141] But now that God and my Lord Jesus Christ is tested among you, he is doing such signs and wonders through me for the conversion of his sinners. And now in the sight of them all, O Lord, in thy power raise up through my voice the man whom Simon killed with his touch!' And Peter said to the boy's master, 'Come, take his right hand, and you shall have him alive and (able to) walk with you.' And Agrippa the prefect ran and came to the boy and taking his hand restored him to life. And when the crowds saw it they all cried out, 'There is but one God, the one God of Peter!'

27. (p. 74) Meanwhile the widow's son also was brought in on a stretcher by the young men; and the people made way for them and brought them to Peter. And Peter lifted up his eyes towards heaven and held out his hands and said, 'Holy Father[142] of thy Son Jesus Christ, who hast given us thy power, that through thee we may ask and obtain, and despise all that is in this world, and follow thee alone; thou who art seen by few, and wouldst be known by many; shine thou about (us), Lord, give light, appear, and raise up the son of (this) aged widow who cannot help herself without her son. Now I take up the word of Christ my master, and say to thee, Young man, arise and walk[143] with thy mother, so long as thou art useful to her. But afterwards thou shalt offer thyself to me in a higher service, in the office of deacon and bishop.' And immediately the dead man stood up, and the crowds were astonished at the sight, and the people shouted, 'Thou art God the Saviour, thou, the God of Peter, the invisible God, the Saviour!' And they spoke among themselves, being truly astonished at the power of a man that called upon his Lord by his word; and they accepted it to their sanctification.

28. So while the news spread round the whole city, the mother of a senator approached and pressing through the middle of the crowd she threw herself at Peter's feet, saying, 'I have heard from my household that you are a servant of the merciful God, bestowing his grace to all who desire this light. Bestow then this light on (my) son, for I have heard that you are not ungenerous towards anyone; if (even) a lady entreats you do not turn away!' Peter said to her, 'Do you believe my God, by whom your son shall be restored to life?' But his mother cried aloud and said with tears, 'I believe, Peter, I believe.' The whole people shouted, 'Grant the mother her son!' Then Peter said, 'Let him be brought here before all these.' And Peter turned to the people and said, 'You men of Rome, seeing that I too am one of you, wearing human flesh, and a sinner, but have obtained mercy, (p. 75) do not look at me, as though by my own power I were doing what I do;[144] (the power is) my Lord Jesus Christ's,

who is the judge of the living and of the dead. Believing in him and sent by him, I dare to entreat him to raise the dead. Go then, lady, let your son be brought here and restored to life.'

Then the woman made her way through the crowd and went out into the street with haste and great joy, and believing in her heart she reached her house and made her young men carry him and came to the forum. And she told her young men to put their caps on their heads and walk in front of the bier, and all that was to be used for the body of her son (i.e. for the funeral) should be carried in front of the bier so that Peter should see it and have pity on the dead man and on herself. So with them all as mourners she came to the assembly; and a crowd of senators and ladies followed her to see the wonderful works of God. Now Nicostratus, the dead man, was much respected and liked among the senate; so they brought him in and laid him down before Peter. Then Peter called for silence and said with a loud voice, 'Men of Rome, let there now be a just judgment between me and Simon, and consider which of us believes in the living God, he or I. Let him revive the body which lies here; then (you may) believe in him as an angel of God. But if he cannot, then I will call upon my God; I will restore her son alive to his mother, and then you (shall) believe that this is a sorcerer and a cheat, this guest of yours!'

And they all heard this and accepted Peter's challenge as just; and they encouraged Simon, saying, 'Now, if there is anything in you, bring it out! Spite him, or be spited! Why are you waiting? Go on, begin!' But Simon, seeing them all pressing him, stood there silent; (however), when he saw that the poeple had become silent and were looking at him, Simon raised his voice and said, 'Men of Rome, if you see the dead man restored to life, will you throw Peter out of the city?' And all the people said, 'We will not only throw him out, but that self-same hour we will burn him with fire.'

Then Simon went to the dead man's head, and stooped down three times and stood up three times (p. 76), and showed the people that (the dead man) had raised his head and was moving, opening his eyes and bowing towards Simon.[145] And at once they began to look for wood and kindling, in order to burn Peter. But Peter gaining the strength of Christ raised his voice and said to the men who were shouting against him, 'Now I see, people of Rome, that I must not call you foolish and empty-headed, so long as your eyes and ears and hearts are blinded. So long as your sense is darkened, you do not see that you are bewitched, since you believe that a dead man has been revived when he has not stood up. I would have been content, you men of Rome, to keep silent and die without a word and leave you among the illusions of this world. But I have before my eyes the punishment of unquenchable fire.[146] If you agree, then, let the dead man speak, let him get up if he is alive, let him free his jaw of its wrappings with his own hands, let him call for his mother, and when you call out, let him say, "What is it you are calling?" Let him beckon to you with his hand. Now (if) you wish to see that he is dead and you are spell-bound, let this man withdraw from the bier - this man who has persuaded you to withdraw from Christ, - and you will see that the (young) man is (still) in the same state as (when) you saw him brought in.'

But Agrippa the prefect could not contain himself, but got up and pushed Simon away with his own hands. And so the dead man lay there again as he was before. And the people were enraged and turned away from Simon's sorcery, and began to call out, 'Hear (us), Caesar! If the dead man does not stand up, let Simon be burnt instead of Peter, for he has truly blinded us.' But Peter held out his hand and said, 'Men of Rome, have patience! I am not telling you that Simon should be burnt when the boy is restored; for if I tell you, you will do it.' The people shouted 'Even if you will not have it, Peter, we will do it!' Peter said to them, 'If you are determined on this, the boy shall not return to life. For we have not learnt to repay evil with evil;[147] but (p. 77) we have learnt to love our enemies and pray for our persecutors.[148] For if even this man can repent, that is better; for God will not remember evil (deeds). So let him come into the light of Christ. But if he cannot, let him possess the inheritance of his father the devil; but your hands shall not be stained.'

And when he had said this to the people, he went up to the boy, and before he revived him he said to his mother, 'Those young men whom you set free in honour of your son, are they to do service to their master as free men, when he is alive? For I know that some will feel injured on seeing your son restored to life, because these men will become his slaves once again. But let them all keep their freedom and draw their provisions as they drew them before, for your son shall be raised up, and they must be with him' And Peter went on looking at her, to see what she thought. And the boy's mother said, 'What else can I do? So I will declare in the presence of the prefect: all that I meant to lay out for my son's funeral shall be their property.' And Peter said to her, 'Let the remainder be distributed to the widows.' But Peter rejoiced in his heart, and said in the spirit, 'Lord who art merciful, Jesus Christ, appear to thy (servant) Peter who calls upon thee, as thou hast always shown mercy and goodness; in the presence of all these men, who have obtained their freedom so as to do service, let Nicostratus now arise!' And Peter touched the boy's side and said, 'Stand up.' And the boy stood up and gathered up his clothes and sat down and untied his jaw and asked for other clothes; and he came down from the bier and said to Peter, 'I beg you, sir, let us go to our Lord Jesus Chirst whom I saw talking with you; who said to you, as he showed me to you, "Bring him here to me, for he is mine."' When Peter heard this from the boy he was yet more strengthened in mind by the help of the Lord; and Peter said to the people, 'Men of Rome, this is how the dead are restored to life, this is how they speak, this is how they walk when they are raised up, and live for so long as God wills. Now therefore, you people who have gathered to (see) the show, if (p. 78) you turn now[149] from these wicked ways of yours and from all your man-made gods and from every kind of uncleanness and lust, you shall receive the fellowship with Christ through faith, so that you may come to everlasting life.'

29. From that same hour they venerated him as a god, and laid at his feet such sick people as they had at home, so that he might heal them. But the prefect, seeing that such a great number (p. 79) were waiting upon Peter, made signs to Peter that he should withdraw. But Peter invited the people to come to Marcellus' house. But the boy's mother entreated Peter to set foot in her house.[150] But Peter had arranged to go to[151] Marcellus on the Lord's day, to see the widows as Marcellus had promised, so that they should be cared for by his own hands. So the boy who had returned to life said, 'I will not leave Peter.' And his mother went joyfully and gladly to her own house. And on the next day after the sabbath she came to Marcellus' house bringing Peter two thousand pieces of gold and saying to Peter, 'Divide these among the virgins of Christ who serve him.' But when the boy who had risen from the dead saw that he had given nothing to anyone, he went home and opened the chest and himself brought four thousand gold pieces, saying to Peter, 'Look, I myself, who am restored to life, am bringing a double offering, and (present) myself as a speaking sacrifice[152] to God from this day on.'

III. Martyrdom of the holy Apostle Peter (Aa I, 78-102)[153]

30 (1). Now on the Lord's day Peter was preaching to the brethren and encouraging them to faith in Christ. Many of the senators were present and a number of knights and wealthy women <and> matrons, and they were strengthened in the faith. But there was present a very wealthy woman who bore the name of Chryse (the golden), because every utensil of hers was made of gold - for since her birth she had never used a silver or glass vessel, but only golden ones; she said to Peter, 'Peter, servant of God, there came to me in a dream the one you say is God; and he said to me, "Chryse, bring my servant Peter (p. 80) 10,000 pieces of gold; for you owe them to him." So I have brought them, for fear lest I should suffer some harm from him who appeared to me, who has gone away into heaven.' So saying, she laid down the money and departed. But Peter when he saw it gave praise to the Lord, because the afflicted could now be relieved. Now some of those who were present said to him, 'Peter, you were wrong to accept this money from her; for she is notorious all over Rome for fornication and (they say) that she does not consort with one man only; indeed she even goes in to her own (house-) boys. So have no dealings with the "golden" table (i.e. Chryse's table), but let her (money) be returned to her.' But Peter, when he heard this, laughed and said to the brethren,

'I do not know what this woman is as regards her usual way of life; but in taking this money I did not take it without reason; for she was bringing it as a debtor to Christ, and is giving it to Christ's servants; for he himself has provided for them.'

31 (2). And they brought the sick people also to him on the sabbath, entreating him that they might be cured of their diseases. And many paralytics were healed, and many sufferers from dropsy and from two- and four-day fevers, and they were cured of every bodily disease, such as believed in the name of Jesus Christ, and very many were added every day to the grace of the Lord.[154]

But after a few days had elapsed Simon the magician promised the rabble that he would show Peter that he had not put his faith in the true God but in a deception. Now while he performed many false miracles, he was laughed to scorn by those disciples who were already firm (in the faith). For in their living-rooms he caused certain spirits to be brought in to them, which were only appearances without real existence. And what more is there to say? After he had spoken at length about his magic art, he made the lame appear to be sound for a short time, and the blind likewise, and once he appeared to make many who were dead come alive and move, as he did with Nicostratus.[155] But all the while Peter followed him and exposed him to the onlookers. And as he was now always out of favour and derided by the people of Rome and discredited, as not succeeding in what he promised to do, it came to such a point that he said to them, 'Men of Rome, at present you think that Peter has mastered me, as having greater power, and you attend to him rather (than me). (But) you are deceived. For tomorrow I shall leave you, who are utterly profane and impious, and fly up to God, whose power I am, although enfeebled. If then you have fallen, behold I am He that Standeth.[156] And I am going up (p. 82) to my Father[157] and shall say to him, "Even me, thy Son that Standeth, they desired to bring down; but I did not consent with them, and am returned to myself."'

32 (3). And by the following day a large crowd had assembled on the Sacred Way to see him fly. And Peter, having seen a vision, came to the place, in order to convict him again this time; for when (Simon) made his entry into Rome, he astonished the crowds by flying; but Peter, who exposed him, was not yet staying in Rome, (the city) which he so carried away by his deceptions that people lost their senses through him.

So this man stood on a high place, and seeing Peter, he began to say: 'Peter, now of all times, when I am making my ascent before all these onlookers, I tell you: If your god has power enough - he whom the Jews destroyed, and they stoned you who were chosen by him[158] - let him show that faith in him is of God; let it be shown at this time whether it be worthy of God. For I by ascending will show to all this crowd what manner of being I am.' And lo and behold, he was carried up into the air, and everyone saw him all over Rome, passing over its temples and its hills; while the faithful looked towards Peter. And Peter, seeing the incredible sight, cried out to the Lord Jesus Christ, 'Let this man do what he undertook, and all who have believed on thee shall now be overthrown, and the signs and wonders which thou gavest them through me shall be disbelieved. Make haste, Lord, with thy grace; and let him fall down from (this) height, and be crippled, but not die; but let him be disabled and break his leg in three places!' And he fell down from that height and broke his leg in three places. Then they stoned him and went to their own homes; but from that time they all believed in Peter.

But one of Simon's friends named Gemellus, from whom Simon had received much (support), who was married to a Greek woman, came along the road shortly afterwards and seeing him with his leg broken said, (p. 84) 'Simon, if the Power of God is broken, shall not the God himself, whose power you are, be proved an illusion?' So Gemellus also ran and followed Peter, saying to him, 'I too desire to be one of those that believe in Christ.' But Peter said, 'Then what objection (can there be), my brother? Come and stay with us.' But Simon in his misfortune found some (helpers) who carried him on a stretcher by night from Rome to Aricia; and after staying there he was taken to a man named Castor, who had been banished from Rome to Terracina on a charge of sorcery; and there he underwent an operation; and thus Simon, the angel of the devil,[159] ended his life.

33 (4). But Peter stayed in Rome and rejoiced with the brethren in the Lord and gave thanks night and day for the mass of people who were daily added to the holy name by the grace of the Lord.[160] And the concubines of the prefect Agrippa also came to Peter, being four in number, Agrippina and Nicaria and Euphemia and Doris. And hearing the preaching of purity and all the words of the Lord they were cut to the heart and agreed with each other to remain in purity (renouncing) intercourse with Agrippa; and they were molested by him. Now when Agrippa was perplexed and distressed about them - for he loved them passionately - he made inquiries, and when he sent (to find out) where they had gone, he discovered that (they had gone) to Peter. And when they came (back) he said to them, 'That Christian has taught you not to consort with me; I tell you, I will both destroy you and burn him alive.' They therefore took courage to suffer every injury from Agrippa, (wishing) only to be vexed by passion no longer, being strengthened by the power of Jesus.

34 (5). (p. 86) But one woman who was especially beautiful, the wife of Albinus the friend of Caesar, Xanthippe by name, came with the other ladies to Peter, and she too separated from Albinus. He therefore, filled with fury and passionate love for Xanthippe, and amazed that she would not even sleep in the same bed with him, was raging like a wild beast and wished to do away with Peter; for he knew that he was responsible for her leaving his bed. And many other women besides fell in love with the doctrine of purity and separated from their husbands, and men too ceased to sleep with their own wives, since they wished to worship God in sobriety and purity. So there was the greatest disquiet in Rome; and Albinus put his case to Agrippa, and said to him, 'Either you must get me satisfaction from Peter, who caused my wife's separation, or I shall do

so myself'; and Agrippa said that he had been treated in the same way by him, by the separation of his concubines. And Albinus said to him, 'Why then do you delay, Agrippa? Let us find him and execute him as a trouble-maker, so that we may recover our wives, and in order to give satisfaction to those who cannot execute him, who have themselves been deprived of their wives by him.'

35 (6). But while they made these plans Xanthippe discovered her husband's conspiracy with Agrippa and sent and told Peter, so that he might withdraw from Rome. And the rest of the brethren together with Marcellus entreated him to withdraw, But Peter (p. 88) said to them 'Shall we act like deserters, brethren?' But they said to him, 'No, it is so that you can go on serving the Lord.' So he assented to the brethren and withdrew by himself, saying, 'Let none of you retire with me, but I shall retire by myself in disguise.' And as he went out of the gate he saw the Lord entering Rome; and when he saw him he said, 'Lord, whither (goest thou) here?'[161] And the Lord said to him, 'I am coming to Rome to be crucified.' And Peter said to him, 'Lord, art thou being crucified again?' He said to him, 'Yes, Peter, I am being crucified again.' And Peter came to himself; and he saw the Lord ascending into heaven; then he returned to Rome rejoicing and giving praise to the Lord, because he said, 'I am being crucified'; (since) this was to happen to Peter.

36 (7). So he returned to the brethren and told them what had been seen by him; and they were grieved at heart, and said with tears, 'We entreat you, Peter, take thought for us that are young.' And Peter said to them, 'If it is the Lord's will, it is coming to pass even if we will not have it so. But the Lord is able to establish you in your faith in him, and he will lay your foundation on him and enlarge you in him, (you) whom he himself has planted, so that you may plant others through him. But as for me, so long as the Lord wills me to be in the flesh, I do not demur; again, if he will take me, I rejoice and am glad.'

And while Peter was saying this and (p. 90) all the brethren were in tears, four soldiers arrested him and took him to Agrippa. And he in his distemper ordered that he be charged with irreligion and be crucified.

So the whole mass of the brethren came together, rich and poor, orphans and widows, capable and helpless, wishing to see Peter and to rescue him; and the people cried out irrepressibly with a single voice, 'What harm has Peter done, Agrippa? How has he injured you? Answer the Romans!' And others said, 'If this man dies, we must fear that the Lord will destroy us too.'

And when Peter came to the place (of execution) he quietened the people and said, 'You men, who are soldiers of Christ,[162] men who set their hopes on Christ, remember the signs and wonders which you saw through me, remember the compassion of God, how many healings he has performed for you. Wait for him that shall come and reward everyone according to his deeds.[163] And now do not be angry with Agrippa; for he is the servant of his father's influence; and this is to happen in any event, because the Lord has showed me what is coming. But why do I delay and not go to the cross?'

37 (8). Then when he had approached and stood by the cross he began to say, 'O name of the cross, mystery that is concealed! O grace ineffable (p. 92) that is spoken in the name of the cross! O nature of man that cannot be parted from God! O love (Φιλία) unspeakable and inseparable, that cannot be disclosed through unclean lips! I seize thee now, being come to the end of my release from here. I will declare thee, what thou art; I will not conceal the mystery of the cross that has long been enclosed and hidden from my soul. You who hope in Christ, for you the cross must not be this thing that is visible; for this (passion), like the passion of Christ, is something other than this which is visible. And now above all, since you who can hear, can (hear it) from me, who am at the last closing hour of my life, give ear; withdraw your souls from every outward sense and from all that appears but is not truly real; close these eyes of yours, close your ears, withdraw from actions that are outwardly seen; and you shall know the facts about Christ and the whole secret of your salvation. Let so much be said to you who hear as though it were unspoken. But it is time for you, Peter, to surrender your body to those who are taking it. Take it, then, you whose duty this is. I request you therefore, executioners, to crucify me head-downwards - in this way and no other. And the reason, I will tell to those who hear.'

38 (9). (p. 94) And when they had hanged him up in the way which he had requested, he began to speak again, saying 'Men whose duty it is to hear, pay attention to what I shall tell you at this very moment that I am hanged up. You must know the mystery of all nature, and the beginning of all things, how it came about. For the first man, whose likeness I have in (my) appearance, in falling head-downwards showed a manner of birth that was not so before; for it was dead, having no movement. He therefore, being drawn down - he who also cast his first beginning down to the earth - established the whole of this cosmic system, being hung up as an image of the calling, in which he showed what is on the right hand as on the left, and those on the left as on the right, and changed all the signs of their nature, so as to consider fair those things that were not fair, and take those that were really evil to be good. Concerning this the Lord says in a mystery, "Unless you make what is on the right hand as what is on the left and what is on the left hand as what is on the right and what is above as what is below and what is behind as what is before, you will not recognize the Kingdom."[164] This (p. 96) conception, then, I have declared to you, and the form in which you see me hanging is a representation of that man who first came to birth. You then, my beloved, both those who hear (me) now and those that shall hear in time, must leave your former error and turn back again; for you should come up to the cross of Christ, who is the Word stretched out, the one and only, of whom the Spirit says, "For what else is Christ but the Word, the sound of God?"[165] So that the Word is this upright tree on which I am crucified; but the sound is the cross-piece, the nature of man; and the nail that holds the cross-piece to the upright

in the middle is the conversion (or turning point) and repentance of man.

39 (10). Since then thou hast made known and revealed these things to me, O Word of life, which name I have just given to the tree, I give thee thanks, not with these lips that are nailed fast, nor with the tongue, through which truth and falsehood issues forth, nor with this word that comes forth by the skill of physical nature; but I give thee thanks, O King, with that voice which is known in silence, which is not heard aloud, which does not come forth through the bodily organs, which does not enter the ears of the flesh, that is not heard by corruptible substance, that is not in the world or uttered upon earth, nor is written in books, nor belongs to one but not to another; but with this (voice), Jesu Christ (p. 98) I thank thee, with silence of the voice, with which the spirit within me, that loves thee and speaks to thee and sees thee, makes intercession. Thou art known to the spirit only. Thou art my Father, thou art my Mother, thou my Brother, thou art Friend, thou art Servant, thou art House-keeper; thou art the All, and the All is in thee; thou art Being, and there is nothing that is, except thou.

'With Him then do you also take refuge, brethren, and learning that in him alone is your real being, you shall obtain those things of which he says to you, "What eye has not seen nor ear heard, nor has it entered the heart of man."[166] We ask then, for that which thou hast promised to give us, O Jesus undefiled; we praise thee, we give thanks to thee and confess thee, and being yet men without strength we glorify thee; for thou art God alone and no other, to whom be glory both now and for all eternity, Amen.'

40 (11). But as the crowd that stood by shouted Amen with a resounding cry, at that very Amen, Peter gave up his spirit to the Lord.

But when Marcellus saw that the blessed Peter had given up his spirit, without taking anyone's advice, since it was not allowed, he took him down from the cross with his own hands (p. 100) and washed him in milk and wine;[167] and he ground up seven pounds of mastic, and also fifty pounds of myrrh and aloe and spice and embalmed his body, and filled a trough of stone of great value with Attic honey and laid it in his own burial-vault.[168]

But Peter visited Marcellus by night and said, 'Marcellus, you heard the Lord saying, "Let the dead be buried by their own dead"?'[169] And when Marcellus said, 'Yes', Peter said to him, 'The things which you laid out for the dead, you have lost; for you who are alive were like a dead man caring for the dead.' And Marcellus awoke and told the brethren of Peter's appearing; and he remained with those whom Peter had strengthened in the faith of Christ, gaining strength himself yet more until the coming of Paul to Rome.

41 (12). But when Nero later discovered that Peter had departed this life, he censured the prefect Agrippa because he had been put to death without his knowledge; for he would have liked to punish him more cruelly and with extra severity; for Peter had made disciples of some of his servants and caused them to leave him; so that he was greatly incensed and for some time would not speak

to Agrippa; for he sought to destroy all those brethren who had been made disciples by Peter. (p. 102) And one night he saw a figure scourging him and saying, 'Nero, you cannot now persecute or destroy the servants of Christ. Keep your hands from them!' And so Nero, being greatly alarmed because of this vision, kept away from the disciples from the time that Peter departed this life.

And thereafter the brethren kept together with one accord, rejoicing and exulting in the Lord,[170] and glorifying the God and Saviour of our Lord Jesus Christ with the Holy Spirit, to whom be the glory for ever and ever. Amen.

Notes:

* In the translation the earlier works of Parrott (for the Coptic text), C. Schmidt, Ficker, Vouaux and Erbetta (for the Act. Verc.) have been used. Conjectures by Lipsius and Turner (JTS 32, 1931, 119ff.) in the Latin text of the Act. Verc. are sometimes noted, sometimes adopted without comment. Titles of individual sections, apart from the Martyrdom, are not derived from the tradition. Biblical quotations and allusions are noted, without claim to completeness. Peter's speeches in particular are pervaded by biblical expressions and trains of thought. Further references in Ficker, Vouaux and Erbetta. Act. Verc. = Actus Vercellenses (see above, pp. 277f.); VA = Vita Abercii (see above, p. 276); PapOx = Papyrus Oxyrhynchus 849 (see above, p. 278); ( ) = explanatory additions by the translator; < > = restorations.

1. Cf. Mk. 6:55; Mt. 4:24; Acts 5:16, etc.
2. Cf. Mt. 11:5.
3. On the whole scene cf. Mk. 2:1-12 and pars.
4. The content of the two missing pages is outlined by Parrott (op. cit. 484f.) on the basis of the passage from Augustine quoted above, p. 276 as follows: 'Ptolemy, in his passionate desire, apparently abducted the girl and was about to force her to have intercourse with him (thus making her his wife without the parents' consent - Deut. 22:28-29), when she was suddenly paralysed by a divine act that had been sought by Peter in prayer.'
5. Cf. 1 Tim. 5:2.
6. Cf. 1 Cor. 12:13.
7. Here C. Schmidt assumes a lacuna (*Die alten Petrusakten*, 1903, 21f.).
8. So according to Brashler-Parrott, op. cit. 490.
9. Cf. Acts 5:1-11.

II. Actus Vercellenses
1. Cf. Rom. 16:23.
2. Turner: *permisit.*
3. Turner: *constituti.*
4. Cf. Acts 20:25, 38.
5. Turner: *Christum esse eum.*
6. Cf. Col. 2:8, 16, 22.
7. Lipsius: *urgebant.*
8. On the eucharist with bread and water cf. APl, above p. 252.
9. Turner: *utique.*
10. Turner: *corpore.*
11. Cf. Acts 1:24, 15:8.
12. Cf. 1 Jn. 1:9.
13. Cf. Mt. 25:30.

14. The story of Rufina is mentioned also in ps.-Titus, see above p. 55.
15. V.A.: 'You men, who have now come to believe and wish to do Christ's (war-) service.'
16. V.A.: 'Then God through his holy Son, on whom you now believe, will forgive you what you did in ignorance before you knew him.' Cf. Acts 3:17, 17-30.
17. Cf. Col. 1:15.
18. V.A.: Then you shall find grace and mercy with God who is loving towards men, and with our commander, the first-born of all creation and power, our Lord Jesus Christ.'
19. Turner: *qui vinculum inligatum <homini confregisti, qui lumen> omni saeculo.*
20. Cf. 1 Tim. 1:13.
21. Turner: *sed <et>.*
22. Cf. Phil. 4:22.
23. Lipsius proposes: *adiecerunt quia*. Since *quia* could render ὅτι, the direct speech would begin here.
24. Cf. Acts 8:10.
25. Cod. Verc.: 'But this woman (or this man, *hic*?) seeks for contention, we know.' The translation given above uses Bonnet's conjecture: *quae sit dimicatio nescimus.*
26. Cf. Acts 19:22; Phil. 2:19ff.
27. Cf. Kerygma Petri, Fragm. 3, above, p. 39.
28. Turner's punctuation.
29. Cf. Wis. 7:13: lit. 'grudging'.
30. Turner: *ex insperato casu.*
31. Cf. Acts 2:11.
32. Turner: *diaconii*; James's punctuation.
33. Cf. Jn. 20:19, 21, 26.
34. Lipsius: *lotus.*
35. Turner: *qui aperte adventum tuum.*
36. 1 Cor. 16:13.
37. Cf. Rev. 12:9.
38. Cf. Rom. 16:20.
39. Cf. Mk. 9:42 and pars.
40. The text is corrupt. The sense is: Peter could not, like Simon, cause temptation, but again he could not meet his end far away from the Roman church (*sc.* - presumably - until he had convicted Simon).
41. Cf. Rom. 16:11.
42. Turner: *discentem domini* (?).
43. Cf. Jn. 3:17.
44. V.A.: 'You men, who have put your hope in Christ, learn why God revealed his Son through the holy Virgin Mary and sent him into the world.'
45. Vouaux: *procuratio* = οἰκονομία.
46. Turner: *volens <tollere>.*
47. V.A.: 'before our Lord Jesus shone out in his world'.
48. V.A.: omits: 'Because . . . weaknesses.'
49. Turner: *ambulavi* is correct, and not to be changed, with Lipsius, to *ambulavit.*
50. Cf. Mt. 14:22ff.
51. Cf. Mk. 14:66ff. and pars.
52. Turner: *sicut ait prophetes*; cf. Ps. 21:17 (LXX).
53. Lk. 22:61.
54. Cf. the usage in Acts (9:2 and often); W. Michaelis, TDNT V, 88ff.; G. Schneider, *Die Apostelgeschichte*, II.Teil, 1982, 25f.
55. Cf. Jn. 17:12; 2 Thess. 2:3.
56. Cf. Jn. 1:18, 6:46; but there it is the Son, here the believers, who can see God.

56. Cf. Jn. 1:18, 6:46; but there it is the Son, here the believers, who can see God.
57. Turner (following Lipsius): *non sunt mea, quia cui vis ea donas.*
58. Turner: *maledixit* = ὠνείδισεν.
59. Cf. *inter alia* Rom 2:5.
60. Cf. Mt. 7:15; Acts 20:29.
61. Cf. Mk 15:2 par., noting however the different account given: Jesus is handed over not to Pilate but to the 'throng', i.e. the Jews.
62. Turner: *eris ab ecclesia.*
63. Turner: *ianuas* (for *tunicas*).
64. Cf. Jn. 10:12.
65. Cf. Acts 2:47.
66. CodVerc: *synagoga.*
67. Turner: *quacumque.*
68. Turner: *ilico.*
69. Cf. Mt. 5:44.
70. Cf. Justin, Apol. 26:2. ('Young', *iuveni*, no doubt represents νέῳ, 'new'. - G.C.S.).
71. Cf. Mk. 8:36 and pars.
72. Cf. Mt. 17:20.
73. Cf. Mt. 14:30f.
74. Turner's punctuation.
75. Cf. Jn. 10:11ff.
76. Turner: *hoc audito iuveni expulit se*; the demon is the subject.
77. Cf. Philostratus, *Vita Apoll.* IV 20.
78. Cf. Mk. 10:27 and pars.
79. Cf. 2 Pet. 2:16.
80. Cf. Mt. 8:12.
81. Turner's punctuation and reading: *angele et apostole dei veri, Petre.*
82. We cannot say what kind of fish is meant. The word *sarda* used here (a loan-word from the Greek Σάρδα) was probably originally descriptive of a sardine (or small herring), but was then employed for other salted or smoked fish also (e.g. tunny). Cf. D'Arcy W. Thompson, *A Glossary of Greek Fishes*, London 1947, 229.
83. Turner: *totum comedebat.*
84. Turner: *offenderant.*
85. Cf. Mt. 13:55.
86. Turner: *reversa est per te ad me et per quae signa.*
87. Cf. Jn. 8:44.
88. Turner: *cui nomen est autem 'numen domini'* (= δύναμις θεοῦ, cf. Acts 8:10).
89. Cf. Acts 2:11.
90. Turner: *lecto.*
91. Turner: *invenias.*
92. *refrigerium* (= ἀνάπαυσις?).
93. Cf. 2 Cor. 12:7. *Lit.* 'angel'.
94. Turner: *et quidem.*
95. Cf. 1 Tim. 6:16.
96. Cf. Isidore of Pelusium II 99 (PG 78, 544): ἃ ἐχωρήσαμεν ἐγράψαμεν.
97. Vouaux: *inferri.*
98. V.A.: 'God's mercy and kindness to men'.
99. Cf. Mk. 9:2ff. and pars.; 2 Pet. 1:18.
100. Is. 53:4.
101. Jn. 10:38.
102. V.A.: 'He ate and drank for our sakes, (and) for our sakes endured all things, because

he is kind towards men and good, who also strengthens me, who desire and require him in all things for his greatness and for the knowledge of him.'

103. Turner: *videtur*.

104. Turner: *passionem exterum et nunc est tamquam nos*.

105. V.A. (continuing from 'knowledge of him', above note 102): 'He likewise encourages you also, that you may know him and love and fear him, who is little to those who are ignorant, but great to those who know him, who is beautiful to those who understand but (appears) ugly to the ignorant, who is both old and young, who appears in time and exists for ever, who is everywhere, yet is in nothing that is unworthy of him; whom no human hand has held, yet himself holds all things, whom the flesh has not seen to this day, yet is seen with the eyes of the soul by those who are worthy of him, the Word that was proclaimed by the prophets and has now been shown forth, who is untouched by sins yet was handed over to powers and authorities, who always takes thought for us and for all who love him. This Jesus we call the door', etc.

106. V.A. (instead of 'the resurrection . . . Amen'): 'Him we also call the repose (ἀνάπαυσις), the vine, the grace, the Word (Logos) of the Father; he has indeed many names, but is in truth the one only-begotten Son of God.'

107. *refrigerium*.

108. On the individual titles cf. Jn. 10:7, 9; 3:19; 8:12; 14:6; 6:35; 4:10; 7:38; 14:6; 11:25; Mt. 11:28; 13:46; 44, 24 [refs. listed in order of titles]; 13:31; Jn. 15:1; Lk. 9:62; Jn. 1:1, 14.

109. Turner: *surgentes* (for *credentes*).

110. V.A.: 'We too entreat our Master and Lord Jesus Christ to show through you his merciful kindness to us also.'

111. Turner: *interiores* (for *non omnes*).

112. V.A.: 'If your faith is as you say, established in him, then see him with the eyes of your heart, and if these your outward eyes be satisfied, then those of your soul shall be opened. And if now those eyes of yours are opened, they shall be closed again, and recovering their sight they shall see nothing but outward things, that is men and cattle and other animals and stones and sticks; but Jesus, who is truly God, these eyes were not designed to see.'

113. In V.A. only one widow returns each answer; but the answers largely correspond with the text of the Act. Verc.

114. Turner: *constat*.

115. Vouaux: *conlocutio dei* = προσηγορία θεοῦ.

116. Bonnet: *sordidis pannis*.

117. Cf. Acts 8:18ff.

118. Cf. Mt. 16:17-19(?).

119. Cf. Mk. 6:3 and pars.

120. Is. 53:8.

121. Is. 53:2 ('form nor comeliness', AV).

122. Unknown quotation.

123. Cf. Tertullian, *de Carne Christi* XXIII 2; Clem. Alex. *Strom.*, VII 16.94; NTApo[2] 388.

124. Turner: part of the quotation from Isaiah 7:13 has been omitted.

125. Is. 7:14.

126. Ascension of Isaiah 11:13f. (see below, p. 618).

127. Unknown; cf. Vouaux, p. 369.

128. Dan. 2:34.

129. Ps. 118:22; cf. Mk. 12:10 and pars.

130. Is. 28:16.

131. Dan. 7:13; cf. Mk. 13:26 and pars.

132. Cf. Lk. 7:11ff.

133. Vouaux: *duc te* = ὕπαγε.

134. Turner: *illa autem hoc audiens*.

135. PapOx (which begins here): '<inspected the boy's nostrils, to see> if . . . '
136. Pap Ox: 'the old woman' (in place of 'his mother').
137. Pap Ox: 'Now if you are willing, mother, and have confidence in Peter's God'.
138. Pap Ox: 'while they said these things, the prefect looking closely at Peter <. . .> "See, Peter, my servant lies dead."'
139. Pap Ox: 'but I wished to test you, and the God (who is preached) by you, whether you (pl.) are truthful'.
140. Turner: *sed dilectis suis.*
141. PapOx: 'God is not tested or proved, Agrippa; but being loved and entreated he listens to those who are worthy. But since . . .' (here PapOx ends).
142. Cf. Jn. 17:11.
143. Lk. 7:14.
144. Cf. Acts 3:12.
145. Turner: *inclinans se ter, ter erigens ostendit . . . aperientem et inclinantem se Simonem. illi . . .* (?). The passage is still obscure. The essential point is that Simon has to use all kinds of techniques, whereas Peter performs similar actions by a single word of command (cf. Vouaux, pp. 386f., n. 3).
146. Cf. Mk. 9:43.
147. Rom. 12:17; 1 Thess. 5:15.
148. Cf. Mt. 5:44.
149. Turner: *nunc.*
150. Cf. Acts 16:15.
151. Turner: *ire ad.*
152. Cf. Rom. 12:1.
153. On the transmission of this part of the APt, which became independent at an early date, see above, p. 278. A translation is given here of the Greek text published by Lipsius-Bonnet. The numerous deviations in CodVerc, which frequently rest on misunderstandings by the translator, cannot be noted here, any more than the variants in the different versions (Slavonic, Coptic, Armenian etc.), most of which in any case begin only with c. 33 (4).
154. Cf. Acts 2:47.
155. In CodVerc the man raised up is called Nicostratus here as in c. 28, whereas in the Greek version the name is Stratonicus.
156. Cf. Clem. Alex., *Strom.* II. 11.52; Hippolytus, *Ref.* VI. 17.
157. Cf. Jn. 20:17.
158. Cf. Mt. 23:37; Jn. 8:59; Acts 14:19.
159. Cf. 2 Cor. 12:7.
160. Cf. Acts 2:47.
161. Cf. Jn. 13:36.
162. Cf. 2 Tim. 2:4.
163. Cf. Mt. 16:27.
164. Cf. vol. I, p. 213.
165. Quotation of unknown origin; cf. Vouaux, pp. 449f.
166. Cf. 1 Cor. 2:9; Gospel of Thomas, 17; see vol. I, p. 119.
167. Cf. Mk. 15:42ff. and pars.
168. On this passage cp. Cullmann, *Peter*[2], p. 176 (ET 1962, p. 155).
169. Cf. Mt. 8:22.
170. Cf. Acts 2:46.

5. The Acts of Thomas

Han J.W. Drijvers

Introduction[1]

1. Literature: Of the older literature the following are still important: C. Thilo, *Acta S. Thomae Apostoli*, 1823 (an antiquated edition of the text with a valuable commentary); R.A. Lipsius, *Die apokryphen Apostelgeschichten und Apostellegenden* I, 1883 (reprint, Amsterdam 1976), 225-347; W. Bousset, *Hauptprobleme der Gnosis* (FRLANT 10), 1907; id., 'Manichäisches in den Thomasakten', ZNW 18, 1917/18, 1-39; R. Reitzenstein, *Das iranische Erlösungsmysterium*, 1921. Further literature on the ATh in NTApo[1] (473ff.; NTApoHdb 562ff.: R. Raabe and E. Preuschen), NTApo[2] (256ff.: W.Bauer) and NTApo[3] (297ff.: G. Bornkamm [ET 425f.]); R. Söder, *Die apokryphen Apostelgeschichten und die romanhafte Literatur der Antike* (Würzburger Studien zur Altertumswissenschaft 3), 1932; G. Bornkamm, *Mythos und Legende in den apokryphen Thomasakten. Beiträge zur Geschichte der Gnosis und zur Vorgeschichte des Manichäismus* (FRLANT NF 31), 1933. The gnostic interpretation of the ATh is found in G. Widengren's works, *inter alia*: *The Great Vohu Manah and the Apostle of God. Studies in Iranian and Manichaean Religion* (UUA 5), 1945; id., *Mesopotamian Elements in Manichaeism* (UUA 3), 1946; id., 'Der iranische Hintergrund der Gnosis', ZRGG 4, 1952, 98-114; H. Jonas, *Gnosis und spätantiker Geist, I. Die mythologische Gnosis* (FRLANT NF 33), [2]1954; A. Adam, *Die Psalmen des Thomas und das Perlenlied als Zeugnisse vorchristlicher Gnosis* (BZNW 24), 1959. The same position is maintained by E. Plümacher, 'Apokryphe Apostelakten', in PW Suppl. XV, 1978, 'Thomasakten', cols. 34-43, and W. Foerster, *Die Gnosis*, vol. 1, 'Zeugnisse der Kirchenvater', 1969, 430-467 (ET *Gnosis*, 1972, 337-364). The piety and theology of the ATh are discussed by G. Blond, 'L'encratisme dans les actes apocryphes de Thomas', *Recherches et Travaux* I, 1946, No.2, 5-25; C.L. Sturhahn, *Die Christologie der ältesten apokryphen Apostelakten. Ein Beitrag zur Frühgeschichte des altkirchlichen Dogmas*, Theol. Diss. Heidelberg 1952, 51-89, 102-127; A. Hamman, '*Sitz im Leben* des actes apocryphes du Nouveau Testament', *Studia Patristica* VIII (TU 93), 1966, 62-69. For the relation of the ATh to Manicheism cf. P. Nagel, 'Die apokryphen Apostelakten des 2. und 3. Jahrhunderts in der manichäischen Literatur. Ein Beitrag zur Frage nach den christlichen Elementen im Manichäismus', *Gnosis und Neues Testament*, 1975, 149-182; J.-D. Kaestli, 'L'utilisation des actes apocryphes des apôtres dans le manichéisme', in M. Krause (ed.), *Gnosis and Gnosticism* (Nag Hammadi Studies VIII), 1977, 107-116. Thomas's connections with India: A. Dihle, 'Neues zur Thomas-Tradition', JbAC 6, 1963, 54-70; (quite uncritical is J.N. Farquhar in BJRL X, 80-111; XI, 20-50, see J. Vellian (ed.), *The Apostle Thomas in India according to the Acts of Thomas*, Kerala 1972); E. Junod, 'Gli Apocrifi cristiani e cristianizzati', *Augustinianum* 23, 1983, 284f.; Matthias Lipinski, *Konkordanz zu den Thomasakten* (Bonner Bibl. Beiträge 67), 1987; G. Fiaccadorii, 'Tommaso in Etiopia', *Studi Classici e Orientali* 34, 1984, 298-307; M. Bussagli, 'The Apostle Thomas and India', *East and West* NS 3, 1952, 88-94; G. Huxley, 'Geography in the Acts of Thomas', *Greek, Roman and Byzantine Studies* 24, 1983, 76ff.; N. Sorge, 'Le traslazioni delle reliquie dell'Apostolo Tommaso', *Miscellanea A. Pertusi* II, Bologna 1982, 147ff.; L. van Kampen, 'Apostelverhalen. Doel en compositie van de oudste apokriefe Handelingen der apostelen' (Diss. Utrecht 1990): 'De handelingen van Thomas', 165-200.

For the literary and religious symbolism of the ATh cf. J.A. Delaunay, 'Rite et symbolique en ACTA THOMAE *vers. syr. I, 2a et ss.*, in: Ph. Gignoux (ed.), *Mémorial Jean de Menasce*, Acta Iranica, Teheran 1974, 11-34; J.M. LaFargue, *Language and Gnosis: The Opening Scenes of the Acts of Thomas* (Harvard Dissertations in Religion 18), Philadelphia 1985; Y.

Tissot, 'Les Actes apocryphes de Thomas: exemple de recueil composite', in: F. Bovon *et al.*, *Les Actes apocryphes des apôtres. Christianisme et monde païen*, 1981, 223-232.

2. Transmission, editions of the text and translations: the ATh came into being at the beginning of the 3rd century in East Syria, and were originally composed in Syriac. This original version, which was probably at once translated into Greek, as was the case with other writings in this bilingual area, has not survived. In general preference is given to the extant Greek text, published by M. Bonnet on the basis of 21 MSS[2] (*Acta Apostolorum Apocrypha* II 2, 1903; reprint 1959, 99-288). The Syriac version, edited and translated on the basis of a London MS by W. Wright, *Apocryphal Acts of the Apostles*, London 1871 (reprint Amsterdam 1968) I, 171ff. (Syriac), II, 146ff. (English), displays a catholicising revision, but has certainly also preserved much that is original (cf. A.F.J. Klijn, *The Acts of Thomas. Introduction - Text - Commentary*, Suppl. 5 to *Novum Testamentum*, 1962, 1-17; Y. Tissot in *Les Actes apocryphes des apôtres*, 1981, 223-232). P. Bedjan (*Acta martyrorum et sanctorum* III, 1892, 3ff.) prepared a new edition of the Syriac text (on the basis of a Berlin MS). Older fragments in A. Smith Lewis, *Acta mythologica apostolorum*, Hor. Sem. III-IV, 1904; partly already published by F.C. Burkitt, Studia Sinaitica IX, 1900, 24-44. The literary dependence of the ATh on a Syriac version of the Acts of John, assumed by E. Junod and J.-D. Kaestli (*L'Histoire des actes apocryphes des apôtres du IIIe au IXe siècle: Le cas des actes de Jean*, Geneva 1982, 35ff.), can be better explained from the common background of tradition and milieu shared by the two Acts (cf. K. Schäferdiek, ZNW 74, 1983, 249ff.). Some parallels between the ATh and the Acts of Paul are also better explained in this way than on the assumption of literary dependence or influence, with which E. Peterson thinks we must reckon ('Einige Bemerkungen zum Hamburger Papyrusfragment der Acta Pauli', *VigChr* 3, 1949, 142-162 = *Frühkirche, Judentum und Gnosis*, 1959, 183-208; cf. also P. Devos, 'Actes de Thomas et Actes de Paul', *AnalBoll* 69, 1951, 119-130 and Klijn, *The Acts of Thomas*, 24f.).

Comparison of the Syriac and the Greek texts shows that the history of the text and its transmission are extremely complicated, since the various versions of the ATh were continually interpolated, revised and reworked, and in this way adapted to religious developments in the Syriac area and outside of it. The manifold history of the text thus reflects the gradual stratification of orthodoxy and heresy which was set in motion in this East Syrian area particularly by Manicheism (cf. Drijvers, *East of Antioch. Studies in Early Syriac Christianity*, 1984, I. 'Forces and Structures in the Development of Early Syriac Theology').

The ATh belong to the corpus of the five apocryphal Acts which the Manichees incorporated into their canon, rejecting the New Testament Acts. At the end of the 4th century this group of apostolic Acts is attested for the first time by Philaster of Brescia (*de Haer*. 88.6). Photius (*Bibl.* cod. 114) ascribes their authorship to one Leucius Charinus, who probably ranked in Manichean circles from the beginning of the 5th century as their legendary author (cf. K. Schäferdiek, above pp. 92ff. and E. Junod, 'Actes apocryphes et hérésie: le jugement de Photius', in F. Bovon *et al.*, *Les Actes apocryphes des apôtres*, 11-24). At any rate the ATh were intensively read by the Manichees, as is clear from the Manichean Psalm-Book (cf. Nagel, 'Die apokryphen

Apostelakten des 2. und 3. Jahrhunderts in der manichäischen Literatur' 171ff.) and also documented elsewhere (Augustine, *c. Faust.* 22.79; *c. Adimant.* 17.2.5; *de Sermone domini in monte* I 19.65; Turribius of Astorga, *Epist. ad Idac. et Cepon.* 6).

Epiphanius mentions the use of the ATh by encratite sects (*Haer.* 47.1; 61.1). Yet the ATh also enjoyed great popularity in orthodox circles, as is shown by the later revisions in Latin (K. Zelser, 'Zu den latein. Fassungen der Th. Akten', *Wiener Stud.* N.F. V, 1971, 161-179; VI, 1972, 185-212), Armenian, Coptic, Arabic and Ethiopic (cf. Klijn, *The Acts of Thomas*, 8ff.; BHO 260-265; P.-H. Poirier, *La version copte de la Prédication et du martyre de Thomas*, Brussels 1984; M. van Esbroeck, 'Les actes apocryphes de Thomas en version arabe', *Parole de l'Orient* 14, 1987, 11-77).

The ATh have frequently been translated into modern languages. There are German translations in NTApo[1-2-3], an English in James, [6]1955, 364-438, and an Italian in Erbetta II, 1967, 313-374. A.J. Festugière has published a French translation (*Les actes apocryphes de Jean et de Thomas. Trad. française et notes critiques*, Geneva 1983, 45-117) and there is a Dutch one in A.F.J. Klijn (ed.), *Apokriefen van het Nieuwe Testament* II, Kampen 1985, 56-160. The Syriac version has been translated into English by W. Wright, *The Apocryphal Acts of the Apostles* II, 146-298, and by A.F.J. Klijn, *The Acts of Thomas*, 1962, 65-154.[3] A new edition of the Greek text, with due attention to the Syriac, is being prepared for the Corpus Christianorum by P.H. Poirier and Y. Tissot (with translation and commentary). A translation of the Armenian version of the ATh is published in the same Corpus by L. Leloir (CChr SA vol. 4). On the transmission of the Wedding Hymn and the Hymn of the Pearl contained in the ATh, and on their translations, see below, pp. 329ff.; 380ff.

3. The apostle Thomas: in the ATh and related writings like the Coptic Gospel of Thomas and the Book of Thomas the Athlete (cf. vol. 1, pp. 110-133, 232-247), the apostle is called Judas Thomas, Judas the Twin. The name occurs also in the Old Syriac of John 14:22 and in the Abgar legend (cf. vol. 1, pp. 492-500), and indicates that in the East Syrian region Judas, the brother of James the Lord's brother, was identified with Judas 'not Iscariot' and treated as a twin brother of Jesus, who is moreover mentioned as Thomas Didymus in the Fourth Gospel (cf. A.F.J. Klijn, 'John XIV 22 and the Name Judas Thomas', *Studies in John pres. to J.N. Sevenster*, 1970, 88-96; H.-Ch. Puech, *En quête de la gnose*, II. 'Sur l'évangile selon Thomas', 1978, 42ff.; J.J. Gunther, 'The Meaning and Origin of the Name "Judas Thomas"', *Le Muséon* 93, 1980, 113ff.). In the ATh Judas Thomas (the name appears as 'Ιούδας Θωμᾶς, 'Ιούδας ὁ καὶ Θωμᾶς, 'Ιούδας Θωμᾶς ὁ καὶ Δίδυμος) ranks as twin brother of Jesus, whom he is like in appearance (c. 11, 34, 45, 57, 147-153) but also in his destiny and his works (c. 31, 39, 123). As in related literature (Epist. Apost. 42f.; Pistis Sophia 42f.; prologue and logion 13 of the Coptic Gospel of Thomas and preamble to the Book of Thomas the Athlete), Judas Thomas appears in the ATh as the recipient and mediator of special revelations (c. 10, 47, 78 and especially 39: ὁ δίδυμος τοῦ Χριστοῦ, ὁ ἀπόστολος τοῦ ὑψίστου καὶ συμμύστης τοῦ λόγου τοῦ Χριστοῦ τοῦ ἀποκρύφου, ὁ δεχόμενος αὐτοῦ τὰ ἀπόκρυφα λόγια). There are also several other connections in terms of content between the different Thomas documents, which point to an origin in the same area and the same spiritual climate (cf. Puech, *En quête de la gnose* II. 'Sur l'évangile selon Thomas', *passim* and esp. 43ff.; cf. logion 13 and

ATh 47; logion 37 and ATh 14; J.D. Turner, *The Book of Thomas the Contender*, 1975, 233ff.). In the East Syrian region, the centre of which is Osrhoëne and Edessa, there evidently developed a form of Christianity in which the 'twin' motif was a constitutive factor. This central motif occasioned the characteristic naming of the apostle Judas, the twin brother of Jesus, or briefly Judas Thomas. A tradition preserved in Eusebius (*HE* III 1.1) and going back to Origen describes Thomas as the apostle of Parthia, a point which is also attested elsewhere and must rank as the oldest tradition about Thomas's mission area (cf. E. Junod, 'Origène, Eusèbe et la tradition sur la répartition des champs de mission des apôtres', in F. Bovon *et al.*, *Les actes apocryphes des apôtres*, 233-248; Lipsius, *Die apokryphen Apostelgeschichten* I, 225ff.). In full agreement with this tradition the Syriac *Doctrina Addai* reports that, after the Ascension of Jesus, Judas Thomas sent the apostle Addai to Edessa (cf. vol. 1, pp. 492ff.). Edessa was known as the daughter of Parthia (cf. Cureton, *Ancient Syriac Documents*, 41; Rubens Duval, *Histoire d'Edesse*, 29), and belonged culturally and for a time politically to the Parthian realm (cf. Drijvers, ANRW II.8, 885ff.). If Origen is the first to mention the tradition about Thomas as the apostle of Parthia, we are again at the beginning of the 3rd century, in a period in which the Thomas literature came into being in East Syria, the daughter of Parthia. Judas Thomas as the apostle of India, as the ATh describe him, is entirely legendary; this owes its origin to the lively cultural and commercial relations of Edessa and Osrhoëne with North India, which particularly at the beginning of the 3rd century were very intensive (cf. Drijvers, ANRW II.8, 893ff.). According to Porphyry (*FGrHist* III, C 719, F.1) the Edessene philosopher Bardaisan composed a book about India and the customs practised there. He owed his knowledge to an Indian embassy to the emperor Elagabalus (218-222), with whom he had detailed discussions. That is why the ATh in their legendary frame-story show a certain familiarity with historical figures like the Indian king Gundaphorus (cf. v.Gutschmid, *Kleine Schriften* II, 332ff.; A. Dihle, 'Neues zur Thomas-tradition', JbAC 6, 1963, 54-70; id., 'The Conception of India in Hellenistic and Roman Literature', *Proc. Cambr. Phil. Soc.* 1964, 15-23). The Martyrdom of Judas Thomas, which also circulated independently, is likewise attested for the first time in the ATh, as is the transference of his bones to the West, i.e. Edessa, of which Ephraem Syrus also reports (*Carm. Nis.* 42) and which is further attested by the pilgrim Egeria, who visited Edessa in 384 (*Itin. Eger.* 17.1; 19.3; cf. P. Devos in *AnalBoll* 85, 1967, 381-400; Drijvers, TRE IX, 282f.; G. Garitte, 'La passion arménienne de S. Thomas l'apôtre et son modèle grec', *Le Muséon* 84, 1971, 171-195).

4. The literary character of the ATh: the ATh comprise altogether 13 Praxeis and end with the martyrdom of the apostle.[4] In the first Praxeis, which are loosely strung together and also have no uniform scene of action, there is a motley mixture of miracle stories, fantastic deeds of the apostle, conversions, nature miracles and stories of demons, which are akin to the novelistic narrative art of the ancient world (cf. R. Söder, *Die apokryphen Apostelgeschichten und die romanhafte Literatur der Antike, passim*; R. Helm, *Der antike Roman*, 1948, 53-56, 115ff.; Plümacher, op. cit. col. 63; B.P. Reardon, *Courants littéraires grecs de IIe et IIIe siècle après J.-C.*, 1971; cf. also above, pp. 78ff.). To this extent the figure of the apostle Thomas is approximated to the late-antique type of the 'divine man' (cf. L. Bieler, ΘΕΙΟΣ

ANHP. *Das Bild des "göttlichen Menschen" in Spätantike und Frühchristentum*, 1935-36, reprint 1976). In addition the ATh, often in a very subtle fashion, employ biblical motifs and allude to particular Old Testament and New Testament pericopes, which in like manner determine the structure of the narrative and its inherent purpose, and are recognisable only to those in the know or initiates (cf. Delaunay, 'Rite et symbolique en ACTA THOMAE *vers. syr. 1, 2a et ss.*; LaFargue, *Language and Gnosis: The Opening Scenes of the Acts of Thomas*). The different narratives, the sequence of which certainly is not arbitrary, could thus be read and interpreted in a symbolic and typological way, for which every detail has a meaning within the whole, even though much still remains obscure. To this artfully worked out literary structure and arrangement there belongs also the frequent use of particular words and terms in different contexts, which still refer to one another and give to the whole a quite definite meaning, because they shed light on one another. Words and concepts from a narrative often recur in the numerous liturgical passages, in the apostle's sermons, in the prayers and hymns, and through this an interpretation is suggested. The first Praxis may serve as an example. After an introduction in which it is related how the apostles divided the regions of the earth among themselves by lot, and India fell to Judas Thomas (cf. J.-D. Kaestli, 'Les scènes d'attribution des champs de mission et de départ de l'apôtre dans les Actes apocryphes', in F. Bovon *et al.*, *Les Actes apocryphes des apôtres*, 249-264), Thomas declines 'because of weakness of the flesh' to set out on his journey. After an appearance in the night the Lord Jesus sells his slave Judas to the merchant Abban, who had been sent by king Gundaphorus to buy a carpenter, at the price of three pounds (of silver; the Syriac version here reads twenty silver pieces). Jesus brings Judas Thomas to Abban, who asks him: 'Is this your master?' To which the apostle replies: 'Yes, he is my Lord.' Thereupon Abban says: 'I have bought you from him.' And the apostle is silent. Next morning the apostle, carrying only his purchase price with him, goes to the merchant Abban, and together they sail with a favourable wind to Andrapolis, a royal city (the Syriac here reads Sandaruk). The sale of Judas relates to Judas Iscariot, who sold his Lord, and introduces the passion motif which is dominant in the whole of the first Praxis (cf. Delaunay, 'Rite et symbolique'). The roles are reversed, and the Lord sells Judas, but gives him his purchase price (in contrast to Judas Iscariot; cf. 1 Cor. 6:20: 'You are bought with a price').[5] The merchant, who was sent to buy a carpenter (cf. Jesus as a carpenter, as Judas too is a carpenter), is again related to the merchant in the biblical parable of the merchant who bought the pearl, and so the motif of the kingdom of God is introduced. When Jesus, the son of Joseph, sells his brother Judas to a merchant, this also refers to Gen. 37, where Joseph is sold into Egypt as a slave by his brothers (the twenty silver pieces of the Syriac version agree with Gen. 37:28). Thus a central place in the narrative is given to the motif of Egypt and the deliverance from slavery, the Exodus, which played a large role in biblical typology in the patristic period (cf. Daniélou, *Sacramentum Futuri*, 1950, 131ff.). When Judas at first declines to go and then travels by ship to Andrapolis (Man-city), he is like Jonah, who did not want to go to Nineveh. As is well known, the typology of Jonah and Jesus was widespread (cf. Mt. 12:39-41; Lk. 11:30). Read in this way, the first Praxis takes on an almost programmatic form, and announces in very subtle allusions the central theme of the ATh.

It therefore does not seem justified to describe the ATh - as is widely done - as popular literature, in which we can recognise motifs of the ancient novel in a popular and cruder form. Rather they came into being in a learned milieu, to which symbolism and typology were familiar and in which a certain form of biblical exegesis had already developed, which comes to light also in other writings from the same area in space and time (cf. Drijvers, *East of Antioch. Studies in Early Syriac Christianity*, 1984, *passim*). An analysis of the other six first Praxeis could confirm this characterisation of the literary, symbolic and typological structure, which is welded into a unity, as it were subterraneously, by all kinds of allusions.

In the second part of the ATh (7th to 13th Praxeis) the court of king Misdai is the scene of the action, which is aimed solely at conversion to *enkrateia*. There the *kerygma* of the ATh is fully displayed, since ultimately all the personages at the royal court are converted, even king Misdai after the death of the apostle. The ATh thus form a literary unity which was created in a highly artistic manner by a redactor. All the narratives and the liturgical sections connected with them, prayers, sermons, epicleses and hymns, present the mystery of salvation and the way to become a partaker of it. Even if individual narratives may have come into being and circulated separately, the whole is so uniform both in terminology and in motif that we must think of its origin as all of a piece; the author or redactor has employed themes from the realm of the ancient novel and biblical motifs for his symbolic presentation of salvation. This applies also to the two hymns incorporated into the ATh, the bridal hymn in the first Praxis and the Hymn of the Pearl in the ninth, which lay before the author already complete and were incorporated by him at appropriate points because in terms of content they correspond fully with his world of ideas. It is not possible to identify other sources in the ATh, although in c.91 there is an exact parallel to Bardaisan's *Book of the Laws of the Countries*, which might indicate use of this book or origin in related circles, especially there are traces of Bardaisan's world of thought in cc. 32, 82 and 148 also.

5. The theology of the ATh: the apostle Thomas's preaching, in symbolic and exemplary acts and didactic and explanatory sermons and prayers, is resolutely soteriological throughout. Man in this world is subject to death, to sexuality and to earthly appetites, tormented (c. 32) and even slain (cc. 30, 31) by demons, the sons of Satan, the ruler of this world; his whole life can be described as sickness and corruption (c. 15). He lives in darkness and filthy passion (c. 13), and no longer knows how and what he originally was (c. 15). The contrast between his wretched bodily and sexual life and the spiritual, immortal existence in rest is repeatedly painted in the most glaring colours (cc. 28, 38, 124). The earthly existence of mankind is dominated by ignorance and error, and continually exposed to the attacks of the enemy. The enemy symbolises evil in the cosmos and in the creation, over which he has acquired a measure of power (c. 32). He has many forms (c. 44), and appears as the serpent in paradise, makes Cain a murderer, hardens the heart of Pharaoh, brings Judas to the point of delivering Christ to death (c. 32); he has the demons as his sons, and manifests himself in particular in two forms, as an unsightly old man and a seductive youth who sexually threaten the women (cc. 43, 44, 64). The demons fulfil the will of him who sent them, i.e. the enemy (c. 76), who seeks to enter into men and divide their thoughts (c. 160). The enemy is thus the continuing temptation which throws men into doubt, as it did in paradise and thus brought death and the sexuality bound up with it into the world. Adam and Eve made the wrong choice, used their free will wrongly, and thereby became mortal and were compelled to bring forth children in pain and suffering (c. 12). But God has kept immortality and life ready for them as their true nature (c. 15, 43). The original human nature as God intended it is thus immortal, and therefore asexual. The preaching of *enkrateia* has as its aim the restoration of that original condition. Man has freedom of will, and is therefore in a position to make the right choice, to undo the Fall. Here he is aided by Jesus the Redeemer, who is the Helper *par excellence* (c. 60, 66, 81). Jesus in his earthly life overthrew the enemy (c. 10), that is, he did not succumb to temptation (c. 32). In his humble and even unsightly human form he deceived the enemy, and took his power from him (c. 45). Like the enemy, Jesus the Redeemer also has many forms (cf. D.R. Cartlidge, 'Transfigurations of Metamorphosis Traditions in the Acts of John, Thomas and Peter', in D.R. MacDonald, *The Apocryphal Acts of Apostles*, Semeia 38, 1986, 53-66). He can appear as Judas Thomas (c. 34 and elsewhere), but usually manifests himself as a youthfully handsome and radiant young man (cc. 8, 27, 35, 36, 80, 149). Jesus is the helper of those who believe in him, their guide and companion (cc. 10, 80, 37, 39 etc.), the commander of their army (c. 39), the good shepherd (c. 39), their ally in dangers (c. 119), since he himself has fought the enemy in battle (c. 10) and appeared as a true and invincible champion (c. 39). He heals the faithful from death, since he is physician and bringer of life (c. 10, 15, 25, 34 etc.); he is their refuge, their haven and their rest (c. 10, 27, 37 etc.). He reveals to his own the heavenly mysteries (c. 10, 47), is the herald of what is hidden (c.78) and thus the destroyer of error (c. 38, 39, 80). The faithful sin no longer, since sin is mere ignorance (c. 59). They have learned from the Redeemer and his twin brother Judas Thomas (c. 31) how and who the enemy is and how he can be overcome, namely in *enkrateia*, in holiness (c. 12, 28, 85, 86), which sets men again in rest, the paradisal asexual immortality. Instead of bodily wedlock the ATh preach the heavenly marriage, which is contracted in the heavenly bridal chamber of immortality and light with the true Man, i.e. with the Redeemer Jesus (c. 12-14). The broadly depicted stories about the wife of Charisius in the ninth Praxis, Mygdonia in the tenth, the wife of Misdai in the eleventh and about the king's son Vazan and his wife in the twelfth and thirteenth Praxeis make clear the fundamental opposition between the earthly and the heavenly marriage, between death and life, darkness and light, error and truth (cc. 88, 93, 98, 117, 124, 135). The heavenly marriage is union with Christ in the form of the Spirit (cf. 1 Cor. 6:17) or the Word of God, as it is clearly expressed in c. 88, where the apostle Thomas prays 'that the word of God may settle upon all and tabernacle in you'. In c. 93 he uses the image of the Lord rising as the sun in the soul, or being received into the soul, i.e. the Lord unites himself as Spirit with the human soul (cf. c. 98 'Lord Jesus, who is with me and rests in me').

The ATh are thus characterised by a dualism which has primarily an ethical and soteriological orientation, and has human freedom as its centre. The enemy has no power of his own which is independent of God the Creator; he is a fallen angel whose power beneath the heavens is only tolerated and gains prevalence when men submit to it (c. 32). This to my mind is clear from the formulation in c. 32, where the demon says 'I am the son of him who smote the four standing brothers (τοὺς τέσσαρας ἀδελφοὺς τοὺς ἑστῶτας).' The four standing brothers are the four archangels who stand before God's throne (cf. Job 1:6; Lk. 1:19; Jn. 8:44; 2 Enoch 29.4-5; Bousset-Gressmann, *Religion des Judentums im neutestamentlichen Zeitalter* [4]1966, 335f.). They could also be identified with the four elements (*stoicheia*) (2 Enoch 15; 16.7; cf. Diehls, *Elementum*, 1899, 41-57; Bousset- Gressmann, op. cit. 323f.). Then we must assume in addition to early Jewish and Christian angelology the influence of Bardaisan's cosmology (Drijvers, *Bardaisan of Edessa*, 1966, 96ff.), according to which the darkness through chance destroys the harmony of the other elements, as a result of which the origin of the world comes about. Angelology and Bardaisan's cosmology lead to the idea of the four standing brothers, who are injured by the fifth.

The dualism of the ATh has its sphere of validity within the temporally limited frame of the creation, hence within the sphere of freedom, and is also picked up again within the creation. The enemy, the prince of this world, has no power of his own, but evil, death, sickness and temptation only become real when man in the freedom with which he was created surrenders to them (c. 32) and offers them the opportunity to manifest themselves. Hence the acts of the apostle lay open the merely ephemeral existence of death, sickness and the demonic temptations. They are all abolished through the powerful word of the Redeemer and brought to naught, and the original condition of man is thereby restored (c. 14, 15 etc.). This restoration has two aspects. Under the one it is brought about as a process of knowledge. Man comes to know the truth of God and also himself, that he was created for immortality and through a wrong choice has given room within the creation to death and sickness and bodily passions. Under the other it is accomplished as a renunciation of sexuality, i.e. of death, and as a conflict against the demons. Through this man's original likeness to God, his immortality, is restored.

The ATh thus have no soteriology in the strict sense of a doctrine of a redeemer. Terms like sin and grace do not occur. The incarnation, crucifixion, resurrection and ascension of Christ are not mentioned. Every man can freely achieve his own redemption, in so far as he appropriates to himself the knowledge of the truth and renounces sexuality. In this process the redeemer is a teacher, an example of how man was actually intended to be, and how he can again become what he was in the beginning. The beginning and end of the human predicament (man's 'lostness') are an act of human freedom, and hence knowledge of the truth.

This basic structure of the ATh, which is presented in a symbolic and typological way in the deeds of the apostle, is also the principal theme of the two famous hymns in the ATh, the Wedding Hymn in the first Praxis (c. 6f.) and the Hymn of the Pearl in the ninth (c. 108-113).

6a. The Wedding Hymn is sung by the apostle Judas Thomas at the banquet held by the king of Andrapolis in honour of the marriage of his daughter, to which all men are invited by heralds (cf. Mt. 22:1-14). Judas Thomas disguises himself as the suffering Christ while he reclines in the midst of the guests, so that the wedding banquet symbolises both the royal wedding feast and also the Last Supper. Following the prophetic words which he speaks to the cup-bearer who has struck him (cf. Mt. 26:68 par.; Jn. 18:22; 19:3), and which are meant as words from the cross, the apostle sings the Wedding Hymn. After the hymn his appearance has changed (c. 8). He fixes his eyes on the ground and pays no further attention to anyone, 'waiting for the time when he might take his departure'. This last clause refers to the ascension from the cross: the silent apostle, who looks only at the ground, represents the dead Christ on the Cross. Through the insertion of the Wedding Hymn the redactor of the ATh effects a transition from the wedding of the king's daughter to the marriage of Christ and the Church, 'the daughter of light', for which he has given himself (cf. Eph 5:25-27; 2 Cor. 11:2; R. Murray, *Symbols of Church and Kingdom. A Study in Early Syriac Tradition*, 1975, 131ff.; H. Kruse, 'Das Brautlied der syrischen Thomas-Akten', OCP 50, 1984, 291-330). In the Church, which is represented as a cosmic phenomenon, like the heavenly Jerusalem (cf. Rev. 19:6-8; 21:2ff.; 21:9ff.), the bride of the Lamb, the heavenly marriage of the faithful is celebrated. United with Christ, the living Spirit, they praise the Father and the Mother, i.e. God and the Holy Spirit, who in the Syrian tradition is often represented as a mother (cf. Murray, *Symbols of Church and Kingdom*, 142ff.). When in the Syriac version of the Wedding Hymn the maiden, the daughter of light, is described *expressis verbis* as the Church, that is a correct interpretation, which corresponds to the intentions of the poet, although the Syriac text otherwise catholicises throughout. In the text of the Wedding Hymn there are numerous references to the frame-story which could underpin the interpretation of the hymn here proposed. The fingers of the bride open the gates of the *city*, i.e. the heavenly Jerusalem (cf. Rev. 21:9-14). The city however also points to Andrapolis, Man-city, so that the king of Andrapolis also symbolises God, the heavenly King (cf. Rev. 19:6ff.), in whose city the marriage of his daughter is celebrated. The Wedding Hymn has thus been inserted in its correct place in the first Praxis, because it both interprets the events preceding and also sets the following wedding of the king's daughter in its proper context. In other words, the Wedding Hymn with all the allusions it contains is the cardinal point of the first Praxis, and also the interpretative clue which makes it possible to read the whole narrative likewise on two levels.

b. The Hymn of the Pearl is one of the most beautiful products of Syriac literature, and at the same time one of the most hotly debated. A gnostic interpretation of the hymn is usual, although other interpretations have been given (cf. P.-H. Poirier, *L'hymne de la perle des actes de Thomas. Introduction, Texte-Traduction, Commentaire*, 1981, where almost the entire literature is mentioned). In contrast to the Wedding Hymn, it is the Syriac version of the Hymn of the Pearl which has best preserved the original. Although the text of the ATh is handed down in six Syriac and nineteen Greek manuscripts, the Hymn of the Pearl appears only in one Syriac (BM Add. 14645) and one Greek MS (B 35 of the Biblioteca Vallicelliana in Rome) (cf. P.-H. Poirier, '*L'Hymne de la Perle* des Actes de Thomas: Étude de la tradition manuscrite', *OrChrAn* 205, Rome 1978, 19-29). In the Syriac MS BM Add. 14645 a long doxology of the Father and the Son follows the Hymn of the Pearl; it also appears in two other Syriac MSS of the ATh, but is completely lacking in the Greek tradition. In contrast to the Greek MS, the Hymn in BM Add. 14645 is rounded off by a colophon and bears a title of its own. This discovery indicates that the Hymn of the Pearl and also the doxology is an interpolation into the ATh. In the Greek tradition the Hymn has undergone further revision, and in the process lost its title and colophon. The Hymn has preserved its original wording better in the Syriac version, including the title and the colophon. Yet we may assume that the Hymn also circulated separately under the name of Judas Thomas and must be reckoned to the Thomas literature, especially since the content agrees with the message of the ATh.

Contrary to what the usual title suggests, the pearl is not the principal theme of the Hymn. It describes, in the form of a didactic poem, the fate of a king's son who was sent from his parents' home in the East to Egypt to fetch the pearl, which was there guarded by a serpent. Before sending him, his parents had taken from him the splendid robe which he wore in the royal palace, and made a bargain with him, written in his heart, that so soon as he had fetched the pearl he was to put on his splendid robe again and be heir in the kingdom along with his brother, the crown prince. With a burden that was precious yet light, the youth made his way to Egypt, where he established himself in the neighbourhood of the serpent, as a stranger to his fellow-guests in the inn. The unclean Egyptians noted that he was not their countryman, treated him craftily, and gave him of their food to eat, so that he forgot his royal descent and the pearl, and sank into a deep slumber. His parents took note of all this, and resolved that he should not remain in Egypt. They wrote him a letter 'from thy father, the king of kings, and thy mother, the mistress of the East, and thy brother, our other son, to thee our son in Egypt, greeting!', in which they reminded him of his royal descent, the pearl, his splendid robe and the promise that he should rule with his brother in the kingdom.

The letter flew like an eagle and 'became all speech', so that the king's son woke up, and remembered his descent and the pearl. He put the serpent to sleep with a trinitarian formula, and seized the pearl. Then he made his way back to his homeland in the East, led by the letter as by a lamp and drawn on by its love. His parents sent the splendid robe to meet him, and he recognised it as his own reflection and united with it into a single form. The complete likeness of the king of kings was embroidered on the robe. Thus clothed, he came to the court and threw himself down before the majesty of his father who had sent him the robe, whose commands he had carried out, and who himself had fulfilled his promise.

This, briefly summarised, is the content of the Hymn of the Pearl, which is based on the parables of the Prodigal Son (Lk. 15:11-32) and the Pearl (Mt. 13:45-46) but reinterprets them in a quite specific sense. The Hymn is a symbolic portrayal of the life of Adam, the man who of his own free will left his Father's house, Paradise, with a part of his inheritance. His parents, God and the Holy Spirit, sent him out, and took from him the splendid robe, the image of God, which however they kept ready for him for the time when he had robbed the serpent of the pearl, that is, deprived Satan of his power (cf. Gen. 3:15-24). Then the whole process is put into reverse: he recovers his splendid robe, the image of God, and will rule with his brother, his heavenly second self, Jesus (cf. Thomas and Jesus as twins) in the (heavenly) kingdom. Man as an alien in Egypt, the world of the demons, forgets his commission and falls asleep, until a letter is sent to him, i.e. until the Gospel of Jesus takes shape. Then man knows again what his task in the world is, he seizes the pearl, the serpent (Satan) is overpowered in the name of the Father, the Holy Spirit and the Son, and since *his freedom yearns after its nature* (v. 56) he returns as a king's son to his paradisal heavenly homeland. He receives the image of God again, the lost son is once again installed, man becomes again one in a single form (v. 78; cf. ATh 15). The Hymn of the Pearl deals with man's expulsion from and his return to the paradise of God, and describes how man loses the image of God of his own free will and recovers it, how he becomes mortal and again returns to the immortality which God promised him in his covenant and holds ready for him (cf. H. Kruse, 'The Return of the Prodigal. Fortunes of a Parable on its Way to the Far East', *Orientalia* 47, 1978, 163-214). This deliverance from the demonic world is in part described with motifs borrowed from the Exodus story. The letter goes before him on his way to his homeland, and leads him with its light (cf. Exod. 13:21-22). Such borrowings of motifs often occur in early Syriac literature (cf. Drijvers, *East of Antioch* VIII, 168ff.; Daniélou, *Sacramentum Futuri*, Paris 1950, 131f.).

Another central motif in the Hymn of the Pearl is the garment. Man leaves paradise, his Father's house, without his royal robe and receives it again when he has fetched the pearl and returned to his homeland. The robe symbolises the image of God, immortality, which man recovers when he is clothed with his heavenly second self, his twin brother Jesus (cf. S. Brock, 'Clothing Metaphors as a Means of Theological Expression in Syriac Tradition', in *Typus, Symbol, Allegorie bei den östlichen Vätern und ihren Parallelen im Mittelalter*. ed. M. Schmidt (Eichstätter Beiträge 4), 1982, 11-38). The symbolism of departure and return is here combined with that of the wedding garment, which the guests wear at the heavenly bridal feast in which they are united with the heavenly bridegroom (cf. Rev. 3:5; 19:7-9). It is also found in the parable of the Prodigal Son, who on his return receives στολὴν τὴν πρώτην (Lk. 15:22).

Adam in paradise is represented as a child who has not yet quite grown up, and moreover is a king's son. Adam as a child is a familiar idea in the apocryphal Acts (Acta Andreae et Matthiae c. 18; c. 33; Act Joh. c. 73; c. 76; c. 87) and in patristic literature (Iren. *adv. Haer.* III 22.4; IV 38.1; *Demonstr.* c. 12; Theophilus, *ad Autol.* II 25; Clem. Alex. *Protr.* XI 111.1; cf. Peterson, *Frühkirche, Judentum und Gnosis*, 1959, 192ff.; Murray, *Symbols*, 304ff.). Man as a king's son is a fixed element in Syriac literature (cf. Brock, 'Clothing Metaphors', 20f. and Ephraem Syrus, Hymns *de Paradiso*, where the combination of clothing symbolism, bridal symbolism and Adam-Christ typology occurs in almost every hymn; Ephraem, Hymns *c. Haer.* 32.4: since the king had stumbled like a child, the king of kings put on the raiment of an old man).

The geographical descriptions in the Hymn of the Pearl betray acquaintance with the Parthian kingdom, and also with the caravan routes in the region of Syria and Mesopotamia. The Syriac version of the Hymn contains Persian loan-words, which however are also documented at other places in Syriac literature (cf. Widengren, *Iranisch-semitische Kulturbegegnung in parthischer Zeit*, 1960). All this is in harmony with the image of Parthia as the missionary field of Judas Thomas, and with an origin of the Hymn in Edessa, the daughter of Parthia. The milieu, geography and language of the Hymn are at any rate not incompatible with an origin in Christian East Syria about the turn from the 2nd to the 3rd century.

The main theme of the Hymn of the Pearl is exactly that of the ATh, man's return from the demonic world to that condition in which God created him, and his reunion with his brother Christ, with whom he will be heir in the kingdom (lines 15, 48, 78). The Hymn is inserted at an appropriate place in the ATh, where it is reported that the apostle Judas Thomas has been thrown into prison. Immediately after the hymn the ATh describe a dialogue between Charisius and his wife Mygdonia. Mygdonia says to him: 'He whom I love is heavenly and *will take me with him into heaven*.' Charisius *falls asleep*, and Mygdonia goes out secretly. On the way Judas Thomas meets with her. When she sees him, she is afraid, for she thinks *that he is one of the princes; for a great light went before him* (cf. v. 65). In this way the Hymn is redactionally connected in particular turns of phrase with the ATh, with which it also has the brother motif in common.

7. Sacraments and dedicatory prayers: almost all the conversions in the ATh are rounded off with sacramental acts, which normally consist of a sealing with oil, which is poured on the head (c. 27, 121, 132, 157), a water baptism (c. 121, 132. 157), and the eucharist meal with bread alone (c. 27, 29, 49f., 133), with bread and water (c. 121) or with bread and cup (= the body and blood of Christ, c. 158). The actual initiation is thus formed by the sealing with oil and the water baptism, which belong very closely together in all Syrian baptismal rituals (cf. S.P. Brock, *Holy Spirit in the Syrian Baptismal Tradition*, 1979, 23ff.; L. Leloir, 'Symbolisme dans la liturgie syriaque primitive', in J. Ries (ed.), *Le symbolisme dans le culte des grandes religions*, Louvain-la-Neuve 1985, 247-263; id., 'Le baptême du roi Gundaphor', *Le Muséon* 100, 1987, 225-233). The oil signifies the Holy Spirit, which is invoked in the epiclesis (c. 27) and makes the believers new men (Brock, *Holy Spirit*, 16f., 27). Like the king in the OT, the believer is anointed with oil and thereby recovers his original royal status (cf. the Hymn of the Pearl). In the sealing and water baptism, man is clothed with Christ, or Christ takes up his abode in him. The faithful strip off the old man and put on the new (c. 48, cf. Col. 3:9f.; c. 132). The garment symbolism which is predominant in the Hymn of the Pearl also plays an important role in the baptismal ritual, in which man is clothed with Christ, the new Man, or to put it in other terms is united with him as in a marriage. Conversion to *enkrateia*, which is represented as marriage with a heavenly consort, is in this way sealed in the unction with oil and the water baptism, which signifies union with the Spirit of Christ (cf. c. 157; Murray, *Symbols of Church and Kingdom*, 116).

The eucharist is celebrated with bread and water only, which is part of the encratite character of the ATh. In encratite circles communion with bread and water instead of wine was usual, the bread having a stronger significance than the wine. In Syria the rite of the breaking of bread with the accompanying prayers long remained the central point of the eucharistic liturgy (cf. RGG[3] I, art. 'Abendmahl' IVb, col. 40).

The ATh contain in a sacramental framework two epicleses to the Holy Spirit (cf. H. Kruse, 'Zwei Geist-Epiklesen der syrischen Thomas-Akten', *OrChr* 69, 1985, 33-53). The first (c. 27) belongs to the sealing, the second (c. 50) to the eucharist with bread. In these epicleses characteristic features of the trinitarian ideas in the ATh come to light, which have given rise to quite diverse interpretations. The ATh know a trinity which consists of Father, Mother and Son, the Mother assuming the place of the Holy Spirit. The Holy Spirit is called 'Mother of all wisdom' (c. 7) or 'Mother of all creation' (c. 39). The Hymn of the Pearl calls the Spirit 'mother, mistress of the East', a didactic address about baptism 'hidden power which dwells in Christ' (c. 132). A blessing over the bread of the eucharist speaks of the 'mother of the ineffable mystery of the hidden dominions and powers' (c. 133). This last formula is related to the epiclesis of c. 50, which calls the Holy Spirit 'thou that dost know the mysteries of the chosen', the one who reveals the great deeds of the whole greatness, who shows forth the hidden things and makes the ineffable manifest, just as c. 27 has the description 'thou that dost reveal the hidden mysteries'. The Spirit is called 'compassionate mother' (c. 27), 'holy Dove, that bearest the twin young' (c. 50), and is characterised as 'fellowship of the male' (cc. 27, 50). The Holy Spirit, the Mother, thus has two main characteristics: she represents the Wisdom of God, which she also reveals to the faithful, and in communion with God she gives birth to the Son, whose divine Mother she is, and also gives birth to the new man, the twin brother of the Son. The link with the figure of Wisdom, as she appears in Prov. 8:1-9:6, Sir. 24 and Wisd. Sol., emerges clearly in her description as 'Mother of the seven houses, that thy rest may be in the eighth house' (c. 27; cf. W. Staerk, 'Die sieben Säulen der Welt und des Hauses der Weisheit', ZNW 35, 1936, 232-261). The idea of the Holy Spirit as a mother is quite common in early Syrian theology and literature, occurs in the Odes of Solomon and in the writings of Aphraates and Ephraem Syrus, and has left further traces in later literature (cf. Murray, *Symbols of Church and Kingdom*, 142-150, 312-320; Drijvers, 'The 19th Ode of Solomon: Its Interpretation and Place in Syrian Christianity', JTS 31, 1980, 337-355). She has nothing to do with the fallen Sophia of many gnostic systems, but stands for that element of the divine which represents its wisdom and power in outgoing effect, brings it into operation, and hence as it were gives birth to it. The idea of the female Spirit is thus related to more philosophical speculations about the relation of the Pneuma to the divine being (cf. Elze, *Tatian und seine Theologie*, 1960, 65ff.; J. Dillon, *The Middle Platonists*, 1977, 163ff.). On the other side there are certain lines of connection to typical baptismal ideas which were at home in Syria. At his baptism the Holy Spirit descends upon Jesus like a dove, and thereby he becomes Son of God (Mt. 3:16-17 par.), i.e. the Holy Spirit as it were gives birth to the Son of God. In the same way the Spirit gives birth to the new man, in whom the Spirit dwells (cf. Jn. 1:12-13). The spirituality of Syrian Christianity with its inherent emphasis on birth and rebirth, on return to the condition of mankind for which God provided as a thoroughly spiritual process, brings about the salient position of the Holy Spirit as the parent of the life willed by God. Hence the Spirit is much more strongly linked with Christ than with God, since Christ as living spirit dwells within man (c. 7). He is called 'holy name of Christ' (cc. 27, 132), 'power of the Most High' (c. 27), 'power which dwells in Christ' (c. 132), 'ineffable power', 'through which the baptised are renewed' (c. 132). This role of the Holy Spirit in the process of redemption quite consistently carries with it a Spirit-Christology such as is predominant in pre-Antiochene Syrian Christianity (cf. Drijvers, 'Early Forms of Antiochene Christology', *After Chalcedon, Festschrift A. van Roey*, 1985, 99-113).

8. The position of the ATh in the history of religion and spirituality can be fixed fairly accurately on the basis of the theological and soteriological system which underlies the work. The basic idea of the ATh goes back to Tatian, whose *Oratio ad Graecos* contains all the elements which are brought out in symbolic and narrative fashion in the ATh. Right at the beginning of his discussion about the Logos, the first-born Son of the Father, Tatian establishes a relationship between the birth of the Logos and his own rebirth: 'and so I too am reborn in imitation of the Logos and have acquired knowledge of the truth . . .' (*Or.* 5.1-3; cf. the prologue of John). By this he states exactly the main theme of the ATh (cf. H.J.W. Drijvers-G.J. Reinink, 'Taufe und Licht. Tatian, Ebionäerevangelium und Thomasakten', in *Text and Testimony, Festschrift A.F.J. Klijn*, 1988, 91-110). Man can be born again, as the first-born Son was born (κἀγὼ κατὰ τὴν τοῦ λόγου μίμησιν ἀναγεννηθεὶς), and through this they become identical with one another. The term μίμησις signifies a precise reproduction, as the ATh say: the reborn man and the first-born of God are twins. Man was created immortal and with free will after the image of God (*Or.* 7.1), but lost his immortality when he yielded obedience to the first-born of the angels, Satan, who since then with his host of demons has promoted folly in the world (cf. M. Elze, *Tatian und seine Theologie*, 1960, 100ff.). The loss of immortality is brought about by the fact that man loses the stronger or higher Pneuma (*Or.* 7.3), which is the image and likeness of God (*Or.* 12.1). Tatian says quite clearly: 'We are not created for dying, but we die through our own fault (δι' ἑαυτούς). Our freedom has destroyed us. We, the free men, have become slaves; because of sin are we sold' (*Or.* 11.2). Judas Thomas is sold as a slave, but carries his purchase price with him, and through it he again becomes free (cf. 1 Cor. 6:12-20: '. . . your body is a temple of the Holy Spirit that is in you, which you have from God. For you are bought with a price - ἠγοράσθητε γὰρ τιμῆς"; cf. ATh c. 3). Man has however kept his freedom of will, so that he remains capable of undoing sin. 'Nothing evil is created by God; it is we who have raised up wickedness; but he who has raised up something is also capable of rejecting it again' (*Or.* 11.2). The original condition of man is restored when he receives again the Pneuma which he has lost. Tatian puts it thus: 'It is therefore necessary that we now again seek what we possessed and have lost, unite our soul with the holy Pneuma, and bring about the union according to God (τὴν κατὰ θεὸν συζυγίαν)' (*Or.* 15.1). The idea of the union of the soul with the Holy Spirit or Pneuma is symbolically represented as a marriage, which makes man immortal and brings him back to his original status, just as the ATh often describe the true marriage. This divine Pneuma also functions as a guide on the way upwards and as a helper (*Or.* 13.2 συζυγίαν δὲ κεκτημένη τὴν τοῦ θείου πνεύματος οὐκ ἔστιν ἀβοήθητος, ἀνέρχεται δὲ πρὸς ἅπερ αὐτὴν ὁδηγεῖ χωρία τὸ πνεῦμα), a theme which occurs in the Hymn of the Pearl. The divine Pneuma will however only dwell in a pure body as in a temple (*Or.* 15.2: τὸ δὲ τοιοῦτον τῆς συστάσεως εἶδος εἰ μέν ὡς ναὸς εἴη, κατοικεῖν ἐν αὐτῷ θεὸς βούλεται διὰ τοῦ πρεσβεύοντος πνεύματος). This lays the foundation for the encratite ethics of Tatian and the ATh. As in Tatian the Spirit as God's representative will dwell only in a pure body, so the apostle Judas Thomas says: 'Holiness is a temple of Christ, and he who dwells in it receives it as a habitation' (c. 86) (cf. Elze, *Tatian und seine Theologie*, 95f.). The recovery of the Pneuma is also described by Tatian as the gaining of a beautiful mantle, and here we are back with the Hymn of the Pearl: 'It is possible for anyone who is unclothed (i.e. does not have the heavenly Pneuma as a mantle for the mortal soul, which gives it immortality) to obtain the adornment (τὸ ἐπικόσμημα) and hasten up to the original fellowship' (*Or.* 20.2; cf. Elze, *Tatian und seine Theologie*, 95f.). Finally Tatian describes the recovery of immortality as the finding of a treasure in the field in which it is buried (*Or.* 30.1; cf. M. Whittaker, Tatian *Oratio ad Graecos and Fragments*, Oxford 1982, Appendix II, 84ff.; cf. also Mt. 13:44; Gos. Thom. log. 109). This refers beyond a doubt to the pearl as it occurs in the Hymn of the Pearl (cf. Elze, *Tatian und seine Theologie*, 98f.). Exactly as in the ATh, Tatian voices no soteriology in the sense of a doctrine of a Redeemer, just as he does not know any real fall of man as a historical event. Knowledge of the truth and strict *enkrateia*, which means a struggle against the demons, these are salvation, which every man can freely attain.

Christ is here the Helper (cf. *Or.* 13.2), who demonstrates God's power, but for this any man is capable (ATh cc. 39, 60, 66, 81, 85, 119 etc.).

In addition to the unmistakable influence of Tatian's world of thought, which finds expression also in the choice of words in the ATh (cf. Peterson, *Frühkirche, Judentum und Gnosis*, 192ff., 202ff.; H.-Ch. Puech, *En quête de la gnose* II, 1978, 118ff.; Drijvers, *East of Antioch*, 1984, I, 7-18), we can establish also an influence from the philosophy of Bardaisan. In the speech in c. 91 the redactor of the ATh has taken over a fairly long quotation from Bardaisan's 'Book of the Laws of the Countries'. When Satan is described as the one 'who hurt and smote the four standing brothers', we may perhaps discover there an influence from Bardaisan's doctrine of the elements. The epicleses in c. 27 and c. 50 have parallels in the fragments of Bardaisan's hymns which Ephraem Syrus has preserved (*Hymni contra Haereses* LV; cf. Drijvers, *Bardaisan of Edessa*, 1966, 143ff.). The point on which the ATh and Bardaisan are particularly in agreement is the ethically and anthropologically rooted dualism within a strictly monotheistic framework. Although in Bardaisan this does not lead to the rigorous *enkrateia* of the ATh, he too knows no fall of man in the proper sense, and is convinced that man as an at any rate partially free being is in a position to overcome evil. The ATh and Bardaisan know nothing of a matter which in and of itself is evil and wicked. Matter occupies the lowest level of the cosmos, which is entirely in accord with contemporary Middle Platonic philosophy, but is not in itself the origin of evil. For the encratites of the ATh this consists solely in sexuality, which is the result of man's wrong choice. For Bardaisan the world and man represent a mixture of good and evil, light and darkness, which is purified by right conduct until the original harmony is restored. Like Tatian and the ATh, Bardaisan too knows no *Heilsgeschichte* in the proper sense. The Christian faith is an eternal, timeless philosophy of the correct conduct by which salvation and redemption are brought about. Jesus is a spiritual principle, a helper and teacher, in whom the Spirit of God for a short time dwelt.

Both in Tatian's theology with its basically Middle Platonist philosophical structure and also in Bardaisan's philosophical system, which is likewise strongly influenced by Middle Platonism (cf. A. Dihle, 'Zur Schicksalslehre des Bardesanes', *Kerygma und Logos*, FS C. Andresen, 1979, 123-135; id., *The Theory of Will in Classical Antiquity*, 1982, 108ff.), the doctrine of the Spirit occupies a central place. The divine Spirit fashions the world, represents the image of God, i.e. immortality, in man, and is actively at work in world history to refashion man and bring him back to his original condition. We meet this central theme again in a philosophical form in the contemporary philosophy, and it appears in Christian dress in the various developments of the Christian faith in early Syrian Christianity. The ATh proclaim this timeless historical Christian philosophy in a symbolic and narrative garb in the Acts of the apostle, which could be read on different levels. They describe like a novel the apostle's adventures in a foreign land, but contain many allusions which make a symbolic interpretation possible. The Homeric myths and other literary works were also read and interpreted in exactly the same way (cf. e.g. F. Buffière, *Les mythes d'Homère et la pensée grecque*, 1956).

When the milieu in which ideas of this kind flourished, and such writings and systems came into being, is described as gnostic or vulgar gnostic, justice is not done to its peculiar character. Philosophical and religious knowledge plays a central role, not as the actual instrument of redemption but in order to lead to the true action which effects salvation. All the characteristic marks of the classic gnostic systems are completely lacking. There is no mention of a fall in the Pleroma; the creation is not the work of a wicked Demiurge, and matter is therefore not in itself evil. Man's freedom is the primal cause of good and evil, life and death, and this stands in sharp contrast to the gnostic determinism. Of course in such a milieu the boundaries are fluid, and a development in a radically dualistic direction is perfectly possible, as the later history of Syrian Christianity in the course of the 3rd century shows, when Manicheism proclaimed itself the sole legitimate heir of the Christian tradition. The intellectual world of the ATh and related writings had however a manifold influence on later orthodoxy, as represented by Ephraem Syrus and others, and in Syria Tatian like Bardaisan was branded as a heretic only late and with reluctance; for this their appropriation by the Manichees provided the impulse.

The milieu of early Syrian Christianity, in which the ATh are at home, is rather enlightened, and may be characterised as open to the world and 'sophisticated'; it assimilates pagan traditions, which are interpreted in a Christian framework (cf. Drijvers, *Bardaisan of Edessa*, 143ff.), and takes over Jewish writings and ideas in a Christian garb of a philosophical and ascetic colouring (cf. Drijvers, 'The Peshitta of the Wisdom of Solomon: Characteristics of a Translation', *Scripta Signa Vocis*, FS J.H. Hospers, 1986, 15-30). What was thought and written in this milieu is the property of a spiritual elite which was conversant with contemporary culture and found an answer of its own to the questions of human existence. The apostle Judas Thomas, his deeds and his teaching, are a part of the answer, a symbolic and religious composition about the divine Spirit which is the twin brother of man, and with whom he must unite in order to become fully man again.

9. The ATh and Manicheism have many individual motifs in common, but in their structure and orientation they are fundamentally different. In the ATh it is a question of the reunion of man with the Pneuma, the Holy Spirit, who dwells as Christ within him or with whom he contracts an eternal marriage, so that he recovers his original immortality. In Manichean doctrine and practice the central theme is the liberation of the divine particles of light from the world of evil matter and from bodily existence. According to the ATh, God created the world, that man should live there for ever as the image of God, a possibility that is open to him even today if he lives in *enkrateia*. According to Manichean teaching the Demiurge, who in contrast to other gnostic systems plays a positive role, created the world as a counter-measure against the devices of matter, in order to further the liberation of the particles of light. The creation of the world is thus a kind of emergency measure, which is to be broken off as soon as possible. Man on the other hand is a creation initiated by the wicked archons to hinder the deliverance of the particles of light (cf. A. Böhlig, *Die Gnosis*, vol. III. 'Der Manichäismus', 1980, 21ff.). The ATh and Manicheism nevertheless have in common the encratite ethic, which makes it possible to read the ATh, so to speak, with Manichean eyes, although the *enkrateia* in the ATh does not have its origin in hatred for matter and corporality, as is the case in Manicheism (cf. Drijvers, 'Conflict and Alliance in Manicheism', in H.G. Kippenberg (ed.), *Struggles of Gods*, 1984, 99-124).

In particular the idea of the heavenly twin, which dominates the ATh and the picture of the apostle Judas Thomas as the representative of a theological idea, exercised a profound influence on Mani's self-understanding, as is clearly shown by the Cologne Mani Codex (cf. A. Henrichs-L. Koenen, 'Ein griechischer Mani-Codex', ZPE 5, 1970, 161ff.; H.-Ch. Puech, *En quête de la gnose* II. 'Sur l'évangile selon Thomas', 1978, 219-241; P. Nagel, 'Die apokryphen Apostelakten des 2. und 3. Jahrhunderts in der manichäischen Literatur', *Gnosis und Neues Testament*, 1975, 171ff.). The Coptic Manichean texts show acquaintance with the Thomas legend and with the martyrdom of the apostle (MPsB 194.13 etc.; MPsB 142.27-29), although they have taken over only the legend and not gnosticising elements (cf. Nagel, 'Die apokryphen Apostelakten', 172f.). It has often been assumed that the ATh have preserved traces of a Manichean revision (W. Bousset, 'Manichäisches in den Thomasakten', ZNW 18, 1917/18, 1-39; Bornkamm, *Mythos und Legende*, 115-117), and that the Hymn of the Pearl in particular was soon transferred to Mani and provided with individual features from his Vita. It is certainly possible that the Manicheans recognised in the king's son of the Hymn and in his life elements of the Vita of the Apostle of Light, but the differences are too great to make a Manichean revision credible. Rather the figure of the apostle Judas Thomas as the twin brother of Jesus was of decisive influence upon Mani's consciousness of mission, and it is also to be assumed that individual motifs from the ATh were accepted into the legendary Vita of Mani. The apostle concept of the ATh made Mani into an apostle of Jesus Christ, in whom the Paraclete has found a dwelling (cf. A. Böhlig, 'The New Testament and the Concept of the Manichean Myth', *The New Testament and Gnosis*, FS R.M. Wilson, 1983, 90-104). When Bousset ('Manichäisches in den Thomasakten', 1ff.) treats as a Manichean addition the invocation in the epiclesis of c. 27: 'Come, messenger of the five members, understanding, thought, prudence, consideration, reasoning', it has to be observed that this idea of a fivefold Spirit was by no means confined to Manicheism. It occurs in the Letter of Eugnostus and in the Sophia Jesu Christi, basically thus in philosophical texts, and probably belongs to the Middle Platonic school tradition. From there it found its way into the ATh and into Manicheism (cf. M. Tardieu, *Écrits gnostiques. Codex de Berlin*, Paris 1984, 67).

The acceptance of the ATh by Mani and the Manicheans is a constituent element in the total process of the taking-over and radicalising of the literature and theology of early Syrian Christianity which was accomplished in Mani and in the Manichean community, and made Manicheism into a Christian form of religion. How far the ATh in addition represent the religious ideas of Syrian orthodoxy is shown by their use and transmission in later Christian circles, which from time to time subjected the acts and speeches of the apostle to an orthodox revision, which however does not imply the heretical character of an earlier version. These recensions bear witness to a continuing adaptation of the ATh to later developments in doctrine, which come to light particularly in the apostle's prayers and sermons and can be detected in special formulations of the Syriac version. In this way the Manichean use of the ATh and the 'orthodox' recensions reflect the final separation of orthodoxy and heresy in Syrian Christianity, although they nevertheless preserved much in common.

Notes

Introduction

1. In what follows, ATh = Acts of Thomas; EvThom = Gospel of Thomas.
2. Especially important are a Roman codex (Vallicellanus B 35) from the 11th cent., in Bonnet under the siglum U, and a Paris codex (B.N. graec. 1510) of the 11th or 12th cent., in Bonnet under the siglum P. Cf. Klijn, *The Acts of Thomas*, 4ff.
3. The following text is based on Raabe's complete translation, revised and corrected by G. Bornkamm, which has been checked through yet again.
4. The Martyrdom was also transmitted separately, and has some literary connections with the Abgar legend, where for example it is related that Thomas was laid to rest in the royal sepulchre. See also G. Garitte, 'Le martyre géorgien de l'apôtre Thomas', *Le Muséon* 73, 1970, 497-532.
5. The pericope 1 Cor. 6:12-20 appears to play an important role in the theology of the ATh and - as among the Encratites generally - is almost programmatic for the apostle's sermon in the first Praxis.

The Acts of the Holy Apostle Thomas

(Aa II. 2, pp. 99-287)

<First Act of the Apostle Judas Thomas
How the Lord sold him to the merchant Abban, that he might go down and convert India S>*

1. At that time we apostles[1] were all in Jerusalem, Simon called Peter and Andrew his brother, James the son of Zebedee and John his brother, Philip and Bartholomew, Thomas and Matthew the publican, James (the son) of Alphaeus and Simon the Cananaean, (p. 100) and Judas (the brother) of James; and we divided the regions of the world, that each one of us might go to the region which fell to his lot, and to the nation to which the Lord sent him. According to lot, India fell to Judas Thomas, who is also (called) Didymus; but he did not wish to go, saying that through weakness of the flesh he could not travel, and: 'How can I, who am a Hebrew, go and preach the truth among the Indians?' And as he considered and said this, the Saviour appeared to him by night[2] and said to him: 'Fear not, Thomas, go to India and preach the word there, for my grace is with thee.' But he would not obey (p. 101) and said: 'Send me where thou wilt - but somewhere else! For I am not going to the Indians.' 2. And as he thus spoke and thought, it happened that a certain merchant was there who had come from India. His name was Abban and he had been sent by king Gundaphorus, and had received orders from him to buy a carpenter and bring him back to him. Now the Lord saw him walking in the marketplace at noon, and said to him: 'Dost thou wish to buy a carpenter?' He said to him: 'Yes.'

And the Lord said to him: 'I have a slave who is a carpenter, and wish to sell him.' And when he had said this he showed him Thomas from a distance, and agreed (p. 102) with him for three pounds of uncoined (silver),[3] and wrote a <deed of S> sale saying: I Jesus the son of Joseph the carpenter[4] confirm that I have sold my slave, Judas by name, to thee Abban, a merchant of Gundaphorus the king of the Indians. And when the <deed of S> sale was completed the Saviour took Judas, who is also (called) Thomas, and led him to the merchant Abban. And when Abban saw him, he said to him: 'Is this thy master?' And the apostle in answer said: 'Yes, he is my Lord.' But he said: 'I have bought thee from him.'[5] And the apostle was silent.[6]

3. On the following morning the apostle prayed and besought the Lord, and said: 'I go whither thou wilt, Lord Jesus; (p. 103) *thy will be done!*'[7] And he went off to Abban the merchant, carrying with him nothing at all, save only his price. For the Lord had given it to him, saying: 'Let thy price also be with thee, with my grace, whithersoever thou goest!' But the apostle found Abban <.> carrying his baggage aboard the ship, and he too began to carry it with him. And when they had embarked on the ship and sat down, Abban questioned the apostle, saying: 'What manner of trade dost thou know?' And he said: 'In wood (I can make) ploughs and yokes and balances, <goads> and ships and oars for ships and masts and pulleys; and in stone, pillars and temples and royal (p. 104) palaces.' And Abban the merchant said to him: '(It is good), for of such a craftsman are we in need.' So they began their voyage. They had a favourable wind, and sailed prosperously until they arrived at Andrapolis, a royal city.

4. Leaving the ship, they went into the city. And lo, sounds of <flutes> and water-organs and trumpets echoed round about them; and the apostle inquired, saying: 'What is this feast which (is being celebrated) in this city?' The people there said to him: (p. 105) 'Thee too have the gods brought to keep festival in this city. For the king has an only daughter, and now he is giving her to a man in marriage. So it is for the wedding, this rejoicing and this assembly for the feast today which thou has seen. And the king has sent out heralds to proclaim everywhere that all should come to the wedding,[8] rich and poor, bond and free, strangers and citizens;[9] but if any man refuse, and come not to the marriage, he shall be accountable to the king.' When Abban heard it, he said to the apostle: 'Let us also go, then, that we may not give offence to the king, especially since we are strangers.' And he said: 'Let us go.' And after taking quarters at the inn and resting a little they went to the wedding. (p. 106) And the apostle, seeing them all reclining, himself lay down in the midst;[10] and they all looked at him, as at a stranger and one come from a foreign land. But Abban the merchant, as being the master, lay down at another place. 5. But while they dined and drank, the apostle tasted nothing; so those who were round about him said: 'Why didst thou come here neither eating nor drinking?' But he answered and said to them: 'For something greater than food or drink am I come hither,

<for the king's rest S> and that I may accomplish the king's will.[11] For the heralds proclaim the king's (commands) and (p. 107) whoever does not listen to the heralds shall be liable to the king's judgment.' And when they had dined and drunk, and crowns and scented oils were brought, each one took of the oil, and one anointed his face, another his chin (his beard), another again other parts of his body; but the apostle anointed the crown of his head and smeared a little upon his nostrils, dropped some also into his ears, touched his teeth with it, and carefully anointed the parts about his heart; and the crown that was brought to him, woven of myrtle and other flowers, he took and set upon his head; and he took a branch of a reed[12] (p. 108) in his hand and held it. Now the flute-girl, holding her flute in her hand, was going round all the company and playing; but when she came to the place where the apostle was, she stood over him and played at his head for a long time. Now that flute-girl was by race a Hebrew. 6. While the apostle was looking at the ground, one of the cup-bearers stretched out his hand and slapped him.13 But the apostle lifted up his eyes, directed his gaze at the man who had struck him, and said: 'My God will forgive thee this injury in the world to come,[14] but in this world he will show forth his wonders, and I shall even now see that hand that smote me dragged by dogs.' And when he had said this he began to sing this song and to say:[15]

(p. 109) The maiden is the daughter of light,
Upon her stands and rests the majestic effulgence of kings,
Delightful is the sight of her,
Radiant with shining beauty.
Her garments are like spring flowers,
And a scent of sweet fragrance is diffused from them.
In the crown of her head the king is established,
Feeding with his own ambrosia those who are set <under> him.
Truth rests upon her head,
By (the movement of) her feet she shows forth joy.
Her mouth is open, and that becomingly,
<For (with it) she sings loud songs of praise. S>
Thirty and two are they that sing her praises.
Her tongue is like the curtain of the door,
Which is flung back for those who enter in.
<Like steps her neck mounts up S>,
Which the first craftsman wrought.
Her two hands make signs and secret patterns, proclaiming the dance of the blessed aeons,
Her fingers <open S> the gates of the city.
Her chamber is full of light,
Breathing a scent of balsam and all sweet herbs,

(p. 110) And giving out a sweet smell of myrrh and (aromatic) leaves.
Within are strewn myrtle branches and <all manner of sweet-smelling flowers>,
And the <portals> are adorned with reeds.
7. Her <groomsmen> keep her compassed about, whose number is seven,
Whom she herself has chosen;
And her bridesmaids are seven,
Who dance before her.
Twelve are they in number who serve before her
And are subject to her,
Having their gaze and look toward the bridegroom,
That by the sight of him they may be enlightened;
And for ever shall they be with him in that eternal joy,
And they shall be at that marriage
For which the princes assemble together,
And shall linger over the feasting
Of which the eternal ones are accounted worthy,
And they shall put on royal robes
And be arrayed in splendid raiment,
And both shall be in joy and exultation
And they shall glorify the Father of all,
Whose proud light they received
And were enlightened by the vision of their Lord,
Whose ambrosial food they received,
Which has no deficiency at all,
And they drank too of his wine
Which gives them neither thirst nor desire;
And they glorified and praised, with the living Spirit,
The Father of Truth and the Mother of Wisdom.

8. (p. 111) And when he had sung and ended this song, all who were present gazed upon him; and he was silent. They saw also his appearance changed,[16] but they did not understand what he said, since he was a Hebrew and what he said was spoken in the Hebrew tongue. The flute-girl alone heard it all, for she was a Hebrew by race; and moving away from him she played to the others, but often looked back and gazed on him. For she loved him greatly, as a man of her own race; moreover in appearance he was comely above all that were present. And when the flute-girl had <quite> finished <her playing>, she sat down opposite him and looked steadily at him. But he looked at no one at all, nor did he pay attention to anyone, but kept his eyes only on the ground, waiting for the time when (p. 112) he might take his departure.[17] But the cup-bearer who had slapped him went down to the well to draw water. And it happened that

there was a lion there, and it slew him[18] and left him to lie on the spot, after tearing his limbs to pieces. And immediately dogs seized his limbs, and among them a black dog grasped his right hand in its mouth and carried it into the place where the feast was. 9. But when they saw it, they were all amazed and inquired which of them was absent. But when it became evident that it was the hand of the cup-bearer who had struck the apostle, (p. 113) the flute-girl smashed her flute and threw it away, and went to the apostle's feet and sat down, saying: 'This man is either a god or an apostle of God; for I heard him say to the cup-bearer in Hebrew: "Even now shall I see the hand that smote me dragged by dogs" - which you also have now seen; for as he said, so did it come to pass.' And some believed her, but some did not. But when the king heard it, he came and said to the apostle: 'Arise and come with me, and pray for my daughter! For she is my only child, and today I give her in marriage.' But the apostle would not (p. 114) go with him, for the Lord was not yet revealed to him there. But the king led him away against his will into the bridal chamber, that he might pray for them (the bridal pair). 10. And the apostle standing began to pray and to speak thus: '*My Lord and my God*,[19] the companion of his servants, who doth guide and direct those who believe in him, the refuge and rest of the oppressed, the hope of the poor and redeemer of the captives, the physician of the souls laid low in sickness and saviour of all creation, who dost quicken the world to life and strengthen the souls, thou dost know what is to be, who also dost accomplish it through us; thou, Lord, who dost reveal hidden mysteries and make manifest words that are secret;[20] thou, Lord, art the planter of the good tree, and by thy hands are all good works engendered; thou, Lord, art he who is in all and passes through all and dwells in all thy works, and manifest in the working of them all*; Jesus Christ, Son of compassion and (p. 115) perfect Saviour; Christ, *Son of the living God*,[21] the undaunted power which overthrew the enemy, the voice that was heard by the archons, which shook all their powers; ambassador sent from the height who didst descend even to Hell, who having opened the doors[22] didst bring up thence those who for many ages had been shut up in the treasury of darkness, and show them the way that leads up to the height; I pray thee, Lord Jesus, as I bring to thee my supplication for these young people, that thou do for them the things that help and are useful and profitable.' And after laying his hands upon them and saying: 'The Lord shall be with you', he left them in that place and departed.

11. The king required the attendants to go out of the bridal chamber. And when all had gone out and the doors were shut, the bridegroom lifted up the veil of the bridal chamber, (p. 116) that he might bring the bride to himself. And he saw the Lord Jesus in the likeness of the apostle Judas Thomas, who shortly before had blessed them and departed from them, conversing with the bride, and he said to him: 'Didst thou not go out before them all? How art thou now found here?' But the Lord said to him: 'I am not Judas who is also Thomas,

I am his brother.' And the Lord sat down upon the bed and bade them also to sit on the chairs, and began to say to them: 12. 'Remember, my children, what my brother said to you, and to whom he commended you; and know this, that if you (p. 117) abandon this filthy intercourse you become holy temples,[23] pure and free from afflictions and pains both manifest and hidden, and you will not be girt about with cares for life and for children, *the end of which is destruction.*[24] But if you get many children, then for their sakes you become robbers and avaricious, (people who) flay orphans and defraud widows, and by so doing you subject yourselves to the most grievous punishments. For the majority of children become unprofitable, possessed by demons, some openly and some in secret; for they become either lunatic or half-withered (consumptive) or crippled or deaf or dumb or paralytic or stupid. Even if they are healthy, again will they be unserviceable, performing useless (p. 118) and abominable deeds; for they are caught either in adultery or in murder or in theft or in unchastity, and by all these you will be afflicted. But if you obey, and keep your souls pure unto God, you shall have living children whom these hurts do not touch, and shall be without care, leading an undisturbed life without grief or anxiety, waiting to receive that incorruptible and true marriage (as befitting for you), and in it you shall be groomsmen entering into that bridal chamber <which is full of> immortality and light.' 13. But when the young people heard this, they believed the Lord and gave themselves entirely to him, and refrained (p. 119) from the filthy passion, and so remained[25] throughout the night in that place. And the Lord departed from them, saying: '*The grace of the Lord shall be with you!*'[26] When morning broke, the king came to meet them, and after furnishing the table brought it in before the bridegroom and the bride; and he found them sitting opposite one another, the bride with her face unveiled[27] and the bridegroom very cheerful. But her mother came in and said to the bride: 'Why dost thou sit thus, child, and art not ashamed, but dost behave as if thou hadst lived a long time with thine own husband?' And her father said: 'Because of thy great love for thy husband dost thou not even veil thyself?' 14. The bride in answer said: 'Truly, father, I am in great love, and I pray to my Lord that the love (p. 120) which I experienced this night may remain with me, and I will ask for the husband of whom I have learned today. <But that I do not veil myself S> (is) because the mirror <veil S> of shame is taken from me;[28] and I am no longer ashamed or abashed, because the work of shame and bashfulness has been removed far from me. And that I am not alarmed, (is) because alarm did not remain with me. And that I am in cheerfulness and joy (is) because the day of joy was not disturbed. And that I have set at naught this man, and this marriage which passes away from before my eyes, (is) because I am bound in another marriage. And that I have had no intercourse with a short-lived husband, the end of which is <remorse and bitterness> of soul, (is) because I am yoked with <the> true man.'

15. And while the bride was saying yet more than this, the bridegroom answered and said: 'I thank thee, Lord, who through the (p. 121) stranger wast proclaimed and found in us; who hast removed me from corruption and sown in me life; who didst free me from this sickness, hard to heal and hard to cure and abiding for ever, and didst implant in me sober health; who didst show thyself to me and reveal to me all my condition in which I am; who didst redeem me from the fall and lead me to the better, and free me from things transitory but count me worthy of those that are immortal and everlasting; who didst humble thyself[29] to me and my smallness, that setting me beside thy greatness thou mightest unite me with thyself; who didst not withhold thy mercy from me that was ready to perish, but didst show me to seek myself and to recognise who I was and who and how I now am, that I may become again what I was; whom I did not know, but thou thyself didst seek me out; of whom I was unaware, but thou thyself didst take me to thee; whom I have perceived, and now cannot (p. 122) forget; whose love ferments within me, and of whom I cannot speak as I ought, but what I can say about him is short and very little and does not correspond to his glory; but he does not blame me when I make bold to say to him even what I do not know; for it is for love of him that I say this.'

16. But when the king heard this from the bridegroom and the bride he rent his garments[30] and said to those who stood near him: 'Go out quickly and go through all the city, and seize and bring to me that man, the sorcerer who by an evil chance is in this city. For I brought him with my own hands into my house, and told him to pray over my most unfortunate daughter. And whosoever finds and brings him to me, to him do I give <all that he may ask of me>.' (p. 123) So they departed and went about in search of him, and did not find him; for he had set sail. They went also into the inn where he had lodged, and there they found the flute-girl weeping and distressed, because he had not taken her with him. But when they told her what had happened in the case of the young people, she was very glad when she heard it, and setting aside her grief she said: 'Now have I too found rest here!' And rising up she went to them, and stayed with them a long time, until they had taught the king also. And many of the brethren also gathered there, until they heard a report (p. 124) about the apostle, that he had landed in the cities of India and was teaching there. And they went off and joined themselves with him.

Second Act of the Apostle Thomas
Concerning his coming to King Gundaphorus

17. But when the apostle came to the cities of India with Abban the merchant, Abban went off to salute King Gundaphorus, and reported to him concerning the carpenter whom he had brought with him. The king was glad, and commanded that he should come to him. So when (p. 125) he came

the king said to him: 'What kind of trade dost thou understand?' The apostle said to him: 'Carpentry and building.' The king said to him: 'What craftsmanship, then, dost thou know in wood, and what in stone?' The apostle said: 'In wood, ploughs, yokes, balances, pulleys, and ships and oars and masts; and in stone, pillars, temples and royal palaces. And the king said "Wilt thou build me a palace?' And he answered: 'Yes, I will build and finish it; for this is why I came, to build and work as a carpenter.' 18. And the king took him and went out of the gates of the city, and began to discuss with him on the way (p. 126) the building of the palace and how the foundations should be laid, until they came to the place where he wanted the building to be. And he said: 'I wish the building to be here.' And the apostle said: 'Yes, for this place is suitable for the building.' But the place was wooded, and there was much water there. So the king said: 'Begin to build.' But he said: 'I cannot begin to build now at this season.' And the king said: 'When canst thou?' And he said: 'I will begin in November and finish (p. 127) in April.' But the king said in astonishment: 'Every building is built in summer, but thou canst build and establish a palace even in winter?' And the apostle said: 'So it ought to be, and there is no other way.' And the king said: 'Well then, if this is thy resolve, draw me a plan how the work is to be, since I shall come back here (only) after some time.' And the apostle took a reed and drew, measuring the place; and the doors he set toward the east, to face the light, and the windows to the west towards the winds, and the bakehouse he made to be to the south, and the aqueduct for the service to the north. But when the king saw it, he said to the apostle: 'Truly thou art a craftsman, and it is fitting (p. 128) for thee to serve kings.' And leaving much money with him he departed from him.

19. And at appointed times he used to send him money and what was necessary both for his own sustenance and for that of the other workmen. But he took it all and dispensed it, going about the towns and the villages round about, distributing it and bestowing alms[31] on the poor and afflicted, and he gave them relief, saying: 'The king knows that he will receive a royal recompense, but the poor must for the present be refreshed.' After this the king sent (p. 129) an ambassador to the apostle, writing to him thus: 'Show me what thou hast done, or what I should send thee, or what thou dost require.' The apostle sent to him, saying: 'The palace is built, and only the roof remains.' When the king heard this, he sent him again gold and uncoined silver, writing: 'If the palace is built, let it be roofed!' But the apostle said to the Lord: 'I thank thee, Lord, in every respect, that thou for a short time didst die that I might live eternally in thee, and that thou didst sell me in order to deliver many through me.' And he did not cease from teaching and refreshing the afflicted, (p. 130) saying: 'The Lord has dispensed this to you, and himself provides to each his food. For he is the nourisher of the orphans and supporter of the widows,[32] and to all that are afflicted he is relief and rest.'[33]

20. But when the king came to the city he inquired of his friends concerning the palace which Judas who is also Thomas was building for him. But they said to him: 'Neither has he built a palace, nor has he done anything else of what he promised to do, but he goes about the towns and villages, and if he has anything he gives it all to the poor, and he teaches a new God <.> and heals (p. 131) the sick and drives out demons and does many other wonderful things; and we think he is a magician. But his works of compassion, and the healings which are wrought by him without reward, and moreover his simplicity and kindness and the quality of his faith, show that he is righteous or an apostle of the new God whom he preaches. For continually he fasts and prays, and eats only bread and salt, and his drink is water, and he wears one garment[34] whether in fine weather or in foul (winter), and takes nothing from anyone, and what he has he gives to others.' When he heard this, (p. 132) the king smote his face with his hands, shaking his head for a long time. 21. And he sent for the merchant who had brought him, and for the apostle, and said to him: 'Hast thou built me the palace?' And he said: 'Yes, I have built it.' The king said: 'Then when shall we go and see it?' But he answered him and said: 'Now thou canst not see it, but when thou dost depart this life thou shalt see it.'[35] But the king in great wrath commanded (p. 133) both the merchant and Judas who is also Thomas to be put in bonds and cast into prison until he should investigate and learn to whom the king's money had been given, and so destroy him together with the merchant. But the apostle went rejoicing into the prison, and said to the merchant: '*Fear nothing*, but *only believe*[36] in the God who is preached by me, and thou shalt be freed from this world but from the age to come shalt obtain life.'

Now the king was considering with what manner of death (p. 134) he should destroy them. But when he had resolved to flay them alive and then burn them with fire, in the same night Gad the king's brother[37] fell sick, and because of the pain and disappointment which the king had suffered he was greatly depressed. And he sent for the king and said to him: 'My brother the king, my house and my children I commend to thee. For I have been grieved on account of the despiteful usage that has befallen thee and behold, I am dying, and if thou do not come down with vengeance upon the head of that magician, thou wilt give my soul no rest in Hades.' But the king said to his brother: 'The whole night through I was considering how I should put him to death; and this have I resolved, to flay him alive and then burn him with fire, both him and with him the merchant who brought him.' (p. 135) 22. And as they conversed the soul of Gad his brother departed. The king mourned Gad deeply, for he loved him greatly, and commanded him to be buried in royal and costly apparel. But when this happened, angels took the soul of Gad the king's brother and carried it up into heaven, showing him the places there and the dwellings and asking him: 'In what kind of place wouldst thou live?' But when they drew near to the building of Thomas the apostle, which he built for the king, Gad when he saw it said to the angels: 'I pray you, sirs, allow me to live in one of these lower apartments.' But they said to him: (p. 136) 'Thou canst not live in this building.' And he said: 'Why?' They said to him: 'This palace is the one which that Christian built for thy brother.' But he said: 'I pray you, sirs, allow me to go to my brother, that I may buy this palace from him. For my brother does not know of what kind it is, and will sell it to me.' 23. Then the angels let Gad's soul go. And while they were putting the grave clothes on him, his soul entered into him; and he said to those who stood around him: 'Call to me my brother, that I may ask of him one request.' So at once they brought the good news to the king, (p. 137) saying: 'Thy brother is alive again!' The king sprang up and came with a great crowd to his brother, and going in he stood by his bed as if stupefied, unable to speak to him. But his brother said: 'I know and am persuaded, brother, that if anyone asked of thee the half of thy kingdom,[38] thou wouldst have given it for my sake. Wherefore I beseech thee to grant me one favour which I ask of thee, that thou sell me what I ask from thee.' But the king said in answer: 'And what is it that thou dost ask me to sell thee?' But he said: 'Convince me by an oath that thou wilt grant it me.' And the king swore to him: '<Whatever of my possessions thou dost ask for thyself>, (p. 138) I give it thee.' And he said to him: 'Sell me that palace which thou hast in heaven.' And the king said: 'Whence should I have a palace in heaven?' But he said: 'The one that Christian built for thee, who is now in prison - the man the merchant brought thee after buying him from one Jesus. I mean that Hebrew slave whom thou didst wish to punish, as having suffered some deception at his hand - against whom I too was vexed, and died, and now I am alive again.'

24. Then the king, considering the matter, understood (his words) concerning the eternal goods which were more excellent for him and which he was to receive, and said: 'That palace I cannot sell to thee, but I pray that I may enter it and live in it, and be counted worthy <to belong to> its inhabitants. But if thou dost truly wish to buy such a palace, behold the man is alive, and will build thee one better than that.' (p. 139) And immediately he sent and brought the apostle out of the prison, and the merchant who had been shut up with him, saying: 'I entreat thee, as a man entreating the servant of God, to pray for me and beseech him whose servant thou art, that he forgive me and overlook the things that I have done against thee, or thought to do, and that I may become a worthy inhabitant of that dwelling for which I did not labour at all, but thou didst build it for me labouring alone, the grace of thy God working with thee, and that I too may become a servant, and serve this God whom thou dost proclaim.' And his brother also fell down at the apostle's feet and said: 'I pray thee and implore before thy God, that I may become worthy of this ministry and service, and that it may be my lot to be worthy of the things <shown to me by his angels>.' (p.

140) 25. But the apostle, possessed <with> joy, said: 'I praise thee, Lord Jesus, that thou hast revealed thy truth in these men. For thou alone art the God of truth, and no other; and thou art he who knows all that is unknown to the many; thou, Lord, art he who in all things shows <mercy and forbearance to men>. For men because of the error that is in them forsook thee, but thou didst not forsake them. And now as I beseech and supplicate thee, receive the king and his brother and unite them with thy flock, cleansing them with thy washing[39] and anointing them with thy oil from the error which surrounds them. Preserve them also from the wolves, leading them in thy pastures. Give them to drink from thine ambrosial spring which neither is turbid nor dries up. For they pray thee and implore and desire to become thy ministers and servants, and for this cause they are content even to be persecuted by thine enemies, (p. 141) and for thy sake to be hated by them and be despitefully used and put to death,[40] even as thou for our sakes didst suffer all these things that thou mightest preserve us, who art Lord and truly a *good shepherd*.[41] But do thou grant to them that they may have confidence in thee alone, and <obtain> the help which cometh from thee and hope of their salvation, which they expect from thee alone, and that they may be established in thy mysteries and receive of thy graces and gifts the perfect good, and may flourish in thy service, and bring forth fruit to perfection in thy Father.'

26. Being now well disposed to the apostle, King Gundaphorus and his brother Gad followed him, departing from him not at all and themselves supplying those who were in need, giving to all and refreshing all. And they besought him that they also might now receive the seal of the word, saying to him: 'Since our souls are at leisure and we are zealous for God, give us the seal! For we have heard thee say that the God whom thou dost preach knows his own sheep by his seal.'[42] But the apostle said to them: 'I also rejoice and pray you to receive this seal, and to share with me in this eucharist (p. 142) and (feast of) blessing of the Lord, and be made perfect in it. For this is the Lord and God of all, Jesus Christ whom I preach, and he is the Father of truth in whom I have taught you to believe.' And he commanded them to bring oil, that through the oil they might receive the seal. So they brought the oil, and lit many lamps; for it was night. 27. And the apostle rose up and sealed them. But the Lord was revealed to them by a voice, saying: '*Peace be with you*,[43] brethren!' But they only heard his voice, but his form they did not see; for they had not yet received the additional sealing of the seal. And the apostle took the oil and pouring it on their heads anointed and chrismed them, and began to say:

Come, holy name of Christ *that is above every name*;[44]
Come, power of the Most High[45] and perfect compassion;
Come, thou highest gift;
Come, compassionate mother;

Come, fellowship of the male;
Come, thou (fem.) that dost reveal the hidden mysteries;
Come, mother of the seven houses,[46] that thy rest may be in the eighth house;
Come, elder <messenger S> of the five members, understanding, thought, prudence, (p. 143) consideration, reasoning,
Communicate with these young men!
Come, Holy Spirit, and purify their reins and their heart[47]
And give them the added seal in the name of Father and Son and Holy Spirit.

And when they had been sealed there appeared to them a young man carrying a blazing torch, so that the very lamps were darkened at the onset of its light. And going out he vanished from their sight. But the apostle said to the Lord: 'Beyond our comprehension, Lord, is thy light, and we are not able to bear it; for it is greater than our sight.' But when dawn came and it was light, he broke bread and made them partakers in the eucharist of Christ. And they rejoiced and were glad. And many others also, believing, were added (to the faithful) and came into the refuge of the Saviour.

28. But the apostle did not cease preaching and saying (p. 144) to them: 'Men and women, boys and girls, youths and maids, vigorous and aged, whether you are slaves or free, abstain from fornication and avarice and the service of the belly; for in these three heads all lawlessness is comprised. For fornication blinds the mind and darkens the eyes of the soul, and is a hindrance to the right ordering of the body, turning the whole man to weakness and throwing the whole body into sickness. Insatiate desire brings the soul into fear and shame, since it is within the body and plunders the goods of others, and harbours this suspicion, <that if it restore> the goods of others to the owners <it will be put to shame>. And the service of the belly plunges the soul into cares and anxieties and sorrows, <since it becomes anxious lest it come to be in want, and reaches out for what is far from it>. If then you escape from these, you become free from care and sorrow and fear, and there remains with you that which was said by the Saviour: *Be not anxious for the morrow, for the morrow will take care of itself.*[48] Remember also that word which was spoken before: Look at *the ravens* and (p. 145) consider *the birds of the heaven, that they neither sow nor reap nor gather into barns, and God provides for them. How much more for you,*[49] *O ye of little faith!*[50] But do you wait for his coming, and set your hope in him, and believe in his name. For he is *the judge of living and dead,*[51] and he *gives to each one according to his works.*[52] And at his coming and later appearance no man has any word of excuse[53] when he is about to be judged by him, as if he had not heard. For his heralds are proclaiming to the four regions of the

world. Repent, then, and believe the gospel, and receive a yoke of meekness and a light burden,[54] that you may live and not die! These things obtain, these do ye keep. Come out from the darkness, that the light may receive you! Come to him who is truly good, that you may receive grace from him and lay up his sign in your souls.'

29. When he had said this, some of the by-standers said to him: 'It is time for the creditor to receive the debt.' But he said to them: 'The creditor always wishes to receive more than enough, (p. 146) but let us give him what is needful.' And when he had blessed them he took bread and oil and herbs and salt, and blessed and gave to them; but he himself continued in his fasting, for the Lord's day was about to dawn. As he slept in the following night, the Lord came and stood at his head and said: 'Thomas, rise up early and bless them all, and after the prayer and service go down the eastern road two miles, and there I will show in thee my glory.[55] For because of the work to which thou goest out many will take refuge in me, and thou shalt convict the nature and the power of the enemy.' And rising up from sleep he said to the brethren who were with him: 'Children and brethren, the Lord wishes to accomplish something through me today. But let us pray and entreat him, that nothing may become a hindrance for us towards him, but that as at all times so now it may come to pass through us according to his will and desire.' And when he had said this he laid his hands upon them and blessed them. And breaking the bread of the eucharist he gave it to them, saying: 'This eucharist shall be to you for compassion and mercy, and not for judgment and requital.' And they said: 'Amen.'

(p. 147) Third Act
Concerning the serpent

30. And the apostle went out to go whither the Lord had commanded him; and when he was near the second mile(stone) and had turned aside a little from the road he saw lying there the body of a comely youth, and said: 'Lord, was it for this that thou didst bring me out here, that I might see this temptation? Thy will be done, then, as thou wilt.' And he began to pray and say: 'O Lord, *judge of living and dead*,[56] of the living who stand by and the dead who lie (here), thou Lord of all and Father - but Father not of the souls that are in bodies, but of those that are gone out; for of the souls that are in pollutions thou art Lord and judge - come in this hour in which I call upon thee, and show thy glory toward this man who lies here.' And turning to those who followed him he said: 'This thing has not happened to no purpose, but the enemy has been at work, and has wrought this that he may make an attack thereby; and you see that he has made use of no other form and wrought through no other creature than that which is his subject.'

31. And when he had said this a great serpent came out of a hole, darting his head and lashing his tail on the ground, and said with a loud voice to (p. 148) the apostle: 'I will say before thee for what reason I slew him, for to this end art thou come, to put my works to shame.' And the apostle said: 'Yes, speak on.' And the serpent: 'There is a certain beautiful woman in this village over against us. And as she once <passed by my place> I saw her and fell in love with her, and following her I kept watch on her. And I found this young man kissing her, and he had intercourse with her and did other shameful things with her. Now it would be easy for me to disclose them before thee, <but I dare not do it S>. For I know that thou art the twin brother of Christ, and dost ever abolish our nature. But not wishing to disquiet her I did not kill him in that very hour, but watched for him, and as he came by in the evening I smote and slew him, the more especially since he dared to do this on the Lord's day.' But the apostle questioned him, saying: 'Tell me of what seed and what race thou art.' 32. And he said to him: 'I am a reptile of reptile nature, the baleful son of a baleful father; I am son of him who hurt and smote the four standing brothers; I am son of him who sits upon the throne <and has power over the creation S> which is under heaven, who takes his own (p. 149) from those who borrow; I am son of him who girds the sphere about; and I am a kinsman of him who is outside the ocean, whose tail is set in his own mouth; I am he who entered through the fence into Paradise and said to Eve all the things my father charged me to say to her;[57] I am he who kindled and inflamed Cain to slay his own brother,[58] and because of me thorns and thistles sprang up on the earth;[59] I am he who hurled the angels down from above, and bound them in lusts for women, that earth-born children might come from them[60] and I fulfil my will in them; I am he who hardened Pharaoh's heart, that he might slay the children of Israel and enslave them in a yoke of cruelty;[61] I am he who led the multitude astray in the wilderness, when they made the calf;[62] I am he who inflamed Herod[63] and kindled Caiaphas to the false accusation of the lie before Pilate;[64] for this was fitting for me; I am he who kindled Judas and bribed him to betray Christ to death;[65] I am he who inhabits and possesses the abyss of Tartarus,[66] but the Son of God did me wrong against my will, and chose out his own from me; I am a kinsman of him who is to come from the east, to whom also is given power to do what he will on the earth.'

33. When the serpent had said this, in the hearing of all the crowd,* the apostle lifted up his voice on high and said: 'Cease now, most shameless one, and be thou put to shame and (p. 150) entirely done to death! For thine end, destruction, is come. And do not dare to say what thou hast wrought through those who have become subject to thee. I command thee in the name of that Jesus who contends with you until now for the men who are his own, that thou

suck out thy poison which thou didst put into this man, and draw it out and take it from him.' But the serpent said: 'Not yet is the time of our end come, as thou hast said. Why dost thou compel me to take what I have put into this man and die before the time? For indeed if my father draw forth and suck out what he cast into the creation, then is his end.' But the apostle said to him: 'Show now the nature of thy father!' And the serpent came forward and set his mouth against the young man's wound and sucked the gall out of it. And little by little the young man's colour, which was purple, became white, but the serpent swelled up. But when the serpent had drawn up all the gall into himself, the young man sprang up and stood, then ran and fell at the apostle's feet. But the serpent, being swollen, burst and died, and his poison and gall poured out; and in the place where his poison poured out there came a great chasm, and that serpent was swallowed up. And the apostle said to the king and his brother: 'Send workmen and fill up that place, and lay foundations and build houses on top, that it may become a dwellingplace for the strangers.'

34. But the young man said to the apostle, with many tears: 'Wherein have I sinned against thee? For thou art a man that has two forms, (p. 151) and wherever thou wilt, there thou art found, and thou art restrained by no man, as I see. For I saw how that man stood beside thee, and said to thee: "I have many wonders to show through thee, and I have great works to accomplish through thee, for which thou shalt receive a reward; and thou shalt make many live, and they shall be in rest in eternal light as children of God. Do thou, then," he said, speaking to thee of me, "revive this young man stricken by the enemy, and become at all times his guardian." Thou hast done well to come here, and again thou shalt do well to depart to him, for indeed he never leaves thee at all. But I have become free from care and reproach, and the light shone upon me (so that I am free) from the care of the night, and I am at rest from the toil of the day; but I am free also from him who urged me to do these things. I sinned against him who taught me the opposite, and I have lost that kinsman of the night who compelled me to sin by his own deeds; but I found that figure of light to be my kinsman. I have lost him who darkens and blinds his subjects, that they may not know what they are doing and, being ashamed at their works, depart from them and their deeds come to an end; but I found him whose works are light and his deeds truth, of which if a man does them he does not repent. I have been freed (p. 152) from him whose lie is persistent, before whom darkness goes as a veil and behind whom follows shame, shameless in inactivity; but I found him who revealed to me beautiful things that I might take hold of them, the Son of Truth, who is kinsman of concord, who driving away the mist enlightens his own creation, and healing its wounds overthrows its enemies. But I pray thee, man of God, make me to look upon him again, and to see him who is now become hidden from me, that I may also hear his voice, the wonder

of which I cannot express; for it is not of the nature of this bodily organ.' 35. But the apostle answered and said to him: 'If thou art freed from those things of which thou hast received knowledge, as thou hast said, and dost know who it is that has wrought this in thee, and dost learn and become a hearer of him whom now in thy fervent love thou seekest, thou shalt both see him and be with him for ever, and in his rest shalt thou rest, and thou shalt be in his joy. But if thou be lightly disposed towards him, and turn again to thy former doings, and let go the beauty and that radiant countenance which now was shown to thee, and the effulgence of his light which now thou dost desire <be wholly hidden from thee>, not only of this life shalt thou be deprived but also of that which (p. 153) is to come, and thou shalt depart to him whom thou didst say thou hadst lost, and no longer look on him whom thou didst say thou hadst found.'

36. And when the apostle had said this, he went into the city holding fast that young man's hand and saying to him: 'These things which thou hast seen, child, are but a few of the many which God has; for it is not about these visible things that he brings good news to us, but greater things than these he promises us. But so long as we are in the body we cannot speak and declare what he is to give to our souls. If we say that he gives us light, this is <something> visible, and we possess it; and if (we say that he gives us) wealth, <this> both exists and is visible in this world, and we name it, and do not require it, for it has been said: *Hardly shall a rich man enter into the kingdom of heaven.*[67] And if we speak of the mantle of clothing which the luxurious in this life put on, it is named and it has been said: *They who wear soft raiment are in king's houses.*[68] And if (we speak of) costly banquets, concerning these we have received a commandment to *beware* of them (and) *not to be weighed down in intemperance and drunkenness and the cares of this life*[69] (. . .), and it is said: *Be not anxious for your life, what ye shall eat or what ye shall drink, neither for your body, what ye shall put on,* for *the life is more than meat, and the body than raiment.*[70] And if we speak of this rest which is temporal, judgment is appointed for this also. But we speak about the world above, (p. 154) about God and angels, about watchers and saints, about the ambrosial food and the drink of the true vine,[71] about clothing that endures and does not grow old, about things *which eye has not seen nor ear heard, neither have they entered into the heart of* sinful *men, which God has prepared for those who love him.*[72] These things we discuss, and about these we bring good tidings. Do thou also, therefore, believe in him, that thou mayest live, and set in him thy trust, and thou shalt not die. For he is not persuaded by gifts, that thou shouldest offer to him, nor does he need sacrifice, that thou shouldest sacrifice to him. But look thou to him, and he will not disregard thee; and turn to him, and he will not forsake thee. For his comeliness and beauty will make thee very eager to love him, but also it does not allow thee to turn thyself away <from him>.'

37. And when the apostle said this, a large crowd joined that young man

(gathered round him). But as he looked the apostle saw them lifting themselves up that they might see him, and they were going up on high places. And the apostle said to them: 'Ye men who have come to the assembly of Christ and wish to believe in Jesus, take an example (a lesson) from this and see that unless you are lifted up you cannot see me who am small, and though I am like you you cannot observe me. If then you cannot see me, who am like you, unless you raise yourselves (p. 155) a little from the earth, how can you see him who dwells in the height and now is found in the depth, unless you first raise yourselves out of your former condition and your unprofitable deeds, and the desires that do not abide, and the wealth which is left here, and the possession which <comes> of the earth <and> grows old, and the clothing which deteriorates, and the beauty which grows old and vanishes, and indeed the whole body in which all these are stored and which growing old becomes dust, returning to its own nature? For all these things support the body itself. But believe rather in our Lord Jesus Christ, whom we preach, that your hope may be in him and that in him you may have life for ever and ever, that he may become for you a fellow-traveller in this land of error, and may be a haven for you in this turbulent sea. And he shall be for you a spring gushing forth in this thirsty land,[73] and a <house> full of food in the place of the hungry, and a rest for your souls, and also a physician of your bodies.' 38. Then the crowd of those who had gathered together, when they heard this, wept and said to the apostle: 'Man of God, we dare not say that we belong to that God whom thou dost preach, because our works which we have done are alien to him and not pleasing to him. But if he has compassion on us and pities us and saves us, overlooking our former deeds, and (p. 156) frees us from the evils which we wrought when we were in error, and does not reckon them to our account nor make mention of our former sins, we shall become his servants and shall carry out his will to the end.' But the apostle answered them saying: 'He does not condemn you, nor does he count against you the sins which you wrought while you were in error, but overlooks your transgressions which you have done in ignorance.'

Fourth Act
Concerning the colt

39. While the apostle was still standing in the highway and speaking with the crowd, an ass's colt came and stood before him, opened its mouth and said: 'Twin brother of Christ, apostle of the Most High and fellow-initiate into the hidden word of Christ, who dost receive his secret saying, fellow-worker of the Son of God,[74] who being free didst become a slave and being sold didst lead many to freedom; thou kinsman of the great race which condemned the enemy and redeemed his own, who has become a cause of life for many in the land

of the Indians - for thou didst come to the men who erred, and through thine appearance and thy divine words they are now turning to the God of truth who sent thee - mount and sit upon me and rest until thou enter the city.' And in answer the apostle said: 'O Jesus Christ, <son> (p. 157) of the perfect compassion! O peace and quiet, who art now spoken of even among unreasoning beasts! O hidden rest, and revealed by thy working as our Saviour and nourisher, preserving us and giving us rest in alien bodies, the Saviour of our souls, the spring that is sweet and unfailing, the fountain that is secure and pure and never defiled,[75] the defender and helper of thine own servants in the fight, who dost turn aside the enemy and drive him away from us, who in many battles dost fight for us, and make us conquer in them all, our true and invincible champion, our holy and victorious commander, the glorious, and providing for thine own a joy that does not pass away and a relief that contains no affliction at all, the good shepherd who didst give thyself for thine own sheep, and conquer the wolf and redeem thine own lambs[76] and lead them into good pasture; we glorify and praise thee and thine invisible Father and thy Holy Spirit and the Mother of all creation.'

40. When the apostle said this, all the crowd that was present looked at him, expecting to hear what he would answer to the colt. But after the apostle had stood for a long time <as if in a trance>, and had looked up to heaven, he said to the colt: '<Who are thou>, and to whom dost thou belong? For astonishing are the things (p. 158) shown forth by thy mouth, and beyond expectation, such as are hidden from the many.' And the colt in answer said: 'I am of that race that served Balaam[77] and thy Lord and teacher also sat upon one that belonged to me by race.[78] And now am I sent to give thee rest as thou dost sit upon me, and <that these may receive faith> and that to me may be given that portion which I am now to obtain through the service which <I render to thee>, and which if I serve thee <not> is taken from me.' But the apostle said to it: 'He who has bestowed on thee this gift (of speech) is able to cause it to be fulfilled to the end in thee and in those who belong to thee by race; for as to this mystery I am weak and feeble.' And he would not sit upon it. But the colt prayed and entreated that he would bless it <by riding upon it>. Then the apostle mounted and sat, and they followed with him, some going before and some following after. And they all ran, wishing to see the end and how he would dismiss the colt.

41. But when he came near to the gates of the city, he dismounted from it saying: 'Go, and be thou kept safe where thou wert.' But immediately the colt fell down on the ground at the apostle's feet and died. All those who were present were sorrowful, and said to the apostle: 'Bring it to life and raise it up!' But he (p. 159) said in reply: 'I could indeed raise it up through the name of Jesus Christ. But this is <not> expedient at all. For he who gave it speech that it might speak was able also to make it not die. But I do not raise it up, not

because I am not able but because this is what is useful and helpful for it.' And he instructed those who were present to dig a pit and bury its body; and they did as he commanded.

Fifth Act
Concerning the demon that dwelt in the woman

42. The apostle went into the city, all the people following him; and he was thinking of going to the parents of the young man whom he had made alive after he had been killed by the serpent, for they earnestly besought him to come to them and enter into their house. But a very beautiful woman suddenly uttered a piercing cry, saying: 'Apostle of the new God, who art come to India, and servant of that holy and only good God - for by thee is he preached as Saviour of the souls of those who come to him, and by thee are healed the bodies of those who are scourged by the enemy, and thou art he who is become an occasion of life for all who turn to him - command me to be brought before thee, that I may relate to thee what has befallen me, and perhaps from thee there may be hope for me, and these who stand beside thee (p. 160) may become more confident in the God whom thou dost preach. For I am no little tormented by the adversary these five years past. As a woman I formerly sat in quiet, and peace encompassed me on every side, and I had no anxiety over anything, for indeed I took no thought for any other. 43. But it happened one day, as I came out of the bath, there met me <a man like one> troubled and disturbed. His voice and his answer seemed to me to be very faint and weak. And standing in front of me he said: "I and thou shall be in one love, and we shall associate with one another as a man unites with his wife." And I answered saying to him: "With my betrothed I never united, since I declined to marry, and how shall I give myself up to thee, who dost wish to associate with me as in adultery?" And when I had said this I passed on; but I said to the handmaid who was with me: "Didst thou see the youth and his shamelessness, how without shame he spoke with me openly?" But she said to me: "I saw an old man conversing with thee." But when I was in my house and had dined, my soul suggested <.> a certain suspicion to me, and especially since he appeared to me in two forms. And having this in my mind I fell asleep. (p. 161) In that night, then, he came and united with me in his foul intercourse. I saw him also when it was day, and fled from him; but in the night that is akin to him he came and misused me. And now as thou dost see me I have been troubled by him five years, and he has not departed from me. But I know and am persuaded that demons and spirits and avengers are subject to thee, and become all a-tremble at thy prayer. Pray therefore for me, and drive out from me the demon that continually vexes me, <that> I too may be free and may be gathered together into my original nature, and receive the gift that has been given to my kindred.'

44. The apostle said: 'O evil not to be restrained! O shamelessness of the enemy! O envious one, never at rest! O hideous one that dost subdue the comely! O thou of many forms - he appears as he may wish, but his essence cannot be altered. O thou from the crafty and faithless one! O bitter tree, whose fruits are like him! O thou from the devil that fights for the aliens! O thou from the deceit that uses shamelessness! O thou from the wickedness that creeps like a snake and <is akin to it>!' (p. 162) And when the apostle had said this, the enemy came and stood before him, no one seeing him except the woman and the apostle, and with a very loud voice said in the hearing of all: 45. '*What have we to do with thee*, apostle *of the Most High?*[79] What have we to do with thee, servant of Jesus Christ? What have we to do with thee, counsellor of the holy Son of God? Why dost thou wish to destroy us, when our time is not yet come? Why dost thou wish to take our authority? For until this present hour we had hope and time remaining. What have we to do with thee? Thou hast authority in thine own (sphere) and we in ours. Why dost thou wish to exercise despotic rule against us, especially since thou thyself dost teach others not to act despotically? Why dost thou crave what belongs to others, as one not satisfied with his own? Why art thou made like to the Son of God who wronged us? For thou art altogether like him, as if begotten of him.* For we thought to bring him also under the yoke, even as the rest, but he turned and held us in subjection. For we knew him not; but he deceived us by his form most unsightly and by his poverty and need. For as we beheld him, such as he was, we thought that he was a man bearing flesh, not knowing that it is he who gives life to men. But he gave us authority in our own (sphere), and that in our time we should not abandon our own, but live in them; but thou dost wish to obtain above what is due, and what was given thee, and do us violence!' 46. And when the demon had said this, he wept, saying: 'I leave (p. 163) thee, my fairest consort, whom I found <a long time ago> and with whom I rested.[80] I forsake thee, my steadfast sister, my beloved in whom I was well pleased. What I shall do I know not, nor on whom I shall call that he may hear and help me. I know what I shall do: I shall go to places where the fame of this man has not been heard, and for thee, my beloved, I shall perhaps find one with another name.' And lifting up his voice he said: 'Abide in peace, since thou hast taken refuge in one greater than I; but I will depart and seek one like thee, and if I find her not I return to thee again. For I know that while thou art near to this man thou hast thy refuge in him, but when he is gone thou shalt be as thou wert before he appeared, and him shalt thou forget, but for me there shall be opportunity and confidence; but now I fear the name of him who hath saved thee.' And when he had said this, the demon vanished; only as he departed fire and smoke were seen there, and all who stood by there were astounded.

47. When the apostle saw it, he said to them: 'That demon showed nothing strange or alien, but his own nature, in which also he shall be burned up. For

indeed the fire shall consume him utterly, and the smoke of him shall be scattered abroad.' And he began to say: 'Jesus, the hidden mystery that has been (p. 164) revealed to us, thou art he who has made known to us many mysteries; who did set me apart from all my companions and speak to me three words,[81] wherewith I am inflamed, and tell them to others I cannot; Jesus, man, slain, corpse, buried; Jesus, God of God, Saviour who dost quicken the dead and heal the sick; Jesus, who wert in need like <a poor man S>, and dost save as one who has no need; thou who didst catch the fish for the breakfast and the dinner,[82] and didst make all satisfied with a little bread;[83] Jesus, who didst rest from the weariness of the journey like a man,[84] and walk upon the waves like a God;[85] 48. Jesus most high, voice arising (like the sun) from the perfect mercy, Saviour of all, right hand of the light which overthrows the evil one by his own nature, thou who dost gather all his nature into one place; thou of many forms, who art only-begotten, the *first-born of many brethren*;[86] God from God Most High, man despised until now;* Jesus Christ, who dost not neglect us when we call upon thee; who art become <an occasion of life to all mankind>; who for our sakes wast judged and shut up in prison, and dost set free all that are in bonds; who wast called a *deceiver*,[87] and dost deliver thine own from deception; I pray thee for these (p. 165) who stand (here) and believe in thee. For they crave to obtain thy gifts, having good hope in thy help, and having <their> refuge in thy greatness. They have their ears open to hear from us the words which are spoken to them. Let thy peace come and dwell in them, and let it renew them from their former deeds, and let them *put off the old man with his deeds and put on the new*[88] who is now proclaimed to them by me.'

49. And laying his hands upon them he blessed them, saying: '*The grace of our Lord Jesus Christ be upon you for ever!*'[89] And they said: 'Amen.' But the woman besought him, saying: 'Apostle of the Most High, give me the seal, that that enemy may not return to me again!' Then he made her come near to him, and laying his hands upon her sealed her in the name of the Father and of the Son and of the Holy Spirit. And many others also were sealed with her. And the apostle commanded his servant (deacon) to set a table before them; and he set out a stool which they found there, (p. 166) and spreading a linen cloth upon it set on the bread of blessing. And the apostle stood beside it and said: 'Jesus, who has made us worthy to partake of the Eucharist of thy holy body and blood, behold we make bold to approach thy Eucharist, and to call upon thy holy name; come thou and have fellowship with us!' 50. And he began to say:

<Come, gift of the Most High; S>
Come, perfect compassion;
Come, fellowship of the male;
<Come, Holy Spirit; S>

Come, thou that dost know the mysteries of the Chosen;
Come, thou that hast part in all the combats of the noble Athlete;
<Come, treasure of glory; S>
<Come, darling of the compassion of the Most High; S>
Come, silence
That dost reveal the great deeds of the whole greatness;
Come, thou that dost show forth the hidden things
And make the ineffable manifest;
Holy Dove
That bearest the twin young;
Come, hidden Mother;
Come, thou that art manifest in thy deeds and dost furnish joy
And rest for all that are joined with thee;
Come and partake with us in this Eucharist
Which we celebrate in thy name,
And in the love-feast
In which we are gathered together at thy call.

And when he had said this, he marked the Cross upon the bread and broke it, and began to distribute it. And first he gave to the woman, saying: 'Let this be to thee for forgiveness of sins and eternal transgressions!' And (p. 167) after he he gave also to all the others who had received the seal.

Sixth Act

Concerning the youth who had murdered the maiden

51. Now there was a certain young man who had wrought a lawless deed. As he came forward and took the Eucharist with his mouth, his two hands withered up,[90] so that he could no longer put them to his mouth. When those who were present saw him, they informed the apostle of what had happened, and calling him the apostle said to him: 'Tell me, child, and be not ashamed: what (was it) that thou didst and camest here? For the Lord's Eucharist has convicted thee (of an evil deed). For this gift, passing into many, brings healing, especially to those who approach in faith and love, but thee it has withered away, and what has happened has not taken place without some action (on thy part).' But the young man, convicted by the Lord's Eucharist, came and fell at the apostle's feet and besought him, saying: 'An evil deed has been wrought by me, <although> I thought to do something good. I loved a woman who lives outside the city in an inn, and she also loved me. But when I heard (the sermon) from thee (p. 168) and believed that thou dost proclaim (the) living God, I came forward and received the seal from thee with the others. But thou didst say: "Whoever shall unite in the impure union, and

especially in adultery, he shall not have life with the God whom I preach." Since, then, I loved her greatly, I besought her and tried to persuade her to become my consort in chastity and pure conduct, which thou thyself dost teach; but she would not. Since she was unwilling, then, I took a sword and slew her; for I could not see her commit adultery with another.'

52. When the apostle heard this, he said: 'O insensate union, how dost thou run to shamelessness! O desire not to be checked, how didst thou move this man to do this! O work of the serpent, how dost thou rage in thine own!' But the apostle commanded water to be brought to him in a basin. And when the water was brought, he said: 'Come, waters from the living waters, the existent from the existent and sent to us; rest that was sent to us from the Rest; power of salvation that cometh from that power which conquers all things and subjects them to its own will - come and dwell in these waters, that the gift of the Holy Spirit may be perfectly fulfilled in them!' And he said to the young man: 'Go, wash thy hands in these waters!' And when he had washed (p. 169) they were restored, and the apostle said to him: 'Dost thou believe in our Lord Jesus, that he is able to do all things?' And he said: 'Though I be but the least, I believe. But I wrought this deed thinking to do something good; for I besought her, as I told thee, but she would not obey me, to keep herself chaste.'

53. But the apostle said to him: 'Come, let us go to the inn where thou didst commit this deed, and let us see what has come to pass!' And the young man went before the apostle on the way; and when they arrived in the inn they found her lying. And seeing her the apostle was despondent, for she was a comely girl. And he commanded her to be brought into the middle of the inn. And they laid her on a bed, carried her out, and laid her in the middle of the court of the inn. And the apostle laid his hand upon her, and began to say: 'Jesus, who dost appear to us at all times - for this is thy will, that we should ever seek thee, and thou thyself hast given us this right to ask and to receive, and not only didst thou grant this, but also thou didst teach us to pray,[91] - thou who are not seen with our bodily eyes, but art never hidden at all from those of our soul, and in thy form indeed art hidden, but in thy works (p. 170) art manifest to us; and by thy many works we have come to know thee, as we are able, but thou thyself hast given to us thy gifts without measure, saying: *Ask, and it shall be given you, seek and ye shall find, knock and it shall be opened unto you.*[92] We pray now, since we have a fear because of our sins. But we ask thee not for wealth, neither gold nor silver nor possessions nor any other of the things which come of the earth and return again to the earth, but this we beseech of thee and entreat, that in thy holy name thou raise up her who lies here by thy power, to (thy) glory and (the confirmation of) the faith of them that stand by.' 54. And he said to the young man, after sealing him: 'Go, take her hand and say to her: "I with my hands did slay thee with iron, and with my hands by faith in Jesus I raise thee up."' So the young man went and stood beside her, saying: 'I have

believed in thee, Christ Jesus.' And looking at Judas Thomas the apostle, he said to him: 'Pray <for me>, that my Lord, upon whom I call, may come to my help.' And laying his hand upon her hand he said: (p. 171) 'Come, Lord Jesus Christ; unto her grant life, and to me the earnest of thy faith!' And immediately when he drew on her hand she sprang up and sat, looking on the great crowd that stood by. She saw also the apostle standing opposite her, and leaving the bed and springing up she fell at his feet and caught hold of his garments, saying: 'I pray thee, my Lord, where is that other who was with thee, who did not leave me to remain in that dreadful and cruel place, but delivered me to thee, saying: "Take thou this woman, that she may be made perfect, and hereafter be gathered to her place"?'

55. But the apostle said to her: 'Relate to us where thou hast been.' And she answered: 'Thou who wast with me, to whom also I was delivered, dost thou wish to hear?' And she began to say: 'A man received me, hateful of countenance, entirely black, and his clothing exceedingly dirty. And he led me to a place[93] in which there were many chasms,[94] and much ill odour and a hateful vapour was given off thence. And he made me look down into each chasm, and I saw in the (first) chasm a flaming fire, and wheels of fire were running <hither and> thither, and souls were hung upon those wheels, dashed against each other. And there was a cry there and a very great lamentation, but there was none to deliver. And that man said to me: "These souls are kindred to thee, (p. 172) and in the days of reckoning they were delivered for punishment and destruction. And then (when the chastisement of each is ended) others are brought in their stead, and likewise these again to another (chasm). These are they who perverted the intercourse of man and woman." And when I looked, I saw (new-born) infants heaped one upon another and struggling with one another as they lay upon them. And he answered and said to me: "These are their children, and therefore are they set here for a testimony against them." 56. And he led me to another chasm, and looking in I saw mire, and worms[95] welling up, and souls wallowing there, and (heard) a great gnashing break out thence from among them. And that man said to me: "These are the souls of women who forsook their husbands (and men who left their wives) and committed adultery with others, and have been brought to this torment." Another chasm he showed me, and when I looked into it I saw souls, some hanging by the tongue, some by the hair, some by the hands, some by the feet head downwards, and (all) reeking with smoke and brimstone.[96] Concerning these that man who was with me answered me: "These souls which are hung by the tongue are slanderers, and such as utter lying and infamous words and are not ashamed. And those that are hung by the hair are the shameless who have no modesty at all (p. 173) and go about in the world bare-headed. And those which are hung by the hands, these are they who took away and stole the

goods of others, and never gave anything to the needy or gave help to the afflicted, <and> did this because they wished to take everything, and paid no heed whatever to justice and to the law. And those who hang upside down by the feet, these are they who lightly and eagerly run <upon> evil ways and disorderly paths, not visiting the sick and not escorting them that depart this life. And for this cause each several soul receives what was done by it." 57. Leading me away again he showed me a cave, very dark (and) breathing out a great stench, and many souls looked out thence, wishing to get something of the air; but their guards did not allow them to look out. And he who was with me said: "This is the prison of those souls which thou didst see. For when they have fulfilled their punishments for what each one did, others later succeed them. And some are entirely consumed, and <some> are handed over to other punishments." Now those who guarded the souls that were in the dark cave said to the man who had received me: "Give her to us that we may take her in to the others until (p. 174) the time comes for her to be handed over for punishment." But he answered them: "I do not give her to you, for I fear him who delivered her to me; for I was not commanded to leave her here. I am taking her back with me until I receive an order concerning her." And he took me and led me to another place, in which were men who were being tortured cruelly. But he who is like thee took and delivered me to thee, saying to thee: "Take her, for she is one of the sheep that have gone astray." And received by thee I am now before thee. I beseech thee, therefore, and entreat that I may not depart into those places of punishment which I saw.'

58. But the apostle said: 'You have heard what this woman related. But there are not only these punishments, but also others worse than these. And you also, if you do not turn to this God whom I preach, and desist from your former works and from the deeds which you wrought without knowledge, shall have your end in these punishments. Believe therefore in Christ Jesus, and he forgives you the sins committed before this and will cleanse you from (p. 175) all your bodily desires which remain on the earth, and will heal you from the trespasses which follow you and depart with you and are found before you. Each one of you, therefore, put off the old man and put on the new,[97] and abandon your first way of life and conduct. And let them that steal steal no more, but live by labouring and working.[98] Let the adulterers no longer practise lechery, that they may not utterly deliver themselves to eternal punishment; for with God adultery is exceeding wicked, above the other evils. Put away also avarice and falsehood and drunkenness and slander, and do not return evil for evil.[99] For all these things are strange and alien to the God who is preached by me. But walk ye rather in faith and meekness and holiness and hope, in which God delights, that ye may become his kinsmen, expecting from him the gifts which only some few receive.'

59. So all the people believed, and yielded their souls obedient to the living

God and to Christ Jesus, rejoicing in the blessed works (p. 176) of the Most High and in his holy service. And they brought much money for the service of the widows; for he had them gathered together in the cities, and to them all he sent what was necessary by his deacons, both clothing and provision for their nourishment. But he himself did not cease preaching and speaking to them and showing that this is Jesus the Christ whom the Scriptures proclaimed, who came and was crucified and after three days was raised from the dead. And secondly he showed them and explained, beginning from the prophets, the things concerning Christ, that he must come and that in him all that had been prophesied concerning him must be fulfilled.[100] And the fame of him spread into all the towns and villages, and all who had sick or such as were troubled by unclean spirits brought them, and laid them on the road by which he was to pass, and he healed them all in the power of the Lord. Then all who were healed by him said with one accord with one voice: 'Glory be to thee, Jesus, who (to all) alike hast granted healing through thy servant (p. 177) and apostle Thomas! And being in health and rejoicing we beseech thee that we may become (members) of thy flock and be numbered among thy sheep. Receive us therefore, Lord, and do not reckon unto us our transgressions and our <former> errors which we committed while we were in ignorance.'

60. And the apostle said: 'Glory be to *the only-begotten of the Father*,[101] glory to *the first-born of many brethren*,[102] glory to thee, the defender and helper of those who come to thy refuge, the sleepless and the one who awakens those in sleep, who lives and gives life to those who are in death, O God Jesus Christ, Son of the living God, redeemer and helper, refuge and rest of all who labour in thy work, giver of healing to those who for thy name's sake endure *the burden and the heat of the day*:[103] we thank thee for the gifts given to us from thee, and the help bestowed upon us by thee, and thy provision that cometh to us from thee. 61. Perfect these things therefore unto us even to the end, that we may have the confidence that is in thee. Look upon us, because for thy sake we have left our homes and our fathers' goods,[104] and for thy sake have gladly and willingly become strangers. Look upon us, Lord, (p. 178) because we have left our own possessions for thy sake, that we may obtain thee, the possession that cannot be taken away. Look upon us, Lord, because we have left those who belong to us by race, that we may be united with thy kindred. Look upon us, Lord, who have left our fathers and mothers and fosterers,[105] that we may behold thy Father and be satisfied with his divine nourishment. Look upon us, Lord, for for thy sake we have left our bodily consorts and our earthly fruits, that we may share in that abiding and true fellowship and bring forth true fruits, whose nature is from above, which none can take away from us, with whom we abide and they abide in us.'

Seventh Act
Concerning the captain

62. While the apostle Thomas was proclaiming the word of God in all India, a certain captain of king Misdaeus (Mazdai S) came to him and said to him: 'I have heard concerning thee that thou dost not take reward of any man, but whatever thou hast thou dost give to the needy. For if thou didst take rewards, I would have sent much money and would not have come hither myself, for the king takes no action without me. For I have many possessions and am rich, one of the (p. 179) wealthy in India. And I never wronged anyone at all; but the contrary has befallen me. I have a wife, and of her I had a daughter, and I am wholly devoted to her, as indeed nature requires, and have not made trial of another wife. Now it happened that there was a wedding in our city, and those who made the marriage were my very close friends. So they came and asked me (for my consent), in that they were inviting her (my wife) and her daughter. Since they were my good friends, I could not refuse. So I sent her, although she did not wish to go, and with them I sent many servants also. So off they went, dressed in great finery, she and her daughter. 63. But when evening came and it <was> time to come away from the wedding, I sent lamps and torches to meet them. And I stood in the street watching when she should come and I see her with my daughter. And as I stood I heard a sound of wailing. "Woe for her!" was heard from every mouth. And the servants came to me with their clothes torn and told me what had happened. "We saw", they said, "a man and a boy with him. And the man laid his hand upon thy wife and (p. 180) the boy upon thy daughter, but they fled from them. We wounded them with our swords, but our swords fell to the ground. And in the same hour they (the women) fell down, gnashing their teeth and dashing their heads on the ground; and when we saw this we came to tell thee." And when I heard this from the servants I rent my clothes and struck my face with my hands, and ran down the street like one gone mad; and when I came I found them prostrate in the market-place. And I took them and brought them to my house, and after a long time they came to themselves, and when they were calmed they sat down. 64. So I began to question my wife: "What has happened to thee?" And she said to me: "Dost thou not know what thou hast done to me? For I prayed thee that I might not go to the wedding, since I was not in a good state of body. And as I went along the street and drew near the channel in which the water was flowing, I saw a black man standing opposite me, <nodding his head at me S>, and a boy like him standing beside him. And I said to my daughter: Look at these two ugly men, whose teeth are like milk but their lips like soot. And we left them by the aqueduct and went on. But when the sun had set and <we came away> from the wedding (p. 181) <and> were going through (the town) with the young men, <and> had come very near the aqueduct, my daughter saw

them first and stealthily took refuge with me. And after her I too saw them coming against us, and we fled from them; and the servants who were with us <fled likewise>. <But they (the two men) struck us and threw us down, me and my daughter.' And when she had told me this, the demons came upon them again and threw them down. And from that hour they cannot go outside, but are shut up in one room or another. And on their account I suffer much and am distressed. For they throw them down wherever they find them, and strip them naked. I pray thee and entreat before God: help me and have pity on me. For it is three years now since a table was set in my house, and my wife and daughter have not sat at table. And especially (I pray thee) for my unhappy daughter, who has seen no good at all in this world.'

65. And when the apostle heard this from the captain (p. 182) he was greatly grieved for him; and he said to him: 'Dost thou believe that Jesus will heal them?' And the captain said: 'Yes.' And the apostle: 'Commit thyself then to Jesus, and he will heal them and bring them help.' But the captain said: 'Show me him, that I may entreat him and believe in him. But the apostle said: '<Stretch thy mind upward as much as thou canst, for S> he does not appear to these bodily eyes, but with the eyes of the mind is he found.' So the captain lifted up his voice and said: 'I believe in thee, Jesus, and I pray thee and entreat: help thou my little faith[106] which I have in thee.' But the apostle commanded Xenophon the deacon to assemble all at one place, and when the whole crowd was gathered the apostle stood in the midst and said: 66. 'My children and brethren who have believed in the Lord, abide in this faith, preaching Jesus who was proclaimed to you by me and having your hopes in him. And <do not forsake him>, and he will not forsake you. While you lie asleep in this slumber that weighs down the sleepers, (p. 183) he being sleepless keeps watch; and when you sail on the sea and are in danger, and none can help, he walking upon the waters[107] rights <your ship S> by his help. For I am now going from you, and it is uncertain whether I shall see you again according to the flesh. Be ye not, therefore, like the people of Israel, who <when their shepherd departed from them> for a short time stumbled.[108] But I leave with you Xenophon the deacon in my place, for he also preaches Jesus, even as I do. For neither am I anything, nor is he, but Jesus. For indeed I too am a man clothed with a body, a son of man like one of you. Neither have I riches such as are found with some, which convict their possessors since they are utterly useless, and are abandoned upon the earth from which they came. But the transgressions which come upon men because of them, and the stains of sins, <they carry away> with them. But seldom are rich men found in acts of mercy; but the merciful (p. 184) and the lowly in heart, they shall inherit the kingdom of God.[109] For it is not beauty that is enduring with men; for those who rely upon it, when old age takes hold of them, shall be suddenly put to shame. All things have their season; so at one time there is loving and at another hating.[110] Let your hope therefore be

in Jesus Christ the Son of God, who is ever loved and ever desired. And remember us, as we do you. For we <ourselves>, if we do not <bear> the burden of the commandments, are not worthy to be preachers of this name, and shall later suffer punishment there.' 67. And when he had prayed with them, remaining a long time in prayer and supplication, he commended them to the Lord and said: 'Lord, who rulest over every soul that is in a body; Lord, Father of the souls that have their hope in thee and await thy mercies, thou who dost deliver thine own men from error and set free from slavery and corruption those who are subject and come to thy refuge; be thou with Xenophon's flock, anoint it with holy oil, heal it from the wounds and preserve (p. 185) it from the ravening wolves.'[111] And laying his hand upon them he said: 'The peace of the Lord be upon you and go with us.'

Eighth Act
Concerning the wild asses

68. So the apostle went out to depart on his way. And they all escorted him, weeping and adjuring him to remember them in his prayers and not <forget> them. When he had mounted and taken his seat on the wagon, and all the brethren were left behind, the captain came and aroused the driver, saying: 'I pray and entreat that I may become worthy to sit beneath his feet, and I shall become his driver along this road, that he may become my guide to that road by which few travel.' 69. Now when they had journeyed about two miles, the apostle begged of the captain and made him rise and sit with him, allowing the driver to sit in his own place. But when they went off along the road, it befell that the beasts became weary with the great heat, and <could> not move at all. The captain was vexed and altogether in despair, and thought of going on his own feet (p. 186) and bringing other animals for the wagon. But the apostle said: 'Let not thy heart be troubled or afraid,[112] but believe in Jesus Christ whom I declared to thee, and thou shalt see great wonders.' And looking about he saw a herd of wild asses grazing beside the road. And he said to the captain: 'If thou <dost believe> in Jesus Christ, go to that herd of wild asses and say: "Judas Thomas, the apostle of Christ the new God, says to you, Let four of you come, of whom we have need."'

70. And the captain went, although he was afraid; for they were many. And as he went, they came to meet him. And when they drew near he said to them: 'Judas Thomas, the apostle of the new God, commands you: Let four of you come, of whom I have need.' When the wild asses heard this, they came to him with one accord at a run, and having come they did him reverence.* But the apostle said to them: 'Peace be with you! Yoke four (of you) in place of these beasts that have come to a stand.' And every one of them came and pressed to be yoked. Now there were four there, stronger <than the rest>, and these were

yoked. (p. 187) As to the others, some went before and some followed. But when they had travelled a short distance he dismissed <them>, saying: 'To you dwellers in the wilderness I say, Go to your pastures! For if I needed all, you would all come with me. But now go to your place in which you <were dwelling>.' But they went off quietly until they were out of sight.

71. Now as the apostle, the captain and the driver <took their seats S>, the wild asses pulled the wagon quietly and evenly, that they might not disturb the apostle of God. And when they came near the gate of the city they turned aside and stood before the doors of the captain's house. And the captain said: 'It is not possible for me to relate what has happened, but when I see the end then I will speak,' So the whole city came, when they saw the wild asses yoked; moreover they heard the report about the apostle, that he was to stay there. But the apostle asked the captain: 'Where is thy dwelling, and whither art thou taking us?' And he said to him: 'Thou thyself dost know that we stand before the doors, and these that are come with thee by thy command know it better than I.'

72. Saying this, he dismounted from the wagon. So the apostle began to say: 'Jesus Christ, <the knowledge of whom is blasphemed in this land S>, Jesus Christ, whose fame is strange in this city, Jesus who dost receive all (p. 188) the apostles in every land and in every city, and all who are worthy of thee are glorified in thee; Jesus, who didst take shape and become as a man, and didst appear to us all,[113] that thou mightest not separate us from thine own love; thou, Lord, art he who gave himself for us and by thy blood bought us[114] and gained us as a precious possession. But what have we to give thee, Lord, in exchange for thy life[115] which thou didst give for us? <For what we have is thy gift.> <And thou dost ask of us nothing S> but this, that we entreat of thee and (thereby) live.' 73. And when he said this, many gathered together from all sides to see the apostle of the new God. But the apostle said again: 'Why stand we idle? Lord Jesus, the hour is come. What dost thou require to be done? Command therefore that that be fulfilled which must come to pass.' . . . And the apostle said to one of the wild asses that were yoked on the right side: 'Go into the court and stand there, call the demons and say to them: "Judas Thomas, the apostle and disciple of Jesus Christ, says to you: Come out here! (p. 189) For because of you was I sent, and against those who belong to you by race, to destroy you and pursue you to your place, until the time of fulfilment comes and you go down to your depth of darkness."' 74. And that wild ass went in, a great crowd accompanying him, and said: 'To you I speak, the enemies of Jesus who is called Christ; to you I speak, who shut your eyes that you may not see the light - for the nature most evil cannot be transformed to the good; to you I speak, the children of Gehenna and of destruction, of him who does not cease from evil until now, who ever renews his workings and the things that fit his substance; to you I speak, the most shameless, who are being destroyed by yourselves; but what I shall say of your destruction and end, and what I shall

advise, I know not. For there are many things and innumerable for the hearing. But greater are your deeds than the punishment that is reserved for you. But to thee I speak, thou demon, and to thy son who follows with thee, for now am I sent against you - but why do I make a long story of your nature and root, which you yourselves know and are unashamed? But Judas Thomas says to you, the apostle of Christ Jesus who out of great love and good will has been sent here: (p. 190) Before all the crowd that stands here come out and tell me of what race you are.'

75. And immediately the woman came out with her daughter, <like> people dead and dishonoured. And when the apostle saw them he was grieved, especially for the girl, and said to the demons: 'God forbid that there be propitiation or sparing for you, for you know not sparing or compassion. In the name of Jesus, depart from them and stand by their side.' When the apostle said this, the women fell down and died;[116] for they neither had breath nor uttered a sound. But the demon in answer said with a loud voice: 'Art thou come hither again, thou that mockest our nature and race? Art thou come again, thou that dost blot out our crafty devices <traces S>? And as I think, thou dost not consent to our being on earth at all. But this thou canst not do now at this time.' But the apostle recognised that this was the demon who had been driven out of that woman. 76. But the demon said: 'I pray thee, give me leave to go and dwell where thou wilt, and to receive commandment from thee, and I fear not the mighty one who has authority over me. For even as thou didst come to preach the Gospel, so did I come to destroy. And even as, if thou fulfil not (p. 191) the will of him who sent thee, he brings punishment upon thy head, so I also, if I do not do the will of him who sent me, am sent back before the time and appointed season to my nature. And as thy Christ helps thee in what thou dost perform, so my father helps me in what I perform. And as he prepares for thee vessels worthy of thy habitation, so also he (my father) seeks out for me vessels through which I may accomplish his deeds. And as he nourishes and provides for his subjects, so for me also (my father) prepares punishments and tortures with those who have become my dwellings. And as to thee he gives eternal life as reward for thy working, so for me he (my father) provides in requital for my works eternal destruction. And as thou art refreshed by thy prayer and good works and spiritual hymns, so am I refreshed by murders and adulteries and sacrifices wrought with wine at the altars. And as thou dost convert men to eternal life, so do I pervert those who obey me to destruction and eternal punishment. And thou dost receive thine own <reward>, and I mine.'

77. When the demon had said this and much more (p. 192), the apostle said: 'Jesus commands thee and thy son through me to enter no more into the habitation of man, but go out and depart and live wholly outside the dwelling of men.'[117] But the demons said to him: 'A hard command hast thou given us.

But what wilt thou do against those who are now hidden from thee? For those who have wrought < . . . > the images rejoice in them more than thee, and the many worship them <.> and do their will, sacrificing to them and bringing food in libations <of> wine and water and <offering oblations>.' And the apostle said: 'They also shall now be abolished, together with their works. And suddenly the demons became invisible; but the women lay prostrate on the ground like dead people, without a sound.

78. And the wild asses stood together and did not separate one from another; but while all were silent and watched to see what they would do, that wild ass to whom speech was given by the power of the Lord (p. 193) said to the apostle: 'Why dost thou stand idle, apostle of Christ the Most High, who looks for thee to ask of him the fairest learning? Why then dost thou delay? For thy teacher wishes to show his mighty works by thy hands. Why dost thou stand, herald of the hidden one? For thy master wishes to make known the ineffable things through thee, preserving them for those who are worthy to hear them from him. Why dost thou rest, thou who dost perform mighty works in the name of the Lord? For thy Lord urges thee on, engendering boldness in thee. Fear not, therefore; for he will not forsake the soul that belongeth to thee by race. Begin then to call upon him, and he will readily hear thee. Why dost thou stand wondering at all his deeds and workings? For these things are small which he has shown through <thee>. And what wilt thou tell concerning his great gifts? For thou wilt not be sufficient to declare them. And why dost thou wonder at his bodily healings, <which come to nought S>, especially when thou dost know that sure and abiding healing of his which he offers to <his own possession>? And why dost thou look to this temporal life, and take no thought of the eternal? 79. (p. 194) But to you crowds who stand by and expect those that are cast down to be raised up I say: Believe the apostle of Jesus Christ! Believe the teacher of truth! Believe him who shows you the truth! Believe in Jesus! Believe in Christ, who was born that the born might live through his life, who <became a child and was raised up> that <the perfect manhood> might become manifest <through him>. He taught his own <teacher>,[118] for he is the teacher of truth and the wisest of the wise, who also offered the gift in the temple[119] to show that all offering is sanctified <through him>. This man is his apostle, the revealer of truth. This is he who performs the will of him who sent him. But there shall come false apostles and prophets of lawlessness, whose end shall be according to their deeds,[120] who preach indeed and ordain that men should flee from impieties but are themselves at all times found in sins; *clothed* indeed *with sheep's clothing, but inwardly ravening wolves*.[121] Not satisfied with one wife, they corrupt many women; saying they despise children, they <ruin> many children, (p. 195) for which they pay the penalty; who are not <content> with their own possession but wish that everything <useful> should minister to them alone, and yet profess themselves as his (Christ's) disciples.

And with their mouth they utter one thing, but in their heart they think another; they exhort others to secure themselves from evil, but they themselves accomplish nothing good; who are thought to be temperate, and exhort others to abstain from fornication, theft and avarice, but <secretly practise all these things themselves>, although they teach others not to do them.'

80. As the wild ass <said> this, they all looked at him. And when he fell silent the apostle said: 'What I am to think about thy beauty, Jesus, and what I am to tell about thee, I do not know. Or rather, I am not able. For I have no power to declare it, O Christ who art at rest and only wise, who alone knowest what is in the heart and understandest the content of the thought - to thee be glory, merciful and tranquil; to thee be glory, wise word;* glory to thy compassion that was poured out upon us; glory to thy pity that was spread out over us; glory to thy majesty which for our sakes was made small; glory to thy most exalted kingship which (p. 196) for our sakes was humbled; glory to thy strength which for our sakes was made weak; glory to thy Godhead which for our sakes was seen in the likeness of men; glory to thy manhood which for our sakes died that it might make us live; glory to thy resurrection from the dead, for through it rising and rest come to our souls; glory and honour to thine ascent into the heavens, for through it thou has shown us the ascent to the height, having promised us that we shall *sit* on thy right hand *and* with thee *judge the twelve tribes of Israel.*[122] Thou art the heavenly word of the Father, thou art the hidden light of the understanding, he who shows the way of truth, pursuer of the darkness and obliterator of error.' 81. When he had said this, the apostle stood over the women, saying: 'My Lord and my God, I doubt not concerning thee, nor in unbelief do I call upon thee, who art ever our helper and defender and restorer, who dost breathe thine own power into us[123] and encourage us and furnish boldness in love to thine own servants; I pray thee, let these souls rise healed, and become as they were before they were smitten by the demons.' And when he said this, the women turned (p. 197) and sat up. And the apostle charged the captain that his servants should take them and lead them inside. But when they had gone in, the apostle said to the wild asses: 'Follow me.' And <they followed him S> until they were outside the gates. And when they came out he said: 'Depart in peace to your pastures.' So the wild asses went off readily. But the apostle stood and watched over them, that they might not be harmed by anyone, until they were far off and out of sight. And the apostle returned with the crowd to the captain's house.

Ninth Act
Concerning the wife of Charisius

82. Now it happened that a certain woman whose name was Mygdonia, the wife of Charisius, the close kinsman of the king, came to see and behold <the

new phenomenon of the new God who was being proclaimed>, and the new apostle who had come to stay in their land. She was carried by her own slaves, and because of the great crowd and the narrow space they were not able to bring her to him. But she sent to her husband, that he might send her more of their servants; and they came and <went ahead of her>, pressing upon the people (p. 198) and cuffing them. But when the apostle saw it, he said to them: 'Why do you trample on those who come to hear the word, and are eager for it? But you wish to be beside me, when you are yet far off - as it was said of the crowd that came to the Lord: *Having eyes, you see not, and having ears, you do not hear.*'[124] And he said to the crowds: '*He that hath ears to hear, let him hear.*'[125] And: *Come unto me, all ye that labour and are heavy-laden, and I will give you rest!*'[126]

83. And looking on those who carried her, he said to them: 'This blessing and this admonition[127] which was promised to them is now for you who are heavy laden. You are they who bear burdens grievous to be borne, you who <are driven forward> at her command. And though you are men they lay burdens on you, as on unreasoning beasts, while (p. 199) those who have authority over you think that you are not men such as they are. <And they know not that all men are alike before God S>, be they slaves or free.[128] <And righteous is the judgment of God which comes upon all souls on earth, and no man escapes it S>. For neither will possession at all profit the rich, nor poverty deliver the poor from the judgment. <For> we have not received a command which we cannot fulfil, nor has he laid upon us burdens grievous to be borne, which we cannot carry. Nor has he <imposed upon us> such a building as men build, nor to hew stones and prepare houses as your craftsmen do by their knowledge; but we have received this commandment from the Lord, that what does not please us when it is done by another, this we should not do to any other man.[129] 84. Abstain then first from adultery, for of all evils this is the beginning, <and from murder, because of which the curse came upon Cain[130] S>, (p. 200) then also from theft, which ensnared Judas Iscariot and brought him to hanging,[131] <and from intemperance, which cost Esau his birthright,[132] and from avarice S>, for those who <yield themselves to avarice> do not see what is done by them; and from ostentation <and from slander S> and from all disgraceful deeds, especially those of the body, <and from the horrid intercourse and couch of uncleanness S>, whose outcome is eternal condemnation. For this (impurity) is the mother-city of all evils. And likewise it leads those who walk proudly into slavery, dragging them down to the depth and subduing them under its hands that they may not see what they do; wherefore their deeds are unknown to them. 85. But do you <walk in holiness, for this is choice before God, more than any other good S>, and become thereby pleasing to God; <and in sobriety, for this shows commerce with God S>, and gives eternal life and sets death at nought. And (walk) in

friendliness, <. . . .> for this conquers the enemies and alone receives the crown of victory. And in <goodness> and (p. 201) <in stretching out of the hand to the poor and supplying> the want of the needy, bringing to them (of your goods) and distributing to the needy, especially those who walk in holiness. For this is choice before God, and leads to eternal life. For this before God is the mother-city of all good. For those who do not contend in Christ's stadium shall not attain holiness. And holiness appeared from God, abolishing fornication, overthrowing the enemy, well pleasing to God. For she is an invincible athlete, standing in honour with God and glorified by man. She is an ambassador of peace, proclaiming peace. <But temperance - > if anyone gains it, he remains without care, pleasing the Lord, awaiting the time of redemption. For it does nothing unseemly, and gives life and rest and joy to all who gain it. 86. But meekness has overcome death, bringing it under authority. Meekness (p. 202) has enslaved the enemy.[133] Meekness is a good yoke. Meekness fears no man and does not offer < . . . > resistance. Meekness is peace and joy and exultation of rest. Abide therefore in holiness, and receive freedom from care, and be near to meekness; for in these three heads is portrayed the Christ whom I proclaim to you. Holiness is a temple of Christ,[134] and he who dwells in it receives it as a habitation. <And temperance is the refreshing of God S>; for forty days and forty nights he fasted, tasting nothing.[135] And he who observes it (temperance) shall dwell in it as in a mountain. But meekness is his boast, for he said to Peter our fellow-apostle: *Turn* back *thy sword and restore it* again *to its sheath!* For if I wanted to do this, *could I not have brought more than twelve legions of angels* from *my Father?*'[136]

87. When the apostle said this in the hearing of all the crowd, they pressed and trampled one another. But the wife of Charisius the king's kinsman sprang from the litter and threw herself on the ground before the apostle, and catching his feet she said in entreaty: 'Disciple of the living God, thou art come into a desert country. For we live in a desert, like unreasoning beasts in our conduct; but now by thy hands shall we be saved. I pray thee, then, take thought for me and pray for me, that the compassion of the God whom thou dost preach may come upon me, and that I may become (p. 203) his dwelling-place and <have part with you> in the prayer and hope and faith in him, and that I too may receive the seal and become a holy temple, and he dwell in me.'[137] 88. And the apostle said: 'I pray and entreat for you all, brethren, who believe on the Lord, and for you sisters who hope in Christ, that the word of God may settle upon all and tabernacle in you;[138] for we have no power over you.' And he began to say to the woman Mygdonia: 'Rise up from the ground and compose thyself. For this added adornment shall profit thee nothing, nor the beauty of thy body, nor thy garments. But neither the fame of the honour that surrounds thee, nor the power of this world, nor this sordid communion with thy husband shall avail thee if thou be deprived of the true communion. For the pomp of

adornment comes to nothing, and the body grows old and changes, and garments become worn out, and authority and lordship pass away, accompanied by punishment for the manner in which each has conducted himself in it (lordship). And the fellowship of procreation also passes away, as being indeed matter of condemnation. Jesus alone abides for ever, and they who hope in him.' Having thus spoken he said to the woman: (p. 204) 'Depart in peace,[139] and the Lord will make thee worthy of his own mysteries.' But she said: 'I fear to depart, lest thou forsake me and go to another nation.' But the apostle said to her: 'Even if I go, I will not leave thee alone, but Jesus because of his compassion will be with thee.' And she falling down did him obeisance and departed to her house.

89. But Charisius the kinsman of king Misdaeus came back after bathing and sat down to dine. And he asked concerning his wife, where she was; for she had not come from her own chamber to meet him as she was wont. Her handmaids said to him: 'She is not well.' And he sprang up and went into the chamber, and found her lying on the bed and veiled; and unveiling her he kissed her, saying: 'Why art thou sorrowful today?' And she said: 'I am not well.' And he said to her: 'Why didst thou not have regard to thy position as a free woman and remain in thy house, but go out and listen to vain words and look upon magic works? But rise up and dine with me, for without thee I cannot dine.' But she said to him: 'I pray thee, today excuse me; for I am sore afraid.' 90. When Charisius heard this from Mygdonia, he did not want to go out to dinner, but commanded his servants to bring her to dine with him. (p. 205) So when they brought her he asked her to dine with him, but she excused herself. Since she was unwilling, he dined alone, saying to her: 'For thy sake I declined to dine with king Misdaeus, and wert thou unwilling to dine with me?' But she said: 'Because I am not well.' When he rose, Charisius wanted as usual to sleep with her, but she said: 'Did I not tell thee that for today I have declined?'

91. When he heard this, he went and slept in another bed. But when he awoke from sleep he said: 'My lady Mygdonia, listen to the dream which I have seen. I saw myself reclining near king Misdaeus, and a full-laid table was set beside us. And I saw an eagle coming down from heaven and carrying off from before me and the king two partridges, which he bore off to his <nest>. And again he came upon us, flying round above us; but the king commanded a bow <to be brought> to him. And the eagle again snatched from before us a pigeon and a dove. But the king shot an arrow at him, and it passed through him from one side to the other, and did him no harm; and he rose up quite unscathed to his nest. And now that I am awake I am afraid and sore troubled, because I had tasted of the partridge, and he did not allow me to put it to my mouth again.' But Mygdonia said to him: 'Thy dream is good, for thou dost eat partridges daily, but this eagle had not tasted of a partridge until now.'

92. (p. 206) But when morning came, Charisius went off and dressed, and he bound his left sandal on his right foot.[140] And pausing, he said to Mygdonia: 'Now what is the meaning of this? For see - the dream and <this business>!' But Mygdonia said to him: 'This too is nothing bad, but seems to me very good; for from a bad business it will come to the better.' But he after washing his hands went away to salute king Misdaeus. 93. And likewise Mygdonia also rose up early and went to salute Judas Thomas the apostle. And she found him conversing with the captain and all the crowd; and he was exhorting them, speaking about the woman who had received the Lord in her soul (and asking)[141] whose wife she was. <The captain said>: 'She is the wife of Charisius, the kinsman of king Misdaeus', and 'Her husband is a very hard man, and in all that he says to the king he obeys him.[142] And he will not allow her to continue in this opinion which she has avowed. For indeed he has often praised her before the king, saying that there is no other like her for love. So all that thou dost discuss with her is strange to her.' But the apostle said: 'If the Lord has truly and surely risen in her soul, and she has received the seed sown, she will neither take thought (p. 207) for this transient life nor fear death, nor will Charisius be able in any way to harm her. For greater is he whom she has received into her soul, if she has truly received him.' 94. When Mygdonia heard this, she said to the apostle: 'Truly, my lord, I have received the seed of thy words, and will bring forth fruit like to such seed.' The apostle said: '<These souls which are thy possession> praise and thank thee, Lord; the bodies thank thee, which thou hast held worthy to become dwelling-places of thy heavenly gift.' And he said also to all those who stood by: 'Blessed are the holy, whose souls have never condemned them; for having gained these (souls) they are not divided against themselves. Blessed are the spirits of the holy, and those who have received the heavenly crown intact from the aeon appointed for them. Blessed are the bodies of the holy, because they have been counted worthy to become temples of God, that Christ may dwell in them. Blessed are ye, because you have power to forgive sins.[143] Blessed are ye if you lose not what is committed to you, but with joy <and gladness> bring it with you. Blessed are you holy, for to you it is given to ask and to receive.[144] *Blessed are* you *meek*,[145] because God has counted you worthy to become *heirs* of the heavenly kingdom. *Blessed are* you *meek*, for you are (p.208) they who have conquered the enemy. Blessed are you *meek*, because you *shall see* the face of the Lord.[146] *Blessed are* you who *hunger*[147] for the Lord's sake, because for you is rest preserved and from now on your souls rejoice. Blessed are you quiet, (because you have been counted worthy) to be freed from sin <......>.' When the apostle had said this in the hearing of all the crowd, Mygdonia was the more confirmed in the faith, and in the glory and majesty of Christ.

95. But Charisius the king's kinsman and friend came to breakfast, and did not find his wife in the house. And he inquired of all in the house: 'Where did

your mistress go?' And one of them said in reply: 'She is gone to that stranger.' But when he heard this from his slave he was angry with his other servants, because they did not at once report to him what had happened; and he sat down and waited for her. And when it was evening and she came into the house, he said to her: 'Where wert thou?' And she said in answer: 'At the doctor.' But he said: 'Is that stranger a doctor?' And she said: 'Yes, a physician of souls. For most doctors heal bodies which are dissolved, but he souls which are not destroyed.' When Charisius heard this, he was very angry at heart against Mygdonia because of the apostle, but he made her no answer, for he was afraid; for she was better than he both in wealth and in understanding. But he went off (p. 209) to dinner, and she went into her chamber. And he said to the servants: 'Call her to dinner!' But she would not come. 96. When he heard that she would not come out of her chamber, he went in and said to her: 'Why wilt thou not dine with me, and perhaps not sleep with me as usual? And on this point I have the greater suspicion, for I have heard that that magician and deceiver teaches that a man should not live with his own wife, and what nature requires and the deity has ordained he overthrows.' When Charisius said this, Mygdonia remained silent. He said to her again: 'My lady and consort Mygdonia, be not led astray by deceitful and vain words, nor by the works of magic which I have heard this man performs in the name of Father, Son and Holy Spirit. For never was it heard in this world that anyone raised a dead man; but as I hear, <it is rumoured of him> that he raises the dead. And that he neither eats not drinks, do not think that it is for righteousness' sake that he neither eats not drinks; but this he does because he possesses nothing. For what should he do, who does not even have his daily bread? And he has one garment because he is poor. As for not taking anything from anyone, (p. 210) (he does that) because he knows <that no one is really healed by him.>' 97. But when Charisius said this, Mygdonia was silent like a stone; but she prayed that when it was day she might go to the apostle of Christ. And he departed from her, and went off to dinner despondent; for he was anxious to sleep with her as usual. But when he had gone, she bowed her knees and prayed, saying: 'Lord God, Master, merciful Father, Saviour Christ, do thou give me strength that I may overcome Charisius' shamelessness, and grant me to keep the holiness in which thou dost delight, that I too through it may find eternal life.' And when she had so prayed she laid herself veiled on the bed. 98. But Charisius when he had dined came upon her, and she cried out, saying: 'Henceforth thou hast no place with me, for my Lord Jesus who is with me and rests in me is greater than thou.' But he laughed and said: 'Well dost thou mock, saying these things about that sorcerer, and well dost thou deride him when he says: Ye have no life with God unless ye sanctify yourselves.' And when he had said this he attempted to sleep with her; and she did not endure it, but crying out bitterly said: 'I call upon thee, Lord Jesus, forsake me not! For with thee I have made my refuge. For as I learned that thou art he who seeks out those imprisoned in ignorance, and delivers those held fast in error, so now I pray thee whose fame (p. 211) I have heard and believed: Come thou to my help and deliver me from Charisius' shamelessness, <that> his foulness may not gain the mastery over me!' And striking her hands <against her face> she fled from him naked; and as she went out she tore down the curtain of the chamber, and throwing it about her went away to her nurse and slept there with her. 99. But Charisius all through the night was in despair, beating his hands against his face. And he wanted to go off in that very hour and bring the king the news of the violence that had come upon him; but he reflected, saying to himself: 'If the great despair that is about me should compel me to go now to the king, who will bring me in to him? For I know[148] that an evil report has overthrown me from my proud bearing and vainglory and grandeur, and cast me down to this pettiness, and separated my sister Mygdonia from me.[149] Even if the king himself stood before the doors in this hour, I could not have gone out and given him answer. But I will wait until it is day; and I know that whatever I ask of the king he grants me. I will tell of the madness of that stranger, which tyrannously casts down the great (p. 212) and notable into the depth. For it is not this that grieves me, that I am deprived of her company, but I am grieved for her, because her great soul is humbled. Noble lady as she is, whom none of her house ever charged <with impropriety S>, she has fled naked from her chamber and run outside, and I know not where she has gone. And perhaps, maddened by that sorcerer, she has in her frenzy gone into the market-place in search of him. For indeed nothing seems lovable to her but that man and the things said by him'.

100. When he had said this he began, lamenting, to say: 'Woe to me, my consort, and to thee also! For I have been too quickly deprived of thee. Woe is me, most beloved, for thou art better than all my race! Neither son nor daughter have I of thee, that I might rest upon them; nor didst thou live with me <a full> year,[150] but an evil eye has snatched thee from me. <.> Would that the violence of death had taken thee, and I should have <reckoned myself> among kings and chieftains! But that I should suffer such a thing at the hands of a stranger! And perhaps he is a slave who has run away, to my hurt and that of my most unhappy soul. (p. 213) May there be for me no hindrance until I destroy him and avenge this night; and may I not be well-pleasing before king Misdaeus if he does not give me satisfaction with the head of the stranger, and in the matter of Siphor the captain, who was the cause <of her loss S>. For through him did he appear here, and with him he lodges; and many are they who go in and come out, whom he teaches a new doctrine, saying that none can live except he give over all his possessions and become a renouncer like himself; and he is zealous to make many partners with himself.'[151]

101. While Charisius thought on these things, day dawned. And having watched all night he put on mean clothing, bound on his sandals, and went

gloomy and despondent to salute the king. But when the king saw him, he said: 'Why art thou sorrowful, and come in such attire? And I see that thy face too is changed.' But Charisius said to the king: 'I have a new thing to tell thee, and a new desolation, which Siphor (p. 214) has brought into India: a Hebrew man, a sorcerer, whom he has sitting in his house and who does not depart from him; and many are they who go in to him, whom he teaches a new God, and lays on them new laws which were never yet heard, saying: "It is impossible for you to enter into the eternal life which I proclaim to you, except you rid yourselves of your wives, and likewise the women of their husbands." But it happened that my ill-fated wife also went to him, and became a hearer of his words; which she believed, and leaving me in the night she ran to the stranger. But send both for Siphor and for that stranger who is hidden with him, and visit them with death, that all who are of our race may not perish.' 102. When his friend Misdaeus heard this, he said to him: 'Be not grieved or disheartened, for I will send for him and avenge thee, and thou shalt have thy wife again. <For if I avenge others S> who cannot avenge <themselves>, <thee above all S> will I avenge.' And going out the king sat down on the judgment seat; and when he was set he commanded Siphor the captain to be called.

So they went to his house, and found him sitting (p. 215) at the apostle's right hand, and Mygdonia at his feet listening to him with all the crowd. And those who were sent from the king came up to Siphor and said: 'Dost thou sit here listening to vain words, and king Misdaeus in his wrath is thinking to destroy thee because of this magician and deceiver whom thou hast brought into thy house?' When Siphor heard this he was dejected, not because of the king's threat against him but because of the apostle, because the king had pronounced adversely concerning him. And he said to the apostle: 'I am distressed about thee. For I told thee from the beginning that that woman is the wife of Charisius, the king's kinsman and friend, and he does not allow her to do what she promises, and all he asks of the king he grants him.' But the apostle said to Siphor: 'Fear nothing, but believe in Jesus, who plays the advocate for us all. For to his refuge are we gathered together.' When Siphor heard this, he flung his cloak about him and went off to king Misdaeus. 103. But the apostle inquired of Mygdonia: 'What was the reason that thy husband was angry and devised this against us?' And she said: 'Because I did not give myself to his destruction. For last night he wanted to subdue me, and subject me to that passion which he serves; and he to whom I (p. 216) have committed my soul delivered me out of his hands. And I fled from him naked and slept with my nurse. But what has come upon him that he has contrived this, I do not know.' The apostle said: 'These things will not harm us; but believe in Jesus, and he will overthrow Charisius' anger and his madness and his passion. And he shall be a companion for thee in the fearful way, and himself shall guide thee into his kingdom. And he shall bring thee into eternal life, granting thee the confidence which neither passes away nor changes.'

104. But Siphor stood before the king, and he questioned him: 'Who is he and whence, and what does he teach, that magician whom thou hast lurking in thy house?' And Siphor answered the king: 'Thou art not ignorant, O king, what trouble and grief I had, with my friends, concerning my wife, whom thou also dost know and many others remember; and concerning my daughter, whom I value above all my property, what a time and trial I have suffered. For I became a laughing-stock and a curse to all our country. But I heard the report of this man, went to him and besought him, and took him and brought him here. And as I came along the road (p. 217) I saw wonderful and astonishing things, and here many heard the wild ass, and about the demon whom he drove out; and he healed my wife and daughter, and now they are whole. And he did not ask for reward, but demands faith and holiness, that (men) may become partakers with him in what he does. This he teaches, to worship and fear one God, the Lord of all, and Jesus Christ his Son, that they may have eternal life. What he eats is bread and salt, and his drink is water from evening to evening, <and> he makes many prayers; and whatever he asks of his God, he gives him. And he teaches that this God is holy and powerful, and that Christ is life and giver of life. Therefore he charges those who are with him to approach him (God) in holiness and purity and love and faith.' 105. When king Misdaeus heard this from Siphor, he sent many soldiers to the house of Siphor the captain to bring Thomas the apostle and all who were found there. And when those who were sent went in, they found him teaching a great number; and Mygdonia was sitting at his feet. But when they saw the great crowd around him, they were afraid and went back to their king and said: 'We did not dare to say anything to him, for there was a great crowd (p. 218) around him; and Mygdonia, sitting at his feet, was listening to what was said by him.' When king Misdaeus and Charisius heard this, Charisius sprang up from the king's presence and taking a large crowd with him said: 'I will bring him, O king, and Mygdonia, whose understanding he has taken away.' And he went to the house of Siphor the captain, greatly perplexed. And he found him teaching; but Mygdonia he did not catch, for she had returned to her house, having learned that it had been reported to her husband that she was there.

106. But Charisius said to the apostle: 'Stand up, thou wicked man and destroyer and enemy of my house! For me thy magic does not harm; for I will visit thy magic upon thy head!' But when he said this, the apostle looked at him and said to him: 'Thy threats shall return against thee, for me thou wilt not harm in any way. For greater than thou and thy king and all your army is the Lord Jesus Christ in whom I have my hopes.' But Charisius took a kerchief of one of his slaves and threw it round the apostle's neck, saying: 'Hale him off and take him away! Let me see if his God can deliver him out of my

hands.' And they dragged him off and brought him to king Misdaeus. <But when the apostle stood> before the king, the king said to him: 'Tell me who thou art, and *by what power*[152] thou dost perform these things.' But the apostle remained silent.[153] And the king commanded his subjects that he should be scourged with a hundred and twenty-eight lashes and flung in bonds (p. 219) into the prison. And they put him in chains and led him away. But the king and Charisius considered how they might put him to death. But the crowd worshipped him as a god. And they had it in mind to say: 'The stranger insulted the king, and is a deceiver.'

107. And as the apostle went away to the prison he said, rejoicing and exulting: 'I praise thee, Jesus, that thou hast made me worthy not only of faith in thee, but also of suffering much for thy sake. I thank thee therefore, Lord, that thou hast taken thought for me, and given me patience. I thank thee, Lord, that for thy sake I have been called a sorcerer and a magician. <May I> therefore <receive> of the blessing of the humble, and of the rest of the weary, and of the blessings of those whom men hate and *persecute* and *revile*, speaking evil words of them.[154] For lo, for thy sake am I hated; lo, for thy sake am I cut off from the many, and for thy sake they call me such as I am not.' 108. And as he prayed all the prisoners looked at him, and besought him to pray for them. And when he had prayed and sat down, he began to utter a psalm in this fashion:[155]

1 When I was a little child
And dwelt in the <kingdom>, the house of my father,
2 And enjoyed the wealth and the <luxuries>
Of those who brought me up,
3 From the East, our homeland,
My parents provisioned and sent me;
4 And from the wealth of our treasury
They had already bound up for me a load.
5 Great it was, but (so) light
That I could carry it alone:
6 Gold from the house of the high ones (Beth 'Ellaye)
And silver from great (p. 220) Ga(n)zak
7 And <chalcedonies from> India
And <opals of> the realm of Kushan.
8 And they girded me with adamant,
Which crushes iron.
9 And they took off from me the <splendid robe>
Which in their love they had wrought for me,
10 And the purple toga,
Which was woven to the measure of my stature,

11 And they made with me a covenant
And wrote it in my heart, that I might not forget:
12 'If thou go down to Egypt
And <bring> the one pearl
13 Which is in the midst of the sea,
In the abode of the loud-breathing serpent,
14 Thou shalt put on (again) thy splendid robe
And thy toga which lies over it,
15 And with thy brother, our next in rank,
Thou <shalt be heir> in our kingdom.'
109 16 I quitted the East and went down,
Led by two <couriers>,
17 For the way was dangerous and difficult
And I was very young to travel it.
18 I passed over the borders of Maisân (Mesene),
<The meeting-place of the merchants> of the East,
19 And reached the land of Babel,
And entered in to the walls of Sarbûg.
20 I went down into Egypt,
And my companions parted from me.
21 I went straight to the serpent,
Near by his abode I stayed,
22 Until he should slumber and sleep,
That I might take my pearl from him.
23 And since I was all alone
I was a stranger to my companions of my hostelry.
24 <But> one of my race I saw there,
A nobleman out of <the East>,
25 A youth fair and lovable,
26 An <anointed one>,
And he came and attached himself to me (p. 221)
27 And I made him my intimate friend,
My companion to whom I communicated my business.
28 I (He?) warned him (me?) against the Egyptians
And against consorting with the unclean.
29 But I clothed myself in garments like theirs,
That <they might> not <suspect> that I was come from without
30 To take the pearl,
And so might <waken> the serpent against me.
31 But from some cause or other
They perceived that I was not their countryman,
32 And they dealt with me treacherously

And gave me to eat of their food.
33 And I forgot that I was a king's son
And served their king.
34 And I forgot the pearl
For which my parents had sent me.
35 And because of the heaviness of their <food>
I fell into a deep sleep.
110 36 <And all this> that befell me
My parents observed and were grieved for me.
37 And a proclamation was published in our kingdom
That all should come to our gate,
38 The kings and chieftains of Parthia
And all the great ones of the East.
39 They made a resolve concerning me,
That I should not be left in Egypt,
40 And they wrote to me a letter
And every <noble> set his name thereto:
41 'From thy father, the king of kings,
And thy mother, the mistress of the East,
42 And from thy brother, our other son,
To thee, our son in Egypt, greeting!
43 <Awake> and rise up from thy sleep,
And hearken to the words of our letter.
44 Remember that thou art a son of kings.
See the slavery - him whom thou dost serve!
45 (p. 222) Remember the pearl
For which thou didst journey into Egypt.
46 Remember thy splendid robe,
And think of thy glorious toga,
47 That thou mayest put them on and <deck thyself therewith>,
<That> thy name <may be read> in the book of the heroes
48 And thou with thy brother, our crown prince,
<Be heir> in our kingdom.'
111 49 And the letter was a letter
Which the king <had sealed> with his right hand
50 Against the wicked, the people of Babel
And the <rebellious> demons of Sarbûg.
51 It flew in the form of an eagle,
The king of <all> birds,
52 It flew and alighted beside me
And became all speech.
53 At its voice and the sound <of its rustling>

I awoke and stood up from my sleep,
54 I took it and kissed it,
Broke <its seal> and read.
55 And even as it was engraven in my heart
Were the words of my letter written.
56 I remembered that I was a son of kings
And my noble birth asserted itself.
57 I remembered the pearl
For which I was sent to Egypt,
58 And I began to cast a spell
On the terrible loud-breathing serpent.
59 I brought him to slumber and sleep
By naming my father's name over him,
60 And the name of our next in rank
And of my mother, the queen of the East.
61 And I snatched away the pearl
And turned about, to go to my father's house.
62 And their dirty and unclean garment
I took off and left in their land,
63 And directed my way <that I might come>
To the light of our homeland, the East.
64 And my letter, my awakener,
I found before me on the way;
65 As with its voice (p. 223) it had awakened <me>,
(So) it led me further with its light,
66 (Written) on Chinese tissue with ruddle,
Gleaming before me with its aspect
67 And with its voice and its guidance
Encouraging me to speed,
68 And <drawing> me with its love.
69 I went forth, passed through Sarbûg,
Left Babel on my left hand
70 And came to the great (city) Maisân (Mesene),
The haven of the merchants,
71 <Which lies> on the shore of the sea.
72 And my splendid robe which I had taken off,
And my toga with which it was wrapped about,
73 From the heights <of> Warkan (Hyrcania)
My parents sent thither
74 By the hand of their treasurers,
Who for their faithfulness were trusted therewith.
112 75 Indeed I remembered no more its dignity,

For I had left it in my childhood in my father's house,
76 But suddenly, when I saw it over against me,
The <splendid robe> became like me, as my reflection in a mirror;
77 I saw it <wholly> in me,
And in it I saw myself <quite> apart <from myself>,
78 So that we were two in distinction
And again one in a single form.
79 And the treasurers too
Who had brought it to me, I saw in like manner,
80 That they were two of a single form,
For one sign of the king was impressed upon them,
81 (His) who restored to me through them
<The honour G>, my pledge and my riches,
82 My splendid robe adorned
<Gleaming> in glorious colours,
83 With gold and beryls,
Chalcedonies and <opals>,
84 And <sardonyxes> of varied <colour>,
This also made ready in its grandeur,
85 And with stones of adamant
(Were) all its seams fastened.
86 And the likeness of the king of kings
Was <completely> embroidered all over it
87 <And like> stones of sapphire again in its
Grandeur resplendent with manifold hues.
113 88 (p. 224) And again I saw that all over it
The motions of <knowledge> were stirring.
89 And I saw too
That it was preparing as for speech.
90 I heard the sound of its songs
Which it whispered <at its descent>:
91 'I belong to the most valiant servant,
For whom they reared me before my father,
92 And I <perceived> also in myself
That my stature grew according to his labours.'
93 And with its royal movements
It poured itself entirely toward me,
94 And in the hands of its bringers
I hastened, that I might take it;
95 And my love also spurred me
To run to meet it and receive it,
96 And I stretched out and took it.

With the beauty of its colours I adorned myself.
97 And my toga of brilliant colours
I drew <completely> over myself.
98 I clothed myself with it and mounted up
To the gate of greeting and homage.
99 I bowed my head and worshipped
The splendour of the father <who> had sent it (the robe) to me,
100 Whose commands I had accomplished,
As he also had done what he promised.
101 And at the gate of his satraps
I mingled among his great ones.
102 For he rejoiced over me and received me,
And I was with him in his kingdom.
103 And with the sound <of the organ>
All his servants praised him.
104 And he promised me that to the gate
Of the king of kings I should journey with him again
105 And with my gift and my pearl
With him appear before our king.

114. Charisius went off home rejoicing, thinking that his wife would be with him again and that she <would be S> as (p. 225) of old, before she heard the divine word and believed in Jesus. But when he went, he found her with <her hair shorn S> and her garments rent. And seeing this he said to her: 'My lady Mygdonia, why does this cruel sickness hold thee fast? And why hast thou done these things? I am thy husband from thy virginity, and both the gods and the laws give me (the right) to rule over thee. What is this great madness of thine, that thou art become a laughing-stock in all our nation? But put away the care that comes from that sorcerer; and I will take away the sight of him from our midst, that thou mayest see him no more.' 115. But when Mygdonia heard this, she gave <herself> up to <her grief>, groaning and lamenting. And Charisius said again: 'Have I then so much wronged the gods, that they have compassed me about with such a sickness? What offence have I committed so great that they have flung me into such a humiliation? I pray thee, Mygdonia, do not torment my soul at the pitiful sight of thee, and thy mean appearance, and do not burden my heart with care over thee! I am Charisius thy <husband>, whom all the nation honours and fears. What must I do? I know not how to <conduct> myself. And what am I to think? Shall I keep silent and endure? And who will bear it when people take his treasure? But who would endure <to be robbed> of thy sweet ways? < . . . > Thy fragrance is in my nostrils, and thy radiant face is fixed in my eyes. They are taking away (p. 226) my soul, and the beautiful body in which I rejoiced when I saw it they are destroying; the

sharpest of eyes they are blinding, and they are cutting off my right hand. My joy is turned to grief and my life to death, and the light <is plunged> in darkness. <Let> none of my kinsmen look on me henceforth, they from whom no help has come to me, nor will I worship henceforth the gods of the East, who have compassed me about with such evils. In truth, I will neither pray to them any more nor sacrifice to them, if I am robbed of my spouse. But what else should I ask of them? For all my glory is taken away. I am a prince, second to the king in authority. But all this Mygdonia <by rejecting me> has taken away. <Would that someone would strike out my eyes, if thou wouldst turn thine eyes upon me as of old!>'

116. While Charisius said this with tears, Mygdonia sat silent and looking on the ground. But he came to her again and said: 'My lady, most beloved Mygdonia, remember that out of <all> the women in India I chose thee as the fairest and took thee, when I could have joined to myself in marriage others far <more beautiful> than thee. But rather do I lie, Mygdonia. For by the gods it <is> not possible that another like thee should be found in the land of the Indians. But woe is me for ever more, that thou wilt not (p. 227) answer me at all. Revile <me> if thou please, that I may but be granted <a word> from thee! Look upon me, for I am <far better and more handsome S> than that sorcerer! <I have riches and honour, and all recognise that none has such a lineage as I. But thou art my riches and my honour>, thou art my family and kinship - and lo, he is taking thee away from me!' 117. When Charisius said this, Mygdonia said to him: 'He whom I love is better than thee and thy possessions. For thy possession is of the earth and returns to earth; but he whom I love is heavenly, and will take me with him into heaven. Thy wealth shall pass away, and thy beauty shall vanish, and thy robes and thy many works; but thou (shalt remain) alone with thy transgressions <. . .> Remind me not of thy deeds towards me; for I pray the Lord that thou mayest forget, so as to remember no more the former pleasures and the bodily intimacy, which will pass away like a shadow; but Jesus alone abides for ever, and the souls which hope in him. Jesus himself will set me free from the shameful deeds which I did with thee.' And when Charisius heard this (p. 228) he turned broken-hearted to sleep, saying to her: 'Consider this by thyself all through this night! If thou wilt be with me, such as thou wast before thou didst see that sorcerer, I will do all thy desires, and if because of thy friendship for him thou shouldst wish it, I will take him out of the prison and set him free, and he may go to another country. And I will not vex thee, for I know that thou art greatly attached to the stranger. And it was not with thee first that this matter came about, but he has also deceived many other women along with thee. But they have come to their senses and returned to themselves. So do not set my words at nought, and make me a reproach among the Indians.'

118. As Charisius was saying this he fell asleep. But she took ten denarii

and went out secretly to give them to the gaolers, that she might go in to the apostle. <But on the way Judas Thomas met her, coming to her>, and seeing him she was afraid; for she thought he was one of the rulers, for a great light went before him. And she said to herself as she fled: 'I have destroyed thee, unhappy soul! For thou wilt not again see Judas, the apostle <of the living God>, and as yet (p. 229) thou hast not received the holy seal.' And as she fled she ran into a narrow place and there hid herself, saying: 'It is better to be <taken> by the poorer, whom it is possible to persuade, than to fall in with this powerful prince, who despises gifts.'

Tenth Act
How Mygdonia receives baptism

119. As Mygdonia was considering this by herself, Judas came and stood over her. And seeing him she was afraid, fell down in terror, and lay like one dead. But standing beside her and taking her hand he said to her: 'Fear not, Mygdonia. Jesus will not desert thee, nor will thy Lord to whom thou hast committed thy soul overlook thee. His compassionate rest will not forsake thee. He who is kind will not forsake thee, because of his great kindness, and he that is good, because of his goodness. Rise up then from the earth, since thou art become wholly above it. See the light, for the Lord does not allow those who love him to walk in darkness. Look upon the fellow-traveller of his servants, for he is to them an ally in dangers.' And Mygdonia stood up and looked at him, and said: 'Where wert thou going, my Lord? And who is he who brought thee out of the prison to behold the sun?' Judas Thomas says to her: 'My Lord Jesus is more powerful than all powers and kings and rulers.'[156]

120. And Mygdonia said: 'Give me the seal of Jesus Christ, and I will receive a gift from thy hands (p. 230) before thou depart from life.' And taking him with her she went into the court and wakened her nurse, saying to her: 'My mother and nurse Marcia (Narcia S), all the services and refreshments thou hast rendered me from childhood to my present age are vain, and for them I owe thee (only) temporal thanks. But do me now also a favour, that thou mayest for ever receive the recompense from him who bestows the great gifts.' At these words Marcia said: 'What dost thou wish, my daughter Mygdonia, and what is to be done for thy pleasure? The honours which thou didst promise me <before>, the stranger did not allow thee to bring to fulfilment, and thou hast made me a reproach in all the nation. And now what is the new thing which thou dost command me?' And Mygdonia said: 'Become my partner in eternal life, that I may receive from thee a perfect nourishment. Take bread and bring it me, and a mixture of (wine and) water, and have regard for my free birth.' And the nurse said: 'I will bring many loaves, and instead of water gallons

(*metretai*) of wine, and fulfil thy desire.' But she says to the nurse: 'Gallons I do not need, nor the many loaves, but bring this only: a mixture of (wine and) water, and one loaf, and oil.'

121. And when Marcia had brought these things, Mygdonia stood before the apostle with her head bare; and he taking the oil poured it on her head, saying: 'Holy oil given to us for sanctification, hidden mystery in which the Cross was shown to us, thou art the straightener of (p. 231) the <crooked> limbs; thou art the humbler of hard works; thou art he who shows the hidden treasures; thou art the shoot of goodness. Let thy power come; let it be established upon thy servant Mygdonia; and heal her through this <unction>!' And when the oil had been poured out he bade the nurse unclothe her and gird a linen cloth about her. Now there was there a spring of water, and going to it the apostle baptized Mygdonia in the name of the Father and the Son and the Holy Spirit. And when she was baptized and clothed, he broke bread and took a cup of water, and made her partaker in the body of Christ and the cup of the Son of God,[157] and said: 'Thou hast received thy seal, and <obtained> for thyself eternal life.' And straightway there was heard from above a voice saying: 'Yea, Amen.' And when Marcia heard this voice she was startled, and besought the apostle that she too might receive the seal. And giving it to her the apostle said: 'The zeal of the Lord be about thee, as about <the others>.'

122. When the apostle had done this he returned to the prison; but he found the doors open and the guards still asleep. And Thomas said: 'Who is like thee, O God, who dost withhold from none thy tender love (p. 232) and zeal? Who is like thee <in compassion>, who hast delivered thy <creatures> from evil? Life that has mastered death, rest that has ended toil! Glory be to the only-Begotten of the Father,[158] glory to the compassionate who was sent from his heart!' And when he said this, the guards woke up and saw all the doors open, and the prisoners within. And they said among themselves: 'Did we not secure the doors? And how are they now open, and the prisoners inside?'

123. But Charisius as soon as it was dawn went to Mygdonia, and he found them praying and saying: 'New God, who through the stranger didst come to us here: God, who art hidden from the dwellers in India; God who hast shown thy glory through thine apostle Thomas; God whose fame we heard and believed in thee; God to whom we came to be saved; God who through love for men and through pity didst descend to our littleness; God who didst seek us out when we knew thee not; God who dost dwell in the heights and dost not remain hidden <from the> depths: turn thou away Charisius' madness from us!' But when Charisius heard this he said to Mygdonia: 'Justly dost thou call me evil and mad and base! For if (p. 233) I had not borne thy disobedience and made thee a gift of freedom, thou wouldst not have invoked <the witchcraft of that man S> against me and made mention of my name before God. But believe me, Mygdonia, that with that sorcerer there is no profit, and what he

promises he cannot perform. But I do for thee before thine eyes all that I promise, that thou mayest believe and bear with my words and become to me as thou wert before.' 124. And drawing near he besought her again, saying: 'If thou wilt listen to me, there will be no grief for me henceforth. Remember that day on which thou didst meet me first. Tell me the truth: was I more beautiful to thee at that time, or Jesus at this?' And Mygdonia said: 'That time required its own, and this time also. That was the time of beginning, but this of the end. That was the time of a transitory life, but this of eternal. That was of a passing pleasure, but this of one that abides for ever; that, of day and night, but this of day without night. Thou hast seen that marriage, which passed away <and remains here (on earth)>, but this marriage abides for ever. That fellowship was one of corruption, but this of life eternal. Those attendants are short-lived men and women, but these now remain to the end. <That marriage was founded on earth, where there is a ceaseless pressure; but this on the fiery bridge, whereon grace is sprinkled. S> That bridal chamber is taken down, but this remains for ever. That bed was spread <with coverlets>, but this with love and faith. Thou art a bridegroom who passes away and is destroyed, (p. 234) but Jesus is a true bridegroom, abiding immortal for ever. That bridal gift was money and robes that grow old, but this is living words which never pass away.'

125. When Charisius heard this, he went away to the king and told him everything. And the king commanded Judas to be brought, that he might judge and destroy him. But Charisius said: 'Have patience a little while, O king. First terrify the man with words <and persuade him>, that he may persuade Mygdonia to become to me as formerly.' And Misdaeus sent for the apostle of Christ, and had him brought from the prison. But all the prisoners were grieved because the apostle was departing from them. For they yearned after him, saying: 'Even this comfort which we had they have taken from us.' 126. But Misdaeus said to the apostle: 'Why dost thou teach this new doctrine, which both gods and men hate and <in which there is no profit>?' And Judas said: 'What evil do I teach?' And Misdaeus said: 'Thou dost teach that <it is not possible for men to have life with God, if they do not keep themselves pure> for the God whom thou dost preach.' Judas says: 'Thou speakest truly, O king; thus do I teach. For tell me: art thou not vexed with thy soldiers if they escort thee in dirty garments? If thou then, who art an earthly king and dost return to earth, (p. 235) dost require that thy subjects be seemly <in their appearance>, how canst thou be wrathful and say I teach ill when I say: Those who serve my king must be holy and pure and free from all grief and care for children and useless riches and from vain trouble? For indeed thou dost wish thy subjects to follow thy behaviour and thy ways, and thou dost punish them if they scorn thy commands. How much more must those who believe in my God serve him with great holiness and purity and <chastity>, free from all

bodily pleasures, adultery and prodigality, theft and drunkenness and service of the belly and (other) shameful deeds?'

127. When Misdaeus heard this he said: 'See, I set thee free. So go and persuade Mygdonia, the wife of Charisius, not to desire to part from him.' Judas says to him: 'Do not delay, if thou hast anything to do (against me). For if she has rightly received what she has learned, neither iron nor fire nor anything else stronger than these will be able to harm her or cut away him who is held in her soul.' Misdaeus says to Judas: 'Some drugs make other drugs ineffective, and an antidote makes an end of the viper's bites; and thou if thou wilt canst give release from those poisons, and bring peace and concord to this (p. 236) marriage. For by doing so thou dost spare thyself; for thou hast not yet thy fill of life. But know that if thou do not persuade her I will pluck thee out of this life <that is desirable> to all.' And Judas said: 'This life is given in usufruct, and this time changes; but that life which I teach is incorruptible. But the beauty and the youth which is seen shall soon be no more.' The king says to him: 'I have advised thee what is expedient, but thou knowest thine own affairs.' 128. But as the apostle was departing <from the> king, Charisius came up and said to him in entreaty: 'I pray thee, O man: never have I sinned at all, neither against thee or any other, nor against the gods. Why hast thou stirred up so great an evil against me? And why hast thou brought such confusion on my house? And what profit is there for thee from this? But if thou dost think to gain anything, tell me what kind of a gain it is, and I will procure it for thee without trouble. For what reason dost thou drive me out of my mind, and cast thyself into destruction? For if thou persuade her not, I will both slay thee and finally take myself out of life. And if, as thou sayest, after <our release from life here> there is yonder life and death, and also condemnation and victory and a tribunal, I too will go in there to be judged with thee. And if the God whom thou dost preach is just, and awards the punishments justly, I know that I shall obtain justice (p. 237) <against thee>. For thou hast injured me, though thou hast suffered no wrong at my hands. For indeed here I am able to avenge myself <for all that> thou hast done against me. Therefore listen to me and come home with me, and persuade Mygdonia to become with me as formerly, before she saw thee!' But Judas says to him: 'Believe me, child, if men loved God as much as (they love) each other, they would receive from him all they asked, without anyone constraining him.'

129. As Thomas said this, they went into Charisius' house and found Mygdonia sitting, and Marcia standing beside her with her hand laid on Mygdonia<'s cheek>; and (Mygdonia) was saying: 'May the remaining days of my life be cut short for me, mother, and may all the hours become as one hour, and may I depart from life, that I may go the more quickly and see that beautiful one whose fame I have heard, that living one and giver of life to those

who believe in him, where there is neither day and night, nor light and darkness, nor good and evil, nor poor and rich, male and female, no free and slave, no proud that subdues the humble.' As she said this, the apostle stood beside her; and at once she stood up and did him reverence. Then Charisius (p. 238) said to him: 'Dost thou see how she fears and honours thee, and does willingly all that thou dost command?' 130. But as he said this, Judas says to Mygdonia: 'My daughter Mygdonia, obey what brother Charisius says!' And Mygdonia said: 'If thou couldst not <name> the deed in word, <how> dost thou compel me to endure the act? For I heard from thee that this life is a loan <.>, and this rest temporary, and these possessions transitory. And thou didst say again that he who renounces this life shall receive the eternal, and he who hates the light of day and night <shall see> a light that is not <extinguished>, and that he who despises these goods shall find other, eternal goods. But now <thou sayest this S> because thou art afraid. But who that has done something and been praised for the work changes it? <Who builds a tower S> and again overthrows it from the foundations? Who when he has dug a well of water in a thirsty place fills it in again? Who finding a treasure does not make use of it?' But when Charisius heard this, he said: 'I will not imitate you nor hasten to destroy you. <But since it is in my power I will put <thee> in fetters, and will not allow thee to converse with this sorcerer. And if thou obey me <not>, I know what I must do'

131. But Judas departed from Charisius' house and went away to the house of Siphor, and stayed there with him. And Siphor said: 'I will prepare for Judas a room (*triclinium*) in which he <may> teach.'[159] (p. 239) And he did so; and Siphor said: 'I and my wife and daughter will live henceforth in holiness, in purity, and in one disposition. I pray thee, that we may receive the seal from thee, that we may become servants to the true God, and be numbered among his sheep and lambs.' But Judas says: 'I am afraid to say what I think. But I know something, and what I know it is not possible for me to declare.' 132. And he began to speak about baptism: 'This baptism is forgiveness of sins.[160] It brings to new birth a light that is shed around. It brings to new birth the new man,[161] <renews the thoughts, mingles soul and body S>, raises up the new man in three-fold manner, and is partaker in forgiveness of sins. Glory be to thee, hidden power that is united with us in baptism! Glory be to thee, ineffable power that is in baptism! Glory be to thee, renewal through which are renewed the baptised who take hold of thee with affection!'[162] And when he had said this he poured oil upon their heads and said: 'Glory be to thee, the love of compassion! Glory be to thee, (p. 240) name of Christ! Glory be to thee, the power established in Christ!' And he commanded a basin to be brought, and baptized them in the name of the Father and the Son and the Holy Spirit. 133. And when they were baptized and clothed, he set bread upon the table and blessed it and said: '<Bread> of life, those who eat of which remain incorrupt-

ible; bread which fills hungry souls with its blessing - thou art the one <thought worthy> to receive a gift, that thou mayest become for us forgiveness of sins, and they who eat thee become immortal. We name over thee the name of the mother of the ineffable mystery of the hidden dominions and powers, we name <over thee the name of Jesus>.' And he said: 'Let the power of blessing come and <settle upon the bread>, that all the souls which partake of it may be washed of their sins!' And breaking it he gave to Siphor and his wife and daughter.

Eleventh Act
Concerning the wife of Misdaeus

134. After king Misdaeus had set Judas free, he went off home <to dine S>. And he told his wife what had befallen their kinsman Charisius, saying: 'See what has happened to that unhappy man! But thou thyself dost know, my sister Tertia, that there is nothing (p. 241) <fairer> to a man than his own wife, by whom he rests. But it happened that his wife went away to that sorcerer, of whom thou hast heard that he is come to the land of the Indians, and fell a victim to his potions and was parted from her husband; and he is at a loss what he should do. But when I wished to destroy the malefactor, he would not have it. But do thou go and advise her to incline to her husband, and to keep away from the vain words of the sorcerer.'

135. And Tertia at once arose and went away to the house of Charisius her husband's kinsman; and she found Mygdonia lying on the ground in abasement. Ashes and sackcloth were spread under her, and she was praying that the Lord might forgive her her former sins, and she depart quickly from life. And Tertia said to her: 'Mygdonia, my dear sister and companion, < . . . . . > what is the sickness that has taken hold of thee? And why dost thou do the deeds of madmen? Know thyself, and return to thine own way! Come near to thy many kinsfolk, and spare thy true husband Charisius, and do not do what is alien to thy free birth!' Mygdonia says to her: 'O Tertia, thou hast not yet heard the preacher of life! Not yet has (his message) fallen upon thine ears, (p. 242) not yet hast thou tasted the medicine of life and been freed from corruptible groaning. Thou standest in the transient life, the eternal life and salvation thou knowest not; and perceiving not the incorruptible fellowship <thou art afflicted by a corruptible fellowship S>. Thou standest clothed in robes that grow old, and dost not desire the eternal; and thou art proud of this beauty that vanishes, but takest no thought of the ugliness of the soul. And in a multitude of servants thou art rich, <but hast not freed thine own soul from slavery S>; and thou dost plume thyself in thy glory before the many, but dost not redeem thyself from the condemnation unto death.' 136. When Tertia heard this from Mygdonia she said: 'I pray thee, sister, take me to that stranger who teaches these great things, that I too may go and hear him, and be taught to worship the

God whom he preaches, and become a sharer of his prayers and a partaker in all the things of which thou hast told me.' But Mygdonia says to her: 'He is in the house of Siphor the captain. For indeed he is become an occasion <of life> for all who are saved in India.' But when Tertia heard this, she went off in haste to Siphor's house, that she might see the new apostle who had come to the country. But when she went in Judas said to her: 'What hast thou come to see? A strange man and poor and contemptible and beggarly, who has neither wealth nor possession?[163] But one possession have I obtained which (p. 243) neither king nor rulers can take away, which neither perishes nor comes to an end, which is Jesus, the Saviour of all mankind, the Son of the living God, who has given life to all who believe in him and take refuge with him, and is known in the number of his servants.' Tertia says to him: 'May I become a partaker in this life which thou dost promise all shall receive who come together to God's hostelry!' And the apostle said: 'The treasury of the holy king is open wide, and those who worthily partake of the goods there do rest, and resting reign.[164] <.> But no man comes to him who is unclean and vile; for he knows our inmost hearts and the depths of our thought, and none can escape his notice. Thou too, then, if thou dost truly believe in him, shalt be made worthy of his mysteries; and he shall magnify thee and enrich thee and make thee heir of his kingdom.'[165]

137. When Tertia heard this, she went back home rejoicing; and she found her husband <awaiting her>, without having broken his fast. And when he saw her Misdaeus said: 'Whence is thy coming in today more beautiful? And why didst thou come on foot, which is not fitting for free-born women like thee?' And Tertia says to him: 'I owe thee the greatest thanks that thou didst send me to Mygdonia. For when I went I heard of a new life, and I saw the apostle of the <new> God who gives life (p. 244) to those who believe in him and fulfil his commands. I ought therefore myself to requite thee for this favour and admonition with good advice. For thou shalt be a great king in heaven if thou obey me and fear the God who is preached by the stranger, and keep thyself holy to the living God. For this kingdom passes away, and thy comfort shall be turned into affliction. But go to that man, and believe him, and thou shalt live unto the end!' When Misdaeus heard this from his wife, he smote his face with his hands and rent his clothing, and said: 'May the soul of Charisius find no rest, because he has hurt me to the soul; and may he have no hope, because he has taken my hope away.' And he went out greatly troubled.

138. And he found Charisius his friend in the market-place and said: 'Why hast thou thrown me <as thy companion S> into Hades? Why hast thou robbed and defrauded me to gain no profit? Why hast thou hurt me at no benefit to thyself? Why hast thou slain me, and thyself not lived? Why hast thou wronged me without thyself obtaining what is rightful? Why didst thou not consent to my destroying that sorcerer, before he ruined my house with his <sorcery>?'

And he <was upbraiding Charisius S>. But Charisius said: 'What has befallen thee?' Misdaeus said: 'He has bewitched Tertia.' (p. 245) And they both went away to the house of Siphor the captain, and found Judas sitting and teaching. Now all who were there stood up for the king, but he (Judas) did not rise. But Misdaeus recognised that he was the man, and taking hold of the chair overturned it, and lifting up the chair with both hands he struck him on the head so that he wounded him. And he handed him over to his soldiers, saying: 'Take him away, and drag him roughly and without restraint, that his insolence may be manifest to all.' And they dragged him off and brought him to a place where Misdaeus used to sit in judgment. And there he stood, held fast by Misdaeus' soldiers.

Twelfth Act
Concerning Vazan (Vîzan), the son of Misdaeus

139. But Vazan, the son of Misdaeus, went to the soldiers and said: 'Give him to me, that I may converse with him until the king comes.' And they gave him up, but he led him in where the king used to sit in judgment. And Vazan said: 'Dost thou not know that I am the son of king Misdaeus, and that I am free to say to the king what I wish, and <if I tell him> he will let thee live? Tell me, then, who is thy God, and (p. 246) to what power dost thou cling, and glory in it? For if it is a magic power and craft, tell it and teach me, and I will set thee free.' Judas says to him: 'Thou art the son of king Misdaeus, who is a king for a season; but I am the servant of Jesus Christ, <the> eternal king. Thou art free to speak to thy father to save whom thou wilt in this transient life, in which men do not continue, which thou and thy father give; but I pray my Lord and cry aloud on behalf of men, and he gives them a new life which is altogether <enduring>. Thou dost boast of possessions and slaves and robes and luxury and beds impure; but I boast of poverty and love of wisdom (*philosophia*) and humility and fasting and prayer and fellowship with the Holy Spirit and with my brethren who are worthy of God; and I boast of eternal life. And thou hast sought refuge with a man who is like thee, who cannot save his own soul from judgment and from death; but I have sought refuge with the living God, the Saviour of kings and rulers, who is judge of all. And you are, perhaps, for today, but tomorrow no more; but I have taken refuge with him who abides for ever, who knows all our seasons and times. But if thou wilt become a servant of this God, thou shalt do so quickly. And that thou wilt be a servant worthy of him, <thou shalt> show by these tokens: first by holiness, which is the chief of all good things; then by fellowship with this God whom I preach, and by love of wisdom (*philosophia*), and by simplicity and love and faith, and by <hope in him>, and by <simplicity of pure living>.'

(p. 247) 140. But the young man, persuaded by the Lord, sought occasion how he might help Judas to escape. But while he was considering, the king <arrived>, and the soldiers took Judas and led him out. And Vazan went out with him and stood beside him. And when the king was seated he commanded Judas to be brought in with his hands bound behind him. And he was brought into the midst and stood there. And the king said: 'Tell me who thou art, and *by what power*[166] thou dost do these things.' But Judas says to him: 'I am a man like thee, and by the power of Jesus Christ I do these things.' And Misdaeus says: 'Tell me the truth before I destroy thee.' And Judas says: 'Thou hast no power against me, as thou dost think,[167] and thou wilt not hurt me at all.' But the king, annoyed at these words, gave orders to heat (iron) plates and set him on them barefoot. And as the soldiers took off his shoes he said: 'The wisdom of God is better than the wisdom of men. Do thou, Lord and King, resist his wrath!' And they brought the plates, which were like fire, and set the apostle upon them; and immediately water gushed abundantly from the ground, so that the plates were swallowed up. And those who held him let him go and fell back. 141. But when the king saw the abundance of water, he said to Judas: 'Pray thy God that he deliver me from this death, that I may not perish in the flood.' And the apostle prayed and said: 'Thou who didst bind this nature and gather it (p. 248) into one place, and dost send it out to different countries; thou who out of disorder didst bring into order; thou who givest mighty works and great wonders by the hands of thy servant Judas; thou who hast compassion on my soul, that I may always receive thy light; who givest reward to those who have laboured; thou saviour of my soul, who dost restore it to its own nature, to associate no more with the hurtful; thou who art ever an occasion of life - restrain this element, that it may not rise up and destroy! For *there are some of those here standing who shall live*,[168] when they have believed in thee.' But when he had prayed, the water was in a short time consumed, and the place became dry. And when Misdaeus saw it, he commanded him to be taken into the prison 'until I consider how we must deal with him'.

142. But as Judas was led away to the prison they all followed him, and Vazan the king's son walked at his right hand and Siphor on his left. And going into the prison he sat down, and Vazan and Siphor with him, and he (Siphor) persuaded his wife and daughter (also) to sit down; for they too had come to hear the word of life. For indeed they knew that Misdaeus would slay him because of the extremity of his anger. But Judas (p. 249) began to say: 'Liberator of my soul from the bondage of the many, because I gave myself to be sold; behold, I rejoice and <exult>, knowing that the times are fulfilled for me to enter in and receive <thee S>. Behold, I am set free from the cares on earth. Behold, I fulfil my hope and receive truth. Behold, I am set free from grief, and put on only joy. Behold, I become carefree and unpained, dwelling in rest. Behold, I am set free from slavery, and called to liberty. Behold, I have served times and seasons, and am lifted <above> times and seasons. Behold,

I receive <my reward S> from the requiter who gives without reckoning, <because his wealth is sufficient for his gifts>. <Behold, I unclothe myself and clothe myself S>, and shall not again be unclothed. Behold, I sleep and awake, and shall not again fall asleep. Behold, I die and come to life again, and shall not again *taste of death.*[169] Behold, they await rejoicing, that I may come and be united with their kindred, and be set as a flower in their crown. Behold, I reign in the kingdom on which even here I have set my hope. <Behold, the wicked shall be put to shame, who thought that they would subject me to their powers S>. Behold, the rebellious fall before me, because I have escaped them. Behold, peace has come, and all go to meet it.' 143. As the apostle said this, all who were there listened, thinking that <in that hour> he <would> depart from life. And again he said: 'Believe in the physician of all, both visible and invisible, and in the <saviour> of the souls that need his help. This is the free man, (scion) of kings. This is the physician of his <creatures>. This is he (p. 250) who was reviled by his own servants. This is the Father of the height and Lord and Judge of nature. Most high is he become from the Greatest, the only-begotten son of Depth; and he was called son of Mary a virgin, and was termed son of Joseph a carpenter.[170] He whose lowliness <we beheld> with the eyes of the body, but his greatness we received by faith, and saw it in his works; whose human body *we handled* even *with our hands*, and his appearance *we saw* transfigured *with our eyes*,[171] but his heavenly form we could not see upon the mount;[172] who baffled the rulers and overpowered death; he who is truth that does not lie, and paid tribute <and S> poll-tax for himself and his disciples;[173] <he whom> the Archon feared when he saw him, and the powers that were with him were confounded. And the Archon <asked> who and whence he was, and did not know the truth, for indeed he is alien to the truth.[174] He, though he has authority over the world and the pleasures in it, and the possessions and the indulgence, <has rejected> all these things, and incites his subjects to make no use of them.'

144. And when he had finished this he stood up and prayed thus: '*Our Father who art in heaven, hallowed be they name; thy kingdom come; thy will be done, as in heaven so on earth; <give us constantly our daily bread S>; and forgive us our debts, as we also have forgiven our debtors; and lead us not into temptation, but deliver us from evil.*[175] (p. 251) *My Lord and my God*,[176] hope and confidence and teacher and <my comforter S>, thou hast taught me to pray thus. Behold, I pray this prayer and fulfil thy command. Be thou with me unto the end. Thou are he who from childhood has sown life in me, and preserved me from corruption. Thou art he who brought me into the poverty of the world, and invited me to true riches. Thou art he who made himself known to me, and showed me that I am thine; and I withheld myself from woman, that what thou dost require might not be found in defilement. 145 (p. 252). My mouth does not suffice to render thanks unto thee, nor my understanding to ponder on <thy

zeal for me>, who when <I wished> to be rich and possess < . . . > didst show me that <for many> on earth riches are a loss. But I believed thy revelation and remained in the poverty of the world, until <thou>, the true riches, didst appear and fill with riches both me and those worthy <of thee>, and didst free us from want and care and avarice. Behold, therefore, I have fulfilled thy work and accomplished thy command; and I have become poor and needy and a stranger and a slave, despised and a prisoner and hungry and thirsty and naked and weary. Let not my trust, then, (p. 253) come short (of its fulfilment), and let not my hope in thee be put to shame! Let not my labours become vain! Let not my continual prayers and fastings perish, and let my works to thee-ward not be diminished! Let not the devil snatch away the seed of wheat <from the> land, and <let not his tares be found upon it;[177] for thy land cannot receive his tares, neither can they be laid in the barns of thy husbandmen.' And again he said: 146. 'Thy vine have I planted in the land S>; may it send its roots into the depth, and the spread of its branches up to heaven! And may its fruits be seen on the earth, and may they delight in it who are worthy of thee, and whom thou hast acquired! Behold, the money which thou hast given me I have laid (p. 254) on the table (of the money-changers);[178] demand it and return it to me with interest, as thou didst promise! With thy mina I have gained another ten;[179] may they be added to me (to my property) as thou didst ordain! I remitted the mina to the debtors;[180] may that not be demanded from me which I have remitted! When called to dinner I have come, released from field and wife; may I not, then, be cast out, but blamelessly taste of it![181] To the wedding have I been invited, and have put on white robes; may I be worthy of them and not go out, bound hand and foot, into outer darkness![182] My lamp shines with its light;[183] may its Lord preserve it (keep it burning) until he leaves the bridal house and I receive him; may I not see it (p. 255) extinguished for lack of oil!> Let mine eyes behold thee and my heart rejoice, because I have fulfilled thy will and accomplished thy command! <Let me be like the wise and God-fearing servant, who with careful diligence did not neglect his vigilance!>[184] Watching all the night I have wearied myself, to guard my house from the robbers, that they might not break in.[185] 147.[186] *My loins have I girded with truth*[187] and my shoes have I bound to my feet,[188] that I may not see their thongs loosened altogether. My hands have I put to the yoked plough, and have not turned away backward,[189] that the furrows may not be crooked. The field is become white and the harvest is at hand,[190] that I may receive my reward. My garment that grows old (p. 256) I have worn out, and the laborious toil that leads to rest I have accomplished. I have kept the first watch and the second and the third,[191] that I may behold thy face and worship thy holy radiance. I have pulled down the <barns> and left them desolate on earth, that I may be filled from thy treasures.[192] The abundant spring within me I have dried up, that I may find thy living spring.[193] The prisoner whom thou didst commit to me I have slain, that the freed man in me may not lose his trust. The inside I have made outside, and the outside <inside>,[194] and thy whole fullness has been fulfilled in me. I have not turned back to what is behind, but have advanced to what is before, that I may not become a reproach. The dead I have brought to life and the living I have put to death, and what was lacking I have filled up, that (p. 257) I may receive the crown of victory and the power of Christ be perfected in me. Reproach have I received on earth, but give me recompense and requital in heaven! 148. Let not the powers and dominions perceive me, and let them form no plan concerning me! Let not the tax-gatherers and the exactors busy themselves with me! Let not the base and the wicked mock at <me, the brave and kind>! And when I am borne upward, let them not venture to stand in my way, by thy power, Jesus, which enwreathes me. For they flee and hide themselves; they cannot look thee in the face. For suddenly do they fall upon their subjects, and the portion of the sons of the evil one itself cries out and convicts them. (p. 258) And none of them remains hidden, for their nature is made known. The children of the evil one are separated; <the tree of their fruit is bitterness S>. Grant me now, Lord, that in quietness I may pass by, and in joy and peace cross over and stand before the judge. And let not the devil look upon me; let his eyes be blinded by thy light which thou hast made to dwell in me. Stop up his mouth, for he has nothing against me.'

149.[195] And he said again to those who were about him: '<Believe, my children, in this God whom I proclaim; believe in Jesus Christ, whom I preach; believe in the giver of life and helper of his servants S>; believe in the saviour of those who have grown weary in his service! For my soul already rejoices, because my time is near to receive him. For being beautiful he leads me to speak ever of his beauty, of what manner it is, although I am neither able nor sufficient to speak of it worthily. Thou who art the light of my poverty and supplier of my deficiencies and nourisher of my need: be thou with me until I come and receive thee for ever more.'

(p. 259) Thirteenth Act
How Vazan receives baptism with the others

150. But the youth Vazan besought the apostle, saying: 'I pray thee, O man, <holy man S>, apostle of God, allow me to go, and I will persuade the gaoler to permit thee to come home with me, that through thee I may receive the seal, and become thy servant and a keeper of the commandments of the God whom thou dost preach. For indeed formerly I walked in those things which thou dost teach, until my father constrained me and joined me to a wife named Mnesara; for although I am (only) twenty-one years old I have already been seven years married. But before I was joined in marriage I knew no other woman; and therefore was I reckoned useless in my father's eyes. Nor has either son or

daughter ever been born to me of this wife: but indeed my wife has lived with me in chastity during this time, and today (p. 260) had she been in health and had listened to thee, I know that I should be at rest and she would receive eternal life. But she is in peril, and tried by much sickness. So I will persuade the guard, if thou promise to come with me, for I live alone by myself; and at the same time thou shalt heal that unhappy one.' When Judas the apostle of the Most High heard this, he said to Vazan: 'If thou dost believe, thou shalt see the wonders of God, and how he saves his servants.'

151. But while they were discussing these things, Tertia and Mygdonia and Marcia were standing at the door of the prison, and after giving the gaoler 363 staters of silver they went in to Judas. And they found Vazan and Siphor and his wife and daughter and all the prisoners sitting and hearing the word. And as they stood before him he said to them: 'Who allowed you to come to us? And who opened the sealed door for you to come out?' Tertia says to him: 'Didst thou not open the doors for us, bidding us go to the prison (p. 261) that we might meet our brethren who were there, and then the Lord might show his glory in us? And when we were near the door, I know not how, thou didst separate from us, and hiding thyself didst come here before us, where indeed we heard the noise of the door as thou didst shut us out. So we gave money to the guards and came in: and lo, we are here, praying thee that thou wilt be persuaded and we help thee to escape until the king's wrath against thee shall abate.' Judas said to her: 'Tell us first how you were shut up.' 152. And she said to him: 'Thou wast with us, and didst never leave us for a single hour, and dost thou ask in what manner we were shut up? But if thou dost desire to hear, hear. King Misdaeus sent for me and said: "Not yet has that sorcerer prevailed over thee, for as I hear he bewitches men with oil and water and bread, and thee he has not yet bewitched. But obey thou me, for otherwise I will shut thee up and crush thee, but him I will destroy. For I know that <so long as> he has not given thee oil and water and bread he has not gained the power to prevail over thee." (p.262) But I said to him: "Over my body thou hast authority; do to it all that thou wilt. But my soul I will not destroy with thee." But when he heard this he shut me up in a room. And Charisius also brought Mygdonia, and shut her in with me. And thou didst lead us out and bring us to those here (assembled). But give us the seal quickly, that the hopes of Misdaeus, who is plotting thus, may be cut off.'

153. When the apostle heard this, he said: 'Glory be to thee, Jesus of many forms, glory to thee who dost appear in the guise of our poor manhood! To thee be glory, who dost encourage us and strengthen us and give <joy> and comfort us, and stand by us in all our dangers and strengthen our weakness!' But as he was saying this the gaoler came and said: 'Put away the lamps, lest anyone accuse <us> to the king.' And then, extinguishing the lamps, they turned to sleep. But the apostle conversed with the Lord: 'Now it is time, Jesus, for thee

to make haste; for behold, the children of darkness <make us to sit> in their darkness. Do thou therefore enlighten us <through the light of thy nature>!' And suddenly the whole prison was as bright as the day. But while all who were in the prison slept in a deep slumber, only those who had believed in the Lord were just then awake. 154. (p. 263) So Judas says to Vazan: 'Go ahead and make ready for us the things we need.' Vazan says: 'And who will open the doors of the prison for me? For the gaolers have shut them and gone to sleep.' And Judas said: 'Believe in Jesus, and thou shalt find the doors open!' But as he went away to go out, all the others followed behind him. And since Vazan had gone ahead, his wife Mnesara met him, on her way to the prison. And recognising him she said: 'My brother Vazan, is it thou?' And he said: 'Yes; and art thou Mnesara?' And she said: 'Yes.' Vazan said to her: 'Whither goest thou, and especially at such an untimely hour? And how wast thou able to get up?' But she said: 'This young man laid his hand upon me and raised me up, and I saw in a dream that I was to go where the stranger is sitting, and become perfectly healthy.' Vazan said to her: 'What young man is with thee?' And she said: 'Dost thou not see the one on my right hand leading me?'

155. (p. 264) But while they were conversing thus, Judas with Siphor and his wife and daughter, and Tertia and Mygdonia and Marcia, came to Vazan's house. And when she saw (him), Mnesara the wife of Vazan made obeisance and said: 'Art thou come, our Saviour from the troublesome disease? Thou art he whom I saw in the night delivering to me this young man to lead me to the prison. But thy goodness did not allow me to grow weary, but thou thyself didst come to me.' And saying, this, she turned about, and saw the young man no more; and since she did not find him she said to the apostle: 'I cannot walk alone; for the young man is not here whom thou gavest me' And Judas said: 'Jesus shall lead thee by the hand henceforth.' And after this she went <before them S> at a run. But when they went into the house of Vazan the son of king Misdaeus, although it was still night, a great light shone, shed round about them. 156. And then Judas began to pray and to speak thus: 'Companion and ally, hope of the weak and confidence of the poor, refuge and lodging of the weary, <voice that came forth from the height>, comforter who (p. 265) dwellest in <our> midst, lodging and haven of those who pass through <regions of darkness S>, physician (who healest) without payment, who among men wast crucified for many, who didst descend into Hades with great power, the sight of whom the princes of death did not endure, and thou didst ascend with great glory, and gathering all those who took refuge in thee thou didst prepare a way, and in thy footsteps they all journeyed whom thou didst redeem, and thou didst bring them to thine own flock and unite them with thy sheep; son of compassion, the son sent to us out of love for men from the perfect fatherland above; Lord of possessions <undefiled S>; thou who dost serve thy servants, that they may live; thou who hast filled creation with

thy riches; the poor, who was in need and hungered forty days;[196] who dost satisfy thirsty souls with thine own good things; be thou with Vazan the son of Misdaeus, and Tertia, and Mnesara, and gather <them> into thy fold and (p. 266) unite them with thy number. Be thou their guide in a land of error; be thou their physician in a land of sickness; be thou their rest in a land of the weary; sanctify them in a land <polluted>; be the physician of their bodies and souls; make them the holy temples, and let thy Holy Spirit dwell in them!'[197]

157. When the apostle had thus prayed for them, he said to Mygdonia: 'Unclothe thy sisters!' And she unclothed them, girded them with girdles, and brought them. But Vazan had come forward before, and they came after him. And Judas took oil in a silver cup, and spoke thus over it: 'O fruit fairer than the other fruits, with which no other can be compared at all; thou altogether merciful; fervent with the force of the word; power of the tree which if men put on they conquer their adversaries; thou that crownest the victors; symbol and joy of the weary; who hast brought to men glad tidings of their (p. 267) salvation; who dost show light to those in darkness; who in thy leaves art bitter, <but in thy fruit most sweet>; who in appearance art rough, but soft to the taste; who seemest weak, but by the greatness of thy power dost carry the power that sees all things; < . . . > Jesus, let <thy> victorious power come, and <let it settle> in this oil as then it settled in the wood that is its kin < . . . > and they who crucified thee did not endure its word; let the gift also come by which, breathing upon <thine> enemies, thou didst make them draw back and fall headlong,[198] and let it dwell in this oil, over which we name thy holy name!' And when the apostle had said this, he poured it first on Vazan's head, then on the heads of the women, saying: 'In thy name, Jesus Christ, let it be to these souls for remission of sins, and for the turning back of the adversary, and for salvation of their souls!' And he commanded Mygdonia to anoint them (the women), but he himself anointed Vazan. And when he had anointed them he led them down to the water in the name of the Father and of the Son and of the Holy Spirit. (p. 268)

158. But when they had come up from the water he took bread and a cup, and blessed and said: 'Thy holy body which was crucified for us we eat, and thy blood which was poured out for us for salvation we drink. Let thy body, then, become for us salvation, and thy blood for remission of sins! For the gall which thou didst drink for our sakes, let the gall of the devil be taken away from us; and for the vinegar which thou hast drunk for us,[199] let our weakness be made strong; for the spitting which thou didst receive for our sakes,[200] let us receive the dew of thy goodness; and for the reed with which they smote thee for our sakes,[201] let us receive the perfect house! Because thou didst receive a crown of thorns for our sakes,[202] let us who have loved thee put on a crown that does not fade away; and for the linen cloth in which thou wast wrapped,[203] let us be girt about with thine unconquerable power; and for the new grave[204] and

burial let us receive renewal of soul and body! Because thou didst rise (p. 269) and come to life again, let us come to life again and live and stand before thee in righteous judgment!' And breaking (the bread of) the Eucharist he gave[205] to Vazan and Tertia and Mnesara and Siphor's wife and daughter, and said: 'Let this Eucharist be to you for salvation and joy and health for your souls!' And they said: 'Amen.' And a voice was heard saying: 'Amen. Fear not, but only believe.'[206]

Martyrdom of the holy and esteemed apostle Thomas[207]

159. And after these things Judas went away to be imprisoned. And not only so, but Tertia and Mygdonia and Marcia too (p. 270) went away to be imprisoned. And Judas said to them: 'My daughters, handmaids of Jesus Christ, hear me in this my last day <on which> I shall accomplish my word among you, to speak no more (with you) in the body. For behold, I am taken up to my Lord Jesus who had mercy on me, who humbled himself even to my littleness and led me to a service of majesty, and counted me worthy to become his servant. But I rejoice that the time is near for my release from hence, that I may go and receive my reward (p. 271) in the end. For righteous is my requiter, he knows how recompense must be made. For he is not grudging, but he is lavish with his goods, since he is confident <that his possessions are unfailing>. 160. I am not Jesus, but a servant of Jesus. I am not Christ, but I am a minister of Christ. I am not the Son of God, but I pray to be counted worthy with him. But abide in the faith of Jesus Christ! Wait for the hope of the Son of God! Do not shrink in afflictions, neither be ye doubtful when ye see me insulted and imprisoned and dying. For in these I fulfil what has been appointed for me by the Lord. For <.> if I <wished> not to die, <you know S> that I am able. But this apparent death is not death, but deliverance and release from the body. (p. 272) And this I shall await gladly, that I may go and receive that fair one, the merciful. For I am altogether worn out in his service, and what I have done by his grace, and now he will certainly not forsake me. But do you see to it that that one come not upon you, who comes in by stealth and divides the thoughts (casts into doubt); for stronger is he whom you have received. Look then for his coming, that when he comes he may receive you; for ye shall see him when ye depart.'

161. But when he had completed his word to them, he went into (the) dark house, and said: 'My Saviour, who didst endure much for our sakes, let these doors become as they were, and <let them be sealed> with their seals!' And leaving the women he went away to be shut up. But they were grieved and wept, since they knew that king Misdaeus would destroy him.

162. But Judas, when he <returned>, found the guards fighting and saying: 'What sin have we committed against that sorcerer, that by magic art he opened

the doors of the prison, and wishes all the prisoners to escape? But let us go and inform the king, and <let us tell him also> about his wife and son!' But while the gaolers were saying this, Judas was listening in silence. And as soon as day broke they arose and went off (p. 274) to king Misdaeus, and said: 'Lord, release that sorcerer, or command him to be kept in custody somewhere else. For <twice> has thy good fortune kept the prisoners together. Though we shut the doors at the proper time, yet when we wake we find them open. And moreover, thy wife and thy son, together with those others, do not stay away from the man.' When he heard this, the king went to inspect the seals which he had set upon the doors; and he found the seals as they were (before). And he said to the gaolers: 'Why do you lie? For indeed these seals are still intact. And how say you, that Tertia and Mygdonia went into the prison?' And the guards said: 'We told thee the truth.'

163. (p. 275) After this the king went into the <judgment hall S> and sent for Judas. But <when he came>, they stripped him and girded him with a girdle, and set him before the king. And Misdaeus said to him: 'Art thou a slave or a free man?' And Judas said: 'I am a slave, <but thou hast no authority over me at all>' And Misdaeus said: 'How didst thou come as a runaway to this country?' And Judas said: 'I came here to save many, and that I (p. 276) might at thy hands depart from this body.' Misdaeus says to him: 'Who is thy master? And what his name? And of what country?' 'My Lord', says Thomas, 'is my master and thine, since he is Lord of heaven and earth.' And Misdaeus said: 'What is his name?' Judas said: 'Thou canst not hear his true name at this time, <. . . > but the name which was bestowed upon him for a season is Jesus, the Christ.' And Misdaeus said: 'I have not hastened to destroy thee, but have restrained myself. But thou hast made addition to thy deeds, so that thy sorceries are reported (p. 277) in all the land. But now I will <so> deal with thee <that> thy sorceries may perish with thee, and our nation <be cleansed> from them.' And Judas said: 'These sorceries, as thou dost call them, <. . . shall never depart from hence>.' 164. During these words Misdaeus was considering in what manner he should put him to death; for he was afraid of the crowd which stood around, since many believed him, and even some of the leading people.[208] And rising up he took Judas with him outside the city; and a few armed soldiers followed him. But the <.> crowds supposed that the king wished (p. 278) to learn something from him; and they stood and observed him. But when they had advanced three stadia, he handed him over to four soldiers and one of the officers, commanding them to take him to the mountain and despatch him with spears. And he himself returned to the city.

165. The bystanders ran to Judas, eager to snatch him away. But he was led away, the soldiers escorting him two on either side, holding their spears, and the officer (p. 279) holding his hand fast and leading <him>. And as they went, Judas said: 'O thy hidden mysteries, <which> even to life's end are fulfilled

in us! O riches of thy grace, who dost not allow <that we should feel the sufferings of the body>! For behold, how four have laid hold of me, since from the four elements I came into being! And one leads me, since I belong to one, to whom I depart < . . . > But now I learn that my Lord, since he was of one, to whom I depart and who is ever invisibly with me, was smitten by one;[209] but I, since I am of four, am smitten by four.' 166. (p. 280) But when they came to the place where they were to slay him, Judas said to those who held him: 'Listen to me now at least, because I stand at the point of departure from the body! And let not the eyes of your understanding be darkened, nor your ears stopped that they do not hear < . . . >! Believe in the God whom I preach! Released form the arrogance of the heart, conduct yourselves in a manner of life befitting free men, and in esteem among men and in life with God!' 167. (p. 281) But to Vazan he said: 'Son of the earthly king, but servant of Jesus Christ, give to those who attend on the command of king Misdaeus what is due, that I may be released by them and go and pray.' And when Vazan had persuaded the soldiers, Judas turned to prayer; and it was this: '*My Lord and my God*,[210] and hope and redeemer and leader and guide in all the lands, be thou with all who serve thee, and lead me today, since I come to thee! Let none take my soul, which I have committed unto thee. Let not the tax-collectors see me, and let not the exactors lay false charge against me! Let not the serpent see me, and let not the children of the dragon hiss me! Behold, (p. 282) Lord, I have fulfilled thy work and accomplished thy command. I have become a slave; therefore today do I receive freedom. Do thou now give it to me <completely>! But this I say not as one doubting, but that they may hear who ought to hear.'

168. And when he had prayed, he said to the soldiers: 'Come and fulfil <the command> of him who sent you!' And at once the four smote him and slew him. But all the brethren wept. And wrapping him in fine robes and (p. 283) many fine linen cloths they laid him in the tomb in which the kings of old <were buried>. 169. But Siphor and Vazan were unwilling to go down into the city, but after spending the whole day there they passed the night there also. And Judas appeared to them, and said: 'I am not here.[211] Why do you sit here and watch over me? For I have gone up and received what was hoped for. But arise and walk, and after no great time ye shall be gathered to me.' But Misdaeus and Charisius brought great pressure to bear on Tertia and Mygdonia, but did not persuade them to depart from their belief. And Judas appeared and said to them: (p. 284) 'Forget not the former things! For Jesus the holy and living will himself help you.' And those about Misdaeus and Charisius, being unable to persuade them, allowed them to live according to their own will. And all the brethren there used to assemble together; for Judas on the mountain had made Siphor a presbyter and Vazan a deacon, when he was being led off to die. (p. 285) But the Lord helped them, and increased the faith through them.

170. But after a long time had passed it <befell> that one of Misdaeus' sons

was possessed by a demon; and since the demon was stubborn, no one was able to heal him. But Misdaeus pondered and said: 'I will go and open the tomb, and take <one of the bones of the apostle> of God, and fasten it upon my son, and I know that he will be healed.' And he went away to do what he had in mind. (p. 286) And Judas appeared to him and said: 'Since thou didst not believe in the living, how dost thou wish to believe in the dead?[212] But fear not! Jesus the Christ, because of his great goodness, acts humanely towards thee.' But Misdaeus did not find the bones; for one of the brethren had stolen them away, and carried them to the regions of the West. But taking dust from the place where the bones of the apostle had lain, (p. 287) he attached it to his son and said: 'I believe in thee, Jesus, now when he has left me, who ever confuses men that they may not look upon thy rational light.' And when his son was in this manner restored to health, he (Misdaeus) came together with the other brethren, becoming submissive to Siphor. And he besought all the brethren to pray for him, that he might find mercy from our Lord Jesus Christ.

The acts of Judas Thomas the apostle are completed, which he wrought in the land of the Indians, fulfilling the command of him who sent him; to whom be glory for ever and ever. Amen.

Notes

* Brackets are used as follows:
( ) explanatory additions by the translator.
< > conjecture or emendation.
< S> correction or restoration on the basis of the Syriac text.
< G> correction or restoration on the basis of the Greek text (in the Hymn of the Pearl).
<. . . . . > deletion.
The bracketed page numbers refer to Bonnet's edition.

1. Cf. Mk. 3:16-19; Mt. 10:2-4; Lk. 6:14-16; Acts 1:13.
2. Cf. Acts 18:9; 23:11.
3. Cf. Mt. 26:15 par.; S reads 'twenty silver pieces'; cf. Gen. 37:28.
4. Cf. Mk. 6:3.
5. Cf. 1 Cor. 6:20.
6. Cf. Mt. 26:63 par.
7. Mt. 6:10; Lk. 22:42.
8. Cf. Mt. 22:3-14.
9. Cf. Gal. 3:28.
10. Cf. Mt. 26:26-29 par.
11. Cf. Jn. 4:34.
12. Cf. Mt. 27:29 par.
13. Cf. Mt. 26:68; Mk. 14:65; Jn. 18:22; 19:3.
14. Cf. Lk. 23:39-43.
15. See G. Hoffmann, 'Zwei Hymnen der Thomasakten', ZNW 4, 1903, 295-309; E. Preuschen, *Zwei gnostische Hymnen*, 1904, and H. Kruse, 'Das Brautlied der syrischen Thomas-Akten', OCP 50, 1984, 291-330 for numerous suggestions for altering and improving the text.
16. Cf. Mt. 17:2 par.

17. Cf. Jn. 20:17; Acts 1:2.
18. Cf. Gos. Thom. log. 7; vol. 1, p. 118.
19. Jn. 20:28.
20. Cf. Gos. Thom. log. 1; vol. 1, p. 117.
* Here the Syriac has: 'Thou art the beginning, and didst put on the first man. Thou art the power and wisdom, understanding, will and rest of thy Father, through whom thou art hidden in glory and through whom thou art revealed in thy doings. And ye are one in two names. And thou didst appear as one that was weak, and those who saw thee thought of thee that thou wast a man who had need of help, and thou didst show the glory of thy godhead through the forbearance of thy Spirit with our humanity, in that thou didst cast down the evil one from his power and call with thy voice upon the dead, that they might live, and didst promise to those who live and hope in thee an inheritance in thy kingdom. Thou didst become an ambassador and wast sent from the heights above, since thou canst do the living and perfect will of him who sent thee. Blessed be thou, Lord, in thy might, and thy government works with renewing power in all thy creatures and in all the works which thy godhead has accomplished, and no other can make the will of thy majesty of none effect and stand up against the nature of thine eminence, as thou art. Thou didst descend to Hell. . . . '
21. Mt. 16:16.
22. Cf. Ps. 107:16; Mt. 16:18; Ps. 9:14.
23. Cf. 1 Cor. 6:19.
24. Cf. Phil. 3:19.
25. Cf. 1 Cor. 7:26.
26. 1 Cor. 16:23.
27. Cf. 2 Cor. 3:7-18.
28. Cf. Gen. 3:7, 21; Gos. Thom. log. 37; vol. 1, p. 123.
29. Cf. Phil. 2:6-8.
30. Cf. Mt. 26:65 par.
31. Cf. Mt. 6:1-4 par.
32. Cf. Ps. 68:6.
33. Cf. Mt. 25:35-37.
34. Cf. Mt. 10:9.
35. Cf. Mt. 6:19-21 and Lk. 18:22, the treasure in heaven.
36. Mk. 5:36.
37. The Semitic name Gad means 'fortune, lot' and in this context perhaps has a symbolic sense: Gad the brother symbolises his brother's lot, a variant of the 'twin' motif.
38. Cf. Mk. 6:23.
39. Cf. Eph. 5:26.
40. Cf. Mt. 5:11-12.
41. Cf. Jn. 10:12, 14; Mt. 10:22; Jn. 17:14-18.
42. Cf. Jn. 10:1-18, esp. 14.
43. Jn. 20:19, 21, 26.
44. Phil. 2:9.
45. Cf. Lk. 1:35; 24:49.
46. Cf. Prov. 9:1.
47. Cf. Ps. 26:2.
48. Mt. 6:34.
49. Mt. 6:26; cf. Lk. 12:24.
50. Mt. 6:30 par.
51. Acts 10:42.
52. Mt. 16:27.
53. Cf. Kerygma Petri, frag. 3b, above p. 39.

54. Cf. Mt. 11:29-30.
55. Cf. Jn. 2:11.
56. Acts 10:42. Cf. Rom. 14:9
57. Cf. Gen. 3:1ff.
58. Cf. Gen. 4:5ff.
59. Cf. Gen. 3:18.
60. Cf. Gen. 6:1-4.
61. Cf. Exod. 1ff.
62. Cf. Exod. 32.
63. Cf. Mt. 2; Lk. 23:6-16.
64. Cf. Mt. 26:3ff.; 27:11ff.; Jn. 18:28ff.
65. Cf. Mt. 26:14-16.
66. Rev. 9:11.
* Here according to the Syriac the crowd says: "One is (God), the God of this man, who has taught us about his God and through his word has commanded this fearful beast to reveal its nature to us." Then the narrative continues: And they prayed him that, as he by his word had commanded it to speak like a man, he should also kill it by his word.
67. Mt. 19:23.
68. Mt. 11:8.
69. Lk. 21:34.
70. Mt. 6:25.
71. Cf. Jn. 15:1.
72. Cf. 1 Cor. 2:9.
73. Cf. Gos. Thom., log. 13.
74. Cf. 1 Cor. 3:9; Col. 4:11.
75. Cf. Gos. Thom, log 13; vol. 1, p. 119.
76. Cf. Jn. 10:11f.
77. Cf. Num. 22:21ff.
78. Cf. Mk. 11:1ff. pars.
79. Mk. 5:7.
* Here the Syriac has: 'Why art thou like God thy Lord, who hid his majesty and appeared in a body (flesh)? And we thought regarding him that he was mortal. But he turned and did us violence; art thou, then, born of him?' Cf. Jn. 1:12, 13; 3:5.
80. The whole of c. 46 is based on Lk. 11:23-26.
81. Cf. Gos. Thom. log. 13; vol. 1, p. 119.
82. Cf. Jn. 21:6, 11f.
83. Cf. Mk. 6:34ff. pars.
84. Cf. Jn. 4:6; Mk. 4:35-41.
85. Cf. Mk. 6:45ff. pars.
86. Rom. 8:29; cf. Jn. 1:12, 13, 18.
* Here the Syriac has: 'Jesus, right hand of the Father, who hast hurled down the evil one under his nature (other MSS: 'to the lowest limit') and hast gathered his possessions into a blessed place of assembly; Jesus, king over all, who dost subdue all; Jesus, who art in the Father and the Father in thee; and ye are one in power, will, glory and essence, and for our sakes thou wast named by name and art the Son and didst put on a body; Jesus, who didst become a Nazirite, and thy grace provides for all like God; Son of the Most High God, who didst become a despised man . . . '
87. Mt. 27:63.
88. Col. 3:9f.; Rom. 6:6; Eph. 4:22-24.
89. Rom. 16:20.
90. Cf. 1 Cor. 11:27-30
91. Cf. Mt. 6:5ff.; Lk. 11:1ff.

92. Mt. 7:7.
93. Cf. Apoc. Petri, below pp. 620ff.
94. Cf. Lk. 16:26.
95. Cf. Mk. 9:48.
96. Cf. Rev. 21:8.
97. Cf. Col. 3:9.
98. Cf. Eph. 4:28.
99. 1 Pet. 3:9.
100. Cf. Lk. 24:27.
101. Jn. 1:14.
102. Rom. 8:29.
103. Mt. 20:12.
104. Cf. Mt. 19:27, 29.
105. Cf. Mt. 10:37; Lk. 14:26.
106. Cf. Mk. 9:24.
107. Cf. Mk. 6:45ff. par.
108. Cf. Exod. 32.
109. Cf. Mt. 5:7; 11:29.
110. Cf. Eccles. 3:1-8.
111. Cf. Mt. 7:15.
112. Cf. Jn. 14:27.
* Here the Syriac has the following hymn from the apostle: 'Blessed be thou, God of truth and Lord of all being, that thou didst will with thy will and make all thy works and finish all thy creations and bring them to the rule of their nature and lay thy fear upon them all, that they might be subject to thy command. And thy will trod the way from thy secrecy to revelation, and cared for every soul which thou didst make. And he was proclaimed by the mouth of all the prophets in all visions, sounds and voices. But Israel did not obey because of their evil inclination. And since thou art Lord of all, thou dost take care of all thy creatures, so that thou dost spread out thy mercy upon us in him who came by thy will and put on the body, thy creature; whom thou didst will and form in thy blessed wisdom; whom thou didst appoint in thy secrecy and establish in thy revelation; to whom thou didst give the name of Son; who is thy will and the power of thy thought; so that ye are in various names, Father, Son and Spirit, because of the government of thy creatures, for the nourishing of all natures, while ye are one in glory, power and will. And ye are divided without being separated, and one although divided; and all subsists in thee and is subject to thee, since all is thine. And I trust in thee, Lord, and through thy command have I subjected these dumb beasts, that thou mightest rule us and them, because it is necessary (one MS that thou mightest minister to us and them with what is needful), and that thy name might be glorified in us and the dumb beasts.'
113. Cf. Phil. 2:7-8.
114. Cf. Rev. 5:9; 1 Cor. 6:20.
115. Cf. Mk. 8:37 pars.; 2 Clem. 1.
116. Cf. Mk. 9:26.
117. Cf. Lk. 11:24-26.
118. Cf. Infancy Gospel of Thomas 6-8; 14 and 15; 19; vol. 1, pp. 444ff. Cf. Lk 2:46
119. Cf. Mt. 17:27; Lk. 2:23f.
120. Mt. 7:15; 24:11 parr.; 2 Pet. 2:1; 2 Cor. 11:13, 15.
121. Mt. 7:15.
*Here the Syriac has: 'How I am to name thee, I know not. O noble one, silent, tranquil and speaking, seer who art in the heart, seeker who art in the understanding. Glory to thee, the gracious; glory to thee, the living word; glory to thee, who hast many forms; glory to thy compassion. . . .
122. Mt. 19:28; cf. 20:23.

123. Cf. Jn. 20:22.
124. Mk. 8:18 (Jer. 5:21; Ezek. 12:2).
125. Mt. 11:15 par.
126. Mt. 11:28.
127. The following is according to the Rome MS. U, here however very corrupt. The Paris MS. P is very much shorter.
128. Cf. Gal. 3:28.
129. Cf. Did. 1. 2; Tob. 4. 15; Mt. 7:12.
130. Cf. Gen. 4:11f.
131. Cf. Jn. 12:6; Mt. 27:5; Acts 1:18.
132. Cf. Gen. 25:29-34.
133. From this point again according to the two MSS P and U.
134. Cf. 1 Cor. 6:18f.
135. Cf. Mt. 4:2.
136. Mt. 26:52f.
137. Cf. 1 Cor. 6:19.
138. Cf. Col. 3:16.
139. Cf. Lk. 7:50.
140. Cf. Gos. Thom. log. 22; vol. 1, p. 120.
141. The following according to U. P differs.
142. From this point again according to the two great MSS.
143. Cf. Jn. 20:23; Mt. 16:19; 18:18.
144. Cf. Mt. 7:7-8.
145. Mt. 5:5.
146. Mt. 5:8; cf. Rev. 22:4.
147. Mt. 5:6.
148. The following according to U. P differs.
149. From this point again according to the two great MSS.
150. The following according to U. P differs and is very much shorter.
151. From this point again according to the two great MSS.
152. Acts 4:7.
153. Cf. Lk. 23:9.
154. Cf. Mt. 5:11.
155. The German translation is by and large identical with that of G. Hoffmann ('Zwei Hymnen der Thomasakten', ZNW 4, 1903, 273ff.), which was also taken over by E. Preuschen (*Zwei gnostische Hymnen*, 1904). A. Adam (*Die Psalmen des Thomas und das Perlenlied*) made a translation of his own, which has been consulted at particular points, as has that of M.R. James (*The Apocryphal New Testament*, 411ff.). R. Köbert ('Das Perlenlied, *Orientalia* 38, 1969, 447-456) offers a new German translation with valuable notes. H. Kruse ('The Return of the Prodigal', *Orientalia* 47, 1978, 177-184) gives a new English translation with an important commentary. P.H. Poirier (*L'Hymne de la Perle des actes de Thomas*, Louvain 1981) composed a new French version. (The following English version is based on that prepared for the earlier English translation of this book, which Prof. M. Black kindly checked against the Syriac text; the whole has been revised in the light of Prof. Drijvers' version.)
156. Cf. Eph. 1:21; Col. 2:10.
157. Cf. 1 Cor. 10:16.
158. Cf. Jn. 1:14.
159. Cf. Acts 19:9.
160. The following in the main according to U; P differs. Cf. Acts 2:38.
161. Cf. Jn. 3:4f.
162. From here on again according to both MSS.

163. Cf. Mt. 11:7.
164. Cf. the Gospel of the Hebrews 4ab; 2; vol. 1, p. 177. Cf. also next note.
165. Cf. Gos. Thom. log. 2; vol. 1, p. 117. Cf. also the previous note.
166. Acts 4:7.
167. Cf. Jn. 19:11.
168. Cf. Mk. 9:1 pars.
169. Mk. 9:1.
170. Cf. Lk. 3:23.
171. 1 Jn. 1:1.
172. Cf. Mk. 9:2ff. pars.
173. Cf. Mt. 17:24-27.
174. Cf. Jn. 8:44.
175. Mt. 6:9ff. From this point the two MSS U and P diverge considerably. P (with 3 and in part even 4 other MSS) presents this long prayer (from *My Lord and my God* to c. 148) only in the Martyrdom (after c. 167) and with a very divergent text. S on the other hand agrees by and large with U. James (p. 364) considers the position and textual tradition of this chapter presented by P (and the parallel MSS) the more original. (Cf. also what is said below on the Martyrdom.) The above text on the whole follows the substantially shorter form of U and its arrangement.
176. Jn. 20:28.
177. Cf. Mt. 13:25.
178. Cf. Mt. 25:27.
179. Cf. Lk. 19:13ff.
180. Cf. Mt. 18:23ff.
181. Cf. Lk. 14:16ff. par.
182. Cf. Mt. 22:1ff.
183. Cf. Mt. 25:1ff.
184. Cf. Mt. 24:45ff.
185. Cf. Mt. 24:43.
186. C. 147 has been supplemented according to the tradition presented by P and S. U here has only two sentences.
187. Cf. Eph. 6:14.
188. Cf. Eph. 6:15.
189. Cf. Lk. 9:62.
190. Cf. Jn. 4:35.
191. Cf. Lk. 12:38.
192. Some Greek MSS have here: 'All my goods have I sold, that I may gain thee, the pearl.'
193. Cf. Gos. Thom. log. 13; vol. 1, p. 119.
194. Cf. the Gospel of the Egyptians, vol. 1, p. 213; Gos. Thom. log. 22; vol. 1, p. 120.
195. U and S alone have c. 149. In chapters 150-158 the great Greek MSS are in fairly close agreement.
196. Cf. Mt. 4:2.
197. Cf. 1 Cor. 6:19.
198. Cf. Jn. 18:6.
199. Cf. Mt. 27:34, 48.
200. Cf. Mt. 27:30.
201. Cf. Mt. 27:30.
202. Cf. Mt. 27:29.
203. Cf. Mt. 27:59.
204. Cf. Mt. 27:60.
205. Cf. Mt. 26:26.
206. Cf. Mk. 5:36 parr.

207. In the tradition of the Martyrdom the great Greek MSS U and P diverge considerably, even apart from the insertion in P of the great prayer (cf. on this p. 410, n. 175 above). There is much to be said for the view that the Martyrdom had a textual history of its own. Thus James (pp. 434ff.) prefers the text of P (and its parallel MSS). Here again we present the text of U (like Rabbe, cf. also Bonnet).

208. Cf. Lk. 20:19; 22:2; Acts 5:26.

209. Cf. Jn. 19:34.

210. Cf. Jn. 20:28.

211. Cf. Lk. 24:6.

212. Cf. Gos. Thom. log. 52; vol. 1, p. 125.

XVI. The Acts of Peter and the Twelve Apostles

Hans-Martin Schenke

1. Literature: *Facsimile: The Facsimile Edition of the Nag Hammadi Codices*, published under the auspices of the Department of Antiquities of the Arab Republic of Egypt in conjunction with the United Nations Educational, Scientific and Cultural Organization, Codex VI, Leiden 1972, pl. 5-16.

Editions: M. Krause, *Gnostische und hermetische Schriften aus Codex II und Codex VI* (= Abhandlungen des Deutschen Archäologischen Instituts Kairo, Koptische Reihe 2), 1971, (24-26, 36-41) 107-121; R.McL. Wilson/D.M. Parrott, 'The Acts of Peter and the Twelve Apostles, VI 1: 1.1-12.22', in: D.M. Parrott (ed.), *Nag Hammadi Codices V, 2-5 and VI with Papyrus Berolinensis 8502, 1 and 4* (= Nag Hammadi Studies XI), Leiden 1979, 197-229.

Translations: D.M. Parrott/R.McL. Wilson, 'The Acts of Peter and the Twelve Apostles (VI, 1)', in: J.M. Robinson (ed.), *The Nag Hammadi Library in English*, San Francisco 1977, 265-270 (3rd ed. 1988, 287-294); H.-M. Schenke, '"Die Taten des Petrus und der zwölf Apostel" - Die erste Schrift aus Nag-Hammadi-Codex VI', ThLZ 98, 1973, cols. 13-19.

Select further **Literature** (for complete coverage of the literature cf. D.M. Scholer, *Nag Hammadi Bibliography 1948-1969* (= Nag Hammadi Studies I), Leiden 1971, 182f. and the annual supplements as 'Bibliographia Gnostica' in *Novum Testamentum* since vol. 13, 1971): G.M. Browne, 'Textual Notes on Nag Hammadi Codex VI', *Zeitschrift für Papyrologie und Epigraphik* 13, 1974, 305f.; C. Colpe, 'Heidnische, jüdische und christliche Überlieferung in den Schriften aus Nag Hammadi I', JAC 15, 1972, 8-11; J.E. Furman, 'Leading to Light: A Christian Reading of a Nag Hammadi Text', *Coptic Church Review* 6/I, 1985, 22-26; M. Krause, 'Die Petrusakten in Codex VI von Nag Hammadi', in M. Krause (ed.), *Essays on the Nag Hammadi Texts in Honour of A. Böhlig* (= Nag Hammadi Studies III), Leiden 1972, 36-58; J. Kubinska, 'L'ange Litakskuel en Nubie', *Muséon* 89, 1976, 451-455; P. Perkins, *The Gnostic Dialogue. The Early Church and the Crisis of Gnosticism* (Theological Inquiries), New York 1980, 125-130; H.-M. Schenke, 'Zur Faksimile-Ausgabe der Nag-Hammadi-Schriften. Nag-Hammadi-Codex VI', OLZ 69, 1974, cols. 229f.; H.-M. Schenke, review of Parrott's edition of Nag Hammadi Codices V,2-5 and VI, OLZ 79, 1984, cols. 460-464; E. Segelberg, 'Prayer Among the Gnostics? The Evidence of some Nag Hammadi Documents', in: M. Krause (ed.), *Gnosis and Gnosticism. Papers read at the Seventh International Conference on Patristic Studies* (Oxford, September 8-13, 1975)(= Nag Hammadi Studies VIII), Leiden 1977, 62-64.[1]

2. Transmission: for this short document, which bears the somewhat curious title 'The Acts of Peter and the Twelve Apostles' (abbreviated: ActPt), there is no external evidence of any sort in early Christian literature. Down to the accidental discovery of its text it was itself completely unknown. This text which has been recovered is admittedly only a Coptic translation, and also is extant in but a single copy. It is the first of eight tractates in what is now numbered as Codex VI in the Cairo corpus of the Nag Hammadi papyri (Coptic Museum, Department of Manuscripts, inv. 10549). This is a single-quire papyrus codex (27.9 x 14.8 cm), which has come down to us together with its sheepskin binding and contains 78 paginated pages (owing to damage to the upper margin on many leaves, the original page numbers are often no longer extant). ActPt stands in this codex on pages 1 (line 1) to 12 (line 22). As in the rest of the codex, the pages of our text are written in one column, with no text divisions, marginal aids, or decoration. As to the time of manufacture of the codex, which is important as the *terminus post quem non* for the composition of ActPt, the fragments of documents in the papyrus cartonnage of its binding, as with those from other Nag Hammadi bindings, especially that of Codex VII, point to the first half of the 4th century.

The copy of ActPt contained in Codex VI unfortunately does not present the text in an undamaged form. The copy has indeed been made with great care, but this copy itself is not perfect; for there are mistakes - even if only a few. Where the copyist or a corrector has noticed them, they have been corrected. Frequently, however, they have been overlooked. In the following translation the necessary corrections to these passages are presupposed, duly marked and/or provided with a reference to this effect, or an explanation, in the notes. Angled brackets < > indicate emendatory interchanges or additions, while curly braces { } mark deletions. The real defect of this single witness to the text is however that pages 1-8 have suffered considerable damage at the top and the text thus shows fairly large lacunae, which are marked as usual by square brackets [ ]. Because of the transparent plot, however, most of them can be restored relatively easily and with a high degree of certainty (and agreement among the specialists). But passages remain for which no obvious reconstruction has yet been achieved. Among these external and material defects which impair the value of this witness and make its use difficult there is finally the fact that on pages 2-6 the text has been rendered obscure by the mirror-image imprint of parts of the column on the facing page (blotting). On the other hand the round brackets ( ) which occasionally appear in the translation are not an indication of imperfections in our witness. The words enclosed within them are merely paraphrases or explanations intended to elucidate the understanding of the text which is presupposed.

3. Original language, place and time of origin: the Coptic language, in which by chance the ActPt have been preserved, cannot be the language in which the tractate was originally composed. As with most works of Coptic literature, we have to do with a translation from the Greek. Occasionally this Greek substratum can still be clearly recognised beneath the Coptic surface. The clearest indication is the two Greek vocatives (ὦ) Πέτρε which have been retained (p.9[.15][2] and 10[.23]). Since there is no reason for going back behind the Greek, we may probably assume that Greek was the original language of our tractate.

The next question, *where* the prototype of ActPt may have come into being, cannot be answered - or at least not without more ado or not at the moment. The text contains no direct indication of any kind as to its place of origin. However, there may perhaps be some other traces which the original homeland has left in the text, only we cannot yet 'read' them. In this regard three points are perhaps worthy of consideration: a) from the content and tenor of the text it is difficult to understand it as a product of the Great Church; it is much more likely that it belongs to a quite specific variety of Christianity, and came into being within a relatively small closed group. The special way in which the ideal of poverty is presented in ActPt makes one instinctively think of the Ebionites. b) The most important clue is perhaps the figure of Lithargoel which dominates the text, that is, if Lithargoel is properly and originally the key figure in a quite specific tradition, as yet still scarcely tangible, but originally Jewish. c) The way in which the text propagates asceticism, and gives voice to this asceticism, recalls the Syrian itinerant ascetics, and thus leads our thoughts to the wide area of Syria.

There is also scarcely any serviceable indication in the text for answering the question of the date of composition, i.e. how long before the first half of the 4th century, the *terminus post quem non*, the ActPt was composed. We are practically entirely reduced to estimates. Thus scholars speak in quite general terms of the 2nd and/or 3rd century. To my mind we ought by all means to reckon with the possibility that ActPt could already have come into being in the 2nd century. In any case the stance adopted in ActPt with regard to the New Testament is important for attempts at dating. Naturally one can discover and note down many cross-connections (as Krause and Furman especially have done). What is really striking however is that direct and unambiguous reference to particular passages in the New Testament is quite rare, or scarcely present at all. The sources from which ActPt essentially drew its ideas and material were evidently not New Testament writings, but apocryphal traditions of one kind or another.

4. Genre and title: our tractate is an extremely curious text. If we attempt to classify it, we are immediately plunged into deep perplexity. It displays a manifold variety of aspects. We are reminded of Lucian's 'True Histories', and might also be tempted to think of our author as an early Christian Münchhausen. What is related appears to be half reality and half a dream, half history and half fable, half apostolic legend and half portrayal of a vision, or allegory; paraenesis and church order also play a part. The story is unnatural, shot through with doublets, contradictions and absurdities. Yet the composition can convey the effect of a self-contained unity. The problematic relationship to reality of what is reported in this document, its surrealism, may in fact be described as its most striking feature. And yet again it is much closer to reality (for example in its reference to asceticism, poverty and riches) than many another well-told and much more probable story.

Should we wish to bring these observations and impressions to the point, we might say two things: a) our tractate does not belong at all to any natural genre of text which actually existed; it is a hybrid which has come into being through the forced combination of individual texts which each belong to different kinds of text. b) In order to understand and evaluate our tractate properly, in respect of the message which it seeks to proclaim, we must evidently read it (as Sallust did the Attis myth) under the rubric: ταῦτα δὲ ἐγένετο μὲν οὐδέποτε, ἔστι δὲ ἀεί (Sallust, *de Diis et mundo*, c. 4).

So far as the title is concerned, it at any rate offers no assistance in any attempt to find a form-critical definition of the text. Moreover it is equally inappropriate as the starting-point for a literary understanding (for which it is used by Krause). The title indeed covers only one of several aspects of the text. If an author had wanted to write an 'Acts of Peter and the Twelve Apostles', his work would have had to have a quite different appearance. This means however that the title must be secondary. On the other hand it can be readily understood as a title given later, by which somebody sought to give a name to the already finished work, and in so doing attained only a *pars pro toto*. In this perspective the 'and' in the title, or the mention of the number twelve after it, is not really at all surprising. Wherever Peter is singled out from the group of the twelve apostles, and yet the group as such is named thereafter, such formulations can readily be created. What is meant is in any case: the acts of Peter in particular, and at the same time of the group of the twelve as a whole.

The title of our document almost automatically gives rise to the question whether we may perhaps with justice assume - as for the 'Act of Peter' at the end of Papyrus Berolinensis 8502 (cf. above, pp. 285f.) - that we have here a part, transmitted separately, of the lost first third of the ancient Acts of Peter. Krause - to the disapproval of all others who have concerned themselves with ActPt - immediately answered this question positively, and would see in our text the original beginning of these Acts of Peter. Now in this area of literature one cannot simply exclude such a possibility. But without doubt the text is not really favourable to such a hypothesis. The sub-title as it now stands, with its '*and* the Twelve Apostles', already seems to forbid our seeking the home of this text in the apocryphal tradition relating to Peter alone. And if in answering the question we must even set him aside - because he is not original - then no basis remains any longer for such an assessment. Likewise we may scarcely regard our text as part of other apocryphal Peter documents which are known in their structure or through fragments. In general we cannot really conceive it rightly as part of a larger whole.

5. Internal character: In ActPt we have to do with a Christian text. The particular nature of its Christianity is however problematic, or at least scholars are of different minds on this question. It is a matter of the alternatives, whether the text must be described as Christian *gnostic* (this is the view of Krause, Perkins, Segelberg), or is to be assigned to the growing Great Church, i.e. is so to speak orthodox or popular Christian (Furman, Schenke, Wilson/Parrott). Whichever side one may incline to, the simple fact that ActPt belongs to the Nag Hammadi discovery, the *so-called* Coptic gnostic library of Nag Hammadi, ought not to prejudice the issue. It is indeed one of the fundamental insights of present-day Nag Hammadi research that not indeed the majority but still a quite imposing number of the Nag Hammadi texts is not gnostic at all. So far as the internal character of a document is concerned, and especially in regard to the question whether it is gnostic or non-gnostic, each must be examined in itself, and called to bear witness for itself.

In regard to the difference of opinion about ActPt in particular, it is really almost solely a conflict about words. For there must be agreement on this point - or it ought to be possible to achieve it - that ActPt is one of those Nag Hammadi texts which contain no unambiguous and specific gnostic views. There thus remains only the question whether such a text in its nature and under the surface can still be gnostic. On the other hand scholars are really also of one mind in holding that the text as it now is, when read with gnostic eyes, could very easily *become* a gnostic text.

But even if ActPt is not of gnostic origin and gnostic nature, which I myself still consider the only right view, this does not automatically mean that from the beginning it always belonged to the Great Church. It is a special form of Christianity, even if not a gnostic one, that finds a voice here. But since it does not advocate any heretical teachings, this group's literary product could very quickly have become an edifying book for a larger Church public - before it became interesting for Christian Gnosticism also and finally found its way into the Coptic gnostic library of Nag Hammadi.

6. Content: when we now turn to the content of ActPt, not to recapitulate it but from various points of view to analyse and elucidate it, attention may be drawn at the outset to the fact that here we are talking of a text not insignificantly different from the one which is the subject of the other discussions about ActPt. The most important point is that in ActPt two cities (an island city and the heavenly city), and the names of these cities, occur in a central position and with an important function, but that so far as the names are concerned a misunderstanding has inexplicably maintained itself from the initial phase of the interpretation of the text down to today. These cities in reality are not simply called 'Gorg' or 'Habitation', or 'Nine Gates'. The surest indication of this is provided by the grammar. First of all it is a matter of a single letter, an epsilon. Where the name of the island city is introduced, and shortly after the word which Wilson/Parrott render 'Habitation', there is mention of a ruler (ἡγεμών; p. 2[.5]). The point here is that that epsilon stands between what looks like the masculine singular of the Coptic definite article and this noun. That is, in this prefix we have the corresponding *possessive* article for the second person singular of the feminine. What actually stands there is thus: '*thy* ruler (O city)!' Accordingly it is here the city itself that is addressed. In the name of the heavenly city (p. 6[.23f.]) three letters are decisive, namely those which stand before the numeral 9, and which cannot possibly represent the indefinite plural article (as is assumed), but only the preposition 'in'. In order to see that something is out of harmony here, however, we do not need to concern ourselves only with the grammar. For behind the catch-words of the city names, or round about them, there stand all kinds of elements which are not intended to yield any proper sense, and at any rate do not carry on the narrative at all. In short, the two cities in reality bear very remarkable longer and evidently symbolic names, just as the cities themselves are symbols for the world and the kingdom of heaven.[3] In the case of the island city, the name of which is mentioned three times, the reference is made in a shortened form and with slight variation, after the full name has once been introduced. What is essential and the constant element in this name is at any rate the admonition: '(O city,) be founded on endurance!', i.e. 'Let your foundation, O city, be endurance!'

We can now attempt in various ways to grasp and understand the total content of our difficult document. A promising approach is for example the question of the scope of the text. The disparate individual elements are not indeed all equally important, but have a certain validity and move toward a goal. If we inquire of the text in this respect, we could receive the answer: everything focusses on the heavenly command to mission; the concern of the text is with the commissioning of Peter and the other apostles, effected by Jesus in heaven above, with a Gospel for the poor to be proclaimed and practised in all the world, and how this came about. We might also say that what has come out is a kind of exaggeration or spinning out of Mt. 5:3 and 28:16-20.

The motif that the apostles receive their charge for world mission *in heaven* also occurs elsewhere, interestingly enough, in the Book of the Installation of the Archangel Michael.[4] The crucial passage runs: 'The Saviour said to them (the apostles): "Arise, let us go to the Father, that he may bless you and you depart and preach in all the world." And we betook ourselves into the heaven with Michael and our Saviour. We came to the first gate. The angels worshipped him (*sc. the Saviour*), and he brought us to all the gates. All the angels worshipped him and praised him. He set us before his Father, who blessed us.'[5] This text can at the same time serve as an illustration of the symbolic name of the heavenly city in our ActPt (p.6[.23-26]): 'In nine gates let us praise him, mindful that the tenth is the chief gate.' In the background there evidently stands, both here and there, a conception the peculiarities of which may have come about through the transposition of Jerusalem and its sanctuary into heaven.

In general such analyses of motifs are an essential approach to the understanding of our document. However, instead of repeating what has already been said, let us move on at once to the outlining of a higher form of motif-analysis, the analysis of the text in terms of clusters of motifs and whole complexes of motifs. This will be done as we proceed along a road which Krause has already opened up. It is a question of understanding our text on the basis of its origins. Complicated texts like this are better understood when one (also) sees how they have been put together. The author of our text - fortunately for us - has left behind ample traces of his literary work. Admittedly all the contradictions, absurdities and doublets are not of equal relevance for our investigation, but altogether a clear picture emerges.

ActPt must have come into being through the combination of three different *texts*, each of which belonged to a different *kind* of text. What is common to all three, and could arouse the temptation to form such a hybrid, was *probably* that in all of them a city stood mysteriously at the centre, and *possibly* also that all three, although in different ways, may have been Peter texts. The second and third must also have been bound together through the name Lithargoel, which the central figure in each case bears. Each text was marked by characteristic clusters of motifs, specific to the genre or peculiar to that text, and here it is not difficult to recognise where they really belong, even when they have been displaced in the weaving-together of the texts.

The first text was the legendary narrative of a marvellous voyage by Peter and the other apostles, which brings them out of time and space to an imaginary small island, which signifies the world and is accordingly symbolically and mysteriously named. Its high points are the imparting of this name, the wonderful display of the truth of this name, since the island city still endures although it ought properly to be swallowed up by the sea, the conversation about the significance and power of endurance, and a kind of application in the style of the peroration of a sermon. The original end of this text (with the catch-word 'kingdom of heaven') may still be clearly recognisable at p. 7[.18].

The second text was not *added* to the first, but inserted into it. It could be interpreted as the description of a vision (by Peter?) of the appearance of a mysterious pearl-merchant named Lithargoel in a strange city, and the reaction of rich and poor to his offer; all this (transparent as an allegory) as a symbol for Jesus' preaching of salvation and its outcome in the world. That this second text can originally have had nothing at all to do with the first becomes clear through the breakdown of the internal logic of the imagery: on the sea there are no black dogs, wolves, lions or bulls. The city in which Lithargoel offers his pearls which cannot be displayed must be conceived as lying in the midst of the (desert) land. The description is made considerably less clear by the fact that the author of the whole makes Peter (the recipient of the vision?) himself intervene in the action of the vision. The only logical sequence - and so it may originally have been related - is that the poor themselves ask the pearl-merchant his name and that of his city, and also about the way to that city. Another disturbing element is part of the in any case inconceivable clothing of Lithargoel. On the other hand it is perfectly conceivable that the motif of the grave-clothes which leave the wounds exposed and thus draw attention to them, through which people can recognise the crucified Jesus, has migrated here from the third text, and that we have to imagine the pearl-merchant as equipped originally only with the linen cloth, golden belt, book-cover and staff. To relate how anyone actually travels the dangerous road to Lithargoel's city must seem like a μετάβασις εἰς ἄλλο γένος. Accordingly the theme of the second text must in principle run out at p.6[.26], and the thread there come to an end.

The third text betrays its original character by the piling-up of motifs such as are elsewhere known only in Easter stories. An idea of its former specific character, now hidden beneath the present surface, emerges from the circumstance often noted, that the central figure now wears one disguise too many: the physician, who is supposed to be Lithargoel, makes himself known not as the latter but as Jesus. We can well imagine that this text, as an Easter and Pentecost story, had its setting before one of the gates of the real Jerusalem, where the eleven disciples under Peter's leadership were to meet the risen Jesus. But instead of Jesus a physician comes with an assistant, and at first presents himself as Lithargoel but finally, laying aside his physician's garments, makes himself known as the crucified and risen Jesus by means of the grave-clothes which draw attention to the wounds and which he wears underneath. The equipment with power from on high for the world mission (cf. Lk. 24:49; Acts 1:8) takes place in a two-fold way: for the healing of souls the disciples receive from the hand of Jesus the contents of the small medicine chest which he carries himself, for the miraculous healing of bodily sicknesses the contents of the large medicine chest which the assistant carries. At any rate things must have been ordered in some such way if the bringing and handing-over of the *two* medicine containers was to have any meaning.

Finally, the most characteristic feature of the material would also be important for our understanding of the content of ActPt as a whole. This is the figure and name of Lithargoel himself, under which Jesus here appears (twice over). This name, as it appears, is so far only rarely attested. Apart from ActPt there are only two cases, but the first of them is extremely instructive in so far as it relates not only to the name but to the substance. In the Book of the Installation of the Archangel Gabriel (probably originating in the 7th cent.) the name occurs, only slightly modified, as that of the fifth and last of a group of five angelic princes (1. Uriel; 2. Surathiel; 3. Daveithael; 4. Ieremiel; 5. Litharkuel) who along with other angelic princes appear before Jesus and the apostles and introduce themselves. The crucial passage runs: 'The fifth angel answered: "I am Litharkuel, in whose hand is the medicine chest, filled with the medicine of life - I heal every soul . . . "!'[6] The second piece of evidence even presents along with the name, which again appears in a slightly variant form, a picture of this angel; more precisely, only the remains have survived, namely the feet and the lower part of his garment (we thus unfortunately do not know what he had in his hands). That the figure portrayed actually was an angel is certain; for immediately after it was laid bare the excavators could observe the outline of a wing in addition to the blurred halo. This evidence, a fresco and dedicatory inscription (the main text in Greek, from the donor's name on in Coptic) derives from the beginning of the 11th century, and was found in the cathedral of Faras in Nubia.[7] The inscription belonging to the picture, which identifies the figure portrayed, runs: 'Lord Jesus Christ (and) *Litaxkuel*, guard, bless, protect, confirm and stand by thy servant Martere, daughter of Isusinta. So be it. Amen.'[8]

The relevance of the two 'parallels' to ActPt for our understanding of its content naturally depends on our view of the - undoubtedly problematic - religio-historical relationship between the three witnesses. Because of the chronological disparity (and spatial proximity) of the two 'parallels', the solution closest to hand would seem to be to explain the veneration of Litharkuel/Litaxkuel in the Coptic Church as simply the result of an intensive reading of ActPt in Egypt (Krause). In the Gabriel book and in the cathedral at Faras we should then have to do with the history of the *influence* of ActPt. In this case, of the two complexes in which the name Lithargoel occurs (our second and third 'texts'), the story of the pearl-merchant might be the natural and original context of this name in ActPt also; indeed the name could have originated in connection with it, as an *ad hoc* formation by the author (Wilson/Parrott). This view however implies that a mysterious name of Jesus has become an actual angel - which of course is not impossible. On the other hand we cannot exclude the possibility - and from the point of view of the history of religions it may perhaps rank as more probable - that the later witnesses, despite their great chronological remoteness from ActPt, have preserved the true and original significance of the name Lithargoel and the religio-historical background of ActPt (something of its *pre*-history). For then Lithargoel must have been the genuine name of an angel, already Jewish, who would have had the special task of the healing of body and soul. Lithargoel would then have been something like a Jewish Asclepius. And this again means that within ActPt (or its source 'texts') Lithargoel in terms of tradition history is firmly rooted in the third and last complex, where he appears precisely as a physician.

Notes

1. In addition to the generally accessible literature mentioned, use has been made in what follows of two very important internal memoranda of the Coptic Gnostic Library team for Parrott's edition, a short one by G.M. Browne and a long one by S. Emmel.
2. Although, for ease of reading, the lines of the codex pages are not marked in the following translation, here in the introduction the line numbers have been added in brackets in the references, to facilitate checking with an edition and for further work.
3. For the principle of such names, cf. for example Is. 1:26; 60:18; 62:4,12; Jer. 3:17; 33:16; Ezek. 48:35; 2 Tim. 2:19.
4. C.D.G. Müller (ed.), *Die Bücher der Einsetzung der Erzengel Michael und Gabriel* (=

CSCO 225/226; Scriptores Coptici 31/32), Louvain 1962.
5. Translation after Müller, CSCO 226, p. 71.7-13; Coptic text, CSCO 225, p. 59.7-12.
6. Translation after Müller, CSCO 226, p.86.23-25; Coptic text, CSCO 225, p. 71.3-5.
7. K. Michalowski, *Faras. Die Wandbilder in den Sammlungen des National-museums zu Warschau*, Warsaw/Dresden 1974, pp. 66, 249, 250, 253, 311.
8. Translation after S. Jakobielski (K. Michalowski, *Faras*, 311). After inspection of the original in Warsaw, the reading of the letter Xi in the angel name seems to me personally to be not beyond all doubt; perhaps the letter concerned was only a somewhat unusually written Rho.

*The Acts of Peter and the Twelve Apostles**

[wor]ds (?) which [the occ]asi[on] as follows: It ha[ppene]d w[hen] we [had] out to [the] apostolic [.], that w[e] and travelled by ship, being [ ] of the body with other [ ] who were anxious in [the]ir [hearts].

And from now on (?) we were of one mi[nd] and agreed to fulfil the ministry to which the Lord had appointed us. We made an agreement with one another, and went down to the sea - at an opportune moment which came about for us through (the counsel of) the Lord. We found a ship at anchor by the shore, ready to put to sea. And we spoke with the sailors of the ship, that we should embark with them. They showed us great friendliness, as was (already) ordained by the Lord.

Now it happened, after we had put to sea, that we sailed for a day and a night, and after that a storm came up against the ship and drove us to a small city which was in the midst of the sea.

But I, Peter, asked about the name of this city from some people of that place who were standing on the quay. [One] of [them] **(p. 2)** answered, [saying: 'The name] of this [city is "Dwell - that] is, establish yourself - [on end]urance! So your[1] leader who is in [you[1] will] the palm branch[2] [ ] at the end of the [ ]"'

Now it happened, when we had gone ashore [with the] baggage, that I went into [the] city, enquiring of that [man] about a lodging. There came out a man wearing a linen cloth bound about his waist, and with a golden belt buckled about [it]; there was a napkin tied upon [his] chest, extending over his shoulders and covering his head and his hands.

I was looking at this man, because he was handsome both in form and bearing. There were four parts of his body that I saw: the soles of his feet, a part of his chest, the palms of his hands and his face.[3] These are (the parts) which I could see.

There was a book cover like that of an official[4] in his left hand, and a staff of styrax wood in his right hand. His voice resounded as he spoke slowly, crying aloud in the city: 'Pearls! Pearls!'

Now I was thinking that he was a ma[n of] that city, and said to him: 'My brother and my friend!' **(p. 3)** [He answered] me th[en, saying:] '[Rig]htly did you sa[y so, O (you) *my* brother and *m]y* friend! What is it that you [seek] from me?' I said to him: '[I wish to ask] you [about] a lodging for myself [and] my brethren, for we are strangers here.' He said [to] me: '[That] is why [I] too said (to you) before, "My brother and my friend", because I too am a fellow stranger like you.' And when he had said this, he cried out (again): 'Pearls! Pearls!'

The rich men of that city heard his voice. They came out of their hidden chambers: now some were looking (through the door) out of the chambers in their houses, others looked from their lofty windows. And they did not see anything in him; for there was no pouch upon his shoulder, nor was there any bundle in his linen cloth or napkin. Because of their contempt of men they did not even ask him who he was;[5] and he also did not make himself known to them. So they went back into their chambers, saying: 'Is this man making mock of us?'

And the poor **(p. 4)** of th[at city] heard [his voice, they came to] the man [who offered this pe]arl for sale and s[aid to him:] 'Take the trouble and show [us the] pearl, even if [we can see] it only with our eyes; for we are [poor] and do not have this [great sum] to pay for it. But [show (it) to us], that we may say to our friends that [we have seen] a pearl with our own eyes.'

He answered and said to them: 'If it is possible, come to my city, that I may not only show it to your eyes but give it to you freely.'

But the poor of that city heard (this) and they said: 'Since we are beggars, we also know that nobody gives a pearl to a beggar, but it is bread and money that they are wont to receive. So now the charity that we wish to receive from you (is) that you show the pearl to our eyes, that we may say proudly to our friends that we saw a pearl with our (own) eyes; for it is not found among the poor, especially such beggars (as we are).'

He answered and said to them: 'If it is possible, come yourselves to my city, that I may not only show it to you but give it to you freely.' The poor and the beggars rejoiced because of **(p. 5)** the [one who gives for] nothing.

[The peo]ple [asked Peter] about the hardships. P[et]er an[swe]red [and told th]em the things about which he had heard on the way, because they were themselves end[ur]ers of hardsh[ips] in their service.

He s[ai]d to the man who offered his[6] pearl for sale: 'I wish to know your name, and the hardships of the way to your city. For we are strangers and servants of God. We must spread the word of God obediently, (and that) in every city.'

He answered and said: 'If you ask my name, Lithargoel is my name, the interpretation of which is "the light bright stone".[7] And also (as to) the way to this city, about which you asked me, I will tell you about it. No one is able to go on that way if he does not renounce all his possessions and fast daily from one night's lodging to the next. For many are the robbers and the wild beasts which are on that road. He who takes bread with him on the road, the black dogs kill him because of the bread. He who takes a costly garment of this world with him, the robbers kill him **(p. 6)** [because of the gar]ment. H[e who] takes water [with him, the wolves kill him] be[cause of the] water, for which they were thirsty. [He who] is concerned about [meat] and [veg]etables, the lions eat him because of the meat; [if] he escapes the lions, the bulls trample him because of the vegetables.'

When he had said [these] things to me, I groaned within myself and said: 'O the great hardships on the way! Would that Jesus would give us power to walk upon it!'

He saw that my face was sad as I groaned, and said to me: 'Why do you groan if you indeed know this name "Jesus" and believe in him? He is a power great enough to give strength. For I also believe in the Father who sent him.'[8]

I asked him again: 'How is the {name of the} place called to which you are going (as) to your city?'[9] He said to me: 'This is the name of my city: "In *nine* gates let us praise God, reflecting that the *tenth* is the chief (gate)."'[10] After this I went away from him in peace, to go and call my companions.

I saw waves and great high walls (of water) surrounding the banks of the city, and marvelled at these wonders which I saw. I saw an old man sitting there and asked him the name of the city, if its name really **(p. 7)** [was the one] he had gi[ven it, when he named it] 'Dw[ell on endur]ance!' He sa[id] to me: '[ ] truly.[11] We dwe[ll] here [be]cause [we] endure.'

I a[ns]wered and said: 'Rightly [ ] have men named it (endurance) "[the fir]st (virtue)". For all [who] bear their temptations with endurance, (by them) cities are inhabited and from them comes a noble kingdom, because they endure in the midst of the waves[12] and the difficulties of the storms. And this serves as a parable (to show)[13] that the city of everyone who bears the burden of his yoke of faith is inhabited, and he is reckoned to the kingdom of heaven.'[14]

I went quickly away and called my companions, that we might go to the city to which Lithargoel had directed us. In a bond of faith we abandoned everything, as he had said. We escaped the robbers, for they did not find the garment they were looking for with us. We escaped the wolves, for they did not find with us the water for which they thirsted. We escaped the lions, for they did not find with us the meat which they desired. **(p. 8)** [We escape]d the [bulls, for , they did not find any] vegetables. [There came upon u]s a great joy [and] free[dom] from care in pea[ce in (?)] our Lord. We [rested] in front of the gate. A[nd] we conversed with one another; [t]hat was not a conversation about this world, but we were continually in eager discussion about the faith, as we recalled the robbers on the road whom we had escaped.

Behold, Lithargoel came out, in another form than the one we knew, (namely) in the form of a physician who carried a medicine chest under his armpit, and there was a young disciple following him carrying a pouch full of medicines. We did not recognise him. Peter began to speak and said to him: 'We wish you to do us a favour, for we are strangers, and take us to the house of Lithargoel before evening comes.' He said: 'In uprightness of heart I will show it to you. But I wonder how you know this good man. For he does not show himself to every man, because he is himself the son of a great king. Rest yourselves a little while I go and treat this man (to whom I am now on the way), and then come back.' He hurried, and came back **(p. 9)** [qu]ickly.

He said to Peter: '[P]eter!' But Peter was startled that he knew that his name was Peter. Peter answered the Saviour: 'Whence do you know me, that you called my name?' Lithargoel answered: 'I wish to ask you: Who gave you this name "Peter"?' He said to him: 'It was Jesus Christ, the son of the living God - he gave this name to me.'[15] He answered and said: 'It is I! Recognise me, Peter!' He loosened the garment which clothed him, and by which he had made himself unknown to us.

When he had (in this way) truly revealed to us that it was he, we prostrated ourselves on the ground and worshipped him - we were eleven disciples.[16] He stretched out his hand and made us stand up. We spoke with him humbly. Our heads were bowed down shamefacedly as we said: 'What you wish, we will do! But give us power that we may do what pleases you at all times.'

He gave them the medicine chest[17] and the pouch which was in the disciple's hands, and commanded them in this manner, **(p. 10)** saying: 'Return to [the] city from wh[i]ch you came, which is called "Dwell and continue in endurance!", and teach all those who have come to believe in my name that I (too) have endured in hardships of the faith. I myself will give you your reward. To the poor of that city you are to give what they need that they may live, until I give them that which is better,[18] of which I told <them>:[19] "I will give it to you freely."'

Peter answered and said to him: 'Lord, you have taught us to renounce the world and all that is in it. We have abandoned them for your sake. The food for a single day is what we are concerned about. Where shall we be able to find what is needful, which you ask us to give to the poor?' The Lord answered and said: 'O Peter, it was necessary that you understand the parable which I (once) told you![20] Do you not know that my name which you teach is worth more than all riches, and the wisdom of God worth more than gold and silver and precious stones?'

He gave them the pouch with the medicines and said: 'Heal all the sick of this city who believe **(p. 11)** [in] my name!' Peter was afraid to raise an objection to him a second time. He motioned to the one who stood nearest to him,[21] who was John: 'You speak this time!'

John answered and said: 'Lord, we are afraid in your presence to speak many words. But it is you who ask us to practise this skill. We have not been taught it, to be physicians. How then shall we know to heal bodies, as you have told us?'

He answered him: 'Well did you (once) say, John: "I know that the physicians of this world heal (only) worldly (sicknesses),[22] but the physicians of souls heal the heart."[23] Heal therefore the bodies first, that through these demonstrable wonders of the healing of their bodies, (which is wrought) without medicine of this world, they may believe in you, that you have power to heal the sicknesses of the heart also.'

'But the rich men of this city, those who did not even think it necessary to ask me who I am,[24] but rejoiced in their riches and their arrogance - with such as these **(p. 12)** do not eat with them in their houses, neither have fellowship with them at all, [and so it will] not befall you to show partiality to them;[25] for many have (already) shown partiality to the rich! For (where there are rich people) in the churches, they sin themselves and also lead others astray into sinning. But judge them in uprightness, that your ministry may be glorified, and that my name also may be glorified in the churches!'

The disciples answered and said: 'Yes, truly! This is what it is fitting to do.' They threw themselves on the ground and worshipped him. He made them stand up, and departed from them in peace.

Amen.

Notes

Text

* In the manuscript the title appears only in the subscription.

1. It is the second person singular of the *feminine*, i.e. the city itself is addressed.
2. 'Palm branch' here could mean 'crown of victory'. Cf. 1 Cor. 9:24, where in the Bohairic version this Coptic word appears as an equivalent for βραβεῖον.
3. As evidence that εἰκών can actually be used in Coptic with the meaning 'face', cf. ostracon No. 1133 of the Hermitage in Leningrad (ed. O. von Lemm, *Kleine Koptische Studien*, 671-680; H. Quecke, *OrChrP* 40, 1974, 46-60), verso line 3.
4. The reading and interpretation here are problematic. Both that of Krause and that of Wilson/Parrott ['like (those of) my books'] are quite unsatisfactory. I still think it possible, or even probable, that in the text the word ἄρχων is used, the chi being represented by the letter *djandja*; such substitution is nothing unusual in Coptic texts. What else can still be seen in the manuscript between *djandja* and omega may then be an impress from the opposite page.
5. Literally 'they did not even ask after his *face*' (i.e. his *person*). Another possibility would be the nuance 'they did not even examine him'. At any rate the construction in question also occurs in the Gospel of Truth (NHC I 3), p. 37.36f.
6. Both Krause and Wilson/Parrott read 'this'. The relevant expression seems to me however to have been corrected into 'his'.
7. Lit. 'the light *gazelle* stone'. What is meant is a light stone which gleams like the eye of a gazelle (and which from that has its Greek name δόρκας [here however the Coptic equivalent is used]). Here 'gazelle stone' or 'bright stone' is the proper interpretation of the name Lithargoel (leaving out the element -el), namely as containing λίθος ἀργός. The element 'light' is added only by virtue of the context, to establish the link with the pearl, of which Lithargoel is here taken to be in charge (and which is indeed lighter than a real precious stone). Perhaps the text really meant: 'the <(angel) of the> light bright stone(s)', i.e. the angel of the pearl(s).

8. The expression 'the Father who sent . . . ' recalls the Gospel of John; cf. Jn. 5:23 and often.
9. Here there might be a corruption in the text. The scribe made an error, and himself corrected his mistake. At any rate one would expect 'What is your city called, to which you are now going?'
10. Lit. 'head'; we have thus to envisage κεφαλή in the Greek original.
11. The relation of the extant fragments presupposed here at the beginning of p. 7 differs considerably from that in Krause and Wilson/Parrott.
12. The Coptic word used here does indeed look like the normal (Sahidic) term for 'a lie' (so Krause: 'in the midst of the lies'; Wilson/Parrott: 'in the midst of the apostasies'). Since however this is completely out of keeping with the context, we have to interpret our word as a homonym resulting from the influence of a lower Egyptian dialect (B,F), with the meaning 'wave'.
13. 'And this serves as a parable (to show) that': lit. 'that in this way' (or 'that in the same manner').
14. The expression 'kingdom of heaven' recalls the Gospel of Matthew - in so far as one sees our text against the background of the New Testament.
15. Cf. Mt. 16:16, 18.
16. On eleven as the number of the disciples (after Easter and in Easter stories) cf. Mt. 28:16; Mk. 16:14; Lk. 24:9, 33; Acts 1:26.
17. Lit. 'box of the physician's craft'. In the word for 'physician' the copyist has committed an error without noticing it (the last of the five Coptic letters is wrong). The outcome of this error means 'box of fame'.
18. I.e. what was meant by the metaphor of the 'pearl' (eternal salvation, or the like).
19. The manuscript has 'you'. If however we wish to do justice to the text, we must assume a scribal error or mistake in translation (and accordingly regard the end of the sentence as *direct* speech and not, with Krause and Wilson/Parrott, as *indirect*; this 'you' refers to the poor).
20. A search for this parable *within* our text leads to no obvious result. It is therefore better to assume that reference is being made to some Peter tradition lying *outside* of ActPt, especially since the following 'parallel', Jesus' reply to John, also seems to be introduced by such a reference extending beyond the narrative framework.
21. The wording of the text recalls Jn. 13:23, 24, but this may be pure chance. At any rate a completely different situation is presupposed here: 'him' in 'who stood nearest to him' (which in itself could mean 'who was lying close to his breast') refers to Peter, not to Jesus.
22. Lit. 'the (things) which belong to the world' or 'what is worldly'; i.e. we could even directly paraphrase by using 'bodies'.
23. Understanding of this sentence up to now is on closer examination unsatisfactory in several respects. To my mind, light is only shed upon the situation when we recognise that Jesus begins his answer to John with a statement which John himself once made (and which the reader, it is assumed, already knows from some other source), and then for his part gives it concrete application. 'Well' or 'Rightly' as Jesus' reaction to John's question is just as out of place as the 'I know' on the lips of Jesus.
24. Lit. 'to ask me after my face (i.e. my person)'; or generally 'to examine me' (cf. n. 5).
25. Lit. 'so their regard for persons (their προσωπολημψία) will not happen for you', where the possessive corresponds to an objective genitive; hence 'so it will not happen to you that you have regard for their persons'.

XVII. Later Acts* of Apostles

Aurelio de Santos Otero

* *Preliminary note by the Editor*: The five apocryphal apostolic Acts of the 2nd and 3rd centuries are only partly preserved in their original form (cf. above, pp. 75ff.). For the reconstruction of these texts a special importance attaches to the later 'apostolic Acts'. In addition we can observe in the later Acts, which are reported on in this section, the development from the texts of the early centuries which belong to the category of the New Testament apocrypha (see vol. 1, pp. 61ff.) to the hagiographical literature which took shape in connection with the spread of the cult of the saints from the 4th century on.

Texts from this later literature cannot be presented here. But A. de Santos Otero's survey is a necessary supplement to chapter XV. At the same time it is a valuable aid for work on this literature, which in terms of its *Gattung* grew out of the ancient apocryphal Acts of apostles. (*W. Schn.*)

Synopsis:
Introduction

1.1 Acta Iohannis (Prochorus)
1.2 Historia Iohannis (syriaca)
1.3 Virtutes et Passio Iohannis (latinae)
2.1 Martyrium Petri (Ps.-Linus)
2.2 Doctrina Petri (syriaca)
2.3 Historia Petri (syriaca)
2.4 Vita Petri (slavica)
2.5 Passio Petri et Pauli (Ps.-Hegesippus)
3.1 Martyrium Pauli (Ps.-Linus)
3.2 Historia Pauli (syriaca)
4.1 Acta Petri et Pauli (Ps.-Marcellus)
4.2 Acta Petri et Pauli (orientalia)
4.3 Passio Petri et Pauli (latina)
5.1 Acta Andreae et Matthiae apud anthropophagos
5.2 Acta Petri et Andreae
5.3 Acta Andreae et Bartholomaei (coptica)
5.4 Acta Pauli et Andreae (coptica)
5.5 Acta Andreae et Philemonis (coptica)
6.1 Acta Bartholomaei (coptica)
6.2 Passiones Bartholomaei
7.1 Acta Thomae
7.2 Acta Thomae minora
8.1 Martyrium Matthaei
8.2 Passio Matthaei (Ps.-Abdias)
8.3 Acta Matthaei in Kahenat (coptica)
9.1 Martyrium Marci
9.2 Acta Marci
10.1 Acta Barnabae (Ps.-Marcus)
10.2 Acta Bartholomaei et Barnabae
11.1 Passio Lucae
12.1 Acta Philippi
12.2 Historia Philippi (syriaca)
12.3 Acta Philippi et Petri (coptica)
13.1 Acta Iacobi Zebedaei (coptica)
13.2 Passio Iacobi Zebedaei (latina et armeniaca)
14.1 Acta Iacobi Minoris (coptica et latina)
15.1 Acta Simonis Cananaei (coptica)
15.2 Acta Thaddaei (coptica)
15.3 Acta Thaddaei (graeca)
15.4 Passio Simonis et Iudae (latina)

Introduction

In this section we are concerned with the very numerous writings which came into being as revisions, imitations or adaptations of the five ancient apostolic Acts already discussed - the Acts of John, Peter, Paul, Andrew and Thomas - as well as those of which the subject is the deeds and/or martyrdom of other apostles. Although the multiplicity of the material scarcely allows of any characterisation that would be universally valid, we may adduce their later time of origin - from about the 4th century - and the relative poverty in ideas of their content as the most important distinguishing marks of this literature in comparison with the five ancient apostolic Acts.

The significance of these later texts lies above all in the fact that the writings thus associated demonstrate the survival of ancient apostolic Acts through the centuries in the most diverse linguistic areas and cultures, and occasionally transmit the core of primitive traditions in the form of a legend.

Over and above this, the study of this literature deserves especial attention because at least important elements of it, in the form that has come down to us, show very close connections with the five ancient Acts - the wording of which is often known only in fragments. Thus, for example, the 'textological symbiosis' between two writings so different in age and character as AJ and the Acts of Prochorus (see below, 1.1) is so close that without the textual tradition of the latter substantial constituents of the ancient Acts of John - as we now know them in their fragmentary condition - would have been lost. In terms of tradition history and of theme the ancient Acts of Peter also are closely connected with their later off-shoots, for it is only on the basis of lengthy investigation and sifting in the area of the Peter literature handed down in the Latin, Coptic and Greek languages, the results of which have not infrequently had to be corrected, that it has become possible to discern, at least approximately, the probable content of these Acts. With the ancient Acts of Andrew in particular this process of sifting is not yet completed, and it must often remain an open question to what extent the numerous episodes about Andrew which have come down scattered about in later texts are connected with the original Acts. The situation is different with the ancient Acts of Thomas, since we have the complete text at our disposal in Syriac and in Greek. This makes possible an instructive comparison between the content of these Acts, as it is now known to us, and the revisions and adaptations which developed out of it in the course of time (see below, p. 457). In the process we can recognise certain features in the reworking which appear to be applicable not only to the 'later Acts of Thomas' but also to the off-shoots of other ancient apostolic Acts, and give rise to the suspicion that the ATh played a major role as the model for a series of later apostolic Acts - no matter which apostle was concerned.

This dovetailing between the ancient and the later apostolic Acts, conditioned by their tradition history and in terms of their Gattung, is only indicated in outline here, but beyond doubt justifies a nuanced consideration of the two complexes in a work devoted to the New Testament apocrypha.

It has already been indicated above that it is scarcely possible to discern any universally valid features for the literature here discussed. The old theory of R.A. Lipsius, who ascribed to the ancient Acts a gnostic origin and saw in the later works predominantly 'catholic' versions, i.e. versions purged of heterodox influence, has rightly been abandoned, and in fact is of no assistance. Reference has frequently been made to the enhancement of the teratological element and the free rein given to fancy as a typical characteristic of these legends in contrast to their models. At first sight this observation does hold good in some cases, particularly in legends of oriental origin. On closer examination however it proves that in many other cases this 'craze for miracles' is not so much a primary feature of this literature but a secondary phenomenon connected with the manner in which the several writings came into being. For example, where we can identify revisions of ancient apostolic Acts, the most important concern of the reviser seems to have been to make the text of his model, usually very extensive and burdened with all kinds of speculations, ritual acts, covert allusions, constant repetitions and endless monologues, 'readable' for a wider public. This has resulted in most cases not only in a stylistic simplification but also in a partial or complete elimination of the ideological 'ballast' and an excerpting of individual episodes, while at the same time preserving the edifying and entertainment values inherent in the original work (hence the heaping-up of adventure and miracle stories) and also its general tendency (e.g. encratism).

There are other features, chiefly of a formal nature, which might be adduced in this connection - again not without qualification. One of them concerns the pericope about the assigning of the apostles to the different regions of the world after the Resurrection of Jesus. This passage in fact became commonplace, and is found in innumerable variations in almost all the later Acts, whereas in the ancient ones - except for the Acts of Thomas - it is missing. The fragmentary condition in which four of the five classical apostolic Acts are handed down is however enough to show that this criterion can be applied only with qualifications. On the problems underlying this pericope, see the discussions of E. Junod and J.-D. Kaestli, in F. Bovon et al. (ed.), *Les actes apocryphes des apôtres*, Geneva 1981, 233-248; 249-264.

More reliable is another feature, which points a certain contrast between the ancient and the later Acts. Whereas in the former the central point is the deeds (with or without the martyrdom) of a single apostle, in the latter we can see an increasing tendency to introduce the participation of other members of the apostolic college. This departure from the ancient models does indeed have its exceptions - e.g. in the Acts of Prochorus - but in general points to a progressive assimilation to the structure of the canonical Acts.

Apart from the features so far listed, the legends which form the stock of the Coptic corpus known as the *Certamen apostolorum* - the collection of apostolic legends consisting partly of translations from the Greek, partly of original Coptic revisions and adaptations, handed down in fragmentary form in various Coptic dialects and complete in Arabic and Ethiopic translations from the Coptic - and the Latin so-called Ps.-Abdias collection are distinguished by a series of parallel regularities which, despite the very diverse origin and quality of the material there assembled, are typical for the two collections mentioned. In this connection we should note above all the effort in these two collections to increase the number of the Acts, so that each member of the apostolic college is given a legend of his own. The creation of 'new' Acts displays a confusing variety of forms, which will be discussed at the relevant place in the present survey. It is also one of the peculiarities of these two compilations that each Act is divided into two parts: the first describes the 'deeds' of the apostle concerned (= *praedicatio* in the Coptic, *virtutes* in the Latin), while the second is devoted to the *'martyrium'* or *passio*. That this arrangement can occasionally lead to hybrid combinations of text, doublets and confusions, will also be noted later.

Finally, the local colour which attaches to a large number of the legends belonging to the compilations just mentioned is connected with their origin. While in the Coptic Acts we may note a constant concern to 'Africanise' the original setting of the legend in view, and the modes of action connected with it, in the Latin it is striking what a considerable role is played by the various local traditions about individual apostles which were domiciled in the West. This local background is however not a characteristic exclusive to the Coptic and Latin legends, but also applies to other Acts handed down outside of such compilations.

In the following study an attempt will be made to present a comprehensive survey of the material which in the light of the discussion above belongs in this group of texts. The emphasis in this presentation will be on the tradition history of the legends in question, according to the present state of research. That in the process - in contrast to chapter XV - we must renounce any reproduction of the texts transmitted will be evident to anyone who takes into consideration the character of the present work and the mass of the material that comes into question. We shall likewise refrain from pursuing the various traditions, not infrequently contradictory and sometimes interchangeable, which have been brought into connection with a particular apostle on the basis of isolated accounts - on these chapter XIII reports in detail - in so far as such traditions have not taken on the form of a coherent and textually tangible legend.

In the treatment of the individual themes a special significance will be accorded to the primary and secondary literature in question. Hence the corresponding bibliographical material will be incorporated into the body of the relevant section. This may lead to frequent repetition, but has the advantage for the reader that he can easily find and survey the material adduced for the tradition history of a particular legend together in one place.

The 'general bibliography' usual in comparable works of reference has therefore been omitted. As the only exception to this rule - apart from the known works of R.A. Lipsius and M. Bonnet - reference may be made at this point to the various series of the Bollandist Bibliotheca hagiographica (= BHG[3] by F. Halkin, vols. I-III, 1957, Auctarium 1984; BHL vols. I-II, 1898/99-1900/01, reprint 1949; BHO by H. Peeters 1910, reprint 1954), which as ever are an essential starting-point and at the same time a valuable resource for any further investigation in this field.

1.1 Acta Iohannis (Prochorus)

The Πράξεις τοῦ ἁγίου ἀποστόλου καὶ εὐαγγελιστοῦ 'Ιωάννου τοῦ θεολόγου current under the name of Prochorus (BHG II, 916-917) have little to do with the ancient AJ, which are extant only in fragments. The manuscript tradition of the two documents is however closely connected, for a large part of the AJ episodes so far known in their original version is handed down exclusively in Greek manuscripts of the Prochorus recension.

The Prochorus Acts are a novelistic account of alleged events in which the author - a disciple of John, who is described in some Greek manuscripts as 'one of the seventy disciples and the seven deacons of Jerusalem' (cf. Acts 6:5) and even as 'nephew of the proto-martyr Stephen' - is supposed to have participated at his master's side from the partition of the mission fields among the apostles in Jerusalem until John's death in Ephesus. What distinguishes this writing from most of the later apostolic Acts - apart from the question of the author, just mentioned - is above all the absence of the otherwise usual ascetic and encratite tendencies, and the fact that it is not a reworking of older Acts (in particular the AJ) but is to be regarded as essentially an original creation by its author. The Prochorus Acts do indeed presuppose the AJ, as is shown by the μετάστασις (Zahn, 162_{10}-165_{5}), shaped in imitation of the AJ (cc. 106-115), and the episode of the destruction of the Artemis temple (Zahn 33_{1}-35_{23}; 42_{1-23}), inspired by the AJ (cc. 38-47), but are not an attempt to replace or counter them. There is here no basis for ideological debate with the AJ, since Prochorus in his work is interested only in the narrative and displays a great indifference with regard to speculative questions. Whether in this connection we can go so far as to deny him any direct knowledge of the AJ seems to me in the present state of the textual tradition questionable - despite the arguments of E. Junod and J.-D. Kaestli to the contrary (*Acta Iohannis*, CChrSA 1/2, Turnhout 1983, 718-736).

The action is concentrated - this too in contrast to the AJ - upon the island of Patmos, and here the author betrays a great ignorance of the stage-setting and its geography and also, in opposition to the ancient Ephesian tradition, makes John dictate his Gospel there (Zahn 154_{1}-158_{6}). Other traditions which from ancient times governed the portrayal and the career of John - such as for example his virginity or his martyrdom in oil - find no echo here. There is just as little reason to think of local traditions as a source of information, when we take into account the scant familiarity the author shows with the island of Patmos.

Despite the preponderant role which fancy has played in the shaping of this work, we cannot overlook certain reminiscences of particular episodes in other apostolic Acts, as Lipsius already emphasised in the case of the AA (*Die apokr. Apostelgeschichten* I, 400-402) and Junod-Kaestli have done more recently (*Acta Iohannis, 737-738*). The episode of the changing of sea-water into drinking-water (Zahn 54_{21}-55_{14}) offers in addition clear analogies with a similar episode in the Acta Pauli et Andreae (see below, pp. 449f.). The narrative of John's shipwreck before his arrival in Ephesus (Zahn 8_{9}-9_{8}; 13_{4}-14_{13}) probably reflects an old tradition which turns up again in the Acta Timothei (ed. H. Usener, Bonner Universitätsprogramm, 1877, 9_{24-28}). The more clearly emergent points of contact with the Syriac Historia Iohannis (BHO 468), of which no Greek original is known, are not sufficient to allow us to postulate a relationship of dependence - no matter in which direction; they are however to be taken as an indication that alongside the Prochorus Acts there must have been similar efforts, even if not so successful.

For the time of origin of this document we may with Th. Zahn (*Acta Joannis*, 1880, LVIII-LIX) put forward the reign of the emperor Theodosius the Great (end of 4th cent.) as the terminus post quem, and the nascence of the Chronicon Pascale (beginning of 7th cent.), which has taken from Prochorus the numbers for the biography of John, as the terminus ante quem. Although there are no firm clues for a more precise dating, among other things because of uncertainties in the textual tradition, we may treat the 5th century as a probable time of origin within the range mentioned. There can be no doubt about the enormous success which these Acts enjoyed, particularly in the Byzantine sphere of influence. It is attested not only by the widely branching textual tradition but also by the zealous use which was made of the statements of Prochorus by the hagiography of the Eastern Church (menologies, Nicetas of Paphlagonia, Nicephorus, Symeon Metaphrastes) and its iconography (cf. on this J. Martinov's contribution in *Revue de l'Art chrétien* 28, 1879, 197-216). There are ancient versions of these Acts in Latin and in almost all oriental languages.

For the literary assessment of this document - in addition to the works of Zahn (III-LX) and Lipsius (I, 348-446) already mentioned - see the new contribution by Junod/Kaestli (*Acta Iohannis* 3-11; 718-749), in which an attempt is made, on the basis of linguistic observations, to solve the riddle of the author's personality. There is a modern translation in Erbetta's Italian edition (II, 71-110).

The manifold problems which the textual tradition of these Acts throws up remain for the most part unsolved. There is a permanent interest in pressing forward with research in this area, not only for the sake of the text before us but also because new finds in the Greek Prochorus Acts and their oriental versions could bring in their train new discoveries of lost fragments of the ancient AJ, as the contribution by E. Junod and J.-D. Kaestli shows (*Museum Helveticum* 31, 1974, 94-104; *Acta Iohannis* 93-96).

With Zahn's contribution, already mentioned, and the edition by the Russian archimandrite Amphilochios, based on three Greek manuscripts, which appeared shortly before it ('Choždenie po voznesenii gospoda nasego I.X. sv. apostola i evangelista Ioanna' [Izd. obščestva ljubitelej drevnej pis'menosti, vol. 31], St Petersburg 1878), we have since 1880 possessed a complete and 'readable' edition of the original Greek text, and here the merits of Zahn's work in comparison with that of the archimandrite Amphilochios are manifest. Still deserving of attention is the editio princeps of the Greek Prochorus, published with a Latin translation by Melanchthon's pupil Michael Neander as an appendix to the Greek translation of the Catechesis Martini Lutheri parva (3rd ed., Basel 1567, 526-663). The fundamental merit of this edition is that it is based on a valuable witness (Vatic. Palat. gr. 37 of the 10th cent., which Zahn [op.cit. IX] erroneously thought lost), which apart from one gap (Zahn 13_4-56_{21}) reproduces the entire text. The editions published after Neander (Grynaeus, Birch) have merely a historiographical value, since they are only a partial reprint of the editio princeps.

Zahn's Greek edition did indeed meet with violent criticism (cf. inter alia the arguments of M. Bonnet in *Revue critique d'histoire et de litérature* 14, 1880, 449-454), but down to the present there has been nothing to replace it. The fact that in addition to him and Amphilochios numerous notable editors like J.C. Thilo, M.H. Usener, C. Tischendorf and even M. Bonnet worked at similar projects without any visible success is clear evidence of the difficulties which such an undertaking carries with it. These difficulties are connected above all with the fact that in consequence of the wide diffusion of this writing and its popular character there was a considerable amount of 'running wild' in the manuscript witnesses. Particularly badly affected was the so-called μετάστασις (Zahn 162_{10}-165_4), which - as already indicated -

presents a shortened version of the corresponding part in the AJ. In the oriental versions in particular the Prochorus μετάστασις was supplanted by that of the AJ, which had a tradition of its own with several redactions (on this see K. Schäferdiek's discussion, pp. 152ff. above); in some Greek witnesses on the other hand (e.g. Paris gr. 1468 = Zahn 191_{1}-192_{12}) there was a contamination of the text.

The essential presupposition for us to be able to resolve the text-critical problems of the Prochorus Acts is a comprehensive consideration of the available manuscript material. Over and above the defects in Zahn identified in this connection by Bonnet (art. cit.) and Lipsius (op. cit. I, 357-358; Ergänzungsband, 25-26), A. Ehrhard (*Überlieferung und Bestand,* vol. I, 155^{8}, 160^{15}, 164^{7}, 169^{7}; 206^{51}; 255^{4}; 323^{40}; 350^{18}; 381^{7}; vol. III, 760, note 1; 884^{22}) and F. Halkin (BHG II, 916-917 and Auctarium) give information about additional manuscript material, mostly fragmentary. A. Musikides reports on a codex in the Greek Patriarchate in Jerusalem (*Nea Sion* 42, 1947, 245-246; 43, 1948, 51-53; 121-122). On other discoveries see Junod/Kaestli (*Acta Iohannis* 887-889) and the study promised in that work (p. 3, note 2) on the manuscript tradition of the Greek Prochorus Acts.

The evidence of the ancient versions of Prochorus was imperfectly taken into account by Zahn - in consequence of the state of research at that time. In the following compilation of the material that has become known in the interval, reference is made in brackets to the corresponding passages in the Greek text according to Zahn's edition.

Apart from the translation prepared in the 16th century by S. Castellio and appended to Michael Neander's editio princeps, there is an ancient Latin version of the Acts before us (BHL I, 4323), the text-critical value of which is highly rated, although we do not have any secure knowledge either about its exact age or about its original textual form. It is however certain that the text used by Zahn for his edition - a printed Vorlage which goes back to the first edition by M. de la Bigne (*Sacra Bibliotheca Sanctorum Patrum,* Paris 1575, II cols. 185-230) - is only an interpolated form of the ancient version and truncated at the end (cf. Zahn, VI-VII; XVI-XX). The interpolation relates - according to the chapter division also secondarily introduced here - to chapters 8-11 of the Latin text, and contains the episode of John's martyrdom in oil in Rome under the emperor Domitian, deriving from Western tradition. The insertion is of later date (about 15th cent.), and most probably goes back directly to the Passio Johannis of ps.-Mellitus (BHL I, 4320) - cf. on this Lipsius, op. cit. I, 358; 415-417. Since some manuscripts of older date remained immune to such manipulations of the text (cf. BHL I, 4323), the need to prepare a reliable edition of the text of this version is self-evident, that we may be able the better to evaluate its testimony.

Of the Coptic version numerous fragments have become known. The scraps published together with a Latin translation by I.A. Mingarelli (*Aegyptiorum codicum reliquiae Venetiis in bibliotheca Naniana asservatae,* Bononiae 1785, fasc. II, 302; 304-313) are the only Coptic evidence which Zahn (XX; 128_{9}-133_{20}) took into account for his Greek edition. Shortly after Mingarelli, A.A. Giorgi (*De miraculis Sancti Coluthi et reliquiis actorum Sancti Panesniv martyrum thebaica fragmenta duo,* Rome 1793, 119-122) published a fragment from the Roman Codex Borgianus 134 (= Zahn 145_{10}-147_{3}). The fragments published by I. Guidi (*Rendiconti della R. Accademia dei Lincei,* Serie IV vol. III/2, Rome 1887, 252-264; = Zahn 39_{17}-44_{15}; 104_{12}-106_{13}; 109_{2}-117_{4}; 125_{5}-126_{16}; 148_{7}-149_{12}; 156_{3}-158_{9}) derive from the same

Codex Borgianus 134 and from 135; Guidi himself translated them into Italian (*Giornale della Società Asiatica Italiana* 2, 1888, 56-66). Larger fragments from the Prochorus Acts (= Zahn 75_{15}-77_{2}; 99_{13}-101_{6}; 135_{6}-136_{13}; 17_{12}-19_{9}; 161_{13}-163_{12}) are contained in the diplomatic edition of the Vienna Coptic manuscripts edited by Carl Wessely (*Studien zur Paläographie und Papyruskunde* XV [Griechische und koptische Texte theologischen Inhalts, IV], 1914, 24-25; 26-27; 28-29; 129-130; 133-134). On the other hand the fragments published by W.E. Crum (*Catalogue of the Coptic Manuscripts in the British Museum*, London 1905, 129 No. 294; 413 No. 996) are of smaller compass (= Zahn 101_{6}-102_{15}; 111_{8-14}). Several paper fragments in the Bohairic dialect, presumably of the 13th century (Cairo, Coptic Museum Nos.5-6), were discovered and edited bilingually by H.G. Evelyn White (*The Monasteries of the Wadi 'n Natrun*, Part I, New York 1926, 28-34); they correspond to the Greek text of Zahn 12_{14}-14_{6}; 16_{16}-19_{14}; 20_{16}-23_{8}; 24_{13}-27_{18}; 37_{3}-40_{14} and 43_{16}-44_{8}. In addition there are further fragments of the same origin (two leaves), which were published some years later by their then owner W.H.P. Hatch (*Coptic Studies in Honor of W.E. Crum*, Boston 1950, 312-315). Finally, Codex 576 of the Pierpont Morgan Library in New York contains on fol. 1-65 an extensive Coptic witness to the text, which has not so far been closely examined.

This mosaic of various fragments does not indeed yield any complete picture of the Coptic version, but is a valuable indication that there must have been a complete draft of it. In view of the defective condition of the Arabic and Ethiopic witnesses, which are commonly treated as off-shoots from a Coptic original, this conclusion is of considerable significance.

Of the Arabic version, a part of the Prochorus Acts (from the beginning to the exile on Patmos = Zahn 3-44) was edited with an English translation from a manuscript of the 14th century by A. Smith Lewis (*Horae Semiticae* III-IV, London 1904, 31-46; 37-53). I. Guidi (*Giornale della Società Asiatica Italiana* 2, 1888, 10-13) had previously published smaller fragments according to Codd. Vatic. arab. 171 and 694. On further Arabic manuscripts see G. Graf, *Geschichte der christlichen arabischen Literatur* I (Studi e Testi 118), Rome 1944, 261; 263-264.

Of the Ethiopic version also the first part of the Acts (= Zahn 3-44) has been made known through the bilingual edition by E.A. Wallis Budge (*The Contendings of the Apostles* I-II, London 1899-1901, 189-213; 186-211) and through the preceding translation by S.C. Malan (*The Conflicts of the Holy Apostles*, London 1871, 117-137).

It is typical for the published witnesses of the Arabic and Ethiopic versions that they round off the part of the Acts mentioned with a text of the μετάστασις which derives not from Prochorus but from the AJ. A similar combination of texts can be identified in the extant fragments of the Bohairic version (text of the AJ μετάστασις in Evelyn White, op. cit. 35-48), whereas the Coptic remains of the older Sahidic version adhere to the text of the Prochorus μετάστασις (see a fragment of it in Wessely, op. cit. 133_{b14}-134_{b30} = Zahn 162_{10}-163_{12}). This is a clear indication that the combination of texts observed in the Arabic and Ethiopic versions is of a secondary character and is to be traced back to a Bohairic model.

In the Armenian literature also we meet with individual episodes from the Prochorus Acts in more or less loose association with the μετάστασις deriving from the AJ and widely disseminated among the Armenians (BHO 474), as F. Emin's contribution shows (*Pravoslavnoe obozrenie*, January 1876). A coherent text of the Armenian Prochorus - without the μετάστασις - has been published by K. Tsherakhian (*Thesaurus litterarum armeniarum* III, Venice 1904, 190-292). In it there is an episode (pp. 219-221) which has been translated by L. Leloir and very probably belongs to the ancient AJ (cf. E. Junod-J.-D. Kaestli, *Museum Helveticum* 31, 1974, 96). All the Armenian texts published in this connection by Tsherakhian (BHO 458-467) have recently been investigated and translated into French by L. Leloir (CChrSA 3/1, Turnhout 1986, 295-407).

The Georgian version has been published by C. K'urc'ikidze (['Les versions géorgiennes des actes apocryphes des apôtres'], Tiflis 1959, 55-91) on the basis of one coherent witness (Cod. Tiflis A-19, 10th cent.) and one fragmentary one (Cod. Tiflis A-95 = Zahn 3-57_8). In comparison with the Greek textus receptus this version shows a gap (= Zahn 78_{10}-116_7) and a somewhat confused arrangement of the individual episodes. In Cod. Tiflis A-19 a version of the μετάστασις is accommodated, as an alleged homily of Chrysostom, as an appendix to the Prochorus Acts; as in most of the oriental versions, it derives from the AJ, and represents a separate redaction in the Georgian area. Cf. on this the discussion of M. van Esbroeck (*AnalBoll* 93, 1975, 5-19), with an edition and Latin translation of the μετάστασις mentioned.

Apart from this version, which for the rest is a faithful reproduction of the Greek *Vorlage*, and several Prochorus episodes which appear sporadically in various Georgian manuscripts of later date, there is a Georgian compilation with extensive material from the Acts before us which goes back to a translation from the Greek prepared by Euthymius Athonites (955-1028). On this cf. the discussion of van Esbroeck in the article mentioned (pp. 6-8) and the remarks of Junod/Kaestli (*Acta Johannis*, 42-43). Van Esbroeck has published a French translation of the Georgian text (*Bedi Kartlisa* 33, 1975, 73-109).

The Prochorus Acts are particularly extensively documented in the Old Slavonic literature. Zahn in his introduction (XX-XXIII) used only the testimony of the Russian manuscript of the 15th-16th century published by the archimandrite Amphilochios as an appendix to his Greek edition mentioned above. A Glagolitic fragment from the 13th cent. (= Zahn 37_{14}-40_{17}) had already been published before that by I. Berčič (*Čitanka Staroslovenskoga jezika*, Prague 1864, 36-38) and a Serbian one from the 12th cent. (= Zahn 146_{13}-150_{10}) by I. Sreznevskij (Svedenija i zametki o maloizvestnych i neizvestnych pamjatnikach LXVI (*Zapiski Akademii Nauk*, vol. 28), St Petersburg 1875, 393-396). The variants of the latter fragment were examined by the archimandrite Amphilochios (op. cit. V-VI) in comparison with the codex which he himself published and with another fragmentary witness (Moscow, Troice-Sergieva-Lavra Cod. No. 36, fol. 55-60). The differences between Amphilochios' frequently mentioned codex and the Russian manuscript No. 110 in folio from the collection of Prince P.P. Vjazemskij (16th cent.) were the subject of an investigation by N. Barsukov (*Pamjatniki Drevnej Pis'mennosti* 4, 1879, 102-139). Over and above that, the complete text of the Slavonic Prochorus is contained in the Menaea of the Metropolitan Makarios of the 16th century and was published on the basis of the Codex Uspenskij Sobor No. 784 (986) - with variants from the two other exemplars of this work - by the Archeografičeskaja Kommissija (*Velikie Minei četii*, 25-30 September, St Petersburg 1883, cols. 1584-1660).

Both the two first-mentioned fragments from the 12th and 13th centuries and also the witnesses from the 15th and 16th centuries published by Amphilochios and the Archeograficeskaja Kommissija are without any doubt to be treated as the product of a single Slavonic translation from the Greek, which came into being probably about the 11th century. Typical features of this Slavonic version are inter alia the episodes of the sojourn in Epicurus (= Zahn 51_7-53_{15}), the transforming of sea-water into drinking-water (= Zahn 54_{21}-56_9), and the origin of the Apocalypse (= Zahn 184_6-185_{19}). The last-named episode is treated by Zahn as an interpolation - against the evidence of a Greek witness so important as Palat. gr. 37 from the 10th century (Neander), as well as the Latin and Slavonic versions.

With regard to the Slavonic textual tradition, the question arises whether the extensive manuscript material is to be traced back ultimately to the 11th century translation just mentioned. Amphilochios already (op. cit. VII-IX) identified hints of another Slavonic version in a Prochorus text published in 1795 by the Old Believers as well as in other manuscripts in his collection from the 18th century. To what extent this version - or these versions - should be thought of as based on a different original translation from the Greek is a question to which we can for the moment just as little give an answer as for many other questions relating to the Slavonic Prochorus; all the more so, in that of the mass of witnesses to the text which exist in the Slavonic area (cf. A. de Santos Otero, *Überlieferung*, I, 99-123; II, 244-246) only a fraction has so far been investigated.

The text frequently published (e.g. in I. Franko, *Apokrify i legendy* III, L'vov 1902, 49-56 and E.I. Demina, *Tichonravovskij Damaskin* II, Sofia 1971, 81-88) under the title *prestavlenie* (= μετάστασις), which appears in many Slavonic manuscripts, is simply a summary of the Prochorus Acts intended for liturgical purposes (= BHG II, 919e) and has little to do with the authentic text of the μετάστασις.

In terms of the history of art a great significance attaches to the Slavonic Prochorus Acts - above all in the Russian area. This is connected in the main with a series of manuscripts in which the Prochorus text is illustrated with the aid of valuable miniatures. The first to be published was an illuminated codex from the collection of Prince P.P. Vjazemskij (*Izdanija Obščestva ljubitelej drevnej pis'mennosti*, vol. 23, St Petersburg 1878). The 130th volume in the same series was the Facsimile Edition of N.P. Lichačev (*Choždenie sv. apostola i evangelista Ioanna Bogoslova po licevym rukopisjam XV i XVI vekov*, St Petersburg 1911), which contains a part of Codex No. 71 from the former collection of N.P. Lichacev and another of Codex 34.3.5 from the collection of the Academy of Sciences - both today in Leningrad. On the connection between the book-illumination of the Prochorus Acts and the great development of Russian icon painting during the 15th and 16th centuries, cf. the contribution by G.V. Popov (*Trudy otdela drevnerusskoj literatury 22*, Moscow-Leningrad 1966, 208-211).

1.2 Historia Iohannis (syriaca)

A legend is handed down in Syriac as the History - or Teaching - of John (BHO 468) which, as already indicated, shows some points of contact with the Prochorus Acts.

The original text was published with an English translation by W. Wright (*Apocryphal Acts of the Apostles* I-II, London 1871, 1-65, 3-60) on the basis of a Leningrad manuscript of the 6th century and a London codex of the 9th. A. Baumstark (*Geschichte der syrischen Literatur*, 1922, 68, note 6) reports on further witnesses to the Syriac text. Although this legend in its manuscript tradition is linked with the text of the AJ μετάστασις (see Wright, op. cit. 66-72; 61-68), it shows just as few traces of the ancient Acts of John as the Prochorus Acts already discussed. What is striking about it, however - in contrast to Prochorus - is the large proportion of doctrinal content with an unmistakable post-Nicene character woven into the narrative. The episodes which run parallel to Prochorus - e.g. John in the bath-house and the destruction of the Artemis temple (cf. the detailed analysis of the contents by R.A. Lipsius, *Die apokr. Apostelgeschichten* I, 433-441, esp. 435-438) - show such peculiar features that we cannot deduce any relationship of dependence from them. In terms of its character this History appears to be a Syrian compilation which inter alia has worked up material also present in the Greek Prochorus. It is significant in this connection that a translation of Prochorus is unknown to Syriac literature. The time of origin may lie between the 5th and the 6th centuries (further details on this in E. Junod-J.-D. Kaestli, *Acta Iohannis*, 705-711).

An Arabic translation of the Historia Iohannis according to Codex Sinaiticus arab. 539 of the 16th century, which in its editor's opinion is a more original version of the legend than the Syriac text just discussed, was published with an English translation by A. Smith Lewis (*Horae Semiticae* III-IV, London 1904, 134-144; 157-167). A. Baumstark (op. cit. 68, note 6) reports on a further witness to the text of the Arabic version.

1.3 Virtutes et Passio Iohannis (latinae)

(See on this the discussion by K. Schäferdiek on the Acts of John, above p. 154).

2.1 Martyrium Petri (Ps. Linus)

A Latin Passio, which frequently bears the title *Martyrium beati Petri apostoli a Lino conscriptum* (BHL II, 6655), is current under the name of Linus - according to ancient tradition Peter's successor as bishop of Rome (cf. Irenaeus, adv. Haer. III 3.3). Both the widely branching manuscript tradition (cf. Aa I, XIV-XXIII) and also its wide diffusion according to the first edition, prepared in 1512 by J. Lefèvre d'Étaples, testify to the pre-eminent position of this document in the Western Peter literature, although critical attitudes towards it were not lacking, especially after the Reformation (on this cf. G. Poupon in F. Bovon et al., *Les actes apocryphes des apôtres*, Geneva 1981, 27ff.).

Overrated by R.A. Lipsius (*Die apokr. Apostelgeschichten* II/1, 84-93) in regard to its significance for textual criticism, and even considered more original than the Actus Vercellenses, ps.-Linus is simply a Roman revision of the ancient Acts of Peter closely connected with the Greek Martyrium Petri (BHG II, 1483-84; cf. above pp. 311f.), in which the typical encratite features of the Peter literature are just as little lacking as other motifs known from ancient times, e.g. the reproach of magic. Particularly valuable is inter alia Peter's address before his crucifixion (c. XI: Aa I, p.13).

The origins of this Passio may go back to the concern to bring the statements of the ancient Acts of Peter about the activity and death of the prince of the apostles in the eternal city into conformity with local Roman tradition. Other revisions of the Acta Petri are in larger or smaller measure dependent on ps.-Linus, e.g. the Acts of Nereus and Achilleus (BHG II, 1327; cf. Lipsius, op. cit. 106; 109), ps.-Abdias (Book I: BHL II, 6663-64; cf. Lipsius, op. cit. 101; 387-388) and the so-called ps.-Hegesippus (see 2.5). On the basis of these observations the 5th century may be considered the probable period of origin. Text (apart from Aa I, 1-22) in A.H. Salonius, *Martyrium beati Petri* (Commentationes humanarum litterarum I 6: Societas Scientiarum Fennica), Helsingfors 1926. Further literature: A. Harnack, *Geschichte d. altchristl. Literatur* I/1, 133; E. Amman in *Dictionnaire de la Bible*, Suppl. I, 1928, col. 499; Erbetta II, 170-177 (Italian translation).

2.2 Doctrina Petri (syriaca)

A Syriac Peter legend has survived, under the title *Doctrina Simonis Kepha in urbe Roma* (BHO 936), which in addition to an episode from the Actus Vercellenses (c. 28: Aa I, 74_{18}-78_{4}) contains further narrative material of later origin with dogmatic statements of a post-Nicene character. The text was published with an English translation by W. Cureton (*Ancient Syriac Documents relative to the Earliest Establishment of Christianity in Edessa*, London 1864, 35-41). On the basis of predominantly philological considerations the time of origin has been conjectured as about the turn from the 4th to the 5th century (cf. A. Baumstark, *Die Petrus- und Paulusacten in der litterar. Überlieferung der syrischen Kirche*, 1902, 38-40; id. *Geschichte der syrischen Literatur*, 1922, 69) or even earlier (cf. P. Peeters, *AnalBoll* 21, 1902, 129). The dogmatic statements which it contains however point rather to the period of the later Christological controversies (5th-6th century). Further literature: R.A. Lipsius, *Die apokr. Apostelgeschichten* II/1, 206-207; F. Haase, *Apostel und Evangelisten in den orientalischen Überlieferungen* (Neutestamentl. Abhandlungen IX/1-3), 1922, 205.

2.3 Historia Petri (syriaca)

A Syriac legend was edited by P. Bedjan (*Acta Martyrum et Sanctorum* I, Paris 1890, 1-44) as History of Saints Peter and Paul; it describes the activity and martyrdom of the two apostles - separately from one another. The basis of this edition is the copy, transmitted by I Guidi, of a Syriac manuscript then in Koj-Kerkûk (cf. on this the discussion of I. Guidi, *Zeitschrift der deutschen morgenländischen Gesellschaft* 46, 1892, 744-746). On a probable further witness to the text from Mosul, see A. Baumstark, *Geschichte der syrischen Literatur*, 1922, 69, note 3.

The Historia Petri transmitted as part of this document (BHO 935 = Bedjan, op.

cit. 1-33) proves to be a compilation which first appears in the later Nestorian tradition, and in which alongside canonical material ancient Peter legends from the Actus Vercellenses are worked over, as well as excerpts from the Pseudo-Clementine literature and from the Doctrina Petri (BHO 936) just discussed (cf. on this I. Guidi, art. cit. 745 and F. Haase, *Apostel und Evangelisten in den orientalischen Überlieferungen* (Neutestamentl. Abhandlungen IX/1-3), 1922, 214).

On Syriac Peter legends of later date see F. Nau (*Revue de l'Orient Chrétien* 3, 1898, 39-57) and A. Baumstark (*Die Petrus- und Paulusacten in der litter. Überlieferung der syrischen Kirche*, 1902, 35-38).

2.4 Vita Petri (slavica)

This is a Peter legend the most important witnesses to which are to be found in Old Slavonic manuscripts. Only in the fifties did E. Follieri (*AnalBoll* 74, 1956, 115-130) draw attention to a Greek version (BHG II, 1485f.) - to my knowledge as yet unprinted - which is contained in a Vatican codex of the 16th-17th century.

This legend has only the outer framework (Peter's stay in Rome and martyrdom under the emperor Nero) in common with the rest of the Peter literature. Otherwise it shows peculiar features (e.g. Peter's five-year sojourn in a Syrian desert and his subsequent embarkation for Rome with Jesus or the archangel Michael as helmsman; the appearance of Jesus in the form of a child, who is later sold as a slave to Peter; the sprouting of the tree on which Peter is crucified) which occur in this or a modified form in other apostolic Acts (e.g. Acta Thomae c. 2 [Aa II/2. 101f.], Martyrium Matthaei cc. 1, 7 [Aa II/1, 217, 225], Acta Andreae et Matthiae c. 5 [Aa II/1, 69], Acta Bartholomaei coptica (see below), Historia Pauli syriaca [cf. Italian trans. in L. de Stefani, *Giornale della Società Asiatica Italiana* 14, 1901, 216], Acta Philippi c. 147 [Aa II/2, 88]).

In view of these parallels the 'gnostic' origin of this Vita postulated by I. Franko (ZNW 3, 1902, 315-333), probably under the influence of Lipsius, is untenable, as J. Flamion among others emphasised (*Les actes apocryphes de l'apôtre André*, Louvain 1911, 302-303). E. Follieri (op. cit.) subjected the Greek version of the 16th-17th century which she discovered to a thorough analysis, drawing upon the only Slavonic witness known to her, and came to the conclusion that the origin of this Vita is to be sought in the Syrian monastic milieu about the 5th or 6th century.

This conclusion is indeed more plausible than Flamion's hypothesis (op. cit.) of the 'Egyptian' origin of this document, but its credibility is put in question above all by the fact that the underlying text-critical question is still not resolved. In addition we must bear in mind that what Signora Follieri and her predecessors Franko and Flamion describe as the 'Slavonic version' relates only to the fragmentary witness from the 16th century published by A.S. Archangel'skij (*Izvestija Otdelenija Russkago Jazyka i Slovesnosti Imp. Akademii Nauk* 4, St Petersburg 1899, 112-118). A witness from the 16th century published by V.N. Močul'skij (*Trudy X-go Archeologičeskago S'ezda v Rige*, Moscow 1896) and another from the 14th century which K.F. Radcenko published shortly afterwards (*Izvestija Otdelenija Russkago*

Jazyka i Slovesnosti Imp. Akademii Nauk 8/4, St Petersburg 1903, 199-211) have remained unnoticed. Without the evidence of these already-published witnesses and of others still unpublished (on this cf. A. de Santos Otero, *Überlieferung* I, 54 No.1; 57 No.19; 58 No. 26) we cannot pronounce any definitive judgment on the origin of the Vita Petri, the Slavonic attestation of which is a good two centuries older than the Greek one so far known.

2.5 Passio Petri et Pauli (Ps.-Hegesippus)

What is meant here is the Latin reworking of the De bello judaico of Flavius Josephus, which is known inter alia as *de excidio urbis hierosolymitanae libri quinque* (PL 15, 2062-2310; V. Ussani, CSEL 66, vols. I-II, 1930 [=1960]) and is current falsely under the name of Ambrose of Milan. This document devotes a chapter (III/2) to the conflict between Peter and Simon Magus - with the inclusion of Paul - and briefly mentions the martyrdom of the two apostles under Nero.

Parallel to this account, the dependence of which on ps.-Linus has been indicated above (cf. R.A. Lipsius, *Die apokr. Apostelgeschichten* II/1, 103-105), there is a Greek narrative, transmitted inter alia in the Byzantine Chronicle of Gregory Hamartolos (Lib. III, c. 121; PG 110, 436ff.), which had a wide circulation in the Old Slavonic literature under the title 'Prenie s Simonom Volchvom'. The Slavonic text has been published by V.M. Istrin (*Chronika Georgija Amartola v drevnem slavjanorusskom perevode t.I*, Petrograd 1920). On further witnesses to the text cf. O.V. Tvogorov (*Drevnerusskie chronografy*, Leningrad 1975, 267; 279; 293) and V.F. Pokrovskaja et al. (*Opisanie rukopisnogo otdela Biblioteki AN SSSR* III/1, Leningrad 1959, 46; 56; 82; 123).

3.1 Martyrium Pauli (Ps.-Linus)

In some manuscripts entitled simply Passio sancti Pauli apostoli, in others Martyrium Pauli apostoli a Lino conscriptum (BHL II, 6570), this Latin legend is a reworking of the final part of the Acts of Paul (= Hamburg Greek papyrus, pp. 9-11, and Heidelberg Coptic papyrus, pp. 53-58; cf. W. Schneemelcher above, pp. 260ff.). In contrast to the view advocated by R.A. Lipsius (*Die apokr. Apostelgeschichten* II/1, 142-162), this legend is to be regarded as an imitation of the so-called Passio Pauli brevior (BHG II, 1451-52; BHL II, 6571), which very probably came into being as a counterpart to the Martyrium Petri of ps.-Linus already discussed (see 2.1 above). There is a modern Italian translation in Erbetta II, 290-296.

The Bohairic parchment fragment (Cairo, Coptic Museum No. 17 Add.) published as part of ps.-Linus by H.G. Evelyn White (*The Monasteries of the Wadi 'n Natrun*, Part I, New York 1926, 225) - exactly like the Arabic version published by A. Smith Lewis (*Horae Semiticae* III-IV, London 1904, 184-189; 217-222) - corresponds not to the wording of ps.-Linus but to that of the Passio Pauli brevior just mentioned (Aa I, 110-111).

3.2 Historia Pauli (syriaca)

This legend was published together with the more extensive Historia Petri (see above, p. 437f.) by P. Bedjan (*Acta martyrum et sanctorum* I, Paris 1890, 34-44), as a component of the Syriac 'History of Saints Peter and Paul'. Here too it is a case of a compilation concerning the life and martyrdom of Paul, in which various canonical (from Acts and Paul's letters) and apocryphal elements are mixed together. The compiler however does not seem to have had direct access to the relevant sources, since he can be shown to have made fairly large borrowings from the exegetical works of the Greek grammarian Euthalios (PG 85, cols. 693-713). Cf. in this connection the study by L. De Stefani (*Giornale della Società Asiatica Italiana* 14, 1901, 201-216), with an Italian translation of the Syriac text. For other Syriac revisions of the Acts of Paul cf. the literature to the Historia Petri (syriaca), pp. 437f. above.

4.1 Acta Petri et Pauli (Ps.-Marcellus)

The effort to unite the apostles Peter and Paul in their missionary activity and in their martyrdom - already clearly recognisable in ps.-Hegesippus - finds its most important literary expression in the so-called Acta Petri et Pauli (BHG II, 1490-91), which because of the statements of some manuscripts of the Latin version (BHL II, 6659) are also know as ps.-Marcellus. This tendency, which when all is said and done signifies a rejection of the traditions contained in the ancient Acts of Peter and of Paul, and of which the veneration and iconography of the two apostles unmistakably bear witness as early as the 2nd century but especially from the 4th in the Roman sphere of influence, comes clearly to expression in the Decretum Gelasianum c. III 2: 'Addita est etiam societas beatissimi Pauli apostoli [. . .], qui non diverso - sicut heresei garriunt - sed uno tempore uno eodemque die gloriosa morte cum Petro in urbe Roma sub Caesare Nerone agonizans coronatus est' (E. von Dobschütz, TU 38/4, 1912, 7). The origins of our present document evidently belong in this chronological context, although we cannot determine any exact date of composition. The letter of Pilate to the Roman emperor Claudius - instead of Tiberius - which is contained in the Greek recension (c. 40-42; Aa I, 196-197) and in the ancient versions can scarcely be used as a clue in regard to this question, since its own date of composition is unknown - assuming that it is a case of an interpolation. The same holds for several changes and additions in the manuscript tradition, the origin of which is probably to be ascribed to the zeal and local patriotism of some copyist.[1]

The number of the Greek and Latin texts edited by Lipsius (Aa I, 118-222) and of the extant ancient versions cannot deceive us as to the fact that all the witnesses to the text of these Acts, transmitted in Greek, Latin, Armenian, Coptic, Georgian, Old Slavonic, Irish and Arabic, go back ultimately to one basic document which according to present-day knowledge is best represented by the so-called Πϱάξεις τῶν ἁγίων ἀποστόλων Πέτϱου καὶ Παύλου (BHG II, 1490 = Aa I, 178-222). This recension rests not only - with a single exception - on the entire number of the Greek manuscripts so far known, but also on the testimony of the Armenian and Old Slavonic versions, the wording of which shows a great conformity with the Greek text.

A different redaction is presented on the other hand by the Latin version known as *Passio sanctorum apostolorum Petri et Pauli* (BHL II, 6659), which Lipsius examined text-critically, drawing upon a large number of manuscripts, and edited in parallel with the Greek text of a Venetian codex of the 16th century, which shows a great similarity with it (Aa I, 119-177).[2] Apart from the Greek witness just mentioned, the Arabic and Irish versions, and so far as we can see from the few extant fragments the Coptic, stand close to the Latin version.

The chief difference between the Greek 'Praxeis' and the Latin 'Passio' is already indicated by their titles. While the latter confines itself to the controversy of the two apostles with Simon Magus and the emperor Nero in Rome, with the following martyrdom, the Praxeis in their first 21 chapters set before these the description of Paul's journey from Malta to Rome by way of Puteoli and other intermediate stations. A further difference is the absence of sections 46 and 62-66 (Aa I, 158; 172-176) in the Praxeis and of sections 80 a-c and 84 in the Passio. Otherwise the two recensions to a large extent agree with one another. In view of such differences, it would be appropriate - instead of speaking of different redactions of the Acta Petri et Pauli - to distinguish between Acta (handed down in Greek, Armenian, Georgian and Old Slavonic) and Passio (transmitted mainly in Latin, Arabic and Irish).

Lipsius raised objections against the authenticity of the first 21 chapters of the Acta, and disposed of the relevant section, in which various stations in Paul's journey are described, as an interpolation of South Italian origin dating from the 9th century. His arguments are predominantly of a philological nature, but their effect is anything but convincing when we consider the differences in the various manuscripts and versions at the points named by him. There are certainly traces of occasional interpolations, which could be connected with the origins of the manuscript concerned and the local patriotism of some copyist. This does not seem to represent any obstacle to the unity of the Acta as transmitted.

Numerous other versions in addition to the Latin already mentioned testify to the diffusion of this document. The Armenian (BHO 959) was first edited by P. Vetter (*Oriens Christianus* 3, 1903, 16-53; 324-383) on the basis of four manuscripts from the National Library in Paris, and then by Kh. Tsherakhian (*Thesaurus litterarum armeniarum* III, Venice 1904, 1-29) on the basis of six manuscripts from the library of the Mechitarists of S. Lazzaro. Vetter further added to his edition a Greek retroversion of the Armenian text. This Armenian version adheres strictly to the wording of the Greek Acta, and is accordingly an important witness for the age of this text. Less significance is to be attributed on the other hand to another 'shorter' Armenian version (BHO 962), which Tsherakhian published as an appendix to the text he edited (op. cit. 30-45). In the opinion of P. Vetter, who produced a German translation of it (*Theologische Quartalschrift* 1906, 162-186), this is a later reworking of the original Armenian version. All the Armenian texts published by Tsherakhian in this connection (BHO 959, 962-63) have recently been examined and translated into French by L. Leloir (CChrSA 3/1, Turnhout 1986, 7-63).

Of the Georgian version a fairly long fragment from the 11th century is known, accommodated in Codex H 1708 of the Manuscript Institute in Tiflis. From what G. Garitte says (*Le Muséon* 74, 1961, 404 No.1), this text is a translation from the Greek Acta.

Of the Coptic version various fragments have been published in the contributions of A. Jacoby (*Recueil de travaux relatifs à la philologie et à l'archéologie égyptiennes et assyriennes* 24, 1902, 43-44), E.O. Winstedt (*Proceedings of the Society of Biblical Archaeology* 28, 1906, 233-236) and T. Orlandi (*Papiri copti di contenuto teologico* [Mitteilung aus der Papyrussammlung der Österr. Nationalbibliothek NS, IX. Folge], Vienna 1974, 120-125). On the last-mentioned contribution cf. the remarks of G.M. Browne (*Enchoria* 6, 1976, 121). It is certain that these fragments are the remnants of a Coptic translation from the Greek, although some of their readings appear to show more similarity with the text of the Latin Passio that with that of the Greek Acta.

The brevity of the extant fragments certainly stands in the way of any final judgment on the Coptic version. For the clarifying of this question, however, scholars have so far neglected to consult the evidence of the Arabic version (BHO 960), which is without doubt to be treated as a translation from a Coptic *Vorlage*. The Arabic text was published with an English translation by A. Smith Lewis on the basis of a late manuscript with no date (*Horae Semiticae* III-IV, London 1904, 165-178; 193-209). It is clearly a question of a Passio - as also with the Latin version - which shows a great conformity with the Coptic fragments mentioned. On further Arabic witnesses to the text cf. G. Graf, *Geschichte der christl. arabischen Literatur* I (Studi e Testi 118) 261, 263.

With the Old Slavonic version we are not dependent on isolated fragments, but have a large number of witnesses, which in general reproduce the complete text of the Greek Acta. Two of them (Chludov No. 105 of the 15th century and Čudovskij Monastyr' No. 62/264 of the 16th) were published by A.N. Popov (*Bibliografičeskie Materialy* No.15 [Čtenija 1889 kn.3], 1-19; 20-41), and seem to go back to two different *Vorlagen* of the Greek Acta. On further witnesses to the text cf. A. de Santos Otero, *Überlieferung* I, 60-66; II, 242-243

Notes 4.1

1. The allusions to a 'Praedicatio Pauli' or 'Petri et Pauli' which appear in ps.-Cyprian (3rd cent.?) and in Lactantius (3rd-4th cent.) are not substantially more informative (on these see the discussion by W. Schneemelcher, pp. 32f. above), for the statements associated with them betray no agreement with the present Acts beyond the mere similarity of their titles.
2. A small fragment of this Latin Passio from the 10th-11th century [= Aa I, $137_{20\text{-}21}$; $139_{1\text{-}12}$], completely irrelevant for textual criticism, has recently been published by R. Somerville (*VigChr* 40, 1986, 302-303).

4.2 Acta Petri et Pauli (orientalia)

The Acta Petri et Pauli just discussed are not to be confused with another document of the same title, which is transmitted in Syriac, Arabic, Garshuni and Ethiopic manuscripts. These Acts, which inter alia describe the activity of the two apostles in Ephesus and Rome, as well as their controversy with Simon Magus and the emperor Nero, in a particularly markedly fabulous fashion (detailed analysis of the contents in Moraldi II, 1640-1644), seem to have only their theme in common with the Greek Acts of the same name.

The oldest witness to the text may be a short Palestinian Syriac fragment contained in a palimpsest presumably of the 6th century and published by A. Smith Lewis (*Horae Semiticae* VIII, Cambridge 1909, 190-193). Some years earlier the same author had published a substantially more extensive Arabic witness to this recension according to Codex Sin. O of the 12th-13th century (*Horae Semiticae* III-IV, London 1904, 150-164; 175-192 [BHO 965]). Here belongs also a Garshuni Arabic text - i.e. in Syriac script - edited by A. van Lantschoot according to Codex Vat. Syr. 199 (*Le Muséon* 68, 1955, 219-233). Finally the Ethiopic text, which A. van Lantschoot also edited (op. cit. 17-46) on the basis of an extensive fragment from Codex Vat. Aeth. 268, goes back to Arabic sources.

The Coptic origin of this cycle of legends can be taken as probable at least for the Arabic and Ethiopic versions, since A. van Lantschoot identified several Coptic fragments with similar content in the palimpsest codex British Mus. Or. 8802, presumably of the 10th century (*Le Muséon* 41, 1928, 230-232; 242-244).

4.3 Passio Petri et Pauli (latina)

The *Passio apostolorum Petri et Pauli*, also in Latin (BHL II, 6667), is to be distinguished from the Latin Passio of ps.-Marcellus already discussed (see above, p. 441). This is a later compilation, the sources of which are to be sought in ps.-Marcellus and ps.-Hegesippus. The Latin text was published by R.A. Lipsius (Aa I, 223-234) on the basis of two manuscripts from the 9th and 11th centuries. There is an Italian translation in Erbetta II, 194-198. For further information see Lipsius, *Die apokr. Apostelgeschichten* II/1, 366-380.

5.1 Acta Andreae et Matthiae apud anthropophagos

The question of the relation between the Πράξεις 'Ανδρέου καὶ Ματθεία εἰς τὴν πόλιν τῶν ἀνθρωποφάγων (BHG I, 109ff.) and the ancient Acts of Andrew is still debated - despite the contrary opinion of M. Hornschuh (NTApo[3] ET 397) - and requires further investigation. The old view of Lipsius (*Die apokr. Apostelgeschichten* I, 546), according to which our Acts are to be treated as remnants of the ancient Acts of Andrew, could not be entirely replaced by the opposing thesis, maintained above all by J. Flamion (*Les actes apocryphes de l' apôtre André*, Louvain 1911, 310ff.) and his precursor S. Reinach (*Revue d' histoire et de littérature religieuse* 9, 1904, 305-320), which assigns to them a quite different origin. This is shown inter alia by the attitudes and the contributions of O. Bardenhewer (*Geschichte der altkirchl. Literatur* I, 1913, 570-571), F. Blatt (*Die lateinischen Bearbeitungen der Acta Andreae et Matthiae apud anthropophagos*, 1930, 16), M. Blumenthal (TU 48/1, 1933, 38-57), P.M. Peterson (*Novum Testamentum* - Suppl. 1, 1958, 26ff.), as well as the full discussion of this theme between D.R. MacDonald and J.-M. Prieur, which has recently appeared ('The Apocryphal Acts of Apostles', *Semeia* 38, 1986, 9-39). Cf. also Prieur, p. 106f. above.

Lipsius' theory of the 'gnostic origin' of the ancient Acts of Andrew and of their 'gnostic remnants' in the present document is undoubtedly untenable (see on this the relevant arguments of Flamion, op. cit. 301-309); this does not however mean that we must deny any affiliation between the two texts, assigning to the one a 'Greek' and to the other an 'Egyptian' origin, as Flamion does (see 310-324). The arguments brought forward for this (e.g. the appearance of the 'Sphinx' and the 'Ethiopians', the alleged Egyptian monastic character etc.) are in fact so weak that their demonstrative force is doubted even by those who share Flamion's general conception of the origin of the Acts of Andrew (see e.g. F. Dvornik, *The Idea of Apostolicity in Byzantium and the Legend of the Apostle Andrew*, Cambridge/Mass. 1958, 202). The separate treatment of the two apocrypha in editorial practice - usual since Lipsius-Bonnet - is indeed justified on various grounds, but for lack of the pertinent argumentation does not presuppose any final solution of the question in view.

The witness of Gregory of Tours points in a quite different direction. According to the unanimous opinion of all scholars in this field, he was one of the last who read the original Acts of Andrew (probably in a Latin translation) and towards the end of the 6th century excerpted them, before they were for the most part lost. The result of his work is extant in the form of an epitome *de miraculis beati Andreae* (ed. M. Bonnet, *MGH, Scriptores rerum Merovingicarum* vol. I, 1884, 821-846; Italian translation as part of the Abdias collection in Moraldi II, 1363-1395). Among other episodes which in the interval have proved to be genuine constituents of the ancient Acts of Andrew, it contains a description of the sojourn of Andrew and Matthias among the cannibals (Gregory calls them *diri*) and the journey thither, in agreement with our Acts. Since Gregory does not specify any other relevant source of information for his summary, apart from the *liber de virtutibus sancti Andreae apostoli* which he expressly used, it would be at least illogical to separate off the episode mentioned from the whole complex of the Acts of Andrew there described, and accepted as such by scholars, and assign to it a different origin, without some compelling reason. On the contrary, it looks as though at the time when Gregory wrote (i.e. the end of the 6th century) the Acta Andreae et Matthiae apud anthropophagos - just as they have come down to us - were a fixed element in the Acta Andreae in a Latin translation.

There is certainly no lack of references which speak for a great antiquity for the elements contained in this apocryphon. We may refer first of all to the tradition (παράδοσις) attested by Eusebius (HE III 1.1) and probably going back to Origen (185-253), according to which the apostle Andrew's sphere of work is to be sought among the Scythians. This reference fits particularly well with our Acts (since Herodotus the 'man-eaters' were located according to the hellenistic world-view on the north coast of the Black Sea), and not so much with the remaining episodes in the ancient Acts of Andrew which are regarded as genuine, which are played out in various towns of Achaea, Macedonia and Thrace (cf. the contribution of E. Junod in F. Bovon et al., *Les actes apocryphes des apôtres*, Geneva 1981, 233-248).

A further indication of age is provided by a passage in the Coptic Vita of Shenute written by Besa (BHO 1074-75), to which O. von Lemm drew attention (*Bulletin de l'Académie Impériale des Sciences de St.-Pétersbourg* NS I [XXXIII], 1890, 580-581. This passage offers a clear parallel to c. 5 (= Aa II/1, 69) of our Acts, in which Jesus, accompanied by two angels, appears as helmsman of a ship which speeds

Andrew to his goal. Since Shenute was born in 333 and his biographer and successor Besa lived in the 5th century, it is to be assumed that the latter in composing the Vita of his master laid hold of legends which were in circulation in Egypt during the 4th century. One of these legends now proves to be an essential constituent of our Acts, and this date should accordingly be treated as the terminus ante quem for the origin of our present document.

To these indications of age we may add the fact that the Acta Andreae et Matthiae are not complete Acts, calculated to replace the ancient Acts of Andrew in a revised form, as is occasionally the case with later Acts, but simply contain an episode in the missionary activity of Andrew which redactionally and in terms of content could easily be inserted into the traditional framework of the ancient Acts of Andrew, which are not exactly marked by their heretical character.

This naturally does not exclude the possibility that this episode, which because of its popularity shows an extremely extensive and wide-branching textual tradition, was also at some time the subject of expansions and elaborations, the time of origin of which we cannot establish. The differences which are present in the transmitted forms of the text point to this. So far as concerns the length of the Greek version, of which we have an excellent edition (Aa II/1. 65-116), it is for example worthy of note that a papyrus fragment published by J.B. Bauer (*Jahrbuch der österreichischen Byz. Gesellschaft* 16, 1967, 35-38), which presumably derives from the 7th century, seems to point to a more extensive wording than our textus receptus - just as is in part the case with the Latin version - whereas the Syriac, Coptic, Arabic, Ethiopic and in part the Old Slavonic witnesses in general offer a significantly shorter text.

Equally uncertain is the form of the name of Andrew's companion, which varies between Matthaeus and Matthias. Both forms appear in the Greek and Latin witnesses, so that while Bonnet in his edition decided for Matthias, Lipsius gave preference to the form Matthaeus (above all because of the parallelism with the Latin version of the Passio Matthaei, in which it is said that Matthew went *in regionem Medorum qui homines manducabant* [Aa II/1, 217-218]). The form Matthaeus is also attested in the Syriac and Old Slavonic witnesses, in which a confusion of the two names can particularly easily occur, while the remaining versions (Coptic, Arabic and Ethiopic) hold firmly to Matthias. Despite this uncertainty it is probable that the latter form, as the more difficult, is the original.

As already indicated, our Acts with their 33 chapters represent only an episode, in which the fictitious adventure of Matthias and Andrew in the city of the cannibals and the latter's marvellous journey there are described in iridescent colours. There is a detailed analysis of the contents in Lipsius, *Die apokr. Apostelgeschichten* I, 550-553, and Moraldi II, 1613-1615; modern translations in James, 453-458 [extracts] and Erbetta II, 495-505; further details on the textual tradition in J. Gil (*Habis* 6, 1975, 177-194) and D.R. MacDonald/J.-M. Prieur in the discussion already mentioned (*Semeia* 38, 1986, 9-39).

Although the stigmatizing of cannibalism associated with the theme of these Acts can also be interpreted as a renunciation of any consumption of meat - in contrast to the man-eaters the apostles feed exclusively on figs - there are here no pronounced encratite tendencies as in other episodes of the ancient Acts of Andrew. There are also no corresponding protracted speeches in this or other directions. The narrative element which is here dominant cannot however conceal several typical features of the Acts of Andrew, such as the conflict with the demons (see c. 24ff.) or the epiphany of Jesus in the form of a child (see cc. 18, 33).

The testimony of Gregory of Tours, mentioned at the beginning, must go back to a translation into Latin already in existence at the end of the 6th century. Because of this a special significance attaches to the Latin version of the Acta Andreae et Matthiae apud anthropophagos. However, only scant witnesses of it are known. A fragment, which with some gaps matches cc. 16-18 of the Greek text, was already discovered by Bonnet in a Roman palimpsest of the 11th century, and published (Aa II/1, 85-88). It is however F. Blatt (*Die lateinischen Bearbeitungen der Acta Andreae et Matthiae apud anthropophagos*, 1930) to whom we owe the first thorough investigation of the entire Latin tradition, together with the edition of two further witnesses. The Codex Casanatensis No.1104 of the 12th century (text op. cit. 32-95) reproduces the wording of the Greek version in a somewhat expanded form, while the Codex Vaticanus 1274 of the 11th century (text op. cit. 96-148) is a Latin revision in rhythmic prose, which can be regarded as a connecting-link for the 'Legend of St Andrew' disseminated in the Anglo-Saxon area (see on this K.R. Brooks, *Andreas and the Fates of the Apostles*, London/New York 1961). A hallmark common to all the Latin witnesses (including the epitome of Gregory of Tours) is that in contrast to the extant Greek witnesses, which for the most part contain no statement to this effect, they describe the land of the cannibals as Mermidona civitas, Mermedonia or Mirmidonia provincia. These names recall the place-names Μύρνη or Μυρμένη [τὴν πόλιν τῶν ἀνθρωποφάγων], which appear in the Passio Matthaei (Aa II/1, 220_6 and 227_2), and could be identified with the Scythian town of Μυρμηκίων (cf. Pauly-Wissowa, art. 'Myrmekeion', vol. 16/1, 1933, col. 1105). The Latin witnesses at any rate point to a Greek *Vorlage* which in this as in other details departed from the wording of our present textus receptus.

Of the Coptic version two important fragments have been published, which roughly match cc. 1-8 and 10-13 of the Greek version in a shortened form. The first (BHO 735) derives from the Codex Copt. Tischendorfianus VI (fragments 6-8) in the present Saltykov-Scedrin library (formerly the Publicnaja Biblioteka) in Leningrad, is written in the Fayyumic dialect, and was published by O. von Lemm with a German translation and commentary (*Bulletin de l'Académie Impériale des Sciences de St.-Pétersbourg* NS I [XXXIII], 1890, 558-576). O. von Lemm conjectured the existence of an older Sahidic version behind this Fayyumic text. The second fragment testifies to the correctness of this conjecture - Codex Vindobonensis K9576 [fol.75], which is composed in the Sahidic dialect and was first published by C. Wessely (*Studien zur Paläographie und Papyruskunde*, vol 18 [= Griechische und koptische Texte theologischen Inhalts, vol.5], 1917, 72-73) in a diplomatic edition. This text, which is not unquestionably a continuation of the one just mentioned and has finally been examined, translated and reprinted by E. Lucchesi and J.-M. Prieur (*AnalBoll* 96, 1978, 339-350), could be regarded as a remnant of the original Sahidic version of our Acts. On another Coptic papyrus fragment (Amherst-Morgan No.17), the brevity of which prevents our establishing with any certainty whether it belongs to our apocryphon, cf. E. Lucchesi and J.-M. Prieur, art. cit. 340-341.

The various Arabic (BHO 736, 738) and Ethiopic (BHO 734, 747, 739) versions, which likewise present a shortened text, took shape later, probably on the basis of the Coptic version. Text in A. Smith Lewis (*Horae Semiticae* III, Cambridge 1904, 109-118, 83-91) and E.A. Wallis Budge (*The Contendings of the Apostles* I, London 1899, 307-335, 225-242, 101-113), with corresponding English translation in the companion volumes.

The Acta Andreae et Matthiae were also translated from the Greek into Syriac: original text according to a codex of the 10th century with an English translation in W. Wright, *Apocryphal Acts of the Apostles* I-II, London 1871 (repr. 1968), 102-126; 93-115. The wording of the Syriac version is shorter than that of the textus receptus, especially from c. 7 (= Aa II/1, 72.12ff.), and names the city of the cannibals "city of the dogs, which is called 'Irka'". This version is important because of its age, and because it served as the Vorlage for the Armenian revisions (BHO 740-741: text in K. Tsherakhian, *Thesaurus litterarum armeniarum* III, Venice 1904, 168-173; 124-145; French translation in L. Leloir, CChrSA 3/1, 260-265; 205-227). On the secondary character of the Armenian versions as witnesses to the text see the discussions of L. Leloir (*New Testament Studies* 22, 1976, 115-139 and *Orientalia Christiana Analecta* 205, 1978, 137-148).

There is also a Georgian version of our Acts under the somewhat misleading title of 'Dispersio apostolorum'. The text - according to Codex H 341 of the 11th century in the Manuscript Institute in Tiflis - was edited by C. K'urc'ikidze ([Les versions géorgiennes des actes apocryphes des apôtres], Tiflis 1959, 21-42). See on this the discussion by G. Garitte (*Le Muséon* 74, 1961, 393 No.13).

Among the ancient versions the Old Slavonic beyond doubt displays the most witnesses to the text. Some of them have been published by St. Novakovič (*Starine* 8, 1876, 55-69), M.N. Speranskij (*Drevnosti: Trudy Moskovskogo Archeologičeskogo Obščestva* 15, 1894, 64-75), P.A. Lavrov (*Apokrifičeskie teksty*: Sbornik ORJS 67, St Petersburg 1899, 40-51), I. Franko (*Apokrify i legendy* vol. III, L'vov 1902, 126-141), R. Strohal (*Stare hrvatske apokrifne priče i legende*, Bjelovar 1917, 43-47) and B. Grabar (*Radovi Staroslavenskog Instituta*, knj. 6, Zagreb 1967, 186-200 [with special consideration of the Glagolitic manuscripts). On numerous other witnesses to the text see A. de Santos Otero, *Überlieferung* I, 70-83; II, 243-244.

From the investigation of the texts which have become known, it emerges that the Slavonic witnesses derive from at least two different Greek *Vorlagen*, which were very literally translated and for the most part offer a shorter wording than the "textus receptus" - exactly as in the case of the Coptic and Syriac versions. Not to be confused with the witnesses to the Old Slavonic version just discussed is the legend of the Christianising of Russia by the apostle Andrew (see bibliography in A. de Santos Otero, op. cit.). Based inter alia on the statements of Epiphanius Monachus in his Vita Andreae (PG 120, 218-260) and the so-called "Laudatio" (ed. M. Bonnet, *AnalBoll* 13, 1894, 311-352), which themselves go back in part to our Acts, it met with a wide diffusion in various monuments of early Russian literature. On this complex of themes cf. F. Dvornik (*The Idea of Apostolicity in Byzantium . . .*, Cambridge/Mass. 1958, 225ff.; 263-264) and L. Müller ('Drevnerusskoe skazanie o choždenii apostola Andreja v Kiev i Novgorod', Letopisi i chroniki [*Sbornik statej*, 1], Moscow 1974, 48-63).

5.2 Acta Petri et Andreae

The Acts known under the title Πράξεις τῶν ἁγίων ἀποστόλων Πέτρου καὶ Ἀνδρέα (BHG II, 1489) represent a continuation of the Acta Andreae et Matthiae apud anthropophagos (see above, pp. 443ff.). The scene of the action is here 'the city of the barbarians', and Peter and also Andrew's disciples Alexander and Rufus appear as leading figures beside Andrew and Matthias. In addition to a strong passion for adventure and the miraculous, other motifs known from the ancient apostolic Acts (e.g. the reproach of magic and of hostility to marriage directed against the apostle) are conspicuous in this legend.

For the restoration of the imperfectly transmitted Greek text M. Bonnet (Aa II/1, 117-127) drew, in addition to the only two Greek manuscripts as yet known, upon the evidence of the Ethiopic version (according to S.C. Malan's translation, *The Conflicts of the Holy Apostles*, London 1871, 221-229) and the Old Slavonic (according to the edition by N. Tichonravov, *Pamjatniki otrečennoj russkoj literatury* II, Moscow 1863, 5-10 [translated by N. Bonwetsch, ZKG 5, 1882, 506-509]).

In the Coptic tradition this legend is current as the 'Acta Thaddaei' (for further details on this see below, p. 480). Our knowledge of the Old Slavonic version has in the meantime been enlarged by the valuable contribution of B. Grabar (*Radovi Staroslavenskog Instituta*, knj. 6, Zagreb 1967, 162-185; 200-206), in which the text of a new Glagolitic witness to the text (Cod. glagol. VII 30 of the Jugoslav Academy of Sciences in Zagreb) is published together with an investigation of the available manuscript material.

For a detailed analysis of the content of this legend see R.A. Lipsius (*Die apokr. Apostelgeschichten* I, 553-555) and Moraldi II, 1618-1619. There are modern translations in James 458-460 (extracts) and Erbetta II, 530-534.

5.3 Acta Andreae et Bartholomaei (coptica)

It is certain that these Acts, long known only from Coptic (BHO 57), Arabic (BHO 55) and Ethiopic (BHO 56) sources, came into being in association with the Acta Andreae et Matthiae apud anthropophagos. Relying on the witnesses known to him, the content of which he analysed in detail, Lipsius further pleaded for an Egyptian origin (*Die apokr. Apostelgeschichten* II/2, 76-86). It was the researches of A. Ehrhard (*Überlieferung und Bestand der hagiographischen Literatur* ... III, 1939, 771 No. 54; 858-59 No. 7) and F. Halkin (*Silloge bizantina in onore di S.G. Mercati*, Rome 1957, 225 [reprint: *Subsidia hagiographica* No. 51, Brussels 1971, 121-122]) which first demonstrated the existence of two Greek witnesses of the 15th century, which show great agreement with part of the content of our Acts - e.g. the appearance of Andrew and Bartholomew together with Andrew's disciples Alexander and Rufus and their mission among the Parthians, the conversion of the fabulous monster 'Kynokephalos' and his renaming as 'Christianos' or 'Christomaios', etc. Since the Greek texts (BHG III, 2056), which in any case cover only a part of our Acts, are not yet published, we cannot say anything final about their relation to the Coptic, Arabic and Ethiopian sources; but even if the Greek version should prove to be the *Vorlage* for the other versions, it does not appear that the Egyptian origin of this apocryphon must be called in question.

The Coptic version consists in the main of two fragments contained in the Roman codices Borgiani 132 and 133 (about 9th cent.), which belong to two different recensions and were published (*Rendiconti della R. Accademia dei Lincei*, Serie IV vol. III/2, Rome 1887, 117-190; 179-184) and translated into Italian (*Giornale della Società Asiatica Italiana* 2, 1888, 46-55) by I. Guidi. Some folios which are missing from the Codex Borgianus 133 (siglum Bibl. Vaticana, Borgia 109, cassette XXVI No. 133) and contain further pieces of the present Acts have recently been identified as the Coptic fragments preserved in the British Museum under the siglum Or. 3581 B (1) and in the National Library in Paris under the siglum 129[18] fol. 115 and 165. The corresponding texts have been edited and translated into French by their discoverers E. Lucchesi and J.-M. Prieur (*AnalBoll* 96, 1978, 347-350 and 98, 1980, 75-82).

The Arabic translation (BHO 55) came into being from a Coptic *Vorlage*, probably in the second half of the 13th century. Two witnesses to the text in particular, from the 14th and 16th centuries, are known through the edition of A. Smith Lewis (*Horae Semiticae* III-IV, London 1904, 11-23; 11-25). On further Arabic witnesses to the text see G. Graf, *Geschichte der christl. arabischen Literatur* I, 1944, 263. Finally the Arabic text of the Coptic Synaxarium (ed. R. Basset, *Patrologia Orientalis* I/3, 1904, 224-226) presents - as part of the Coptic 'Acta Bartholomaei' (see below, pp. 451f.) - a brief summary of this legend. The Ethiopic version (BHO 56) goes back to Arabic sources and despite its inaccurate and secondary character presents the same content as these. In addition to the English translation by S.C. Malan (*The Conflicts of the Holy Apostles*, London 1871, 76-99), the Ethiopic version is accessible in the bilingual edition of E.A. Wallis Budge (*The Contendings of the Apostles* I-II, London 1899-1901, 156-183; 183-214).

Lipsius already (loc. cit.) convincingly showed that the 'Acta Andreae et Matthiae apud anthropophagos' played the godfather in the origins of this document. In addition to the imitation of this model, however, there is at the same time an increasingly conspicuous tendency to 'Africanise' the stage-setting and the place-names. This also explains the differences which appear in the Coptic, Arabic and Ethiopic texts in the description of the mission field. Andrew's voyage with Jesus as the helmsman is replaced in these Acts - borrowing from the OT - by a journey in the belly of a fish. What is new here is the appearance and conversion of the fabulous monster 'Kynokephalos', which is without doubt of Egyptian origin.

5.4 Acta Pauli et Andreae (coptica)

The description 'Acta' fits this document only with qualifications. The text has survived only in two Coptic fragments in the Codex Borgianus 132 in Rome (BHO 917). The first was first edited by G. Zoega *(Catalogus codicum copticorum manu scriptorum qui in Museo Borgiano Velitris adservantur*, Rome 1810, 230-235). Some decades later Guidi published the second, substantially shorter, fragment from the same codex (*Rendiconti della R. Accademia dei Lincei*, Serie IV vol. III/2, Rome

1887, 80-81) and translated it into Italian (*Giornale della Società Asiatica Italiana* 2, 1888, 45-46).

The interest of scholars has focused especially on the first fragment, of which in the course of the years partial reprints (e.g. G. Steindorff, *Koptische Grammatik*, 1930³, 34*-46*; id. *Kurzer Abriß der koptischen Grammatik*, 1921, 43*-47*; I. Guidi, *Elementa linguae copticae*, Naples 1924, 36-39) and partial translations (e.g. E. Dulaurier, *Fragment des révélations apocryphes de saint Barthélemy*, Paris 1835, 30-35; F.H. Hallock, *Journal of the Society of Oriental Research* 13, 1929, 190-194; J. Zandee, *Nederlands Theologisch Tijdschrift* 9, 1954-55, 158-174) have frequently been published.

It was only the contribution of X. Jacques, 'Les deux fragments conservés des Actes d'André et de Paul' (*Orientalia* N.S. 38, 1969, 187-213), with a complete and critical edition of the original text and a translation, also in French (reprinted a year later in *Recherches de Science Religieuse* 58, 1970, 289-296), bibliography and commentary, that finally replaced the earlier partial editions and translations.

Particular interest was aroused among scholars by the passage in which it is narrated that 'Andrew with a beaker of sweet water put asunder the salt sea-water and so made it possible for Paul to ascend again from Hell.' This motif has been associated inter alia with ancient Egyptian magical texts: so for example F. Lexa, *La magie dans l'Égypte antique* I, Paris 1925, 150-151 and A.M. Kropp, *Ausgewählte koptische Zaubertexte* III, Brussels 1930, 61-62. S. Morenz (ThLZ 79, 1947, cols. 295-297) considers such explanations questionable, and suggests comparing the miracle of the dividing of the waters accomplished by Andrew with an act ascribed by Aelius Aristides to the hellenistic-Egyptian god Sarapis, according to which 'in the midst of the sea he called forth drinkable water'. On this view we should here have before us a syncretistic text in which - in Morenz' words - the apostle Andrew would appear as νέος Σάραπις. That this conclusion is not valid is already clear from the fact that the alleged parallelism between the two motifs is at least just as imperfect as others which might be drawn from the Egyptian magical texts previously mentioned, or even from biblical sources (e.g. Exod. 15:22ff., the bitter water at Mara). There appears to be a clearer analogy with an episode in the Prochorus Acts (= Zahn 54_{21}-56_{9}), which speaks of a transformation of sea-water into drinking-water. The motif of the dividing of the waters seems however to be deeply rooted in Egypt, and could - with the inclusion of other circumstances in the tradition - be taken as a sign that our present document originated in Egypt. For other indications in this direction, see Jacques, art. cit. passim.

A striking feature of these 'Acts' is the hybrid character of their contents: this is chiefly a matter of an alleged episode of the Acts of Andrew (i.e. the raising-up of a child through the apostle's intercession, as in the Acta Andreae et Philemonis; see below, 5.5) into which the apocalyptic interlude of Paul's journey to Hell is interwoven (with great reliance on the known Apocalypse of Paul [BHG II, 1460] and the Gospel of Bartholomew [BHG I, 228]). This is without doubt an indication of a late time of origin. For a detailed analysis of the contents cf. Lipsius (*Die apokr. Apostelgeschichten* I, 616-617; Ergänzungsheft 96), James, 472-475 and Moraldi II, 1616-1617.

5.5 Acta Andreae et Philemonis (coptica)

This is again a matter of an alleged episode from the Acts of Andrew, which is preserved only defectively in two different Coptic fragments (Cod. copt. Parisinus 129[17] fol. 87 and Cod. copt. Leidensis [Insinger No. 51]). The subject of the action is the raising-up, accomplished through the prayer of Andrew (with Philemon's assistance), of a child to whom a wicked mother had given birth just before and whom she wished to give to a dog to devour. Edition of the Coptic text with German translation in O. von Lemm, 'Koptische Miscellen LXVIII' (*Bulletin de l'Académie Impériale des Sciences de St.-Pétersbourg*, VI série, vol. IV, St Petersburg 1910, 61-69.

6.1 Acta Bartholomaei (coptica)

According to the Arabic text of the Coptic Synaxary (ed. R. Basset, *Patrologia Orientalis* I/3, 1904, 224-226), the missionary activity of the apostle Bartholomew took place at first - at the instance of Peter - in the Egyptian oases. From there he goes in company with Andrew to the Parthians and finally suffers his martyrdom, being stuffed into a hairy sack filled with sand and cast into the sea in the neighbourhood of a town on the coast. Since the second episode (the mission among the Parthians) forms the subject of the Acta Andreae et Bartholomaei already discussed (see above, pp. 448f.), only the Praedicatio Bartholomaei in Oasi (BHO 152-155) with the associated Martyrdom (BHO 157-158) is taken into consideration under the present rubric.

Several fragments of the Coptic original of these Acts are known through the editions of W.E. Crum (*Catalogue of the Coptic Manuscripts in the British Museum*, London 1905, 126-127), O. von Lemm (*Bulletin de l'Académie Impériale des Sciences de St.-Pétersbourg* NS I [XXXIII], 1890, 513-519) and H.G. Evelyn White (*The Monasteries of the Wadi 'n Natrun*, Part I, New York 1926, 43-45). The text is however preserved complete only in the Arabic version (ed. A. Smith Lewis, *Horae Semiticae* III-IV, London 1904, 58-63; 69-75) and in the Ethiopic which followed from it (ed. E.A. Wallis Budge, *The Contendings of the Apostles* I-II, London 1899-1901, 83-92; 93-103).

The scene of the action according to the witnesses before us is unmistakably the land of the oases in Egypt. Other descriptions common since Zoega - e.g fines Ichthyophagorum - which led Lipsius to many a speculation (see *Die apokr. Apostelgeschichten* II/2, 84), rest solely on a false interpretation of the Coptic text, as O. von Lemm (op. cit. 518-519) has shown. Of interest is the passage which describes how Bartholomew is sold by Peter to a merchant, to all appearance as a slave, that he may be able to gain entry to the towns of the oases. This passage recalls inter alia the well-known episode in the Acts of Thomas (c. 2), and together with other parallels to this document (e.g. the story of the talking serpent which at the bidding of the apostle is compelled to suck out the poison it has squirted into a wound) is proof that the author of the present Acts used the ancient Acts of Thomas and adapted them to the Egyptian situation. There is a sign of this effort at adaptation, for example, in the fact that Bartholomew in our Acts performs his slave's work as a wine-grower in the oasis, whereas Thomas in the Acts of that name is active as a craftsman and architect in the king's service.

The complete text of the Martyrdom has survived only in Arabic (A. Smith Lewis, op. cit. 64-66; 76-79) and Ethiopic (E.A. Wallis Budge, op. cit. 93-100; 104-110). From the conclusion of a Coptic fragment (text in O. von Lemm, op. cit. 515) it emerges that the scene of the event is the town of Nintos (= Andinus [Arabic] or Naidas [Ethiopic]) on the coast. Whether the still unpublished Passio Bartholomaei contained in the Coptic codex 635 (fol. 4^{r2}-5^{v2}) in the Pierpont Morgan Library in New York (cf. F. Morard, *Revue de Théologie et de Philosophie*, 113, 1981, 411) belongs in this context has still to be investigated.

6.2 Passiones Bartholomaei

The Passiones meant here, in Latin and Armenian, have no relation of any kind either with one another or with the Martyrdom connected with the Acta Bartholomaei coptica (see above, pp. 451f.).

The Latin Passio Bartholomaei forms chapter VIII of ps.-Abdias, and was critically edited by M. Bonnet (Aa II/1, 128-150). The Greek text previously edited by Tischendorf (BHG I, 227) goes back, as M. Bonnet proved (*AnalBoll* 14, 1895, 353), to this Latin *Vorlage*, with which an early Irish translation is also to be associated (cf. M. McNamara, *The Apocrypha in the Irish Church*, Dublin 1975, 93-94). The subject of the present legend is Bartholomew's missionary activity in India, in which the destruction of the heathen idols and the conflict with the demons connected with it are the motifs which almost exclusively dominate the action. At the end Bartholomew suffers martyrdom by beheading under king Astriges. For modern translations of the Latin text see Erbetta II, 583-588 and Moraldi II, 1568-1576. In contrast to the Coptic Acts of Bartholomew this legend presents few points of contact with the ancient Acts of Thomas. The most striking feature here is the absence of encratite traits, which in most apostolic Acts provide the cause that triggers off the inevitable martyrdom. Only with the Latin Passio sancti Thomae apostoli (BHL 8136), a later reworking of the Acta Thomae, can some common elements, chiefly of a stylistic nature, be identified (cf. K. Zelzer, *Die alten lateinischen Thomasakten*, TU 122, 1977, XXX-XXXII). A. Dihle ('Neues zur Thomastradition', JbAC 6, 1963, 54-70) uses the evidence of this Latin Passio to underpin his theory about the alleged original 'Bartholomew mission' in south-west India, according to Eusebius (HE V.10) - in opposition to the familiar Thomas tradition. In view of the large number of apocryphal Acts which concern themselves with Bartholomew's mission, and their very diverse statements with regard to it, one cannot to my mind set too much store on the demonstrative force of this evidence.

The Armenian Passio consists of several reports (BHO 156, 159) which have been edited by I.B. Aucher (*Sanctorum acta pleniora* vol. IX, Venice 1813, 447-449), L. Alishan (*Bibliotheca armenia* fasc. XIX, Venice 1861, 5-30), Kh. Tsherakhian (*Thesaurus litterarum armeniarum* vol. III, Venice 1904, 333-357, 367-368) and in the collection *Vitae et Passiones sanctorum* vol. I (Venice 1874, 200-

211). For the most part the content of such texts has been made accessible through the Latin translation of G. Mosinger (*Vita et Martyrium sancti Bartholomaei apostoli*, Innsbruck 1877), which Lipsius (*Die apokr. Apostelgeschichten* II/2, 92ff.) used as the basis for his detailed analysis of this document. In this Passio it is a question of a later compilation, the sources of which lie in part in local Armenian tradition and may be of Syrian - hence the association of Bartholomew and Judas Thaddaeus (BHO 160) - and Greek origin. In this connection it is interesting to discover that according to some early Irish reports the martyrdom of Bartholomew took place in 'Armenia, that is a certain realm in India' (cf. M. McNamara, op. cit. 85, 94).

7.1 Acta Thomae

In view of the particularly complicated textual tradition, the question of the reworkings of the Acta Thomae and their relation to the original document is difficult to elucidate. Everything speaks for the view that such reworkings to a larger or smaller extent are already to be placed immediately after the apocryphon came into being. The Syriac version, known through W. Wright's edition (BHO 1186-1204), which - in all probability - may stand nearest to the Syriac original of these Acts, already shows according to the general opinion clear traces of redaction. The Greek textus receptus (Aa II/2, 99-288) has for its part best transmitted the original content of these Acts, but at the same time is the result of at least one translation from the Syriac, in which again various redactions are reflected. Moreover the several Greek witnesses to the text provide an impressive example of the carefree way in which the individual copyists dealt with the wording of these Acts: omissions, alterations and transpositions of the text very frequently occur, and are the seeds for later reworkings.

Apart from these occasional interferences, the tendency to excerpt the extensive text of this document appears to have established itself very early. Of the thirteen acts of which the apocryphon consists, nos. 1, 2 and 13 are attested in nearly all known manuscripts, whereas for the other ten only very few witnesses to the text are available. It was evidently not ideological criteria that were decisive in this preference for excerpts, but rather practical considerations, such as the attempt to reduce the extent of the text by offering only isolated episodes, including the obligatory martyrdom. In this connection it is interesting to observe that both the episode of the so-called punitive miracle, already felt obnoxious by Augustine, and also the hymn of the bridal chamber, which is close to gnostic ideology - quite apart from the encratite admonitions - are contained in the first act (c. 6ff.: Aa II/2. 108ff.), which normally belongs among these excerpts. A reflection of this tendency, the long influence of which is demonstrated by the Modern Greek witness from Sparta published only a few years ago by S. Agourides (*Deltion biblikon meleton* 1, 1971, 126-147), is provided not only by the editions of the Greek text which preceded that of M. Bonnet (Thilo 1823, Tischendorf 1851) but also by numerous ancient versions of this apocryphon - e.g. the Armenian, Georgian and Slavonic - which go back to a Greek Vorlage.

On the other hand, the abundant manuscript material brought together by M. Bonnet for his edition (cf. his discussion in Aa II/2. XVff. and that of Lipsius, *Die apokr. Apostelgeschichten* I, 230ff.) shows at the best attested places considerable differences, which point to several redactions of the Greek text and are of significance for the transmission of the Acts of Thomas in the oriental literatures. From c. 6 on, for example, the Greek witnesses for the first and second acts (= cc. 1-29: Aa II/2, 99-146) fall into two clearly distinct groups with a correspondingly different text, which Bonnet printed separately (the one above, the other below). Do these two Greek versions represent two different translations from Syriac Vorlagen, as the Syriacisms identified in both redactions by A.F.J. Klijn (*The Acts of Thomas* [Suppl. Nov. Test. 5], Leiden 1962) appear to indicate, or has the one developed from the other through abbreviation or expansion? The fact that the version printed by Bonnet on the lower part of the page is shorter than the other might support the second hypothesis, although we cannot supply any unambiguous proof for it. What is certain is the significance which this 'short version' has as a *Vorlage* for other versions. In this connection prominence should be given in particular to the Old Slavonic, which boasts a very large number of manuscripts - cf. in A. de Santos Otero's list (*Überlieferung* I, 84-96) the witnesses marked with a reference to BHG II 1800 - and has so far scarcely attracted the interest of scholars.

As with the first and second acts, the Greek witnesses which contain the thirteenth act with the martyrdom (= cc. 159-171: Aa II/2. 269-288) fall into two different groups with a different wording. This time also M. Bonnet printed the corresponding versions separately (the one above, the other below). In contrast to the section just discussed, however, the differences between the two versions here are to be seen not so much in the extent of the texts concerned but rather in other details. Among these there is in the first place the different positioning of the great prayer uttered by Thomas shortly before his martyrdom, which in the one redaction forms cc. 144-148 (Aa II/2, 251-258) and in the other is inserted between cc. 167/178.

This second redaction, which is represented by the Greek manuscripts P F L S Z and today, in opposition to Bonnet (Aa II/2, 269-288), is regarded by some scholars as the more original (cf. for example E. Junod, J.-D. Kaestli, *L'histoire des actes apocryphes des apôtres du IIIe au IXe siècle*, Lausanne 1982, 37), is of great significance in relation to the wider textual tradition - as with the first section. For to it belongs inter alia a witness known to Bonnet only in extracts, the Codex Vaticanus graecus 1608 (fol. 7-12) from the beginning of the 11th century, which was first published in recent years by G. Garitte (*Le Muséon* 84, 1971, 158-195) and contains a version of the martyrdom which in compass corresponds roughly to the wording of cc. 155-170 of the textus receptus. Apart from the above-mentioned positioning of the great prayer between cc. 167/168, which is a feature common to all the manuscripts of this redaction, what is striking in this text of the martyrdom is that the narrative begins abruptly with the last sentence of c. 155 (Aa II/2, 264_{14}) and offers only a brief summary of the circumstantial c. 157 (Aa II/2, 266_7-267_{18}). On the basis of these typical features and a systematic analysis of the text, G. Garitte has shown (art. cit. 151-158 and *Le Muséon* 83, 1970, 497-532) that it was this very version which served as the *Vorlage* for the Armenian version of the martyrdom (BHO 1215: text in K. Tsherakhian, *Thesaurus litterarum armeniarum* III, Venice 1904, 388-400), and indirectly also for the Georgian (text in C. K'urc'ikidze, [Les versions géorgiennes des actes apocryphes des apôtres], Tiflis 1959, 14-20), which issued from the Armenian. From Garitte's investigation, which includes not only the publication of the Greek Vorlage but also that of the Armenian and Georgian texts with corresponding Latin translations prepared by the author himself, it emerges that the Armenian version is a faithful translation of the Greek original mentioned.

Is the *De miraculis beati Thomae apostoli* (= c. IX of the ps.-Abdias collection; cf. BHL 8140), so important for the Latin tradition, also to be considered an offshoot from this Greek source? This question may at first sound somewhat strange when we reflect that this book (a critical edition, following the defective one by M. Bonnet [*Supplementum codicis apocryphi* I, 1893, 96-132], has recently been supplied by K. Zelzer [*Die lateinischen Thomasakten*, TU 122, 1977]) is a comprehensive reworking of this apocryphon, whereas the Greek version under discussion contains only the martyrdom. Moreover, the posing of this question seems to stand in contradiction to the thesis advanced by K. Zelzer, that the Latin Acts of Thomas are 'no translation of an extant Greek version of the text or of individual sections' (op. cit. XII; cf. similar formulations in his other contributions on this theme: *Wiener Studien* 84, NF 5, 1971, 161-179 and 85, NF 6, 1972, 188-211, as well as *Studia Patristica* 12, 1975, 190-193).

The differing compass of the texts in question does indeed restrict the material for comparison to the parts they share, but is no obstacle to the justifying of the question raised, especially since the Greek martyrdom with its abrupt beginning at the last sentence of c. 155 conveys the impression of a fragment torn from a more complete text. On the general marks of redaction in the 'Miracula' relative to the Greek textus receptus and the improbable - not to say: impossible - authorship of Gregory of Tours, see K. Zelzer's arguments in his edition quoted (XII-XXIX). The basis of my reflections is a comparison between the Codex Vaticanus graecus 1608 (fol. 7-12) already mentioned, according to Garitte's edition, and the corresponding text of the 'Miracula' (in Zelzer, 68_{20}-77_{5}).

Bonnet, with the edition of Codex P (= Parisinus graecus 1510) in his *Supplementum Codicis apocryphi* I, 1883, already showed that the Latin version is in some form related to the redaction represented by the Greek manuscripts P F L S Z. The new witness to the text confirms that they belong together, and in addition reveals a dependence of the Latin text on its Greek wording, which in some respects amounts to that of a free translation. This is shown inter alia by two of the three marks of identity which hold for the Armenian translation (see above, p. 454) - the third mark, relating to the beginning of the two texts, does not apply here, for obvious reasons - and also a great mass of verbal agreement, which is to be observed particularly at passages with a predominantly narrative character. Deviations in the Latin text can be identified chiefly where the corresponding parts of the Greek Vorlage are especially repetitive or circumstantial, e.g. in the great prayer (Zelzer, 73_{21}-75_{12}) or in the extended dialogues which precede it (Zelzer, 72_{3}ff.). Such deviations however do not normally represent any change to the content of the text, but are rather a stylistic simplification, achieved through omissions in long-winded enumerations, by changing the dialogues into indirect sentences, or by other stylistic means. Such liberties underline the dependence of the Latin text upon the Greek original and characterise the work of the translator, whose starting-point was an already excerpted and evidently widely disseminated Greek version of the Acts of Thomas; the brief summary of c.157 in both texts points to that. Ideological points of view, oriented towards orthodoxy, do not appear to have stood in the foreground in the preparation of this work. Whether the validity of the above observations extends beyond the limits of the material for comparison at our disposal will only be shown when the complete text of the Greek *Vorlage*, as yet only fragmentarily known, can be taken into consideration.

The so-called *Passio sancti Thomae apostoli* (BHL 8136: text in K. Zelzer, op. cit. 1-42), which along with the book De Miraculis enjoyed a wide diffusion in the Latin Middle Ages, is to be assessed differently. Here materials of diverse origin, which are connected with the Acts of Thomas, have been worked up and enriched with later insertions of an ecclesiastical character. One of the sources of this reworking may have been the book De Miraculis.

It is difficult to find any certain clue for the dating of the 'Miracula'. The punitive miracle to which Augustine objected in various writings towards the end of the 4th century (e.g. *contra Adimantum* 17; *de Sermone domini in monte* 1; 20; 65), which is also contained in the text of the 'Miracula' (cf. Zelzer, op. cit. 47_{22}-48_{7}), could be taken as an indication that a Latin translation of the Acta Thomae already existed at this time. There is however nothing at all to suggest an identification of such a translation with the book De Miraculis. This question is further complicated by the existence of some Latin fragments of the Acta Thomae which clearly derive from an older translation - e.g. the hymn handed down in the Irish palimpsest commentary of Codex Clm 14429 in the Bavarian Staatsbibliothek (= cc. 49-50: Aa II/2. $166_{4\text{-}18}$); cf. on this M. McNamara, *The Apocrypha in the Irish Church*, Dublin 1975, 118-119. Still more problematic in my opinion is the attempt to set the origin of the book De Miraculis about the middle of the 4th century by means of a coupling with the Passio already mentioned (cf. Zelzer, op. cit. XXIV-XXVI).

Finally, the Martyrium Thomae contained in Old Slavonic and Arabic witnesses is also dependent on the redaction represented by the manuscripts P F L S Z - although here we cannot describe the source more precisely. The Old Slavonic Martyrium was first edited as an element in the great Menaea of the Metropolitan Makarios by the Archeografičeskaja Kommissija (*Velikie Minei Četii*, 4-18 October, St Petersburg 1874, cols. 822-827). A second text according to the Codex L'vov [Universitätsbibliothek] I F-15, in which a large part of the prayer inserted between cc. 167/168 is omitted, became known through I. Franko's collection of apocrypha (*Apokrify i legendy*, vol. III, L'vov 1902, 98-101). This martyrdom, of which numerous other witnesses are extant (see in A. de Santos Otero, op. cit., the manuscripts provided with a reference to BGH II 1831), begins at c. 163 of the textus receptus (Aa II/2, 275ff.).

The Arabic version of the Martyrium, published by A. Smith Lewis (*Horae Semiticae* III-IV, London 1904, 79-83; 94-99) after two different codices from the 14th century, is contaminated at the beginning by other sources, but then reproduces the wording of cc. 159-171 (Aa II/2, 269-288) of the textus receptus according to the redaction mentioned. The same holds for the Ethiopic Martyrium (see S.C. Malan, *The Conflicts of the Holy Apostles*, London 1871, 214-220 and E.A. Wallis Budge, *The Contendings of the Apostles*, London 1899-1901, 287-295; 346-356). For further witnesses of the Arabic Martyrium see G. Graf, *Geschichte der christl. arabischen Literatur* I, 264.

The Coptic version underlying the Arabic and Ethiopic Martyrium is preserved in numerous fragments, which have recently been published and translated by P.-H. Poirier (*La version copte de la Prédication et du Martyre de Thomas* [Subs. hagiographica 67], Brussels 1984, 53-66; 69-90; 95-100; 101-107). The most extensive of them is contained in Codex 635 (fol. 6-14) of the Pierpont Morgan Library in New York (text ibid. 73-90; 103-107).

7.2 Acta Thomae minora

In addition to the reworkings so far discussed, which in general came into being through major or minor manipulations of the text of the original document, as well as through free translation, there are others which may be considered as independent imitations of the ancient Acts of Thomas. The most important and influential example is the so-called Πράξεις τοῦ ἁγίου ἀποστόλου Θωμᾶ (BHG II, 1833-1834) - also called Acta Thomae minora - handed down in Greek, Ethiopic, Coptic, Arabic and Old Slavonic witnesses. The background of the action is acts 1 and 2 of the ancient Acts of Thomas, particularly the episodes of the sending of the apostle as a slave to India and the building of the palace. Within this framework some of the old narrative elements have been preserved, while others have been altered, reinterpreted or introduced de novo from later apostolic Acts (e.g. the presence of Peter and Matthew). The encratite tendency typical for the ancient Acts of Thomas comes to the fore here also, no longer however in the form of long-winded speeches and admonitions but on the basis of episodes which are either new and introduced after long-known patterns, or simply transformed, such as that of Arsinoe and Leucius or that of the young man who was killed together with his brothers because he had refused to enter into a marriage. The miraculous destruction of the heathen idols plays a prominent role here - exactly as in other Acts of Egyptian origin. This motif could be taken as an indication that the episode of the sun-god inserted into the Latin book De Miraculis (ed. Zelzer, *Die lateinischen Thomasakten*, TU 122, 1977, 62_2-64_4), and also appearing in the Passio (ib. 37_5-40_{10}), could derive from Greek sources. Also characteristic for the present Acts is their conclusion: Thomas at the end does not suffer any martyrdom, but is healed from the effects of his earlier torturings, carried off in the living body, and brought to the company of the other apostles. The absence of the obligatory martyrdom has in some Greek witnesses and in the Arabic version led to contamination of the text from the ancient Acts of Thomas.

The elements identified by M.R. James (*Apocrypha anecdota* II, Cambridge 1897, XXXVIII-XLIV) which are shared with the so-called Egyptian corpus of Acts suggest an Egyptian origin for these Acts, although we cannot conclude from this - just as in the case of the Acta Andreae et Bartholomaei already discussed (above, pp. 448f.) - that the original was of necessity Coptic. It is however certain that by reason of its wide diffusion and as an alternative to the ancient Acts of Thomas this document played a role in the Byzantine and Coptic sphere of influence similar to that of the oft-mentioned book De Miraculis in the West.

The Acts first became known through the translation of the Ethiopic version published by S.C. Malan (*The Conflicts of the Holy Apostles*, London 1871, 187-

214). E.A. Wallis Budge later published the original text in his bilingual edition (*The Contendings of the Apostles* I-II, London 1899-1901, 265-287, 265-286). A great significance attaches to the Arabic version, edited by A. Smith Lewis (*Horae Semiticae* III-IV, London 1904, 67-78; 80-93), as the *Vorlage* for the Ethiopic version. The Coptic *Vorlage* which underlies the Arabic and Ethiopic versions is preserved in several fragments, which have recently been published and translated by P.-H. Poirier (*La version copte de la Prédication et du Martyre de Thomas* [Subs. hagiographica 67], Brussels 1984, 41-52; 67-68; 91-95; 100); cf. in addition the discussion by F. Morard in *Augustinianum* 23, 1983, 73-82.

Several witnesses have been published of the Greek version. M.R.James (op. cit. 28-45) led the way by publishing a text from the codex Br. Mus. Add. 10073 of the 15th century, the wording of which is contaminated at the end by brief extracts from the ancient Acts of Thomas. D. Tamila (*Rendiconti della R. Accademia dei Lincei/* Classe di scienze morali, storiche e filologiche. Serie V vol. 12, Rome 1903, 387-408) then published a more reliable text on the basis of two better manuscripts (Chigi R VI 39 and Bibl. Naz. 20, both from Rome). Finally A. Mancini (*Atti della R. Accademia delle scienze di Torino*, vol. 39, Turin 1904, 743-758) drew attention to the Codex Messinensis Bibl. Univ. No.30 of the year 1307, which - just like the British Museum codex Add. 10073 - is contaminated towards the end.

The Old Slavonic version has so far scarcely been taken into account, although at least two witnesses of it have been published: one from the 14th century by V. Jagič (*Starine* 5, 1873, 95-108) and another from the 16th century by I. Franko (*Apokrify i legendy* vol. III, L'vov 1902, 101-111). Both texts in general follow the wording of the Greek version represented by the codices Chigi R VI 39, Br. Mus. Add. 10073 and Messinensis 30, but in contrast to the last two manuscripts show no kind of contamination of the text at the end. For further witnesses see the manuscripts marked with a reference to BHG II 1833 in A. de Santos Otero (*Überlieferung* I, 84-96).

Although the present Acts were also transmitted as an element in (non-metaphrastic) menologies, as the example of the Codex Messinensis shows, they have nothing to do with the menological epitome (BHG II, 1836), which presents a summary of cc. 3-29 of the ancient Acts of Thomas and also occurs in Armenian and Old Slavonic synaxaries. They show just as little in common with the revisions of the Acts of Thomas ascribed to archbishop Nicetas of Thessalonica (11th cent.). On this see the arguments, probably still valid, of M. Bonnet (*Supplementum codicis apocryphi*, 1883, VIII-IX; *AnalBoll* 20, 1901, 159-164) and R.A. Lipsius (*Die apokr. Apostelgeschichten* I, 241).

8.1 Martyrium Matthaei

The document handed down as Μαρτύριον τοῦ ἁγίου Ματθαίου τοῦ ἀποστόλου (BHG II, 1224-25) was first edited in its Greek original by C. Tischendorf (*Acta apostolorum apocrypha*, 1851, 167-189), and then by M. Bonnet (Aa II/1, 217-262). The lengthy discussions of R.A. Lipsius on these Acts (*Die apokr. Apostelgeschichten* II/2, 109-141) are based solely on Tischendorf's edition. There is an Italian translation of the Greek text after Bonnet's edition in Erbetta (II, 511-517); extracts in English in James (460-462).

The Martyrium Matthaei portrays Matthew's activity and martyr's death in a manner which is very strongly reminiscent of the Acta Andreae et Matthiae already discussed (see above, pp. 443ff.) - above all in regard to the mission 'in the land of the man-eaters'. However, the identity of the person, or persons, acting under the name of Matthias or Matthew is not entirely clear, for the two names are often confused with one another in the manuscript tradition of both documents. In the Acta Andreae et Matthiae it appears that despite such confusion of names Matthias, who according to Acts 1:26 became an apostle in the place of Judas Iscariot, is intended as Andrew's companion, whereas in the present Martyrium it is unmistakably a question of the evangelist and former tax-collector Matthew. If this distinction of the persons applies to both apocrypha, which is the most likely, we can count the Martyrium Matthaei among those independent writings the prototype of which is to be sought in the Acta Andreae et Matthiae. Otherwise - i.e. if as Lipsius thought it is a question of the same person in both documents - we must regard the present Martyrium as a continuation and conclusion of the aforesaid Acts.

Apart from the relation to the Acta Andreae et Matthiae just mentioned, there are in cc. 1-5 of the Greek version of this martyrdom (= Aa II/1, 217-221) numerous parallels to the Vita Petri slavica already discussed (see above, pp. 438f.) - e.g. Matthew's sojourn in the desert and the appearance of Jesus in the form of a child.

A text of the Latin version which belongs here (BHL II, 5689) was printed by M. Bonnet along with the Greek original. Typical for this Latin version and for the texts so far published of the Old Slavonic version, still to be mentioned, is inter alia the absence of the early chapters with the parallels noted to the Vita Petri slavica: in both versions the narrative begins only from c. 9 of the Greek text. A further common factor is that both versions show numerous points of contact with one another and with the Greek manuscript group characterised as Δ by Bonnet (Aa II/1, XXXIII; 217), which very often signifies a deviation from Codex Paris gr. 881, the chief witness to the text in Bonnet's edition. It is certain that the versions mentioned (contrary to the view of Lipsius, op. cit. II/2, 123, so far as the Latin version is concerned) are not reworkings of the Greek original, but go back to *Vorlagen* which in all probability are to be located in the neighbourhood of the text cited in BHG II 1225_c under the somewhat misleading description 'epitome'. A closer examination of this complex of questions, drawing upon the Greek manuscripts Weimar Q. 729 (formerly W. Froehner; on this cf. J. Noret, *AnalBoll* 87, 1969, 79-83) and Oxford Bodl. Selden Arch. supra 9 (= BHG II, 1225_c) would be instructive for the textual history of our present document.

Two texts of the Old Slavonic version from the 16th century have been edited. The version published by I. Franko (*Apokrify i legendy* III, L'vov 1902, 156-164) according to Codex No.38 of the Ossolinski Library in Breslau shows features more original than the sporadically corrected wording of the Menologion of the Metropolitan Makarios (ed. by the Archeografičeskaja Kommissija, *Velikie Minei Četii* [16 November], Moscow 1910, cols. 2068-2079). On numerous other Slavonic witnesses, whose character and significance for textual criticism have still to be investigated, cf. A. de Santos Otero, *Überlieferung* I, 130-135.

Finally, various texts of an Armenian Passio (BHO 725-728) have been edited by Kh. Tsherakhian (*Thesaurus litterarum armeniarum* III, Venice 1904, 437-448).

8.2 Passio Matthaei (ps.-Abdias)

The Passio Matthaei handed down in Latin as Book VII of ps.-Abdias (BHL II, 5690) has nothing to do with the Martyrium just discussed. In agreement with Rufinus' statement in his Latin translation of Eusebius' Historia ecclesiastica (III 1; X 9; on this cf. E. Junod in F. Bovon et al., *Les actes apocryphes des apôtres*, Geneva 1981, 233ff.), Ethiopia is assigned to Matthew in this Passio as his mission field.

For further discussion on the origin and content of this legend see R.A. Lipsius, *Die apokr. Apostelgeschichten* I, 147-149; 166-168; II/2, 134-141. Italian translations are offered by Erbetta (II, 519-526) and Moraldi (II, 1554-1567). See further the bilingual edition by G. Talamo Atenolfi (*I testi medioevali degli Atti di S. Matteo l'Evangelista*, Rome 1958 [see review by A. Pratesi, *Studi Medievali* ser. III 1, 1960, 235-237], in which in addition to the Passio other texts connected with local traditions in the Salerno area are taken into consideration.

8.3 Acta Matthaei in Kahenat (coptica)

These Acts, the text of which is known almost exclusively through the Arabic version (text in A. Smith Lewis, *Horae Semiticae* III-IV, London 1904, 83-94; 100-112) and the Ethiopic version which is probably dependent on it (text in E.A. Wallis Budge, *The Contendings of the Apostles* I-II, London 1899-1901, 101-118; 93-114), presuppose the Acta Andreae at Matthiae (above, pp. 443ff.) - exactly like the Martyrium Matthaei just discussed. We can see an indication that there is a Coptic *Vorlage* underlying these versions in the fact that the Coptic Synaxary, handed down in Arabic (ed. R. Basset, *Patrologia Orientalis* I/3, 1904, 330-332), contains various elements of this legend. In Coptic however only a short fragment of this presumed *Vorlage* has been published, relating to the Passio still to be mentioned (BHO 722-724).

The Acts of Matthew in Kahenat are probably connected with the Greek Martyrium mentioned above (cf. pp. 458f.) through numerous points of contact, which point to a common narrative framework, but not through any kind of textual relationship. The view advocated by Lipsius (*Die apokr. Apostelgeschichten* II/2, 109ff.), according to which our present Acts are the complete text of a catholic revision of the original 'gnostic' Acta Matthaei, with the associated arguments about the relation of the various extant texts to one another, suffers from the fact that this renowned investigator of the apocrypha was inadequately acquainted with the textual attestation of the Greek Martyrium (see above, pp. 458f.). In addition, he knew only the secondary Ethiopic version of the present Acts, according to S.C. Malan's inadequate translation (*The Conflicts of the Holy Apostles*, London 1871, 43-60).

The Acta Matthaei in Kahenat contain two episodes in particular which are missing in the Greek Martyrium, and were possibly elements of the Acta Matthaei in their original form. These are Matthew's meeting with Peter and Andrew (text in

A. Smith Lewis, op. cit. 83-85; 100-101) - with a clear allusion to the Acts of the same name already discussed (above, p. 448) - and the pericope included in association with it and known from other apostolic Acts, about the division of the mission areas among the apostles (cf. on this J.-D. Kaestli in F. Bovon et al., *Les actes apocryphes des apôtres*, Geneva 1981, 249-264).

Apart from these two episodes, the remains of our present Acts rather convey the impression that it is a question of a reshaping and expansion of the narrative material contained in the Greek Martyrium, a phenomenon often to be observed in the Coptic apocrypha (see on the Acta Andreae at Bartholomaei [above, pp. 448f.] and Acta Bartholomaei coptica [above, pp. 451f.]). As examples of this manner of reworking we may adduce the transformation of the Greek scene of action, 'the land of the man-eaters', into 'the land of the Kahenat' (= the land of the priests or sooth-sayers), the replacing of Matthew's sojourn in the desert and the vision associated with it by the apostle's rapture into Paradise, and the change in the motive for the conversion of king Fulbanos [the raising-up of the king's son by Matthew becomes a deliverance from demons]. Whether this revision had its starting-point in the Coptic area or in an earlier Greek source unknown to us - as in the case of the Acta Thomae Minora (above, pp. 457ff.) - cannot for the present be determined.

In relation to the Greek Martyrium, the expansion of these Acts comes most clearly to light in the appended Passio (text in A. Smith Lewis, op. cit. 91-94; 110-112 and E.A. Wallis Budge, op. cit. 114-118; 109-114). In agreement with the Greek text the apostle does indeed, according to our present Acts, suffer the punishment by fire decreed by king Fulbanos, but he does not die thereby; he travels further to Parthia, and ends his life with a martyr's death by beheading under king Festus.

A Coptic fragment of this Passio (Cod. Br. Mus. Or. 3581 B [12]) has become known through W.E. Crum's contribution (*Catalogue of the Coptic Manuscripts in the British Museum*, London 1905, 130-131, No. 297). Despite its brevity and the inevitable textual variants, this fragment admits of no doubt whatever as to its belonging to the present Passio. It is however interesting to observe that the Coptic text begins with a pericope about the division of the world among the apostles which does not occur in the Arabic and Ethiopic texts of the Passio and is distinct from that found within the Acts (see above, p. 460). This fact could confirm Lipsius' view (op. cit. 128-132) about the secondary character of the compilation in the Acta Matthaei in Kahenat. A similar example has already been identified in the Prochorus Acts with regard to the μετάστασις of John (see above, pp. 433f.).

Whether the still unpublished Passio Matthaei contained in the Coptic codex 635 [fol. 14^{v2}-15^{r12}] in the Pierpont Morgan Library in New York (cf. F. Morard, *Revue de Théologie et de Philosophie* 113, 1981, 411) belongs in this context has still to be investigated.

9.1 Martyrium Marci

The missionary activity of the Evangelist Mark in Egypt - especially in Alexandria - rests upon a very old tradition, of which inter alia the Church History of Eusebius (II.16) at the beginning of the 4th century bears witness. There is no doubt at all that the document underlying our present Μαρτύριον τοῦ ἁγίου ἀποστόλου καὶ εὐαγγελιστοῦ Μάρκου (BHG II, 1035, 1036) links up with this tradition - it is significant in this connection that the series of Mark's disciples named in this document [Anianus, Milaeus, Sabinus, Cerdo] largely agrees with the list adduced by Eusebius of Mark's successors in the bishop's chair at Alexandria (HE II 24; III 14, 21; IV 1, 4) - although only later witnesses can be brought forward for the existence of the text transmitted. The oldest of them comes from Paulinus of Nola (353-431), who in his Carmen XIX, 84-86 (ed. W. Hartel, CSEL 30, Vienna 1894, 21) refers to Mark's conflict with the cult of Sarapis in Alexandria: this cult plays an essential role in our present Martyrium (cc. 5, 9: PG 115, cols. 168A; 169B). The Passio Petri Alexandrini, which probably originated in the 6th century, contains a similar reference to the former sanctuary of Sarapis in Alexandria (τὰ Βουκόλου) in connection with Mark's death as a martyr (c. 11: text in P. Devos, *AnalBoll* 83, 1965, 171). The report about the death of the evangelist contained in the Chronikon Paschale from the beginning of the 7th century (ed. L. Dindorf, *Corpus Scriptorum Historiae Byzantinae* 4/1, Bonn 1832, 471) is with a high degree of certainty inspired by our Martyrium. Finally we may refer in this connection to the encomium contained in the Coptic papyrus fragment Amherst Morgan No.15 - also of the 7th century (text in W.E. Crum, *Theological Texts from Coptic Papyri*, Oxford 1913, 65-68) - in which there is an allusion to the healing of Anianus by Mark described in c. 3 of our Martyrium (= PG 115, col. 165A-B). For further discussion of other testimonia of later date, as well as a detailed analysis of the contents, see R.A. Lipsius, *Die apokr. Apostelgeschichten* II/2, 321-353.

Two Greek witnesses to the text of this document have been edited: one according to Codex Vatic. gr. 866 (*Acta Sanctorum*, April vol. III, Antwerp 1675, XLVI-XLVII) and another according to Codex Paris gr. 881 (PG 115, cols. 164-169). It is certain that despite their differences both witnesses go back to a common *Vorlage*, which is also to be regarded as the starting-point for the available versions. It is equally certain that the version represented by Codex Paris gr. 881, although it is accommodated in Migne among the works of Simeon Metaphrastes, is not a metaphrastic text (on this cf. A. Ehrhard, *Überlieferung und Bestand*, II, 674[143]). Among its peculiarities are the erroneous confusion of the name of Mark's disciple Anianus with Ananias (cc. 4-5: PG 115, cols. 165D-167A), the absence of the portrait of Mark inserted at the end of the text in Vatic. gr. 866 (*Acta Sanctorum*, loc. cit. XLVII-B), and the mutilation of the words found at the beginning in the same codex (XLVI-A). In both Greek versions Mark's missionary activity in Egypt, Libya, the Pentapolis and in other provinces - with the city of Alexandria as the central point - is portrayed in meagre terms. Prominent events are the friendship, formed through a miracle, between Mark and the former cobbler Anianus, and the martyr death of the evangelist, brought about by the worshippers of Sarapis.

The testimony of Paulinus of Nola adduced above gives reason to conjecture that a Latin version of this Martyrium must have come into existence shortly after the formation of the Greek original. Whether the various extant versions (cf. BHL 5276-5280) go back ultimately to this Latin *Vorlage* must remain an open question, particularly in view of the brevity of Paulinus' allusion. Among these versions the one edited in *Acta Sanctorum* (April vol. III, Antwerp 1675, 347-349) on the basis of various manuscripts deserves special notice: its wording betrays a literal translation of the Greek text, which is not always free from misunderstandings (cf. on this Lipsius, op. cit. 331, note 2).

The 7th century encomium already mentioned, contained in the papyrus fragment Amherst Morgan No.15, speaks for the age of the Coptic version. Among the pieces which have become known in the Sahidic dialect there is in the first place the parchment fragment Br. Mus. Or.3581 B (12) - cf. W.E. Crum, *Catalogue of the Coptic Manuscripts in the British Museum*, London 1905, No. 297/II, p. 131 - which contains only the initial words about the division among the apostles, and is therefore not very informative. More extensive is the fragment Br. Mus. 3581 B (13) - cf. W.E. Crum, op. cit. No. 298, pp. 131-132 - which contains the detailed description of the martyrdom in agreement with the Greek text (cc. 7-8: PG 115, 168C-D). According to Crum's statement (op. cit., note* to No. 300, p. 132) there is also in Codex 129^{14} of the National Library in Paris a fragment with the Anianus episode, narrated in cc. 4-5 of the Greek text. Still unpublished to my knowledge is a more extensive text of the Passio Marci, which is contained in the Coptic codex 635 (fol. 24^{r1}-33^{v2}) in the Pierpont Morgan Library in New York (on this cf. F. Morard, *Revue de Théologie et de Philosophie* 113, 1981, 411). In some Sahidic fragments occasionally adduced under the rubric 'Acta Marci' (cf. W. Grossouw's list, *Studia Catholica* 11, 1934-35, 35) it is predominantly a matter of pieces of encomia or homilies, which have nothing to do with our present Martyrium.

On the other hand a Bohairic text of the 13th century (Cairo, Coptic Museum Cod. No. 5-6) is very informative. It was published by H.G. Evelyn White (*The Monasteries of the Wadi 'n Natrun*, Part I, New York 1926, 46-47) and consists of several fragments,[1] which correspond roughly to cc. 1-2 and 5-6 of the Greek text (PG 115, col. 164A-B; cols. 165D-168B). In this text it is interesting that the 'Sabinus' who comes forward as Mark's disciple in the Greek and Latin witnesses appears under the name of 'Primus'. Since this name already turns up in the same capacity in Eusebius (HE IV 1, 4), and later in a form of the Ethiopic version (BHO 599 [= 'Barimus']), there is reason to conjecture that behind the Coptic textual tradition there lies a Greek *Vorlage* other than the one we know from the Greek witnesses at our disposal. This conjecture is reinforced when we consider that the agreement between the Bohairic text and the Ethiopic version mentioned extends to other readings which are not represented in the known Greek texts.

The Arabic version of the Martyrium (BHO 597) is known above all through the text published by A. Smith Lewis (*Horae Semiticae* III-IV, London 1904, 126-129; 147-151). This version reflects the Greek original with a strong affinity to the wording of Codex Vatic. gr. 886 (*Acta Sanctorum*, April vol. III, Antwerp 1675, XLVI-XLVII). Another Arabic version (BHO 598), contained in the 'History of the Patriarchs of Alexandria' of Severus ibn al-Muqaffa' (10th cent.), shows such strong signs of reworking that it is impossible to incorporate it into the history of the transmission of our present Martyrium (see the bilingual edition of B. Evetts, *Patrologia Orientalis* vol. 1, 1904, 141-148; detailed information about other editions and manuscripts of this 'History' in G. Graf, *Geschichte der christl. arabischen Literatur*, II, 301-306).

Of the Ethiopic version several texts have survived. The form BHO 599 made known through the translation by S.C. Malan (*The Conflicts of the Holy Apostles*, London 1871, 181-187) and the bilingual edition of E.A. Wallis Budge (*The Contendings of the Apostles* I-II, London 1899-1901, 257-264; 257-264) shows, as already mentioned, a fundamental agreement in all details with the Bohairic fragments published by H.G. Evelyn White, which distinguishes the Coptic textual tradition from the Greek. Hence the Arabic version mentioned above (BHO 597) is excluded as the *Vorlage* for it. Another Ethiopic version has recently been published by G. Haile (*AnalBoll* 99, 1981, 117-134) from a manuscript of the 14th century. It goes back - without an Arabic intermediary, in its editor's opinion - to a Greek *Vorlage* which must have had a great similarity to the wording of Codex Paris gr. 881 [PG 115, 164-169].

Of the Old Slavonic version the text of the great Menaea of the Metropolitan Makarios of the 16th century has been made known (ed. by the Archeografičeskaja Kommissija, *Velikie Minei Četii*, 20-30 April, Moscow 1916, cols. 958-963). This version represents a literal translation of a Greek *Vorlage* which must have been closely related with the wording of the Codex Paris gr. 881 just mentioned. Among the typical peculiarities which link these two texts are the confusion of the names Anianus and Ananias, already mentioned, and the absence of the portrait of Mark at the end of the Martyrium.

Notes

9.1 Martyrium Marci

1. A further fragment of the same origin, consisting of one leaf, was published some years later by its owner at that time, W.H.P. Hatch (*Coptic Studies in Honor of W.E. Crum*, Boston 1950, 316-317).

9.2 Acta Marci

The dryness of the 'Martyrium Marci' just discussed evidently stimulated the emergence of new 'Acts', in which other sources have been worked in alongside the latter document.

Among them is in the first place the Πράξεις καὶ θαύματα καὶ μαρτύριον τοῦ ἁγίου . . . εὐαγγελιστοῦ Μάρκου (BHG II, 1036m), which was edited for the first time after a Greek codex from the Stávronikita monastery on Mt Athos (13th cent.) by F. Halkin (*AnalBoll* 87, 1969, 346-371). What is striking is above all the verbose and rhetorical style of this extensive document, in contrast to the rather prosaic language of most later apostolic Acts. A large part of its contents (cc. 16-35; Halkin 358-371) is a long-winded paraphrase, enriched with additional teratological material, of the Martyrium already mentioned. The remains contain numerous statements about Mark's life before his mission in Egypt. Some such details - e.g. Mark as a disciple of John the Baptist (c. 5), as a Levite (c. 2), at his baptism by Peter (c. 4) and as author of the Gospel in Rome (c. 9) - are known especially through the Gospel prologues and arguments (on which see J. Regul, *Die antimarcionitischen*

Evangelienprologe, 1969, 30; 47-50) and in part go back to an ancient interpretation of specific biblical passages (e.g. Acts 4:36 and 1 Peter 5:13). The statements about Mark's relations with his mother Mary (c. 4) and with Paul and Barnabas (c. 6) derive mainly from Acts (12:12; 13:5-14), the conflict between Paul and Barnabas because of Mark there mentioned (Acts 15:37-39) being passed over in silence. F. Halkin (art. cit. 345, 354) sees a clear indication of the use of the Acta Barnabae by the author of the present document in the description of Mark's stay on the island of Pityusa (see Aa II/2. 296_{10}). A further pointer in the same direction is provided by the enigmatic statement of c. 8 about Mark's intention of going 'to the west, to the Gauls'; the counterpart to that is in c. 5 of the Acts of Barnabas (Aa II/2. $293_{25\text{-}27}$).

A similar attempt to supplement the Martyrium Marci hagiographically is the legend of Mark (BHO 596) prefaced to the above-mentioned Arabic version of the Martyrium (see above, p. 463) in the 'History of the Patriarchs of Alexandria' of Severus ibn al-Muqaffa'. The text has been published bilingually inter alia by B. Evetts (*Patrologia Orientalis* I, 1904, 134-140).

10.1 Acta Barnabae (Ps.-Marcus)

The Acts of Barnabas known as Περίοδοι καὶ μαρτύριον τοῦ ἁγίου Βαρνάβα τοῦ ἀποστόλου (BHG I, 225) do not in the first place, like most later Acts, serve purposes of edification or entertainment, but pursue an unambiguously Church-political aim: the under-pinning of the efforts of the Church of Cyprus to achieve autonomy. In the background is the conflict between the patriarchate of Antioch and the island hierarchy, brought into the open for the first time at the Council of Ephesus (431), over the authority of the Cypriote Church in the consecration of its own bishops. Although the Council declared itself against the interference of Antioch in this affair (ACO I/1.7, 118-122; Mansi IV, 1465-1470), the Cypriotes continued their efforts for independence until at the end of the 5th century they obtained from the emperor Zeno (474-475) the confirmation of their prescriptive rights (cf. on this the 'Laudatio in apost. Barnabam' of Alexander Monachus [6th cent.]: *Acta Sanctorum*, 11 June, [3]1867, 445-446; PG 87.3, cols. 4101-4104). In this debate the so-called apostolicity question was of decisive significance, and according to the contemporary conception it included not only the apostolic origin of the Church concerned, but also the possession of an 'apostle's grave' in its territory. The Acts of Barnabas were composed under the false authorship of John Mark, probably towards the end of the 5th century, as proof that in the case of Cyprus both conditions were fulfilled. The author, evidently an islander who is very well acquainted with the geography of his homeland, presupposes the Cyprus mission of Paul and Barnabas described in Acts (13:4-13), with John Mark as a helper, and reports in close association with the canonical document on the second missionary journey to the island by Barnabas, this time without Paul but with Mark (cf. Acts 15:39). The Acts are rounded off with Barnabas' death as a martyr in the island capital Salamis and the burying of his ashes - together with a copy of the Gospel of Matthew. Both John Mark's role as reporter and that of the copy of Matthew's Gospel (see cc. 15, 22, 24) are inventions of the author as a guarantee of the authenticity of the relics of the apostle Barnabas discovered centuries later in the neighbourhood of the town of Salamis (cf. the "Laudatio" of Alexander Monachus already mentioned: *Acta Sanctorum*, 11 June, [3]1867, 444-445). For a detailed examination of these Acts see R.A. Lipsius, *Die apokr. Apostelgeschichten* II/2, 270-320. There is a modern Italian translation in Erbetta II, 597-600.

The Greek text was finally edited by M. Bonnet (Aa II/2, 292-302) on the basis of six different witnesses, taking the Latin version into consideration. In this connection it is interesting to note that cc. 6-7 (= Aa II/2, $294_{4\text{-}25}$), which report on the penance which John Mark is said to have done as a result of the conflict between Paul and Barnabas which arose because of him (cf. Acts 13:13; 15:37-39), have been omitted in Codex Vatic. gr. 1667 (ed. *Acta Sanctorum*, 11 June, [3]1867, 425-429). We can observe a similar state of affairs in some witnesses of the Latin and Old Slavonic versions. This disagreement in the textual tradition of the passage mentioned is without doubt connected with the various attempts at interpretation which the conflict between Paul and Barnabas called into being in the hagiographical and apocryphal literature. Examples of this are the Greek 'Laudatio in apostolum Barnabam' of Alexander Monachus (cc. XV-XVII [22-24]: *Acta Sanctorum*, 11 June, [3]1867, 438D-F) and the Coptic encomium on Mark, of which some fragments have been published according to Codex Borgianus 274 by I. Guidi (*Atti della R. Accademia dei Lincei/ Rendiconti*, Serie V/2, Rome 1893, 517-521). On other Coptic codices with a similar content to Borgianus 274 (= Br. Mus. Or. 3581 B (15) and Paris Bibl. Nat. 129[14] fol. 102) see W.E. Crum, *Catalogue of the Coptic Manuscripts in the British Museum*, London 1905, No. 300, p. 132.

Several witnesses of the Latin version of the Acts of Barnabas are known. In these our present legend may appear either as an independent document (BHL I, 983) or as part of a compilation along with other reports about Barnabas' missionary activity in Rome and Milan (BHL I, 985). It is a common mark of all the Latin witnesses that they are strongly excerpted, and particularly in the last section show traces of redaction which presuppose the 'Laudatio' of Alexander Monachus (see above, p. 465), which came into being in the 6th century. For further information cf. Lipsius, op. cit. II/2, 277-280, 316-320.

One witness of the Old Slavonic version from the 15th century (Codex No. 164 of the library of the Rumanian Academy of Sciences in Bucharest) has been published by E. Kalusnjackij (*Sbornik Otdelenija Russkago Jazyka i Slovesnosti Imp. Akademii Nauk* vol. 83/2, St Petersburg 1907, 50-57). The kinship of the version there represented with that of Codex Vatic gr. 1667 is shown inter alia by the fact that both witnesses have omitted the cc. 6-7 mentioned above (= Aa II/2, $294_{4\text{-}25}$). On further Slavonic manuscripts see A. de Santos Otero, *Überlieferung* I, 136-137 and Chr. Hannick, *Maximos Holobolos in der kirchenslavischen homiletischen Literatur*, Vienna 1981, 221.

10.2 Acta Bartholomaei et Barnabae

The Περίοδοι καὶ μαρτύριον τῶν ἁγίων ἀποστόλων Βαρθολομαίου καὶ Βαρνάβα (BHG III, 2057), published by B. Latysev (*Menologii anonymi byzantini saeculi X quae supersunt*, II, Petropoli 1912, 34-40), are not apostolic Acts in the usual sense but two artificially combined encomia in which various traditions about Bartholomew (pp. 34-35) and Barnabas (pp. 36-40) have been used. The longer encomium on Barnabas is very strongly influenced by the 'Laudatio in apostolum Barnabam' of Alexander Monachus (BHG I, 226), mentioned in the preceding section.

11.1 Passio Lucae

There are numerous extant encomia on Luke which make use of reports about the evangelist, chiefly from canonical sources. Although one of them bears the title Περίοδοι καὶ τελείωσις (cf. text by Ph. Meyer, *Jahrbücher f. protest. Theologie* 16, 1890, 423-434), there is no indication at all that there ever was an 'Acts of Luke' in the proper sense of the term. That no Passio Lucae is known from Greek and Latin sources is probably connected with the view, widespread in these linguistic areas, that Luke the evangelist died a natural death (cf. on this R.A. Lipsius, *Die apokr. Apostelgeschichten* II/2, 354-371 and J. Regul, *Die antimarcionitischen Evangelienprologe*, 1969, 15-16; 45-47; 197-202).

Our present Passio, hitherto known only from oriental sources (BHO 567-569), stands in opposition to this view. The scene of the action is Rome and the neighbouring coastal region, which is not more precisely described. Luke is accused of magic, among other things, and suffers martyrdom under the emperor Nero. The author evidently knows the Martyrium Petri and the Martyrium Pauli - separate from one another, according to the old oriental tradition - and builds his narrative in association with these legends. The inclusion of Titus as Luke's fellow-disciple and companion probably goes back to the opening words of the Martyrium Pauli (Aa I, $105_{2\text{-}3}$). The author of this Passio also appears to have had before his eyes several details from c. 1 of the Acta Pilati (e.g. the name of the High Priest, the bowing of the standards before Jesus).

Whether the origin of this legend is ultimately to be sought in the Coptic area, as Lipsius thought, appears doubtful, since a witness from the 10th century to the text of the Syriac version has become known through F. Nau's contribution (*Revue de l'Orient chrétien* 3, 1898, 39-42; 151-167).

The known Coptic witnesses to the text - without exception Bohairic - fall into two different versions. The first of them, extant in full, is represented by the Codex Vatic. 68, fol. 16-21 (= LXI = Mus. Borg. Copt. 118 [J.VII, 13]), the original text of which was first published with an Italian translation by G. Balestri (*Bessarione*, Ser. 2/vol. 8, 1905, 128-140). The same text, this time provided with a Latin translation, was printed by I. Balestri and H. Hyvernat as part of the Acta Martyrum (C.S.C.O. Script. coptici vol. VI, 1924 [=1953], 1-8; vol. XV, 1950, 1-6). That this version is a revision of the original Passio is shown inter alia by the numerous abbreviations made to the text.

More valuable from a text-critical point of view is the second Bohairic version, of which only two fragments from the 13th century are known. These are the Codex Cairo Coptic Mus. No. 5-6 (ed. H.G. Evelyn White, *The Monasteries of the Wadi 'n Natrun*, Part I, New York 1926, 47-50) and a leaf belonging to the same codex (ed. S. Gaselee, JTS 19, 1908, 52-53) which is preserved in Cambridge (Univ. Libr. Add. 1886.3). The basic agreement of the known Arabic and Ethiopic witnesses with the wording of the fragments named suggests the conjecture that this Bohairic version must have been very closely related to the Coptic *Vorlage* from which the Arabic version was produced.

Apart from the Coptic Synaxary handed down in Arabic (ed. R. Basset, *Patrologia Orientalis* I/3, 358-360; [144]-[146]), which contains a short summary of our present legend, the Arabic version of the Passio is extant complete in Codex Sinait. Arab. 539 (ed. A. Smith Lewis, *Horae Semiticae* III-IV, London 1904, 130-133; 152-156). The Ethiopic counterpart to it has been made known through the English translation by S.C. Malan (*The Conflicts of the Holy Apostles*, London 1871, 60-66) and the bilingual edition of E.A. Wallis Budge (*The Contendings of the Apostles* I-II, London 1899-1901, 119-121; 115-117).

12.1 Acta Philippi

Among the later apostolic Acts the Πράξεις τοῦ ἁγίου καὶ πανευφήμου ἀποστόλου Φιλίππου (BHG II, 1516-1526) occupy a special place because of their age, their encratite character, their symbol-laden content, and not least the role which the apostle Philip played in heterodox works of early Christian literature.

In the Greek text form handed down - to the materials published by M. Bonnet (Aa II/2. 1-98) after the preliminary work of C. Tischendorf and P Batiffol there are still to be added the sections recently discovered by B. Bouvier and F. Bovon and not yet published, according to the codices Xenophontos 32[1] and Athens, Bibl. Nat. 346 - the Acta Philippi are a compilation of fifteen different acts, of which the tenth and part of the eleventh are still missing. The present arrangement of the document recalls very strongly that of the ancient Acts of Thomas (Aa II/2, 99-288) and is probably to be regarded as the work of a compiler who has strung together very diverse and often unconnected acts of Philip, and to some extent edited them himself. The lack of any internal structure and the numerous chronological and geographical absurdities which result from that - particularly in the route of Philip's travels - are indeed manifest even after the latest discoveries, but with this kind of literature and in view of the state of the textual tradition they ought not to be overestimated, as Zahn did in his time (*Forschungen zur Geschichte des ntl. Kanons* VI, 1900, 18-24).

What a problematic picture the Acts of Philip present in their extant form is shown, for example, by the fact that for the fifteenth act (cc. 107-148; Aa II/2. 41-90), in which the martyrdom is described, there are numerous witnesses to the text and several ancient versions, whereas the remaining acts are attested only by one or at best two manuscripts in each case (cf. the exposition by F. Bovon/B. Bouvier in F. Bovon et al., *Les actes apocryphes des apôtres*, Geneva 1981, 302-303). To this disparity we may add the splintering of the witnesses so far known into divergent redactions with considerable differences, three for the fifteenth act (on this cf. J. Flamion in *Mélanges d'histoire offerts à Charles Moeller* [Recueil de travaux publ. par les membres de l'Université de Louvain, fasc. 40], Louvain-Paris 1914, 215-225) and two - as many as the witnesses to the text - for acts 1 and 3-8.

Despite the deficiency in the textual tradition just shown, two elements can be identified in the present Acts which give to the extant narrative material a certain cohesion. One of them is the central figure in the legend, Philip. He appears everywhere as an apostle, but at the same time is endowed with attributes which pertain both to the apostle in the four Gospels and also to the deacon and evangelist in Acts (Acts 6:5; 8:5-13, 26-40; 21:8-9). This confusion of persons is not an original feature in the Acts of Philip (cf. on this the discussions of H.O. Stölten, *Jahrbücher für prot. Theologie* 17, 1891, 149-160 and K. Smyth, *Irish Ecclesiastical Record* 97, 1962, 288-295), and occurs substantially more often in the first seven acts - catchwords 'land of the Candaces', 'Azotus' - than in the remaining acts.

The second connective element is the encratite character of the material handed down. It is not only a question of a general tendency in the direction of an emphasis on sexual continence, which can easily be observed here, exactly as in the AJ, AA, ATh and APt, but of the outward characteristics of an encratite sect, the traces of which are clearly visible, again particularly in the first seven acts. Such features relate to clothing, names, customs in eating and drinking and in assemblies, abstinence from marriage and the vagrant way of life of the persons involved, and show a bewildering similarity with the phenomena of an encratite movement in Asia Minor which was condemned at the Council of Gangra in 342 (Mansi II, 1097-1100), as E. Peterson impressively showed (ZNW 31, 1932, 97-111). Epiphanius evidently had the same movement in mind when between 374 and 377 he wrote his Panarion, and there (Haer. 47; Holl II, 215-219) located the 'Encratites' above all in Phrygia. In the same passage a special fondness for apocryphal apostolic Acts - especially the AA, AJ and ATh - is attested for the adherents of this sect (for further details see G. Blond, art. 'Encratisme', in *Dictionnaire de Spiritualité* IV/1, 1960, cols. 628-642).

From these observations we may conclude with a high degree of probability that the version of the Acta Philippi which has come down to us originated in encratite circles in Asia Minor somewhere about the middle of the 4th century. Since this version is however an artificial conglomeration of very diverse and sometimes contradictory material, the question of the authorship and origin of individual parts remains open.

The report included at the beginning of the eighth act, about the division of the world among the apostles and the sending of Philip together with Bartholomew and Mariamne to the 'city of the serpent', forms a clear break after the preceding first seven acts, and signals the beginning of the 'Acta Philippi in Hierapolis' with the appended martyrdom (cc. 94-148: Aa II/2, 36-90). This part is without doubt the most important - in terms of volume also - and oldest section of the Acta Philippi, and is conspicuous both for its stylistic unity and also for its depth of thought - in contrast to the episodes of the first seven acts, which are often intermixed without continuity, full of adventures and poor in ideas.

The scene of the action here is the Phrygian town of Hierapolis, which is given the nickname 'Ophioryme' (= the town which the serpent protects), with its religio-historical and geographical background. The 'serpent' referred to here is no other than the embodiment of the goddess Cybele, whose cult originated in Phrygia and had a long tradition in Hierapolis (cf. the articles 'Hierapolis' and 'Ophioryme' in Pauly-Wissowa VIII/2, 1913, cols. 1404-1405; XVIII/1, 1939, col. 647). In this connection it is worthy of note that in Philip legends in other languages also, which show no kind of relation with our Greek text, the motif of the 'serpent' or dragon plays a central role.

The associations of the apostle Philip with the town of Hierapolis are rooted in a very ancient tradition, which is already attested at the end of the 1st century by the witness of Papias of Hierapolis and at the end of the 2nd by that of Polycrates of Ephesus (cf. Eusebius, HE III 39.8; III 31.3 and V 24.2). Since in both witnesses there is reference to the 'daughters' of Philip, and he is described in the same breath as the 'apostle', it is clear that the confusion of persons mentioned above and taken over by the Acts of Philip was already current in this period (cf. Th. Zahn, *Forschungen zur Geschichte des ntl. Kanons* VI, 1900, 158-175).

The fact that not all the elements of this old tradition found their way into the 'Acta Philippi in Hierapolis' - e.g. there is not a word about Philip's daughters, and instead the apostle is given his 'sister' Mariamne as a companion - and that (against this tradition) a martyrdom embellished with rich symbolism and profound trains of thought was added already signals the relationship of our present Acts to the five older Acts of the Manichean corpus, although we cannot always demonstrate a direct dependence upon them.

The famous logion in c. 140 (Aa II/2, $74_{8\text{-}9}$) appears for example in this or a similar form not only in the Acts of Peter (Actus Vercellenses 38: Aa I, $95_{10\text{-}13}$), which is often cited as the source for it, but also in the Coptic Gospel of Thomas (log. 22; cf. vol. 1, p. 120 and p. 213), in the Acts of Thomas (c. 147: Aa II/2, $256_{12\text{-}15}$), in Julius Cassianus (Clem. Alex. Strom. III 13.92) etc., and could without more ado be interpreted according to Valentinian categories (cf. A. Orbe, *Cristología gnóstica* II, Madrid 1976, 548-549).

The episode of Peter's crippled daughter (c. 142: Aa II/2, $81_{3\text{-}7,\ 11\text{-}14}$), which is close to encratite ideology, does indeed probably derive from the Acts of Peter (cf. the discussion of W. Schneemelcher above, pp. 278f.), but is attested only in two of the three extant redactions of this passage. The crucifixion of Philip and his address on the cross (c. 124ff.: Aa II/2, 52ff.) also offer certain analogies to the corresponding episode in the APt (Actus Vercellenses 37ff.: Aa I, 91ff.), but there are serious differences between the two passages.

We might adduce the episode of the 'communicating animals', recently discovered in Codex Xenophontos 32 (act 12; cf. F. Bovon/B. Bouvier in F. Bovon et al., op. cit. 303), as a parallel to the baptised lion of the Acts of Paul (on this cf. W. Schneemelcher in *Mullus*, FS Th. Klauser, 1964, 316-326). Moreover, from act 8 of our present Πράξεις 'Mariamne', who is assigned to the apostle as sister and companion, plays a role similar to that of Thecla at the side of Paul.

The dialogue between Mariamne and Nicanora, in which the two women are described as 'twin sisters, daughters of the same mother' (c. 115: Aa II/2, 45_{15}-46_{13}), could in A. Orbe's opinion (op. cit. vol. I, 546-547; vol. II, 440-441) contain an esoteric interpretation of the Heilsgeschichte according to the Valentinian myth with clear analogies to the Acts of Thomas (c. 50: Aa II/2. 116ff.). The waiting period of forty days before entry into Paradise, which Philip is given as a punishment for his impatience (c. 137; 147-148: Aa II/2. 69; 88-89), is strongly reminiscent of the likewise forty days during which Adam too according to the myth of the Ophites is detained outside of Paradise (Anonymous treatise in Nag Hammadi Codex II, 163.3-14; 25-30 [Böhlig; = 115.3-14 Layton, cf. NHLE[3] 182]; cf. A. Orbe, op. cit. vol. I, 457-458; vol. II, 373-374, 529).

In this connection the wrathful character (ὀργίλος) which is ascribed to Philip in the present Acts is striking (c. 95: Aa II/2, 37_6), whereas the Manichean Psalm-book extols 'his patience when he was in the land of the man-eaters' (ed. C.R.C. Allberry, Part II, 1938, 192_{10}). This contradiction evidently reflects different Philip traditions, and to my mind cannot be resolved by referring to the second act (c. 22: Aa II/2, 11_{24}), in which a change of character is attributed to Philip (υἱὸς ποτὲ βροντῆς, νῦν δὲ πρᾳότητος). This passage is rather to be understood as a gloss inserted by the redactor of the first seven acts (not conversant with the Bible) in order to explain the enigmatic statement of the Martyrium about Philip's 'wrathful character'. How awkwardly he went about it is shown by the predicate 'son of thunder' (Mk. 3:17) wrongly conferred on Philip in this connection, completely in opposition to the Martyrium (cf. c. 129: Aa II/2, $58_{9,20,28}$), in which this designation is correctly addressed to the apostle John.

The presence of John during the martyrdom (cf. cc. 129ff.), apart from its possible roots in local traditions of Asia Minor, takes on a new light through the discovery of the - still unpublished - eleventh act in the Codex Xenophontos 32, since this fragment contains a reworking of the gnostic hymn in the Acts of John (cc. 94-96; cf. E. Junod and J.-D. Kaestli, *L'histoire des actes apocryphes des apôtres du IIIe au IXe siècle*, Geneva 1982, 30).

These references do not indeed provide any justification for the old theory of Lipsius (*Die apokr. Apostelgeschichten* II/2, 1-53; Ergänzungsband 64-73) about the gnostic origin of the Acts of Philip, but they do show that the author of the 'Acta Philippi in Hierapolis' (acts 8-15) readily availed himself of an encratite and gnostic symbolism which was current during the 3rd century both in the five apostolic Acts of the Manichean corpus and also outside this sphere of literature. The encratite ideology which comes to light in this part of the Acta Philippi is of a different quality from that of which the external marks are particularly clearly visible in the first seven acts, as is shown for example by the episode, pregnant with symbolism, of the sprouting at Philip's cross of a vine, from which wine for the celebration of the eucharist is to be obtained (c. 143; Aa II/2. 84_{2-5}). This episode is incompatible with the views of the encratites of the 4th century, which have left their traces in the section mentioned (cf. e.g. c. 3: Aa II/2. 2_{27-28}).

The interpretation thus far advanced contradicts the theory of E. Peterson (*Oriens Christianus* 20, 1932, 172-179), who held acts 8-15 to be a 'Messalian' revision of the original Acta Philippi. The starting-point for Peterson's argument was the contrast already mentioned, between the episodes of the first seven acts, poor in ideas and loosely strung together, and the coherent narrative of the 'Acta Philippi in Hierapolis' with its ideological significance and the symbol-laden martyrdom. Even after the discovery of the new manuscript material, in which more speculative matter comes to light, particularly of a ritual nature, this contrast remains essentially unaffected, and can be adequately explained by the arguments above. On the other hand, one can scarcely detect any typically 'Messalian' element in the section referred to, if we disregard abstract concepts, images and turns of phrase which can be found everywhere in monastic literary circles in this period. The example adduced by Peterson to underpin his theory (*Theologische Quartalschrift* 113, 1932, 289-298), namely the Armenian Synaxary, which offers a very sober adaptation of the Greek

Martyrium, is a particularly weak argument in this connection, for as is well known the Synaxaries as a rule presuppose the ancient Acts and are merely short biographical extracts from them for liturgical purposes, mostly without any kind of ideological ballast.

The motif of the 'storm at sea' is one of the most familiar topoi of the apocryphal apostolic Acts, and appears also - in a more or less unnatural context - in the third act of the present Acta Philippi (cc. 33-36: Aa II/2. 16_{31}-17_{36}). Despite the variants which the newly discovered version of Codex Xenophontos 32 offers for this episode (cf. F. Bovon and B. Bouvier, in F. Bovon et al., op. cit. 302), this description of the storm conforms with the model of the Synoptic Gospels (Mt. 8:23-27; Mk. 4:35-40), whereas a similar episode in the Acts of Peter (Actus Vercell. 5: Aa I, 49_{20}-51_{13}) is inspired by chapters 1-2 of the book of Jonah (cf. on this J. Rougé, *Nuovo Didaskaleion* 12, 1962, 55-69).

The present version of the Acta Philippi contains numerous formulae of address or prayer, which are often uttered in connection with the conversion of some person (e.g. cc. 61 and 117: Aa II/2, 25_{22-33}, 47_{9-17}). It is sometimes a question of monologues or prayers the literary structure of which is known from various works of Jewish-hellenistic missionary literature, such as 'Joseph and Asenath' (cf. K. Berger, *Kairos* 17, 1975, 232-248), although we cannot deduce from this any literary dependence of the Acta Philippi upon such works.

In contrast to the first seven acts, of which so far no ancient translation has become known, the 'Acta Philippi in Hierapolis' are extant - complete or in extracts - in several ancient versions, which in general require further investigation. An Armenian text (BHO 980-981) has been edited by K. Tsherakhian (*Thesaurus litterarum armeniarum* III, Venetiis 1904, 300-302). Reference has been made above to a study by E. Peterson on the Armenian Synaxary. A text of the Georgian version according to Codex H 341 of the Manuscript Institute of the Academy of Sciences in Tiflis (11th cent.) has been edited by C. K'urc'ikidze ([Les versions géorgiennes des actes apocryphes des apôtres], Tiflis 1959, 3-13), and may be related to that of the Armenian version just mentioned (on this cf. G. Garitte, *Le Muséon* 74, 1961, 392 No. 11). Finally the document is preserved by way of extracts in numerous Old Slavonic witnesses (cf. A. de Santos Otero, *Überlieferung* I, 124-129), of which one has been edited by the Archeografičeskaja Kommissija (*Velikie Minei Četii*, 13-15 Nov., St Petersburg 1899, cols. 1996-2002) and one by I. Franko (*Apokrify i legendy* III, L'vov 1902, 174-179).

Astonishingly, no ancient Latin version of the Acta Philippi, or part of it, has yet become known. The theory of the Latin origin of our present Greek text, advanced by A. Kurfess (ZNW 44, 1952/53, 145-151) on the basis of purely stylistic points of view, is indeed absolutely untenable in the light of the arguments above, but many indications tell in favour of the view that the Acts of Philip - like the five older Acts of the Manichean corpus - had become known relatively early in the West. The Decretum Gelasianum of the 6th century expressly mentions *actus nomine Philippi apostoli* (ed. E. von Dobschütz, TU 38/4, 49-50), and is accordingly one of the oldest external witnesses so far known for the existence of the Acta Philippi. Another witness from the 7th century, which comes from Spain, is not to be rejected out of hand. This is a representation in relief of the apostle Philip, which is to be found on the east side of a capital in the West Gothic church of San Pedro de la Nave (Zamora). The figure is marked by the inscription *SCS Filippus apostolus* and wears on his head a crown adorned with precious stones. Since of the Philip legends so far known only the Martyrium contained in our present Greek Acts (c. 144: Aa II/2. 85_4-86_2), in all its versions, refers to a 'crown of victory', for which Philip asks in his solemn prayer immediately before his death, it is to be assumed that this portrayal of Philip is inspired by a Latin translation of our Acts (cf. on this H. Schlunk and Th. Hauschild, 'Die Denkmäler der frühchristlichen und westgotischen Zeit': *Hispania Antiqua* I, Mainz 1978, 226, plate 137c).

A detailed analysis of the content of this apocryphon on the basis of the Greek text so far published is offered - after R.A. Lipsius (op. cit. and contribution in *Jahrbücher für prot. Theologie* 17, 1891, 459-473) - by James (439-450) and Moraldi (II, 1625-1631). There is a complete Italian translation in Erbetta (II, 457-485). For further details on the structure of the Greek Acts of Philip and their environment cf. the comprehensive study of F. Bovon ('Les Actes de Philippe', ANRW II.25.6, 1988, 4431-4527), the proofs of which were kindly made available to me by W. Schneemelcher after the completion of the present study.

The Vita Philippi handed down as book 10 of the ps.-Abdias collection (BHL II, 6814-6817), despite occasional points of contact with the motif of the 'dragon' already mentioned, shows no textual relationship of any kind with the Greek Acts of Philip. The traditions about Philip which are used in this legend come for the most part from canonical sources and from Eusebius' Church History. The Latin text in its various forms has been edited several times (precise details at the point mentioned in BHL), and has recently been translated into Italian by M. Erbetta (op. cit. 489-490) and L. Moraldi (op. cit. 1604-1606). This Latin Vita is one of the chief sources for the Irish Passio Philippi, found in a compilation from the beginning of the 15th century (ed. R. Atkinson, *The Passions and the Homilies from Leabhar Breac*, Dublin 1887, 110-113, 356-358). Further details about the Irish Philip legends in M. McNamara, *The Apocrypha in the Irish Church*, Dublin 1975, 113-118.

Notes

12.1 Acta Philippi

1. Cf. A. Ehrhard, *Überlieferung und Bestand* (TU 50-52) III/1, 971[3].

12.2 Historia Philippi (syriaca)

A Syriac legend has come down to us as the 'wonderful story of Philip' (BHO 972). It was edited by W. Wright (*Apocryphal Acts of the Apostles* I-II, London 1871, 74-79, 69-72) from a manuscript of the Royal Asiatic Society in London of the year 1569. Although this document also shows older witnesses to its text (cf. on this A. Baumstark, *Geschichte der syrischen Literatur* 1922, 68, note 9) everything speaks for the view that we have here a later Philip legend, which has only isolated points of contact with the Greek Acta Philippi and other ancient apostolic Acts.

Philip's missionary goal is specified by the enigmatic - not to say nonsensical - designation 'city of Carthagena, which lies in Azotus'. Apart from the probable confusion of the word 'Carthagena' for 'Carthage', which is possibly to be charged to some copyist, this description of the place recalls a similar geographical formation 'land of the Candace/Azotus', which occurs in the Greek Acts of Philip (c. 33: Aa II/2, 16_{31-34}) and evidently links up with the statements of Acts 8:27, 40, with little knowledge of the facts. In fact the geographical descriptions mentioned are simply the necessary frame for the sea adventure which is attached in both apocrypha, and takes a different course in each. In the Greek Acts (c. 33: Aa II/2, 16_{31}-17_{32}) it is a question of the episode of the storm, already mentioned, the significance of which is confined to its slavish imitation of the canonical model. In the Syriac Historia Philippi on the other hand - as in the Acts of Peter (Actus Vercell. 5: Aa I, 49_{20}-51_{13} - it is a case of a miraculous triumph over a calm during Philip's voyage.

More important than this detail is the fact that this episode, because of the events described in it, prepares the way for the great diatribe against the Jews, which forms the real subject of this legend. Although isolated motifs like those already mentioned, and others which could be added (such as the picture of the Jew Ananias, who remains hanging head downwards from the ship's sail until at Philip's instigation he confesses Jesus, or the obedient and talking oxen and dolphins, etc.), recall older apostolic Acts, it is clear that the Syriac 'story of Philip' is both stylistically and chronologically far removed from this genre of literature, because of its completely polemical character and because of the rhetorical erudition displayed in this connection.

12.3 Acta Philippi et Petri (coptica)

Like the Syriac Historia Philippi, the Coptic Acts of Philip presuppose the Greek Acta Philippi and at the same time show some points of contact with them. Here however the typical Coptic method of redaction emerges very clearly, namely to adapt the old Greek scheme to the Egyptian situation and fill it with new and autochthonous narrative material.

The Acta Philippi in Hierapolis (Aa II/2, 36-90) - without their ideological loading - are clearly the starting-point for this legend. This is already indicated by the scene of the action, which is described in all the Coptic witnesses as 'Fricia' (= Phrygia). That in the later Arabic and Ethiopic offshoots this has become 'Africa' is easily explained, and needs no further discussion. The city of Hierapolis is not mentioned by name in this legend, but the incidents described in connection with the nature of the land - earthquakes, the inhabitants taking refuge in natural caves, etc. - agree with the corresponding scene of action in the Greek Acts, and find their explanation in the volcanic region around Hierapolis, which was visited by earthquakes from ancient times.

In contrast to its Greek precursor and in agreement with other Coptic re-workings - e.g. Acta Bartholomaei coptica (above, pp. 451f.), Acta Thomae minora (above, pp. 457f.), Acta Matthaei in Kahenat (above, pp. 460f.) - Philip here receives the apostle Peter as his companion. In place of the 'serpent' in the Greek Acts, the embodiment of the goddess Cybele, the 'golden sparrow-hawk' appears in the Coptic witnesses, evidently in association with Egyptian mythology. The address by one who just before had been possessed, from a pillar which stands at the city gate and readily allows itself to be raised or lowered or transposed at the apostle's command, presents a certain similarity with the debate between Peter and Simon Magus (Martyrium Petri 3: Aa I, $82_{15\text{-}27}$), and at the same time bears unmistakably Egyptian features which recall the Coptic version of the Apophthegmata Patrum (= Symeon Stylites) and the Coptic Acta Pauli et Andreae (above, p. 449). For further parallels to the last-named Acts, see O. von Lemm, *Bulletin de l'Académie Impériale des Sciences de St.-Pétersbourg* NS I (XXXIII), 1890, 550-557.

As is often the case in Coptic apostolic Acts, this legend falls into two parts: 'Praedicatio' and 'Martyrium'. The Martyrium - exactly like the Praedicatio - presupposes the Acta Philippi in Hierapolis, as is shown by the manner of Philip's death and the symbolism of the apostle's outpoured blood, but otherwise it exhibits few features in common with the Greek legend.

Various fragments have survived of the Coptic original of this document, and together they cover a substantial part of the original form. A Sahidic fragment, according to Codex Borgianus 126 (fol. 72-76), was published first by I. Guidi (*Rendiconti della R. Accademia dei Lincei*, Serie IV vol. IV/2, Rome 1887, 20-23) and translated into Italian (*Giornale della Società Asiatica Italiana* 2, 1888, 27-29). Further smaller fragments - British Mus. Or. 3581 B 3, 7, 24 - were edited by W.E. Crum (*Catalogue of the Coptic Mss. in the British Museum*, London 1905, No. 288 pp. 126-127; No. 292 p. 128; No. 310 pp. 137-138). There are other Coptic fragments also in Codex 129^{18} (fol. 102-102, 160^{v}) of the National Library in Paris and in Codex 635 (fol. 2^{v}-4^{r}) of the Pierpont Morgan Library in New York (on these cf. W.E. Crum, op. cit. No. 288 p. 126 and F. Morard, *Revue de Théologie et de Philosophie* 113, 1981, 408, 411).

An extensive Fayyumic fragment, according to the badly damaged Codex Tischendorfianus VI in the present-day Saltykov-Ščedrin Library in Leningrad, was edited by O. von Lemm (op. cit. 521-549) parallel to the Codex Borgianus 126 already mentioned, with a German translation. Finally the Bohairic fragments, published with an English translation by H.G. Evelyn White according to Cod. No. 5-6 of the Coptic Museum in Cairo (*The Monasteries of the Wadi 'n Natrun*, Part I, New York 1926, 38-43), are important as a connecting link between the Coptic Vorlage and the Arabic version.

In contrast to the fragmentary state of the Coptic witnesses so far mentioned, the Arabic (ed. A. Smith Lewis, *Horae Semiticae* III-IV, London 1904, 51-58; 60-68) and Ethiopic versions (ed. E.A. Wallis Budge, *The Contendings of the Apostles* I-II, London 1899-1901, 126-139; 122-136 [BHO 978; 983]) offer a complete text of the Acta Philippi et Petri. The starting-point for both versions is very probably to be sought in a Bohairic *Vorlage*. In this case we cannot demonstrate any dependence of the Ethiopic version upon the Arabic on the basis of the known editions of the text. At any rate the Ethiopic text in places offers more original features than the Arabic. Among these is for example the reproduction of the idol described in the Coptic fragments as a golden sparrow-hawk: the Ethiopic version still refers to an 'eagle', whereas the Arabic text mentions merely an idol 'in human form' (cf. A. Smith Lewis, op. cit. III, p. XVII). The scene of the Martyrium given as 'Martagena' (= Carthagena) is completely foreign to the Coptic and Ethiopic tradition of this legend. This suggests the conjecture that here we have to do with an interpolation from the Historia Philippi syriaca (above, p. 473). The conjecture is confirmed when we reflect that the Arabic manuscript used by A. Smith Lewis comes from the Dair-as-Suryan, a monastery in the Wadi Natrun in Egypt, from which a large number of Syriac manuscripts was brought to the British Museum in the middle of the 19th century. Whether other Arabic witnesses (cf. for these G. Graf, *Geschichte der christl. arabischen Literatur* I, 257, 264) reflect a more original version from which the present Ethiopic version could have originated has still to be investigated.

13.1 Acta Iacobi Zebedaei (coptica)

Although the name of John's brother James certainly appears to have played a role in certain gnostic circles as that of a conveyor of mysteries, there are no Acta Iacobi of any kind to which we can ascribe a significant age. An explanation for this is very probably to be found in the apostle's early martyr death under Herod Agrippa I in A.D. 44 (cf. Acts 12:1-2), hence at a time when the legend of the division of the world among the apostles had not yet come into being. The brief account in Acts about the beheading of James was indeed the subject of an expansion (ἱστορία) at an early date - cf. Clem. Alex. Hypotyp. book VII according to Eusebius, HE II 9.2-3 - but our present Acts of James came into being substantially later.[1]

The Coptic Acta Iacobi are handed down in fragments in several Sahidic pieces, and complete in Arabic and Ethiopic translations. They consist - like the other apostolic Acts of Egyptian origin - of two parts: the 'Praedicatio' and the 'Martyrium'. The Praedicatio is a freely invented and stereotyped narrative, in which the characteristics typical for the Coptic corpus of Acts repeatedly appear (e.g. the presence of Peter, the destruction of the heathen idols, reports of miracles, the charge of magic). The Martyrium makes the apostle evangelise 'the twelve tribes of Israel scattered in all the world', which beyond doubt goes back to a confusion with James the Lord's brother (James 1:1). Such absurdities, not uncommon in the Coptic version, are frankly multiplied in the extant Arabic and Ethiopic translations, which for example make James preach 'in the towns of India' (instead of 'Lydia'), and set the emperor Nero, quite anachronistically, alongside Herod Agrippa I.

The most important witnesses to the Coptic version are contained in the Codd. Borgiani 126 and 127 in Rome (BHO 415-416, 420), and were edited (*Rendiconti della R. Accademia dei Lincei*, Serie IV vol. III/1, Rome 1887, 54-60) and translated into Italian (*Giornale della Società Asiatica Italiana* 2, 1888, 15-20) by I. Guidi. The codices named contain two different recensions of the Praedicatio in a fragmentary condition. The section of the Praedicatio missing in Borgianus 127 is very probably to be found in Codex Paris BN 129[18], 139 (cf. F. Morard, *Revue de Théologie et de Philosophie* 113, 1981, 408). The Martyrium is preserved complete in Codex Borgianus 127 (fol. 4^v-5^v). The Vienna parchment leaf K 361 (No. 196a-b according to the diplomatic edition by C. Wessely, *Studien zur Paläographie und Papyruskunde* XIV, 1914, 7-8) contains a corresponding text - down to the last missing lines.

A further witness to the text of the Martyrium is contained in the Coptic codex 635 (fol. 1^{r1}-2^{r2}) in the Pierpont Morgan Library in New York (cf. F. Morard, art. cit. 411). Finally, a small fragment with the end of this text (Or. 3581 B [7]) is preserved in the British Museum (cf. W.E. Crum, *Catalogue of the Coptic Mss in the Br. Mus.*, London 1905, No. 292 p. 128).

The Arabic version of the Acta Iacobi was bilingually edited by A. Smith Lewis (*Horae Semiticae* III-IV, London 1904, 26-29, 30-36) according to a manuscript from the Dair-as-Suryan (14th cent.). The Ethiopic version published by S.C. Malan (*The Conflicts of the Holy Apostles*, London 1871, 172-181) and E.A. Wallis Budge (*The Contendings of the Apostles* I-II, London 1899/1901, 247-256; 246-256) agrees in essentials with the Arabic text and accordingly represents a recension, expanded by a few details, of the Coptic *Vorlage* known to us.

Notes

13.1 Acta Jacobi Zebedaei

1. Beyond the *Coptic* and *Latin* Acts of James here considered [13. 1-2], there are only a few Greek texts extant which report in a comprehensive form about the apostolic activity and the martyrdom of James. Among these are in the first place the Acts published in 1902 by J. Ebersolt (BHG I, 767) - presumably end of the 8th century - and the menological notice from 1034-1041, largely dependent on them and published by F. Halkin (*Biblica* 64, 1983, 565-570). These legends, in which information deriving from canonical sources plays a key role, show few elements in common with the Acts in other languages.

13.2 Passio Iacobi Zebedaei (latina et armeniaca)

A Passio Iacobi is handed down as Book IV of the ps.-Abdias collection (BHL I, 4057), but shows no points of contact of any kind with the Coptic legends just discussed. In addition to details which appear to be inspired by the canonical Acts, and others which are completely free inventions (e.g. the narrative of the Magus Hermogenes and his demons), it contains an episode which represents an expanded reworking of the ἱστορία attested by Clement of Alexandria (Hypotyp. book VII according to Euseb. HE II 9.2-3), about the conversion of James's accuser and his death along with the apostle. A further indication of age, in the view of R.A. Lipsius (*Die apokr. Apostelgeschichten* II/2. 202-208), is to be seen in the fact that a speech by James contains quotations from the OT which agree only in part with the Vulgate. Such deviations from the Vulgate text can however also be explained on the assumption that our present Latin version goes back to a Greek original. On an Irish version of this Passio, which appears inter alia in the compilation 'Leabhar Breac' from the beginning of the 15th century (ed. R. Atkinson, *The Passions and the Homilies from Leabhar Breac*, Dublin 1887, 102-106; 346-351), cf. M. McNamara, *The Apocrypha in the Irish Church*, Dublin 1975, 94. Italian translations of the Latin text have been published by Moraldi (II, 1498-1506) and M. Erbetta (II, 544-548).

The Armenian legend known as 'Historia Iacobi apostoli' (BHO 419), about James's mission to Spain, is a later compilation from various sources, which here and there - above all in cc. 8-23 - agrees with the Passio of ps.-Abdias just mentioned. The text has been published by Kh. Tsherakhian (*Thesaurus litterarum armeniarum* III, Venetiis 1904, 174-189; French translation in L. Leloir, CChrSA 3/1, Turnhout 1986, 270-288).

The oldest written witnesses about James's mission in Spain (BHL I, 4056) go back to the 7th century. The documents for the transfer of the relics to Compostella (BHL I, 4058ff.), which forms the essential part of the Spanish James tradition, are very numerous, but not older (see on this R.A. Lipsius, op. cit. 214-227 and J. Guerra Campos, art. 'Santiago', in *Diccionario de Historia Eclesiástica de España* IV, Madrid 1975, 2183-2191, with abundant information about sources and literature).

14.1 Acta Iacobi Minoris (coptica et latina)

Various ancient traditions, which for the most part derive from Jewish Christian circles, report about James 'the righteous, brother of the Lord and bishop of Jerusalem' (cf. the discussion by W. Bienert, vol. 1, pp. 473-479 [The Relatives of Jesus]). One of the chief witnesses to such traditions in the 2nd century was Hegesippus, whose report about James's ascetic way of life and his martyrdom in Jerusalem is handed down in the Church History of Eusebius (HE II 23.4-18). This report forms the basis for the legends about James extant in various languages.

The Coptic Acts of James practically confine themselves to expanding Hegesippus' narrative with additional reports of miracles (e.g. the expulsion of demons in an old man's house, or the healing of a barren woman). A fragment of the Praedicatio from the Coptic original version is contained in the parchment leaf No. 9231 of the Coptic Museum in Cairo (ed. H. Munier, *Manuscrits coptes*, Cairo 1916, 25-26). The text of the Martyrium which I. Guidi published according to the Codex Borgianus 127 (fol. 6^{r}-6^{v1}) in Rome (*Rendiconti della R. Accademia dei Lincei*, Serie IV vol. III/1, Rome 1887, 60-61), and translated into Italian (*Giornale della Società Asiatica Italiana* 2, 1888, 20), is codicologically connected with this fragment. A further witness to the text of the Martyrium is contained in Codex 635 (fol. 20^{r1}-24^{r1}) of the Pierpont Morgan Library in New York (cf. F. Morard, *Revue de Théologie et de Philosophie* 113, 1981, 409).[1] The complete text of the Coptic Acts of James is known only through the translations into Arabic (ed. A. Smith Lewis, *Horae Semiticae* III-IV, London 1904, 120-126, 140-147) and Ethiopic (ed. S.C. Malan, *The Conflicts of the Holy Apostles*, London 1871, 15-24 and E.A. Wallis Budge, *The Contendings of the Apostles* I-II, London 1899/1901, 73-82, 65-75).

The Latin Passio Iacobi comprises cc. 1-6 of Book VI of the ps.-Abdias collection, and is handed down in several versions (BHL I, 4089-4097). As the basis for his narrative the compiler took over Hegesippus' report according to Rufinus' Latin translation. In addition other testimonia about James, which derive from the Pseudo-Clementine literature (e.g. Recog. I 44; 66; 68-73) or from Eusebius (e.g. HE II 1.1-5), turn up in some versions (on this cf. R.A. Lipsius, *Die apokr. Apostelgeschichten* I, 145-146; II/2, 253-257). There is an Italian translation of the Passio in Erbetta (II, 554-557) and Moraldi (II, 1534ff.).

Finally, the Georgian 'Martyrium Iacobi fratris Domini' published by K. Kekelidze (*Monumenta hagiographica georgica* II, Tiflis 1946, 98-100) according to Codex H 535 (11th cent.) of the Manuscript Institute in Tiflis is likewise a translation of Hegesippus' report (cf. G. Garitte, *Le Muséon* 74, 1961, 398).

Notes

14.1 Acta Iacobi Minoris

1. A *Coptic* version of the Martyrium, independent of Hegesippus, has been found in Codex V of Nag Hammadi (cf. A. Böhlig/P. Labib in *Zeitschr. d. M. Luther-Universität* 1963, 57ff.; see W.-P. Funk in vol. 1, p. 327ff.).

15.1 Acta Simonis Cananaei (coptica)

In contrast to the Latin tradition, which unites Simon the Canaanite and Judas Thaddaeus in their missionary activity and in their martyrdom (see below, pp. 481f.), the Coptic tradition has fundamentally different legends for the two apostles.

The Coptic Acta Simonis (Praedicatio et Martyrium) identify the apostle Simon the Canaanite (see NTApo³ II, ET 61) with Simon 'son of Cleopas, surnamed Judas, i.e. Nathanael, called Zelotes'. In association with the role assigned to him in the Coptic legend as the successor of James the Just on the bishop's throne in Jerusalem (cf. on this the account of Hegesippus in Eusebius, HE III 32.1-2), his sphere of work is located in Samaria and Jerusalem. Accused of magic, he suffers martyrdom by crucifixion at the command of the emperor Trajan. The remainder of the Acts is filled up with the usual commonplaces of the Coptic corpus of Acts (reports of miracles, the assistance of Peter, the founding of churches, etc.).

Like other apostolic Acts of similar provenance, this legend is handed down in fragmentary form in Coptic and complete in Arabic and Ethiopic translations. A Sahidic fragment from the Codex Borgianus 127 (fol. 6^{v2}) in Rome, in which the beginning of the Praedicatio and probably the last lines of the Martyrium are preserved, was edited (*Rendiconti della R. Accademia dei Lincei*, Serie IV vol. III/1, Rome 1887, 62) and translated into Italian (*Giornale della Societá Asiatica Italiana* 2, 1888, 20-21) by I. Guidi. A more extensive fragment of the Praedicatio, in which the raising-up of a young man is described, is contained in a parchment leaf from Akhmim (Br. Mus. Or. 3581 B [25]), which was published by W.E. Crum (*Catalogue of the Coptic Manuscripts in the British Museum*, London 1905, No. 311 p. 138). An abbreviated Sahidic version of the Martyrium according to the Coptic codex 274 of the National Library in Naples was edited by I. Guidi (*Rendiconti della R. Accademia dei Lincei*, Serie V vol. II/2, Rome 1893, 513-515) with an Italian translation. Except for a few variations the Martyrium contained in Br. Mus. Or. 3581 B (27) (see on this W.E. Crum, op. cit. No. 313 p. 139) agrees with this version. Finally, another witness to the text of this Martyrium is contained in Codex 635 (fol. 17^{r1}-18^{r1}) of the Pierpont Morgan Library in New York (cf. F. Morard, *Revue de Théologie et de Philosophie* 113, 1981, 411).

It was only through the translations into Arabic (ed. A. Smith Lewis, *Horae Semiticae* III-IV, London 1904, 96-100, 115-119) and Ethiopic (ed. S.C. Malan, *The Conflicts of the Holy Apostles*, London 1871, 24ff. and E.A. Wallis Budge, *The Contendings of the Apostles* I-II, London 1899/1901, 67-72, 58-64) that a continuous version of these Acts became known.

Another legend about the 'Martyrium of the apostle Simon', in which the famous episode of the virgin Theonoe plays a prominent role, shows only scant points of contact with our Acts. This Martyrium, handed down exclusively in Coptic (BHO 1112), is a local continuation of the "Acta Simonis" which is evidently intended to document the link between this apostle and Egypt. The task there promised to the virgin Theonoe, to take vengeance on king "Adrianus" for the apostle's death, is inspired by the OT book of Judith. A large fragment of the original Coptic version is known from the Codex Borgianus 137 in Rome (fol. 33-36), which I. Guidi edited (*Rendiconti della R. Accademia dei Lincei*, Serie IV vol. III/2, Rome 1887, 76-80) and translated into Italian (*Giornale della Società Asiatica Italiana* 2, 1888, 41-44). A further, substantially shorter fragment was published by W.E. Crum (op. cit. No. 312 pp. 138-139) from a parchment leaf in the British Museum (Or. 3581 B [26]).

15.2 Acta Thaddaei (coptica)

There is a Coptic legend (BHO 1141) about the apostle Judas, 'brother of the Lord, who preached in Syria and Mesopotamia', which shows no points of contact either with the Greek (see below) or with the Latin Acta Thaddaei (see below, p. 481). In fact it is not a question of a new text, but of a Coptic translation of the Greek Acta Petri et Andreae (see above, p. 448), in which Thaddaeus takes over the role of Andrew in the Greek *Vorlage*. This present case has little to do with other Coptic attempts at adaptation - cf. for example the Acts of Bartholomew already discussed (above, pp. 451f.) - since here the wording of the Greek Acts is taken over almost literally.

A Sahidic fragment with the beginning of the legend, from the Codex Borgianus 127 (fol. 7^{r}) in Rome, was edited (*Rendiconti della R. Accademia dei Lincei*, Serie IV vol. III/1, Rome 1877, 62-63) and translated into Italian (*Giornale della Società Asiatica Italiana* 2, 1888, 21-22) by I. Guidi. Further Coptic fragments which presumably also belong to these Acts are to be found in Codex 129^{18} (fol. 98; 101^{v} and 114) in the National Library in Paris (cf. on this F. Morard, *Revue de Théologie et de Philosophie* 113, 1981, 410). A Passio Judae Thaddaei which is preserved in Codex 635 (fol. 16^{r1}-17^{r1}) in the Pierpont Morgan Library in New York (cf. F. Morard, op. cit. 411) is on the other hand hardly connected with them.

The complete text of this legend is known through the translations into Arabic (ed. A. Smith Lewis, *Horae Semiticae* III-IV, London 1904, 101-109, 120-125) and Ethiopic (ed. S.C. Malan, *The Conflicts of the Holy Apostles*, London 1871, 221ff. and E.A. Wallis Budge, *The Contendings of the Apostles* I-II, London 1899/1901, 296-306; 296-306).

15.3 Acta Thaddaei (graeca)

A legend is handed down under the title Πράξεις τοῦ ἁγίου ἀποστόλου Θαδδαίου (BHG II, 1702-1703), the starting-point for which is the saga of the origins of Christianity in Edessa, known from Greek (Euseb. HE I 12.3; I 13.1-22; II 1.6) and Syriac sources (Doctrina Addaei: BHO 24)(on this see the discussion by H.J.W. Drijvers in vol.1, p. 492 ff.). The Greek text was first published by C. Tischendorf (*Acta apostolorum apocrypha*, 1851, 261-265) and then - with a few variations - by R.A. Lipsius (Aa I, 273-278). Erbetta (II, 577-579) has provided an Italian translation.

In comparison with the oldest witnesses of the Abgar legend the corresponding parts of our present Acts show specific features which point to a further development of the original legend in the Byzantine milieu. Among these are the identity of the central character - Thaddaeus or Addaeus in the Greek sources ranks throughout as 'one of the seventy disciples', whereas here the apostle Thaddaeus or Lebbaeus according to Mt. 10:3 and Mk. 3:18 is unmistakably meant - and the prominent role played in our present Acts by the portrait of Christ (ἀχειροποίητος), which came into being through a miracle and was allegedly brought to Edessa by the messenger Ananias. This last episode (= Aa I, 274_{11}-275_{2}) - differently presented in the Doctrina Addaei and completely ignored by Eusebius in his report - is connected with the known discussions about the cult of images within the Byzantine Church, and in all probability has a direct relationship with the portrait of Christ which turned up in the year 544 during the siege of the city of Edessa by the Persians (cf. on this E. von Dobschütz, *Christusbilder*: TU 18 [= NF 3], 1899. 102-196; 163*-249* and C. Schneider, art. 'Acheiropoietos': RAC I, cols. 68-71). These observations suggest an origin for the Greek Acta Thaddaei only in the middle of the 6th century or later.

In this legend - employing the stylistic methods usual in the later apostolic Acts - the apostle's missionary work is extended beyond the bounds of the city of Edessa over the whole of Syria and Mesopotamia. His death takes place in Phoenicia, in the city of Beirut. Further discussion in R.A. Lipsius, *Die apokr. Apostelgeschichten* II/2, 178-200.

15.4 Passio Simonis et Iudae (latina)

Book VI of the ps.-Abdias collection (cc. 7-23) contains a Passio Simonis et Iudae (BHL II, 7749-7751) which reflects an entirely different tradition about the deeds and the martyrdom of the apostles Simon the Canaanite and Judas Thaddaeus from the legends already discussed on pp. 479f. above. Over and above its significance within the Acts collection mentioned, this Passio has a historiographical importance because of a report contained in c. 20 about a certain Abdias, who is presented as the companion of the two apostles on the way to Persia and as first bishop of Babylon. For since 1552 (the edition of W. Lazius) people have deduced from this notice the authorship of the entire compilation *Virtutes apostolorum*, in favour of the above-mentioned Abdias, and fixed it in the following editions through manipulations of the text (on this cf. R.A. Lipsius, *Die apokr. Apostelgeschichten* I, 117-178).

In terms of content the present legend, which purports to be a brief excerpt from a comprehensive work composed originally in Greek by the apostles' disciple Craton, presents a detailed description of the missionary work of the two apostles in the twelve provinces of the Persian kingdom and in Babylon, as well as their debates with the magi Zaroes and Arfaxat, who are already known from the Latin Passio Matthaei (see above, pp. 460f.), down to the martyrdom they suffered in the town of Suanir.

The choice of Babylon as an important scene of the action could be brought into relation with 1 Peter 5:13, if we take as the point of departure for it an accidental or deliberate confusion of Simon Peter and Simon the Canaanite. The debate between Simon and Judas on the one side and the Persian magi on the other - a dominant element in this legend - is very strongly reminiscent of the debate between Peter and Simon Magus in the ancient Acts of Peter. The impression that this ancient apocryphon played the godfather in the origin of our present Passio may be strengthened by the circumstance that the real hero of the Latin legend is Simon the Canaanite, whereas Judas plays a very modest role at his side.

The author certainly shows himself thoroughly familiar with the details of the Persian kingdom in the 4th century in regard to ruler, religion and the position of the magi. Although the whole treatment is dominated by the adventure element and even encratite tendencies are hardly given a voice, views are ascribed to the magi Zaroes and Arfaxat which come close to the Manichean ideology (e.g. rejection of the OT, the dichotomy of man into a good and an evil principle, docetism, etc.). For the origin of this Passio the 4th century is accordingly the terminus post quem. There are no unambiguous clues for a more precise determination of the date.

The martyrdom suffered by the two apostles at the hands of the priests of the temple of the sun in Suanir is described in a manner which shows a great similarity to the corresponding episodes in the Latin Passio Thomae and the book 'De Miraculis beati Thomae' (ed. K. Zelzer, *Die lateinischen Thomasakten* [TU 122], Berlin 1977, esp. 37_5-40_{10}; 62_2-64_4). It is evidently a case of a common motif which originally - in opposition to the arguments of R.A. Lipsius (op. cit. II/2. 172-175) - appears to be connected with the Thomas tradition (on this see above, pp. 453ff.). Italian translations of this Passio have been published by Erbetta (II, 563-571) and Moraldi (II, 1534ff.). There are extracts in English in James (464-466).

XVIII. The Pseudo-Clementines

Johannes Irmscher and *Georg Strecker*

Introduction

Georg Strecker

1. Literature: G. Uhlhorn, *Die Homilien und Rekognitionen des Clemens Romanus*, 1854; P.A. de Lagarde, *Clementis Romani Recognitiones Syriace*, 1861; id. *Clementina*, 1865; H. Waitz, *Die Pseudoklementinen, Homilien und Rekognitionen. Eine quellenkritische Untersuchung* (TU 25.4), 1904; O. Stählin, *Die altchristliche Literatur*, [6]1924; W. Frankenberg, *Die syrischen Clementinen mit griechischem Paralleltext* (TU 48.3), 1937; B. Rehm, 'Zur Entstehung der pseudoklementinischen Schriften', ZNW 37, 1938, 77-184; id. *Die Pseudoklementinen II*, zum Druck besorgt durch F. Paschke (GCS 51), 1965; id. *Die Pseudoklementinen I*, zum Druck besorgt durch J. Irmscher/F. Paschke (GCS 42), [2]1969; G. Quispel, 'L'Évangile selon Thomas et les Clémentines', *VigChr* 12, 1958, 181-196; K. Beyschlag, 'Das Jakobusmartyrium und seine Verwandten in der frühchristlichen Literatur', ZNW 56, 1965, 149-178; id. *Simon Magus und die christliche Gnosis* (WUNT 16), 1974; F. Paschke, *Die beiden griechischen Klementinen-Epitomen und ihre Anhänge. Überlieferungsgeschichtliche Vorarbeiten zu einer Neuausgabe der Texte* (TU 90), 1966; A.F.J. Klijn, *A Survey of the Researches into the Western Text of the Gospels and Acts* II, 1969; O. Kresten, 'Zu griechischen Handschriften des Francisco Torres SJ', *Römische Historische Mitteilungen* 12, 1970, 179-196; L.L. Kline, *The Sayings of Jesus in the Pseudo-Clementine Homilies* (SBL Dissertation Series 14), 1975; id. 'Harmonized Sayings of Jesus in the Pseudo-Clementine Homilies and Justin Martyr', ZNW 66, 1975, 223-241; A. Faivre, 'Les Fonctions ecclésiales dans les écrits pseudo-clémentins', *Revue des Sciences Religieuses* 50, 1976, 97-111; J. Rius-Camps, 'Las Pseudoclementinas. Bases filológicas para una nueva interpretación', *Revista Catalana de Teologia* 1, 1976, 79-158; J.L. Martyn, 'Clementine Recognitions I, 33-71. Jewish Christianity and the Fourth Gospel', *God's Christ and His People* (FS N.A. Dahl), 1977, 265-295; G. Strecker, 'Eine Evangelienharmonie bei Justin und Pseudoklemens?', NTS 24, 1978, 297-316; id. 'Judenchristentum und Gnosis', in K.W. Tröger (ed.), *Altes Testament - Frühjudentum - Gnosis*, 1980, 261-282; id. art. 'Judenchristentum', TRE 17, 1988, 310-325; F.S. Jones, 'The Pseudo-Clementines, A History of Research', *The Second Century* 2, 1982, 1-33; 63-96; A. Stötzel, 'Die Darstellung der ältesten Kirchengeschichte nach den Pseudoklementinen', *VigChr* 36, 1982, 24-37; G. Lüdemann, *Paulus, der Heidenapostel* II. *Antipaulinismus im frühen Christentum* (FRLANT 130), 1983; J. Wehnert, 'Literarkritik und Sprachanalyse. Kritische Anmerkungen zum gegenwärtigen Stand der Pseudoklementinen-Forschung', ZNW 74, 1983, 268-301; J. v. Amersfoort, 'Het Evangelie van Thomas en de Pseudo-Clementinen' (Diss. Utrecht),

1984; G. Ory, 'Réflexions sur les écrits clémentins. Qui était Clément?', CCER 32, 1984, 33-39; W. Pratscher, *Der Herrenbruder Jakobus und die Jakobustradition*, 1987. Further literature will be found in G. Strecker, *Das Judenchristentum in den Pseudoklementinen* (TU 70), [2]1981.

Abbreviations used in what follows: Cont. = Contestatio (Διαμαρτυρία); Ep. Pet. = Epistula Petri; Ep. Clem. = Epistula Clementis; (Ep. Pet., Cont. and Ep. Clem. = introductory writings handed down in the Greek recension of the Clement romance); G = Pseudo-Clementine basic document (which can be reconstructed from H and R); H = Homilies (first Greek recension of the Clement romance, ed. B. Rehm-J. Irmscher, GCS 42); KΠ = Κηρύγματα Πέτρου; ΠΠ = Πράξεις Πέτρου; R = Recognitions (second recension of the Clement romance, originally in Greek, extant in Rufinus' Latin translation, ed. B. Rehm-F. Paschke, GCS 51).

2. Content: the Pseudo-Clementines is the name given to a series of writings which deal with the life of St Clement of Rome and name him as their author. In their principal traits their contents are everywhere cast in the same mould.

Clement is born of an aristocratic family belonging to the city of Rome. Great misfortune breaks in upon it because Clement's mother, as directed in a vision, leaves the city secretly along with the narrator's two older twin brothers. When all inquiries after her fail, the father himself finally goes in search of her. He likewise does not come back. Clement, who meanwhile has grown to be a young man, busies himself in a complete devotion to religious problems. To these the doctrines of the philosophers fail to give him any satisfactory answer. Accordingly, immediately on hearing of the appearance of the Son of God in Judaea, he proceeds on a journey. He makes contact with Peter, who makes known to him the word of God, which does away with his doubts. From this time onwards he attaches himself to the apostle as a disciple on missionary journeys which take him into the cities in the region of the Syrian coast. As a preacher, as a missionary and as an apologist, Peter is here able to display an abundant activity, of special significance being his contests with the Simon Magus known to us from the Acts of the Apostles (8:9-24), who appears with his magical arts as Peter's opponent and is finally refuted by him in word and deed. In the end also Clement's family is reunited; as becomes apparent, its several members have been far scattered, but all have continued to live. These recognitions (ἀναγνωρισμοί, ἀναγνώσεις, *recognitiones*) as also other motives of the story bring the Clementines into intimate connection with the profane romances in which precisely such developments are usual (W. Bousset, ZNW 5, 1904, 18-27; K. Kerényi *Die griechisch-orientalische Romanliteratur*, 1927, pp. 67ff.; R. Helm, *Der antike Roman*, 1948, p. 61; A. Salac, 'Listy filologické 7', *Eunomia* 3, 1959, 45ff.; N. Holzberg, *Der antike Roman*, 1986, 28ff.).

The Epistula Petri and the Contestatio were placed in front of one of the source documents of the Pseudo-Clementines - the Κηρύγματα Πέτρου. According to the statements of the Epistula Petri, Peter sends the books of his Kerygmata to 'bishop' James, with a request for special circumspection in handing them on, to prevent the falsification of his teaching by the adherents of the 'hostile man'. The following Contestatio describes the making known of the letter before the seventy presbyters and the appointing of the required precautions, and then follows the text of the engagement pledge. The Epistula Clementis provides an introduction to the Clement romance, and reports on Clement's ordination by Peter as bishop of Rome.

But the mere telling of a story is only one concern of this literature, at least in its original state. Side by side with it there is a purpose to communicate the Christian doctrine or certain outward forms of it apologetically and systematically. This sets the Clementines at a certain distance from the apocryphal Acts, which aim first and foremost at being *acta*, πράξεις, accounts (O. Stählin, *Literatur*, 1924, 1200f.; cf. however pp. 78ff. above), and through just this theological tendency the Clementines at the same time held out an incentive to remodellings and revisions of many sorts.

3. History of the text: the Clementines have not come to us as they were originally composed. Today the view is widely entertained that they go back to a basic document (B. Rehm, Entstehung 155ff.). The basic document has not survived, but its main features can be deduced from the recensions derived from it. The decisive components of the Clement romance already belong to it. Its main attitude is the *rationalismus* of the age of the apologists. Just conduct on earth is the guarantee of a successful undergoing of the last judgment; *rationabiliter vivere* is the demand that results from such practical philosophy. Belief plays only a subordinate role; the death of Jesus has no religious significance; the Christological problem scarcely exists. The guarantor of the metaphysical notions is the true prophet, whose call has to be proved by the coming true of his predictions. The basic document belongs to Coele-Syria, where it may have come into existence in the middle of the 3rd century (Waitz, *Pseudoklementinen*, 72ff.; Strecker, *Judenchristentum*, 255-267; cf. also below, pp. 492f.). It certainly was not widely disseminated, and underwent a first revision at the hands of an Arian theologian, the Homilist. To a profound ethical interest he joined one that was metaphysical, which permitted him to develop a 'doctrinal system' (Uhlhorn, *Homilien*, 153-230) entirely his own, but this, it is true, he was not able to press home everywhere in an entirely consistent way upon the material that already lay before him. The doctrine of the syzygies, the opposite pairs, which the Homilist finds everywhere in the world, even in the being of God, provides a foundation for that opposition of Peter to Simon which becomes the leading motif of the story. The critical position which the Homilist occupies in reference to the OT is noteworthy (Rehm, Entstehung 159). His attitude to the Trinitarian question (XVI 16; XX 7) ties him down to the time before the Nicene Creed, probably to the first two decades of the 4th century; he too may have written in Coele-Syria.

The Recognitions came into being independently of the Homilies - probably about A.D. 350 - in Syria or Palestine. Their author feels himself less bound than the Homilist to the content of the basic document. What has the appearance of heterodoxy is deleted, and the anti-Paulinism of the basic document is largely removed. We may thus conjecture that the Recognitionist was an orthodox catholic.

The Recognitions however had the misfortune to be interpolated by heretics so as to authenticate their irregular teaching. In a way that is nothing short of ingenious a disciple of Eunomius knew how to make room there for his own conception of the Trinity (III 2-11), with the result that the Recognitions also became suspect in the Great Church and gradually disappeared from it. Rufinus, Jerome's opponent, who translated the Recognitions into Latin, secured for them acceptation and circulation in the West, omitting in his rendering the portions that gave offence; and no difference was made to this by the fact that these portions were later brought back by another translator.

4. Tradition: the Homilies (Κλήμεντος τοῦ Πέτρου ἐπιδημιῶν κηρυγμάτων ἐπιτομή) together with two epistles to James, one of Peter and one of Clement, as also the instructions for the right use of the book (Διαμαρτυρία περὶ τῶν τοῦ βιβλίου λαμβανόντων) are preserved in Greek in two codices, the *Parisinus Graecus* 930, which is incomplete from XIX 14, and the *Vaticanus Ottobonianus* 443 discovered in 1838 by A.R.M. Dressel. The first complete edition comes from Dressel and appeared at Göttingen in 1853 (reproduced in Migne, PG 2, cols. 19-468). It has now been superseded by the editions of P.A. de Lagarde and B. Rehm.

The Recognitions have come down to us only in the Latin rendering of Rufinus, without the Διαμαρτυρία and the two epistles, of which the translator had published that of Clement separately (edited by O.F. Fritsche, *Universitäts-Programm Zürich* 1873). The book, which was preceded by a dedication to bishop Gaudentius, was widely disseminated in the West, as is proved by over a hundred manuscripts that have been preserved. They have all been drawn upon for Bernhard Rehm's edition in GCS, whereas the previous edition by E.G. Gersdorf (Leipzig 1838, reprinted in Migne, PG 1, cols. 1201-1474) no longer satisfies present-day requirements.

Both the Homilies and the Recognitions were early translated into Syriac. A manuscript from Edessa (British Museum Add. 12150) of the year 411 contains a collection of texts from R I-IV 1, 4 and H X-XIV 12 from the pen of two different translators. Following Lagarde (Leipzig 1861) this text with a reconstruction of the Greek original has been edited by W. Frankenberg, TU 48. 3 (1937).

The interest taken in the narrative portion of the Clementines by a wide circle of readers gave occasion to the drawing-up of summaries in which the dogmatic discussions were relegated to the background. We possess in Greek two such epitomes (edited by Dressel, 1859). Particularly the older of the two, which has been handed down in about thirty manuscripts, is of importance for the state of the text of the Homilies; on the other hand, the so-called Cotelierian epitome, which is entered in numerous codices, represents simply a paraphrase of the older summary. Finally, in addition to the Sinai-epitome composed in Arabic (ed. by M. Gibson, *Studia Sinaitica* 5, 1896), which presents a text of the Recognitions independent of Rufinus, we possess Clementine fragments in Ethiopic (Stählin, *Literatur*, p. 1213).

5. History of Research: since the time of Ferdinand Christian Baur ('Die Christuspartei in der korinthischen Gemeinde', TZTh 1831, 61-206) the question of Jewish-Christian elements has occupied the central place of interest in the Pseudo-Clementines. The so-called (later) Tübingen School names the Clement romance as a witness for the thesis that the catholic Church arose out of Petrinism and Paulinism. According to this thesis the Jewish-Christian colouring is an expression of an Ebionitism which, in spite of its anti-Pauline attitude, has taken over from Paulinism its universalistic tendency, and so represents a step in Ebionitic thought in the direction of catholicism. Later scholars linked with the question as to the character and significance of the Pseudo-Clementine Jewish Christianity a consideration, much more thorough than that of the Tübingen School, of literary-critical arrangement in the Clement romance: Adolf Hilgenfeld (*Die klementischen Recognitionen und Homilien nach ihrem Ursprung dargestellt*, Jena 1848) reconstructed from R I 27-72, according to the 'table of contents' in R III 75, a Jewish-Christian source document which was originally joined to the Epistula Petri and the Contestatio and is called the Κηρύγματα Πέτρου. The Jewish Christianity of the *kerygmata* was associated with the Essenes. That was followed by further Ebionite adaptations (R II-III, R IV-VII and R VIII-X). Finally the Homilist reviewed the romance that had thus grown together and gave to it an anti-Marcionite alignment. Gerhard Uhlhorn (*Homilien*) maintains against Hilgenfield that, as compared with the Recognitions, the Homilies are primary. Nevertheless he had to recognise that in some passages the Recognitions have primitive features. He was thus forced to assume a Pseudo-Clementine basic document which lay before the Homilist and the Recognitionist, who used the Homilies as well. The basic document and the Homilies represent a Jewish Christianity of which the ultimate root reaches back to the Elkesaites. In the Recognitions, on the other hand, the Jewish-Christian element steps into the background.

Richard Adelbert Lipsius (*Die Quellen der römischen Petrussage*, Kiel 1872) asserted the existence of Ebionite Πράξεις Πέτρου, which depicted the discussions between Peter and the magician Simon from Palestine to Rome and must have been accessible to the author of the basic document through the likewise Ebionite Kerygmata. In opposition to him Hans Waitz, (*Pseudo-klementinen*) for the first time clearly distinguishes between catholic and Jewish-Christian originals in the Clement romance: the author of the basic document used a catholic-antignostic source in the Πράξεις Πέτρου, a Jewish-Christian and anti-Pauline source that was independent of that in the Kerygmata. The *KΠ*-source found entrance into the basic document in a form that had been touched up by Marcionites. The (according to R III 75) 'Seventh' Book of the Kerygmata R I 54-69, which delineates Jerusalem disputations of the apostle with the Jews, was originally independent. The genuine Kerygmata are a product of syncretistic Jewish Christianity; their author was of Elkesaite extraction.

A return to the Tübingen school is marked by the names of Cullmann and Schoeps. Oscar Cullmann (*Le problème littéraire et historique du roman Pseudo-Clémentin*, Paris 1930) understands the ΠΠ-document as Περίοδοι Πέτρου, which on literary-historical grounds he files between the Kerygmata and the basic document. The KΠ-document, as he sees it, stands in the sphere of influence of Jewish gnosis and of the Baptist sects. From this point of view numerous parallels to the earliest literary pronouncements of early Christianity can be pointed out. The explanation of these is found by going back to an environment that was common to the early Church and the Kerygmata. For his presentation of the *Theologie und Geschichte des Judenchristentums* (Tübingen 1949) Hans Joachim Schoeps draws essentially upon the Pseudo-Clementine romance. The KΠ-source, which is to be reconstructed in a measure beyond what Waitz allows on the basis of R III 75, originated in the conflict against the Marcionite gnosis and defends early Church traditions. With these it associates Essene ideas. Schoeps seeks to deduce from the Kerygmata literary units that lie still farther back;

as such there are mentioned a commentary of Symmachus on the Gospel of the Ebionites and also an 'Ebionite Acts of Apostles', which combined with a narrative of the occurrences in Jerusalem according to R I 27-72 a Jewish-Christian description of the conversion of Saul and other anti-Pauline material.

In this way it was claimed that there is a close connection between the Pseudo-Clementine circle of writings and early Christianity, and so a significance was given to the Clementines such as hitherto had been given them only by the Tübingen scholars. But a counter-stroke did not fail. John Chapman ('On the Date of the Clementines', ZNW 9, 1908, 21-34; 147-159) had already disputed the presence of Ebionite elements in the Clementines, and Eduard Schwartz ('Unzeitgemässe Betrachtungen zu den Clementinen', ZNW 31, 1932, 151-199) reinforced the negative-critical position by referring to parallel literary phenomena in the Greek romances. Bernhard Rehm ('Entstehung') strove in a special way to secure a foundation for the critical trend in research, going back to Uhlhorn in his approach to source-analysis and assuming for the Recognitionist a double dependence, both upon the basic document (G) and upon the Homilies. Ebionite elements in the Clementines are not denied, but Rehm understands them on the basis of his own source-critical approach as interpolations, which intruded into the Homilies and from there influenced the Recognitions also; for the orthodox Recognitionist succeeded only imperfectly in restoring by means of omissions and polishings the orthodox character of the Clement romance.

If the table of contents is fictitious and not to be drawn upon for the reconstruction of the Jewish-Christian elements, the Ebionite insertions can still be recognised from their linguistic style, and accordingly the introductory writings (Ep. P., Cont.), the James motive in H XI 35. 3-36. 1 par., the anti-Pauline section H XVII 13-19 and the like can be indentified as Ebionite.

6. The Kerygmata Petrou:. *a) The Starting-point for Reconstruction*: the presence of Jewish-Christian elements in the Pseudo-Clementines has not been doubted any more since Rehm made his investigations. On the other hand, the literary-historical classification is disputed. It must proceed from a settlement of the relation of the two recensions H and R to one another and to the basic document. Since Rehm's attempt to prove a double dependence of the Recognitions on G and H must be regarded as having failed (see Strecker, *Judenchristentum* 35-38), it is to be assumed as more likely that H and R go back independently of one another to the basic document. On the basis of this source-analytical starting-point it can be concluded, from the fact that H and R hand down Jewish-Christian ideas, that the basic document already comprised Jewish-Christian elements.

The author of the basic document did not himself create the genuine 'Ebionitisms'. From him comes the Epistula Clementis, which was fashioned after the Jewish-Christian Epistula Petri. But if the Letter of Peter lay before the author of the basic document, then that is also to be assumed for the Contestatio, which is placed after the Epistula Petri, and further for all Jewish-Christian elements of the Clementines which together with the Epistula Petri and the Contestatio constitute an entity. In conformity with what is mentioned in Ep. Pet. 1.2; Cont. 1.1 and frequently, this source-document bears the name Κηρύγματα Πέτρου.

If R III 75, the so-called Table of Contents of the Kerygmata, is to be recognised (with Rehm) as a literary fiction, then in reconstructing the KΠ-source we must proceed only from the introductory writings, the Epistula Petri and the Contestatio, isolating on the basis of conceptual and material parallels those contexts in the Pseudo-Clementines which display the same trend or tendency. Admittedly it is always only portions of the basic document that are thus laid hold of; statements regarding the Kerygmata cannot be wholly freed from the relativity that is theirs through their having been selected and interfered with by the author of the basic document.

This approach to reconstruction does not allow of the section R I 33-44.2 and 53.4b-71 being connected with the Kerygmata. Since as compared with the KΠ it has an independent character, it is to be regarded as a second Jewish-Christian source-writing which the author of the basic document worked up side by side with his remaining texts and expanded by a dialogue between Clement and Peter (R I 44.3ff). This writing comprised a sketch of the history of salvation - from Abraham to the Church in Jerusalem - disputations of the twelve apostles and of James with the factions of Judaism and a discussion with Paul. Because of its parallelism with the 'Αναβαθμοὶ Ἰακώβου according to Epiphanius (= AJ I; Epiph. *Haer*. 30.16.6-9), with which it has a basis (= AJ) in common, it is called the AJ II-source (cf. Strecker, *Judenchristentum* 221-254; Beyschlag, 'Jakobusmartyrium'; Martyn, 'Recognitions'; Pratscher, *Jakobus*, 124-129). Lüdemann (*Paulus* II, 242) assumes a 'R I-source' which corresponds to the AJ, and excludes R I 55-65 from it. This section is ascribed to the redaction (G or R; against this cf. Stötzel, 'Darstellung', 28).

The existence of KΠ is doubted by Lüdemann (*Paulus* II, 229) and Wehnert ('Literarkritik'). Wehnert points *inter alia* to the lack of linguistic agreements between Ep. Pet./Cont. and the other chapters assigned to the KΠ, and the absence of significant linguistic features in these sections as compared with the remaining parts of the Homilies (see also Rius-Camps, 'Pseudoclementinas'). The Ep. Pet. and the Cont. are ascribed like the Ep. Clem. to the Homilist, and the KΠ are said to be a literary fiction (against this cf. Pratscher, *Jakobus* 122-124).

b) Contents: The Epistula Petri and the Contestatio were prefixed to the KΠ document. There can be no doubt about the fictitious character of the introductory writings. Not only are the statements about sender and recipient imaginary, but the same literary tendency appears also in the characteristic archaizing style; it determines among other things the mention of the college of the seventy in the Jerusalem community (Ep. Pet. 2.1; Cont. 1.1ff., following Lk. 10:1; Num. 11:25; cf. Ep. Pet. 1.2), the requirement of a six-year probation period (Cont. 1.2), and the prohibition of swearing, which is in fact abandoned in what follows (cf. Cont. 1.2 with 4.3). It is, however, in the literary motives that the real concern of the author comes to expression. The introductory writings are intended to arouse the interest of the reader and make good the claim which the 'proclamation of Peter' makes. Moses already made known the 'word of truth' and by Jesus it was confirmed (Ep. Pet. 2.5, cf. 2.2). Peter now testifies to the true 'lawful proclamation' in opposition to the 'lawless doctrine' of the 'hostile man' (Ep. Pet. 2.3). The tradition of the Jews provides a precedent; they have preserved a uniform norm of exposition which is employed in dealing with the 'ambiguous utterances of the (Biblical) prophets', and in that they can serve the Christians by way of example (Ep. Pet. 1.3ff.). Such statements permit us to recognise the outline of a theological system which is to be defined exactly in what follows on the basis of the original KΠ-sections within the basic document.

The dominating entity in the Kerygmata is 'the true prophet' (cf. above all H III 17-28), the bearer of the divine revelation, who has manifested himself since the beginning of the world in a continuous series of changing characters (H III 20.2). Adam represents the first incarnation of 'the prophet'; he was anointed with the oil of the tree of life (R I 47) and possessed the Spirit of God (H III 17.3); accordingly, contrary to the report in Genesis, he committed no sin (H III 17, 21.2; II 52.2). Beside him as figures in whom the true prophet was manifested prominence is given to the lawgiver Moses (H II 52.3) and the Lord Jesus (H III 17-19; cf. Ep. Pet. 2.5). The true prophet has the task of proclaiming the 'lawful knowledge' which shows the way to the future aeon (H XI 19.3).

Female prophecy appears as the opponent of the true prophet (cf. also H II 15-17); she accompanies him as a negative, left-hand syzygy-partner in his passage through time. Her first representative is Eve, the mother of mankind, who was created at the same time as Adam (H III 22.25). What she proclaims suits the taste of the transitory cosmos (H II 15.2); she pretends to possess knowledge, but leads all who follow her into error and to death (H III 24.3f.).

The knowledge which the true prophet brings to men is identified with the law (on the following, see: H II 37-52; III 39, (42), 43-56; H. XVI 5-15 ~ R II 38-46). Adam already taught an eternal law (H VIII 10.3). It is identical with the law of Moses. Moses transmitted it orally to the seventy elders (H III 47.1). Thus it has been preserved on the 'chair of Moses' through the ages (Ep. Pet. 1.2ff.). Now it rests in the hands of the Pharisees and scribes, to whom Jesus expressly referred (Mt. 23:2f.). But the representatives of Judaism have failed in passing it on (Mt. 23:13). Consequently the sending of the true prophet has become necessary (H III 18f.). He points out the false pericopes (H III 49.2) which were worked into the written formulation of the law in the Pentateuch (H II 38.1). He who is instructed by him is able to recognise that those Scripture passages which speak of God as a being afflicted with human passions cannot be original (H II 43f.; III 39.43ff.), and likewise those pericopes which speak of many gods (H XVI 5ff.). A portion also of the utterances of the Old Testament prophets (Ep. Pet. 1.4; H III 53.2), the references to sacrifice (H II 44.2; III 52.1), to the temple (H II 44.1f.) and to kingship (H III 52.1; 53.2) are to be reckoned to the falsified elements of Scripture.

The consequence of the 'lawful proclamation' of the true prophet is an anti-Paulinism. That is how the Kerygmata, directly or indirectly, have expressed it (cf. H II 15-17; H XI 35.3-6 ~ R IV 34.5-35.2; H XVII 13-19). It is true that in the basic document the statements in question are directed against Simon Magus, and in this way veiled; nevertheless the allusions to citations from the Pauline letters, above all to the discussion between Paul and Peter in Antioch (Gal. 2:11ff.: H XVII 19), the inapposite designation of the magician as a missionary to the Gentiles (H II 17.3; XI 35.4-6), and not least the scarcely disguised attitude of the Epistula Petri (2.3f.) show that in the KΠ source they are levelled against Paul.

Paul is Peter's antagonist; the two are mentioned as the last pair of the series of syzygies, Paul as the representative of female prophecy (H II 17.3). There is also a polemical emphasis in the discussion about revelation, in which the possibility of genuine visions is disputed (cf. Acts 9; Gal. 2:2; 1 Cor. 15:8; 2 Cor. 12:1ff.), and over against that the true apostolicity of Peter is substantiated by the promise of Jesus (Mt. 16:17: H XVII 18f.).From the fact that Jesus chose only twelve apostles it is to be concluded that Paul does not rightly call himself an apostle (cf. R IV 35). Since moreover his proclamation of the dissolution of the law cannot be approved by James, it is to be recognised as false doctrine (cf. H XI 35.4-6; Ep. Pet. 2.3f.).

The teaching about baptism presents a confirmation of this standpoint (cf. on this H XI 21-33 ~ R IV 6-14). The KΠ author attaches himself to the Christian gnostic school of thought. In baptism 'rebirth' comes about (H XI 26.1), 'likeness to God' being attained (H XI 27.2) through 'living water' (H XI 26.4). In the teaching about baptism, however, the emphasis lies on the requirement of good works; the *pneuma* associated with the water of baptism has the task of offering the good works of the person baptized as gifts to God (H XI 26.3). Stress is laid on the exhortation to the candidate for baptism to perform good works analogous to the sins that were passed over in the time of 'ignorance'. This counsel is based on the instructions of the Sermon on the Mount (Mt. 5: H XI 32.1). In addition observance of the Jewish law of purity is called for (H XI 28f.). The requirements apply generally to Jews and Gentiles and in this respect are in conformity with the universalistic tendency of the Kerygmata, of which there is independent evidence (cf. Ep. Pet. 2.3 and often).

c) Religio-historical character: the religio-historical position of the KΠ source can be recognised fairly exactly in spite of the literary setting. The milieu in which this writing came into being presupposes gnostic influence. The anthropological statements (e.g. H III 27.3; 28.1f.) point to that. The baptism terminology comprises gnostic elements. The true prophet's appearance in different manifestations has parallels in gnostic literature. The dualism of the two prophecies, which is determinative for the whole of the Kerygmata, also points on its materialistic-cosmological side to a gnostic background (cf. H II 15.3; XIX 23.3).

Side by side with that there are found close contacts with Judaism. That the KΠ author was in contact with Jewish theology follows no doubt from his emphatically positive estimation of the religion of Moses (Ep. Pet. 1.2ff.). But actual connections can also be observed. To the rational substantiating of the false-pericope theory (H II 40.1: 'All that is said or written against God is lies') the interpretation of Scripture in late Judaism presents similar tendencies and, especially in the Targumim, near parallels. Admittedly the radicalism of the Kerygmata can no longer be understood on the basis of Jewish presuppositions, and only in the gnostic sphere are there parallels to it (cf. e.g. Ptolemy, *ad Floram* 4.1f.). If here elements of Jewish origin have been worked in under gnostic influence, on the other hand the nomism of the Kerygmata interprets the originally gnostic dualism in a Jewish or Jewish-Christian light. The opposition of two cosmic principles is interpreted as opposition between the true prophet, the content of whose proclamation is the law, and the female prophecy, which teaches the dissolution of the law (H III 23.3). A Jewish or Jewish-Christian environment also determines the detailed instructions of the true prophet, for example in the ceremonial-legal requirements of the counsel given at baptism. The anti-Paulinism, which is attested for different kinds of Jewish-Christian groups ('Ebionite': Iren. *Adv. Haer.* I 26.2; 'Cerinthian': Epiph. *Haer.* 28.5.3; 'Elkesaite': Eusebius, *HE* VI 38; 'Encratite': Origen, *c. Cels.* V 65 and often), certainly comes from Jewish-Christian tradition. To this there belongs the corresponding understanding of Peter and James respectively. That the author stood in a Jewish-Christian tradition follows from the motif of different manifestations, which evidently already lay before him as fixed tradition, the identification of the true prophet with Jesus being assumed as a matter of course. This idea - parallels are found in the doctrine of Mani and in Mandaeism - is attested for the Elkesaites among others (Hippol. *Ref.* IX 14.1). There is also a reminder of Elkesaitism in the wording of the oath in Cont. 2.1; 4.1 (cf. Hippol. *Ref.* IX 15.2; Epiph. *Haer.* 19.1.6; 6.4), which, however, serves only literary ends in the Contestatio and therefore does not permit more than a passing acquaintance with the Elkesaite system to be inferred. Since important differences from the Elkesaite theology can be pointed out, a relationship of dependence cannot be concluded from the remaining analogies, but it must be assumed that the author of the Kerygmata and Elkesai, the founder of the sect, worked in similar circumstances. The author writes in a Jewish-Christian-gnostic milieu. His work is influenced by a universalistic tendency and presupposes the writings of the New Testament canon: in the land of its origin the great Church and heresy do not yet appear to have been marked off the one from the other.

7. Country of origin and date: for answering the question of the country of origin and date of the Pseudo-Clementines we may start from the KΠ document. In recent scholarship there is widespread agreement in the opinion that this written source of the Pseudo-Clementine basic document cannot have originated in the West, but only in the East. The same applies to the composition of the basic document. This will have been composed in Coele-Syria (cf. above, p. 485). There the relationship between Judaism and Christianity is for a long time not clear, and the separation not yet final. This situation explains the Jewish sympathies of the author of the basic document. The pseudonym 'Clemens Romanus' was also frequently employed in Coele-Syria. Since the Kerygmata do not appear to have been widely disseminated, we must seek the homeland of the KΠ-author in the neighbourhood of the land of origin of the basic document. Something more precise can be deduced from the citation of the New Testament writings. Here the conjecture that the apologist Justin composed a harmony of the Gospels, which lay before both the Pseudo-Clementine basic document and the Diatessaron of Tatian (L.L. Kline, *The Sayings*), may be regarded as disproved (Strecker, 'Evangelienharmonie'); the attempt to demonstrate that a Jewish-Christian gospel was used in common for both the Gospel of Thomas and Pseudo-Clement (so Quispel, 'L'Évangile'; Amersfoort, 'Evangelie'; against this see Klijn, *Survey*) is also scarcely successful. Yet the use of a canon which does not include the Catholic Epistles and the Apocalypse of John points to Syria (on the formation of the Syrian canon cf. Th. Zahn, *Geschichte des neutestamentlichen Kanons* I, 1888, 373ff.). This location may also be deduced from the fact that the KΠ-author quotes among the Pauline letters only Galatians and (indirectly) First Corinthians, and the Syrian corpus of the Pauline letters begins with just these two letters - granted that an abridged canon lies behind the Kerygmata. The Kerygmata source was composed in Greek, not in Aramaic; hence for its land of origin we may think of the Greek-speaking Syria which bordered on Osrhoene. Numerous Jewish Christians lived there - in the time of Epiphanius (*Haer.* 29.7) and Jerome (*de Vir. Ill.* 3) they were still living in Beroea.

The *terminus a quo* for the origin of the basic document is Bardesanes' work Περὶ Εἱμαρμένης, to which the section R IX 19-29 goes back. The earliest possible time of origin is thus A.D. 220. Establishing the *terminus ad quem* is substantially more difficult. The use of the basic document by Epiphanius takes us back at the earliest to the middle of the 4th century. There thus remains as the most obvious clue only the time of composition of the Homilies in the first two decades of the 4th century (cf. above, p. 485), which results in a range from 220 to 300 with the year 260 A.D. as the arithmetical mean. This is also the lower limit for the origin of the KΠ document. For the latter there is no firm foundation for establishing the *terminus a quo*. We may not go too far back into the 2nd century, since then we should not be able to understand why there is no evidence for the Kerygmata outside of the basic document. Over and above that, we can obtain an indication of the possible dating through comparison with the time of composition of the other sources of the basic document: if Bardesanes' dialogue, which the author of the basic document copied, was composed about the year 220, an ordination schema which that author used (in Ep. Clem., H III 60-72; XI 36; R III 65-66; VI 15) also came into being about 200. The same dating may be assumed for the Kerygmata.

1. *Introductory Writings*

Letter of Peter to James
(Epistula Petri)

1. 1. Peter to James, the lord and bishop of the holy church: Peace be with you always from the Father of all through Jesus Christ.

2. Knowing well that you, my brother, eagerly take pains about what is for the mutual benefit of us all, I earnestly beseech you not to pass on to any one of the Gentiles the books of my preachings which I (here) forward to you, nor to any one of our own tribe before probation. But if some one of them has been examined and found to be worthy, then you may hand them over to him in the same way as Moses handed over his office of a teacher to the seventy.[1] 3. Wherefore also the fruit of his caution is to be seen up to this day. For those who belong to his people preserve everywhere the same rule in their belief in the one God and in their line of conduct, the Scriptures with their many senses being unable to incline them to assume another attitude. 4. Rather they attempt, on the basis of the rule that has been handed down to them, to harmonise the contradictions of the Scriptures, if haply some one who does not know the traditions is perplexed by the ambiguous utterances of the prophets. 5. On this account they permit no one to teach unless he first learn how the Scriptures should

be used. Wherefore there obtain amongst them one God, one law and one hope.

2. 1. In order now that the same may also take place among us, hand over the books of my preachings in the same mysterious way to our seventy brethren[2] that they may prepare those who are candidates for positions as teachers. 2. For if we do not proceed in this way, our word of truth will be split into many opinions. This I do not know as a prophet, but I have already the beginning of the evil before me. 3. For some from among the Gentiles have rejected my lawful preaching and have preferred a lawless and absurd doctrine *of the man who is my enemy.*[3] 4. And indeed some have attempted, whilst I am still alive, to distort my words by interpretations of many sorts, as if I taught the dissolution of the law and, although I was of this opinion, did not express it openly.[4] But that may God forbid![5] 5. For to do such a thing means to act contrary to the law of God which was made known by Moses and was confirmed by our Lord in its everlasting continuance. For he said:[6] '*The heaven and the earth will pass away, but one jot or one tittle shall not pass away from the law.*' 6. This he said *that everything might come to pass.* But those persons who, I know not how, allege that they are at home in my thoughts wish to expound the words which they have heard of me better than I myself who spoke them. To those whom they instruct they say that this is my opinion, to which indeed I never gave a thought. 7. But if they falsely assert such a thing whilst I am still alive, how much more after my death will those who come later venture to do so?

3. 1. In order now that such a thing may not happen I earnestly beseech you not to pass on the books of my preachings which I send you to any one of our own tribe or to any foreigner before probation, but if some one is examined and found to be worthy, let them then be handed over in the way 2. in which Moses handed over his office of a teacher to the seventy, in order that they may preserve the dogmas and extend farther the rule of the truth, interpreting everything in accordance with our tradition and not being dragged into error through ignorance and uncertainty in their minds to bring others into the like pit of destruction.

3. What seems to me to be necessary I have now indicated to you. And what you, my lord, deem to be right, do you carry fittingly into effect. Farewell.

Testimony regarding the Recipients of the Epistle *(Contestatio)*

1. 1. Now when James had read the epistle he called the elders together, read it to them and said: 'As is necessary and proper, our Peter has called our attention to the fact that we must be cautious in the matter of the truth, that we should pass on the books of his preachings that have been forwarded to us not indiscriminately, but only to a good and religious candidate for the position of a teacher, a man who as one who has been circumcised is a believing Christian, and indeed that we should not pass on all the books to him at once, so that, if he shows indiscretion in handling the first, he may not be entrusted with the others. 2. He ought therefore to be proved for not less than six years. Thereafter, according to the way of Moses, let him be brought to a river or a fountain where there is living water and the regeneration of the righteous takes place; not that he may swear, for that is not permitted,[7] but he should be enjoined to stand by the water and to vow, as we also ourselves were made to do at the time of our regeneration, to the end that we might sin no more.

2. 1. And let him say: "As witnesses I invoke heaven, earth and water, in which everything is comprehended, and also in addition the all-pervading air, without which I am unable to breathe, that I shall always be obedient to him who hands over to me the books of the preachings and shall not pass on to any one in any way the books which he may give to me, that I shall neither copy them nor give a copy of them nor allow them to come into the hands of a copyist, neither shall I myself do this nor shall I do it through another, and not in any other way, through cunning or tricks, through keeping them carelessly, through depositing them with another or through underhand agreement, nor in any other manner or by means of any other artifice will I pass them on to a third party. 2. Only if I have proved someone to be worthy - proving him as I myself have been proved, or even more, in no case for less than six years - if he is a religious and good candidate for the position of a teacher, I will hand them over to him as I have received them and certainly in agreement with my bishop.

3. 1. Otherwise, though he be either my son or a brother or a friend or any other relation, if he is unworthy, I shall keep information away from him since it does not befit him. 2. I shall allow myself neither to be frightened by persecutions nor to be deceived by gifts. And even if I should ever come to the conviction that the books of the preachings which have been handed to me do not contain the truth, then also I shall not pass them on but shall hand them back. 3. When I am on a journey, I shall carry with me all the books that are in my possession. And if I purpose not to take them with me, I shall not leave them behind in my house, but shall consign them to the care of my bishop, who is of the same faith and of like extraction. 4. If I am sick and see death before me, I shall, if I am childless, proceed in the same way. I shall do the like if at the time of my death my son is not worthy or is not yet of age. I shall deposit the books with my bishop that if, when my son has come of age, he should prove to be worthy of the trust he may hand them over to him as a father's legacy according to the terms of the vow.

4. 1. And that I shall proceed in this way, I again invoke as witnesses heaven, earth and water, in which everything is comprehended, and also in addition the all-pervading air without which I am unable to breathe: I shall be obedient to him who hands over to me the books of the preachings, I shall keep them in every respect as I have vowed and even beyond that. 2. If now I observe the agreements, then will my portion be with the saints; but if I act against my vow, then may the universe and the all-pervading ether and God, who is over all and is mightier and more exalted than any other, be hostile to me. 3. And if even I should come to believe in another god, then I swear also by him, whether he now is or is not, that I shall not proceed otherwise. In addition to all that, if I am false to my word, I shall be accursed living and dead and suffer eternal punishment." - And thereupon let him partake of bread and salt with him who hands over the books to him.'

5. 1. When James had said this, the elders were pale with fright. Accordingly, observing that they feared greatly, James said, 'Hear me, brethren and fellow-servants. 2. If we pass on the books to all without discrimination and if they are falsified by audacious men and are spoiled by interpretations - as indeed you have heard that some have already done - then it will come to pass that even those who earnestly seek the truth will always be led into error. 3. On this account it is better that we keep the books and, as we have said, hand them with all caution only to those who wish to live and to save others. But if any one, after that he has made such a vow, does not adhere to it, then will he rightly suffer eternal punishment. 4. For why should he not go to ruin who has been guilty of the corruption of others?' Then were the elders pleased with James's conclusion and said, 'Praised be he who has foreseen all things and destined you to be our bishop.' - And when they had said this, we rose up and prayed to God the Father of all, to whom be glory for ever. Amen.

Notes

Letter of Peter to James
Translation after G. Strecker.

1. Cf. Num. 11:25.
2. Cf. Lk. 10:1.
3. Cf. Mt. 13:28.
4. Cf. Gal. 2:11-14.
5. Cf. Gal. 2:17.
6. Mt. 24:35; 5:18.
7. Cf. Mt. 5:34; Jas. 5:12

Letter of Clement to James
(Epistula Clementis)

1. 1. Clement to James, the lord and bishop of bishops, who governs the holy church of the Hebrews at Jerusalem and those which by the providence of God have been well founded everywhere, together with the presbyters and deacons and all the other brethren. Peace be with you always.

2. Be it known to you, my lord, that Simon, who because of the true faith and the most secure basis of his teaching was appointed to be a foundation stone of the Church, and for that very reason was surnamed Peter[1] by the mouth of Jesus which cannot lie, 3. the first-fruit of our Lord, the first of the apostles, to whom the Father first revealed the Son,[2] whom Christ with good reason called 'blessed', the called and chosen, table companion and fellow-traveller, the good and proven disciple, who as the most capable of all was commanded to enlighten the darkest part of the world, the West,[3] and was enabled to achieve it - 4. but to what end do I prolong my address, not wishing to report what is grievous, which of necessity, though reluctantly, I must yet speak out? - 5. this very man, who because of his abundant love towards mankind made known to all the world the future good king, clearly (and) publicly in the face of the present evil,[4] who came even here to Rome, saving men by his God-willed teaching, has by violence exchanged this present way of life for life.

2. 1. In those very days when he was about to die, the brethren being assembled together, he suddenly grasped my hand, and standing up said to the congregation: 'Listen to me, brethren and fellow-servants. 2. Since the days of my death are at hand, as I was taught by our Lord and Teacher Jesus Christ who sent me,[5] I appoint to you Clement here as bishop and to him I entrust my teacher's chair. 3. He has accompanied me from the beginning even to the end, and so has heard all my homilies. To put it briefly, he has shared in all my trials and been found persevering in the faith. I have proved him more than any other - devout, a lover of mankind, pure, learned, prudent, good, righteous, patient and one who knows how to bear nobly the ingratitude of some of the catechumens. 4. Wherefore I convey to him the authority to bind and to loose,[6] that all that he ordains on earth shall be decreed in heaven. For he will bind what must be bound and loose what must be loosed, as one who knows the canon of the Church. 5. Hearken then to him, knowing that he who grieves the president of truth sins against Christ and provokes the wrath of the Father of all;[7] wherefore he shall not live. 6. And so the president himself must occupy the place of a physician, and not have the passion of an irrational animal.'

3. 1. When he said this, I fell at his feet and besought him, seeking to decline the honour and authority of the chair. 2. But he answered: 'About this make no requests of me; for I have decided that this should be, and all the more if you seek to decline. For such a chair does not require an ambitious man who is eager to take it, but one who is reverent in manner and learned in the word.[8] 3. Give me a better man, who has travelled with me more than you and heard my words and thoroughly learned the governing of the Church, and I will not compel you to do what is right against your will. 4. But you will not be able now to produce one who is better than you; for you are the better first-fruits among the Gentiles who are saved through me. 5. But consider this other thing also: if in fear of the danger of sinning you do not accept the governing of the Church, then be very well aware that you sin the more, if when you are able you are unwilling to help the faithful when they are, as it were, on a voyage and running into danger, because you are looking only to your own interest and not to the common good. 6. You know very well[9] that you must by all means accept the danger, when I do not cease asking this of you for the help of all. 7. The sooner you consent with me, the more you will lighten my discouragement.

4. 1. But I know myself, O Clement, that I am bestowing on you sorrows and discouragement, dangers and reproaches from uneducated multitudes, which you will be able to bear nobly if you look to the great reward for endurance that is given to you by God. 2. But consider with me also, justly: When does Christ have need of your assistance? Now, when the evil one has begun a war against his bride, or in the future, when having conquered he reigns, no longer having need of any help? Is it not clear even to one that has a small mind, that it is now? 3. Hasten then with all determination to ally yourself in the time of the present distress with the good king who is able after victory to give great rewards. 4. Take up the bishop's office then gladly - the more fittingly since you have learned the governing of the Church from me - for the salvation of the brethren who have taken refuge with us.

5. 1. But in the presence of all and for the sake of all I would remind you briefly of the things of government. 2. You must live irreproachably,[10] and with the utmost zeal shake off all the occupations of this life, being neither guarantor nor advocate, nor becoming involved in any other affair of this life.[11] 3. For Christ does not wish to appoint you as judge or arbiter in matters of money or other business affairs which belong to this present life,[12] that entangled in the transitory cares of men you should have no time (to do what should be your task, namely) to separate with the word of truth the better of men from the worse. 4. These things let the laity[13] provide for one another, and not hinder you[14] from speaking the words which are able to save. 5. For as it is impious for you to accept worldly concerns and neglect to do what you are commanded, so it is for every layman a sin if they do not stand by one another in the needs of this life. 6. And if they all do not think to act in regard to those things with which you should have no concern, let them learn from the deacons, that you may take thought only for the Church, to govern it rightly and to hold forth the words of truth.

6. 1. For if you devote your time to the cares of this life, you will ensnare both yourself and your hearers. Since for lack of time you have been unable to supply what is profitable, you will be punished as not having taught what is profitable, and they, not having learned, will perish by reason of ignorance. 2. Wherefore become their president without delay, that in due season you may hold forth the words which can save them; 3. and let them listen to you, knowing that whatever the emissary of the truth shall bind on earth is also bound in heaven, and what he looses is loosed. But you will bind what must be bound, and loose what must be loosed. 4. Now these and the things like them are what concern you as the presiding (bishop).

7. 1. The things concerning the presbyters shall be thus. Above all let them speedily unite the young people in marriage, forestalling the snares of youthful passion. 2. But let them not neglect those already grown old in the matter of marriage; for in some even when they are old there is an intense passion. 3. Therefore, that harlotry may not find pasture among you and bring this same plague upon you, take precautions and investigate, lest the fire of adultery be secretly kindled among you. 4. For adultery is very dangerous, so much so that it occupies the second place in the penal catalogue; for the first is reserved for those who are in error, even when they live chastely. 5. Wherefore do you as presbyters of the Church train the bride of Christ to chastity - by bride I mean the totality of the Church.[15] 6. For if she is found to be chaste by the royal bridegroom, she will obtain the greatest honour and you as wedding guests will enjoy great gladness. 7. But if she is detected as having sinned, she will be cast out but you will pay the penalty, lest the sin should have come about through your neglect.

8. 1. Therefore above all be concerned for chastity. For before God harlotry is accounted an exceedingly great evil. 2. Now there are many forms of harlotry, as Clement himself will explain to you. The first is adultery, for a man not to have intercourse with his own wife only, and a woman with her own husband. 3. If anyone is chaste, he can also become philanthropic, and for this cause will obtain eternal mercy. 4. Now as adultery is a great evil, so philanthropy is the greatest good. 5. Therefore love all your brethren with respectful and compassionate eyes, doing for orphans the duties of parents, for the widows those of their husbands,[16] providing them nourishment with all gladness; 6. (arrange) marriages for those in the bloom of their powers, and for those unskilled among them devise pretexts for them to obtain the necessary food through (suitable) occupations, give work to the craftsman, compassion to the helpless.[17]

9. 1. I know that you will do these things, if you establish love in your minds. To ensure its entrance, there is one sufficient occasion: the common partaking of salt. 2. Therefore be zealous to become more frequently sharers at table with one another, as you are able, that you may not lose your grasp of it. For it is the cause of well-doing, and well-doing of salvation. 3. Do you all then hold out your livelihood in common to all the brethren in God, knowing that in giving temporal things you shall receive eternal. 4. All the more, feed the hungry and provide drink for the thirsty, clothing for the naked, visit the sick, show yourselves to the prisoners and as you are able to help them, receive strangers with all readiness into your houses.[18] 5. But - that I do not lose myself in details - philanthropy will teach you to do all that is good, as misanthropy points the way to evil-doing for those who do not wish to be saved.

10. 1. If brethren have disputes, let them not be judged before the (worldly) authorities, but let them be reconciled in every way by the presbyters of the Church, readily obeying them.[19] 2. Moreover flee from covetousness, which under the pretext of temporal gain can rob you of the eternal goods. 3. As to balances, measures and weights, preserve carefully the just ones in your places, and deal faithfully with what is entrusted to you. 4. But this and all that is similar you will continue to do to the end, if you are unceasingly mindful in your hearts of the judgment which comes from God. 5. For who will sin who is convinced that the righteous God, who now is only long-suffering and good, has appointed at the end of life a judgment, that the good hereafter may enjoy eternally the ineffable good things, but the sinners who have been found to be wicked will meet with unspeakable punishment for ever? 6. And that this is so it might well be easy to doubt, if the prophet of truth had not affirmed under oath that it will be.

11. 1. Wherefore, being disciples of the true prophet, lay aside the doubt from which comes evil-doing, and welcome eagerly the doing of good. 2. But if any one of you doubts whether what has been said will happen, let him confess it without shame, if he is concerned for his soul, and he will be fully convinced by the leader. If however he has believed correctly, let him live his life with confidence, as escaping the great fire of judgment and entering into the eternal good kingdom of God.

12. 1. Now as to the deacons of the Church, let them be the eyes of the bishop,[20] going about wisely, much concerned with the deeds of each (member) of the Church, (that they may find out) who is on the point of sinning, that by the admonition of the president when he is detected he may perhaps not carry through with the sin. 2. Deserters from the ranks let them turn (to repentance), that they may not leave (the company of) those who assemble to hear the words, that by the word of truth they may be able to purge away the discouragements which ever descend upon the heart, both from the accidents of this life and from evil conversations. For if they are left untended for a long time, they become matter for the fire. 3. Let them learn who are sick in body, and bring it to the notice of the multitude who do not know, that they may visit them and provide what is needful in accordance with the judgment of the president. Even if they do this without his knowledge, they do not sin. These and the things like them are what the deacons should take thought for.

13. 1. Let the catechists give instruction, having first been instructed; for the work concerns the souls of men. The teacher of the (saving) words must attune himself to the many opinions of those who learn. 2. Hence the catechist must be learned, irreproachable, mature and dauntless,[21] as you yourselves will find Clement, who is about to become your catechist after me. 3. For there is (too) much for me to say now in brief compass. But if you are of one mind, you will be able to attain to the haven of rest, where the great king's peaceful city is.

14. 1. The whole business of the Church is like a great ship[22] which through a violent storm bears men who are from many places and wish to dwell in some one city of a good king. 2. Let God then be for you its captain, and let the helmsman be likened to Christ, the look-out at the bow to the bishop, the sailors to the presbyters, the overseers of the rowers to the deacons, the pursers to the catechists, to the passengers the multitude of the brethren, 3. to the sea the world, the contrary winds to the trials, but the persecutions and dangers and all kinds of afflictions to the triple waves, the violent streams that come from the land (and the)[23] gales to the speeches of the deceivers and false prophets, 4. the rocky promontories and reefs to the judges in high places who utter dreadful threats, the shoals[24] and wild places to irrational men who doubt the promises of the truth. Let the hypocrites be considered like to the pirates. 5. But consider violent eddies, the whirlpool of Tartarus, murderous wrecks, and deadly shatterings to pieces to be no other than sins. 6. So then, that sailing with a favourable wind you may be brought without danger to the harbour of the city you hope for, offer prayers that will be heard. Now prayers that are heard are offered with good works.

15. 1. Let the passengers then remain quietly and steadfastly sitting in their places, that they may not through disorderly behaviour cause any upheaval or listing. 2. Let the pursers keep their payments in mind. The deacons are not to neglect any of the things entrusted to them. Let the presbyters, like sailors, make ready carefully what each requires. Let the bishop, keeping watch as the look-out at the bow, give heed to the words of the helmsman only. 3. Let Christ our[25] saviour as a helmsman be loved, and let him alone be trusted in what he says. But let all pray to God to sail with a favourable wind. 4. Let the voyagers expect every affliction, as sailing across a great and turbulent sea, this world; sometimes disheartened, persecuted, scattered abroad, hungry, thirsty, naked, distressed, and again (at other times)[26] united, in fellowship together, and at peace; 5. but also falling victim to sea-sickness, vertigo and nausea (that is, confessing their transgressions like poisons which cause sickness. I mean the sins which come from bitterness and the evils which are heaped up through disorderly passions - by confessing them, as if you had vomited, you are relieved of the disease and approach the saving health that comes from careful attention).

16. 1. But you all know that the bishop labours more than all of you, because each of you suffers his own affliction, but he (suffers) both his own and that of each one (of you). 2. Wherefore, O Clement, show yourself in your precedence a helper to each one, so far as in you lies, bearing the burden of the cares of all. I know that I have received a gift, not given one, when you accept this stewardship. 3. But be of good cheer and bear it nobly, as knowing that God will give you the greatest of goods, a reward that cannot be taken away, when you arrive in the haven of rest, inasmuch as you have accepted the greater labour for the salvation of all. 4. So if many of the brethren should hate you because of righteousness carried to its peak, their hatred will in no way harm you, but the love of the righteous God will profit you greatly. 5. So strive to shake off the praise that comes from unrighteousness, and through just administration to capture that beneficial praise which comes from Christ.'

17. 1. When he had said this, and more than this, he looked again on the multitude and said: 'And you, my beloved brethren and fellow-servants, be subject in all things to the president of truth, knowing that he who grieves him has not accepted Christ, with whose chair he is entrusted; and he who has not accepted Christ is reckoned as having set the Father at naught,[27] for which cause he will be cast out from the good kingdom.[28] 2. Because of this, strive to come to all assemblies, that you may not as deserters incur the charge of sin through the ill-will of the commander. 3. Therefore, all of you, think above all of the things concerning him, in the knowledge that because of each of you the evil one, hating him the more, wages war on him alone. 4. Do you then endeavour to continue in love toward him and goodwill to one another, and to obey him, that his burden may be lightened and you be able to be saved.

18. 1. Some things you ought to think of for yourselves, because he cannot speak openly because of the intrigues. For example, if he is at enmity with anyone, do not wait for him to say 'Do not associate with this man', but prudently follow his counsel, being enemies to those with whom he is at enmity, and not consorting with those with whom he does not consort. 2. Anyone who wishes to have all as friends should be reconciled with him and may be saved, if he hearkens to his instruction. 3. But if anyone remains a friend to those with whom he (the bishop) is at enmity, and speaks with those with whom he does not consort, he is himself one of those who wish to destroy the Church. 4. For he who is with you in the body, but in his mind is not with you, he is against you,[29] far more dangerous than the enemies who are visible outside, since with seeming friendship he scatters those within.'

19. 1. And when he had said this he laid his hands upon me publicly, in the presence of all, and constrained me to sit in his chair. 2. And when I had sat down, he immediately said this to me: 'I request of you, in the presence of all my brethren here attending, that when I depart from this present life, as is appointed for me, you will not delay in sending to James the Lord's brother a written summary both of your reflections since your youth and of how from the beginning until now you have accompanied me, listening to the words proclaimed by me in every city and (seeing) the deeds; and then at the end set forth also the reason of my death, as I said before. 3. Nor will this grieve him too much, since he knows that I have piously fulfilled what it was altogether necessary for me to suffer, and he will obtain the greatest consolation when he learns that after me it is not an unlearned man who is ignorant of the life-giving words and does not know the canon of the Church who has been entrusted with the teacher's chair. 4. For deceptive instruction destroys the souls of the crowds who hear.'

20. 1. Wherefore, my lord James, having promised when he said these things, I have not delayed, as I was bidden, to put together in summary fashion the great mass of the speeches (which he delivered) in every city, which were already written out for you and sent by him in books, and thus to send them to you with the title: Extract of the travel addresses of Peter, by Clement. Now as I was commanded I shall begin with the story.

Notes

1. Cf. Mt. 16:17f.
2. Cf. 1 Cor. 15:5.
3. Cf. 1 Clem. 5.7; Mt. 5:14.
4. Cf. Gal. 1:4.
5. Cf. Jn. 21:18f.
6. Cf. Ep. Clem. 6.3; H III 72.4; Mt. 16:19; Jn. 20:23.
7. Cf. Mt. 10:40; Mk. 9:37; Jn. 13:20.
8. Cf. 1 Tim. 3:1ff.
9. Conjecture after Schwegler.
10. Cf. Const. Apost. II 6.1.
11. Cf. 1 Cor. 6:1, 3.
12. Cf. Lk. 12:14.
13. Literally 'the learners'; translation after Rufinus (*discentes id est laici*); see also what follows.
14. Conjecture after Schwegler.
15. Cf. Mt. 25:1.
16. Cf. Sir. 4:10.
17. Cf. Const. Apost. IV 2.1.
18. Cf. Mt. 25:35f.; Is. 58:7; Const. Apost. IV 2.1.
19. Cf. Const. Apost. II 46.1.
20. Cf. Const. Apost. II 44.4.
21. Conjecture after Schwegler; PO 'clear'.
22. Cf. Const. Apost. II 57.2-4; Hippol. *de Antichr.* 59; Clem. Alex. *Paed.* II 59.2; Epiph. *Haer.* 61.3.4; Egyptian Church Order 32.38 etc.
23. Conjecture after Rehm.
24. Cf. Acts 27:41.
25. With O; P etc. otherwise: 'as'.
26. Conjecture after Schwegler.
27. Cf. Mt. 10:40; Jn. 5:23; 13:20.
28. Cf. Mt. 8:12; 22:13; 25:30.
29. Cf. Mt. 12:30.

2. *The Clement Romance**

Clement's Spiritual Development (H I)

1. 1. I Clement, a Roman citizen, was able even in my youth to pursue a circumspect line of conduct, whilst my pensiveness from childhood held down my desires and brought me much affliction and tribulation. 2. Again and again there came to me - whence I cannot tell - thoughts of death. After my departing this life, would I be no more and no one remember me, 3. seeing that time, which knows no limits, brings every thing, even every thing, into oblivion? I wondered too if I would be without existence and without knowledge of those to whom existence belongs.... 4. Did the world begin at some time? I asked further. And what was then before its beginning? If it has always existed, then it will also continue to exist; if, however, it has come into being, then it must also pass away. 5. And what will be then after its dissolution but silence perhaps and oblivion? Or can there then be something which at the present time we cannot even conceive? **2.** 1. With such and such-like thoughts I concerned myself continually - why I know not - and was so painfully distressed by them that I fell ill with anaemia and consumption. And the worst of it was that when at any time I sought to drive these thoughts away as futile, I had to suffer all the more severely. 2. That embittered me, for I did not yet know that in these thoughts I had good companions who would provide for me an introduction to immortality, 3. as later my experience in life showed me, and for that I have been thankful to God, the Lord of all things. For by these anxieties which at the beginning I felt as oppressive I was made to probe things to their foundation and to find this foundation; 4. then I pitied those whose happiness I in my ignorance formerly thought should be praised. **3.** 1. As then onwards from childhood I occupied myself with such problems, I resorted to the lectures of the philosophers that I might learn something definite. Dogmas refuted and anew established fought and wrangled with one another; deductions that had been puzzled out were produced and new conclusions devised; I was unable to catch a glimpse of anything else. 2. To give an instance, at one time it was said that the soul is immortal, at another time that it is mortal. When the view prevailed that it is immortal, then I was glad; when on the other hand it was said that it is mortal, then I was grieved on that account. 3. Still greater, I confess, was my despair over my inability to make my own either the one or the other opinion; rather I had the impression that the hypotheses put forward are regarded as false or correct according to the person who champions them and are not set forth as they actually are. 4. As soon, however, as I had once grasped the truth that conclusions are not drawn according to the measure of the facts that are advocated but that opinions usually gain ground according to the personality of their champions, my confusion regarding these questions increased still more. At this I groaned in the bottom of my heart. For neither was I able to come to a firm decision nor had I power to free myself altogether from these thoughts, although, as I have already said, I had a will thereto.

(R I 6)

6. 1. While a flood of such reflections laid hold of me, there got through to us in the reign of the emperor Tiberius a report which took its rise in the East; it spread everywhere and finally, like a good message from God, it filled the whole world, not willing to permit that the will of God should remain unproclaimed. 2. It reached the remotest corners, and this was its content: There is a Man in Judaea who since the beginning of spring has been proclaiming to the Jews the kingdom of God; those, he states, will attain it who keep the demands of his commandments and of his doctrine. 3. As proof that his speech is worthy of credit and is from the divine Spirit, he performs, so it is said, by his mere word many signs and singularly miraculous deeds, 4. so that, as it were in the power of God, he makes the deaf to hear and the blind to see, makes the infirm and lame to stand erect, expels every weakness and all demons from men, yea even raises dead persons who are brought before him, and besides brings healing to lepers whom he sees from a distance, and there is nothing at all that is impossible for him. 5. In the course of time we came to know such things no longer through the numerous rumours that were in circulation; rather they were confirmed by the trustworthy reports of travellers who came from that quarter, and the truth of the story became clearer with every passing day.

7. 1. At length meetings took place here and there in Rome, there were discussions about these reports and interest manifested itself as to who this might be who had appeared there and what message he had delivered to men. 2. That went on until in the same year a man appeared in a very busy place in the city and addressed himself to the multitude in the following terms: 3. 'Hear me, ye citizens of Rome! The Son of God has appeared in the land of Judaea and promises eternal life to everyone who will hear, provided that he fashions his doings according to the will of God the Father, by whom he has been sent. 4. Wherefore turn ye from evil things to good, from what is temporal to what is eternal! 5. Recognise that there is one God, who rules heaven and earth and in whose righteous sight ye unrighteous populate the world that belongs to him! 6. If ye repent you and act according to his will, ye will enter into a new era, will become immortal and participate in his unspeakably delightful treasures and gifts.' 7. The man who thus spoke to the multitude came from the East, was a Hebrew by name Barnabas, and stated that he belonged to the circle of the disciples of that Son of God and had been sent to the end that he might proclaim this message to those who would hear it. 8. On learning that, I followed him with the rest of the people and heard further what he said. Then it was clear to me that in the case of this man words were not of a mere rhetorical finery, but that he made known simply and without circumlocution what he had heard from the Son of God or had seen of him. 9. For he supported his assertions not with plausible arguments, but brought forward, even from the circle of the bystanders, numerous witnesses of the sayings and marvels which he proclaimed. **8.** 1. But while the simple people willingly assented to such sincere words, and welcomed his simple manner of speech, those who fancied themselves scholars and philosophers began to laugh at Barnabas and to scoff at him and to direct against him the snares of their syllogisms as their heaviest weapons. 2. But he did not allow himself to be confused by that, regarded their sophistry as foolery and deemed them not even worthy of an answer, but courageously pursued the way on which he had entered. 3. Once when he was speaking someone interrupted him with the question why the gnat, which is merely a tiny creature, is so made that it has six feet and wings besides, whereas the elephant, in spite of its extraordinary size, has no wings at all and only four feet; 4. to that, however, he paid no attention whatever, but with persistent attentiveness went on with his discourse which the inappropriate remark had interrupted, merely uttering the one admonition every time he was interrupted: 5. 'We have the commission to proclaim to you the words and miraculous doings of him who has sent us and to confirm the trustworthiness of our proclamation not by ingenious arguments but by testimony from your own ranks. 6. For I see standing among you very many who, as I know, have heard along with us what we have heard and have seen along with us what we have seen. It lies with you to decide to accept or to repudiate our preaching. 7. We cannot hold back what, as we know, is profitable to you. For not to mention it would be hurt to us, and not to receive what we proclaim is destruction to you. 8. But as regards your absurd objection - I have in mind the difference between a gnat and the elephant - I could answer it without difficulty if you asked to learn the truth; but it would be foolish to speak to you now about creatures when you do not know the Creator and Founder of all things.' **9.** 1. Scarcely had he ended when all of a sudden, as with one consent, they all started an unrestrained laughter, by which they aimed at overawing him and putting him to silence, and called him a barbarian who was out of his senses. 2. As I had to witness all this, I was suddenly seized - I know not how - holy indignation burned in me, I could no longer hold myself in check, but declared with all frankness: 3. 'Very rightly has Almighty God hid his will from you, foreseeing your unworthiness to know him, an unworthiness that is too manifest to every discerning person from your present behaviour. 4. For whilst you see among you heralds of God's will whose manner of discourse gives no evidence of schooling in grammar, but who communicate to you the divine commands in simple, artless words so that all hearers can follow and understand what is said, 5. you deride the executors and bearers of your salvation, not knowing that to you, who fancy yourselves clever people and excellent speakers, it means sentence of condemnation that the truth is recognised by barbarous and uncivilised men. 6. For after it has come to you, it finds no hospitable reception although, had your rebellion and dissoluteness not stood against it, it would have been your beloved fellow-citizen. 7. In consequence it is made a reproach to you that you are not friends of truth and philosophers, but boasters and braggarts who think that the truth is to be found not in simple but only in subtilising ingenious speech, and who chatter many thousands of words, which yet cannot compensate for a single true one. 8. What think ye then, all ye Greeks, what will happen to you if there takes place the judgment of God of which this man speaks? 9. Wherefore at once give up laughing at him to your own destruction, and let any one of you explain to us why by your bleating you seek to deafen the ears of those who desire to be saved, and why by your hubbub you entice to fall into unbelief minds that are ready to believe. 10. How can there be pardon for you if you deride and ill-treat the messenger of God who promises you the knowledge of God? 11. In any case, even if he had no sort of truth to bring to you, he ought, merely because of his good-will towards you, to be received and welcomed.'

10. 1. Whilst I was expressing myself in these and such-like terms, violent discussions started among the bystanders. Some were moved with compassion on Barnabas, who after all was a visitor of theirs, and in consequence they regarded my speech as altogether justified. Others attempted in impudence and stupidity to wreak their anger upon me as much as upon Barnabas. 2. But as soon as evening drew on, I took Barnabas by the right hand and, paying no attention to his reluctance, brought him to my house and would not let him out any more lest some rowdy should lay violent hands upon him. 3. Thus we spent several days together; he succinctly expounded to me the word of truth, and at the same time I was his willing hearer. 4. Yet he hastened his departure since, as he said, he wished by all means to keep an approaching feast of his religion in Judaea; and there also he would remain with his own countrymen and brethren. Thereby he clearly indicated that he was grievously agitated by the wrong that he had suffered.

11. 1. At last I said to him, 'Only expound to me the doctrine of the Man whose appearing you proclaim! I shall then introduce your words into my discourses and preach the kingdom and righteousness of Almighty God; and after that, if you wish it, I shall travel with you. 2. For I desire extremely to become acquainted with Judaea that, if possible, I may always remain with you.' 3. To that Barnabas replied: 'If you wish to see our fatherland and to learn what you desire to know, then sail right now with me! 4. If, however, something still keeps you here, I shall give you particulars that identify our dwelling, so that you may easily find us when you please to come. For tomorrow morning I shall set out on my way.' 5. As it was clear to me that he would not reverse this decision, I accompanied him to the harbour and had him make quite clear to me the particulars of which he had spoken that would identify his dwelling. At the same time I said to him: 6. 'Had I not to demand from debtors the payment of a sum of money, I would not delay for another moment, but I shall soon follow you.' 7. When I had said that and had very warmly commended Barnabas to the ship-owners, I returned in sadness, for I had an intense longing for this esteemed guest and good friend.

12. 1. Having for the most part settled the question of the money that was owing to me - in this connection, that I might not be turned aside from my purpose, I overlooked a great deal in my haste - I set sail some days later direct for Judaea and after a voyage of fifteen days landed at Caesarea Stratonis, the largest city in Palestine. 2. On landing I made enquiries for a lodging and got to know from what was told me by the people that a certain Peter, a very highly approved disciple of the Man who had appeared in Judaea and wrought with divine power many signs and wonders among the people, was to hold a disputation on the following day with Simon a Samaritan from the village of Gittha. 3. On hearing this, I asked to be shown Peter's quarters. 4. When I had found them and was standing at the door, I told the door-keeper who I was and whence I came. 5. And, behold, Barnabas came out and, as soon as he saw me, fell into my arms with tears of joy. Then he took me by the hand and led me to Peter. 6. Having pointed him out to me from a distance, he said: 'That is Peter, of whom I have told you that he has penetrated most deeply into the divine wisdom. I told him about you without delay. 7. You can therefore face him as one well known to him. 8. For he has an accurate knowledge of all your good qualities and has attentively followed your purpose; on which account he very much wishes to get to know you. 9. And thus I present you to him today as a great gift.' Then, presenting me, he said: 'This, beloved Peter, is Clement!' **13.** 1. When this good man Peter heard my name, he stepped towards me and remained standing for a little before me; then, having invited me to sit down, he said: 2. 'You did well in receiving Barnabas, a herald of the truth, into your house, not fearing the fury of the raving mob. You will be blessed. 3. For as you received the messenger of truth, so will the truth itself receive you, a pilgrim and a stranger, and bestow upon you the citizen rights of her own city. You will greatly rejoice when, because now you show a small favour, you are appointed heir of good things that are eternal. 4. You need not now trouble yourself to provide me with an explanation of yourself. For Barnabas has truthfully told me everything about you and the qualities of your character, and almost every day without ceasing he has praised your good deeds.'

Clement's Outward Fortunes (H XII)

8. 2. There are (related to me) many important men who belong to the emperor's family. Indeed the emperor gave a relative of his own as wife to my father because he had grown up with him. She bore three sons, the two other brothers before me. Moreover they were twins and were quite like one another, as my father himself told me. For I knew neither them nor my mother, but carry in me merely a dim, dream-like picture of them. 3. My mother was called Mattidia, my father Faustus, of my brothers the one Faustinus and the other Faustinianus. 4. Now after I was born as the third, my mother had on one occasion a dream - such at all events is the story told me by my father: unless, along with her twin sons, she immediately left the city of Rome for a period of ten years, she would, together with them, die a fearful death. **9.** 1. Then my father, who very much loved his children, provided them amply with all essentials, put them with male and female slaves on board a ship and sent them to Athens, where the sons would have an opportunity of being educated; me alone he retained as a single child to be a comfort to him. And I am very thankful that the dream had not ordered me also to leave Rome in company with my mother. 2. For when a year had passed, my father sent money for his sons to Athens and ordered that inquiries be made as to how things were going with them. But those who set out on the journey did not return. 3. In the third year my father in his despair sent other messengers also with money for their support, and in the fourth year they came back with the report that they had seen neither my mother nor my brothers, indeed that they had never reached Athens and that no trace could be found of those who had accompanied them. **10.** 1. On hearing that, my father almost passed away in his great grief, for he no longer knew where he should turn and seek his own. Eventually he took me with him and went down with me to the harbour. There again and again he put the question, now to one person and now to another, whether he had seen or heard where there had been a shipwreck four years ago. To that he obtained many answers. He inquired further whether the dead bodies of a woman and her children had been seen washed up on the shore. 2. When those questioned answered that they had seen numerous dead bodies in different places, my father sighed at the information. Nevertheless, bewildered by his great heart-burnings, he raised the insane question of his attempting to search the sea, far as it might extend; and it must be put down to his credit that it was out of his love for those he missed that he entertained such vain hopes. Finally he placed me, at that time twelve years of age, under the care of tutors and thus left me behind in Rome, whilst he himself, weeping, went down to the harbour, boarded a ship, put to sea and set out on his quest. 3. And from that day until now I have never had a letter from him, nor do I know precisely whether he is alive or dead. 4. But I do regard it as more likely that in some way or other he also has perished; possibly anguish has overwhelmed him or he has fallen a victim in a shipwreck. For this conjecture there speaks the fact that twenty years have already gone past since I had any sure account of him.

The True Prophet (H I)

18. 1. (Peter says to Clement:) The will of God has fallen into oblivion for many sorts of reasons, 2. above all in consequence of inadequate instruction, careless upbringing, bad company, unseemly conversation and erroneous statements. 3. Thence there comes ignorance, and there come also dissoluteness, unbelief, unchastity, avarice, vanity and innumerable vices of this kind, which have occupied the world as it were a house which, like a cloud of smoke, they have filled; they have thus made muddy the eyes of those who dwell in the house and have prevented them from looking up and recognising the Creator God from his works and inferring his will. 4. Therefore the friends of truth who are in the house must cry from the depth of their heart for help for their truth-seeking souls, that if someone is outside the smoke-filled house, he may come and open the door, so that the sunlight from outside may invade the house and that the smoke within may be dissipated. **19.** 1. Now the man who can help here, I call the true prophet; he alone can enlighten the souls of men that with their own eyes they may be able to see the way to eternal salvation. 2. That is not possible in any other way, as indeed you yourself know; only just now you said 3. that every view has its friends and opponents and counts as true or false according to the qualification of its advocate, and in consequence different opinions do not come to light as what they are, but receive the semblance of worth or worthlessness from their advocates. 4. Wherefore the world needs the godly efforts of the true prophet that he may describe things to us as they actually are and tell us what we have to believe regarding everything. 5. First of all then we must examine the prophet with all seriousness and arrive at the certainty that he is a true prophet, 6. and then we should believe him in all matters and ought not to quibble at the least small particular in his teaching, but should accept all his words as valid, as it may appear in faith, yet actually on the ground of the sound examination that we have made. 7. For by proof at the outset and an extensive, meticulous examination everything is received with right deliberation. 8. Therefore it counts above all things to find the true prophet, for without him there cannot possibly be anything certain among men.

The Doctrine of the Pairs of Opposites or Syzygies (H II)

15. 1. (Peter:) Now that he might bring men to the true knowledge of all things, God, who himself is a single person, made a clear separation by way of pairs of opposites, in that he, who from the beginning was the one and only God, made heaven and earth, day and night, life and death. 2. Among these he has gifted free-will to men alone so that they may be just or unjust. For them he has also permuted the appearing of the pairs of opposites, in that he has set before their eyes first the small and then the great, first the world and then eternity, this world being transitory, but the one to come eternal; so also ignorance precedes knowledge. 3. In the same way he has ordered the bearers of the prophetic spirit. For since the present is womanly and like a mother gives birth to children, but the future, manly time on the other hand takes up its children in the manner of a father, 4. therefore there come first the prophets of this world (who prophesy falsely, and) those who have the knowledge of eternal things follow them because they are sons of the coming age. 5. Had the God-fearing known this secret, then they would never have been able to go wrong, and also they would even now have known that Simon, who now confounds all, is merely a helpmate of the feeble left hand (of God, i.e. the evil one). **16.** 1. As regards the disposition of the prophetic mission the case is as follows. As God, who is one person, in the beginning made first the heaven and then the earth, as it were on the right hand and on the left, he has also in the course of time established all the pairs of opposites. But with men it is no longer so - rather does he invert the pairs. 2. For as with him the first is the stronger and the second the weaker, so with men we find the opposite, first the weaker and then the stronger. 3. Thus directly from Adam, who was made in the image of God, there issued as the first son the unrighteous Cain and as the second the righteous Abel. 4. And in the same way from the man who amongst you is called Deucalion two symbols of the Spirit, the unclean and the clean, were sent out, the black raven and after it the white dove. 5. And also from Abraham, the progenitor of our people, there issued two sons, the older Ishmael and then Isaac, who was blessed by God. 6. Again from this same Isaac there sprang two sons, the godless Esau and the godly Jacob. 7. Likewise there came first, as first-born into the world, the high priest (Aaron) and then the law-giver (Moses). **17.** 1. The syzygy associated with Elias, which ought to have come, willingly held off to another time, being resolved to take its place when the occasion arises. 2. Then in the same way there came first he who was *among them that are born of women* [1] and only after that did he who belongs to the sons of men appear as the second. 3. Following up this disposition it would be possible to recognise where Simon belongs, who as first and before me went to the Gentiles, and where I belong, I who came after him and followed him as the light follows darkness, knowledge ignorance and healing sickness.

4. Thus then, as the true prophet has said,[2] a false gospel must first come from an impostor and only then, after the destruction of the holy place, can a true gospel be sent forth for the correction of the sects that are to come. 5. And thereafter in the end Antichrist must first come again and only afterwards must Jesus, our actual Christ, appear and then, with the rising of eternal light, everything that belongs to darkness must disappear. **18.** 1. Since now, as has been said, many do not know this conformity of the syzygies with law, they do not know who this Simon, my forerunner, is. For were it known, no one would believe him. But now, as he remains unknown, confidence is wrongly placed in him. 2. Thus he who does what haters do finds love; the enemy is received as a friend; men long for him who is death as a bringer of salvation; although he is fire, he is regarded as light; although he is a cheat, he obtains a hearing as a proclaimer of truth.

Simon's Former Life (H II)

22. 2. (Aquila [see p. 527] relates:) The father of this Simon is called Antonius, his mother Rachel. By nationality he is a Samaritan and comes from the village of Gittha, which is six miles distant from the capital. 3. During a stay in Egypt he acquired a large measure of Greek culture and attained to an extensive knowledge of magic and ability in it. He then came forward claiming to be accepted as a mighty power of the very God who has created the world. On occasion he sets himself up for the Messiah and describes himself as the Standing One. 4. He uses this title since he is to exist for ever and his body cannot possibly fall a victim to the germs of corruption. 5. He also denies that the God who created the world is the highest, nor does he believe in the resurrection of the dead. Turning away from Jerusalem, he sets Mount Gerizim in its place. 6. In the place of our true Christ he shows himself (as the Christ). The content of the law he interprets according to personal arbitrariness. He speaks indeed of a future judgment, but he does not reckon with it in earnest; for were he convinced that God will call him to account, he would not have ventured in his wickedness to turn against God Himself. 7. Thus there are ruined not a few who do not know that Simon uses piety merely as pretence in order to steal secretly from men the fruits of truth, and who believe in him, as though he were himself pious, in his manifold promises and in the judgment promised by him.

23. 1. Simon's contact with the tenets of religion came about in the following way. There appeared a certain John the Baptist, who according to the disposition of the syzygies was at the same time the forerunner of our Lord Jesus. 2. And as the Lord had twelve apostles according to the number of the solar months, so also there gathered about John thirty eminent persons according to the reckoning of the lunar month. 3. Among these was a woman Helena by name, and herewith a significant disposition prevailed. For the woman, who makes up only the half of the man, left the number 30 incomplete, precisely as in the case of the moon, the revolution of which is not altogether a month in duration. 4. Of these thirty Simon counted with John as the first and most distinguished; and indeed he was prevented after the death of John from assuming the leading place for a reason which we shall hear directly. **24.** 1. John was made away with at the very time when Simon had journeyed to Egypt to study magic; therefore a certain Dositheus, who aimed at becoming the head of the school, was able to spread abroad a false report that Simon was dead and to take over the leadership of the sect. 2. When now a little later Simon returned, he did not, on meeting Dositheus, demand of him his post, much as he desired it for himself, for he knew quite well that the man who had forestalled him in this office could not be removed against his will. 3. For this reason he made a pretence of friendship and for a while rested content with the second place after Dositheus. 4. When, however, after a time he met his thirty fellow-disciples, he began to circulate slanders against Dositheus. This man, he asserted, hands down the doctrines incorrectly, and does so less because of an evil intent and more out of ignorance. 5. Dositheus observed that Simon's well-calculated slanders were shaking his own standing among the great multitude so that they no longer regarded him as the Standing One; then on one occasion when Simon arrived for the ordinary meeting, he struck out at him with indignation. The stick seemed to go through Simon's body as if it were smoke. 6. Affrighted at this, Dositheus shouted to him, 'If thou be the Standing One, I also shall pay homage to you.' 7. As Simon answered in the affirmative Dositheus, knowing that he himself was not the Standing One, fell down and did homage to Simon and, associating himself with the twenty-nine others, set him in his own place. Then Dositheus died a few days after Simon had attained to standing but he himself had suffered downfall.

25. 1. Simon then took Helena to himself, and since then he moves about with her and up to the present day, as you yourself see, he upsets the people. 2. Of Helena herself he asserts that he brought her down to the world from the highest heaven, of which she is the mistress as the mother of all being and Wisdom. Because of her, he says, there came about a conflict between the Greeks and the barbarians; although they clung only to an image of the reality, for the true Helena dwelt at that time with the supreme God. 3. Giving thus a new interpretation to other concoctions of the Greek saga, he deceives many in a plausible manner, and at the same time he performs numerous wonderful deeds, by which we would ourselves have been imposed on, had we not known that he works them only by sorcery. . . . **26.** 1. He has also burdened himself with bloodguiltiness and has even related among his friends that he separated the soul of a boy from its body by means of secret magical invocations and keeps it in the interior of his house, where his bed is, to assist him in his performances, having in this connection drawn a likeness of the boy. 2. This boy, he asserts, he at one time fashioned out of air by a divine transformation and then, having put his appearance on record, he returned him again to air. 3. That came about in the following way. In his way of thinking the human spirit, which tends to what is warm, first imbibes the surrounding air in the manner of a cucumber and sucks it in; having infiltrated into the interior of the human spirit, this air then changes into water. 4. Since now the water in the human spirit cannot be drunk in consequence of its consistency, it has to undergo a transformation into blood. Let the blood coagulate and the flesh is fashioned. Then the flesh becomes solid, and so man comes into being not from the earth but out of air. 5. And so Simon persuaded himself that in such a way he had been able to fashion a new man; of him he asserted that he had returned him to air, having reversed the changes that had taken place.

Disputation between Simon and Peter in Caesarea (H II)

35. 1. Towards morning Zacchaeus came in with the following communication for Peter: 2. 'Simon wishes the disputation postponed until tomorrow; 3. for today is his tenth-day Sabbath.' 4. To that Peter answered: 'Inform Simon that he may use his own discretion and be assured that we hold ourselves in readiness, when he pleases, to confront him in a way well-pleasing to God.' 5. When Zacchaeus heard that, he went on his way to deliver the answer.

(H III)

29. 1. Zacchaeus returned and said: 'Beloved Peter, now it is about time to go to the disputation. 2. For a great crowd has assembled in the courtyard and awaits you, and in its midst Simon stands like a commander, surrounded by the people as by his guardsmen.' 3. When Peter heard that, he invited me, as I had not yet received the baptism that is necessary for salvation, to go aside for a little; for he desired to say his prayers. But to those who were already perfect (through baptism) he said: 4. 'Let us rise to our feet and pray that God in his unending mercy may support me in my conflict for the deliverance of the men whom he has created.' 5. Thereafter he prayed and betook himself to the great, open courtyard in which many were assembled out of curiosity, the impending decision having increased their wish to listen to it. **30.** 1. There then Peter entered; and when he had looked on the multitude, every eye in which was fixed upon him in breathless stillness, and on the magician Simon, who stood in the midst, he began to discourse as follows. 2. 'Peace be with you all who are ready to commit yourselves to the truth of God, this his great and incomparable gift to our world! He who has sent us, the true prophet of good principle, has commissioned us, by way of salutation and before any instruction, to speak to you of this truth. 3. If then there be among you any son of peace, then by virtue of our instruction peace will enter into him. But if any one among you does not accept peace, then for a testimony thereto we *shall shake off from us the dust of the street* which through the hardships of the way we have carried on ourselves and brought to you for your salvation, and shall go into other houses and cities . . . '[3]

38. 1. When Peter had thus spoken, Simon at a distance from the multitude cried aloud: 'Will you by your lies deceive the simple people who surround you, persuading them that one ought neither to believe nor to assert that there are gods, although the literature of the Jews mentions many gods? 2. For now in the presence of all I would argue with you from these very books that one must necessarily assume the existence of gods. It is in the first place a question of the God of whom you speak. With regard to him I prove that he cannot be the supreme and almighty power, being unable to foresee the future, and that he is imperfect, not without needs, not good, and is subject to innumerable dubious passions. 3. But once that is proved from Holy Scripture, then there remains, I assert, yet another god not mentioned in Scripture who foresees the future and is perfect, without needs, good and free from all dubious passions. . . . **39.** 1. Thus then forthwith Adam, who came into being after that image, is created blind and knows, as it is said, neither about good nor about evil, he proves himself disobedient, is expelled from Paradise and is punished with death. 2. In the same manner his Creator, being unable to see everywhere, says at the time of the fall of Sodom, *Come, let us go down and see whether or not they do according to their cry that comes before me, that I may know it,*[4] thus making his ignorance notorious. 3: When it is said of Adam: *Let us send him forth lest perhaps he stretch out his hand, touch the tree of life, eat thereof and live for ever,*[5] the *perhaps* manifests his ignorance; moreover the phrase *lest he eat thereof and live for ever* manifests his jealousy. 4. And if it stands written: *It repented God that he had made man,*[6] then that points to a change of mind and to ignorance. For *he repented* signifies reflection through which one who does not know what he will do attempts to fix his purpose, or is characteristic of one penitent at something which has not gone as he has wished. 5. And if it stands written: *And the Lord smelled a pleasing odour,*[7] that does not indicate freedom from need, and the fact that he enjoyed the smell of the flesh of the sacrifice is not exactly a proof of his goodness. His making trial - why, it is said: *And the Lord tried Abraham*[8] - allows a being to be inferred who is wicked and does not foresee the end of his patience.'

40. 1. In such a way Simon produced from Holy Scripture seemingly manifold evidences that God is subject to all passions. To that Peter replied:

'Is a scoundrel or malefactor ready to admit his offence to himself? Answer me that!' - 'No', Simon replied, 'he is not.' 2. Peter proceeded: 'How then can God be bad and wicked if the shameful actions ascribed to him are imputed to him with his consent in all publicity?' - Simon: 'It is to be assumed that the charges against him were formulated by another power against his will.' 3. Again Peter: 'Let us first of all investigate that! If of his own will he has incriminated himself, then, as you have just allowed, he cannot be wicked; but if it has come about through the action of another power, then we need to ask and by all means to investigate whether someone has not subjected him, who alone is good, to all these evils.' **41.** 1. To that Simon: 'Apparently you would ignore the charges which emerge from Holy Scripture against your God.' Again Peter: 'I believe that that is precisely what you do. For he who will not stick to the order of the discussion clearly does not wish a real investigation to take place. 2. If then I advance in file and wish first to consider the author, it is clear that I decide for the straight way.' . . . **42.** 2. Again Simon: 'How can one know the truth when of the books of Scripture some describe God as wicked and others describe him as good?' 3. To that Peter: 'Those statements of the Holy Scriptures which are in keeping with the creation wrought by God must be counted as genuine and those which contradict them as false.' 4. Simon: 'How can you prove that there is contradiction in Holy Scripture?' To that Peter: 'Of Adam you assert that he was created blind, but that he was not. For to a blind man God would not have given the commandment: *Of the tree of the knowledge of good and evil thou shalt not eat.*'[9] 5. Simon: 'He has described his mind as blind.' Peter: 'How could he be blind in mind who, before he ate of the fruit and with the approval of his Creator, gave appropriate names to all living things?' 6. Simon: 'Why did Adam, if he could see into the future, not suspect beforehand the serpent's deception of his wife?' 7. Peter: 'How could Adam, if he was not able to see into the future, give to his sons at the time of their birth names according to their future deeds? For he named his first son Cain, which means jealousy: for out of jealousy he slew his brother Abel, whose name means mourning, for his parents mourned for him, the first to be murdered. **43.** 1. And now if Adam, who was yet a creature of God, was able to see into the future, by how much more then must God who created him be able to do so? 2. Also that is incorrect which stands written: *It repented God*[10] as if out of ignorance he had to reflect; likewise the statement: *The Lord tried Abraham*[11] in order to find out whether he would hold his ground . . . 3. All these passages . . . are shown to be false and are overturned by others which assert the opposite.'

58. 2. This disputation lasted for three days. In the night before the fourth day dawned, Simon made off in the direction of Tyre.

The Appointment of Zacchaeus (H III)

59. 1. On the following night Peter called the multitude of his followers together. As soon as they had assembled, he said to them: 2. 'Whilst I betake myself to the heathen, who say that there are many gods, to preach and proclaim the one only God, who made heaven and earth and all that is therein, that they may love him and be saved, wickedness has anticipated me according to the law of the syzygies, and has sent Simon ahead, 3. in order that those men who, rejecting the gods assumed to exist on the earth, speak no more of their great number, may believe that there are many gods in heaven. Thus would men be brought to dishonour the monarchy of God and to meet severe punishment and eternal perdition . . . 5. But I must hasten after him that his lying assertions may not find a footing and establish themselves everywhere. **60.** 1. Since now some one must be appointed to fill my place, let us all with one accord pray God to make known the ablest among us who may set himself in the chair of Christ and lead his church in the spirit of godliness. 2. Who then is to be decided upon? By the decree of God that man is described as blessed whom his lord *will appoint* to serve his fellow-servants, *to give them their meat at the proper time*,[12] without thinking in himself: *My lord delays his coming*[13] . . . **61.** 1. But should one of those present who is able to restrain the ignorance of his fellow-citizens withdraw from this duty simply out of a care for his own personal peace, then he must be prepared to hear the words: *Thou wicked, slothful servant, you ought to have deposited my money with the bankers, that on my return I might have had my gain; cast out the worthless servant into the uttermost darkness*.[14] 2. And that rightly. For it is your duty - he would say therewith - to bring my words as money to the bankers and to regard them as values that you possess. 3. The community of believers must be obedient to one particular person that their unity may be preserved. 4. For a finally emerging leadership through a single organ of government, in the likeness of the monarchy of God, brings those who yield themselves to it into the delights of peace, . . . **62.** 1. And beyond that the things that are happening before our eyes should certainly instruct us that at the present time wars are constantly being waged because many kings reign in all the world; for each of them the lordship of another is reason enough for war. 2. But if there is one head of the whole, he has no occasion for war and therefore maintains perpetual peace. 3. For in the end, for those who are held to be worthy of eternal life, God anoints one king over all in this world that in consequence of this monarchy there may prevail a peace that is not to be disturbed. 4. In short, all must follow a single person as their leader, honouring him as the likeness of God; but the leader must know well the way that goes to the holy city.[15] **63.** 1. But among those present whom else should I choose for this but Zacchaeus, in whose house even our Lord stayed and rested,[16] holding him worthy to be saved?' With these words he laid his hand upon Zacchaeus, who was standing before him, and invited him to be seated on his stool. 2. But Zacchaeus fell at Peter's feet and besought him to release him from ruling,declaring emphatically: 'All that a ruler must do I shall attend to, only permit me to renounce this name! For I hesitate to adopt this designation; indeed it involves bitter envy and danger.' **64.** 1. Peter replied, 'If you are apprehensive of that, then allow yourself to be designated not ruler but commissioner, a designation which the Lord himself coined when he said: *Blessed is the man whom the Lord will commission to serve his fellow-servants.*[17] 2. But if you absolutely refuse to be regarded as the holder of an administrative office, then you are apparently unaware that the recognised status of a president can contribute much towards keeping the multitude in check; for everyone obeys the office-bearer, since conscience very much constrains him to do so. 3. And is it not sufficiently clear to you that you have not to wield the sceptre as do the rulers of the nations, but as a servant who ministers to them as a father who cares for them, as a physician who visits them, as a shepherd who watches over them - in short as one who is concerned for their well-being in every respect? Can you possibly think that I do not know what a charge I impose upon you in requiring that you suffer yourself to be criticised by the rabble that no one can please? . . . 4. Wherefore I beseech you to undertake it confidently in God's name and in Christ's, for the salvation and blessing of the brethren and for your own benefit. **65.** 1. Consider also this other point, that the more troublesome and the more dangerous it is to govern the Church of Christ the greater is the reward, but the greater also is the punishment of him who is in a position to do so and refuses. 2. I desire then that you, of whom I know that you are more educated than the others present, make the most of the excellent attainments with which God has entrusted you, that some day it may be said of you: *Well done, my good and faithful servant!*[18] and that you be not rebuked and declared liable to punishment as was the man who hid his talent.[19] 3. If, however, you do not wish to be a good shepherd of the Church, then name another in your stead who is more learned and more trustworthy than you are! This indeed you cannot do, for you associated even with the Lord, saw his miraculous deeds and learned how to govern the Church. **66.** 1. Your work then is to command what needs to be done, that of the brethren to conform and not be disobedient. If they conform, then they will be saved; if they abide in disobedience, then they will be punished by Christ, for the place of Christ is entrusted to the president. 2. Therefore the honour or defamation of the president lights upon Christ and from Christ upon God. 3. This I have said that the brethren also may recognise the danger into which disobedience to you leads them. For he who disobeys your command resists Christ, and he who is disobedient to Christ makes God angry.[20]

67. 1. The church as *a city built on a hill*[21] must have an order pleasing to

God and good administration. Above all the bishop as the authoritative leading spokesman must be heard. 2. The elders have to attend to the carrying-through of his orders. The deacons should walk about, looking after the bodies and souls of the brethren, and report to the bishop. 3. All the rest of the brethren should be ready even to suffer wrong. But if they desire an inquiry into a wrong that has been done to them, then they should be reconciled in the presence of the elders, and the elders should submit the agreement to the bishop. **68.** 1. They should urge on to marriage not only the young people but also those who are older, in order that lust may not flare up and infect the church with unchastity and adultery. 2. For God hates the committing of adultery more than any other sin because it destroys not only the sinner himself but also those who feast and keep friends with him; it is like canine madness for it has the capacity to spread farther its own frenzy. 3. For the sake of morality not only the elders but also all the other members of the Church should encourage marriage; for the sin of the man who is lewd necessarily comes upon all the rest. 4. To urge the brethren to morality is love's highest service, for it is the saving of the soul, whereas the nourishing of the body is only refreshment. **69.** 1. But if you love your brethren, take nothing of what is theirs, but rather give them of what you possess; for *you should feed the hungry, give drink to the thirsty, clothe the naked, visit the sick, do your best to help those in prison,*[22] receive strangers willingly into your dwellings and *hate no man.*[23] 2. How you have to manifest your piety, that, if you are sufficiently wise, your own intelligence should show you. Above all, if indeed I need to say it, you must assemble very frequently, where possible hourly, but by all means on the appointed days of assembly. 3. When you do that, you find yourselves within the walls of a place of refuge. For perdition begins with eccentric ways. 4. Therefore let no one keep himself away from the community out of a petty attitude of mind towards a brother. For if one of you abandons the community, then he will be counted in the number of those who scatter the Church of Christ,[24] and he will find his punishment as a leader of the enemies of Christ. 5. He will be rejected together with the adulterers. For like an adulterer, through the spirit that dwells in him and on some pretext or other he has separated himself and has given place to the evil one against himself, to steal the sheep that he has found ostensibly outside the fold. **70.** 1. Moreover, hear your bishop and do not become weary in showing him all honour; for you must know that, by showing it to him, it is carried over to Christ and from Christ to God; and to him who shows it, it is requited manifold. 2. Hold then the chair of Christ in honour,for you are also bidden to honour *the chair of Moses,*[25] although its occupants may have to reckoned sinners. 3. Therewith I have perhaps said enough to you. On the other hand it is not necessary to say to Zacchaeus how he must live without stain, for he is a true disciple of him who taught me also. **71.** 1. There are assuredly some things, beloved brethren, which you should not have to wait to be told, but which you should recognise of yourselves. Zacchaeus alone is wholly absorbed in service for you. He also has his necessities of life, but no time for himself. How then can he procure the support he needs? 2. Is it not then the right thing that all of you should attend to his necessities without waiting for him to ask you to do so? For that means begging, and he would rather die of hunger than condescend to that. 3. And how can you not be culpable if you do not give a thought to this, that *the labourer is worthy of his hire*?[26] And let no one say: "Then *the word that is freely received* is sold![27] That is not at all the case! 4. If one who possesses the means of living takes something, he sells the word; but he who possesses nothing and takes the necessities of life does no wrong. For the Lord also accepted at dinner-parties and among friends at a time when he, who later was to possess all things, possessed nothing. 5. Accordingly you ought to honour elders, catechists, competent deacons, widows whose conduct is respectable, and orphans as children of the Church. And when outlays become necessary for some purpose, you should contribute all of you together. 6. Be kind to one another and do not delay to undertake whatever conduces to your salvation.'

72. 1. After these words he laid his hand upon Zacchaeus and said: 'Ruler and Lord of all, Father and God, guard Thou the shepherd with the flock. 2. Thou art the cause, Thou art the power. We are that for which help is intended. Thou art the helper, the physician, the saviour, the wall, the life, the hope, the refuge, the joy, the expectation, the rest; in a word: Thou art everything. 3. Help, deliver and preserve us unto eternal salvation. Thou canst do all things. Thou art the Sovereign of sovereigns, the Lord of lords, the Ruler of kings. 4. Give Thou power to the president to loose what is to be loosed and to bind what is to be bound.[28] Through him as thine instrument preserve the Church of thy Christ as a beautiful bride. For thine is eternal glory. 5. Praise to the Father and to the Son and to the Holy Spirit to all eternity. Amen.'

The Appion Disputation (H IV)

1. 1. From Caesarea Stratonis I betook myself with Nicetas and Aquila to Tyre in Phoenicia, and, as instructed by Peter who had sent us forth, we lodged with Berenice, the daughter of Justa the Canaanitess, who received us very courteously.... **6.** 2. But in the morning there came a relative of Berenice who told us that Simon had set sail for Sidon, but had left behind him the following from the circle of his disciples: Appion Pleistonices of Alexandria, a grammarian by profession, in whom I recognised a friend on my father's side, Annubion of Diospolis, an astrologer, and Athenodorus of Athens, an Epicurean. 3. On learning this about Simon, we wrote it down in a letter which we despatched to Peter; after that we went for a walk.

7. 1. While we were doing so Appion met us. He was accompanied not only by the two above-mentioned companions but in addition by about thirty other men. 2. As soon as he caught sight of me, he saluted and kissed me. 'This', he said, 'is Clement of whose noble birth and superior culture I have told you much; he belongs to the family of the Emperor Tiberius and is well read in all the departments of Grecian learning, only he has allowed himself to be deceived by a barbarian named Peter with the result that he now thinks and acts after the manner of the Jews. 3. Therefore I beseech you to give me your help in my endeavour to correct him, and in your presence I ask him. Since he thinks that he has devoted himself to the culture of piety, let him tell me if he has not sinned exceedingly in forsaking the ancestral traditions and turning to the customs of the barbarians.' **8.** 1. To that I answered: 'I acknowledge the kindly inclination toward me of which you give evidence, but I take exception to your ignorance.' . . . 2. Appion said: 'Does it seem to you to be ignorance to retain the ancestral customs and to accord with the Greek way of thinking?' 3. I answered: 'The man who makes up his mind to be godly should never on principle cling to the ancestral customs, but must preserve them if they are pious and renounce them if they are impious. For it is quite conceivable that a man may be the son of an impious father but himself desire to be pious and therefore may not be prepared to follow his father in his principles.' 4. To that Appion replied: 'What? do you then impute to your father a bad course of life?' 'It was not his course of life that was bad', I answered, 'but his religious conviction.' 5. Appion: 'I would like to know then what it was that was so bad in his views.' To that I replied: 'That he believed in the false, bad myths of the Greeks.' 'What then', Appion asked, 'Are these false, bad myths of the Greeks?' 'Their false conception of God', I replied. . . . **11.** 1. 'Then, my beloved Greek friends, there is a great difference between truth and custom. For where truth is honestly sought for, there also it is found, but custom, be it true or false, maintains its ground undisputed, just as it was taken over, and he who takes it over has no joy in it if it is true, nor is he angry with it if it is false. . . . 2. And it is not easy to cast off the ancestral garment, even when it seems to the bearer of it to be worn out and ridiculous. **12.** 1. Accordingly I assert outspokenly that Greek culture is in its entirety a most malicious concoction of the evil spirit. 2. For some Greeks have brought in many gods, gods that are evil and guilty in manifold respects, in order that he who wishes to do similar things himself may not need to be ashamed, as man naturally is, being able to plead as an example the bad, sinful conduct of the mythical gods. . . . 3. Others again have brought in fate . . . contrary to which no one can do or suffer anything. 4. Here the situation is the same as in the first case; for when a man believes that he can do nothing and suffer nothing contrary to his fate, it is easy for him to be ready to sin. . . .

13. 1. Others again believe in unforeseen chance and think that everything takes its course of itself without the supervision of a ruler. This view is . . . of all conceptions the worst. 2. For if there is no being who directs all things and cares for all things and duly assigns to every man his portion, then men, having nothing to fear, are quickly prepared for all possibilities. . . . 3. On the other hand, the doctrine of the barbarian Jews, as you call them, is the most godly. It accepts one Father and Creator of all things who in his nature is good and righteous, good in that he pardons those who repent of their sins, righteous in that he rewards every one who knows no repentance according to his deeds. . . . **15.** 1. Nevertheless I return to the first view of the Greeks, which speaks of the existence of many gods who have become culpable in manifold respects. 2. Only I shall not spend much time on things that are known and tell the stories of the vicious doings of every one of these so-called gods . . . with which through your Greek education you are well acquainted; **16.** 1. but I may well make a beginning with the very kingly Zeus. . . . 2. He put his own father in irons and imprisoned him in Tartarus and punishes the other gods! For those who desire to practise unmentionable indecencies he swallowed Metis after he had begotten her. For Metis means seed, it being impossible to swallow a child. 3. As an excuse for sodomites he carried off Ganymede. As a help to adulterers he himself is often exposed as an adulterer. He has incited to incest with sisters by cohabiting with his own sisters Hera, Demeter and Aphrodite Urania. . . . 4. To those who wish to have sexual intercourse with their daughters he proves a bad mythical example in his cohabiting with Persephone. And in addition to that he has wrought impiously in manifold other ways. . . . **17.** 1. That men of no learning do not worry much about such notions may well be understood, but what ought cultured men to say of them? Now many among them, who profess to be grammarians and sophists, assert that such doings are compatible with the dignity of the gods. 2. For they themselves live an uncontrolled life and readily lay hold on the myth as an excuse that they may be able to commit their iniquities without hesitation after the example of the higher powers. . . . **19.** 3. We must then shun such myths of the Greeks, as also their theatres and their books, yea, if it be possible, their cities also. For their inhabitants are full of false doctrine and this they transmit as a plague. . . . **20.** 1. Some among them who even pass themselves off as philosophers, represent these offences as indifferent and call those who are indignant at such doings blockheads. . . . **22.** 1. Let us regard that as enough for the present! This much at all events we all know, that only too frequently men fly into uncontrolled passion about it and that on its account wars have broken out, houses have been overthrown, and cities taken possession of, and many other evils come about. 2. Therefore have I taken refuge with the holy God and the law of the Jews, having attained, after I had made positive examination, to the conviction that the law has been prescribed on the basis of the righteous judgment of God and that in all cases the soul receives some day what befits it according to its deeds.'

Peter on his Mission Journeys (H VII)

1. 1. In Tyre not a few people from the neighbourhood and numerous inhabitants of the city came to Peter and cried to him: 'May God have mercy upon us through you, and may he through you bring us healing!' And Peter, having mounted a high rock that he might be seen of all, greeted them in a godly way and began as follows: **2.** 1. 'God, who has made heaven and the universe, is not wanting in power to save those who desire to be saved. . . . **4.** 2. And what is pleasing to God is this, that we pray to him and ask from him as the one who dispenses everything according to a righteous law, that we keep away from the table of devils,[29] that we do not eat dead flesh, that we do not touch blood, that we wash ourselves clean from all defilement.[30] 3. Let the rest be said to you also in one word, as the God-fearing Jews heard it, while you show yourselves, many as you are, of one mind: "What good a man wishes for himself, let him confer the same also on his neighbour!"[31] ' . . .

5. 1. After they had thus been instructed for some days by Peter and had been healed, they were baptized. At the time of his other miraculous deeds the rest sat beside one another in the middle of the market-place in sackcloth and ashes and did penance for their former sins. 2. When the Sidonians heard this, they did likewise; and because they themselves were not able on account of their diseases to come to Peter, they sent a petition to him. 3. After he had stayed for some days in Tyre and had instructed all the inhabitants and freed them from numerous sufferings, Peter founded a church and appointed a bishop for them from the number of the elders who were accompanying him; then he set out for Sidon.

6. 1. When Peter entered Sidon, the people brought many sick folk in beds and set them down before him. 2. And he said to them: 'Do not on any account believe that I, a mortal man, myself subject to many sufferings, can do anything to heal you! But I greatly desire to tell you in what way you can be delivered. . . . **7.** 1. For I mention to you two ways,[32] showing you in the first place in what way men fall into misfortune and in the second place in what way under God's guidance they are delivered. 2. The way of those who perish is broad and very easy, but it leads straight away to misfortune; the way of those who are delivered is narrow and rough, but in the end it leads to salvation those who have taken its burdens upon themselves. Before these two ways there stand belief and unbelief.' . . .

8. 3. Such were the addresses that Peter gave in Sidon. There also within a few days many were converted and believed and were healed. So Peter founded a church there and enthroned as bishop one of the elders who were accompanying him. He then left Sidon.

9. 1. Immediately after the arrival of Peter in Berytus an earthquake took place; and people came to Peter saying: 'Help, for we greatly fear that we shall

all together perish!' 2. Then Simon dared, along with Appion, Annubion, Athenodorus and his other comrades, to turn against Peter in the presence of all the people: 'Flee, ye people, from this man; 3. for he is a magician - you may believe me - and has himself occasioned this earthquake and has caused these diseases to frighten you, as if he himself was a god!' 4. And many other false charges of this sort did Simon and his followers bring against Peter, suggesting that he possessed superhuman power. 5. As soon as the multitude gave him a hearing, Peter with a smile and an impressive directness spoke the words: 'Ye men, I admit that, God willing, I am capable of doing what these men here say and in addition am ready, if you will not hear my words, to turn your whole city upside down.' **10.** 1. Now when the multitude took alarm and readily promised to carry out his commands, Peter said: 'Let no one of you associate with these magicians or in any way have intercourse with them.' 2. Scarcely had the people heard this summons when without delay they laid hold of cudgels and pursued these fellows till they had driven them completely out of the city. . . .

12. 1. After he had stayed for several days with the inhabitants of Berytus, had made many conversant with the worship of the one God and had baptized them, Peter enthroned as bishop one of the elders who were accompanying him and then journeyed to Byblus. 3. On coming there he learned that Simon had not waited for him even for a single day, but had started at once for Tripolis. Accordingly Peter remained a few days with the people of Byblus, effected not a few healings and gave instruction in the Holy Scriptures. He then journeyed in the track of Simon to Tripolis, being resolved to pursue him rather than to make room for him.

(H VIII)

1. 1. Along with Peter there entered into Tripolis people from Tyre, Sidon, Berytus, Byblus and neighbouring places, who were eager to learn, and in numbers that were not smaller people from the city itself crowded about him desiring to get to know him. . . . **4.** 1. Astonished at this eagerness of the multitudes, Peter answered: 'You see, beloved brethren, how the words of our Lord are manifestly fulfilled. For I remember how he said: *Many will come from east and west, from north and south, and repose in the bosom of Abraham, Isaac and Jacob.*[33] Nevertheless *many are called, but few are chosen.*[34] 2. In their coming in response to the call so much is fulfilled. 3. But since it rests not with them but with God who has called them and permitted them to come, on this account alone they have no reward. . . . 4. But if after being called they do what is good, and that rests with them themselves, for that they will receive their reward. **5.** 1. For even the Hebrews who believe in Moses

. . . are not saved unless they abide by what has been said to them. 2. For their believing in Moses lies not with a decision of their own will but with God, who said to Moses: *Behold, I come to thee in a pillar of cloud that the people may hear me speaking to thee and believe for ever*![35] 3. Since then it is granted to the Hebrews and to them that are called from the Gentiles to believe the teachers of truth, whilst it is left to the personal decision of each individual whether he will perform good deeds, the reward rightly falls to those who do well. 4. For neither Moses nor Jesus would have needed to come if of themselves men had been willing to perceive the way of discretion. And there is no salvation in believing in teachers and calling them lords. **6.** 1. Therefore is Jesus concealed from the Hebrews who have received Moses as their teacher, and Moses hidden from those who believe Jesus. 2. For since through both one and the same teaching becomes known, God accepts those who believe in one of them. 3. But belief in a teacher has as its aim the doing of what God has ordered. 4. That that is the case our Lord himself declares, saying: *I confess to thee, Father of heaven and earth, that thou hast hidden this from the wise and elder, but hast revealed it to simpletons and infants*.[36] 5. Thus has God himself hidden the teacher from some since they know beforehand what they ought to do, and has revealed him to others since they know not what they have to do. **7.** 1. Thus the Hebrews are not condemned because they did not know Jesus . . . provided only they act according to the instructions of Moses and do not injure him whom they did not know. 2. And again the offspring of the Gentiles are not judged, who . . . have not known Moses, provided only they act according to the words of Jesus and thus do not injure him whom they did not know. 3. Also it profits nothing if many describe their teachers as their lords, but do not do what it befits servants to do. 4. Therefore our Lord Jesus said to one who again and again called him Lord, but at the same time did not abide by any of his commands: *Why sayest thou Lord to me and doest not what I say*?[37] For it is not speaking that can profit any one, but doing. 5. In all circumstances good works are needed; but if a man has been considered worthy to know both teachers as heralds of a single doctrine, then that man is counted rich in God. . . . '

From the Recognition Scenes (H XII)

12. 1. One of us took courage and in the name of all directed a request to Peter that on the following day early in the morning we should set sail for the island Aradus which lay opposite to us. . . . **13.** 1. Peter, who alone had not thought it necessary to take a view of the sights that were there, observed attentively a woman who sat outside before the doors and got her livelihood by begging. 2. 'Dear woman', he said to her, 'what limb fails you that you have submitted to such disgrace - I mean that of begging - and do not rather earn your livelihood by working with the hands that God has given you ?' 3. She answered with a sign, 'Had I only hands that could work! Now they have merely the appearance of hands and are actually dead. . . . ' 4. To Peter's question, 'For what reason do you suffer so grievous a misfortune?' 5. she answered, 'Weakness in my soul and nothing else. For had I had the heart of a man, then there would have been a precipice, there would have been waves of the sea into which I would have cast myself and so have been able to make an end of my life.'

19. 1. Whilst the woman related her life's story, it appeared as if Peter's thought drew him sometimes here and sometimes there. . . . 3. Finally he asked, 'Dear woman, tell me your family, your native place and the names of your children!' . . . 4. But the woman stated that she came from Ephesus and that her husband was a Sicilian; and in the same way she changed the names of her three sons. 5. Being of opinion that she spoke the truth, Peter said, 'What a pity! I thought, dear woman, that today I would be able to bring you great joy, supposing you to be a certain person whose life's story I know very well from hearsay.' 6. Then she implored him with the words: 'I beseech thee, tell me that I may know if among all women there is one more unfortunate than I!' **20.** 1. And Peter, who could not lie, out of pity for her began to tell her the truth: 'Among my companions there is a young man who willingly takes part in religious discussions, a Roman citizen, who, as he has told me, has besides his father two twin brothers, and on no one of these latter has he set eyes. 2. For according to his father's account his mother had a dream and thereupon left Rome for a time together with her twin sons lest she should die an evil death; but since she left the city with them, it has been impossible to find her. 3. Her husband, the father of the narrator, went in search of her, and since that time he has not been heard of.'

21. 1. At these words of Peter the woman, who had listened attentively, started in amazement. Then Peter approached her, supported her, and called upon her to maintain her upright bearing, advising her to say openly what was going on in her. 2. And whilst her body was still stricken as with intoxication, she yet recovered consciousness and was able to estimate the greatness of the joy that was awaiting her. Rubbing her eyes, she asked, 'Where is this young man?' 3. Then Peter, who saw through everything, answered, 'First speak your mind, for otherwise you cannot see him.' Then she made haste, saying: 'I am the mother of the young man.' Peter: 'What is his name?' She: 'Clement.' 4. Thereupon Peter: 'It is so.' . . . 5. She: 'I am ready for anything, only let me see my only son! For in him I shall again recognise my two children who died here.'

(H XIII)

1. 3. The next day we reached Laodicea. And, think of it! there met us before the gates Nicetas and Aquila, who greeted us and brought us to the inn. 4. When Peter saw the large, beautiful city, he said: 'It is worth while to stay here for some days.' 5. And Nicetas and Aquila asked who the strange woman was. I answered them, 'My mother! God has granted to me through my lord Peter to recognise her again.' **2.** 1. After I had spoken these words, Peter told them the whole story in its main features. . . . **3.** 1. At that Nicetas and Aquila were startled and cried out: 2. 'O Lord and Ruler of all things, is this truth or a dream?' Peter answered: 'Provided we are not asleep, it is the truth.' 3. For a little the two of them paused to recover their senses, and then they said: 'We are Faustinus and Faustinianus.'

7. 1. Thereupon Nicetas began the following account: 'On that night in which, as you know, the ship went to pieces, we were sheltered by some men whom no inner restraints kept from being pirates. They put us in a boat and . . . brought us to Caesarea Stratonis. 2. As we wept because of hunger and fear and the blows we received, they sold us, after changing our names that we might not say all of a sudden something that was unacceptable to them. 3. A very respectable woman, who had become a convert to Judaism, Justa by name, bought us and adopted us and brought us up very attentively in all the departments of Greek learning. 4. When we came to the age of discretion, we became fond of worship, and found delight in study that through discussions with other peoples we might be able to convince them of their error. We also made ourselves thoroughly familiar with the doctrines of the philosophers, especially with the most godless, those of Epicurus and of Pyrrho, that we might be able all the better to refute them. **8.** 1. We were school-fellows of Simon the magician, and through this friendship we ran the risk of becoming victims to deceit.'

(H XIV)

2. 1. Peter . . . related . . . : 2. 'Whilst you were withdrawing, an old workman came on the scene, who kept himself curiously aloof in order that, ere he himself was seen, he might be able to make out what we would do. . . . 3. He then followed us farther that he might come upon a fitting opportunity to address me. "For long", he said, "I have been following you and would have spoken to you, but I was afraid that you might be angry with me because of my curiosity. But now I say to you, if you will please hear it, what appears to me to be the truth." . . . **3.** 5. And I asked, "What then is it that you have had to suffer?" "That I do not need to say now", he replied, "perhaps you will get to know later who I am, whence I originate and into what circumstances I have fallen. For the present I would like it to be clear to you that everything depends on nativity." **4.** 1. Thereupon I said, "If everything depends on nativity, and you are convinced that that is the case, then your present reflections are contrary to your basic conceptions. 2. For if it is not possible so much as to fashion a thought contrary to nativity, why do you trouble yourself in vain as to whether something can take place which yet cannot possibly take place? 3. Even if nativity has its significance, you do not need to go to any trouble at all to dissuade me from worshipping him who is even the Lord of the stars; if he wills that a thing should not take place, then its coming to pass is impossible. For of necessity the subordinate part must always obey the superior part.' . . . **6.** 1. To that the old man answered, "To a certain extent that sounds likely enough, but in its entirety my experience of life is opposed to your incomparable arguments. 2. For earlier I lived as an astrologer in Rome, came there into touch with a member of the emperor's house and obtained information about the nativity of this man and of his wife; and having seen that their fate turned out in actual agreement with their nativity, I can no more allow myself to be convinced by your exposition. 3. The constellation of the wife's nativity pointed to this, that she would commit adultery, love her own slaves and meet her death abroad in the sea. And that is precisely what came about. For she fell in love with her slave, fled with him, being unable to bear the reproach, went to a foreign land, cohabited with him there and finally perished in the sea." **7.** 1. At that I asked, "Whence do you know that after her flight she married the slave in the foreign land and after this marriage met her death?" To that the old man replied, 2. "Naturally I do not know accurately about her marriage to him, indeed I knew nothing even of her falling in love with him; but after her departure the man's brother told me the whole story of her amour . . . and also that the wretched woman - for she cannot be blamed seeing that she was obliged to do and to suffer all this in consequence of her nativity - devised a dream, whether true or false I do not know. 3. According to his story she certainly asserted that in the dream a man appeared to her and ordered her to leave Rome immediately with her children. 4. Anxious for the well-being of his wife and children, the husband at once sent them in the company of their mother and several slaves to Athens for their education; only the third, the youngest, son he kept with him, the person who had appeared in the dream having granted that this son should remain with him. 5. Receiving in the course of a long time no word from his wife, although he himself had frequently sent to Athens, he called me to himself as the nearest of his friends and with me set out in search of her. 6. In this journey I willingly endured with him many hardships, remembering that earlier he had permitted me to share in all his prosperity, for he loved me more than all his other friends. 7. Leaving Rome, we came here to Syria. We landed at Seleucia; and after we had left the ship, it came about that after a few days my friend died of despair, whilst I came to this place, hired myself out, and up till this day have earned my bread by the work of my hands."

8. 1. Whilst the old man told this story it became clear to me that the man of whom he said that he had died was himself, your father. But I did not wish to confront him with your lot until I had unbosomed myself to you.'

The Installation of Clement (Epitome II)

144. Thus we, I Clement, Aquila and Nicetas, remained together with the apostle Peter and in the service of God proclaimed the word of truth in very many villages and cities. Peter, the apostle of Christ, attended many who were sick, healed those who were possessed, and through the power of the Lord Jesus Christ raised to life again numerous persons who were dead; he led me through cities and villages and finally betook himself even to Rome that there also he might proclaim the word of truth. Arriving in the city, he taught the word of truth daily in the synagogues and in private houses and through holy baptism brought much people, important and unimportant, to Christ, and finally also the influential among the women of rank, so that in a short time almost all came to holy baptism and through the teaching of the apostle believed in God.

145. . . . When the brethren were assembled, Peter suddenly seized me by the hand, rose and said in presence of the Church: **146.** 'Hear me, brethren and fellow-servants. Since I have been taught by our Lord and Master Jesus Christ, who sent me, that the time of my death is near, I appoint Clement to be your bishop. To him I commit my teacher-ship; for from the beginning to the end he has been my companion and has thus listened to all my discourses. He has shared in all my temptations, and always it was evident that he could hold his ground in the faith. I have proved him to be more than all others god-fearing, sober-minded, humane, good, learned, pure, upright, patient and capable of tolerating calmly the bad conduct of some catechumens. Therefore I transfer to him the power to *bind* and to *loose* in order that all he orders on earth may be decreed in heaven.[38] He will bind what is to be bound, and loose what is to be loosed, knowing the rule of the Church. Hearken to him and be assured that he who grieves the teacher of the truth sins against Christ and provokes the anger of the Father of all things; therefore he will not live. But the president himself must assume the place of a physician and not show the nature of a savage beast.'

147. During this discourse I fell at Peter's feet and besought him earnestly to release me from the honour and power of the bishop's office. But Peter answered: 'Ask me not about this. It is thus decreed, for this bishop's chair needs no thoughtless, ambitious person but one who is distinctively trustworthy and spiritually refined. Or give me one who is better than you are, who has travelled more with me, who has heard more of my discourses, and has learned more thoroughly how to lead the Church, and I will not constrain you to do good against your will. . . . The sooner then you consent, the more you will ease my difficult situation.' **158.** After these words he laid his hands upon me in the sight of all and called me to take my place in his own chair.

Notes

Translated after Johannes Irmscher

1. Mt. 11:11.
2. Cf. Mt. 24:24; 7:15.
3. Cf. Mt. 10:12ff.; Mk. 6:11; Lk. 10:5.
4. Gen. 18:21.
5. Gen. 3:22.
6. Gen. 6:6.
7. Gen. 8:21.
8. Gen. 22:1.
9. Gen. 2:17.
10. Gen. 6:6.
11. Gen. 22:1.
12. Mt. 24:45ff.; Lk. 12:42.
13. Mt. 24:48; Lk. 12:45.
14. Mt. 25:26f., 30; Lk. 19:23.
15. Cf. Rev. 3:12; 21:10.
16. Lk. 19:5, 9.
17. Cf. Mt. 24:45f.; 25:21; Lk. 12:42f.
18. Mt. 25:21.
19. Cf. Mt. 25:27, 30.
20. Cf. Lk. 10:16.
21. Mt. 5:14.
22. Cf. Mt. 25:35ff.
23. Didache 2, 7.
24. Cf. Mt. 12:30.
25. Mt. 23:2f.
26. Lk. 10:7.
27. Cf. Mt. 10:8.
28. Cf. Mt. 16:19; 18:18.
29. Cf. 1 Cor. 10:21.
30. Cf. Acts 15:20, 29; 21:25.
31. Cf. Tobit 4.15; Mt. 7:12; Lk. 6:31.
32. Cf. Mt. 7:13f.
33. Mt. 8:11; Lk. 13:29.
34. Mt. 22:14.
35. Ex. 19:9.
36. Mt. 11:25; Lk. 10:21.
37. Cf. Mt. 7:21; Lk. 6:46.
38. Cf. Mt. 16:19; 18:18.

3. *Kerygmata Petrou*

The true Prophet (H III 17-21)

17.1. 'If any one denies that the man (= Adam) who came from the hands of the Creator of all things possessed the great and holy Spirit of divine foreknowledge, but acknowledges that another did this who was begotten of impure seed, how does he not commit a grievous sin? 2. I do not believe that such an one will find pardon even if he has been misdirected to this affront to the Father of all things by a forged passage of Scripture. . . .

20. 2. On the other hand, he executes a godly work who acknowledges that no other possesses the Spirit but he who from the beginning of the world, changing his forms and his names, runs through universal time until, anointed for his toils by the mercy of God, he comes to his own time and will have rest for ever.

21. 1. He, who alone is the true prophet, has, in the place of the Creator, given a suitable name to every living thing according to the measure of its nature;[1] for if he gave a name to anything, then that was also the name given it by him who had created it. 2. How then was it yet necessary for him to eat of a tree that he might know what is good or evil? (Assuredly it stands written:) "He commanded."[2] But this undiscerning men believe, who think that a dumb brute is more generous than God, who created them and all things.'[3]

(H III 26)

1. 'He who is among the sons of men has prophecy innate to his soul as belonging to it, and as a male being he announces in clear words the hopes of the world to come. Therefore he called his son by the name Abel, which without any ambiguity is translated "grief". 2. For he directs his sons to grieve over their deluded brethren. With no deceit he promises them consolation in the world to come.[4] 3. He exhorts them to pray to one God alone. He neither speaks himself of gods nor does he believe any other who speaks of them. He keeps and increases the good that he has.[5] He hates sacrifices, bloodshed and sprinklings, he loves pious, pure and holy men, he puts out the altar fire, 4. puts a stop to wars, preaches peace, commends temperance, does away with sins, orders marriage, permits abstinence and leads all men to purity. 5. He makes men compassionate, commends justice, seals the perfect, publishes the word of peace. He prophesies what is intelligible and speaks what is certain. 6. He frequently calls attention to the eternal fire of punishment, he constantly proclaims the kingdom of God. He makes reference to the heavenly riches, promises imperishable glory and indicates the forgiveness of sins by what he does.'

(H XI 19)

1. 'Since the prophet of the truth knew that the world had fallen into error and associated itself with wickedness, he did not cherish peace[6] with it, whilst it continued in error; but to the end he occasions wrath against all those who consent to wickedness. 2. Thus he brings knowledge in place of error; among those who are sober he kindles wrath like a firebrand[7] against the insidious serpent. He draws the word like a sword and by knowledge slays ignorance, cutting and separating the living from the dead. 3. Whilst wickedness is vanquished by lawful knowledge, war fills the universe. For the sake of salvation the son who is obedient is separated from his obstinate father, or the father from the son, or the mother from the daughter, or the daughter from the mother, relatives from their people and friends from their companions.'[8]

Female Prophecy (H III 22)

1. 'Along with the true prophet there has been created as a companion a female being who is as far inferior to him as *metousia* is to *ousia*, as the moon is to the sun, as fire is to light. 2. As a female she rules over the present world, which is like to her, and counts as the first prophetess; she proclaims her prophecy with all *amongst those born of woman. . . .* '[9]

(H III 23-25)

1. 'There are two kinds of prophecy, the one is male . . . 2. the other is found *amongst those who are born of woman.* Proclaiming what pertains to the present world, female prophecy desires to be considered male. 3. On this account she steals the seed of the male, envelops them with her own seed of the flesh and lets them - that is, her words - come forth as her own creations. 4. She promises to give earthly riches gratuitously in the present world and wishes to exchange <the slow> for the swift, the small for the greater. **24.** 1. She not only ventures to speak and hear of many gods, but also believes that she herself will be deified; and because she hopes to become something that contradicts her nature, she destroys what she has. Pretending to make sacrifice, she stains herself with blood at the time of her menses and thus pollutes those who touch her. 2. When she conceives, she gives birth to temporary kings and brings about wars in which much blood is shed. 3. Those who desire to get to know the truth from her, are led by many opposing and varied statements and hints to seek it perpetually without finding it, even unto death. 4.For from the beginning a cause of death is certain for blind men; for she prophesies errors, ambiguities

and obscurities, and thus deceives those who believe her. **25.** 1. Therefore has she also given an ambiguous name to her first-born son; she named him Cain, which word has a two-fold meaning; for it is interpreted both "possession" and "envy" (and indicates) that later he was to envy (his brother Abel) a woman, or a possession, or the love of his parents. 2. But if it be none of these, then it was well ordered that he should be called "possession", for he was her first possession; which was profitable for her (= false prophecy). For he was a *murderer* and a *liar*[10] and did not wish to cease to sin once he had begun to do so. 3. Moreover, his descendants were the first adulterers. They made harps and lyres and forged instruments of war.[11] 4. Therefore also is the prophecy of his descendants full of adulterers and harps, and secretly and sensually excites to war.'

The Law and False Pericopes (H III 47)

1. . . . 'Moses delivered the law of God orally to seventy wise men[12] that it might be handed down and administered in continuous sequence. After the death of Moses, however, it was written not by Moses himself, but by an unknown person; 2. for in the law it is said: *And Moses died and was buried near the house of Phogor, and no one knows of his sepulchre unto this day.*[13] 3. But how, after his death, could Moses write: *And Moses died . . .* ? And as in the time after Moses - about five hundred or more years later - it was found in the temple that had lately been built,[14] after a further five hundred years it was carried away, and in the reign of Nebuchadnezzar it was consumed by fire.[15] 4. And since it was written in the time after Moses and was repeatedly destroyed, the wisdom of Moses is shown in this; for he did not commit it to writing, foreseeing its disappearance. But those who wrote the law, since they did not foresee its destruction, are convicted of ignorance and were not prophets.'

(H II 38)

1. 'The prophet Moses having by the order of God handed over the law with the elucidations to seventy chosen (men) that they might prepare those who were willing among the people, after a short time the law was committed to writing. At the same time some false pericopes intruded into it. These defamed the only God, who made heaven and earth and all that is in them. The wicked one dared to do this for a good purpose, 2. namely, that it might be ascertained which men are shameless enough to hear willingly what is written against God and which, out of their love of him, not only do not believe what is said against him, but do not bear to hear even the beginning of it, even should

it be true, (men therefore) who are of the opinion that it is safer to expose oneself to danger on the ground of a well-meaning belief than in consequence of defamatory words to live with a bad conscience.'

(H III 48-52)

48.2. . . . 'In the providence of God a pericope was handed down intact in the written law so that it might indicate with certainty which of the things written are true and which false.' 49. 1. . . . 'In the conclusion of the first book of the law it stands written: *A ruler shall not fail from Judah nor a leader from his loins, until he come whose it is, and him will the Gentiles expect.*[16] 2. Now he who sees that the leaders out of Judah are past and that a ruler and leader has appeared and is expected by the Gentiles, is able on the ground of the fulfilment to recognise that the passage of Scripture is true and that the promised one has appeared. And if he accepts his doctrine, then will he learn which portions of the Scriptures answer to the truth and which are false.'

50. 1. And Peter said: 'That what is true is mixed with what is false, follows also from this, that when on one occasion - as I remember - he was attacked by the Sadducees, he answered: *Wherefore ye do err, because ye do not know the true things of the Scriptures, and on this account also ye know nothing of the power of God.*[17] If then he assumes that they did not know the true things of the Scriptures, then clearly there are false portions contained in them. 2. Also his utterance, *Be ye good money changers*,[18] refers to the genuine and non-genuine words of Scripture. And in saying: *Wherefore do ye not understand what is reasonable in the Scriptures*?[19] he strengthens the understanding of him who already on his own reflection judges prudently. 51. 1. That he alluded to the scribes and the teachers of the existing Scriptures[20] because they knew about the true, genuine law, is known. 2. And in saying: *I am not come to destroy the law*,[21] and yet destroying something, he indicated that what he destroyed had not belonged originally to the law. 3. His declaration: *The heaven and the earth will pass away, but one jot or one tittle shall not pass from the law*[22] shows that what passes away earlier than heaven and earth does not belong to the true law. 52. 1. For whilst heaven and earth still exist, sacrifices, kingdoms, the prophecies of those *among them that are born of women*[23] and such like, have passed away, not going back to the ordinance of God.'

(H II 43-44)

1. 'On this account be it far from us to believe that the Lord of all, who has made heaven and earth and all that is in them, shares his authority with others

or that he *lies*[24] (for if he lies, who then is truthful?) or that he *puts to the test*[25] as if he was ignorant (for who then has foreknowledge?). 2. If he *is grieved*[26] or *repents*,[27] who then is perfect and of immutable mind? If he is *jealous*,[28] who then is satisfield with himself? If he *hardens hearts*,[29] who then makes wise? 3. If he *makes blind*[30] and *deaf*,[31] who then has given sight and hearing? If he counsels robberies,[32] who then requires that justice be done? If he *mocks*,[33] who then is without deceit? If he is powerless, who then is omnipotent? If he acts unjustly, who then is just? If he *makes what is wicked*,[34] who then will work what is good? 44. 1. If he longs for a *fertile hill*,[35] to whom then do all things belong? If he *lies*,[36] who then is truthful? If he dwells in a *tabernacle*,[37] who then is incomprehensible? 2. If he craves after the steam of fat, *sacrifices*,[38] *offerings*,[39] *sprinklings*,[40] who then is without need, holy, pure and perfect? If he takes delight in *lamps* and *candlesticks*,[41] who then set in order the luminaries in the firmament? 3. If he dwells in *shadow*, *darkness*, *storm* and *smoke*,[42] who then is light and lightens the infinite spaces of the world? If he draws near with *flourish of trumpets*, *war-cries*, *missiles* and *arrows*,[43] who then is the rest that all long for? 4. If he loves *war*,[44] who then desires peace? If he *makes what is wicked*,[45] who then brings forth what is good? If he is cruel,[46] who then is kind? If he does not make good his promises,[47] who then will be trusted? 5. If he loves the unjust, *adulterers* and *murderers*,[48] who then is a just judge?'

Polemic against Paul (H II 16-17)

16.1. 'As in the beginning the one God, being as it were a right hand and a left, created first the heavens and then the earth, so also has he assembled in pairs everything that follows. In the case of man, however, he has no longer proceeded in this way, but has reversed every pair. 2. For whereas he created what was stronger as the first and what was weaker as the second, in the case of man we find the opposite, namely, first what is smaller and in the second place what is stronger. 3. Thus from Adam, who was created in the image of God, there sprang as the first the unrighteous Cain, as the second the righteous Abel. 4. Again from him whom you call Deucalion there were sent forth two prototypes of spirits, one clean and one unclean, namely, the black raven and as second the white dove.[49] 5. And from Abraham, the forefather of our people, there issued two firsts,[50] Ishmael first and then Isaac, who was blessed of God. 6. From Isaac again there originated two, the godless Esau and the pious Jacob. 7. According to this order there followed as a first-born in the world the high priest (= Aaron), then the lawgiver (= Moses).[51]

17. 1. Similarly - for the pair with respect to Elias was, as it would seem, set aside for another time... - 2. there came as the first the one who was *among* *those that are born of women*,[52] and after that there appeared the one who was among the sons of men. 3. He who follows this order can discern by whom Simon (= Paul), who as the first came before me to the Gentiles, was sent forth, and to whom I (= Peter) belong who appeared later than he did and came in upon him as light upon darkness, as knowledge upon ignorance, as healing upon sickness.'

(H XVII 13-19)

1. When Simon heard this, he interrupted with the words: ' . . . You have stated that you have learned accurately the teaching of your master because you have heard and seen him directly (ἐναργείᾳ) face to face, and that it is not possible for any other to experience the like in a dream or in a vision.[53] 2. I shall show you that this is false: He who hears something directly is by no means certain of what is said. For he must check whether, being a man, he has not been deceived as to what appears to him. On the other hand, vision creates together with the appearance the certainty that one sees something divine. Give me an answer first to that.'

16. 1. And Peter said: ' . . . 2. We know . . . that many idolaters, adulterers and other sinners have seen visions and had true dreams, and also that some have had visions that were wrought by demons. For I maintain that the eyes of mortals cannot see the incorporeal being of the Father or of the Son, because it is enwrapped in insufferable light. 3. Therefore it is a token of the mercy of God, and not of jealousy in him, that he is invisible to men living in the flesh. For he who sees him must die. 6. . . . No one is able to see the incorporeal power of the Son or even of an angel. But he who has a vision should recognise that this is the work of a wicked demon.

17. 5. . . . For to a pious, natural, and pure mind the truth reveals itself; it is not acquired through a dream, but is granted to the good through discernment. **18.** 1. For in this way was the Son revealed to me also by the Father,[54] Wherefore I know the power of revelation; I have myself learned this from him. For at the very time when the Lord asked how the people named him[55] - although I had heard that others had given him another name - it rose in my heart to say, and I know not how I said it, *Thou art the Son of the living God*.[56] 6. You see now how expressions of wrath have to be made through visions and dreams, but discourse wth friends takes place from mouth to mouth, openly and not through riddles, visions and dreams as with an enemy.

19. 1. And if our Jesus appeared to you also and became known in a vision and met you as angry with an enemy, yet he has spoken only through visions and dreams or through external revelations. But can any one be made competent to teach through a vision? 2. And if your opinion is, "That is possible", why then did our teacher spend a whole year with us who were awake? 3. How can we believe you even if he has appeared to you, and how can he have appeared to you if you desire the opposite of what you have learned? 4. But if you were visited by him for the space of an hour and were instructed by him and thereby have become an apostle,[57] then proclaim his words, expound what he has taught, be a friend to his apostles and do not contend with me, who am his confidant; for you have in hostility *withstood*[58] me, who am a firm rock, the foundation stone of the Church.[59] 5. If you were not an enemy, then you would not slander me and revile my preaching in order that I may not be believed when I proclaim what I have heard in my own person from the Lord, as if I were undoubtedly *condemned*[60] and you were acknowledged. 6. And if you call me *condemned*,[60] then you accuse God, who revealed Christ to me, and disparage him who called me blessed on account of the revelation.[61] 7. But if you really desire to co-operate with the truth, then learn first from us what we have learned from him and, as a learner of the truth, become a fellow-worker[62] with us.'

The Doctrine of Baptism (H XI 25-33)

25. 1. Wherefore come readily as a son to a father that God may reckon your ignorance as the original cause of your transgressions. But if, after you have been invited, you will not come or delay to do so, then by the just judgment of God you will perish because you have not been willing. 2. And do not believe that you will ever have hope if you remain unbaptized, even if you are more pious than all the pious have been hitherto. Rather you will then suffer a punishment all the more severe because you have done good works not in a good way. 3. For to do good is good only when it takes place as God has commanded. But if in opposition to his will you will not be baptized, then you serve your own will and despise his decree.

26. 1. But someone may say: "What good results to piety when a man is baptized with water?" In the first place, that you do the will of God. And in the second place, when you are born again for God of water, then through fear you get rid of your first birth which came of lust, and thus can attain to salvation. But that is not possible in any other way. 2. For thus has the prophet appealed to us with an oath: *Verily I say unto you, if you are not born again of living water . . . you cannot enter into the kingdom of heaven.*[63] 3. Wherefore come! For from the beginning there has been associated with the water something that shows mercy;[64] it knows those who are baptized in the thrice holy name and delivers them from future punishment, bringing as gifts to God the good works of the baptized done after baptism. 4. Wherefore flee to the water; for that alone can quench the violence of fire. He who has not yet been willing to come still bears in himself the spirit of passion and for that reason does not desire to approach the living water for his own salvation. **27.** 1. Come then now, be you a righteous or an unrighteous man. For if you are righteous, you need only to be baptized for salvation, but an unrighteous man ought not only to submit to baptism for the forgiveness of the sins he has committed in ignorance, but should also do good according to the measure of his past godlessness, as baptism requires. 2. Therefore hasten, be you at present righteous or unrighteous, that soon you may be born unto God the Father, who begets you of water. For postponement brings danger with it, because the hour of death is hidden. Prove your likeness to God by good works, loving the truth and honouring the true God as a father. To honour him means to live as he, who himself is righteous, desires you to live. 3. The will of a righteous man is directed to the doing of nothing that is wrong. But wrong is murder, adultery, hatred, avarice, and the like; and there are many kinds of wrongdoing. **28.** 1. Besides these instructions there is to be observed what is not for all men in common, but is peculiar to the worship of God. I mean the keeping of one's self pure, that a man should not have intercourse with his wife during her monthly courses, for so the law of God commands.[65] 2. But what? If the keeping of one's self pure (καθαρεύειν) did not belong to the (true) worship of God, would you wallow gladly in filth like dung-beetles (κάνθαροι)? Therefore cleanse your hearts from wickedness by heavenly thoughts, as men who as rational beings stand above dumb brutes, and wash your bodies with water. 3. For to keep one's self pure is truly worth aspiring after not because purity of the body precedes purity of the heart, but because purity follows goodness. 4. Therefore our teacher convicted some of the Pharisees and scribes among us, who are separate and as scribes know the law better than others, and (described) them as hypocrites because they kept clean only what is visible to men, but neglected purity of the heart, which is visible to God alone.

29. 1. The following expression he rightly used with reference to the hypocrites among them, not (however) with reference to them all; for of some he said that they should be heard because to them *the seat of Moses*[66] had been assigned. 2. But to the hypocrites he said: *Woe unto you, ye scribes and Pharisees, hypocrites, for ye make clean only the outside of the cup and the platter, but the inside is full* of dirt. *Thou blind Pharisee, cleanse first the inside of the cup and the platter that their outside may be clean also.*[67] 3. And truly: for if the mind is enlightened by knowledge, he who has been instructed can be good, and then purity follows thereupon. For out of the mental attitude within there comes right care for the body without, as indeed out of neglect of the body care for one's mental attitude cannot come. 4. Thus the man who is pure can cleanse both what is within and what is without. But he who cleanses only what is without, does this to obtain praise of men; and whilst lookers-on lavish praise upon him, he obtains nothing from God.[68]

30. 1. But to whom does it not seem to be better not to have intercourse with a woman during her monthly course, but only after purification and washing? And one should also wash himself after intercourse. 2. If you hesitate to do this, recall to mind how you observed a portion of the purification instructions when you served inanimate idols. Be ashamed that you now hesitate when you ought to commit yourselves, I do not say to more but to the whole of purity. Remember him who made you, and you will recognise who he is who now puts hesitation in your way with respect to purity.

31. 1. But some one of you may ask, "Is it necessary that we now do everything that we did in the service of the idols?" I answer you, Not everything; but what you did in a good way, that you should do now even more. For whatever is done well in error comes from the truth, just as (conversely) if anything is done badly in the truth, it comes of error. 2. Receive then from every quarter what belongs to you, not what is alien to you, and say not: "If those who are in error do something good, then we are not under an obligation to do it." For according to this contention, if any one who worships idols does not kill, then we ought to kill because he who is in error does not become a murderer.

32. 1. No; but (we should do) more: if those living in error *do not kill*, let us never *be angry*;[69] if he who is in error *does not commit adultery*, let us avoid even the beginning and never *lust*.[70] If he who is in error *loves his friends*, let us also love those who *hate* us.[71] If he who is in error *lends* to those who have possessions, let us do so to those also who have no possessions.[72] 2. In a word: we who hope to inherit the endless age are under obligation to complete better works than those who know only this present world. 3. For we know that if in the day of judgment their works, being compared with ours, are found equal in well-doing, we shall then suffer shame, but they perdition, because in consequence of error they have done good not to their own benefit.[73] But we shall be ashamed, as I said, because we have done no more than they although we have had a greater knowledge. 4. And if we are ashamed because we are equal to them in well-doing and do not surpass them, by how much more shall we be so if we have not so many good works to show as they have?

33. 1. That in truth in the day of judgment the deeds of those who have known the truth will be found equal to the good works of those living in error, the infallible (prophet) has taught us, saying to those who did not wish to come to him and hear him: '*The queen of the south shall rise up with this generation and shall condemn it, because she came from the ends of the earth to hear the wisdom of Solomon. And behold! here is more than Solomon*, and ye believe not.'[74] 2. And to those among the people who, confronted with his preaching, would not repent he said: '*The men of Nineveh will rise up with this generation* *and will condemn it, because they repented at the preaching of Jonah; and behold! here is more than Jonah*, and no one believes.'[75] 3. And thus he set over against their godlessness the Gentiles who have done (good) - in condemnation of all who possess the true religion and never have so many good works to show as they have who live in error. And he exhorted the judicious to accomplish good works not only in the same way as the Gentiles, but to do more than they.

4. I have adduced this because of the necessity of observing the monthly courses and of washing after sexual intercourse and of not making objection to such purity, though it is practised by those living in error. For the men who do good in error will judge those who have the true religion without however being saved themselves. 5. For they observe purity because of error, and not as service rendered to the true Father and God of the universe.'

Notes

Translated after Georg Strecker

1. Cf. Gen. 2:20.
2. Gen. 2:16.
3. Cf. Gen. 3:1ff.
4. Cf. Mt. 5:4.
5. Cf. Mt. 25:14ff.
6. Cf. Mt. 10:34.
7. Cf. Lk. 12:49.
8. Mt. 10:35; Lk. 12:53.
9. Cf. Mt. 11:11.
10. Gen. 4:6ff.; Jn. 8:44.
11. Cf. Gen. 4:21f.
12. Num. 11:16ff.
13. Deut. 34:5f.
14. Cf. 1 Kgs. 8f. (Solomon's temple), contaminated with 2 Kgs. 22:8; 2 Chron. 34:14.
15. Cf. 2 Kgs. 24:11-13; 25:8f.
16. Gen. 49:10.
17. Cf. Mk. 12:24 (Mt. 22:29).
18. A frequently attested uncanonical saying; cf. Resch, *Agrapha*[2] (TU 30.2), 1906, 112-122.
19. Non-canonical, instanced only here in the patristic literature.
20. Mt. 23:2f.
21. Mt. 5:17.
22. Mt. 24:35; 5:18; cf. Ep. Pet. 2.5.
23. Mt. 11:11.
24. Ps. 89:35; 1 Kgs. 22:22f.
25. Gen. 22:1; Ex. 15:25; 16:4 and often.
26. Gen. 6:6f.
27. 1 Sam. 15:35; 1 Chron. 21:15; Ps. 110:4.
28. Deut. 32:19; Ex. 20:5 and often.
29. Ex. 4:21; 7:3 and often.
30. Ex. 4:11; 2 Kgs. 6:18.
31. Ex. 4:11.

32. Ex. 3:21f. and often.
33. Ex. 10:2.
34. Is. 45:7.
35. Ps. 68:15f.
36. Cf. note 24.
37. Ex. 40:34.
38. Gen. 4:3 and often.
39. Ex. 29:28 and often.
40. Cf. Ex. 24:6 and often.
41. Ex. 25:31ff.
42. Deut. 4:11; Ex. 10:22; 19:18; 20:21.
43. Ex. 19:13, 16; Num. 24:8; Deut. 32:23, 42 and often.
44. Ex. 15:3; Deut. 21:10.
45. Is. 45:7.
46. Cf. Job 30:21; Is. 13:9.
47. Cf. Gen. 18:13ff.
48. 2 Sam. 12:13; Gen. 4:15; Ex. 2:12ff.
49. Gen. 8:6ff.
50. Ishmael and Elieser; not adduced in what follows; but cf. R I 33f.
51. Ex. 6:20; 7:7; 1 Chron. 23:13f.
52. Mt. 11:11.
53. Cf. H XVII 5, 6b.
54. Mt. 16:17.
55. Mt. 16:13f.
56. Mt. 16:16.
57. Cf. Acts 9:3ff.; 1 Cor. 15:8.
58. Gal. 2:11.
59. Cf. Mt. 16:18.
60. Gal. 2:11.
61. Mt. 16:17.
62. 1 Cor. 3:9.
63. Jn. 3:5.
64. The Spirit of God; cf. Gen. 1:2.
65. Lev. 15:24; 18:19.
66. Mt. 23:2f.
67. Mt. 23:25f.
68. Cf. Mt. 6:1ff.; 23:4ff.
69. Mt. 5:21f.
70. Mt. 5:27f.
71. Mt. 5:43ff.; Lk. 6:27ff.
72. Cf. Lk. 6:34f.
73. Cf. H XI 27. 1 above.
74. Mt. 12:42; Lk. 11:31.
75. Mt. 12:41; Lk. 11:32.

C. APOCALYPSES AND RELATED SUBJECTS

Introduction

Philipp Vielhauer † and *Georg Strecker*

Literature (general): *Texts*: R.H. Charles (ed.), *The Apocrypha and Pseudepigrapha of the Old Testament* I-II, 1913. - J.H. Charlesworth (ed.), *The Old Testament Pseudepigrapha* I-II, Garden City 1983-1985; E. Kautzsch (ed.), *Die Apokryphen und Pseudepigraphen des Alten Testamentes* I-II, 1921; W.-G. Kümmel (ed.), *Jüdische Schriften aus hellenistisch-römischer Zeit*, 1973ff; P. Rießler, *Altjüdisches Schrifttum außerhalb der Bibel*, [2]1966; J.M. Robinson (ed.), *The Nag Hammadi Library in English*, San Francisco 1977 (3rd ed. 1988); D.S. Russell, *The Old Testament Pseudepigrapha. Patriarchs and Prophets in Early Judaism*, Philadelphia 1987; H.F.D. Sparks (ed.), *The Apocryphal Old Testament*, New York 1984.

Studies: H. Althaus (ed.), *Apokalyptik und Eschatologie* 1987; J.M. Baumgarten, 'The Heavenly Tribunal and the Personification of Sedeq in Jewish Apocalyptic', ANRW II 19/1, 1979, 219-239; W. Bousset, *Die Offenbarung Johannis* (KEK 16) [6]1906 (reprint 1966); id./ H. Greßmann, *Die Religion des Judentums im späthellenistischen Zeitalter* (HNT 21), [4]1966; R. Bultmann, *Geschichte und Eschatologie*, 1958; J.H. Charlesworth/J.R. Mueller, *The New Testament Apocrypha and Pseudepigrapha: a guide to publications with excursuses on apocalypses* (ATLA 17), London 1987; J.J. Collins (ed.), *Apocalypse. The Morphology of a Genre* (Semeia 14), 1979; id. *The Apocalyptic Imagination. An Introduction to the Jewish Matrix of Christianity*, New York 1984; F. Dexinger, *Henochs Zehnwochenapokalypse und offene Probleme der Apokalyptikforschung* 1977; U. Fischer, *Eschatologie und Jenseitserwartung im hellenistischen Diasporajudentum* (BZNW 44), 1978; J. Geffcken, 'Christliche Sibyllinen', NTApo[2] 399-422; I. Grünwald, 'Jewish Apocalyptic Literature', ANRW II 19/1, 1979, 89-118; id. *Apocalyptic and Merkavah Mysticism*, 1979; W. Harnisch, *Verhängnis und Verheissung der Geschichte* (FRLANT 97), 1969; D. Hellholm (ed.), *Apocalypticism in the Mediterranean World and the Near East*, 1983; K. Koch, *Ratlos vor der Apokalyptik*? 1970; id. 'Sabbatstruktur der Geschichte. Die sogennante Zehn-Wochen-Apokalypse (1 Hen 93, 1-10; 91, 11-17) und das Ringen um die alttestamentlichen Chronologien im späten Israelitentum', ZAW 95, 1983, 403-430; id./J.M. Schmidt, *Apokalyptik* (WdF 365), 1982; H.-W. Kuhn, *Enderwartung und gegenwärtiges Heil* (StUNT 4), 1966; G. Lanczkowski, art. 'Apokalyptik/Apokalypsen I. Religionsgeschichtlich', TRE 3, 1978, 189-191; J. Lebram, art. 'Apokalyptik/Apokalypsen II. Altes Testament', TRE 3, 1978, 192-202; J. Maier, *Antikes Judentum* (GKT 2, Urban TB 422), 137-184; K. Müller, art. 'Apokalyptik/ Apokalypsen III. Die jüdische Apokalyptik. Anfänge und Merkmale', TRE 3, 1978, 202-251; M. Noth, 'Das

Geschichtsverständnis der alttestamentlichen Apokalyptik', in id. *Gesammelte Studien zum AT*, 1957, 248-273; id. 'Die Heiligen des Höchsten', ibid. 274-290; M. Philonenko-M. Simon, *L'Apocalyptique*, 1977; O. Plöger, art. 'Baruchschriften, apokryphe', RGG[3] I, 1957, cols. 900-903; id. *Theokratie und Eschatologie* (WMANT 2), [2]1962; G. von Rad, *Theologie des Alten Testaments* I, 1957 ([6]1969 = 1987); II, 1960 ([5]1968 = 1987); C. Rowland, *The Open Heaven. A Study of Apocalyptic in Judaism and Early Christianity*, London [2]1985; D. Rößler, *Gesetz und Geschichte. Untersuchung zur Theologie der jüdischen Apokalyptik und der pharisäischen Orthodoxie* (WMANT 3), [2]1962; D.S. Russell, *The Message and Meaning of Jewish Apocalyptic*, London [2]1971; J.M. Schmidt, *Die jüdische Apokalyptik. Die Geschichte ihrer Erforschung von den Anfängen bis zu den Textfunden von Qumran*, [2]1976; W.H. Schmidt, 'Altes Testament A. Einleitung und Theologie', in GKT 1, Urban TB 422, 1989, 9-88; W. Schmithals, *Die Apokalyptik. Einführung und Deutung*, 1973; H. Stegemann, 'Some Aspects of Eschatology in Texts from the Qumran Community and in the Teaching of Jesus', *Bibl. Arch. Today*, Jerusalem 1985, 405-426; J.C. Vanderkam, *Enoch and the Growth of an Apocalyptic Tradition*, Washington 1984; J. Vermeylen, *Du prophète Isaie à l'apocalyptique* I-II, Paris 1977/78; P. Vielhauer, *Geschichte der urchristlichen Literatur*, 1975, 485-528; P. Volz, *Die Eschatologie der jüdischen Gemeinde im neutestamentlichen Zeitalter*, [2]1934 (repr. 1966); T. Willet, *Eschatology in the Theodicies of 2 Baruch and 4 Ezra*, 1988.

Christianity commenced its career as an eschatological and enthusiastic movement and gave expression to its faith largely in the language of *Apocalyptic* and of *Prophecy*. From the end of the 1st century to the beginning of the Middle Ages it produced an extensive apocalyptic literature, to which the Sibyllines also belong. Christian prophecy was not similarly productive of literature, but, in the combination 'Apocalypses and Related Subjects', it must be taken into account by reason of its actual historical significance.

While the Gospels represent a literary genre created by primitive Christianity itself, and the apocryphal Acts of apostles - as distinct from the canonical Acts - belong within the tradition of the hellenistic romance, Christianity took over the genre of the apocalypse from Palestinian Judaism and that of the Sibyllines from Hellenistic Judaism. It was able to do this because the earliest community was influenced in the highest degree by apocalyptic ideas and expectations and repeated these in its mission; that this led ultimately to the composition of books of apocalypses was only natural. In addition, early Christianity adopted Jewish apocalypses; it employed them as Holy Scripture (cf. for example, the apocryphal quotations in Jude 9 and 14) and, by reworking of various kinds, christianised them. Furthermore, it is due to this process of adoption that this Jewish literature (like almost the entire extant non-Rabbinic literature) was saved from destruction by the 'orthodox' Judaism, i.e. by the party which asserted itself successfully after A.D. 70.

In view of these circumstances, Jewish Apocalyptic must be described in the following introduction in order that the affinities and differences between the Jewish and the Christian may become clear; consequently we begin with the literary phenomenon, not with general features of the period. Moreover, a description of Jewish and Christian prophecy is necessary in order that their relation to one another and to Apocalyptic may be made clear; in this case it is certainly not possible to begin with larger literary evidences, and we are left to testimonies concerning them and to inferences.

1. Apocalyptic

1.1 Name and Idea

Literature (supplementary): T. Holtz, art. ἀποκαλύπτω, ἀποκάλυψις Apokalypto, Apokalypsis', in EWNT 1, 1980, 312-317; A. Oepke, art. ἀποκαλύπτω, ἀποκάλυψις, in ThWNT III, 1938, 565-597 (TDNT III, 563-592); M. Smith, 'On the History of ΑΠΟΚΑΛΥΠΤΩ and ΑΠΟΚΑΛΥΨΙΣ', in D. Hellholm, *Apocalypticism*, 9-20; H. Stegemann, 'Die Bedeutung der Qumranfunde für die Erforschung der Apokalyptik', in D. Hellholm, *Apocalypticism*, 495-530.

The verb ἀποκαλύπτω first occurs in Greek literature in Herodotus (I 119), with the meaning 'uncover, reveal'. Plato uses it in figurative language (*Protag.* 352a; *Gorgias* 455d). The beginnings of a theological significance can be traced in non-Christian literature in the Corpus Hermeticum (XIII 1). The Neoplatonist Iamblichus also employs the word, to describe not only human but divine 'revelations' (*de Myst.* III 17; VI 7). He is presumably not influenced by the Christian terminology (M. Smith, 18). In LXX the verb mostly appears as a translation of the Hebrew גָּלָה (pi.). If the secular usage stands in the foreground here (e.g. 1 Kings 20:2; 22:8, 17), the theological use (e.g. 1 Kings 3:7; Isa. 56:1) is not yet firmly impressed (against Oepke's question, p. 573: 'whether the extra-biblical use of our terms in a technical sense does not derive directly or indirectly from the Greek Bible', cf. M. Smith, 10). The substantive ἀποκάλυψις appears for the first time in the Epicurean Philodemus (*Vitia* 22) in the sense of 'being uncovered' (of the head), in Plutarch as 'unclothing' (of the body: *Cato Maior* 20) or in a figurative sense of 'exposure' (of a fault: Plut. *Adulat.* 32). Towards the end of the 4th century Synesius uses it as a technical term of the soothsayer (*Ep.* 54). In LXX and in hellenistic Jewish literature the word is very rare (1 Kings 20:3; Sirach), and is not attested in its theological significance (M. Smith, 10). At the beginning of the terminological use presupposed in what follows stands the New Testament Apocalypse of John, for the content of the book is characterised (1:1) as 'Αποκάλυψις 'Ιησοῦ Χριστοῦ, ἣν ἔδωκεν αὐτῷ ὁ θεός, δεῖξαι τοῖς δούλοις αὐτοῦ ἃ δεῖ γενέσθαι ἐν τάχει. The word ἀποκάλυψις is here for the first time used with the meaning of 'revelation of what must shortly take place'. It occurs for the first time as the designation of a book in the title of the Johannine Apocalypse: 'Αποκάλυψις 'Ιωάννου. Because of the significance of this Apocalypse, the word ἀποκάλυψις also became a literary title and the designation of related Christian books - about A.D. 200 the Muratorian Canon mentions *apocalypse . . . johannis et petri* (lines 71f.) - and was then transferred, and that by Christians, to Jewish works of this kind. Admittedly the word also appears in the title of a Jewish apocalypse, the Syriac Baruch: 'Book of the revelation of Baruch, son of Neria, translated from Greek into Syriac' (Kautzsch, *Pseudepigraphen*, 410; Charles, *Pseudepigrapha*, 481). This title however evidently does not belong to the original form of the apocalypse; the book is translated from Greek, and perhaps goes back to a Hebrew or Aramaic original which must have come into being between A.D. 70 and 132 (O. Plöger, RGG[3] I, col. 302); consequently we may regard the influence of Christian usage on the title of the Syriac translation as possible or even probable. The same holds for the title of the Greek Baruch. At any rate the term 'revelation' as a designation for these literary works cannot be proved pre-Christian. This kind of literature appears originally to have had no common designation at all.

1.2 Literary character

Literature (supplementary): K. Berger, 'Hellenistisch-heidnische Prodigien und die Vorzeichen in der jüdischen und christlichen Apokalyptik', ANRW II 23/2, 1980, 1428-1469; L. Hartman, 'Functions of some So-Called Apocalyptic Timetables', NTS 22, 1975, 1-14; A.P.Hayman, 'Problem of Pseudonymity in the Ezra Apocalypse', JSJ 6, 1975, 47-56; M. Hutter, '"Halte diese Worte geheim" - Eine Notiz zu einem apokalyptischen Gebrauch', *BibNot*25, 1984, 14-18; C. Münchow, *Ethik und Eschatologie. Ein Beitrag zum Verständnis der frühjudischen Apokalyptik mit einem Ausblick auf das Neue Testament*, 1981; R. Meyer, art. Προφήτης κτλ. C. Prophetentum und Propheten im Judentum der hellenistisch-römischen Zeit', ThWNT VI, 1959, 813-828 (TDNT VI, 812-828); C. Rowland, 'The Visions of God in Apocalyptic Literature', JSJ 10, 1979, 137-154; H. H. Rowley, *The Relevance of Apocalyptic*, ²1955.

In most of the Jewish apocalypses definite formal peculiarities recur, and these we must regard as fixed features, as elements in the style of this literary genre.

1.2.1. *Pseudonymity.*

The apocalyptist does not write under his own name, but under that of one of the great personages of the past (e.g. Daniel, Elijah and Isaiah, Moses and Ezra, Enoch and Adam). He has not sufficient authority of his own, as the writing prophets had, but has to borrow it from these great men. Together with pseudonymity, fictitious antiquity is found as an element in the style of the apocalyptic writer. In this case, it has to be made clear why the book has just recently become known and not a long time ago. This happens because of the sealing-up of the book, or because of the command for its secret preservation till the end of days (Dan. 12:9; 4 Esd. 12:35-38; 14:7f., and often). Such a sealing, and also the breaking open of the sealed book (cf. Rev. 5:1ff.), demonstrates at the same time the 'elite' character of the apocalyptic knowledge, which is made accessible to the seer or to a limited readership (cf. M. Hutter, 18).

1.2.2 *Account of the Vision.*

The apocalyptist receives his revelations mostly in visions, whereas they were granted to the prophets mostly through auditions. But just as the prophets had visions as well, so the apocalyptists also occasionally have auditions, but the visions predominate so strongly that the apocalypses are generally presented in the form of an account of a vision. The apocalyptic vision takes place in various ways; first, through a dream (Dan. 7:1ff., cf. also 2:1; 4:2; eth. Enoch 83f.; 85ff.; slav. Enoch 1:3ff.; 4 Esd. 11:1; 12:1; 13:1, 13, etc.), and then through visionary ecstasy. The visions of Dan. 10-12 will have been experienced by the seer in a waking state. Cf. syr. Bar. 13:1f., and particularly 22:1:

'And afterwards, the heavens opened, and I saw . . . and a voice was heard from the height, and it said unto me . . .

In the Johannine Apocalypse there are no dream-visions, only ecstatic visions (1:10; 4:2; cf. 17:3; 21:10). Bousset is of the opinion that Jewish Apocalyptic 'tended more and more to move away from the simple dream-vision to ecstatic vision' (*Offenbarung*, 4). Eventually the apocalyptic vision takes place through visionary rapture. In his ecstasy the seer experiences changes of location and wanders through strange and mysterious regions on earth and in heaven. Rapture of this kind is found for the first time in Ezekiel, who, on the whole, has had a very strong influence on apocalyptic (Ez. 8:3ff.). The prophet Habakkuk (the dragon in Babylon) and Baruch (syr. Bar. 6:3ff.) were enraptured. Raptures into heaven were experienced by Enoch (eth. Enoch 70f.), by Paul (2 Cor. 12:3) and by John the Apocalyptist (4:1). The idea of the journey to heaven, originally only a means to an end, becomes the theme of a special literature in which cosmological, astrological and other-worldly secrets in general are disclosed (slav. Enoch; cf. G. Strecker, art. 'Entrückung', RAC V, 1962, cols. 461-476; G. Lohfink, *Die Himmelfahrt Jesu. Untersuchungen zu den Himmelfahrts- und Erhöhungstexten bei Lukas* [StANT 26], 1971, 32-74; O.Betz-H. Wißmann, art. 'Entrückung, I. Religionsgeschichtlich, II. Biblische und frühjüdische Zeit', TRE 9, 1982, 680-690).

The vision itself is a picture: either a picture which represents the occurrences themselves directly, or a picture which portrays them indirectly, in the form of symbols and allegories.

In the last-mentioned instance, an explanation is essential. This is given by a mediator of the revelation. Thus Daniel explains the dream of Nebuchadnezzar. Generally an interpreting angel, an *angelus interpres*, takes over this role, as, for example, in Dan. 7 where the seer experiences the vision and its interpretation in a dream. In eth. Enoch there is quite a number of these *angeli interpretes*. In 4 Esd. the interpreting angel plays only a minor role, and he is completely absent from syr. Bar., in which the seer communicates directly with God. Sometimes, as in the vision of Beasts in eth. Enoch, no explanation is given and the interpretation is left to the reader.

The imagery in the visions is, in the main, traditional, but often an image taken over ready coined resists a completely allegorical interpretation. Sometimes the seer adds to an image taken over a new and subordinate one which will restore the connection with the actual situation. According to Bousset, it is the small allegorical vision which is the germ-cell of the apocalypse; in it either a number of individual features are woven into an allegorical pattern or a number of small and separate images are set side by side. Considering the traditional character of the imagery and the manner of its composition, the question arises how far the apocalyptic visions are true to experience. Apocalyptic is book-wisdom, a 'literature', and in fact collected literature, but the ardour of the expectation and the strength of the hope are genuine. Moreover, it cannot be denied that the apocalyptists had visions, but it is quite another question how far these experiences have been deposited in the literature. Even with the aid of the psychology of religion and of type-psychology, the work of distinguishing neatly between actual experience and literary activity in the apocalypses will scarcely be successful

'There is in fact an apocalyptic culture which transmits to the ecstatics visions and experiences which are to a certain degree fixed, - however much it may appear as a psychological curiosity that someone gives frenzied expression to what someone else has previously communicated to him in a frenzied state, and that people are raptured, not independently, but in something like a process of borrowing, and according to a mechanical routine. Nevertheless this is the position.' (Th. Mann, *Doctor Faustus*, p. 567)

1.2.3. *Surveys of history in future-form*

Related to the fiction of antiquity is the fact that the apocalyptic writers frequently present the history of the past right up to their own present time in the form of prophecies. This is always followed by a prediction of the End, and on this the emphasis lies: the present of the actual (not the fictional) author is always the last time. This imminent expectation can also be formulated from the standpoint of the fictional author: 'The history of the world is divided into twelve parts; we have come to the tenth, to the middle of the tenth; but there remain two parts, in addition to the half of the tenth' (4 Esd. 14:11f.). The description naturally does not employ clear references (names of people, countries, etc.), but uses a code with images, symbols and allegories, and it generally has attached to it a comprehensive interpretation. 'This method often permits the dating of apocalypses; the point at which the history loses precision and accuracy is the moment of writing' (C.K. Barrett, *The Background of the New Testament: Selected Documents*, 1957, p. 231).

We can distinguish two types of such historical description: first, that which takes in its view world-history as a whole, and secondly, that which begins from a definite point of time within history, generally the time of the imaginary author, and from that point traces the picture to the End. Occasionally both may be found in the same apocalypse (Dan. and syr. Bar.). To the first type belong the picture of the four world-empires (Dan. 2 and 7) which represent in their number the whole of world-history; the Vision of Clouds (syr. Bar. 53-71) which depicts world-history from Adam till the appearance of the Messiah and his rule; and also the Vision of the Beasts and the Apocalypse of Ten Weeks in Enoch (eth. Enoch 85-90 and 93; 91:12-17). To the second type belong the visions of Dan. 8-12 which begin with the Persian empire and the last of which (10:11-11:45) opens into a very precise description of contemporary events as being the eschatological period; also the so-called Vision of Cedars (syr. Bar. 35-40) which sketches the entire course of history from the time of the biblical Baruch, from the exile of Judah at the hands of the Babylonians, using in an entirely different manner the schema of the four kingdoms in Daniel; in addition, the apocalypse in the Testament of Levi 16-18 (commencing with Aaron), the Vision of Eagles at 4 Esd. 11f., which begins with the fourth kingdom of Daniel and reinterprets it with specific reference to Rome, Ass. Mos. 2-10 and Apoc. Abr. 27-30. Sometimes these outlines of history are divided into periods: the history of the world in four empires in Daniel, in ten weeks in Enoch (cf. Sib. 4:47ff.), in twelve parts in 4 Esd. and in the Vision of Clouds in syr. Bar; the history of Israel in seven Jubilees (Test. Levi 17); the division of Israel's internal history into periods, in terms of the seventy shepherds (eth. Enoch 89:59ff.), is not carried through clearly. Although these divisions into periods may often appear so multifarious and frivolous, they pursue the same aim as the historical surveys, that is, to express and to awaken the consciousness of the imminent end.

The apocalyptic writers employ this description of history in future form in order to arouse confidence in their own predictions of the future. If the imaginary author has so precisely predicted the past which can be checked from the standpoint of the reader, then the future also will come to pass as he predicts it. However, we must not fail to appreciate the fact that behind the *pia fraus* of this stylistic method there stands the religious conception of God's determining the course of the world.

This presentation of history as *vaticinium ex eventu* has only very remote OT parallels in the Blessing of Jacob (Gen. 49) and of Moses (Deut. 33), or in the Oracles of Balaam (Num. 23f.). These scarcely come into the question as models. It has been suggested that the Sibylline oracles of the hellenistic-Roman period which, as prophecy, bring us to the actual present, have served as models for the apocalyptic descriptions of history. Moreover a Sibylline model has been assumed for the apocalyptic pseudonymity: the ancient Sibyl, active throughout the ages, has provided the stimulus for figures of salvation-history to be made in Apocalyptic the guarantors of these predictions (R. Meyer, TDNT VI, 828).

1.2.4. *Forms and combinations of forms*

As has been said, there was in pre-Christian times no common title for the genre of the Apocalypse. In the eth. Enoch we meet several times the characterisation *Symbolic Utterances* (1:2; 37:5; 38:1; 45:1; 58:1); sometimes this is parallel to *Vision* (1:2; 37:1) and *Blessings* (1:1), *Wisdom sayings* and *Sacred sayings* (37:2). The term *Symbolic Utterance* does not always designate the symbolic or allegorical character of the statements (eth. Enoch 1-6), but the report of the vision is generally given in symbolic form.

Not all apocalypses are reports of visions. The Ass. Mos., for example, purports to be a speech of Moses, given shortly before his death to Joshua in order to install him as his successor and to teach him about Israel's future destiny. This apocalypse has the form of a farewell discourse and displays all the marks of this genre. Likewise the slav. Enoch is a farewell discourse which Enoch, on the day of his rapture, delivers to his son and in which he describes his journey into the beyond, undertaken on that very day. Slav. Enoch is therefore a report of a vision in the form of a farewell discourse. Similar features may be seen in many parts of eth. Enoch, except that there Enoch is not expressly characterised as being about to depart; but, since he refers there to visions long past, we may doubtless presume that he is recounting his revelations shortly before his rapture. He narrates to his son Methuselah the two dream-visions concerning the coming judgment by flood (83f.) and concerning the fate of Israel (the Vision of Beasts 85-90); likewise the paraenetic book (91-105) claims to be a speech of Enoch to his son; the astronomical book (72-82) is also composed for Methuselah (76:14), like the small final Warning (108). Here again, then, we have a combination of an account of a vision and a farewell discourse. Nevertheless, it is not the latter but the former which is the real apocalyptic type. We must distinguish precisely between the two genres, even if in farewell discourses like the Test. XII Patr. eschatological texts and even small apocalypses are occasionally present (Test. Levi 18, cf. D. Rößler, *Gesetz*, 43).

Very frequently the apocalyptic writers include prayers in their books. It is not unusual for these to appear between a vision and its interpretation, and sometimes they rise to hymn-forms of great beauty (cf. Dan. 9:4-19; eth. Enoch 84:2-6; syr. Bar. 38; 48; 54, etc.). 4 Esd. is especially rich in prayers: before the first four visions the seer each time expounds his questions in prayer (3:4-36; 5:23-39; 6:38-59; 9:29-37) and receives an answer in a vision and

and interpretation; at times his book produces the impression of being a collection of prayers (8:6-19, 20-36; 13:14-20; 14:18-22).

Finally all apocalypses include paraenesis, both exhortations to repentance and conversion in view of the imminent end and of judgment, and also paraenesis in the form-critical sense of the word, i.e. traditional ethical exhortations in the form of maxims and series of aphorisms which are sometimes arranged thematically. In eth. Enoch the paraenesis appears at the beginning and at the end (2-5; 91-105; 108), while in slav. Enoch it forms the last part of the book (43-65). In 4 Esd. and syr. Bar. the paraenesis is inserted in the prophecies. Paraenesis may also be given in the form of a farewell discourse (eth. Enoch 91-105; slav. Enoch 43-65; syr. Bar. 44f.).

1.3 The world of ideas

Literature (supplementary): O. Böcher, 'Die heilige Stadt im Völkerkrieg. Wandlungen eines apokalyptischen Schemas', in *Josephus-Studien* (FS O. Michel), 1974, 55-76; J.H. Charlesworth, 'The Concept of the Messiah in the Pseudepigrapha', ANRW II 91/1, 1979, 188-218; J. Duhaime, 'La Règle de la Guerre de Qumran et l'apocalyptique', *Science et Esprit* 36, Montreal 1984, 67-88; J.G. Gammie, 'Spatial and Ethical Dualism in Jewish Wisdom and Apocalyptic Literature', JBL 93, 1974, 356-385; D.E. Gowan, 'The Fall and Redemption of the Material World in Apocalyptic Literature', *Horizons in Biblical Theology* 7, Pittsburgh 1985, 83-103; E.-M. Laperrousaz, *L'attente du Messie en Palestine à la veille et au début de l'ère chrétienne*, 1982; U. Luck, 'Das Weltverständnis in der jüdischen Apokalyptik, dargestellt am äthiopischen Henoch und am 4 Esra', ZThK 73, 1976, 283-305; J. Neusner (ed.) *Judaism and their Messiahs at the turn of the Christian Era*, 1987; W. Schmithals, 'Eschatologie und Apokalyptik', VuF 33, 1988, 64-82; M.E. Stone, 'Coherence and Inconsistency in the Apocalypses: The Case of "the End" in 4 Ezra', JBL 102, 1983, 229-243.

The apocalypses contain not only revelations on the Last Things (including the termination of history), but also on other *Secrets*, on the Beyond, Heaven and Hell and their inhabitants, on astronomy, meteorology and geography (especially eth. and slav. Enoch), as well as on the origin of sin and evil in the world (4 Esd. and syr. Bar.). The main interest, however, does not lie in problems of cosmology or theodicy, but in eschatology. We may therefore designate Apocalyptic as a special expression of Jewish eschatology. Even if we cannot assume any absolute separation from the national eschatology represented by the rabbis (so rightly K. Müller, TRE 3, 1978, 244ff.), there is yet a quite different understanding of God, the world and man. The world of ideas in Apocalyptic is very varied and anything but uniform; in the following discussion we must characterize only its most important common features.

1.3.1. *The doctrine of the Two Ages*

The essential feature of Apocalyptic is its dualism which, in various expressions, dominates its thought-world. Above all, in the doctrine of the Two Ages, in the dualistic time-scheme of world eras (ὁ αἰὼν οὗτος and ὁ αἰὼν μέλλων), the entire course of the world is comprehended. *This Age* is definitely detached from the *Age to come*, and therefore the words *this* and *to come* are not simply time-divisions, but have a qualitative significance: *this Age* is temporary and perishable, the *Age to come* is imperishable and eternal. This idea first becomes explicit as a theory in the later Apocalyptic (4. Esd. and syr. Bar.), but it is in fact present already in the oldest apocalypses. It finds symbolic expression as early as Daniel, in the contrast between the four kingdoms and the stone, or Son of man, who destroys the former and so brings in the eternal kingdom (Dan. 2 and 7). The national eschatology also is acquainted with the Two-Ages doctrine, but here, up to the 2nd century A.D., *the coming Olam* is the continuation within the world of *this Olam* in the glorious earthly kingdom of the Messiah (cf. Volz, *Eschatologie*, pp. 64ff., 71f., 166f.). According to the apocalyptic conception, on the other hand, the new Age is of a transcendent kind: it breaks in from the beyond in supernatural fashion, through divine intervention and without human activity, and puts an end to this world-era. This thought finds expression, in a particularly impressive fashion, in the image of the stone which 'broken off without the action of human hand, struck the iron and clay feet of the image and crushed them', and its interpretation, 'The God of heaven shall set up a kingdom which shall remain for ever indestructible, and the dominion shall not be left to other people. It will crush and destroy all these kingdoms, but itself shall stand for ever' (Dan. 2:34; 44; cf. 7:11-14, 18). This end is extreme: it is judgment, a destruction of this world and the simultaneous appearance of a new one, a 'new heaven and a new earth' (eth. Enoch 45:4f.; 91:16, etc.), a 'new creation' (eth. Enoch 72:1; 4 Esd. 7:75; syr. Bar. 32:6, etc.). The dualism of the Two-Ages doctrine recognises no continuity between the time of this world and of that which is to come: 'For behold, the days are coming when everything that has come into being will be given over to destruction, and it will be as if it had never been' (syr. Bar. 31:5). Between the two Ages there is a qualitative difference, and this comes to its clearest expression in Dan. 7 with the contrast of the beasts rising from the sea and the 'man' coming from heaven (cf. also 4 Esd. 7:52-61).

This eschatological dualism of the Two Ages is the essential characteristic of Apocalyptic so far as its contents are concerned: it distinguishes it fundamentally even from those texts which possess a formal similarity to Apocalyptic and have enriched its language and imagery (e.g. Ezekiel). The old must first entirely pass away before the new, the holy, can be established as the final state. This dualism is not absolute or metaphysical, but temporal, and is thereby different from the dualism of Gnosis. God is Creator and Lord of both Ages (see below, 1.3.4.).

1.3.2. *Pessimism and hope of the beyond*

The other-worldly character of the coming Age implies an extreme devaluation of this Age, the so-called apocalyptic pessimism.

The real baseness and transitoriness of this world-era is symbolised mythologically by the idea of the dominion over it of Satan and evil powers, but it is conveyed also by the notion of its growing physical and moral *degeneration*. On the physical decline, see the image of the four metals in Dan. 2 or the statement of Esra:

> For the world has lost its youthfulness,
> The times draw near to old age.
> (4 Esd. 14:10; cf. 5:55; syr. Bar. 85:10)

The moral degeneration is represented for the apocalyptic writers by a decay of all morality and the increase of godlessness, which culminates in an assembling of the hostile powers to struggle with the saints and with God himself in a final conflict (Dan.

7:19-25; eth. Enoch 93:9; 4 Esd. 13, and often). The apocalyptic writers devote their special interest to the final evil time (the so-called *Messianic Woes*), which is their own present and immediate future, and elaborate it in various ways. The natural ageing of the world and the moral and religious decay of mankind culminate in a cosmic catastrophe in which *this Age* perishes in order to make way for the new:

> 'Then the world shall return to the silence of old for seven days, like as in the first beginning, so that no man shall remain. After the seven days, the Age which still sleeps shall awake and that which is transitory shall perish.' (4 Esd. 7:30f.)

In this pessimism the basic thought of apocalyptic dualism is clearly expressed: it indicates the radical discontinuity between *this Age* and *the Age to come*, and consequently the strict other-ness of the latter.

To the depreciation of this Age there corresponds an intensification of the desire for and speculation about the Beyond. The apocalyptic writers compensate for their sorrow at the affliction of *this world* by fantastic pictures of the after-life, the glory of the blessed and the torments of the impious. It is intended that knowledge concerning the other-ness of the divine world should be conveyed in this fantasy. As it is brought about in wonderful ways - in which resurrection and judgment form the chief acts (4 Esd. 7:32-38) - so it is itself wonderful and divine. We need only refer in passing to the various images of the *coming Age* (new creation, new heaven and new earth, heavenly Jerusalem, Paradise). Its characteristics are incorruptibility (4 Esd. 7:31) and eternity (Dan. 2:44; eth. Enoch 91:17; slav. Enoch 65:7f.; syr. Bar. 44:11f.).

1.3.3. *Universalism and Individualism*

With what has been said up to this point another feature of Apocalyptic has already become clear, namely, its universalism. Its temporal horizon is incomparably wider than that of the national eschatology, for it reaches from the creation to the dissolution of the world, and the sphere in which the events take place is not limited to the earth, with Palestine and Jerusalem as the focal points, but includes earth, heaven and the underworld (cosmological speculations, the idea of judgment on the angels). Within this cosmic-universal framework the Jewish people does not play the central and sustaining role it does in the national eschatology, not even when a strong Jewish national colouring can be traced in many apocalypses. The trend in apocalyptic modes of thought is unmistakably universalistic. Daniel can symbolise the whole of world-history in a statue made of four metals or in four beasts, without even mentioning Israel;and even when Israel's history is narrated, it is done in a framework which is as universal as possible, through a kind of regression to the creation (Vision of Bulls, eth. Enoch 85-90; Apocalypse of Ten Weeks, eth Enoch 93; 91.12-17; Vision of Clouds, syr. Bar. 53-71). This universalistic trend explicitly influences the description of the eschatological events, for three of them - resurrection, world judgment, world dissolution - are on a cosmic scale. The apocalyptic writer sees the world and mankind as a unity and as a whole, and therefore as something over against God.

Just as the fate of all mankind is drawn into the apocalyptic drama, so man no longer stands as a member of the sacred Jewish race or of the heathen nations, but as an individual before God. From this stems the thought of individual resurrection and of individual judgment (Dan. 12:1ff., etc.). Hence there is a demand in this Age to observe the law and to practise righteousness, always as an individual (cf. the ethical exhortations in the apocalypses; see above, 1.2.4.). Man must prove his righteousness as an individual in order to stand firm in the judgment.

1.3.4. *Determinism and imminent expectation*

Alongside dualism, the outstanding characteristic of the apocalyptic thought-world is determinism. God has fore-ordained everything: all that happens happens precisely according to the fixed plan of God, which human plans and actions can neither advance nor hinder.

He said to me: In the beginning of the world,
Before the portals of heaven stood,
Before the blast of the wind blew,
Before the peals of thunder sounded,
Before the flashes of lightning shone,
Before the foundations of Paradise were laid,
Before the beauty of its flowers was seen,
Before the powers of the earthquake were established,
Before the innumerable hosts of angels were gathered,
Before the heights of the air were lifted,
Before the spaces of heaven were named,
Before the footstool of Zion was established,
Before the years of the present were reckoned,
Before the designs of sin were repudiated,
But those who gather the treasure of faith were sealed, -
Then did I consider all this, and through me
And none other it came into being:
So also shall the End come through me and none other!
(4 Esd. 6:1-6)

God created both Ages ('The Most High created not one Age, but two', 4 Esd. 7:50; 'The Most High created this world for man, but the future age for a few', 4 Esd. 8:1). In fact, he created all things at the same time, even the Eschata, the coming Age 'which now sleeps' (4 Esd. 7:31), the sacred persons and the sacred joys of the Age to come; they are pre-existent and the seer can see them either in the world above or descending from it (Dan. 7:13; eth. Enoch 39:3ff.; 48:3, 6; 49:2; 4 Esd. 13:36).

For everything God has set its *measure*, and everything proceeds without interference or recall:

God has weighed the world in the balance,
By measure has he measured the hours
And by number has he numbered the times (seasons),
He will not disturb nor stir them,
Until the said measure be fulfilled. (4 Esd. 4:36ff.)

Since everything has its time precisely determined, the end of this Age can be calculated, either by reckoning its entire duration from the creation (in which case different conclusions may be arrived at; cf. Volz. op. cit., pp. 143f.), or by reckoning from a point within history (in which case information is provided by the apocalyptic writers from Daniel on in complex and obscure tricks with numbers), or by observing the *signs of the times*. But these calculations are always determined by the conviction that the End is very near at hand.

This conviction about the predetermined character of all that happens and about the nearness of the End also stands behind the division of history into periods (cf. pp. 547f. above). From the standpoint of the imminent End, the apocalyptist sees history complete, just as it was seen by God in the very beginning, as a unity and as a whole, so much so indeed that all the movements of history are levelled out and become of no interest, and the division of history into periods lies in the free choice of the individual writer. Whether he takes history in his view by applying the Four-Ages doctrine of Hesiod or by using the Biblical accounts, whether he gives Israel prominence or not, whether he divides it into four, seven, ten or twelve periods, is of no importance. What matters is not history itself nor the activity of God within it - one knows, of course, that it proceeds according to his pre-historic plan - but solely the demonstration of its completedness and so of one's own historical position as immediately preceding the End. 'Apocalyptic really was concerned only with the last generation of Israel which, according to its own conviction, was on the point of entering into the last things. Therefore it is comparatively unimportant whether the history of God's people is described at one time in detail, at another in concise terms' (G. von Rad, *Theologie* II, 317).

This imminent expectation is expressed in the most varied ways: not only in surveys and divisions of history, in reflections on the world's duration, in observation of the *signs of the times* and calculations of the end, but also in the existence and publication of apocalypses; for these books by figures of past history were to be made public only at the End of Days (Dan. 12:4, 9; eth. Enoch 105:1; 4 Esd. 12:37f.; 14:7f. etc.). All this, however, does not mean that the imminent expectation had to be stimulated: it is in fact completely genuine. It is expressed with convincing directness in the passionate questions concerning the End which extend through all the apocalypses (Dan. 8:13; 12:5ff.; 4 Esd. 6:59; syr. Bar. 26; 81:3, etc.) and often bear upon them the marks of eschatological impatience:

> 'And I answered and said: How long? When shall these things come to pass? Wherefore is our life so short and miserable? But he answered and said: Art thou not wanting to hasten more than the Most High? For thou desirest haste for thine own sake, but the Most High for the sake of many.' (4 Esd. 4:33f.; cf. eth. Enoch 97:3, 5; 104:3)

The distresses of the present (the Maccabean period, the destruction of Jerusalem, etc.) are reflected in this kind of impatience; but these, however, are only the occasion, not the cause, of the apocalyptic mood of the End, else the latter would have disappeared with the former; rather this mood is general (Dan. 2; 7;

11:21-12:4; eth. Enoch 93:9f.; 4 Esd. 4:48-50; 5:55).

> 'For the youth of the world is past; the strength of the creation has long ago come to its end, and the approach of the times is (already) at hand and (indeed already) passed by. For the pitcher is near to the well, the ship to harbour, the caravan to the city, and life to its conclusion.' (syr. Bar. 85:10)

This cosmological statement makes it clear that the conviction concerning the nearness of the End is rooted in the deep levels of the apocalyptic understanding of the world.

G. von Rad raises the question 'whether Apocalyptic has still, in general, an existential relation to the dimension of history' and 'whether this conception is not the signal for a serious loss of history, whether, behind this gnosticizing understanding of the termination which people can measure and even calculate, there does not stand a fundamentally unhistorical type of thought, since it has eliminated even the phenomenon of contingency' (op. cit., 317; 318f.). His question really implies its answer. He might even speak, like R. Bultmann (*Geschichte und Eschatologie*, 1958, 35) of a 'complete de-historicizing of history through Apocalyptic'.* In contrast to this, D. Rößler puts forward the thesis that the real interest of Apocalyptic lies in history, and that the history of Israel. This however ignores typical apocalyptic ideas such as imminent expectation, dualism and the doctrine of the Two Ages, to name only the most important. This theory has therefore provoked widespread opposition (most recently: J. Maier, GKT 2, 164).

1.3.5 *Lack of uniformity*

In view of what has been said, the fact that the apocalyptic world of ideas is uniform only in its basic structure, but lacks that uniformity and harmony in its expressions, requires no further emphasis. By way of example we need refer only to the variations in the conception of the Saviour-figure. That this question, important for the Christian interpretation of Apocalyptic, plays no primary role in the apocalyptic literature itself is shown by the fact that the central figure of the national eschatology, the Davidic Messiah, is completely absent from many of the apocalypses. Here it is God or his angels who bring in salvation and judgment and replace the old Age by the new (Dan 2:7; 12:1-4; eth. Enoch 93.3-10; 91.11-17. Cf. S. Uhlig, JSHRZ V 6, 1984, 709ff.; also Ass. Mos.).

Where world-judgment plays such an important role the figure of the national, earthly Saviour-King is out of place. It is replaced occasionally by the pre-existent, transcendent Judge and Redeemer figure, the Son of Man (eth. Enoch 37-71; 4 Esd. 13) who draws to himself many of the titles and traits of the Davidic Messiah, without our being permitted to speak of a fusion of the two figures. Of course, the expectation of the Davidic Messiah is not allowed to disappear completely. He appears in the Vision of Bulls in eth. Enoch, completely without motive, suddenly and without his having anything to do, after the judgment of the world has already been consummated and the new world brought in (90.37). In 4 Esd. 7 the national and transcendent expectations are combined in such a way that, at the end of this Age, a Messianic interregnum lasting 400 years is inserted; at the end of this period, the Messiah and all men die, whereupon this Age sinks back into the silence of the Beginning, the judgment of the world takes place and the new Age appears (7:26-31). Less successful combinations are found in syr. Bar. (cf. the perspicuous analysis in Volz, op. cit. 38-41, which is not surpassed by more recent descriptions, such as A.F.J. Klijn, JSHRZ V 2, 1976, 116f.). Test. Levi 18 promises the figure of a priestly Messiah, and this has parallels in the Qumran texts but, in contrast, is of a transcendent kind (1 QS 9.11; 1 QSa 2.11-21; cf. M. Burrows, *More Light on the Dead Sea Scrolls*, 1958, pp. 308ff.; A. Dupont-Sommer, *The Essene Writings from Qumran*, 1961, p. 94 n. 3; pp. 108f.). How far this lack of uniformity in the conception of the Saviour is due to literary compilation or to the reworking of heterogeneous traditions would require detailed investigation. The same is true of the complexity of other apocalyptic themes.

1.4 Origin

Literature (supplementary): J.J. Collins, *The Apocalyptic Imagination. An Introduction to the Jewish Matrix of Christianity*, New York 1984; G. Couturier, 'La vision du conseil divin: étude d'une forme commune au prophétisme et à l'apocalyptique', *Science et Esprit* 36, Montreal 1984, 5-43; P.D. Hanson, *The Dawn of Apocalyptic. The Historical and Sociological Roots of Jewish Apocalyptic Eschatology*, Philadelphia 1975; P. von der Osten-Sacken, *Die Apokalyptik in ihrem Verhältnis zu Prophetie und Weisheit* (ThEx 157), 1969; H. Weinel, 'Die spätere christliche Apokalyptik', ΕΥΧΑΡΙΣΤΗΡΙΟΝ, *FS H. Gunkel, 2. Teil. Zur Religion und Literatur des NT*, 1923, 141-173.

The problem as to the origin or the rise of Apocalyptic and the *Sitz im Leben* of the apocalypses is still unresolved and can be treated only briefly here.

Without doubt the influx of foreign ideas, especially the cosmological dualism of Iranian origin (the doctrine of the Two Ages, determinism), played an important role in the rise of Jewish Apocalyptic. But the essential problem of how far an understanding of God, the world and mankind so opposed to the basic convictions of the OT could have been taken over by Israel has not been answered, but only presented, especially since this influx must have taken place in post-exilic times (the Persian and Hellenistic periods) when 'Israel' consolidated itself as a theocracy and sought to shield itself from all foreign influences. O. Plöger (*Theokratie*) has investigated this problem and he concludes that it was eschatologically-stimulated circles in the post-exilic community (*c.* 400-200 B.C.), who stood in a certain opposition to the non-eschatological theocracy and who were therefore more and more forced into the role of sectarians, who were the 'soft spots' on which the foreign ideas had influence. It is in these circles, to which he traces back the 'anonymous additions' to the prophetic books (e.g. Is. 24-27; Zech. 12-14, etc.) that he thinks the beginnings of Apocalyptic are located; it then unfolded itself powerfully in the distresses of the Maccabean period. Its origin accordingly coincides chronologically with the spread of hellenistic thought. It is therefore understandable that P. Vielhauer describes Apocalyptic as 'a product of Hellenism': 'It is a *Jewish reaction to the advancing hellenistic culture*, and seeks by harking back to wisdom and revelation to strengthen the self-consciousness of Judaism. Although itself a syncretistic phenomenon, it is an act of Jewish self-affirmation, directed against the syncretistic dissolution of Judaism such as was making headway in some circles of Judaism at the beginning of the second century before Christ' (*Lit. gesch.* 493).

While acknowledging foreign influence, other scholars have seen in Apocalyptic the continuation of prophecy (so H.H. Rowley, *Relevance*). Here we must ask whether it was so in the intention of the apocalyptists, and whether it is actually the case. The first question is to be answered in the affirmative. The 'anonymous additions' to the prophets are without doubt intended to be understood as continuing interpretation. However, the fact that these additions are not characterised as such, but are 'ascribed' to the prophets in the proper sense of the word, so that anonymity borders on pseudonymity, is a sign that the authors concerned did not consider themselves as prophets. The same is shown in the real, pseudonymous, Apocalyptic. When, for instance, Daniel interprets the seventy years mentioned in Jer. 25:11ff.; 29:10 as seventy weeks of years, and when the angel says to Daniel, ' Seventy weeks of years are fixed for thy people . . . till vision and prophet are sealed' (Dan. 9:2, 10-27), the apocalyptic writer's understanding of himself is clear: he is not himself a prophet, but rather the authentic interpreter of prophecy, and as such is the legitimate successor to the prophets. That such a self-understanding is not the property of Daniel alone is shown by syr. Bar., in which a conscious reflection on the relation to prophecy is shown. Here we find the well-known sentence which can easily be interpreted as an admission of decadence ('But now . . . the prophets have lain down to sleep': 85:3), but this provides only a partial view; the rest is made clear by the book as a whole. Baruch conveys to Jeremiah God's command to leave Jerusalem (2:1ff.; 5:5ff.), likewise, after the destruction, to remove to Babylon with the prisoners, while he himself (Baruch) remains in Jerusalem at the divine bidding.

> 'Say to Jeremiah that he go forth and take care of the prisoners of the people to Babylon. But do thou linger here in the ruins of the city and I will make known to thee after these days what will happen at the end of days. (syr. Bar. 10.2f.)

Baruch receives his comprehensive vision, acts as the messenger of God to the elders (44-46) and people (77), writes to the exiles, not only like Jeremiah to those in Babylon (Jer. 29) but also to those in Assyrian captivity (78-86), and is convinced that he knows and says better things than the prophets (10:3; 85:4f.). The self-awareness of the apocalyptic writer might then be described as follows: the prophets have disappeared; the apocalyptists have taken their place and continue their work in other, but better ways.

The other question, whether Apocalyptic is actually a continuation of OT prophecy, has been answered in the negative by M. Buber (*Kampf um Israel*, 1933, 50-67) and G. von Rad (*Theologie des AT* II, 316-331). The dualism, determinism and pessimism of Apocalyptic form the gulf which separates it from prophecy.

> 'The prophetic belief in the End is in all essentials autochthonous, whereas the apocalyptic is really built up from elements of Iranian dualism. Accordingly, the former predicts a completion of creation, the latter its dissolution, its replacement by another world of a completely different kind; the former allows the now aimless powers, 'evil', to find their way to God and change to good, the latter sees good and evil finally separated at the end of days, the one redeemed, the other unredeemed for ever; the former believes in the sanctification of the earth, the latter despairs of it as hopelessly ruined; the former allows the original creative will of

> God to be fulfilled without remainder, the latter makes the faithless creation powerful over the Creator, in that it compels him to surrender Nature. . . .
>
> The apocalyptic writers wish to assume an irrevocably fixed future event; therefore they are rooted in Iranian ideas which divided history into equal thousand-year cycles and fixed, with numerical accuracy, the end of the world, the final triumph of good over evil. It was otherwise with the prophets of Israel: they prophesied 'to the converted', that is to say, they did not state something which would happen in any event, but something which would happen, if those summoned to conversion were not converted.' (M. Buber, op. cit., pp. 61-63).

On the basis of a penetrating analysis of the prophetic tradition, von Rad comes to the same conclusion: he summarises the irreconcilable difference in the pregnant formula of 'the incompatibility of the understanding of history in Apocalyptic with that in the prophets' op. cit., p. 316). However (with P. von der Osten-Sacken, *Apokalyptik*) it should not be disputed that not only is a prophetic claim made by the apocalyptic 'seer', but also there are in fact lines of connection to the Old Testament Jewish prophecy. Thus P. Hanson has shown for the later prophetic texts of the OT the presuppositions and starting points for apocalyptic forms of thought; and it must be stated as a point of principle that 'the future reference, probably the hall-mark of Apocalyptic, is beyond doubt inherited from the prophets' (W.H. Schmidt, GKT 1, 68).

The earlier theories on the spiritual home of Apocalyptic - the apocalypses are 'folk-books' (W. Bousset, E. Stauffer) or the esoteric literature of the Rabbis (A. Schlatter, J. Jeremias) - would scarcely be advocated today. Attention may be given rather to the increasing tendency, under the influence of the discoveries from the Dead Sea, to establish an 'Essene' origin for Apocalyptic. Among the texts found at Qumran are fragments of the Book of Enoch, the Testaments of the XII Patriarchs (Levi and Naphtali) and of Jubilees. In terminology and ideas there are points of connection: the characteristically broken dualism, which marks the apocalyptic doctrine of the Two Ages, also marks the Qumran teaching on the Two Spirits, and here and there a strong expectation of the imminent End is alive. Admittedly the material is not yet sufficient for convincing conclusions. The fact that the Book of Enoch was read in Qumran does not prove that it originated there. The eschatological texts of the Qumran community differ, in form and content, from the Jewish apocalypses. The relevant passages in the Manual of Discipline, the War Scroll, the commentaries on the prophetic books, are not apocalypses in the 'form-historical' sense of the word. J. Carmignac finds the literary 'genre' of Apocalyptic only in some few isolated pieces: in the texts about the new Jerusalem (1Q 32; 2Q 24; 5Q 15), also in the angelic liturgy (4QSirSabb), in the Prayer of Nabonidus (4QPrNab), the visions of 'Amram (4Q'Amram) and in some sections of 1 QapGen and 1 QH ('Qu'est-ce que l'Apocalyptique? Son emploi à Qumran', *RevQum* 10, 1979, 3-33). Differences in content appear for one thing with regard to the saving figures - the Teacher of Righteousness, the Prophet and the Two Messiahs are to be found in this combination in none of our apocalypses - and also with regard to the nature of the events of the End - in the Qumran texts, these are earthly; in Apocalyptic, and even in those parts of the Book of Enoch known in Qumran, they are transcendent. So some considerations resist the acceptance of the theory of an

Essene origin of Apocalyptic.

Von Rad has vigorously tried to make probable the view that *Wisdom* (Hochmah) is 'the real native-soil' of Apocalyptic op. cit., pp. 319ff.): Daniel, Enoch and Ezra are characterised as 'wise' (Dan. 1:3ff.; 2:48; eth. Enoch 32:2-4; 4 Esd. 14:50; dream-interpretation is the domain of the wise, Dan. 2:30; 5:11; Gen. 41:8, 39); the genre of the figurative utterances is a 'traditional Sapiential form of teaching'; the material also is, to a large extent, of Wisdom character: the knowledge of the cosmos which eth. Enoch 8:72-79 in particular displays, and of history, i.e. more precisely the kind of 'presentation which is empty of interest in salvation-history and only enumerates the events', of which Sir. 44-50 is the first example. If one can scarcely avoid the force of von Rad's arguments, still the fact that there is no eschatology and imminent expectation in the Wisdom literature corresponding to the presence of Wisdom-motifs in the apocalypses forms an insurmountable objection to his thesis. The eschatological ideas and expectations are doubtless primary and so fundamental that the Wisdom elements must be evaluated as colouring, and not as the basis. But the fact that connections with 'Wisdom' exist - cf. also eth. Enoch 42; 4 Esd. 5:9f. - is undeniable and this would make intelligible the association of Apocalyptic with Gnosis which von Rad has also stressed.

With all necessary reserve and with proper readiness to revise opinions, we may accept the view that the home of Apocalyptic is in those eschatologically-excited circles which were forced more and more by the theocracy into a kind of conventicle existence (O. Plöger). In their eschatological expectation, dualistic ideas and esoteric thought these have a certain connection with the Qumran community; in their organisation, materials and forms they have a certain connection with 'Wisdom' circles. The origin and, in particular, the history of these circles are not yet clear.

The apocalypses represent the literature of these conventicles. They were frequently written out of actual distresses and for the strengthening of the community in them (Dan., Ass. Mos., 4 Esd., syr. Bar), not for the instruction of an interested public in knowledge and prudence, as Wisd. Sol. and Sir. were, even though many apocalypses include an 'encyclopaedic erudition' (large parts of eth. Enoch. gk. Bar., slav. Enoch); their wisdom is a secret wisdom. This esotericism and the real concern with the strengthening and comforting of the particular community mark out these works as the literature of conventicles.

1.5 Continuation in the Christian period

Literature (supplementary): A. Böhlig, 'Der judenchristliche Hintergrund in gnostischen Schriften von Nag Hammadi', *Mysterion und Wahrheit* (AGSU 6), 1968, 102-111; M. Krause, 'Die literarischen Gattungen der Apokalypsen von Nag Hammadi', in D. Hellholm (ed.). *Apocalypticism*, 621-637; W. Pratscher, *Der Herrenbruder Jakobus und die Jakobustradition*, 1987; K.-H. Schwarte, art. 'Apokalypsen V. Alte Kirche', TRE 3, 1978, 257-275; G. Strecker, art. 'Judenchristentum', TRE 17, 1988, 310-325; H. Weinel, in ΕΥΧΑΡΙΣΤΗΡΙΟΝ, Teil II, 1923, 141-173. For the texts from Nag Hammadi cf. D.M. Scholer, *Nag Hammadi Bibliography 1948-1969* (NHS 1), Leiden 1971, 174 and the annual continuation as 'Bibliographia Gnostica' in *NovTest* since vol. 13 (1971).

The thought-world and temper of Jewish Apocalyptic were shared, to a large extent, by the early Christian movement as well, especially the Palestinian and hellenistic-Jewish Christian wing. In fact, as has already been said, it took over the literary documents of the former, the apocalypses, and 'christianised' them by means of a rewriting of varying kinds and intensity. It took over also the literary form and produced numerous works of its own in this genre. The Christian apocalypses presented in the following sections are the oldest and the most characteristic; but the stock is much greater. H. Weinel and K.H. Schwarte provide a survey. Since a report on this group of writings would strain the limits of an 'introduction', reference may be made to the discussions mentioned. Cf. also Chapter XXI, pp. 691ff. below.

The number of the Christian or Christian-gnostic writings which bear the designation 'apocalypse' has been increased by the discoveries of Nag Hammadi. This designation is however misleading, since the title 'apocalypse' largely means the same as 'revelation'. That such revelation documents are not to be assigned to the genre of 'apocalypses' follows also from the recession of Jewish content, the more so in that the conjecture of Jewish-Christian substrata is in most cases extremely problematic (cf. G. Strecker in TRE 17, 322f.). Thus the two so-called 'Apocalypses of James' (NHC V 3-4) are not to be reckoned to this literary genre; as revelation-speeches of Jesus in conversation with James the Lord's brother, they are appropriately included in vol. 1 (pp. 313ff.) under the heading of 'Dialogues of the Redeemer'.

The situation is different with the 'Apocalypse of Adam' (NHC V 5), which not only presents pseudonymity, the report of a vision and a survey of history in future form, but also contains dualistic ideas (death and life, the wrath of God and the glorification of man), so that the designation 'apocalypse' is very natural. However, important constituents of the Jewish apocalyptic world of ideas are missing. Since Christian elements also cannot be proven, we may ask whether this writing should be understood as a document of the transition from Jewish to gnostic Apocalyptic (so G.W. MacRae, NHLE 256 [3rd ed. 1988, 277]).

There are problems about assigning the 'Apocalypse of Paul' (NHC V 2; cf. below, pp. 695ff.) to the apocalyptic literature, since it does indeed contain traditional elements of apocalyptic style (pseudonymity, vision report, aspect of judgment), but on the other hand there is no orientation to history. One fundamental motif is the (non-apocalyptic) rapture of Paul, according to 2 Cor. 12. The 'Apocalypse of Peter' (NHC VII 3; cf. below, pp. 700ff.) is also frequently reckoned to our genre. It likewise contains apocalyptic elements (pseudonymity, visions and auditions, the imparting of secret knowledge), but its survey of history does not have a universalistic orientation; it is conceived as a debate with groups outside the Church and with the Great Church, showing strong links with Mt. 21-28. Since essential elements of the apocalyptic system are missing, we must have reservations about including it in the genre of the apocalypses. On the other hand its gnostic (docetic) character is clear (cf. 81.3-14).

There is also debate as to whether 'The Thought of our great Power' (NHC VI 4) may be called an 'apocalypse', although despite the absence of typical elements there is at any rate a presentation related to history, and the figure of the 'Anti-Christ' is known (44.14f.). The same holds for the 'Paraphrase of Shem' (NHC VII 1), which does indeed contain elements of Apocalyptic and also bears Old Testament Jewish features, but is to a considerable extent distinct from Jewish and Christian apocalypses. In addition there are isolated pieces which are parts of larger entities and are described as apocalypses (cf. M. Krause, 'Gattungen', 634f.).

Christian Apocalyptic, like the Jewish, is pseudepigraphical. The author of the Johannine Apocalypse also does not write under his own name. The situation is different with the Shepherd of Hermas, but his book - as will be shown below (Chapter XIX) - is not a genuine apocalypse. All the others are presented under the authority of great names: Jesus (e.g. the Synoptic Apocalypse, the Testamentum Domini), various Apostles (Peter, Paul, Thomas, John, Bartholomew, Philip, etc.), the mother of Jesus, Mary; even OT figures were used as authorities for Christian apocalypses (Abraham, Ezra, Zephaniah and Elijah). Visions and raptures are the usual means of revelation.

So far as content is concerned, these Christian books took over, on the widest scale, Jewish material, whether it existed in 'traditions' (fixed ideas, imagery and schemata) or in written documents. But through its concern with the Parousia of Christ there occurs a concentration on this one theme, which means a sharp reduction in the Jewish materials and devices. Above all, the surveys of history disappear; they pass over from Apocalyptic to Apologetic (e.g. Luke and Theophilus of Antioch) and exchange the eschatological function for that which is concerned with salvation-history. On the other hand, Christian Apocalyptic takes over much non-Jewish, heathen and gnostic material, especially ideas concerning the Beyond (Ascens. Isaiah, Apocalypse of Peter).

The themes of Christian Apocalyptic became more limited the longer it continued. At first, the imminent expectation of the Parousia was the organising principle, but then, with the delay of the return of Christ, interest moved to the Anti-Christ and things associated with him, and to the Beyond, to Heaven and its blessedness, to Hell and its miseries. The Anti-Christ and the After-life, which in the New Testament are only subsidiary themes of the Parousia expectation, are the two main themes around which Christian Apocalyptic revolves from the middle of the 2nd century.

2. The Sibyllines

Literature: see below, section XX 2 (pp. 652ff.).
The Sibyllines represent the Apocalyptic of hellenistic Diaspora Judaism. In the second half of the 2nd century B.C. it seized on the Greek Sibylline literature as a means of literary debate. The Greek Sibyllines, which reach back to the 7th century B.C. and in the hellenistic age had attained to a new florescence as a means of religious and political propaganda against the rulers of the time, had already in pre-Christian times found their definitive form: - hymns, in hexameters, which continued prophecies of disastrous content, and which were attributed to the ancient Sibyl who kept prophesying through the ages. In these prophecies it was a matter of *vaticinium ex eventu*, of 'a kind of Greek history in future form' (J. Geffcken, NTApo[2], 400). Diaspora Judaism adopted this literary genre in such a way that it inserted in the pagan texts prophecies for Israel and events of the actual recent past and present, also attacks on polytheism, propaganda for monotheism, even eschatological promises and threats, or it even created entirely new Sibyllines for this content. In various respects this "propaganda literature in a trivial sense" (A. Dihle, *Griechische Literaturgeschichte*, 1967, 414) is related to the apocalypses: formally, in respect of pseudonymity, that is,

by the attributing of the statements to an ancient sacred authority, and in respect of the description of history in the future; then, as far as content is concerned, in respect of the eschatological material. There is, however, a basic difference in the function of the two genres. While the apocalypses are fundamentally a conventicle-literature designed to strengthen a particular community, the Jewish Sibyllines originated as missionary propaganda writings which were turned, from the very beginning, towards those outside; their *Sitz im Leben* is originally the mission of Diaspora Judaism to the heathen.

In the second half of the 2nd century A.D. the Christians took over from hellenistic Diaspora Judaism this literary genre, which seemed very suitable for the struggle to maintain and assert their faith in a pagan world. In their reception of the Jewish Sibyllines they proceeded in the same way as the Jews had done with the pagan. Details of the early history and development of Christian Sibyllines are found in XX 2 below.

3. Prophecy

The prophecy of the period in question (*c.* 200 B.C.-A.D. 200) cannot be treated in the same way as Apocalyptic or the Sibyllines because, unlike these and unlike the writing prophets of the Old Testament, it has left behind no literary documents. Nevertheless, its significance in Judaism and certainly in early Christianity should not be underestimated. For knowledge concerning it we are dependent on reports about it, on literary-critical and form-historical analyses, and on sparse testimonies.

3.1 Jewish prophecy

Literature (supplementary): D.E. Aune, *Prophecy in Early Christianity and the Ancient Mediterranean World*, Grand Rapids/Mich. 1983, 103-152; O. Böcher, art. 'Johannes der Täufer', TRE 17, 1988, 172-181; E. Fascher, ΠΡΟΦΗΤΗΣ, 1927; J. Giblet, 'Prophétisme et attente d'un Messie Prophète dans l'ancien Judaisme', *L'Attente du Messie*, ed. L. Cerfaux, Paris 1954, 85-130; F. Lang, 'Erwägungen zur eschatologischen Verkündigung Johannes des Täufers', *Jesus Christus in Historie und Theologie, FS H. Conzelmann*, 1975, 459-473; R. Meyer, *Der Prophet aus Galiläa*, 1940; O. Michel, 'Spätjüdisches Prophetentum', *Neutestamentliche Studien für R. Bultmann*, 1954, 60-66; O. Plöger, 'Prophetisches Erbe in den Sekten des frühen Judentums', ThLZ 79, 1954, cols. 291-296; P. Vielhauer, art. 'Johannes der Täufer', RGG[3] III, 1959, cols. 804-808; J. Ernst, Johannes der Täufer, BZNW 53, 1989; also E. Lupieri, Giovanni Battista fra storia e leggenda, Brescia 1988.

While W. Bousset maintained the thesis that the 'late hellenistic period' of Judaism was marked by the quenching of the Spirit and the absence of prophets (*Religion*, 394), R. Meyer contradicted this by showing that the individual witnesses (Zech. 13:2ff.; Ps. 74:9; 1 Macc. 4:6; 9:27; 14:41) are not sufficient to prove that this conception was universally held (ThWNT VI, 813-828 [TDNT VI, 812-828]). Yet it is not only in the rabbinic tradition that the tendency to limit the appearance of prophets to an ideal age in antiquity first makes itself felt. The apocalyptic authors too are marked by a post-prophetic consciousness, as the pseudonymity of their writings shows, not to mention the fact that they did indeed wish to continue the old prophecy, but did not consider themselves as prophets (see above, pp. 555ff.). According to Josephus, prophetic figures are to be found in almost all the groups of the Jewish people. In his admittedly by no means objective report he says of the Essenes that they possessed and cultivated the gift of prophecy (*Bell.* 2. 159), and he records the names of Essene prophets and the contents of many of their prophecies. Moreover he mentions prophetically-gifted Pharisees at the court of Herod (*Ant.* 17. 43ff.), tells of a Zealot 'pseudo-prophet' in the last hours of the Temple (*Bell.* 6. 283-286), of a mass ecstasy of priests (ibid. 299) and of the peasant Jesus ben Chananiah who alarmed Jerusalem for years with his sinister prophesying of disaster (ibid. 300-309). Rabbinic sources ascribe to many scholars the gift of prophecy, as well as other wonderful abilities, and it is well known that R. Akiba appeared as a prophet of the Messiah Simon bar Cosiba.

In spite of the variety of the of the phenomena and in spite of the tendentious description in Josephus, we can recognise some types of prophecy (the vision of the future which many Rabbis were supposed to have had on their death-beds is here left out of consideration).

First, there is the spiritual and topical interpretation of the prophetic writings, as it was practised by the Essenes (Jos. *Bell.* 2.159; an example is the Habakkuk 'Commentary' from Qumran; particularly instructive for the spiritual understanding of what God actually wanted to say through the prophets is 1QpHab. 7:1-5; a similar phenomenon is found at Dan. 9:1-3, 20-27). The fact that this kind of interpretation was not purely academic and was not confined to the Essenes is shown by the following: in the time of the Jewish war 'an ambiguous oracle which was found in Holy Scripture' - one readily thinks of Dan. 7:13f. - and which prophesied world-dominion 'to one from this country' was openly and violently disputed, and people differed in their answers to the question whether it signified salvation or disaster for Israel (Jos. *Bell.* 6. 312f.). In both cases an eschatological occurrence is seen in the fulfilment of the prophecy.

Then there are the different kinds of active prophecy, the vision into the future. We may divide these into prophecy concerned with salvation and that concerned with catastrophe, but that brings us no nearer to its essence.

Professional prophesying, which a man may learn, is represented, alongside the first-mentioned, among the Essenes. The Essene Judas, who prophesied destruction to Antigonus, was accompanied 'by his followers and confidants who stayed with him in order to learn how to predict the future' (Jos. *Ant.* 13. 311). Prophets like these announced their fate to individuals, and in particular to rulers (Menachem to the young Herod, *Ant.* 15. 373ff.), sometimes in the form of the interpretation of a dream (*Ant.* 17. 345ff.).

A special type is to be seen in the 'messianic prophets' (R. Meyer) or the prophetic pretenders to messiahship, who promised to the people a startling authentication of their case and the arrival of the imminent salvation. To this type belong the Samaritan who promised to show to his followers the Temple-furniture which had been hidden by Moses on Gerizim (Jos. *Ant.* 18. 85ff.), Theudas, who promised to the people the repetition of Joshua's miracle in the cleaving of Jordan (*Ant.* 20. 97f.; Acts 5:36), the 'false leaders', the 'impostors' who again and again led the people into the wilderness (*Bell.* 2. 258ff., *Ant.* 20. 167f.) and the prophet from Egypt who held out the prospect of a repetition of the Jericho miracle at Jerusalem (*Ant.* 20. 169ff.; Acts 21:38). These prophets were convinced that the eschatological age of salvation would correspond to the early history of Israel (hence the wilderness and Moses typologies), that the age of salvation was imminent and that they were called as the second Moses or Joshua to bring things to a head. These messianic pretenders are exponents of the imminent expectation of the national eschatology.

Finally a type of prophet which seems to come closest to those in the Old Testament - men who, in a definite political situation, brought messages from God. The most impressive figure among these is that Jesus ben Chananiah who, on the Feast of Tabernacles in A.D. 62, four years before the outbreak of the war, appeared in Jerusalem and by his woeful pronouncements threw into panic a city which was completely at peace. Insensitive to cruelties and kindnesses alike, he continued his disastrous prophesying unflinchingly for seven years and five months till he fell, shortly before the taking of the city (Jos. *Bell.* 6. 300ff.). Perhaps also the Zealot who, a few hours before the burning of the Temple, urged 6000 men to their death was no 'false prophet', but a prophet filled with the imminent eschatological expectation, who dragged the despairing masses along with him by means of an oracle of deliverance. How inextricably religious enthusiasm and national fanaticism were bound up in the Messianic hope of Judaism, especially in times of crisis, is shown by the figure of R. Akiba who allied himself, religiously and politically, to the rebellion against Hadrian, and who, with the pledge of his entire personal authority, advanced the cause of Simon ben Cosiba as Messiah.

There were certainly even more types of prophets, but the tendency of Josephus to give a hellenised picture of Judaism and to conceal Jewish messianism as much as possible makes it difficult to find out the personal awareness of those figures who are called and characterised by him as false leaders, cheats and bandits. He presents with sympathetic understanding only the Essene and Pharisaic soothsayers and the prophets of disaster.

For this reason we are poorly informed concerning the form of prophetic statements. Josephus gives the prophecy mostly in indirect speech, and only twice, so far as I can see, in direct speech. The first is the oracle of Menachem to the young Herod, which is linked with a corroborating sign (*Ant.* 15. 374ff.). In this he predicts the elevation of Herod to kingship, refers to the inconstancy of fortune, exhorts him to righteousness, piety and gentleness, foretells his wickedness and threatens him with the wrath of God. In view of the Hellenistic terminology, it seems likely that Josephus is not citing the oracle verbatim, but has formulated it independently. On the other hand, he may have reproduced the calamitous cry of Jesus ben Chananiah in a literal translation:

A voice from the sunrise,
A voice from the sunset,
A voice from the four winds:

Woe to Jerusalem and the Temple!
Woe to bridegroom and bride!
Woe to the whole people! (*Bell.* 6. 301.).

The rhythmical and metrical form of the two three-lined parts, the *parallelismus membrorum* and the Semitisms argue for its originality (cf. R. Meyer, *Prophet aus Galiläa*, 46f.). This is a threatening message, without any word of rebuke at its base and without any call to repentance, which in the second strophe proclaims the unavoidability and the completeness of the destruction, and in the first asserts with uncanny impressiveness the divine origin of the oracle. The prophecies of the messianic pretenders and of the Zealot prophets of salvation can be reconstructed only roughly as far as content is concerned, but not in their formal structure. The prophetic propaganda of Akiba for Simon worked with the contemporary interpretation of the 'Star of Jacob' (Num. 24:17) in terms of this leader, but even more significant than this interpretation of a traditional messianically understood prophecy in terms of a figure of the present is the statement of Akiba concerning Simon ben Cosiba, 'This is the King, the Messiah!' (jer. Taan. 4.8 (68d, 50) cited by R. Meyer, ThWNT VI, 825 and note 306 [TDNT VI 824 n. 306]). The sentence has the structure and the sense of an acclamation.

These observations may suffice to show how lively and many-sided prophecy was in Judaism at this time. These prophets believed that they were commissioned by God (as did the Essene soothsayers as well). In their messianic hopes they were religiously and politically active, but unlike the apocalyptic writers they were not productive of literature. Their prophecy is entirely determined by the national eschatology and stands beside Apocalyptic as the expression, today difficult to grasp, but then at least as powerfully effective, of the eschatological expectation of Judaism.

John the Baptist occupies a special position. However, the tradition has largely distorted the historical picture of this undoubtedly prophetic figure. Josephus portrays him as an ethical teacher (*Ant.* 18. 116-119), and thereby has made himself guilty of a 'hellenising re-interpretation' (P. Vielhauer, RGG[3] III, col. 804). The overlay of legend, as for example in the Slavonic Josephus (II 7.2; 9.1), has also contributed to making him unrecognisable. This holds not least for the Christianised portrayal in the New Testament Gospels: it goes back to no small extent to controversy with the Baptist's sect, and shows the tendency to incorporate and subordinate John to the Christian portrait of Jesus (e.g. Mk. 9:12ff.; Mt. 3:13ff.). The Baptist's adherents revered their master as the prophet Elijah returned to life again (cf. Lk. 1:17; 7:27), and can still be traced at a later period (cf. Mk. 2:18; Acts 19:3; Jn. 3:23ff.; ps.-Clem., Rec. I 54, 60). The historical core in the Synoptic Gospels informs us that John appeared in the wilderness (Mk. 1:4; Mt. 11:7, which is possibly to be interpreted in the sense of a 'wilderness typology'; cf. Hos. 2:14ff.; 12:10) and led an ascetic life (cf. Mk. 1:6; his clothing with a garment of camel hair with a leather belt, and his diet of locusts and wild honey, cannot be interpreted with sufficient certainty in terms either of a Bedouin way of life or of the Old Testament prophet Elijah, but have a close parallel in the emergence of the Jewish ascetic Banus in Jos. *Vita* 2). John proclaims the coming of 'one stronger', to whom he is subordinate as in the role of a slave (Mk. 1:7). If this figure had no name, which for Christian tradition simplified the application to Jesus, he was at any rate expected as a judge who would baptize with fire (Mt. 3:12 par.). In prophesying the final judgment in the immediate future, John at the same time summoned to baptism, described as a 'baptism of repentance' (Mk. 1:4), which in association with confession of sins had the function of preparing for confrontation with the Coming One (cf. Mt. 3:10 par.). Even if analogies to John's baptism can be found in a widespread and not only Jewish Baptist movement, both his baptismal practice and his preaching of repentance stand in close connection with the Baptist's radical eschatology and are not to be separated from it.

3.2 The early Christian prophecy

Literature (supplementary): D.E. Aune, op. cit. (above, 3.1), 153-346; M.E. Boring, *Sayings of the Risen Jesus. Christian Prophecy in the Synoptic Tradition* (SNTS MS 46), Cambridge 1982; R. Bultmann, *Die Geschichte der synoptischen Tradition* (FRLANT 29), [9]1979 (with supplement [5]1979; ET *The History of the Synoptic Tradition* 1968); E. Fascher, art. 'Propheten III B. In der alten christlichen Kirche', RGG[3] III, cols. 634f; E. Käsemann, 'Sätze heiligen Rechtes im Neuen Testament', *Exegetische Versuche und Besinnungen* II, [2]1965, 69-82 (ET *New Testament Questions of Today*, 1969, 66-81); U.B. Müller, *Prophetie und Predigt im Neuen Testament. Formgeschichtliche Untersuchungen zur urchristlichen Prophetie* (StNT 10), 1975; M. Sato, *Q und Prophetie* (WUNT II 29), 1988; F. Schnider, art. 'προφήτης', EWNT III, cols. 442-447; S. Schulz, *Q - Die Spruchquelle der Evangelisten*, Zürich 1972; P. Vielhauer, art 'Propheten III A. Im NT', RGG[3] III, cols. 633f.

Jesus of Nazareth can also be understood as an exponent of the Jewish prophetic tradition, in so far as he continued the proclamation of his teacher John (on this see below, XIX). Over against this, *primitive Christian prophecy* starts from the Easter event. Its representatives are charismatics, like the Jewish prophets, but in contrast to them form an 'estate' largely bound to the local community, which ranks in authority under the apostles and above the teachers (1 Cor. 12:28; Eph. 2:20; 3:5; 4:11; Rev. 18:20; Acts 13:1). If they exercise their function chiefly in worship (1 Cor. 11:4; 14:23f., 29ff.; also Didache 10.7, 11.9), it is yet not to be schematically restricted, and moreover the question whether there were itinerant prophets in addition to the resident ones should not be answered in terms of an alternative. The texts just mentioned do indeed attest the presence of an 'estate' of prophets in the Christian communities, but it can be shown that there were also prophets not tied to any location. Thus according to the Lucan account, which is doubtless based on older tradition, the prophet Agabus travels from Jerusalem to Antioch, to proclaim there a Spirit-inspired prophecy (Acts 11:27f.; cf. 21:10: Caesarea). For the prophet mentioned in the Didache it is indeed conceivable that, in contrast to the itinerant apostles (Did. 11.4f.), he should settle in the community and be supported by it, but in this very context it is said that he appears as not tied to any location (13.1). This follows also from the warnings against 'false prophets', which are documented not only in the apocalyptic texts but generally in early Christian literature. These false prophets are expected for the end-time (Mk. 13:22 par.), but already threaten the churches in the present (Mt. 7:15; Acts 13:6; 2 Pet. 2:1; also Jn. 5:43; Rev. 16:13; 19:20; 20:10). According to 2 Jn. 7 they appear as 'deceivers', and are identified with the Antichrist. Similarly 1 Jn. 2:18f. and 4:1-3, according to which they 'have gone out into the world'. Since such an expectation does not relate to the final drama, it is to be concluded that for the early Christian communities the appearance of itinerant prophets was a familiar idea. Here it is to be assumed (with M.E. Boring, *Sayings*, 58) that primitive Christian prophecy was not anchored either to a particular geographical area or to a sociologically restricted group or to a particular theological tradition.

Paul gives a relatively clear picture of the function of the prophets in his churches. He counts 'prophecy' among the charismata which are to be used in proportion to one's faith (Rom. 12:6). If in 1 Cor. 13:2 it is adduced beside 'knowledge of mysteries' and 'gnosis', it is yet not to be treated on the same level with them. According to 1 Cor. 14:3 Paul distinguishes the prophecy which has up-building, comfort and exhortation for its object from the ecstatic speaking with tongues; in contrast to glossolalia it is a matter of intelligible speech. When prophetic preaching takes place in ordered sequence and with rational argument, it can convince outsiders (1 Cor. 14:15f., 24f., 29ff.). Since Paul can describe his own apostolic preaching by the words 'comfort' or 'exhort' (1 Cor. 1:10; 2 Cor. 1:3ff.; Rom. 12:1 etc.), or again by 'edification' (2 Cor. 10:8; 12:19), the content of the primitive Christian prophetic speech can scarcely be distinguished from the apostle's preaching, especially since the attempts which have been made to reconstruct the early Christian prophets' manner of speech more clearly through form-critical criteria, drawing *inter alia* on the formulaic language of Old Testament prophecy, have not yet proved convincing. At any rate primitive Christian prophecy has the character of revelation, and is distinct from the instruction of the community by Christian teachers or scribes (Mt. 13:52), which is more strongly bound to tradition. Frequently eschatological statements (e.g. Rom. 11:25f.; 1 Cor. 15:51f.; Gal. 5:21; 1 Thess. 3:4; 4:2-6) are described as prophetic maxims (cf. D.E. Aune, *Prophecy*, 261); in the given text they are characterised as tradition and as Paul's apostolic claims, and are not ascribed to early Christian prophets. According to E. Käsemann, 'sentences of holy law' which lay down the eschatological *ius talionis* (1 Cor. 3:17; 14:38; 16:22) go back to the prophets. If we accept this suggestion, then it becomes understandable why in the Pauline churches the Christian prophets possessed an authority comparable to that of the apostle.

From the *Synoptic Gospels* we can gain some information about primitive Christian prophecy. These books - as reports about Jesus - do not indeed concern themselves directly with Christian prophets; but, as was said above, the express warning against false prophecy (Mk. 13:22 par.), which relates not to Jewish but to Christian messianic pretenders (Mk. 13:6 par.), presupposes that Christian prophets were a well-known and widespread phenomenon. Analysis of the Synoptic tradition by source and form criticism allows us to recognise the work of Christian prophets in older strata of the tradition, that is, for earlier periods and for the Syro-Palestinian area. According to S. Schulz, we can identify 'a prophetic-apocalyptic enthusiasm in Palestinian Jewish Christianity', which advocated a 'fervent imminent expectation awakened by Easter'. Fundamental materials of the Q tradition are traced back to this 'prophetic post-Easter enthusiasm' (Schulz, op. cit. 33f.). Even if the religio-historical and literary assignment may remain debated in point of detail, we must in general start from the fact that in the early Christian literary tradition numerous 'inauthentic' sayings of the Lord were handed down, which cannot be understood as distortions of authentic sayings, as literary forgeries or as emanating from discussions with the Jews or from controversies within the Church; they must be considered as the utterances of men who spoke 'in the name', that is, at the command and with the authority of the exalted Lord, and whose words were heard and respected as words of the exalted Lord himself, and were repeated in the accounts of his earthly life as words of the earthly Lord. These are the people who are meant by the designation Christian prophets. For the understanding of their prophetic consciousness, reminiscences of Old Testament aphorisms such as we find in the letters of Rev. 2 and 3 are instructive, as are the words of the Revealer in Rev. 16:15:

See, I come like a thief. Blessed is he who is awake and keeps his garments, that he may not walk naked and people see his shame.

The well-known word in Od. Sol. 42.6 is also characteristic:

And I have arisen and am among them,
And I speak through their mouth.

Prophetic utterances which are placed on the lips of Jesus are found especially in that genre of dominical sayings which Bultmann calls 'Prophetic and Apocalyptic Sayings', but also under 'Legal Sayings and Church Rules' (cf. Bultmann, *The History of the Synoptic Tradition*, ET 1968, pp. 108ff., 130ff.). The different forms are naturally very varied. We may distinguish: preaching of salvation, words of threat, words of exhortation, apocalyptic predictions; the 'sentences of holy law' already mentioned (e.g. Lk. 12:8 par.) should also be noted here. These are not to be altogether restricted to the first-person speech of the exalted Lord: it is presupposed that 'the prophetic word which actually lies before us . . . is a word of the exalted Christ' (U.B. Müller, *Prophetie und Predigt*, 17). These observations compel us to conclude that Palestinian Christianity already had a strongly pneumatic colouring (cf. Mk. 3:29 par.; 13:11 par.) and that the prophets must have had a considerable significance in the leading of the early Christian communities. This last point emerges not least from the fact that not a few 'legal' sayings of Jesus and community rules were newly formulated by the mouth of the prophets, even if one should acknowledge that the boundaries with the early Christian teachers were fluid.

The Christian prophecy of Palestine stands in sharp contrast to the Jewish prophecy of the same period. It is largely separated from the national eschatology and Messianology and pays homage, like the primitive Church as a whole, to apocalyptic ideas. Here we find for the first time the union of prophecy and Apocalyptic, a union which finds expression again and most impressively in the author of the Apocalypse of John. As far as their vocation is concerned, the prophets were not apocalyptists, but charismatic leaders of the churches who stood out among their fellow-Christians through their prophetic way of speaking. John the 'seer' (Rev. 22:8) also composed his work with prophetic self-consciousness; but he is essentially an apocalyptist - the other prophets mentioned by him (11:18; 16:6; 18:20; 22:6,9) wrote no such books; presumably it is for this very reason that he uses the pseudonym 'John' familiar in Johannine circles; he thus became the first Christian writer who adorned his apocalypse with the name of a disciple of Jesus (cf. also below, Chapter XIX, Introduction).

By the end of the 1st century prophecy has lost its original significance; but in Asia Minor it seems still to play a part, as the statements of the Johannine Apocalypse make probable. Later it fell more and more into the twilight of the discussion about true and false prophets (Did. 11.7ff.; Herm. Mand. XI; Justin, *Dial.* 35.3; 51.2; 69.1; 82.1f.). In a Church which was building more and more on the hierarchical offices and the normative tradition, it soon had no place; as such, it was suspected of being gnostic, and about the middle of the 2nd century was forced into heresy by an orthodoxy which was in process of consolidating itself. It flourished occasionally on the edge of the Church, in Elchasai at the beginning of the 2nd century (cf. below, pp. 685ff.) and in Montanus at its end, and here also created a literary deposit. These are the only literary witnesses to early Christian prophecy that we possess.

Notes

* The earlier English edition of this work, *History and Eschatology*, 1957, does not contain this exact phrase; but for the idea of which it is a convenient summary, see there pp. 27-37, esp. 37. - Trans.

XIX. Apocalyptic in Early Christianity

Introduction

Philipp Vielhauer † and Georg Strecker

Preliminary Note

In what follows the apocalyptic materials and sketches in the early Christian literary tradition are described, from the New Testament to the formation of the oldest apocryphal apocalypses, in order to make clear the background of this literature in the history of tradition. In this survey a larger amount of space is devoted to those texts which present special problems. For general literature the lists in the preceding chapter (see above, pp. 542ff.) should be drawn upon. The lists in the following sub-sections are chosen from the point of view of whether further information may be obtained from them.

1. Jesus

Literature (supplementary): R. Bultmann, *Theologie des Neuen Testaments* [9]1984 (ET London 1952-55); C.C. Caragounis, *The Son of Man. Vision and Interpretation* (WUNT 38), 1986; A.J.B. Higgins, *The Son of Man in the Teaching of Jesus* (SNTS MS 39), 1980; R. Kearns, *Das Traditionsgefüge um den Menschensohn*, 1986; id. *Die Entchristologisierung des Menschensohns*, 1988; W.G. Kümmel, 'Jesus der Menschensohn?' (*Sitzungsber. der wiss. Ges. der J.W. Goethe-Universität Frankfurt a.M.*, vol. XX.3), 1984; K.L. Schmidt, art. 'βασιλεύς κτλ.', ThWNT I, 576-583 (TDNT I, 576-583); G. Strecker, 'Die Leidens- und Auferstehungsvoraussagen im Markusevangelium', ZThK 64, 1967, 16-39 (= id. *Eschaton und Historie. Aufsätze*, 1979, 52-75); P. Vielhauer, 'Gottesreich und Menschensohn in der Verkündigung Jesu', in id. *Aufsätze zum Neuen Testament* (TB 31), 55-91; ANRW II 25.1, 1982 (contributions by M. Wilcox, R. Leivestad, H. Bietenhard, J.H. Charlesworth *et al.*).

In the preaching of *Jesus*, in so far as it can still be recovered by critical methods from the Synoptic tradition, it is the concepts 'Kingdom of God' and 'Son of Man' which provide the strongest link with Apocalyptic. The Synoptic tradition contains three groups of *Son of Man sayings*: they relate to the Son of Man as coming, as active in the present, or as suffering and rising again. If the last group, which is largely to be traced back to Marcan redaction, probably developed out of community tradition, the authenticity of the other two groups also is debated in critical research. P. Vielhauer exercised a great influence on the discussion with his theory that the ideas of the Kingdom of God and the Son of Man are mutually exclusive in the history of tradition, and that the Son of Man tradition does not go back to the historical Jesus. Alongside that the conservative view maintains that the Son of Man title, deriving from Jewish Apocalyptic (Dan. 7:13; eth. Enoch, 4 Esd.), was taken over by Jesus and applied to his own person (so e.g. A.J.B. Higgins, C.C. Caragounis). Even if we do not overrate the possibilities of translation back into Aramaic, or of interpreting 'Son of Man' in a general way ('mankind') or in a specific sense (a particular 'man'), it is still clear from the Baptist's proclamation of a 'stronger one' (see above, p. 564) that there was in Jesus' immediate surroundings an expectation of a 'coming one'; it was of significance for Jesus' message and his self-understanding as the 'prophet of the end-time', even if the details of its attribution must remain in dispute.

The *Kingdom of God* is proclaimed in the Synoptic parable tradition as an imminent event which is graphically realised in the coming of Jesus. If this tradition is to be traced back to the historical Jesus, the same holds for the understanding of the Kingdom of God as the essential content of the preaching of Jesus, as it is expressed in the secondary summary in Mk. 1:14f., and also for the prayer for the coming of the Kingdom in the Lord's Prayer (Mt. 6:10 par.). The sovereignty of God is not a familiar apocalyptic concept, but corresponds in some measure to the 'Age to come', the 'new creation', the 'new heaven and new earth', and expresses what these ideas intended. Jesus' preaching of the Kingdom and his vocation presuppose the apocalyptic dualism in so far as he understands the coming of God's rule not as an event within the world, but as a divine miracle which puts a definitive end to this world and to time and brings in the eternal world of God. Nonetheless, the differences from Jewish Apocalyptic are unmistakable. They are already revealed in the choice of the central concept of *the sovereignty of God*, in terms of which Jesus replaces the popular apocalyptic notions of the eschatological salvation by the thought that God is king and assumes Lordship over all things. The rigour and clarity of this concept put an end to all descriptions of the *spectaculum mundi* and of the glory of the Beyond; only the image of a banquet as the symbol of community with God is retained. The imminent expectation also seems to link Jesus with Apocalyptic. But in addition to the statements concerning the nearness of the reign of God are those concerned with its contemporaneity, and this characteristic juxtaposition of future and present shatters the time-scheme of the Two-Ages doctrine. The question about the actual point in time then drops out, for the meaning of the expectation consists 'in the qualifying of the human situation in view of the coming of the Kingdom. Now one can no longer watch and ask about the terminal event, but only prepare oneself immediately for the Kingdom, i.e. repent' (Conzelmann, RGG³, II, col. 667). Consequently surveys and divisions of history, numerical speculation and divination are absent drom the preaching of Jesus. The authority with which Jesus makes his appearance is not that of an apocalyptic seer, applying to himself the name of some figure of the past. The historical features of his coming contradict any characterisation of him as an apocalyptic figure (such as an angel). These very points are enough to shatter the conventional eschatological expectation. In that Jesus combines apocalyptic and

Wisdom sayings in his message, he makes the claim that his proclamation of the sovereignty of God and his actions, as signs of this Lordship, are the final summons of God, on the acceptance or rejection of which eternal salvation or damnation depends. To this extent, the preaching of Jesus 'implies' a Soteriology, even if he did not make his person the object of faith (Bultmann, *Theologie* 8 [ET i.9]).

2. Apocalyptic Material in the New Testament

2.1 Point of departure:

Literature: E. Käsemann, 'Die Anfänge christlicher Theologie', in id., *Exegetische Versuche und Besinnungen* II, ³1970, 82-104 (ET *New Testament Questions of Today* 1969, 82-107); id. 'Zum Thema der urchristlichen Apokalyptik', ibid. 105-131 (ET op. cit. 108-137); W. Kramer, *Christos Kyrios Gottessohn* (AThANT 44), 1963; E. Lohse, 'Apokalyptik und Christologie', in id. *Die Einheit des Neuen Testaments*, ²1976, 125-144; A. Sand, 'Zur Frage nach dem Sitz im Leben der apokalyptischen Texte des Neuen Testaments', NTS 18, 1972, 167-177; P. Vielhauer, 'Ein Weg zur neutestamentlichen Christologie?', in id. *Aufsätze zum Neuen Testament* (TB 31), 1965, 141-198.

The primitive Church could not reproduce the proclamation of Jesus without alteration, but had to include his death and resurrection in its preaching. It understood both as eschatological and soteriological events, which had taken place *according to the Scriptures* (1 Cor. 15:3ff.), i.e. as eschatological fulfilment of the prophecies of Scripture. While they first of all interpreted his death in cultic-juridical categories as an atoning sacrifice (1 Cor. 15:3; Rom. 3:25; 4:25, etc.) they interpreted his resurrection as an exaltation to God, an installation into the dignity of an eschatological Saviour. In place of the expectation of the reign of God there now appears the expectation of the Parousia of Christ, and at this point the momentous influx of apocalyptic ideas takes place. The conception of the Son of Man, now sojourning with God and coming at the end of time as Saviour and Judge from Heaven, was best suited to bring together the heavenly dignity of the Exalted One and the eschatological crisis-character of the earthly person. The national expectation of the Davidic Messiah could not, on account of Jesus' preaching and fate, be used for this purpose. The apocalyptic Son of Man ideas dominate and shape the early Christian expectation of the Parousia, even when the title *Son of Man* is replaced by other titles of dignity, for example, by *Son of God* (1 Thess. 1:10), *Kyrios* (1 Thess. 4:15ff.) or *Soter* (Phil. 3:20), which do not stem from Apocalyptic.

2.2 Bearers and Forms:

Literature: K. Berger, *Die Amen-Worte Jesu. Eine Untersuchung zum Problem der Legitimation in apokalyptischer Rede* (BZNW 39), 1970; A.F.J. Klijn, '1 Thessalonians 4, 13-18 and its Background in Apocalyptic Literature', *Paul and Paulinism* (FS C.K. Barrett), London 1982, 67-73; G. Lohr, '1 Thess. 4,15-17: Das "Herrenwort"', ZNW 71, 1980, 269-273; M.E. Boring, *Sayings of the Risen Jesus* (SNTS MS 46), 1982.

The oldest form of Apocalyptic communication is the saying of Jesus. This is demonstrated not only by the numerous 'non-genuine' words of Jesus with apocalyptic content which are found in the Synoptic tradition, but also by the 'word of the Lord' cited by Paul in 1 Thess. 4:16f. In this fact we might discover an analogy with the pseudonymity of the apocalypses. However, in these words it is evidently a matter of utterances of early Christian prophets which were understood as utterances of the Exalted Lord (see above, pp. 566f.); the situation is different in the composition of such sayings and other material into an apocalyptic 'address' of Jesus (on the Synoptic Apocalypse see below pp. 579ff.); here pseudonymity lies before us.

Instruction on the Parousia of Christ belonged to the main articles of the missionary preaching to the heathen (1 Thess. 1:9f.) and the bearers of this instruction were thus the apostles and missionaries. But they were essentially transmitters, not elaborating the thought further. Paul, at any rate, speaks on this matter in his genuine epistles in a very reserved manner, bound by tradition and only twice thematically; thus, the description of the Parousia in 1 Thess. 4:15ff. is a citation which stands in association with comforting instruction on the destiny of deceased Christians; likewise, the picture of the Parousia in 1 Cor. 15:20-28 appears in the context of instruction on the resurrection of the body. In so far as we can judge from his letters Paul gave apocalyptic instruction of major dimensions only in connection with the resurrection and existence 'with Christ' (see below, 2.3). His reluctantly given report of the visionary experience of rapture into Paradise and into the third heaven (2 Cor. 12:1-4) had a literary sequel, the Apocalypse of Paul (see below, pp. 712ff.).

Only in the post-apostolic generation do 'the apostles of the Lord' become the bearers and the guarantors of apocalyptic tradition (Jud. 17); and so the fictitious apostolic letter is the form of their communication (2 Thess.; 2 Pet.), providing a parallel to the apocalypses with apostolic names.

In the course of the long and by no means straight path from the simple form of the apocalyptic saying of Jesus to the developed apocalypse there may be observed an increase in the subject-matter: first it was the Parousia and the events following it (resurrection and judgment), then it included the time immediately preceding the Parousia (with its 'signs', apostasy and Antichrist), and finally a complete apocalyptic outline embracing the time from the present right to the End. The fact that the use of apocalyptic material and forms reflects very clearly the ups and downs of the early Christian expectation is self-evident.

2.3 The Parousia:

Literature: J. Baumgarten, *Paulus und die Apokalyptik* (WMANT 44), 1975; J.C. Beker, *Paul's Apocalyptic Gospel. The Coming Triumph of God*, 1982; G. Klein, 'Apokalyptische Naherwartung bei Paulus', *Neues Testament und christliche Existenz* (FS H. Braun), 1972, 241-262; G. Lüdemann, *Paulus der Heidenapostel I. Studien zur Chronologie* (FRLANT 123), 1980, 213-271; U. Luz, *Das Geschichtsverständnis des Paulus* (BevTh 49), 1968; W. Radl, *Ankunft des Herrn. Zur Bedeutung und Funktion der Parusieaussagen bei Paulus* (BET 15), 1981; H.H. Schade, *Apokalyptische Christologie bei Paulus* (GTA 18), [2]1984; W. Schmithals, 'Eschatologie und Apokalyptik', VuF 33, 1988, 64-82; W. Trilling, *Der zweite Brief an die Thessalonicher* (EKK XIV), 1980.

The apocalyptic utterances of Jesus on the coming Son of Man vary in their intention: sentences of holy law (Mk. 8:38; Lk. 9:26; 12:8f.; Mt. 10:32f.), comfort (Mt. 10:23), warning (Mt. 24:26f.; Lk. 17:23f.) and threat (Mt. 24:37ff.; Lk. 17:26f.).

The themes developed vary accordingly: the Parousia takes place suddenly and unequivocally, hence the challenge to constant preparedness (Mt. 24:37 and par.) and the warning against deception (Mt. 24:26f. and par.); the Son of Man is saviour of his people (Mt. 10:23) and the judge who judges according to the eschatological *ius talionis* (Mk. 8:38; Lk. 12:8 and par.). On the other hand, the word of the Lord, 1 Thess. 4:16f. - the original text of which cannot be reconstructed with certainty (cf. G. Lüdemann, *Paulus* I, 242-263) - is a miniature apocalypse which describes the event of the Parousia itself; it presents this in three acts, succeeded by the resurrection and the rapture of the faithful to meet the Lord. This, the oldest apocalyptic text in the New Testament, shows that the primitive Church had already, at a very early stage, pictured the Parousia with the aid of apocalyptic material (examples in A.F.J. Klijn, see above, 2.2).

The association of the Parousia and the resurrection of the dead is naturally very frequent, and this corresponds to the Jewish eschatology and the apocalyptic Son of Man ideas. It is understandable that the event of the Parousia was more and more richly endowed with apocalyptic colouring and requirements, and indeed was described by taking over Jewish texts. This is for example the case with Mk. 13:24-27 and par. (cosmic catastrophes, the appearing of the Son of Man, the gathering of the elect). Behind the description of the Parousia of Christ in the deutero-Pauline 2 Thess. (1:5-10) there lies perhaps, as M. Dibelius and others have suggested, the Jewish text of a judgment-theophany:

> '(This is) a sign of the righteous judgment of God: . . . for it is right in the sight of God to repay with affliction your oppressors and (to give) liberation to you who are oppressed, at the revelation of the Lord . . . from heaven with the angels of his might in flaming fire, who grants pardon to all who do not know God . . . They shall receive as punishment eternal destruction from the presence of God and from the glory of his might, when he comes . . . on that day to be glorified among his saints and to be extolled among all the faithful.' (2 Thess. 1:5-10; cf. Dibelius, *An die Thessalonicher I.II. An die Philipper* (HNT 11), [3]1937, 40-43).

This text may be the first example of the literary expression of early Christian Apocalyptic. However, to trace it back to a Jewish *Vorlage* is not convincing, since the section 2 Thess. 1:5-10 stylistically does not stand in tension to the letter as a whole, and can therefore be assigned to the author of the letter as an apocalyptic development (W. Trilling, *2 Thess.* 42).

In addition to what has been said, the question arises for the Pauline letters whether the apocalyptic statements in 1 Thess. 4:13-18; 1 Cor. 15:20-28, 50-58; Rom. 13:11-14 are simply a traditionally conditioned framework beside the eschatology determined by faith in Christ, or whether the Pauline Christology is not to be thought of without any apocalyptic stamp (so H.H. Schade). Two things must be ruled out: 1 Thess. 4:15-18 and Rom. 13:11-12a are not to be excised as post-Pauline pieces (W. Schmithals, 'Eschatologie'). Similarly the apocalyptic statements mentioned are not to be paralysed with the aid of the assumption of a development in Pauline thinking (hellenising of the eschatology). The expectation of the Parousia is the definitive horizon of the earliest Pauline letter (1 Thess. 2:19; 3:13; 4:15; 5:23; cf. also 1 Cor. 15:23), but it is also attested in the late letter to the

Philippians (1:6, 10; 2:16; 3:10, 20f.; 4:5). To this extent the Pauline eschatology is apocalyptically oriented.

The idea of the Messianic interregnum attested in 1 Cor. 15:23-28 deserves special attention. The expression εἶτα τὸ τέλος (v. 24a) marks the closing period of the final drama: the handing over of Christ's kingdom, the destruction of every dominion, including that of death as the 'last enemy'. This τέλος is not yet given with the Parousia, which will bring the resurrection of those who believe in Christ (v. 23c; so G. Sellin, *Der Streit um die Auferstehung der Toten* (FRLANT 138), 1986, 272-275), and certainly not with the enthronement of Christ. The chronological sequence is underlined by ἔπειτα - εἶτα (vv. 23c-24) and is implied in the word τάγματι (v. 23a; cf. also O. Böcher, 'Das tausendjährige Reich', in id. *Kirche in Zeit und Endzeit. Aufsätze zur Offenbarung des Johannes*, 1983, 133-143; id. art. 'Chiliasmus I', TRE 7, 1981, 727; contrast H.-A. Wilcke, *Das Problem eines messianischen Zwischenreiches bei Paulus* (AThANT 51, Zürich 1967). In this Paul links up with Jewish apocalyptic ideas (syr. Bar. 30; 4 Esd. 7:26-44 etc.) which have also stamped the eschatological expectation in other Pauline letters (1 Cor. 6:2f.; 2 Cor. 5:10).

2.4 The Signs:

Literature (supplementary): K. Berger, 'Hellenistisch-heidnische Prodigien und die Vorzeichen in der jüdischen und christlichen Apokalyptik', ANRW II 23.2, 1428-1469; O. Betz, 'Der Katechon', NTS 9, 1962/63, 276-291; O. Cullmann, 'Le caractère eschatologique du devoir missionaire et de la conscience apostolique de S. Paul. Étude sur le "Katechon" de II Thess 2, 6-7, RHPhR 16, 1936, 210-245; J. Ernst, *Die eschatologischen Gegenspieler in den Schriften des Neuen Testaments* (BU 3), 1967, 24-79; J. Munck, *Paulus und die Heilsgeschichte*, Copenhagen 1954 (ET *Paul and the Salvation of Mankind*, London 1959); B. Rigaux, *Saint Paul. Les épitres aux Thessaloniens* (EtB), Paris/Gembloux 1956; W. Trilling, Der zweite Brief an die Thessalonicher (EKK 14), 1980; id., 'Die Briefe des Paulus an die Thessalonicher', ANRW II 25.4, 3365-3403 (pp. 3402f.: lit. on 2 Thess. 2:1-12).

While the NT authors exercise remarkable reserve in describing the events which follow on the Parousia, they have devoted all the greater attention to the time preceding it. Being an eschatological community, the early Church understood its present and its immediate future as the End-time, and the events which befell it as being in essential connection with the Christ who had come and would come again. The expression of this awareness in terms of the Mysteries and of gnostic ideas may be left out of account here, since we are dealing only with Apocalyptic. The grievous experiences of the Church were connected with the theme, common to the entire Jewish eschatology, of a final evil period (the 'Woes of the Messiah') before the appearance of the Saviour. This connection, which was equivalent to an extensive retention of traditional Jewish eschatology, was in itself natural, and moreover it was encouraged by the fact that the Church found certain features of Jewish eschatology corroborated in her own experiences (persecution; the appearance of political and religious seducers). Consequently the motifs of wars and famine, the ruin of families, the increase of tribulation to the point of excess, the appearance of the last great adversary, all find acceptance within the apocalyptic ideas of early Christianity. This linking of traditional Jewish elements with actual Christian experience has its literary deposit in the 'words of the Lord', Mk. 13:5-23 and par.; Mt. 10:17-36, and - with various modifications - in the epistolary literature.

Even in the preaching of Jesus and of the Church in its earliest period (Paul), 'the signs of the times' had played a part, certainly with the aim of providing knowledge of the time, but not of calculating it; that is to say, with the aim of making clear that the present is the period of decision with reference to the End, but not of outlining a picture of the future. Hence the exhortations to vigilance and constant preparedness for the reign of God in Jesus' teaching and for the Parousia of Christ in Paul (1 Thess. 5:1ff. and often).

The systematising of this idea into an apocalyptic picture of the future presupposes that people do not believe any more that the End is immediately impending, even though a relatively imminent expectation may still exist (on the Synoptic and Johannine Apocalypses, see below, pp. 579ff.; 583ff.).

The way in which such an outline, and in particular the corroboration of definite signs of the time, may even be turned against the imminent expectation is shown by the apocalypse in 2 Thess. 2:1-12. Because of its significance and its problems this passage will be treated here in a somewhat more detailed fashion. As against the opinion that the day of the Lord is immediately impending, the author claims that the great apostasy must come first and the Antichrist appear; only then will Christ come again. In fact, 'the mystery of lawlessness' is already at work, but the appearing of the Antichrist is still delayed by a restraining power (τὸ κατέχον v. 6, ὁ κατέχων v. 7), and can follow only upon its elimination. All the features in this picture are traditional, but the stress, in the sense of a quenching of the imminent expectation, is new. For that reason, the restraining power becomes a matter of special interest.

The great apostasy is, along with the assault of the enemy on the people of God, a constant feature of Jewish (national and apocalyptic) eschatology (Dan. 11:31; Jubil. 23.14-23; eth. Enoch 91.7; Ass. Mos. 5; 4 Esd. 5:1f.; Damas. Doc. 1.20; 5.21; 8.19; 19.5, 32; 1 QpHab. 2.1-6, etc.).

The restraining factor, once described by the neuter τὸ κατέχον, once by the masculine ὁ κατέχων, in both cases without any object, is a present entity, which the Thessalonians know:

> 'But now you know what is restraining, that he (i.e. the Man of lawlessness) may be revealed (only) in his time. For the mystery of lawlessness is already at work. Only (it lasts) until he who restrains is removed'. (2 Thess. 2:6-7; translation after W. Trilling, op. cit. 68)

The identity of the Katechon is uncertain. Although it has been dominant for a long time and goes back to the Apologists and their kingdom- ideology, the political explanation of the κατέχον as the *imperium Romanum* and the κατέχων as the Roman emperor has scarcely an advocate today; it is not likely on Jewish presuppositions, since for apocalyptic and nationally minded Jews the Roman state and emperor are the epitome of hostility to God; nor is it likely on Christian presuppositions since, despite Rom. 13, the Christians of the 1st century had no political philosophy, and since the Antichrist according to Rev. 13 is embodied in the Roman emperor, and in 2 Thess. 2:4 also shows political features. One widespread view is the interpretation in terms of salvation history, ingeniously worked out by O.

Cullmann and championed in particular by J. Munck (op. cit. 28-34; ET 36-42): τὸ κατέχον is the Gospel, which 'must first be preached to all nations' (Mk. 13:10) before the End comes, and ὁ κατέχων is the apostle to the Gentiles, Paul, whose death forms the prelude to the appearance of the Antichrist. B. Rigaux however, assuming the authenticity of 2 Thess., has raised serious doubts against this interpretation:

> 'Either Paul, at the time of his sojourn among the Thessalonians, did not confine himself to teaching that the day of the Lord must be preceded by two signs, but added that the manifestation of the Anti-Christ was delayed by the apostolic preaching and his own activity. In this first case we can no longer understand that, some months after Paul's departure, the Thessalonians could have believed that the Gospel had been carried to the ends of the earth, or forgotten that the Parousia could not come so long as Paul was preaching. Or he spoke in Thessalonica only of apostasy and of the man of sin, and adds by letter that this coming of the impious one is delayed by the Christian preaching and his own. In this second case they had need of an exegete to discover beneath Paul's phrases a prophecy touching on the Christian preaching or the activity of Paul himself. Finally, against those who identify Paul with the κατέχων and make his death the condition for the dawn of the eschatological struggle, we have every right to affirm that in this case there is a flagrant contradiction between our pericope and 1 Thess. 4:13-18, where Paul expresses the hope of being alive at the Parousia'. (op. cit. 276f.)

On the assumption that 2 Thess. is not authentic, this interpretation is quite certainly not possible: after Paul's death the Antichrist has not come, and the author believes that his appearance lies still in the distant future. The mythological interpretation of the Katechon sees in him a divine or heavenly power which holds the mythical monster bound until the hour appointed by God. As in an Egyptian prayer Horus is called ὁ κατέχων δράκοντα, and Michael in a magical papyrus is ὁ κατέχων, ὃν καλέουσιν δράκοντα, so in Rev. 20:1-10 it is an angel who holds the Devil captive. In analogy with this, one might conjecture that 2 Thess. 2:6f. makes the Antichrist, the Devil in human form, 'bound'. On this understanding, however, the statement that the 'binding' heavenly power will be 'removed' is difficult. It also remains obscure whom the author understands by this. Assuming the authenticity of the letter, we can see 2:6f. as a new piece of teaching, namely *that* there is still an obstacle to the coming of the Antichrist, but we are not told in what it consists. On the assumption that it is not authentic we must further say that this change of gender is a deliberate veiling, and thus an apocalyptic stylistic device.

The allusive and mysterious manner of expression in v. 5-7 corresponds with this, whereas there is precise instruction in the traditionally controlled statements about the Antichrist in v. 3b-4; 8-10a. The function of the stylistic device of veiling becomes clear when we observe that positively the Katechon holds back the hostile power, but in a negative way the mystery of evil is at the same time active in him. Hence W. Trilling (92) understands the Katechon as a purely formal concept, and identifies it with the delay of the Parousia itself.

The dating of this little apocalypse is uncertain. The tendency to play down the imminent expectation puts it into post-Pauline times. Other indications are not unambiguous: the theme of Temple-profanation does not prove an origin before A.D. 70, since it is a frequent feature in the apocalypses even after the destruction of the

Temple (cf. Trilling, op. cit. 86f.); the self-deification does not necessarily point to the Flavian period - worship of the living emperor as divine became customary only under the Flavians - since this feature may reflect the hellenistic ruler-cult or be a reminiscence of Ezek. 28, and is evidently not yet a reality. The letter belongs in a period in which the delay of the Parousia had become a problem, and is directed against enthusiasts who wished to revive the imminent expectation artificially by appealing to Paul.

2.5 The Antichrist:

Literature (supplementary): O. Böcher, art. 'Antichrist II', TRE 3, 1978, 21-24; id. 'Die Teuflische Trinität', in id. *Die Johannesapokalypse* (EdF 41), ²1980, 76-83; W. Bousset, *Der Antichrist*, 1895; J. Ernst, *Die eschatologischen Gegenspieler in den Schriften des Neuen Testaments* (BU 3), 1967; D. Flusser, 'The Hybris of the Antichrist in a Fragment from Qumran', *Immanuel* 10, 1980, 31-37; S.S. Hartmann, art. 'Antichrist I', TRE 3, 1978, 20f; E. Lohmeyer, art. 'Antichrist', RAC I, 1950, cols. 450-457; B. Rigaux, *L'Antéchrist et l'opposition au royaume messianique dans l'Ancien et le Nouveau Testament*, Paris 1932; H. Schlier, 'Vom Antichrist. Zum 13. Kap. der Offenbarung Johannis', *Theologische Aufsätze*, FS Karl Barth 1936, 110-123; id. *Die Zeit der Kirche. Exegetische Aufsätze und Vorträge*, 1956, 16-29; J. Schmid, 'Der Antichrist und die kommende Macht (2 Thess. 2, 1-12)', ThQ 129, 1949, 323-343; G. Stählin, 'Die Feindschaft gegen Gott und ihre Stelle in seinem Heilsplan für die Welt', *Die Leibhaftigkeit des Wortes*, FS Adolf Köberle, 1958, 47-62; G. Strecker, 'Der Antichrist. Zum religionsgeschichtlichen Hintergrund von 1 Joh 1,18.22; 4,3 und 2 Joh 7', *Text and Testimony*, FS A.F.J. Klijn, 1958, 247-254; G. Widengren, *Religionsphänomenologie*, 1969; R. Yates, 'The Antichrist', EvQ 46, 1974, 42-50.

The Antichrist represents a Christian variant on the eschatological opponent of God in Apocalyptic. This opponent must be of mythological origin, as Bousset, Gunkel and Dibelius have shown: he is a mythical monster, the adversary of God in the Creation, who, according to the ancient Eastern conception of the return of primordial time at the end of time, appears again at the End and takes up afresh his struggle against God, but is finally destroyed; in the conflict of primordial times, he was only defeated and bound. As the opponent of God or the Messiah he appears in the End-time as Satan or a dragon, but can also be distinguished from 'the Devil', 'Beliar' etc, and appear in human form as a tyrant or a prophet hostile to God. The experiences under pagan rulers, especially in the time of the Maccabees (Antiochus IV Epiphanes), caused the mythical monster to be historicised into the representative or envoy of the Devil. The figure does not appear in all Jewish apocalypses. It is for example described as an anti-Messiah in the Syriac Apocalypse of Baruch (*c.* 100-130 A.D.), in which 'the last ruler' is judged and slain by the Anointed.

In the NT the title 'Antichrist' appears only in 2 Jn. 7; 1 Jn. 2:18, 22; 4:3. It is either a word created by the presbyter or derives from the tradition that lay before him. Through the prefix ἀντί- it describes both a 'being in the place of' and also a hostile confrontation. The figure however also appears in other New Testament writings. Here two strands of tradition may be distinguished. For one thing, early Christianity knows as an apocalyptic figure one or more false prophets (Mk. 13:22; 2 Thess. 2:9f.; 1 Jn. 2:18, 23; 4:1-3; 2 Jn. 7; Rev. 13:11-18; 16:13; 19:20; 20:10), who - except in the Johannine literature - is expected in association with 'signs and wonders'.

Through these he causes men to fall away (cf. also Did. 16.3f.; Sib. III 63ff.; Asc. Is. 4.5 etc.). Possibly a Jewish tradition about the false prophet of the end time as the opponent of the true prophet lies at the base of this idea (so E. Lohmeyer, Antichrist, 453); but for this conjecture there is as yet no unambiguous evidence. For another, the New Testament - apart from the Johannine literature, where the ἀντίχριστος is the proclaimer of a false teaching - attests a conception of the Antichrist as an eschatological world-ruler. Here Jewish apocalyptic elements appear, largely borrowed from Daniel (cf. Mk. 13:9-13 with Dan. 7:25; 8:10, 24; Mk. 13:14 with Dan. 8:13; 9:27; 12:11; Mk. 13:19 with Dan. 12:1; 2 Thess. 2:4 with Dan. 11:36; Rev. 13:1-11 with Dan. 7). The statements which in Daniel refer to the Seleucid empire or to Antiochus Epiphanes are reinterpreted in terms of the Roman empire and its emperor.

The two strands of tradition are combined in a systematised form in Rev. 13. The first beast from the sea is the antitype of Christ, and accordingly in the stricter sense Antichrist, while the second beast appears as the false prophet of the first beast and thus likewise represents an anti-Christ figure. In Mk. 13, if the βδέλυγμα τῆς ἐρημώσεως in v. 14 is to be related to the activity of Antichrist and v. 22 gives concrete form to the false-prophet expectation in several figures, the two forms of the Antichrist are described one after the other. In 2 Thess. 2:3-12 the two Antichrist traditions are fused into a single figure. V. 4 employs the motif of the arrogant despot from Dan. 11:36, while v. 9f. take up the false-prophet tradition which ultimately goes back to Deut. 13:2-6. The differing weight given to the two Antichrist expectations in Rev., Mk. par. and 2 Thess. is explained by the actual situation in which author and community saw themselves in each case (more a political threat in Rev., more a threat from apostasy to false teaching in Mk., 2 Thess. and 1-2 Jn.).

2.6 The dogmatising of apocalyptic ideas:

Literature: R.J. Bauckham, '2 Peter: An Account of Research', ANRW II 25.5, 3713-3752; K. Berger, 'Streit um Gottes Vorsehung. Zur Position der Gegner im 2. Petrusbrief', *Tradition and Re-Interpretation, FS J.C.H. Lebram*, Leiden 1986, 136-149; E. Käsemann, 'Eine Apologie der urchristlichen Eschatologie', *Exegetische Versuche und Besinnungen* I, 1970, 135-157 (ET *Essays on New Testament Themes*, London 1964, 169-193); K.H. Schelkle, *Die Petrusbriefe - Der Judasbrief* (HThK XIII/2), [2]1980; C.H. Talbert, 'II Peter and the Delay of the Parousia', *VigChr* 20, 1966, 137-145.

The author of 2 Pet., the latest NT document, coming from the middle of the 2nd century, attacks Gnostics who jeer at the delay of the Parousia and impress part of the community with their arguments. He characterises them as those whose appearance was predicted by the OT prophets and NT apostles.

> 'In the last days, scoffers will come with scoffing, who follow their own passions, saying, Where is the promise of his coming? For ever since the fathers fell asleep all things have continued as they were from the beginning of the world.' (3:3f.)

The author defends the traditional apocalyptic eschatology of early Christianity and lays particular emphasis on the sudden and spectacular dissolution of the world (3:10); he delineates the goal as 'the victorious entry of the faithful into the eternal kingdom and the destruction of the godless' (Käsemann, 'Apologie' 157 [ET 194-195]; cf. 1:11; 2:9; 3:7). He presents arguments for the imminent hope: (1) concepts of time are not adequate when referred to the action of God (3:8), (2) the matter in question is not delay, but forbearance (3:9) and (3) the faithful can and should hasten the coming of the Parousia by holy conduct (3:11f.). The apocalyptic eschatology is retained as *locus de novissimis* and the imminent hope is repeated artificially as dogma, without either having any living relationship to Christian existence; it belongs simply to the traditional picture of the future and as such is made into dogma.

3. The Synoptic Apocalypse

Literature: H. Conzelmann, 'Geschichte und Eschaton nach Mc. 13', in id. *Theologie als Schriftauslegung* (BevTh 65), 1974, 62-73; J. Dupont, 'La ruine du temple et la fin des temps dans le discours de Marc 13', in: *Apocalypses et théologie de l'espérance*, LeDiv 95, 1977, 207-269; id. *Les trois apocalypses synoptiques* (LeDiv 121), Paris 1985; L. Gaston, *No stone on another*, NovTest Supp. 23, 1970; F. Hahn, 'Die Rede von der Parusie des Menschensohnes Markus 13', *Jesus und der Menschensohn, FS A. Vögtle*, 1975, 240-266; G. Harder, 'Das eschatologische Geschichtsbild der sogenannten kleinen Apokalypse Markus 13', *ThViat* 4, 1952, 71-107; L. Hartman, *Prophecy Interpreted* (CB. NT 1), 1966; G. Hölscher, 'Der Ursprung der Apokalypse Markus 13', ThBl 12, 1933, 193-202; W.G. Kümmel, *Verheissung und Erfüllung*, [3]1956 (ET *Promise and Fulfilment*, London 1957); J. Lambrecht, *Die Redaktion der Markus-Apokalypse* (AnBib 28), 1967; W. Marxsen, *Der Evangelist Markus* (FRLANT 67), 1956, 101-140 (ET *Mark the Evangelist*, Nashville 1969); R. Pesch, *Naherwartungen. Tradition und Redaktion in Markus* 13, 1968; N. Walter, 'Tempelzerstörung und synoptische Apokalypse', ZNW 57, 1966, 38-49.

3.1. The Synoptic Apocalypse at Mk. 13 presents a detailed summary of the events of the End. Mark represents this apocalypse formally as esoteric teaching of Jesus to his four intimate friends who, after his prediction of the destruction of the Temple (v. 2), raised the question, 'When will this happen? And what is the sign when these things are all to be accomplished?' (v. 4). In his answer Jesus first of all sketches a picture of the future: many false leaders will appear who will claim to be Christ; wars, earthquakes and famines will occur (v. 6-8); oppression of the disciples, persecution by Jewish and pagan courts, divisions in families, hatred for the sake of Jesus (v. 9-13); then the last great affliction: the profanation of the Temple, flight to the mountains (v. 14-20) and the appearance of false prophets and Messiahs (v. 21-23); finally the End, with the appearing of the Son of Man amid cosmic catastrophes, and the gathering of the elect (24-27). Then Jesus concludes his answer with a detailed exhortation on observing the signs and on constant preparedness, for the fixed time of the End is unknown, but is near (v. 28-37).

This 'address' is composed, as critical analysis has shown, of larger and smaller fragments of various origin and often of divergent purpose which the evangelist has furnished with his own additions and formed into a whole. Side by side with the pieces which reflect the situation of the Christian community (v. 5f., 9, 11, 13, 21-22, 28-32, 34-36) stand those of a Jewish-apocalyptic kind which reveal nothing Christian (vs. 7f., 12, 14-20, 24-27); verse 10 (and perhaps v.13 also) as well as vv.23, 33, and 37 and many of the notes of time may go back to the evangelist. Especially controversial is the question whether he brought together the whole discourse from separate fragments, or whether in vs. 7f., 12, 14-20, 24-27 a connected Jewish apocalypse or connected parts of one were available to him. G. Hölscher considers the verses mentioned to be an apocalyptic pamphlet from the year A.D. 40 when Caligula demanded that his statue be set up in the Temple at Jerusalem. But W.G. Kümmel objects that this 'apocalypse' is too short and colourless (*Promise and Fulfilment* (ET), 1957, pp. 98ff.). Nevertheless the two fragments, v. 14-20 and 24-27, are so coherent in themselves and with one another that we must see in them a literary prototype. The critical revisions which Mark applies in v. 5-13 (see below) permit us to conclude that he is not here arranging collected material with complete independence, but that there was available to him in this complex a connected tradition which, if it was not in literary form, was yet already fixed. We may thus infer that there existed, even before Mark, a Christian apocalypse which was assembled out of the Jewish fragments mentioned and Christian elements - that is, an apocalypse which included not only the Parousia and the events immediately preceding it, but also events even earlier, reaching down to the time of the evangelist and his community. However, the extent of this apocalypse cannot be reconstructed from Mk. 13 with certainty.

It is significant that the present text exhibits a temporal arrangement and an objective emphasis. It is widely recognised that the time-references are not all of equal value. Opinions diverge widely on particulars and especially on the question as to where the actual events of the End begin in Mark's view, whether it is at v. 14 or at v. 24. Support for the first view is provided by the well-founded assumption that v. 14-20 and 24-27 originally formed a connected text. W. Marxsen (op. cit. 112ff. [ET 166ff.]) claims that the real events of the End begin at v. 14. On the other hand, H. Conzelmann stresses, on good grounds, the fact that Mark makes two definite incisions, one at v. 14 where he intervenes with the description of the last epoch of history, and then at v. 24 where he begins ('after that tribulation'!) with the description of the actual eschaton, which is no longer an historical, but a supernatural Parousia. Conzelmann affirms that Mark makes a fundamental distinction between the historical and the supernatural instead of that gradual transition into the future which is represented in Apocalyptic. 'The essential *novum* in the Marcan description lies in this . . . that here (so far as we can see, for the first time) the future (!) events are consciously divided into two groups, certainly related to one another, but nevertheless basically different: there is a contrast between the final epoch of world-history, i.e. the great affliction which, for all its increase, . . . still remains fundamentally within the framework of the existing course of history, and the concluding, cosmic catastrophe which takes place in supernatural form. The latter is the real sign of the Parousia, but in such a way that both sign and in-breaking happen together' (p. 215).

However, the chronological difference is already given in the pre-Marcan Christian stratum of tradition, in which v. 14 - in contrast to the Jewish apocalyptic model - relates not to an event of the present but to the future epoch of θλῖψις (v. 14-23; cf. G. Strecker, ZKG 72, 1961, 141-147). The Marcan redaction, under the impress of the delay of the Parousia, reflects the passing of time more fully. In v. 10 it lays the emphasis on the church's missionary charge, which is valid in the interval leading up to the Parousia.

If this is correct, we can understand the two preceding sections accordingly: v.

5-8 are not so much a 'summary survey' describing the fundamental situation of the world, but rather in association with v. 9-13 a characterisation of the present situation of the Church in this world. The comments, 'But the end is not yet' (v. 7) and 'this is the beginning of woes' (v. 8) may belong to the pre-Markan Christian stratum of tradition, and alongside the temporal arrangement of the future serve as a defence against the hasty explanation of events as events of the End: these events are 'not yet the End', but just 'the beginning of the woes'. It is in this antithesis to traditional apocalyptic ideas, and to a large extent even early Christian ideas, that the reflection on the delay of the Parousia becomes noticeable. This is especially the case with the Marcan v. 10, according to which the present is interpreted in the light of the Parousia as the period of the Christian world mission and as a divinely ordained epoch (δεῖ; G. Strecker, 'Das Evangelium Jesu Christi', *Eschaton und Historie*, 1979, 218-220).

Nevertheless, Mark does not wish to suppress the imminent hope, as the writer of 2 Thess. does, but really to maintain it (v. 30). He seeks 'the balance between the two motifs which belong to the very substance of eschatology: the observing of the signs in which that which is to come is proclaimed, and the expectation of a sudden unsuspected invasion', (Conzelmann, op. cit., p. 220). Accordingly, the apocalyptic teaching is not an end in itself; just as it is interspersed with warnings and exhortations and words of comfort, so it is followed by detailed instruction (v. 28-37); its aim is to exhort to sobriety and constant preparedness.

As to the dating of Mk. 13 as a literary unit, there is no definite clue in the chapter. Apart from the possible Caligula-apocalypse, which might be dated to A.D. 40, the rest of the material, because of its traditional character, is not serviceable for chronology.

We may conjecture, although with reservations, that the destruction of the Temple must have left traces in Mk. 13, and since this is not the case draw the conclusion that the Marcan apocalypse in its present form came into being before A.D. 70; the fact that there are no traces of it in Matthew, although the Gospel of Matthew was written after the Fall of Jerusalem, cannot be adduced as a counter-argument since, unlike Mk. 13, Mt. 24 was composed *en bloc* as a declaration of the future (see below). Since Mk. 13:2 may go back to a Jewish apocalyptic idea (cf. e.g. Jer. 7:14; 9:11; 26:18; Micah 3:12), with which Jesus' saying about the Temple is possibly connected (Mk. 14:58; 15:29; Jn. 2:19), the origin of Mark's Gospel, and therefore of the present form of Mk. 13, is rather to be placed in the period before the destruction of Jerusalem, especially since the statements in Mk. 12:9 and 15:38 must be understood not chronologically but as the proclamation of a change in the history of salvation (from Israel to the new people of God).

3.2 The modification of the Synoptic Apocalypse in Matthew and Luke cannot be treated in detail here; only a few points may be raised. Both evangelists change the private teaching of Jesus into something open, Matthew into general instruction to disciples, and Luke into an address of Jesus to his customary public. Both concentrate their attention more strongly than Mark does on the delay of the Parousia, though they do so in different ways.

In contrast to Mk. 13:4, where the disciples' question relates to the events of the

End which will include the destruction of the Temple, Mt. evidently distinguishes between the destruction of the Temple (24:1-2), which he assumes as a past event (cf. 22:7), and the Parousia which takes place at the end of the world (24:3). Matthew transposes Mk. 13:9-13 to the Mission-charge (Mt. 10:17-21) and replaces the Marcan passage by a series of general and 'apocalyptically' related prophecies on external oppression and internal danger to the community (24:10-12). In this way Jesus' apocalyptic address in the first Gospel has become as a whole a proclamation of the future. The 'beginning of woes' (24:8) no longer relates to the present situation of the community (Mk. 13:5-13), but takes on a purely future character. In agreement with this, Matthew highlights the future character of the 'wars and rumours of wars' by μελλήσετε (24:6 against Mk. 13:7) and stresses the necessity of the proclamation of the Gospel as a future fact (24:14). Consistently, the time of the θλῖψις (24:15-18), like the 'Parousia of the Son of Man' (24:29-31), also lies exclusively in the future. If Matthew has taken over the outline from Mark and enlarged it with sayings from Q which give warnings against false identifications of the Son of Man and refer to the suddenness of his Parousia (24:26-28, 37-41), he yet on the other hand intensifies the paraenetic accent through appended parables which summon to watchfulness (24:37ff.; 25:1ff.); and this under the rubric that the Parousia is delayed (24:48; 25:5, 19: μετὰ πολὺν χρόνον - against Lk. 19:15) and the time of its coming uncertain (24:42; 25:13). In the interim the Church as in Mark is charged with the task of the world mission (24:14); it is an eschatological entity in time, since it knows itself subjected to the will of the exalted Christ, who has already come and is at the same time expected, and who accompanies it on its way through time with his challenge (28:20).

Luke alters the Marcan outline by interventions which are insignificant but go very deep (21:5-36), without however drawing upon an additional source. In particular, by the comment, 'before all this' (v. 12), he advances the persecution of the Church to the beginning of the events which are described in Mk. 13:5-8 = Lk. 21:8-11 and which he augments by cosmic catastrophes (11b), and therefore locates it long before the Parousia. By additions, he alters Mk. 13:14-20 in such a way that out of the final epoch of history comes the episode of the destruction of Jerusalem, out of an eschatological act comes an event of past history. On the other side this event, which from the reader's point of view lies in the past, vouches for the reliability of Jesus' prophecy of the Parousia. So Lk. presents the following sequence: (1) persecution of the community, (2) political and (3) cosmic catastrophes. The tendency is to postpone the Parousia as far as possible and to prevent the eschatological explanation of temporal events. Luke inserts at the very beginning of the address an express rejection of any definite imminent hope (cf. v. 8 with Mk. 13:5f.) and describes its propagators as seducers just as much as the false Messiahs. The essential connection with 2 Thess. 2:1ff. is clear: a judgment is given, and it is in even sharper tones than there, and not with the authority of an apostle, but with that of Jesus himself. Luke does not engage in polemic against the imminent expectation, nor does he renounce it. But he lays great stress on the indirect summons to be constantly prepared. The present is conceived as a necessary interim period of the Church and its world mission (Acts 1:7f.)

4. The Johannine Apocalypse

Literature (supplementary): O. Böcher, *Die Johannesapokalypse* (EdF 41), [2]1980; id. *Kirche in Zeit und Endzeit. Aufsätze zur Offenbarung des Johannes*, 1983; G. Bornkamm, 'Die Komposition der apokalyptischen Visionen in der Offenbarung Johannis', *Studien zu Antike und Urchristentum* (BevTh 28), [3]1970, 204-222; W. Bousset, *Die Offenbarung Johannis* (KEK 16), 1966 (reprint); A. Feuillet, *L'Apocalypse. État de la question* (Studia Neotest. Subs. 3), Paris 1963; F. Hahn, 'Die Sendschreiben der Johannesapokalypse. Ein Beitrag zur Bestimmung prophetischer Redeformen', *Tradition und Glaube, FS K.G. Kuhn*, 1971,357-394; id. 'Zum Aufbau der Johannesoffenbarung', *Kirche und Bibel, FS E. Schick*, 1979, 145-154; M. Karrer, *Die Johannesoffenbarung als Brief* (FRLANT 140), 1986; H. Kraft, *Die Offenbarung des Johannes* (HNT 16a), 1974; id. 'Zur Offenbarung des Johannes', ThR 38, 1974, 81-98; E. Lohmeyer, *Die Offenbarung des Johannes* (HNT 16), [3]1970; U.B. Müller, *Die Offenbarung des Johannes* (ÖTK 19), 1984; id. 'Literarische und formgeschichtliche Bestimmung der Apokalypse des Johannes als einem Zeugnis frühchristlicher Apokalyptik', in Hellholm (ed.), *Apocalypticism*, 599-619; E. Schüssler-Fiorenza, 'Apokalypsis and Propheteia. The Book of Revelation in the Context of early Christian Prophecy', in J. Lambrecht (ed.), *L'Apocalypse johannique et l'Apocalyptique dans le Nouveau Testament* (BEThL 53), Leuven 1980, 77-104; G. Strecker, 'Die Anfänge der johanneischen Schule', NTS 32, 1986, 31-47; A. Strobel, 'Apokalypse des Johannes', TRE 3, 1978, 174-189; J.-W. Taeger, 'Einige neuere Veröffentlichungen zur Apokalypse des Johannes', VF 29, 1984, 50-75; U. Vanni, 'L'Apocalypse johannique. État de la question', in Lambrecht, *Apocalypse* (see above), 21-46.

4.1 Connection with the Johannine Literature: among the writings of the Johannine circle a special significance attaches to the Revelation of John as the only New Testament apocalypse. Since with its presumably pseudonymous authorship (1:4a) it is linked with the Johannine circle, we must inquire into assumptions of apocalyptic thinking in this literature. Here we must mention first of all 2 John, probably along with 3 John, as writings of the presbyter, the oldest document of the Johannine circle. The presbyter's eschatological expectation is directed towards a realistic appearance of Christ in the flesh at the Parousia to set up the messianic kingdom (2 Jn. 7). In this apocalyptic perspective there appears at the same time the deceiver, the Antichrist. If there is consequently a chiliastic position at the beginning of the Johannine school, the apocalyptic statements in 1 John (2:28; 3:2f.; 4:17) and the Fourth Gospel, as later writings of the Johannine circle, can scarcely be traced back (against R. Bultmann) to an ecclesiastical redaction with the aim of assimilation to the general eschatological expectation, but rather represent traces of the apocalyptic orientation which belongs throughout to the traditional material of the Johannine circle. The Revelation of John on the other hand is intended to make clear propaganda for these views in its time.

The Revelation of John is the only Christian apocalypse which has found acceptance as a separate book in the Canon of the New Testament. On the one hand it shows a close relationship to Jewish Apocalyptic in form and materials, but on the other it reveals the not inconsiderable influence of Christian features on the accepted tradition. Nevertheless, it is unique even among the Christian apocalypses, especially since important elements of Jewish Apocalyptic are lacking (e.g. wisdom *ex eventu*, the sealing of the revelations).

4.2 Form: The Apocalypse declares itself, through a meagre epistolary framework (Preface 1:4f., cf. v. 11; closing greeting, 22:21), as a circular letter sent 'to the seven churches in Asia'. The epistolary character is elsewhere prominent only in chs. 2 and 3, which contain a special message for each of the seven Asian churches. M. Karrer accordingly assigns the Apocalypse to the genre of 'church letters' (op. cit. 83 etc.) and, since the author has used the letter form known from Paul (Schüßler-Fiorenza, op. cit. 127), he is appealing to addressees from a Pauline tradition. As a whole the Apocalypse, from 1:9 to 22:20, is the record of a vision, and the author repeatedly stresses his ecstatic state (1:10; 4:2; 17:3; 20:10). One Lord's Day on the isle of Patmos the seer John experienced a visionary call (1:9-20) in which the Exalted Lord commanded him to write what he saw in a βιβλίον and to send it to the seven churches; in this vision he also writes the seven letters (heavenly letters) at the dictate of the Exalted One. At 4:1 a new ecstasy appears to begin in which the seer, raptured to heaven, views what is described in 4:1 to 22:20. At the end of the vision even the writing down of the βιβλίον seems to be complete (22:10). We ought not to ask when he wrote it: this kind of thing belongs to the apocalyptic style (Dan. 12:6).

4.3 Composition: The outline of the book is given in 1:19, 'Write what thou hast seen and what is and what will be hereafter'; hence, the visionary call (1:9-20), the seven letters to the churches on their present state (2f.) and the revelation of future events (4:1-22:5). In the composition of Revelation the number seven plays an important role. The seven churches with their symbols (candlesticks and stars) represent, in the number seven, the totality of the Church. In the apocalyptic section there are 3 seven-fold visions: the vision of the seals (5:1-8:1), of the trumpets (8:2-9:21; 11:15-19) and of the vials (15f.), and even in ch. 14 we can count seven visions. At the same time other numbers come into prominence, three, four and twelve, but the number seven is the most important. Nevertheless it is not the key to the composition of the Apocalypse. More important for the elucidation of this is the understanding of the 'book with the seven seals' (5:1) and the parallelism of certain parts in ch. 6-20 (on this see especially G. Bornkamm, 'Komposition'; F. Hahn, 'Aufbau'; J.W. Taeger, 'Veröffentlichungen', 60-62).

The βιβλίον 'written within and without and sealed with seven seals' (5:1; so according to the probably correct reading) is according to Bornkamm's convincing explanation, 'a document in two parts which, being written in two-fold fashion, comprises one legally valid text and a corresponding second text, unsealed and proffered for the inspection of everyman' (p. 205). The 'outside' designates the unsealed part of the document, and the 'inside' the sealed part. Consequently, the phenomena which accompany the opening of the seven seals (6:1 to 8:1) do not form the contents of the document, for these are first made accessible after the loosing of the last seal and so embrace rather what follows, the visions, 8:2 to 22:5.

Analysis of the composition has to be guided by the principles of division which are recognisable in the Apocalypse itself (F. Hahn, 'Aufbau', 159). The parallelism of the three seven-fold visions has always attracted attention. Bornkamm, however, has pointed out the parallelism of the texts following the visions of the trumpets and the vials (chs. 12-14 and 17-19) and, on the basis of a careful analysis, has drawn the conclusion that in 8:2-14:20 and 15:1-22:5 the same events of the End are being described, first in preparatory fashion and then in a final way, as were described in concise outline in the visions of the seals. Ch. 12-14 and 17-19 do not provide the chronological continuation of the events predicted in the visions of the trumpets and vials, but additional concrete supplements to what was systematically represented in the series of sevens.

The arrangement of the actual apocalyptic section of Rev. (4:1 to 22:6) is therefore governed by the fact that the same eschatological period is predicted three times: in summary form in the vision of the seven seals, 6:1-8:1; in a suggestive but fragmentary way in 8:2-14:20; and finally and completely in 15:1-22:5. The summary description in 6:1-8:1 is to be understood as the list, visible on the outside of the double document, of the contents of the sealed text on the inside, which will be set forth after the loosing of the seventh seal, in 8:2-22:5. The number seven in the visions of the seals, trumpets and vials means on each occasion the totality of time and events. That the author presents the descriptions in chs. 12-14 and 17-19 as additional material instead of working them into the system of sevens is due partly to the fact that his material resists such treatment. Moreover, the various tensions in the general apocalyptic picture are due largely to the traditional material with which the seer is working and also to the historical emphasis he lays upon it. On the whole, however, the Apocalypse is a work of strict arrangement and of magnificent inclusiveness.

4.4 Sources: the complex question concerning sources and the hypotheses offered for its solution cannot be entered upon here, even by way of suggestion. On this we should consult the commentaries and the survey of research by J.W. Taeger (op. cit. 59f.). The Fragment-theory of W. Bousset would seem - with modification in its details - most nearly to do justice to the facts of linguistic and stylistic unity and the effort to attain uniformity of construction on the one hand, and the various tensions of subject-matter on the other. Such fragments taken over are 7:1-8; 11:1-13; 12, or are found in 13f., 17f., 21f. In type and in origin they are very varied: while 11:1f. would seem to be a Jewish pamphlet from the time of the siege of Jerusalem the vision of the queen of heaven, the child and the dragon derives from Eastern mythology (12), and in ch. 17 an older and a more recent version of the Nero redivivus tale seem to be merged. The writer has worked over these fragments with different degrees of intensity in some parts, but in other parts not at all. It is not always clear whether the fragments existed before in a state of written or oral fixity.

The Old Testament served the seer as his 'source'. The Apocalypse is full of OT allusions and images, and basic to it are the chariot vision of Ezek. 1 and the Son of Man chapter, Daniel 7. There are numerous parallels to Jewish Apocalyptic as well, but no direct quotations from which one could infer literary dependence; it is a case of general dependence on the same apocalyptic world of ideas.

This leads one, against H. Kraft, to refrain from overestimating the OT influence or understanding the seer of Revelation as the successor of OT prophecy (op. cit. 16).

4.5 Author: it is debated whether the author writes under the pseudonym of John or whether he is to be identified with the presbyter John mentioned by Papias (so W. Bousset, 42-45; A. Strobel, 186 *et al.*). According to P. Vielhauer (NTApo³ [ET], 623) the author does not write under the disguise and with the borrowed authority of some hero of the past, but under his own name and in his own authority. His self-awareness is based on the fact that he knows he has been called by Christ to be a prophet (1:9-20) and it is revealed by the fact that he calls his writing λόγοι τῆς προφητείας (1:3; 22:7, 10, 18f.) and lays claim to 'canonical' authority for it (22:18f.). On the other side the 'school' connection with the Johannine writings is emphasised (O. Böcher 1-12) and the Apocalypse is understood as a pseudonymous writing (U. Vanni). This would correspond with the apocalyptic genre and makes us question any precise assignment of the Apocalypse to the Johannine circle. All the traditional apocalyptic features associated with antiquity are missing, e.g. the surveys of history in phases given in the form of predictions, and the sealing of the revelation with the obligation to secrecy (22:10, cf. for the contrary Dan. 8:26; 12:4). The author emphatically stresses his contemporaneity with his readers and, instead of a review of history, provides a description and critique of the present situation of the Church (ch. 2f.), which are however kept so general that they could also be understood as apostolic statements belonging to the past. He takes care that his writing should be understood as an ecumenical letter, not as a secret document (1:4, 11, 19; 22:16, 21).

Corresponding to these peculiarities is the relative departure from the practice of making *vaticinia ex eventu* on events of the present or recent past. In spite of the system of sevens, all calculations of the End are absent, for the three and a half years, 42 months or 1260 days (11:2f.; 12:6, 14; 13:5) is a stereotyped apocalyptic number which does not serve a chronological interest. And despite the numerous cosmic phenomena which he describes, the seer's interest does not lie in cosmology.

Finally, amongst the peculiarities of the Johannine Apocalypse, we note the fact that the mode of revelation is not the dream, but visionary ecstasy - a sign of the advanced development of Apocalyptic - and secondly, that the mediator of the revelation is only rarely an *angelus interpres* (17:1ff.; 21:9; cf. 1:1; 22:6ff.), but elsewhere always Christ - an understandable Christian modification - and thirdly, that only rarely is an explanation of the vision given (e.g. ch. 17; otherwise only for details).

4.6 Purpose: according to a widespread view among scholars, who think they can appeal to Irenaeus (*adv. Haer.* V 30.3), the Apocalypse originated in Asia Minor at the beginning of the so-called Domitianic persecution (*c.* A.D. 95), but pseudonymity and other internal reasons, and especially the relation to the Johannine circle, could point to a later period. The aim of the book is to strengthen Christians in this emergency to endure faithfully and to witness to their confession. But does this need such a great display as the composition of an entire apocalypse? The contents of the book go far beyond its actual aim, which makes precise interpretation difficult. It is the codification and, in a certain fashion,the systematisation of apocalyptic expectations such as were cherished in those Jewish-Christian circles in Asia Minor which were eschatologically stimulated. The 'seer' again can be understood as their spokesman (U.B. Müller, 'Bestimmung', 617f.). The author desires not only to strengthen and comfort, but also to enlist sympathy for these ideas. That in fact appears to have been his chief aim. Consequently the apocalyptic material (4-22) outweighs the hortatory (2f.) and at 1:1 the author mentions only the former as the content of this book.

Among his ideas - which are not treated in detail here - some which were evidently specially important to the author may be singled out. Like all apocalyptic writers he is interested, not in the past, but only in the period of time from the present to the End, and this period is very short. The entire Apocalypse is characterised by a strong imminent expectation (1:1, 3; 3:11; 16:15; 22:7, 10, 17, 20), and it is more intense than in the Synoptic Apocalypse of Mk. 13. That means, since traces of the delay of the Parousia are present (e.g. 3:3), that the imminent hope has been awakened afresh, and where it is no longer present the author seeks to arouse it. To achieve this end, he employs, as has been said, no reviews of history in the form of predictions, but uses daring, yet, for the Christian reader of that time, fairly clear allusions to great events and figures of the present and the recent past. Thus in the *vaticinium ex eventu* in 17:3-11, v. 10 predicts, that is, presupposes the short reign of the seventh king (Titus), and v. 11 points to Domitian as the eighth king who is also one of the earlier seven, i.e. it characterises him as Nero redivivus. Domitian may also be intended in the beast from the pit (11:7; 17:8) or from the sea (13:1-10, 18). If the seer lets the beast's persecution of witnesses and Christians extend to the time of the sixth trumpet (11:7; cf. 9:13; 11:15) and of the sixth vial (16:13ff.), then it is clear that he believes the End to be immediately at hand.

He advocates apocalyptic determinism even more clearly than the apocalypses of Mark 13 par. and 2 Thess. 2 do with their δεῖ. The plan of God for history is unalterably laid down in the 'book with seven seals' and, after the opening of this, it is unfolded without obstruction. But - and this is a Christian element - the book is in the hands of the Lamb who alone is able to loose the seal, which means that it is Christ who inaugurates the End. This idea has a certain parallel in Paul (1 Cor. 15:24f.), and something closely corresponding in 2 John. Here the expectation is directed towards the future coming of Christ in fleshly form for the setting up of the messianic kingdom (2 Jn. 7; cf. G. Strecker, 'Anfänge').

Moreover, the apocalyptic dualism is more strongly marked in the Johannine Apocalypse than in the rest of the NT Apocalyptic. It is expressed in the notion that heaven and earth, space and time, must pass away to make room for the new heaven and the new earth (20:11; 10:6f.; 21:1; cf. 2 Pet. 3:12f.). It is expressed in the antagonism between the Christian Church and the pagan world-power, which is but the foreground of the real struggle between Christ and Satan (12-14). It finds expression also in the fact that in the visions of the trumpets and vials numerous catastrophes in history are depicted as catastrophes of nature and their actors are occasionally described as demonic beings; in other words, the End-event is raised to cosmic dimensions (angels and demons). The strict distinction between historical and supernatural event which is found in Mk. 13 is not found here.

In the apocalyptic section of his book the seer wishes to point to two things: first, the End-events which concern the whole world and which are described by him in the seven-fold visions whose scheme makes clear the fixed irresistibility of events; secondly, the events which concern the Church in particular and which he describes in the supplements (12f., 17f.) where the antithesis, Christ-Satan, shows the crisis-situation of the Church. He unites the two groups of themes by inserting motifs from the second in the seven-fold series (11:3-14; 16:13-16; cf. also 6:9-11) and by merging both themes in the final act (world-dissolution and the conquest of the Satanic powers, 16:17-21; 19:11-20:15). So the stress shifts more and more to the second theme, and in this the real interest of the author lies. For this reason he does not include it in the seven-fold visions, but in the supplementary additions.

The motifs of the second group of themes are to a large extent familiar from Mk. 13 and par. and 2 Thess. 2, but they are worked out in the Johannine Apocalypse more broadly and clearly, in a mythological way but also with topical purposefulness. Satan, who is not mentioned at all in Mk. 13 and only briefly in 2 Thess. 2:9, appears in the Apocalypse as the real opponent of Christ and his Church (12-20). The Antichrist, who is mentioned in veiled language in Mk. 13:14 and par. and suggestively described in 2 Thess. 2, is characterised by the seer as the exact image of Satan and the counterpart of the dead and resurrected Christ, and as the representative of the world-dominion of Rome. He possibly identifies him with a figure of political history (contrast Lohmeyer, *Offenbarung*, 115: the contemporary references are deliberately deleted by the author), although the interpretations advanced have not attained to any generally recognised result (cf. the commentaries on 12:18-13:10, 18; 17:3-11; a widespread view refers to the emperor Domitian, seen as Nero redivivus). The false prophets whom 2 Thess. 2 omits but who are a sign of the End at Mk. 13:22ff. par. appear at Rev. 13:11-17 in a single figure, the second beast, the pseudo-prophet (16:13). Whether the seer meant a concrete contemporary person or merely intended a personification cannot be decided. In any case, he combines the Devil, Antichrist and the false prophet into an extremely impressive 'satanic trinity' (12f., 16:13; cf. W. Bousset, *Antichrist*; G. Strecker, The 'Antichrist', see above, 2.5). He makes the cult of Caesar (13:4ff; 12-17) the motive for the persecution of the Church (cf. Mk. 13:9ff.; perhaps hinted at in 2 Thess. 2:4), describes it as the work of Satan (12:13-17) and he allows it to pass over into the great assault of the hostile powers (16:13-16; 17:12-14). Accordingly he describes the Parousia of Christ as a Messianic battle and conquest of these hostile powers, and this he does twice (14:14-20; 19:11-20:3). 2 Thess. also characterises it as the conquest of Antichrist and therefore of Satan, and even at Mk. 13:26 the idea of the conquest is indicated.

With the Parousia the writer connects two other ideas which are unique in the NT but obviously important to him. One is the idea of the thousand-year reign. This is a Messianic reign of peace on this earth taking place between the Parousia and the dissolution of the world. During it the devil is bound, and after it, being loosed again, he leads the powers of the world (Gog and Magog) to the final struggle against the holy city; he is conquered and thrown, for eternity, into the lake of fire and brimstone (20:1-10). There follows then the end of the world, the judgment and the appearing of the new world. This idea of a Messianic interregnum originates in Jewish Apocalyptic (e.g. 4 Esd. 7:28ff.; syr. Bar. 29:3ff.) and is a combination of the national and transcendent eschatological expectations. Then there is the idea of the two resurrections, one before and one after the millennium (20:4-6, 12-15). This is a combination of two Jewish conceptions, the older one of the resurrection of the righteous only, and the later one of the general resurrection of all the dead.

We must however ask whether the author of the Johannine Apocalypse goes back directly to Jewish Apocalyptic or is not rather inspired by early Christian models. Paul too attests the idea of the messianic interregnum (1 Cor. 15:24-26; cf. also 1 Cor. 6:2f. with Rev. 3:21; 20:4). In addition further traces have been assumed in the Johannine school (Jn. 5:17; 9:4). The splendidly coloured description of the new world (21:1-8) and of the new Jerusalem (21:9-22:5) is unique in the New Testament. By means of this the seer offers to his persecuted companions in the faith a glimpse that is full of promise into their glorious future. He forgoes giving a corresponding picture of Hell; later Apocalyptists would make up for this (for details see O. Böcher, Das tausendjährige Reich, in id., *Kirche in Zeit und Endzeit* 133-143).

When the actual cause of its existence was gone, the purpose of the Apocalypse was no longer understood. Detached from its concrete historical reference it really became a 'book with seven seals' which for some was suspect and objectionable, but to others it became an inexhaustible arsenal of apocalyptic speculations (on this see G. Maier, *Die Johannesoffenbarung und die Kirche*, WUNT 25, 1981).

5. The final chapter of the Didache

Literature: *Editions*: K. Bihlmeyer-W. Schneemelcher, *Die Apostolischen Väter* I, [3]1970; W. Rordorf-A. Tuilier, *La Doctrine des douze apôtres (Didache)*. Intr., texte, trad., notes, appendice et index (SC 248), Paris 1978; K. Wengst, *Didache (Apostellehre), Barnabasbrief, 2 Klemensbrief, Schrift an Diognet* (Schriften des Urchristentums II), 1984.

Commentaries: J.-P. Audet, *La Didachè. Instructions des apôtres* (Études Bibliques), Paris 1958; R. Knopf, *Die Lehre der zwölf Apostel...* (HNT Ergbd.), 1923; K. Niederwimmer, *Die Didache* (KEK Erg. Reihe 1), 1989.

Studies: A. Adam, 'Erwägungen zur Herkunft der Didache', ZKG 68, 1957, 1-47; E. Bammel, 'Schema und Vorlage von Didache 16', *Studia Patristica IV* (TU 79), 1961, 253-262; B.C. Butler, 'The Literary Relations of Didache, ch. XVI', in JTS 11, 1960, 265-283; W.-D. Köhler, *Die Rezeption des Matthäusevangeliums in der Zeit vor Irenäus* (WUNT II 24), 1987; E. Peterson, 'Über einige Probleme der Didache-Überlieferung', in id. *Frühkirche, Judentum und Gnosis*, 1959, 146-182.

The Didache, a compilation of Church regulations probably put together in the first decade of the 2nd century in Syria, has at its end a little apocalypse (Did. 16):

> '1. Be ye watchful[1] for your life! Let not your lamps be extinguished nor your loins ungirded,[2] but be ye ready! For ye know not the hour in which your Lord cometh. 2. Assemble yourselves frequently, seeking what is fitting for your souls. For the whole time of your faith will not be profitable to you, if you are not made perfect in the last time.[3] 3. For in the last days the false prophets and corrupters will be multiplied and the sheep will be turned into wolves and love shall be changed into hate.[4] 4. For as lawlessness increases, they shall hate one another and shall persecute and betray,[5] and then the world-deceiver[6] shall appear as a son of God, and shall work signs and wonders, and the earth shall be delivered into his hands, and he shall commit

crimes such as have never been seen since the world began.[7] 5. Then shall created mankind come to the fire of testing,[8] and many shall be offended[9] and perish, but those who have endured in the faith[10] shall be saved by the Curse (?Christ? Audet - from the grave). 6. And then shall the signs of the truth appear,[11] first, the sign of a rift in heaven, then the sign of the sound of a trumpet,[12] and thirdly, a resurrection of the dead,[13] 7. but not of all, but as it was said, "The Lord will come and all his saints with him."[14] 8. Then shall the world see the Lord coming on the clouds of heaven.'[15]

The text commences with an exhortation to wakefulness and constant preparedness in view of the coming of the Lord (v. 1f.) and to this is added an account, as concise as it is clear in construction, of the last things, the main acts of which are indicated from time to time in their historical sequence by a τότε (4b, 5, 6, 8): 1. The increase in 'lawlessness'; the appearance of false prophets and corrupters; the struggle of all against all (3, 4a). 2. The appearance of the 'world-deceiver' (Antichrist) who performs signs and wonders, accomplishes unprecedented crimes and subjects the world to himself (4b). 3. The commencement of the final distress in which only those who endure in the faith shall be saved (5); 4. The appearance of 'the signs of the truth', three apocalyptic acts (6f.). 5. The Parousia of the Lord on the clouds of heaven (8).

The scheme and the details of this apocalypse are found in Mt. 24 and 2 Thess. 2. One feels however that the description of the Parousia in v. 8 is incomplete. The Georgian translation renders 16:8 as follows:

> 'Then will the world see our Lord Jesus Christ, the Son of Man who (at the same time) is Son of God, coming on the clouds with power and great glory, and in his holy righteousness to requite every man according to his works before the whole of mankind and before the angels, Amen.' (Gr. Peradse, '"Die Lehre der zwölf Apostel' in der georgischen Überlieferung', ZNW, 31, 1932, 111-116; quotation from p. 116)

The rendering in the Seventh Book of the Apostolic Constitutions gives a similar ending:

> '. . . with the angels of his power, at the throne of his dominion to judge the world-deceiver, the devil, and to requite each according to his deeds' (Audet, p. 73)

Palaeographical observations on the manuscript of the Bryennios text support the view that the present text of 16:8 is incomplete and should be supplemented by the sense of the two readings noticed above (Audet, pp. 73f.; pp. 473f.; Bammel, p. 259f.; Wengst, *Didache* 20). Admittedly the missing judgment is already included in the statement of v. 7 (if this sentence is not a secondary addition, cf. Bammel, p. 261, n. 3), but still, something is missing in v. 8, if not the judgment, then the gathering of the elect (Mt. 24:31) or the union of the faithful with the Lord (1 Thess. 4:17).

The almost complete absence of specifically Christian features in v. 3-8 is striking. If we disregard the enigmatic κατάθεμα in v. 5, only the description of the world-deceiver as ὡς υἱὸς θεοῦ points to Christian enlargement; however, these words could be erased without damaging the text, and then it would be purely Jewish. For there is nothing in the description of the distress in v. 3-8 which suggests that the persecution is directed against Christians. Nevertheless we can hardly assume that we have here before us a Jewish text with Christian interpolations. As is generally the case with early Christian Apocalyptic the scheme and the material of this apocalypse are of Jewish origin. But the description in v. 3-8 is so strongly indebted to New Testament phraseology, especially Mt. 24 but also 2 Thess. 2, that we should probably assume that these texts provided the *Vorlage*. This holds even if the assumption that Synoptic texts were the author's direct written *Vorlage* in Did. 16 (so B.C. Butler, 'Relations', 265-268, referring to Lk. 12:35-40) cannot be proved with certainty (cf. W.-D. Köhler, *Rezeption*, 51-56).

Unlike the apocalyptic sections of the New Testament the apocalypse at Did. 16. 3-8 has no reference to the period of the author himself. There is no imminent hope. This is not conveyed by the introductory exhortation to constant wakefulness and preparedness for the unknown hour of the Parousia (v. 1f.); for this exhortation is traditional and v. 2 shows clearly that 'the last time', according to the author's interpretation, has not yet commenced. Did. 16 thus does not aim to exhort or comfort a community exposed to eschatological tension and distress, or even (like 2 Pet.) to awaken to a new eschatological hope a Church which has become languid. Did. 16 has also no speculative aim. The text pictures nothing; rather everything is schematised. The author's main concern is evidently to give a general outline of the last things with distinct conciseness and clear arrangement. This suggests that Did. 16 is a fragment of something like a catechism.

As such it fits well into Didache as a whole and possibly belonged to it from the start. Whether it originally formed the end of the Two-Ways catechism is questionable. More important than the question of sources and redaction from our point of view is the observation that an apocalypse - without concrete reference to the present and without interest in the speculative arrangement of the last things - has become a component part of the 'Teaching' and, as a *locus de novissimis*, has found a place in a manual of Church order.

Notes

1. Cf. on the whole verse Mt. 24:42, 44; 25:13.
2. Cf. Lk. 12:35.
3. Barn. 4:9.
4. Cf. Mt. 24:10-12; 7:15; 2 Pet. 3:3; 1 Tim. 4:1.
5. Cf. Mt. 24:24.
6. Cf. 2 Jn. 7; Rev. 12:9.
7. Cf. 2 Thess. 2:3f., 9f.; Rev. 13:1-10, 13f.
8. Cf. Mt. 24:21f. and par.
9. Cf. Mt. 24:10.
10. Cf. Mt. 24:13 and par.
11. Cf. Mt. 24:30.
12. Cf. Mt. 24:31; 1 Cor. 15:52; 1 Thess. 4:16.
13. Cf. 1 Thess. 4:16.
14. Zech. 14:5.
15. Cf. Mt. 24:30; 26:64.

6. The Shepherd of Hermas

Literature: *Editions*: F.X. Funk, *Opera Patr. Apostol.* I, ^{2}1901; O. von Gebhardt-A. Harnack, *Hermae Pastor graece addita versione latina recentiore e codice Palatino* (Patr. Apostol. Opera III), 1877; R. Joly, *Hermas Le Pasteur* (SC 53), Paris ^{2}1968; M. Whittaker, *Der Hirt des Hermas* (GCS 48), ^{2}1967.

Commentaries: M. Dibelius, *Der Hirt des Hermas* (HNT Ergbd.), 1923.

Studies: S. Arai, *Angelus Interpres in the Shepherd of Hermas*, Tokyo 1959; R. van Deemter, *Der Hirt des Hermas. Apokalypse oder Allegorie?*, 1929; M. Dibelius, 'Der Offenbarungsträger im "Hirten" des Hermas', in id. *Botschaft und Geschichte* II, 1956, 80-93; I. Goldhahn-Müller, *Die Grenze der Gemeinde* (GTA 39), 1989; D. Hellholm, *Das Visionenbuch des Hermas als Apokalypse*, Uppsala 1980; E. Peterson, 'Beiträge zur Interpretation der Visionen im "Pastor Hermae"', in id. *Frühkirche, Judentum und Gnosis*, 1959, 254-270; id. Kritische Analyse der fünften Vision des Hermas, ib. 271-284; id. Die Begegnung mit dem Ungeheuer, ib. 285-309; J. Reiling, *Hermas and Christian Prophecy: A Study of the Eleventh Mandate* (NovTest Supp. 37), 1973; A.V. Ström, *Der Hirt des Hermas, Allegorie oder Wirklichkeit*? (Act. Sem. NT Ups. III), 1936; H. Weinel, NTApo^2 II, 1924, 327-384.

6.1 Textual Tradition: the Greek text of Pastor Hermae is not extant in its entirety. The most extensive text (Vis. I 1-Sim. IX 30.2) is provided by the MS 96 from the Monastery of St. Gregory on Athos, which is now in part in Leipzig (14th or 15th cent.; siglum Aℵ Athous, earlier G). Codex Sinaiticus (4th cent.;) provides, after the NT and the letter of Barnabas, the text of Vis. I 1-Mand. IV 3.6. In addition to these earlier known MSS there appeared in 1936 Pap. 129 of the Papyrus collection of the University of Michigan (3rd cent.; siglum M) which contains Sim. II 8-Sim. IX 5.1. The Greek text is also attested by a great number of papyrus and parchment fragments which include larger or smaller pieces from all sections of the book.

Of the translations, the two into Latin are the most important: the so-called Vulgata, an old-Latin translation which exists in a number of MSS and which includes the end of the book, not extant in Greek (L^1); and the so-called Palatina, which exists in two MSS of the 15th century (L^2). Then there is an Ethiopic version (probably 6th cent.: E; possibly there is also a further Ethiopic version, see R. Joly, *Hermas*, 47) and two Coptic versions, an Achmimic (C^1) and a Sahidic (C^2), which are only fragments, and finally a fragmentary middle-Persian version (Mpers).

For textual criticism ps.-Athanasius, *Praecepta ad Antiochum* (ed. G. Dindorf, 1857) and Antiochus Monachus, *Homiliae* (PG 89, 1413ff.) are also drawn upon (cf. also R. Joly, *Hermas*, 58-68).

The attempt to bring the Greek witnesses and the versions into a relation of dependence and to draw up a stemma has not yet been successful. Nevertheless, the textual criticism of the Pastor Hermae has been greatly advanced by the discovery of the Michigan papyrus M.

The witnesses differ in the headings they use and in their numbering system. The latter is meaningless in the case of the Visions. The edition of M. Whittaker replaces the traditional division into 5 visions, 12 mandates and 10 similitudes, with their subdivisions into chapters and paragraphs, by a continuous numbering of the chapters, which are arranged, for their part, in the traditional paragraphs. This new system of numbering is certainly shorter than the more laborious earlier system, but it is by no means more convenient or even clearer. Since it is not suitable for our purposes, we abide by the customary method of citation (so also R. Joly, *Hermas*).

6.2 Contents: the book is an Apocalypse in its form and style, but not in its contents, since it includes no disclosures of the eschatological future or of the world beyond. Two heavenly figures, an old lady and a shepherd, mediate to Hermas, in and around Rome, revelations on the possibility of Christian repentance. The book takes it name from the second bearer of revelation, the shepherd, to whom some four-fifths of the book go back.

Vision I comprises the early part of the story: Hermas sees his former mistress bathing in the Tiber and desires to have such a beautiful woman for his wife. Then follows the account of the actual vision. Some days later, Hermas, while journeying to Cumae, is raptured by the Spirit into a strange region, and he sees his former mistress as a heavenly figure who proceeds to tell him that his desire was a sin of thought. There then appears to him an old lady in gleaming raiment, with a book in her hand and sitting on a great white seat; she preaches repentance to Hermas and his house and reads to him a song of praise to God (2, 3); after that the angels carry away the chair and then the old lady departs (4).

Vision II takes place a year later at the same place. The aged lady gives to Hermas a heavenly letter, which he, without understanding it, copies; it then mysteriously vanishes (1). Only fifteen days later, after prayer and fasting, can Hermas read the letter; it contains the divine message that contemporary Christianity has still the possibility of a single repentance, and charges Hermas to impart this message to the leaders of the Church (2 and 3). There follow two additional visions: while sleeping, Hermas receives the revelation that the old lady is not the Sybil, as he had thought, but the Church; then the old lady appears in his house and gives him instructions for the circulation of the heavenly letter (4).

Vision III, concerning the building of the tower. After long prayer and fasting, Hermas is commanded by the old lady to go to his farm, and he finds there an ivory couch on which the old lady sits and appoints to him the place on her left hand. She shows him six young men building an enormous tower, raised upon the waters, using white stones which were being brought by thousands of men (1 and 2); she explains the building of the tower as an allegory of the Church (3-7). She then lets him see seven young women around the tower and interprets these as the virtues (8.1-7) and she mediates to him exhortations for the Church (8.11-9.10). In a long addition, which still reports on two visions, we learn that the old lady, in the three encounters up to the present, has appeared in successively rejuvenated form. Hermas receives an allegorical explanation of these three figures (10-13).

Vision IV, the vision of the Beast. Twenty days later, on his way to his farm, Hermas meets a gigantic sea-monster (1) and the old lady, who has changed into a young girl. She explains the monster to him in terms of the coming affliction (2.1-3.6) and then, in mysterious fashion, vanishes for ever.

Vision V. Introduction to the Mandates and Similitudes. The new bearer of revelation, the Shepherd, appears to Hermas in his house and reveals his identity as he 'to whom he was delivered', while Hermas recognises him as 'the angel of repentance'. The Shepherd instructs Hermas to write down his commandments and parables.

Mand. I: Faith, Fear and Continence.
II: Purity.
III: Truth.
IV: Chastity, Divorce and Second Marriage (including at 2.1-3.7, Christian repentance).
V: Patience and Violent Anger.
VI: The two kinds of faith.
VII: The two kinds of fear.
VIII: The two kinds of continence.
IX. Doubt.
X: Sorrow.
XI: The false prophet: true and false prophecy.
XII: 1.1-3.1: Two-fold kinds of desire.
3.2-6.5: Epilogue to the Mandates.

Sim. I: The foreign and the home city.
II: Elm and Vine.
III: The wintry wood.
IV: The summer wood.
V: The faithful slave (1, 2); application to works (3), to Christ (4-6) and the preservation of the flesh (7).
VI: The angel of revelry and the angel of punishment.
VII: The effect of the angel of punishment on Hermas.
VIII: Willow-tree; allegorical explanation.
IX: The twelve mountains in Arcadia (1); repetition of the vision of the tower (2-4); testing and cleansing of the tower (5-11); the meaning of the building (12-16) and of the mountains (17.1-31.3). Final exhortation (31.4-33.3).
X: Appearance of Christ to Hermas and the Shepherd; Concluding exhortation and promise.

6.3 Composition: the division of the book into Visions, Mandates and Similitudes does not correspond to its arrangement in composition. The fifth Vision does not belong with the four preceding, but is the introduction to the following Mandates and Similitudes. The Shepherd appears in Vision V and acts as mediator of the commandments and parables, while the old lady is the bringer of revelation only in Visions I-IV. From this distinction in the mediators of revelation it is obvious that there is a caesura in the construction between Visions IV and V, but there does not seem to be one between the Mandates and the Similitudes. There is indeed a long Epilogue to the 12 Mandates (Mand. XII 3.2-6.5), but the Shepherd plays the main part both before and after. Sim. I brings no new declaration of situation, but begins with the sequence-formula, 'He saith to me', and the headings ('Parables which he spake to me' etc.) do not come from the author, but have grown up in the manuscript tradition (as the Ethiopic version clearly reveals by placing a corresponding heading at Mand. XII 3.4). Add to this the fact that the author seems to have understood the commandments and the parables as a unity: in the introductory vision (Vis. V 5f.) he speaks of them three times in such a way that they must be understood as very closely related (the first time, the nouns ἐντολαί and παραβολαί are linked by a personal pronoun used only once, while the other two cases link them by the use of the article only once); the same is true at Sim. IX 1.1. Furthermore, the first Similitudes are closely associated with the Mandates (cf. Dibelius, commentary, pp. 493f., p. 546, pp. 550f.) and Sim. VII 7 speaks of the παραβολαί as ἐντολαί. The difference between them is so fluid that it cannot be evidence for the arrangement of the book. Dibelius suggests, probably quite correctly, that the division into Mandates and Similitudes was first produced in accordance with the two-fold expression, and that the epilogue to Man. XII was 'joined on as an addition' (op. cit., p. 493). The book falls into two parts of very different size: Visions I-IV on the one hand, and the commandments and parables on the other.

Obviously the second part originally ended with Sim. VIII. Sim. IX 1.1 begins entirely afresh ('When I had written down the commandments and parables of the shepherd, the angel of repentance' - Hermas has followed the instruction of the Shepherd at Vis. V 5 - 'he came to me and said to me, I wish to show thee all things which the Holy Ghost, which spake with thee in the form of the Church, has shown to thee'), and 1.4-33.3 provides an excessively circumstantial and allegorised repetition of the vision of the tower in Vis. III ('And yet must thou learn everything more accurately from me' Sim. IX 1.3). This repetition is in fact a supplement and is clearly recognisable as such. The shepherd's statement in Vis. V 5a ('For I was sent . . . to show thee again all that thou didst see before, which is especially important and profitable for you') is an addition which is meant to prepare the way for this supplement (Dibelius, op. cit., p. 421, p. 493, pp. 601f.).

These observations support the hypothesis advanced by Dibelius and others that (i) the book of Visions (Vis. I-IV) and the book of commands and parables (Vis. V-Sim. VIII) originated and existed independently of one another, that (ii) the book of Visions is the older of the two, and that (iii) at the time when the two were combined, Sim. IX and X were added, Sim. IX to emphasise what the author considered particularly important and profitable, Sim. X to form the conclusion to the whole composition.

Both the books, as well as their linking-together, are probably the work of the same author. At any rate the composition does not suggest more than one author (so S. Giet, *Hermas et les Pasteurs*, Paris 1963; against this, see R. Joly, 'Hermas et le Pasteur', *VigChr* 21, 1967, 201-218). The many discrepancies, as Dibelius and Joly have shown, are better resolved by tradition criticism than by literary criticism. The epilogue alone, Mand XII. 3.2-6.5, may be an interpolation. Some of the headings, and particularly their numbering, have been added in the course of the manuscript tradition.

6.4 Literary character: the form of the book is apocalyptic in so far as *angeli interpretes* reveal and explain the entire contents to Hermas. The fixed outlines (visions and raptures), the first-person narrative throughout the whole and the many dialogues, all comply with this form.

But the two bearers of revelation are not anonymous, as they are in Jewish apocalypses and in the Johannine Apocalypse, nor are they even specially named angels who are absorbed in the task of interpreting, but, as Dibelius in particular has shown, figures with several layers. In Vis. II 4.1 and III 3.3 the old lady is identified with the Church; this is an entirely secondary feature which conflicts with the fact that the Church is the recipient of the message of repentance from the old lady and that its condition is dealt with by her in Vis. III.

The Sibyl has provided the model for this figure. Certain features clearly show that the old lady is really the Sibyl with whom Hermas at first identified her (great old age, the journey to Cumae, written communication of revelation, the seat; Peterson, p. 267, even refers the schema of the three stages of life to the Sibyl). An analogous situation obtains in the case of the Shepherd. He is designated as the angel of repentance, but he is also the one to whom Hermas 'has been delivered', and he 'who will live with him the rest of the days of his life', i.e. a protecting angel. The dress of the Shepherd is associated with this role and this points to a non-Jewish origin for the figure, to Hermes; and that is suggested also by the mention of Arcadia (Sim. IX 1.4; further evidence in Dibelius, op. cit., pp. 495f., and and W. Schmid, Eine frühchristliche Arcadien-Vorstellung, *Convivium* 1954, 121ff.). The appearing of the Shepherd in Vis. V displays the typical features of the epiphany of a divine being. Both figures are clearly of pagan origin: a Sibyl and a protecting angel; furthermore they take upon themselves the function of *angeli interpretes* and, in the end, become allegories of Christian realities, the Church and the angel of repentance. In both the main figures of the book one feature which is prominent, and which is remarkable throughout the entire work, is the artificial linking and allegorising of different figures and motifs. The author is particularly concerned with allegory in order that, with its help, he may adapt his heterogeneous and diverging pictorial and conceptual material to his own purpose.

Hermas no doubt wishes to write an apocalypse, but the apocalyptic framework embraces no apocalyptic picture. The Mandates include exhortation, traditional ethical sayings which the author arranges thematically, works out in an interpretative fashion and casts partly in the form of dialogue. Reference has been made in the survey of contents to the repetition, with commentary, of the three themes of Mand. I in Mand. VI-VIII. 'The clothing of these rules in a heavenly revelation is not to be discovered in the content in general; for many an early Christian teacher could, and in fact did, speak like this angel of repentance' (Dibelius, commentary, 496). Only Mand. IX falls out of the paraenetic framework, but with its topical warning against false prophets it fits in with the ethical tendency of the Mandates.

The 'parables' Sim. I-V are marked by strong allegorical tendencies and possess a 'precept-character' (Dibelius), and are thus used likewise for exhortation. Even the christological passage at Sim. V 4-6 is ethically oriented. Eschatological ideas are scarcely to be found: the Parousia is mentioned quite by the way and without emphasis in V 5.3, and occasionally the Shepherd promises eternal life to the righteous who follow his commandments. Sim. VI-IX are 'visionary parables' (Dibelius), allegories in visionary form on the effect of repentance. The visionary form is at its clearest in Sim. IX (rapture) but it is unmistakable in Sim. VI and VIII as well (appearance of the angels: the elegant Shepherd = the angel of revelry; the dishevelled Shepherd = the angel of punishment, Sim. VI; the appearing of the angel of the Lord, Sim. VIII). Sim. X is not a parable, but an account of the ephiphany of God's Son; it is actually an addition to the introductory vision, Vis. V.

The presence of paraenesis and allegory would not in itself argue against the apocalyptic character of the book, for both appear in apocalypses. Allegory, in particular, is a stylistic feature in Apocalyptic, while every early Jewish and Christian apocalypse has a paraenetic angle. But in that case, paraenesis and allegory are eschatologically determined, whereas this eschatological determination is absent from the Pastor Hermae.

The same is true also of the book of Visions (Vis. I-IV). In spite of Apocalyptic items, there are no revelations on the Eschaton or on the Beyond. The book belongs, if at all, only to a limited extent to the visionary literature (cf. the list in M. Buber, *Ekstatische Konfessionen*, 1921). All four visions (the preaching of penitence by the old lady, Vis. I; the heavenly letter on Christian repentance, Vis. II; the allegory of the building of the tower, Vis. III; the vision of the beast, Vis. IV) have no eschatological purpose, but rather a moral one. Vis. III and IV are intricate allegories, but not well harmonised; the author makes traditional material serve his own ends, which do not correspond to the original meaning (cf. Dibelius, op. cit., pp. 454ff., 482ff.). This is particularly clear in Vis. IV, which is the only section of the book where Hermas works with apocalyptic material. For that reason we quote it here.

'The fourth vision which I beheld, brethren, twenty days after the former vision, a type of the impending tribulation. I was going into the country by the Campanian way. From the high road it is about ten stades away, and the place is easily reached. While I was walking alone, then, I entreated the Lord to accomplish the revelations and the visions which he showed me through his holy church, that he might strengthen me and grant repentance to his servants who have stumbled, that his great and glorious name might thus be extolled, for that he held me worthy to be shown his marvels. While I was giving praise and thanksgiving, a kind of voice came to me in answer, "Do not doubt, Hermas." I began to ponder within myself and to say, "What have I to doubt about, seeing that the Lord has established me on firm ground and has allowed me to behold glorious things?" And I went on a little farther, brethren, and behold I perceived a cloud of dust rising as it were to heaven and I began to ask myself, "Is it perhaps cattle coming which are raising the dust?" for it was just about a stade from me. As the cloud became greater and greater, I perceived that it was something supernatural. Then the sun broke through a moment, and behold, I saw a huge beast like some sea-monster, and from its mouth fiery locusts issued forth. It was about a hundred feet long and its head was like a barrel (?). And I began to weep and to entreat the Lord to rescue me from it, and I remembered the word which I had heard, "Hermas, do not doubt." So, brethren, I gained new faith in the Lord; I placed before my eyes the mighty things he had taught me and courageously went to meet the beast. But it was coming on with such a rush that it could have destroyed a city. As I came near to it, the huge monster stretched itself on the ground and did no more than put forth its tongue and did not stir at all till I had passed by. And the beast bore on its head four colours: black, red like fire and blood, gold and white. After

I had passed by and had gone forward about thirty feet, there met me a virgin adorned like a bride going forth from a bride-chamber, all in white, with white sandals, veiled up to her forehead and with a turban as her head-covering; and her hair was white. I recognized from the former visions that it was the Church and so I became more cheerful. She greeted me, saying "Good day, my good man", and I replied, "Lady, good day." She asked me, "Did you meet nothing?" "Lady," I answered, "such a huge beast as might have destroyed whole peoples. But I escaped, thanks to the grace and power of the Lord." "Thou didst escape fortunately", said she, "for thou didst cast thy care upon God and hast opened thy heart to the Lord, certain in the faith that thou canst attain deliverance by no other means than by his great and glorious name. Therefore the Lord has sent his angel, to whom the beasts are subject - his name is Segri - and has shut its mouth that it should not hurt thee. Thou hast escaped a great tribulation because thou hast believed and at the sight of such a huge beast hast not doubted. Go therefore and declare to the elect of the Lord his mighty deeds and say to them that this beast is a type of the great tribulation which is to come. If ye therefore prepare yourselves and with your whole heart turn to the Lord in repentance, then shall ye be able to escape it, if your heart be pure and blameless and if, for the future days of your life, ye serve the Lord without blame. Cast your cares upon the Lord and he will bring them to a right end. Trust in the Lord, ye doubters, for he can do all things: he can turn away his wrath from you and can send his punishments on you who doubt. Woe to them who hear these words and ignore them! It were better for them that they had not been born." Then I asked her about the four colours which the beast wore on its head. She answered me, "Again thou art curious about such things." "Yes, lady", said I, "make known unto me what these things are." "Listen", said she, "the black is this world in which ye dwell; the fire and blood colour shows that this world must perish by blood and fire. The golden colour stands for you who have escaped from this world. For as the gold is tested by fire and becomes useful, so ye also who dwell in it are being tested. And all ye that endure and undergo the fiery trial in it will become pure. As the gold loses its dross, so shall ye also cast away all sorrow and anxiety and shall be pure and useful for the building of the tower. The white colour stands for the future world, in which the elect of God will dwell; for they will be blameless and pure whom God has chosen for eternal life. Therefore cease not thou to speak in the ears of the saints. Now ye know the symbol of the great tribulation to come. But if ye are willing, it shall be nothing. Remember the things pointed out beforehand." After these words she departed without my seeing in which direction she went. For there was a noise, and I turned back in fear because I thought that the beast was coming.'

The most important results of the analysis carried out by Dibelius (pp. 482ff.) and Peterson (pp. 285ff.) may be briefly noted. The fact that the locusts are not explained and that the interpretation of the four colours is artifical - how could the wicked beast bear the colours of the Christians and the World to come? - make it clear that Hermas did not form the picture by himself, but took it over from elsewhere. This picture and its figures are of apocalyptic origin. The sea-monster is the mythical demon who is fettered from Creation and will be released at the end of the world; the locusts are eschatological plagues and the four colours, originally cosmic colours, are characteristics of apocalyptic figures (Rev. 6:1ff.). All these are fixed traits in the picture of the future End-time which threaten the whole of mankind. But in Vis. IV they are not used for apocalyptic description; they are 'de-eschatologised' and reinterpreted. Hermas 'does not catch sight in advance, in a visionary way, of a fragment of the End-time but, on a walk in the neighbourhood of Rome, experiences in a vision phenomena of the End-time as personal menaces in the present . . . The peculiar character of the Beast-vision is thus explained by the fact that the author has individualized apocalyptic terrors' (Dibelius, op. cit., p. 485). In a modification of this kind a new understanding of existence seeks expression. 'This process of individualization corresponds to an alteration in the Christian hope which was significant for that time: it is not the fate of mankind at the end of days, but the fate of the individual at the end of his life that is the centre of interest' (Dibelius, op. cit., p. 486). The description of the heavenly journey of the individual takes on features of the final fate of the cosmos.

This example shows particularly clearly how Hermas gives a new interpretation to traditional material. As well as making apocalyptic material serve his own ends, he has done the same with the apocalyptic form. In his case, the literary form of the apocalypse is no longer the sufficient expression of its declarations, as is the case still with the later Apocalypse of Paul. We should reckon the Pastor Hermae as falling in the genre of Apocalypse only in a non-literal sense, and must therefore designate it as a pseudo-apocalypse.

6.5 Intention: the intention of the book is paraenetic throughout and directed towards repentance. This follows not only from the Mandates and from Sim. I-IV, which comprise in the main only exhortation, but from the remaining parts as well, for they are clearly oriented towards paraenesis and have as their aim repentance, whether they illustrate repentance itself (Sim. V) or its effects (Sim. VI-VIII) or its meaning for the church (Vis. III, Sim. IX). Vis. II proclaims this repentance by a heavenly letter and Vis. I introduces the general theme.

In the repentance propagated by Hermas it is a question of the possibility opened up by God that Christians, after repentance at their conversion and baptism, may still have a last chance to do penance, and this possibility is offered to them in the message of Hermas. He is commissioned by the letter from heaven to make know to the Church this opportunity for repentance on the part of Christians.

> 'After thou hast made known unto them all these words which the Lord commanded me to reveal to thee, then all the sins they sinned aforetime are forgiven them; also to all the saints that have sinned up to this day, if they repent with their whole heart and banish doubt from their heart. For the Lord has sworn this oath by his own glory concerning the elect, that if, now that this day has been set as a limit, sin shall hereafter be committed, they shall have no more deliverance. For repentance for the righteous has an end: the

> days of repentance are accomplished for all the saints, whereas for the Gentiles repentance is open till the last day.' (Vis. II 2.4f.)

With this programme Hermas is set apart from the earlier Christian conceptions which knew only of a repentance at conversion (Heb. 6:4ff.; 10:26-31; 12:16f.; 1 Jn 3:6; 5:16f.). That is how I. Goldhahn-Müller has recently presented it in a penetrating investigation of the early Christian understanding of repentance (*Grenze der Gemeinde*). Only the revelation-book of the Jewish Christian Elkesai anticipated the Shepherd in proclaiming the possibility of a second repentance (cf. G. Strecker, 'Elkesai', in id. *Eschaton und Historie*, 1979, 320-333; L. Cirillo, *Elchasai e gli Elchasaiti*, Cosenza 1984; J. Irmscher, below pp. 685ff.). The sins of Christians had never assumed the proportions of a theological problem - though the actual presence of sins in Christians made any theory of sinlessness impossible - and so neither had the repentance of Christians. This was a result of the eschatological expectation. With the weakening of this expectation which resulted from the continuing existence of the world, the sins and the repentance of Christians became a problem. Hermas is aware of the novelty of his solution to the problem, in which he diverges from the early Christian radicalism which he himself considered fundamentally correct:

> 'I said, "I have heard from certain teachers that there is no other repentance save that which took place when we went down into the water and obtained remission of our former sins." He (the Shepherd) answered me: "Thou hast heard rightly, for so it is. For whoever received remission of sins was pledged to sin no more, but to abide in purity. But since thou enquirest all things accurately, I will declare this also to thee, for I do not wish to mislead (into sin) those who in the future will believe or those who have already believed on the Lord. For they that have already believed, or will believe in the future, have no further chance to repent of their (future) sins, but have only remission of their former sins. But for all them that were called before these days the Lord has appointed repentance. For the Lord, the discerner of hearts, who knows all things beforehand, perceived the weakness of men and the craftiness of the devil, that he will be doing some mischief to the servants of God and will commit evil against them. The Lord then, being compassionate, had mercy upon his creation and appointed this repentance, and to me was transmitted the discharge of this repentance. But I say (now), saith he, If after this great and holy calling anyone, being tempted by the devil, falls into sin, there shall be only one repentance for him. But if he sin over and again and repent, it is unprofitable for him: he will reach life with difficulty." I said to him: "I have come alive again since I have heard this so precisely from thee. For I know that, if I add no more to my sins, I shall be saved." "Thou shalt be saved", said he, "thou and all, if they do this."' (Mand. IV 3)

In the fixing of a time for repentance we must see an echo of the eschatological expectation. God grants to his own 'a final hour of grace' (Dibelius). Hermas bases the extension of time (Man. IV 3.5) on the merciful character of God, just as the almost contemporary 2 Pet. (3:9) bases it on his forbearance. But the eschatology is given a new interpretation in terms of the ethical (the 'day' which originally designated the End is, for example, according to Vis. II 2.4f. the last opportunity for repentance in the message of Hermas).

Hermas is aware that he stands in opposition to the earlier eschatology just as much as he does to the earlier theory and practice of repentance. He intentionally allows the relation between the coming great tribulation and the End to remain unclear. Because his theory of repentance is a result of the non-appearance of the End of the world and the extension of time, he lengthens the period of repentance. The publication of the heavenly letter is delayed (Vis. II 4.2f.) and reference is expressly made to a 'pause' in the building of the tower of the Church (Sim. IX 5.1; 14.2). 'For it is on your account that the building is interrupted, for unless ye hasten to do right, the tower will be completed and ye will be shut out' (Sim. X 4.4). How little life there is in this theoretically fixed expectation is shown by Vis. III 8.9f., a passage which rejects the question about the End as foolishness and directs the questioner to the 'reminder' and to the 'renewal of the spirit', to repentance:

> 'I asked her concerning the times, whether the End is even now. But she cried with a loud voice, "Foolish man, seest thou not that the tower is still being built? Whenever the tower is completed, then is the End: but it will soon be ready. Ask me no more questions. This reminder and the renewal of your spirit is enough for you and for the saints. But it was not revealed for thee alone, but that thou mightest make it know to all. . . . "'

The position of Hermas is very clear here. The traditional motif of the imminent hope and the actual problem of the life of Christians in the continuing world, as well as of the Church as a *Corpus permixtum*, conflict with one another. He escapes from this collision by means of his theory and message concerning a Christian repentance which is limited to one occasion. The problem which occupies him is not the non-appearance of the end of the world, but the relation of the ideal and the empirical Church. The latter must be purified and in this way perfected - the interpretation of the parable of the weeds among the wheat (Mt. 13:36ff.) has a broadly casuistic continuation in the allegory of the building of the tower (Vis. III, Sim. IX). Cf. also the allegory of the willow tree, Sim. VIII. Only when the ideal and the empirical Church coincide, 'only when the tower is completed, then comes the End' (Vis. III 8.9).

6.6 The significance of the form: the significance of the form can be understood if we remember Hermas' position and programme and that he was aware of their opposition to the earlier rigorous ideas. 'A breaking through of radical demands is . . . generally only possible if God himself gives the impetus' (Dibelius, op. cit., p. 511). Consequently the opportunity of a single repentance after baptism is first proclaimed in the form of a letter from heaven and is then repeated in detail by the Shepherd, 'the angel of repentance'. Hence the apocalyptic form of the book as a whole: it lends to it the character of a revelation, that is, a divine authority for the claims put forward in it, an authority which the author could not lay claim to for himself.

6.7 Author; place and time of composition: the author is not an apocalyptist, for he presents no disclosures on the End of the world or the life to come. Moreover he is not a prophet, for the alleged adoption of the 'old prophetic summons to repentance' does not mark him out as such (*contra* Weinel, NTApo[2] 327f.), and the early Christian prophets produced no apocalyptic literature (even if the Apocalyptist John counts himself among the prophets, see above, p. 586); compare also the descriptions of false and true prophecy (Man. XI). Hermas may have been a visionary and have received his illumination concerning the possibility of a single repentance for Christians in an ecstatic state. But he was well versed in the ideas of Apocalyptic and of the magical papyri, and probably in the related literature as well; in any case, he knew how to mould this material to suit his own ends. The evidence for this strongly traditional element in Hermas has been conclusively provided by Dibelius and Peterson. The attempt by R. van Deemter and A.V. Ström to prove that the author was a genuine apocalyptic visionary, and in addition one of a particular psychological type, has, against their will, only confirmed the former evidence.

It is a debated question whether and how far we can trust the numerous autobiographical details in Hermas concerning himself and his family. Discounting such of these details as may have been intended typologically (cf. Dibelius, op. cit., pp. 419f. and *passim*), it seems that Hermas was a small-business man in Rome. The Muratori Canon affirms that he was the brother of the then bishop of Rome (ll.73ff.; cf. vol. 1, p. 36), so also the *Catologus Liberianus* (A. Harnack, *Chronologie* I, 145) and the *Liber Pontificalis* (Dibelius, op. cit.). The truth of these assertions has been placed in doubt by the fact that the Muratori Canon impugns the canonicity of the 'Shepherd' by giving to it an obviously tendentious late date (Hermas composed the book 'quite lately in our time, when on the throne of the church of the city of Rome the bishop Pius, his brother, sat'). E. Peterson declares that this comment is 'false ascription' and that it is 'a fixed form of school-polemic' in the circles of the Roman 'teachers' of the 3rd century against the apocalypses handed down in the Church. But only the dating is polemical: the late date of the 'Shepherd' makes it unsuitable for use in worship; but the person of its author remains untouched. It has been demonstrated by Dibelius (op. cit., pp. 421f.) that this particular dating of the book to Pius' tenure of office does not exclude the possibility of the relationship of the author to the Roman bishop or, more correctly, presbyter. We may therefore accept this statement. Peterson wants to dissociate the entire work from Rome and sees Hermas as a Palestinian-Jewish Christian and his 'house' as a *chaburah* of Jewish-Christian ascetics. Against this and similar views, however, we must urge the methodological considerations which Dibelius raised as far back as 1923: 'There is no justification for explaining the strong connections of the book with Jewish tradition by postulating a Jewish-Christian origin for the author. Customary Semitisms based on Bible reading, Jewish cult-formulae and Jewish paraenesis were taken over as their inheritance by 2nd-century Christians in such measure that we cannot interpret every trustee of the inheritance as a relative of the testator' (op. cit., p. 423).

On the basis of internal criteria, we may place the composition of the book in the third, or, at the outside, in the fourth decade of the 2nd century (Dibelius, op. cit., p. 422; J. Reiling, *Hermas* 24; R. Staats, art. Hermas, TRE 15, 1986, 103: "well before 150")

1. The Ascension of Isaiah

C. Detlef G. Müller

Introduction

1. Editions and literature: *Texts: a. Ethiopic*: R. Laurence, *Ascensio Isaiae vatis*, Oxford 1819; A. Dillmann, *Ascensio Isaiae*, 1877; R.H. Charles, *The Ascension of Isaiah*, London 1900 (complete critical edition with Greek and Latin fragments, Latin trans. of the Slavonic version and English translation). *b. Latin*: A. de Fantis, *Liber gratiae spiritualis*, Venice 1522; J.K.L. Gieseler, *Vetus translatio latina Visionis Isaiae*, 1832; E. Tisserant, *Ascension d'Isaïe*, Paris 1909. *c. Greek*: c. II.4-IV.4, ed. Grenfell-Hunt, *The Amherst Papyri I*, 1900, 1-22; O. von Gebhardt in *Zeitschr. f. wiss. Theol.* 1878, 330-358 published a Greek reworking of the whole Asc. Is. into a Christian sacred legend (cf. on this Charles and Tisserant). *d. Slavonic*: A. Vaillant, *Textes vieux-slaves*, Paris 1968. vol. I, 87-98 and vol. II, 73-82 (edition of text and French trans.). *e. Coptic*: L.Th. Lefort, *Le Muséon* 51, 1938, 24-30; 52, 1939, 7-10; P. Lacau, *Le Muséon* 59, 1946, 453-467.

A new critical edition is announced by A. Acerbi.

Translations: *French*: R. Basset, *Les apocryphes éthiopiens trad. en Français* III, 1894; Tisserant (see above); *Le livre de l'ascension du prophète Isaïe*... Préf. de F. Bardeau (Les portes de l'étrange), Paris 1978; A. Caquot, 'Martyre d'Isaïe', in A. Dupont-Sommer/M. Philonenko, *La Bible: écrits intertestamentaires*, Paris 1987, 1017-1033. *English*: Charles (see above); G.H. Box (J.J. Landsman), *The Apocalypse of Abraham and the Ascension of Isaiah*, London 1919 (cf. M. Dibelius, ThLZ 47, 1922, col. 544); M.A. Knibb, 'Martyrdom and Ascension of Isaiah', in J.H. Charlesworth, *The Old Testament Pseudepigrapha*, II, London 1985, 143-176. *Danish*: E. Hammershaimb, in *De Gammeltestamentlige Pseudepigrafer*, Heft 3, Copenhagen-Oslo-Lund 1958, 303-315. *Modern Greek*: Σ. 'Αγουρίδης, Τὸ μαρτύριον 'Ησαΐα, in 'Επιστομοννικὴ 'Επέτηρις τῆς Θεολογικῆς Σχολῆς, Athens 1976, 427-465. *Italian*: Erbetta III, 175-208 (with bibliography). *German*: J. Flemming-H. Duensing, NTApo[3] II, 454-468 (ET 644-663).

Literature: D. Flusser, 'The Apocryphal Book of Ascensio Isaiae and the Dead Sea Sect'. *Israel Exploration Journal* 3, 1953, 30-47; Joh. Michael Schmidt, *Die jüdische Apokalyptik*, 1969, *passim*. F. Buck, 'Are the "Ascension of Jesaiah" and the "Odes of Solomon" witnesses of an early cult of Mary?' in *De primordiis cultus mariani* 4, Rome 1970, 371-399; A.K. Helmbold, 'Gnostic Elements in the "Ascension of Isaiah"', NTS 18, 1971-72, 222-227; A. Caquot, 'Bref commentaire du Martyre d'Isaïe', *Semitica* 23, 1973,65-93; M. Delcor, 'L'"Ascension d'Isaïe" à travers la prédication d'un évêque cathare en Catalogne au quatorzième siècle', *Revue de l'histoire des religions* 185, 1974, 157-178; A. Renoux, 'Note sur l'Ascension d'Isaïe dans la tradition liturgique hiérosolymitaine', *Cristianesimo nella storia* 2, 1981, 367-370; E. Turdeanu, 'La vision d'Isaïe', *Apocryphes slaves et roumains de l'Ancien Testament*, Leiden 1981, 145-172; A.G. Kossova, 'Osservazioni sulla tradizione paleoslava della Visione di Isaia; coincidenze e divergenze con la tradizione testuale dell'Ascensione di Isaia', *Atti 8° Cong. int. studi sull'alto medioevo*, Spoleto 1983, 167-186; M. Pesce (ed.), *Isaia, il Diletto e la Chiesa. Visione ed esegesi profetica cristiano-primitiva nell'Ascensione di Isaia. Atti del Convegno di Roma, 9-10 Aprile 1981*, Brescia 1983 (Testi e ricerche di Scienze Religiose 20). A. Acerbi, 'Antonio de Fantis', *Aevum* 57, 1983, 396-415; E. Schürer, *History of the Jewish People* III 1, rev. ed., Edinburgh 1986, 335-341; detailed bibliography in J.H. Charlesworth, *The Pseudepigrapha and modern Research, with a Supplement*, Ann Arbor 1981, 125-130.

2. Transmission: the Ascension of Isaiah is transmitted complete only in Ethiopic. Separate fragments or parts of it are preserved in old Coptic versions, in Greek and in Old Slavonic. Alexandria with its good connections on the one side with the Sudan, on the other with Constantinople, could be its place of origin. It was however particular groups, increasingly persecuted as heretical, who from the 3rd century on zealously made use of this document - such as Hieracas, the Archontics, the Arians, the Manicheans, the Messalians and the Bogomiles, and in the West the Cathari. A.K. Helmbold pleads with general arguments for 'Christian gnostic' circles as the originators of the work. That the document was disseminated in Egypt and Ethiopia, with their interest in additional revelations, is not surprising.

The original must have been composed in Greek. The Ethiopic version, which alone is complete, has probably reproduced the original correctly in essentials, if we disregard some small roughnesses.

The Coptic fragments, which come from a papyrus roll, are composed in an archaic dialect (Proto-Subachmimic, also called Proto-Lycopolitan; on this cf. J. Vergote, *Grammaire copte* Ia, Louvain 1973, 57; id. 'Le dialecte copte P <Pap. Bodmer VI: Proverbes>, essai d'identification', *Revue d'Égyptologie* 25, 1973, 50-57, here pp. 54f.) and not in the later literary language. The roll form and the dialect certainly point to splinter groups. These Coptic fragments comprise I 1-5; III. 25-28; V 7-8; VI 7-11; VII 12-15, 28-32; VIII 16-17; IX 9-11, 28-30; X 9-11, 27; XI 14-16, 35-37 (cf. the editions by Lefort and Lacau). The manuscript is however badly damaged. There is also a version of the Ascensio Isaiae in Sahidic, the later literary language of Coptic. The text of III 3-6, 9-12 and XI 24-32, 35-40 is extant. According to Lefort the manuscript derives from the last third of the 4th century (cf. his edition).

The Greek fragment (Amherst Papyri I) contains the text of II 4-IV 4.

The Latin text of the ascension or vision in VI-XI, published in 1522 by Antonio de Fantis, who was interested in the apocrypha and in occult sciences, may derive from the circles of the Cathari, perhaps through the medium of Lombard inquisitors (cf. A. Acerbi, 'Antonio de Fantis', where at pp. 414f. there is also a discussion of the theories of E. Turdeanu and others). The Latin text probably goes back to a Greek version. There is debate as to its relation to the Slavonic versions and the role of the Bogomiles in its transmission.

3. Composition and date: in its present form the Ascensio Isaiae is a Christian work, which was put together at the earliest in the second half of the 2nd century. It was intended to combat, in the manner of an ancient apocalypse, certain contemporary evils, the lack of discipline and the divisions in the Church. One cannot however fail to recognise that the work takes up traditions already in existence and makes them serve its purpose.

Chapters I to V present the martyrdom of the prophet Isaiah. The activity of Sammael, the prince of this world, is there portrayed in all its wickedness for all to see. III 13-V.1 interrupts the narrative, already hints at the prophet's ascension, and then presents an apocalypse which is indisputably Christian. It refers to the Saviour and his twelve apostles. This part must be put to the account of the Christian author of the work as a whole. Here too, naturally, he will be dependent on traditions in circulation. In chapters VI to XI we then have the second main section, which presents the ascension or vision of the prophet Isaiah. Here also there is an interruption in the flow of the narrative, at XI 2-22, which again proves to be an interpolation; it reports on Mary and Joseph, the birth of the Saviour and his crucifixion.

The book thus uses old tradition and interpolates it with Christian material. We therefore cannot in any case affirm a uniform origin for the Ascension of Isaiah. A literary unity, such as Vacher Burch still postulates (JTS 21, 1920, 249-265), can only relate to the activity of the compiler, who naturally adapted the material - so far for example as the prophet's martyrdom is concerned - to his own purposes. The oldest part may be this martyrdom of Isaiah - a document of Jewish origin which uses material the existence of which is attested by Heb. 11:37. For the transmission of the document and its prestige the most important factor was without doubt the prophet's ascension or vision, which portrays the seven heavens and refers to the coming deliverance by the Redeemer. Here XI 2-22 is an additional interpolation which makes more precise an already Christian document of the 2nd century. The martyrdom must have been prefaced to the ascension only later, and on this occasion expanded by the Christian apocalypse.

In the Latin version edited by Antonio de Fantis in Venice in 1522 and in the six Slavonic versions only the ascension is handed down, without any insertion, while XI 34 offers the expansion assumed by Jerome to be known in the Iberian peninsula. A hitherto unknown Occitan version (cf. M. Delcor) may go back to the Latin (the de Fantis version is late, and not the only one).

There is much to be said for the view that the first part of the work, which reports the martyrdom of Isaiah, derives from the circles of the Qumran community. Manichean circles come into question for its wider dissemination (cf. Flusser, Delcor). A. Caquot also argues cautiously, but in the same direction - with a recapitulation of the whole history of research.

Explanation of signs: ( ) addition to text; < > restoration; [ ] supplement in the translation for better comprehension.

The Ascension of the Prophet Isaiah

1. 1. It came to pass in the twenty-sixth (*Coptic*: sixteenth) year of the reign of Hezekiah, king of Judah, that he called Manasseh his son who was the only son he had. 2. And he called him into the presence of the prophet Isaiah, the son of Amoz, and into the presence of Jasub, the son of Isaiah, in order to deliver to him the words of righteousness (or of salvation = the truth) which he, the king, himself had seen,[1] 3. and the eternal judgments and the punishments of Hell and of the prince of this world, and of his angels, authorities and powers; 4. and the words of the faith concerning the Beloved which he himself had seen in the fifteenth year of his reign during his illness. 5. And he delivered to him the recorded words which Sebna, the scribe, had written and that which Isaiah the son of Amoz had given to him together with the prophets, that they might write down and store with him what he himself

had seen in the king's house concerning the judgment of the angels and the destruction of this world, concerning the garments of the righteous, and concerning the going forth, the transformation, the persecution and ascension of the Beloved. 6. And in the twentieth year of the reign of Hezekiah, Isaiah had seen the words of this prophecy and had delivered them to his son Jasub. And whilst the former gave commands, with Jasub the son of Isaiah present, 7. Isaiah said to king Hezekiah, but not in the presence of Manasseh, alone did he say it to him, 'As truly as the Lord liveth, whose name has not been sent into this world, and as truly as the Beloved of my Lord liveth, and the spirit which speaketh in me liveth, all these commands and these words will have no value for thy son Manasseh, and by the outrage of his hands I shall depart amid the torture of my body. 8. And Sammael Malkira will serve Manasseh and execute all his desires, and he will be a follower of Beliar rather than of me. 9. And many in Jerusalem and in Judah will he cause to depart from the true faith, and Beliar will dwell in Manasseh, and by his hand shall I be sawn asunder.' 10. And when Hezekiah heard these words, he wept very bitterly, rent his clothes, cast dust upon his head and fell on his face. 11. And Isaiah said to him, 'The design of Sammael against Manasseh is [already] settled: nothing will help thee.' 12. On that day Hezekiah resolved within himself to kill his son. 13. But Isaiah said to Hezekiah, 'The Beloved will make thy purpose fruitless and the thought of thy heart will not be accomplished, for with this calling have I been called, and I must have my portion with the inheritance of the Beloved.'

2. 1. And after Hezekiah died and Manasseh became king, he remembered no more the commands of his father Hezekiah, but forgot them, and Sammael settled upon Manasseh and clung fast to him. 2. And Manasseh ceased from serving the God of his father and served Satan and his angels and powers. 3. And he caused the house of his father, which had been under the eye of Hezekiah, to depart (from) the words of wisdom and from the service of God. 4. And Manasseh altered his purpose and became a servant of Beliar, for the prince of unrighteousness who rules this world is Beliar, whose name is Matanbukus. Now this Beliar rejoiced in Jerusalem over Manasseh and strengthened him in his leading to apostasy and in the lawlessness which was spread abroad in Jerusalem. 5. Witchcraft and the practice of magic increased, and predictions from the flight of birds, divination, fornication (and adultery), the persecution of the righteous by Manasseh (and by Belchira) and by Tobia the Canaanite, John of Anathoth and <Zadok> the overseer of works. 6. The rest of the narrative is recorded in the book of the kings of Judah and Israel.[2] 7. And when Isaiah the son of Amoz saw the evil which was taking place in Jerusalem, the worship of Satan and its wantonness, he withdrew from Jerusalem and settled in Bethlehem-Judah. 8. But there was much lawlessness there also; so he withdrew from Bethlehem and settled on a mountain in desert country. 9. And Micaiah the prophet and Ananias the aged, and Joel, Habakkuk

and Jasub his son, and many of the faithful who believed in the ascension to heaven withdrew and settled on the mountain. 10. And they all put on sackcloth and all were prophets; they had nothing with them, but were naked and they bitterly lamented the apostasy of Israel. 11. And they had nothing to eat except wild herbs which they gathered on the mountains, and after they had cooked them, they ate them in the company of the prophet Isaiah. And thus they spent two years on the mountains and hills. 12. And after this, while they were in the desert, a man appeared in Samaria named Belchira, of the family of Zedekiah, the son of Chenaan, a false prophet who had his dwelling place in Bethlehem; now Hezekiah, the son of Chanani, his father's brother, was in the days of Ahab king of Israel the teacher of the 400 prophets of Baal, and he [Zedekiah] smote and abused the prophet Micaiah, the son of Imlah. 13. And he, Micaiah, was (also) abused by Ahab and was thrown into prison. And the people of the false prophet Zedekiah belonged to (the party of) Ahaziah the son of Ahab in Semmoma.[3] 14. But Elijah the prophet from Thisbe in Gilead rebuked Ahaziah and Samaria, and prophesied concerning Ahaziah that he would die on his bed of a sickness, and that Samaria would be delivered into the hand of Salmanasser, because he had slain the prophets of God. 15. And when the false prophets who were with Ahaziah, the son of Ahab, and their teacher Jallarias from Mount Joel (Israel?) heard - 16. now he (i.e. Jallarias; elsewhere Belchira) was a brother of Zedekiah - when they heard, they prevailed upon Ahaziah, king of Gomorrah, and (slew) Micaiah.

3. 1. But Belchira found and saw the whereabouts of Isaiah and the prophets who were with him, for he lived in the region of Bethlehem and was an adherent of Manasseh. And he appeared as a false prophet in Jerusalem and many in Jerusalem joined with him, although he was from Samaria. 2. And it came to pass when Salmanasser, king of Assyria, came and captured Samaria and led the nine (and a half) tribes into captivity, and dragged them off to the mountains of the Medes and to the river Gozan, 3. this man, while still a youth, escaped and reached Jerusalem in the days of Hezekiah, king of Judah; but he walked not in the ways of his father of Samaria, for he feared Hezekiah. 4. And he was found in the days of Hezekiah delivering impious speeches in Jerusalem. 5. And the servants of Hezekiah accused him and he fled to the region of Bethlehem, and they persuaded (*Coptic and Ethiopic*: he persuaded). . . . 6. Now Belchira accused Isaiah and the prophets who were with him in these words, 'Isaiah and his companions prophesy against Jerusalem and against the cities of Judah that they shall be laid waste, and (against the children of Judah) and Benjamin, that they shall go into captivity, and against thee also, O lord my king, that thou shalt go (bound) with hooks and iron chains;[4] 7. but they prophesy falsely concerning Israel and Judah. 8. And Isaiah himself has said, "I see more than the prophet Moses." 9. Now Moses said, "There is no man who can see God and live", but Isaiah has said, "I have seen God and behold I live".[5]

10. Know therefore, O king, that he is a liar. Moreover he has called Jerusalem Sodom and the princes of Judah and Jerusalem he has declared to be the people of Gomorrah.'[6] And he brought many accusations against Isaiah and the prophets before Manasseh. 11. But Beliar abode in the heart of Manasseh and in the hearts of the princes of Judah and Benjamin, of the eunuchs and councillors of the king. 12. And the speech of Belchira pleased him (exceedingly) and he sent and seized Isaiah.

13. For Beliar harboured great wrath against Isaiah on account of the vision and of the exposure with which he had exposed Sammael, and because through him the coming forth of the Beloved from the seventh heaven had been revealed, and his transformation, his descent and the likeness into which he was to be transformed, namely, the likeness of a man, and the persecution which he was to suffer, and the tortures with which the children of Israel were to afflict him, and (the coming) of the twelve disciples (and the) instruction, (and that he should before the Sabbath be crucified on the tree) and that he was to be crucified together with criminals, and that he would be buried in a sepulchre, 14. and that the twelve who were with him would be offended because of him, and the watch of the guards of the grave, 15. and the descent of the angel of the church which is in the heavens, whom he will summon in the last days; 16. and that the angel of the Holy Spirit and Michael, the chief of the holy angels, would open his grave on the third day, 17. and that the Beloved, sitting on their shoulders, will come forth and send out his twelve disciples, 18. and that they will teach to all the nations and every tongue the resurrection of the Beloved, and that those who believe on his cross will be saved, and in his ascension to the seventh heaven, whence he came; 19. and that many who believe in him will speak in [the power of] the Holy Spirit, 20. and that many signs and wonders will take place in those days; 21. and afterwards, when he is at hand, his disciples will forsake the teaching of the twelve apostles and their faith, their love and their purity, 22. and there will arise much contention about (his coming and) his appearing. 23. And in those days there will be many who will love office though they are devoid of wisdom, 24. and many elders will be lawless and violent shepherds to their sheep and will become ravagers [of the sheep], since they have no holy shepherds. 25. And many will exchange the glory of the garment of the saints for the garment of the covetous, and respect for persons will be common in those days, and such as love the honour of this world. 26. And there will be much slandering and boasting at the approach of the Lord and the Holy Spirit will depart from many. 27. And in those days there will not be many prophets nor such as speak reliable words, except a few here and there, 28. on account of the spirit of error, of fornication, of boasting and of covetousness which shall be in those who yet will be called his servants and who receive him. 29. Great discord will arise among them, between shepherds and elders. 30. For great jealousy will prevail

in the last days, for each will say what seems pleasing in his own eyes. 31. And they will set aside the prophecies of the prophets which were before me and also pay no attention to these my visions, in order to speak [forth from the] torrent of their heart.

4. 1. And now, Hezekiah and Jasub, my son, these are the days of the completion (?) of the world. 2. And after it has come to its consummation, Beliar, the great prince, the king of this world who has ruled it since it came into being, shall descend; he will come down from his firmament in the form of a man, a lawless king, a slayer of his mother, who himself (even) this king 3. will persecute the plant which the Twelve Apostles of the Beloved have planted; and one of the twelve will be delivered into his hand. - 4. This ruler will thus come in the likeness of that king and there will come with him all the powers of this world and they will hearken to him in all that he desires. 5. And at his word the sun will rise in the night and he will cause the moon to shine at the sixth hour. 6. All that he desires he will do in the world; he will act and speak in the name of the Beloved and say 'I am God and before me there has been none else.' 7. And all the people in the world will believe in him, 8. and will sacrifice to him and serve him saying, 'This is God and beside him there is none other.' 9. And the majority of those who have united to receive the Beloved will turn aside to him, 10. and the power of his miracles will be manifest in every city and region, 11. and he will set up his image before him in every city, 12. and he shall rule three years, seven months and twenty-seven days. 13. And many believers and saints, after they have seen him for whom they hoped, Jesus Christ the crucified - after I, Isaiah, have seen him who was crucified and ascended - who thus believed in him, of these [only] a few will remain as his servants, fleeing from desert to desert and awaiting his coming.[7] 14. And after (one thousand) three hundred and thirty-two days the Lord will come with his angels and with the hosts of the saints from the seventh heaven with the glory of the seventh heaven, and will drag Beliar with his hosts into Gehenna,[8] 15. and he will bring rest to the pious who shall be found alive in the body in this world (and the sun shall grow red with shame),[9] 16. and to all who through faith in him have cursed Beliar and his kings. But the saints will come with the Lord in their garments which are stored on high in the seventh heaven; with the Lord they will come, whose spirits are clothed, they will descend and be present in the world, and those who are found in the body will be strengthened by the image of the saints in the garments of the saints, and the Lord will minister to those who were watchful in the world.[10] 17. And afterwards they will turn themselves upwards in their garments but their body will remain in the world. 18. Then the voice of the Beloved will in wrath rebuke this heaven and this dry place [= the earth] and the mountains and hills, the cities, the desert and the forests, the angels of the sun and of the moon and all things wherein Beliar manifests himself and acts openly in this world, and

resurrection and judgment will take place in their midst in those days, and the Beloved will cause fire to go forth from himself, and it will consume all the impious and they will be as if they had not been created.

19. The remainder of the words of the vision is recorded in the vision concerning Babylon.[11] 20. And the rest of the vision of the Lord, behold, it is recorded in parables in my words which are written in the book which I openly proclaimed. 21. Moreover the descent of the Beloved into the realm of the dead is recorded in the section where the Lord says 'Behold, my servant is prudent.'[12] And behold, all these things are written (in the Psalms) in the poems of David, the son of Jesse, in the sayings of his son Solomon, in the words of Korah and Ethan, the Israelite, and in the words of Asaph and in the remaining Psalms which the angel of the spirit caused to be written by those whose name is not recorded, and in the words of Amoz, my father, and of the prophets Hosea and Micah, Joel, Nahum, Jonah, Obadiah, Habakkuk, Haggai, Zephaniah, Zechariah and Malachi, and in the words of Joseph the Just, and in the words of Daniel.

5. 1. On account of this vision, therefore, Beliar grew angry with Isaiah and he dwelt in the heart of Manasseh, and Isaiah was sawn asunder with a tree-saw. 2. And when Isaiah was being sawn asunder, Belchira his accuser and all the false prophets stood there, laughing and expressing their malicious joy over Isaiah. 3. And Belchira stood with Mekembukus before Isaiah, mocking him.[13] 4. And Belchira said to Isaiah: 'Say "In all that I have spoken, I have lied: the ways of Manasseh are good and right, 5. also the ways of Belchira and his companions are right."' 6. This he said to him when they were beginning to saw him asunder. 7. But Isaiah [was absorbed] in a vision of the Lord, and although his eyes were open, he did not see them. 8. And Belchira spoke thus to Isaiah, 'Say what I say to thee and I will alter their purpose, and I will prevail upon Manasseh and the princes of Judah and the people and all Jerusalem to reverence thee [upon their knees].' 9. And Isaiah answered and said 'So far as I am concerned, so to speak, damned and cursed be thou, all thy powers and thy whole house, 10. for thou canst take no more than the skin of my flesh.' 11. So they seized and sawed asunder Isaiah the son of Amoz, with a saw. 12. And Manasseh, Belchira, the false prophets and the princes and the people all stood and looked on. 13. And to the prophets who were with him he said before he was sawn asunder: 'Go to the region of Tyre and Sidon; for me alone has God mingled the cup.' 14. But while he was being sawn asunder Isaiah neither cried out nor wept, but his mouth conversed with the Holy Spirit until he had been sawn apart.

15. This did Beliar to Isaiah through Belchira and Manasseh, for Sammael cherished fierce anger against Isaiah from the days of Hezekiah king of Judah, on account of the things which he had seen concerning the Beloved, 16. and because of the destruction of Sammael, which he had seen through the Lord, while his father Hezekiah was still king. And he acted according to the will of Satan.

The vision which Isaiah the son of Amoz saw.

6. 1. In the twentieth year of the reign of Hezekiah, king of Judah, Isaiah the son of Amoz and Jasub the son of Isaiah came from Gilgal to Jerusalem to Hezekiah. 2. And (after he [Isaiah] had entered) he sat down on the king's couch and [although] they brought him a chair, he refused to sit on it. 3. So Isaiah began to speak words of faith and righteousness with Hezekiah, while all the princes of Israel sat [around] with the eunuchs and the king's councillors. And there were there forty prophets and sons of the prophets who had come from the neighbouring districts, from the mountains and from the plains,when they heard that Isaiah had come from Gilgal to Hezekiah. 4. They had come to greet him and to hear his words, 5. and that he might lay his hands upon them and that they might prophesy and that he might hear their prophecy; and they were all before Isaiah. 6. When Isaiah was speaking to Hezekiah the words of truth and faith, they all heard (the door which [someone] had opened, and) the voice of the (Holy) Spirit. 7. Then the king called all the prophets and the entire people who were found there, and they came [in], and Micaiah and the aged Ananias, and Joel and Jasub sat on his right hand (and on his left). 8. And it came to pass when they all heard the voice of the Holy Spirit they all fell upon their knees in worship and glorifed the God of righteousness, the Most High in the highest world who as the Holy One has his seat on high and rests among his saints,[14] 9. and they gave honour to him who had granted [such] a door (*Slav*: excellence of words) in the alien world, and had granted it to a man. 10. And while he was speaking by the Holy Spirit in the hearing of all, he [suddenly] became silent and his consciousness was taken from him and he saw no [more] the men who were standing before him: 11. his eyes were open, but his mouth was silent and the consciousness in his body was taken from him; 12. but his breath was [still] in him, for he saw a vision. 13. And the angel who was sent to make him behold it belonged neither to this firmament nor to the angels of the glory of this world, but had come from the seventh heaven. 14. And the people who were standing around, with the exception of the circle of prophets, did (not) think that the holy Isaiah had been taken up. 15. And the vision which he saw was not of this world, but from the world which is hidden from (all; *Ethiopic also*: his) flesh. 16. And after Isaiah had beheld this vision, he imparted it to Hezekiah, his son Jasub, and the remaining prophets. 17. But the leaders, the eunuchs and the people did not hear, with the exception of Sebna the scribe, Joachim and Asaph the chronicler, for they were doers of righteousness and the sweet fragrance of the spirit was upon them. But the people did not hear, for Micaiah and Jasub his son had caused them to go forth, when the knowledge of this world was taken from him and he became as a dead man.

7. 1. Now the vision which he had seen Isaiah narrated to Hezekiah, his son

Jasub, Micaiah and the rest of the prophets saying, 2. 'In that moment when I was prophesying according to things heard by you, I saw a sublime angel and he was not like the glory of the angels which I was accustomed [already] to see, but he possessed great glory and honour, so that I cannot describe the glory of this angel. 3. And he took hold of me by my hand and then I saw (*Slav*: he led me on high); and I said to him, "Who art thou, and what is thy name, and wherefore dost thou lead me on high?", for strength was granted to me to speak with him. 4. And he said to me: "When I have led thee on high by degrees and have shown thee the vision for which I have been sent to thee, then wilt thou know who I am, 5. but my name thou shalt not find out, since thou must return to this thy body. But whither I would raise thee on high, thou shalt see, since for this purpose I have been sent." 6. And I rejoiced because he spoke amiably with me. 7. And he said to me: "Dost thou rejoice because I have spoken amiably to thee?"; and he went on, "Thou wilt see one who is greater than I, who will speak amiably and peaceably with thee; 8. and his Father also who is greater wilt thou see, because for this purpose have I been sent from the seventh heaven to explain all these things for thee." 9. And we ascended to the firmament, I and he, and there I saw Sammael and his hosts, and a great struggle was taking place against him, and the angels *(so Mai's first Latin fragment: L^1)* of Satan were envious of one another. 10. And as it is above, so is it also on the earth, for the likeness of that which is in the firmament is also on the earth. 11. And I said to the angel, "(What is this struggle) and what is this envy?" 12. And he said to me, "So it has been, since this world began until now, and this struggle [will continue] till he whom thou shalt see shall come and destroy him [Satan]." 13. And after this he brought me up above the firmament, which is the (first) heaven. 14. And there I saw a throne in the midst, and on the right and on the left of it were angels. 15. And (the angels on the left) were not like the angels who stood on the right, for those on the right possessed a greater glory, and they all praised with one voice; and there was a throne in the midst; and likewise those on the left sang praises after them, but their voice was not such as the voice of those on the right, nor their praise like their praise. 16. And I asked the angel who led me and said unto him, "To whom is this praise given?" 17. And he said to me, "[It is] for the praise (of him who is in) the seventh heaven, for him who rests [in] eternity among his saints, and for his Beloved, whence I have been sent unto thee. (Thither is it sent)." 18. And again he caused me to ascend to the second heaven, and the height of that heaven is the same as from heaven to earth (and to the firmament). 19. And (I saw there as) in the first heaven, angels on the right and on the left and a throne in the midst and the praise of the angels in the second heaven; and he who sat on the throne in the second heaven had a greater glory than all [the rest]. 20. And there was much [more] glory in the second heaven, and their praise was not like the praise of those in the first heaven. 21. And I fell on my face to worship him, and the angel who conducted me did not allow me, but said to me, "Worship neither angel nor throne which belongs to the six heavens - for this reason was I sent to conduct thee - till I tell thee in the seventh heaven. 22. For above all the heavens and their angels is thy throne set, and thy garments and thy crown which thou shalt see." 23. And I rejoiced greatly that those who love the Most High and his Beloved will at their end ascend thither by the angel of the Holy Spirit. 24. And he brought me up to the third heaven, and in like manner I saw those on the right and on the left, and there stood there also a throne in the midst but the remembrance of this world is not known there. 25. And I said to the angel who was with me, for the glory of my countenance was being transformed as I ascended from heaven to heaven, "Nothing of the vanity of that world is here named." 26. And he answered and said to me, "Nothing is named by reason of its weakness, and nothing is hidden here [of what] took place." 27. And I desired to find out how it is known, but he answered and said to me, "When I have brought thee to the seventh heaven whence I was sent, high above these, then shalt thou know that nothing is hidden from the thrones and from those who dwell in the heavens and from the angels." And great were the praises they sang and the glory of him who sat on the throne, and the angels on the right and on the left possessed a greater glory than those in the heaven beneath them. 28. And again he carried me upwards to the fourth heaven, and the distance from the third heaven to the fourth is greater than that from earth to the firmament. 29. And there once more I saw those on the right and on the left, and he who sat on the throne was in the midst, and here also they sang their praises. 30. And the praise and glory of the angels on the right was greater than that of those on the left, 31. and again the glory of him who sat on the throne was greater than that of the angels on the right, and their glory was greater than that of those who were below. 32. And he brought me up to the fifth heaven. 33. And again I saw those on the right and those on the left and him who sat on the throne, possessing greater glory than those in the fourth heaven. 34. And the glory of those on the right surpassed that of those on the left. 35. And the glory of him who sat on the throne was greater than the glory of the angels on the right, 36. and their praises were more glorious than those in the fourth heaven. 37. And I praised the unnamed one and the only one, who dwells in the heavens, whose name is unfathomable for all flesh, who has bestowed such a glory from heaven to heaven, who makes great the glory of the angels and makes greater the glory of him who sits on the throne.

8. 1. And again he raised me up into the air of the sixth heaven, and I saw there a glory such as I had not seen in the fifth heaven, 2. as I ascended, namely, angels in greater glory; 3. and there was a holy and wonderful song of praise there. 4. And I said to the angel who conducted me, "What is this that I see, my Lord?" 5. And he said, "I am not thy Lord, but thy companion." 6. And once more I asked him saying, "Why are the angels not [any longer] in two groups?"

7. And he said, "From the sixth heaven and upwards there are no longer any angels on the left, nor is there a throne in the midst, but (they receive their arrangement) from the power of the seventh heaven, where the unnamed one dwells and his Elect one whose name is unfathomable and cannot be known by the whole heaven, 8. for it is he alone to whose voice all the heavens and thrones give answer. Thus I have been empowered and sent to bring thee up here to see the glory, 9. and to see the Lord of all those heavens and these thrones 10. being transformed till he comes to your image and likeness. 11. But I say to thee, Isaiah, that no one who has to return to a body in this world has ascended or seen or perceived what thou hast perceived and what thou shalt [yet] see; 12. for it is appointed unto thee in the lot of the Lord (the lot of [the cross of] wood,) to come hither (, and from hence comes the power of the sixth heaven and the air).;" 13. And I extolled my Lord with praise that I through his lot should come hither. 14. And he said, "Hear then this from thy companion: when thou by the will of God hast ascended here from the body as a spirit, then shalt thou receive the garment which thou shalt see, and the other garments as well, numbered and stored up, thou shalt see; 15. and then shalt thou resemble the angels in the seventh heaven." 16. And he brought me up into the sixth heaven and there was no one on the left and no throne in the midst, but all had one appearance and their song of praise was the same. And (power) was given to me and I sang praise with them , and that angel also, and our praise was like theirs. 18. And there they all named the primal Father and his Beloved, Christ, and the Holy Spirit, all with one voice, 19. but it was not like the voice of the angels in the fifth heaven, 20. nor like their speech, but another voice resounded there, and there was much light there. 21. And then, when I was in the sixth heaven, I considered that light which I had seen in the five heavens as darkness. 22. And I rejoiced and praised him who has bestowed such light on those who wait for his promise. 23. And I besought the angel who conducted me that he would no more take me back to the world of the flesh. 24. I say to you, Hezekiah and Jasub my son and Micaiah, that there is much darkness here. 25. And the angel who conducted me perceived what I thought and said, "If thou dost rejoice already in this light, how much wilt thou rejoice when, in the seventh heaven, thou seest that light where God and his Beloved are, whence I have been sent, (who in the world will be called 'Son'. 26. Not yet is he revealed who shall be in this corrupted world), and the garments, thrones and crowns which are laid up for the righteous, for those who believe in that Lord who shall descend in your form. For the light there is great and wonderful. 27. As far as thy [wish] not to return to the flesh is concerned, thy days are not yet fulfilled that thou mayest come here." 28. When I heard that, I was sad; but he said, "Do not be sad."

9. 1. And he conveyed me into the air of the seventh heaven and I heard again a voice saying, "How far shall he ascend who dwells among aliens?" And

I was afraid and began to tremble. 2. And when I trembled, behold, there came another voice, sent forth thence, and said, "It is permitted to the holy Isaiah to ascend hither, for his garment is here." 3. And I asked the angel who was with me and said, "Who is he who forbade me, and who is this who has permitted me to ascend?" 4. And he said unto me, "He who forbade thee is he who [is placed] over the praise of the sixth heaven, 5. and he who gave permission is thy Lord, God, the Lord Christ, who will be called Jesus on earth, but his name thou canst not hear till thou hast ascended out of thy body." 6. And he caused me to ascend into the seventh heaven and I saw there a wonderful light and angels without number. 7. And there I saw all the righteous from Adam. 8. And I saw there the holy Abel and all the righteous. 9. And there I saw Enoch and all who were with him, stripped of the garment of the flesh, and I saw them in their higher garments, and they were like the angels who stand there in great glory. 10. But they did not sit on their thrones, nor were their crowns of glory on their heads. 11. And I asked the angel who was with me, "How is it that they have received their garments, but are without their thrones and their crowns?" 12. And he said to me, "Crowns and thrones of glory have they not yet received, [but] only when the Beloved shall descend in the form in which you will see him descend; - 13. that is to say, in the last days the Lord, who will be called Christ, will descend into the world. - Nevertheless, they see the thrones and know to whom they shall belong and to whom the crowns shall belong after he has descended and become like you in appearance, and it will be thought that he is flesh and a man. 14. And the god of that world will stretch forth his hand against the Son, and they will lay hands on him and crucify him on a tree, without knowing who he is. 15. So his descent, as thou wilt see, is hidden from the heavens so that it remains unperceived who he is. 16. And when he has made spoil of the angel of death, he will arise on the third day and will remain in that world 545 days; 17. and then many of the righteous will ascend with him, whose spirits do not receive their garments till the Lord Christ ascends and they ascend with him. 18. Then indeed will they receive (their garments and) thrones and crowns when he shall have ascended into the seventh heaven." 19. And I said unto him, "As I asked thee in the third heaven, 20. show me (*Ethiop*. instead: And he said to me) how what happens in the world becomes known here." 21. And while I was still talking with him, behold, [there came] one of the angels who stood by, more glorious than the glory of that angel who had brought me up from the world, 22. and he showed me books (but not like books of this world) and he opened them and the books were written, but not like books of this world. And he gave them to me and I read them and behold, the deeds of the children of Israel were recorded therein, and the deeds of those whom I know (*Eth*.: thou knowest) not (*missing in Eth.*), my son Jasub. 23. And I said, "Truly there is nothing hidden in the seventh heaven of that which happens in the world."

24. And I saw there many garments stored up, and many thrones and many crowns, 25. and I said to the angel who conducted me, "To whom do these garments and thrones and crowns belong?" 26. And he said to me, "These garments shall many from that world receive, if they believe on the words of that one who, as I have told thee, shall be named, and observe them and believe therein, and believe in his cross. For them are these laid up." 27. And I saw one standing whose glory surpassed that of all, and his glory was great and wonderful. 28. And after I had beheld him, all the righteous whom I had seen and all the angels whom I had seen came unto him, and Adam, Abel and Seth and all the righteous appraoched first, worshipped him and praised him, all with one voice, and I also sang praise with them, and my song of praise was like theirs. 29. Then all the angels drew near and worshipped and sang praise. 30. And [again] I was transformed (*Eth.*: he transformed) and became like an angel. 31. Then the angel who conducted me said to me, "Worship this one"; so I worshipped and praised. 32. And the angel said to me, "This is the Lord of all glory whom thou hast seen." 33. And while he [the angel] was still speaking, I saw another glorious one, like to him, and the righteous drew near to him, worshipped and sang praise, and I too sang praise with them, but my glory was not transformed in accordance with their appearance. 34. And thereupon the angels approached and worshipped. 35. And I saw the Lord and the second angel, and they were standing; but the second one whom I saw was on the left of my Lord. 36. And I asked, "Who is this?", and he said to me, "Worship him, for this is the angel of the holy Spirit, who speaks (*Eth.*: has spoken) through thee and the rest of the righteous." 37. And I beheld the great glory, for the eyes of my spirit were open, and I was not thereafter able to see either the angel who was with me or all the angels whom I had seen worshipping my Lord. 38. But I saw the righteous beholding with great power the glory of that One. 39. So my Lord drew near to me, and the angel of the Spirit, and said, "Behold, now it is granted to thee to behold God, and on thy account is power given to the angel with thee." 40. And I saw how my Lord worshipped, and the angel of the Holy Spirit, and how both together praised God. 41. Thereupon all the righteous drew near and worshipped, 42. and the angels approached and worshipped, and all the angels sang praise.

10. 1. And thereupon I heard the voices and the hymns of praise which I had heard ascending in each of the six heavens (and they were audible) here. 2. And they were all directed to the glorious One whose glory I could not see. 3. And I myself heard and saw the praise for him. 4. And the Lord and the angel of the spirit beheld all and heard all; 5. and all the praises which were sent forth from the six heavens were not only heard but were also visible. 6. And I heard the angel who led me, how he said, "This is the Most High of the High ones, who dwells in the holy world and rests with the holy ones, who will be called by the holy Spirit, through the mouth of the righteous, the Father of the Lord." 7. And

I heard the words of the Most High, the Father of my Lord, as he spoke to my Lord Christ who shall be called Jesus: 8. "Go and descend through all the heavens; descend to the firmament and to that world, even to the angel in the realm of the dead; but to Hell thou shalt not go. 9. And thou shalt become like to the form of all who are in the five heavens; 10. and with carefulness thou shalt resemble the form of the angels of the firmament and the angels also who are in the realm of the dead. 11. And none of the angels of this world will know that thou, along with me, art the Lord of the seven heavens and of their angels. 12. And they will not know that thou art mine till with the voice of heaven I have summoned their angels and their lights, and the mighty voice be made to resound to the sixth heaven, that thou mayest judge and destroy the prince and his angels and the gods of this world and the world which is ruled by them, 13. for they have denied me and said 'We alone are, and there is none beside us.' 14. And afterwards thou wilt ascend from the angels of death to thy place, and thou wilt not be transformed in each heaven, but in glory thou wilt ascend and sit on my right hand. 15. And the princes and powers of this world will worship thee." 16. Thus I heard the great glory give command to my Lord. 17. Then I saw that my Lord went forth from the seventh heaven to the sixth heaven. 18. And the angel who conducted me (from this world was with me and) said, "Attend, Isaiah, and behold, that thou mayest see the transformation of the Lord and his descent." 19. And I beheld and when the angels who are in the sixth heaven saw him they praised and extolled him, for he had not yet been transformed into the form of the angels there, and they praised him, and I also praised with them. 20. And I saw how he descended into the fifth heaven, and in the fifth heaven took the appearance of the angels there, and they did not praise him, for his appearance was like theirs. 21. And immediately he descended into the fourth heaven and took the form of the angels there; 22. and when they saw him, they did not praise and laud him, for his appearance was as theirs. 23. And again I beheld how he descended into the third heaven and took the form of the angels of the third heaven. 24. And the guardians of the gate of this heaven demanded the pass-word and the Lord gave it to them in order that he should not be recognised, and when they saw him they did not praise and extol him, for his appearance was as theirs. 25. And again I beheld how he descended into the second heaven, and again he gave the pass-word there, for the door-keepers demanded it and the Lord gave it. 26. And I saw how he took the form of the angels in the second heaven; they saw him but did not praise him, since his form was like theirs. 27. And again I beheld how he descended into the first heaven and also gave the pass-word to the door-keepers there, and took the form of the angels who are on the left of that throne; and they did not praise or laud him, for his appearance was as theirs. 28. But no one asked me, on account of the angel who conducted me. 29. And again he descended into the firmament where the prince of this world dwells, and he gave the pass-word to those on the left, and his form was like theirs, and they did not praise him there, but struggled with one another in envy, for there the power of evil rules, and envying about trifles. 30. And I beheld, how he descended and became like the angels of the air and was like one of them. 31. And he gave no pass-word for they were plundering and doing violence to one another.

11. 1. And after this, I beheld, and the angel who talked with me and conducted me said to me, "Attend, Isaiah, son of Amoz, because for this purpose have I been sent from God." 2. And I saw of the family of David the prophet a *woman named Mary*, who was a *virgin, and betrothed to a man called Joseph*,[15] a carpenter, and he also was of the seed and family of the righteous David, of Bethlehem in Judah. 3. And he came to his portion. And *when she was betrothed, it was found that she was with child*, and *Joseph*, the carpenter, *wished to put her away*. 4. But the *angel* of the Spirit *appeared* in this world, and after that Joseph did not put Mary away, but kept her; but he did not reveal the matter to anyone.[16] 5. And he did not approach Mary, but kept her as a holy virgin, although she was with child. 6. And he did not [yet] live with her for two months. 7. And after two months, when Joseph was in his house, and his wife Mary, but both alone, 8. it came to pass, while they were alone, that Mary straightway beheld with her eyes and saw a small child, and she was amazed. 9. And when her amazement wore off, her womb was found as it was before she was with child. 10. And when her husband Joseph said to her, "What made thee amazed?" his eyes were opened and he saw the child and praised God, that the Lord had come to his portion. 11. And a voice came to them: "Tell this vision to no one." 12. And the report was noised abroad in Bethlehem. 13. Some said, "The virgin Mary has given birth before she was married two months", 14. and many said, "She has not given birth: the midwife has not gone up [to her] and we have heard no cries of pain." And they were all in the dark concerning him, and they all knew of him, but no one knew whence he was. 15. And they took him and came *to Nazareth* in *Galilee*.[17] 16. And I saw, O Hezekiah and Jasub my son, and declare before the other prophets who stand [here] that this was hidden from all the heavens and all the princes and every god of this world. 17. And I saw: in Nazareth he sucked the breast like a baby, as was customary, so that he would not be recognised. 18. And when he grew up he performed great signs and wonders in the land of Israel and in Jerusalem. 19. And after this the adversary envied him and roused the children of Israel against him, not knowing who he was, and they delivered him to the king and crucified him, and he descended to the angel [of the underworld]. 20. In Jerusalem indeed I saw how he was crucified on the tree, 21. and how he was raised after three days and remained [still many] days. 22. And the angel who conducted me said to me, "Attend, Isaiah." And I saw how he sent out his twelve apostles and ascended. 23. And I saw him and he was in the firmament, but he had not

changed to their form, and all the angels of the firmament and the Satan saw him, and they worshipped him. 24. And great sorrow was occasioned there, while they said, "How did our Lord descend in our midst and we perceived not the glory (which was upon him) which, as we see, was found on him from the sixth heaven?" 25. And he ascended into the second heaven and was not changed, but all the angels on the right and on the left and the throne in the midst 26. worshipped him and praised him saying "How did our Lord remain hidden from us when he descended, and we perceived not?" 27. And in like manner he ascended to the third heaven and they sang praise and spoke in the same way. 28. And in the fourth and the fifth heavens they spoke exactly in the same manner; 29. there was rather one song of praise and [even] after that he was not changed. 30. And I saw how he ascended to the sixth heaven, and they worshipped him and praised him, 31. but in all the heavens the song of praise increased. 32. And I saw how he ascended into the seventh heaven, and all the righteous and all the angels praised him. And then I saw how he sat down on the right hand of that great glory, whose glory, as I told you, I was not able to behold. 33. And also I saw the angel of the holy Spirit sitting on the left. 34. And this angel said to me, "Isaiah, son of Amoz, it is enough for thee, for these are great things; for thou hast seen what none born of flesh has yet seen,[18] 35. and thou wilt return into thy garment till thy days are fulfilled: then thou wilt come hither." This have I seen.' 36. And Isaiah told it to all who stood before him, and they sang praise. And he spoke to king Hezekiah and said, 'Such things have I spoken, 37. and the end of this world 38. and all this vision will be consummated in the last generation.' 39. And Isaiah made him swear that he would not tell this to the people of Israel, nor permit any man to write down the words. 40. (So far as ye understand from the king what is said in the prophets), so far shall ye read. And ye shall be in the holy Spirit so that ye may receive your garments and the thrones and crowns of glory which are preserved in the seventh heaven.

41. On account of these visions and prophecies Sammael Satan sawed asunder the prophet Isaiah the son of Amoz, by the hand of Manasseh. 42. And all these things Hezekiah delivered to Manasseh in the twenty-sixth year. 43. But Manasseh did not remember them nor take them to heart, but after becoming the servant of Satan, he went to ruin.

Here endeth the vision of the prophet Isaiah with his ascension.

Notes

1. The Ascension of Isaiah

1. Is. 7:3.
2. 2 Kings 21:17; 2 Chron. 33:18.
3. Arguments for this translation in André Caquot, *Semitica* 23, 1973, 80. Cf. 1 Kings 22:25-

28, 52-54; 2 Kings 1:1-18.
4. Cf. 2 Chron. 33:11.
5. Ex. 33:20; Is. 6:5.
6. Is. 1:10.
7. Cf. 1 Cor. 1:7.
8. Cf. 2 Thess. 1:7ff.
9. Cf. Is. 24:23.
10. Cf. Lk. 12:37.
11. Cf. Is. 13:1 (LXX).
12. Is. 52:13 (LXX).
13. Arguments for the translation in André Caquot, *Semitica* 23, 1973, 89f.
14. Cf. Is. 57:15 acc. to LXX.
15. Lk. 1:27.
16. Mt. 1:18-20.
17. Mt. 2:23; Lk. 2:39.
18. Latin addition: *a saeculo non audierunt neque auribus perceperunt* (cf. 1 Cor. 2:9) = Jerome, *In Isaiam* XVII 64 (Migne, PL XXIV cols. 622-623). - Cf. also M. Delcor, *Revue de l'histoire des religions* 185, 1974, 169f.

2. Apocalypse of Peter

C. Detlef G. Müller

Introduction

1. Literature: *Editions and Translations: a) Greek text from Akhmim*: U. Bouriant, 'Fragments du texte grec du livre d'Énoch et de quelques écrits attribués à saint Pierre' (*Mémoires publiées par les membres de la Mission Archéologique Française au Caire*, vol. IX), Paris 1892 (*editio princeps*); A. Lods, photogravures of the manuscript (in same volume, fasc. 3) 1893; O. von Gebhart, *Das Evangelium und die Apokalypse des Petrus*, 1893; E. Preuschen, *Antilegomena*, [2]1905, 84-88 (with patristic citations) and 188-192 (German trans.).

Greek fragment in the Bodleian Library in Oxford: M.R. James, JTS 12, 1911, 367-369.

Greek fragment in the Erzherzog Rainer Papyrus Collection in Vienna: M.R. James, JTS 32, 1931, 270-279.

b) *Ethiopic text*: S. Grébaut, 'Littérature éthiopienne ps.clémentine. La second venue du Christ et la résurrection des morts', ROC 1907, 139-151; 1910, 198-214; 307-323; 425-439 (with French trans.); H. Duensing, 'Ein Stücke der urchristlichen Petrusapokalypse enthaltender Traktat der äthiopischen pseudoclementinischen Literatur', ZNW 14, 1913, 65-78 (German trans. with philological notes).

Translations: NTApo[2] 314-327 (H. Weinel); NTApo[3] 468-483 (Ch. Maurer and H. Duensing; ET 663-683); James, 505-524; Michaelis, 469-481; Erbetta III, 209-233; Moraldi II, 1803-1848.

Studies: On the basis of the Akhmim text: A. Harnack, *Bruchstücke des Evangeliums und der Apokalypse des Petrus* (TU 9), 1893; id. *Die Petrusapokalypse in der abendländischen Kirche* (TU 13), 1895; A. Dieterich, *Nekyia*, 1893 ([2]1913); F. Spitta, 'Die Petrusapokalypse und der zweite Petrusbrief', ZNW 12, 1911, 237-242; Th. Zahn, *Grundriß der Geschichte des ntl. Kanons* [2]1904, 24.

Since the appearance of the Ethiopic text: M.R. James, 'A New Text of the Apocalypse of Peter', JTS 12, 1911, 36-54; 362-383; 573-583; id. 'The Rediscovery of the Apocalypse of Peter', *The Church Quarterly Review*, April 1915, 1-37; O. Bardenhewer, *Geschichte der altkirchlichen Literatur* I, [2]1913, 610-615; K. Prümm, 'De genuino apocalypsis Petri textu, examen testium iam notorum et novi fragmenti Raineriani', *Biblica* 10, 1929, 62-80; J.R. Harris, 'The Odes of Solomon and the Apocalypse of Peter', *Expository Times* 42, 1930, 21f.; C.M. Edsman, *Le baptême de feu* (Acta Seminarii Neotest. Upsal. 9), 1940, 53-63; G. Quispel/R.M. Grant, 'Note on the Petrine Apocrypha', *VigChr* 6, 1952, 31f.; K. Berger, 'Unfehlbare Offenbarung. Petrus in der gnostischen und apokalyptischen Offenbarungsliteratur', *Kontinuität und Einheit, FS F. Mußner*, 1981, 261-326 (Lit.).

( ) = explanatory additions by the translator
[ ] = words to be deleted in the text
< > = restoration of the text

2. Textual tradition: during the excavations instigated by S. Grébaut in the winter of 1886/87 in cemetery A at al-Hawāwīs in the desert necropolis of Akhmim (K.P. Kuhlmann, *Materialien zur Archäologie und Geschichte des Raumes von Achmim*, 1983, 53 and 62), parchment leaves of the Greek version of the Revelation of Peter were discovered in the grave of a Christian monk. In addition to this fragment of text, some further unpaginated leaves were found with parts of the Book of Enoch and the Gospel of Peter (see vol. 1, pp. 216ff.). The three texts, which are today in Cairo, are all from the same hand and were written in the 8th or 9th century. U. Bouriant gave to the Greek pages of the Apocalypse of Peter the pagination 13 to 19. The text of the Apocalypse, which occupies not quite half of the original book, was divided by Harnack into 34 verses. The identification of the text results from a quotation of the Apocalypse of Peter adduced by Clement of Alexandria in the *Eclogae propheticae* (41.2), which agrees with v. 26.

The Ethiopic translation has been known since 1910. A. Dillmann (NGWG 1858) and P. de Lagarde (*Mitteilungen* IV, 1891) had already referred to the extensive Ethiopic translation of the Corpus Clementinum, which may go back to the 7th-8th century. E. Bratke sought for possible Arabic precursors of the Ethiopic Apocalypse of Peter, but was unsuccessful in his search (see 'Handschriftliche Überlieferung und Bruchstücke der arabisch-äthiopischen Petrusapokalypse', ZwTh 36, 1893, 454-493). S. Grébaut finally published Pseudo-Clementine literature from MS No 51 of the Abbadie collection, and added a French translation (*Revue de l'Orient chrétien*, 1907/10). It was however M.R. James who in a fundamental study first succeeded in classifying the text correctly (JTS 12, 1911, 36-54; 362-383; 573-583). A German translation with detailed philological commentary was published by H. Duensing (ZNW 14, 1913, 65-78). Depending on Grébaut's section divisions, H. Weinel divided the text into 17 chapters (NTApo^{2} 318-327).

There are also two other small Greek fragments. One contains verses 33f., comes from the 5th century, and was bought in Egypt in 1894/95. It is today in the Bodleian Library in Oxford. The other fragment belongs to the Erzherzog Rainer papyrus collection in Vienna and contains the 14th chapter. Wessely ascribed it to the 3rd/4th century. James however recognised that these two fragments derive from one and the same manuscript (see 'The Rainer Fragment of the Apocalypse of Peter', JTS 32, 1931, 270-279, esp. 278).

For the identification of the Apocalypse of Peter and the assessment of its significance and influence, the citations in the Church Fathers are particularly important. Theophilus of Antioch about 180 alludes to v. 15 of the Akhmim fragment (*ad Autolycum* II 19); Clement of Alexandria († before 215) twice quotes chapters 4 and 5; Methodius of Olympus († about 311) once quotes chapter 8, Macarius Magnes (about 400) chapters 4 and 5 once each. Reference is made to these citations at the appropriate points in the notes to the translation.

From this Apocalypse of Peter we must distinguish the Ethiopic Apocalypse of Peter II (cf. on this Bratke, see above), the Arabic Apocalypse of Peter I (cf. Bratke again), the Arabic Apocalypse of Peter II (cf. A. Mingana, *The Apocalypse of Peter*, Woodbrooke Studies 3.2, Cambridge 1931, 93-152, 209-282, 349-407; reviewed by M.R. James in JTS 33, 1932, 311ff.) and also the Coptic Apocalypse of Peter (cf. Werner, pp. 700ff. below). K. Berger offers a general survey ('Unfehlbare Offenbarung' 261-326). In Berger's list the Apocalypses of Peter bear the numbers 42-47.

3. Period of origin and circulation: we do not know the original text of the Apocalypse of Peter. The translation below makes it clear that the Greek and Ethiopic texts frequently diverge from one another. The Ethiopic version contains a series of linguistic obscurities which are evidently to be traced back to lacunae and defects in the transmission of the text. In this respect it deserves attention that Clement of Alexandria regards the Apocalypse of Peter as Holy Scripture (cf. Euseb. *HE* VI 14.1), which is proof of an origin at least in the first half of the 2nd century. The *terminus a quo* can be more precisely determined through the time of origin of 4 Esd. (about 100 A.D.), which was probably used in the Apocalypse of Peter (cf. 4 Esd 5.33 with c. 3), and 2 Peter, the priority of which was demonstrated by F. Spitta. We thus come, with H. Weinel, to approximately the year 135 as the probable time of origin, if in interpreting the parable of the fig-tree in c. 2 we also relate the Jewish Antichrist who persecutes the Christians to Bar Cochba.

The Apocalypse presumably came into being in Egypt (cf. Clement of Alexandria); the reference to the Egyptian worship of animals also points in this direction, in so far as this passage belongs to the original content. In this connection however we must refer above all to the ancient Egyptian Peter tradition (cf. esp. Berger, 275). Starting from a first rendering into Coptic, the Ethiopic translation probably came into being - as usual - through the medium of Arabic versions. To this extent our Ethiopic text, linguistically not altogether unexceptionable, is only the last in a series, with all the imponderables that entails.

Except in broad-minded Ethiopia, the Apocalypse of Peter was later evidently suppressed almost everywhere so far as the Church was concerned. The numerous references and citations in any case show that this apocryphal book once enjoyed considerable esteem both in East and West, which is connected with the significance of the apostle Peter. Methodius of Olympus still reckons the Apocalypse of Peter among the inspired writings. The Stichometry of Nicephorus counts it among the Antilegomena. Macarius Magnes and Eusebius (*HE* III 3.25) however relegate it to the spurious writings. In the West the Muratorian Canon knows it as a text the canonicity of which is debated. A Latin sermon ascribed to the 4th century (edited by Dom Wilmart) quotes the Apocalypse of Peter for its interpretation of the parable of the ten virgins (cf. James, JTS 12, 1911, 383; further Western witnesses in Harnack, *Die Petrusapokalypse in der alten abendländischen Kirche*, 71ff.).

4. The problem of the original Text: only the Ethiopic version offers a complete text, although certainly not one free from error. The Greek version is so fragmentary that its original dimensions can no longer be deduced with any certainty. Also in the parallel passages the considerable differences in the portrayal of heaven and hell catch the eye. In the description of the torments of hell the statements essentially agree in substance, but there are differences in the diction and the Greek text is in part incomplete (cf. c. 8 and then from c. 11, where the Greek text is completely lacking). In the description of paradise on the other hand we come upon far-reaching differences of content. The Ethiopic version strictly mentions the place of the elect only in c. 14. Then follows in cc. 15 and 16 a broad description of the transfiguration of Jesus, where the figures of Moses, Elijah and other OT saints also appear. Jesus declares that his disciples will attain to the same honour and glory. The Greek version offers no parallel to the transfiguration story in the Ethiopic version (c. 14), but makes it into a real description of paradise. The disciples expressly ask for a glimpse of the world of the departed saints, and the text then depicts it in detail. Here the form of the presentation is the same in both texts. Peter reports in the past tense on the vision of the world of the righteous which Jesus imparted on the holy mountain. The Greek places the portrayal of hell also in this context, whereas the Ethiopic tradition presents it as a prediction of the future by Jesus. In addition the *altered sequence* of the descriptions should be noted. While the Ethiopic tradition places the description of hell in the context of Christ's prophecy about his return, the resurrection of the dead and the last judgment and only then brings in the transfiguration story, the Greek version does exactly the opposite.

On reading the two versions, one can easily establish their close relationship, but in the parallel accounts we cannot observe any real identity between the two texts. Taking up and developing the suggestions of Dieterich and Zahn, James already comes to the conclusion that the Ethiopic version must present tolerably well the original version of the Apocalypse of Peter, but the Greek in contrast belongs to the Gospel of Peter. James and Zahn agree that the original Apocalypse of Peter did not develop from the Gospel of Peter, as Dieterich suggested, but conversely was worked into it. The Greek text from Akhmim is to be understood as a recasting of the original apocalypse into a kind of apocalyptic address by Jesus in the manner of Mk. 13. Despite several difficulties, Weinel pleads for a later dating of the Ethiopic version and for the priority of the Greek tradition. According to him the paradise story is actually a further development of the older Greek text from Akhmim. However, so long as we do not have further evidence in Coptic, Arabic or Ethiopic literature at our disposal we can hardly attain to any final solution of this problem. Thus Berger under numbers 42 to 47 in his list of the Petrine revelation literature has adduced separately not only the two Ethiopic (42/43) and Arabic fragments (45/46) and the Coptic gnostic text (47) but also the Greek tradition (44), and has refrained from any decision as to the relation of the texts and fragments to one another.

It is however possible to find some firm conclusions: 1. The Ethiopic version must approximately correspond to the original length of the Apocalypse of Peter, since it goes only a little beyond the figures given by the Stichometry of Niçephorus (300 lines) and the Codex Claromontanus (270 lines). 2. All the old citations are to be found in the Ethiopic version, distributed over chapters 4, 5, 8, 10, 12 and 14. This speaks for the view that, apart from linguistic errors and minor alterations, we have here the original text of the apocalypse. 3. The papyrus fragment in the Rainer collection shows that the original text has suffered considerably on its way from Greek through Coptic and Arabic to Ethiopic, so that we must reckon with numerous translation and scribal errors. That the Ethiopic translation could be very old, and made directly from the Greek, remains a possibility. The extant manuscript material does not allow any conclusive statement on this point. 4. The description of hell in the Ethiopic version is supported by evidence from three quarters, and shown to be original. Moreover the Clement citation and the Bodleian fragment attest its 'prediction' form. Chapter 8b is guaranteed by Clement and Methodius as part of the original Apocalypse of Peter.

Problems remain however with regard to the content of the transfiguration and paradise stories and the sequence of the accounts of heaven and hell. Ch. Maurer (NTApo[3] 470 [ET 666]) understood the Greek fragment from Akhmim as a reworking by someone who knew only chapters 7-10 and 15-16a of the Apocalypse of Peter. From the 'I' form in chapters 15 and 16a he was able to recognise that it belonged to the Apocalypse of Peter. Since he did not have 16b, he could not observe that the transfiguration story fitted in at this point, and that this again in chap. 17 changed into the account of a heavenly journey. He therefore had to assume that he had before him the clear counterpart of the other fragment, namely the actual description of paradise. This new picture he rounded off by means of some material additions: the disciples' request to see the departed brethren and their world; the extended description of the place of light and its inhabitants; the transformation of the OT 'fathers' into NT 'high priests (brothers?)'. He conceived the first words of chap. 15 as the introduction to the whole, and from this the change in the sequence results. We have however a secondary witness for the original sequence in Orac. Sibyl. II 238-338 (3rd cent.; see below, p. 660-663), where the Apocalypse of Peter is used. On this view the parallel passages in the Akhmim text, vv. 17f and 21 (angels of light or of punishment; bright or obscure air; the pregnant designation of heaven or hell as the 'place', which occurs only here), belong to the transition effected by the redactor, as do vv. 1-3, which are taken from 2 Pet. 2:1ff.

Dieterich, Zahn and James regarded the Akhmim fragments as parts of the Gospel of Peter, since the texts were all found together in the same grave and in addition proved to be linguistically related to one another. This conjecture is supported by the observation that the two most important parallels occur precisely in the secondary redactional work: the absolute title 'the Lord' appears often in the Gospel of Peter (v. 2, 3, 6 etc.), whereas in v. 4, 6, 12, 15 and 20 of the Akhmim text it is peculiar to the Greek over against the Ethiopic tradition, which never employs this expression. Also 'We, the twelve disciples' occurs in the Gospel of Peter (v. 59) and in the Greek version of the Apocalypse (v. 5), whereas the Ethiopic does not know this phrase. Maurer however objects against this view that the ancient witnesses always speak of the Gospel and the Apocalypse of Peter as two different writings. He therefore assumes, not that the author of the Gospel assimilated the Apocalypse (Zahn, James), but that only later someone who had the two texts before him adapted the Apocalypse to the Gospel. Maurer even goes so far as to suggest that this redactor was the copyist in the 8th/9th century.

This ingenious hypothesis, based on accurate observation of the text, cannot be verified without further textual discoveries. That the Ethiopic version is authentic and offers the original text of the Apocalypse of Peter, albeit in parts somewhat distorted, can scarcely be contested any longer today. The Akhmim fragments are either actually such revised extracts or at least the remains of a rich Petrine revelation literature, which had an independent circulation and naturally show some parallels in content.

4. The significance of the Apocalypse of Peter as an important witness of the Petrine literature is not to be underestimated. Peter is the decisive witness of the resurrection event. Hence he is also deemed worthy of further revelations, which he hands on (in revelation documents) with authority. *Revelatio* and *traditio*, *receiving* and *handing on*, the chain of transmitters, are the central ideas of this understanding of revelation (Berger). Peter's disciple Clement (2 Clem. 5) plays the decisive role here, as witnessed by the Ethiopic version of the Apocalypse, which belongs in the framework of the Clement literature in which Peter hands on the secret revelation to Clement (on Peter as a recipient of revelation cf. Berger, 379ff.). As compared with the Canon, the eschatological functions of Peter are new (Berger, 325). In its description of heaven and hell the Apocalypse draws on the abundance of ideas from the East which has also left its deposit in the writings of late Jewish Apocalyptic and the mystery religions. The motif of the river of fire, which is one of the pregnant eschatological ideas among Egyptian Christians, certainly goes back to ancient Egypt. In view of the abundance of traditions in Egypt and the prestige of the Petrine tradition there (veneration of Peter's disciple Mark), an origin in Egypt is probable. The Apocalypse of Peter brings together divergent traditions, for which it has not yet been possible to discover any uniform source.

The Apocalypse of Peter

Ethiopic Text[1]

1. *And when he was seated on the Mount of Olives*, his own *came unto him*,[2] and we entreated and implored him severally[3] and besought him, saying unto him, 'Make known unto us what are *the signs of thy Parousia and of the end of the world*,[4] that we may perceive and mark the time of thy Parousia and instruct those who come after us, to whom we preach the word of thy Gospel and whom we install in thy Church, in order that they, when they hear it, may take heed to themselves that they mark the time of thy coming.' And our Lord answered and said unto us, '*Take heed that men deceive you not*[5] and that ye do not become doubters and serve other gods. *Many will come in my name saying "I am Christ."*[6] *Believe them not and draw not near unto them.*[7] For *the coming of the Son of God will not be manifest, but like the lightning which shineth from the east to the west*,[8] so shall I *come*

on the clouds of heaven with a great host in my *glory*;[9] with my cross going before my face[10] will I come in my glory, shining seven times as bright as the sun will I *come in my glory, with* all *my saints, my angels*,[11] when my Father will place a crown upon my head, that I may *judge the living and the dead*[12] and *recompense every man according to his work.*[13]

2. And ye, *receive ye the parable of the fig-tree* thereon: as soon as *its shoots* have gone forth and *its boughs* have *sprouted*, the end of the world will come.'[14] And I, Peter, answered and said unto him, 'Explain to me concerning the fig-tree, and how we shall perceive it, for throughout all its days does the fig-tree sprout and every year it brings forth its fruit [and] for its master. What (then) meaneth the parable of the fig-tree? We know it not.' - And the Master answered and said unto me, 'Dost thou not understand that the fig-tree is the house of Israel? Even as a man *hath planted a fig-tree in his garden* and it brought forth no fruit, and he *sought its fruit for* many *years*. When he *found it not, he said to the keeper of his garden*, "*Uproot the fig-tree* that *our land may* not be *unfruitful for us*." And the gardener *said* to God, "We thy servants (?) wish to clear it (of weeds) and to *dig*[15] the ground around it and to water it. *If it does not then bear fruit*, we will immediately *remove* its roots from the garden and plant another one in its place." Hast thou not grasped that the fig-tree is the house of Israel? Verily, I say to you, when its boughs have sprouted at the end, then *shall deceiving Christs come*,[16] and awaken hope (with the words): "*I am the Christ*,[17] who am (now) come into the world." And when they shall see the wickedness of *his* (the false Messiah's) deeds, they shall turn away after them and deny him to whom our fathers gave praise (?), who crucified the first Christ and thereby sinned exceedingly. But this deceiver is not the Christ. And when they reject him, he will kill with the sword (dagger) and there shall be many martyrs. Then shall the boughs of the fig-tree, i.e. the house of Israel, sprout, and there shall be many martyrs by his hand: they shall be killed and become martyrs. Enoch and Elias will be sent to instruct them that *this is the deceiver who must come into the world*[18] *and do signs and wonders in order to deceive.*[19] And therefore shall they that are slain by his hand be martyrs and shall be reckoned among the good and righteous martyrs who have pleased God in their life.'

3. And he showed me in his right hand the souls of all (men) and on the palm of his right hand the image of that which shall be fulfilled at the last day; and how the righteous and the sinners shall be separated and how those will do (?) who are upright in heart, and how the evil-doers will be rooted out for all eternity. We saw how the sinners wept in great distress and sorrow, until all who saw it with their eyes wept, whether righteous, or angels or himself also. And I asked him and said, 'Lord, allow me to speak thy word concerning these sinners: "*It were better for them that they had not been created.*"' And the Saviour answered and said 'O Peter, why speakest thou thus, "*that not to have*

been created were better for them"?[20] Thou resistest God. Thou wouldest not have more compassion than he for his image, for he has created them and has brought them forth when they were not (*probably an error for*: and has brought them forth from not-being into being). And since thou hast seen the lamentation which sinners shall encounter in the last days, therefore thy heart is saddened; but I will show thee their works in which they have sinned against the Most High.

4. Behold now what they shall experience in the last days, when the day of God comes. On the day of the decision of the judgment of God, all the children of men from the east unto the west shall be gathered before my Father who ever liveth, and he will command *hell* to open its bars of steel and to *give up* all *that is in it*.[21] And the beasts and the fowls shall he command to give back all flesh that they have devoured, since he desires that men should appear (again); for nothing perishes for God, and nothing is impossible with him, since all things are his. For all things (come to pass) on the day of decision, on the day of judgment, at the word of God, and as all things came to pass when he created the world and commanded all that is therein, and it was all done[22] - so shall it be in the last days; for everything is possible with God and he says in the Scripture: "*Son of man, prophesy upon the several bones*, and say to the bones - *bone unto bone* in joints, *sinews, nerves, flesh* and *skin* and hair thereon." And *soul* and *spirit*[23] shall the great Uriel[24] give at the command of God. For him God has appointed over the resurrection of the dead on the day of judgment. Behold and consider the corns of wheat which are sown in the earth.[25] As something dry and without a soul does a man sow (them) in the earth; and they live again, bear fruit, and the earth gives (them) back again as a pledge entrusted to it. And this which dies, which is sown as seed in the earth and shall become alive and be restored to life, is man. How much more shall God raise up on the day of decision those who believe in him and are chosen by him and for whom he made (the earth); and all this shall the earth give back on the day of decision, since it shall also be judged with them, and the heaven with it.[26]

5. And these things shall come to pass in the day of judgment of those who have fallen away from faith in God and have committed sin: cataracts of fire shall be let loose; and obscurity and darkness shall come up and cover and veil the entire world, and the waters shall be changed and transformed into coals of fire, and all that is in it (the earth?) shall burn and the sea shall become fire; under the heaven there shall be a fierce fire that shall not be put out and it flows for the judgment of wrath. And the stars shall be melted by flames of fire,[27] as if they had not been created, and the fastnesses of heaven shall pass away for want of water and become as though they had not been created. And the lightnings of heaven shall be no (?) more and, by their enchantment, they shall alarm the world (*perhaps*: the heaven will turn to lightning and the lightnings will alarm the world). And the spirits of the dead bodies shall be like to them

and at the command of God will become fire. And as soon as the whole creation is dissolved, the men who are in the east shall flee to the west <and those in the west> to the east; those that are in the south shall flee to the north and those in the <north to the> south, and everywhere will the wrath of the fearful fire overtake them; and an unquenchable flame shall drive them and bring them to the judgment of wrath in the stream of unquenchable fire[28] which flows, flaming with fire, and when its waves separate one from another, seething, there shall be much *gnashing of teeth*[29] among the children of men.

6. And all *will see how I come upon an* eternal shining *cloud, and the angels* of God who *will sit with me on the throne of my glory at the right hand of my heavenly Father*. He will set a crown upon my head. As soon as *the nations* see it, they *will weep*,[30] each nation for itself. And he shall command them to go into the *river of fire*,[31] while the deeds of each individual one of them stand before them. *<Recompense shall be given> to each according to his work*.[32] As for the elect who have done good, they will come to me and will not see (?) death by devouring fire. But the evil creatures, the sinners and the hypocrites will stand in the depths of the darkness that passes not away, and their punishment is the fire, and angels bring forward their sins and prepare for them a place wherein they shall be punished for ever, each according to his offence. The angel of God, Uriel,[33] brings the souls of those sinners who perished in the flood, and of all who dwell in all idols, in every molten image, in every love and in paintings, and of them that dwell on all hills and in stones and by the wayside, (whom) men call gods: they shall be burned with them (i.e. the objects in which they lodge) in eternal fire. After all of them, with their dwelling places, have been destroyed, they will be punished eternally.

Ethiopic	*Akhmim*
	21. But I saw also another place, opposite that one, very gloomy; and this was the place of punishment, and those who were punished there and the angels who punished had dark raiment, clothed according to the air of the place.
7. Then will men and women come to the place prepared for them. By their tongues with which they have blasphemed the way of righteousness will they be hung up. There is spread out for them unquenchable fire. . . .	22. And some there were there hanging by their tongues: these were those who had blasphemed the way of righteousness; and under them was laid fire, blazing and tormenting them.
And behold again another place:	23. And there was a great lake full

this is a great pit filled, in which are those who have denied righteousness; and angels of punishment visit (them) and here do they kindle upon them the fire of their punishment. And again two women: they are hung up by their neck and by their hair and are cast into the pit. These are they who plaited their hair,[34] not to create beauty, but to turn to fornication, and that they might ensnare the souls of men to destruction. And the men who lay with them in fornication are hung by their thighs in that burning place, and they say to one another, 'We did not know that we would come into everlasting torture.'

And the murderers and those who have made common cause with them are cast into the fire, in a place full of venomous beasts, and they are tormented without rest, as they feel their pains, and their worms are as numerous as a dark cloud. And the angel Ezrael will bring forth the souls of them that have been killed and they shall see the torment <of those who> killed <them> and shall say to one another, '*Righteousness and justice is the judgment of God.*[35] For we have indeed heard, but did not believe that we would come to this place of eternal judgment.'

8. And near this flame there is a great and very deep pit and into it there flow all kinds of things from everywhere: judgment (?), horrifying things and excretions. And the women (are) swallowed up (by this) up to their necks and are punished with great pain. These are they who have procured abortions and have ruined

of burning mire in which were fixed certain men who had turned away from righteousness, and tormenting angels were placed over them.

24. And there were also others there: women hanging by their hair over that boiling mire. These were they who had adorned themselves for adultery. But those (men) who had united with them for the adulterous defilement <were hanging> by their feet <and> had their heads in the mire, and with <loud voice> cried out, 'We did not believe that we would come to this place.'

25. And I saw the murderers and their accessaries cast into a gorge full of venomous reptiles and tormented by those beasts, and thus writhing in that torture, and worms oppressed them like dark clouds. But the souls of those who had been murdered stood and watched the punishment of those murderers and said, '*O God, righteous is thy judgment.*'[35]

26. And near that place I saw another gorge in which the discharge and the excrement of the tortured ran down and became like a lake. And there sat women, and the discharge came up to their throats; and opposite them sat many children, who were born prematurely, weeping. And from them went forth rays of fire and smote the women on the

the work of God which he has created. Opposite them is another place where the children sit, but both alive, and they cry to God. And lightnings go forth from those children which pierce the eyes of those who, by fornication, have brought about their destruction.[36] Other men and women stand above them naked. And their children stand opposite to them in a place of delight. And they sigh and cry to God because of their parents, 'These are they who neglected and cursed and transgressed thy commandment. They killed us and cursed the angel who created (us) and hung us up. And they withheld from us the light which thou hast appointed for all.' And the milk of the mothers flows from their breasts and congeals and smells foul, and from it come forth beasts that devour flesh, which turn and torture them for ever with their husbands, because they forsook the commandment of God and killed their children. And the children shall be given to the angel Temlakos.[37] And those who slew them will be tortured for ever, for God wills it to be so.

9. Ezrael, the angel of wrath, brings men and women with the half of their bodies burning and casts them into a place of darkness, the hell of men; and a spirit of wrath chastises them with all manner of chastisement, and a worm that never sleeps consumes their entrails. These are the persecutors and betrayers of my righteous ones.

And near to those who live thus were other men and women who chew their tongues, and they are tormented with red hot irons and have their eyes

eyes.[36] And these were those who conceived children outside marriage and who procured abortions.

27. And other <men> and women stood in flames up to the middle of their bodies and were cast into a dark place and were scourged by evil spirits and had their entrails consumed by worms which never wearied. These were those who persecuted the righteous and handed them over.

28. And near to them again were men and women who bit through their lips and were in torment, with heated iron in their eyes. These were

burned. These are the slanderers and those who doubt my righteousness.

Other men and women - whose deeds (were done) in deception - have their lips cut off and fire enters into their mouths and into their entrails. <These are those> who slew the martyrs by their lying.

In another place situated near them, on the stone a pillar of fire (?), and the pillar is sharper than swords - men and women who are clad in rags and filthy garments, and they are cast upon it, to suffer the judgment of unceasing torture. These are they which trusted in their riches and despised widows and the woman (with) orphans . . . in the sight of God.

10. And into another place near by, saturated with filth, they throw men and women up to their knees. These are they who lent money and took usury.

And other men and women thrust themselves down from a high place and return again and run, and demons drive them. These are the worshippers of idols, and they drive them to the end of their wits (the slope?) and they plunge down from there. And this they do continually and are tormented for ever. These are they who have cut their flesh as apostles of a man, and the women who were with them . . . and thus are the men who defiled themselves with one another in the fashion of women.

And beside them . . . *(an untranslatable word)*, and beneath them the angel Ezrael prepares a place of much fire, and all the golden and silver idols, all idols, the works of

those who blasphemed the way of righteousness and slandered it.

29. And opposite these were still other men and women who bit through their tongues and had flaming fire in their mouths. These were the false witnesses.

30. And in another place were glowing pebbles, sharper than swords or any spit, and men and women, clad in filthy rags, rolled upon them in torment. These were they who were rich and trusted in their riches and had no mercy upon orphans and widows, but despised the commandment of God.

31. And in another great lake, full of discharge and blood and boiling mire, stood men and women up to their knees. These were those who lent money and demanded compound interest.

32. Other men and women who cast themselves down from a high slope came to the bottom and were driven by their torturers to go up the precipice and were then thrown down again, and had no rest from this torture. These were those who defiled their bodies, behaving like women. And the women with them, these were those who behaved with one another as men with a woman.

33. And near that precipice was a place filled with powerful fire. And there stood men who, with their own hands, had fashioned images in place of God.

men's hands, and what resembles the images of cats and lions, of reptiles and wild beasts, and the men and women who manufactured the images, shall be in chains of fire; they shall be chastised because of their error before them (the images) and this is their judgment for ever. And near them other men and women who burn in the flame of the judgment, whose torture is for ever. These are they who have forsaken the commandment of God and followed . . . (*unknown word*) of the devils.[38]

And beside them were other men and women who had glowing rods and smote one another and had no rest from this torture.

34. And near to them still other men and women who were burned and turned (in the fire) and were baked. These were those who forsook the way of God.[38]

11. And another very high place . . . (*some unintelligible words*), the men and women who make a false step go rolling down to where the fear is. And again, while the (fire) that is prepared floweth, they mount up and fall down again and continue their rolling. They shall be punished thus for ever. These are they who have not honoured their father and mother, and of their own accord withdrew themselves from them. Therefore shall they be punished eternally. Furthermore the angel Ezrael brings children and maidens to show to them those who are punished. They will be punished with pain, with hanging up (?) and with many wounds which flesh-eating birds inflict. These are they that have confidence in their sins, are not obedient to their parents, and do not follow the instruction of their fathers and do not honour those who are older than they. Beside them, maidens clad in darkness for raiment, and they shall be seriously punished and their flesh will be torn in pieces. These are they who retained not their virginity till they were given in marriage; they shall be punished with these tortures, while they feel them.

And again other men and women who ceaselessly chew their tongues and are tormented with eternal fire. These are the slaves who were not obedient to their masters. This then is their judgment for ever.

12. And near to this torment are blind and dumb men and women whose raiment is white. They are packed closely together and fall on coals of unquenchable fire. These are they who give alms and say, 'We are righteous before God', while they yet have not striven for righteousness.

The angel of God Ezrael allows them to come forth out of this fire and sets forth a judgment of decision (?). This then is their judgment. (And) a stream of fire flows and all judgment (= all those judged)[39] are drawn into the midst of the stream. And Uriel sets them down (there). And there are wheels of fire, and men and women hung thereon by the power of their whirling. Those in the pit burn. Now these are the sorcerers and sorceresses. These wheels (are) in all decision by fire without number (?).

13. Then the angels brought my elect and righteous, who are perfect in all righteousness, bearing them on their hands, clothed with the garments of eternal life. *They shall see* (*their desire*) *on those who hated*[40] them, when he punishes them. Torment for every one (is) for ever according to his deeds. And all those who are in torment will say with one voice, 'Have mercy upon us, for now we know the judgment of God, which he declared to us beforehand, and we did not believe.' And the angel Tatirokos (= Tartarouchos) will come and chasten them with even greater torment and will say unto them, 'Now do ye repent when there is no more time for repentance, and nothing of life remains.' And all shall say, '*Righteous is the judgment of God*: for we have heard and perceived that *his judgment is good*,[41] since we are punished according to our deeds.'

14. Then will I give to my elect and righteous the baptism and the salvation for which they have besought me, in the field Akrosja (= Acherusia)[42] which is called Aneslesleja (= Elysium). They shall adorn with flowers the portion of the righteous and I will go.... I will rejoice with them. I will cause the nations to enter into my eternal kingdom and show to them that eternal thing to which I have directed their hope, I and my heavenly Father. I have spoken it to thee, Peter, and make it known to thee. Go forth then and journey to the city in the west in the vineyard which I will tell thee of . . . by the hand of my Son who is without sin, that his work . . . of destruction may be sanctified. But thou art chosen in the hope which I have given to thee. Spread thou my gospel throughout the whole world in peace! For there will be rejoicing (?) at the source of my word, the hope of life, and suddenly the world will be carried off.[43]

Ethiopic	*Akhmim*
	1. Many of them shall be false prophets and shall teach ways and diverse doctrines of perdition. 2. And they shall become sons of perdition.[44] 3. And then God will come to my faithful ones who hunger and thirst[45] and are afflicted and prove their souls in this life, and shall judge the sons of iniquity.
15. And my Lord Jesus Christ, our King, said to me, 'Let us *go into the holy mountain*.' And his disciples went with him, *praying*.[46]	4. And the Lord continued and said, 'Let us *go to the mountain and pray*.'[46] 5. And we, the twelve disciples, went with him and entreated him to show to us one of our righteous brethren who had departed from the

And behold, there were *two men*, and we could not look on their *faces*, for a light came from them which *shone more than the sun*, and their *raiment* also *was glistening*[47] and cannot be described, and there is nothing sufficient to be compared to them in this world. And its gentleness . . . that no mouth is able to express the beauty of their form. For their aspect was astonishing and wonderful. And the other, great, I say, shines in his appearance more than hail (crystal). Flowers of roses is the likeness of the colour of his appearance and his body . . . his head. And upon his shoulders and on their *(plural!)* foreheads was a crown of nard, a work woven from beautiful flowers; like the rainbow in water was his hair. This was the comeliness of his countenance, and he was adorned with all kinds of ornament. And when we suddenly saw them, we marvelled.

16. And I approached God Jesus Christ and said to him, 'My Lord who is this?' And he said to me, 'These are *Moses and Elias*.'[48] And I said to him, '(Where then are) Abraham, Isaac, Jacob and the other righteous fathers?'

And he showed us a great open *garden*. (It was) full of fair *trees* and blessed *fruits*,[49] full of the fragrance of perfume. Its fragrance was beautiful and that fragrance reached to us. And of it . . . [51] I saw many fruits.

world that we might see in what form they are, and taking courage might encourage the men who should hear us.

6. And as we prayed, suddenly there appeared *two men*, standing before the Lord, on whom we were not able to look. 7. For there went forth from their *countenance a ray, as of the sun*, and their *raiment was shining, such as* the eye of man *never*[47] <saw. For> no mouth can describe nor <heart conceive> the glory with which they were clad nor the beauty of their countenance. 8. And when we saw them we were astonished, for their bodies were whiter than any snow and redder than any rose. 9. But the redness of them was mingled with the whiteness, and I simply cannot describe their beauty. 10. For their hair was curled and charmingly suited their faces and their shoulders like some garland woven of blossom of nard and various coloured flowers, or like a rainbow in the air; so beautifully formed was their appearance. 11. When we saw their beauty, we were astonished before them, for they had appeared suddenly.

12. And I approached the Lord and said, 'Who are these?' 13. He said to me, 'These are your righteous brethren whose form ye did desire to see.' 14. And I said to him, 'And where are all the righteous, and what is the nature of that world in which these are who possess such glory?' 15. And the Lord showed me a widely extensive place outside this world,[50] all gleaming with light, and the air there flooded by the rays of the sun, and the earth itself budding with flowers which

And my Lord and God Jesus Christ said unto me, 'Hast thou seen the companies of the fathers? As is their rest, so also is the honour and glory of those *who will be persecuted for my righteousness' sake*.'[52]

fade not, and full of spices and plants which blossom gloriously and fade not and bear blessed fruit. 16. So great was the fragrance of the flowers that it was borne thence even unto us. 17. The inhabitants of that place were clad with the shining raiment of angels and their raiment was suitable to their place of habitation. 18. Angels walked there amongst them. 19. All who dwell there had an equal glory, and with one voice they praised God the Lord, rejoicing in that place. 20. The Lord said unto us, 'This is the place of your high-priests <brothers?>, the righteous men.'

<And I was joyful and believed> and understood that which is written in the book of my Lord Jesus Christ. And I said to him, '*My Lord, wilt thou that I make here three tabernacles, one for thee, one for Moses and one for Elias*?'[53] And he said to me in wrath, '*Satan* maketh war against thee, and has veiled *thine understanding*,[54] and the good things of this world conquer thee. Thine eyes must be opened and thine ears unstopped that . . . a tabernacle, which the hand of man has not made, but which my heavenly Father has made for me and for the elect.' And we saw (it) full of joy.

17. And behold there came suddenly a *voice from heaven* saying, '*This is my Son, whom I love and in whom I have pleasure*,[55] and my commandments. . . . And there came a great and *exceeding white cloud* over our heads and *bore away our Lord*[56] and Moses and Elias. And I trembled and was afraid, and we looked up and the heavens opened and we saw men in the flesh, and they came and greeted our Lord and Moses and Elias, and went into the second heaven. And the world of Scripture was fulfilled: *This generation seeketh him and seeketh the face of the God of Jacob*.[57] And great fear and great amazement took place in heaven; the angels flocked together that the word of Scripture might be fulfilled which saith: *Open the gates, ye princes*![58] After that the heaven was shut, that had been opened. And we prayed and *went down from the mountain, and we praised God*[59] who *hath written the names* of the righteous in heaven *in the book of life*.[60]

Notes

2. Apocalypse of Peter

1. Edition by S. Grébaut (see Lit. above). H. Duensing in ZNW 14, 1913, 65ff. published a German translation with detailed notes on difficult passages, which he then presented in

revised form in NTApo³ 472-483 (ET 668-683). For the present edition this translation has been subjected to a thorough revision according to the Ethiopic text.
2. Mt. 24:3 and par. In general, all additional revelations by the Saviour are transferred to the Mount of Olives in the period between the Resurrection and the Ascension.
3. Perhaps a wrong translation of κατ' ἰδίαν, Mt. 24:3 and par.
4. Mt. 24:3.
5. Mt. 24:4 and par.
6. Mt. 24:5 and par.
7. Mt. 24:26; Lk. 17:23.
8. Lk. 17:20; Mt. 24:27.
9. Mk. 13:26 and par.
10. Cf. Mt. 24:30.
11. Lk. 9:26 and par.; Mt. 16:27.
12. 1 Pet. 4:5; 2 Tim. 4:1.
13. Mt. 16:27; Ps. 62:12 (= 61:13 LXX).
14. Mk. 13:28f. and par.
15. Lk. 13:6ff.
16. Mk. 13:22 and par.
17. Mt. 24:5.
18. 2 Jn. 7; Rev. 12:9.
19. Mk. 13:22 and par.
20. Mk. 14:21 and par.
21. Rev. 20:13.
22. Cf. Gen. 1:3; Ps. 33:9 (= 32:9 LXX).
23. Cf. Ezek. 37:4ff.
24. Cf. Enoch 20:1; C. Detlef G. Müller, *Die Engellehre der Koptischen Kirche*, 54-58, esp. note 409.
25. Cf. 1 Cor. 15:36ff.
26. Cf. Macarius Magnes, *Apocritica* IV 6.16: 'By way of superfluity let this word also be quoted from the Apocalypse of Peter. He introduces the view that the heaven will be judged along with the earth in the following words, "*The earth will present before God on the day of judgment all men who are to be judged and itself also will be judged with the heaven that encompasses it.*"' On the author, A.v. Harnack, *Geschichte der altchristlichen Literatur bis Eusebius* I, 2, ²1958, 873 and 947; O. Bardenhewer, *Geschichte der altkirchlichen Literatur* IV, 1924 (1962), 189-194.
27. Cf. Macarius Magnes, *Apocritica* IV 7: 'And again he says (i.e. Peter in the Apocalypse) this statement which is full of impiety, saying "*And every power of heaven shall burn, and the heaven shall be rolled up like a book and all the stars shall fall like leaves from a vine and like the leaves from the fig-tree.*" - Probably the pagan writer whom Macarius opposes read not only the first part but also the continuation from Is. 34:4 (Heb.), 'and the heaven shall be rolled up . . . fig-tree' in his text of the Apocalypse. Cf. 2 Pet. 3:10ff.
28. The river of fire which every dead person must cross is a legacy from ancient Egypt; cf. C. Detlef G. Müller, *Die Engellehre der Koptischen Kirche*, 1959, 97-100; Jean Doresse, *Des Hiéroglyphes à la Croix*, Istanbul 1960 (Uitgaven van het Nederlands Historisch-archaeologisch Instituut te Istanbul), 51; in general E. Hornung, *Altägyptische Höllenvorstellungen* (Abhandlungen der Sächsischen Akademie der Wissenschaften zu Leipzig, Philologisch-historische Klasse, Band 59, Heft 3), 1968.
29. Mt. 8:12 etc.
30. Mt. 26:64 and par.; Mt. 24:30 and par.; Mt. 16:27; Lk. 9:26 and par.
31. Cf. Dan. 7:9f. and note 28 above.
32. Mt. 16:27, Ps. 62:12 (= 61:13 LXX).

33. Cf. above n. 24.
34. Cf. 1 Pet. 3:3.
35. Ps. 19:9 (= 18:10 LXX); Rev. 16:7; 19:2.
36. Cf. Clement of Alexandria, *Ecl.* 41: 'The Scripture says that the children exposed by parents are *delivered to a protecting* (= *temelouchos*) *angel*, by whom they are brought up and nourished. And they shall be, it says, as the faithful of a hundred years old here (cf. Is. 65:20; Wisd. Sol. 4:16). Wherefore Peter also says in his Apocalypse, "*and a flash of fire, coming from their children and smiting the eyes of the women*".'
37. Cf. for this:
(*a*) Clement of Alexandria, *Ecl.* 48f.: 'For example Peter in the Apocalypse says *that the children born abortively* receive the better part. These *are delivered to a care-taking* (*temelouchos*) *angel*, so that after they have reached knowledge they may obtain the better abode, as if they had suffered what they would have suffered, had they attained to bodily life. But the others shall obtain salvation only as people who have suffered wrong and experienced mercy, and shall exist without torment, having received this as their reward. 49. *But the milk of the mothers which flows from their breasts and congeals*, says Peter in the Apocalypse, *shall beget tiny flesh-eating beasts and they shall run over them and devour them* - which teaches that the punishments will come to pass by reason of the sins.'
(*b*) Methodius, *Symposium* II 6: 'Wherefore have we received it handed down in Scriptures inspired by God *that children who are born before their time, even if they be the offspring of adultery, are delivered to care-taking angels. . . . How could they* have confidently summoned *their parents* before the judgment seat of Christ *to bring a charge against them*, saying, "*Thou, O Lord, didst not grudgingly deny us this light that is common (to all), but these have exposed us to death, despising thy commandments*."'
On the punishment angel and doorkeeper Temelouchos cf. also C. Detlef G. Müller, *Die Engellehre der Koptischen Kirche*, 1959, 314 and J. Michl in RAC V, no. 239 on col. 237.
38. Cf. the Bodleian Fragment (James, JTS 1911, pp. 367ff.): "*<Men and women> who hold chains and scourge themselves before the deceitful images, and will ceaselessly experience the torment: and near to them other men and women . . . these are they who have <utterly> forsaken the way of God . . .* "
39. Cf. the sermon on the parable of the Ten Virgins in the Epinal MS from the 4th century (cited by James, JTS, 1911, 383): '*The closed door is the river of fire by which the ungodly will be kept out of the kingdom of God, as it is written in Daniel* (Dan. 7:9f.) *and by Peter in his Apocalypse*', and '*That party of the foolish shall also rise and find the door shut, that is, the river of fire lying before them.*'
40. Ps. 54:7 (= 53:9 LXX); 59:10 (= 58:11 LXX).
41. Ps. 19:9 (= 18:9 LXX); Rev. 16:7; 19:2.
42. Erik Peterson, 'Die "Taufe" im Acherusischen See', in id. *Frühkirche, Judentum und Gnosis*, Rome-Freiburg/Breisgau-Vienna 1959, 310-332 and in *VigChr* 9, 1955, 1-20.
43. Cf. the Rainer Fragment (PO XVII, 1924, 482f.; K. Prümm, *Biblica* X, 1929, 77ff.; M.R. James, JTS 1931, 270-279): '*Then will I grant to my called and chosen whomsoever they shall ask me for out of torment* (so James, who reads ὃν ἐὰν αἰτήσωνται instead of the difficult θεὸν ἐὰν στέσωνται = I shall grant to them God, if they call to me in the torment) *and I will give to them a precious baptism unto salvation from the Acherusian lake, which men say* (*is situated*) *in the Elysian field, the portion of the righteous with my holy ones. And I shall depart, I and my exulting chosen, with the patriarchs, into my eternal kingdom, and I will fulfil for them my promises which I have given to them, both I and my Father in heaven. Behold, I have manifested all unto thee, Peter, and expounded it. Go into the city which rules over the west* (so James, who reads δύσεως instead of ὀπύσεως = over fornication) *and drink the cup which I have promised thee* (cf. Mk. 10:39 and par.) *at the hands of the son of him who* (*is*) *in Hades, that his destruction* (cf. 2 Thess. 2:3, 8) *may begin and thou mayest be worthy of the promise* (?) . . . ' The transference

of men from the fiery torment to the Acherusian lake by means of the intercession of the blessed is found particularly in Or. Sib. II 330-339.
44. Cf. 2 Pet. 2:1ff.; Jn. 17:12; 2 Thess. 2:3.
45. Cf. Mt. 5:6.
46. 2 Pet. 1:18; Mk. 9:2ff. and par.; Lk. 9:28.
47. Cf. Mk. 9:2ff. and par.
48. Mk. 9:4 and par.
49. Gen. 2:8ff.; Rev. 22:2.
50. On the following cf. Theophilus of Antioch, *ad Autolycum* II 19, 'God chose for Adam as paradise "*a place in the eastern region, marked out by light, illumined by shining air, with plants of wondrous beauty*"'.
51. *Eth.*: *Mänker*; what is meant is probably 'wonderful'.
52. Mt. 5:10.
53. Mt. 17:4 and par.
54. Mt. 16:23 and par.
55. Mt. 17:5 and par.; Mt. 3:17 and par.
56. Mt. 17:5; Acts 1:9.
57. Ps. 24:6 (= 23:6 LXX).
58. Ps. 24:7-9 (= 23:7-9 LXX). E. Kähler, *Studien zum Te Deum und zur Geschichte des 24. Psalms in der alten Kirche*, 1958, pp. 53-55, finds in ch. 17 of the Apocalypse of Peter a description of the post-Easter triumphal ascension to heaven, in which the opposition of hostile powers is broken by the angels, and the righteous, in the train of the Redeemer, are led into the second, i.e. the real heaven.
59. Mk. 9:9 and par.; Lk. 24:52f.
60. Dan. 12:1; Rev. 17:8, etc.

XX. Apocalyptic Prophecy in the Early Church

Introduction

Wilhelm Schneemelcher

1. Despite the labours of many scholars, the relation to one another of Apocalyptic, the Sibyllines and Prophecy, already discussed above (pp. 555ff.), is still by no means finally settled.[1] It is however clear from the sources that all three phenomena were influential in early Christianity, although in different ways. Here a special significance attaches to the association of Apocalyptic and Prophecy (cf. above, pp. 561ff.). Early Christian prophets, who were probably above all charismatic community leaders, made use - so far as we can discover from the fragmentary tradition - of apocalyptic terminology and ideas. Since however these prophets were soon replaced by other officers, Apocalyptic also took on a different standing in the Church: it became a book-wisdom (which indeed it probably was originally), directed towards the portrayal of the details of the end-time in conjunction with paraenesis and admonitions to repentance. As a result of its early association with prophecy, Apocalyptic remained a marginal phenomenon in a Church led by officials, but one which repeatedly came to expression.

2. The appearance of prophetic figures in the 2nd century was evidently not restricted to the Jewish-Christian area. In his treatise against Christianity, Celsus reports concerning such prophets:

> Many people and (indeed such) without names act as soothsayers with the greatest readiness, for some incidental cause, outside and inside temples; others go around begging in cities and camps. It is common practice and customary for each to say, 'I am God or a child of God or a divine Spirit. But I have come: for already the world is passing away, and you, O men, go hence by reason of your iniquities. But I wish to save you, and you will see me coming again with heavenly power. Blessed is he who has worshipped me now, but upon all the rest will I inflict eternal fire, upon cities and country places. And those men who knew not their penalties shall repent in vain and groan, but those who obey me will I preserve for ever.' ... Having uttered these sayings abroad, they even add unintelligible, half-crazy and utterly obscure words, the meaning of which no intelligent person can discover.
>
> (Origen, *c. Celsum* VII 9)

The question whether Celsus at this point has in view Christian, Christian gnostic, Montanist or heathen prophets cannot be answered with any certainty. There is much to be said for the view that he is not speaking about Christian charismatics. However that may be, it is clear from the text that in the 2nd century there was the phenomenon of prophetic-apocalyptic figures of this kind. The preaching of these men (and women?) evidently only rarely assumed a literary form.

Montanism also has left no literature behind. Only the few prophetic maxims of Montanus and his prophetesses which have been handed on throw some light upon this movement. The interpretation of these sayings however, despite much effort, is just as much in dispute as many other questions which Montanism poses for us.[2] We need not enter into further details here. For present purposes it is sufficient to establish that the representatives of the 'Phrygian prophecy' appeared in the first generation as prophets, whose preaching contained eschatological and apocalyptic elements to an extent which can only be determined with difficulty.

3. When in this collection of 'New Testament apocrypha' texts are included which derive from the area of 'apocalyptic prophecy' thus sketched, this requires a brief justification. In the case of the three texts here presented, it is certainly not a matter of writings which - like the Apocalypse of Peter for example (see above, pp. 620ff.) - belong to the New Testament apocrypha in the proper sense (cf. vol. 1, pp. 50ff.). Nor can we regard them as a continuation of the genre of the 'apocalypse' which is represented by the Revelation of John in the NT. They are chosen here because in them 'prophets', men filled with the Spirit, proclaim their message in apocalyptic images and concepts.

- In 5 and 6 Esra an apocalyptist speaks in the guise of an Old Testament prophet.

- In the Christian parts of the Sibylline Oracles the 'age-old seer' speaks and - linking up with heathen and Jewish oracular sayings - offers of her own accord her words stamped by Jewish and Christian Apocalyptic.

- Finally the prophet Elchasai, who even today poses many a riddle, but whose significance is to be seen not least in his influence upon Mani, has left a book with prophetic-apocalyptic speeches, which suggest that we should include him in the group of the apocalyptic prophets (with syncretistic elements).

These three texts do not form a unity in terms either of their genre or their religio-historical stamp. But they convey an impression of the spiritual environment in which the phenomenon of Christian Apocalyptic in the early centuries is rooted. Even if they are to be reckoned only with reservations to the 'apocalypse' category, they may contribute something to the understanding of the works of early Christian Apocalyptic and its later descendants, and therefore they are included here

Notes

Introduction

1. Cf. David Hellholm (ed.), *Apocalypticism in the Mediterranean World and the Near East* (Proceedings of the International Colloquium on Apocalypticism, Uppsala, August 12-17, 1979), Tübingen 1983.
2. On Montanism cf. P. de Labriolle, *Les sources de l'histoire du Montanisme*, 1913; N.

Bonwetsch, *Texte zur Geschichte des Montanismus* (KlT 129), 1914; K. Aland, 'Bemerkungen zum Montanismus und zur frühchristlichen Eschatologie', *Kirchengeschichtliche Entwürfe*, 1960, 105-148. On the significance of Montanism for the history of the Canon, see vol. 1, p. 24ff.

1. The Fifth and Sixth Books of Esra

(*Hugo Duensing* † and *Aurelio de Santos Otero*)

Introduction

Tradition: in the texts of the Latin Bible, the Fourth Book of Esra has two additional chapters at the beginning and at the end; these are missing in the Oriental translations. Chapters 1 and 2 are a Christian Apocalypse which is introduced in the MSS before or after 4 Esra, and is known to some extent as the Fifth Book of Esra. Chapters 15 and 16 form an appendix: these chapters, in point of style, are prophecies filled with sayings of woe in the fashion of the OT, and, like the introductory chapters as a whole, they are available only in Latin.[1] Linguistic observations point to a Greek original[2] and this is confirmed for chs. 15-16 by the discovery of a small Greek fragment of ch. 15, vv. 57-59, among the Oxyrhynchus papyri. The manuscript tradition is divided into two groups: a Frankish, represented by S, the Codex Sangermanensis of the year 822, and the Codex A = Ambianensis, also from the 9th century; and a Spanish, represented by C = Complutensis from the 9th-10th century and M = Mazarinaeus, from the 11th-12th century, and in addition some other secondary witnesses among which the C. Legionensis = L has a sharply divergent text; according to Violet, this text is indebted to the modifying treatment of a writer of independent spirit. The group S A as a rule has a higher value than C M (NVL).

2. Contents: the prophecy of the two introductory chapters falls into two parts. The first turns against the Jewish people, the second is concerned with the Christians who must take their place. It is possible that in the first section material from a Jewish text has been used and has been worked over by a Christian hand (see 1.11; 1.24; 1.30 and especially 1.35-40) to provide an invective against the Jewish people. On the other hand, the second part, 2.10-48, which brings comforting promises to the Christians, is purely Christian, in spite of 2.33, 42, etc., which are decoration. The Sixth Book of Esra, comprising chs. 15 and 16, contains descriptions of the dissolution of the world which comes to its fulfilment in terrible wars and natural events by which Babylon, Asia, Egypt and Syria in particular are threatened, but which will admonish, strengthen and comfort the people of God who will have suffered the afflictions of persecution.

3. Time of composition: in 2.42-47 an innumerable company of Christian martyrs are crowned. This takes us beyond the 1st century. The young man of great stature has a parallel in the Gospel of Peter, in the Acts of Perpetua and Felicitas, and also in the Shepherd of Hermas. This feature points to the 2nd century, but, since the argument with Judaism still clearly possesses topical significance, we ought not to place the writing too late. We may adhere to a date around A.D. 200.[3]

It is different with the appendix, chs. 15-16. In this a persecution is assumed, stretching over the entire eastern half of the Roman empire, a persecution in which the Christians, driven from their homes, robbed of their goods and imprisoned, are compelled to eat flesh offered to idols. For this there is available the long space of time from about 120 to the end of the persecutions under Constantine. On the basis of some particular features which it has been thought possible to fix in time, the writing has been dated in the 3rd century. But a precise decision as to the time of writing is no more possible than is a fixing of the place of origin, although the western regions of the Orient have the greatest degree of probability.

4. Significance: the extent to which the apocalyptic material of 5th Esra attracted Christians in later times can be seen - in addition to other references and reminiscences in the offical Roman Catholic liturgy - in the fact that in a fragment of a Missal from the 11th century the passage 2.42-48 is communicated in complete text as the epistle for the Mass *de communi plurimorum martyrum.* Many separate points as well have special significance: the twelve angels with flowers 1.40; the people of God who come from the east, 1.38; the tree of life in Paradise, 2.12; the twelve fruit-trees in 2.18; the resurrection in 2.31 and the exceedingly tall son of God in 2.43 (on the growth-motif, cf. the material in E. Hammerschmidt, *Studies in the Ethiopic Anaphoras*, 1961, p. 98).

On the other hand, 6th Esra provides threats of judgment, comfort and exhortation within the definite circumstances of a period of persecution. Everything is earth-bound here. Nevertheless this work was also deemed suitable for use in warning and exhortation, as is shown by the letter of the Anglo-Saxon writer Gildas (dated in the 7th or 6th century), in which the text of ch. 15.21-27 and 16.3f., 5-12 is reproduced

5. Literature: O.F. Fritzsche, *Libri apocryphi Veteris Testamenti*, Leipzig, 1871 (pp. 640ff.); R.L. Bensly, *The Fourth Book of Ezra* (with an introduction by M.R. James), Texts and Studies III 2, 1895; the above-mentioned Fragment of 4 Esra 15.57-59 in *The Oxyrhynchus Papyri*, Part VII (ed. A. Hunt), 1910, 11ff.; older literature in E. Schürer, *The Jewish People in the time of Jesus Christ*, ET, Div. II, vol. III, 113f. (German ed.[4] 1909, III 330f.; rev. English ed. 1986, III 1, 301ff.); in addition, M.J. Labourt, 'Le cinquième livre d'Esdras', *Rev. Bibl.* 17, 1909, 412-434; D. de Bruyne, 'Fragments d'une apocalypse perdue', *Rev Bénéd.* 33, 1921, 97-109; A. Oepke, 'Ein bisher unbeachtetes Zitat aus dem 5. Buche Esra', *Coniect. Neotestament.* XI, 1947, 179-195 (reprinted in ZNW 42, 1949, 158-172); O. Plöger, Article 'Das 5. and 6. Esrabuch', in RGG[3] II, 1958, cols. 699f.; also the introduction to 4 Esra (chs. 3-14) by B. Noack in *De Gammeltestamentlige Pseudepigrapher*, Heft I, 1953, 1-13. W. Schneemelcher, art. 'Esra', RAC 6, 1966, cols. 604-606; *Biblia Sacra iuxta Vulgatam Versionem*, ed. R. Weber *et. al.*, 1969; Moraldi II, 1917ff. (Italian trans.); M.D. Brocke, 'On the Jewish Origin of the "Improperia"' (V Ezra 1, 5-25), *Immanuel* 7, 1977, 44-51.

Fifth Esra[1]

1. 4. The word of God which came to Esra, the son of Chusis, in the days of Nebuchadnezzar, thus: 5. Go and make known to my people their misdeeds, and to their sons the evil which they have committed against me, that they may recount it to their children's children. 6. For the sins of their fathers are increased in them (still); they have forgotten me and sacrificed to strange gods.

7. Have not I brought them out of the land of Egypt, out of the house of bondage? But they have provoked me to wrath and despised my counsels. 8. Shake thou therefore the hair of thy head and let all evils fall upon them, for they have not obeyed my law, the stiff-necked people!

9. How long shall I tolerate them? So many benefits have I shown to them! 10. Many kings have I overthrown for their sakes; Pharaoh and his servants and all his hosts have I thrown violently down. 11. Have I not for your sake destroyed the city of Bethsaida and burned with fire two cities in the east, Tyre and Sidon? 12. Speak thou then unto them: Thus saith the Lord: 13. Of a truth, I have brought you through the sea and in the pathless desert I provided for you prepared roads. As a leader I gave to you Moses and Aaron as a priest. 14. Light have I granted you by the pillar of fire and great wonders have I done among you. But you have forgotten me, saith the Lord. - 15. Thus saith the Lord, the Almighty: The quails were for a sign to you; a camp did I give you for shelter; and there you murmured. 16. And you triumphed not in my name over the destruction of your enemies; no, even to this day, you still murmur. 17. Where are the benefits which I have shown to you? Have you not cried unto me in the desert, when you suffered hunger and thirst: - 18. 'Why hast thou brought us into this desert to kill us? Better that we had been slaves to the Egyptians than to die in this desert!' 19. Your sufferings made me sorrowful and I gave you manna for food; the bread of angels have you eaten. 10. When you suffered thirst, did I not cleave the rock and water flowed to your fill? Because of the heat I covered you with leaves of the trees. 21. Fertile lands did I apportion to you; the Canaanites, the Perizites, the Philistines did I cast out before you. What shall I yet do for you? saith the Lord. - 22. Thus saith the Lord, the Almighty: When you were in the wilderness, thirsting at the bitter waters and blaspheming my name, 23. there I let not fire rain upon you for your blasphemies, but casting a tree into the waters, I made the river sweet. - 24. What shall I do to thee, Jacob? Thou wouldst not obey me, Judah! I will turn to other nations and give to them my name, that they may keep my statutes. 25. Since you have forsaken me, I will also forsake you. When you implore me for mercy, I will have no mercy upon you. 26. When you call on me, I will not hear. For you have defiled your hands with blood and your feet are swift to commit acts of murder. 27. You have not, as it were, left me in the lurch, but your own selves, saith the Lord.

28. Thus saith the Lord, the Almighty: Have I not admonished you with prayers, as a father his sons, as a mother her daughters, as a nurse her infants, 29. that you should be a people for me and I should be your God, that you should be sons to me and I a father to you? 30. I gathered you together as a hen gathereth her chickens under her wing.

But now, what shall I do to you? I will cast you forth from my presence! 31. When you bring offerings to me, I will turn my face from you; for your feasts and new moons and circumcisions of the flesh have I not asked. 32. I sent to you my servants the prophets, whom you have taken and slain and torn their bodies in pieces. Their blood will I visit upon you again, saith the Lord. - 33. Thus saith the Lord, the Almighty: Your house is desolate; I will cast you forth as the wind does stubble. 34. And your children will not produce offspring, for they have with you despised my commandment and done that which is evil in my sight.

35. I will give your dwellings to a people which shall come, who, though they have not heard of me, yet believe; to whom I have shown no wonderful signs. They will do what I have commanded. 36. They have not seen the prophets, but they will hold in remembrance their history. 37. I testify to the grace which shall meet the people to come, whose children jump for joy, though they see me not with the eyes of the body, yet in their spirit they believe what I have said. 38. And now, O Father, behold in glory and see thy people who come from the rising of the sun! 39. To them will I give the dominion with Abraham, Isaac and Jacob, Elias and Enoch, Zachariah and Hosea, Amos, Joel, Micah, Obadiah, 40. Zephaniah, Nahum, Jonah, Mattathias, Habakkuk and the twelve angels with flowers.

2. 1. Thus saith the Lord: I have brought this people out of bondage and have given them commandments by my servants the prophets, but they would not hear them, but threw my counsel to the wind. 2. The mother who bare them saith to them, Go, my sons, for I am widowed and forsaken. 3. I have brought you up with joy, and with sadness and sorrow have I lost you, since you have sinned before the Lord and done what is evil in my sight. - 4. But now, what shall I do to you? I am widowed and forsaken. Go, my children, and ask the Lord for mercy. 5. But I call upon thee, O Father, as a witness upon the mother of these children, for they would not keep my covenant: 6. Let destruction come upon them, and looting upon their mother, so that no offspring may come after them. 7. Let them be scattered among the heathen, let their names be banished from the earth, for they have despised my covenant. 8. Woe to thee, Asshur, who shelterest in thee the unrighteous. Wicked city, remember what I have done to Sodom and Gomorrah, 9. whose land lies in clods of pitch and heaps of ashes; thus will I do to those who have not listened to me, saith the Lord, the Almighty.

10. Thus saith the Lord unto Esra: Tell my people that I will give to them the kingdom of Jerusalem which I would have given to Israel. 11. I will take unto me the glory of these (the Israelites) and give to those (my people) *the everlasting tabernacles*[2] which I had prepared for them (Israel). 12. *The tree of life*[3] will be to them for an ointment of sweet fragrance and they shall not labour nor weary. 13. *Ask and ye shall receive*;[4] plead for few days for yourselves, that they may be shortened. The kingdom is already prepared for you: watch!

14. I call heaven and earth to witness: I have given up the evil and created the good for (= so surely as) I live, saith the Lord. 15. (Good) mother, embrace

thy children, bring them up with joy like a dove (CM: give them joy like a dove who tends her young), establish their feet; for I have chosen thee, saith the Lord. 16. I will raise up the dead from their places and bring them forth out of the tombs,[5] for I have known my name in them. 17. Fear thou not, O mother of the children, for I have chosen thee, saith the Lord. 18. I will send for thy help my servants Isaiah and Jeremiah (CM + and Daniel) according to whose counsel I sanctified (CM + thee) and have prepared for thee twelve trees, heavy laden with many kinds of fruit, 19. and as many fountains which *flow with milk and honey*,[6] and *seven* measureless *mountains*,[7] filled with roses and lilies, wherein I will fill thy children with joy.

20. Do right to the widow, assist the fatherless to his right; give to the needy; protect the orphan, clothe the naked; 21. tend the cripple and the feeble, laugh not at the lame, defend the frail and let the blind man behold my glory.[8] 22. Guard the aged and the young within thy walls, preserve thy little children, let thy slaves and freemen rejoice and thy whole company live in cheerfulness. 23. Wherever thou findest the dead, there commit them to a grave, marking it; so will I give to thee the first place in my resurrection. 24. Rest and be at peace, my people, for your repose will come.[9]

25. Good nurse, nourish thy children, and establish their feet. 26. The (SA: servants) which I have given thee - none of them shall perish,[10] for I will require them according to thy number. 27. Be not anxious; for when the day of affliction and anguish is come, others will weep and be sorrowful, but thou shalt be gay and rich. 28. The nations will envy thee, and prevail not against thee, saith the Lord. 19. My hands will shelter thee, that thy children see not Gehenna. 30. Be joyful, O mother, with thy children, for I will deliver thee, saith the Lord. 31. Remember thy sleeping children, for I will bring them from the hidden graves in the earth and show mercy to them: *for I am merciful, saith the Lord.*[11] 32. Embrace thy children till I come, and proclaim mercy to them, for my wells run over and my grace will not cease.

33. I, Esra, received the command of the Lord on the mountain Horeb that I should go to Israel: when I came to them, they rejected me and received not the commandment of God. 34. Therefore I say unto you, ye nations (= heathen), you who hear and understand: Wait for your shepherd! He will give you everlasting rest, for he is near who shall come at the end of the world. 35. Be ready for the rewards of the kingdom, for everlasting light shall shine upon you for evermore. 36. Flee the shadow of this world; receive the joy of your glory; I call to witness my Saviour openly. 37. Receive that which is offered you by the Lord and be joyful, giving thanks to him *who has called you to his* heavenly *kingdom.*[12]

38. Arise and stand and behold the number of those who are sealed at the banquet of the Lord.[13] 39. Those who have withdrawn from the shadow of this world have received shining garments from the Lord.[14] 40. Receive, O Zion, thy number (see 26) and embrace *those who are clothed in white*,[15] who have

fulfilled the law of the Lord. 41. The number of thy children, whom thou desirest, is complete; beseech the rule of the Lord that thy people, whom I have called from the beginning, may be sanctified.

42. I, Esra, saw upon mount Zion a great company, which I could not number, and they all praised the Lord with songs. 43. In the midst of them was a young man, tall of stature, towering above all the rest, and he set a crown upon the head of each one of them and he waxed ever taller. But I was absorbed by the wonder.[16] 44. So I asked the angel, saying, 'Who are these, Lord?' 45. He answered and said to me, 'These are they who have laid aside their mortal clothing and put on the immortal and have confessed the name of God.[17] Now are they crowned and receive *palms*.' 46. And I said to the angel, 'Who is that young man who setteth crowns upon them and giveth them *palms in their hands*?'[18] 47. He answered me and said, 'This is the Son of God whom they have confessed in the world.' And I began to praise them who had appeared so valiant for the name of the Lord.

48. Then the angel said unto me, 'Go! Proclaim to my people what wonders of the Lord thy God thou hast seen and how great they are.'

Sixth Esra

15. 1. Behold, speak thou in the ears of my people words of prophecy which I will put in thy mouth, saith the Lord, 2. and let them be written on paper, for they are faithful and true. 3. Fear not the schemes (which are devised) against thee; let not the unbelief of the adversary perplex thee, 4. for he who is unbelieving will die in his unbelief.

5. Behold I will bring evils on the whole round earth, saith the Lord, sword, famine, death and destruction, 6. since wickedness has covered the whole earth and their abominable works are completed. 7. Therefore saith the Lord: 8. No more will I be silent on their wickedness which they outrageously commit, nor will I tolerate the unrighteousness they practise. Behold innocent and righteous blood cries out unto me, and the souls of the righteous cry unceasingly. 9. Terrible vengeance will I exact from them and all innocent blood will I visit upon them. 10. Behold my people is led like a flock to the slaughter. No longer will I let them dwell in the land of Egypt, 11. but I will bring them out with a strong hand and an upraised arm, and will visit Egypt with plagues as before, and destroy its entire land. 12. Let Egypt mourn and her foundations for the shock of the chastisement and punishment which the Lord will bring upon her. 13. Let the husbandmen mourn who till the soil, for their grain shall fail and their trees be destroyed by burning and hail and a terrible storm. 14. Woe to the world and all who dwell therein! 15. For the sword and its destruction draws near. And one nation shall rise up against another in battle with their swords in their hands. 16. For dissension shall break out among men: they shall rise

up one against another, and in the consciousness of power they will not be concerned for their king and the leader of their rulers. 17. For a man shall desire to go into a city and he will not be able to do so. 18. For on account of their arrogance will the cities be brought into confusion, their houses will be destroyed, the men afraid. 19. No man shall show pity to his neighbours; they will break into their houses with the sword to plunder their goods by reason of hunger for bread and great tribulation.

20. Behold, saith the Lord, I call together all kings of the earth, to rouse those who come from the north and from the south, and from the east and from the west, that they may turn against one another and give back (in recompense) what they have given to the former. 21. As they have done till this present to my chosen, so will I do and recompense in their bosom. Thus saith the Lord God: 22. My right hand will not spare the sinners and my sword will not cease from those who shed innocent blood on the earth. 23. And a fire shall go forth from his wrath and consume the foundations of the earth, and sinners like kindled straw.

24. Woe to them that sin and keep not my commandments, saith the Lord. 25. I will not spare them. Away from me, rebellious sons! Defile not my sanctuary! 26. For the Lord knoweth all who trespass against him; therefore hath he delivered them to death and destruction. 27. For now hath evil come upon the whole round earth and ye must remain therein, for God will not deliver you, since you have trespassed against him.

28. Behold a vision, and it was terrible! And the appearance of it came from the East. 29. And the nations of the dragon of Arabia shall set forth in many chariots, and from the day of their setting forth, their hissing shall sound over the earth, so that all who hear them fear and tremble. 30. The raging Carmonians shall break forth in fury, like a boar from the wood; they shall come with great power and struggle with them in a conflict and shall waste a part of the land of the Assyrians. 31. And then shall the dragons, remembering their origin, have the upper hand, and if they shall turn to pursue them, snorting with great power, 32. then these latter shall be troubled and shall keep silent before their power and turn their feet to flight. 33. And from the land of the Assyrians shall he who lies in wait for them lay an ambush and shall destroy one of them. Then will fear and trembling fall on their hosts and powerlessness on their kings.

34. Behold - clouds from the east and from the north right to the south! And their appearance was exceeding terrible, full of wrath and storm. 35. And they will dash against one another and they shall pour a mighty storm over the earth. And the blood from the swords shall reach even to the belly of the horses, 36. to the thighs of a man, to the hocks of a camel. And great fear and trembling will be upon the earth. 37. All who see that wrath shall be terrified and fear shall take hold of them. And after that many clouds 38. from the south and from the north and another part from the west shall rise up. 39. But mighty winds will

come from the east and shall shut it up and the clouds which he had allowed to rise in wrath; and the storm which arose from east and west to cause destruction will be damaged. 40. And there shall rise up great and strong clouds, full of wrath and storm, to destroy the whole earth and its inhabitants. They will pour out over every high and exalted one terrible storms, 41. fire, hail, flying swords and great streams of water, so that all fields and valleys are filled with the abundance of their waters. 42. And they will destroy cities and walls, mountains and hills, the trees of the wood, the hay of the meadows and their corn. 43. And they will rush on their course even unto Babylon and destroy it. 44. They shall be gathered about it, and shall encircle it and pour out all their storm and all their anger upon it till they rase it to the ground. Then will the dust and smoke rise to the heaven and all around will bewail it. 45. And those who survive will be the servants of those who have destroyed it.

46. And thou, Asia, who sharest in the splendour of Babylon and in the glory of her station, 47. woe to thee, thou wretch! For thou hast become like to her, thou hast decked thy daughters for works of obscenity that thou might be pleased and praised among thy lovers who always desire thee. 48. The hateful harlot hast thou copied in all her works and devices. Therefore saith God: 49. I will send evils upon thee, widowhood, poverty, famine, sword and pestilence, which will waste thy houses, will destroy and slay. 50. And the glory of thy power will fade like a flower, when the heat shall arise which is sent against thee. 51. Thou wilt become weak and miserable by blows and bruised by stripes, so that thou wilt not be able to receive thy mighty ones and lovers. 52. Would I have been jealous against thee, saith the Lord, 53. if thou hadst not on every occasion slain my chosen, exulting with clapping of hands, and laughing at their death, when thou wast drunken? 54. Deck out the beauty of thy countenance; 55. the reward of harlotry dost thou bear in the bosom of thy raiment; therefore shalt thou receive recompense in thy bosom! 56. As thou doest to my chosen, saith the Lord, so will God do to thee and will cast thee down into suffering. 57. Thy children will die of hunger, thou wilt fall by the sword, thy cities will be destroyed and all thy servants shall fall by the sword in the field. 58. And all who are in the mountains shall perish of hunger; they shall eat their own flesh and drink their own blood, because of hunger for bread and thirst for water. Unhappy one! 59. Miserable shalt thou become above all others, and suffering shall fall upon thee for recompense. 60. As they pass by, they will fall on the hated city and will destroy a portion of thy land and a portion of thy glory, when they return again from Babylon. And when thou art destroyed 61. and wasted, thou wilt be to them as straw, and they to thee as fire! 62. They will consume thee and thy cities, thy land and thy mountains, all thy woods and thy fruit trees will they burn with fire. 63. Thy children will be carried away captive, thy treasure will they take for booty and destroy the glory of thy splendour.

16. 1. Woe to thee, Babylon and Asia! woe to thee, Egypt and Syria! 2. Gird

yourselves with sackcloth and fabric of hair, and bewail your children, and lament, for your destruction is near. 3. The sword is sent against you! 4. Who is there that shall ward it off? The fire is sent against you, 5. and who is there that shall quench it? Sufferings are sent against you, and who is there that shall drive them away? 6. Can a man drive away the hungry lion in the wood, or quench the fire when the straw is kindled? 7. Can a man turn back the arrow which is shot by a strong archer? 8. God the Lord sends the evils and who can drive them away? 9. Fire shall go forth from his wrath and who is there that may quench it? 10. He shall send his lightning, and who will not be afraid? He shall thunder and who will not be alarmed? 11. The Lord shall threaten and who will not utterly dissolve before his face? 12. The earth and its foundations quake, and the sea rises up from the deep, its waves will be troubled and its fish, at the presence of the Lord and the glory of his power. 13. For strong is his right hand which bends the bow! Sharp the arrows which are sent by him! They shall not turn back when he begins to send them upon the earth. 14. Behold, evils are sent forth and shall not return till they come upon the earth. 15. Fire has been kindled and will not be quenched till it consumes the foundations of the earth. 16. As the arrow, shot by the mighty archer, turns not back, so will the evils not turn back which are sent on the earth.

17. Woe is me! woe is me! who will deliver me in these days? 18. The beginning of sorrows (comes) - and many groan; the beginning of famine - and many will perish; the beginning of wars - and powers are alarmed; the beginning of evils - and all will tremble. 19. What will they do (then) when the suffering (itself) comes? 20. Behold, hunger and plagues, confusion and affliction, are sent as scourges to bring amendment. 21. But in all this, they will not turn from their wickedness, nor ever remember the scourges.

Behold corn will be cheap in the earth, so that they will believe that peace has been granted them. 22. But then will evils spring forth on the earth, sword, famine and great confusion. 23. Most of the inhabitants of the earth will die of hunger, and the sword will destroy the others who have survived the famine. 24. The dead will lie on the streets like dung and no one will be there to lament (?) them. For the earth will be left desolate and its cities will be cast down. 25. There will be no one left to till the soil and sow seeds in it. 26. The trees will yield their fruit, but who will harvest it? 27. The grapes will ripen, but who will tread them? For there will be deep desolation everywhere. 28. For a man will passionately desire to see another man, and to hear his voice. 29. For of a city there shall be ten left surviving, and of a hamlet two who had hidden themselves in thick woods and in the clefts of the rocks. 30. As three or four olives remain on the several trees in an olive-garden, 31. and as in a vineyard, after the harvesting, some berries are left by those who carefully search through the yard, 32. so in these days, three or four will be left by those who search their houses with the sword. 33. And the land will be left desolate and its fields will be for briers; its paths and its ways let thorns grow up, for no flock of sheep will pass through any more. 34. The young women will weep because they have no fiancés; the women will weep because they have no husbands; their daughters will weep, because they are robbed of their helpers. 35. The fiancés will be destroyed in the war and the husbands will be destroyed by famine.

36. But hear this and understand it, ye servants of the Lord. 37. Behold, a word of the Lord (it is); receive it! Do not doubt what the Lord has said. 38. Behold, evils come and are not long time in coming! 39. As a woman who is pregnant with child in the ninth month, when the hour of her delivery draws near, for two or three hours before feels woeful pains in her body, and when the child leaves her body, there is not a moment of delay - 40. so shall the evil not tarry to come upon the earth. and the world will suffer misery and sorrows will encompass it.

41. Hear the word, O ye my people! Prepare yourselves for the struggle, and in the evils behave yourselves as strangers on the earth. 42. He that selleth, let him be as one in flight; he that buyeth as he who is about to lose; 43. he that dealeth as he who has no more profit; he that builds as he who will not inhabit; 44. he that soweth as he that will not reap; likewise he that prunes (his vines) as he that will not gather the harvest; 45. they that marry as those who will not beget children; and they that marry not as those who are widowed. 46. Hence they that work, work in vain. 47. Strangers will harvest their fruits and they will deprive them of their property, destroy their houses and take their children into captivity. Therefore those who marry should know that they will bring forth their children in captivity and famine. 48. Those who traffic in business do it as those who plunder. For the more they adorn their cities and houses and their possessions and their persons, 49. the more will I be angry with them because of their sins, saith the Lord. 50. For as a beautiful and noble woman hates a harlot, 51. so shall righteousness hate iniquity when she adorns herself, and accuses her to her face, when he comes that defends her, seeking out every sin on the earth. 52. Therefore be not like to them and their works! 53. For behold, a moment, and iniquity will be destroyed from the earth and righteousness will reign among us. 54. Let not the sinner say that he has not sinned, nor the unrighteous man that he has acted righteously; for coals of fire will burn on the head of him who says, 'I have not sinned, before God and his glory!' Behold the Lord knoweth all the works of men, 55. their imaginations, their aspirations, their thoughts and their hearts. 56. (He) who said, 'Let the earth be made' and it was made, 'let the heaven be made' and it was made, 57. through whose word the stars were established, who knoweth the number of the stars - 58. who searches the deeps and their treasures - who hath measured the sea and its contents - 59. who has shut up the world in the midst of the waters and hath hung the earth over the waters by his word - 60. who has stretched out the heaven like a chamber and founded it upon the waters - 61. who has made in the desert

springs of water and pools on the peaks of the mountains, to send forth rivers from on high to water the earth - 62. who has formed man and given him a heart in the midst of the body, and has poured into him breath and life and understanding, 63. even the breath of Almighty God who made all things and has sought out the hidden things in hidden places: 64. surely he knoweth our imaginations and aspirations and what you think in your hearts! Woe to the sinners and to those who would hide their sins. 65. For the Lord will certainly search out all your works and openly put you all to shame. 66. And you will be put to confusion when your sins are brought before the eyes of men and your iniquities will rise up as accusers on that day. 67. What will ye do? How will you hide your sins before God and his angels? 68. Behold, God is the judge! Fear him! Cease from your sins and forget your inquities to do them now for ever, so God will lead you forth and deliver you from all tribulation. 69. For behold, the wrath of a great multitude will burn against you and they will carry away captive some of you and make you eat food that is offered to idols. 70. And those who are led astray by them will be ridiculed, reproached and mistreated. 71. For there shall be . . . in adjoining cities a great rebellion against those who fear God. 72. For men will suffer want and, through their need, will be like madmen, sparing none, that they may plunder and destroy those who fear God. 73. For they shall destroy and plunder their goods, and banish them from their homes. 74. Then shall the tried quality of my elect come to the light, like gold which is tried by fire.

75. Hear, my elect, saith the Lord! Behold, the days of tribulation are near and I will deliver you from them. 76. Fear not and flinch not; for God is your leader. 77. And you who observe my commandments and precepts, saith the Lord God, let not your sins gain the upper hand over you, nor your iniquities lord it over you. 78. Woe to them that are bound fast by their sins and over-run by their iniquities, like as a field, to which no one goes, is fast bound with bushes, and its corn overgrown with thorns: it is rooted out and thrown into the fire, that it may be utterly consumed.

Notes

Introduction

1. The fact that such texts are also to be found in the Armenian versions of the Bible (cf. M.E. Stone, *The Apocryphal Literature in the Armenian Tradition* [The Israel Acad. of Sciences and Humanities - Proceedings IV, 4], Jerusalem 1969, [6]64), is not in conflict with the above statement, since the Armenian versions concerned go back to Latin sources.
2. Following Labourt (see Lit.), J. Daniélou on the contrary pleads for a Latin original for 5th Esra (*Studies in the History of Religions* [Supplement 21 to *Numen*], 1972, 162-171). His argument however presents no new proofs, but concentrates on the noting of certain analogies which are supposed to link this document with other Latin works from the end of the 2nd century (e.g. *Passio Perpetuae* and the *adv. Judaeos* of ps.-Cyprian)

3. G.N. Stanton recently argues (JTS 28, 1977, 67-83) for an origin as early as the middle of the 2nd century in a Jewish-Christian milieu for 5th Esra. The arguments for this he draws from the supposed exclusive influence which - within the NT - the Gospel of Matthew has exercised upon this document, and from the typically Jewish-Christian features of the community in which 5th Esra came into being.

Fifth Esra

1. No Biblical citations and references are given for the following section (1.4-2.9), for the text is nothing but a mosaic of innumerable OT passages.
2. Lk. 16:9.
3. Rev. 22:2.
4. Cf. Mt. 7:7 and par.
5. Cf. Is. 26:19.
6. Exod. 3:8, etc.
7. Enoch 24.
8. Cf. Is. 1:17; 58:6f.; Jer. 7:5f.; James 1:27; Tob. 1:17.
9. Cf. Heb. 4:9.
10. Cf. Jn. 17:12; also 10:28.
11. Jer. 3:12.
12. 1 Thess. 2:12.
13. Cf. Rev. 7:4ff.; Lk. 14:15.
14. Cf. Rev. 6:11; 7:9.
15. Cf. ibid.
16. Cf. Hermas, Sim. IX 6.1.
17. Cf. Rev. 7:13f.
18. Rev. 7:9.

2. Christian Sibyllines

Ursula Treu

1. Literature: Editions: S. Rzach, *Oracula Sibyllina*, 1891; J. Geffcken, *Die Oracula Sibyllina* (GCS 8), 1902 (reprint 1967); P. Lieger, *Christus im Munde der Sibylle (Or.Sib. III), Programm des Schottengymn.*, Vienna 1911; A. Kurfess, *Sibyllinische Weissagungen (I-VIII and IX)*, Tusculum Bücherei, 1951.

Translations: J.H. Friedlieb, *Die sibyllinischen Weissagungen*, 1852; NTApo[1] 1904, 322-345 (J. Geffcken); NTApo[2] 1924, 402-422 (Geffcken); NTApo[3] 1964, 502-528 (Kurfess; ET 1965, [2]1974, 709-745; there also [ET 703] the titles of Kurfess' numerous articles on the Or. Sib. 1939-1958); Erbetta III, 486-540 (Lit., commentary).

Studies: E. Sackur, *Sibyllinische Texte und Forschungen*, 1898; J. Geffcken, *Komposition und Entstehungszeit der Oracula Sibyllina* (TU 23.1), 1902; W. Bousset, art. 'Sibyllen und Sibyllinische Bücher', in RE[3] 18, 1906, 265-280; A. Rzach, art. 'Sibyllen', in PWRE II A, 1923, cols. 2073-2103; id., art. 'Sibyllinische Orakel', ibid. cols 2103-2183 (Lit. to 1920); J. Bidez and F. Cumont, *Les Mages hellénisés*, Paris 1931 (*passim*); M.J. Wolff, 'Sibyllen und Sibyllinen', *Archiv für Kulturgesch.* 14, 1934, 312-325; H. Fuchs, *Der geistige Widerstand gegen Rom in der antiken Welt*, 1938; H. Erbse, *Fragmente griechischer Theosophien*, 1941; K. Latte, *Römische Religionsgeschichte*, 1950, 160f.; B. Bischoff, 'Die lateinischen Übersetzungen und Bearbeitungen der Oracula Sibyllina', in FS J. de Ghellinck I, Gembloux 1951, 121-147; P. Dalbert, *Die Theologie der hellenistisch-jüdischen Missionsliteratur*

(Theol. Forschung 4), 1954; M.P. Nilsson, *Geschichte der griechischen Religion* I, [2]1955, 620; II, [2]1961, 109f.; J.B. Bauer, 'Die Gottesmutter in den Oracula Sibyllina', *Marianum* 18, 1956, 118-124; F. Dornsieff, 'Die sibyllinischen Orakel in der augusteischen Dichtung', in J. Irmscher and K. Kumaniecki (eds.), *Römische Literatur der Augusteischen Zeit* 1960, 43-51; J. Michl, art. 'Sibyllinen', in LThK[2] 9, 1964, cols. 728f.; P.J. Alexander, *The Oracle of Baalbeck* (Dumbarton Oaks Studies 10), Washington 1967; V. Nikiprowetzky, *La troisième Sibylle* (Études juives 9), Paris 1970 (Or. Sib. III, text and French trans.); G. Salanitro, 'Osservazioni critiche al testo degli Oracoli sibillini', *Boletin de Inst. de Estudios helénicos*, Barcelona, 6, 1972, 75-78; J.J. Collins, *The Sibylline Oracles of Egyptian Judaism* (SBL Diss. 13), Missoula/Montana 1972 (cf. Delling, ThLZ 101, 1976, cols. 762f.); G. Radke, art. 'Sibyllen', *Der kleine Pauly* 5, 1975, cols. 158-161 (Lit.); J. Schwarz, 'L'Historiographie impériale des Oracula Sibyllina', *Dialogues d'Histoire ancienne* 2, 1976, 413-420; M. Simon, 'Sur quelques aspects des Oracles Sibyllins juifs', in D. Hellholm (ed.), *Apocalypticism in the Mediterranean World and the Near East*, 1983, 219-233.

On the Coptic Sibyl: B.A. Pearson, 'The Pierpont Morgan Fragments of a Coptic Enoch Apocryphon', in G.W.E. Nickelsburg (ed.), *Studies in the Testament of Abraham* (SBL Septuagint and Cognate Studies 6), Missoula/Montana 1976, 227-283 (esp. 235; 239ff.).

2. Extant remains: the so-called Oracula Sibyllina are preserved in a collection of twelve 'books' of very differing length, from 162 to 829 hexameters. Book VI, the Christ hymn, is an extreme case with only 28 verses. Altogether there are over 4000 verses of the Sibylline Oracles. The Sibyl constantly speaks in the first person, and the tense is almost always the future. Since Book VIII originally appears in three separate parts, we find occasionally, especially in earlier scholars, a reckoning of fourteen books. We can only conjecture as to the details of who combined the poems into a unity, and when and where this was done.

3. Description of the Sibyl: the figure of the prophetic virgin and her name are not originally Greek, but come from Asia, perhaps from the region of Persia. The Sibyl and her oracular art were however known very early, as a famous citation from Heraclitus about 500 B.C. shows (fr. 92 Diels): 'By uttering things not to be laughed at, unadorned, unscented, the Sibyl penetrates with her voice through the millennia with the aid of the godhead.' There was thus already a Greek Sibyl, who spoke with divine authority and possessed a more than human age. These qualifications she retained for all time. The next mention is in Aristophanes (*Peace* 1095; 1116, in 421 B.C.); Plato (*Phaedrus* 244B) assumes the Sibyl to be generally known, and takes her and her oracles seriously.

In Aristotle (*Probl.* 954 a 36) the one Sibyl has become a whole series, who are named after the sites of their oracles, and then in Roman literature the number grows to ten in the historian Varro. Those of Marpessos and Erythrae in Asia Minor were particularly renowned. In the Greek West the Sibyl of Kyme (Cumae) attained the greatest significance, and the famous Sibylline books on the Capitol were traced back to her. It can scarcely now be determined whether there actually was originally a Chaldean Sibyl, and not just from hellenistic times an oracle placed under her aegis.

We know of Greek-speaking Jewish Sibylline literature from the 3rd century before Christ onwards. It took over much from its Greek models, but gave to the Sibylline oracles a new content. A direct taking-over of the form of the Sibyl from the Alexandrian enigmatic poem 'Alexandra' by Lycophron (3rd cent. B.C.), such as

Kurfess assumed, is unlikely. The Jewish Sibyl, as a non-Jewess, 'put her verses at the service of the propaganda of monotheism' (Kurfess), and in terms of form she like her Greek sisters proclaimed the past as future, in order thereby to lend more weight to her actual prophecies. The characteristic mark of the Jewish Sibyl, as of the Christian who is dependent on her, is the call to repentance, and then the prophecy and portrayal of future punishments down to the last Judgment. The Sibyl is not consulted for advice like the Pythia at Delphi, for example, although in later times she comes into conflict with her over spheres of influence; she speaks of her own accord when moved by God. She sets herself, so to speak, outside of world events from before the beginning of world history, indeed even before the creation. As these texts were taken over or edited by Christians, we can no longer determine for certain what is purely Jewish. The hymns, taken over in the main from the Jewish tradition, also contain Christian elements. Appeal to the Septuagint is at a certain period common to Jews and Christians.

4. Time of origin: the several books came into being somewhere in the period from 180 B.C. to the 3rd Christian century. This has to be deduced from the persons and events mentioned in the poems themselves, which leaves room for many an error, insofar as quotations in other writers of this period do not provide a *terminus ante quem*. Here of course we can only deal, briefly, with the texts in the present selection, and Books IX-XII are also left aside. Book III in its original Jewish form was probably the first to be composed, in Alexandria; Book VI, as purely Christian, certainly came into being later, while VII and VIII are predominantly Christian. In Book VIII there is a famous acrostic (lines 217ff.): *Jesus Christ Son of God Saviour Cross*. According to Eusebius (*Constant. or.* c. 18, Euseb. I, p. 179, GCS 1902) the emperor Constantine quoted this, and Augustine also cites it in a Latin translation (*Civ. Dei* XVIII c. 23).

5. Content: the extracts here presented convey a more coherent impression than the separate poems. Reading them as a whole, one is particularly struck by the abruptness with which ideas break off or dissolve, or completely different motives are introduced. The Oracula Sibyllina are neither a Christian history of doctrine nor an outline of world history, although the course of history is repeatedly stressed. They are very different from one another, and the only common element is their spokeswoman. Occasionally she addresses herself to her own person, mostly at the beginning or the end, as for example in Book II from lines 339 on. She is throughout a penitent sinner, and does not belong to the chosen people.

Common to all the books is the *method* of the prophecy proclaimed in them. First of all the Sibyl prophesies what has already happened in the lifetime of her hearers, and then what is yet to come, which is ordinarily doom and fearful punishment for sin and for apostasy from the one God. The narration of past events relates both to Jewish history and also to that of other peoples. The course of world history proceeds according to the old Greek sequence of the world states, the beginnings of which are already found in Herodotus (*c.* 450 B.C.) and which was taken over by Jewish apocalyptic from the time of Daniel: Egypt, Assyria, Babylon, Media, Persia, the empire of Alexander, that of the Diadochi, Rome. In some passages Egypt, and particularly the rule of the Ptolemaic kings, is dealt with in considerable detail; is this in itself enough to locate the origin of all these very disparate pieces in Alexandria?

The Sibyl accords special attention to the Roman empire and its leaders; individual personages however, according to ancient oracular tradition - and as we approach the writer's own period - are named only in cryptic fashion. The possession and circulation of Sibylline writings was very severely punished in Rome in the time of the emperors. In the several books the accents are quite differently placed (the sequence of the books is not chronological): if the last books (IX-XII) show no special hostility towards Rome, Book VIII in particular, which probably presupposes the Apocalypse of John, is a veritable hymn of hatred against Rome.

What is important for the Sibyl is not the course of world history, however broadly it is often depicted, but the End, the judgment as a punishment for action against God's grace, for polytheism, for covetousness; here there is occasionally a sharp polemic on behalf of the poor and defenceless against the propertied classes. This basic idea, closely related to Jewish apocalyptic, is repeatedly brought out.

6. Metre and language: the metre is the epic hexameter, according to Greek literary tradition obligatory for oracles, but in a late and very free form with many breaches of prosody. The language is epic, but from the period of the late epic, shot through with many unusual and difficult expressions. The complicated manuscript tradition contributes not a little to the general difficulty; Geffcken divides it into three classes with fourteen manuscripts of varying forms of text, and in addition the excerpt manuscripts and the numerous quotations in early Christian writers like Theophilus, (ps.-)Justin's *Cohortatio* and above all Clement of Alexandria, which often show a better recension than the late manuscripts: despite all these difficulties the text often shows a poetic fire, and even more often a genuine inspiration. The Sibyllines do not deserve the uniformly severe judgment pronounced upon them and the related literature - apocalyptic - by the representatives of classical philology: it is indeed not a question of the classical authors protected by grammarians and historians of literature or of sacred writings safe-guarded by a canon, but of 'a piece of popular literature, which in view of its obscure origins and manifold ramifications and also expansions is by no means to be treated as a unity' (so already Geffcken XXVI). Through their early translation into Latin the Oracula Sibyllina became very well known in the West, as we may recognise from Lactantius and Augustine.

7. Transmission: the Oracula Sibyllina were not much read and copied in the Byzantine Middle Ages, but the oracular literature was alive in Byzantium and the old poetic oracles passed into prose proverbs, which in their turn called forth the Erythraean Sibyl and also influenced the West.

The Byzantine Renaissance again took pleasure in the Sibyllines, so that almost all known manuscripts are late (15th cent.). The first printed edition by Xystus Betuleius (Birken) of Augsburg appeared in Basel in 1545, after a manuscript acquired by the Augsburg councillor in Venice: he printed the manuscript above all because with his pupils he was reading Lactantius, who often cites the Sibyllines. The *Latin translation* had already long been known, and now they had the original text at least of Books I-VIII 485. It was only in 1814 that Angelo Mai found the so-called Book XIV (XII), and in addition VI and fragments of VIII in a quite unknown recension, and later also the hitherto unknown Books XI-XII (today IX, X).

The influence of the Sibyllines is attested by a Latin *prophetia Sibyllae magae*, two of the three manuscripts of which derive from the 9th century. The poem begins with three distichs, and is written in very irregular hexameters. The language bears little similarity to classical Latin. A corresponding Greek *Vorlage* is not known.

Translations or adaptations of the Sibylline maxims in *Coptic* are not known, and the figure of the Sibyl has undergone a transformation: she appears on numerous tomb inscriptions alongside Enoch as his virgin sister.

Translation[1]
Oracula Sibyllina
End of Book I

Yea, then shall the Son of the great God come to men,
Clothed in flesh, like unto mortals on earth.
Four vowels he has, twofold the consonants in him,
And now will I declare to thee also the whole number:
Eight monads, and to these as many decads,
And eight hundreds also his name will show
To unbelieving men; but think thou in thy heart
Of Christ, the Son of the immortal, most high God.
He will fulfil God's law, and not destroy,
Offering a pattern for imitation, and will teach all things.
To him shall priests bring and offer gold
And myrrh and frankincense; for indeed all these he will make.
But when a voice shall come through a desert place
Bringing tidings to men, and shall call upon all
To make straight the ways and to cast out
All evil from the heart, and that every body among men
Be illumined by the waters, that born from above
They may no more in any way at all forsake the paths of right,
Then one of barbarous mind, ensnared by the dancer's art,
Shall give in reward the head of him that cried, and a sudden portent
Shall be to men, when from the land of Egypt
Shall come, safe guarded, a precious stone; upon it
The people of the Hebrews shall stumble, but Gentiles shall gather
By his guidance; for indeed God who rules on high
They shall come to know through him, and a path in a common light.
For he shall show eternal life to men
Elect, but on the lawless he will bring the inextinguishable fire.
Then shall he heal the sick and all the afflicted,
As many as put their trust in him.
And the blind shall see, and the lame walk,

And the deaf shall hear, and they that speak not shall speak;
Demons he shall drive out, and there shall be resurrection of the dead;
On the waves he shall walk, and in a desert place
From five loaves and fish from the sea
Shall feed five thousand; and the remains of these
Shall fill twelve baskets for a hope of the peoples.
. . . [*Lacuna*]
. . .

Then Israel in her intoxication shall not perceive,
Nor yet, weighted down, shall she hear with delicate ears.
But when the wrath of the Most High comes on the Hebrews
In raging fury and takes away faith from them,
Because they ill-used the heavenly Son of God,
And then indeed blows and poisonous spitting
Shall Israel give him with their polluted lips,
And for food gall, and for drink unmixed vinegar
They shall impiously give him, smitten they by evil frenzy
In breast and heart; but not seeing with their eyes,
Blinder than moles, more dreadful than creeping beasts
That shoot poison, shackled in deep slumber.
But when he stretches out his hands and measures all things,
And wears the crown of thorns, and his side
They pierce with spears, three whole hours
There shall be night of monstrous darkness in the midst of the day.
And then shall Solomon's temple show to men
A mighty wonder, when to the house of Aidoneus
He goes down, proclaiming a resurrection to the dead.
But when in three days he comes again to the light,
And shows to mortals a token, and teaches all things,
Ascending in clouds will he journey to the house of heaven,
Leaving to the world the ordinance of the Gospel.
Called by his name, a new shoot shall blossom forth
From the Gentiles guided by the law of the Mighty.
And moreover after this there shall be wise guides,
And then shall be thereafter a cessation of prophets.
Then when the Hebrews reap the bitter harvest,
Much gold and silver shall a Roman king carry off
In plunder. And thereafter other kingdoms
Shall follow without remission, as kingdoms perish,
And shall afflict men. But there shall be to those men
A mighty fall, when they rule in unrighteous arrogance.

But when Solomon's temple falls to the holy earth,
Cast down by men of barbarian speech
And brazen breastplates, and the Hebrews are driven from the land
Wandering and plundered, and they mingle many tares
With the wheat, then shall there be an evil discord
For all men; and the cities despoiled on either side
Shall mourn each other, since they transgressed by an evil deed,
And received the wrath of great God to their bosoms.

Book II

And then shall God thereafter make a great sign.
For like a radiant crown a star shall shine,
Radiant and brightly beaming from the brilliant heaven
For not a few days; for then he will show from heaven
A victor's crown for men who contend in the contest.
And then shall come the time of the great triumphal entry
Into the heavenly city, and it shall be universal
For all men, and have the renown of immortality.
And then shall every people in immortal contests
Contend for glorious victory; for there shall none
Be able shamelessly to purchase a crown for silver.
For Christ the holy shall adjudge to them just rewards,
And crown the excellent, and a prize immortal he will give
To martyrs who endure the contest even unto death.
And to virgins who run their course well a prize incorruptible
He will give, and to all among men who deal justly
And to nations from far-distant lands
Who live holy lives and recognise one God.
And those who love marriage and abstain from stolen unions,
Rich gifts will he give to them also, and eternal hope.
For every soul of men is a gift of God,
And it is not lawful for men to defile it with all manner of shame.

* * *

This is the contest, these the prizes, these the awards;
This is the gate of life and entry to immortality
Which the heavenly God appointed for righteous men
As guerdon of victory. They who receive
The crown nobly shall enter it by it.
But when this sign appears throughout all the world,

Children grown grey at the temples from birth,
And afflictions of men, famines and plagues and wars,
And change of seasons, lamentations, many tears -
Ah, how many children in all lands, bitterly wailing,
Shall devour their parents, wrapping the flesh
In shrouds, and foul with blood and dust
Bury them in earth, the mother of peoples! Poor wretches,
Men of the last generation, dreadful transgressors,
Children who do not understand that, when the race of women
Do not give birth, the harvest of mortal men is come!
Near is the end, when instead of prophets
False deceivers approach, spreading reports on earth.
And Beliar too shall come and do many signs
For men. Then indeed a confusion among holy men,
Elect and faithful, and there shall be a plundering
Of them and the Hebrews. Dread wrath shall come upon them,
When a ten-tribe people shall come from the East
Seeking a people which Assyria's shoot destroyed,
Their kindred Hebrews; thereupon nations shall perish.
Later again shall rule over men exceeding mighty
Elect and faithful Hebrews, when they have brought them
To slavery as of old, for power shall never leave them.
And the Most High, the all-surveying who dwells in the ether,
Shall send sleep upon men, veiling their eyelids.
O blessed servants, whom the master when he comes
Shall find wakeful, who all kept watch,
Ever expectant with sleepless eyes.
Come he at dawn or dusk, or in the midst of the day,
Yet come he will for certain, and it shall be as I declare.
He shall appear to the sleepers, when from the starry heaven
All the stars shall be seen of all in the midst of the day,
With the two great lights as time presses on.
And then the Tishbite, speeding the heavenly chariot
From heaven and descending to earth, shall show three signs
To all the world, signs of a life that is perishing.
Woe to all those who in that day are found to be
Great with child, all those who give milk
To infant children, all those who dwell upon the wave;
Woe to all those who look upon that day!
For a murky cloud shall cover the boundless earth,
From East and West and North and South.
And then a great river of burning fire

Shall flow down from heaven and consume every place,
Earth and great ocean and the grey-blue sea,
Lakes and rivers, springs and relentless Hades
And the heavenly sphere. And the lights of heaven
Shall be dashed together into a form all-desolate;
For the stars shall all fall from heaven into the sea.
And all souls of men shall gnash with their teeth,
Burning in the river of pitch and the raging fire
On a glowing plain, and ashes shall cover all things.
And then shall all the elements of the world be desolate,
Air, earth and sea, light, heaven, days and nights.
No more shall unnumbered birds fly in the air,
No more the swimming creatures swim the sea,
Nor laden ship voyage upon the waves,
Nor guided cattle plough the earth;
No sound of trees beneath the wind. But in an instant all
Shall fuse together, and be separated into purity.
But when the undying messengers of the immortal God,
Barakiel, Ramiel, Uriel, Samiel and Azael,
Who know full well what evils a man did before,
Shall bring the souls of men from the cloudy darkness
To judgment all, at the seat of God
Great and immortal - for one only is undying,
The Almighty himself, who shall be the judge of mortals -
Then to the dead shall the heavenly give souls
And breath and speech, bones fitted together
With all manner of joints, flesh and nerves,
And veins and skin about the flesh, and hair of the head.
Divinely compacted, breathing and set in motion,
Bodies of earthly men shall rise on one day.
Cruel, unbreakable and inflexible are the monstrous bars
Of the gates of Hades, not forged of metal;
Yet Uriel, the great angel, shall burst and fling them open,
And shall bring all the shapes deeply mourning into judgment:
The phantoms especially of Titans, born long ago,
And giants too, and all whom the Flood carried off,
And whom on the deep the wave of the sea destroyed,
And all whom beasts and creeping things and birds
Devoured, all these shall he call to the judgment-seat;
And again, whom the flesh-devouring fire destroyed in flame,
These too shall he gather and set before God's judgment-seat.
But when he raises the dead, loosing the bond of destiny,

And Sabaoth Adonai the high-thundering shall sit
On a heavenly throne and establish a great pillar,
There shall come on a cloud to the eternal, eternal himself,
Christ in glory with his blameless angels,
And shall sit on the right hand of Majesty, judging on his throne
The life of the pious and the ways of impious men.
There shall come also Moses, the great friend of the Most High,
Clothed in flesh; great Abraham too shall come,
Isaac and Jacob, Joshua, Daniel and Elias,
Habakkuk and Jonah, and they whom the Hebrews slew.
And those after Jeremiah, all, he shall destroy at the throne,
Hebrews indicted, that they may receive fitting works
And pay the price for all that any did in mortal life.
And then shall all pass through the burning river
And unquenchable flame; and the righteous
Shall all be saved, but the impious shall perish
For whole ages, as many as wrought evil aforetime
And committed murders, and all their accomplices,
Liars and thieves, the treacherous, grim destroyers of houses,
Parasites and adulterers, spreaders of evil reports,
The wickedly insolent, the lawless, the idolaters;
And all those who forsook the great immortal God,
And became blasphemers, ravagers of the pious,
Destroyers of faith and slayers of righteous men;
And all those who with crafty and shameless dissembling
As presbyters and reverend deacons had more regard
For the wealth than for the person and were not ashamed
By unrighteous judging to do injustice to others, relying on false reports,
More deadly than leopards and wolves . . .
And all inordinately proud, and usurers,
Who heaping up usury out of usury in their houses
Wrought sore harm to orphans and to widows;
And all who give to widows and to orphans
From ill-gotten gains, and all who revile others
Who live from honest toil; and all who forsook their parents
In old age, not requiting at all nor as children to parents
Supplying in their turn; and those who did not obey,
But answered savage words to them that begat them;
And all who receiving pledges denied it,
And all servants who turned against their masters,
And again those who defiled their flesh with lewdness,
And all who loosed the maiden girdle

In stealthy union, and women who slay the burden
Of the womb, and all who lawlessly cast out their offspring;
Wizards and witches with them, them also
The wrath of the heavenly and incorruptible God
Shall bring to the pillory, where in circle all about
Flows unwearied the fiery stream, and all of them together
The angels of the immortal, everlasting God
Shall punish fearfully with flaming whips,
Binding them tightly about with fiery chains
And unbreakable fetters; then in the dead of night
Shall they be flung into Gehenna among the beasts of Tartarus,
Many and fearful, where darkness has no measure.
But when they have laid many torments upon all
Whose heart was evil, later again the fiery wheel
From the great river shall close in upon them,
Because wicked works were all their concern.
Then shall they lament, one here, one there, from afar
At their piteous lot, fathers and infant children,
Mothers too, and little ones weeping at the breast.
Neither shall there be for them surfeit of tears, nor shall the voice
Of them that wail bitterly, now here, now there, be hearkened to,
But far beneath Tartarus dark and dank
Afflicted they shall howl; in places unhallowed
They shall pay threefold for every evil deed they wrought,
Burning in a mighty fire. They shall gnash with their teeth,
All wasting away with violent and consuming thirst,
And shall call death fair, and it shall flee from them.
For neither death nor night shall give them rest any more.
Many an appeal, but in vain, shall they make to God who rules on high,
And then will he openly turn away his face from them.
For seven age-long days of repentance did he give
To erring men, by the hand of a holy virgin.
But the others, all who took thought for justice and noble works,
And piety and righteous ways of thinking,
Angels shall bear them through the burning river
And bring them to light and to a carefree life,
Where runs the immortal path of great God
And there are threefold springs of wine and milk and honey.
Earth the same for all, not divided by walls
And fences, will then bear fruits more abundant
Of its own accord; livelihood held in common, wealth unapportioned!
No pauper is there, no rich man, nor any tyrant,

No slave, nor again any great, nor shall any be small,
No kings, no rulers; but all share in common.
No longer shall any say 'Night fell', nor again 'Tomorrow'
Nor 'It happened yesterday', nor be concerned with many days,
Nor spring nor harvest, nor winter nor autumn,
Nor marriage nor death, nor buying nor selling,
Nor sunset and sunrise; for all is one long day.
And for them will almighty, eternal God provide yet more.
To the pious, when they ask eternal God,
He will grant them to save men out of the devouring fire
And from everlasting torments. This also he will do.
For having gathered them again from the unwearying flame
And set them elsewhere, he will send them for his people's sake
Into another life and eternal with the immortals,
In the Elysian plain, where are the long waves
Of the ever-flowing, deep-bosomed Acherusian lake.
Ah, unhappy me, what will become of me in that day!
For that in my folly, labouring more than all,
I sinned, taking thought neither for marriage nor for reason;
Yea more, in my house I shut out the inferiors
Of a wealthy man; and lawless things I did aforetime
Knowingly. But thou, Saviour, deliver me the shameless
From my scourgers, though I have wrought unspeakable things!
And I pray thee, let me rest a little from my song,
Holy Giver of manna, king of a great kingdom.

Book VI: Hymn to Christ

I sing from the heart the great son and famous of the Immortal,
To whom the Most High, his begetter, gave a throne to take
Ere he was born; for according to the flesh he was raised up
The second time, after he had washed in the stream of the river
Jordan, which is borne along on silvery foot, drawing its waves.
Who first, escaping from fire, shall see God
Coming in sweet spirit, on the white wings of a dove.
And a pure flower shall blossom, and springs gush forth.
He shall show ways to men, he shall show heavenly paths;
And he shall teach all with wise speeches.
He shall bring to judgment and persuade a disobedient people,
Proudly declaring the praiseworthy race of his heavenly Father.
He shall walk the waves, and deliver men from sickness,
He shall raise up the dead, and banish many pains.

And from one wallet there shall be sufficiency of bread for men
When David's house puts forth its shoot. In his hand
Is all the world, and earth and heaven and sea.
He shall flash like lightning on the earth, as at his first appearance
Two saw him, begotten from each other's side.
It shall be, when earth shall rejoice in the hope of a Son.
But for thee alone, land of Sodom, evil woe lies waiting;
For thou in thy folly didst not perceive thy God
When he came in the eyes of men. But from the thorn
Thou didst weave a crown, and bitter gall didst thou mingle
For an insulting drink. This will bring thee evil woe.
O tree most blessed, on which God was stretched out,
Earth shall not have thee, but thou shalt see a heavenly home,
When thy fiery eye, O God, shall flash like lightning.

Book VII

O Rhodes, unhappy thou; for thee first, thee shall I weep.
Thou art first of cities, and first shalt thou perish,
Widowed of men and utterly bereft of life.
Delos, thou shalt set sail and be unstable on the water.
Cyprus, thee shall the wave of the grey-blue sea one day destroy.
Sicily, the fire that blazes beneath thee shall burn thee up.
This, I say, is God's terrible oncoming water.
Noah alone of all men came forth and escaped.
Earth swims, the mountains swim, the ether also swims,
All things shall be water,and all shall perish in the waters.
The winds shall stand still, and there shall be a second age.
Phrygia, thou first shalt shine above the surface of the water;
But first for impiety thou shalt deny God,
Pleasing dumb idols which, unhappy one,
Shall destroy thee as many years go round.
Unhappy Ethiopians, still suffering bitter pains,
Ye shall be smitten with swords, deep wounded in your flesh.
And fertile Egypt, ever concerned for its grain,
Which the Nile waters freely with its seven-fold flooding streams,
Intestine discord shall destroy; bereft of hope
Men then shall drive out Apis, baneful to men.
Woe, Laodicea, thou that hast never seen God!
Audacious, thou liest; but the wave of Lycus surges over thee.
Great God himself, the Begetter, shall create many stars,
And hang the axis in the midst of the ether,

And shall set up, a great dread for men to behold, on high
A pillar gigantic in great fire, whose sparks
Shall destroy races of men who have wrought evil mischief.
For there shall be that occasion, once and for all, when men
Shall propitiate God, but shall not put end to their fruitless troubles.
But through David's house shall all be accomplished,
For to him God himself gave a throne for his own possession
But the messengers shall lie down to sleep beneath his feet,
They who bring fires to light and pour forth rivers,
Who keep safe cities and send the winds.
But upon many men shall harsh life come,
Entering into their souls and changing the hearts of men.
But when from the root of the new branch . . .
And this shall be in the fulness of time. But when others
Rule, the race of the warlike Persians, there shall be forthwith
Awesome bridals in consequence of lawless deeds.
For mother shall have her son as husband; son
Shall unite with mother; daughter lying with father
Shall sleep according to this barbarian use. But later
The Roman Ares shall flash upon them from many a lance,
And with human blood they shall knead much earth to a bloody paste.
But then shall Italy's leader flee from the force of the spear,
But they shall leave on the ground the lance inlaid with gold
Which ever in the onset bears ahead the sign of destiny.
Verily the time shall be when the wicked, woefully ill-fated
Ilias shall celebrate burial, not a wedding, where deeply
The brides shall mourn, because they knew not God
But ever with drums and cymbal gave forth sound.
Prophesy, Colophon; for a great and terrible fire hangs over thee.
Thessaly ill-wedded, thee shall earth see no more,
Nor yet thine ashes, but thou shalt set sail alone, an exile from the mainland;
Thus, poor wretch, thou shalt be the sorry refuse of war,
Falling to swift-flowing streams and to swords.
O wretched Corinth, grievous war shalt thou have about thee,
Unhappy one, and ye shall perish at each other's hand.
Tyre, thou so great shalt be found alone; for of pious men
Widowed, thou shalt be distracted by them of small understanding.
O Coelesyria, last abode of Phoenician men,
Where the sea of Berytus laves the shore,
Wretch, thou didst not know thy God, whom once Jordan
Washed in its streams, and the Spirit flew like a dove;

Who was aforetime master both of earth and the starry heavens,
Logos with the Father and the Holy Spirit,
And putting on flesh he flew swiftly to the house of the Father.
Three towers did great Heaven establish for him,
Therein now dwell the noble guides of God,
Hope and Piety and Holiness much desired,
Who delight not in gold or silver but in reverence,
And the offerings of men and righteous thoughts.
Thou shalt sacrifice to God, immortal, great and lordly,
Not by melting a lump of incense in fire, nor with the knife
Slaying the shaggy lamb, but together with all
Who bear thy blood thou shalt take a wild dove,
And having prayed thou shalt send it forth, straining thine eyes to heaven.
Water then shalt thou pour on pure fire, crying out thus:
'As the Father begot thee as Logos, I send forth the bird,
Swift messenger of words, as Logos, with holy water
Sprinkling thy baptism, through which thou didst come out of fire.'
Nor shalt thou shut thy door when a stranger shall come to thee
Begging thee to ward off poverty and hunger from him.
But taking this man's head and sprinkling with water
Pray three times; cry to thy God in such fashion:
'I do not lust after riches; but, a suppliant, I receive a suppliant.
Give thou to both, O Father, leader of the heavenly choir, hear us.'
When thou prayest, he will give thee, but when the other has gone out . . .
'Afflict me not, holy and righteous majesty of God,
Hallowed, indomitable greatness, tested even in Gehenna!
Strengthen my poor heart, Father; unto thee have I looked,
Unto thee the immaculate, whom no hands wrought.'

*   *

Sardinia, powerful now, thou shalt be changed into ashes;
Thou shalt no more be an island, when the tenth Time comes.
Sailing on the waters they shall seek thee that art no more,
Sea-birds shall wail over thee a bitter lamentation.
Rugged Mygdonia, hard-to-pass beacon of the sea,
Thou shalt plume thyself for an aeon, through aeons shalt thou perish
All in a hot breath, and be maddened by many sufferings.
Land of the Celts, by the great mountain, the impassable Alp,
Deep sand shall cover thee altogether; no more shalt thou pay tribute,
No grain, no fodder; all-desolate shalt thou be of people
For ever, but thick with icy crystals

Thou shalt pay, unholy one, for the outrage thou didst not perceive.
Rome the stout-hearted, after Macedonian warfare
Thou shalt hurl lightning upon Olympus; but God shall make thee utterly
Unheard of, when thou thinkest to stand firm
For a yet greater onset. Then will I cry to thee thus:
'Perishing, thou shalt lift up thy voice, thou that once gleamed in splendour.
A second time, O Rome, a second time again will I cry against thee.'
And now, unhappy Syria, thee do I bitterly deplore.
Thebes of ill counsel, an evil sound is upon you
Of piping flutes, for you the trumpet shall sound
An evil sound; ye shall see all the land destroyed.
Woe to thee wretched, woe malevolent sea!
Thou shalt be wholly consumed by fire, and with brine shalt destroy a people.
For there shall be as much fire raging upon earth
As water, it shall rush and destroy all the land.
It shall burn up mountains, set rivers afire, empty the springs.
The world shall be no world, when men are destroyed.
Dreadfully burning, then shall the wretches look
To heaven, lit no more with stars but with fire.
Nor shall they perish quickly, but dying in the flesh
Yet burning in spirit for years of ages
They shall know that God's law is not to be deceived,
And other things hard to be borne, and that earth is oppressed
Because greatly daring she received the altars of the gods
And deceived by the smoke grown dark in the ether
<Did not obey the noble commands of great God.>
But those shall undergo great hardship, who for the sake of gain
Utter base prophecies, prolonging an evil time,
Who putting on the shaggy hides of sheep
Falsely call themselves Hebrews, although that is not their race;
Inveterate talkers, profiting only in sorrows,
They will not change their life nor will they persuade the righteous,
Who faithfully propitiate God in their hearts.
But in the third assignment as the years go round
Of the first Ogdoad, again another world is seen.
Night shall be everywhere over earth, long and hateful.
And then shall the dread odour of brimstone spread around,
Announcing murders, when those shall perish
In a terror of the night. Then will he beget a pure mind

Of men, and set up thy race as it was before.
No more shall any cut the deep furrow with the crooked plough,
No cattle plunge the guiding iron downward;
Thorns and thistles shall there be no more, but at the same time all
Shall eat with white teeth the dewy manna.
Then God too shall be with them and shall teach them
As he taught unhappy me! What evils did I do aforetime
Knowing! And many other things I wrought wickedly, taking no thought.
Countless couches have I known, but never recked of marriage.
Upon all I, utterly faithless, imposed the holy oath.
Suppliants I shut out, and in my halls
Sinned against blood-relatives, disregarding the word of God.
Wherefore fire shall devour and consume me. For I myself
Shall not live, but an evil time will destroy me. Then
Men shall come and prepare a grave for me thrice-wretched,
Or destroy me with stones; for of my own father conceiving
I abandoned the dear child. Stone me, stone me, all of you!
For thus shall I pay the penalty, and fix my eyes on heaven.

Book VIII

The great wrath that is coming on a disobedient world
At the last age, the outburst of God's anger, I show forth,
Prophesying from city to city to all mankind.
Since the tower fell, and the tongues of mortal men
Were divided into many dialects, first there arose
The royal house of Egypt, then of the Persians,
Medes and Ethiopians, Assyria, Babylon,
Then of Macedonia, vaunting great pride,
Then fifth the small and lawless kingdom of Italians
Last of all shall display to all mortals many evils,
And shall expend the labours of every land of men.
It shall lead unwearied kings of nations to the west,
Appoint ordinances for peoples, and subdue all things.
The mills of God grind slowly, but they grind exceeding small.
Fire then will crush all things, and reduce to fine powder
The high-crested peaks of mountains and all flesh.
For all, the beginning of evils is love of money and want of understanding.
For there shall be desire for treacherous gold and silver;
For nothing do mortals prefer more than these.
Not the light of the sun, nor heaven, nor sea,

Nor earth broad-backed, whence all things spring,
Nor God the all-giver, the begetter of all,
Not faith and piety do they prefer to these.
This is the source of impiety and vaunt-courier of disorder,
Contriver of wars, grievous foe of peace,
Making parents hostile to children, children to parents.
Nor shall marriage ever be held in honour apart from gold.
Earth shall have bounds, and every sea its watchers,
Each craftily partitioned among all those who have gold.
And as if they wished to hold for ages the earth that feeds many
They shall despoil the poor, that procuring more land
They may themselves become slaves to vainglory.
And did not the wide earth have its seat
Afar from the starry heaven, the light would not be common to men,
But bought for gold would belong to the rich
And for the beggars God would be preparing another aeon.
But on thee one day shall come from above, proud Rome,
A like heavenly stroke, and thou shalt first bow the neck;
Thou shalt be rased to the ground, and fire shall consume thee wholly,
Laid low to thy foundations; thy wealth shall perish,
And thy foundations shall be the home of wolves and foxes.
And then shalt thou be wholly deserted, as if thou hadst never been.
Where then the Palladium? What manner of god shall save thee,
Of gold or stone or brass? Or where then thy Senate's decrees?
Where the race of Rhea and of Cronos,
And of Zeus and all whom thou didst reverence?
Lifeless demons, phantoms of the dead departed,
Whose tombs ill-fated Crete shall have for a boast,
Solemnly celebrating enthronement for the unfeeling dead.
But when thou, the voluptuous, hast had thrice five kings,
Who enslaved the world from the east unto the west,
There shall be a ruler grey-headed having the name of the near-by sea,
Touring the world with nimble foot, furnishing gifts,
Possessed of abundant gold and silver and from his foes
Gathering more; having stripped them he will return.
He will have part in all mysteries of forbidden magic,
Displaying a boy as a god, and cast down all objects of worship,
And open to all the mysteries of ancient error.
Then follows a woeful time, when the 'woeful' himself shall perish,
And the people one day shall say: 'Thy great power, O city, shall fall'
Knowing straightway that the evil day to come is upon them.

Then shall they mourn together, fathers and infant children,
Foreseeing thy most lamentable destiny.
Plaintive dirges shall the mournful raise by the banks of Tiber.
After him three shall rule in the last day of all,
Fulfilling the name of heavenly God
Whose power is both now and to all ages.
One, an old man, shall wield the sceptre far and wide,
A most pitiable king, who shall shut up and guard in his house
All the wealth of the world, that when from the ends of the earth
The fugitive fierce mother-slayer shall come again
Giving these to all he may set great wealth in Asia.
Then shalt thou mourn, stripping off the purple-bordered
Patrician robe and wearing a mourning garment,
Thou haughty queen, offspring of Latin Roma;
No more shalt thou have fame for thine arrogance.
Nor shalt thou ever, ill-starred, be set upright, but bowed down;
For indeed the glory of the eagle-bearing legions shall fall.
Where then is thy power? What land shall be ally,
Lawlessly enslaved to thy frivolities?
For then shall there be confusion among men of all the earth,
When he comes, the Almighty himself, to judge on his throne
The souls of living and dead, and all the world.
Nor shall parents be dear to children, nor children
To parents, because of impiety and hopeless affliction.
Then shall be gnashing of teeth, dispersion and captivity,
When comes the fall of cities, and chasms in the earth;
And when the purple dragon comes upon the waves
With a host in its belly, and afflicts thy children,
While there is famine, yea, and civil war,
Near is the end of the world and the last day,
And judgment of immortal God for the proved elect.
But first there shall be implacable wrath of the Romans,
A time blood-drinking and a wretched life shall come.
Woe to thee, land of Italy, thou great barbarian nation,
Thou didst not know whence thou didst come, naked and unworthy,
To the light of the sun, that to the same place again
Thou mightest naked go, and later come to judgment
As having judged unjustly . . . (*lacuna*)
By giant hands alone against all the world
Descended from the height thou shalt dwell beneath the earth.
With naphtha and asphalt, brimstone and abundant fire,
Thou shalt be utterly destroyed and shalt be dust burning

For ages; and everyone who beholds shall hear a bellowing
Great and mournful out of Hades, and gnashing of teeth,
And thee beating godless breasts with thy hands.
Upon all there shall be night, alike to those who have riches
And to the beggars; naked from earth, and naked again to earth,
They come, and end their life, when they have completed the time.
None is a slave there, nor lord, nor tyrant,
No kings, no princes swollen with conceit,
No orator skilled in the law, no ruler judging for money;
They pour no blood on altars in sacrificial libations;
Drum does not sound, nor cymbal clash, . . . (*lacuna*)
Nor much-pierced flute with its frenzied note,
No sound of pipe bearing likeness to crooked serpent,
No trumpet, messenger of wars, with barbaric sound;
No drunkards in lawless revels or in dances,
No sound of lyre, no mischievous device;
No strife, no wrath of many forms, no sword
Is there among the dead, but a new age common to all.
. . . <All are dragged> by the keeper of the dungeon to God's throne.
Go on now building your cities and adorn them nobly
With statues of gold and silver and stone,
Ripe are you now, to come to the bitter day,
Beholding thy punishment first, O Rome,and gnashing of teeth.
No more beneath thine enslaving yoke shall bow the neck
Syrian or Greek or barbarian or any other race.
Thou shalt be utterly ravaged, and done by as thou hast done;
Lamenting thou shalt give in fear, until thou hast paid in full.
Thou shalt be a triumph-spectacle for the world, and a reproach to all.

* *

Again when the limit of time comes on of the phoenix,
There will come the ravager of a race of peoples, countless tribes, (and)
The Hebrew nation. Then shall Ares lead Ares captive,
The presumptuous threat of the Romans he himself will destroy.
Ended is Rome's dominion, once so flourishing,
Ancient mistress to neighbouring cities.
No more shall the land of luxuriant Rome be victorious
When from Asia he comes in sovereign power with Ares.
And when he has wrought all this he will come booted to the city.
Thrice three hundred and forty and eight
Years shalt thou fulfil, when upon thee shall come ill-fated

A destiny violent fulfilling thy name.
  Alas, thrice unhappy me, when shall I see that day,
Bringing to thee destruction, Rome, bitter especially to the Latins?
Sing in his honour, if thou wilt, that man of hidden origin,
From the land of Asia riding on a Trojan chariot
With the heart of a lion. But when he cuts through the isthmus,
Gazing about, ready to go against all, exchanging the sea,
Then shall black blood follow after the great beast.
But the lion that destroyed the herds a dog pursued.
The sceptre they will take away, and he will pass to Hades.
  To Rhodes also shall come a final evil, but the greatest,
And for Thebes there was hereafter a dire captivity.
Egypt shall be destroyed by the wickedness of rulers.
But when thereafter mortals escaped utter ruin,
Thrice happy was that man, and fourfold blessed.
Rome shall be an alley, Delos invisible,
Samos a sandheap. . . . (*lacuna*)
Later again thereafter, evil shall lay hold on the Persians
Because of arrogance, and all wanton insolence shall perish.
  Then shall a holy ruler wield the sceptre of all earth
For all ages, he who raised up the dead.
Three shall the Most High bring at Rome to a pitiful fate,
And all men shall perish in their own halls.
But they will not be obedient, which would be far better.
But when for all the evil day grows longer
Of famine and plague intolerable, and of the din of war,
Then once again the wretched ruler of old time
Summoning a council shall deliberate how he may destroy . . .

*   *   *

The dry shall blossom, appearing with leaves together.
But the heavenly floor shall bring on the solid rock
Rain and fire and violent wind upon earth,
And abundance of rust-ruined crops throughout every land.

*   *   *

But again they will do shameless things, full of boldness,
Not fearing the wrath of God or of men,
Abandoning modesty, yearning for effrontery,
Rapacious tyrants and violent sinners,

Liars, faithless friends, evil-doers, in nothing true,
Breakers of faith, inventive of words, pouring out slander;
Nor will they know any surfeit of wealth, but shamelessly
Gather yet more; under the sway of tyrants shall they perish.
The stars shall all fall headlong into the sea;
Many new stars shall come forth, and a radiant comet
Men call the star, sign of much trouble
Yet impending, of war and mortal conflict.
Might I live no more when the polluted woman shall reign,
But at the time when heavenly grace shall rule,
And when a holy child one day shall utterly destroy
All wickedness, opening for baleful mortals the abyss,
And suddenly a wooden house shall compass about the pious.
But when the tenth generation goes down to the house of Hades,
Thereafter shall be great power of woman; to whom many evils
Will God himself increase, when crowned she has obtained
A royal honour; a whole year shall become a gentle aeon.
The sun shall appear by night, running its arid course;
The stars shall leave heaven's vault; and raging with many a gale
He shall make earth desert. But there shall be resurrection of the dead,
And swift running of the lame, and the deaf shall hear
And the blind see, and they that speak not shall speak,
And to all shall life be common, and riches too.
Earth the same for all, not divided by walls
Or fences, will bear fruits more abundant.
Springs of sweet wine and white milk
And of honey will it give . . . (*lacuna*)

* * *

But when God changes the seasons . . .
Making winter summer, then are all the oracles fulfilled.
But when the world has perished <and then the Eternal comes,
Fire shall hold sway in the darkness, and silence in the midst of the night.>

* * *

JESUS CHRIST, SON OF GOD, REDEEMER, CROSS[2]

Earth shall sweat, when the sign of judgment shall appear.
From heaven shall come the eternal king who is to be;

When he comes, he shall judge all flesh and the whole world.
And mortals, faithful and faithless, shall see God
Most High with the saints at the end of time.
He shall judge on his throne the souls of flesh-clothed men
When all the world becomes dry land and thorns.
Men shall cast down their idols and all their wealth.
And the fire shall burn up earth, heaven and sea,
Ranging abroad; he shall break the gates of Hades' prison.
Then shall all flesh of the dead come to the light of freedom,
That is, the saints; the lawless the fire shall torment for ages.
Whatever a man wrought secretly, then shall he speak all openly;
For God will open dark breasts with his lights.
There shall be wailing from all, and gnashing of teeth.
The light of the sun shall be eclipsed, the dances of the stars;
Heaven he will roll up; and the light of the moon shall perish.
He will raise aloft the chasms, lay low the high places of the hills;
No more shall baneful height be seen among men.
Mountains shall be level with plains, and all the sea
Shall no more have voyages. For earth shall then be parched
With its springs, and the foaming rivers run dry.
A trumpet from heaven shall send forth a sound of great lamentation,
Mourning defilement of limbs and a world's calamity.
Then shall a gaping earth display the abyss of Tartarus.
All kings shall come to God's judgment seat.
From heaven shall flow a river of fire and brimstone.
Then shall be a sign for all mortals, a notable seal,
The wood among the faithful, the horn long desired,
Life for pious men, but a stumbling-block for the world,
With its waters enlightening the elect in twelve springs;
A staff of iron, shepherding, shall hold sway.
This is our God now proclaimed in acrostics,
Saviour, immortal King, who suffered for our sakes.

Him Moses typified, extending holy arms,
Conquering Amalek by faith, that the people might know
That with God the Father elect and precious is
The staff of David, and the stone which he promised,
He who believes on which shall have eternal life.
For not in glory but as a mortal shall he come into the world,
Pitiable, dishonoured, unsightly, to give hope to the pitiable.
And to corruptible flesh he will give form, and heavenly faith
To the faithless, and he will take the form of the man
Moulded in the beginning by God's holy hands,

Whom the serpent led astray by guile, to go to a destiny
Of death and receive knowledge of good and of evil,
So that forsaking God he was subject to mortal customs.
For him first of all did the Almighty take as counsellor
265 In the beginning, and say: 'My child, let us two make
The tribes of mortals, modelling them from our image!
Now I with my hands, and thou thereafter with the logos,
Shall tend our figure, that we may produce a common creation!'
Mindful of this resolve, then, will he come into the world
270 Bringing a corresponding copy to a holy virgin,
At the same time enlightening with water by older hands,
Doing all with a word and healing every disease.
With a word shall he make the winds to cease, and calm the sea
While it rages, walking on it with feet of peace and in faith.
275 And from five loaves and fish of the sea
He shall feed five thousand men in the desert,
And then taking all the fragments left over
He will fill twelve baskets for a hope of the people.
He shall call the souls of the blessed, and love the pitiable,
280 Who when scoffed at return good for evil,
Beaten and scourged and yearning for poverty.
Perceiving all and seeing all and hearing all
He shall spy out the inmost parts and lay them bare for scrutiny;
For he himself of all is hearing and understanding and vision.
285 And the Word that creates forms, whom all obey,
Saving the dead and healing every disease,
Shall come at the last into the hands of lawless and unbelieving men,
They shall give to God blows with their unclean hands
And with their polluted mouths poisonous spitting.
290 Then shall he expose his back and submit it to the whips,
292 And buffeted shall keep silence, lest any should know
Who and of whom he is and whence he came to speak to the dying.
And he shall wear the crown of thorns; for of thorns
295 Is the crown of the elect, their eternal glory.
They shall pierce his sides with a lance because of their law.

299 But when all is accomplished which I have spoken,
300 Then in him shall all the law be dissolved, which from the beginning
Was given to men in ordinances because of a disobedient people.
He shall stretch out his hands and measure the whole world.
But for food they gave him gall, and to drink, sour wine;
This table of inhospitality will they display.

But the veil of the temple shall be rent, and in the midst of day
There shall be night dark and monstrous for three hours.
For no longer by secret law and in hidden temple to serve
The phantoms of the world, the hidden truth was again revealed
When the eternal Master came down upon earth.
But he shall come to Hades, announcing hope to all
The saints, the end of ages and the final day,
And shall fulfil death's destiny when he has slept three days;
And then returning from the dead he shall come to the light,
The first to show them that are called the beginning of resurrection,
Having washed away the former iniquities in the waters
Of an immortal spring, that born from above
They may no more be in thrall to the lawless customs of the world.
First to his own will the Lord then openly appear
In flesh, as he was before, and show in his hands and feet
Four nail-prints pierced in his own limbs,
East and west and south and north;
So many kingdoms of the world shall accomplish
The lawless, blameworthy deed as our example.
Rejoice, holy daughter of Sion, that hast suffered so much!
Thy king himself shall come, mounted on a gentle colt.
Meek, behold, he will come to take away our yoke
Of slavery, hard to bear, that rests upon our neck,
And godless ordinances will he dissolve, and oppressive fetters.
Him know thou for thy God, who is God's Son.
Glorifying him and having him in thy breast
Love him with all thy soul and exalt his name!
Put away the old ways and wash thyself of his blood;
For he is not propitiated by thy songs or by thy prayers,
Nor gives he heed to corruptible sacrifices, being incorruptible.
But offering a holy hymn from understanding mouths
Know who this is, and then shalt thou see thy begetter.

* * *

Then shall all the elements of the world be desolate,
Air, earth and sea, and the light of blazing fire;
And the heavenly sphere, and night, and all the days
Shall be dashed together into one, into a form all-desolate.
For the stars of the luminaries shall all fall from heaven.
No more shall the plumed birds fly on the air
Nor is there step on earth; for the wild beasts shall all perish.

No sounds of men or beasts or winged things.
A world in disorder shall hear no useful echo;
But the deep sea shall ring forth a great sound of menace
And the swimming creatures of the sea shall all trembling die;
And ship bearing cargo shall no more sail upon the waves.
But earth shall bellow, blood-stained by wars,
And all souls of men shall gnash with their teeth,
Consumed with thirst and hunger, pestilence and slaughters,
And they shall call death fair, and it shall flee from them;
For no more shall death give them rest, nor night.
Many an appeal, but in vain, shall they make to God who rules on high,
And then will he openly turn away his face from them.
For seven age-long days of repentance did he give
To erring men, by the hand of a holy virgin.
God himself has made known to me all these things in my mind,
And he will accomplish all that is spoken by my mouth:
'I know the number of the sand and the measures of the sea,
I know the inmost parts of earth, and murky Tartarus,
I know the numbers of the stars, the trees, and how many tribes
Of things four-footed and swimming and of winged birds,
And of men, that are and shall be, and of the dead.
Myself I moulded the forms and the mind of men,
And gave them right reason, and taught them knowledge;
I who formed eyes and ears, seeing and hearing
And perceiving every thought, and privy to all,
Lurking within I keep silence, and later myself will convict them.

* * *

The dumb I understand, he that speaks not I hear,
And how great is the whole height from earth to heaven,
Beginning and End I know, I who made heaven and earth.
For I alone am God, and other god there is none.
They seek oracles of my image, wrought from wood,
And shaping with their hands a speechless idol
They honour it with prayers and unholy ritual.
Forsaking the Creator, they render service to wantonness;
Worthless the gifts men have, to useless beings they give them,
And as it were for my honour they think all these useful,
Celebrating a steaming banquet, as for their own dead.
For they burn flesh, and bones full of marrow,
Sacrificing on their altars, and to the demons pour out blood;

And lights they kindle for me, the giver of light,
And as if God were athirst men pour libations of wine
On their useless idols, getting drunk to no purpose.
I need no sacrifice or libation at your hand,
No foul reek of fat, no hateful blood.
For these things will they do in memory of kings
And tyrants, for dead demons, as if they were heavenly,
Performing a ritual godless and destructive.
And gods do the godless call their images,
Forsaking the Creator, thinking that from them they have
All hope and life, trusting to their hurt
In the dumb and speechless, that know not the good end.
I myself set forth two ways, of life and death,
And I set it in their mind to choose the good life;
But they turned eagerly to death and eternal fire.
Man is my image, possessed of right reason.
For him set thou a pure and bloodless table,
Filling it with good things, and give to the hungry bread
And to the thirsty drink, and to the naked body clothing,
Of thine own labours providing it with holy hands!
Receive the afflicted, come to the aid of the weary,
And present this living sacrifice to me, the living God,
Sowing now on the water, that I one day may give thee
Immortal fruits, and thou shalt have light eternal
And life unfading, when I bring all men to proof by fire.
For I shall smelt all things, and separate them into purity.
Heaven I shall roll up, earth's crannies I shall open,
And then shall I raise up the dead, destroying fate
And death's sting, and later shall I come to judgment,
Judging the life of pious and of impious men;
And I will set ram with ram, shepherd with shepherd,
And calf with calf, hard by one another for the testing.
All who were exalted, convicted in the trial,
And stopped the mouth of every man, that they full of envy
Might enslave all alike those who act in holy fashion,
Bidding them keep silence, eager for gain,
All these shall then depart, as not approved in my presence.
No more thereafter shalt thou say in sorrow "Will it be tomorrow?"
Nor "It happened yesterday"; thou art not concerned for many days,
Nor spring nor winter, nor harvest nor autumn,
Nor sunset and sunrise; for I will make day long.
But the light of Majesty shall be desired for ever. . . (lacuna)'

* * *

Self-begotten, immaculate, everlasting and eternal,
He is able to measure the fiery breath of the heaven,
Wields thunder's sceptre with the flaming chariot,
And softens the peals of crashing thunders,
Convulsing the earth, he knows the rolling . . . [of the sun?]
Tempers the fiery scourges of the lightning;
Incessant streams of rain he has, and storms of hail
Ice-cold, the discharge of the clouds, the assaults of winter storms.

* * *

Born before all creation in thy bosom,
Counsellor, moulder of men and founder of life,
Whom thou didst address with the first sweet sound of thy mouth:
'Behold, let us make man all like to our semblance,
And let us give him life-supporting breath to possess;
Him, mortal though he be, shall all earthly things serve,
And to him, moulded of earth, shall we subject all things.'
Thus didst thou speak to the Logos, and all was done to thy purpose.
The elements were all alike obedient to thy command,
The everlasting creation was subjected to the mortal likeness,
Heaven, air, fire, earth, land and the flow of the sea,
Sun, moon, the choir of the heavenly stars . . . (*lacuna*)
Night and day, sleep and waking, spirit and impulse,
Soul and understanding, craft, voice and strength;
And the wild tribes of animals, the swimming and the winged
And those of the land, the amphibious, the creeping and those of double nature;
For in all respects he was in concord with thee beneath thy guidance.
And in the last times he changed his abode, and coming as a child
From the womb of the virgin Mary he arose, a new light.
From heaven he came, and put on mortal form.
First then the holy, mighty form of Gabriel was displayed.
And second the archangel addressed the maiden in speech:
'In thine immaculate bosom, virgin, do thou receive God.'
Thus speaking, God breathed grace into the sweet maiden.
But she then was seized with alarm and wonder together as she listened,
And stood trembling; her mind was in turmoil,
Her heart leaping, at such unheard-of tidings.

But again she rejoiced and her heart was warmed by the saying,
And the maiden laughed, her cheeks flushed scarlet,
Gladly rejoicing and touched in her heart with shame;
Then took she courage. The Word flew into her body,
Made flesh in time and brought forth to life in her womb,
Was moulded to mortal form and became a boy
By virgin birth-pangs; this, a great wonder to mortals,
Is no great wonder to God the Father and to God the Son.
When the child was born, delight came upon the earth,
The heavenly throne laughed, and the world rejoiced,
A new-shining star, God-appointed, was revered by the Magi.
478 Bethlehem was chosen the homeland, divinely elect, of the Logos
477 And the swaddled child was shown to God's obedient in a manger,
479 To herdsmen of cattle and goats and shepherds of sheep.

* * *

. . . to be lowly in heart, and hate malignant deeds,
And wholly to love one's neighbour as oneself;
To love God with all one's soul, and serve him.
Wherefore we, sprung of the holy race of Christ
In heaven, are surnamed brethren,
Having the remembrance of gladness in our rituals
And walking the paths of piety and justice.
Never are we allowed to approach the inner shrines of temples
Or pour libations to images, or honour them with prayers,
Or with the manifold fragrance of flowers or with the gleam
Of torches, nor yet to furnish them with offerings of loaves;
Nor to send up the flame of the altar with vapours of incense,
Nor upon libations of bull-sacrifice to send the blood of slaughtered sheep,
Rejoicing in deliverance, to atone for earthly penalty,
Nor with reeking smoke from the flesh-devouring pyre
And with foul vapours to pollute the light of ether;
But with holy understandings, rejoicing with merry heart,
With abundant love and with generous hands,
In gracious psalms and songs meet for God
To hymn thee the immortal and faithful are we bidden,
God, the Creator of all, the Omniscient . . .

The Latin Sibyl[*]
(*Mundus origo mea est*)

The world is my origin, but soul have I drawn from the stars.
My body inviolate God makes to tremble altogether.
[*perhaps*: What God sets in my heart, that will I proclaim]
If abundant faith adjudge truly devout.
Many a song have my songs uttered aforetime,
But the songs which now I write, these God knows.
The heavenly homeland's citadel first God created with a word
As a divine and perfect work and a great service,
At the beginning of light, before chaos, God himself.
Beginning without end is God, God author of all.
He set chaos aside, separate from kindly night,
Commanded the day to stand, and night and day
To exchange in succession with their lights and move with the stars
By which the ages of all things are renewed in cycle.
A deluge he poured on earth, and a gift from above.
But after God had confined the waters by banks
The first born of heaven in his own right
To earth came down as man, the child of a virgin inviolate,
Bearing on purple neck for ever the crown.
And the Father himself drew near to his own self at the birth,
And one was the soul, one the spirit of his Son,
The name divided, undivided the sovereign power.
The Magus told of his birth in the name of the stars,
And the Lamb descended, whom scarce earth's circle could contain.
He willed to asume the limbs of a human body,
But vigorous in strength of soul and a chaste body
Ever in the bloom of youth he knows not how to grown old.
Alone all-powerful, he shall himself rid the world of sin,
And the shoot is the Father himself; in the two one spirit,
One power, one will, nor any division of will.
He shall rule a world pacified by his father's virtues,
Thereafter returning to heaven and his father's golden house.
Praise him fervently with a loud voice, the Mighty!
Me he allows to speak, he who encompasses all the sea.
Most High God, < . . . > Father and hope of thine own,
Most High Son of the Father, whose origin is seed of the word,
Who graciously bestow your commands on souls,
In mortal hearts secret things are spoken by you.
The wisdom of the Most High forbids us know - they are too great -

What is and has been, and what is foretold for the future,
What fear stirs which heart, what spirit afflicts the soul,
What fortune rules kings, or divine power.
The souls of kings also are controlled by your dominion,
That peoples and nations may fall, nor times of peace arise,
But pestilence and fever and baneful heat of climate,
And waning as of the moon, eclipses of the sun,
And inroads of the surging sea with its ebb and flow.
You have given names to the stars and signs to the constellations,
You command the hot springs to boil in the depths of the earth,
Burning streams flow in like manner in the inward parts.
To you is known the fire of the sun, you who can know
The thoughts of men, and crimes but contemplated.
Say, what doest thou, mortal man, who dost lose part of the body?
God Most High, leave me not to blood and fire,
When thou dost save the soul but destroy the body,
And I know that my form returns to me again.
I look for the fire, and fire does not suffice for fire;
Twice burning I bear threats and mighty wrath.
Fear him, when he arises, whom highest air shall serve.
That day shall come, whose hour the Most High knows,
Which <the Father> forbids us to know, and denied to the Son.
Nor shall I say so much, for himself too knows the day;
Who father to himself is not at variance with the Father,
The same can know, because the power is decreed.
Then we all pay the varied penalties, to our deserts.
Then will he fear the Most High and raise up groans and tears
When he sees men tortured in the eddy of flame,
When fire lays hold on men and no end is set to the punishment.
Then are kingdoms of no avail, nor all the purples
And dyed robes of kings, nor crowns adorned with jewels.
Nor sceptres entrusted to their hands, nor length of reign.
Of no avail the arts, no soothsayer comes to assist.
All things wearily stumble: honour, power, kingship.
The Father himself, hidden in the realm of the snowy world,
Shall give to his saints splendour for their abode.
All implore in supplication that the wrath may cease.
A few gather together, saints of proven heart,
Who ever with upright heart worshipped almighty God,
In whose mind dwelt the nursling spirit,
And who with sincere intent willed to fulfil his precepts.
Thee ever did they name as God, and humbly they prayed

With their voices, and day and night they groaned to thee.
Thus he addresses you, ye saints, with a gracious heart:
'Lo, I am he who made the frame of heaven and the stars,
Who commanded the world to shine with a twofold light,
Who founded earth and the seas, and poured forth souls,
Who with my hands led limbs through the members,
Added body to bones, and in the bones marrow,
Made firm the sinews, and veins filled with blood,
Who formed the gleaming skin from glutinous mud
And inserted souls and added senses to minds,
Who gave nourishment to souls and food for the body,
And riches I gave to the streams, and to the fields metals,
And pure springs, and waters meet for fountains,
And cattle, the race of flocks, the natures of birds,
Who shut up milk in the udders, separating the blood,
Who willed the grass to grow green in the furrows on the dry ground,
Who enclosed the fragile grain in spiked seed,
Who painted the earth with flowers in varied bud,
Who cared for the sweet souls of bees and their homes,
Who commanded the globes on the fruit-trees to swell with moisture,
Who gave vineyards, and made veins in the body.
These I provided and gave to man, nor denied him invention.
Yet am I unthanked, these thanks another receives.
This work is compared with deserts, rewards with deeds.
They worship mountains, rocks, sheep, bulls and caves,
Statues, springs, altars and an empty sepulchre!
Birds give augury, they acknowledge sun and moon,
The author of the works they despise, and forsake the Almighty.
Look upon me; why have I redeemed all with my blood
If they have exchanged the kingdom for an earthly seat of men?
Their greed was greater than their terror of the darkness.
That the soul may be mine, it will seek me in due time (?).'
Receive these precepts with righteous heart in a pure body!
You who shed tears, prove yourselves worthy of reward!
The years press on, the centuries run to their end,
Which God knows, and refused to let me know.
This alone I know, what is and what is foretold for the future.
All that is ours diminishes; the stars grow dim,
Earth is dissolved, the poor air overturned.
If the blood is withdrawn, the whole race is scattered (?).
Deeds burden men, (crimes) planned destroy the guilty;
But he perishes exulting, that faith may purge his crimes.

Then all the race shall renew what it restores from itself (?).
The pure he will command to abide in eternal splendour,
To the chaste who merit the palm he appoints habitations.
Under such a Lord the rich shall have no place;
The poor man shall be rich, who believed in the depth of his heart.
Sinners find no grace, receive no reward (?).
To have done well beyond measure, this is the short way to life,
To say what is dear and the great Author loves (?),
To strive (?) after what the simple nature has for nourishment.
Lo, a mortal, I have sung the songs I knew,
That the last avenging day may not cast me down, nay,
If I be worthy, snatch me away and establish my soul in heaven.
Short is man's life, and when ended dissolves with the years.

Notes

2. Christian Sibyllines

1. The translation is based on Geffcken's edition (GCS 8). Text-critical notes have had to be largely dispensed with. Only at a few places did it seem appropriate to refer to problems of transmission. The numbers of the notes relate to those of the verses.

I 332. Cf. Mt. 5:17. **334f.** Cf. Mt. 2:11. **345f.** Cf. Mt. 21:43; Rom. 9:33 (Is. 8:14; 28:16); 1 Pet. 2:4. **348.** After Friedlieb. **353f.** Cf. Mt. 11:5 par. **356.** Cf. Mk. 6:48 par. **357ff.** Cf Mk. 6:38ff.; Mt. 14:17ff.; Jn. 6:7ff.
359. Rzach after VIII 278. **365.** Cf. Mt. 26:67 par. **369.** Cf. Is. 6:9f.; Mt. 13:14; Mk. 4:12; Jn. 12:40; Acts 28:26. **375ff.** Cf. Mt. 27:54; Mk. 15:38; Lk. 23:44f.
396f. Cf. Mt. 13:25.

II 56-148. (Geffcken) are transmitted only in the MS group Ψ, and are not translated here.
165f. Cf. Mt. 24:11. **171** 'Twelve-tribe' in the MS groups Φ and Ψ.
179. Cf. Mt. 24:46. **190f.** Cf. Mt. 24:19; Mk. 13:17; Lk. 21:23
242f. Cf. Mt. 25:31; 19:28.

VI 7. Cf. Mt. 3:16; Mk. 1:10. **13.** Cf. Mt. 14:25; 6:48; Jn. 6:19.

VII 24. 'Begetter', 'begotten' or 'unbegotten'? **38.** A lacuna follows.
72. 'Guides' for 'mothers': conjecture by Friedlieb.
134. Cf. Mk. 7:15
161. Passage corrupt.

VIII 4f. Cf. Gen. 11:7ff.
59. Conjecture by Hase; cf. Geffcken's apparatus *ad loc.*
88. Cf. Rev. 12.3f.
119. After 'device' some instrument could be mentioned, e.g. the organ.
121ff. Here lacunae must be assumed. **130-139.** Here eight verses have been omitted, which are probably secondary; cf. Geffcken, App. *ad loc.*

165f. A play on words which cannot be imitated in English.
177. Here follows a lacuna (cf. Geffcken). **181.** Another lacuna (cf. Geffcken). **190.** Cf. Is. 34:4; Mk. 13:25; Mt. 24:29; Rev. 6:13.
214-217. Cf. Geffcken, App. *ad loc.*

2. Lines 217-250 form an acrostic, of which the initial letters in the Greek make up the words 'Ιησοῦς Χρειστὸς Θεοῦ Υἱὸς Σωτὴρ Σταυρός. Retention of the acrostic form proved impossible to reconcile with accuracy in translation, and has therefore not been attempted (R. McL. W.). On the acrostic, cf. Geffcken App.
224. Cf. Is. 2:18
231. Cf. Mt. 8:12; Lk. 13:28. **234ff.** Cf. Is. 40:3ff.; Bar. 5.7. **239.** Cf. 1 Thess. 4:16. **245.** Cf. Lk. 1:69 (1 Sam 2:10; Ps. 132:17). **248.** Cf. Rev. 2:27; 12:5; 19:15. **251f.** Cf. Exod. 17:11. **254.** Cf. 1 Pet. 2:6. **255.** Cf. Jn. 3:36.
266. Cf. Gen. 1:26. **273.** Cf. Mt. 14:32. **275ff.** Cf. Mk. 6:38ff. par. **288f.** Cf. Mt. 26:67 par. The lines **291, 297, 298, 351, 371, 372, 376** (Geffcken) are probably to be deleted. **294.** Cf. Mt. 27:29.
296. Cf. Jn. 19:34. **303.** Cf. Ps. 69:21; Mt. 27:34. **325.** Cf. Is. 62:11; Zech. 9:9; Mt. 21:5; Jn. 12:15.
353. Cf. Rev 9:6
402. Cf. Gen. 1:26. **415.** Cf. Hos. 13:14; 1 Cor. 15:55.
428, 429. We must assume a lacuna between these two verses. **432f.** Text obscure. **433.** Restoration after Friedlieb. **442f.** Cf. Gen. 1:26; 2:7.
476. Cf. Mt. 2:2. **477f.** Cf. Lk. 2:7ff. **479.** After this verse a lacuna. **481.** Cf. Mt. 22:39 par. **482.** Cf. Mt. 22:37 par.
* Translation of the text published by Bischoff (see Lit. above).
60f. Cf. Mk. 13:32

3. The Book of Elchasai

Johannes Irmscher

1. Name and tradition: Hippolytus (*Ref.* 9.13-17 and 10.29), Epiphanius (*Haer.* 19 and 30) and Origen (ap. Euseb. *HE* VI 38) all mention the book of a certain Elchasai, which was used by several sects and in particular by the Elchasaites, who were named after this Elchasai. Hippolytus and Epiphanius, the latter clearly uninfluenced by the former, adduce extracts from this book, the only remains that we possess. One of these fragments (No. 9) contains a cryptogram which, reading outwards from the middle word and inverting the order of the letters, produces an Aramaic formula; such a play upon words pre-supposes readers who understood Aramaic, and makes it probable that the book in its original form was written in that language. The author's name is given as Elchasai by Hippolytus or his authority Alcibiades, the disciple of Elchasai, and also later by the Arabic writer en Nedîm in the Fihrist (cf. D. Chwolson, *Die Ssabier und Ssabismus* 2, 1856, 543), while Epiphanius has Elxai; the first and better-attested form deserves the preference. Both forms of the name go back to the Aramaic חיל כסי, which Epiphanius (*Haer.* 19.2.10) correctly translates as 'hidden power'. It is not possible to decide whether Elchasai was his own name or a sobriquet (like that, for example, of Simon Magus in Acts 8:10).

2. Content: when Hippolytus states (*Ref.* 9.14.3) that he intends to go through the

Book of Elchasai, we may conclude that he presents his extracts in the sequence in which he found them in his source. Checking through these extracts, we come upon a meaningful and progressive development of thought; thus the Book of Elchasai must have been more than a mere collection of aphorisms. The introduction may have related that it was imparted to Elchasai by divine revelation. Following this vision and connected with it was the proclamation of a remission of sins. This is valid in particular for even the gross sinners, and is linked to a re-baptism. Ritual immersions are also commended as a means of healing for all kinds of sickness, and in addition a Jewish legalistic way of life is prescribed. Sacrifice and the sacerdotal actions associated with it are forbidden. Thereafter the apocalyptist promises a war among the powers of godlessness; if the adherents of Elchasai should fall into danger during it, an outward denial will be forgiven them provided only that they remain constant at heart. In such a case one need only pray a magic formula, Elchasai's promise: 'I will be witness over you on the day of the great judgment.' For the rest, it is essential to keep the book hidden from the eyes of intruders.

3. The basic character of the book is Jewish, but it is a syncretistic and not a pure Judaism. Jewish elements are in particular the requirements of circumcision, of sabbath observance, and of prayer in the direction of Jerusalem (Epiph. *Haer.* 19.3.5). Contrary to Judaism are the rejection of sacrifice and also the criticism of the OT associated with it (ib. 19.3.6). Christian with a strong tinge of Gnosticism are the ideas of the Son of God or Christ and the Holy Spirit as heavenly beings (see frags. 1 and 2), and in addition the promises of the forgiveness of sins and of eternal salvation, as well as the ethical requirements of sanctification. Contrary to the usage of ecclesiastical Christianity is the prescription of a second baptism. Of heathen origin are the immersions with the invocation of the seven elements (see frags. 2 and 4), and also the astrological conceptions of the influence of malevolent stars.

4. Origin and dissemination: according to his own account (frag. 2) Elchasai came forward with his message in the third year of Trajan (101); he seems to have composed his book during the reign of the same emperor, as is suggested by the prophecy, given in frag. 7 but not fulfilled, of a universal conflict blazing up three years after the Parthian war (114-116) but still under Trajan's rule. The reports about Elchasai's homeland are contradictory; the most worthy of credit are some references in Epiphanius (*Haer.* 19.2.10ff.; 53.1.1ff.), which point to the region east of Jordan. The work was dedicated to the 'Sobiai', the 'baptised' (from צבע), as the adherents of Elchasai called themselves (not a person of that name, as Hippolytus, *Ref.* 9.13.1-3 = Frag. 1a wrongly assumed). It was however disseminated also among other religious groups, both Jewish and Jewish-Christian, and for this Epiphanius once again affords the evidence (*Haer.* 19.1; 30.18; 53). It was brought to the congregation of Callistus in Rome about 220, and that in a Greek version, by the above-mentioned Alcibiades of Apamea, who was active as a missionary in the imperial capital. A propagandist advance by the sect to Caesarea in the year 247 is mentioned by Eusebius (*HE* VI 38). It seems to have met with only slight success, and in any case we cannot speak of a wide diffusion of the sect. The influence of the Elchasaites upon Mani - as we now know from the Cologne Mani Codex -

must however have been quite considerable. Down to his twenty-fourth year Mani lived in an Elchasaite community, and his own independent teaching developed in controversy with this baptist group.

Literature: Fragments and testimonia in A. Hilgenfeld, *Novum Testamentum extra canonum receptum* III 2², 1881, 227-240; W. Brandt, *Elchasai, ein Religionsstifter und sein Werk*, 1912 (a comprehensive monograph); H. Waitz, 'Das Buch des Elchasai', *Harnack-Ehrung*, 1921, 87-104; J. Thomas, *Le mouvement baptiste en Palestine et Syrie*, 1935; H.J. Schoeps, *Theologie und Geschichte des Judenchristentums*, 1949, 325ff.; id. article '*Elkesaiten*' in RGG³ II, col. 435; G. Strecker, article '*Elkesai*' in RAC V, 1959, cols. 1171-1186; K. Rudolph, *Antike Baptisten*, 1981, 13ff.; G.P. Luttikhuisen, *The Revelation of Elchasai*, 1985.

On the Cologne Mani Codex: L. Koenen and C. Römer, *Der Kölner Mani-Codex. Über das Werden seines Leibes*. Kritische Edition aufgrund der von A. Henrichs und L. Koenen besorgten Erstedition hrsg. und ubers. (Abh. Rhein.-Westf. Akademie der Wissenschaften, Sonderreihe Papyrologica Colonensia XIV), 1988. Cf. further A. Henrichs/L. Koenen, 'Ein griechischer Mani-Codex (P. Colon. inv. nr. 4780)', *Zeitschrift für Papyrologie und Epigraphik* 5, 1970, 97-216; R. Merkelbach, *Mani und sein religionssystem* (Rhein.-Westf. Akademie der Wiss., Vorträge G 281), 1986.

Fragments

1. A certain Alcibiades, who lived in Apamea in Syria . . . came to Rome and brought with him a book. Of it he said that Elchasai, a righteous man, had received it from Seres in Parthia and had transmitted it to a certain Sobiai. It had been communicated by an angel, whose height was 24 *schoinoi*, which is 96 miles, his breadth four *schoinoi*, and from shoulder to shoulder six *schoinoi*, and the tracks of his feet in length 1½ *schoinoi*, which is 14 miles, and in breadth 3½ *schoinoi*, and in height half a *schoinos*. And with him there was also a female figure, whose measurements Alcibiades says were commensurate with those mentioned; and the male figure was the Son of God, but the female was called Holy Spirit.

(Hippol. *Ref.* 9.13.1-3)

'And whence', he said, 'did I know the measurements?' 'Because', he said, 'I saw from the mountains that their heads reached up to them, and when I had learned the measure of the mountain I knew the measurements both of Christ and of the Holy Spirit.'

(Epiph. *Haer.* 30.17.7)

2. He affirms the following: That the gospel of a new forgiveness of sins was preached to men in the third year of Trajan's reign. And he appoints a baptism . . . of which he says that through it anyone who is defiled by any licentiousness and pollution and lawlessness receives forgiveness of sins . . . if he be converted and listen to the book and believe in it.

(Hippol. *Ref.* 9.13.3-4)

'If then, children, anyone has had relations with any animal whatsoever, or a male or a sister or a daughter, or has practised adultery or fornication, and wishes to receive forgiveness of his sins, let him, as soon as he has heard this book, be baptized a second time in the name of the great and most high God, and in the name of his Son, the great king. And let him purify himself and sanctify himself, and call to witness the seven witnesses written in this book, heaven and water and the holy spirits, and the angels of prayer, and the oil and the salt and the earth.'

(Hippol. *Ref.* 9.15.1-2)

3. Again I say, ye adulterers, adulteresses and false prophets, if you wish to be converted, that your sins may be forgiven you, to you also there will be peace and a share with the righteous, from the time you hear this book and are baptized a second time with your clothing.

(Hippol. *Ref.* 9.15.3)

4. If then any man or woman or youth or maid is bitten, torn or touched by a mad and raving dog, in which is a spirit of destruction, let him run in the same hour with all he wears, and go down into a river or spring, wherever there may be a deep place, and let him baptize himself with all he wears and pray to the great and most high God with a faithful heart. Then let him call to witness the seven witnesses written in this book: 'Behold, I call to witness the heaven and water and the holy spirits, and the angels of prayer and the oil and the salt and the earth. These seven witnesses I call to witness, that I will no more sin, nor commit adultery, nor steal, nor do wrong, nor claim more than is due, nor hate, nor transgress, nor take pleasure in any wickedness.' Let him, then, say this and baptize himself with all he wears, in the name of the great and most high God. . . . The consumptive also are to baptize themselves in cold water forty times in seven days, and likewise also those possessed by demons.

(Hippol. *Ref.* 9.15.4-16.1)

5. He forbids prayer towards the east, saying that one ought not to pray thus, but from every region have one's face towards Jerusalem,[1] those in the east to turn westwards to Jerusalem, those in the west eastwards to the same place, those in the north southwards, and those in the south northwards, so that from every quarter the face may be opposite Jerusalem.

(Epiph. *Haer.* 19.3.5)

6. He rejects sacrifices and priestly rites as being alien to God and never offered to God at all according to the fathers and the law. . . . But that water is acceptable to God and fire alien, he explains in the following words: 'Children, go not according to the form of the fire,[2] because ye go astray; for

such is error. For you see it, he says, very near and yet it is far away. Go not according to its form, but go rather according to the sound of the water.'

(Epiph. *Haer*. 19.3.6f.)

7. These are evil stars of godlessness. This now is spoken to you, ye pious and disciples: Beware of the power of the days of their dominion, and do not make a start to your works in their days! Baptize neither man nor woman in the days of their authority, when the moon passes through from them and travels with them. Await the day when it departs from them, and then baptize and make a beginning with all your works! Moreover, honour the day of the Sabbath, for it is one of these days! But beware also not to begin anything on the third day of the week, for again when three years of the emperor Trajan are complete, from the time when he subjected the Parthians to his own authority, when these three years are fulfilled, the war between the godless angels of the north will break out; because of this all kingdoms of godlessness are in disorder.

(Hippol. *Ref.* 9.16.2-4)

8. He says that it is not a sin even if a man should chance to worship idols in a time of imminent persecution, if only he does not worship in his conscience, and whatever he confesses with his mouth he does not in his heart. . . . Phineas,[3] a priest of the tribe of Levi and Aaron and the ancient Phineas, in Babylon in the time of the captivity worshipped Artemis in Susa, and so escaped death and destruction in the time of Darius the king.

(Epiph. *Haer*. 19.1.8-9)

9. Let none seek after the interpretation, but let him only say in his prayer these words . . . : '*Abar anid moib nochile daasim ana daasim nochile moib anid abar. Selam.*'

(Ephiph. *Haer*. 19.4.3)

If we read from the middle outwards in either direction, the result is an Aramaic sentence:

אנא מסהד עליכון ביום דינא רבא

'I am witness over you on the day of the great judgment.' Cf. M.A. Levy, ZDMG 12, 1858, 712.

10. Do not read this word to all men, and keep these commandments carefully, because not all men are faithful, nor all women upright.

(Hippol. *Ref.* 9.17.1)

Notes

3. The Book of Elchasai

1. Cf. Dan. 6:10; Ezek. 8:16ff.; Berakoth 4.5.
2. Greek τέκνα, μὴ πρὸς τὸ εἶδος τοῦ πυρὸς πορεύεσθε. Perhaps 'follow not the will-o'-the-wisp of the fire'? (R.M.W.).
3. Cf. Num. 25:7; Ecclus. 45:23.

XXI. Later Apocalypses

Introduction

Wilhelm Schneemelcher

Literature: H. Weinel, 'Die spätere christliche Apokalyptik', in ΕΥΧΑΡΙΣΤΗΡΙΟΝ, Gunkel-FS, 1923, II, 141-173; H. Gross and J. Michl, art. 'Apokalypsen', LThK² I, 1957, cols. 698-708; Vielhauer/Strecker, above pp. 542ff.; K.-H. Schwarte, art. 'Apokalyptik/Apokalypsen V. Alte Kirche', TRE III, 1978, 257-275; K. Berger, *Die griechische Daniel-Diegese, Ein altkirchliche Apokalypse* (Studia Post-Biblica 27), Leiden 1976, esp. XI-XXIII; Erbetta III, 397-481.

Apocalyptic, originally taken over as an inheritance from Judaism, exercised an influence in the Church right through the early centuries and produced divers works which in terms both of literary genre and of content stand in the tradition of the Jewish and early Christian Apocalyptic. In comparison with the early period of the Church, however, many elements are changed. The later 'outlines of the future' (Schwarte) were indeed not only determined by traditional ideas of Jewish-Christian origin, but also had as something given the Canon of the New Testament - with the ideas about the last times which it contains - and its understanding of time. 'The field of the questions of detail which could still be answered through new and additional "revelations" grew ever smaller, and the themes of the later Christian apocalypses became predominant in this area' (Schwarte, op. cit. 257). The insistence on repentance now comes even more strongly into the foreground than in early Christian works of this genre.

'Apocalypses' appear in Gnosis also, as the texts from Nag Hammadi show (cf. Schwarte, op. cit. 265f.). Here however it must be observed that the title 'apocalypse' is not in itself enough for us to allocate a work to this kind of text (see the two Apocalypses of James, vol. 1, pp. 313-341. Cf. also M. Krause, 'Die literarischen Gattungen der Apokalypsen von Nag Hammadi', in D. Hellholm (ed.), *Apocalypticism in the Mediterranean World and the Near East*, 1983, 621-637). A complete survey of all the later apocalypses of this kind cannot be given here (cf. the works of Weinel, Schwarte and Berger mentioned above). Two texts from the Nag Hammadi library (Apoc. Paul and Apoc. Peter) are presented below in full, as well as the two Christian apocalypses of Paul and Thomas, important because they were particularly influential. For a few other apocalypses brief references may be given.

1. Apocalypse of Sophonias (Zephaniah)

A Book of the Prophet Sophonias (Zephaniah), or a Revelation of S., is rejected as apocryphal in the Stichometry of Nicephoros and in the Catalogue of the Sixty Canonical Books (cf. vol. 1, pp. 41ff.). Clement of Alexandria gives a quotation out of a Book of Sophonias in *Strom.* V 11.77. We cannot ascertain from what work this quotation came because the Coptic text of the Apocalypse of Sophonias does not contain it. Probably the quotation of Clement came from a Jewish writing, whereas the Coptic text represents a Christian redaction (of this Jewish text?). The description of the place of punishment occupies a great part of the extant Coptic text. In regard to its relation to the Apocalypse of Paul, that apocalypse must be considered dependent on the Apocalypse of Sophonias (cf. below, p. 714f. and Harnack, *Gesch. der altchristl. Lit.* II 1, 573). The assigning of the 'anonymous apocalypse' (in Steindorff) to the Apocalypse of Sophonias is hardly correct. The Coptic translation of the presumed Greek original probably did not take place before 400. Text and Translation: G. Steindorff, *Die Apokalypse des Elias, eine unbekannte Apokalypse und Bruchstücke der Sophonias-Apokalypse* (TU 17.3a) 1899; P. Riessler, *Altjüdisches Schrifttum ausserhalb der Bibel*, 1928, 168-177. Cf. Harnack, op. cit. I. 2, 854; II. 1, 572f.; Weinel, op. cit. 163f.

2. Apocalypse of Elijah

Editions and translations: Steindorff op. cit. (see above under no. 1); *The Apocalypse of Elijah, based on P. Chester Beatty 2018*, Coptic text ed. and trans. by Albert Pietersma and Susan Turner Comstock with Harold W. Attridge, Chico, CA 1981; Jean-Marc Rosenstiehl, *L'Apocalypse d'Élie.* Introduction, Traduction et Notes (Textes et Études pour servir à l'histoire du Judaisme intertestamentaire I), Paris 1972; Wolfgang Schrage, 'Die Elia-Apokalypse', in *Jüdische Schriften aus hellenistisch-römischer Zeit*, Bd. V, 1980, 193-288 (German trans. with introduction and commentary; detailed bibliography).

An Apocalypse of Elijah (Apoc. El.) is rejected in the Catalogue of the Sixty Books and probably also in the Stichometry of Nicephorus (cf. vol. 1, pp. 41f.). An apocryphon of Elijah is frequently mentioned in early Church literature, mostly in connection with the saying in 1 Cor. 2:9, of which Origen already affirms that it comes from an apocryphon of Elijah (cf. Schrage, op. cit. 195). Now on the one hand this saying is evidently a logion which frequently crops up (cf. Gos. Thom. log. 17; on this see H.-Ch. Puech in NTApo[3] I, 217). On the other hand this logion does not occur in the extant Elijah apocrypha.

The following Elijah texts may be mentioned here:

a) In the apocryphal *Letter of Titus* is is said: 'The prophet Elias bears witness to a vision, in which he claims to have seen what follows' (see above, p. 64). We cannot tell the source of the quotation thus introduced, in which the punishments of Hell are described. This text has nothing to do with the Coptic Apoc. El.

b) In a *Greek* fragment reference is made to an Elijah apocryphon 'On the Antichrist' (ed. F. Nau; cf. Schrage, op. cit. 196). We cannot recognise any connection with the extant Elijah texts.

c) The *Hebrew Apocalypse of Elijah* (ed. Moses Buttenweiser, 1897) is a Jewish writing from the 3rd century A.D.; there are no connections with the Coptic Apoc. El. (cf. Schrage, op. cit. 197f.)

d) Since 1885 the text of an Apoc. El. has gradually become known through some Coptic manuscripts. Since the publication of the Chester Beatty Papyrus 2018 this work is now accessible almost complete (cf. Schrage, op. cit. 198ff). The Coptic (Sahidic and Achmimic) versions go back to a Greek original text, of which we possess a papyrus fragment with six lines; but with this nothing much can be done. The papyri were written in the 4th or 5th century.

The Coptic Apoc. El. presents admonitions, predictions of the terrors of the end-time, a description of the Antichrist and his annihilation, etc.; it ends with the creation of a new heaven and a new earth and the thousand-year reign of Christ. Many elements of the older Apocalyptic are lacking, but on the other hand ancient conceptual material is abundantly used. The work is a typical example of later apocalypses: a Christian description of the end-time (to some extent with contemporary references) has been created on a Jewish foundation.

The dating of the Coptic Apoc. El. is difficult. There is much to be said for the view that the Jewish basic document originated in the second half of the 3rd century, and was taken over and reworked by Christians at the beginning of the 4th century (cf. Schrage, op. cit. 220ff.).

3. Apocalypses of John

Three later apocalypses are known under the name of John.

a) 'Αποκάλυψις τοῦ ἁγίου 'Ιωάννου τοῦ θεολόγου (Text in Tischendorf, *Apa*, 70-94). This is a disclosure by means of question and answer of many details of the next world: Anti-Christ is described, the fate of individuals in the resurrection is discussed in detail, the punishments of Hell and the joys of Heaven are represented. 'Quite apart from its literary quality, the dialogue structure of the work indicates the change in the apocalypses from the making known of visionary "revelations" into convenient clothing for theological tractates. For this Apocalypse of John is exactly that, its aim directed even more strongly than that of ApcThom towards the sketching of a consistent and conclusive picture of the course of the end of the world' (Schwarte, op. cit. 262). The writing probably makes use of Ephraem (cf. Bousset, *Der Antichrist*, 1895, 26) and consequently was probably first composed in the 5th century. The oldest testimony to it comes from the 9th century. Cf. Weinel, op. cit. 149-151. Erbetta III, 409-414; Moraldi II, 1951-1966. On the Slavonic tradition cf. A. de Santos Otero, *Überlieferung* I, 197-209; II 253f. On the Arabic versions cf. Graf I, 273.

b) F. Nau has published a shorter Apocalypse of John: 'Une deuxième Apocalypse apocryphe grecque de S. Jean' (*Rev. Bibl.* 23, 1914, 209-221). According to Nau this Apocalypse had its origin in Cyprus between the 6th and 8th centuries.

c) A third apocalyptic writing under the name of John has been preserved in a Coptic manuscript of the 11th century which E.A.W. Budge has published (*Coptic Apocrypha in the Dialect of Upper Egypt*, 1913, 59-74; English translation, 241-257). The title is: 'These are the mysteries of John the apostle and holy virgin, which he learned in heaven'. On a heavenly journey John sees the mysteries of the world. Up to now there has been no careful investigation of whether this Coptic writing goes back to a Greek substratum; similarly the date of its composition is unknown. Cf. E. Burmester in *Orientalia* 1938, 355ff.; Erbetta III, 417-424.

4. Apocalypses of Mary

There are two writings ascribed to Mary the mother of God which concern us:

a) 'Ἀποκάλυψις τῆς ἁγίας θεοτόκου περὶ τῶν κολάσεων; this is preserved in Greek, Armenian, Ethiopic and Old Slavonic versions. Its nature is that of a revelation in which Mary is shown the tortures of the damned, for whom she then asks pardon. The book 'represents an attempt to draw into a more rigid system the tortures of Hell of the older Apocalypses' (Weinel, op. cit. 156). It appeared probably in the 9th century and is dependent on the Apocalypses of Paul and Peter. Text: M.R. James, *Apocrypha anecdota*, 1893, 115-126; samples of the text in Tischendorf, *Apa* xxvii-xxx; Erbetta III, 447-454. On the Slavonic tradition cf. A. de Santos Otero, *Überlieferung* I, 188-195; II, 252f. A Cretan version in R.M. Dawkins, Κρητικὴ 'Ἀποκάλυψις τῆς Παναγίας (Κρητ. Χρονικά 2, 1948, 487-500). Weinel, op. cit. 156f.; L. Müller, 'Die Offenbarung der Gottesmutter über die Höllenstrafen', *Die Welt der Slaven* 6, 1961, 26-39.

b) Likewise dependent on the Apocalypse of Paul is the Ethiopian *Apocalypsis seu Visio Mariae Virginis*, which may have originated in the 7th century, but is probably later. Edition by M. Chaine, CSCO, Ae 22, 1909 (repr. 1955), 51-80 (text); Ae 23, 1909 (repr. 1955), 43-68 (Latin trans.). Cf. Erbetta III, 455-470.

The *Liber Johannis de dormitione Mariae* printed by Tischendorf (Apa 95-102) is not an apocalypse but a legend.

5. Apocalypse of Stephen

A *Revelatio sancti Stephani* is rejected as apocryphal in the so-called Decretum Gelasianum (cf. vol. 1, pp. 39f.). Nothing more is known about this apocalypse. It has been suggested, perhaps correctly, that there is a misunderstanding here: the reference in the Decr. Gel. does not relate to an apocalypse but to an account of the discovery of the relics of Stephen which was composed in Greek by the Presbyter Lucian of Kaphar Gamala in the year 415 and afterwards translated into Latin in two different recensions, of which one was made by Avitus of Braga. Text of this account: PL 41, 805-815; S. Vanderlinden, 'Revelatio S. Stephani' (*Revue des études byzantines* I, 1946, 178-217); Erbetta III, 397-408. Cf. J. Martin, 'Die revelatio S. Stephani und Verwandtes', in HJ 77, 1958, 419-433.

6. Apocalypse of Bartholomew

The Apocalypse of Bartholomew, which continues to reappear in modern literature, is not an apocalypse. The texts in question are rather later compilations belonging to the category of Gospels, even though many pieces may derive from apocalyptic tradition. These texts have therefore already been dealt with in vol. I, pp. 537ff

1. The Coptic gnostic Apocalypse of Paul

Wolf-Peter Funk

Introduction

1. Literature: ***Facsimile***: *The Facsimile Edition of the Nag Hammadi Codices* published under the Auspices of the Department of Antiquities of the Arab Republic of Egypt in Conjunction with the United Nations Educational, Scientific and Cultural Organization, Codex V, Leiden 1975, plates 25-32.

Editions: W.R. Murdock/G.W. MacRae, 'The Apocalypse of Paul', in D.M. Parrott (ed.), *Nag Hammadi Codices V, 2-5 and VI with Papyrus Berolinensis 8502, 1 and 4* (= Nag Hammadi Studies 11), Leiden 1979, 47-63; A. Böhlig/Labib, *Koptisch-gnostische Apokalypsen aus Codex V von Nag Hammadi im Koptischen Museum zu Alt-Kairo*, Wiss. Zeitschr. der Martin-Luther-Universität Halle-Wittenberg 1963, Sonderband, 15-26.

Translations: German by A. Böhlig in Böhlig/Labib, *Koptisch-gnostische Apokalypsen*, 34-54. English: G.W. MacRae/W.R. Murdock, 'The Apocalypse of Paul (V, 2)', in J.M. Robinson (ed.), *The Nag Hammadi Library in English*, Leiden 1977, 239-241 (3rd ed. 1988, 256-259); W.R. Murdock/G.W. MacRae, 'The Apocalypse of Paul', in D.M. Parrott (ed.), *Nag Hammadi Codices V, 2-5 and VI with Papyrus Berolinensis 8502, 1 and 4*, 51-63.

Further Literature: R. Kasser, 'Textes gnostiques', *Le Muséon* 78, 1965, 76-78; 300; W.R. Murdock, 'The Apocalypse of Paul from Nag Hammadi' (unpublished Th. D. dissertation, School of Theology at Claremont, 1968); H.-M. Schenke, review of Böhlig/Labib, *Koptisch-gnostische Apokalypsen*, OLZ 61, 1966, cols. 25f.

2. Attestation and transmission: When reference is made to an 'Apocalypse of Paul', what is meant is as a rule the well-known Apocalypse of Paul (see below, pp. 712ff.), which circulated widely in the early Church. That there was also another literary work under this title (and possible several) was not known before the Nag Hammadi discovery. There are no concrete clues for an identification of this document with the 'Ascension of Paul' mentioned by Epiphanius (*Pan.* 38.2.5; tr. Williams [NHS 35] 250).

In Codex V from Nag Hammadi (inventory number 10548 of the Coptic Museum in Old Cairo), the Coptic gnostic Apocalypse of Paul (Apoc. Pl.) stands on pages 17 (line 19) to 24 (line 9), as the first of a series of four writings, all described as 'apocalypses' - before the two Apocalypses of James and the Apocalypse of Adam. If this sequence is more than pure chance, the principle of arrangement can only have been a very superficial one, for in terms of content these texts are entirely different. The title of the Apoc. Pl. appears in the manuscript both at the beginning (here badly damaged) and at the end of the document. For details about the papyrus codex, the manufacture of which can be placed about the middle of the 4th century, cf. vol. 1, pp. 313f. (on 1 Apoc. Jas.). Since the codex has suffered very severe damage as far as its ninth leaf, the text on the opening pages shows considerable gaps. The later pages are slightly damaged only at the upper margin and in their lower parts; most of the lacunae resulting from this can be restored with a fair degree of certainty.

3. Original language, place and time of origin: it is generally assumed that - as with almost all other texts of the oldest Coptic tradition - the version of Apoc. Pl. extant in NHC V is a translation from the Greek; there are however no sure indications of this in the text. We can say just as little in regard to the question whether the text corresponds in extent to the presumed Greek original, or has been more heavily marked by deletions or additions within the Coptic tradition.

With regard to the time of origin, it has been suggested (Murdock/MacRae) that the text should be located in the context of the marked interest in the 2nd century, especially among the Valentinians, in the figure of the apostle Paul (and in the interpretation of 2 Cor. 12:2-4). With greater circumspection, however, we can only suggest the period from the middle of the 2nd century to the beginning of the 4th as the possible time of origin. Nothing can be said about its geographical origin.

4. Nature of the text and literary character: the Apoc. Pl. is an 'apocalypse' in the traditional sense of the revelation of matters relating to individual eschatology in a mixture of vision and dialogue - packaged in literary terms as the report of a heavenly journey which the Revealer and the recipient undertake together and which is introduced by an epiphany scene 'on the mount of Jericho'. It is accordingly a question of a free delineation of the rapture of which Paul himself reports in bare allusions in 2 Cor. 12:2-4; it is here embedded in the context of the apostle's journey from Damascus to Jerusalem after his conversion (for the literary linking-up with this situation cf. also the Acts of Paul). The 'little child' whom Paul meets in this introductory scene has to be identified as an epiphany of Jesus. His role in the following heavenly journey strongly resembles that of an *angelus interpres*; he is not however described as an 'angel', but always as 'the Spirit' (or occasionally 'the Holy Spirit').

Much remains obscure with regard to the continuity of the narrative presented by the text, both in individual scenes and also in relation to the action as a whole. For example, Paul originally wished to visit the twelve apostles in Jerusalem but to his surprise he already meets them here upon the way. It is not immediately clear whether they accompany him on his ascent (so Böhlig, similarly Murdock/MacRae) or remain on the earth - where Paul repeatedly sees them (and himself in their circle) when he looks downwards (so Schenke). Both interpretations entail difficulties at several points in the text: the first is most readily suggested by such passages as 20.4f.; 22.1 ('the Spirit' accompanies the whole group), the second by 20.1-4 (Paul when he looks down sees the whole group 'in the creation'). For all that, it would be difficult to see just what is the special quality of this revelation journey, clearly intended for Paul, if it was shared at the same time by the other twelve.

The lacunae in the papyrus at the beginning of the text are probably to be held responsible only in part for its obscurities; another part, but perhaps only a very small one, is due to errors or omissions by the copyist of the extant manuscript. We do not know what irregularities may have arisen in the course of the transmission of this short text in Greek or in Coptic, or how much should actually be put down to the account of the original author; we can only conjecture that in this case the text as it lay before the Coptic translator was perhaps already of inferior literary quality. Among other things, the cohesion of the text is also (slightly) impaired by the fact that at the beginning Paul is at first referred to in the third person, then suddenly at 19.10 in the first person, and at 19.18 again in the third person, whereas the remainder of the narrative (from 20.5 on) is consistently in the 'I' style.[1] Kasser would see here an indication of tampering by a later hand - an interference consisting particularly in the abbreviation of a 'complete' heavenly journey of Paul (composed originally in the 'I' style) in which each separate heaven was given its own description. The change of persons is however too widespread in comparable literature for conclusions to be drawn from this alone, and on the whole it probably speaks for too little rather than too much redactional work.

The whole sequence of the journeys by one and the same person to hell and to heaven (after the example of Christ: Eph. 4:8-10) is in Apoc. Pl. transposed into the various heavens; in the process the *descensus ad inferos*, located in the fourth heaven, is very concisely connected - by movement from one station to another - with the heavenly journey proper, the crossing of the boundary (seventh heaven) and the ascent into the transcendent sphere (eighth to tenth heavens). We may ask whether the author, when he makes the heavenly journey begin - not end - in the third heaven of 2 Cor. 12:2, wished to see the paradise mentioned in 2 Cor. 12:4 in one of the higher heavens. According to the description given here, this would not be conceivable before the eighth heaven, the ogdoad; but precisely from here on there is no detailed description (for example, it is nowhere said that Paul heard the ἄρρητα ῥήματα). If the text originally had the aim of transforming the journey which Paul intended to Jerusalem into a journey to the heavenly Jerusalem (Murdock/MacRae), there is no longer much to be seen of this in the form of the text before us.

That Paul on his heavenly journey is 'out of the body' (cf. 2 Cor. 12:2f.) is sufficiently clear from the use of the rapture terminology and his dealings with 'spirits'. Possibly the author wished to interpret the phrases of Gal. 1:16f. in strictly complementary terms: if the apostle did not go to Jerusalem, and did not confer with 'flesh and blood', then in this period his communication was therefore with a spirit (or spirits).

5. Theological emphasis: one of the few significant theological features of this document must be the function assigned to the figure of God the Father from Dan. 7:9f. The 'old man' enthroned in the seventh heaven evidently embodies the Creator, downgraded in gnostic eyes, who attempts to prevent any further ascent, but is powerless in the face of the gnostic's proof of identity (here 'the sign'). To see here an expression of 'anti-Jewish tendency' is probably to go too far; rather this concept seems to be based on a very simple and indeed natural gnostic interpretation of the peaceful handing-over of power from Dan. 7:13f. (understood in Christian terms).

***Preliminary note to translation*:** there is as yet no recognised chapter division of the text. The numbers prefaced by 'p.' announce the beginning of a new page in the Codex (citation usually always by page and line of Codex V). [. . .] indicates a lacuna within a line (usually of one or more words). [. . . . .] means that several lines are missing (in most cases presumably more than a sentence). Words in angled brackets < . . . > rest upon corrections of defective passages (mostly omissions). Words in round brackets (. . .) are aids to interpretation supplied by the translator.

The Apocalypse of Paul

[. . . . .] . . . [. . . . .] (*several sentences are missing*) (*p. 18*) [. . . . .] . . . [. . . on] the way. And [he asked him], saying: '[By what] road [do I go] up to Jerusalem?' The little child [answered]: 'Say (first) your name, that [I may show] you the way!' [The little child] knew [very well] who Paul [was]. He wished by these words to make conversation with him, that he might find an excuse to speak with him.[2]

The little child answered and said: 'I know who you are, Paul. For it is you who are blessed from his mother's womb. Since now I [saw] that you were about to [go up to Jerusalem] to your fellow-[apostles], [I have . . .]. That is why you were [called (?)]. I am the Spirit [who accompanies (?)] you. Give [me therefore your] hand (?), Paul [. . . . . *several sentences are missing*)] (*p. 19*) [. . . . .] . . . before (?) the rulers [and] these authorities - both archangels and also powers - together with the whole race of the demons. [Understand (?)] him who reveals bodies to a soul-seed.'

After he had ended this speech, he answered[3] and said to me: 'Awaken your mind, Paul, and see that this mountain on which you are standing is the mount of Jericho - that you may recognise the things that are hidden in those that are visible! The twelve apostles to whom you will go <. . .>.[4] For they are chosen spirits, and they will welcome you.' He lifted up his eyes and saw how they greeted him.

Then the Holy [Spirit] who was speaking with [him] carried him up as far as the third heaven, and he went further on into the fourth [heaven].

The [Holy] Spirit answered and said: 'Look here and see your likeness upon the earth!' And he looked downwards and saw those [who were] on the earth. He stared [upwards (?) and saw] those who were on [. . .]. [Then] (*p. 20*) he (again) looked [downwards (?) and] saw the twelve apostles [on] his right [and] on his left in the creation, and the Spirit walked before them.

Now I saw in the fourth heaven angels resembling gods in race,[5] and I beheld how these angels brought a soul from the land of the dead. They set it at the gate of the fourth heaven. And the angels were scourging it. The soul answered and said: 'What sin have I done in the world?' The toll-collector who sits in the fourth heaven answered, saying: 'You had no right to commit all these lawless deeds which are (usual) in the world of the dead.'[6] The soul answered, saying: 'Bring forward witnesses and let them [declare] before you in what body I have committed lawlessness. [. . . . . .][7] bring a book, [to read] from it.'

And there came [the] three witnesses. The first answered and said: 'Was I not [in] the body? About the second hour [I came and] rose up against you, (*p. 21*) until [you fell] into a rage [and] wrath and envy.' And the second answered and said: 'Was I too not in the world? And I came about the fifth hour, and I saw you and desired you. And behold: now I accuse you because of the murders which you committed.' And the third answered and said: 'Did I not come to you about the twelfth hour of the day, when the sun was on the point of going down? I bestowed darkness upon you, until you had completed your sins.'

When the soul heard these things, it looked down dismayed. Then it looked up again, and was cast down. When the soul was cast down, [it went into a] body which had been prepared [for it]. With that its witnesses were at an end.[8]

I [looked] upward and [saw the] Spirit saying [to me]: 'Come, Paul, step [forward to] me!' Now as I [went] the gate opened [and] I came up to the fifth [heaven]. And I saw my fellow-apostles travelling [with me], (*p. 22*) and the Spirit was travelling with us.

And I saw a great angel in the fifth heaven, holding an iron staff in his hand, and with him were also three other angels. I looked them in the face. They were contending with one another, with scourges in their hands, driving the souls to judgment.

But I was walking (further) with the Spirit, and the gate opened to me. Then we went up to the sixth heaven, and I saw my fellow-apostles travelling with me, and the Holy Spirit was leading me before them.[9] I gazed aloft, and saw (there) a great light shining down even to the sixth heaven.

I answered and said to the toll-collector who is in the seventh heaven: '[Open] to me and to the [Holy] Spirit [who goes] before [me]!' He opened [for us. Then we went up][10] to the seventh [heaven].

[I saw in the midst] of the light an old man [in] white [raiment. His throne], which stood in the seventh heaven, was [seven] times brighter than the sun. The old man (*p. 23*) answered and said [to me]: 'Where are you going, Paul, you blessed one, set apart from his mother's womb?'[11] But I looked up to the Spirit, and he made a movement of his head and said to me: 'Speak with him!' And I answered and said to the old man: 'I am going to the place from which I am come.' The old man answered me: 'From whence do you come?' I answered for my part and said: 'I will go down into the world of the dead, to take captivity captive - the one that was led captive in the captivity of Babylon.'[12] The old man answered me, saying: 'How will you be able to escape me? Look here and see these rulers and authorities!' [The] Spirit answered and said: 'Give him [the] sign which you have, and [he will] open for you.' Then I gave [him] the sign. He turned his face downwards to his creation and to those that were his own of the authorities.

Then the (way out of) the <seventh>[13] heaven opened, and we went up [to] (*p. 24*) the Ogdoad. And I saw the twelve apostles; they greeted me. Then we went up to the ninth heaven. I greeted all those who were in the ninth heaven. Then we went up to the tenth heaven, and I greeted my fellow-spirits.

The Apocalypse of Paul

Notes

1. The Coptic Gnostic Apocalypse of Paul

1. Also strange is the repeated use of the verb 'answer, reply' (Coptic *ouōšb*) in situations where there cannot be any question of an answer or reply (pp. 18.13; 19.9, 26; 20.13, 26; 21.3, 9; 22. 19, 30). It seems to me very doubtful whether an extension of the meaning of this verb (e.g. in the sense of 'add' or 'begin to speak') can be documented in the rest of Coptic literature; hence any such glossing over has been deliberately avoided in the translation.
2. Perhaps there is a corruption in the text here: the Coptic expressions chosen in the two clauses would logically fit together better if we could understand something like: 'He intended to have a conversation with him; (these) words of his <had merely the purpose> of providing the occasion for a discussion with him.'
3. See above, note 1.
4. For syntactical reasons it is to be assumed that something has fallen out here; perhaps: <are already here>, <are not in Jerusalem>, <I will show to you> or the like.
5. For several lines here the manuscript text is evidently not quite in order. The rearrangement and modification follow a suggestion by Murdock and MacRae.
6. Böhlig conjectures that what was originally meant was: 'in the world of mortals'.
7. Murdock and MacRae restore: '[Do you wish] to bring a book . . . ?' Schenke conjectures: '<The toll-collector answered;> "[I will have] a book brought . . . " ' There is no further reference to the book.
8. I.e. the witnesses against it.
9. Text possibly corrupt; a very slight alteration would yield the more plausible: 'the Holy Spirit was leading the way before them'.
10. Or: 'He opened [to me. Then I went] up . . . ' In consequence of the peculiar diction and punctuation of the manuscript, one ought really to translate: ' . . . and said to the toll-collector who was in the sixth heaven: "[Open] to me!" And the Holy Spirit, [who went] before [me], opened [to me].' But this will scarcely have been the original sense.
11. Cf. Gal. 1:15.
12. Cf. Eph. 4:8-10. The following view of the text would also not be entirely out of the question: 'I will go into the world of the dead, in order to become a (fellow-) prisoner in the captivity which was led captive in the captivity of Babylon.'
13. MS: 'of the sixth heaven'.

2. The Coptic gnostic Apocalypse of Peter

Andreas Werner

Introduction

1. Literature: ***Facsimile***: *The Facsimile Edition of the Nag Hammadi Codices* published under the Auspices of the Department of Antiquities of the Arab Republic of Egypt in Conjunction with the United Nations Educational, Scientific and Cultural Organization, Codex VII, Leiden 1972.

Editions: M. Krause-V. Girgis, 'Die Petrusapokalypse', in F. Altheim-R. Stiehl (eds.), *Christentum am Roten Meer*, II, 1973, 152-179 (200-229); J.A. Brashler, 'The Coptic Apocalypse of Peter. A Genre Analysis and Interpretation', Diss. Claremont Graduate School 1977.

Translations: *German:* M. Krause, 'Die Petrusapokalypse' (edition of text, see above); 'Die Apokalypse des Petrus. Die dritte Schrift von Nag-Hammadi-Codex VII, eingeleitet und übersetzt vom Berliner Arbeitskreis für koptisch-gnostische Schriften' (federführend: A. Werner), ThLZ 99, 1974, cols. 575-584. *English:* J. Brashler-R.A. Bullard-F. Wisse, 'Apocalypse of Peter', *The Nag Hammadi Library in English*, 1977, 339-345 (3rd ed. 1988, 372-378); S.K. Brown-G.W. Griggs, 'The Apocalypse of Peter. Introduction and translation', *Brigham Young University Studies* 15, 1974, 131-145.

Further literature: T. Baumeister, 'Die Rolle des Petrus in gnostischen Texten', in T. Orlandi-F. Wisse (eds.), *Acts of the Second International Congress of Coptic Studies*, Rome 1985, 3-12; K. Berger, 'Unfehlbare Offenbarung. Petrus in der gnostischen und apokalyptischen Offenbarungsliteratur', in *Kontinuität und Einheit, FS F. Mussner*, 1981, 261-326; A. Böhlig, 'Zur Apokalypse des Petrus', *Göttinger Miszellen* 8, 1973, 11-13 (=id. *Gnosis und Synkretismus*, 2. Teil (WUNT 48), 1989, 395-398); J.-D. Dubois, 'Le préambule de l'Apocalypse de Pierre (Nag Hammadi VII, 70.4-20)', in J. Ries-Y. Janssens-J.M. Sevrin (eds.), *Gnosticisme et monde hellénistique: Actes du Colloque de Louvain-la-Neuve (11-14 mars 1980)* (Publications de l'Institut Orientaliste de Louvain 27), Louvain-la-Neuve 1982, 384-393; F.T. Fallon, 'The Gnostic Apocalypses', in J.J. Collins (ed.), *Apocalypse. The Morphology of a Genre*, Semeia 14, 1979, 123-158; A. Guillaumont, 'Textes de Nag Hammadi: "L'Apocalypse de Pierre"', *Annuaire du College de France 1979-1980*, 80 (1980), 471-473; H. Havelaar, 'An Intertextual Study of the Apocalypse of Peter (VII, 3)', *IVe Congrès International des Études Coptes* (to appear in Louvain-la-Neuve); K. Koschorke, *Die Polemik der Gnostiker gegen das kirchliche Christentum.* Unter besonderer Berücksichtigung der Nag-Hammadi-Traktate 'Apokalypse des Petrus' (NHC VII, 3) and 'Testimonium Veritatis' (NHC IX, 3): NHS 12, Leiden 1978; id. 'Paulus in den Nag-Hammadi-Texten. Ein Beitrag zur Geschichte der Paulusrezeption im frühen Christentum', ZThK 78, 1981, 177-205; M. Krause, 'Die Petrusakten in Codex VI von Nag Hammadi', *Essays on the Nag Hammadi Texts in Honour of Alexander Böhlig* (NHS 3), Leiden 1972, 36-58; id. 'Die literarischen Gattungen der Apokalypsen von Nag Hammadi', in D. Hellholm (ed.), *Apocalypticism in the Mediterranean World and the Near East.* Proceedings of the International Colloquium on Apocalypticism (Uppsala 1979), 1983, 621-637; E.H. Pagels, 'Gnostic and Orthodox Views of Christ's Passion. Paradigms for the Christian's Response to Persecution?', in *The Rediscovery of Gnosticism*, I, Leiden 1980, 262-283; Ph. Perkins, *The Gnostic Dialogue. The Early Church and the Crisis of Gnosticism*, New York/Ramsay 1980; id. 'Peter in Gnostic Revelation', SBL 110 Annual Meeting, Seminar Papers 2, Cambridge 1974, 1-13; H.M. Schenke, 'Bemerkungen zur Apokalypse des Petrus', in *Essays on the Nag Hammadi Texts* (NHS 6), Leiden 1975, 277-285; id. 'Zur Faksimile-Ausgabe der Nag-Hammadi-Schriften. Die Schriften des Codex VII', ZÄS 102, 1975, 123-138 (on VII 3: 130-133); C. Scholten, *Martyrium und Sophiamythos im Gnostizismus nach den Texten von Nag Hammadi*, JAC Erg.-bd. 14, 1987, esp. 80-90; E. Schweizer, 'Zur Struktur der hinter dem Matthäusevangelium stehenden Gemeinde', ZNW 65, 1974, 139; id. 'The "Matthean" Church', NTS 20, 1974, 216; F. Siegert, 'Selbstbezeichnungen der Gnostiker in den Nag-Hammadi-Texten', ZNW 71, 1980, 129-132; T. Smith, *Petrine Controversies in Early Christianity* (WUNT 2.R.15), 1985; G.N. Stanton, '5 Ezra and Matthean Christianity in the Second Century', JTS 28, 1977, 67-83; K.W. Tröger, 'Die Passion Jesu Christi in der Gnosis nach den Schriften von Nag Hammadi', Theol. Diss. (B), Humboldt-Universität Berlin 1978, esp. 208-234.

2. Attestation: in all probability the Coptic gnostic Apocalypse of Peter[1] has only its title in common with the Apocalypse of Peter[2] preserved above all in an Ethiopic translation. So far as it is not a question of citations, in which the matter can in any case be settled beyond a doubt, it is likely that when a Revelation of Peter is mentioned in the early Christian literature of the first centuries it is not the Coptic gnostic Apoc. Pet. that is meant.

3. Tradition: the Greek title stands at the beginning (p. 70. 13) and end (p. 84. 14) of the document. From a palaeographical point of view the text handed down in NHC VII 3 is relatively well preserved. The good state of preservation of the papyrus codex cannot however conceal the fact that the copyist of the present exemplar of Apoc. Pet. evidently did not work with the same care throughout, or perhaps a series of errors was already contained in his *Vorlage*. This leads to numerous obscurities, which make interpretation of the text difficult.

In the following translation the attempts to improve such passages in the text are marked in the usual way: words restored (or parts of words) are enclosed in square brackets [ ]; angled brackets < > indicate additions which would be expected either from the context or on the basis of Coptic grammar, but are missing in the text without any recognisable gaps. To facilitate understanding of the document, explanatory additions are occasionally inserted in round brackets ( ).

4. Language, date and place of origin: we may with some probability postulate Greek as the original language for the Apoc. Pet. also. This is suggested not only by the title, preserved in Greek, but by various Greek words which are only in part translated into Coptic, as well as by numerous Greek particles and conjunctions which have remained unchanged in the Coptic translation.

When such a translation was made cannot be said with any certainty. The manuscript of Codex VII probably derives from the 4th century (middle or end?); at this period a translation must therefore already have been available. Since it has evidently already been transcribed before, we may assume an earlier time of origin, which is further confirmed by the assumption of translation from the Greek. If the text itself, with its mention of the name 'Hermas' at p. 78.18, engages in polemic against the possibility of repentance advocated in the Shepherd of Hermas, this would yield a *terminus post quem* on grounds of content in the middle of the 2nd century. Apoc. Pet. presupposes and criticises the structures of a Great Church in process of consolidation, and the appropriation of Peter as the inaugurator of Gnosis is probably also directed against this; these points together with the controversy with other gnostics suggest placing the document at the end of the 2nd century or the beginning of the 3rd.[3]

With regard to its homeland. Apoc. Pet. provides no clear information. The dominant role of Peter as the mediator of revelation and various points of contact with Jewish-Christian traditions could make an origin in the area of Syria or Palestine probable.

5. Literary character: the Apoc. Pet. claims for itself the name of the literary genre 'apocalypse'. It is a 'revelation' in the literal sense, to the extent that in the frame-story Jesus the Saviour reveals to Peter, the sole recipient and mediator of the revelation, his true nature. This takes place in the form of visions and auditions. Some of the motifs here used are only hinted at, but in essence we can recognise the following: In Passion-week Peter receives from Jesus in the Temple at Jerusalem the revelations necessary for him to understand and comprehend, from a gnostic point of view, the sufferings and death of Jesus. In the process, the Passion story in the canonical Gospels is subjected to explicit and implicit gnostic criticism. This presentation forms the framework of the document. In the central section (p. 73.14-80.23) phenomena, personages and opinions of early Church history are critically dealt with. This too ministers to a correct understanding of the events by Peter and his adherents, but above all to strengthen and comfort them, as is emphasised at various points. Here Apoc. Pet. takes up in a special way the literary traditions of apocalyptic writings, which sought to raise the courage of their readers in a concrete situation of controversy and look forward to the temporal limits of that situation and its imminent termination. At least two sections of evidently different literary origin, best characterised as 'excursuses', are inserted more or less smoothly into the continuous text (p. 75.7-76.20 [24?]; 77.1-22; in the frame story possibly also p. 83.30-84.4); in each case they are taken up by catch-word links to provide further support for the train of thought. The two parts of the Apoc. Pet. are clamped together not only by the person of Peter but also by correspondences in the attitude of the opponents in each case. If in the gnostic portrayal of the Passion story it is the priests and people who rush against the Saviour, in the 'history of heresy'[4] the advocates of a different theology and Church practice are described in the same formulae.[5] It is quite obvious that here too the intention is to encourage. If the enemy were unable to get at the Saviour, Peter and his followers also will overcome all hostility.

6. Main problems and theological emphasis: *a) The controversy:* Beyond a doubt Apoc. Pet. stands in the midst of a debate, for which its readers are to be given assurance. But against whom is the controversy directed? Is it a question of a uniform front which stands in opposition to the gnostics of this document, or are there several directions in which critical argument takes place? The theory which regards the catholic Great Church as the sole opposition in Apoc. Pet. (so K. Koschorke) is attractive because of its apparent persuasive power, but this is sometimes at the expense of an accurate interpretation of the polemic in detail. It seems more in keeping with the facts to see the debate as carried on in different directions. Here we should not exclude the possibility that it is in part a question of views such as established themselves at a later period in the catholic Great Church. The formulation and the argument of Apoc. Pet. favour the view that we should assume several points of conflict and several opponents.[6] Among these are evidently other gnostics, if the interpretation of 74.27-34 as referring to Simon Magus and the heavenly figure personified as Helena in the heresiologists is correct. For the explanation of such a phenomenon it may be helpful to bear in mind that Christian gnostics, from whom Apoc. Pet. came, regarded themselves as the true Christians, and hence could criticise other gnostics (as well as other Christians). The Christian Gnosis of the Apoc. Pet. has a Jewish-Christian colouring; from this came evidently the taking-up of other positions: the (presumed) criticism of Paul (p. 74.16ff.);[7] the rejection of dreams and visions (p. 74.31-75.7); the disparagement of a different form of community as a 'sisterhood' (p. 78.31-79.21). It is striking that the 'official' representatives of the Great Church, 'bishop' and 'deacon', are only mentioned quite late in the course of the polemic (p. 79.21ff.) and disposed of with only a very general criticism. It is not clear how strongly marked the persecution situation already is for the gnostics of Apoc. Pet. When there is reference to judicial proceedings (p. 73.30) and to 'executioners' (p. 74.6), and the taking captive of the 'little ones' is lamented (p.74.2; 79.20f.), this makes one think of martyrdoms. We should however expect a clearer formulation if this was intended to refer to trials and executions in connection with the Decian and Valerian persecution, especially since the sections in question can also be understood differently.[8]

b) Self-understanding and self-designation: behind the Apoc. Pet. there stands a closed gnostic group of a conventicle type, which considers indispensable a sharp delimitation over against various other movements of Christian faith and life. It understands itself to be in direct personal succession to the Saviour through Peter, its hero and mediator of revelation. This emphasis on the formation of tradition through Peter is no doubt to be seen as analogous to the appeal to James in other gnostic groups, but at the same time represents a clear opposition to the ever-growing claims to Peter made by the Great Church. These gnostics apparently call themselves 'the little ones' (p. 79.19; 80.11), and interpret this in accordance with the Matthean 'little ones' who are to be regarded as the greatest in the kingdom of heaven.[9] The Jewish-Christian character of the Gnosis of the Apoc. Pet. can be observed at various points, and moreover it still does not appear to have any marked interest in the development of themes later broadly worked out in the formation of gnostic systems. All this speaks for a (relatively early) origin in a geographical area such as may be assumed for the Gospel of Matthew. The gnostics of the Apoc. Pet. also regard themselves as the 'strangers',[10] who are 'not of this aeon'. They are 'immortal', were 'chosen on the basis of (their) immortal nature', and are therefore also 'strong enough' to receive the secret teaching of Peter.

c) Christology: One special concern of Apoc. Pet is to lead the reader to a right 'knowledge' in regard to the Saviour, hence 'to teach Christology'.[11] This is done in narrative form, particularly through the frame story, in which aids to understanding are provided for a gnostic view of the events of the Passion. Through the varied emphases of the narrative the Christological statements there made seem to become independent, and at first sight have a confusing effect. A basic pattern can however be recognised, which is only varied in the sequel. A clear distinction is made first of all between the 'Son of Man who is enthroned above the heavens' (p. 71.11ff.) and the 'imitator' (p. 71.22f.). The Son of Man, through the 'I' of the Saviour, is in point of fact identified with him, although this is not said *expressis verbis*. However, the redeeming activity which is asserted regarding the Son of Man admits of only one conclusion: the Saviour is as it were a function of the Son of Man.[12] Behind the 'imitator', against whom Peter is urgently warned, lies concealed 'the fleshly (image)' of the 'living Jesus', which came into being 'after his likeness' (p. 81.17-24). That Peter may understand all this, the Saviour must unite with his heavenly pneuma which, conceived as (a garment of) light,[13] descends upon him (p. 72.23-27; cf. also 83.8-12: 'I . . . am the Spirit, perceptible only spiritually, filled with radiant light. Him you saw coming to me'). The same structure is found in the statements about the event of the Cross. The Saviour stands beside the Cross and laughs at the fact that the body of flesh is nailed up in his stead. 'The son of their vain glory instead of my servant have they put to shame' (p. 82.1-3). The 'servant' here functions as the name - interchangeable with other designations - of the Saviour, with whom the heavenly garment of light unites in the context while heavenly hosts sing out their hymns of praise (p. 82.4ff.). Altogether then a divine and a human nature stand over against one another in the Christological statements of

Apoc. Pet. The divine nature is graded into the Son of Man (= the garment of light, the pneuma) and the living Jesus, the Saviour (= the servant, the bodiless body).[14] The human nature alone is capable of suffering; it is the 'fleshly (likeness)', 'the ransom', the 'firstborn', the 'house of the demons' (p. 81.18-24; 82.21-26), with which the divine heavenly figure has for a time united.[15]

With these Christological statements Apoc. Pet. has probably succeeded - amid all the motley variety of the portrayal in point of detail - in making clear the essential concerns of gnostic thinking in this area. The distancing of the Saviour from all that is earthly, from the world and from all suffering, is manifestly emphasised, and from this point of view the criticism of the Great Church's worship of 'a dead man' (p. 74.14; 78. 17) becomes fully comprehensible.

Apocalypse of Peter

(p. 70) As the Saviour sat in the Temple, in the three hundredth[16] (year) of the foundation and (in the month) of the accomplishment of the tenth pillar and (on the day) when he (God) rested on the number of the living and undefiled majesties, he said to me:

'Peter! Blessed are those who belong to the Father <who>[17] is above the heavens, he who has revealed life through me to those who come from life, since I have reminded (them of it). They are indeed (the stones) which are built up[18] into the solid (building), for they will listen to my teaching and will learn to distinguish between words of unrighteousness and transgression of law and (words of) righteousness which **(p. 71)** come from above, (that they may know) every word of this fullness of truth. For they have readily allowed themselves to be enlightened by him whom the powers sought and did not find, who also was not proclaimed by any seed of the prophets, since he has (only) now made his appearance openly among these (children) - that is the Son of Man who is enthroned above the heavens - (revealed) before men of the same nature.[19]

But do you yourself, Peter, become as one perfect according to your name along with me, the one who has chosen you, for through you have I made a beginning for the remnant whom I have called to knowledge. Be therefore steadfast, that the imitator of righteousness, (i.e. the imitator) of him who called you as the first, and indeed called you that you might know him as it is fitting to do, (may be duly recognised by you. Such knowledge is necessary) because of the difference which exists between him and that one. (You can recognise him by . . .) and (by) the (fettered) joints of his hands and feet and by his crowning by the (beings) of the midst and (by) his sh[in]ing body, when they bring h[im in[the hope of (your?) **(p. 72)** service for a reward of honour, that he may move you three times in this night to fall away'.[20]

But when he said this, I saw (in a vision) the priests (take counsel) and the people run towards us with stones as if to slay us. And I was afraid that he would die. And he said to me:

'Peter, I have said to you many times that they are blind and have no leader. If you wish to know their blindness, lay your hands upon the eyes of your garment (= your body)[21] and say what you see.'

But when I did so, I saw nothing. I said: 'No one sees anything (in this way).'

Again he said to me: 'Do it again!'

And fear and joy came upon me, for I saw a new light, which was brighter than the light of day, and afterwards it came down upon the Saviour. And I told him the things I had seen. And again he said to me:

'Lift up your hands (to your ears) and listen to what **(p. 73)** the priests and the people are saying.'

And I heard the priests as they sat with the scribes, <while> the multitude (outside) were crying out with a loud voice.

When he heard these things from me, he said to me:

'Prick up your ears and listen to the things which they are saying!'

And I heard again[22] <. . . . . and said to him:>

'While you sit (here), they are praising you.'

And when I said this, the Saviour said:

'I have told you that they are blind and deaf.

So hear now the things I say to you in secret and keep them. Do not say them to the sons of this age! For in this age you will be ill spoken of, since they are ignorant concerning you. But you will be honoured where knowledge is. For many will receive our words in the beginning, and will turn away again according to the will of the father of their error; for they have done what pleases him. And he will make the (true) servants of the word a spectacle in his judgment. Those who **(p. 74)** associated with them will become their prisoners if they are without perception, but (every) pure and upright good (person) they deliver up to the executioner. And until these come to dominion, the "renewed" Christ is praised and (at the same time) the founders of this false renewal are praised, those who shall come after you. And they will cleave to the name of a dead man, thinking that (through this name) they will become pure, and will defile themselves the more. And they will deliver themselves to a deceitful name and a wicked deceiver[23] and a teaching of many forms, so that they are dominated by (this) disunion.

For some among them will be blaspheming against the truth and speaking evil words. And they will (all) speak evil against one another.

Some of them will give themselves a name - for they stand under the power of the archons - (after the name) of a man[24] with a naked woman of many forms and many sufferings. And **(p. 75)** those who speak these things shall be enquiring concerning dreams. And when they say that a dream comes from a demon[25] - which is (admittedly) appropriate to their error - then destruction will be given them in place of incorruptibility.

For evil cannot bring forth good fruit. For everyone - wherever he comes from - brings forth what is like him. For neither does every soul derive from the truth nor from immortality. For every soul of these ages has death appointed for it in our view. For it is at all times a servant, since it is created (to serve) its desires. And eternal perdition is their portion, which is that in which they exist and from which they derive, since they love the creatures of the matter which came forth together with them. But the immortal souls are not like these, O Peter. But so long as the (last) hour is not (yet) come, it does indeed become like the dead (souls). But it will not reveal its (true) nature; for it is **(p. 76)** it alone that is immortal and thinks of what is immortal, and believes and desires to forsake these (dead souls). For neither does one gather figs from thistles or thorns - if one is wise - nor grapes from thorn-bushes. For the (fruit) always comes from the (growth) to which it belongs. If it comes from that which is not good, it becomes for it (the dead soul) destruction and death. But that (other soul) comes from the eternal (tree), the (tree) of life and immortality. <And its fruits come from the (tree) of life,[26] which they resemble. So then all that does not exist (in truth) will dissolve into that which does not exist. For the deaf and blind associate only with those like them.

But others will cross over to (?) evil teachings and mysteries, which lead people astray. Some do not know (the true) mysteries (and) speak about things which they do not understand. But they will pride themselves that the mystery of the truth is in their hands alone. And in arrogance **(p. 77)** they will attempt the vanity of envying the immortal soul which became a pledge.[27] For all the authorities, dominions and powers of this age wish to be with these (the immortal souls) in the created world, in order that they who do not come from those that (truly) exist may through those (= the immortal souls) who (truly) exist be given glory, after they have forgotten themselves, without being saved by them or (even) brought upon the road, since at all times they (the powers) wish that they themselves may become the indissoluble ones. For if the immortal soul is strengthened through an understanding spirit, then immediately <the demons> of those (already) led astray rush upon them.

But many others who resist the truth, these are the messengers of error, will lie in ambush with their error and their law against my pure thought, since looking from one (point of view only) they think that good and evil come from one (root), and so traffic **(p. 78)** with my word. And they will appoint a stern Heimarmene, wherein the race of the immortal souls shall vainly walk until my Parousia. For there shall arise from among them <people who deny my words> and my forgiveness of their transgressions, into which they fell through the (activity of the) adversary, although I had taken upon me their redemption from the slavery in which they were, to give them freedom. For they will prepare a mere counterfeit (of the true forgiveness) in the name of a dead man, that is (the forgiveness which is proclaimed in the writings of) Hermas,[28] the firstborn of unrighteousness, that the little ones may not believe in the light which (truly) is. People of this sort are those labourers[29] who shall be cast into outer darkness, outside (the kingdom of) the children of light. For neither will they go in themselves nor will they allow those who wish to go in to reach their goal, to work their destruction.

But others again among them, who endure suffering, think that they are full **(p. 79)** of the wisdom of the brotherhood which truly exists, which is the spiritual fellowship with those who are from the same root, in a communion through which the marriage of incorruptibility will be manifest. (Instead of that) there will appear among them as a counterfeit something of only a similar kind, a sisterhood.[30] These are those who oppress their brethren, saying to them: "Through these our God sends his mercy, since there will be salvation for us (alone) through these." They do not know the punishment of those who rejoiced with those who wrought the deed on the little ones, who looked on (without protest) when they took them (the little ones) captive.

But there are others of those who are outside of your[31] number, who are called "bishop" and "deacon", as if they had received authority from God. They recline (at table, and thus fall) under the judgment of the first places.[32] They are the canals without water.'[33]

But I said: 'I am afraid because of the things which you have said to me. For **(p. 80)** only a few - so far as we see - are those who are beside the mark, while there are many who will lead astray many of the living also, crushing them under them. And when they speak your name, (people) will believe them.'

The Saviour said: 'A time is appointed for them in a number of their error, to rule over the little ones. And after the completion of the (period of) error the (aeon) of the immortal insight, which does not grow old, will become new; and they (the little ones) will rule over those who (now) rule over them. And he will pluck out their error by its root and put it to shame, so that it (the soul) may appear in all freedom, when it has taken it (the insight) to itself. And those of this kind shall be unchanging, O Peter.

Come then, let us go to the fulfilment of the good pleasure of the undefiled Father. For see, those will come who draw upon them(selves) the judgment (that fell on me), and they will be put to shame. But me they could not touch. But you, O Peter, take your stand in their midst. Do not be afraid! (This I say) because of your frailty of heart. **(p. 81)** Their insight will be closed up, for the Invisible has come upon them.'

When he said this, I saw him as if he was laid hold of by them. And I said: 'What is this that I see, O Lord? Is it you alone whom they take, and do you lay hold of me? Or who is this who is glad beside the tree and laughs? And another they strike upon his feet and on his hands?'

The Saviour said to me:

'He whom you see beside the tree glad and laughing, this is the living Jesus. But he into whose hands and feet they drive the nails is his fleshly (likeness), the "ransom", which (alone) they (are able to) put to shame. That came into being after his likeness. But look on him and on me!' But when I had looked, I said:

'Lord, no one sees you, let us flee from here!'

But he said to me:

'I have told you that they (are) blind. Let them be! But you, see how little they know what they say. **(p. 82)** For the son of their (empty) glory have they put to shame in the place of my servant.'[34]

But I saw one about to approach us, like to him and to the one who laughed beside the tree - but it was woven[35] in Holy Spirit, and this was the Saviour. And there was a great ineffable light surrounding them, and the multitude of the ineffable and invisible angels, who were praising them. But it is I who saw him while he was revealed as the one who glorifies.[36]

But he said to me:

'Be strong! For you are the one to whom it was given to know these mysteries openly. For he whom they nailed up is the first-born and the house of the demons and the stone jug[37] in which they dwell, <the man> of Elohim, <the man> of the Cross,[38] who is under the law. But he who stands near to him is the living Saviour, who was formerly in him, and was arrested and (yet) set free again, and (now) stands rejoicing, since [he] sees that those who did evil to him are now divided among themselves. **(p. 83)** Because of this he laughs at their blindness, knowing that they were born blind. So then (only) the one capable of suffering will <suffer>,[39] while the body is the "ransom". But he that was set free is my bodiless body. But I (myself) am the Spirit, perceptible only spiritually, filled with radiant light. Him you saw coming to me. But our spiritual fullness is that (process) which unites this perfect light with my Holy Spirit. These things, then, which you have seen, you are to hand them on to the "aliens" who are not of this age. For a gift <of such a kind> has no place among men who are not immortal, but only in those who were chosen because of their immortal nature, which has shown itself to be strong enough to receive that (Spirit) which imparts its abundance.

That is why I said:[40] "Every-one who has, to him will be given, and he will have abundance. But he who does not have"

- that is the man of this place, who is wholly dead, since he proceeded from the planting of the creation of this race; (these men) **(p. 84)** who when someone from the immortal nature reveals himself think that they can lay hold of him -

"from him it is taken away and added to what is (already with the other)."

Do you then be strong of heart and do not fear anything. For I will be with you, that none of your enemies may have power over you. Peace be with you! Be strong!'

When he had said these things, he (Peter) came to himself.

Apocalypse of Peter

Notes

2. The Coptic Gnostic Apocalypse of Peter

1. NHC VII 3, pp. 70.13-84.14. Hereafter abbreviated as Apoc. Pet. The abbreviations of other Nag Hammadi documents follow the list in *The Nag Hammadi Library in English* (1988) xiiif.
2. See above, pp. 620ff.
3. Cf. K.-W. Tröger, 'Passion' 209 ('roughly in the period at the end of the second century'); K. Koschorke, *Polemik*, 17 ('beginning to middle of the third century')
4. This formulation by Koschorke (*Polemik*, 12; 37ff; and often) fits the situation well, in so far as from the point of view of Apoc. Pet. it is probably not a question of a single heresy only, but of various divergent opinions (cf. the repeated openings with 'many', 'some', 'numerous others' etc.). Koschorke on the other hand sees Apoc. Pet. as directed uniformly against the catholic Church.
5. Cf. the references in Koschorke, *Polemik*, 12f.
6. This might support a relatively early dating - end of the 2nd century or beginning of the 3rd. It seems scarcely conceivable that we could postulate so clear a front against gnostic views already at such a date. Moreover it would have to hold for the homeland of the Greek original version as well as for the Coptic translation.
7. Further references for polemic with respect to Paul in Koschorke, *Polemik*, 40f.
8. C. Scholten, *Martyrium*, 85: 'metaphorical ways of expression, feigning action', which are used in the context of the doctrinal debate. Cf. also Koschorke, who would characterise these formulations as 'marks of the eschatological apostasy', analogous to the Synoptic apocalypse (42f.). Something similar may probably also be said of the opponents who at p. 78.31ff. are attested as 'having suffering'. If it was really a question of martyrdoms here, we should certainly expect a more specific form of words.
9. Cf. Mt. 18:1ff. E. Schweizer has brought out these connections in various ways (see Lit.), and has emphasised the kinship of the Church types. Koschorke quite differently would see the 'little ones' as the ordinary Church members, for whose allegiance Church and Gnosis are in conflict with one another (esp. 60-64; 80-85).
10. P. 83.16. The following characteristics are taken from the section p. 83.15-26, in which Peter receives the charge to hand on the secret doctrine to his own people. At 83.16 the Greek term ἀλλογενής occurs, and behind this another self-designation of the group perhaps lies concealed. The questions arising from this title and from other considerations, about a relationship between Apoc. Pet. and the Arcontics of Epiphanius (*Pan.* 40.1.1-8.2) and a possible controversy with them (ThLZ 99, 1974, cols. 576f.), probably cannot be cleared up; in any case there remains for this document an open confrontation between gnostics and other gnostics.
11. For what follows cf. Tröger, 'Passion' 218-234.
12. Despite this the Saviour who brings the revelation is not described as Son of Man: Tröger, 'Passion' 234.
13. Cf. the 'woven' at p. 82.7 and on this H.-M. Schenke, 'Bemerkungen' 283-285.
14. In connection with the vision narrative the Saviour who brings the revelation is probably also to be identified with him.
15. Apoc. Pet says nothing about the point of time at which the union of the two natures takes place - this is one of the internal concerns of the document. But remarkably the text also makes no precise statement about the time and the process of the separation of the divine and the earthly nature, unless it is to be seen behind the words about grasping and being unable to lay hold (p. 81.3-10).
16. A cryptic dating according to year, month and day appears to lie concealed behind the numbers given here. A convincing explanation for this cannot be given; perhaps these statements are in general to be regarded as stylistic devices of Apocalyptic, and therefore insoluble.
17. Text: 'who are above the heavens'. A description of the Father 'who is above the heavens'

is more natural in the context.
18. Cf. 1 Pet. 2:5.
19. The construction of this sentence is not clear. The translation offered attempts to bring out a meaning such as would be expected from the context.
20. The differences between the true Saviour and the 'imitator' are here described with the aid of a mixture of statements especially from the Passion stories in Matthew and John (cf. H.-M. Schenke, 'Bemerkungen' 277-281). It is questionable whether there is (at the end?) an allusion to appearances of the risen Jesus, which in the gnostic interpretation are then explained as a leading astray into apostasy from the true knowledge (cf. Koschorke, *Polemik*, 29-32).
21. The Greek technical term for 'garment' which is used here seems to tell against understanding the word as a metaphor for 'body'. This assumption, however, still presents the fewest difficulties. Perhaps the sentence is not merely unclear in content, but also linguistically corrupt.
22. The Coptic construction does not yield any clear sense. A crucial phrase must have dropped out. For a solution, the following possibilities present themselves: a) in addition to the earthly rejection of the Saviour by the priests and the people, Peter hears at the same time a heavenly hymn of praise to him (cf. the praises of the heavenly host at the end of the frame story, p. 82.11ff.). b) In the passage which has fallen out, by change of subject or otherwise, a meaning has been produced which interprets the words of the opponents as 'praise' (cf. Gamaliel!). c) Behind the Coptic phrase hitherto understood as 'praise' there stands an unknown expression which is in substance an equivalent to the vision of the advancing opponents - something like: 'While you (still) sit here, they (already) want to lay hands on you.'
23. Possibly this is a polemical allusion to Paul, such as we find widely developed in the Jewish-Christian area; cf. the Pseudo-Clementines, Kerygmata Petrou.
24. In the Coptic sentence there is no term connecting with 'a man'; at the same time it is not clear from the extant text what the opponents in view actually called themselves. The clause 'for they stand under the power of the archons', placed in parenthesis in the translation, is evidently criticism of a designation and cannot be understood as a name. To supply 'after the name' appears to be a meaningful conjecture. The whole is then directed against the Simonians (on the problems here addressed, cf. H.-M. Schenke, 'Bemerkungen' 281-283). Otherwise Koschorke (*Polemik*, 15, 39ff.), who regards 'Simon' as a cipher for Paul.
25. Cf. ps.-Clem *Hom.* XVII 16.2 As in the Pseudo-Clementines in the debate between Peter and Paul, the question of dreams and visions serves for the legitimation of theological opinions. The unrelated 'then' in what follows evidently alludes to the punishment of such erroneous belief in the final judgment. The alternative of oral revelation (= right doctrine = Peter) and dreams and visions (= false doctrine = Paul), clearly expressed in the Pseudo-Clementines (*Hom.* XVII 17.5-197), is here to all appearances obscured or blotted out.
26. There is no term connecting with 'of life', and also no subject for 'they are like'. The restoration attempts to correct an omission - perhaps through homoeoteleuton? All the same, it is a natural assumption that the text here has fallen badly into disorder. This could have been caused by concern to fit the excursus-type section, which here comes to an end, into the on-going text, or have originated through the 'quotation' of Lk. 6:44ff., par. (cf. also Gos. Thom. logion 45)
27. The text could be made intelligible in the translation offered, if we are not to assume, a more extensive corruption (cf. ThLZ 99, 1974, col. 580 and note 16).
28. Through the connection with the problem of the forgiveness of sins, it may be taken as certain that here there is polemic against the possibility of repentance advocated by the Shepherd of Hermas. Naturally it is not Hermas who is meant in the phrase 'in the name of a dead man', but here there is a discrediting of other Christological views; cf. already p. 74.13f., as well as the parallel formulation in Treat. Seth (NHC VII 2), p. 60.22: 'a doctrine of a dead man'.
29. Cf. Mt. 23:13; Lk. 11:52; Gos. Thom. logion 102; Phil. 3:2.
30. Cf. with this the idea of 'female prophecy' (likewise negatively assessed) in the Pseudo-Clementines, esp. *Hom.* III 23ff.

31. The unusual full form of the Coptic possessive article (2 plur. fem.), here used in 'your number' (elsewhere BF!), can be understood as a scribal error or has for its background the full form of the article which occurs in various expressions of time (and number?) (cf. Till, *Dialektgrammatik*, 63, 128). Because of the construction of the 'outside' it is not possible to understand the possessive article as 1 plural ('our number').
32. Cf. Mt. 23:6.
33. Cf. 2 Pet. 2:17.
34. A gnostic inversion of 1 Cor. 2:8? Cf. also Tröger, 'Passion', 230.
35. H.-M. Schenke, 'Bemerkungen', 283-285: the background is the idea of the garment, such as is found in other gnostic texts.
36. From the context, we should expect: 'It is I who saw him as he was manifested as the one who is glorified.' The text however appears to be in disorder; at least a relative pronoun is missing at p. 82.16.
37. Here evidently use is made of a legend according to which Solomon imprisoned demons in pitchers. Cf. Testim. Truth (NHC IX 3, p. 70.10-14) and on this B.A. Pearson, NHS XV, 193 and note.
38. In contrast to other passages, which refer to the Cross by the Coptic word for 'wood', we have here the Greek σταυρός - behind which we may perhaps see a further negative allusion to Paul's theology of the Cross. Cf. also Koschorke, *Polemik*, 21f.
39. Either the verb 'to suffer' has dropped out by homoeoteleuton (?) or the text paraphrases another idea (no longer clearly recognisable in the construction): 'It will only be the one capable of suffering' (i.e. only he will appear or exist).
40. In p. 83.26-84.6, the sense of Mt. 13:12; 25:29 is taken up, but interrupted by a gnostic interpretation of the 'he who does not have'.

3. Apocalypse of Paul

Hugo Duensing†/Aurelio de Santos Otero

Introduction

1. Attestation. - In his *Nomocanon* (VII 9) Barhebraeus introduces a quotation from Origen according to which the Apocalypse of Paul, with other apocalypses and also other early Christian writings enumerated there, was accepted by the Church. If this quotation is not altered, with Zahn, to read Peter instead of Paul, and so is accepted as genuine as it stands, then one might also assume acquaintance at least with the material of our apocalypse in his *Homil. in Psalmos* (ed. Lommatzsch XII. 233), where he gives a description of the destiny of souls after death which is closely related with chs. 13ff. of the Apocalypse of Paul. That he cannot in any case have had our recension before him follows not only on grounds of content but also from *Sozomen (Hist. eccl.* VII 19, ed. Bidez-Hansen, GCS 50, 1960, 331) who says of the Apocalypse of Paul that none of the ancients knew it; rather it was allegedly found under the emperor of the time, by which he alludes to the story of its discovery which it contains, but after inquiry from an ancient presbyter in Tarsus it turned out to be a fraud. If Origen knew a document of the same title, it could not have been the apocalypse in the form in which we now have it. We find a more reliable witness to its existence in Augustine (*In Ioh. tract.* 98.8, ed. R. Willems, CChrSL 36, 1954, 581), who says that some have concocted an Apocalypse of Paul which the true church does not accept. And when in the *Enchiridion* (112-113, CChrSL 46, 109f.) he discusses the idea of the relaxation of the lot of the damned souls on the day of the Lord, he will have drawn that from our document; for at almost the same time (around 402) Prudentius produces this conception in his *Cathemerinon* (V. 125ff., ed. J. Bergman, CSEL 61, 1926, 30). In the Decretum Gelasianum the Apocalypse of Paul appears among the apocryphal books which are not accepted (ed. v. Dobschütz, TU 38.4, 1912, 12). Later testimonies only evidence continued knowledge of this apocryphon and the eventual extension of its influence.

2. Transmission. - The original *Greek* text has come down to us only in an abbreviated form, which is like an extract (see below). It has also received additions, as the versions show, e.g. at 62.5ff. there are statements directed against the Nestorians. The most complete and at the same time oldest witness is the *Latin* translation, as published by M. R. James according to a Paris manuscript; it is found in similar form as a torso in Cod. 317 of the St Gall Stadtbibliothek, and was published from that by Silverstein (*Studies and Documents* IV, London 1935). In addition there is a whole series of Latin recensions. A *Syriac* version was first made known in an English translation from a manuscript in Urmiah, and was published in a German version by Zingerle (in *Heidenheims Vierteljahrsschrift* IV, 1871, 139-183) according to the text of Cod. Vatican. Syriacus 180, later printed by Ricciotti in 1933. From Syria the text, like so many others, travelled to *Armenia*, and is preserved there in four forms[1]. The work has also been preserved in *Slavonic*, in the best form in old Russian tradition. The most important witness next to the Latin is the *Coptic* text, beginning at c.15 and to some extent expanded, which Budge published in 1915 with an English translation. The *Ethiopic Apocalypsis Mariae Virginis* which Chaine published represents an adapted translation of chs. 13-44 (cf. above, p. 694).

The differences between the various texts are so great that it is impossible to put them adequately together. We have to keep to that recension which is most complete and has been transmitted comparatively well, and then use the others to complete and correct it; this means using the Latin text published by James. Casey says correctly (p. 5): 'For most purposes it is sufficient to know the content of the work.'

3. Content and sources: in 2 Cor. 12 Paul tells of being caught up into Paradise and this gave someone who was familiar with the apocalyptic tradition the opportunity of putting in Paul's mouth what he himself knew or thought about the next world. He gets over the difficulty that Paul had described what he heard as unutterable by distinguishing between some things which Paul could not tell and others which he was permitted to relate (cf. ch. 21). The introductory report of the discovery of these important revelations serves to explain how it happened that they were not made public earlier, possibly even in the time of Paul himself. If this account comes from the (first) author himself the date of the work is fixed as the end of the 4th or beginning of the 5th century. In any case the recension which we have must date from that period.

After this introduction, placed at the end in the Syriac, we have the rapture to the third heaven (ch. 3); here Paul is told of the complaints which creation has brought against sinning mankind and about the reason for the delay of final punishment, namely, the divine forbearance (chs. 3-6). In chs. 7-10 we are told of the reports about the deeds of men which the angels give to God every evening and morning. Ch. 11 brings a change of locality so that the apostle may see the souls of the righteous and of sinners at and after their death and observe where they live. So he is able to see how a righteous man dies and what happens to him and to a sinner and a soul which denies but then is confronted with those whom it has sinned against during its life in the body (chs. 11-18). Paul is now brought to Paradise where the doors with golden inscribed tables are the occasion for a question, which the *angelus interpres* answers by saying that the names of the righteous are on it. Both Enoch and Elijah greet Paul at his entrance. From heaven he sees the ocean surrounding the earth, the land of promise and Lake Acherusia, whiter than milk, in which the archangel Michael baptizes repentant sinners so that they can enter the city of Christ. He reaches this city by a voyage in a golden ship over Lake Acherusia. Among other things there are four rivers to be seen, one of honey, one of milk, one of wine, one of oil. At the first the prophets live, at the second the children of Bethlehem and those like them, at the third the Patriarchs, Lot, Job and other saints, at the fourth figures rejoicing and singing Psalms. In the city he also sees and hears David singing Hallelujah (chs. 19-30). In ch. 31 there commences the visitation of Hell with its various places of punishment. Among the damned are found presbyters (ch. 34), bishops (ch. 35), deacons and readers (*anagnosti*) (ch. 36). At the request of Michael and other angels and for the sake of Paul Christ gives to the damned freedom from torture on Sundays (chs. 31-44). Then another visit to Paradise follows (ch. 45). Here a strange sight is seen at the beginning, viz. a tree on which rested the Spirit of Gen. 1, at whose movement the waters of the four rivers of Paradise flow (ch. 45). Paul again meets the Patriarchs (ch. 47), Moses (ch. 48), the prophets, Lot, Job (ch 49), Noah (ch. 50), Elijah and Elisha (ch. 51); only the meeting with Mary (ch. 46) was not mentioned earlier. The text breaks off suddenly in ch. 51 with the words 'I will send rain on the earth.' The Coptic alone goes on. In it Paul is yet again carried up into the third heaven (cf. the summary *infra*, pp. 741f.).

The many doublets in this carelessly compiled work show at once that the author has used material which was already in existence before him. His own individuality appears only in his high estimation of the life of monks and nuns, to whose circle evidently he himself belonged. If his own imagination provides the material relative to this life, he is elsewhere dependent on apocalyptic tradition; this, enriched with Greek ideas of the after-life, e.g. Tartarus, Lake Acherusia, the boat journey, permeated the early Church, and then also the Church of the Middle Ages, in an ever-broadening stream. It is clear that he knew the contents of the Apocalypse of Peter; this is seen above all in the description of the places of punishment and especially in that for those guilty of abortion; this conclusion would be quite incontrovertible if the Coptic has preserved the original ending, in which after his heavenly journey Paul returns to the circle of the apostles gathered on the Mount of Olives. The author would then understandably have altered his source only in so far as he replaces Clement, as in the Apocalypse of Peter, by Paul's disciples Mark and Timothy as those who wrote down what Paul saw. Other borrowings are Lake Acherusia (cf. *supra*), the encounter with the Patriarchs, the fiery stream, the angel Tartaruchus or Temeluchus. The ferrying over Lake Acherusia occurs also in the Apocalypse of Zephaniah (G. Steindorff, TU 17. 3a, 1899); in it we have also the recording angel with the manuscript (*chirographon* - agreeing in the Greek expression!) and the encounter with all the righteous in the heavenly world, in particular with the Patriarchs, Enoch, Elijah and David. There is a striking contact with the Apocalypse of Elijah (TU 17. 3a) at the very beginning in ch. 3, where with very little variation the sentence is repeated: 'The word of the Lord came to me thus: "O son of man, say to this people, 'Why do you heap sin on sin and anger God the Lord, who made you?'."' (Steindorff, 155; Schrage, 231) If the additional material at the end of the Coptic is original, then the author copied from the Apocalypse of Zephaniah, where it says, 'Be strong that you may conquer and be mighty that you may overcome the accuser and come up out of the underworld.' (Steindorff, 170; cf. ibid. p. 55, ch. 12, lines 12ff. of the Apocalypse of Elijah, and p. 153: 'Be triumphant and strong, for you are strong and are overcoming the accuser and coming up out of the underworld and the abyss.' Cf. also the last four lines on the same page.) Casey (pp. 22ff.) draws attention to an agreement with Slavonic Enoch, chs. 8-9 (Morfil-Charles, pp. 7-9), in the description of Paradise; James (p. 552 n. 1) likewise draws attention to a contact with the Testament of Job. It is impossible to say from where the author may have drawn his fantastic representation of the colossal fruitfulness of eternity (ch. 22), which corresponds with the description of Papias (in Irenaeus, V 33. 3f.). All these borrowings render a later date probable.

4. Literature: all the relevant literature up to 1935 is listed in *Studies and Documents* (ed. Lake), vol. IV: *Visio sancti Pauli*, ed. Th. Silverstein, 1935, 219-229. This work carefully clarifies the branches of the Latin tradition and reproduces MS 317 of the Stadtbibliothek of St. Gall. The remaining most important publications are: Tischendorf's edition of the abridged Greek text in his *Apocalypses apocryphae*, 1866, 34-69; M.R. James' edition of the oldest Latin Version[2] in *Texts and Studies*, vol. II. 3, 'Apocrypha Anecdota', Cambridge 1893 (on pp. 4-7 there is a comparison of the Greek, Syriac and Latin); the edition of the Syriac in *Orientalia* II, 1933, 'Apocalypsis Pauli syriace' ed. G. Ricciotti, 1-24 and 120-149, with a Latin translation; it consists of the Syriac text according to Cod. Vatic. syr. 180 compared with and completed according to Cod. Borgianus syr. 39. Zingerle had translated the former into German in 1871; the edition of the Coptic in *Miscellaneous Coptic Texts*, ed. E.A. Wallis Budge (with an English translation, 1043-1084), 1915.

R.P. Casey in JThSt, 1933, 1-32, gives an excellent examination of pertinent questions. The archivist of the Cathedral in Barcelona, José Oliveras Caminal, has published in *Scriptorium*, I, 1946/7, 240-242, from Codex 28 of the Cathedral a text coinciding in essentials with the section of the Vienna Cod. 362 printed by Silverstein (153-155). More recent literature in Altaner-Stuiber, Patrologie[8] 143. Since the appearance of the basic work of Silverstein the following studies of this theme may be picked out: A. Landgraf, ZkTh, 1936, 299-370; Th. Silverstein, 'Did Dante know the Vision of St. Paul?' *Harvard Studies and Notes in Philology and Literature* 19, 1937, 231-247; B. Fischer, *Vig. Chr.* 5, 1951, 84-87 (use by Caesarius of Arles). J.E.C. Williams, 'Welsh Versions of Visio s. Pauli', *Études Celtiques* 10, 1962, 109-126; M.

Tveitane, *Une version norroise de la Visio Pauli*, Bergen/Oslo 1965; A. Olivar, '"Liber infernalis" o "Visio Pauli"', *Sacris Erudiri* 18, 1967/68, 550-554; F. Secret, 'La "Revelación de San Pablo"', *Sefarad* 28/1, 1968, 45-67; M. Erbetta, III 353-386; L. Moraldi, II 1855-1911; W. Myszor, 'Apokalipsa Pawla', *Studia Theol. Varsaviensia* 10, 1972, 163-170; A. di P. Healey, 'The Vision of St Paul', Diss. University of Toronto 1973; A.M. Luiselli Fadda, 'Una inedita traduzione anglo-sassone della "Visio Pauli"', *Studia Medievalia* 15, 1975, 482-485, 486-495; R. McL. Wilson, art. 'Apokryphen' II, TRE III, 353; E. Dassmann, 'Paulus in der "Visio sancti Pauli"', JbAC 9, 1982, 117-128; A. Hilhorst in A.F.J. Klijn (*et al.*), *Apocriefen van het Nieuwe Testament* II, Kampen 1985, 210-249.

Silverstein's great service lies in his most thorough examination of the Western tradition of our Apocalypse[3]. In this tradition he has discovered the best representatives of the alleged original Greek text (Paris, B.N., MS Nouv. acq. lat. 1631 and St. Gall, Stadtbibliothek - Bibl. Vadiana, Cod. 317). Similar work on the individual oriental versions would be exceedingly valuable for the recovery of the original text. James made use of the Syriac and Coptic versions in his translation of the Latin text of Paris.

The Slavonic tradition in particular requires a thorough examination. The manuscript material listed by Bonwetsch (in Harnack, *Geschichte der altchr. Literatur* I/2, 910) comprises only a part of the Slavonic tradition. Cf. E. Turdeanu, 'La "Vision de St Paul" dans la tradition littéraire des slaves orthodoxes', *Die Welt der Slawen* 1, 1956, 410-430, and A. de Santos Otero, *Die handschriftliche Überlieferung der altslavischen Apokryphen* I, Berlin 1978, 170-187; II, Berlin 1981, 250-252. On early Irish versions cf. M. McNamara, *The Apocrypha in the Irish Church*, Dublin 1975, 105-109. H. Ch. Puech shows in *Coptic Studies in Honor of W.E. Crum* (134f.) that our Apocalypse of Paul has nothing to do with the Coptic Apocalypse of Paul from gnostic circles discovered at Nag Hammadi (cf. above, pp. 695ff.); cf. further, R. Kasser, 'L'Apocalypse de Paul', *Revue de théologie et de philosophie* 19, 1969, 259-263; J.M. Robinson (ed.), *The Nag Hammadi Library in English*, 1977, 239-241 (3rd ed. 1988, 256-259). On the relations between the Apocalypse of Paul and the Apocalypse of Elias, cf. W. Schrage, Die Elia-Apokalypse (*Jüd. Schriften aus hellenistisch-römischer Zeit V 3, 1980*).

Apocalypse of Paul

The revelation of the holy apostle Paul: the things which were revealed to him when he went up even to the third heaven and was caught up into Paradise and heard unspeakable words.[4]

1. In the consulate of Theodosiüs Augustus the Younger and of Cynegius[5] a certain respected man was living in Tarsus in the house which had once belonged to St. Paul; an angel, appearing to him by night, gave him a revelation[6] telling him to break up the foundations of the house and to make public what he found. But he thought this was a delusion.

2. However the angel came the third time and scourged him and compelled him to break up the foundations. And when he had dug he discovered a marble

box which was inscribed on the sides; in it was the revelation of Saint Paul and the shoes in which he used to walk when he was teaching the word of God. But he was afraid to open the box (itself?) and brought it to a judge; the judge accepted it and sent it as it was, sealed with lead, to the emperor Theodosius; for he was afraid it might be something else. And when the emperor received it he opened it and found the revelation of Saint Paul. After a copy had been made he sent the original manuscript to Jerusalem.[7] And it was written in it as follows:

3. The word of the Lord came to me thus:[8] Say to this people: 'How long will you transgress and add sin to sin[9] and tempt the Lord who made you, saying[10] that you are Abraham's children[11] but doing the works of the devil? Walking[12] in confidence towards God (L[1]: Christus), boasting only because of your name, but poor because of the substance of sin?[13] Remember therefore and understand, children of men, that the whole creation is subject to God but that mankind alone sins. It rules over every creature and sins more than all nature.

4. For often the sun, the great light, has protested to the Lord, saying: O Lord God Almighty, I watch the ungodliness and unrighteousness of men; permit me to deal with them according to my powers so that they may know that thou alone art God. And a voice came to it, saying: I know all these things; for my eye sees and my ear hears, but my patience bears with them until they are converted and repent. But if they do not return to me I will judge them all.

5. Sometimes indeed the moon and the stars have protested to the Lord, saying: O Lord God Almighty, thou hast given us power over the night;[14] how long shall we watch the ungodliness and fornications and murders which the children of men commit? permit us to deal with them according to our powers so that they may know that thou alone art God. And a voice came to them, saying: I know all these things and my eye sees and my ear hears, but my patience bears with them until they are converted and repent. But if they do not return to me, I will judge them.

6. And the sea has requently cried out, saying: O Lord God Almighty, men have defiled thy holy name in me; permit me to rise up and cover every wood and thicket and all the world that I may blot out all the children of men from before thy face, so that they may know that thou art God alone. And a voice came again and said: I know everything; for my eye sees everything and my ear hears, but my patience bears with them until they are converted and repent. But if they do not return, I will judge them. Sometimes the waters have also protested against the sons of men, saying: O Lord God Almighty, all the children of men have polluted thy holy name. And a voice came saying: I know everything before it happens, for my eye sees and my ear hears everything, but my patience bears with them until they are converted. And if not, I will judge. Often the earth has also cried out to the Lord against the children of men, saying: O Lord God Almighty I suffer more harm than all thy creatures for I

(must) bear the fornications, adulteries, murders, robberies, false oaths, sorceries and evil enchantments of men, and every evil which they commit, so that the father rises up against the son and the son against the father, and stranger against stranger, each to defile his neighbour's wife. The father mounts up on the bed of his son and the son likewise mounts up on the couch of his father; and those who offer a sacrifice to thy name have defiled thy holy place with all these evil deeds. Therefore I suffer more harm than every creature and although I do not wish to, I give[15] to the children of men my wealth and fruit. Permit me to destroy the strength of my fruit. And a voice came and said: I know everything and there is no one who can hide himself from his sin. And I know their ungodliness, but my holiness endures them until they are converted and repent. But if they do not return to me, I will judge them.[16]

7. Behold, children of men, creation is subject to God; but mankind alone sins. Therefore, children of men, bless the Lord God unceasingly every hour and every day; but especially at sunset. For at that hour all the angels go to the Lord to worship him and bring before him all the deeds of men, whether good or evil, which each of them does from morning until evening. And one angel goes forth rejoicing from the man he indwells but another goes with sad face.[17] When then the sun has set at the first hour of the night, in the same hour (come)[18] the angel of each people and the angel of each man and woman, (the angels) which protect and preserve them, because man is the image of God: and similarly at the hour of morning which is the twelfth hour of the night all the angels of men and women meet God to worship him and to bring before him every deed which each man has done, whether good or evil. Every day and (every) night the angels present to God an account of all the actions of mankind. Therefore I tell you, children of men, bless the Lord continually every day of your life.

8. Therefore at the appointed hour all the angels, every one rejoicing, go forth together before God that they may meet to worship at the hour arranged. And, behold, suddenly at the time there was a meeting (?),[19] and the angels came to worship before God, and the Spirit went to meet them; and a voice came forth and said, Whence have you come, our angels, bringing burdens of news?

9. They answered and said: We have come from those who have renounced this world on account of thy holy name; they wander as strangers and live[20] in a (the) cave(s) of the rocks; they weep every hour they dwell on earth, and they are hungry and thirst for the sake of thy name; their loins girt, they hold in their hands the incense of their hearts; they pray and bless at every hour; they are distressed and subdue themselves. More than all others who live on earth they are weeping and mourning. And we, their angels, mourn with them; wherever then it may please thee, command us to go and serve. Command them, Lord, to abide even to the end in righteousness.[21] And the voice of God came to them saying: Know that to you here my grace is established now, and my help, who

is my dearly beloved Son, will be with them and guide them every hour; he will also serve them and never forsake them because their place is his dwelling. (*In Gr the Divine voice speaks briefly at the end of ch. 8*: I have kept them and shall keep them void of offence in my Kingdom.)

10. When these angels had retired, behold, other angels who were weeping came into the meeting to worship in the presence of the Majesty. And the Spirit of God went forth to meet them; and the voice of God came, saying: Whence have you come, our angels, bearing burdens as servants of the world's news? And they answered and said in the presence of God: We have come from those who have called on thy name, whom the difficulties of the world have made miserable; for every hour they devise many opportunities, not making one pure prayer, not even with the whole heart, all the time they live; why therefore must we be present with men who are sinners? And the voice of God came to them: you must serve them until they are converted and repent:[22] but if they do not return to me, I shall judge them. Understand then, children of men, that whatever you do, whether it is good or evil, these angels report (it) to God.

11. And after that I saw one of the spiritual beings beside me and he caught me up in the Holy Spirit and carried me up to the third part of Heaven, which is the third[23] heaven.[24] And the angel answered and said to me: Follow me and I shall show you the place of the righteous where they are brought when they are dead; and after that I shall take you to the abyss and I shall show you the souls of sinners and the kind of place to which they are brought when they are dead. And I went behind the angel and he led me to heaven and I saw the firmament and I saw there the Power,[25] and the forgetfulness which deceives and seduces to itself the hearts of men, and the spirit of slander and the spirit of fornication and the spirit of wrath and the spirit of presumption were there, and the princes of wickedness were there. These I saw under the firmament of heaven. And again I looked and I saw angels who were pitiless, who had no compassion; their faces were full of wrath and their teeth projected from their mouths; their eyes flashed like the morning star in the east, and from the hairs of their head and out of their mouth went forth sparks of fire. And I asked the angel, saying: Who are these, sir? And the angel answered and said to me: These are those who are appointed for the souls of the wicked in the hour of need, for those who did not believe that they had the Lord for their helper and did not hope in him.

12. And I looked into the height and I saw other angels with faces shining like the sun; their loins were girt with golden girdles and they had palms in their hands, and the sign of God;[26] and they were clothed in raiment on which was written the name of the Son of God; and they were filled with all gentleness and pity. And I asked the angel and said: Who are these, sir, who have so much beauty and pity? And the angel answered and said to me: These are the angels

of righteousness; they are sent to lead in the hour of their need the souls of the righteous who believed God was their helper. And I said to him: Must the righteous and the sinners meet the witnesses when they are dead? And the angel answered and said to me: There is one way by which all pass over to God, but the righteous, because they have a holy helper with them, are not troubled when they go to appear before God.

13. And I said to the angel: I wish to see the souls of the righteous and of sinners as they leave the world. And the angel answered and said to me: Look down at the earth. And from heaven I looked down on earth, and I saw the whole world and it was as nothing in my sight. And I saw the children of men as if they were nothing and growing weaker; and I was amazed and I said to the angel: Is this the size of men? And the angel answered and said to me: It is, and these are those who do harm (*Syr.*: sin) from morning to evening. And I looked and I saw a great cloud of fire spread out over the whole world, and I said to the angel: What is this, sir? And he said to me: This is the unrighteousness which is mixed by the princes of sinners (?) (*Gr.*: with the destruction of sinners. *Syr.*: with the prayer of men.)

14. And when I heard this, I sighed and wept; and I said to the angel: I wish to wait for the souls of the righteous and of sinners and observe in what way they go out of the body. And the angel answered and said to me: Look down again at the earth. And I looked and I saw the whole world, and men were as nothing and growing weaker; and I looked and saw a man at the point of death. And the angel said to me: This man whom you see is righteous. And again I looked and I saw all his deeds which he had done for the sake of the name of God; and all his desires, which he remembered and which he did not remember, all of them stood before him in the hour of need. And I saw that the righteous man had progressed and found refreshing and confidence; and before he left the world holy and wicked angels stood together by him; and I saw them all; however the wicked found no dwelling in him, but the holy had power over his soul, directing it until it left the body. And they roused the soul, saying: Soul, take knowledge of your body which you have left, for in the day of resurrection you must return to that same body to receive what is promised to all the righteous. They received therefore the soul from the body and at once kissed it just as if they had known it every day, and said to it: Be of good heart, for you did the will of God while you were on the earth. And the angel that watched over it day by day came to meet it and said to it: Be of good heart, soul; for I rejoice over you because you did the will of God on earth; for I have reported to God of what kind all your deeds were. In the same way also the spirit advanced to meet it and said: Soul, neither be afraid nor troubled until you come to a place which you never knew; I however will be your helper, for I found in you a place of refreshing during the time I dwelt in you while I (?) was on earth. And its spirit strengthened it and its angel took it up and

led it into heaven. [And the angel said]:[27] And there went to meet it the evil powers who are under heaven,[28] and the spirit of error came to it and said (to it; *L*[1]: Whither, soul, do you hasten and dare to enter heaven? Wait and let us see if there is anything of ours in you.) (*S alone continues as follows*:) And the soul was bound there. And there was a fight between the good angels and the evil angels.[29] And when that spirit of error saw (it), he wailed with a (loud) voice and said: Alas for you, because we have found nothing of ours in you. And behold! every angel and spirit helps you against me, and behold, all these are with you and you have passed over from us.[30] And there came forth another spirit, a slandering spirit, and a spirit of fornication, and they came to meet it. But when they saw it, they wept over it and said: How did this soul escape us? It did the will of God on earth. And, behold, the angels indeed helped it and allowed it to pass over from us. - And all the powers and evil spirits came to meet it, even up to it. But they did not find anything of their own in it. And they were not able to do anything for themselves. And they gnashed their tooth (teeth) against this soul and said: How did it escape us? And the angel which led it answered and said to them: Be turned to confusion. There is no way for you to it. Indeed you were very cunning; you flattered it while it was on earth, but it paid no heed to you.

And then I heard the voice of myriad upon myriad of holy angels as they said: Rejoice and exult, O soul, be strong and do not tremble! - And they were greatly amazed at that soul because it had held fast by the sign of the living God.[31] And so they encouraged it and called it happy and said: We all rejoice over you because you have done the will of your Lord.[32] - And they led it until it worshipped in the presence of God. And when it had ceased,[33] at once Michael and all the host of angels fell down and worshipped the footstool of his feet and displayed the soul, saying: This is the God of all[34] who made you in his image and likeness. However an angel ran on ahead of it and declared, saying: Lord, remember its works; for this is the soul on whose deeds I reported to thee daily, acting according to thy judgment. And in the same way the spirit said: I am the spirit of quickening, breathing on it and dwelling in it. For I was refreshed in it during the time I dwelt in it. It behaved according to thy judgment. And the voice of God came and said: As this soul has not grieved me, so I shall not grieve it; as it has had compassion, so I shall have compassion on it. Let it therefore be handed over to Michael, the angel of the covenant, and let him lead it into the paradise of jubilation, that it may be there until the day of resurrection and become also a fellow-heir with all the saints. And after that I heard the voices of a thousand times a thousand angels and archangels and the cherubim and the twenty-four elders who sang hymns and glorified God and cried: Righteous art thou, O Lord, and righteous are thy judgments; there is no respect of persons with thee and thou dost requite every man according to thy judgment.[35] And the angel answered and said to me: Have you believed and understood that whatever each of you has done, he sees it in the hour of his need? And I said: Yes, sir.

15. And he said to me: Look down again at the earth and wait for that[36] other soul of an ungodly man as it comes forth from the body, a soul which has provoked the Lord day and night by saying: I know nothing other than this world; I eat and drink and enjoy[37] what is in the world. For who has gone down into the underworld and coming up has told us that there is a judgment there? And I looked and saw all the scorn of the sinner and all that he had done and that stood before him in the hour of his need. And I saw that that hour was more bitter to him than the future judgment. And that man said: O that I had not been born nor been in the world![38] And then holy and wicked angels came together and the soul of the sinner saw both, and the holy angels found no place in it. The wicked angels had power over it; and when they led it out from the body, the angels admonished it three times, saying: O unfortunate soul, look at your flesh, which you have left. For on the day of resurrection you will have to return into your flesh to receive what is fitting to your sins and your ungodliness.

16. And when they led it out, its familiar angel went before it and said to it: O unfortunate soul, I am the angel who clung to you and reported daily to the Lord the evil deeds which you did night and day. And if it had been in my power I would not have served you one single day, but I was not able to do that (anything of those things). For[39] God is merciful and a righteous judge and he has ordered us not to cease to serve a soul until you repent. But you have wasted the time for repentance. And today I am become a stranger to you, and you to me. Let us then go to the righteous judge; I will not discharge you before I know that from the present day I am become a stranger to you. And the spirit afflicted it and the angel troubled it. However when it had reached the powers, as already it went to enter heaven, there was laid on it one evil burden after another. For error and forgetfulness and tale-bearing met it and the spirit of fornication and the rest of the powers and they said to it: Where are you going, unfortunate soul? do you dare to rush on into heaven? Stop and let us see if we have any of our possessions in you, for we do not see any holy helper with you.

(*S*:) And when they had inspected it, they rejoiced and said: Yes, indeed, there is in you and you belong wholly to us; now we know that even your angel cannot help you and wrest you from us. - But the angel answered and said: Understand that it is a soul of the Lord, and he does not leave it and I also do not leave the image of God[40] in the hands of the evil. For he who supported me all the days of the life of this soul can support and help me and it. And I shall not leave it until it goes up to the throne of God on high. And when he sees it he will have power over it and send it wherever he wishes.[41]

And after that I heard voices in the height of heaven which said: Present the unfortunate soul to God that it may know there is a God whom[42] it has despised. Therefore when it had entered heaven, all the angels, thousands of thousands of them, saw it (and) they all cried with one voice saying: Woe to you, unfortunate soul, for the deeds which you did on earth; what answer will you give God when you approach to worship him? And the angel which was with it answered and said: Weep with me, my beloved ones, for I found no rest in this soul. And the angels answered him and said: Let such a soul be sent away from our midst; for since it came in, its foul stench has[43] gone through to all the angels. And then it was taken away to worship in the presence of God, and the angel showed to it the Lord God who had made it after his own image and likeness.[44] But its angel ran on ahead and said: Lord God Almighty, I am the angel of that soul on whose deeds I reported to thee day and night (not behaving according to thy judgment). Deal with it according to thy judgment. And in the same way the spirit said: I am the spirit which dwelt in it from the time when it was made in the world, and it did not follow my will. Judge it, Lord, according to thy judgment. And the voice of God came forth to it and said: Where is your fruit[45] which you have brought forth corresponding to the good things you received? Did I set even the difference of one day between you and the righteous? Did I not make the sun to rise over you just as over the righteous?[46] It however kept silent because it had nothing to say. And again a voice came saying: God's judgment is righteous and there is no respect of persons with him.[47] For whoever has shown mercy, to him will mercy be shown,[48] and whoever has not been merciful, God will not have mercy on him. Let him therefore be handed over to the angel Tartaruchus,[49] who is appointed over punishments, and let him send him into outer darkness where there is wailing and gnashing of teeth,[50] and let him remain there until the great day of judgment. After that I heard the voice of the angels and archangels who said: Righteous art thou, O Lord, and righteous is thy judgment.[51]

17. I looked again and behold two angels were leading a soul which was weeping and saying: Have mercy on me, O God, righteous judge.[52] For it is seven days today[53] since I came out of my body and was handed over to these two angels and they have led me to places which I had never seen. And God the righteous judge said to it: What have you done? You never showed mercy, and for that reason you have been handed over to such angels as have no mercy; and because you did not do what was right they have not treated you compassionately in the hour of your need. Confess therefore the sins which you committed while you were set in the world. And it answered and said: Lord, I have not sinned. And the Lord God, the righteous judge,[54] burned with anger when it said, 'I have not sinned', because it was lying; and God said: Do you think that you are still living in the world, where each of you sins and conceals it and hides it from his neighbour? Here, however, nothing is hidden. For if souls have come to worship in the presence of the throne then the good works of each and his sins are revealed.[55] And when the soul heard this, it kept quiet, for it had no answer. And I heard the Lord God, the righteous

judge, speaking again: Come, angel of this soul, and stand in the middle. And the angel of the sinful soul came and he had a document in his hands and he said: This, Lord, in my hands is (the account of) all the sins of this soul from its youth up to the present day, from the day of its birth onward; and if thou order (it), Lord, I shall recount its deeds from when it was fifteen years old.[56] And the Lord God, the righteous judge, said: I tell you, angel, that I do not expect from you an account from the time when it was fifteen years old, but set forth its sins for the five years before it died and came here. And again, God, the righteous judge, said: I swear by myself and by my holy angels and my power, that if it had repented five[57] years before it died, because of a conversion one year old the evils which it had formerly done would now be forgotten and it would have remission and pardon of sins;[58] now however let it perish. And the angel of the sinful soul answered and said: Command, Lord, that angel to bring forth those souls.

18. And in that same hour the souls were brought out into the middle and the soul of the sinner recognised them. And the Lord said to the soul of the sinner: I say to you, soul, confess the deeds which you committed against these souls which you see, when they were in the world.[59] And it answered and said: Lord, it is not a full year since I slew this soul and shed its blood on the ground, and with (that) other I committed fornication; but that is not all, for I also injured it greatly by taking away its property. And the Lord God, the righteous judge said: Or did you not know that whoever has done violence to another, if the person who has suffered violence should die first, he is kept in this place until the one who has committed the offence dies and then both stand before the judge, and now each has received (*St. G. and L.*: 'will receive') according to what he did? And I heard the voice of one who said: Let that soul be handed over into the hands of Tartarus,[60] and it must be led down to the underworld. Let it be led into the prison of the underworld and be cast into torments and be left there until the great day of judgment. And again I heard thousands of thousands of angels who were singing a hymn to the Lord and crying: Righteous art thou, Lord, and righteous are thy judgments.[61]

19. The angel answered and said to me: Have you understood[62] all this? And I said: Yes, sir. And he said to me: Follow me again, and I will take you and show you the places of the righteous. And I followed the angel and he lifted me up to the third heaven[63] and he set me at the door of a gate. And I looked at it and saw that it was a golden gate and that there were two golden pillars before it[64] and two golden tables above the pillars full of letters. And again the angel turned to me and said: Blessed are you if you enter in by these gates, because only those are allowed to enter who have goodness and purity of body. And I asked the angel and said: Sir, tell me, for what reason are these letters set on those tables? The angel answered and said to me: These are the names of the righteous who while they dwell on earth serve God with a

whole heart. And again I said: Are then their names written in heaven while they are still on earth? And he said: Not only their names but also their faces are written, and the likeness of those who serve God is in heaven, and the servants of God, who serve him with a whole heart, are known to the angels before they leave the world.

20. And when I had entered within the gates of Paradise there came to meet me an old man whose face shone as the sun. And he embraced me and said: Hail, Paul, dearly beloved of God. And with joyful face he kissed me. And then he began to weep.[65] And I said to him: Father, why are you weeping? And he sighed and wept again, and said: Because we are injured by men and they trouble us much; for there are many good things which the Lord has prepared and his promise is great, but many do not accept them. And I asked the angel and said: Who is this, sir? And he said to me: This is Enoch,[66] the scribe of righteousness. And I entered within that place and immediately I saw Elijah[67] and he came and greeted me with gladness and joy. And when he had seen (me),[68] he turned away and wept and said to me: Paul, may you receive the reward[69] for the work which you have accomplished among mankind. As for me, I have seen the great and numerous good things which God has prepared for all the righteous, and the promises of God are great, but the majority do not accept them; but even with difficulty through many labours do a few (one and another) enter into these places.

21. And the angel answered and said to me: Whatever I now show you here and whatever you will hear, do not make it known to anyone on earth. And he brought me and showed me *and I heard there words which it is not lawful for a man to speak.*[70] And again he said: Follow me further and I shall show you what you ought to tell openly and report.

And he brought me down from the third heaven and he led me into the second heaven and he led me again to the firmament, and from the firmament he led me to the gates of heaven. And he opened an aperture[71] and there was the beginning of its foundation over a river which watered the whole earth. And I asked the angel and said: Sir, what is this river of water? And he said to me: This is the Ocean. And suddenly I came out of heaven and perceived that it is the light of heaven which gives light to the whole land there.[72] That land, however, was seven times brighter than silver. And I said: Sir, what is this place? And he said to me: This is the land of promise. Have you not yet heard what is written, '*Blessed are the meek, for they will inherit the earth*'?[73] The souls of the righteous, however,[74] when they have come out of the body are sent for a while to this place. And I said to the angel: Will then this land come to be seen after a time? The angel answered and said to me: When Christ whom you preach comes to reign, then by the fiat of God the first earth will be dissolved and this land of promise will then be shown and it will be like dew or a cloud; and then the Lord Jesus Christ, the eternal king, will be revealed and he will come with all his saints[75] to dwell in it and he will reign over them for a thousand years[76] and they will eat of the good things which I shall now show you.

22. And I looked round that land and I saw a river flowing with milk and honey;[77] and at the edge of the river were planted trees full of fruit. And each tree was bearing twelve times[78] twelve fruits in the year, various and different. And I saw the creation of that place and all the work of God. And I saw there palm trees, some of twenty cubits and others of ten cubits. Now that land was seven times brighter than silver. And the trees were full of fruit from root (up) to tree-top. (*L*[1] *is incomprehensible here and we replace with C*:) From the root of each tree up to its heart there were ten thousand branches with tens of thousands of clusters [and there were ten thousand clusters on each branch] and there were ten thousand dates in each cluster. And it was the same with the vines. Each vine had ten thousand branches, and each branch had on it ten thousand bunches of grapes, and each bunch had ten thousand grapes.[79] And there were other trees there, myriads of myriads of them, and their fruit was in the same proportion. (*L*:) And I said to the angel: Why does each single tree yield thousands of fruits? And the angel answered and said to me: Because the Lord God of his abundance gives gifts profusely to the worthy, for they, while they were in the world, afflicted themselves of their own will and did everything for his holy name's sake.

And again I said to the angel: Sir, are these the only promises which the Lord God has promised to his saints? And the angel replied and said: No! for there are those which are seven times greater.

I tell you however that when the righteous have come forth from the body and[80] see the promises and good things which God has prepared for them, they will sigh and weep yet again, saying: Why did we utter a word from our mouth to irritate our neighbour even for a single day? I however asked and said again: Are these the only promises of God? And the angel answered and said to me: What you now see is for the married who have kept the purity of their marriages in acting chastely. But to virgins and to those *who hunger and thirst after righeousness*[81] and afflict themselves for the name of the Lord, God will give things seven times greater than what I shall now show you.

And after that he took me up away from that place where I had seen these things and, behold, a river whose waters were very white, whiter than milk. And I said to the angel: What is this? And he said to me: This is Lake Acherusia where the city of Christ is, but not every man is allowed to enter into that city. For this is the way which leads to God; and if there is anyone who is a fornicator and ungodly and who turns and repents and brings forth fruit worthy of repentance, first when he has come forth from the body he is brought and worships God and (he) is handed over from there at the command of God to the angel Michael and he baptizes him in Lake Acherusia. Thus he leads him into the city of Christ with those who have not sinned. And I marvelled and blessed the Lord God because of all I had seen.

23. And the angel answered and said to me: Follow me and I shall lead you into the city of Christ. And he stood by Lake Acherusia and put me in a golden boat and about three thousand angels were singing a hymn before me until I reached the city of Christ. Now the inhabitants of the city of Christ rejoiced greatly over me as I came to them, and I entered and saw the city of Christ;[82] and it was completely golden and there were twelve walls around it and twelve towers in it (*C*: a tower on each wall; *S*: and twelve thousand fortified towers are in its midst), and the individual walls as they encircled were distant from one another a stadium.[83] And I said to the angel: Sir, how much is one stadium? The angel answered and said to me: It is as great as between the Lord God and men on earth, for indeed the city of Christ is uniquely great. And in the circuit of the city there were twelve gates of great beauty, and four rivers which encircled it.[84] Now there was a river of honey and a river of milk and a river of wine and a river of oil. And I said to the angel: What are these rivers which encircle this city? And he said to me: These are the four rivers which flow abundantly for those who are in this land of promise; as for their names: the river of honey is called Phison, and the river of milk Euphrates, and the river of oil Gihon and the river of wine Tigris.[85] As therefore the righteous when they were in the world did not use their power over these things but went hungry without them and afflicted themselves for the name of the Lord God, therefore, when they enter into this city the Lord will give them these above number[86] or measure.

24. And when I entered in through the gate I saw before the doors of the city trees which were big and very high and which had no fruit (but) only leaves. And I saw a few men scattered about among the trees and they wept greatly when they saw anyone enter into the city. And the trees did penance for them by abasing themselves and bowing down and by raising themselves up again. And I saw it and wept with them and asked the angel and said: Sir, who are these who are not allowed to enter into the city of Christ? And he said to me: These are those who fasting day and night have zealously practised renunciation, but they have had a heart proud beyond that of other men in that they have glorified and praised themselves and done nothing for their neighbours. For some they greeted in a friendly way, but to others they did not even say 'Greetings': and to whom they wished they opened the doors of the monastery,[87] and if they did some small good to their neighbour they became puffed up. And I said: What then, sir? Has their pride prevented them from entering into the city of Christ? And the angel answered and said to me: Pride is the root of all wickedness. Are they better than the Son of God who came to the Jews in great humility? And I asked him and said: Why is it then that the trees abase themselves and raise themselves up again? And the angel answered and said to me: All the time these spent on earth serving God they humbled themselves shamefacedly

during that time because men confounded and reproached them, but they were not sorry nor did they repent in order to desist from the pride which was in them. This is why the trees abase themselves and rise up again. And I asked and said: For what reason are they allowed into the gates of the city? The angel answered and said to me: Because of the great goodness of God and because the entrance of all his saints who enter into this city is here. Therefore they have been left in this place so that when Christ the eternal king enters with all his saints, all the righteous at his entry may pray for them; and then they will enter with them into the city; yet none of them can have the same confidence as those who humbled themselves by serving the Lord God all their life.

25. And with the angel leading me I went on, and he brought me to the river of honey; and I saw there Isaiah and Jeremiah and Ezekiel and Amos and Micah and Zechariah, the major and minor prophets, and they greeted me in the city. I said to the angel: What is this way? And he said to me: This is the way of the prophets. Everyone who has grieved his own soul and on account of God has not done his own will, when he has come forth from the world and been led to the Lord God and has worshipped him, then at God's command he is handed over to Michael who leads him into the city to this place of the prophets; and they greet him as their friend and neighbour because he did the will of God.

26. Again he led me where the river of milk was; and there I saw in that place all the infants whom king Herod had slain[88] for the name of Christ, and they greeted me. And the angel said to me: All who preserve their chastity and purity,[89] when they come forth from their bodies, are handed over to Michael after they have worshipped the Lord God, and they are brought to the children and they greet them saying, 'You are our brothers and friends and (fellow) members.' Among them they will inherit the promises of God.

27. Again he took me up and brought me to the north of the city and he led me where the river of wine was, and I saw there Abraham, Isaac and Jacob, Lot and Job and other saints; and they greeted me. And I asked and said: What is this place, sir? The angel answered and said to me: All those who have given hospitality to strangers, when they come forth from the world, first worship the Lord God and are handed over to Michael and by this route are led into the city, and all the righteous greet them[90] as sons and brothers and say to them, 'Because you have kept humanity and hospitality for strangers, come, receive an inheritance in the city of our God.' And each righteous man will receive the good gifts of God in the city in accordance with his own behaviour.

28. And again he brought me to the river of oil to the east of the city. And I saw there men who rejoiced and sang psalms, and I said: Who are these, sir? And the angel said to me: These are those who dedicated themselves to God with the whole heart and had no pride in themselves. For all who rejoice[91] in the Lord God and sing praises to him with the whole heart are brought here into this city.

29. And he brought me into the middle of the city close to the twelfth[92] wall. Now at this place it was higher than the others. And I asked and said: Is there a wall in the city of Christ surpassing this spot in honour? And the angel answered and said to me: The second is better than the first and similarly the third than the second because each one surpasses the other right up to the twelfth wall. And I said: Why, sir, does one surpass another in glory? Explain to me. And the angel answered and said to me: From all who in themselves have only a little slander or envy or pride something is taken away from their glory, although they appear to be in the city of Christ.[93] Look behind you.

And I turned and saw golden thrones which were set at the several gates, with men on them who had golden diadems and gems. And I looked and saw within, between the twelve men, thrones set in another rank which appeared (to be) of greater glory, so that no one was able to declare their praise. And I asked the angel and said: Sir, who are those who shall sit on the thrones?[94] And the angel answered and said to me: These are the thrones of those who had goodness and understanding of heart and (yet) made themselves fools for the Lord God's sake in that they neither knew the Scriptures nor many Psalms but paid heed to one chapter concerning the commandments of God and hearing them acted with great carefulness in conformity to these (commandments) and have (thereby) shown a true zealousness before the Lord God. And admiration of these lays hold on all the saints before the Lord God, for they discuss with one another and say: Wait and see these unlearned men who understand nothing more, how they have merited such a great and beautiful robe and such glory because of their innocence.

And I saw in the midst of the city a great and very high altar; and there was standing alongside the altar one whose face shone like the sun and who held in his hands a psaltery and a harp and who sang saying, 'Hallelujah!'[95] And his voice filled all the city. As soon as all who were on the towers and at the gates heard him they replied 'Hallelujah!', so that the foundations of the city were shaken. And I asked the angel and said: Who, sir, is this here with such great power? And the angel said to me: This is David; this is the city of Jerusalem. But when Christ, the king of eternity, shall have come with the confidence (?) of his kingdom, then he will again step forward to sing and all the righteous will sing in reply at the same time, 'Hallelujah'. And I said: Sir, why is it that David alone begins the singing before all the other saints? And the angel answered and said to me: Because (?) Christ, the Son of God, sits at the right hand of his Father, this David will sing psalms before him in the seventh heaven; and just as it is done in the heavens, so it is done below, because it is not permitted to offer to God a sacrifice without David, but it is necessary for David to sing psalms at the time of the offering of the body and blood of Christ; as it is carried out in the heavens, so also on earth.

30. And I said to the angel: Sir, what is 'Hallelujah'? And he answered and

said to me: You search and inquire into everything. And he said to me: Hallelujah is a word in Hebrew, the language of God and angels. And the meaning of Hallelujah is this: tecel. cat. marith. macha. And I said: Sir, what is tecel. cat. marith. macha? And the angel answered and said to me: Tecel. cat. marith. macha is this: Let us bless him all together. I asked the angel and said: Sir, do all who say 'Hallelujah' bless the Lord? And the angel answered and said to me: That is so; and again, if anyone should sing Hallelujah and there are some present who do not sing (it) at the same time, they commit sin because they do not join in the singing. And I said: Sir, does someone who is doting or very old sin in the same way? And the angel answered and said to me: No, but whoever is able, and does not join in the singing, you know that he is a despiser of the word. And it would be proud and discreditable that he should not bless the Lord God his maker.

31. And when he had ceased speaking to me, he led me forth out of the city through the midst of the trees and back from the sites of the land of good things, and he set me above the river of milk and honey. And then he led me to the ocean that bears the foundations of the heavens. And the angel answered and said to me: Do you understand that you are going away from here? And I said: Yes, sir. And he said to me: Come, follow me, and I shall show you the souls of the godless and sinners that you may know what the place is like. And I set out with the angel and he brought me towards the setting of the sun, and I saw the beginning of heaven, founded on a great river of water, and I asked: What is this river of water? And he said to me: This is the ocean which encircles the whole earth. And when I was beyond the ocean I looked and there was no light in that place, but darkness and sorrow and distress; and I sighed.

And there I saw a river boiling with fire, and in it was a multitude of men and women immersed up to their knees, and other men up to the navel, others up to the lips, and others up to the hair. And I asked the angel and said: Sir, who are these in the river of fire? And the angel answered and said to me: They are those who are neither hot nor cold[96] because they were found neither among the number of the righteous nor among the number of the godless. For these spent the period of their life on earth in passing some days in prayers but other days in sins and fornications right up to their death. And I asked and said: Who are these, sir, who are immersed up to the knees in fire: And he answered and said to me: These are those who when they have come out of church occupy themselves in discussing (in) strange discourses. Those, however, who are immersed up to the navel are those who when they have received the body and blood of Christ go away and fornicate and do not cease from their sins until they die. And those who are immersed up to the lips are those who when they meet in the church of God slander one another. Those immersed up to the eyebrows are those who give the nod to one another and (in that way) secretly prepare evil against their neighbour.

32. And I saw to the north a place of varied and different punishments which was full of men and women, and a river of fire poured over them.[97] And I looked and saw very deep pits and in them there were very many souls together; and the depth of that place was about 3,000[98] cubits, and I saw them sighing and weeping and saying: Lord, have mercy on us. But no one had mercy on them. And I asked the angel and said: Who are these, sir? And the angel answered and said to me: These are those who did not hope in the Lord that they would be able to have him for a helper. And I asked and said: Sir, if these souls remain through thirty or forty generations thus one above another, I believe the pits will not hold them unless[99] they are made to go deeper. And he said to me: The abyss has no measure; moreover there also follows on it the (gulf, void?) which is below it. And it is as if perhaps someone takes a stone and throws it into a very deep well and after many hours it reaches the ground; so is the abyss. For when these souls are thrown in they have scarcely reached the bottom after five hundred years.

33. Now when I had heard that, I wept and sighed for the race of men. The angel answered and said to me: Why do you weep? Are you more compassionate than God?[100] For since God is good and knows that there are punishments, he bears patiently the race of men, permitting each one to do his own will for the time that he lives on earth.

34. And I looked yet again at the river of fire and I saw there a man being strangled by angels, the guardians of Tartarus, who had in their hands an iron instrument with three prongs with which they pierced the intestines of that old man. And I asked the angel and said: Sir, who is that old man on whom such torments are inflicted? And the angel answered and said to me: He whom you see was a presbyter who did not execute his ministry properly. While he ate and drank and fornicated he offered to the Lord the sacrifice on his holy altar.[101]

35. And not far away I saw another old man whom four evil angels brought running in haste and they immersed him up to his knees in the river of fire and they struck him with stones and they wounded his face like a storm and they did not allow him to say: Have mercy on me. And I asked the angel and he said to me: He whom you see was a bishop but he did not execute his episcopal office properly; he did indeed receive a great name but he did not enter into the holiness of him who gave to him that name all his life, for he did not give righteous judgments and he had no compassion on the widows and orphans. But now he is being requited according to his iniquity and his deeds.

36. And I saw another man up to his knees in the river of fire. And his hands were stretched out and bloody, and worms came out of his mouth and from his nostrils and he was groaning and weeping and crying, and he said: Have mercy on me, for I suffer more than the rest who are in this punishment. And I asked: Who is this, sir? And he said to me: He whom you see was a deacon who ate up the offerings and committed fornication and did not do right in the sight of God. Therefore unceasingly he pays his penalty.

And I looked and saw at his side another man who was brought with haste and thrown into the river of fire, and he was (in it) up to the knees. And the angel came who was (appointed) over the punishments and he had a great blazing razor with which he lacerated the lips of that man and in the same way his tongue. And sighing I wept and asked: Who is that, sir? And he said to me: He whom you see was a reader (lector) and he read to the people; but he himself did not keep the commandments of God. Now he also pays his own penalty.

37. And in that place I saw another set of pits and in the middle of it a river full of a multitude of men and women whom worms were devouring. I then wept, and with a sigh I asked the angel and said: Sir, who are these? And he said to me: They are those who exacted usury at compound interest and trusted in their riches[102] and did not hope in God that he would be a helper to them.

And then I looked and I saw another place which was very confined, and there was as it were a wall and fire in its bounds. And in it I saw men and women chewing at their tongues. And I asked: Who are these, sire? And he said to me: They are those who reviled the Word of God in church, paying no attention to it, but counting God and his angels as nothing. Therefore in the same way they now pay their own special penalty.

38. And I looked and I saw another hole below in the pit,[103] and it had the appearance of blood. And I asked and said: Sir, what is this place? And he said to me: All (the) punishments flow together into this pit. And I saw men and women submerged up to their lips and I asked: Who are these, sir? And he said to me: These are magicians who dispensed magical charms to men and women and made it impossible for them to find peace until they died. And again I saw men and women with very black faces in the pit of fire; and sighing and weeping I asked: Who are these sir? And he said to me: These are fornicators and adulterers who although they had their own wives committed adultery; and similarly the women committed adultery in the same way, though they had their own husbands. Therefore unceasingly they pay the penalty.

39. And there I saw girls wearing black clothing and four dreadful angels who had blazing chains in their hands. And they set them (the chains) on their necks and led them into darkness. And again weeping I asked the angel: Who are these, sir? And he said to me: They are those who although they were appointed as virgins defiled their virginity unknown to their parents. For that reason they pay their own particular penalty unceasingly.[104]

And again I saw there men and women set[105] with lacerated hands and feet (*or* with hands and feet cut off) and naked in a place of ice and snow, and worms consumed them. And when I saw it I wept and asked: Who are these, sir? And he said to me: They are those who harmed orphans and widows and the poor,[106] and did not hope in the Lord; therefore they pay their own particular penalty unceasingly.

And I looked and saw others hanging over a channel of water and their tongues were very dry and much fruit was placed within their sight and they were not allowed to take of it; and I asked: Who are these, sir? And he said to me: They are those who broke their fast before the appointed hour; therefore they pay these penalties unceasingly.

And I saw other men and women suspended by their eyebrows and hair, and a river of fire drew (?) them; and I said: Who are these, sir? And he said to me: They are those who did not give themselves to their own husbands and wives but to adulterers, and therefore they pay their own particular penalty unceasingly.[107]

And I saw other men and women covered in dust, and their faces were like blood, and they were in a pit of tar and brimstone, and they were running in a river of fire. And I asked: Who are these, sir? And he said to me: They are those who have committed the iniquity of Sodom and Gomorrah, men with men.[108] Therefore they pay the penalty unceasingly.

40. And I looked and saw men and women clothed in bright clothing, whose eyes were blind, and they were set in a pit of fire;[109] and I asked: Who are these, sir? And he said to me: They are the heathen who gave alms and did not know the Lord God; therefore they pay unceasingly their own particular penalty.

And I looked and saw other men and women on a fiery pyramid and wild animals were tearing them to pieces, and they were not allowed to say: Lord have mercy on us. And I saw the angel of punishments[110] laying punishments most vigorously on them and saying: Acknowledge the judgment of[111] the Son of God! For you were forewarned; when the divine Scriptures were read to you, you did not pay attention; therefore God's judgment is just; for your evil deeds laid hold on you and have led you into these punishments. But I sighed and wept; and I asked and said: Who are these men and women who are strangled in the fire and pay the penalty? And he answered me: They are the women who defiled what God had fashioned in that they gave birth to children from the womb and they are the men who went to bed with them. However their children appealed to the Lord God and the angels who are (set) over the punishments, saying: Defend us[112] from our parents,[113] for they have defiled what is fashioned by God; they have the name of God but they do not keep his commandments, and they gave us for food to dogs and to be trampled by pigs;[114] and they threw others into the river. But those children were handed over to the angels of Tartarus,[115] who were over the punishments, so that they should lead them into a spacious place of mercy. However their fathers and mothers were strangled in an everlasting punishment. And after this I saw men and women clothed in rags full of tar and sulphurous fire, and dragons were wound about their necks and shoulders and feet; and angels with fiery horns confined them and struck them and closed up their nostrils, saying to them: Why did you not know the time in which it was right for you to repent and to serve God, and did not do it? And I asked: Who are these, sir? And he said to me: They are those who seemed to renounce the world by wearing our raiment, but the tribulations of the world made them miserable so that they did not arrange a single[116] Agape and had no compassion on the widows and the orphans; they did not take in the stranger and the pilgrim nor present a gift (oblation) nor show mercy to their neighbour. Not even for one day did their prayer go up pure unto the Lord God. But the many tribulations of the world held them back and they were not able to do right in the sight of God. And angels went round[117] with them to the place of punishments. And those who were being punished saw them and said to them: We, while we were living in the world, neglected God; why have you done the same? And they led them to another place and these also spoke in the same way to them: We, while we were in the world, knew that we were sinners; we saw you in holy clothing and we called you happy and said, 'These are the righteous and the servants of God.' But now we have recognised that in vain were you called by the name of God; therefore you pay the perpetual penalty.

And I sighted and wept and said: Woe to men! woe to sinners! Why were you born? And the angel answered and said to me: Why are you weeping? Are you more compassionate than the Lord God, who is blessed for ever, who has appointed judgment and allowed every man to choose good or evil and act as he wishes? Again I wept even very vehemently, and he said to me: Are you weeping, when you have not yet seen the greater punishments? Follow me and you will see those that are seven times greater than these.

41. And he brought me to the north, to the place of all punishments,[118] and he placed me above a well and I found it sealed with seven seals.[119] And the angel who was with me[120] answered and spoke to the angel of that place: Open the mouth of the well that Paul, God's dearly beloved, may look in, because power has been given him to see all the punishments of the underworld. And the angel said to me: Stand at a distance, for you will not be able to bear the stench of this place. Then when the well was opened there came up immediately a disagreeable and very evil smell which surpassed all the punishments. And I looked into the well and saw fiery masses burning on all sides, and the narrowness of the well at its mouth was such that it was only able to take a single man. And the angel answered and said to me: If some one is sent into this well of the abyss and it is sealed above him, reference is never made to him before the Father and the Son and the Holy Spirit and the holy angels. And I said: Who are these, sir, who are sent into this well? And he said to me: They are those who have not confessed that Christ came in the flesh[121] and that the Virgin Mary bore him, and who say[122] that the bread of the Eucharist and the cup of blessing are not the body and blood of Christ.

42. And I looked from the north towards the west and I saw there the worm that never rests,[123] and in that place there was gnashing of teeth.[124] Now the worm was a cubit in size[125] and it had two heads. And I saw there men and women in the cold and gnashing of teeth. And I asked and said: Sir, who are

these in this place? And he said to me: They are those who say that Christ has not risen from the dead and that this flesh does not rise.[126] And I asked and said: Sir, is there neither fire nor heat in this place? And he said to me: In this place there is nothing other than cold and snow. And again he said to me: Even if the sun were to rise over them they would not become warm because of the excessive coldness of the place and the snow.

When I heard this, I stretched out my hands and wept and with a sigh I said again: It would be better for us if we who are all sinners had not been born.

43. However when those who were in this very place saw me weeping with the angel, they cried out and themselves wept, saying: O Lord God, have mercy on us! And after that I saw heaven opened and the archangel Michael coming down from heaven, and with him the whole host of angels, and they came to those who were placed in the punishments. And seeing him they cried out again with tears, and said: Have mercy on us, archangel Michael, have mercy on us and on the human race, for because of your prayers the earth continues. We have now seen the judgment and known the Son of God. It was impossible for us to pray for this[127] previously before we came to this place. For we did hear that there was a judgment before we came forth from the world, but tribulations and a worldly-minded life did not allow us to repent. And Michael answered and said: Listen when Michael speaks: It is I who stand in the presence of God every hour.[128] As the Lord lives,[129] in whose presence I stand, for one day or one night I do not cease from praying continually for the human race, and I pray for those who are (still) on earth. They, however, do not stop committing iniquity and fornication and they do not help me in what is good while they are placed on earth. And the time during which you ought to have repented you used up in vanity. But I have always thus prayed and now I beseech that God may send dew and that rain may be appointed over the earth, and I continue to pray until the earth bring forth its fruit; and I say that if anyone has done even only a little good I will strive for him and protect him until he escapes the judgment of punishments. Where are your prayers? Where is your repentance? You have squandered time contemptibly. But now[130] weep, and I will weep with you, and the angels who are with me together with the dearly beloved Paul, if perchance the merciful God will show mercy and give you ease. And when they heard these words they cried out and wept much and said all together: Have mercy on us, Son of God. And I, Paul, sighed and said: Lord God, have mercy on what thou hast fashioned, have mercy on the children of men, have mercy on thine own image.

44. And I looked and I saw heaven move[131] as a tree shaken by the wind. And they suddenly threw themselves on their faces before the throne; and I saw the 24 elders and the 4 beasts worshipping God,[132] and I saw the altar and the veil and the throne, and all were rejoicing; and the smoke of a good odour rose up beside the altar of the throne of God, and I heard the voice

of one who said: For what reason do you pray, angels and ministers of ours? And they cried out and said: We pray because we see thy great goodness to the race of men. And after that I saw the Son of God coming down from heaven, and a diadem was on his head. And when those who were placed in the punishments saw him, they all cried out together: Have mercy on us, Son of the most High[133] God; it is thou who hast granted ease[134] to all in heaven and on earth; have mercy likewise on us; for since we have seen thee, we have had ease. And a voice went forth from the Son of God throughout all the punishments, saying: What[135] work have you done, that you ask me for ease? My blood was poured out for your sakes and even so you did not repent. For your sakes I bore the crown of thorns on my head;[136] for you I was slapped on the cheeks, and even so you did not repent. Hanging on the cross I begged for water, and they gave me vinegar mingled with gall;[137] with a spear they laid open my right side.[138] For my name's sake they killed my servants, the prophets and the righteous,[139] and in all these things I gave you the opportunity for repentance, and you were not willing. Now, however, for the sake of Michael, the archangel of my covenant, and the angels who are with him, and for the sake of Paul, my dearly beloved, whom I would not sadden, and for the sake of your brethren who are in the world and present offerings, and for the sake of your children, because my commandments are in them,[140] and even more for my own goodness - on the very day on which I rose from the dead I grant to you all who are being punished a day and a night of ease for ever.[141] And they all cried out and said: We bless Thee, Son of God, because thou hast granted to us ease for a day and a night. For one day's ease is better for us than all the time of our life which we were on earth: and if we had clearly known that this (place) was appointed for those who sin we would have done no other work at all, have practised nothing,[142] and have committed no evil. What need was there for us to be born into the world?[143] For here is our pride comprehended, which rose up out of our mouth against our neighbours. Discomfort and our exceptionally great anguish and tears and the worms which are under us, these are worse for us than the punishments which . . . us.[144] When they said this, the wicked angels and those in charge of the punishments were angry with them and said: How long have you wept and sighed? For you have shown no mercy. This indeed is the judgment of God on him who has shown no mercy. However you have received this great grace - ease for the day and night of the Lord's day for the sake of Paul, the dearly beloved of God, who has come down to you.

45. And after this the angel said to me: Have you seen everything? And I said: Yes, sir. And he said to me: Follow me and I will lead you into paradise, and the righteous who are there will see you: for behold, they hope to see you and are ready to come to meet you with joy and exultation. Impelled by the Holy Spirit I followed the angel and he transferred (*lit.* 'set')

me to (in) Paradise, and said to me: This is Paradise where Adam and his wife sinned.[145] And I entered into Paradise and I saw the origin of the waters; and the angel beckoned to me and said to me: See, he said, the waters; for this is the river Phison which encircles the whole land of Evila, and this other is the Gihon which encircles the whole land of Egypt and Ethiopia, and this other is the Tigris which is opposite Assyria, and this other is the Euphrates which waters the land of Mesopotamia.[146] And going in further I saw a tree planted out of whose roots waters flowed, and the source of the four rivers was in it. And the Spirit of God rested over that tree and when the Spirit breathed the waters flowed.[147] And I said: Sir, is it this tree itself which makes the waters flow? And he said to me: Because in the beginning before heaven and earth appeared everything was invisible, the Spirit of God hovered[148] over the waters; but since the commandment of God brought to light[149] heaven and earth, the Spirit rests over this tree. Therefore when the Spirit has breathed, the waters flow from the tree. And he took me by the hand and led me to the tree of knowledge of good and evil[150] and said: This is the tree through which death entered into the world, and Adam receiving from his wife ate of it and death came into the world. And he showed to me another tree in the middle of paradise, and he said to me: This is the tree of life.[151]

46. While I still considered the wood (= the tree), I saw a virgin coming from a distance, and two hundred angels singing hymns before her. And I asked and said: Sir, who is this who comes in such great glory? And he said to me: This is the Virgin Mary, the Mother of the Lord. And when she had come near, she greeted me and said: Greetings, Paul, of God and the angels and men dearly beloved. For all the saints have implored my son Jesus, who is my Lord, that you might come here in the body so that they might see you before you depart out of the world; and the Lord said to them: Wait and be patient. Just a short time and you will see him and he will be with you for ever. And again all together they said to him: Do not sadden us for we wish to see him while he is in the flesh; through him thy name has been greatly glorified in the world,[152] and we have seen that he has taken on himself all the works both of little and great. From those who come here we inquire saying: Who is it who guided you in the world? And they answer us: There is a man in the world whose name is Paul; he in his preaching proclaims Christ, and we believe that because of the power and sweetness of his speech many have entered into the Kingdom. Behold, all the righteous are behind me coming to meet you. But I say to you, Paul, that I come first to meet those who have done the will of my Son and Lord Jesus Christ, I go first to meet them and I do not leave them to be as strangers until they meet my beloved Son[153] in peace.

47. While she was still speaking I saw coming from a distance three very beautiful men, in appearance like Christ, with shining forms, and their angels; and I asked: Who are these, sir? And he said to me: Do you not know them?

And I said: I do not, sir. And he answered: These are the fathers of the people, Abraham, Isaac and Jacob. And when they had come near to me they greeted me and said: Greetings, Paul, dearly beloved of God and men; blessed is he who endured violence for the sake of the Lord. And Abraham answered me and said: This is my son Isaac, and Jacob my dearly beloved. And we knew the Lord and followed him. Blessed are all those who believed your word, that they might inherit the Kingdom of God through work, renunciation and holiness and humility and love and gentleness and right faith in the Lord. And we also have devoted ourselves to the Lord whom you preach, convenanting that we will assist and serve all the souls that believe in him, just as fathers serve their sons.

While they were still speaking I saw twelve others coming in honour from a distance, and I asked: Who are these, sir? And he said: These are the patriarchs. And they stepped up and greeted me and said: Greetings, Paul, dearly beloved of God and men. The Lord has not saddened us, so that we see you while you are still in the body before you leave the world. And in accordance with their order each of them gave me his name, from Reuben to Benjamin; and Joseph said to me: I am the one who was sold;[154] and I tell you, Paul, that for all that my brothers did against me, I have not behaved in anyway badly towards them, not even in all the labour that they laid on me, nor have I hurt them in any thing for that reason[155] from morning until evening. Blessed is he who for the Lord's sake has been injured in something and has endured, for the Lord will repay him many times when he has come forth from the world.

48. While he was still speaking I saw another beautiful one coming from a distance and his angels were singing hymns, and I asked: Who is this, sir, who is beautiful of face? And he said to me: Do you not know him? And I said: No, sir. And he said to me: This is Moses the lawgiver, to whom God gave the law. And when he had come near me he immediately began to weep, and then he greeted me. And I said to him: Why are you weeping? for I have heard that you excel all men in meekness. And he answered and said: I weep over those whom with trouble I planted, because they have borne no fruit and none of them has made progress. And I saw that all the sheep whom I pastured were scattered and become as those who had no shepherd[156] and that all the labours which I endured for the children of Israel were considered[157] of no value and how many mighty deeds I had done among them and they had not understood; and I am amazed that aliens and uncircumcised and idol-worshippers are converted and have entered into the promises of God, but Israel has not entered. And I tell you, brother Paul, that at that hour when the people hanged Jesus, whom you preach, that the Father, the God of all, who gave me the law, and Michael and all the angels and archangels and Abraham and Isaac and Jacob and all the righteous wept for the Son of God as he hung on the cross. And all the saints turned their attention to me at that time, looking at me and saying: See, Moses, what those of your people have done to the Son of God. Therefore you are

blessed, Paul, and blessed is the generation and people who have believed your word.

49. While he was still speaking twelve[158] others came, and when they saw me they said: Are you Paul, who are extolled in heaven and on earth? And I answered and said: Who are you? The first answered and said: I am Isaiah whose head Manasseh cut off with a wood-saw.[159] And the second likewise said: I am Jeremiah who was stoned by the children of Israel[160] and killed. And the third said: I am Ezekiel whom the children of Israel dragged by the feet over the rocks on the mountain until they dashed out my brains. And we bore all these trials because we wished to save the children of Israel. And I tell you that after the trials which they inflicted on me, I threw myself on my face before the Lord, praying for them, bending my knees until the second hour of the Lord's Day, until Michael came and lifted me up from the earth. Blessed are you, Paul, and blessed the people who have believed through you.

When these had passed on I saw another with a beautiful face and I asked: Who is this, sir? [When he had seen me he rejoiced][161] And he said to me: This is Lot who was found righteous in Sodom. (When he had seen me he rejoiced), and coming up to me he greeted me and said: Blessed are you, Paul, and blessed the generation which you have served. And I answered and said to him: Are you Lot, who was found righteous in Sodom? And he said: I received angels into my house as strangers, and when the men of the city wished to violate them, I offered to them my two virgin daughters who had never known men, and gave to them saying: Use them as you wish, so long as you do nothing evil to these men; for this reason they have entered under the roof of my house.[162] We ought therefore to have confidence and understand that whatever anyone has done God will repay it to him many times over when they come to him. Blessed are you, Paul, and blessed the race which has believed your word.

When then he had ceased speaking to me I saw coming from a distance another man with a very beautiful face and he was smiling, and his angels were singing hymns; and I said to the angel who was with me: Does then each of the righteous have an angel as his companion?

And he said to me: Each of the saints has his own angel who helps him and sings a hymn, and the one does not leave the other. And I said: Who is this, sir? And he said: This is Job. And he approached and greeted me and said: Brother Paul, you have great honour with God and men. For I am Job who suffered much through thirty years from the suppuration of a wound. And at the beginning the sores that came out on (from) my body were like grains of wheat; on the third day, however, they became like an ass's foot; and the worms which fell were four fingers long. And the Devil appeared to me for the third time and said to me: Speak a word against the Lord and die.[163] I said to him: If it is the will of God that I continue in affliction all the time I live until I die, I shall not cease to praise the Lord God and shall receive greater reward. For I know that the trials of this world are nothing in comparison to the consolation that comes afterwards.[164] Therefore, Paul, you are blessed, and blessed is the race which has believed through your agency.

50. While he was still speaking another man came from a distance crying and saying: You are blessed, Paul, and I am blessed because I have seen you, the beloved of the Lord. And I asked the angel: Who is this, sir? And he answered and said to me: This is Noah from the time of the flood. And immediately we greeted one another.[165] And with great joy he said to me: You are Paul, the dearly beloved of God. And I asked him: Who are you? And he said: I am Noah who lived in the time of the flood. And I tell you, Paul, that I spent a hundred years making the ark[166] when I did not take off the shirt I wore nor cut the hair of my head. Moreover I strove after continence, not coming near my wife; and in those hundred years the hair of my head did not grow in length nor were my clothes dirty. And I implored the men of that time, saying: Repent, for a flood of water will come upon you. But they ridiculed me and mocked at my words. And again they said to me: This time is rather for those who can play and would sin as they please,[167] for him to whom it is possible to commit fornication not a little; for God does not see and does not know what is done by us all, and a flood of water will certainly not come on this world. And they did not cease from their sins until God destroyed all flesh which had the spirit of life in itself. But know, God cares more for one righteous man than for a whole generation of the ungodly. Therefore you, Paul, are blessed, and blessed is the people who believed through your agency.

51. And I turned and saw other righteous men coming from a distance and I asked the angel: Who are these, sir? And he answered me: They are Elijah and Elisha. And they greeted me. And I said to them: Who are you? And one of them answered me and said: I am Elijah, the prophet of God. I am Elijah who prayed and because of my word heaven did not rain for three years and six months on account of the unrighteousness of men.[168] God who does the will of his servants is righteous and true. For often the angels prayed the Lord for rain, and he said: Be patient until my servant Elijah prays and begs for this, and I will send rain on the earth. . . . [169]

The suffering which each endures for God's sake, God will repay him twofold. Blessed are you, Paul, and blessed is the people who will believe through you. And as he was speaking another, Enoch, came and greeted me and said to me: The sufferings which a man endures for the sake of God, God does not afflict him when he leaves the world.

As he was speaking to me, behold, two others came up together and another was coming after them crying out to them: Wait for me, that I may come to see Paul the beloved of God; there will be deliverance for us (?) if we see him while he is still in the body. I said to the angel: My lord, who are these? He said to me: This is Zacharias and John his son.[170] I said to the angel: And the other who runs after them? He said: This is Abel whom Cain killed.[171] They greeted me and said to me: Blessed are you, Paul, you who are righteous in all your works. John said: I am he whose head they took off in prison for the sake of a woman who danced at a feast.[172] Zacharias said: I am he whom they killed while I was presenting the offering to God; and when the angels came for the offering, they carried up my body to God, and no man found where my body was taken.[173] Abel said: I am he whom Cain killed while I was presenting a sacrifice to God.[174] The sufferings which we endured for the sake of God are nothing; what we have done for the sake of God we have forgotten. And the righteous and all the angels surrounded me, and they rejoiced with me [because] they had seen me in the flesh.

And I looked and saw another who surpassed them all, very beautiful. And I said to the angel: Who is this, my lord? He said to me: This is Adam, the father of you all. When he came up to me, he greeted me with joy. He said to me: Courage, Paul, beloved of God, you who have brought a multitude to faith in God and to repentance, as I myself have repented and received my praise from the Compassionate and Merciful One.

James considers it possible that the Apocalypse ended here. On the other hand a real conclusion is lacking. When C continues now with a fresh visit to the third heaven with many doublets, this is secondary. However perhaps the conclusion of C with the apostle's return to the circle of fellow-apostles on the Mount of Olives contains the original conclusion and would lead us to assume that the rapture also took place on the Mount of Olives. In what follows we give an abstract of C, with the conclusion, however, in a full translation.

Paul is caught up in a cloud into the third heaven. There he receives the command to reveal to no one the things which he will see. Nevertheless he tells about a seal and an altar with seven angels to its right and left. Many thousands of angels sing to the Father. When Paul falls prostrate the angel who accompanies him raises him up and promises to show him his place. He is now brought into Paradise with its shining inhabitants and its glorious thrones. At his request he is shown his own throne in a tabernacle of light; before it there are two singing angels who are presented as Uriel and Suriel. He is greeted by the inhabitants; the angel explains that these are the plants which Paul planted in the world. After further information from the angel he sees Paradise. Three concentric walls surround it, two of silver and in the middle between them one of gold. In the description of Paradise a remarkable feature is its trees which praise God three times daily, morning, noon and evening. The angel argues Paul out of the idea that he might not be worthy to dwell in Paradise: he will win the victory over the Accuser in the underworld (Amente). Moreover he will have great honour on his return to the world. And whenever the whole human race hears the words of this apocalypse then it will repent and live. Paul then gets a sight of the clothes and crowns of his fellow-apostles on thrones, and yet once more meets David who is singing with his harp. After that he sees the place of the martyrs.

The angel of the Lord took me up and brought me to the Mount of Olives. There I, Paul, found the apostles gathered together. I greeted them and made known to them everything which had happened to me and what I had seen and the honours which would be for the righteous and the ruin and destruction which would be for the ungodly. Then the apostles were glad and rejoiced and blessed God, and they commanded us together, i.e. myself, Mark and Timothy, the disciples of Saint Paul (!) the teacher of the Church, to put in writing this holy apocalypse for the benefit and help of those who will hear it. While the apostles were talking with us the Saviour Christ appeared to us out of the chariot of the cherubim, and he said to us: Greetings, my holy disciples, whom I have chosen out of the world! Greetings, Peter, crown of the apostles! Greetings, John, my beloved! Greetings to all (you) apostles! The peace of my good Father be with you. Then he turned to our father and said to him: Greetings, Paul, honoured letter writer![175] Greetings, Paul, mediator of the covenant! Greetings, Paul, roof and foundation of the Church! Are you fully convinced by the things which you have seen? Are you fully convinced by the things which you have heard? Paul answered: Yes, my Lord. Thy grace and thy love have accomplished for me a great good. The Saviour answered and said: O beloved of the Father, Amen, Amen, I tell you that the words of this apocalypse will be preached in the whole world for the benefit of those who shall hear it. Amen, Amen, I tell you, Paul, that whoever will take care of this apocalypse, and will write it and set it down as a testimony for the generations to come, to him I shall not show the underworld with its bitter weeping, until the second generation of his seed. And whoever reads it with faith, I shall bless him and his house. Whoever scoffs at the words of this apocalypse, I will punish him.[176] And men are not to read therein except on the holy days because I have revealed the whole mystery of my deity to you, O my holy members. Behold, I have already made known everything to you. Now go and go forth and preach the Gospel of my kingdom because indeed your course and your holy contest has drawn near. But you yourself, Paul, my chosen one, will finish your (sing.) course with Peter, my beloved, on the fifth day of the month Epeph.[177] You (sing.) will be in my kingdom for ever. My power will be with you. - And he immediately commanded the clouds to take up the disciples and lead them to the country which he had allotted to (each of) them. And they were to preach the Gospel of the kingdom of heaven in every place for ever because of the grace and love for man of our Lord Jesus Christ, our Saviour, to whom be glory and to his gracious Father and to the Holy Spirit for ever and ever. Amen.

After the words 'And the angels have often prayed that he would give them rain' at the break in ch. 51 the Syriac continues:

until I invoked him anew, and then he gave to them. But you are blessed,

Paul, that your generation and all whom you teach are children of the kingdom. And understand, Paul, that everyone who believes through you is blessed and blessedness is preserved for him. - Then he parted from me. And when he had gone away from me the angel who was with me led me out and said with great seriousness: Paul, the mystery of this revelation has been given to you; as it pleases you, make it known and reveal it to men. - I, Paul, however, came to myself and I knew and understood what I had seen and I wrote it in a roll. And while I lived, I did not have rest to reveal this mystery, but I wrote it (down) and deposited it under the wall of a house of that believer with whom I was in Tarsus, a city of Cilicia. And when I was released from this temporal life (and stood) before my Lord, he spoke thus to me: Paul, have I shown everything to you so that you should put it under the wall of a house? Rather send and reveal it for its sake so that men may read it and turn to the way of truth that they may not come into these bitter torments.

And thus this revelation was discovered.

Then the account of the discovery follows.

Notes

3. Apocalypse of Paul

1. The text (BHO 899-901) was published by Kh. Tsherakhian (*Thesaurus litterarum armeniarum* III, Venice 1904, 62-109) and has recently been investigated and translated into French by L. Leloir (*Revue des Études Arméniennes* n.s. 14, 1980, 217-285; id. in Corpus Christianorum/Series Apocryphorum 3/1 [Turnhout 1986], 87-172).
2. It will be denoted by L^1.
3. Since the appearance of his *magnum opus* in 1935, Silverstein has published further studies on the Latin tradition of the 'Visio Pauli' (see above all: 'The Vision of St. Paul. New Links and Patterns in the Western Tradition', *Archives d' histoire doctrinale et littéraire du Moyen Age* 34, 1959, 199-248; 'Visiones et revelaciones Sancti Pauli', in *Problemi attuali di scienza e di cultura*, quad. 188, Acc. Naz. dei Lincei, Rome 1974; 'The Graz and Zürich Apocalypse of St Paul', in *Medieval Learning and Literature: Essays presented to R.W. Hunt*, Oxford 1976, 166-180). On the basis of the new material, largely discovered by himself, Silverstein postulates *inter alia* the existence of two Old Latin translations independent of one another (L_1 and L_2), which for their part lay claim to two different Greek models. This suggests the existence of at least three different Greek versions of the Visio Pauli (G_1, G_2, G_3), which are to be treated as the starting-point for the whole of the witnesses to the text known to us today.
4. So Gr. Instead of this L^1 quotes 2 Cor. 12:1-5 and connects with what follows by means of the question 'At what time was it made public?'
5. Thus correctly restored by James and calculated as A.D. 388.
6. Gr. passive: "(the angel) was revealed": probably better.
7. The last two clauses are from Gr. L^1 has it the other way round: 'He sent a copy of it to Jerusalem and retained the original.' This account of the discovery appears as a postscript in the Syriac translation. The differences between the Syriac translations have generally been left unconsidered as leading too far afield.
8. L^1 prefixes this with a secondary addition: 'While I was in the body in which I had been

caught up into the third heaven.'
9. Is. 30:1.
10. This word is lacking in L[1], which in consequence has the meaningless sentence: 'You are sons of God.'
11. Cf. Jn. 8:33ff.
12. Lacking in L[1].
13. In accordance with Gr.
14. Cf. Jer. 31:35.
15. So in accordance with S[1].
16. Gr omits the complaint of the waters and the earth; S unites sea and rivers; the Armenian versions are different again.
17. The last few words in accordance with Gr A[1] A[4].
18. Here we should probably insert 'to meet God'.
19. The text is in disorder.
20. 'live' inserted in accordance with S.
21. This sentence is taken from Gr in place of the incomprehensible Latin words: *ne et alii fecerint sed inopes pr(ae)caeteris qui sunt in terra.*
22. Heb. 1:14.
23. Cf. 2 Cor. 12:2.
24. This sentence, which is indispensable for the understanding of the scene, is added in accordance with the Syriac, ed. Ricciotti, p. 9.
25. We should expect the plural, 'the powers', as in the Syriac.
26. Cf. Rev. 7:9; 22:4.
27. The bracketed words should be omitted. What follows is given as in the Syriac.
28. The detailed description of the powers of darkness which the Coptic here introduces is secondary according to the evidence of the other versions.
29. Cf. Rev. 12:7.
30. L[1] has: 'And behold, we have found nothing in you. I see also divine help and your angel, and the spirit rejoices with you because you have done the will of God on earth.' What follows is in accordance with S and St. G.
31. St. G.: 'the cross of the Son of God'.
32. From here on again in accordance with L[1] and St. G.
33. Either restore the singular or correct St. G. to: *Quam cum audissent*, 'when they had heard this'.
34. What follows is mostly in accordance with St. G.
35. Cf. Rev. 4:10; 5:8, 14; 11:16; 19:4.
36. What follows is mostly in accordance with St. G.
37. Cf. Is. 22:13; 1 Cor. 15:32; Lk. 17:26f.
38. The last two sentences after S. Cf. Job 3:3; Jer. 20:14.
39. What follows is mostly in accordance with St. G.
40. Cf. Gen. 1:26.
41. The special material belonging to the Syriac ends here.
42. St. G.
43. In what follows mostly in accordance with St. G.
44. Cf. Gen. 1:27; 9:6.
45. Cf. Lk. 13:6ff.
46. Cf. Mt. 5:45.
47. Cf. Acts 10:34f.
48. Cf. Mt. 5:7.
49. St. G.: of Tartarus; Gr.: Temeluchos.
50. Cf. Mt. 8:12; 22:13.

51. Cf. Rev. 16:7; 19:2.
52. St. G.
53. Cf. Sir. 22. 13.
54. St. G.
55. Sir. 39. 24.
56. St. G.
57. St. G.: 'one'.
58. Cf. Ezek. 18:21.
59. St. G.: you (sing.) were . . . '
60. Gr.: Tartaruchos. C: Temeluchos.
61. Cf. Rev. 19:2.
62. Gr., St. G. 'seen',
63. Cf. 2 Cor. 12:2, 4.
64. St. G., Gr.
65. St. G.
66. Cf. the apocryphal Letter of Titus, *supra*, p. 61.
67. Reading 'Elijah' with S and Vienna Codex 362. The *solem* or *solum* (St. G.) of other manuscripts is explained by the reading of the Greek *Helias* as *Helios*; cf. Silverstein, p. 37.
68. Cf. the apocryphal Letter of Titus, ibid.
69. Inserting *merces* with Vienna Cod. 362.
70. 2 Cor. 12:4.
71. St. G.
72. St. G.
73. Mt. 5:5.
74. St. G.
75. Cf. 2 Thess. 1:10.
76. Rev. 20:2.
77. Cf. Exod. 3:8.
78. St. G. is better: 'twelve times in the year various and different fruits'.
79. Cf. the description of Papias (Irenaeus, V 33. 3f.).
80. 'and' inserted in accordance with S.
81. Mt. 5:6.
82. On what follows cf. Rev. 21:10ff.
83. S Urmiensis: 'and between each of them was a stadium'. C: 'The circumference of each was a hundred stadia.'
84. St. G. without 'which'
85. Cf. Gen. 2:11ff.
86. St. G.
87. St. G.
88. Cf. Mt. 2:16.
89. St. G.
90. In what follows St. G. has been mostly used.
91. Cf. Ps. 68:4.
92. St. G and C.
93. 'Although . . . Christ' according to St. G. L^1 differs.
94. St. G.
95. Cf. Ps. 57:8.
96. Cf. Rev. 3:16.
97. St. G.
98. St. G.: '30,000 stadia'.
99. Altering *si* to *nisi*.

100. Cf. 4 Ezra 8:19.
101. C and S are more original here. C: 'Then I looked at the river of fire; I saw an old man who was dragged (Gr: by two). They immersed him up to his knees. And the angel Aftemelouchos came with a great fork of fire which had three prongs and with it he dragged his entrails out of his mouth.' (St. G. to practically the same effect) - S: 'And I looked and saw again a river of fire which flowed very much more rapidly than those other rivers and an old man whom angels brought and immersed in this river of fire up to his knees. And a servant of the angels came and he had in his hand a rod of iron on which there were three teeth. And he drew the entrails of that old man out of his mouth.'
102. Cf. Sir. 5:1.
103. Reading 'hole' with Gr instead of 'man' as in L[1].
104. The reason for the punishment is given more clearly in C and Gr. C: 'They are those who defiled their virginity before they were given to (their) husbands; before they were grown up, they defiled (it), even their parents did not know about them.' Gr: 'They are those who did not obey their parents but before marriage defiled their virginity.'
105. One would expect 'set' to go with 'in a place of ice and snow'.
106. Cf. Zech. 7:10.
107. The better Coptic text of this paragraph runs: 'And I saw other men and women suspended head downwards; and the great torches of fire were burning before their faces, and dragon-serpents were wound round their bodies and were devouring them. And I said to the angel: Who are these, my Lord, who are suffering in this fearful way? And the angel said to me: They are those who were in the habit of beautifying themselves with the devil's cosmetics and then going to church for the sake of adultery and not because of their husbands. They made God their enemy through their deceitful cosmetics. Therefore they will receive this punishment which will endure for ever.'
108. Cf. Gen. 19:4ff.
109. St. G.
110. C: Aftemelouchos.
111. Thus C.
112. St. G.
113. Gr.: 'Grant us our rights against our mothers.'
114. C adds: 'and they did not permit us to grow up into righteous men and to serve God'. Apoc. Mariae: 'they did not permit us to grow up to do good or evil'.
115. Gr.: 'an angel'. St. G.: 'the angel guarding Tartarus'. Apoc. Mariae: Temliaqos = Temeluchos.
116. St. G., C.
117. In what follows mostly after St. G.
118. St. G., C., S.
119. Cf. Rev. 5:1.
120. In the succeeding St. G. is often followed.
121. Cf. 1 Jn. 4:3.
122. Gr., cf. also St. G.
123. Cf. Mk. 9:48.
124. Cf. Mt. 8:12, etc.
125. St. G.
126. Cf. 1 Cor. 15:12ff.
127. St. G. goes: '(Now have we known júdgment), because it was possible for us previously to meet the Son of God before . . . '
128. Cf. Dan. 12:1.
129. Thus after Gr., S, C.
130 St. G.

131. Perhaps the passive (*moveri* instead of *movere*) should be restored in agreement with the Greek.
132. Cf. Rev. 4:9f.
133. St. G.
134. St. G.: 'dost grant'.
135. Gr. adds 'good'. Similarly C and Cod. Mon. 2625.
136. Cf. Mk. 15:17 and pars.
137. Cf. Mt. 27:34.
138. Jn. 19:34.
139. Cf. Mt. 5:11f.
140. St. G. 'and for the sake of your friends who do my commandments'. Similarly C.
141. Cf. Isr. Lévi, 'Le repos sabbatique des âmes damnées', *Revue des études juives* XXV, 1892, 1-13 and XXVI, 1893, 131-135 (Jewish parallels). For Christian material: Merkle, 'Die Sabbatruhe in der Hölle', in *Röm. Quartalschrift*, 1895, 489-505. Worthy of note are Prudentius, *Cathemerinon* V 125ff. and Augustine, *Enchiridion*, ch. 112; on this cf. *supra* pp. 712f..
142. = 'carried on no trade'.
143. *nasum* is a corruption of *natum esse* as C shows.
144. The passage is corrupt from 'For here'; C gives no assistance.
145. Cf. Gen. 3:1ff.
146. Cf. Gen. 2:11ff.
147. In accordance with a textual emendation.
148. The expression is from the Vulgate of Gen. 1:2.
149. An impossible translation. Perhaps a *per* has fallen out before *praeceptum*; then we could translate 'came' instead of 'brought', taking 'heaven and earth' as the subject.
150. Cf. Gen. 2:17.
151. Cf. Gen. 2:9.
152. Cf. Acts 9:15.
153. 'my beloved son' added from C.
154. Cf. Gen. 37:23ff.
155. C: 'I have never kept any evil feeling in my heart against them, even for a single day.' Accordingly *eos* should be elided and it should be translated: 'nor have I in any way been harmed by them = have I felt myself harmed', etc.
156. Cf. Mt. 9:36.
157. *disputati <sunt>*.
158. Gr. 'three'.
159. Cf. Heb. 11:37; Ascension of Isaiah 1:7; 5:1ff., cf. *supra* pp. 606; 610.
160. Cf. the Spanish Bible of St. Pere of Roda (11th century).
161. The words in square brackets I have transposed to the beginning of the following sentence, where they appear in round brackets.
162. Cf. Gen. 19:1ff.
163. Cf. Job 2:9f.
164. Cf. Rom. 8:18.
165. Reading *nos* instead of *vos*.
166. Cf. Gen. 6:14ff.
167. Cf. Mt. 24:38 and pars.
168. Cf. 1 Kings 17:1ff.
169. At this point the text underlying L, S, and Gr. breaks off suddenly. What follows is the continuation as found in the Coptic. For the way in which the Syriac continues at this break after the words 'And the angels have often prayed that he would give them rain' see the end of the section.
170. Cf. Lk. 1:5ff.

171. Cf. Gen. 4:8.
172. Cf. Mk. 6:24, 25 and pars.
173. Cf. The Protevangelium of James 24:3 (vol. 1, p. 436f.).
174. Cf. Gen. 4:8.
175. Literally 'Letterbearer'.
176. Cf. Rev. 22:18f.
177. = the eleventh Coptic month beginning the 25th June.

4. Apocalypse of Thomas

A. de Santos Otero

For centuries the Apocalypse of Thomas was known only through the notice of it in the Decretum Gelasianum (Item 27, cf. vol. 1, p. 39). In 1908 C. Frick (ZNW 9, 1908, 172) drew attention to another reference which is contained in the Chronicle of Jerome of the Codex Philippsianus No. 1829 in Berlin. In this it says in reference to the 18th year of Tiberius Caesar: *in libro quodam apocrypho qui dicitur Thomae apostoli scriptum est dominum iesum ad eum dixisse ab ascensu suo ad celum usque in secundum adventum eius novem iobeleus contineri.*

Today two versions of the Apocalypse of Thomas exist.

The longer is represented by: *a*) Cod. Clm 4585 fol. 66^v-67^v (9th cent.) of Benediktbeuern. This text has been edited by Fr. Wilhelm in his book: *Deutsche Legenden und Legendare*, 1907; *b*) a manuscript from the Library of the Chapter of Verona (8th cent.) which has been published by M.R. James in JTS 11, 1910, 288-290; *c*) Cod. Vatic. Palat. no. 220, discovered by E. v. Dobschütz and used by Bihlmeyer in his edition of Cod. Clm 4563. An early English form of this version is found in the fifteenth sermon of the famous Anglo-Saxon manuscript of Vercelli (9th cent.), cf. M.R. James, *Apoc. NT*, 556ff. This version consists of two different parts. The first is concerned with the events and signs which are to precede the last judgment. In this it reveals a close dependence on similar descriptions of other apocrypha of an apocalyptic nature, e.g. the Assumption of Moses, the Ascension of Isaiah and the Sibylline Books. This part should be regarded as an interpolation;[1] its origin can be dated to the first or second half of the 5th century because of some historical references in the text (e.g. to the Emperor Theodosius and his two sons Arcadius and Honorius). Cf. Bihlmeyer in *Rev. Bénéd.* 28, 1911, 277.

The second part corresponds in range and content with the shorter version of the Apocalypse of Thomas. This version is represented by: *a*) Cod. Vindob. Palatinus 16 (formerly Bobbiensis) fol. 60^r-60^v from the 5th century. This text was first discovered by J. Bick (SWA 159, 1908, 90-100) and identified by E. Hauler (*Wiener Studien* 30, 1908, 308-340) as a fragment of the Apocalypse of Thomas. It is the oldest witness of all to our Apocalypse; *b*) Cod. Clm 4563 fol. 40^r-40^v (11th/12th century) from Benediktbeuern, discovered and edited by Bihlmeyer (*Rev. Bénéd.* 28, 1911, 272-276). This text agrees basically with Vindob. Palat. 16, has been fully preserved and reveals no interpolations.

The shorter version is our oldest witness to the original Apocalypse of Thomas, which would have been subject in the course of time to various orthodox and heretical revisions. We must associate this development above all with Manichean and Priscillianist currents of thought. In favour of that there is not only the mention of the Apocalypse of Thomas in the Decretum Gelasianum but also some parallel places in Priscillianist writings; cf. De Bruyne (*Rev. Bénéd.* 24, 1907, 318-335) and Bihlmeyer (ibid. 28, 1911, 279). Some typical Manichean ideas, e.g. that of light, appear again and again in our Apocalypse. In this connection Bihlmeyer (ibid. p. 282) points to the name *Thomas* which (according to the Acta Archelai of Hegemonius) was borne by one of the three greatest disciples of Mani. Both the longer and shorter versions (Cod. Vindob. Palat. 16 dates from the 5th century) suggest the conjecture that the Apocalypse of Thomas originated prior to the 5th century. Closely dependent on the canonical Revelation of John, it is the only apocryphal apocalypse which apportions the events of the End into seven days. This clearly recalls the seven seals, the seven trumpets and the seven bowls of the Revelation of John (Rev. 5-8:2; 8:2-11; 16). The numerous variants of the Latin codices point to different versions of an original Greek text.

The basis of our translation is the Latin text of Cod. Clm 4563 in the edition of Bihlmeyer (*Rev. Bénéd.* 28, 1911, 272-276) in which he takes into account the variants of the other codices. There is a complete English translation of both versions in M.R. James.[2]

Apocalypse of Thomas

Hearken, Thomas,[3] for I am the Son of God the Father[4] and I am the father of all spirits.[5] Hear from me the signs which will be at the end of this world, when the end of the world will be fulfilled before my elect come forth from the world.

I tell you openly what now is about to happen to men.[6] When these are to take place the princes of the angels[7] do not know, for they are now hidden from them. Then the kings will divide the world among themselves;[8] there will be great hunger, great pestilences and much distress on the earth.[9] The sons of men will be enslaved in every nation and will perish by the sword.[10] There will be great disorder on earth. Thereafter when the hour of the end draws near there will be great signs in the sky for seven days and the powers of the heavens will be set in motion.[11] Then at the beginning of the third hour of the first day there will be a mighty and strong voice in the firmament of the heaven; a cloud of blood[12] will go up from the north and there will follow it great rolls of thunder and powerful flashes of lightning and it will cover the whole heaven. Then it will rain blood on all the earth. These are the signs of the first day.

And on the second day a great voice will resound in the firmament of heaven and the earth will be moved from its place.[13] The gates of heaven will be opened in the firmament of heaven from the east. The smoke of a great fire[14] will burst forth through the gates of heaven and will cover the whole heaven as far as the west. In that day there will be fears and great terrors in the world.[15] These are the signs of the second day.

And on the third day at about the third hour there will be a great voice in heaven and the depths of the earth will roar out from the four corners of the world.[16] The pinnacles of the firmament of heaven will be laid open and all the air will be filled with pillars of smoke. An exceedingly evil stench of sulphur will last until the tenth hour.[17] Men will say: We think the end is upon us so that we perish. These are the signs of the third day.

And at the first hour of the fourth day the Abyss will melt and rumble from the land of the east; then the whole earth will shake before the force of the earthquake. In that day the idols of the heathen[18] will fall as well as all the buildings of the earth before the force of the earthquake. These are the signs of the fourth day.

But on the fifth day at the sixth hour suddenly there will be great thunderings in the heaven and the powers of the light will flash and the sphere of the sun will be burst[19] and great darkness will be in the (whole) world as far as the west.[20] The air will be sorrowful without sun and moon. The stars will cease their work. In that day all nations will so see as (if they were enclosed) in a sack,[21] and they will despise the life of this world. These are the signs of the fifth day.

And at the fourth hour of the sixth day there will be a great voice in heaven. The firmament of heaven will be split from east to west[22] and the angels of the heavens will look out on the earth through the rents in the heavens and all men who are on earth will see the angelic host looking out from heaven. Then all men will flee into the tombs[23] and hide themselves from before the righteous angels, and say, 'Oh that the earth would open and swallow us.' For such things will happen as never happened since this world was created.[24] Then they will see me as I come down from above in the light of my Father with the power and honour of the holy angels.[25] Then at my arrival the restraint on the fire of paradise will be loosed, for paradise is enclosed with fire.[26] And this is the eternal fire which devours the earthly globe and all the elements of the world.[27] Then the spirits and souls of the saints will come forth from paradise and come into all the earth, and each go to its own body where it is laid up; and each of them will say, 'Here my body is laid up.' And when the great voice of those spirits is heard there will be an earthquake everywhere in the earth and by the force of that earthquake the mountains will be shattered above and the rocks beneath. Then each spirit will return to its own vessel[28] and the bodies of the saints who sleep will rise.[29] Then their bodies will be changed into the image and likeness and honour of the holy angels and into the power of the image of my holy Father.[30] Then they will put on the garment of eternal life:[31] the garment from the cloud of light[32] which has never been seen in this world; for this cloud comes down from the upper kingdom of the heavens by the power of my Father, and will invest with its glory every spirit that has believed in me. Then they will be clothed and, as I said to you before, borne by the hands of the holy angels.[33] Then they will be carried off in a cloud of light into the air,[34] and rejoicing go with me into the heavens and remain in the light and honour of my Father. Then there will be great joy for them in the presence of my Father and in the presence of the holy angels. These are the signs of the sixth day.

And at the eight hour of the seventh day there will be voices in the four corners[35] of heaven. All the air will be set in motion and filled with holy angels. These will make war among themselves for the whole day.[36] In that day the elect will be delivered by the holy angels from the destruction of the world.[37] Then all men will see that the hour of their destruction is come near. These are the signs of the seventh day.

And when the seven days are finished, on the eighth day at the sixth hour there will be a gentle and pleasant voice in heaven from the east. Then that angel who has power over the holy angels will be made manifest. And there will go forth with him all the angels sitting on my holy Father's chariots of clouds, rejoicing and flying around in the air under heaven, to deliver the elect who believed in me; and they will rejoice that the destruction of the world has come.

The words of the Saviour to Thomas about the end of this world are finished.

Notes

4. Apocalypse of Thomas

1. Another view in this respect is advocated by M. Dando ('L'Apocalypse de Thomas', *Cahiers d'études cathares* 28/37, 1977, 3-58), who holds the interpolated version here mentioned to be more original than the shorter one. For him, this apocryphon is further to be regarded as a Jewish-Christian writing which originated presumably in Syria, and was disseminated in the West first through the Spanish Priscillianists and then by the Irish monks; cf. in this connection St. J.D. Seymour, 'The Signs of Doomsday in the "Saltair na Rann"', *Proceedings of the Royal Irish Academy* 36, Section C, 1923, 154-163; W.W. Heist, *The Fifteen Signs before Doomsday*, East Lansing, 1952; M. McNamara, *The Apocrypha in the Irish Church*, Dublin 1975, 119-121.
2. In the interval further complete translations have appeared: M. Erbetta III, 387-395; L. Moraldi II, 1939-1950; M. Dando, op. cit. 13-19.
3. Almost all the representatives of the longer version introduce this piece of writing with the words: *incipit epistula domini ad Thomam.* This is succeeded by a long description of the events which will take place in the last days. This description constitutes the first part of the version and is to be considered an interpolation; it concludes with a series of anathemas and cries of *Vae*. Following on this the description of the last seven days begins. With some variations it takes a similar course to the shorter version.
4. Bihlmeyer (ibid. 280) has seen traces of monarchian influence in the prominent place which the person *Dei Patris* occupies in the course of the work. Otherwise M. Dando, op. cit. 24-25, 29-30.
5. Cf. Priscillian, *Tract.* II: *tu animarum pater . . . tu operatio spirituum, tu princip(i)um archangelorum, tu angelorum opus* (ed. Schepss, SCEL 18, 104).
6. The text appears to be corrupt at this point. The longer version offers no parallel.

7. Cod. Vindob. Palat. n. 16: *principes angelorum.* Cod. Clm 4563: *principes, angeli.* Cf. Mk. 13:32 and pars.
8. Cod Clm. 4563: *Tunc erunt participationes in saeculo inter regem et regem.* This can be understood in dependence on Mk. 13:8, as an allusion to the struggles and wars for world dominion.
9. Cf. Lk. 21:11; Mt. 24:7ff.
10. Cf. Lk. 21:24.
11. Cf. Lk. 21:11, 26; Mt. 24:29; Mk. 13:24f.
12. Cf. Rev. 6:12; Joel 2:30.
13. Cf. Rev. 6:12ff.
14. Cf. Rev. 9:2.
15. Cf. Lk. 21:26.
16. Cf. Rev. 7:1; Ezek. 7:2; 37:9; Mt. 24:31; Lk. 21:25; 4 Ezra 5:7.
17. Cf. Rev. 9:17.
18. The *adornamenta* of Cod. Clm 4563 is replaced by *idolas* in Cod. Clem 4585 and by *monumenta* in Vatic. Palat. n. 220. The meaning at any rate is clear. Cf. Is. 2:18; Pseudo-Matthew 22:2, 23 (Santos[6], 215.); Arabic Infancy Gospel 10 (translated ibid. 308f.).
19. Clm 4563 has *et rota solis aperietur.* Bihlmeyer (op. cit.) proposes *operietur* instead of *aperietur.*
20. Cf. Mt. 24:29; Rev. 6:12.
21. Clm 4563 has, *In illa die omnes gentes ita videbunt, velut in sacculo.* James (p. 560) replaces *sacculo* with *speculo* and translates: 'in that day shall all nations behold as in a mirror', though he does not rule out *sacculo* as a possibility. The manuscripts offer no clue for the understanding of this obscure passage.
22. Cf. Copt. Apocalypse of Elijah (ed. Steindorff, 154) and Apocalypse of John, ch. 17 (ed. Tischendorf, *Apa*, 85).
23. Vat. Palat. no 220 has *speluncas montium* instead of the *monumentis* of Clm 4563. Cf. Rev. 6:15.
24. Cf. Mt. 24:21; Mk. 13:19; Rev. 16:18; Dan. 21:1.
25. Cf. Mt. 24:30; Mk. 13:26f; Lk. 21:27; Dan. 7:13. Mt. 25:31; Lk. 9:26; 1 Thess. 3:13 also refer to the presence of the angels at the Parousia. Cf. Dan. 7:10.
26. It is not clear whether there is an allusion here to the expulsion of Adam from paradise (Gen. 3:24) or rather to the conception of the throne of God as surrounded by fire (cf. Dan. 7:9; Ezek. 1:4; Rev. 4:5). A Priscillianist apocryphon also speaks of 'walls of fire' (*Rev. Bénéd.* 24, 1907, 323). There however they surround 'hell'.
27. Cf. 2 Pet. 3:7.
28. Cf. 1 Thess. 4:4.
29. Cf. Mt. 27:52.
30. Cf. Gen. 1:26; 1 Cor. 15:49; 2 Cor. 3:18.
31. Cf. Ascension of Isaiah 9:2 (Translation *supra* p.615).
32. Cf. Acts of Thomas, chs. 108-114 (*supra* pp. 380ff.). The important role which light plays in our apocalypse reminds us of Manichean and gnostic circles where as is well known the theme of light was very popular. Cf. Bihlmeyer, 281.
33. Cf. Apoc. Moses, ch. 37 (ed. Tishendorf, *Apa*, 20); Story of Joseph the Carpenter 23:2 (S. Morenz, TU, 56, 1951).
34. Cf. 1 Thess. 4:17.
35. Cf. Rev. 7:1.
36. Cf. Rev. 12:7.
37. Palat. Vatic. 220 has *querent electi de toto animo ut liberentur de perditione.* Cf. Rev. 7:3; Mt. 24:31; Mk. 13:27.

Index

Based on the German index prepared by Gregor Ahn

1. Biblical Passages (Selection)

The numbers relate to the pages on which the passages are quoted.

2. Names and Subjects

The numbers refer to the pages, volume II being indicated by the prefixed Roman numeral. Number in **bold** type indicate the main sections in which the subject is discussed in detail.